STANDOFF
ASSAULT ON PLEASANT HILL

S.H.I.E.L.D. Case No. 90168-11
Codename: STANDOFF

WITHDRAWN

Collection Editor: **Jennifer Grünwald**
Associate Editor: **Sarah Brunstad**
Associate Managing Editor: **Alex Starbuck**
Editor, Special Projects: **Mark D. Beazley**
VP, Production & Special Projects: **Jeff Youngquist**
SVP Print, Sales & Marketing: **David Gabriel**
Book Designer: **Adam Del Re**

Editor in Chief: **Axel Alonso**
Chief Creative Officer: **Joe Quesada**
Publisher: **Dan Buckley**
Executive Producer: **Alan Fine**

Avengers created by
Stan Lee & **Jack Kirby**

AVENGERS: STANDOFF. Contains material originally published in magazine form as AVENGERS STANDOFF: WELCOME TO PLEASANT HILL #1; AVENGERS STANDOFF: ASSAULT ON PLEASANT HILL ALPHA #1; AGENTS OF S.H.I.E.L.D. #3-4; UNCANNY AVENGERS #7-8; ALL-NEW, ALL-DIFFERENT AVENGERS #7-8; NEW AVENGERS #8-10; CAPTAIN AMERICA: SAM WILSON #7-8; ILLUMINATI #6; HOWLING COMMANDOS OF S.H.I.E.L.D. #6; and AVENGERS STANDOFF: ASSAULT ON PLEASANT HILL OMEGA #1. First printing 2016. ISBN# 978-1-302-90147-9. Published by MARVEL WORLDWIDE, INC., a subsidiary of MARVEL ENTERTAINMENT, LLC. OFFICE OF PUBLICATION: 135 West 50th Street, New York, NY 10020. Copyright © 2016 MARVEL No similarity between any of the names, characters, persons, and/or institutions in this magazine with those of any living or dead person or institution is intended, and any such similarity which may exist is purely coincidental. **Printed in the U.S.A.** ALAN FINE, President, Marvel Entertainment; DAN BUCKLEY, President, TV, Publishing & Brand Management; JOE QUESADA, Chief Creative Officer; TOM BREVOORT, SVP of Publishing; DAVID BOGART, SVP of Business Affairs & Operations, Publishing & Partnership; C.B. CEBULSKI, VP of Brand Management & Development, Asia; DAVID GABRIEL, SVP of Sales & Marketing, Publishing; JEFF YOUNGQUIST, VP of Production & Special Projects; DAN CARR, Executive Director of Publishing Technology; ALEX MORALES, Director of Publishing Operations; SUSAN CRESPI, Production Manager; STAN LEE, Chairman Emeritus. For information regarding advertising in Marvel Comics or on Marvel.com, please contact Vit DeBellis, Integrated Sales Manager, at vdebellis@marvel. com. For Marvel subscription inquiries, please call 888-511-5480. **Manufactured between 5/6/2016 and 6/13/2016 by R.R. DONNELLEY, INC., SALEM, VA, USA.**

10 9 8 7 6 5 4 3 2 1

Involved Parties

AVENGERS STANDOFF: WELCOME TO PLEASANT HILL
Wrtier: **Nick Spencer**
Penciler: **Mark Bagley**
Inker: **Scott Hanna**
Colorist: **Paul Mounts**
Letterer: **VC's Clayton Cowles**
Cover Art: **Daniel Acuña**
Assistant Editor: **Alanna Smith**
Editor: **Tom Brevoort**

AGENTS OF S.H.I.E.L.D. Nos. 3-4
Wrtier: **Marc Guggenheim**
Artist: **Germán Peralta**
Color Artist: **Rachelle Rosenberg**
Letterer: **VC's Joe Caramagna**
Cover Art: **Mike Norton** & **F.C.O. Plascencia**
Assistant Editors: **Alanna Smith** & **Christina Harrington**
Editor: **Katie Kubert**
Executive Editor: **Tom Brevoort**
Special thanks to **Jeph Loeb, Megan Thomas Bradner** & **Al Ewing**

ALL-NEW, ALL-DIFFERENT AVENGERS Nos. 7-8
Wrtier: **Mark Waid**
Artist: **Adam Kubert**
Color Artists: **Sonia Oback** (#7-8), **Dono Sánchez Almara** (#7), **Romulo Fajardo** (#7), **Edgar Delgado** (#7-8) & **Israel Silva** (#8)
Letterer: **VC's Cory Petit**
Cover Art: **Alex Ross**
Assistant Editors: **Alanna Smith**
Editor: **Katie Kubert** with **Wil Moss**

HOWLING COMMANDOS OF S.H.I.E.L.D. No. 6
Wrtier: **Frank J. Barbiere**
Artist: **Brent Schoonover**
Color Artist: **Nick Filardi**
Letterer: **VC's Joe Caramagna**
Cover Art: **Brent Schoonover** & **Nick Filardi**
Editors: **Katie Kubert** & **Christina Harrington**

ILLUMINATI No. 6
Wrtier: **Joshua Williamson**
Artist: **Mike Henderson**
Color Artist: **John Rauch**
Letterer: **VC's Joe Caramagna**
Cover Art: **Riley Rossmo**
Editor: **Katie Kubert**

AVENGERS STANDOFF: ASSAULT ON PLEASANT HILL ALPHA
Wrtier: **Nick Spencer**
Artist: **Jesús Saiz**
Letterer: **VC's Clayton Cowles**
Cover Art: **Jesús Saiz**
Assistant Editor: **Alanna Smith**
Editor: **Tom Brevoort**

UNCANNY AVENGERS Nos. 7-8
Wrtier: **Gerry Duggan**
Penciler: **Ryan Stegman**
Inkers: **Mark Morales** (#7-8), **Guillermo Ortega** (#7) & **Dave Meikis** (#8) with **Ryan Stegman** (#8)
Colorists: **Richard Isanove** with **Matt Yackey** (#7)
Letterer: **VC's Clayton Cowles**
Cover Art: **Ryan Stegman** & **Richard Isanove**
Assistant Editor: **Alanna Smith**
Editors: **Tom Brevoort** with **Daniel Ketchum**

NEW AVENGERS Nos. 8-10
Wrtier: **Al Ewing**
Artist: **Marcus To** with **Juanan Ramirez** (#10)
Colorist Artist: **Dono Sánchez Almara**
Letterer: **VC's Joe Caramagna**
Cover Artists: **Jeff Dekal** (#8), **Leinil Francis Yu & Sunny Gho** (#9) and **Declan Shalvey** & **Jordie Bellaire** (#10)
Assistant Editor: **Alanna Smith**
Editors: **Tom Brevoort** with **Wil Moss**
Special thanks to **Marc Guggenheim**

CAPTAIN AMERICA: SAM WILSON Nos. 7-8
Wrtier: **Nick Spencer**
Artist, #7 (Steve): **Daniel Acuña**
Artists, #7 (Sam): **Angel Unzueta** & **Matt Yackey**
Artist, #8: **Paul Renaud**
Color Artist, #8 pp. 11-13: **Dono Sánchez Almara**
Letterer: **VC's Joe Caramagna**
Cover Art: **Alex Ross** (#7) & **Paul Renaud** (#8)
Assistant Editor: **Alanna Smith**
Editors: **Tom Brevoort**

AVENGERS STANDOFF: ASSAULT ON PLEASANT HILL OMEGA
Writer: **Nick Spencer**
Artists: **Daniel Acuña** & **Angel Unzueta**
Color Artists: **Daniel Acuña** & **Matt Wilson**
Letterer: **VC's Clayton Cowles**
Cover Art: **Daniel Acuña**
Assistant Editor: **Alanna Smith**
Editor: **Tom Brevoort**

S.H.I.E.L.D. Case No. 90168-11
Codename: STANDOFF

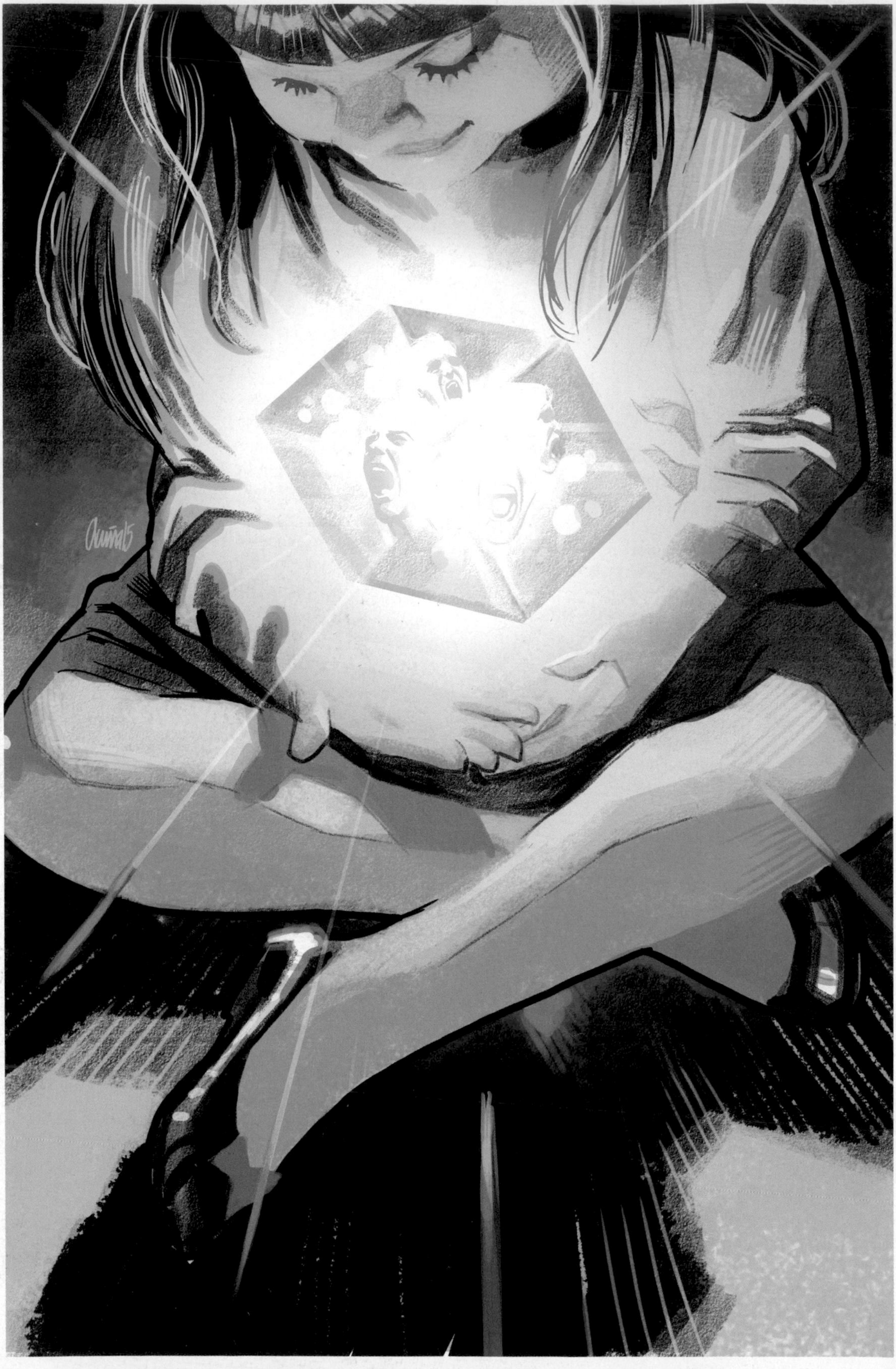

Avengers Standoff:
Welcome to Pleasant Hill

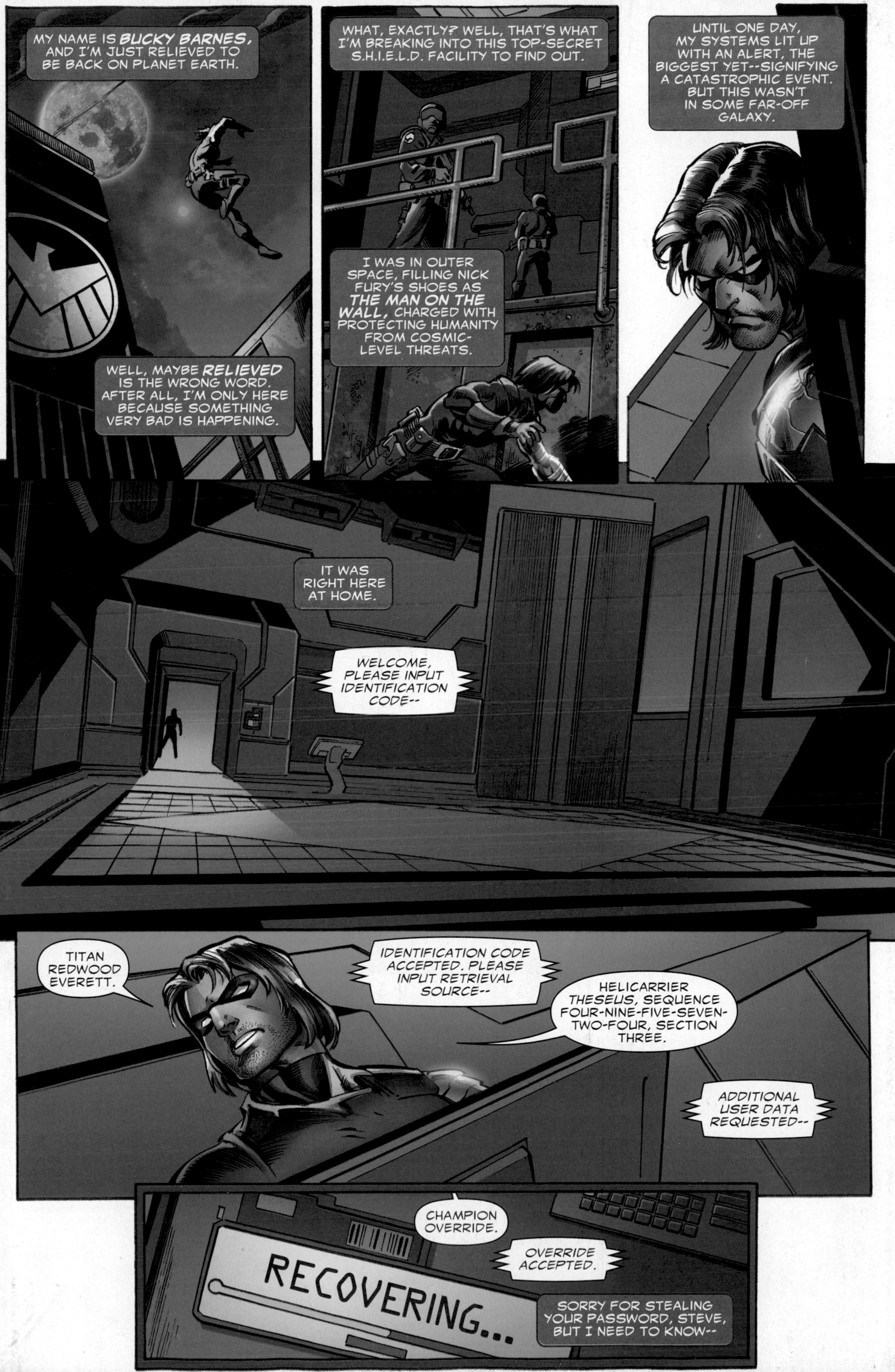

MY NAME IS BUCKY BARNES, AND I'M JUST RELIEVED TO BE BACK ON PLANET EARTH.
WELL, MAYBE RELIEVED IS THE WRONG WORD. AFTER ALL, I'M ONLY HERE BECAUSE SOMETHING VERY BAD IS HAPPENING.
WHAT, EXACTLY? WELL, THAT'S WHAT I'M BREAKING INTO THIS TOP-SECRET S.H.I.E.L.D. FACILITY TO FIND OUT.
I WAS IN OUTER SPACE, FILLING NICK FURY'S SHOES AS THE MAN ON THE WALL, CHARGED WITH PROTECTING HUMANITY FROM COSMIC-LEVEL THREATS.
UNTIL ONE DAY, MY SYSTEMS LIT UP WITH AN ALERT, THE BIGGEST YET--SIGNIFYING A CATASTROPHIC EVENT. BUT THIS WASN'T IN SOME FAR-OFF GALAXY.
IT WAS RIGHT HERE AT HOME.
WELCOME, PLEASE INPUT IDENTIFICATION CODE--
TITAN REDWOOD EVERETT.
IDENTIFICATION CODE ACCEPTED. PLEASE INPUT RETRIEVAL SOURCE--
HELICARRIER THESEUS, SEQUENCE FOUR-NINE-FIVE-SEVEN-TWO-FOUR, SECTION THREE.
ADDITIONAL USER DATA REQUESTED--
CHAMPION OVERRIDE.
OVERRIDE ACCEPTED.
RECOVERING...
SORRY FOR STEALING YOUR PASSWORD, STEVE, BUT I NEED TO KNOW--

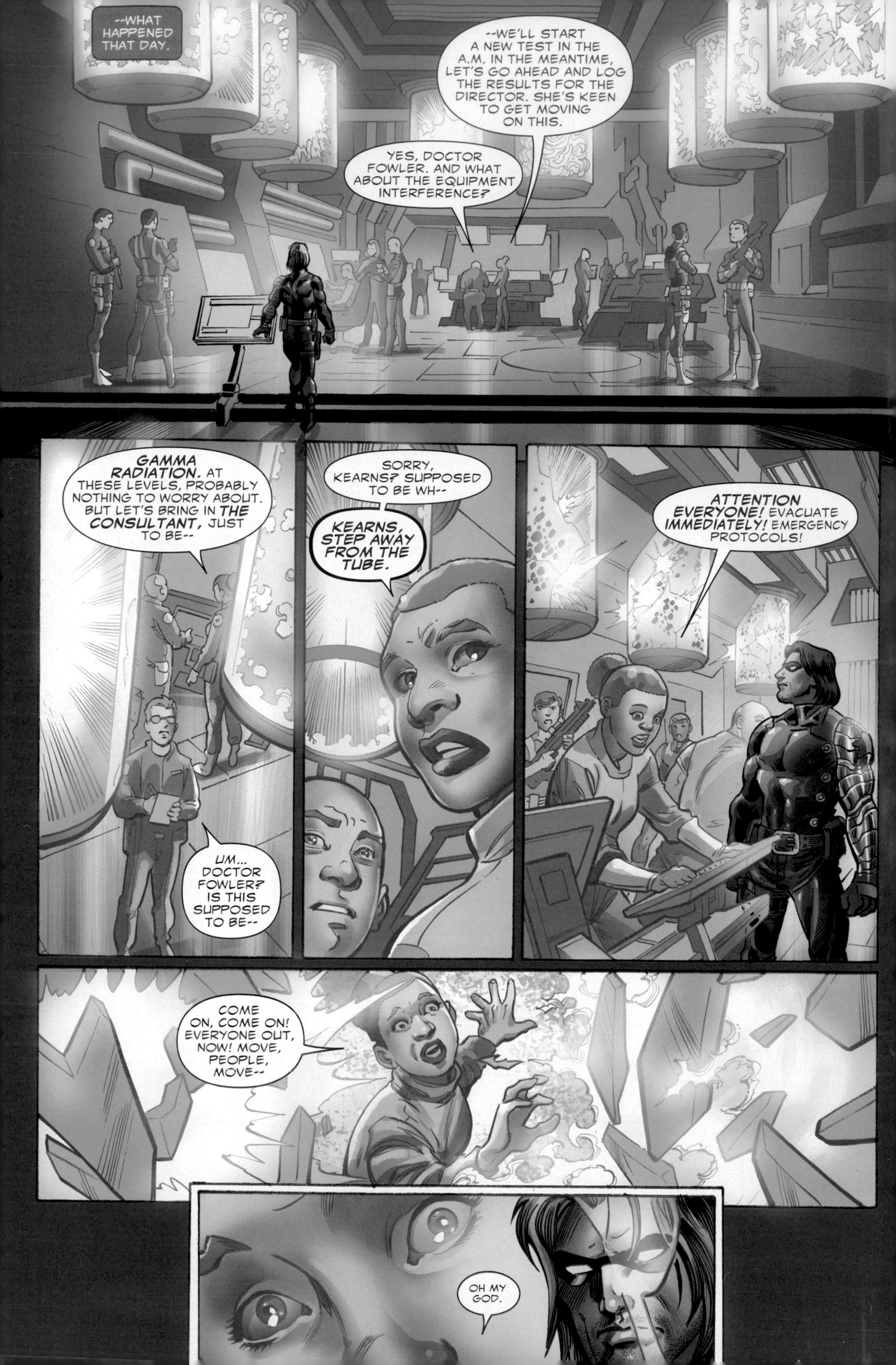
--WHAT HAPPENED THAT DAY.
--WE'LL START A NEW TEST IN THE A.M. IN THE MEANTIME, LET'S GO AHEAD AND LOG THE RESULTS FOR THE DIRECTOR. SHE'S KEEN TO GET MOVING ON THIS.
YES, DOCTOR FOWLER. AND WHAT ABOUT THE EQUIPMENT INTERFERENCE?
GAMMA RADIATION. AT THESE LEVELS, PROBABLY NOTHING TO WORRY ABOUT. BUT LET'S BRING IN THE CONSULTANT, JUST TO BE--
UM... DOCTOR FOWLER? IS THIS SUPPOSED TO BE--
SORRY, KEARNS? SUPPOSED TO BE WH--
KEARNS, STEP AWAY FROM THE TUBE.
ATTENTION EVERYONE! EVACUATE IMMEDIATELY! EMERGENCY PROTOCOLS!
COME ON, COME ON! EVERYONE OUT, NOW! MOVE, PEOPLE, MOVE--
OH MY GOD.

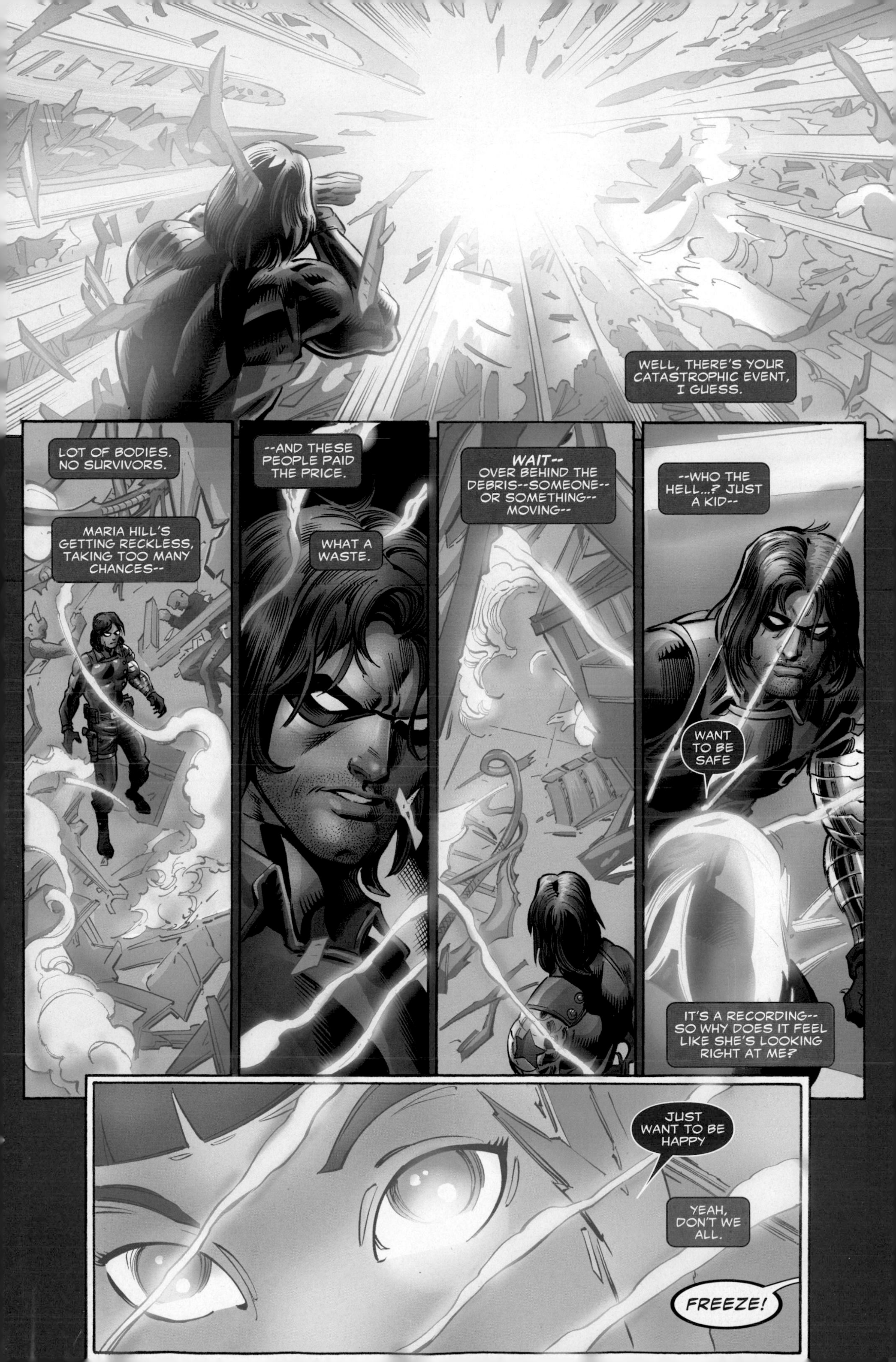
WELL, THERE'S YOUR CATASTROPHIC EVENT, I GUESS.
LOT OF BODIES. NO SURVIVORS.
MARIA HILL'S GETTING RECKLESS, TAKING TOO MANY CHANCES--
--AND THESE PEOPLE PAID THE PRICE.
WHAT A WASTE.
WAIT-- OVER BEHIND THE DEBRIS--SOMEONE--OR SOMETHING--MOVING--
--WHO THE HELL...? JUST A KID--
WANT TO BE SAFE
IT'S A RECORDING--SO WHY DOES IT FEEL LIKE SHE'S LOOKING RIGHT AT ME?
JUST WANT TO BE HAPPY
YEAH, DON'T WE ALL.
FREEZE!

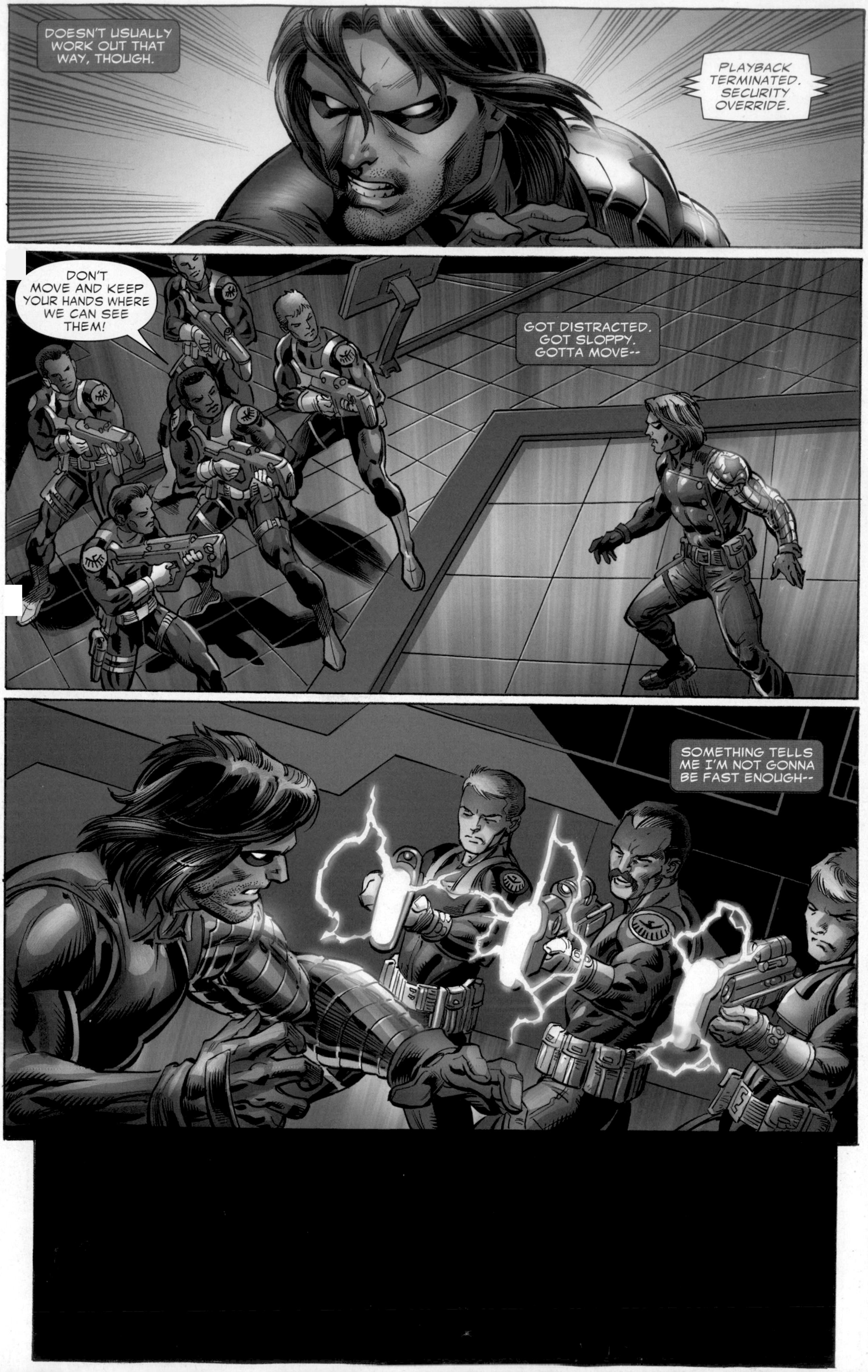
DOESN'T USUALLY WORK OUT THAT WAY, THOUGH.
PLAYBACK TERMINATED. SECURITY OVERRIDE.
DON'T MOVE AND KEEP YOUR HANDS WHERE WE CAN SEE THEM!
GOT DISTRACTED. GOT SLOPPY. GOTTA MOVE--
SOMETHING TELLS ME I'M NOT GONNA BE FAST ENOUGH--

SIX MONTHS AGO, A MYSTERIOUS HACKER KNOWN AS THE WHISPERER LEAKED FILES EXPOSING A TOP SECRET S.H.I.E.L.D. SECURITY PROGRAM, CODENAMED KOBIK, WHICH WOULD ALLOW AUTHORITIES TO USE COSMIC CUBE FRAGMENTS TO MAKE CHANGES IN THE FABRIC OF REALITY WITHOUT PUBLIC KNOWLEDGE.

THIS WAS MARIA HILL'S STATEMENT:

THESE ACCUSATIONS HAVE GOTTEN COMPLETELY OUT OF HAND. FIRST OF ALL, KOBIK WAS A PROPOSAL, NOTHING MORE. I HAVE A LOT OF PROPOSALS ON MY DESK. IT DOESN'T MEAN THEY BECOME REALITY, IF YOU'LL EXCUSE THE CHOICE OF WORDS THERE.
BEYOND THAT, FOR ALL THOSE CRITICIZING EVEN THE INTENT OF THIS PROPOSAL--GIVEN WHAT JUST HAPPENED TO US--THE RECENT INCURSION CRISIS--
IF WE COULD PREVENT THAT KIND OF TRAGEDY--OR WORSE--WITH A MINOR, CAREFULLY CONSIDERED USE OF THIS PROGRAM, SHOULDN'T WE? ISN'T THAT OUR OBLIGATION?
WHAT WE SHOULD BE DISCUSSING TODAY IS THE CRIMINAL WHO LEAKED CLASSIFIED INTELLIGENCE AND, IN DOING SO, PUT LIVES AT RISK.
BECAUSE, REST ASSURED, FINDING WHOEVER DID THIS JUST BECAME MY FAVORITE PRIORITY.

STANDOFF

WELCOME TO PLEASANT HILL

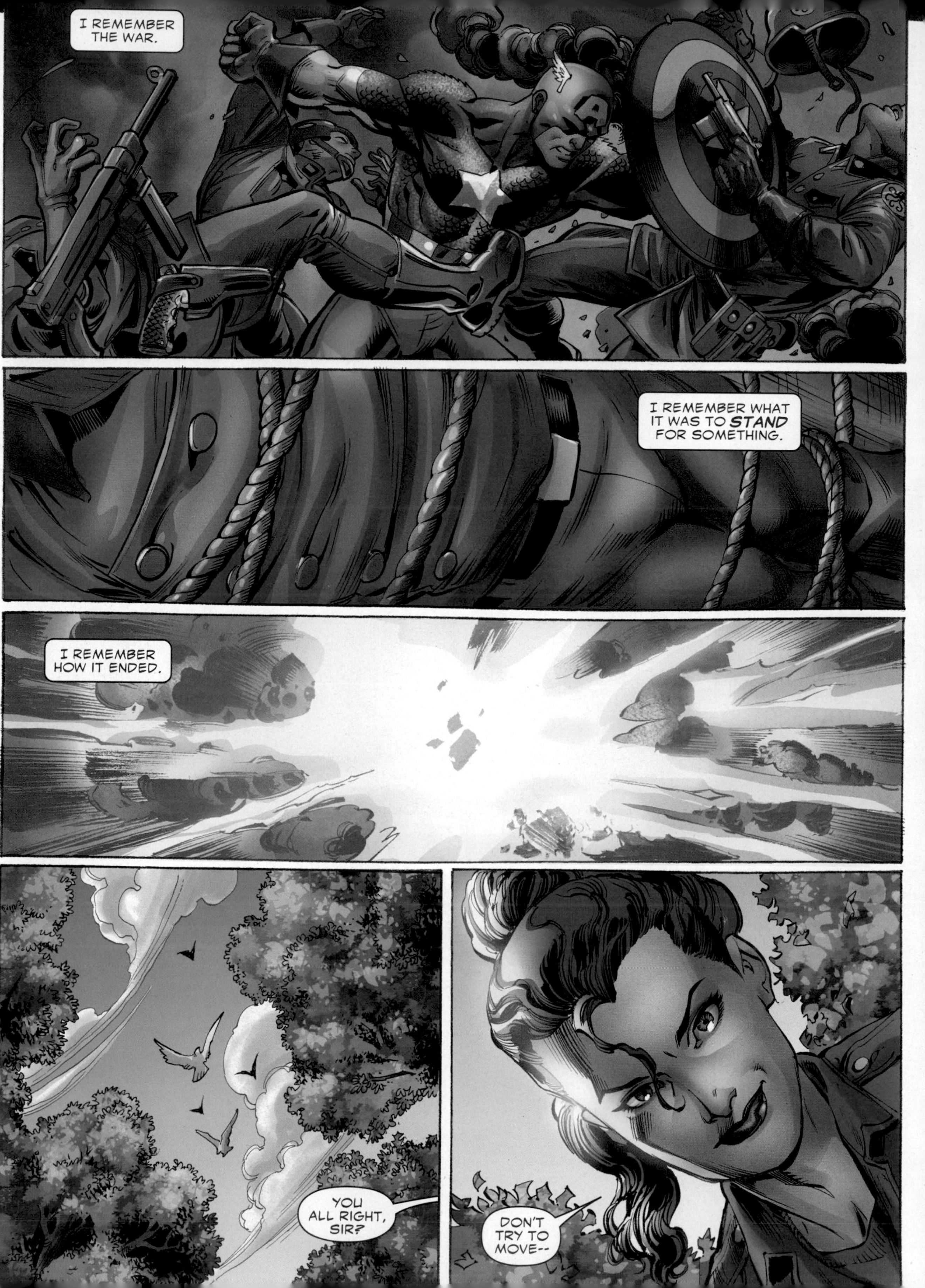
I REMEMBER THE WAR.
I REMEMBER WHAT IT WAS TO STAND FOR SOMETHING.
I REMEMBER HOW IT ENDED.
YOU ALL RIGHT, SIR?
DON'T TRY TO MOVE--

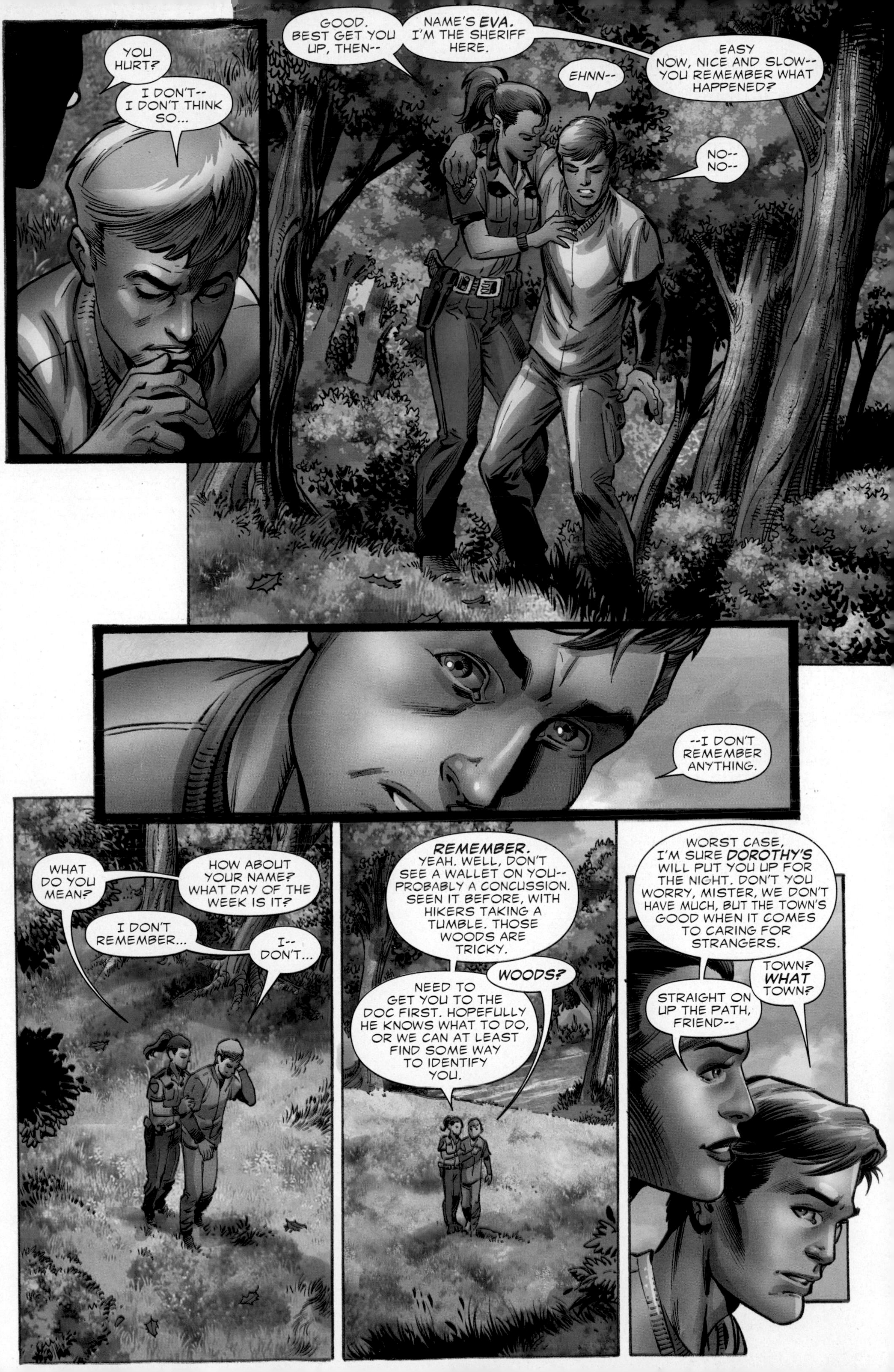
YOU HURT?
I DON'T-- I DON'T THINK SO...
GOOD. BEST GET YOU UP, THEN--
NAME'S **EVA.** I'M THE SHERIFF HERE.
EHNN--
EASY NOW, NICE AND SLOW-- YOU REMEMBER WHAT HAPPENED?
NO-- NO--
--I DON'T REMEMBER ANYTHING.
WHAT DO YOU MEAN?
HOW ABOUT YOUR NAME? WHAT DAY OF THE WEEK IS IT?
I DON'T REMEMBER...
I-- DON'T...
REMEMBER. YEAH. WELL, DON'T SEE A WALLET ON YOU-- PROBABLY A CONCUSSION. SEEN IT BEFORE, WITH HIKERS TAKING A TUMBLE. THOSE WOODS ARE TRICKY.
WOODS?
NEED TO GET YOU TO THE DOC FIRST. HOPEFULLY HE KNOWS WHAT TO DO, OR WE CAN AT LEAST FIND SOME WAY TO IDENTIFY YOU.
WORST CASE, I'M SURE **DOROTHY'S** WILL PUT YOU UP FOR THE NIGHT. DON'T YOU WORRY, MISTER, WE DON'T HAVE MUCH, BUT THE TOWN'S GOOD WHEN IT COMES TO CARING FOR STRANGERS.
TOWN? **WHAT** TOWN?
STRAIGHT ON UP THE PATH, FRIEND--

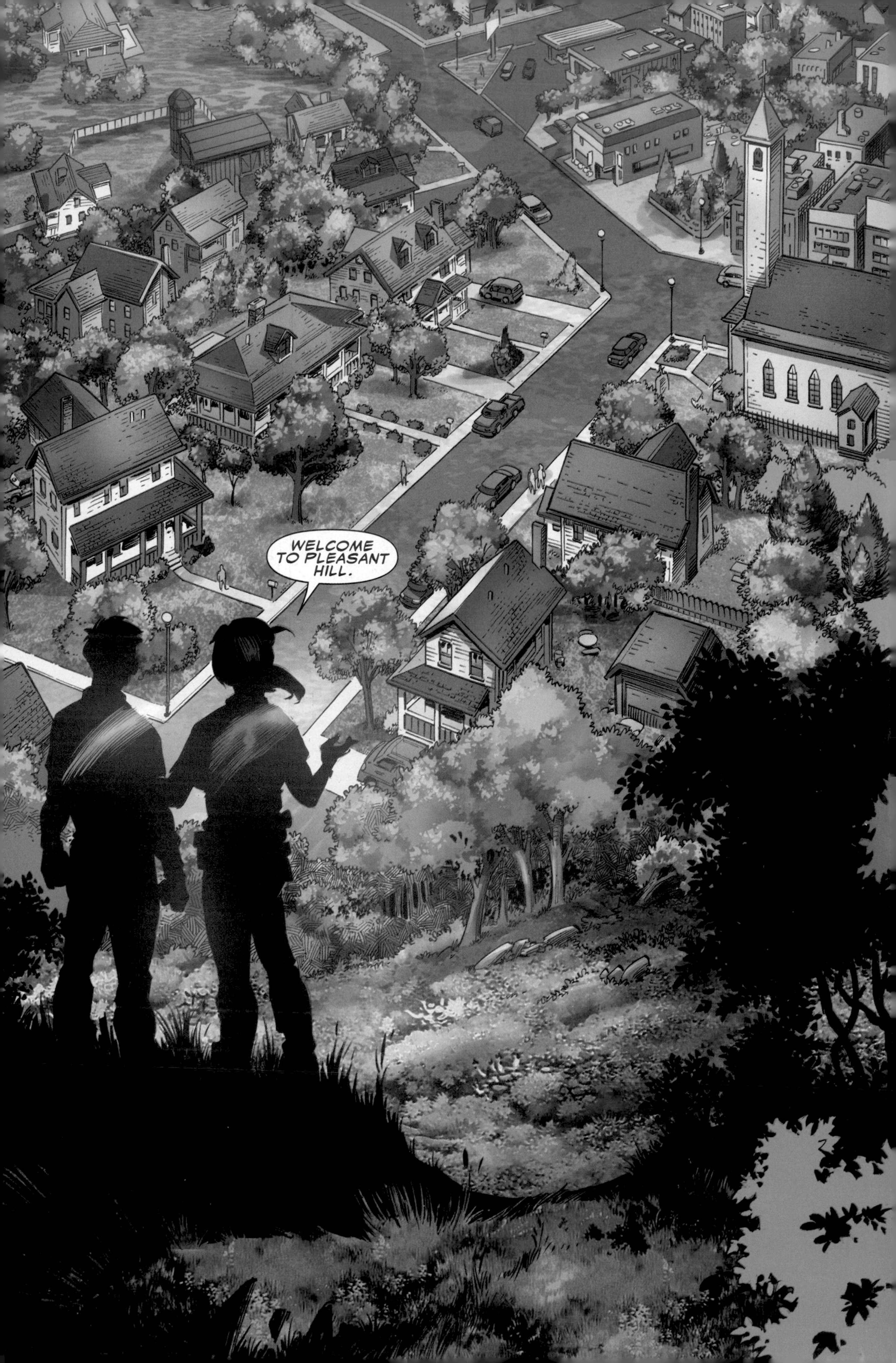
WELCOME TO PLEASANT HILL.

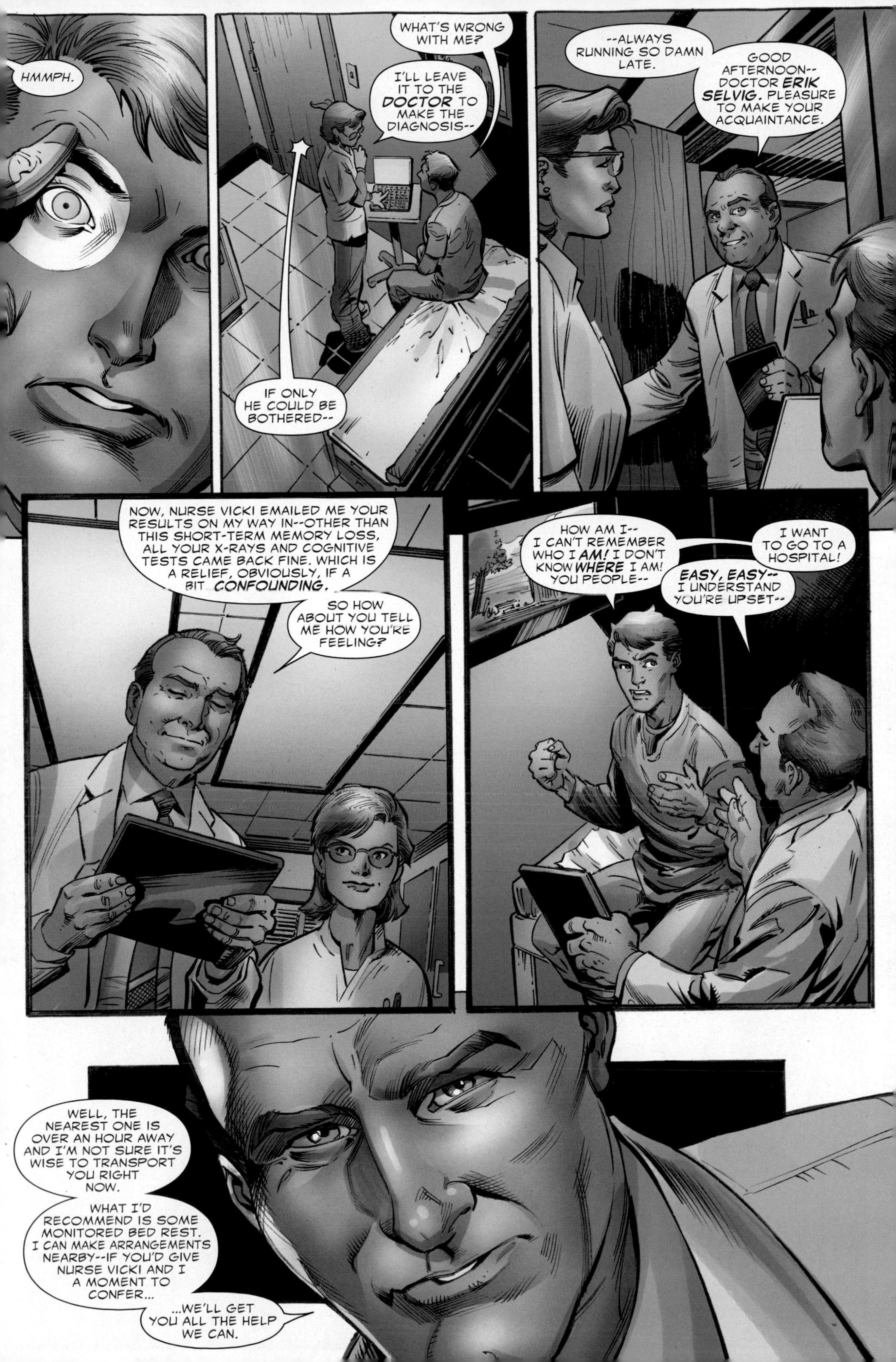
HMMPH.
WHAT'S WRONG WITH ME?
I'LL LEAVE IT TO THE DOCTOR TO MAKE THE DIAGNOSIS--
IF ONLY HE COULD BE BOTHERED--
--ALWAYS RUNNING SO DAMN LATE.
GOOD AFTERNOON--DOCTOR ERIK SELVIG. PLEASURE TO MAKE YOUR ACQUAINTANCE.
NOW, NURSE VICKI EMAILED ME YOUR RESULTS ON MY WAY IN--OTHER THAN THIS SHORT-TERM MEMORY LOSS, ALL YOUR X-RAYS AND COGNITIVE TESTS CAME BACK FINE. WHICH IS A RELIEF, OBVIOUSLY, IF A BIT CONFOUNDING.
SO HOW ABOUT YOU TELL ME HOW YOU'RE FEELING?
HOW AM I-- I CAN'T REMEMBER WHO I AM! I DON'T KNOW WHERE I AM! YOU PEOPLE--
I WANT TO GO TO A HOSPITAL!
EASY, EASY-- I UNDERSTAND YOU'RE UPSET--
WELL, THE NEAREST ONE IS OVER AN HOUR AWAY AND I'M NOT SURE IT'S WISE TO TRANSPORT YOU RIGHT NOW.
WHAT I'D RECOMMEND IS SOME MONITORED BED REST. I CAN MAKE ARRANGEMENTS NEARBY--IF YOU'D GIVE NURSE VICKI AND I A MOMENT TO CONFER...
...WE'LL GET YOU ALL THE HELP WE CAN.

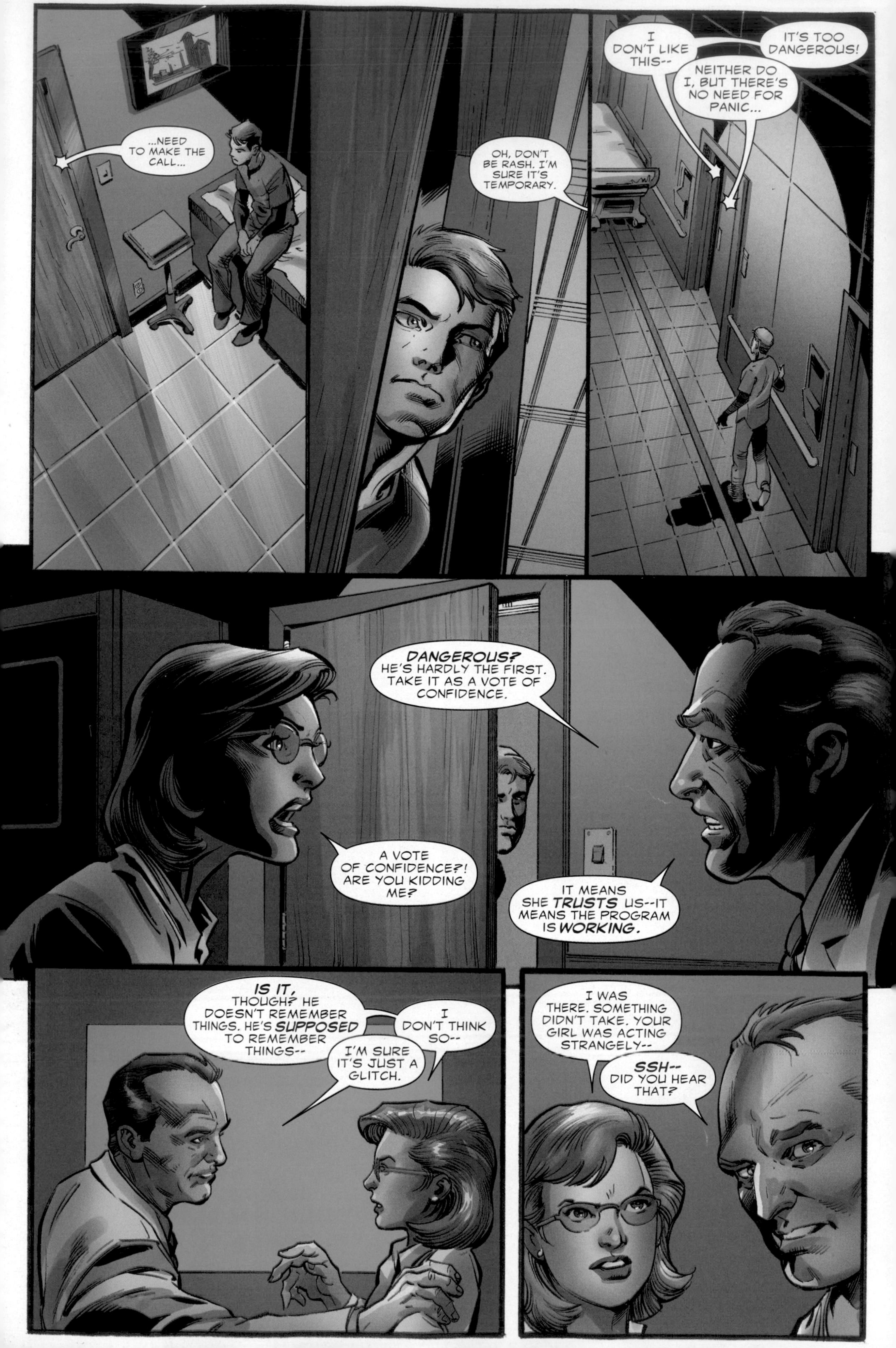
...NEED TO MAKE THE CALL...
OH, DON'T BE RASH. I'M SURE IT'S TEMPORARY.
I DON'T LIKE THIS--
IT'S TOO DANGEROUS!
NEITHER DO I, BUT THERE'S NO NEED FOR PANIC...
DANGEROUS? HE'S HARDLY THE FIRST. TAKE IT AS A VOTE OF CONFIDENCE.
A VOTE OF CONFIDENCE?! ARE YOU KIDDING ME?
IT MEANS SHE TRUSTS US--IT MEANS THE PROGRAM IS WORKING.
IS IT, THOUGH? HE DOESN'T REMEMBER THINGS. HE'S SUPPOSED TO REMEMBER THINGS--
I DON'T THINK SO--
I'M SURE IT'S JUST A GLITCH.
I WAS THERE. SOMETHING DIDN'T TAKE. YOUR GIRL WAS ACTING STRANGELY--
SSH-- DID YOU HEAR THAT?

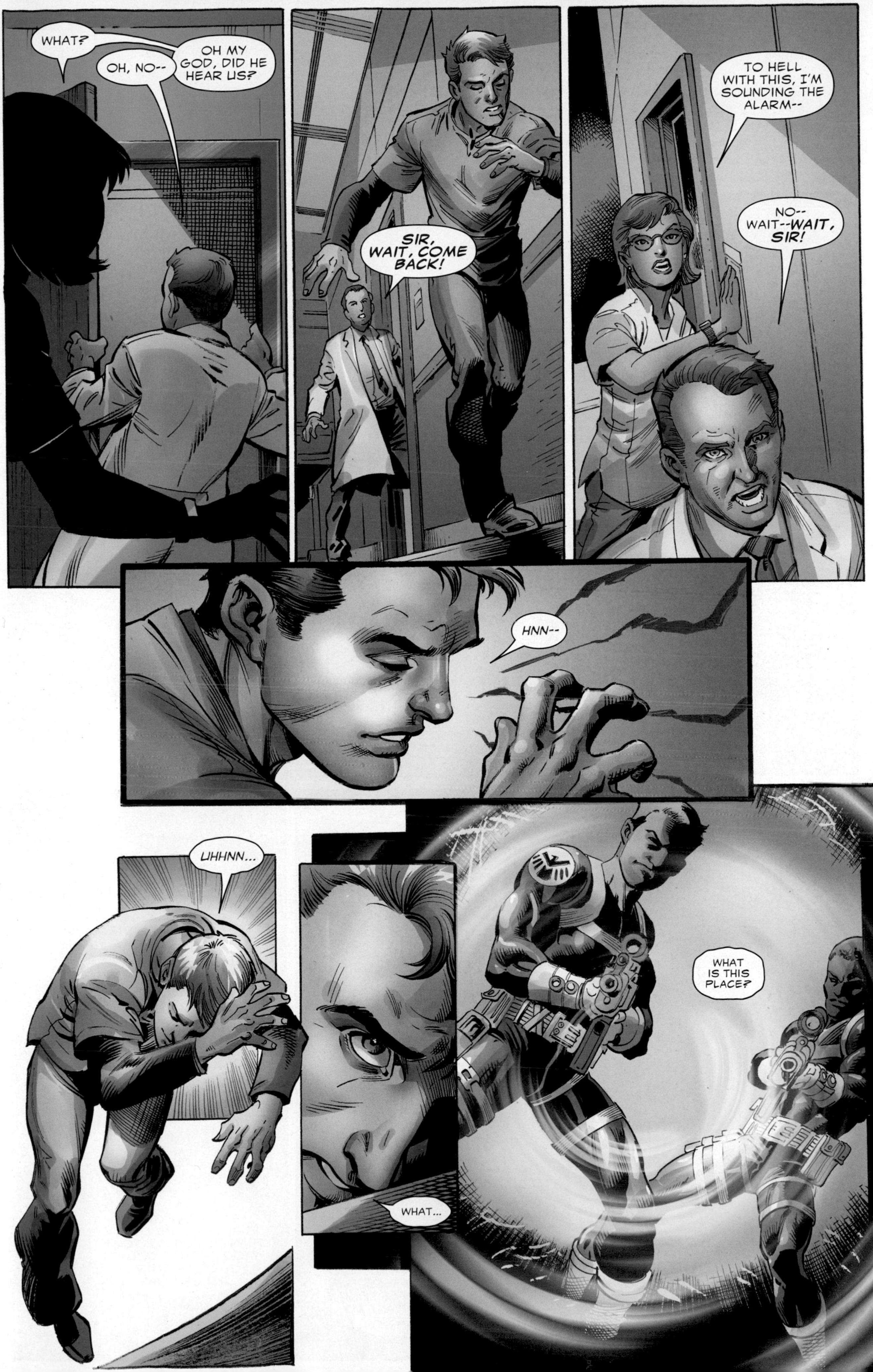
WHAT?
OH, NO--
OH MY GOD, DID HE HEAR US?
SIR, WAIT, COME BACK!
TO HELL WITH THIS, I'M SOUNDING THE ALARM--
NO-- WAIT--WAIT, SIR!
HNN--
UHHNN...
WHAT...
WHAT IS THIS PLACE?

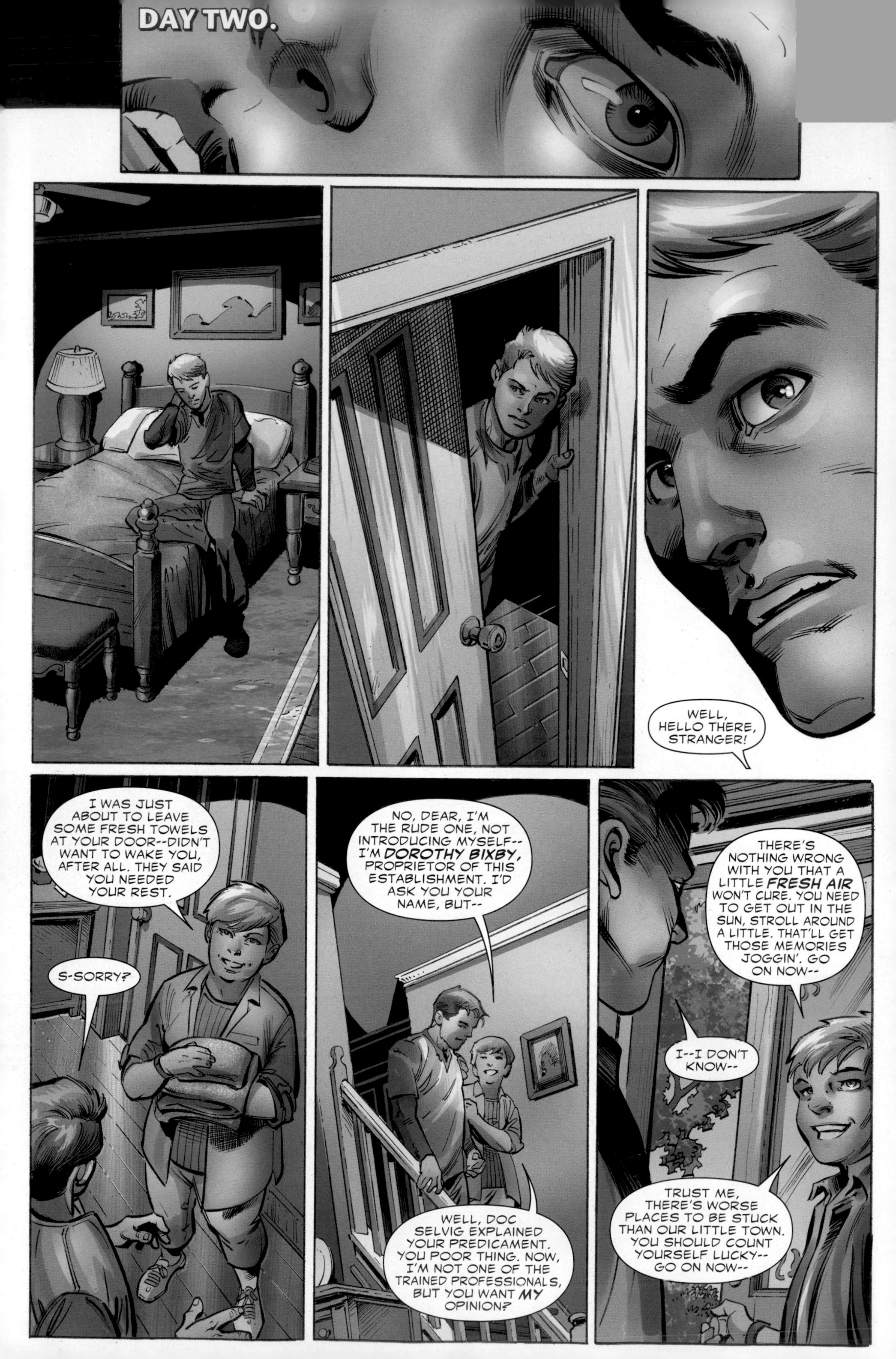
DAY TWO.
WELL, HELLO THERE, STRANGER!
I WAS JUST ABOUT TO LEAVE SOME FRESH TOWELS AT YOUR DOOR--DIDN'T WANT TO WAKE YOU, AFTER ALL. THEY SAID YOU NEEDED YOUR REST.
S-SORRY?
NO, DEAR, I'M THE RUDE ONE, NOT INTRODUCING MYSELF-- I'M DOROTHY BIXBY, PROPRIETOR OF THIS ESTABLISHMENT. I'D ASK YOU YOUR NAME, BUT--
WELL, DOC SELVIG EXPLAINED YOUR PREDICAMENT. YOU POOR THING. NOW, I'M NOT ONE OF THE TRAINED PROFESSIONALS, BUT YOU WANT MY OPINION?
THERE'S NOTHING WRONG WITH YOU THAT A LITTLE FRESH AIR WON'T CURE. YOU NEED TO GET OUT IN THE SUN, STROLL AROUND A LITTLE. THAT'LL GET THOSE MEMORIES JOGGIN'. GO ON NOW--
I--I DON'T KNOW--
TRUST ME, THERE'S WORSE PLACES TO BE STUCK THAN OUR LITTLE TOWN. YOU SHOULD COUNT YOURSELF LUCKY-- GO ON NOW--

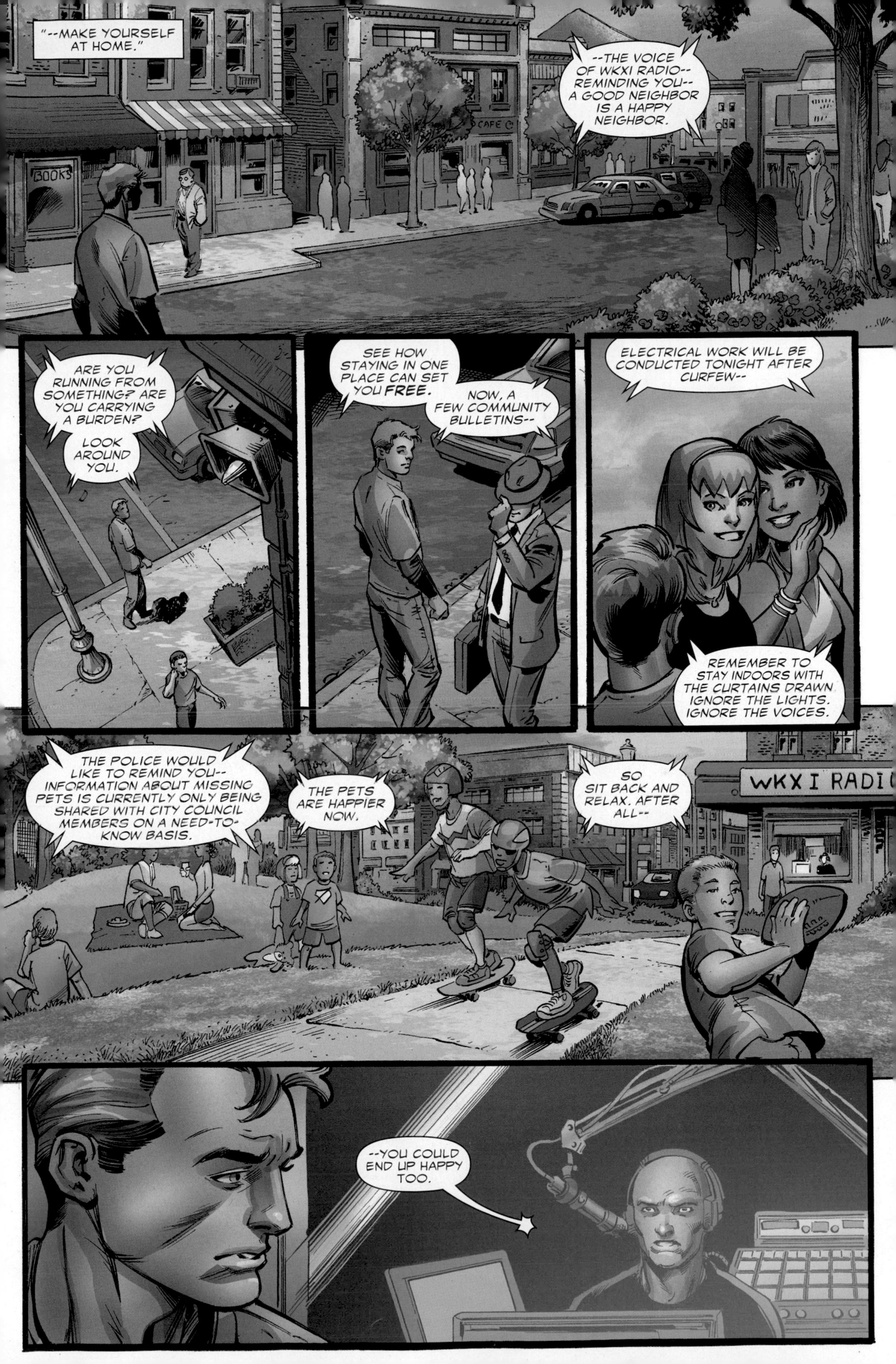
"--MAKE YOURSELF AT HOME."
--THE VOICE OF WKXI RADIO-- REMINDING YOU-- A GOOD NEIGHBOR IS A HAPPY NEIGHBOR.
BOOKS
CAFE
ARE YOU RUNNING FROM SOMETHING? ARE YOU CARRYING A BURDEN?
LOOK AROUND YOU.
SEE HOW STAYING IN ONE PLACE CAN SET YOU **FREE.**
NOW, A FEW COMMUNITY BULLETINS--
ELECTRICAL WORK WILL BE CONDUCTED TONIGHT AFTER CURFEW--
REMEMBER TO STAY INDOORS WITH THE CURTAINS DRAWN. IGNORE THE LIGHTS. IGNORE THE VOICES.
THE POLICE WOULD LIKE TO REMIND YOU-- INFORMATION ABOUT MISSING PETS IS CURRENTLY ONLY BEING SHARED WITH CITY COUNCIL MEMBERS ON A NEED-TO-KNOW BASIS.
THE PETS ARE HAPPIER NOW.
SO SIT BACK AND RELAX. AFTER ALL--
WKXI RADI
--YOU COULD END UP HAPPY TOO.

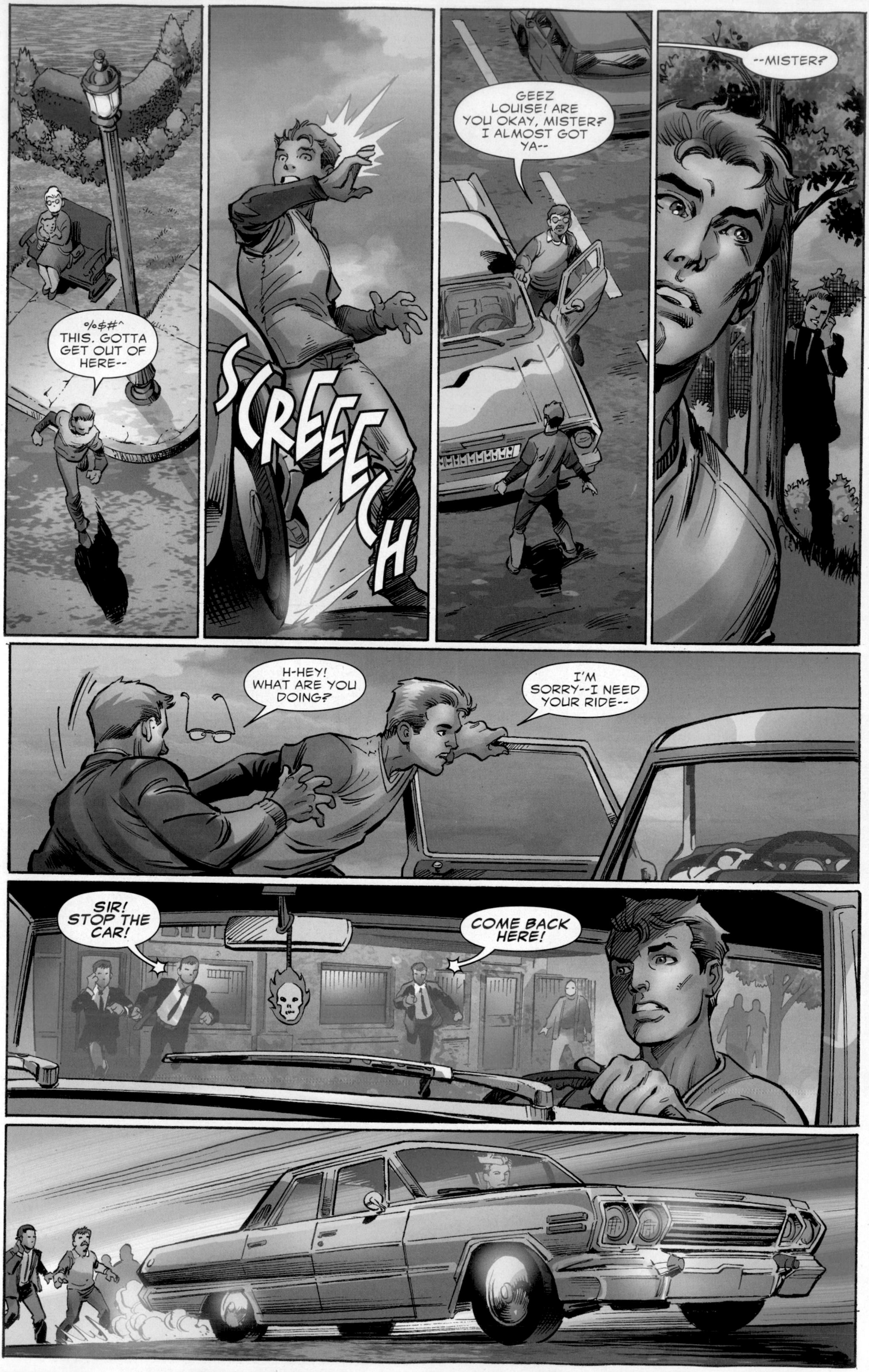
%$#^ THIS. GOTTA GET OUT OF HERE--
SCREEECH
GEEZ LOUISE! ARE YOU OKAY, MISTER? I ALMOST GOT YA--
--MISTER?
H-HEY! WHAT ARE YOU DOING?
I'M SORRY--I NEED YOUR RIDE--
SIR! STOP THE CAR!
COME BACK HERE!

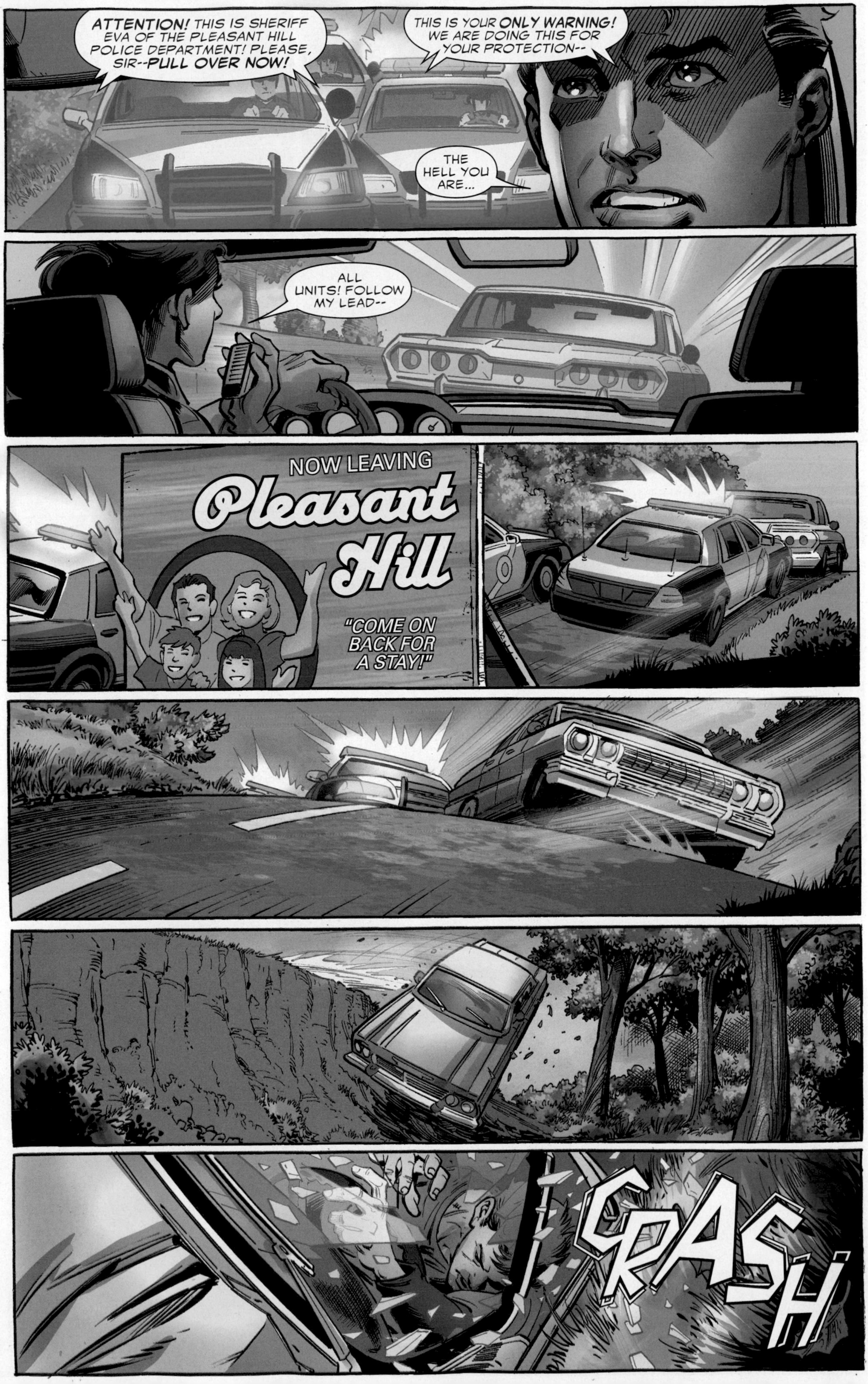
ATTENTION! THIS IS SHERIFF EVA OF THE PLEASANT HILL POLICE DEPARTMENT! PLEASE, SIR--PULL OVER NOW!
THIS IS YOUR ONLY WARNING! WE ARE DOING THIS FOR YOUR PROTECTION--
THE HELL YOU ARE...
ALL UNITS! FOLLOW MY LEAD--
NOW LEAVING
Pleasant Hill
"COME ON BACK FOR A STAY!"
CRASH

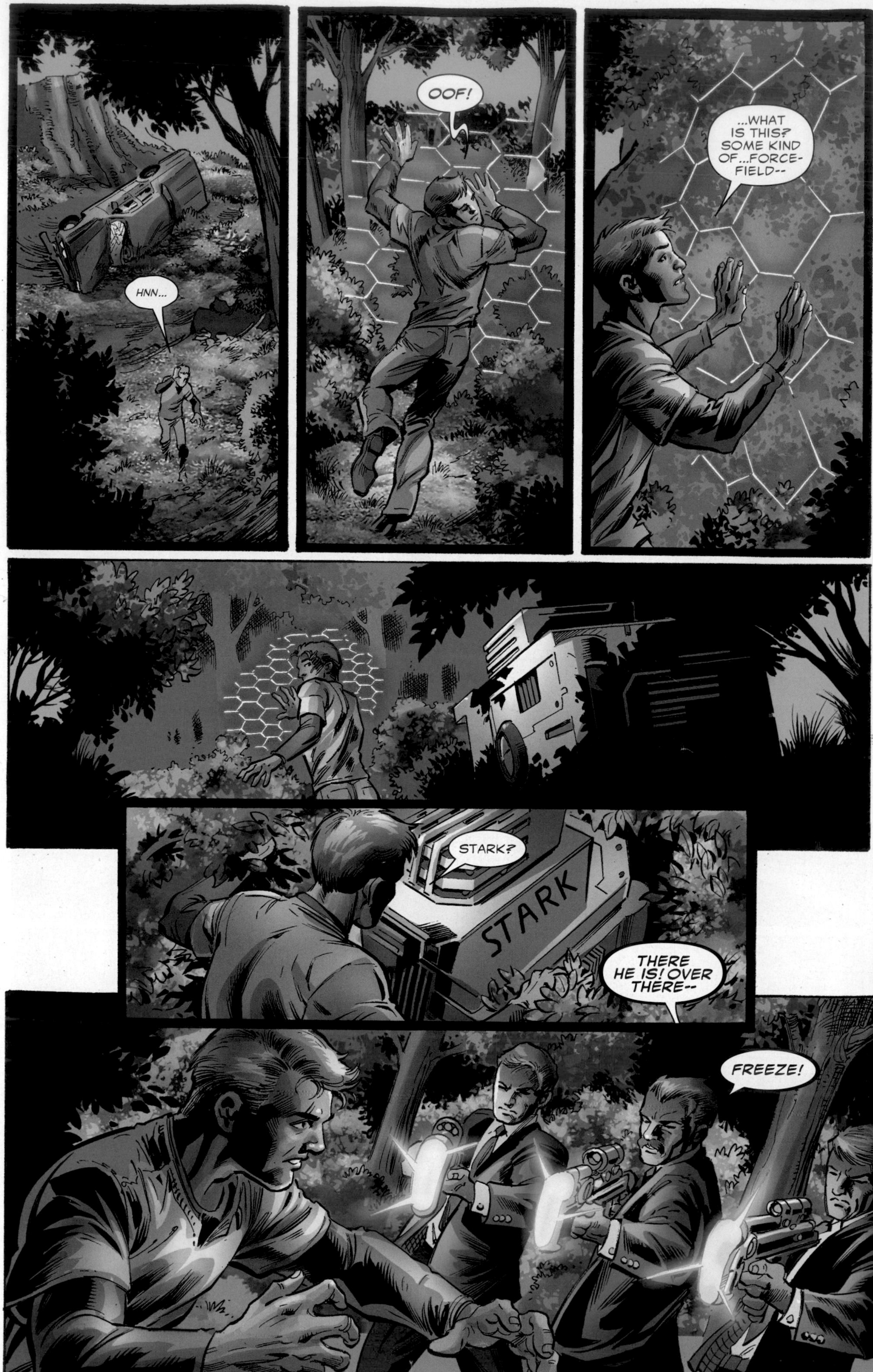
HNN...
OOF!
...WHAT IS THIS? SOME KIND OF...FORCE-FIELD--
STARK?
STARK
STARK
THERE HE IS! OVER THERE--
FREEZE!

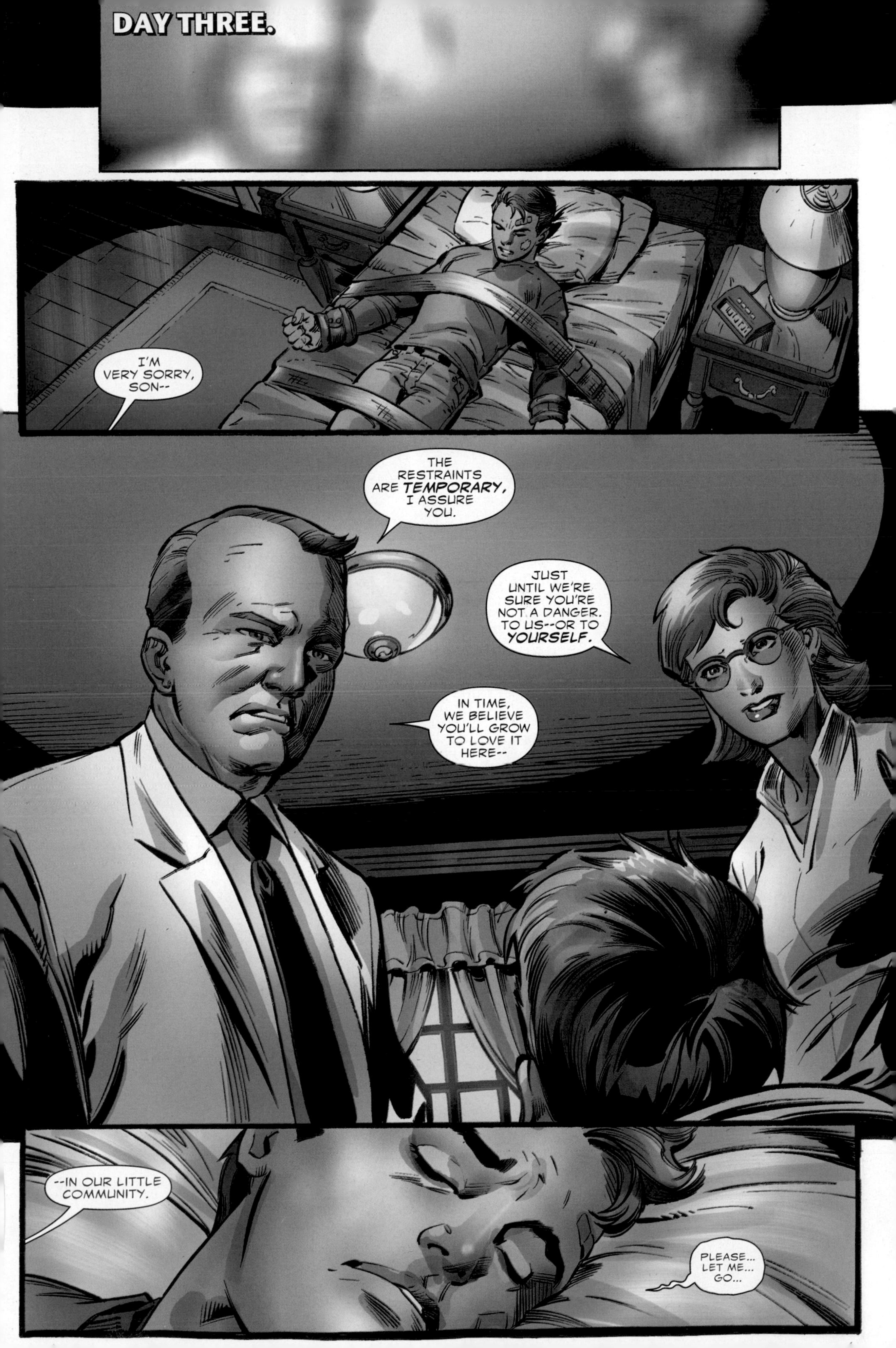
DAY THREE.
I'M VERY SORRY, SON--
THE RESTRAINTS ARE TEMPORARY, I ASSURE YOU.
JUST UNTIL WE'RE SURE YOU'RE NOT A DANGER. TO US--OR TO YOURSELF.
IN TIME, WE BELIEVE YOU'LL GROW TO LOVE IT HERE--
--IN OUR LITTLE COMMUNITY.
PLEASE... LET ME... GO...

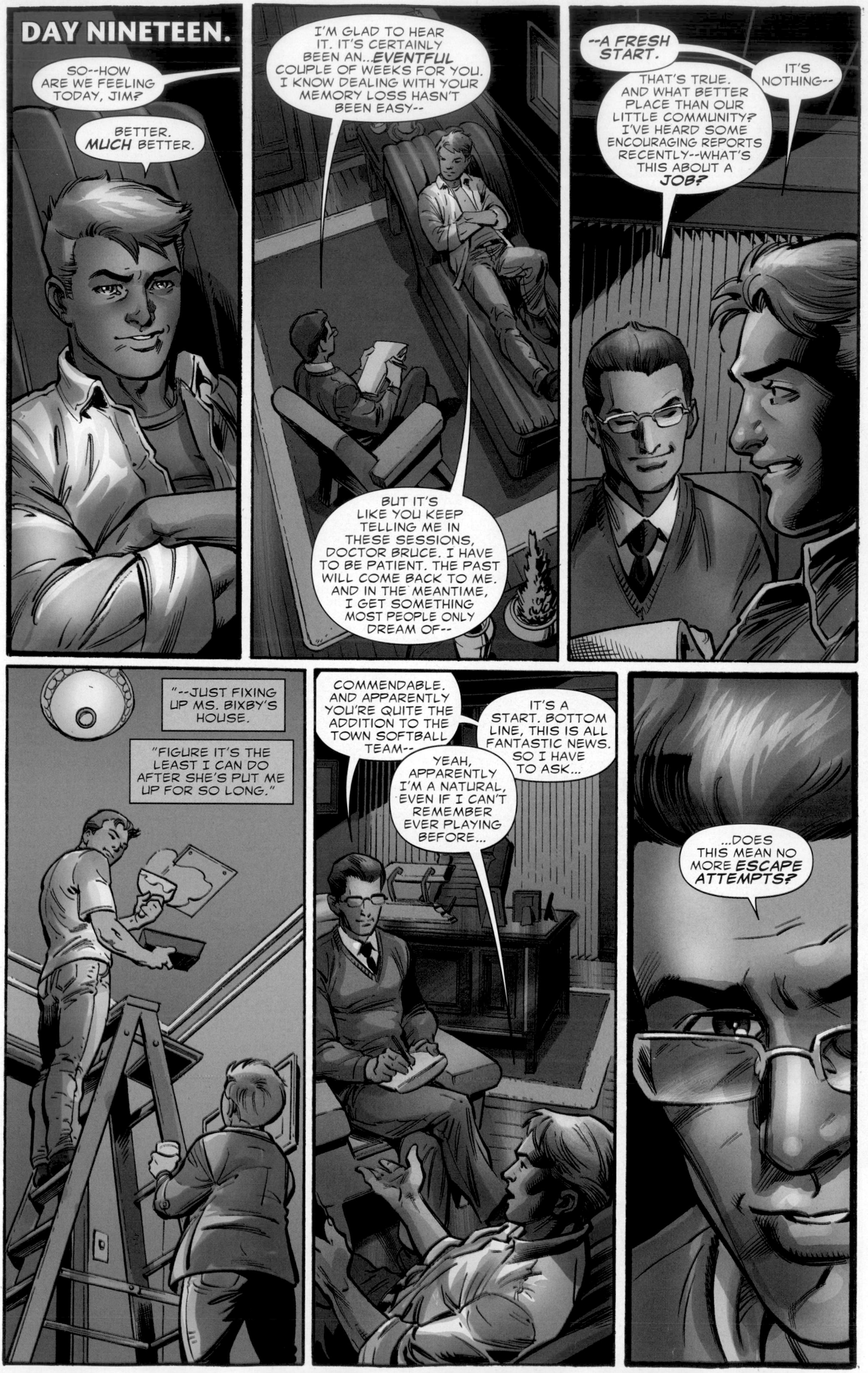
DAY NINETEEN.
SO--HOW ARE WE FEELING TODAY, JIM?
BETTER. MUCH BETTER.
I'M GLAD TO HEAR IT. IT'S CERTAINLY BEEN AN...EVENTFUL COUPLE OF WEEKS FOR YOU. I KNOW DEALING WITH YOUR MEMORY LOSS HASN'T BEEN EASY--
BUT IT'S LIKE YOU KEEP TELLING ME IN THESE SESSIONS, DOCTOR BRUCE. I HAVE TO BE PATIENT. THE PAST WILL COME BACK TO ME. AND IN THE MEANTIME, I GET SOMETHING MOST PEOPLE ONLY DREAM OF--
--A FRESH START.
THAT'S TRUE. AND WHAT BETTER PLACE THAN OUR LITTLE COMMUNITY? I'VE HEARD SOME ENCOURAGING REPORTS RECENTLY--WHAT'S THIS ABOUT A JOB?
IT'S NOTHING--
"--JUST FIXING UP MS. BIXBY'S HOUSE.
"FIGURE IT'S THE LEAST I CAN DO AFTER SHE'S PUT ME UP FOR SO LONG."
COMMENDABLE. AND APPARENTLY YOU'RE QUITE THE ADDITION TO THE TOWN SOFTBALL TEAM--
YEAH, APPARENTLY I'M A NATURAL, EVEN IF I CAN'T REMEMBER EVER PLAYING BEFORE...
IT'S A START. BOTTOM LINE, THIS IS ALL FANTASTIC NEWS. SO I HAVE TO ASK...
...DOES THIS MEAN NO MORE ESCAPE ATTEMPTS?

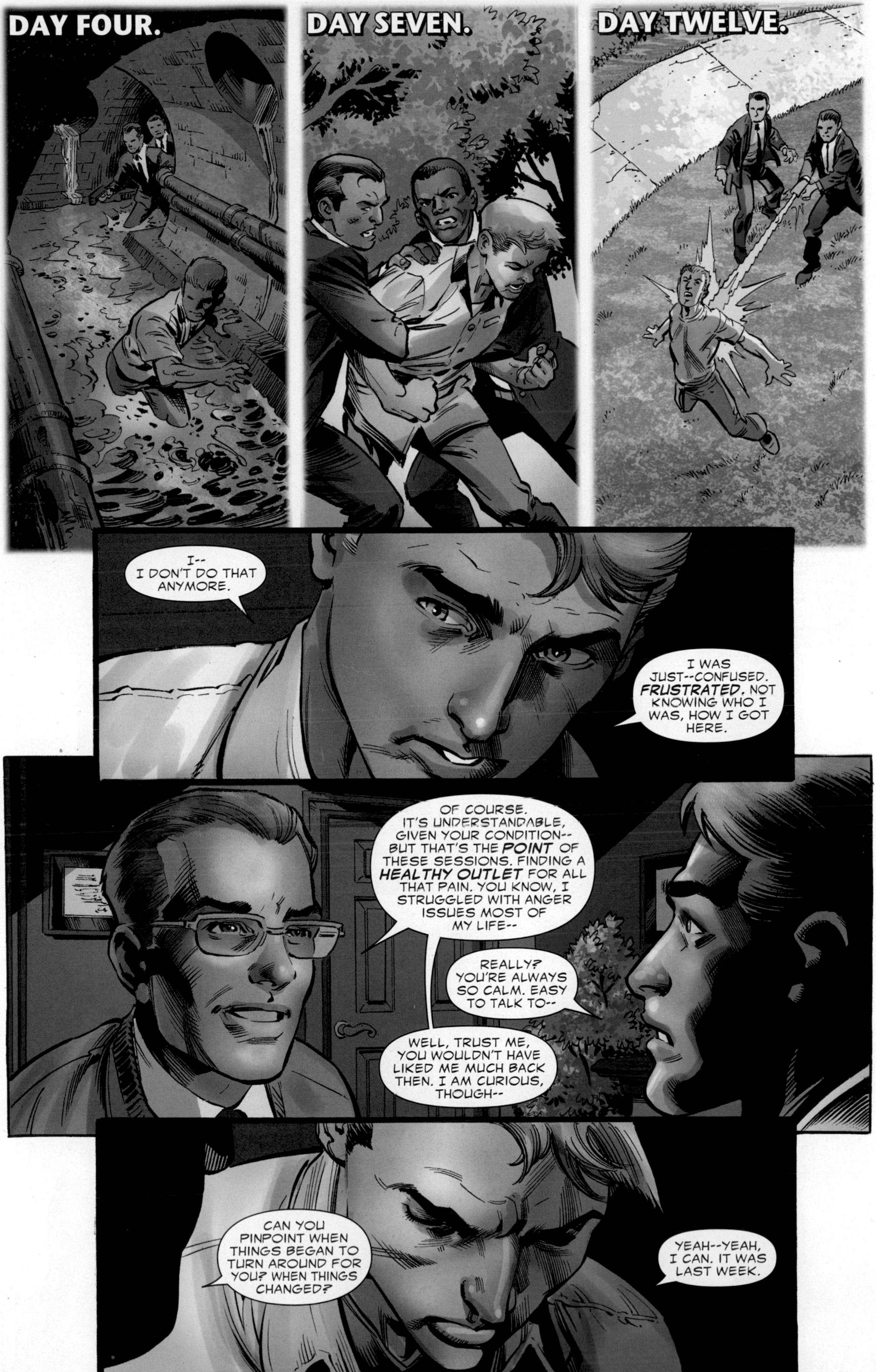
DAY FOUR.
DAY SEVEN.
DAY TWELVE.
I-- I DON'T DO THAT ANYMORE.
I WAS JUST--CONFUSED. FRUSTRATED. NOT KNOWING WHO I WAS, HOW I GOT HERE.
OF COURSE. IT'S UNDERSTANDABLE, GIVEN YOUR CONDITION-- BUT THAT'S THE POINT OF THESE SESSIONS. FINDING A HEALTHY OUTLET FOR ALL THAT PAIN. YOU KNOW, I STRUGGLED WITH ANGER ISSUES MOST OF MY LIFE--
REALLY? YOU'RE ALWAYS SO CALM. EASY TO TALK TO--
WELL, TRUST ME, YOU WOULDN'T HAVE LIKED ME MUCH BACK THEN. I AM CURIOUS, THOUGH--
CAN YOU PINPOINT WHEN THINGS BEGAN TO TURN AROUND FOR YOU? WHEN THINGS CHANGED?
YEAH--YEAH, I CAN. IT WAS LAST WEEK.

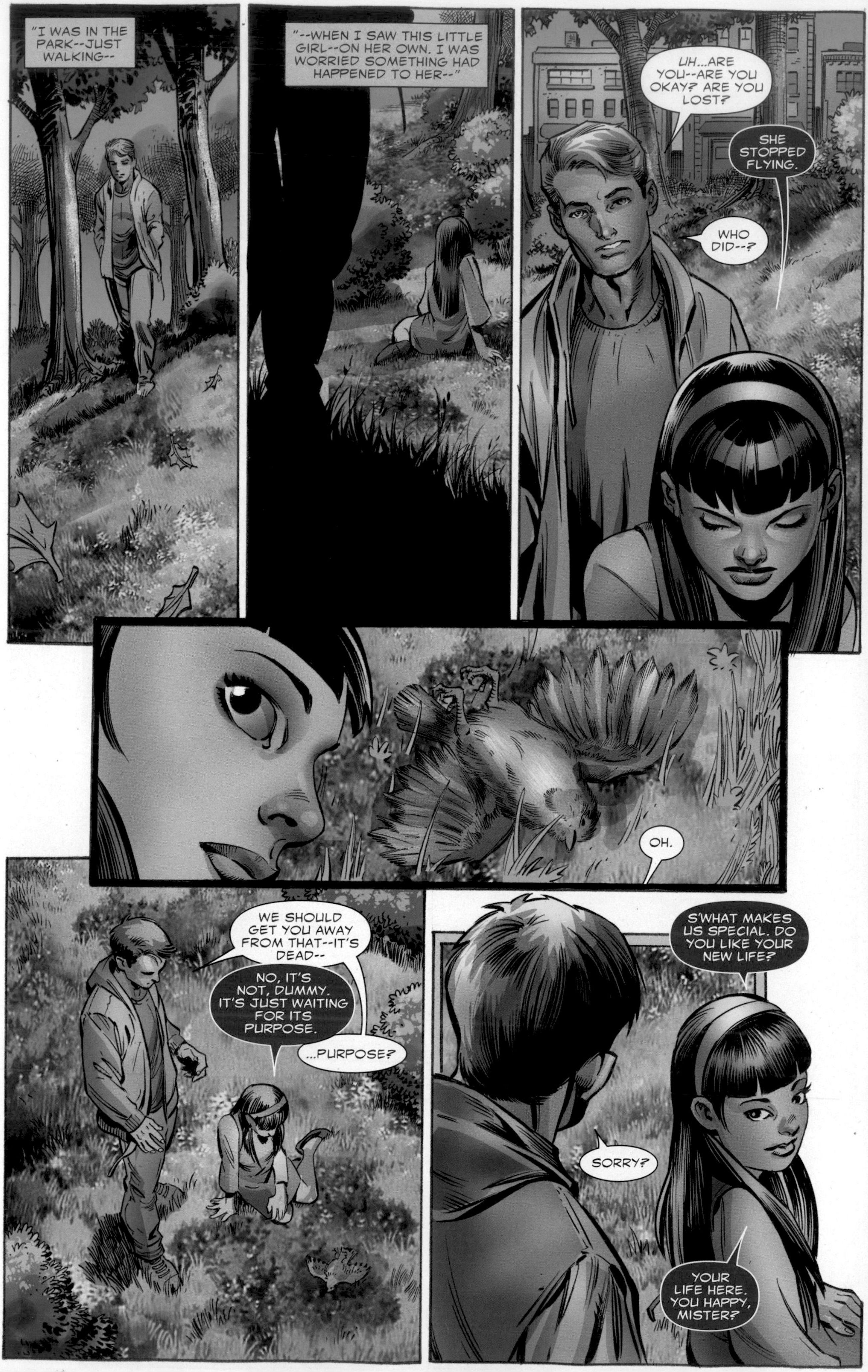

"I WAS IN THE PARK--JUST WALKING--
"--WHEN I SAW THIS LITTLE GIRL--ON HER OWN. I WAS WORRIED SOMETHING HAD HAPPENED TO HER--"
UH...ARE YOU--ARE YOU OKAY? ARE YOU LOST?
SHE STOPPED FLYING.
WHO DID--?
OH.
WE SHOULD GET YOU AWAY FROM THAT--IT'S DEAD--
NO, IT'S NOT, DUMMY. IT'S JUST WAITING FOR ITS PURPOSE.
...PURPOSE?
S'WHAT MAKES US SPECIAL. DO YOU LIKE YOUR NEW LIFE?
SORRY?
YOUR LIFE HERE. YOU HAPPY, MISTER?

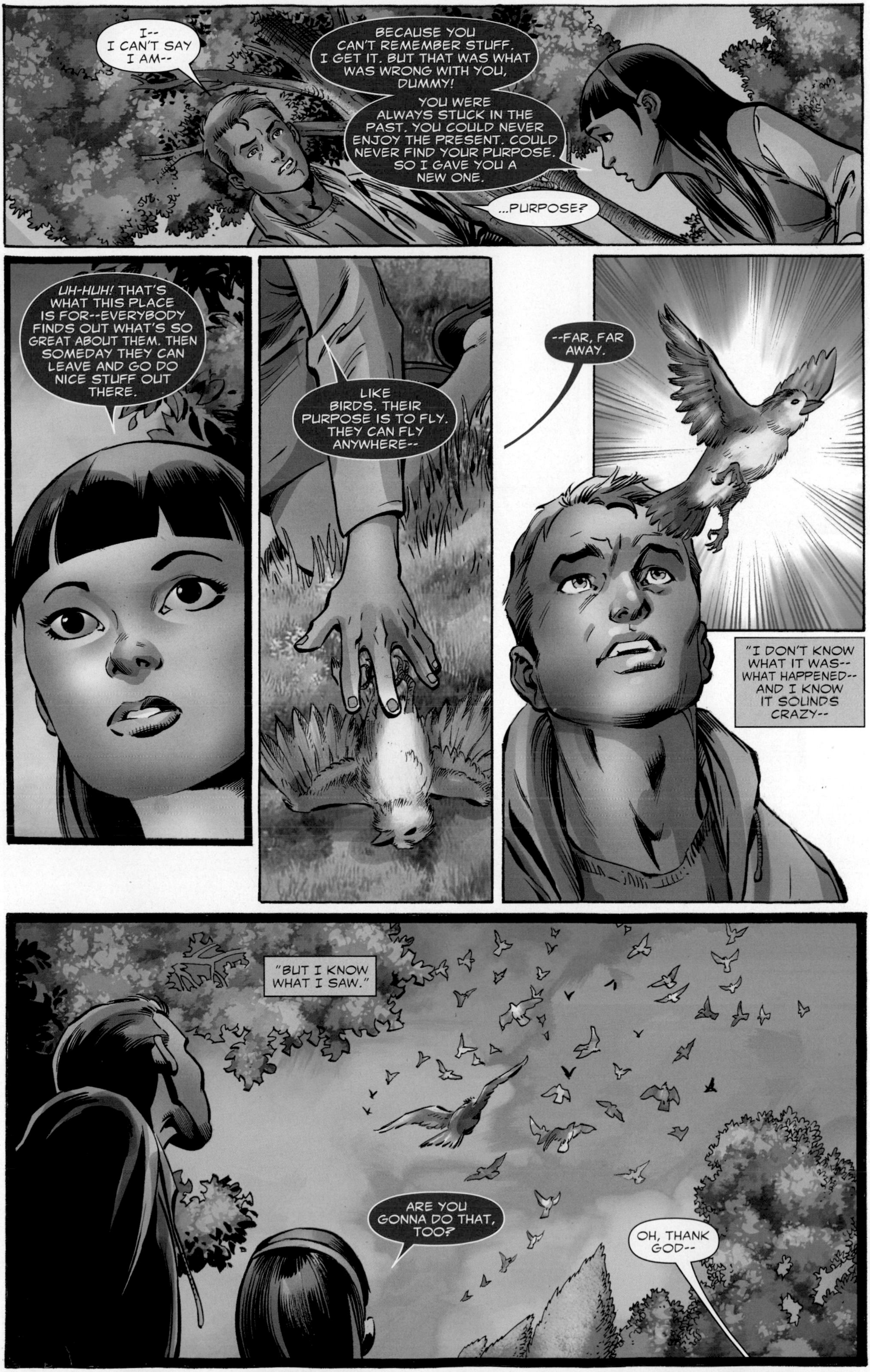
I-- I CAN'T SAY I AM--
BECAUSE YOU CAN'T REMEMBER STUFF. I GET IT. BUT THAT WAS WHAT WAS WRONG WITH YOU, DUMMY!
YOU WERE ALWAYS STUCK IN THE PAST. YOU COULD NEVER ENJOY THE PRESENT. COULD NEVER FIND YOUR PURPOSE. SO I GAVE YOU A NEW ONE.
...PURPOSE?
UH-HUH! THAT'S WHAT THIS PLACE IS FOR--EVERYBODY FINDS OUT WHAT'S SO GREAT ABOUT THEM. THEN SOMEDAY THEY CAN LEAVE AND GO DO NICE STUFF OUT THERE.
LIKE BIRDS. THEIR PURPOSE IS TO FLY. THEY CAN FLY ANYWHERE--
--FAR, FAR AWAY.
"I DON'T KNOW WHAT IT WAS-- WHAT HAPPENED-- AND I KNOW IT SOUNDS CRAZY--
"BUT I KNOW WHAT I SAW."
ARE YOU GONNA DO THAT, TOO?
OH, THANK GOD--

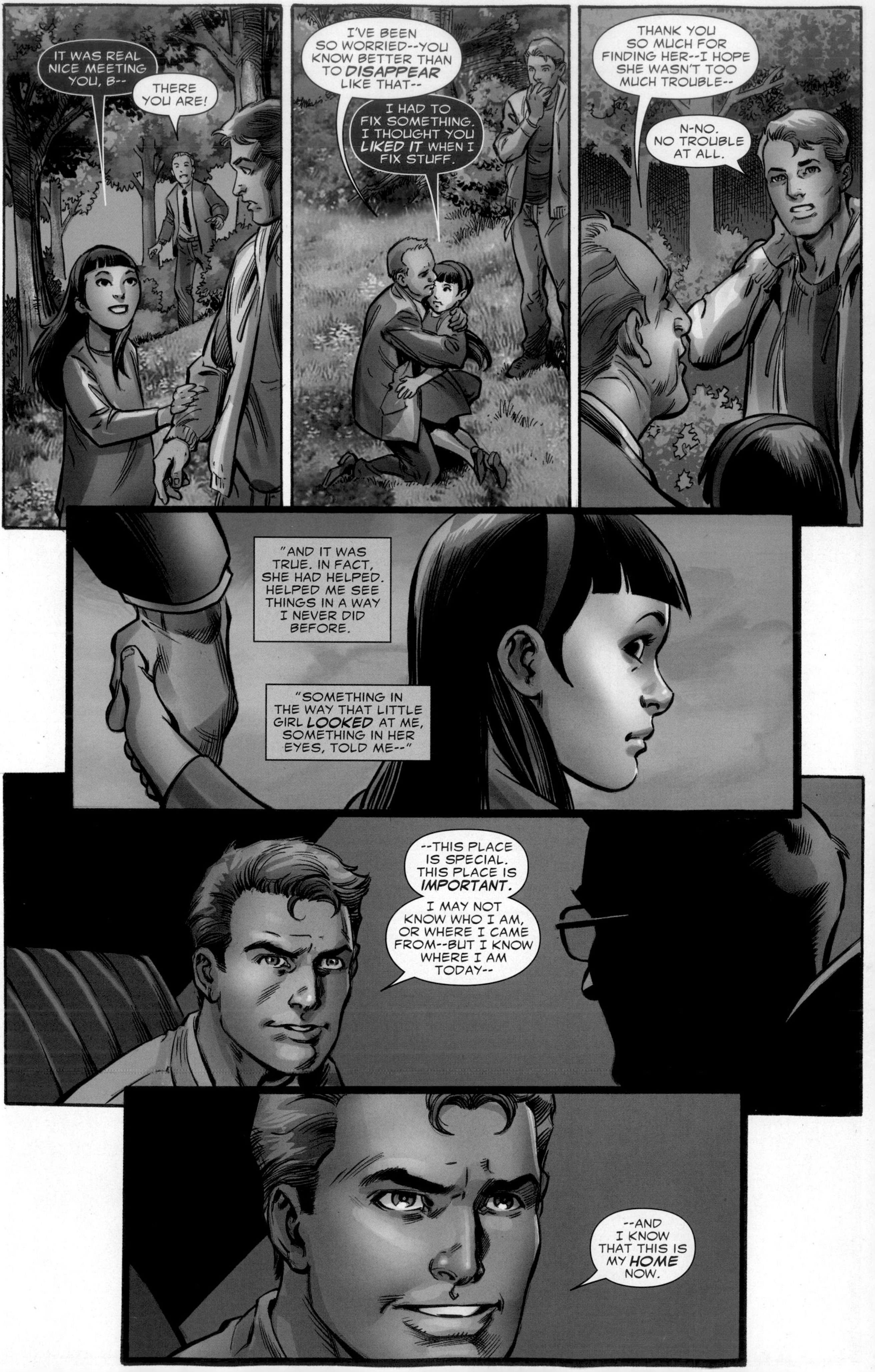
IT WAS REAL NICE MEETING YOU, B--
THERE YOU ARE!
I'VE BEEN SO WORRIED--YOU KNOW BETTER THAN TO DISAPPEAR LIKE THAT--
I HAD TO FIX SOMETHING. I THOUGHT YOU LIKED IT WHEN I FIX STUFF.
THANK YOU SO MUCH FOR FINDING HER--I HOPE SHE WASN'T TOO MUCH TROUBLE--
N-NO. NO TROUBLE AT ALL.
"AND IT WAS TRUE. IN FACT, SHE HAD HELPED. HELPED ME SEE THINGS IN A WAY I NEVER DID BEFORE.
"SOMETHING IN THE WAY THAT LITTLE GIRL LOOKED AT ME, SOMETHING IN HER EYES, TOLD ME--"
--THIS PLACE IS SPECIAL. THIS PLACE IS IMPORTANT.
I MAY NOT KNOW WHO I AM, OR WHERE I CAME FROM--BUT I KNOW WHERE I AM TODAY--
--AND I KNOW THAT THIS IS MY HOME NOW.

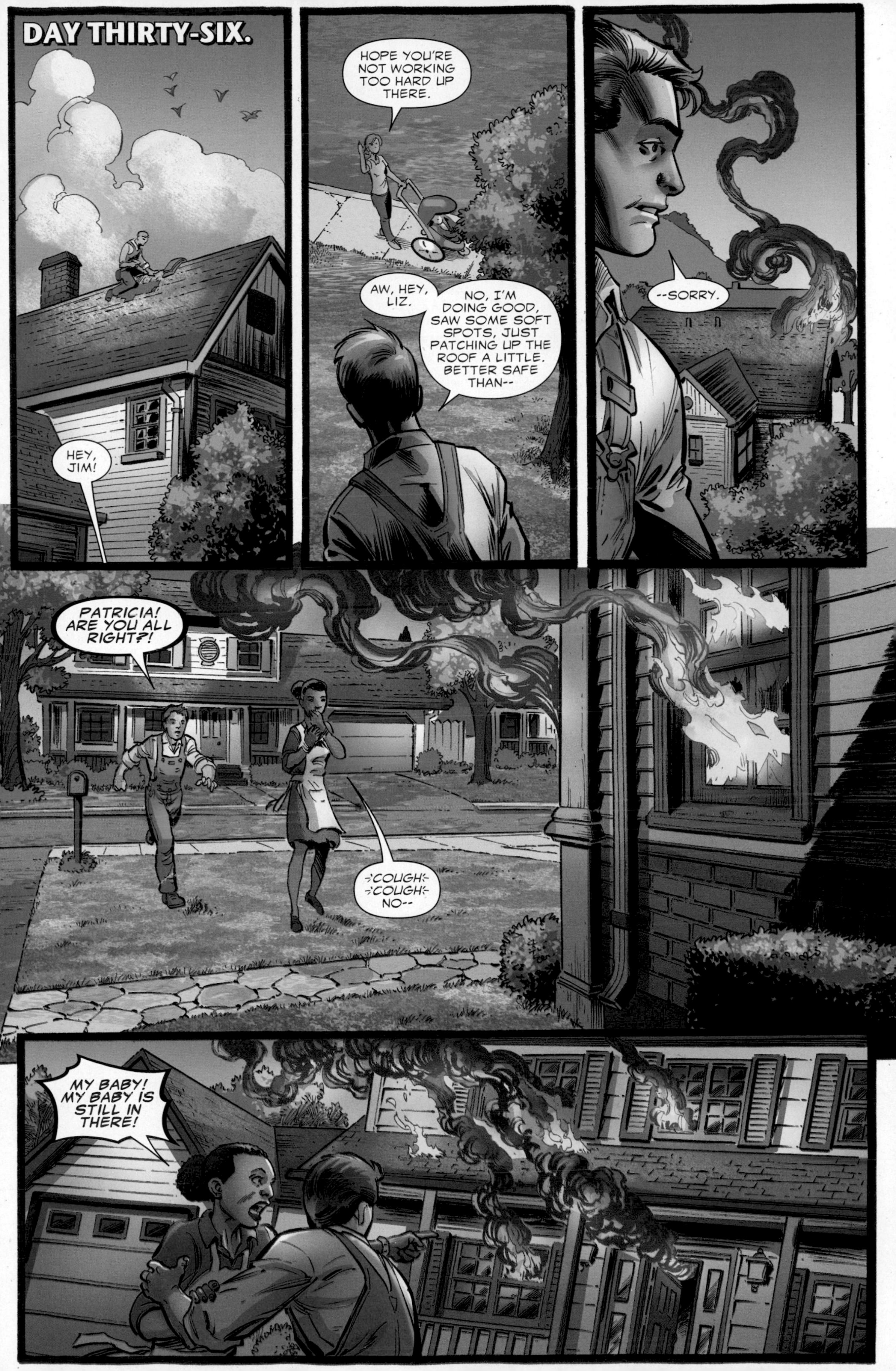
DAY THIRTY-SIX.
HEY, JIM!
HOPE YOU'RE NOT WORKING TOO HARD UP THERE.
AW, HEY, LIZ.
NO, I'M DOING GOOD, SAW SOME SOFT SPOTS, JUST PATCHING UP THE ROOF A LITTLE. BETTER SAFE THAN--
--SORRY.
PATRICIA! ARE YOU ALL RIGHT?!
COUGH COUGH NO--
MY BABY! MY BABY IS STILL IN THERE!

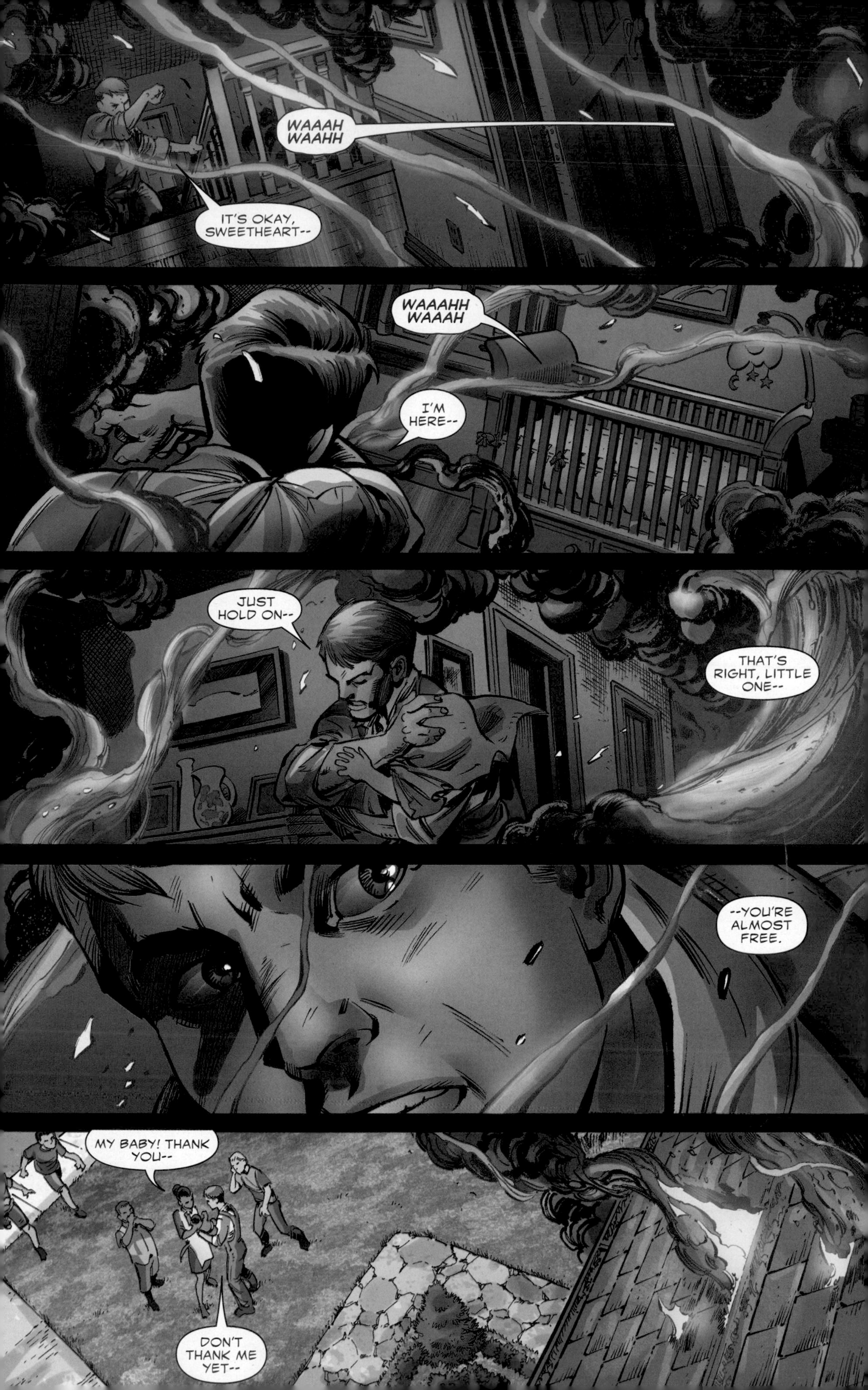
WAAAH WAAHH
IT'S OKAY, SWEETHEART--
WAAAHH WAAAH
I'M HERE--
JUST HOLD ON--
THAT'S RIGHT, LITTLE ONE--
--YOU'RE ALMOST FREE.
MY BABY! THANK YOU--
DON'T THANK ME YET--

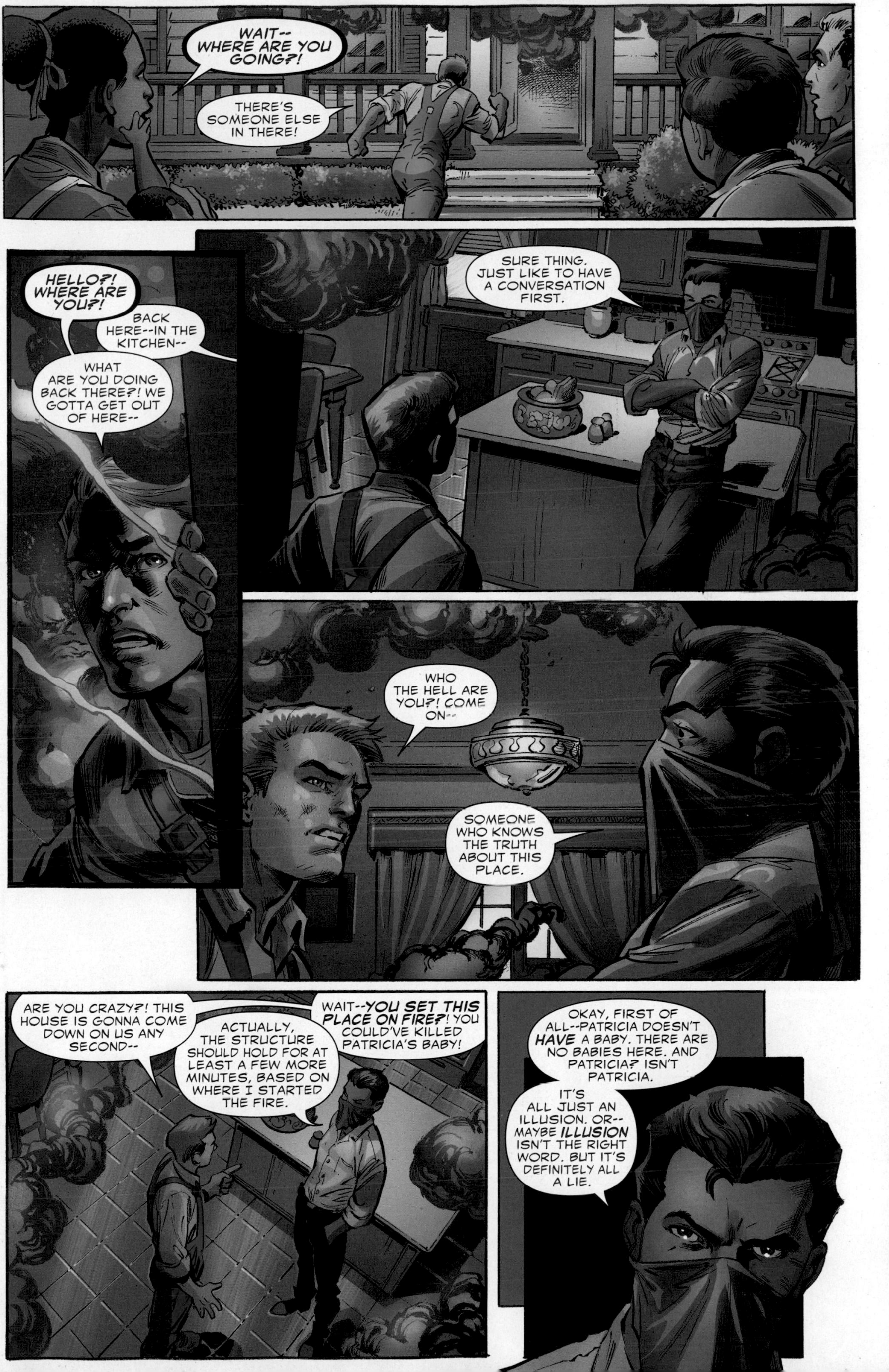
WAIT-- WHERE ARE YOU GOING?!
THERE'S SOMEONE ELSE IN THERE!
HELLO?! WHERE ARE YOU?!
BACK HERE--IN THE KITCHEN--
WHAT ARE YOU DOING BACK THERE?! WE GOTTA GET OUT OF HERE--
SURE THING. JUST LIKE TO HAVE A CONVERSATION FIRST.
WHO THE HELL ARE YOU?! COME ON--
SOMEONE WHO KNOWS THE TRUTH ABOUT THIS PLACE.
ARE YOU CRAZY?! THIS HOUSE IS GONNA COME DOWN ON US ANY SECOND--
ACTUALLY, THE STRUCTURE SHOULD HOLD FOR AT LEAST A FEW MORE MINUTES, BASED ON WHERE I STARTED THE FIRE.
WAIT--YOU SET THIS PLACE ON FIRE?! YOU COULD'VE KILLED PATRICIA'S BABY!
OKAY, FIRST OF ALL--PATRICIA DOESN'T HAVE A BABY. THERE ARE NO BABIES HERE. AND PATRICIA? ISN'T PATRICIA.
IT'S ALL JUST AN ILLUSION. OR-- MAYBE ILLUSION ISN'T THE RIGHT WORD. BUT IT'S DEFINITELY ALL A LIE.

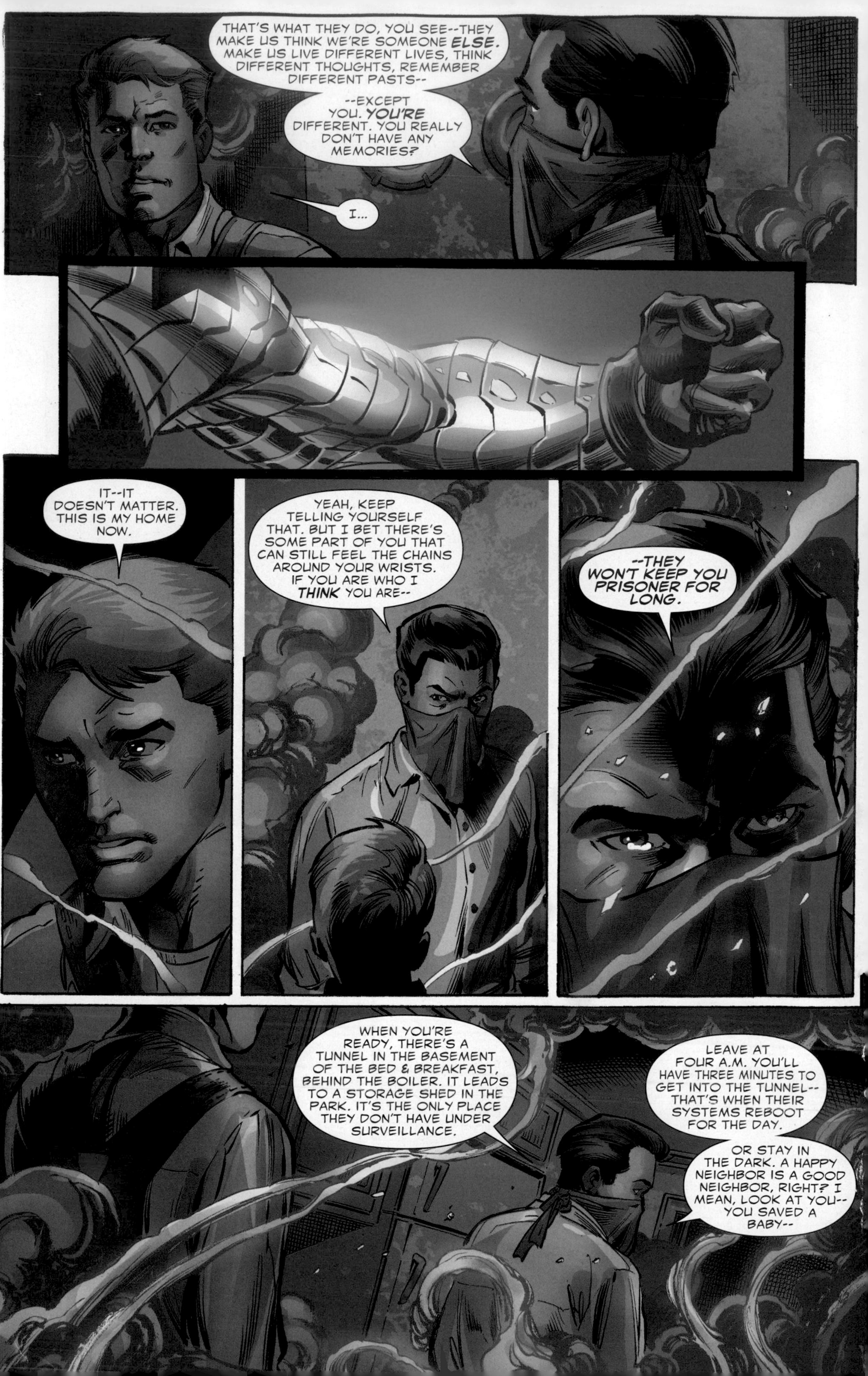
THAT'S WHAT THEY DO, YOU SEE--THEY MAKE US THINK WE'RE SOMEONE ELSE. MAKE US LIVE DIFFERENT LIVES, THINK DIFFERENT THOUGHTS, REMEMBER DIFFERENT PASTS--
--EXCEPT YOU. YOU'RE DIFFERENT. YOU REALLY DON'T HAVE ANY MEMORIES?
I...
IT--IT DOESN'T MATTER. THIS IS MY HOME NOW.
YEAH, KEEP TELLING YOURSELF THAT. BUT I BET THERE'S SOME PART OF YOU THAT CAN STILL FEEL THE CHAINS AROUND YOUR WRISTS. IF YOU ARE WHO I THINK YOU ARE--
--THEY WON'T KEEP YOU PRISONER FOR LONG.
WHEN YOU'RE READY, THERE'S A TUNNEL IN THE BASEMENT OF THE BED & BREAKFAST, BEHIND THE BOILER. IT LEADS TO A STORAGE SHED IN THE PARK. IT'S THE ONLY PLACE THEY DON'T HAVE UNDER SURVEILLANCE.
LEAVE AT FOUR A.M. YOU'LL HAVE THREE MINUTES TO GET INTO THE TUNNEL--THAT'S WHEN THEIR SYSTEMS REBOOT FOR THE DAY.
OR STAY IN THE DARK. A HAPPY NEIGHBOR IS A GOOD NEIGHBOR, RIGHT? I MEAN, LOOK AT YOU--YOU SAVED A BABY--

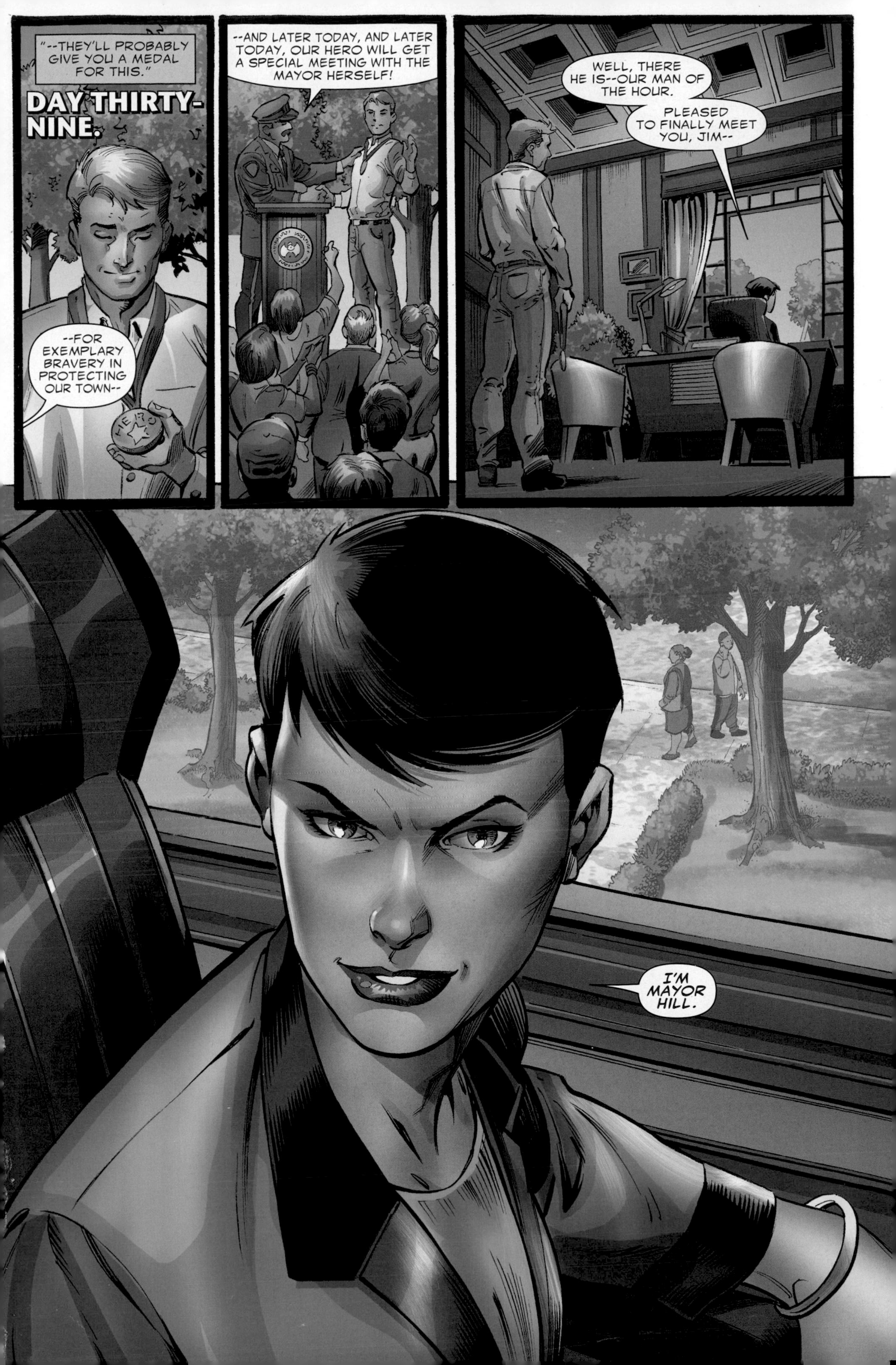
"--THEY'LL PROBABLY GIVE YOU A MEDAL FOR THIS."
DAY THIRTY-NINE.
--FOR EXEMPLARY BRAVERY IN PROTECTING OUR TOWN--
HERO
--AND LATER TODAY, AND LATER TODAY, OUR HERO WILL GET A SPECIAL MEETING WITH THE MAYOR HERSELF!
WELL, THERE HE IS--OUR MAN OF THE HOUR.
PLEASED TO FINALLY MEET YOU, JIM--
I'M MAYOR HILL.

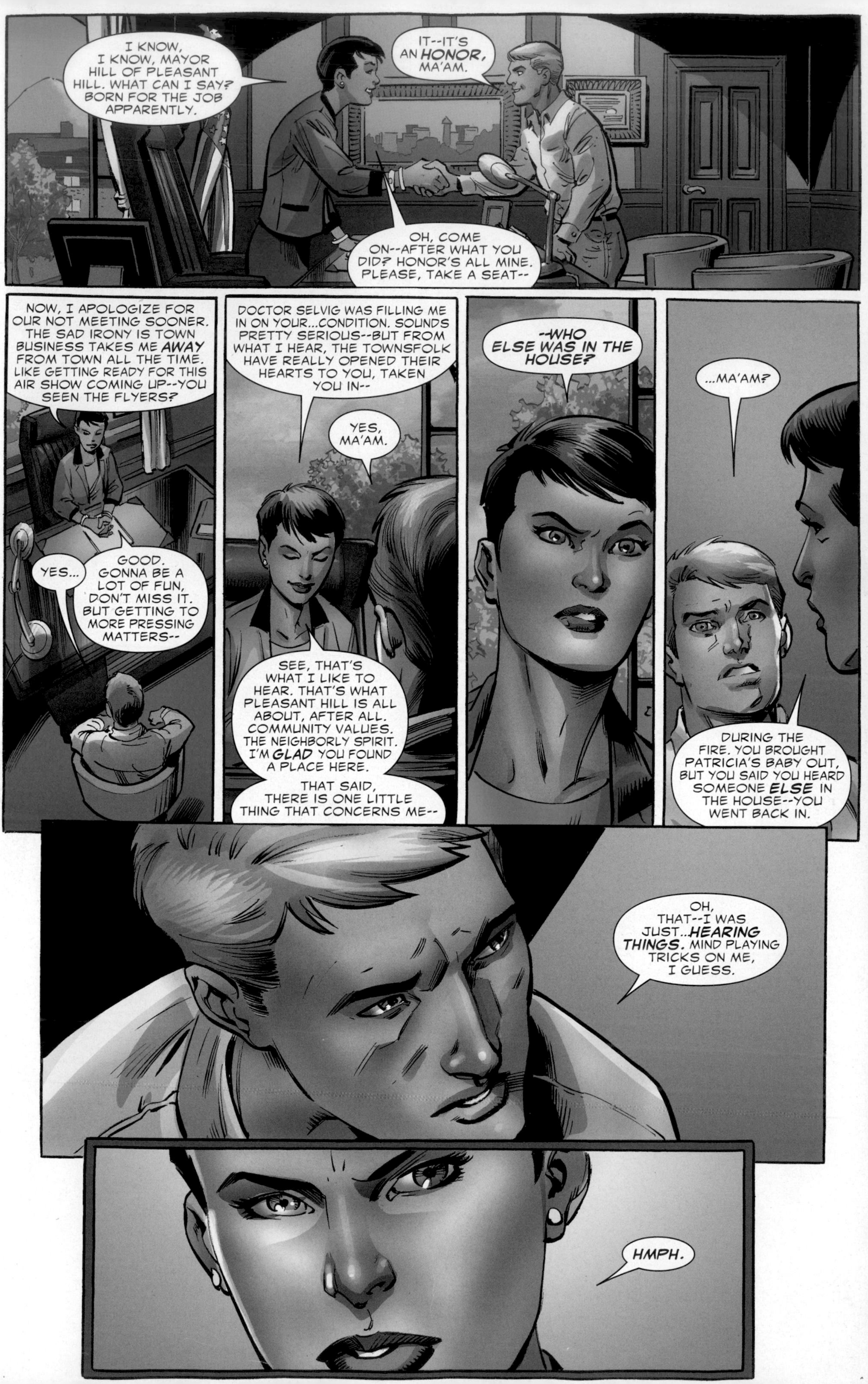
I KNOW, I KNOW, MAYOR HILL OF PLEASANT HILL. WHAT CAN I SAY? BORN FOR THE JOB APPARENTLY.
IT--IT'S AN HONOR, MA'AM.
OH, COME ON--AFTER WHAT YOU DID? HONOR'S ALL MINE. PLEASE, TAKE A SEAT--
NOW, I APOLOGIZE FOR OUR NOT MEETING SOONER. THE SAD IRONY IS TOWN BUSINESS TAKES ME AWAY FROM TOWN ALL THE TIME. LIKE GETTING READY FOR THIS AIR SHOW COMING UP--YOU SEEN THE FLYERS?
YES...
GOOD. GONNA BE A LOT OF FUN, DON'T MISS IT. BUT GETTING TO MORE PRESSING MATTERS--
DOCTOR SELVIG WAS FILLING ME IN ON YOUR...CONDITION. SOUNDS PRETTY SERIOUS--BUT FROM WHAT I HEAR, THE TOWNSFOLK HAVE REALLY OPENED THEIR HEARTS TO YOU, TAKEN YOU IN--
YES, MA'AM.
SEE, THAT'S WHAT I LIKE TO HEAR. THAT'S WHAT PLEASANT HILL IS ALL ABOUT, AFTER ALL. COMMUNITY VALUES. THE NEIGHBORLY SPIRIT. I'M GLAD YOU FOUND A PLACE HERE.
THAT SAID, THERE IS ONE LITTLE THING THAT CONCERNS ME--
--WHO ELSE WAS IN THE HOUSE?
...MA'AM?
DURING THE FIRE. YOU BROUGHT PATRICIA'S BABY OUT, BUT YOU SAID YOU HEARD SOMEONE ELSE IN THE HOUSE--YOU WENT BACK IN.
OH, THAT--I WAS JUST...HEARING THINGS. MIND PLAYING TRICKS ON ME, I GUESS.
HMPH.

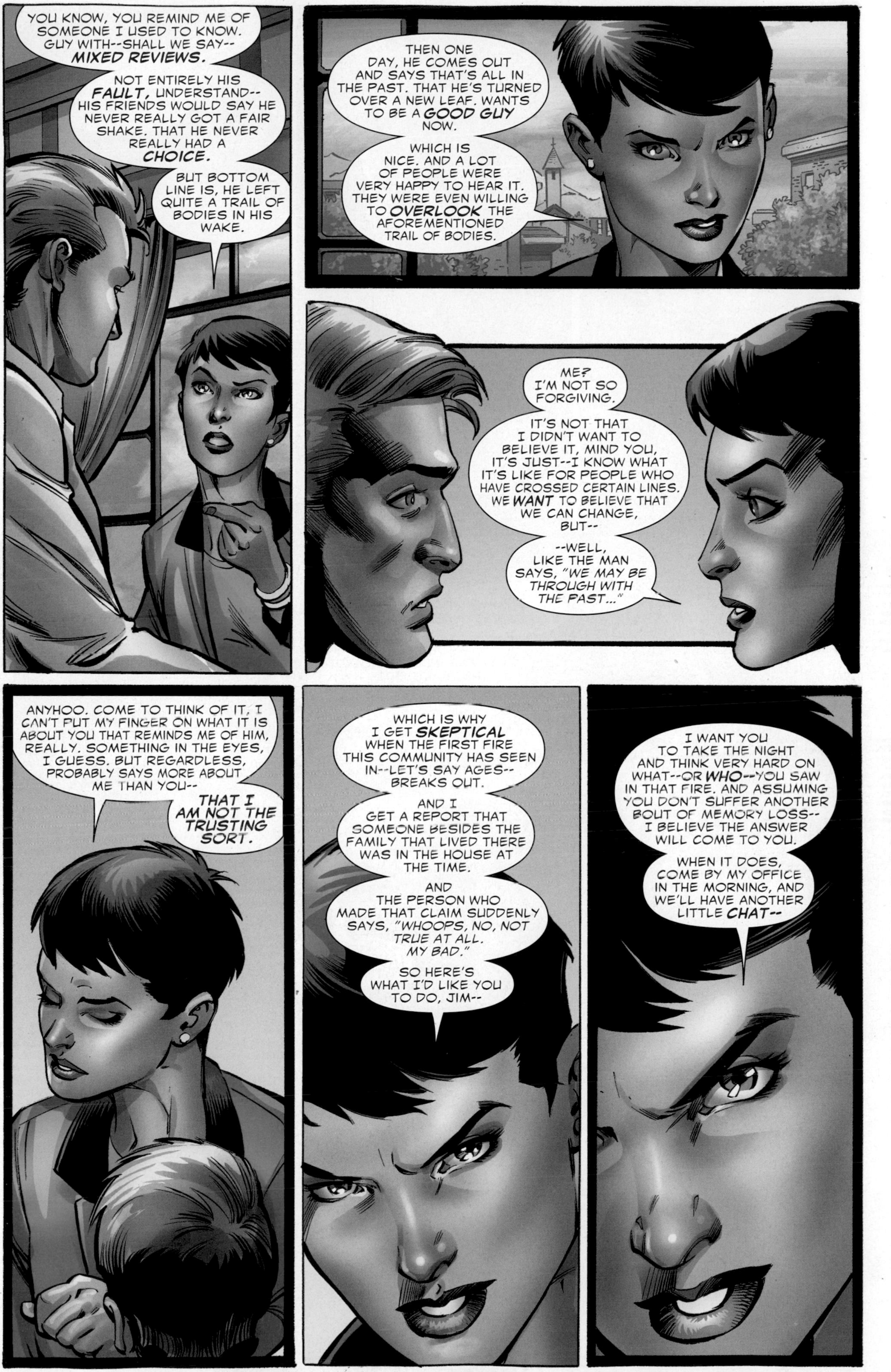
YOU KNOW, YOU REMIND ME OF SOMEONE I USED TO KNOW. GUY WITH--SHALL WE SAY-- MIXED REVIEWS.
NOT ENTIRELY HIS FAULT, UNDERSTAND--HIS FRIENDS WOULD SAY HE NEVER REALLY GOT A FAIR SHAKE. THAT HE NEVER REALLY HAD A CHOICE.
BUT BOTTOM LINE IS, HE LEFT QUITE A TRAIL OF BODIES IN HIS WAKE.
THEN ONE DAY, HE COMES OUT AND SAYS THAT'S ALL IN THE PAST. THAT HE'S TURNED OVER A NEW LEAF. WANTS TO BE A GOOD GUY NOW.
WHICH IS NICE. AND A LOT OF PEOPLE WERE VERY HAPPY TO HEAR IT. THEY WERE EVEN WILLING TO OVERLOOK THE AFOREMENTIONED TRAIL OF BODIES.
ME? I'M NOT SO FORGIVING.
IT'S NOT THAT I DIDN'T WANT TO BELIEVE IT, MIND YOU, IT'S JUST--I KNOW WHAT IT'S LIKE FOR PEOPLE WHO HAVE CROSSED CERTAIN LINES. WE WANT TO BELIEVE THAT WE CAN CHANGE, BUT--
--WELL, LIKE THE MAN SAYS, "WE MAY BE THROUGH WITH THE PAST..."
ANYHOO. COME TO THINK OF IT, I CAN'T PUT MY FINGER ON WHAT IT IS ABOUT YOU THAT REMINDS ME OF HIM, REALLY. SOMETHING IN THE EYES, I GUESS. BUT REGARDLESS, PROBABLY SAYS MORE ABOUT ME THAN YOU--
THAT I AM NOT THE TRUSTING SORT.
WHICH IS WHY I GET SKEPTICAL WHEN THE FIRST FIRE THIS COMMUNITY HAS SEEN IN--LET'S SAY AGES--BREAKS OUT.
AND I GET A REPORT THAT SOMEONE BESIDES THE FAMILY THAT LIVED THERE WAS IN THE HOUSE AT THE TIME.
AND THE PERSON WHO MADE THAT CLAIM SUDDENLY SAYS, "WHOOPS, NO, NOT TRUE AT ALL. MY BAD."
SO HERE'S WHAT I'D LIKE YOU TO DO, JIM--
I WANT YOU TO TAKE THE NIGHT AND THINK VERY HARD ON WHAT--OR WHO--YOU SAW IN THAT FIRE. AND ASSUMING YOU DON'T SUFFER ANOTHER BOUT OF MEMORY LOSS--I BELIEVE THE ANSWER WILL COME TO YOU.
WHEN IT DOES, COME BY MY OFFICE IN THE MORNING, AND WE'LL HAVE ANOTHER LITTLE CHAT--

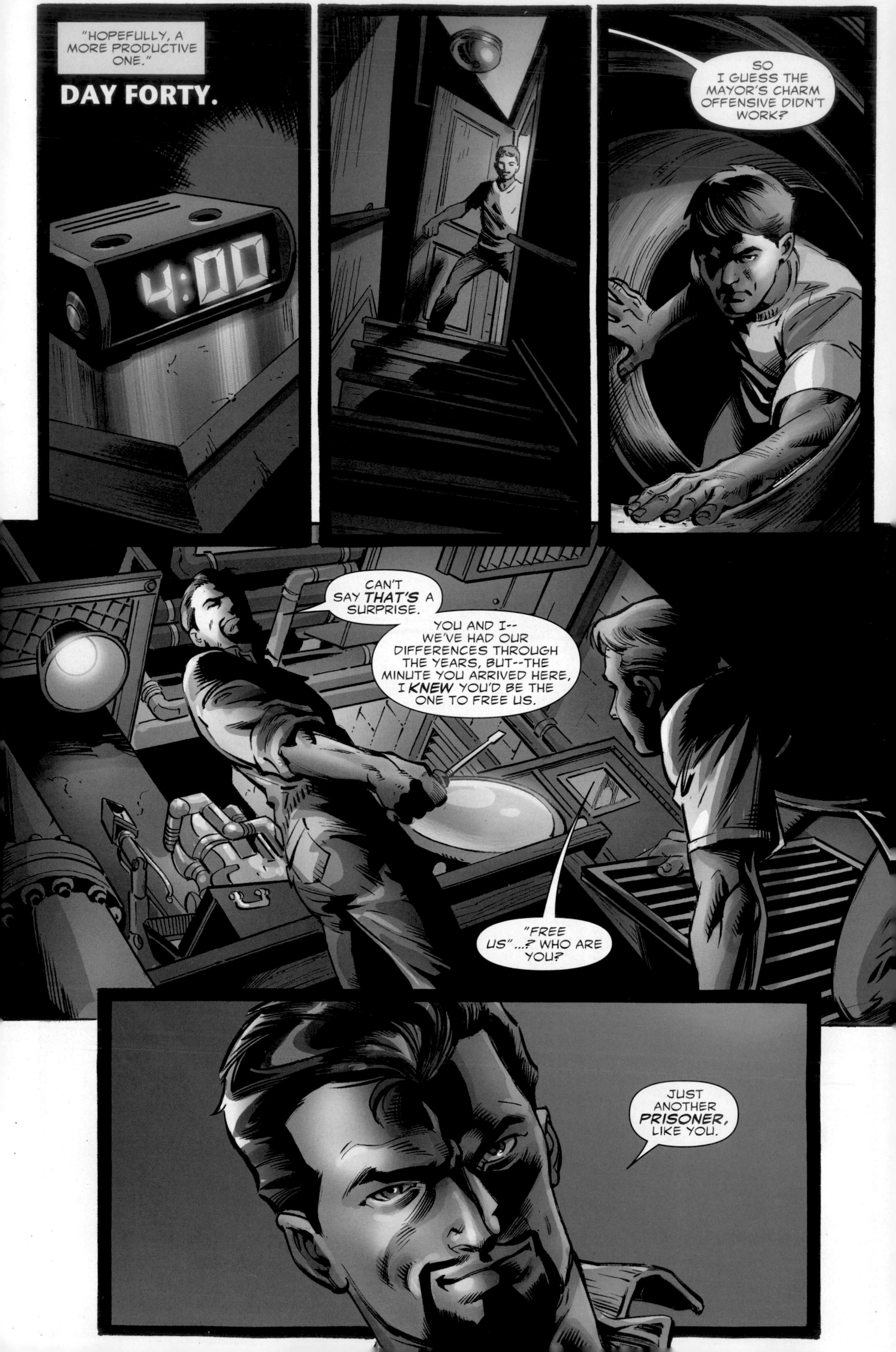

"HOPEFULLY, A MORE PRODUCTIVE ONE."
DAY FORTY.
SO I GUESS THE MAYOR'S CHARM OFFENSIVE DIDN'T WORK?
CAN'T SAY THAT'S A SURPRISE.
YOU AND I-- WE'VE HAD OUR DIFFERENCES THROUGH THE YEARS, BUT--THE MINUTE YOU ARRIVED HERE, I KNEW YOU'D BE THE ONE TO FREE US.
"FREE US"...? WHO ARE YOU?
JUST ANOTHER PRISONER, LIKE YOU.

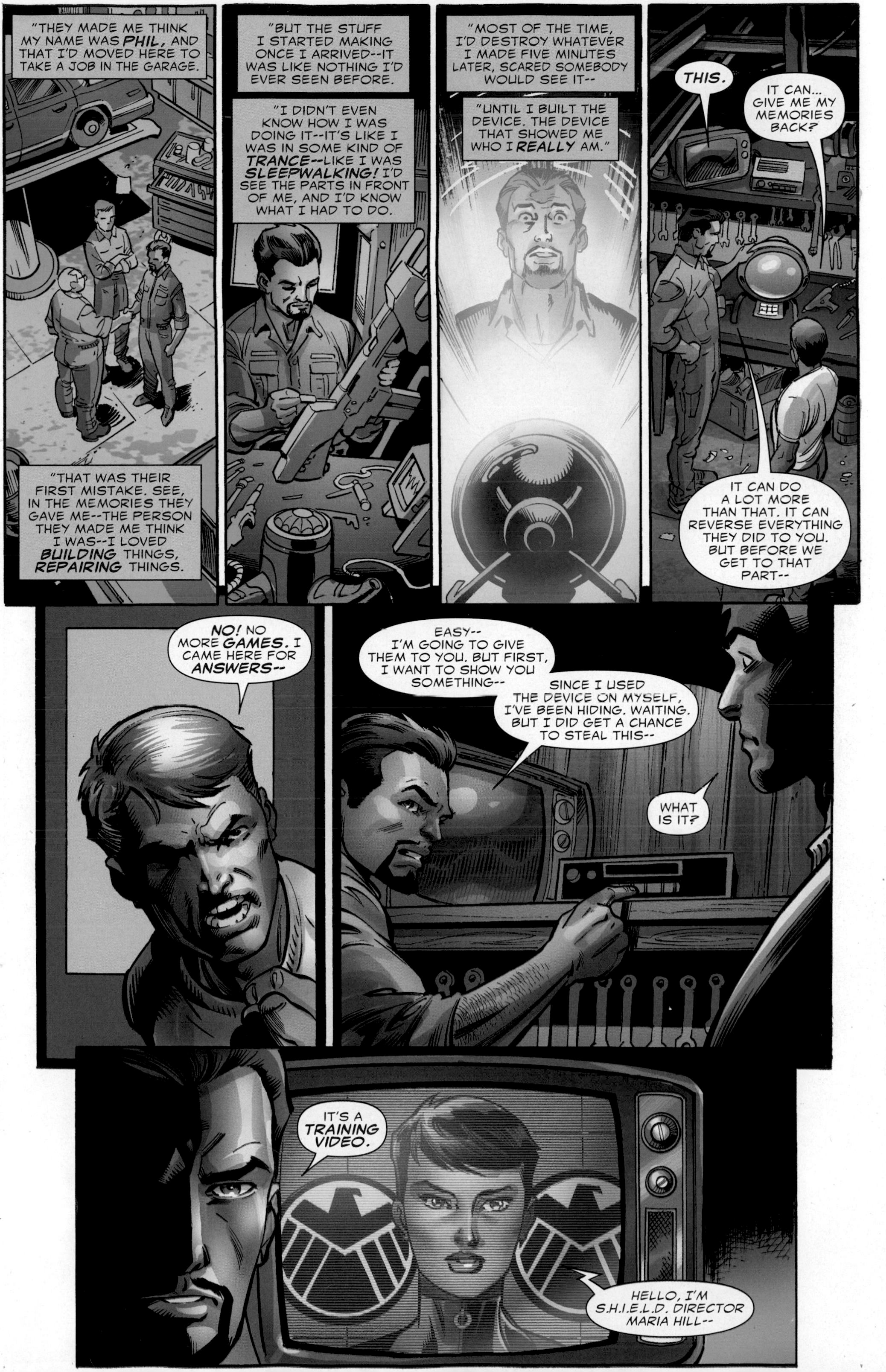
"THEY MADE ME THINK MY NAME WAS PHIL, AND THAT I'D MOVED HERE TO TAKE A JOB IN THE GARAGE.
"THAT WAS THEIR FIRST MISTAKE. SEE, IN THE MEMORIES THEY GAVE ME--THE PERSON THEY MADE ME THINK I WAS--I LOVED BUILDING THINGS, REPAIRING THINGS.
"BUT THE STUFF I STARTED MAKING ONCE I ARRIVED--IT WAS LIKE NOTHING I'D EVER SEEN BEFORE.
"I DIDN'T EVEN KNOW HOW I WAS DOING IT--IT'S LIKE I WAS IN SOME KIND OF TRANCE--LIKE I WAS SLEEPWALKING! I'D SEE THE PARTS IN FRONT OF ME, AND I'D KNOW WHAT I HAD TO DO.
"MOST OF THE TIME, I'D DESTROY WHATEVER I MADE FIVE MINUTES LATER, SCARED SOMEBODY WOULD SEE IT--
"UNTIL I BUILT THE DEVICE. THE DEVICE THAT SHOWED ME WHO I REALLY AM."
THIS.
IT CAN... GIVE ME MY MEMORIES BACK?
IT CAN DO A LOT MORE THAN THAT. IT CAN REVERSE EVERYTHING THEY DID TO YOU. BUT BEFORE WE GET TO THAT PART--
NO! NO MORE GAMES. I CAME HERE FOR ANSWERS--
EASY-- I'M GOING TO GIVE THEM TO YOU. BUT FIRST, I WANT TO SHOW YOU SOMETHING--
SINCE I USED THE DEVICE ON MYSELF, I'VE BEEN HIDING. WAITING. BUT I DID GET A CHANCE TO STEAL THIS--
WHAT IS IT?
IT'S A TRAINING VIDEO.
HELLO, I'M S.H.I.E.L.D. DIRECTOR MARIA HILL--

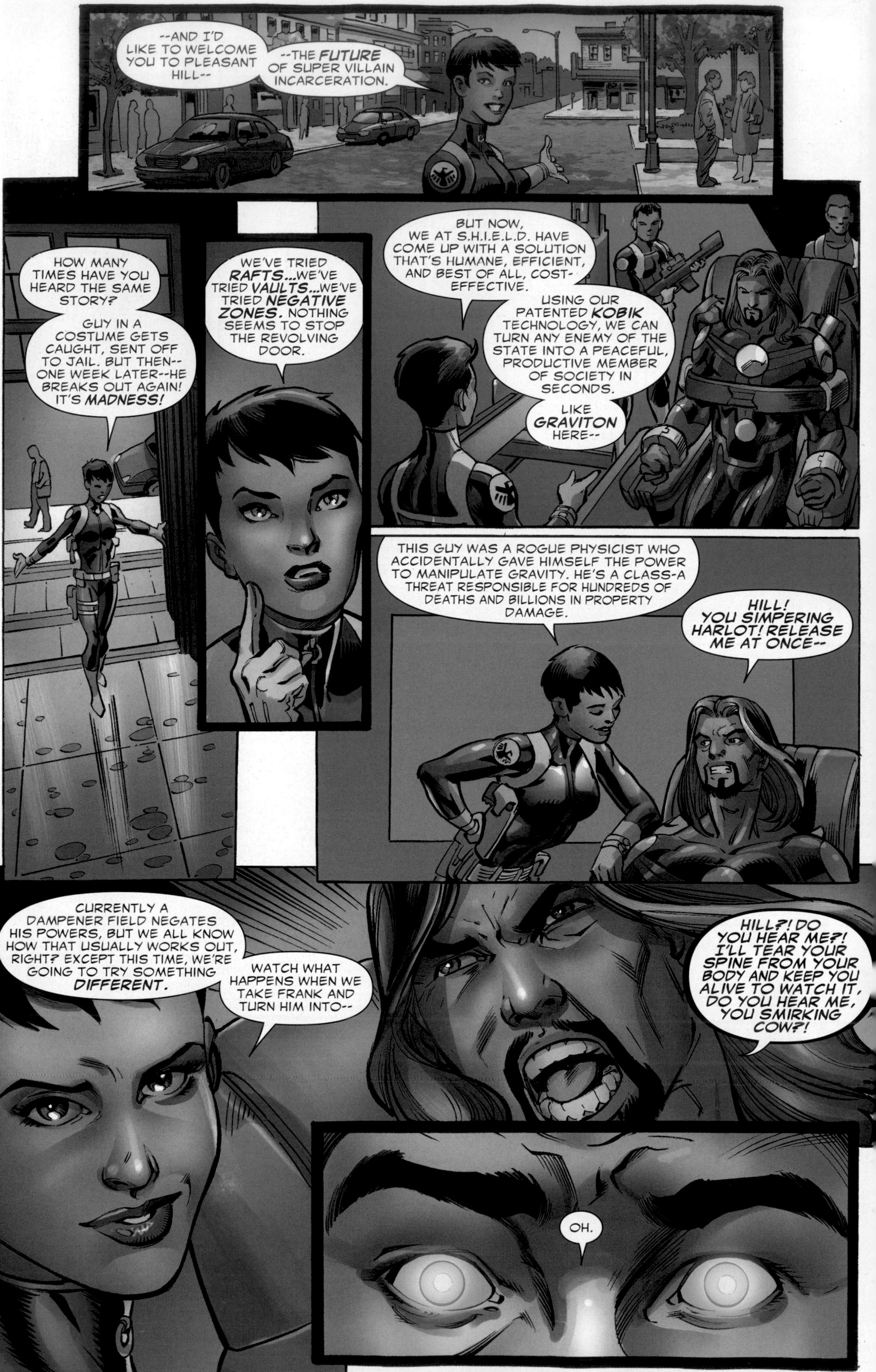
--AND I'D LIKE TO WELCOME YOU TO PLEASANT HILL--
--THE FUTURE OF SUPER VILLAIN INCARCERATION.
HOW MANY TIMES HAVE YOU HEARD THE SAME STORY?
GUY IN A COSTUME GETS CAUGHT, SENT OFF TO JAIL. BUT THEN--ONE WEEK LATER--HE BREAKS OUT AGAIN! IT'S MADNESS!
WE'VE TRIED RAFTS...WE'VE TRIED VAULTS...WE'VE TRIED NEGATIVE ZONES. NOTHING SEEMS TO STOP THE REVOLVING DOOR.
BUT NOW, WE AT S.H.I.E.L.D. HAVE COME UP WITH A SOLUTION THAT'S HUMANE, EFFICIENT, AND BEST OF ALL, COST-EFFECTIVE.
USING OUR PATENTED KOBIK TECHNOLOGY, WE CAN TURN ANY ENEMY OF THE STATE INTO A PEACEFUL, PRODUCTIVE MEMBER OF SOCIETY IN SECONDS.
LIKE GRAVITON HERE--
THIS GUY WAS A ROGUE PHYSICIST WHO ACCIDENTALLY GAVE HIMSELF THE POWER TO MANIPULATE GRAVITY. HE'S A CLASS-A THREAT RESPONSIBLE FOR HUNDREDS OF DEATHS AND BILLIONS IN PROPERTY DAMAGE.
HILL! YOU SIMPERING HARLOT! RELEASE ME AT ONCE--
CURRENTLY A DAMPENER FIELD NEGATES HIS POWERS, BUT WE ALL KNOW HOW THAT USUALLY WORKS OUT, RIGHT? EXCEPT THIS TIME, WE'RE GOING TO TRY SOMETHING DIFFERENT.
WATCH WHAT HAPPENS WHEN WE TAKE FRANK AND TURN HIM INTO--
HILL?! DO YOU HEAR ME?! I'LL TEAR YOUR SPINE FROM YOUR BODY AND KEEP YOU ALIVE TO WATCH IT, DO YOU HEAR ME, YOU SMIRKING COW?!
OH.

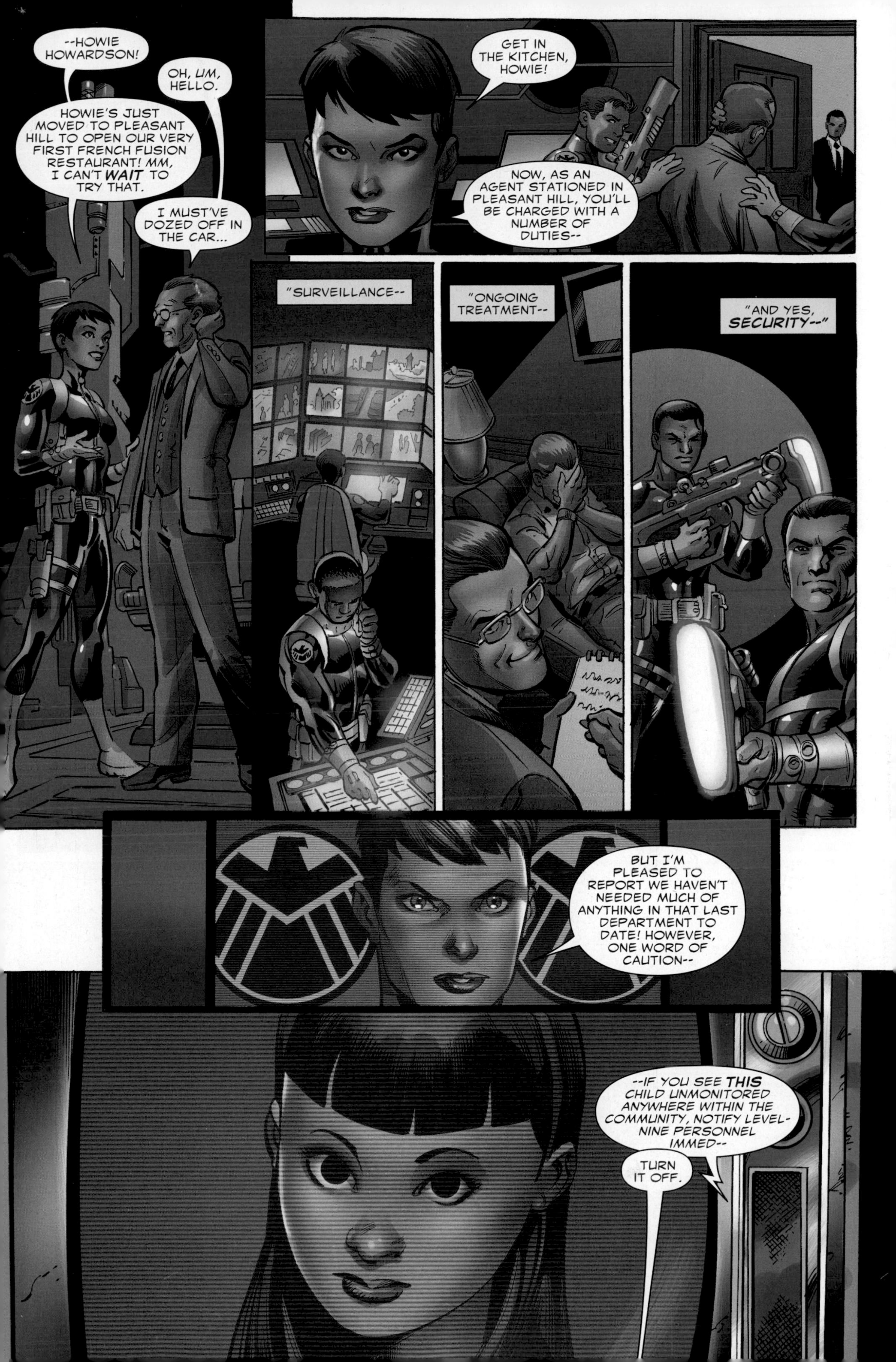
--HOWIE HOWARDSON!
OH, UM, HELLO.
HOWIE'S JUST MOVED TO PLEASANT HILL TO OPEN OUR VERY FIRST FRENCH FUSION RESTAURANT! MM, I CAN'T WAIT TO TRY THAT.
I MUST'VE DOZED OFF IN THE CAR...
GET IN THE KITCHEN, HOWIE!
NOW, AS AN AGENT STATIONED IN PLEASANT HILL, YOU'LL BE CHARGED WITH A NUMBER OF DUTIES--
"SURVEILLANCE--
"ONGOING TREATMENT--
"AND YES, SECURITY--"
BUT I'M PLEASED TO REPORT WE HAVEN'T NEEDED MUCH OF ANYTHING IN THAT LAST DEPARTMENT TO DATE! HOWEVER, ONE WORD OF CAUTION--
--IF YOU SEE THIS CHILD UNMONITORED ANYWHERE WITHIN THE COMMUNITY, NOTIFY LEVEL-NINE PERSONNEL IMMED--
TURN IT OFF.

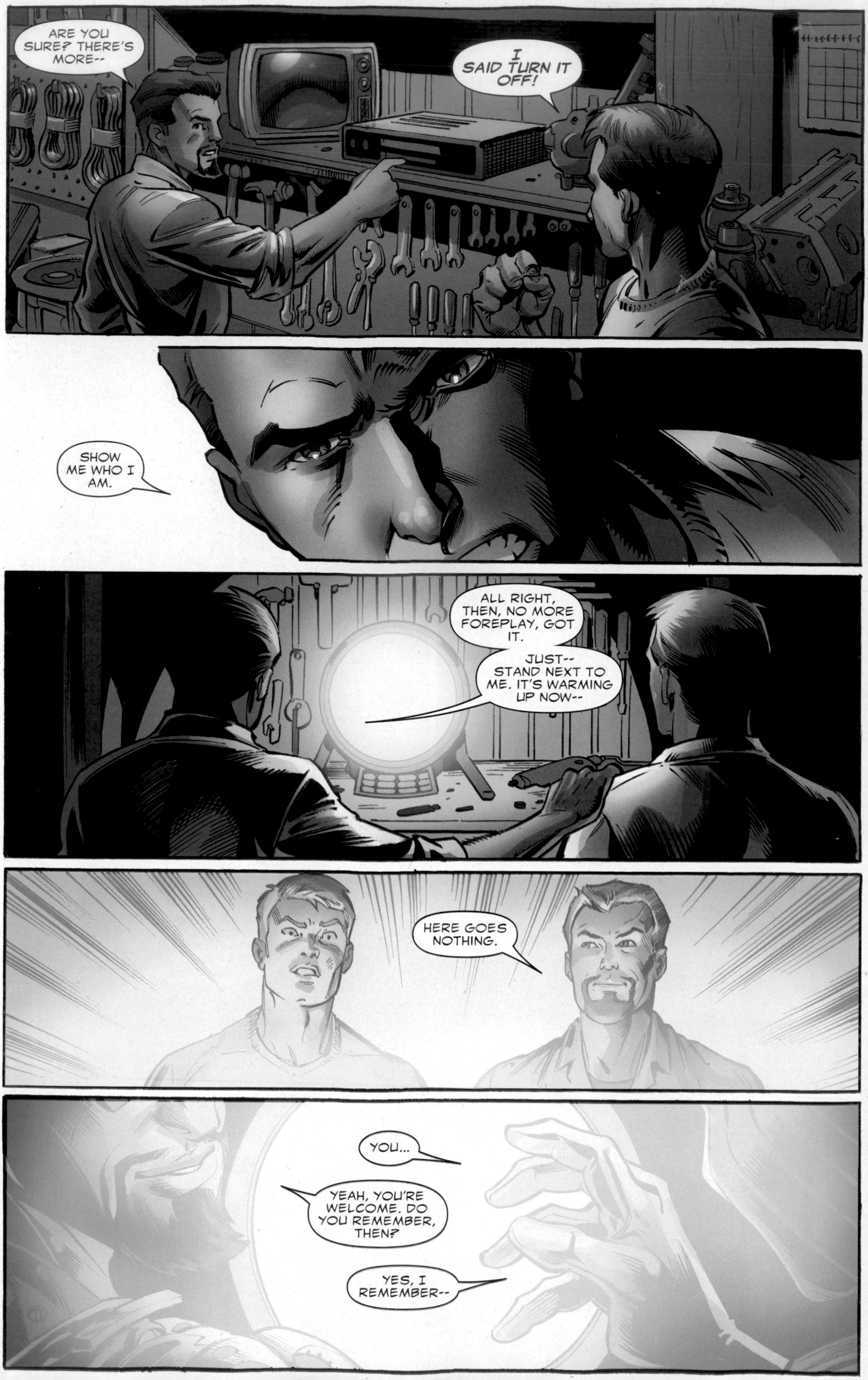
ARE YOU SURE? THERE'S MORE--
I SAID TURN IT OFF!
SHOW ME WHO I AM.
ALL RIGHT, THEN, NO MORE FOREPLAY, GOT IT.
JUST-- STAND NEXT TO ME. IT'S WARMING UP NOW--
HERE GOES NOTHING.
YOU...
YEAH, YOU'RE WELCOME. DO YOU REMEMBER, THEN?
YES, I REMEMBER--

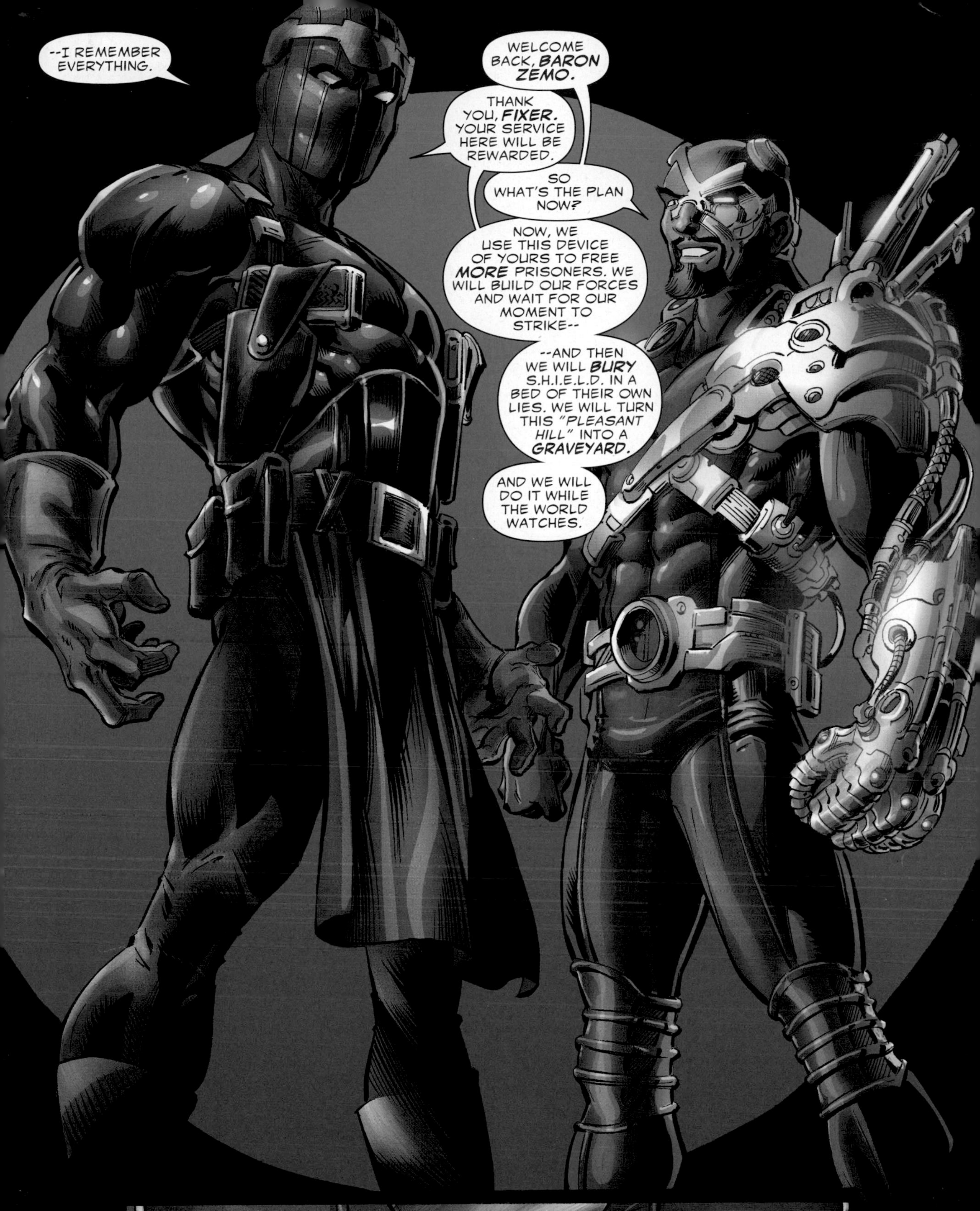
--I REMEMBER EVERYTHING.
WELCOME BACK, BARON ZEMO.
THANK YOU, FIXER. YOUR SERVICE HERE WILL BE REWARDED.
SO WHAT'S THE PLAN NOW?
NOW, WE USE THIS DEVICE OF YOURS TO FREE MORE PRISONERS. WE WILL BUILD OUR FORCES AND WAIT FOR OUR MOMENT TO STRIKE--
--AND THEN WE WILL BURY S.H.I.E.L.D. IN A BED OF THEIR OWN LIES. WE WILL TURN THIS "PLEASANT HILL" INTO A GRAVEYARD.
AND WE WILL DO IT WHILE THE WORLD WATCHES.

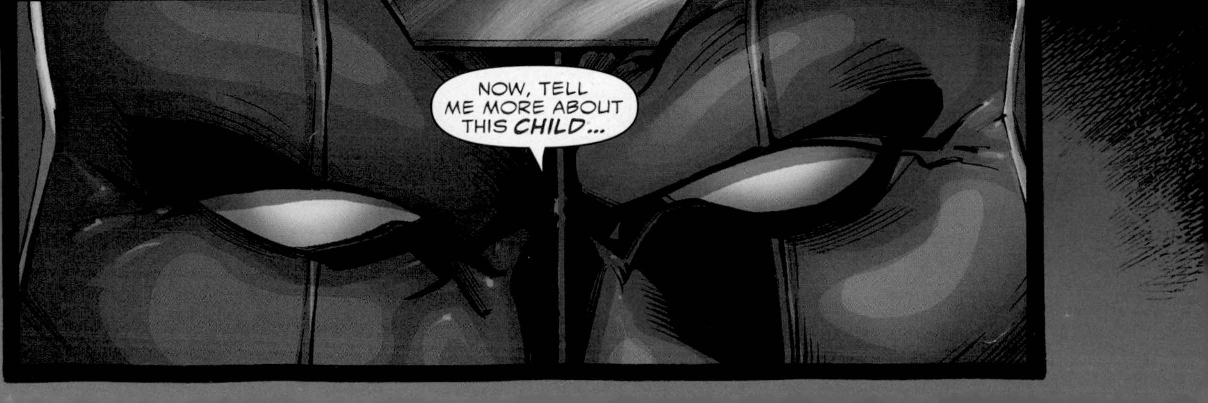
NOW, TELL ME MORE ABOUT THIS CHILD...

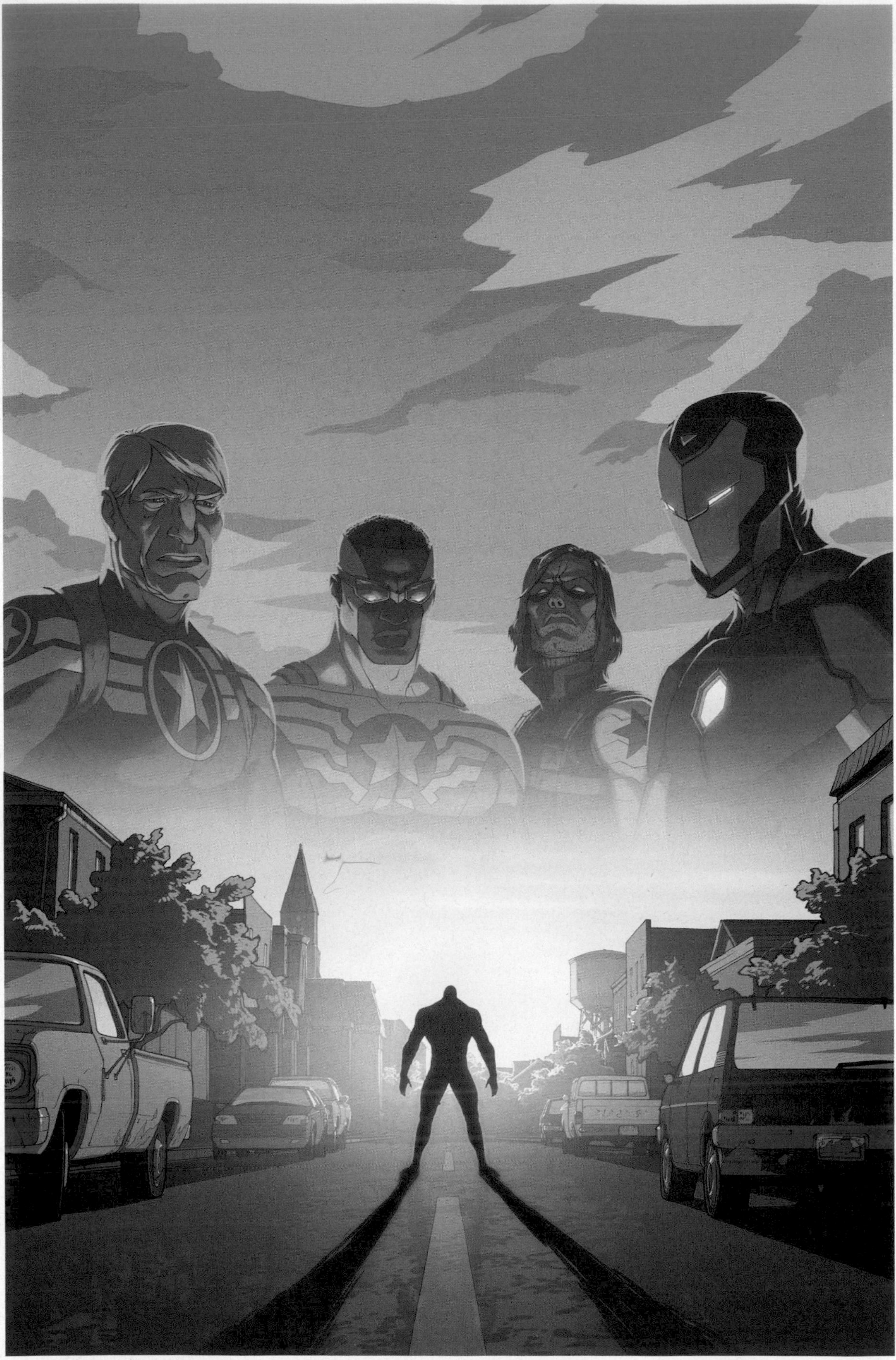

Avengers Standoff: Welcome to Pleasant Hill variant by

MATT RHODES

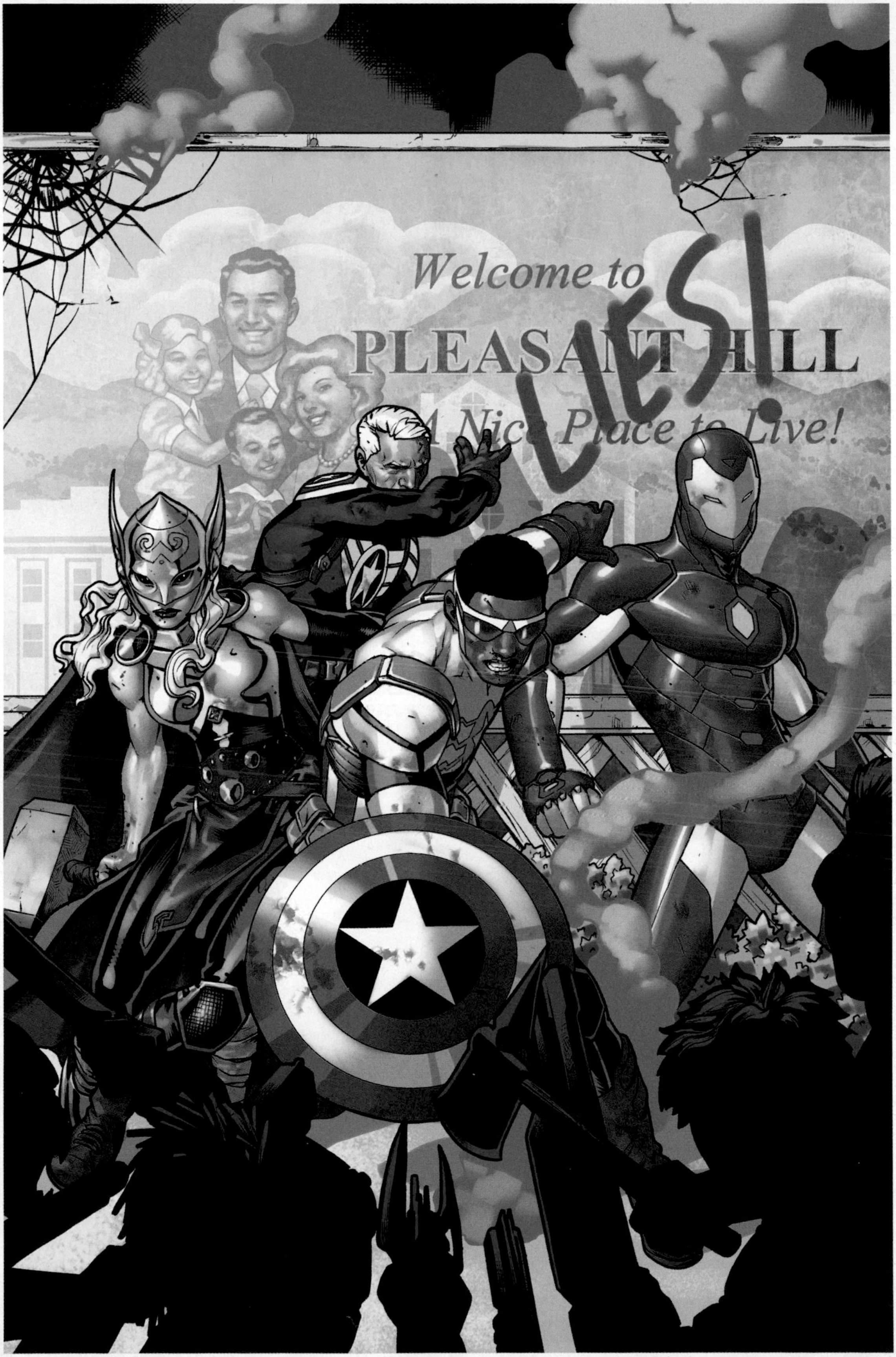
Welcome to
PLEASANT HILL
A Nice Place to Live!
LIES!

Avengers Standoff:
Assault on Pleasant Hill Alpha

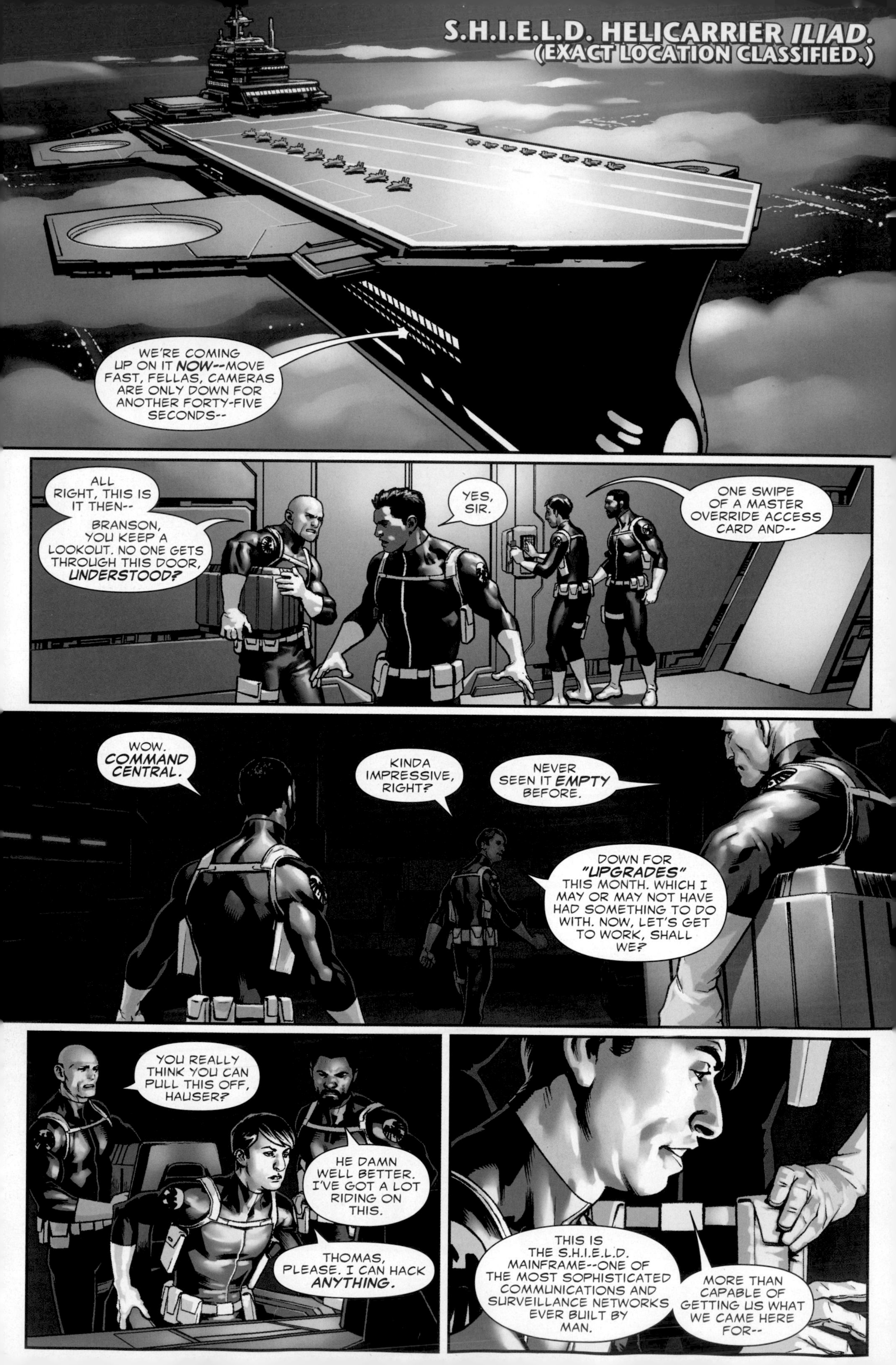
S.H.I.E.L.D. HELICARRIER ILIAD.
(EXACT LOCATION CLASSIFIED.)
WE'RE COMING UP ON IT NOW--MOVE FAST, FELLAS, CAMERAS ARE ONLY DOWN FOR ANOTHER FORTY-FIVE SECONDS--
ALL RIGHT, THIS IS IT THEN--
BRANSON, YOU KEEP A LOOKOUT. NO ONE GETS THROUGH THIS DOOR, UNDERSTOOD?
YES, SIR.
ONE SWIPE OF A MASTER OVERRIDE ACCESS CARD AND--
WOW. COMMAND CENTRAL.
KINDA IMPRESSIVE, RIGHT?
NEVER SEEN IT EMPTY BEFORE.
DOWN FOR "UPGRADES" THIS MONTH. WHICH I MAY OR MAY NOT HAVE HAD SOMETHING TO DO WITH. NOW, LET'S GET TO WORK, SHALL WE?
YOU REALLY THINK YOU CAN PULL THIS OFF, HAUSER?
HE DAMN WELL BETTER. I'VE GOT A LOT RIDING ON THIS.
THOMAS, PLEASE. I CAN HACK ANYTHING.
THIS IS THE S.H.I.E.L.D. MAINFRAME--ONE OF THE MOST SOPHISTICATED COMMUNICATIONS AND SURVEILLANCE NETWORKS EVER BUILT BY MAN.
MORE THAN CAPABLE OF GETTING US WHAT WE CAME HERE FOR--

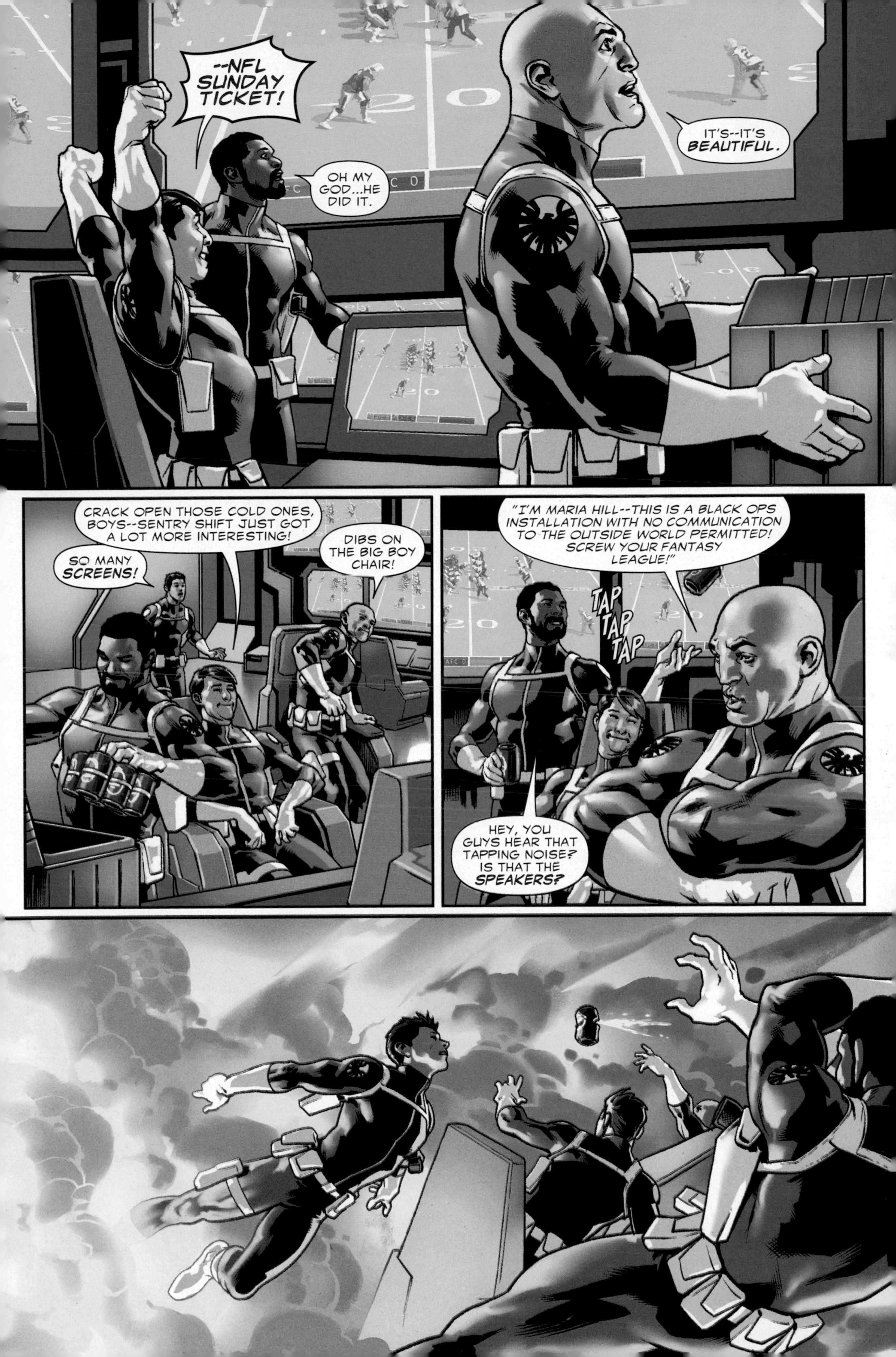
--NFL SUNDAY TICKET!
OH MY GOD...HE DID IT.
IT'S--IT'S BEAUTIFUL.
CRACK OPEN THOSE COLD ONES, BOYS--SENTRY SHIFT JUST GOT A LOT MORE INTERESTING!
SO MANY SCREENS!
DIBS ON THE BIG BOY CHAIR!
"I'M MARIA HILL--THIS IS A BLACK OPS INSTALLATION WITH NO COMMUNICATION TO THE OUTSIDE WORLD PERMITTED! SCREW YOUR FANTASY LEAGUE!"
TAP TAP TAP
HEY, YOU GUYS HEAR THAT TAPPING NOISE? IS THAT THE SPEAKERS?

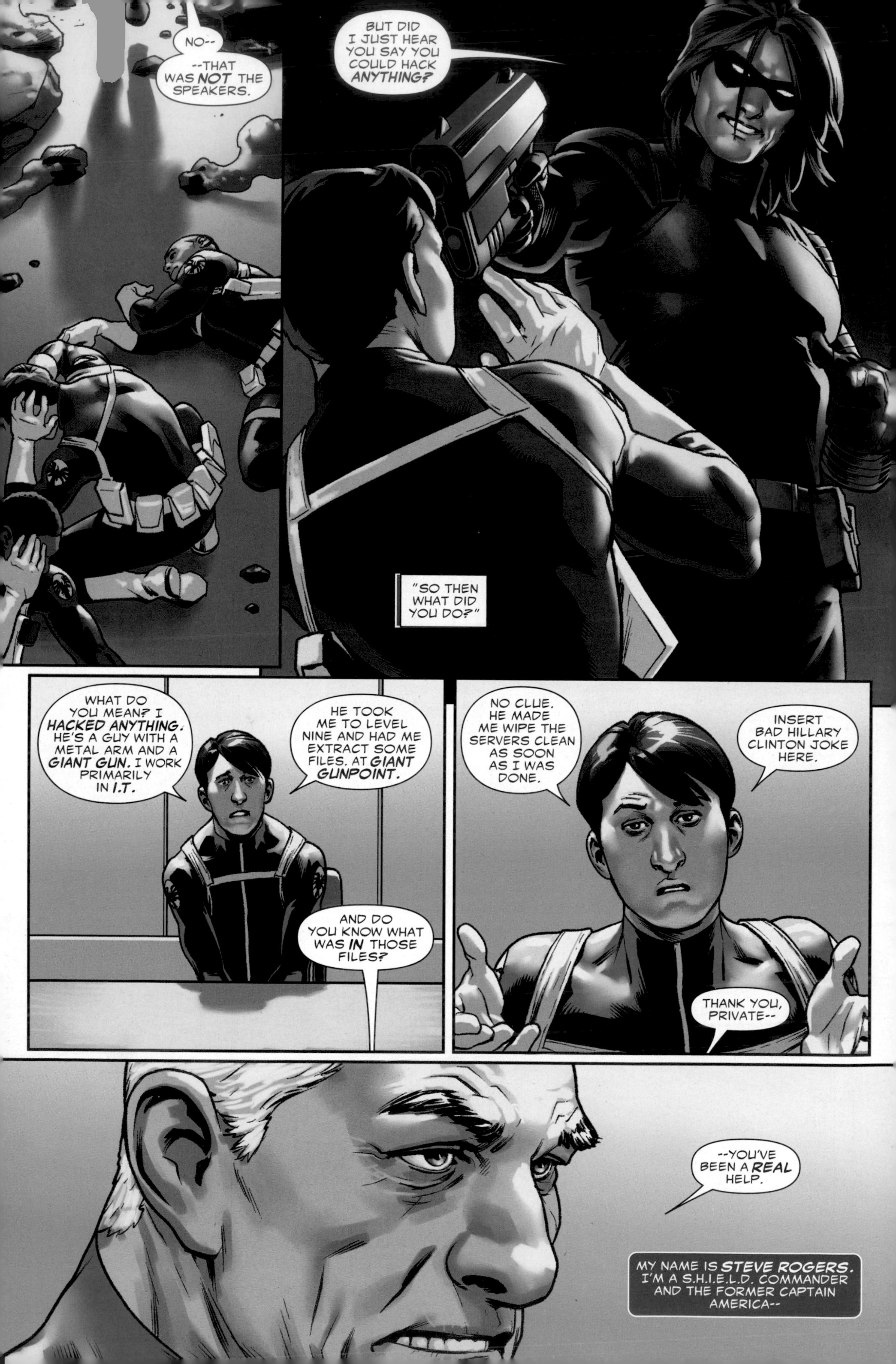
NO--
--THAT WAS NOT THE SPEAKERS.
BUT DID I JUST HEAR YOU SAY YOU COULD HACK ANYTHING?
"SO THEN WHAT DID YOU DO?"
WHAT DO YOU MEAN? I HACKED ANYTHING. HE'S A GUY WITH A METAL ARM AND A GIANT GUN. I WORK PRIMARILY IN I.T.
HE TOOK ME TO LEVEL NINE AND HAD ME EXTRACT SOME FILES. AT GIANT GUNPOINT.
AND DO YOU KNOW WHAT WAS IN THOSE FILES?
NO CLUE. HE MADE ME WIPE THE SERVERS CLEAN AS SOON AS I WAS DONE.
INSERT BAD HILLARY CLINTON JOKE HERE.
THANK YOU, PRIVATE--
--YOU'VE BEEN A REAL HELP.
MY NAME IS STEVE ROGERS. I'M A S.H.I.E.L.D. COMMANDER AND THE FORMER CAPTAIN AMERICA--

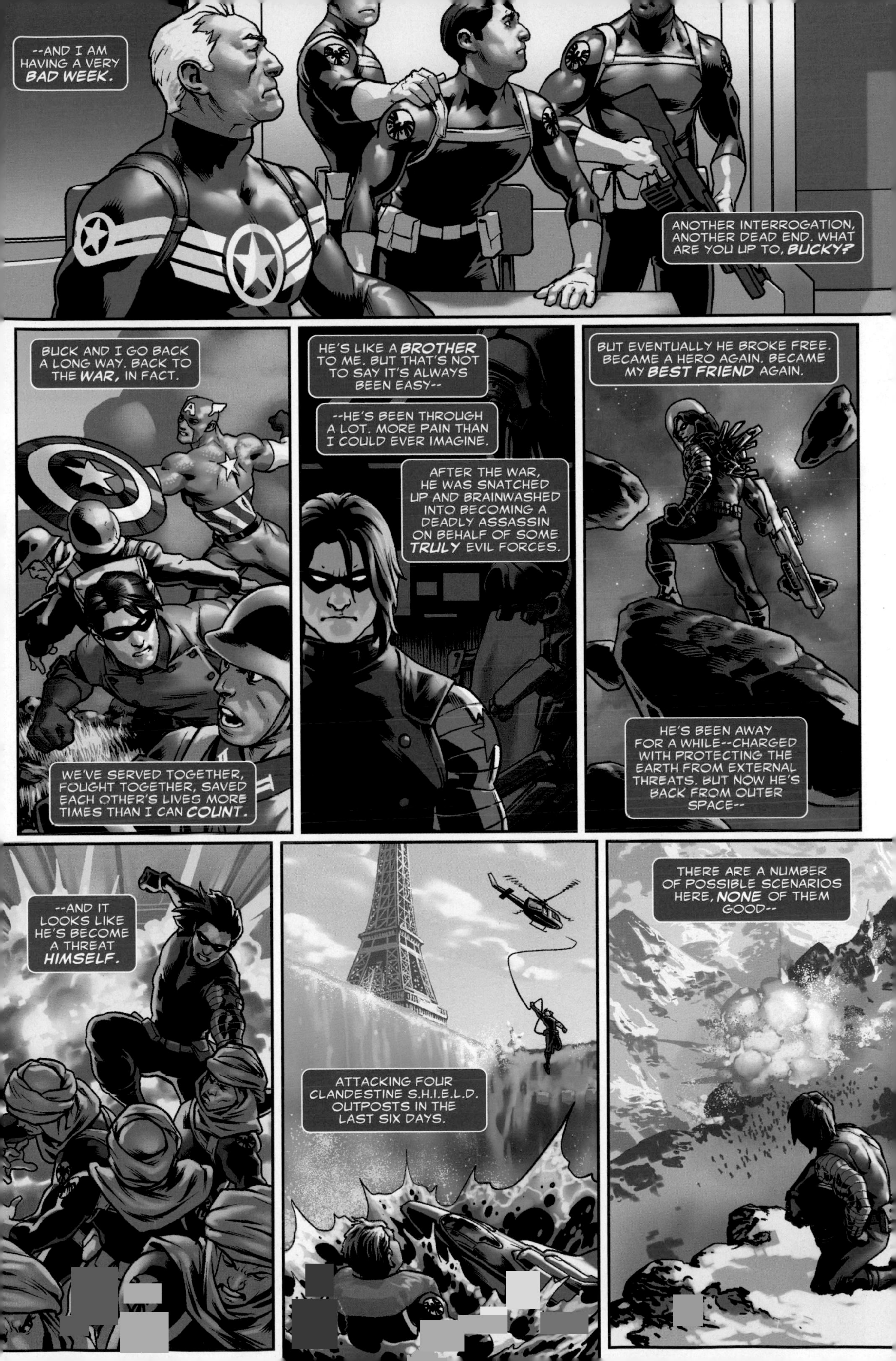
--AND I AM HAVING A VERY BAD WEEK.
ANOTHER INTERROGATION, ANOTHER DEAD END. WHAT ARE YOU UP TO, BUCKY?
BUCK AND I GO BACK A LONG WAY. BACK TO THE WAR, IN FACT.
WE'VE SERVED TOGETHER, FOUGHT TOGETHER, SAVED EACH OTHER'S LIVES MORE TIMES THAN I CAN COUNT.
HE'S LIKE A BROTHER TO ME. BUT THAT'S NOT TO SAY IT'S ALWAYS BEEN EASY--
--HE'S BEEN THROUGH A LOT. MORE PAIN THAN I COULD EVER IMAGINE.
AFTER THE WAR, HE WAS SNATCHED UP AND BRAINWASHED INTO BECOMING A DEADLY ASSASSIN ON BEHALF OF SOME TRULY EVIL FORCES.
BUT EVENTUALLY HE BROKE FREE. BECAME A HERO AGAIN. BECAME MY BEST FRIEND AGAIN.
HE'S BEEN AWAY FOR A WHILE--CHARGED WITH PROTECTING THE EARTH FROM EXTERNAL THREATS. BUT NOW HE'S BACK FROM OUTER SPACE--
--AND IT LOOKS LIKE HE'S BECOME A THREAT HIMSELF.
ATTACKING FOUR CLANDESTINE S.H.I.E.L.D. OUTPOSTS IN THE LAST SIX DAYS.
THERE ARE A NUMBER OF POSSIBLE SCENARIOS HERE, NONE OF THEM GOOD--

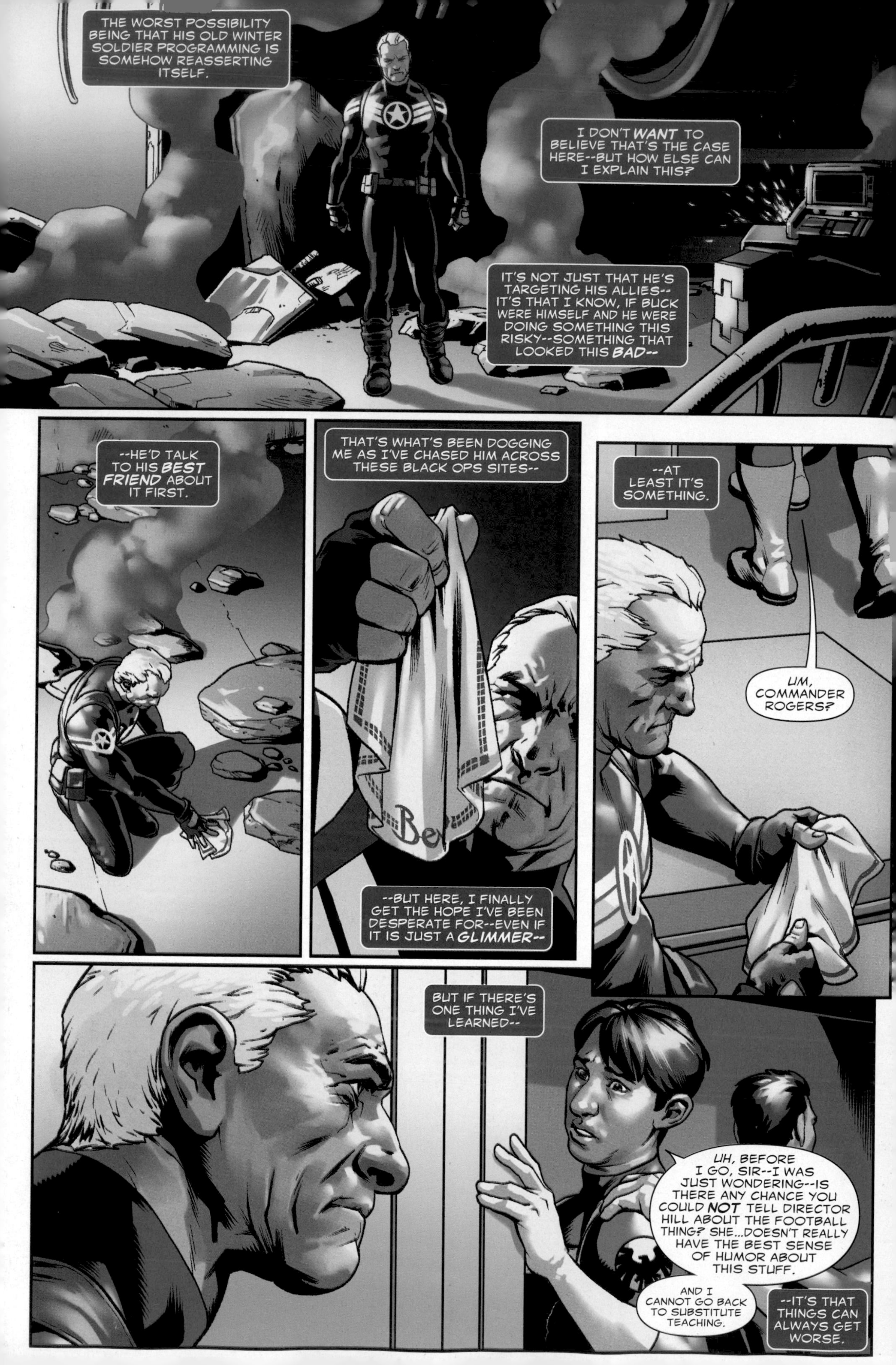
THE WORST POSSIBILITY BEING THAT HIS OLD WINTER SOLDIER PROGRAMMING IS SOMEHOW REASSERTING ITSELF.
I DON'T WANT TO BELIEVE THAT'S THE CASE HERE--BUT HOW ELSE CAN I EXPLAIN THIS?
IT'S NOT JUST THAT HE'S TARGETING HIS ALLIES--IT'S THAT I KNOW, IF BUCK WERE HIMSELF AND HE WERE DOING SOMETHING THIS RISKY--SOMETHING THAT LOOKED THIS BAD--
--HE'D TALK TO HIS BEST FRIEND ABOUT IT FIRST.
THAT'S WHAT'S BEEN DOGGING ME AS I'VE CHASED HIM ACROSS THESE BLACK OPS SITES--
--BUT HERE, I FINALLY GET THE HOPE I'VE BEEN DESPERATE FOR--EVEN IF IT IS JUST A GLIMMER--
--AT LEAST IT'S SOMETHING.
UM, COMMANDER ROGERS?
BUT IF THERE'S ONE THING I'VE LEARNED--
UH, BEFORE I GO, SIR--I WAS JUST WONDERING--IS THERE ANY CHANCE YOU COULD NOT TELL DIRECTOR HILL ABOUT THE FOOTBALL THING? SHE...DOESN'T REALLY HAVE THE BEST SENSE OF HUMOR ABOUT THIS STUFF.
AND I CANNOT GO BACK TO SUBSTITUTE TEACHING.
--IT'S THAT THINGS CAN ALWAYS GET WORSE.

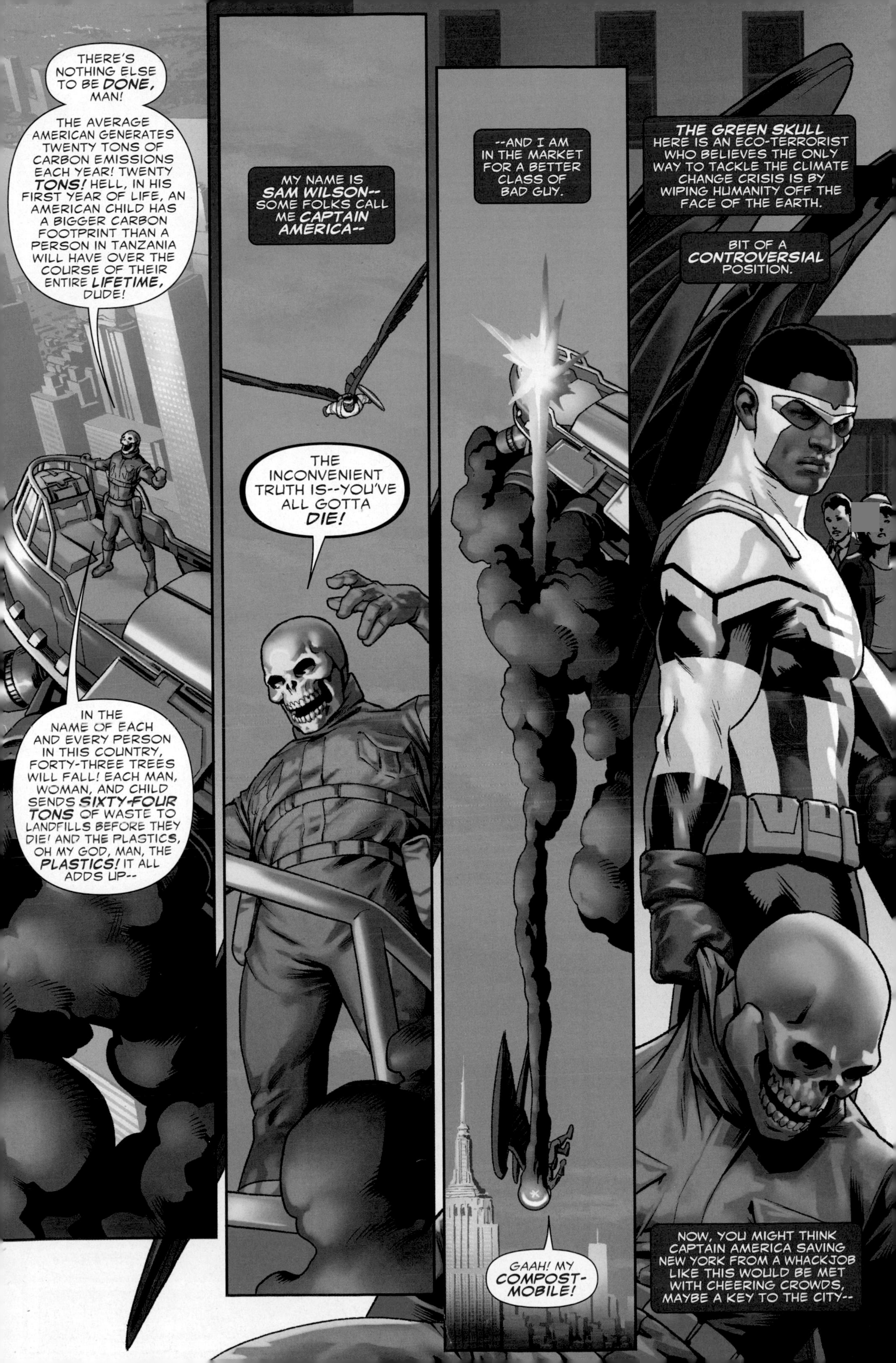

THERE'S NOTHING ELSE TO BE DONE, MAN!
THE AVERAGE AMERICAN GENERATES TWENTY TONS OF CARBON EMISSIONS EACH YEAR! TWENTY TONS! HELL, IN HIS FIRST YEAR OF LIFE, AN AMERICAN CHILD HAS A BIGGER CARBON FOOTPRINT THAN A PERSON IN TANZANIA WILL HAVE OVER THE COURSE OF THEIR ENTIRE LIFETIME, DUDE!
IN THE NAME OF EACH AND EVERY PERSON IN THIS COUNTRY, FORTY-THREE TREES WILL FALL! EACH MAN, WOMAN, AND CHILD SENDS SIXTY-FOUR TONS OF WASTE TO LANDFILLS BEFORE THEY DIE! AND THE PLASTICS, OH MY GOD, MAN, THE PLASTICS! IT ALL ADDS UP--
MY NAME IS SAM WILSON-- SOME FOLKS CALL ME CAPTAIN AMERICA--
THE INCONVENIENT TRUTH IS--YOU'VE ALL GOTTA DIE!
--AND I AM IN THE MARKET FOR A BETTER CLASS OF BAD GUY.
GAAH! MY COMPOST-MOBILE!
THE GREEN SKULL HERE IS AN ECO-TERRORIST WHO BELIEVES THE ONLY WAY TO TACKLE THE CLIMATE CHANGE CRISIS IS BY WIPING HUMANITY OFF THE FACE OF THE EARTH.
BIT OF A CONTROVERSIAL POSITION.
NOW, YOU MIGHT THINK CAPTAIN AMERICA SAVING NEW YORK FROM A WHACKJOB LIKE THIS WOULD BE MET WITH CHEERING CROWDS, MAYBE A KEY TO THE CITY--

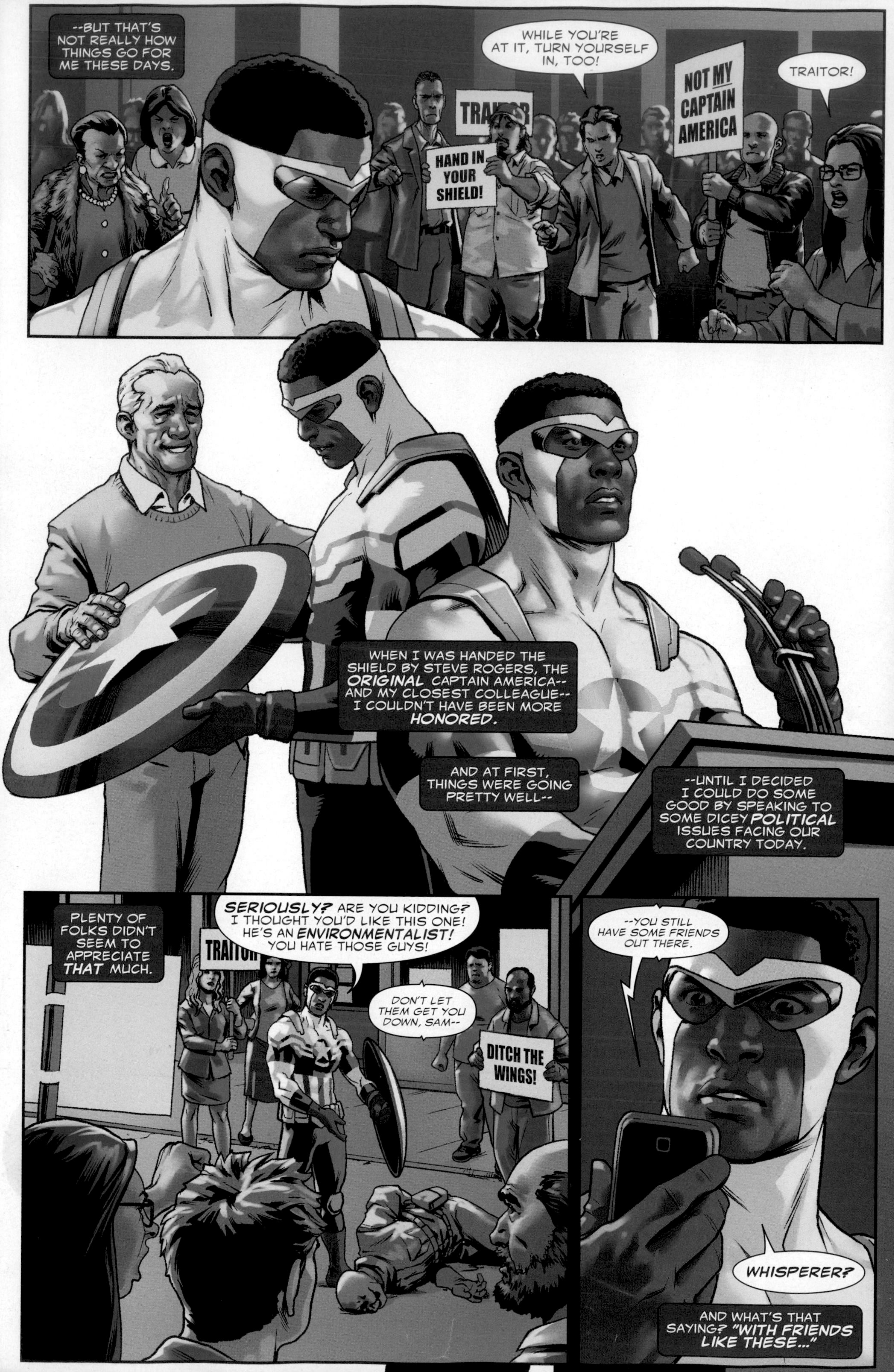
--BUT THAT'S NOT REALLY HOW THINGS GO FOR ME THESE DAYS.
WHILE YOU'RE AT IT, TURN YOURSELF IN, TOO!
HAND IN YOUR SHIELD!
NOT MY CAPTAIN AMERICA
TRAITOR!
WHEN I WAS HANDED THE SHIELD BY STEVE ROGERS, THE ORIGINAL CAPTAIN AMERICA-- AND MY CLOSEST COLLEAGUE-- I COULDN'T HAVE BEEN MORE HONORED.
AND AT FIRST, THINGS WERE GOING PRETTY WELL--
--UNTIL I DECIDED I COULD DO SOME GOOD BY SPEAKING TO SOME DICEY POLITICAL ISSUES FACING OUR COUNTRY TODAY.
PLENTY OF FOLKS DIDN'T SEEM TO APPRECIATE THAT MUCH.
SERIOUSLY? ARE YOU KIDDING? I THOUGHT YOU'D LIKE THIS ONE! HE'S AN ENVIRONMENTALIST! YOU HATE THOSE GUYS!
DON'T LET THEM GET YOU DOWN, SAM--
DITCH THE WINGS!
--YOU STILL HAVE SOME FRIENDS OUT THERE.
WHISPERER?
AND WHAT'S THAT SAYING? "WITH FRIENDS LIKE THESE..."

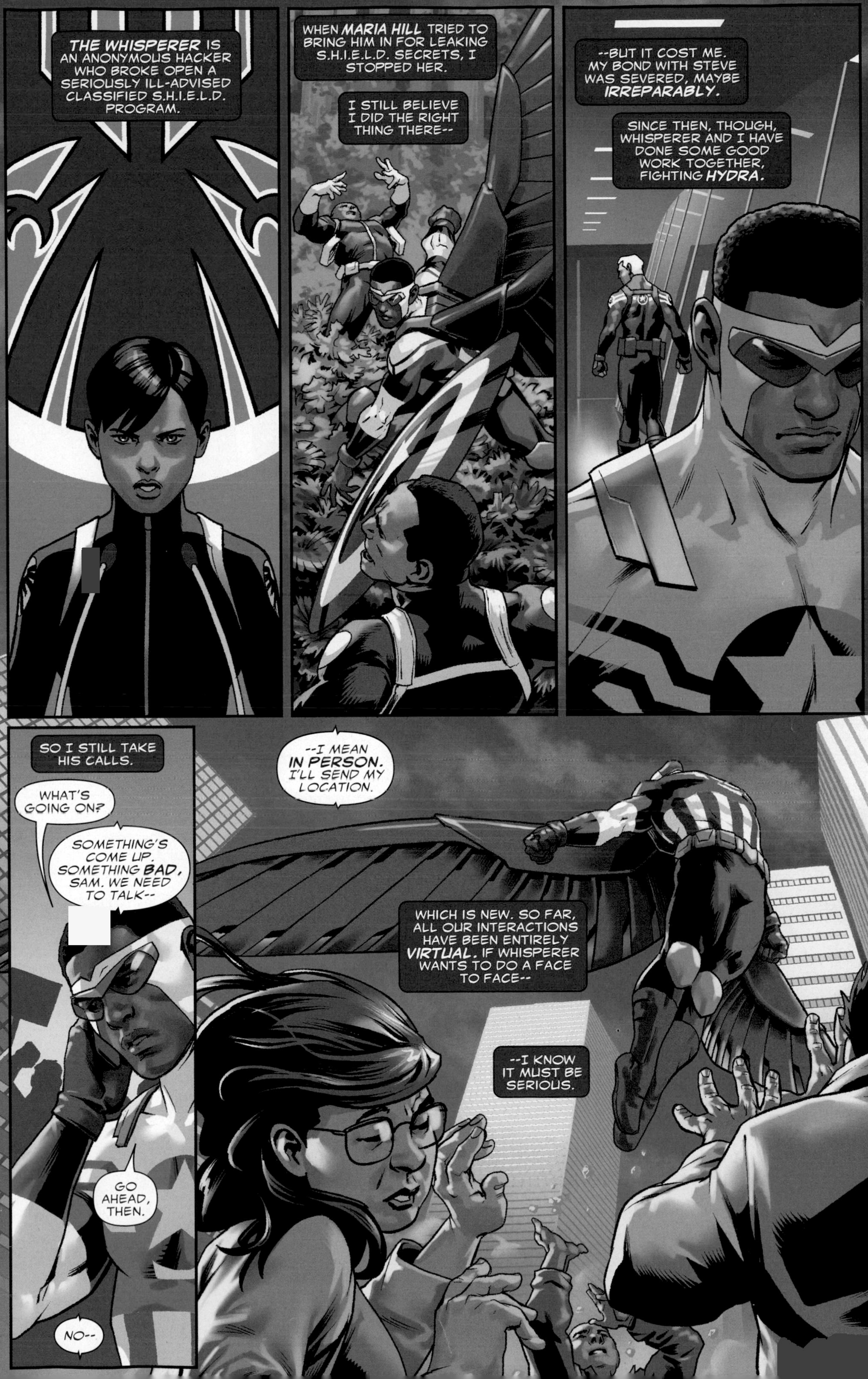
THE WHISPERER IS AN ANONYMOUS HACKER WHO BROKE OPEN A SERIOUSLY ILL-ADVISED CLASSIFIED S.H.I.E.L.D. PROGRAM.
WHEN MARIA HILL TRIED TO BRING HIM IN FOR LEAKING S.H.I.E.L.D. SECRETS, I STOPPED HER.
I STILL BELIEVE I DID THE RIGHT THING THERE--
--BUT IT COST ME. MY BOND WITH STEVE WAS SEVERED, MAYBE IRREPARABLY.
SINCE THEN, THOUGH, WHISPERER AND I HAVE DONE SOME GOOD WORK TOGETHER, FIGHTING HYDRA.
SO I STILL TAKE HIS CALLS.
WHAT'S GOING ON?
SOMETHING'S COME UP. SOMETHING BAD, SAM. WE NEED TO TALK--
GO AHEAD, THEN.
NO--
--I MEAN IN PERSON. I'LL SEND MY LOCATION.
WHICH IS NEW. SO FAR, ALL OUR INTERACTIONS HAVE BEEN ENTIRELY VIRTUAL. IF WHISPERER WANTS TO DO A FACE TO FACE--
--I KNOW IT MUST BE SERIOUS.

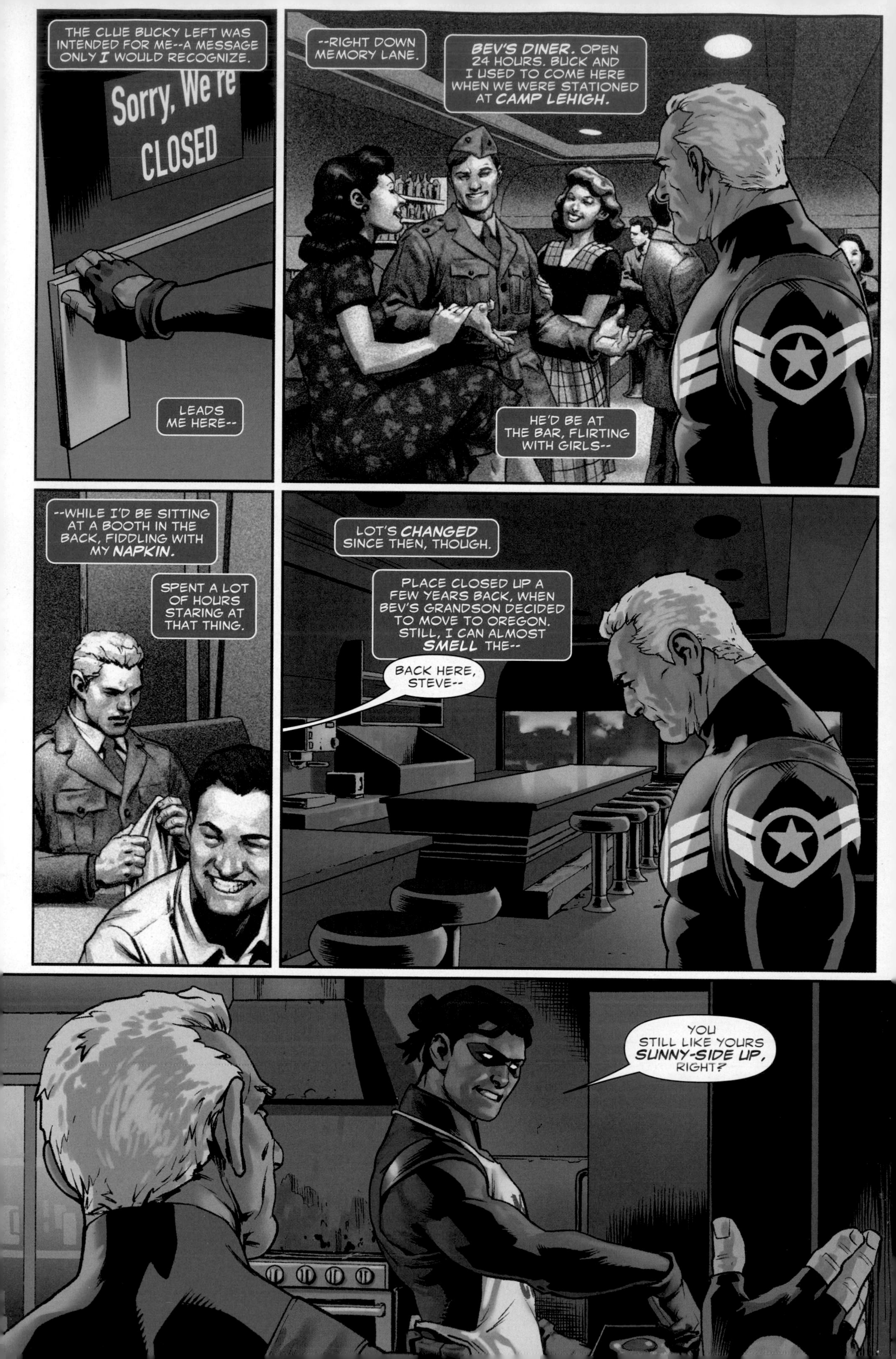
THE CLUE BUCKY LEFT WAS INTENDED FOR ME--A MESSAGE ONLY I WOULD RECOGNIZE.
Sorry, We're CLOSED
LEADS ME HERE--
--RIGHT DOWN MEMORY LANE.
BEV'S DINER. OPEN 24 HOURS. BUCK AND I USED TO COME HERE WHEN WE WERE STATIONED AT CAMP LEHIGH.
HE'D BE AT THE BAR, FLIRTING WITH GIRLS--
--WHILE I'D BE SITTING AT A BOOTH IN THE BACK, FIDDLING WITH MY NAPKIN.
SPENT A LOT OF HOURS STARING AT THAT THING.
LOT'S CHANGED SINCE THEN, THOUGH.
PLACE CLOSED UP A FEW YEARS BACK, WHEN BEV'S GRANDSON DECIDED TO MOVE TO OREGON. STILL, I CAN ALMOST SMELL THE--
BACK HERE, STEVE--
YOU STILL LIKE YOURS SUNNY-SIDE UP, RIGHT?

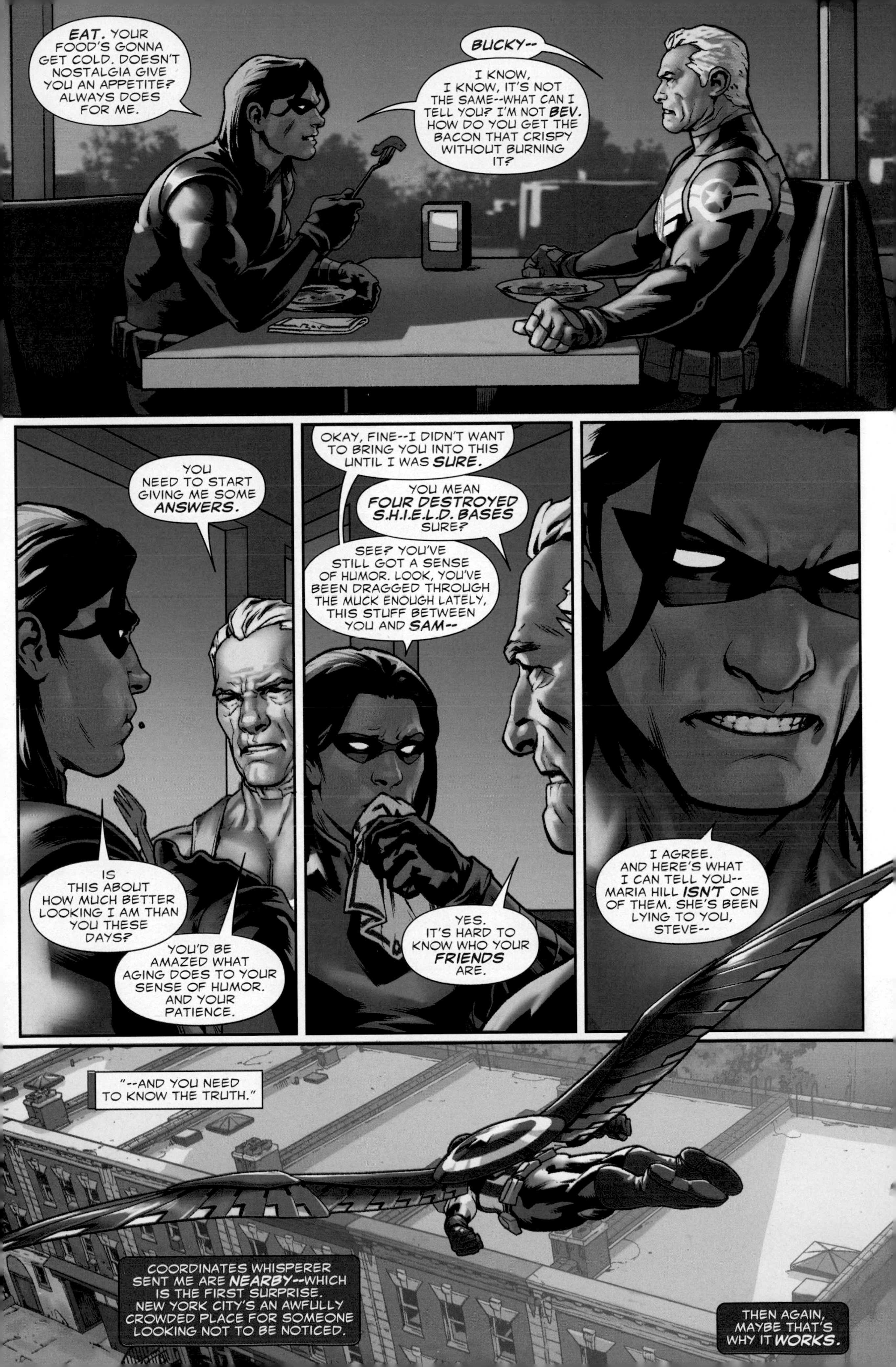
EAT. YOUR FOOD'S GONNA GET COLD. DOESN'T NOSTALGIA GIVE YOU AN APPETITE? ALWAYS DOES FOR ME.
BUCKY--
I KNOW, I KNOW, IT'S NOT THE SAME--WHAT CAN I TELL YOU? I'M NOT BEV. HOW DO YOU GET THE BACON THAT CRISPY WITHOUT BURNING IT?
YOU NEED TO START GIVING ME SOME ANSWERS.
IS THIS ABOUT HOW MUCH BETTER LOOKING I AM THAN YOU THESE DAYS?
YOU'D BE AMAZED WHAT AGING DOES TO YOUR SENSE OF HUMOR. AND YOUR PATIENCE.
OKAY, FINE--I DIDN'T WANT TO BRING YOU INTO THIS UNTIL I WAS SURE.
YOU MEAN FOUR DESTROYED S.H.I.E.L.D. BASES SURE?
SEE? YOU'VE STILL GOT A SENSE OF HUMOR. LOOK, YOU'VE BEEN DRAGGED THROUGH THE MUCK ENOUGH LATELY, THIS STUFF BETWEEN YOU AND SAM--
YES. IT'S HARD TO KNOW WHO YOUR FRIENDS ARE.
I AGREE. AND HERE'S WHAT I CAN TELL YOU--MARIA HILL ISN'T ONE OF THEM. SHE'S BEEN LYING TO YOU, STEVE--
"--AND YOU NEED TO KNOW THE TRUTH."
COORDINATES WHISPERER SENT ME ARE NEARBY--WHICH IS THE FIRST SURPRISE. NEW YORK CITY'S AN AWFULLY CROWDED PLACE FOR SOMEONE LOOKING NOT TO BE NOTICED.
THEN AGAIN, MAYBE THAT'S WHY IT WORKS.

SECOND SURPRISE IS--HONESTLY, I EXPECTED NICER DIGS.

I DON'T KNOW WHY-- I JUST THOUGHT WITH THE WHOLE "INTERNATIONAL MAN OF MYSTERY" VIBE, THERE'D BE MORE OF A JET-SETTER, JAMES BOND LOOK--

--LESS CHINESE TAKEOUT AND BAD CORD MANAGEMENT.

IN HERE, SAM--

BUT NOW I'M ABOUT TO GET TO THE BIGGEST SURPRISE OF THEM ALL--

--THE IDENTITY OF THE WHISPERER.

I'VE HEARD THEORIES IT'S BRUCE BANNER OR DOCTOR DOOM.

LAST I HEARD, VEGAS PICKED A TEENAGE TONY STARK. BUT NOPE, TURNS OUT--

--IT'S RICK JONES.

I KNOW. IT'S A LITTLE ANTI-CLIMACTIC.

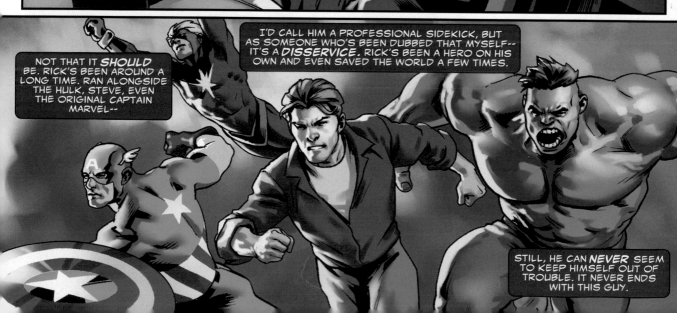

NOT THAT IT SHOULD BE. RICK'S BEEN AROUND A LONG TIME. RAN ALONGSIDE THE HULK, STEVE, EVEN THE ORIGINAL CAPTAIN MARVEL--

I'D CALL HIM A PROFESSIONAL SIDEKICK, BUT AS SOMEONE WHO'S BEEN DUBBED THAT MYSELF-- IT'S A DISSERVICE. RICK'S BEEN A HERO ON HIS OWN AND EVEN SAVED THE WORLD A FEW TIMES.

STILL, HE CAN NEVER SEEM TO KEEP HIMSELF OUT OF TROUBLE. IT NEVER ENDS WITH THIS GUY.

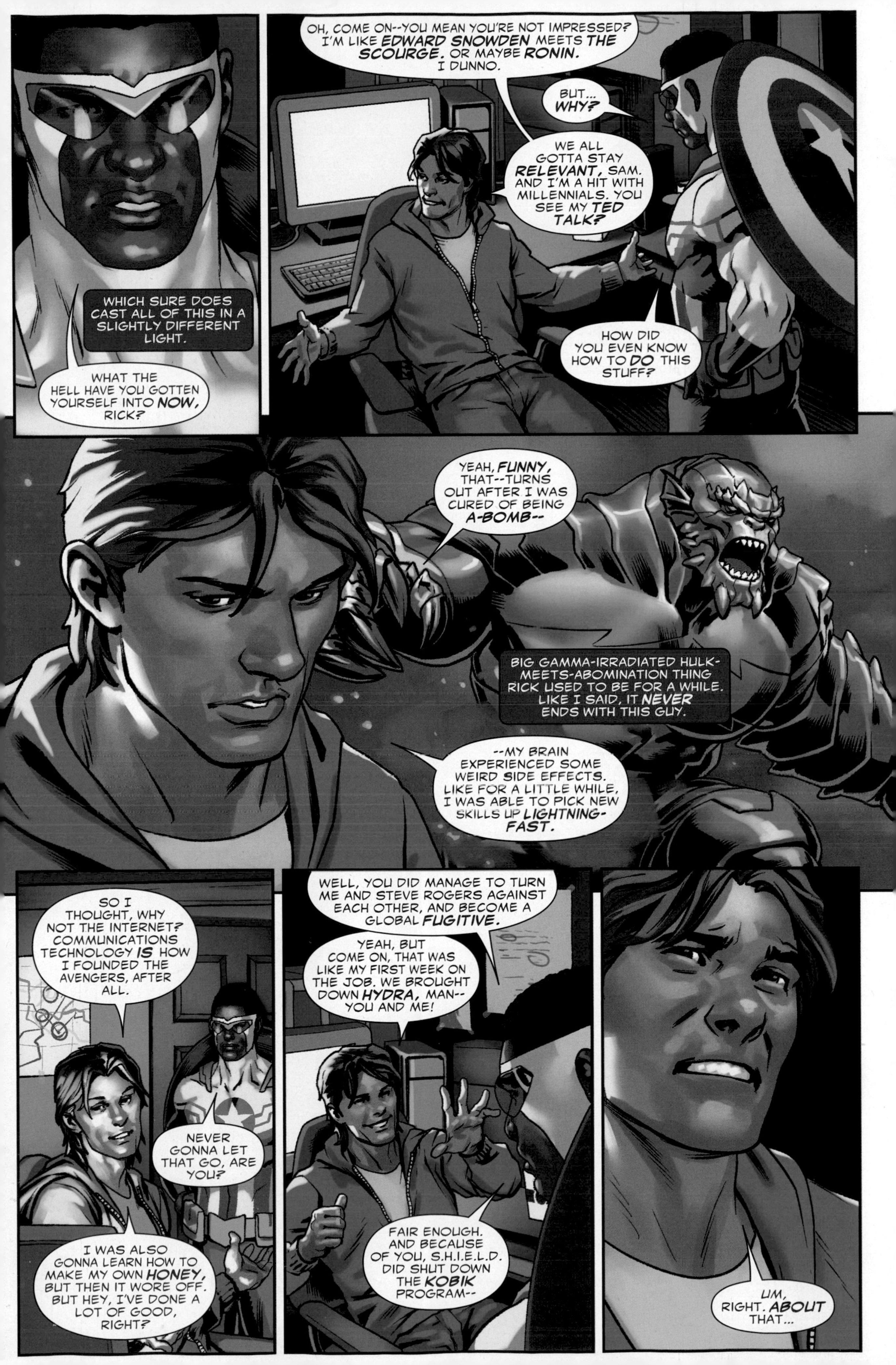
WHICH SURE DOES CAST ALL OF THIS IN A SLIGHTLY DIFFERENT LIGHT.
WHAT THE HELL HAVE YOU GOTTEN YOURSELF INTO NOW, RICK?
OH, COME ON--YOU MEAN YOU'RE NOT IMPRESSED? I'M LIKE EDWARD SNOWDEN MEETS THE SCOURGE. OR MAYBE RONIN. I DUNNO.
BUT... WHY?
WE ALL GOTTA STAY RELEVANT, SAM. AND I'M A HIT WITH MILLENNIALS. YOU SEE MY TED TALK?
HOW DID YOU EVEN KNOW HOW TO DO THIS STUFF?
YEAH, FUNNY, THAT--TURNS OUT AFTER I WAS CURED OF BEING A-BOMB--
BIG GAMMA-IRRADIATED HULK-MEETS-ABOMINATION THING RICK USED TO BE FOR A WHILE. LIKE I SAID, IT NEVER ENDS WITH THIS GUY.
--MY BRAIN EXPERIENCED SOME WEIRD SIDE EFFECTS. LIKE FOR A LITTLE WHILE, I WAS ABLE TO PICK NEW SKILLS UP LIGHTNING-FAST.
SO I THOUGHT, WHY NOT THE INTERNET? COMMUNICATIONS TECHNOLOGY IS HOW I FOUNDED THE AVENGERS, AFTER ALL.
NEVER GONNA LET THAT GO, ARE YOU?
I WAS ALSO GONNA LEARN HOW TO MAKE MY OWN HONEY, BUT THEN IT WORE OFF. BUT HEY, I'VE DONE A LOT OF GOOD, RIGHT?
WELL, YOU DID MANAGE TO TURN ME AND STEVE ROGERS AGAINST EACH OTHER, AND BECOME A GLOBAL FUGITIVE.
YEAH, BUT COME ON, THAT WAS LIKE MY FIRST WEEK ON THE JOB. WE BROUGHT DOWN HYDRA, MAN--YOU AND ME!
FAIR ENOUGH. AND BECAUSE OF YOU, S.H.I.E.L.D. DID SHUT DOWN THE KOBIK PROGRAM--
UM, RIGHT. ABOUT THAT...

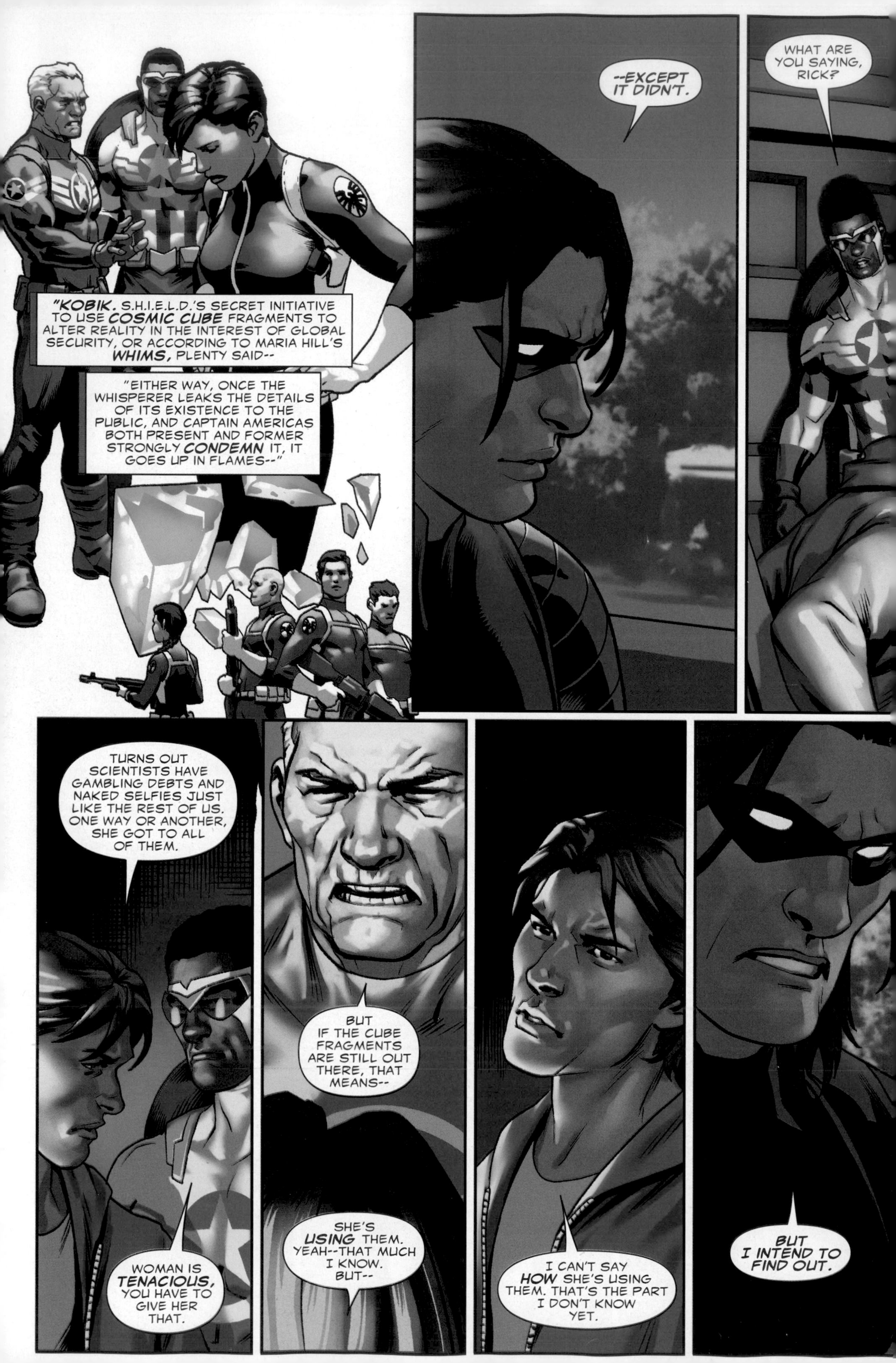
"KOBIK. S.H.I.E.L.D.'S SECRET INITIATIVE TO USE COSMIC CUBE FRAGMENTS TO ALTER REALITY IN THE INTEREST OF GLOBAL SECURITY, OR ACCORDING TO MARIA HILL'S WHIMS, PLENTY SAID--
"EITHER WAY, ONCE THE WHISPERER LEAKS THE DETAILS OF ITS EXISTENCE TO THE PUBLIC, AND CAPTAIN AMERICAS BOTH PRESENT AND FORMER STRONGLY CONDEMN IT, IT GOES UP IN FLAMES--"
--EXCEPT IT DIDN'T.
WHAT ARE YOU SAYING, RICK?
TURNS OUT SCIENTISTS HAVE GAMBLING DEBTS AND NAKED SELFIES JUST LIKE THE REST OF US. ONE WAY OR ANOTHER, SHE GOT TO ALL OF THEM.
WOMAN IS TENACIOUS, YOU HAVE TO GIVE HER THAT.
BUT IF THE CUBE FRAGMENTS ARE STILL OUT THERE, THAT MEANS--
SHE'S USING THEM. YEAH--THAT MUCH I KNOW. BUT--
I CAN'T SAY HOW SHE'S USING THEM. THAT'S THE PART I DON'T KNOW YET.
BUT I INTEND TO FIND OUT.

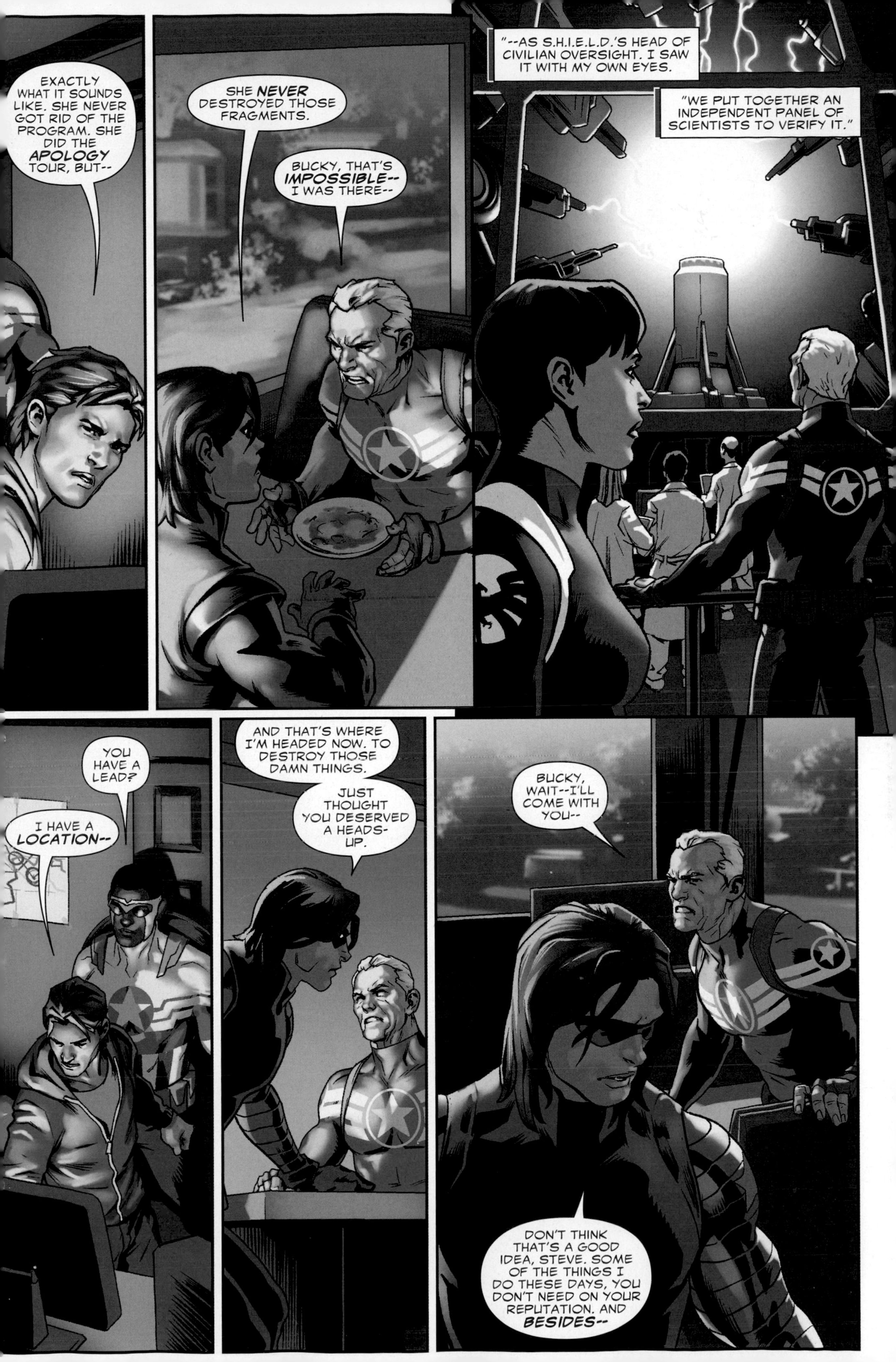
EXACTLY WHAT IT SOUNDS LIKE. SHE NEVER GOT RID OF THE PROGRAM. SHE DID THE *APOLOGY* TOUR, BUT--
SHE *NEVER* DESTROYED THOSE FRAGMENTS.
BUCKY, THAT'S *IMPOSSIBLE--* I WAS THERE--
"--AS S.H.I.E.L.D.'S HEAD OF CIVILIAN OVERSIGHT. I SAW IT WITH MY OWN EYES.
"WE PUT TOGETHER AN INDEPENDENT PANEL OF SCIENTISTS TO VERIFY IT."
YOU HAVE A LEAD?
I HAVE A *LOCATION--*
AND THAT'S WHERE I'M HEADED NOW. TO DESTROY THOSE DAMN THINGS.
JUST THOUGHT YOU DESERVED A HEADS-UP.
BUCKY, WAIT--I'LL COME WITH YOU--
DON'T THINK THAT'S A GOOD IDEA, STEVE. SOME OF THE THINGS I DO THESE DAYS, YOU DON'T NEED ON YOUR REPUTATION. AND *BESIDES--*

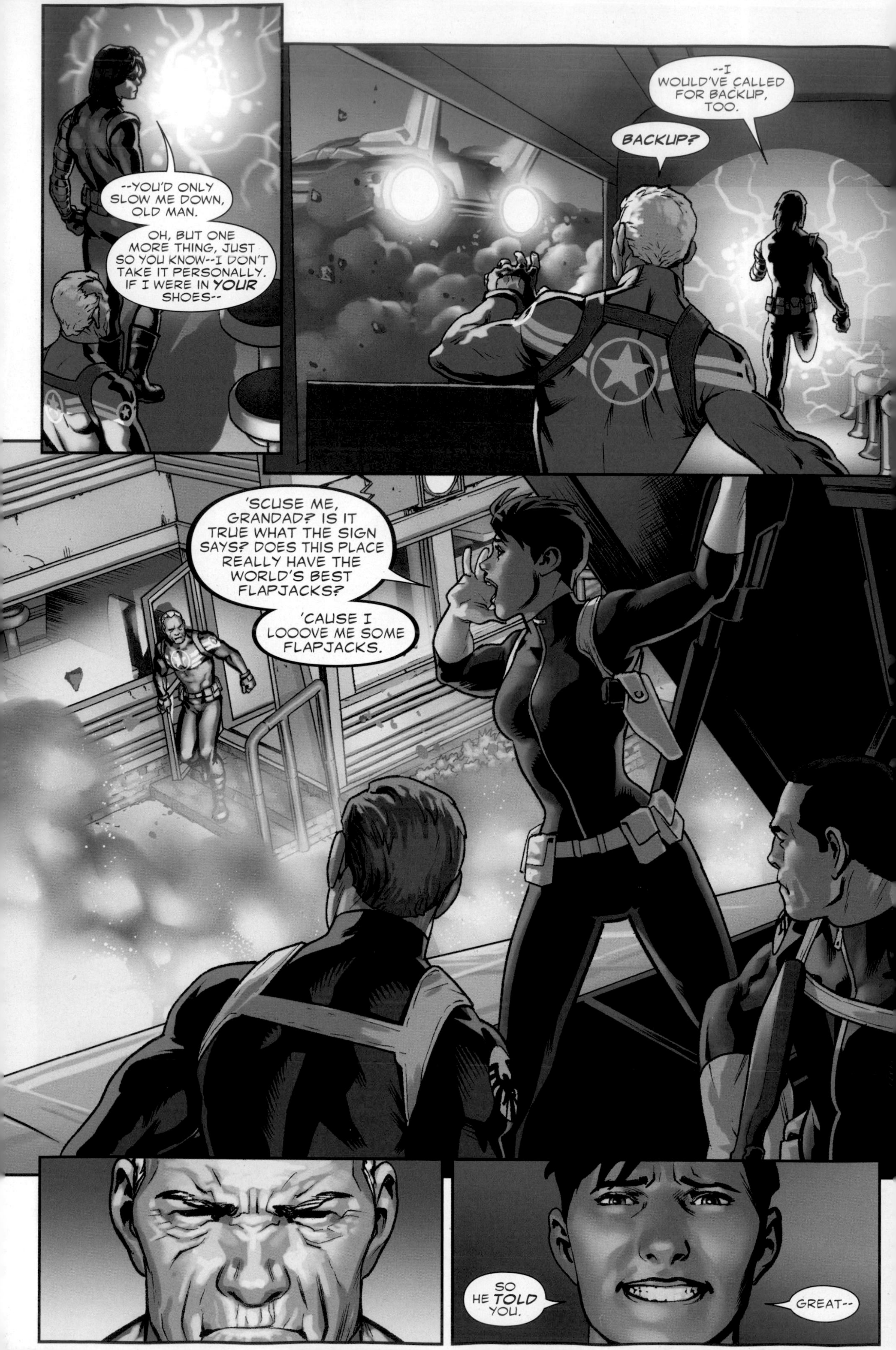
--YOU'D ONLY SLOW ME DOWN, OLD MAN.
OH, BUT ONE MORE THING, JUST SO YOU KNOW--I DON'T TAKE IT PERSONALLY. IF I WERE IN YOUR SHOES--
--I WOULD'VE CALLED FOR BACKUP, TOO.
BACKUP?
'SCUSE ME, GRANDAD? IS IT TRUE WHAT THE SIGN SAYS? DOES THIS PLACE REALLY HAVE THE WORLD'S BEST FLAPJACKS?
'CAUSE I LOOOVE ME SOME FLAPJACKS.
SO HE TOLD YOU.
GREAT--

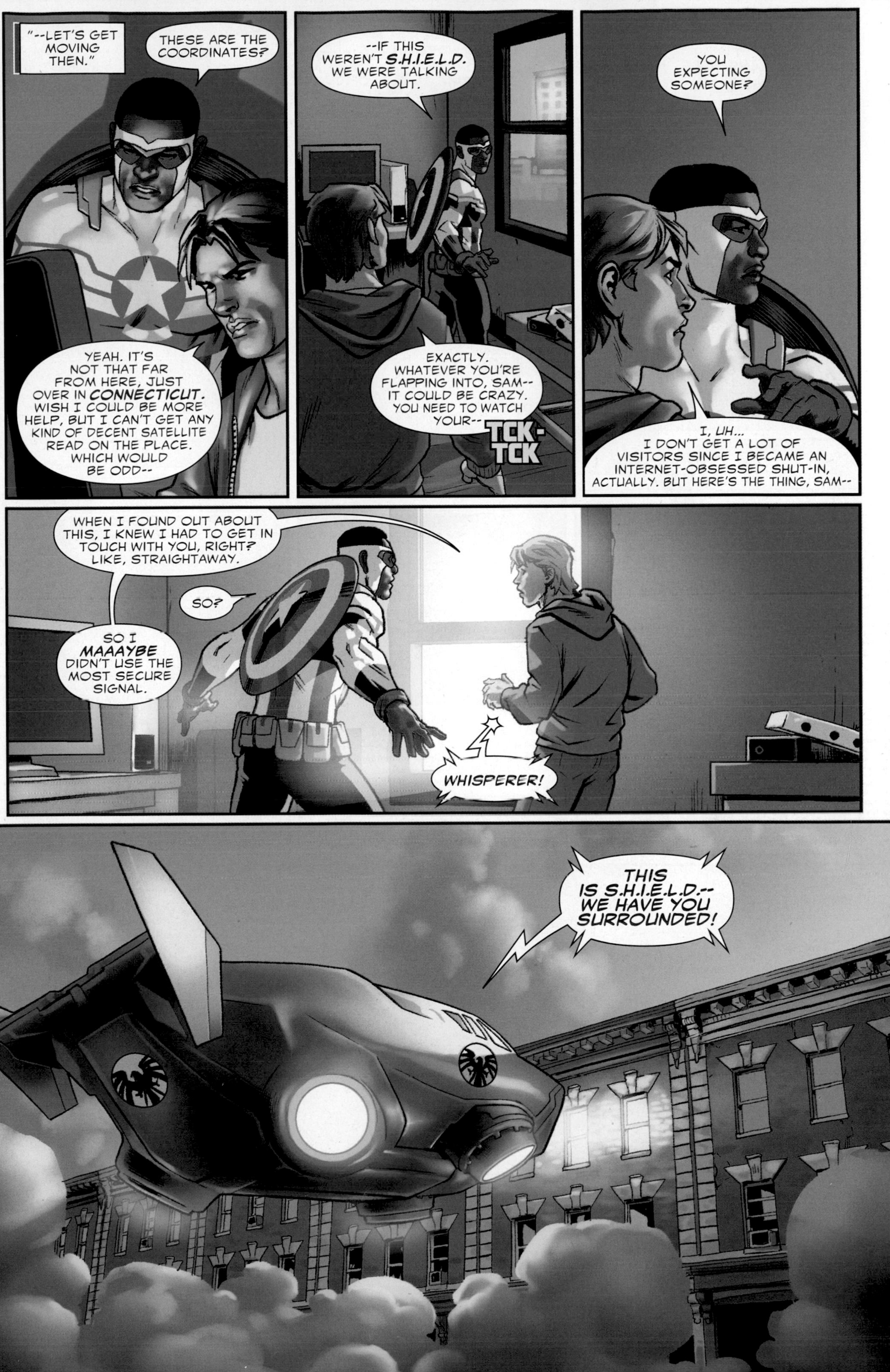
"--LET'S GET MOVING THEN."
THESE ARE THE COORDINATES?
YEAH. IT'S NOT THAT FAR FROM HERE, JUST OVER IN CONNECTICUT. WISH I COULD BE MORE HELP, BUT I CAN'T GET ANY KIND OF DECENT SATELLITE READ ON THE PLACE. WHICH WOULD BE ODD--
--IF THIS WEREN'T S.H.I.E.L.D. WE WERE TALKING ABOUT.
EXACTLY. WHATEVER YOU'RE FLAPPING INTO, SAM-- IT COULD BE CRAZY. YOU NEED TO WATCH YOUR--
TCK-TCK
YOU EXPECTING SOMEONE?
I, UH... I DON'T GET A LOT OF VISITORS SINCE I BECAME AN INTERNET-OBSESSED SHUT-IN, ACTUALLY. BUT HERE'S THE THING, SAM--
WHEN I FOUND OUT ABOUT THIS, I KNEW I HAD TO GET IN TOUCH WITH YOU, RIGHT? LIKE, STRAIGHTAWAY.
SO?
SO I MAAAYBE DIDN'T USE THE MOST SECURE SIGNAL.
WHISPERER!
THIS IS S.H.I.E.L.D.-- WE HAVE YOU SURROUNDED!

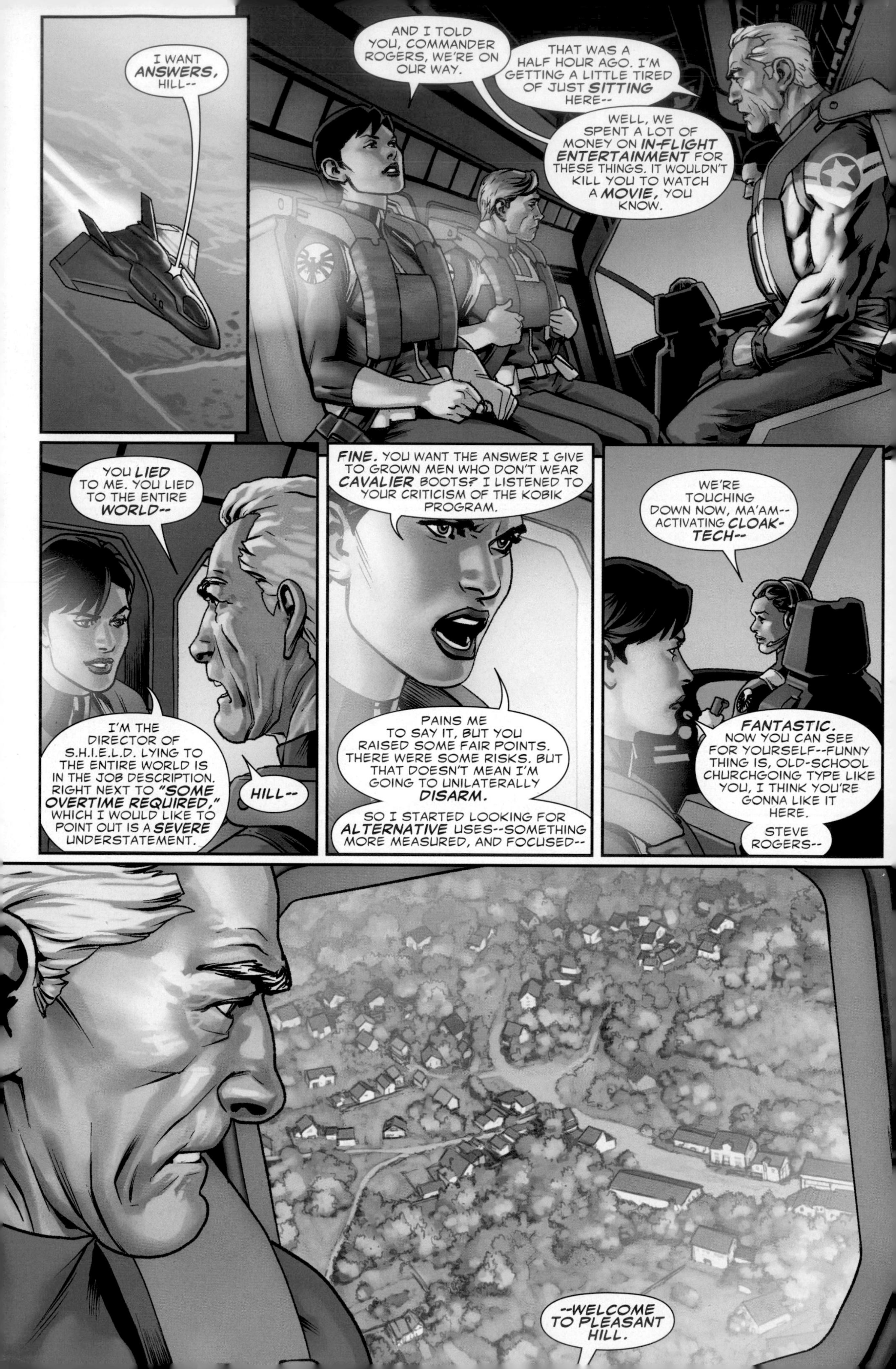
I WANT ANSWERS, HILL--
AND I TOLD YOU, COMMANDER ROGERS, WE'RE ON OUR WAY.
THAT WAS A HALF HOUR AGO. I'M GETTING A LITTLE TIRED OF JUST SITTING HERE--
WELL, WE SPENT A LOT OF MONEY ON IN-FLIGHT ENTERTAINMENT FOR THESE THINGS. IT WOULDN'T KILL YOU TO WATCH A MOVIE, YOU KNOW.
YOU LIED TO ME. YOU LIED TO THE ENTIRE WORLD--
I'M THE DIRECTOR OF S.H.I.E.L.D. LYING TO THE ENTIRE WORLD IS IN THE JOB DESCRIPTION. RIGHT NEXT TO "SOME OVERTIME REQUIRED," WHICH I WOULD LIKE TO POINT OUT IS A SEVERE UNDERSTATEMENT.
HILL--
FINE. YOU WANT THE ANSWER I GIVE TO GROWN MEN WHO DON'T WEAR CAVALIER BOOTS? I LISTENED TO YOUR CRITICISM OF THE KOBIK PROGRAM.
PAINS ME TO SAY IT, BUT YOU RAISED SOME FAIR POINTS. THERE WERE SOME RISKS. BUT THAT DOESN'T MEAN I'M GOING TO UNILATERALLY DISARM.
SO I STARTED LOOKING FOR ALTERNATIVE USES--SOMETHING MORE MEASURED, AND FOCUSED--
WE'RE TOUCHING DOWN NOW, MA'AM--ACTIVATING CLOAK-TECH--
FANTASTIC. NOW YOU CAN SEE FOR YOURSELF--FUNNY THING IS, OLD-SCHOOL CHURCHGOING TYPE LIKE YOU, I THINK YOU'RE GONNA LIKE IT HERE.
STEVE ROGERS--
--WELCOME TO PLEASANT HILL.

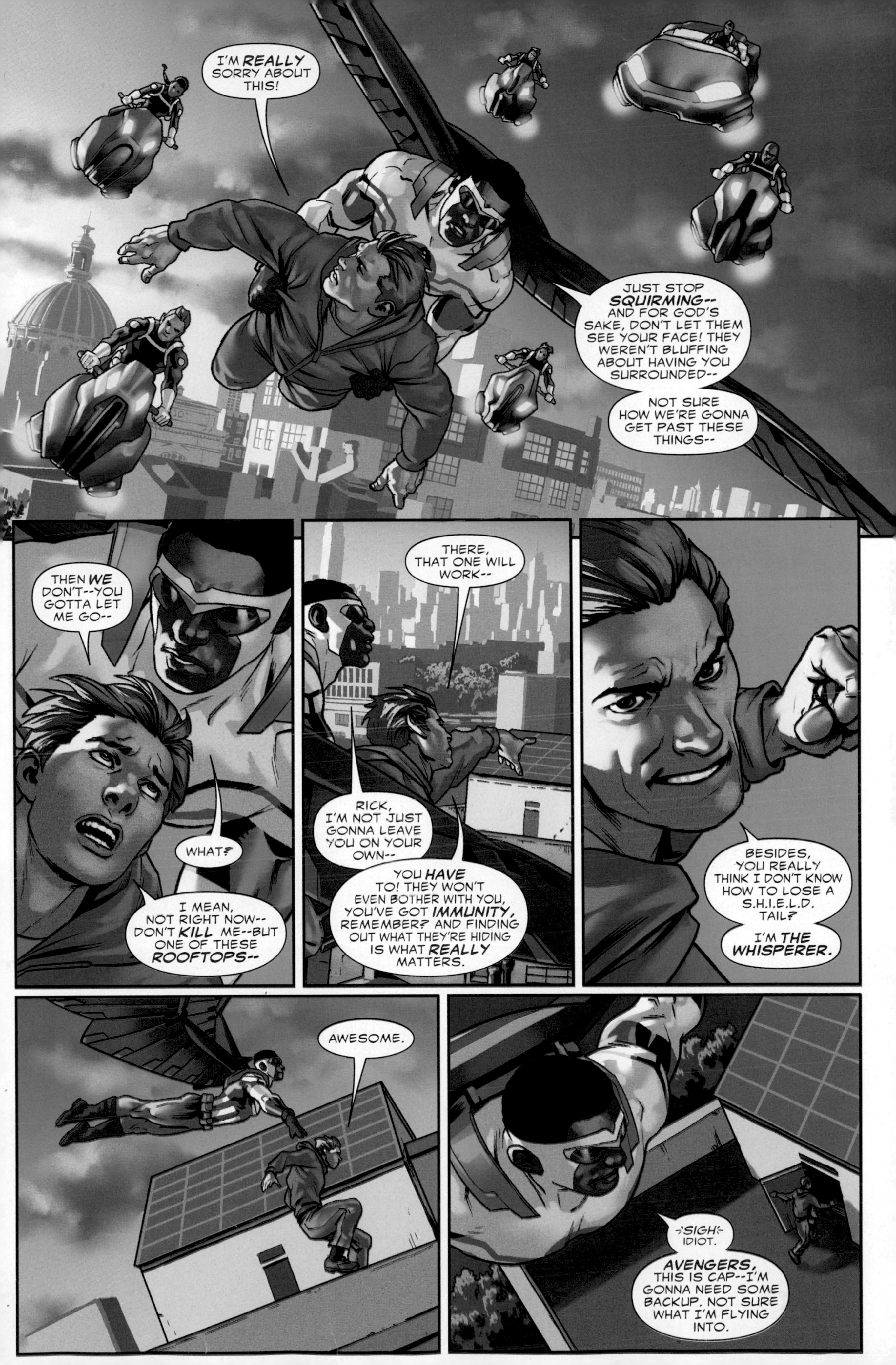
I'M REALLY SORRY ABOUT THIS!
JUST STOP SQUIRMING-- AND FOR GOD'S SAKE, DON'T LET THEM SEE YOUR FACE! THEY WEREN'T BLUFFING ABOUT HAVING YOU SURROUNDED--
NOT SURE HOW WE'RE GONNA GET PAST THESE THINGS--
THEN WE DON'T--YOU GOTTA LET ME GO--
WHAT?
I MEAN, NOT RIGHT NOW--DON'T KILL ME--BUT ONE OF THESE ROOFTOPS--
THERE, THAT ONE WILL WORK--
RICK, I'M NOT JUST GONNA LEAVE YOU ON YOUR OWN--
YOU HAVE TO! THEY WON'T EVEN BOTHER WITH YOU, YOU'VE GOT IMMUNITY, REMEMBER? AND FINDING OUT WHAT THEY'RE HIDING IS WHAT REALLY MATTERS.
BESIDES, YOU REALLY THINK I DON'T KNOW HOW TO LOSE A S.H.I.E.L.D. TAIL?
I'M THE WHISPERER.
AWESOME.
SIGH IDIOT.
AVENGERS, THIS IS CAP--I'M GONNA NEED SOME BACKUP. NOT SURE WHAT I'M FLYING INTO.

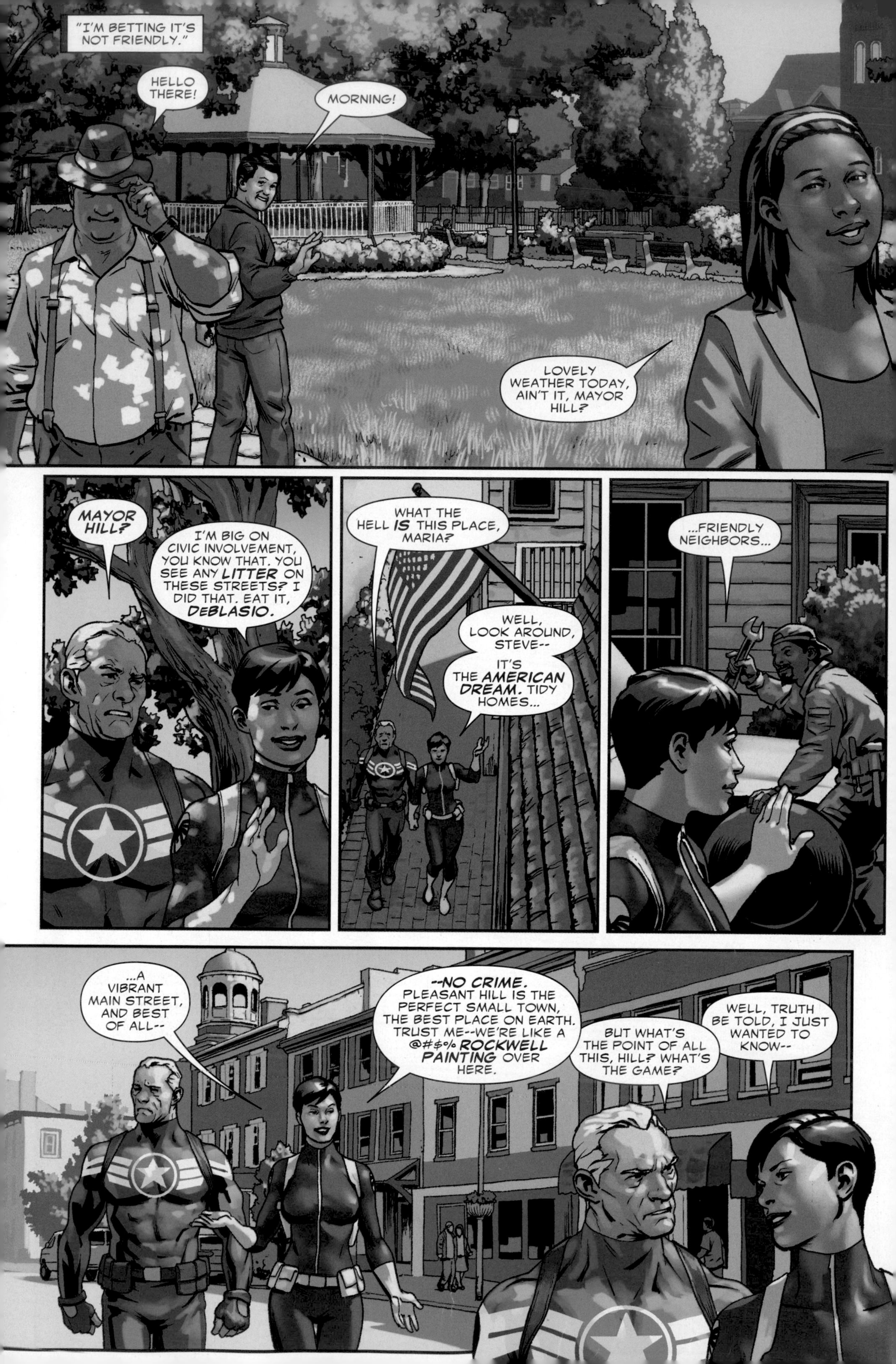
"I'M BETTING IT'S NOT FRIENDLY."
HELLO THERE!
MORNING!
LOVELY WEATHER TODAY, AIN'T IT, MAYOR HILL?
MAYOR HILL?
I'M BIG ON CIVIC INVOLVEMENT, YOU KNOW THAT. YOU SEE ANY LITTER ON THESE STREETS? I DID THAT. EAT IT, DEBLASIO.
WHAT THE HELL IS THIS PLACE, MARIA?
WELL, LOOK AROUND, STEVE--
IT'S THE AMERICAN DREAM. TIDY HOMES...
...FRIENDLY NEIGHBORS...
...A VIBRANT MAIN STREET, AND BEST OF ALL--
--NO CRIME. PLEASANT HILL IS THE PERFECT SMALL TOWN, THE BEST PLACE ON EARTH. TRUST ME--WE'RE LIKE A @#$% ROCKWELL PAINTING OVER HERE.
BUT WHAT'S THE POINT OF ALL THIS, HILL? WHAT'S THE GAME?
WELL, TRUTH BE TOLD, I JUST WANTED TO KNOW--

--WHAT THESE OLD *ICE CREAM PARLORS* WERE LIKE!

NOW, WERE THESE AROUND IN YOUR DAY, OR WERE THEY MORE OF A *FIFTIES* THING? 'CAUSE THERE'S ONE IN IT'S A WONDERFUL LIFE, BUT IT WAS A PHARMACY, TOO? *DO NOT GET.* EITHER WAY, WHAT'D YOU LIKE?

WHAT I'D LIKE IS FOR PEOPLE TO STOP OFFERING ME FOOD AND START GIVING ME *ANSWERS*.

WELL, MAYBE YOU'RE STARTING TO LOOK A LITTLE *THIN*, OLD FELLA, YOU CONSIDER THAT?

MAYOR HILL!

HEY, HAROLD. GOOD TO SEE YOU. HOW'S BUSINESS?

YOU KNOW ME, I CAN'T COMPLAIN.

I DO KNOW YOU, HAROLD. SPEAKING OF--YOU RECOGNIZE *THIS* FELLA?

HMM--NAAH? NAAH, CAN'T SAY I DO. GETUP LOOKS KINDA *MILITARY*, THOUGH--I'M GUESSIN' YOU'RE HERE FOR THE BIG AIR SHOW THIS WEEK?

THAT'S RIGHT, *THE BIG AIR SHOW.*

WELL, ANY FRIEND OF THE MAYOR'S IS A FRIEND OF MINE. TWO MALTEDS COMING RIGHT UP, ON THE HOUSE!

MALTEDS. *HA!* YOU HEAR THAT? *MALTEDS.*

MARIA--

SURE. HEY, HAROLD, BEFORE YOU DO THAT--YOU MIND LETTING ME TAKE A QUICK SCAN?

WHY, 'COURSE NOT! GOTTA KEEP THE TOWN *SAFE* AND ALL--

THAT'S RIGHT, JUST KEEPING US SAFE...

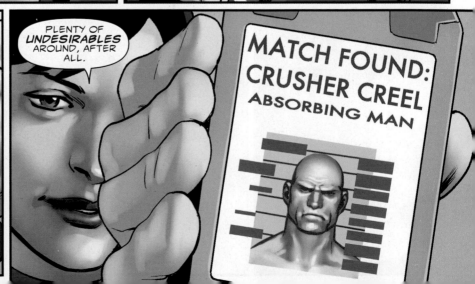

PLENTY OF *UNDESIRABLES* AROUND, AFTER ALL.

MATCH FOUND: CRUSHER CREEL ABSORBING MAN

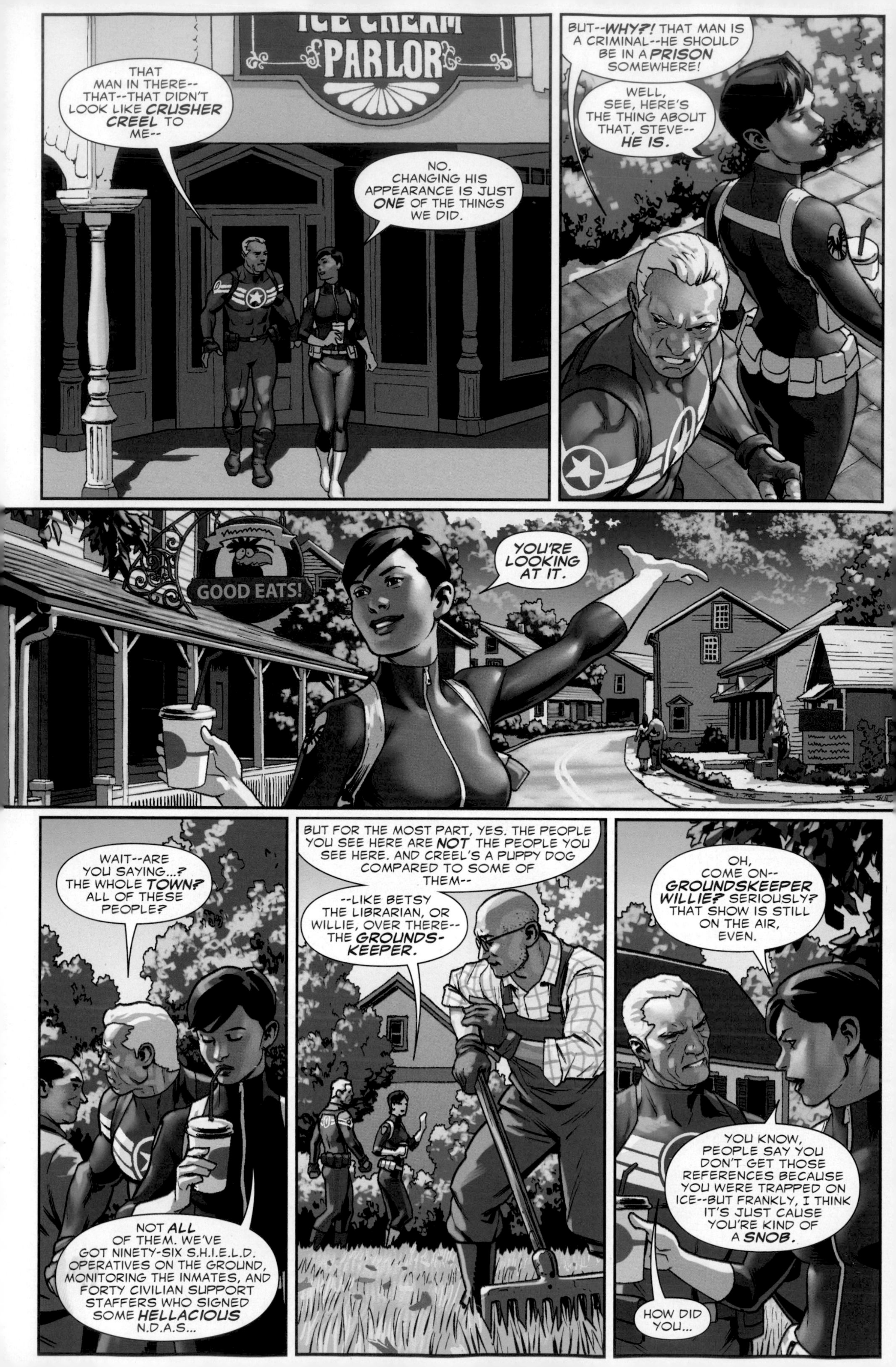
ICE CREAM PARLOR
THAT MAN IN THERE--THAT--THAT DIDN'T LOOK LIKE CRUSHER CREEL TO ME--
NO. CHANGING HIS APPEARANCE IS JUST ONE OF THE THINGS WE DID.
BUT--WHY?! THAT MAN IS A CRIMINAL--HE SHOULD BE IN A PRISON SOMEWHERE!
WELL, SEE, HERE'S THE THING ABOUT THAT, STEVE--HE IS.
GOOD EATS!
YOU'RE LOOKING AT IT.
WAIT--ARE YOU SAYING...? THE WHOLE TOWN? ALL OF THESE PEOPLE?
NOT ALL OF THEM. WE'VE GOT NINETY-SIX S.H.I.E.L.D. OPERATIVES ON THE GROUND, MONITORING THE INMATES, AND FORTY CIVILIAN SUPPORT STAFFERS WHO SIGNED SOME HELLACIOUS N.D.A.S...
BUT FOR THE MOST PART, YES. THE PEOPLE YOU SEE HERE ARE NOT THE PEOPLE YOU SEE HERE. AND CREEL'S A PUPPY DOG COMPARED TO SOME OF THEM--
--LIKE BETSY THE LIBRARIAN, OR WILLIE, OVER THERE--THE GROUNDSKEEPER.
OH, COME ON--GROUNDSKEEPER WILLIE? SERIOUSLY? THAT SHOW IS STILL ON THE AIR, EVEN.
YOU KNOW, PEOPLE SAY YOU DON'T GET THOSE REFERENCES BECAUSE YOU WERE TRAPPED ON ICE--BUT FRANKLY, I THINK IT'S JUST CAUSE YOU'RE KIND OF A SNOB.
HOW DID YOU...

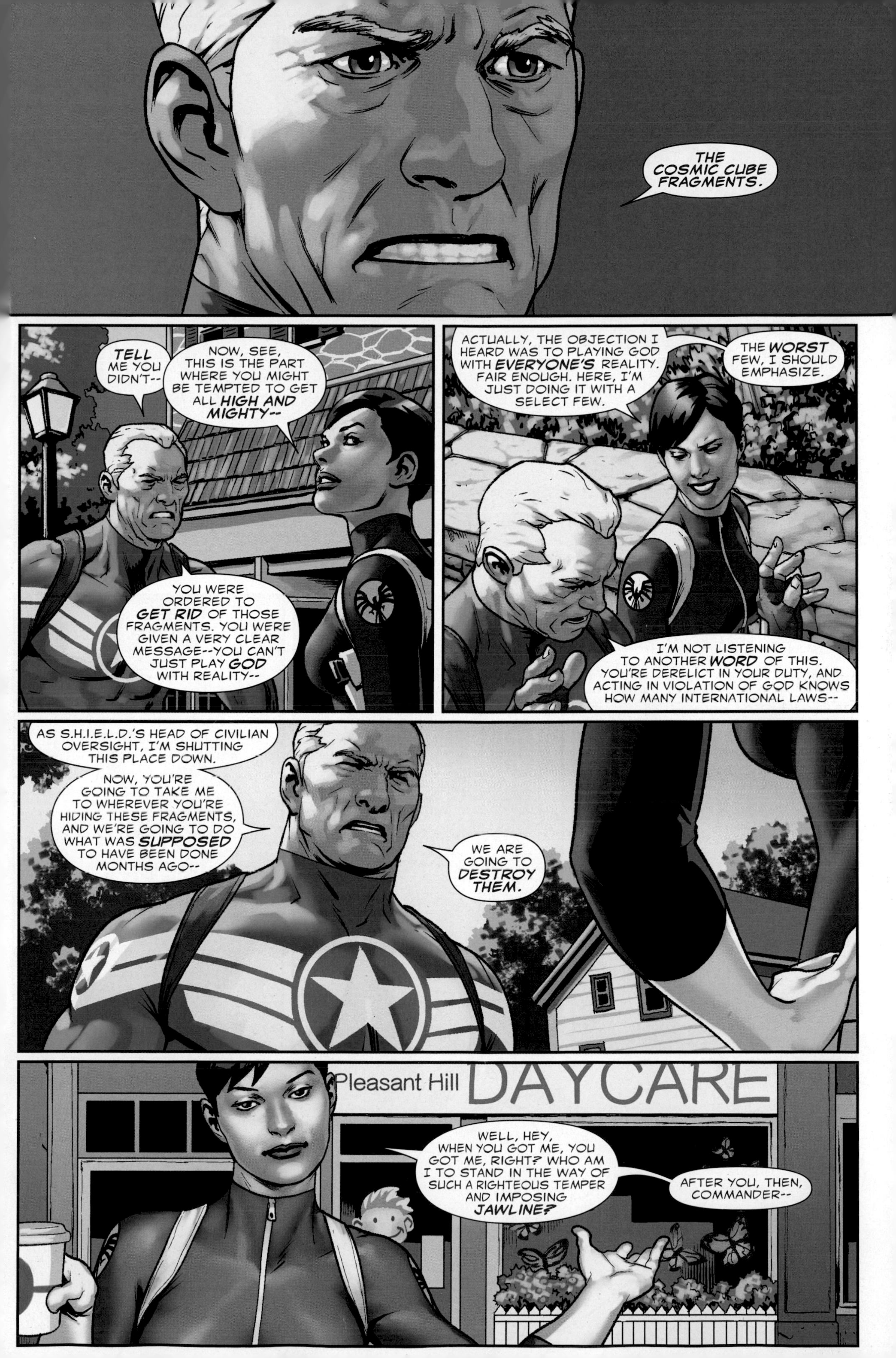
THE COSMIC CUBE FRAGMENTS.
TELL ME YOU DIDN'T--
NOW, SEE, THIS IS THE PART WHERE YOU MIGHT BE TEMPTED TO GET ALL HIGH AND MIGHTY--
YOU WERE ORDERED TO GET RID OF THOSE FRAGMENTS. YOU WERE GIVEN A VERY CLEAR MESSAGE--YOU CAN'T JUST PLAY GOD WITH REALITY--
ACTUALLY, THE OBJECTION I HEARD WAS TO PLAYING GOD WITH EVERYONE'S REALITY. FAIR ENOUGH. HERE, I'M JUST DOING IT WITH A SELECT FEW.
THE WORST FEW, I SHOULD EMPHASIZE.
I'M NOT LISTENING TO ANOTHER WORD OF THIS. YOU'RE DERELICT IN YOUR DUTY, AND ACTING IN VIOLATION OF GOD KNOWS HOW MANY INTERNATIONAL LAWS--
AS S.H.I.E.L.D.'S HEAD OF CIVILIAN OVERSIGHT, I'M SHUTTING THIS PLACE DOWN.
NOW, YOU'RE GOING TO TAKE ME TO WHEREVER YOU'RE HIDING THESE FRAGMENTS, AND WE'RE GOING TO DO WHAT WAS SUPPOSED TO HAVE BEEN DONE MONTHS AGO--
WE ARE GOING TO DESTROY THEM.
Pleasant Hill DAYCARE
WELL, HEY, WHEN YOU GOT ME, YOU GOT ME, RIGHT? WHO AM I TO STAND IN THE WAY OF SUCH A RIGHTEOUS TEMPER AND IMPOSING JAWLINE?
AFTER YOU, THEN, COMMANDER--

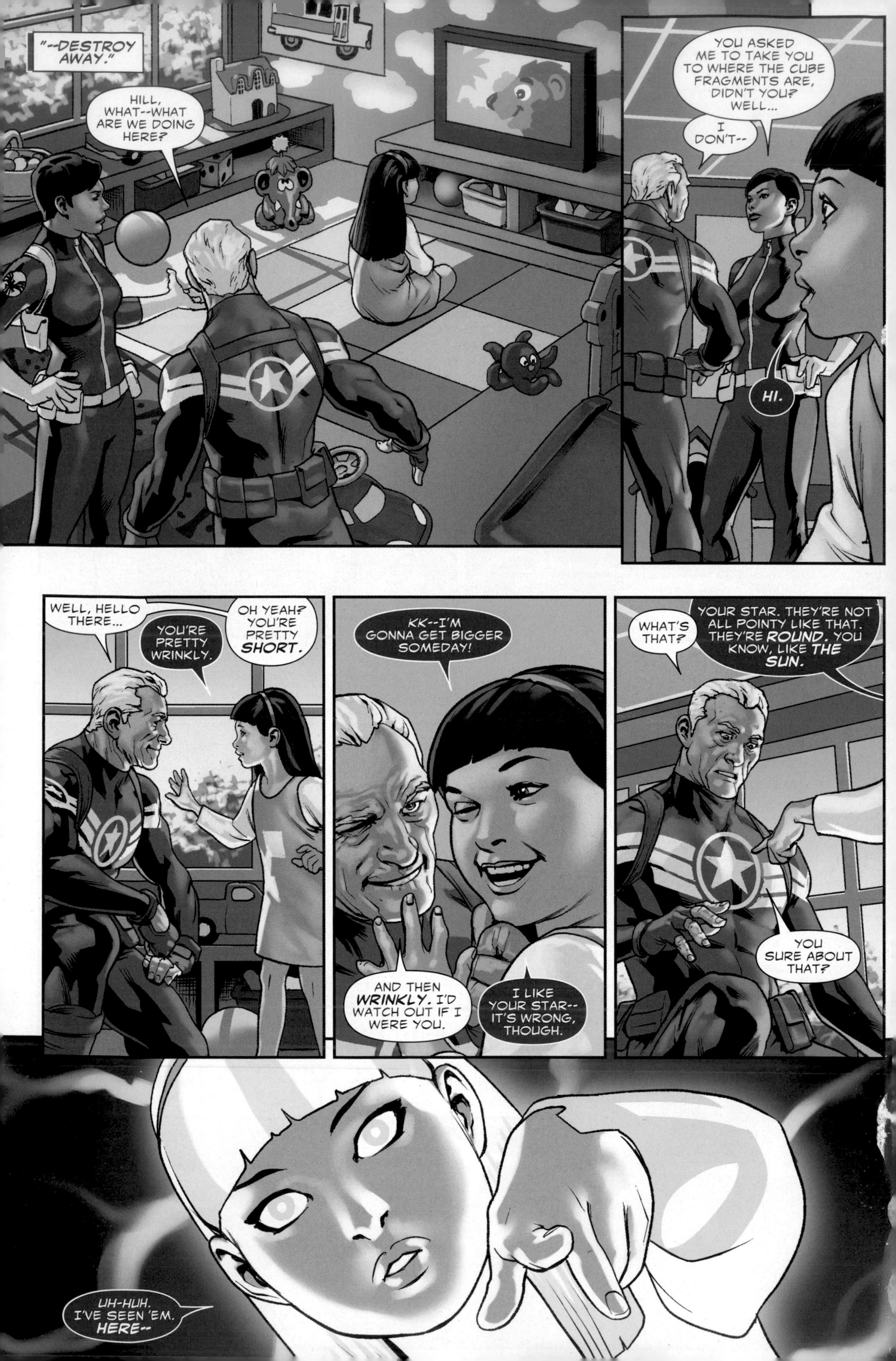
"--DESTROY AWAY."
HILL, WHAT--WHAT ARE WE DOING HERE?
YOU ASKED ME TO TAKE YOU TO WHERE THE CUBE FRAGMENTS ARE, DIDN'T YOU? WELL...
I DON'T--
HI.
WELL, HELLO THERE...
YOU'RE PRETTY WRINKLY.
OH YEAH? YOU'RE PRETTY SHORT.
KK--I'M GONNA GET BIGGER SOMEDAY!
AND THEN WRINKLY. I'D WATCH OUT IF I WERE YOU.
I LIKE YOUR STAR-- IT'S WRONG, THOUGH.
WHAT'S THAT?
YOUR STAR. THEY'RE NOT ALL POINTY LIKE THAT. THEY'RE ROUND. YOU KNOW, LIKE THE SUN.
YOU SURE ABOUT THAT?
UH-HUH. I'VE SEEN 'EM. HERE--

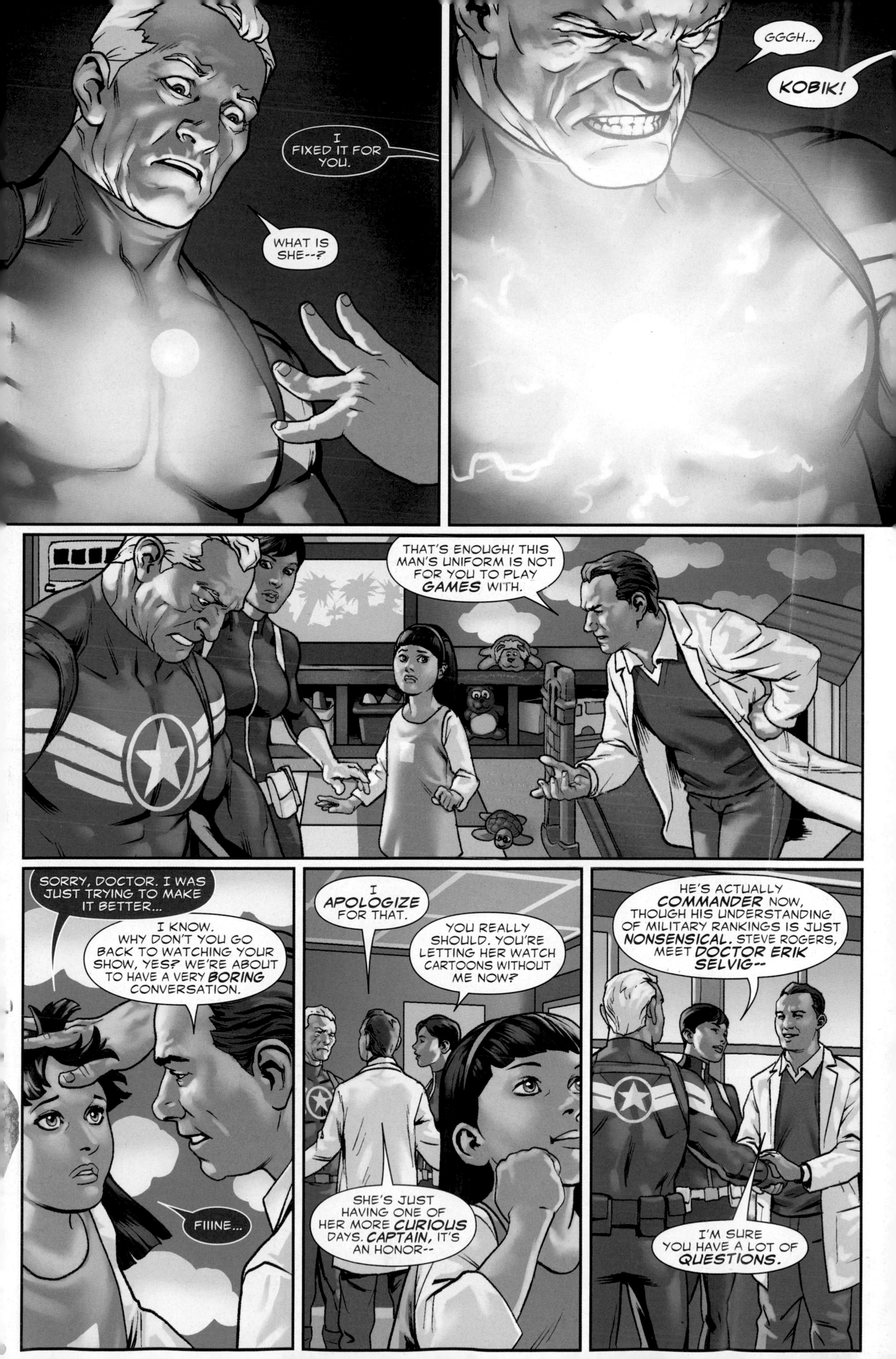
I FIXED IT FOR YOU.
WHAT IS SHE--?
GGGH...
KOBIK!
THAT'S ENOUGH! THIS MAN'S UNIFORM IS NOT FOR YOU TO PLAY GAMES WITH.
SORRY, DOCTOR. I WAS JUST TRYING TO MAKE IT BETTER...
I KNOW. WHY DON'T YOU GO BACK TO WATCHING YOUR SHOW, YES? WE'RE ABOUT TO HAVE A VERY BORING CONVERSATION.
FIIINE...
I APOLOGIZE FOR THAT.
YOU REALLY SHOULD. YOU'RE LETTING HER WATCH CARTOONS WITHOUT ME NOW?
SHE'S JUST HAVING ONE OF HER MORE CURIOUS DAYS. CAPTAIN, IT'S AN HONOR--
HE'S ACTUALLY COMMANDER NOW, THOUGH HIS UNDERSTANDING OF MILITARY RANKINGS IS JUST NONSENSICAL. STEVE ROGERS, MEET DOCTOR ERIK SELVIG--
I'M SURE YOU HAVE A LOT OF QUESTIONS.

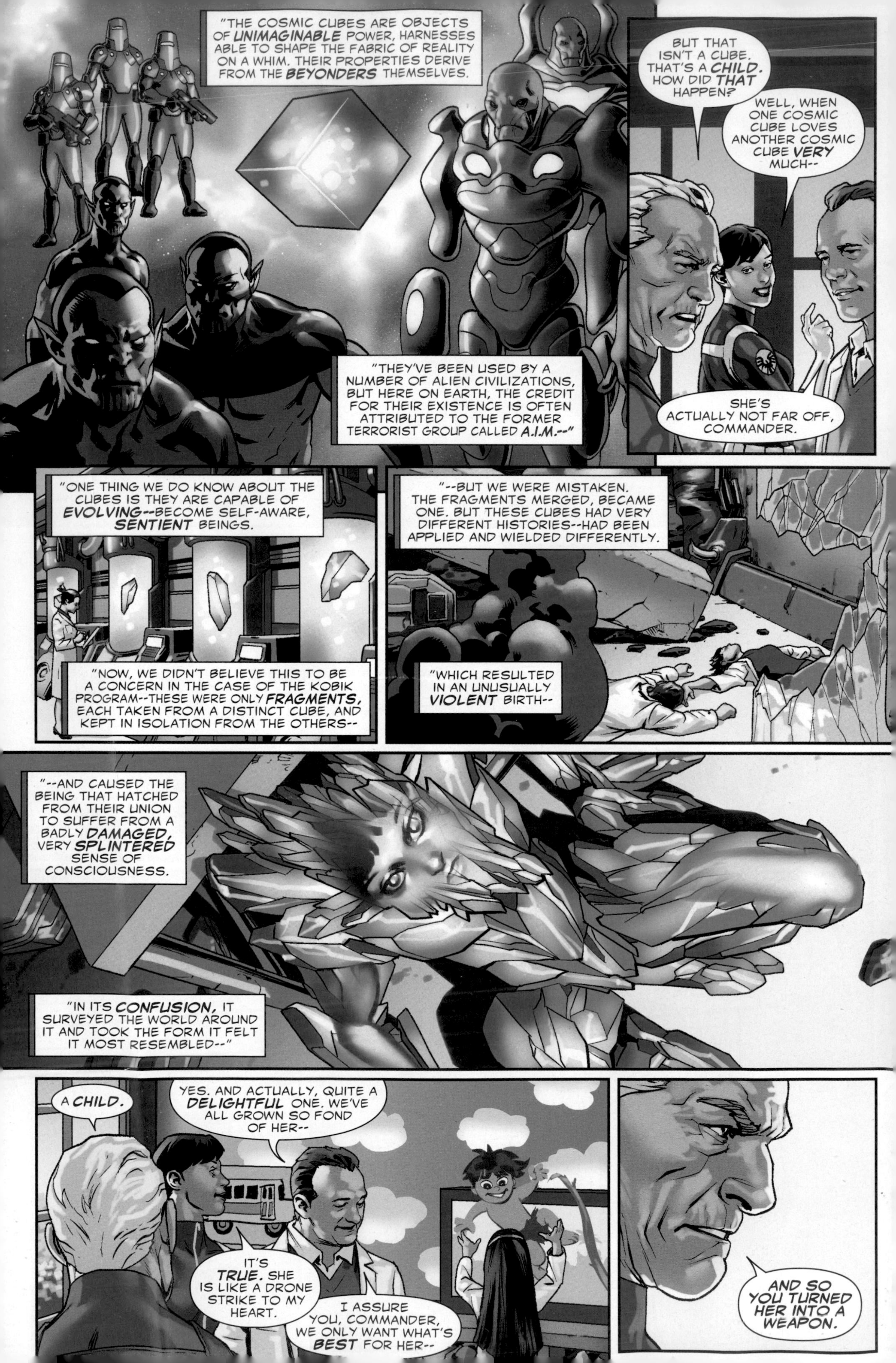
"THE COSMIC CUBES ARE OBJECTS OF UNIMAGINABLE POWER, HARNESSES ABLE TO SHAPE THE FABRIC OF REALITY ON A WHIM. THEIR PROPERTIES DERIVE FROM THE BEYONDERS THEMSELVES.
"THEY'VE BEEN USED BY A NUMBER OF ALIEN CIVILIZATIONS, BUT HERE ON EARTH, THE CREDIT FOR THEIR EXISTENCE IS OFTEN ATTRIBUTED TO THE FORMER TERRORIST GROUP CALLED A.I.M.--"
BUT THAT ISN'T A CUBE. THAT'S A CHILD. HOW DID THAT HAPPEN?
WELL, WHEN ONE COSMIC CUBE LOVES ANOTHER COSMIC CUBE VERY MUCH--
SHE'S ACTUALLY NOT FAR OFF, COMMANDER.
"ONE THING WE DO KNOW ABOUT THE CUBES IS THEY ARE CAPABLE OF EVOLVING--BECOME SELF-AWARE, SENTIENT BEINGS.
"NOW, WE DIDN'T BELIEVE THIS TO BE A CONCERN IN THE CASE OF THE KOBIK PROGRAM--THESE WERE ONLY FRAGMENTS, EACH TAKEN FROM A DISTINCT CUBE, AND KEPT IN ISOLATION FROM THE OTHERS--
"--BUT WE WERE MISTAKEN. THE FRAGMENTS MERGED, BECAME ONE. BUT THESE CUBES HAD VERY DIFFERENT HISTORIES--HAD BEEN APPLIED AND WIELDED DIFFERENTLY.
"WHICH RESULTED IN AN UNUSUALLY VIOLENT BIRTH--
"--AND CAUSED THE BEING THAT HATCHED FROM THEIR UNION TO SUFFER FROM A BADLY DAMAGED, VERY SPLINTERED SENSE OF CONSCIOUSNESS.
"IN ITS CONFUSION, IT SURVEYED THE WORLD AROUND IT AND TOOK THE FORM IT FELT IT MOST RESEMBLED--"
A CHILD.
YES. AND ACTUALLY, QUITE A DELIGHTFUL ONE. WE'VE ALL GROWN SO FOND OF HER--
IT'S TRUE. SHE IS LIKE A DRONE STRIKE TO MY HEART.
I ASSURE YOU, COMMANDER, WE ONLY WANT WHAT'S BEST FOR HER--
AND SO YOU TURNED HER INTO A WEAPON.

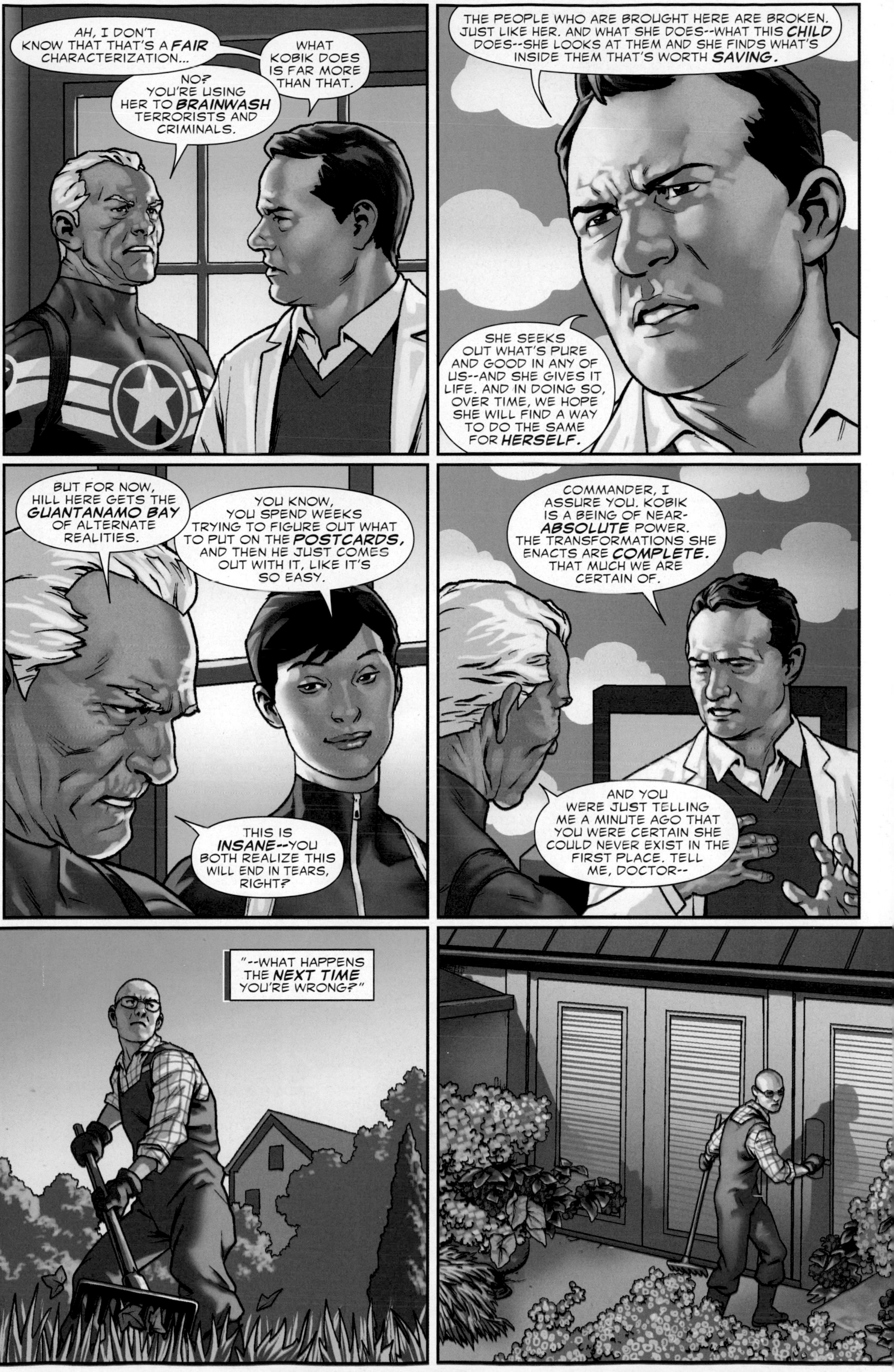
AH, I DON'T KNOW THAT THAT'S A FAIR CHARACTERIZATION...
WHAT KOBIK DOES IS FAR MORE THAN THAT.
NO? YOU'RE USING HER TO BRAINWASH TERRORISTS AND CRIMINALS.
THE PEOPLE WHO ARE BROUGHT HERE ARE BROKEN. JUST LIKE HER. AND WHAT SHE DOES--WHAT THIS CHILD DOES--SHE LOOKS AT THEM AND SHE FINDS WHAT'S INSIDE THEM THAT'S WORTH SAVING.
SHE SEEKS OUT WHAT'S PURE AND GOOD IN ANY OF US--AND SHE GIVES IT LIFE. AND IN DOING SO, OVER TIME, WE HOPE SHE WILL FIND A WAY TO DO THE SAME FOR HERSELF.
BUT FOR NOW, HILL HERE GETS THE GUANTANAMO BAY OF ALTERNATE REALITIES.
YOU KNOW, YOU SPEND WEEKS TRYING TO FIGURE OUT WHAT TO PUT ON THE POSTCARDS, AND THEN HE JUST COMES OUT WITH IT, LIKE IT'S SO EASY.
THIS IS INSANE--YOU BOTH REALIZE THIS WILL END IN TEARS, RIGHT?
COMMANDER, I ASSURE YOU. KOBIK IS A BEING OF NEAR-ABSOLUTE POWER. THE TRANSFORMATIONS SHE ENACTS ARE COMPLETE. THAT MUCH WE ARE CERTAIN OF.
AND YOU WERE JUST TELLING ME A MINUTE AGO THAT YOU WERE CERTAIN SHE COULD NEVER EXIST IN THE FIRST PLACE. TELL ME, DOCTOR--
"--WHAT HAPPENS THE NEXT TIME YOU'RE WRONG?"

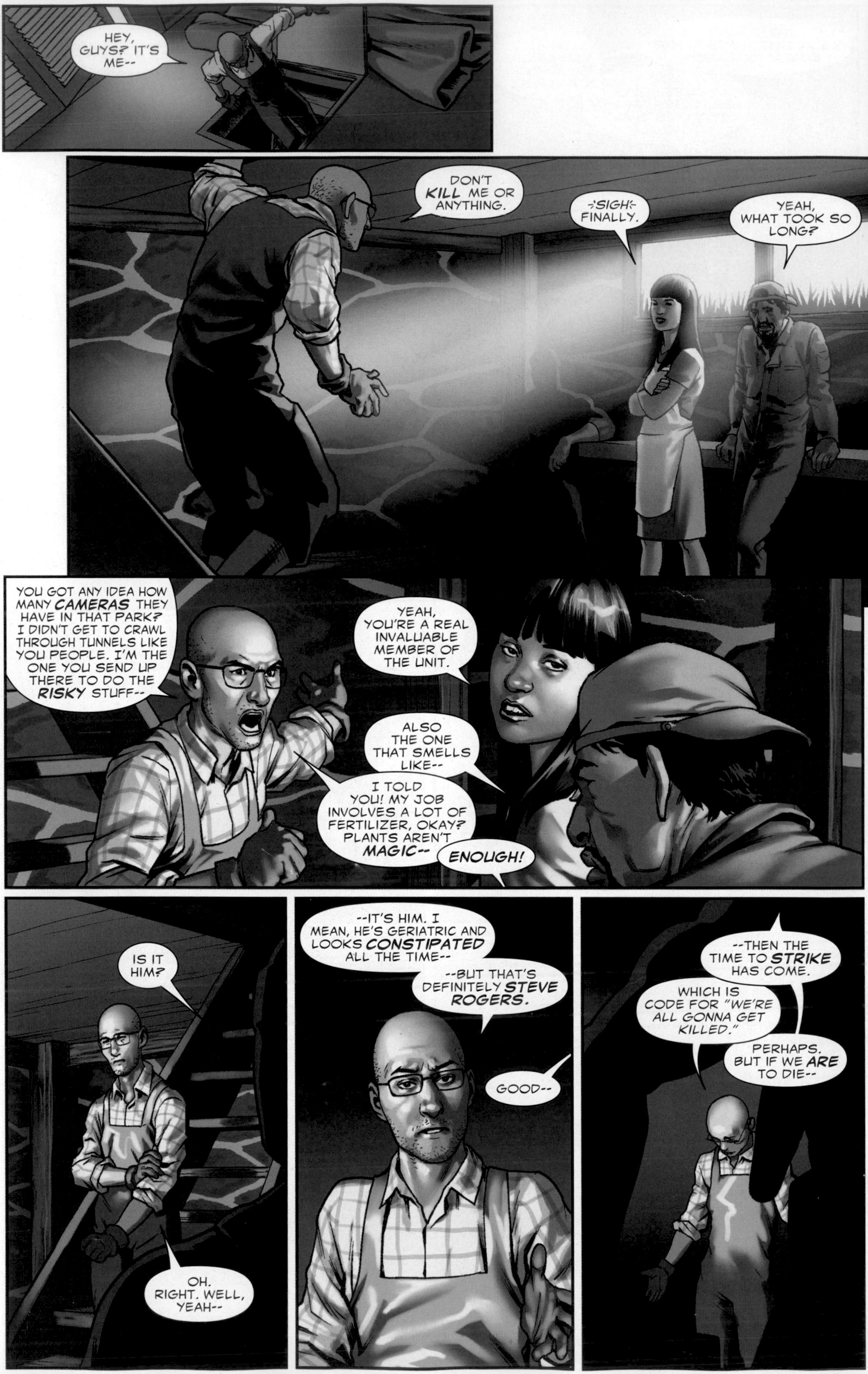
HEY, GUYS? IT'S ME--
DON'T KILL ME OR ANYTHING.
-SIGH- FINALLY.
YEAH, WHAT TOOK SO LONG?
YOU GOT ANY IDEA HOW MANY CAMERAS THEY HAVE IN THAT PARK? I DIDN'T GET TO CRAWL THROUGH TUNNELS LIKE YOU PEOPLE. I'M THE ONE YOU SEND UP THERE TO DO THE RISKY STUFF--
YEAH, YOU'RE A REAL INVALUABLE MEMBER OF THE UNIT.
ALSO THE ONE THAT SMELLS LIKE--
I TOLD YOU! MY JOB INVOLVES A LOT OF FERTILIZER, OKAY? PLANTS AREN'T MAGIC--
ENOUGH!
IS IT HIM?
OH. RIGHT. WELL, YEAH--
--IT'S HIM. I MEAN, HE'S GERIATRIC AND LOOKS CONSTIPATED ALL THE TIME--
--BUT THAT'S DEFINITELY STEVE ROGERS.
GOOD--
--THEN THE TIME TO STRIKE HAS COME.
WHICH IS CODE FOR "WE'RE ALL GONNA GET KILLED."
PERHAPS. BUT IF WE ARE TO DIE--

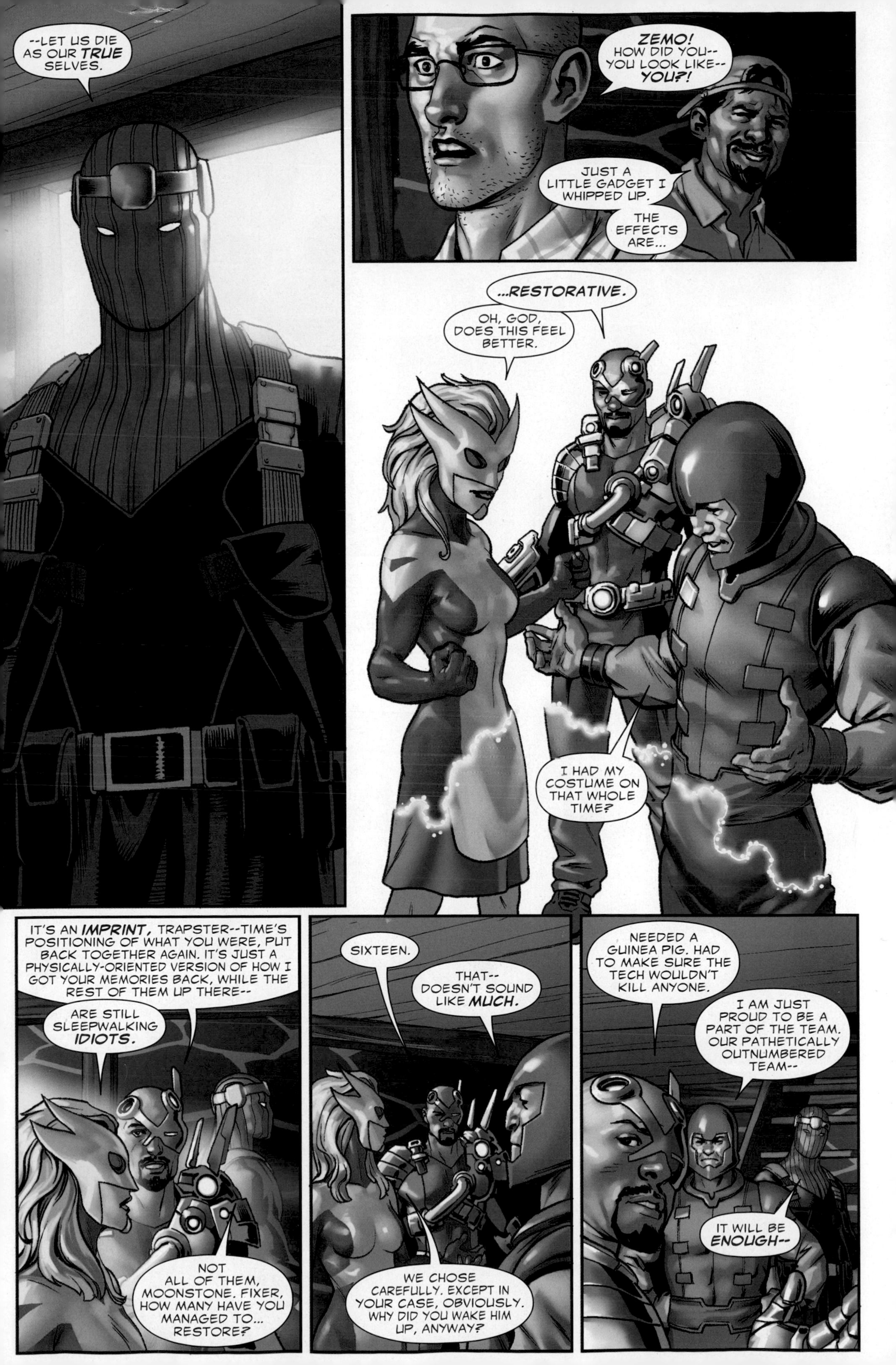
--LET US DIE AS OUR TRUE SELVES.
ZEMO! HOW DID YOU-- YOU LOOK LIKE-- YOU?!
JUST A LITTLE GADGET I WHIPPED UP.
THE EFFECTS ARE...
...RESTORATIVE.
OH, GOD, DOES THIS FEEL BETTER.
I HAD MY COSTUME ON THAT WHOLE TIME?
IT'S AN IMPRINT, TRAPSTER--TIME'S POSITIONING OF WHAT YOU WERE, PUT BACK TOGETHER AGAIN. IT'S JUST A PHYSICALLY-ORIENTED VERSION OF HOW I GOT YOUR MEMORIES BACK, WHILE THE REST OF THEM UP THERE--
ARE STILL SLEEPWALKING IDIOTS.
NOT ALL OF THEM, MOONSTONE. FIXER, HOW MANY HAVE YOU MANAGED TO... RESTORE?
SIXTEEN.
THAT-- DOESN'T SOUND LIKE MUCH.
WE CHOSE CAREFULLY. EXCEPT IN YOUR CASE, OBVIOUSLY. WHY DID YOU WAKE HIM UP, ANYWAY?
NEEDED A GUINEA PIG. HAD TO MAKE SURE THE TECH WOULDN'T KILL ANYONE.
I AM JUST PROUD TO BE A PART OF THE TEAM. OUR PATHETICALLY OUTNUMBERED TEAM--
IT WILL BE ENOUGH--

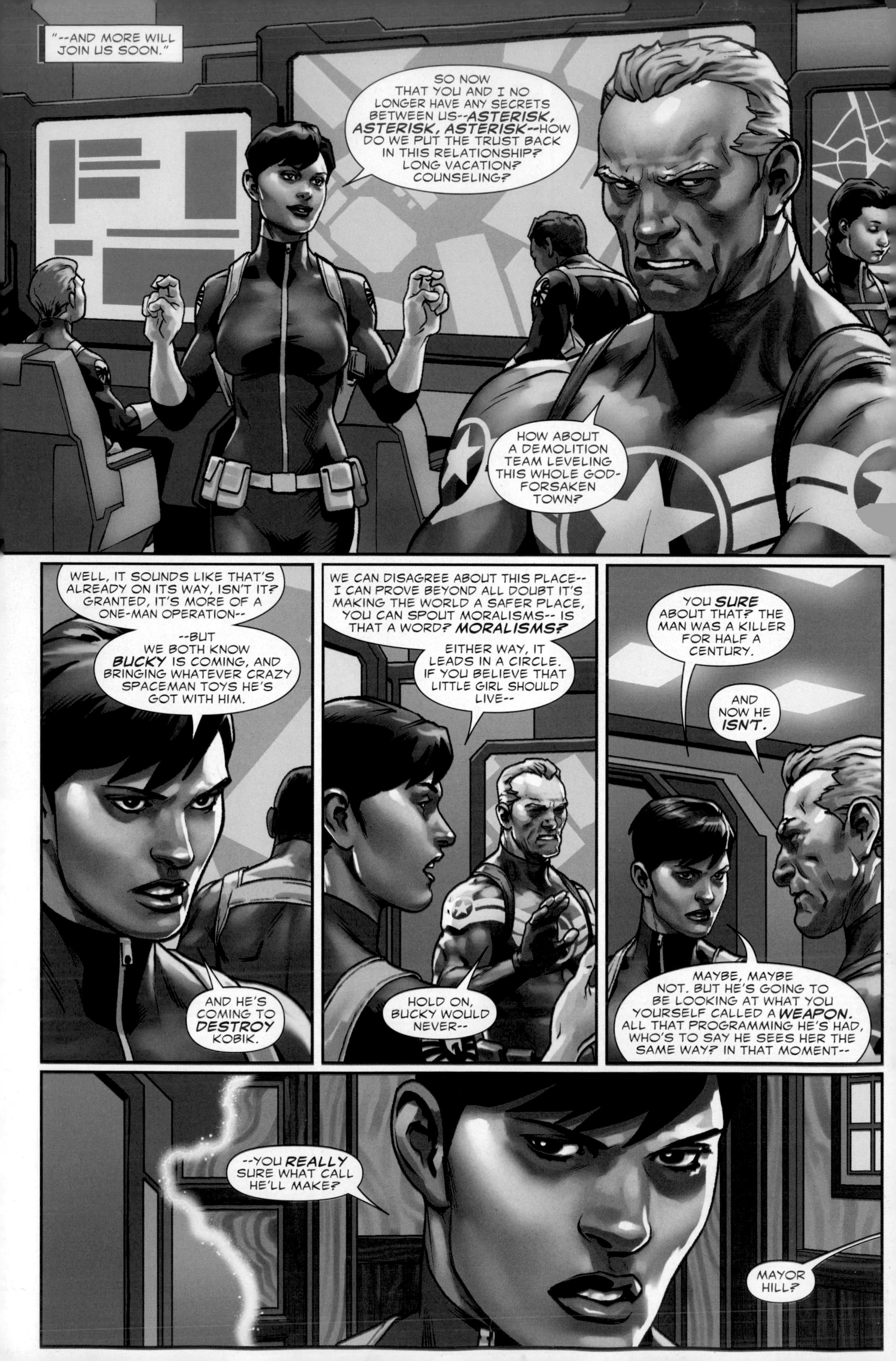
"--AND MORE WILL JOIN US SOON."
SO NOW THAT YOU AND I NO LONGER HAVE ANY SECRETS BETWEEN US--ASTERISK, ASTERISK, ASTERISK--HOW DO WE PUT THE TRUST BACK IN THIS RELATIONSHIP? LONG VACATION? COUNSELING?
HOW ABOUT A DEMOLITION TEAM LEVELING THIS WHOLE GOD-FORSAKEN TOWN?
WELL, IT SOUNDS LIKE THAT'S ALREADY ON ITS WAY, ISN'T IT? GRANTED, IT'S MORE OF A ONE-MAN OPERATION--
--BUT WE BOTH KNOW BUCKY IS COMING, AND BRINGING WHATEVER CRAZY SPACEMAN TOYS HE'S GOT WITH HIM.
AND HE'S COMING TO DESTROY KOBIK.
WE CAN DISAGREE ABOUT THIS PLACE-- I CAN PROVE BEYOND ALL DOUBT IT'S MAKING THE WORLD A SAFER PLACE, YOU CAN SPOUT MORALISMS-- IS THAT A WORD? MORALISMS?
EITHER WAY, IT LEADS IN A CIRCLE. IF YOU BELIEVE THAT LITTLE GIRL SHOULD LIVE--
HOLD ON, BUCKY WOULD NEVER--
YOU SURE ABOUT THAT? THE MAN WAS A KILLER FOR HALF A CENTURY.
AND NOW HE ISN'T.
MAYBE, MAYBE NOT. BUT HE'S GOING TO BE LOOKING AT WHAT YOU YOURSELF CALLED A WEAPON. ALL THAT PROGRAMMING HE'S HAD, WHO'S TO SAY HE SEES HER THE SAME WAY? IN THAT MOMENT--
--YOU REALLY SURE WHAT CALL HE'LL MAKE?
MAYOR HILL?

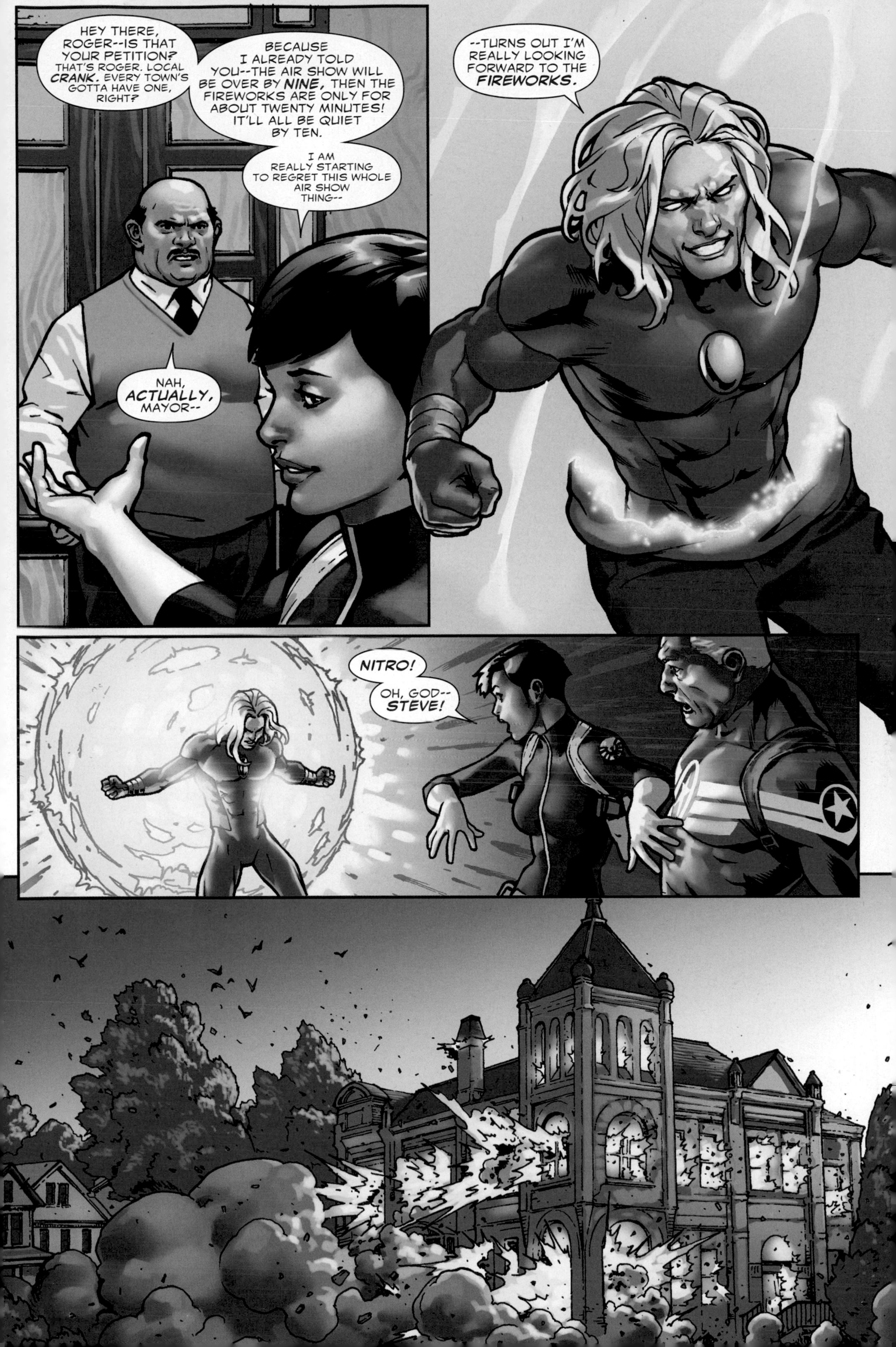
HEY THERE, ROGER--IS THAT YOUR PETITION? THAT'S ROGER. LOCAL CRANK. EVERY TOWN'S GOTTA HAVE ONE, RIGHT?
BECAUSE I ALREADY TOLD YOU--THE AIR SHOW WILL BE OVER BY NINE, THEN THE FIREWORKS ARE ONLY FOR ABOUT TWENTY MINUTES! IT'LL ALL BE QUIET BY TEN.
I AM REALLY STARTING TO REGRET THIS WHOLE AIR SHOW THING--
NAH, ACTUALLY, MAYOR--
--TURNS OUT I'M REALLY LOOKING FORWARD TO THE FIREWORKS.
NITRO!
OH, GOD--STEVE!

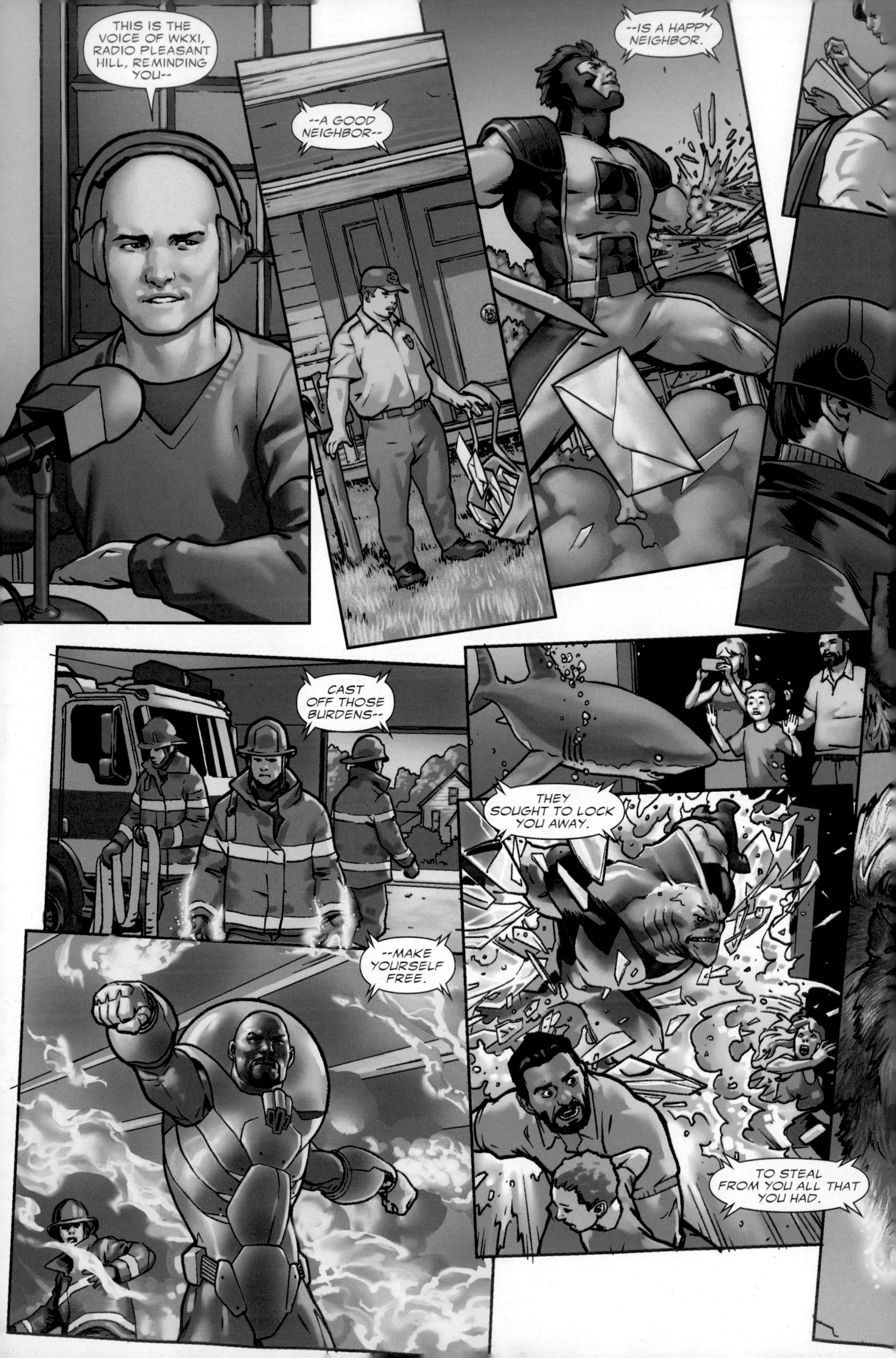
THIS IS THE VOICE OF WKXI, RADIO PLEASANT HILL, REMINDING YOU--
--A GOOD NEIGHBOR--
--IS A HAPPY NEIGHBOR.
CAST OFF THOSE BURDENS--
--MAKE YOURSELF FREE.
THEY SOUGHT TO LOCK YOU AWAY.
TO STEAL FROM YOU ALL THAT YOU HAD.

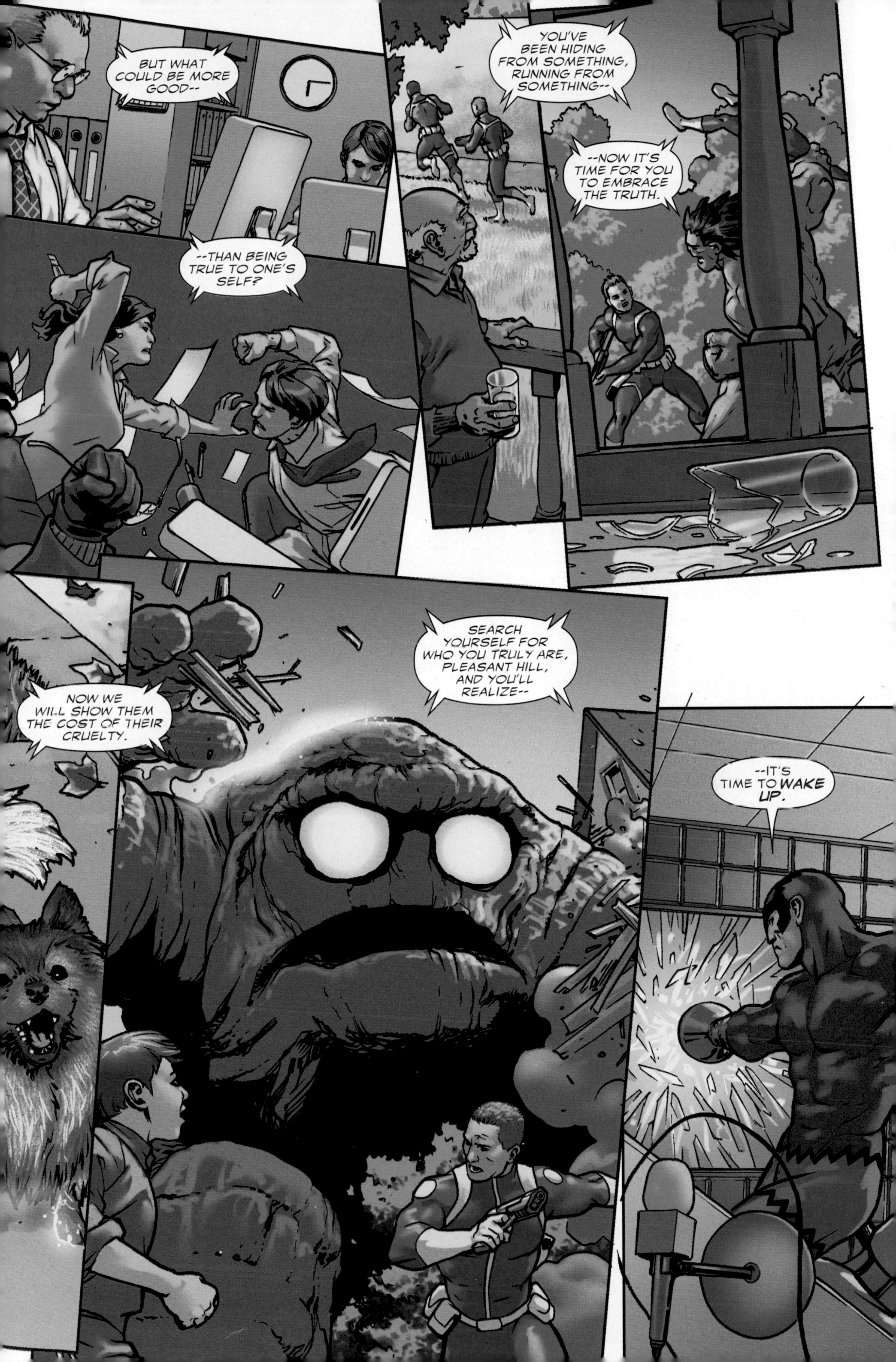
BUT WHAT COULD BE MORE GOOD--
--THAN BEING TRUE TO ONE'S SELF?
YOU'VE BEEN HIDING FROM SOMETHING, RUNNING FROM SOMETHING--
--NOW IT'S TIME FOR YOU TO EMBRACE THE TRUTH.
NOW WE WILL SHOW THEM THE COST OF THEIR CRUELTY.
SEARCH YOURSELF FOR WHO YOU TRULY ARE, PLEASANT HILL, AND YOU'LL REALIZE--
--IT'S TIME TO WAKE UP.

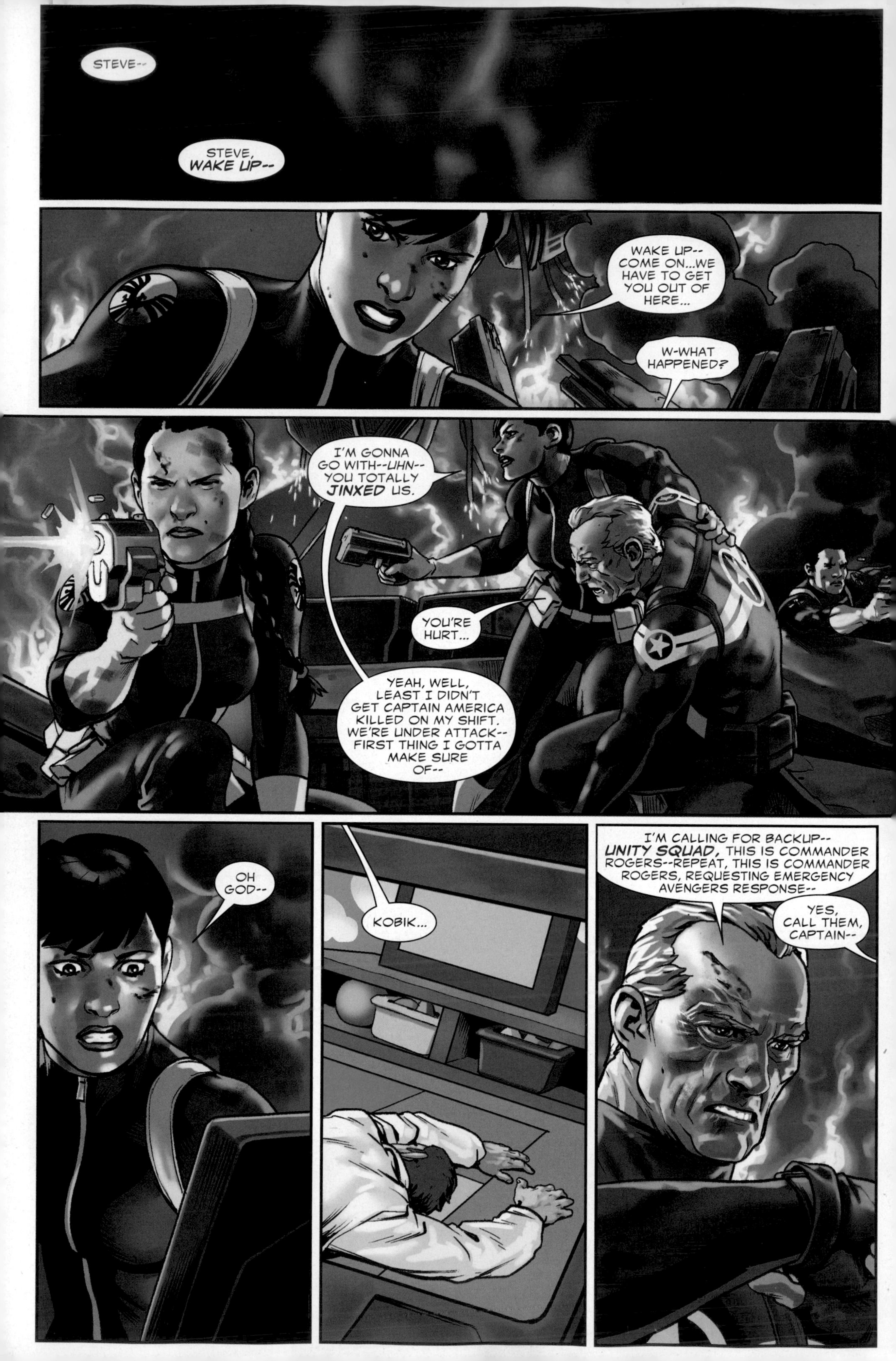
STEVE--
STEVE, WAKE UP--
WAKE UP-- COME ON...WE HAVE TO GET YOU OUT OF HERE...
W-WHAT HAPPENED?
I'M GONNA GO WITH--UHN-- YOU TOTALLY JINXED US.
YOU'RE HURT...
YEAH, WELL, LEAST I DIDN'T GET CAPTAIN AMERICA KILLED ON MY SHIFT. WE'RE UNDER ATTACK-- FIRST THING I GOTTA MAKE SURE OF--
OH GOD--
KOBIK...
I'M CALLING FOR BACKUP-- UNITY SQUAD, THIS IS COMMANDER ROGERS--REPEAT, THIS IS COMMANDER ROGERS, REQUESTING EMERGENCY AVENGERS RESPONSE--
YES, CALL THEM, CAPTAIN--

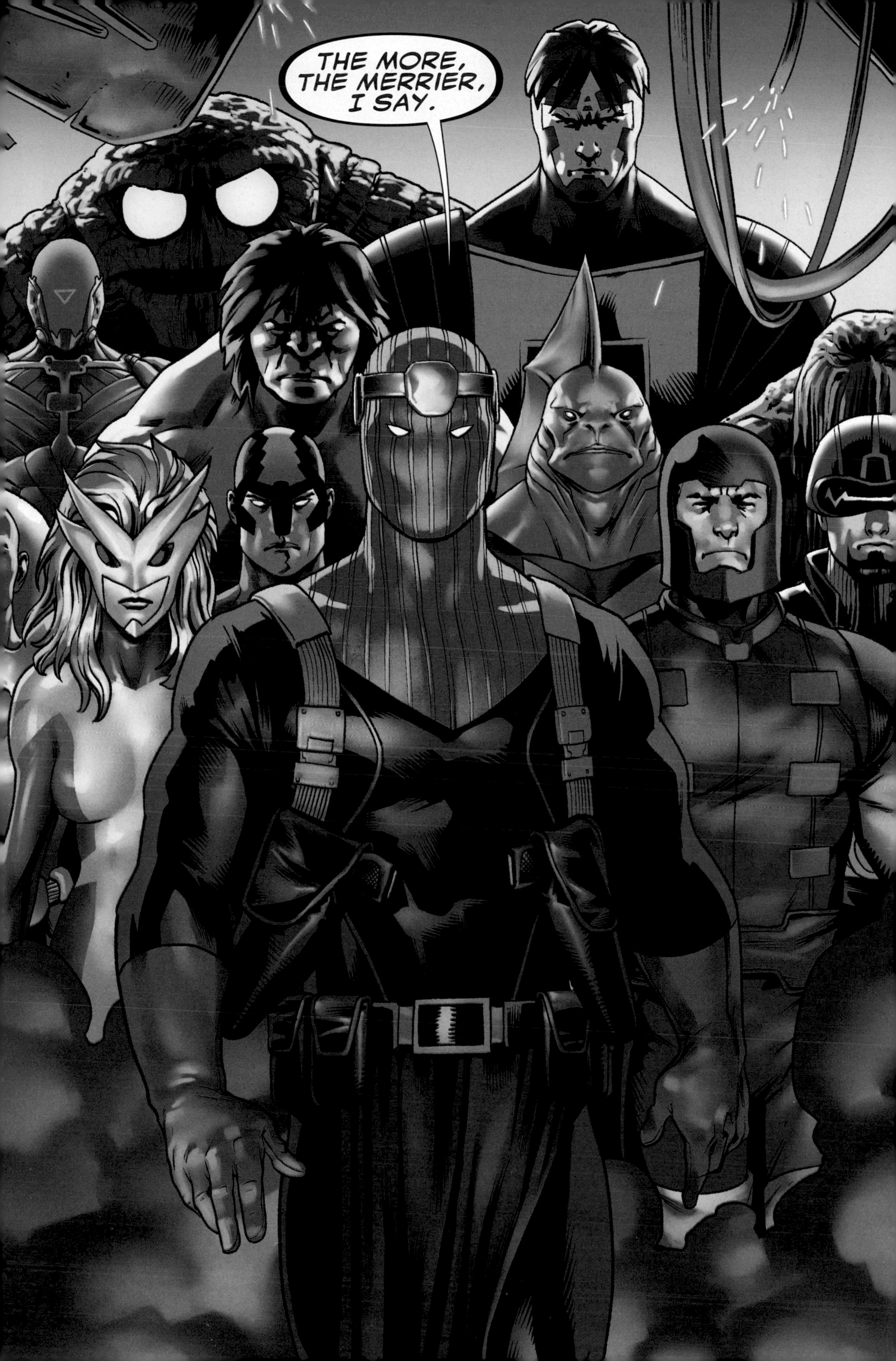
THE MORE, THE MERRIER, I SAY.

Agents of S.H.I.E.L.D. No. 3

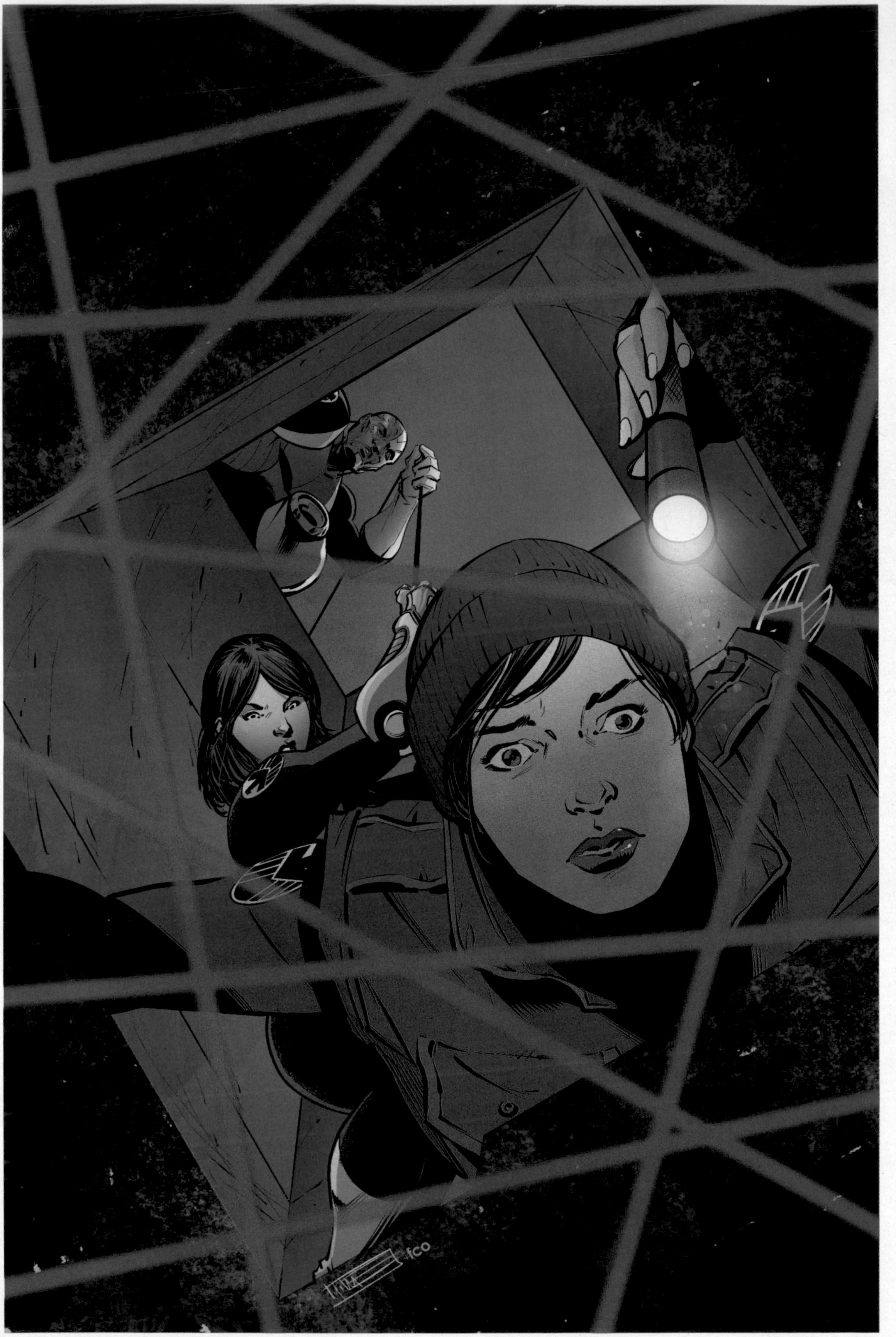

Mission Brief

Phil Coulson and his team have a mission: recover a quantum drive filled with data that endangers the lives of Earth's super heroes. To do that, they're working with Coulson's telepathic ex-girlfriend, Lola, to track down the thief–a mysterious individual in an Iron Man suit who's planning to auction off the drive to the highest bidder.

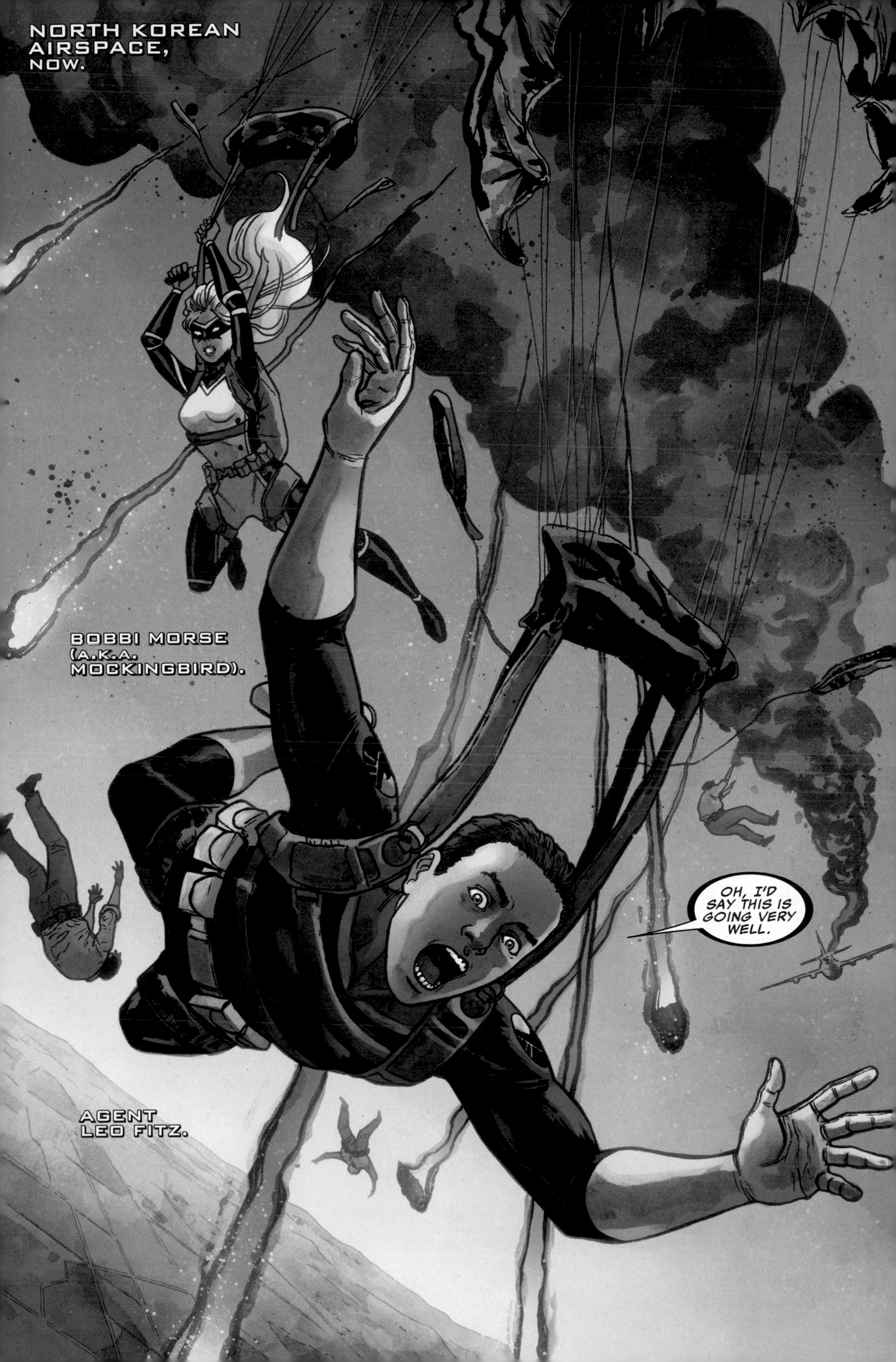
NORTH KOREAN AIRSPACE, NOW.
BOBBI MORSE (A.K.A. MOCKINGBIRD).
AGENT LEO FITZ.
OH, I'D SAY THIS IS GOING VERY WELL.

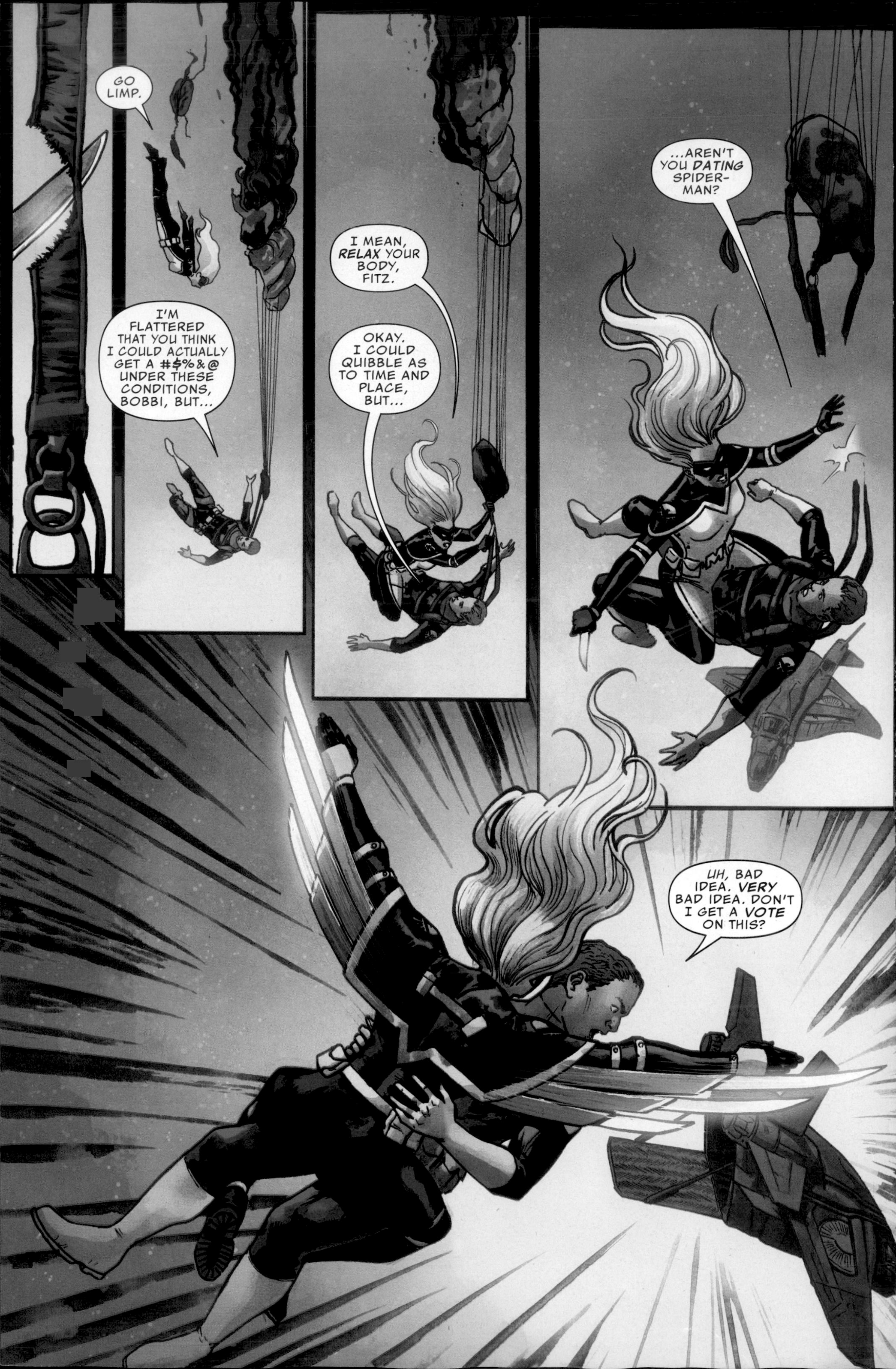
GO LIMP.
I'M FLATTERED THAT YOU THINK I COULD ACTUALLY GET A #$%&@ UNDER THESE CONDITIONS, BOBBI, BUT...
I MEAN, RELAX YOUR BODY, FITZ.
OKAY. I COULD QUIBBLE AS TO TIME AND PLACE, BUT...
...AREN'T YOU DATING SPIDER-MAN?
UH, BAD IDEA. VERY BAD IDEA. DON'T I GET A VOTE ON THIS?

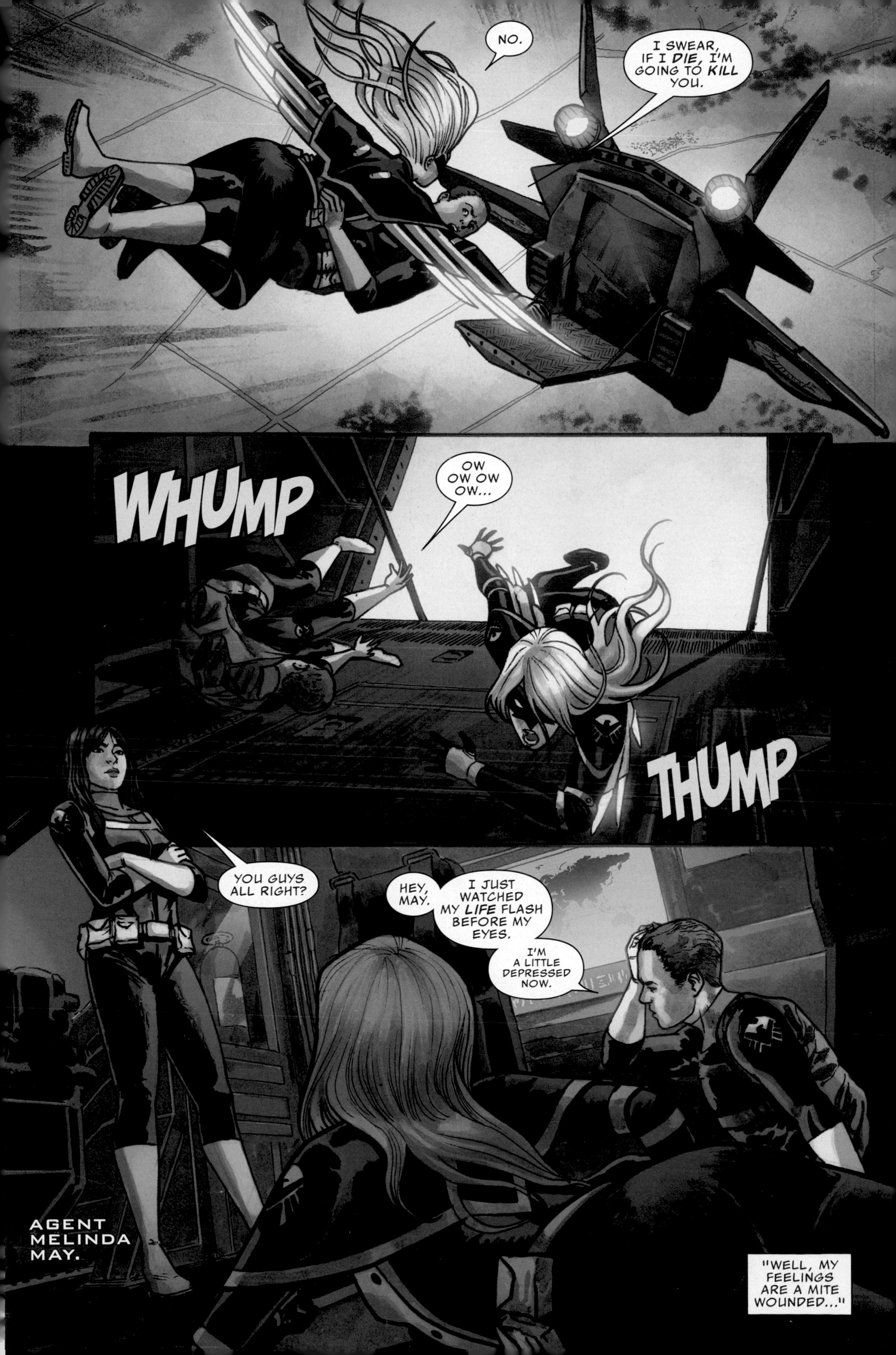

NO.
I SWEAR, IF I DIE, I'M GOING TO KILL YOU.
WHUMP
OW OW OW OW...
THUMP
AGENT MELINDA MAY.
YOU GUYS ALL RIGHT?
HEY, MAY.
I JUST WATCHED MY LIFE FLASH BEFORE MY EYES.
I'M A LITTLE DEPRESSED NOW.
"WELL, MY FEELINGS ARE A MITE WOUNDED..."

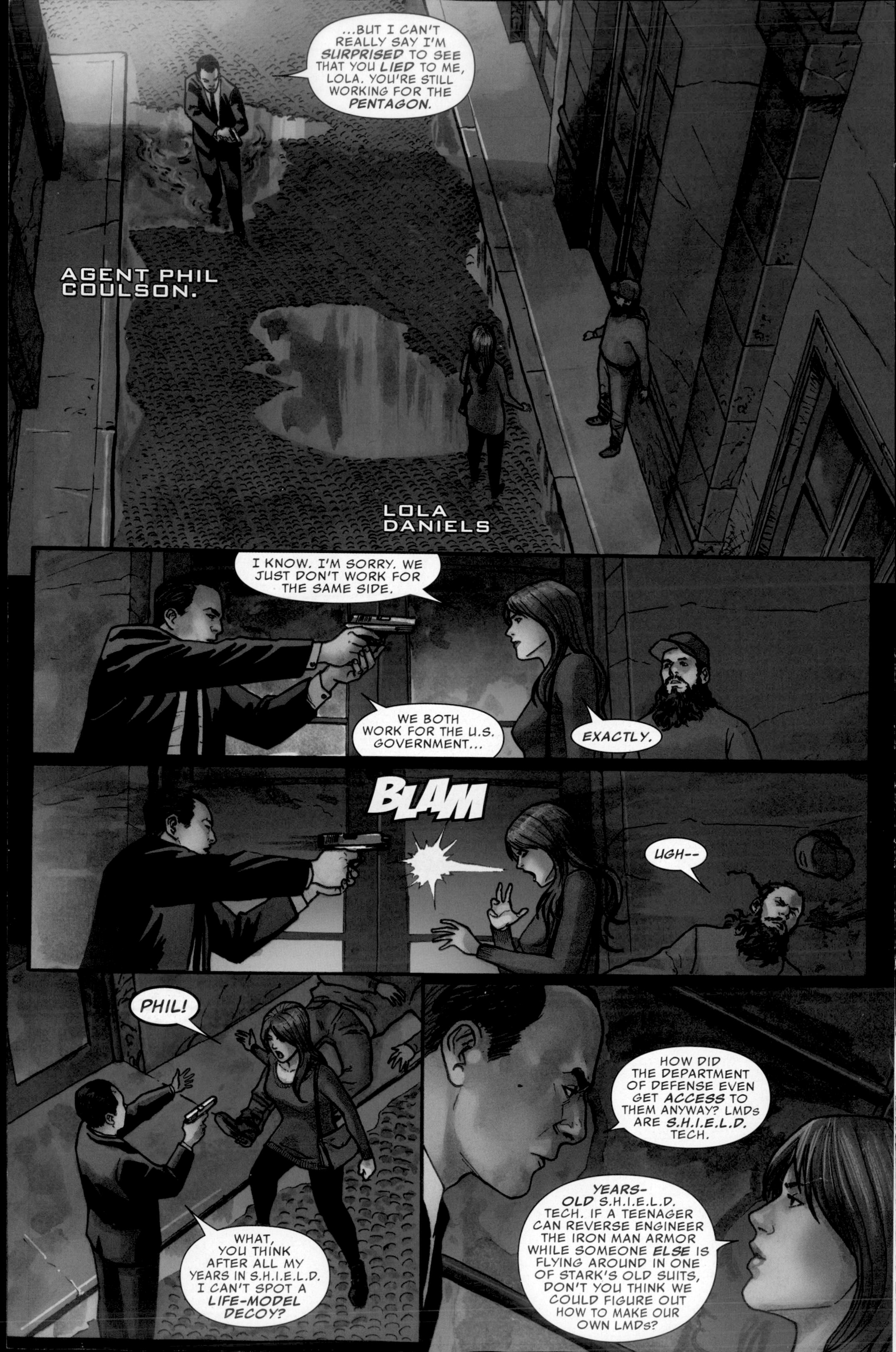
...BUT I CAN'T REALLY SAY I'M SURPRISED TO SEE THAT YOU LIED TO ME, LOLA. YOU'RE STILL WORKING FOR THE PENTAGON.
AGENT PHIL COULSON.
LOLA DANIELS
I KNOW. I'M SORRY. WE JUST DON'T WORK FOR THE SAME SIDE.
WE BOTH WORK FOR THE U.S. GOVERNMENT...
EXACTLY.
BLAM
UGH--
PHIL!
WHAT, YOU THINK AFTER ALL MY YEARS IN S.H.I.E.L.D. I CAN'T SPOT A LIFE-MODEL DECOY?
HOW DID THE DEPARTMENT OF DEFENSE EVEN GET ACCESS TO THEM ANYWAY? LMDs ARE S.H.I.E.L.D. TECH.
YEARS-OLD S.H.I.E.L.D. TECH. IF A TEENAGER CAN REVERSE ENGINEER THE IRON MAN ARMOR WHILE SOMEONE ELSE IS FLYING AROUND IN ONE OF STARK'S OLD SUITS, DON'T YOU THINK WE COULD FIGURE OUT HOW TO MAKE OUR OWN LMDs?

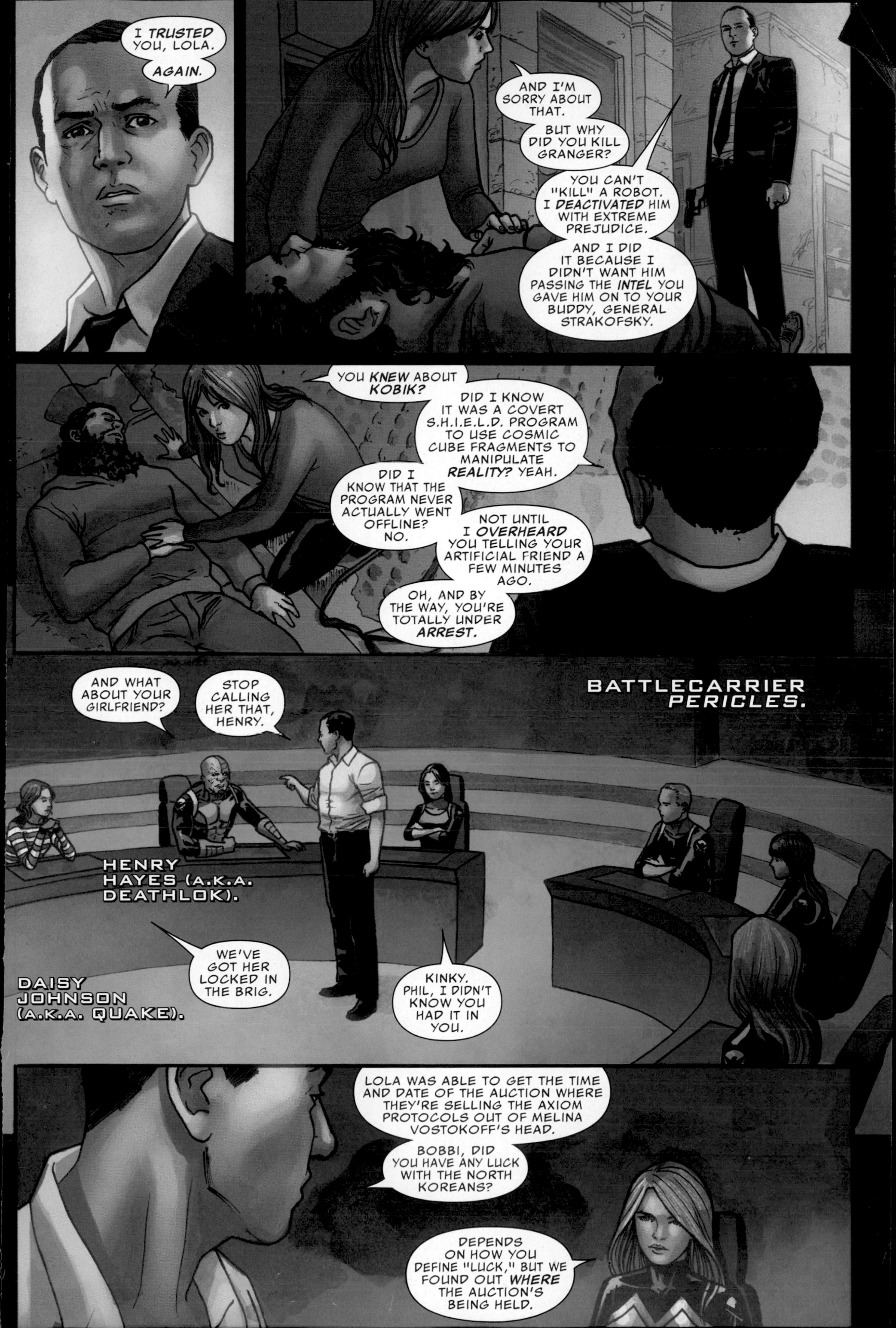
I TRUSTED YOU, LOLA.
AGAIN.
AND I'M SORRY ABOUT THAT.
BUT WHY DID YOU KILL GRANGER?
YOU CAN'T "KILL" A ROBOT. I DEACTIVATED HIM WITH EXTREME PREJUDICE.
AND I DID IT BECAUSE I DIDN'T WANT HIM PASSING THE INTEL YOU GAVE HIM ON TO YOUR BUDDY, GENERAL STRAKOFSKY.
YOU KNEW ABOUT KOBIK?
DID I KNOW IT WAS A COVERT S.H.I.E.L.D. PROGRAM TO USE COSMIC CUBE FRAGMENTS TO MANIPULATE REALITY? YEAH.
DID I KNOW THAT THE PROGRAM NEVER ACTUALLY WENT OFFLINE? NO.
NOT UNTIL I OVERHEARD YOU TELLING YOUR ARTIFICIAL FRIEND A FEW MINUTES AGO.
OH, AND BY THE WAY, YOU'RE TOTALLY UNDER ARREST.
BATTLECARRIER PERICLES.
AND WHAT ABOUT YOUR GIRLFRIEND?
STOP CALLING HER THAT, HENRY.
HENRY HAYES (A.K.A. DEATHLOK).
WE'VE GOT HER LOCKED IN THE BRIG.
DAISY JOHNSON (A.K.A. QUAKE).
KINKY. PHIL, I DIDN'T KNOW YOU HAD IT IN YOU.
LOLA WAS ABLE TO GET THE TIME AND DATE OF THE AUCTION WHERE THEY'RE SELLING THE AXIOM PROTOCOLS OUT OF MELINA VOSTOKOFF'S HEAD.
BOBBI, DID YOU HAVE ANY LUCK WITH THE NORTH KOREANS?
DEPENDS ON HOW YOU DEFINE "LUCK," BUT WE FOUND OUT WHERE THE AUCTION'S BEING HELD.

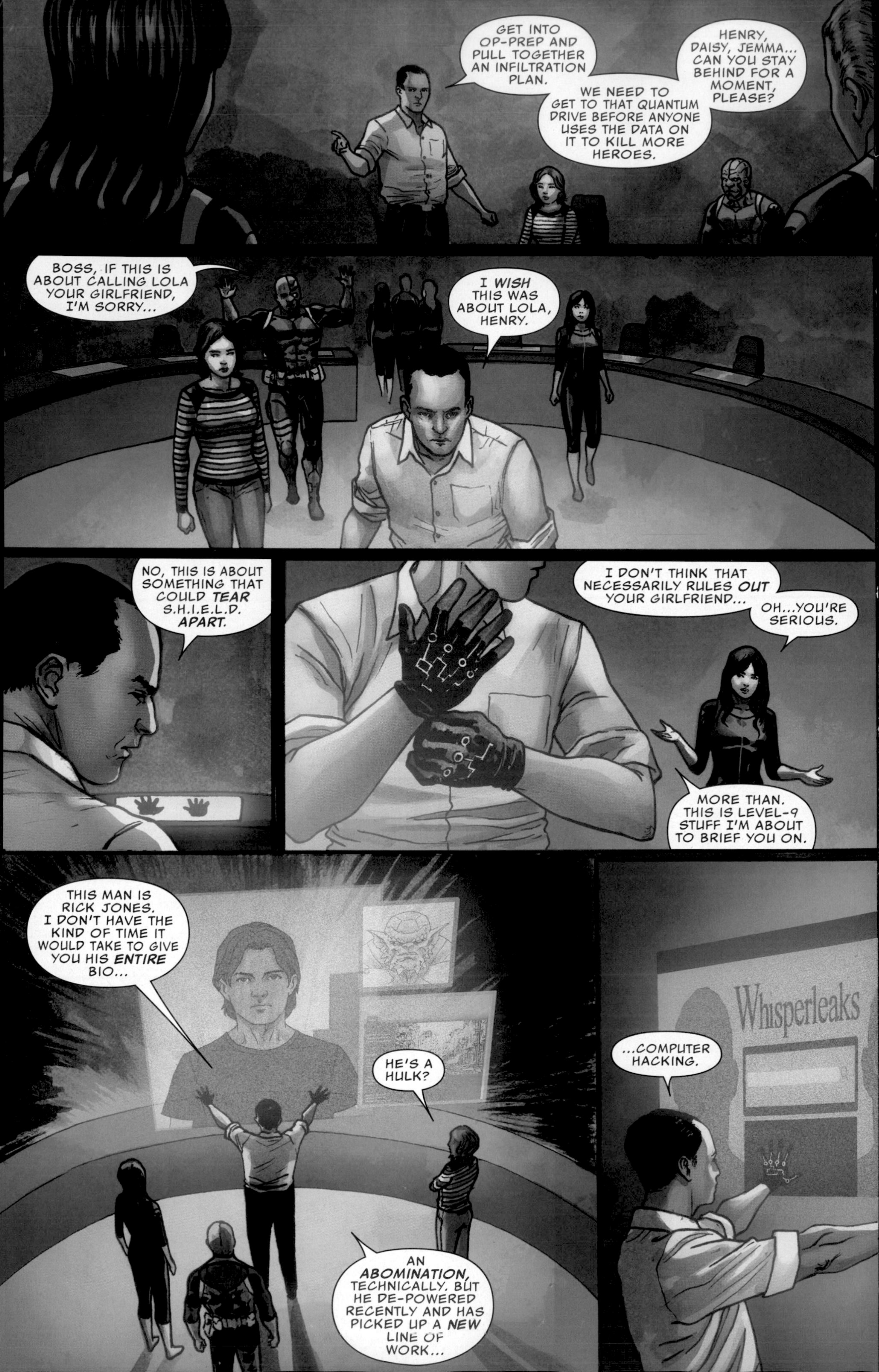

GET INTO OP-PREP AND PULL TOGETHER AN INFILTRATION PLAN.
WE NEED TO GET TO THAT QUANTUM DRIVE BEFORE ANYONE USES THE DATA ON IT TO KILL MORE HEROES.
HENRY, DAISY, JEMMA... CAN YOU STAY BEHIND FOR A MOMENT, PLEASE?
BOSS, IF THIS IS ABOUT CALLING LOLA YOUR GIRLFRIEND, I'M SORRY...
I *WISH* THIS WAS ABOUT LOLA, HENRY.
NO, THIS IS ABOUT SOMETHING THAT COULD ***TEAR*** S.H.I.E.L.D. ***APART.***
I DON'T THINK THAT NECESSARILY RULES ***OUT*** YOUR GIRLFRIEND...
OH...YOU'RE SERIOUS.
MORE THAN. THIS IS LEVEL-9 STUFF I'M ABOUT TO BRIEF YOU ON.
THIS MAN IS RICK JONES. I DON'T HAVE THE KIND OF TIME IT WOULD TAKE TO GIVE YOU HIS ***ENTIRE*** BIO...
HE'S A HULK?
AN ***ABOMINATION,*** TECHNICALLY. BUT HE DE-POWERED RECENTLY AND HAS PICKED UP A ***NEW*** LINE OF WORK...
Whisperleaks
...COMPUTER HACKING.

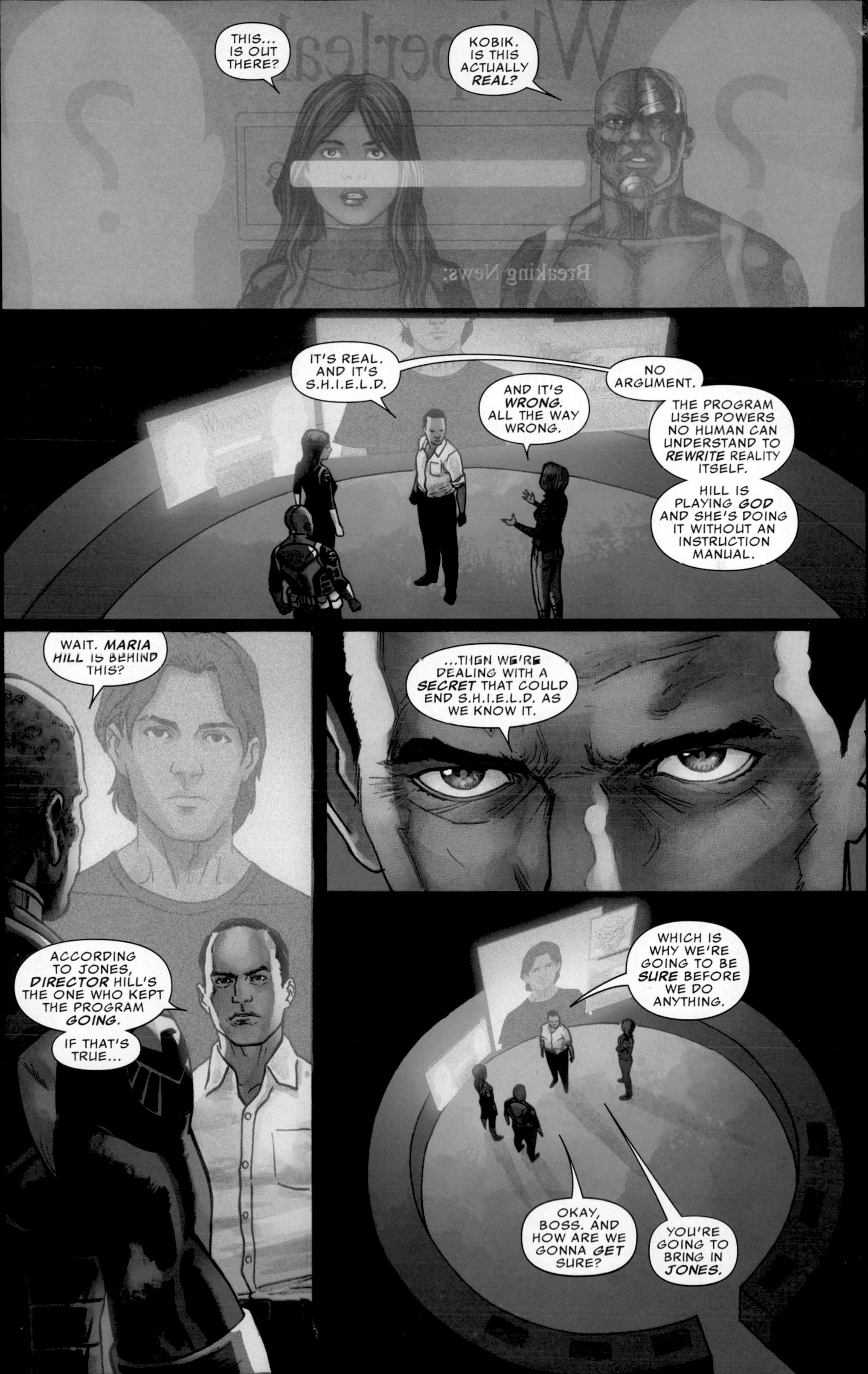
THIS... IS OUT THERE?
KOBIK. IS THIS ACTUALLY REAL?
IT'S REAL. AND IT'S S.H.I.E.L.D.
AND IT'S WRONG. ALL THE WAY WRONG.
NO ARGUMENT.
THE PROGRAM USES POWERS NO HUMAN CAN UNDERSTAND TO REWRITE REALITY ITSELF.
HILL IS PLAYING GOD AND SHE'S DOING IT WITHOUT AN INSTRUCTION MANUAL.
WAIT. MARIA HILL IS BEHIND THIS?
ACCORDING TO JONES, DIRECTOR HILL'S THE ONE WHO KEPT THE PROGRAM GOING.
IF THAT'S TRUE...
...THEN WE'RE DEALING WITH A SECRET THAT COULD END S.H.I.E.L.D. AS WE KNOW IT.
WHICH IS WHY WE'RE GOING TO BE SURE BEFORE WE DO ANYTHING.
OKAY, BOSS. AND HOW ARE WE GONNA GET SURE?
YOU'RE GOING TO BRING IN JONES.

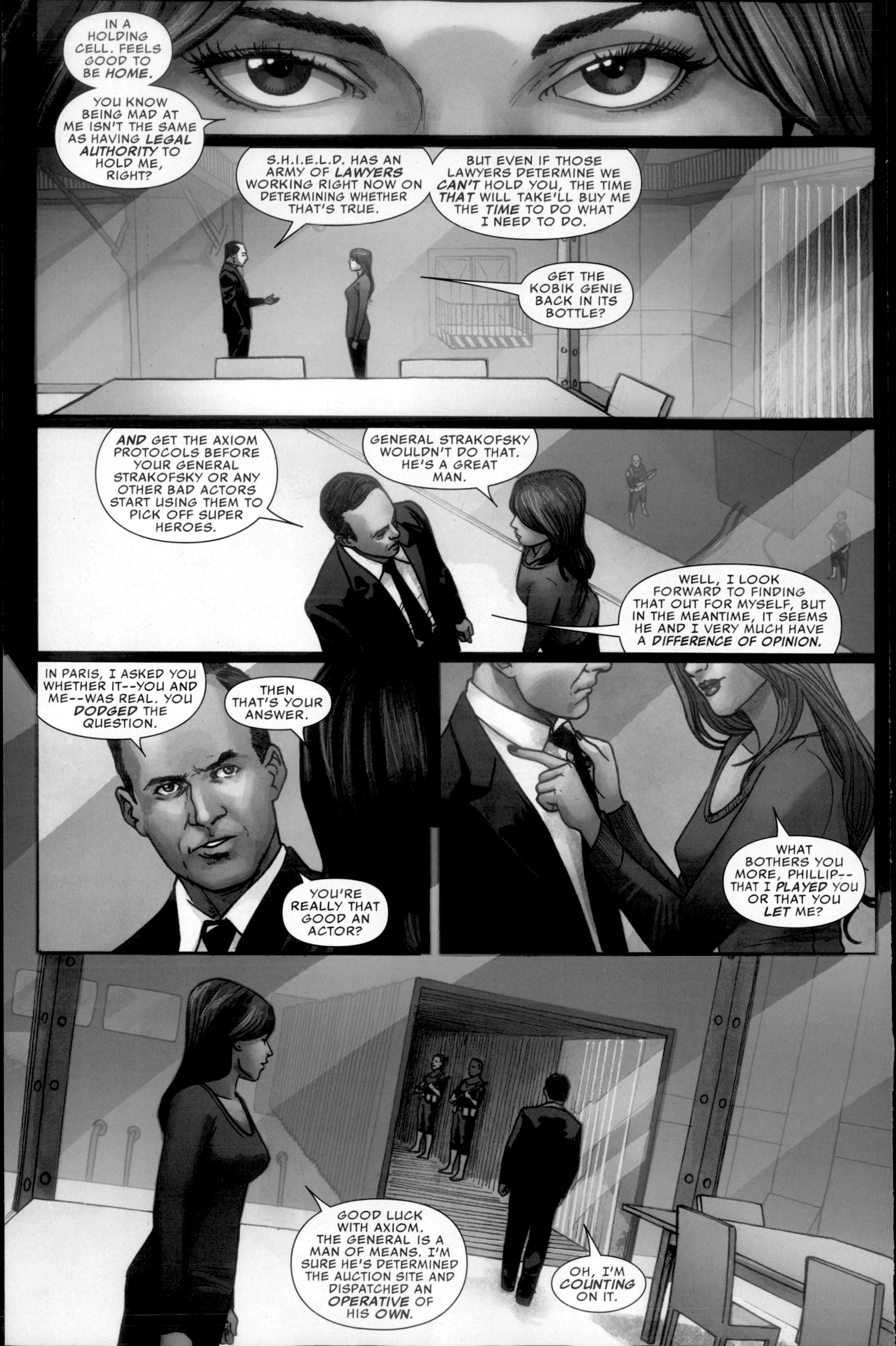
IN A HOLDING CELL. FEELS GOOD TO BE HOME.
YOU KNOW BEING MAD AT ME ISN'T THE SAME AS HAVING LEGAL AUTHORITY TO HOLD ME, RIGHT?
S.H.I.E.L.D. HAS AN ARMY OF LAWYERS WORKING RIGHT NOW ON DETERMINING WHETHER THAT'S TRUE.
BUT EVEN IF THOSE LAWYERS DETERMINE WE CAN'T HOLD YOU, THE TIME THAT WILL TAKE'LL BUY ME THE TIME TO DO WHAT I NEED TO DO.
GET THE KOBIK GENIE BACK IN ITS BOTTLE?
AND GET THE AXIOM PROTOCOLS BEFORE YOUR GENERAL STRAKOFSKY OR ANY OTHER BAD ACTORS START USING THEM TO PICK OFF SUPER HEROES.
GENERAL STRAKOFSKY WOULDN'T DO THAT. HE'S A GREAT MAN.
WELL, I LOOK FORWARD TO FINDING THAT OUT FOR MYSELF, BUT IN THE MEANTIME, IT SEEMS HE AND I VERY MUCH HAVE A DIFFERENCE OF OPINION.
IN PARIS, I ASKED YOU WHETHER IT--YOU AND ME--WAS REAL. YOU DODGED THE QUESTION.
THEN THAT'S YOUR ANSWER.
YOU'RE REALLY THAT GOOD AN ACTOR?
WHAT BOTHERS YOU MORE, PHILLIP--THAT I PLAYED YOU OR THAT YOU LET ME?
GOOD LUCK WITH AXIOM. THE GENERAL IS A MAN OF MEANS. I'M SURE HE'S DETERMINED THE AUCTION SITE AND DISPATCHED AN OPERATIVE OF HIS OWN.
OH, I'M COUNTING ON IT.

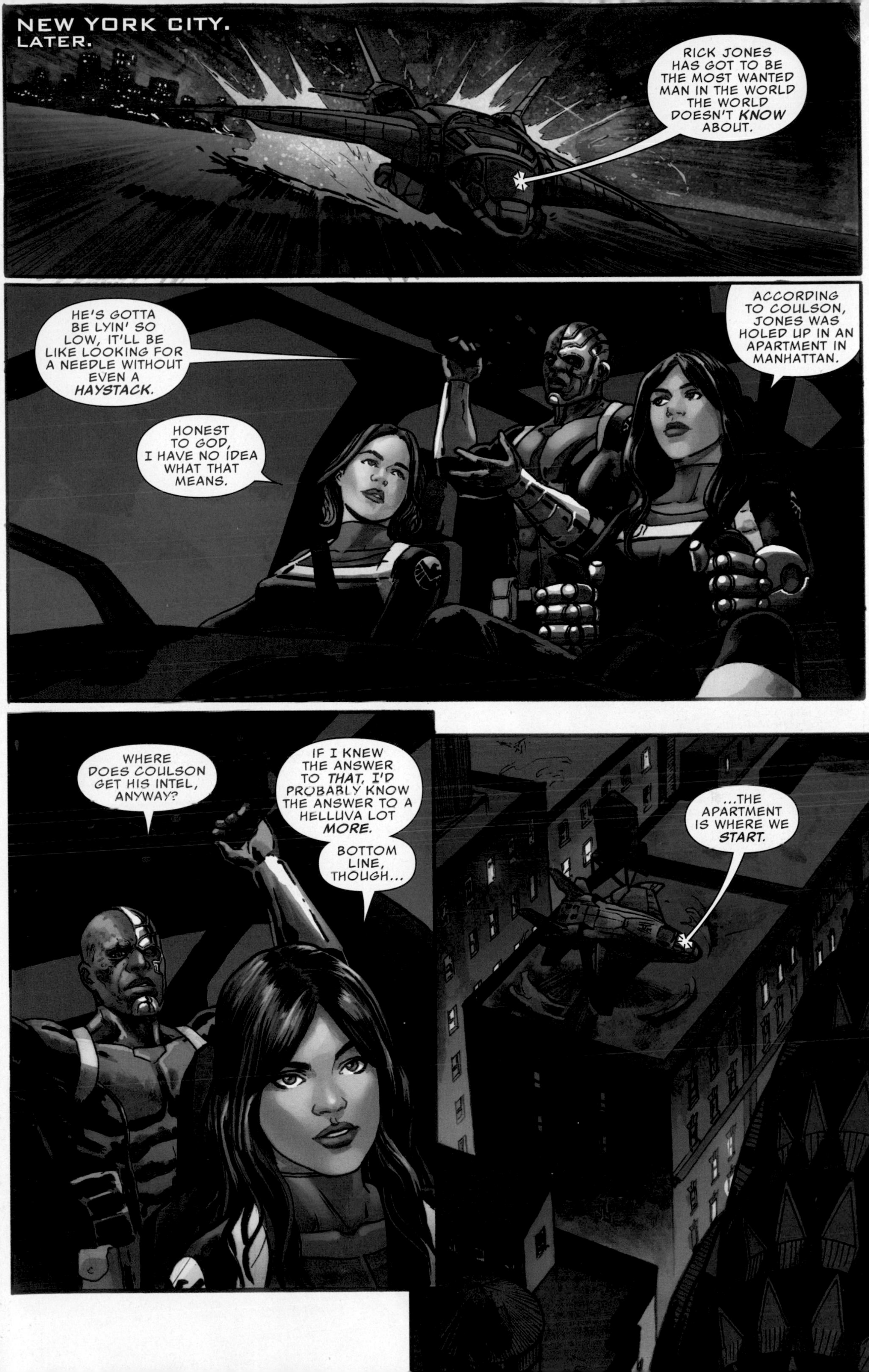
NEW YORK CITY.
LATER.
RICK JONES HAS GOT TO BE THE MOST WANTED MAN IN THE WORLD THE WORLD DOESN'T KNOW ABOUT.
ACCORDING TO COULSON, JONES WAS HOLED UP IN AN APARTMENT IN MANHATTAN.
HE'S GOTTA BE LYIN' SO LOW, IT'LL BE LIKE LOOKING FOR A NEEDLE WITHOUT EVEN A HAYSTACK.
HONEST TO GOD, I HAVE NO IDEA WHAT THAT MEANS.
WHERE DOES COULSON GET HIS INTEL, ANYWAY?
IF I KNEW THE ANSWER TO THAT, I'D PROBABLY KNOW THE ANSWER TO A HELLUVA LOT MORE.
BOTTOM LINE, THOUGH...
...THE APARTMENT IS WHERE WE START.

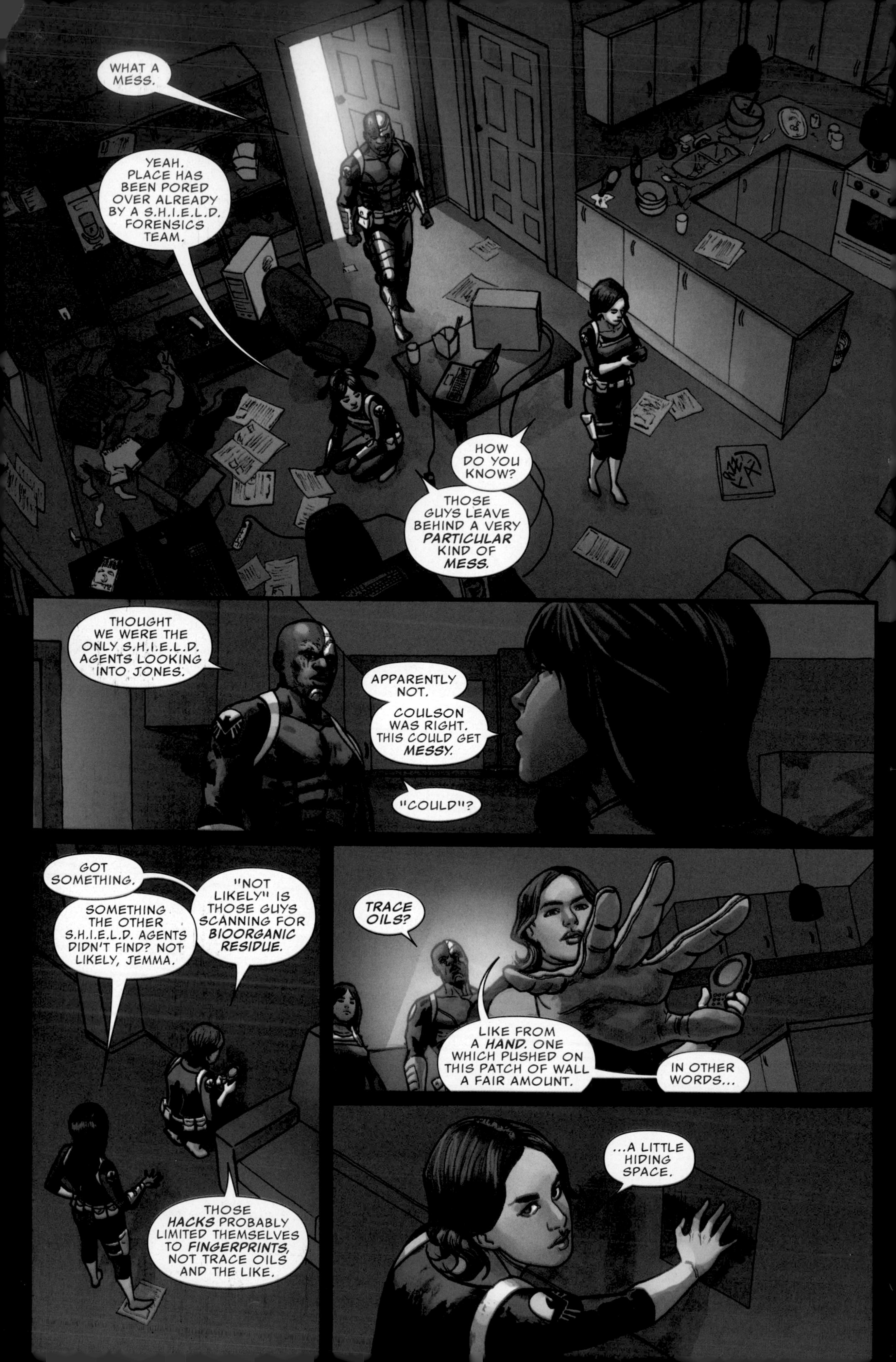
WHAT A MESS.
YEAH. PLACE HAS BEEN PORED OVER ALREADY BY A S.H.I.E.L.D. FORENSICS TEAM.
HOW DO YOU KNOW?
THOSE GUYS LEAVE BEHIND A VERY PARTICULAR KIND OF MESS.
THOUGHT WE WERE THE ONLY S.H.I.E.L.D. AGENTS LOOKING INTO JONES.
APPARENTLY NOT.
COULSON WAS RIGHT. THIS COULD GET MESSY.
"COULD"?
GOT SOMETHING.
SOMETHING THE OTHER S.H.I.E.L.D. AGENTS DIDN'T FIND? NOT LIKELY, JEMMA.
"NOT LIKELY" IS THOSE GUYS SCANNING FOR BIOORGANIC RESIDUE.
THOSE HACKS PROBABLY LIMITED THEMSELVES TO FINGERPRINTS, NOT TRACE OILS AND THE LIKE.
TRACE OILS?
LIKE FROM A HAND. ONE WHICH PUSHED ON THIS PATCH OF WALL A FAIR AMOUNT.
IN OTHER WORDS...
...A LITTLE HIDING SPACE.

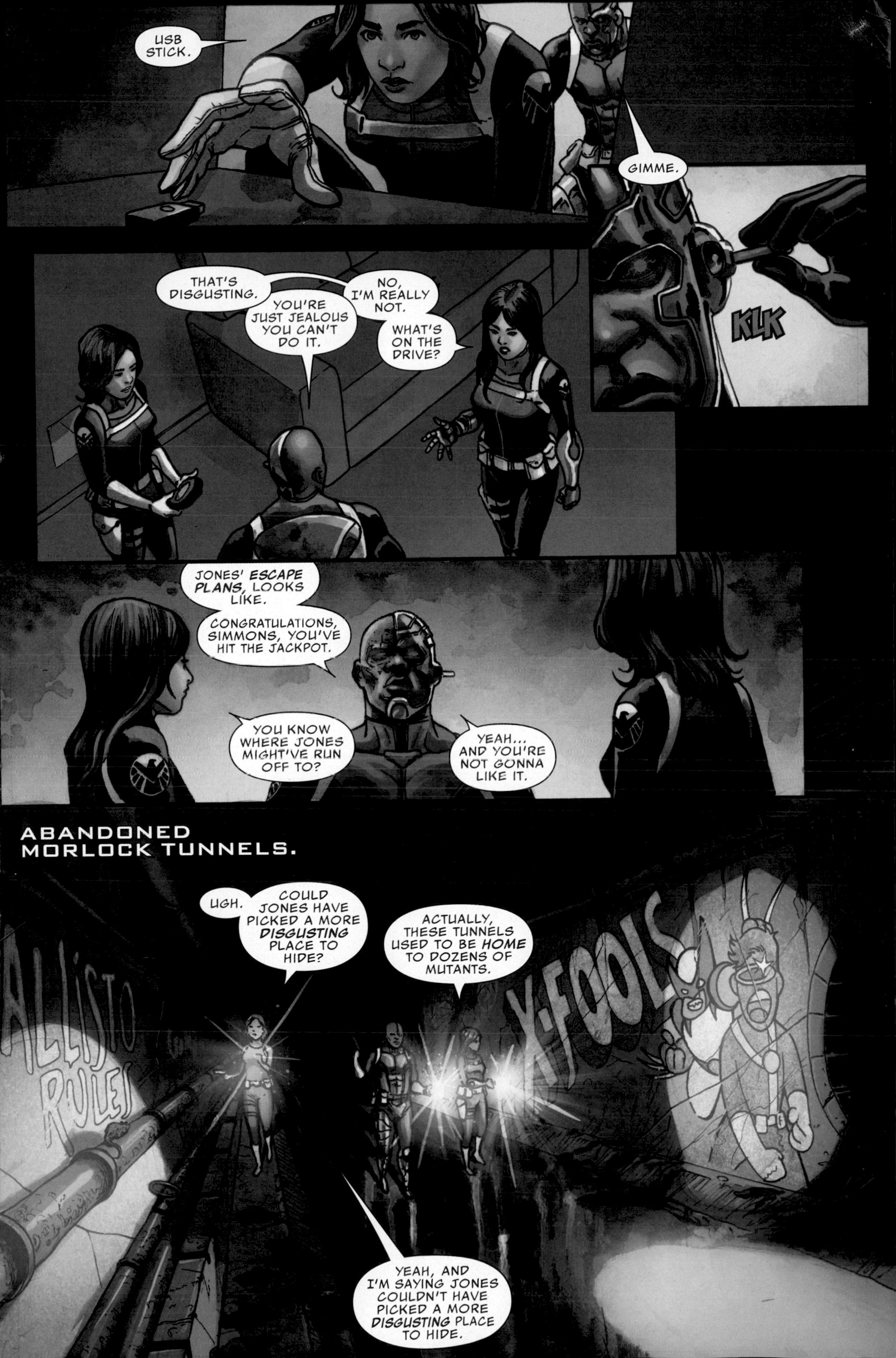
USB STICK.
GIMME.
KLK
THAT'S DISGUSTING.
YOU'RE JUST JEALOUS YOU CAN'T DO IT.
NO, I'M REALLY NOT.
WHAT'S ON THE DRIVE?
JONES' ESCAPE PLANS, LOOKS LIKE.
CONGRATULATIONS, SIMMONS, YOU'VE HIT THE JACKPOT.
YOU KNOW WHERE JONES MIGHT'VE RUN OFF TO?
YEAH... AND YOU'RE NOT GONNA LIKE IT.
ABANDONED MORLOCK TUNNELS.
UGH.
COULD JONES HAVE PICKED A MORE DISGUSTING PLACE TO HIDE?
ACTUALLY, THESE TUNNELS USED TO BE HOME TO DOZENS OF MUTANTS.
YEAH, AND I'M SAYING JONES COULDN'T HAVE PICKED A MORE DISGUSTING PLACE TO HIDE.
X-FOOLS
ALLISTO RULES

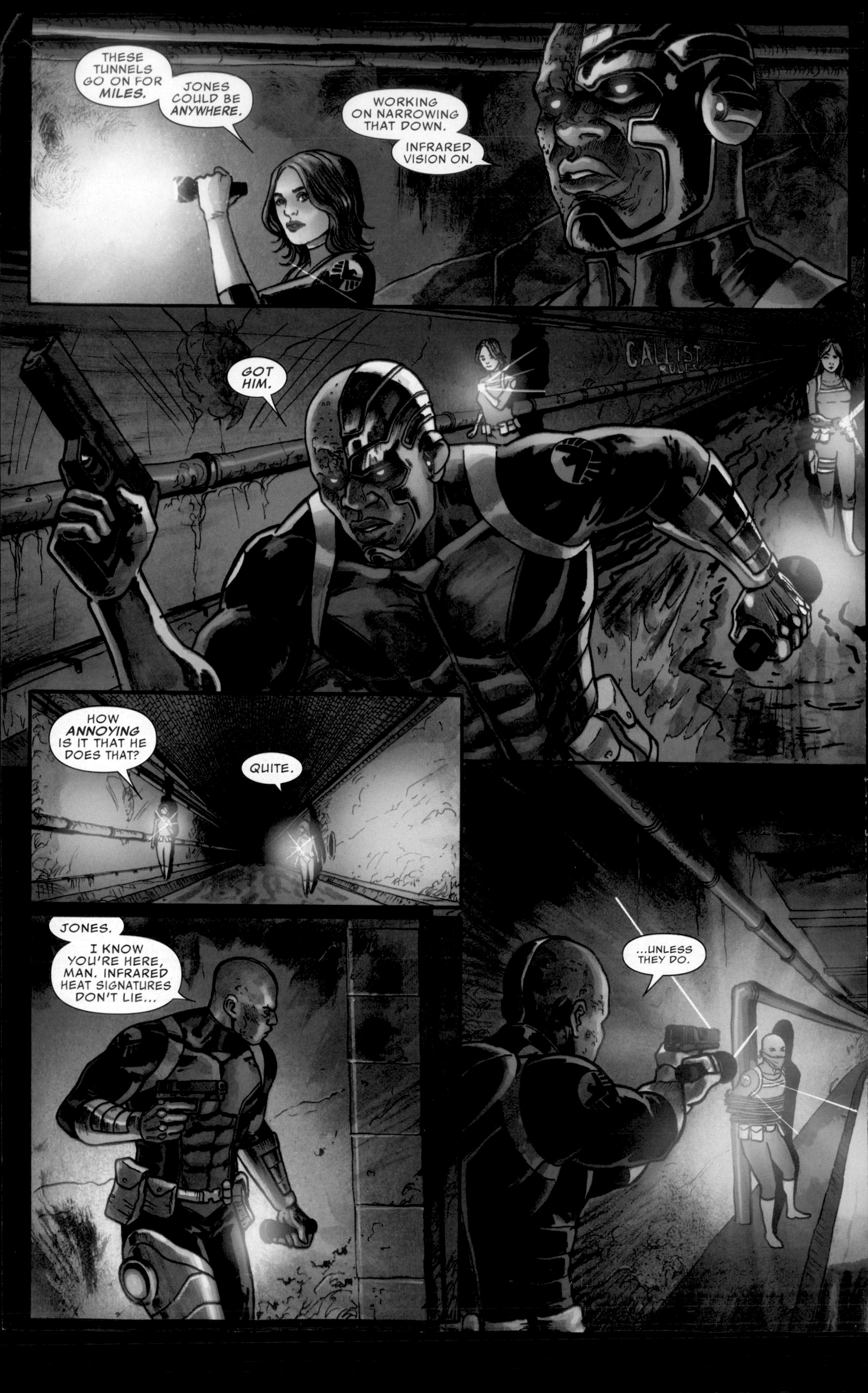
THESE TUNNELS GO ON FOR MILES.
JONES COULD BE ANYWHERE.
WORKING ON NARROWING THAT DOWN.
INFRARED VISION ON.
CALLISTO RULES
GOT HIM.
HOW ANNOYING IS IT THAT HE DOES THAT?
QUITE.
JONES.
I KNOW YOU'RE HERE, MAN. INFRARED HEAT SIGNATURES DON'T LIE...
...UNLESS THEY DO.

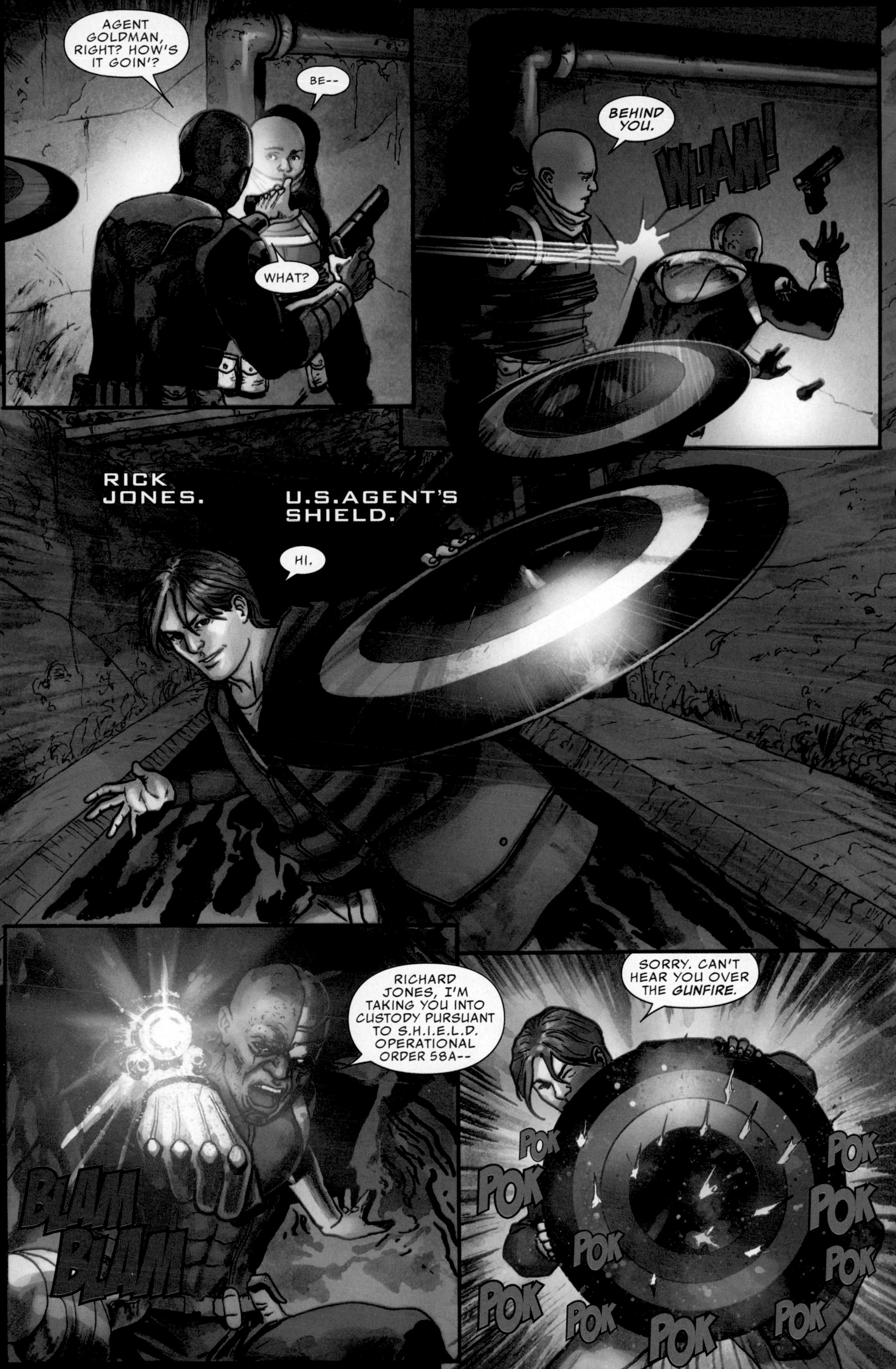

AGENT GOLDMAN, RIGHT? HOW'S IT GOIN'?
BE--
WHAT?
BEHIND YOU.
WHAM!
RICK JONES.
U.S.AGENT'S SHIELD.
HI.
RICHARD JONES, I'M TAKING YOU INTO CUSTODY PURSUANT TO S.H.I.E.L.D. OPERATIONAL ORDER 58A--
BLAM BLAM
SORRY. CAN'T HEAR YOU OVER THE GUNFIRE.
POK POK POK POK POK POK POK POK POK POK POK

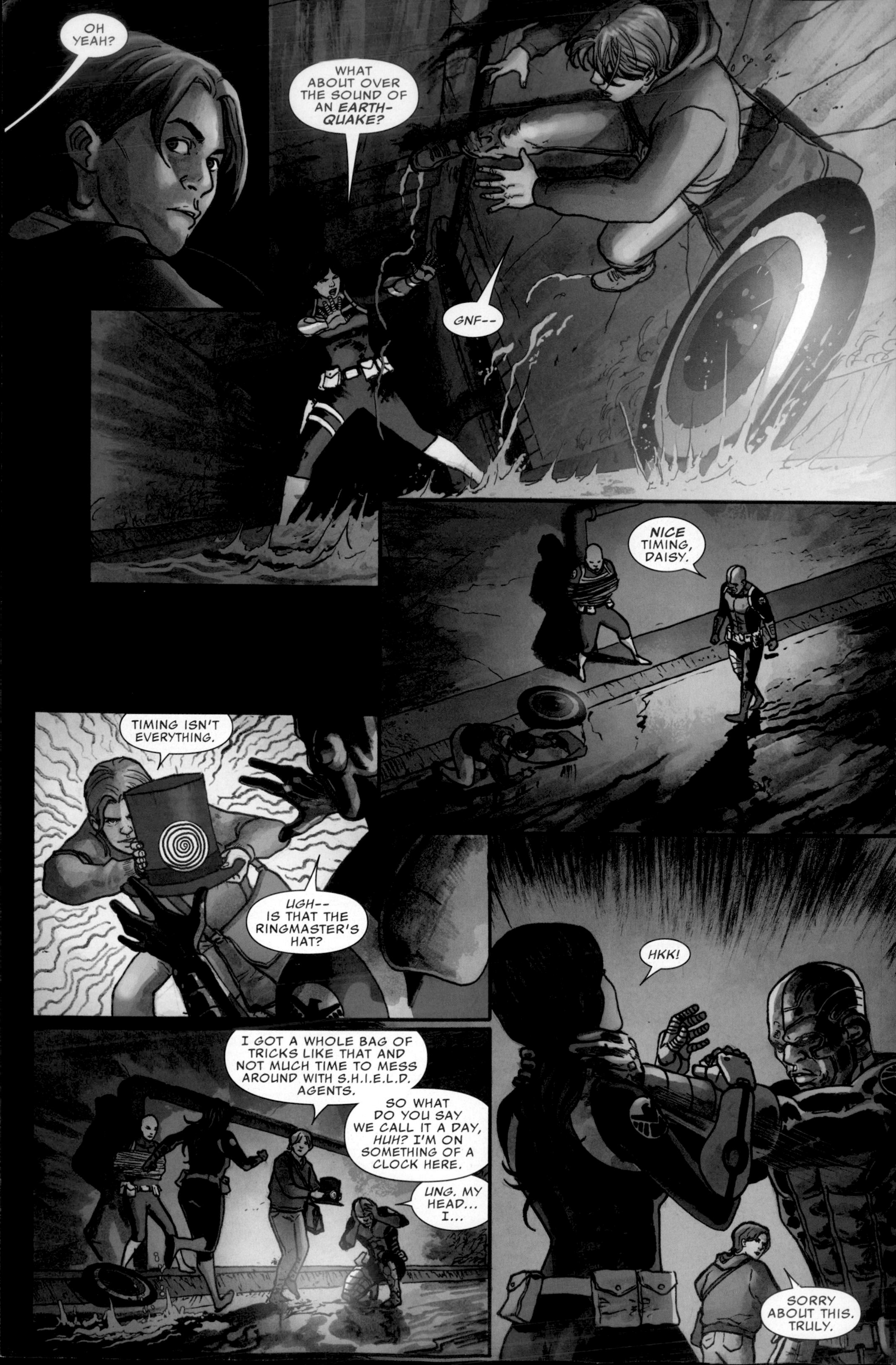
OH YEAH?
WHAT ABOUT OVER THE SOUND OF AN EARTH-QUAKE?
GNF--
NICE TIMING, DAISY.
TIMING ISN'T EVERYTHING.
UGH-- IS THAT THE RINGMASTER'S HAT?
HKK!
I GOT A WHOLE BAG OF TRICKS LIKE THAT AND NOT MUCH TIME TO MESS AROUND WITH S.H.I.E.L.D. AGENTS.
SO WHAT DO YOU SAY WE CALL IT A DAY, HUH? I'M ON SOMETHING OF A CLOCK HERE.
UNG. MY HEAD... I...
SORRY ABOUT THIS. TRULY.

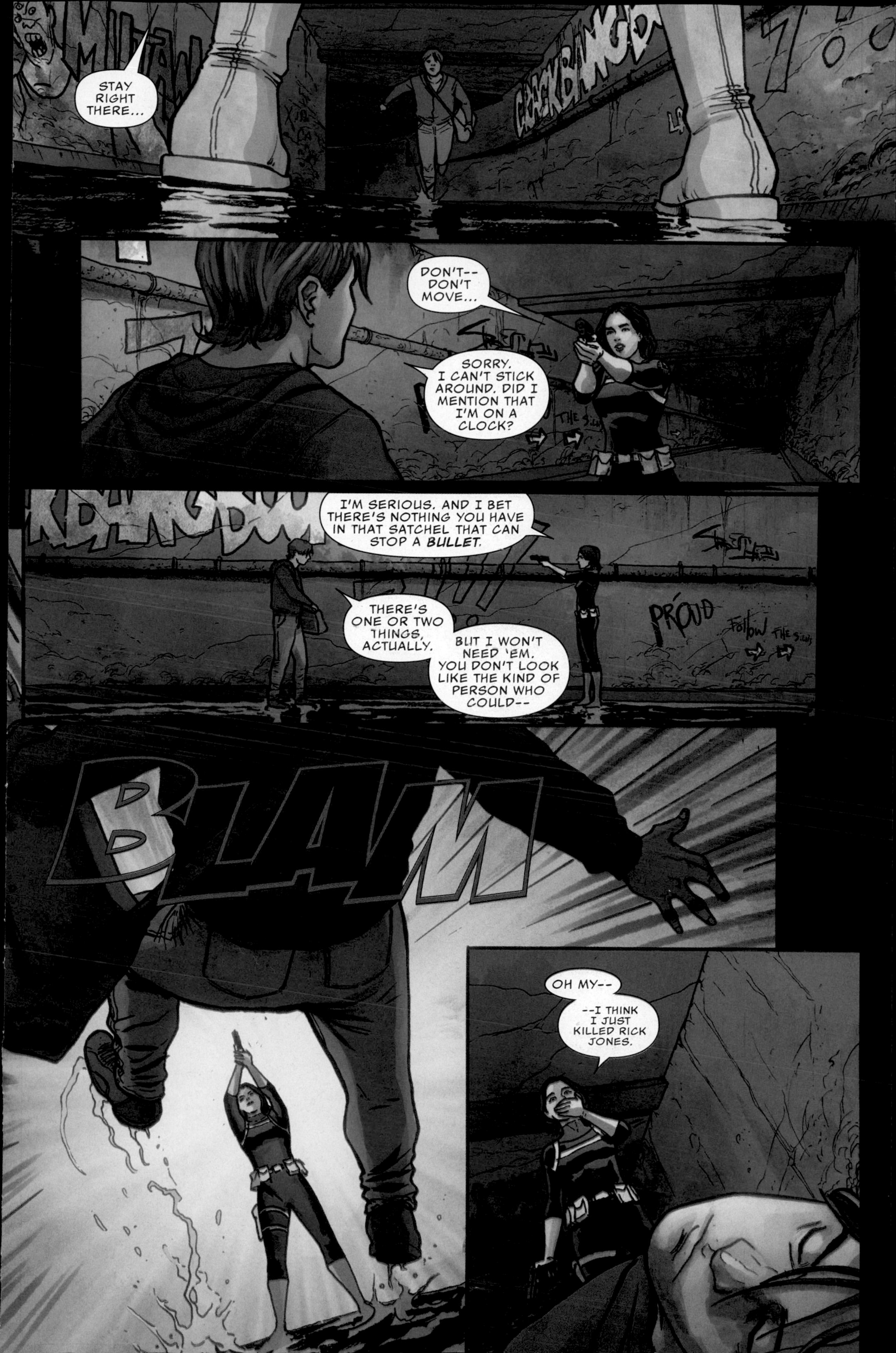
STAY RIGHT THERE...
DON'T-- DON'T MOVE...
SORRY. I CAN'T STICK AROUND. DID I MENTION THAT I'M ON A CLOCK?
I'M SERIOUS. AND I BET THERE'S NOTHING YOU HAVE IN THAT SATCHEL THAT CAN STOP A BULLET.
THERE'S ONE OR TWO THINGS, ACTUALLY.
BUT I WON'T NEED 'EM. YOU DON'T LOOK LIKE THE KIND OF PERSON WHO COULD--
BLAM
OH MY--
--I THINK I JUST KILLED RICK JONES.

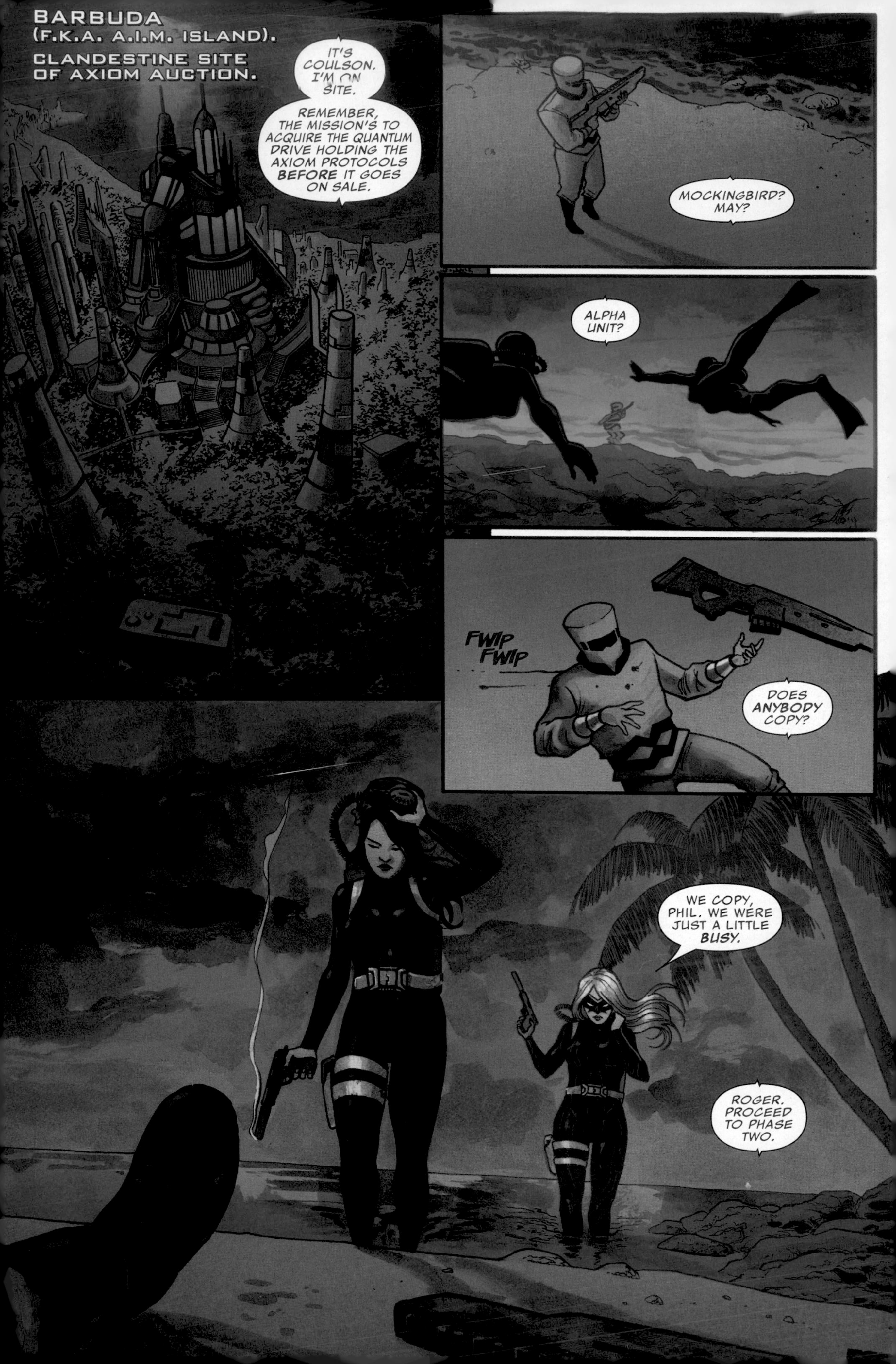
BARBUDA (F.K.A. A.I.M. ISLAND).
CLANDESTINE SITE OF AXIOM AUCTION.
IT'S COULSON. I'M ON SITE.
REMEMBER, THE MISSION'S TO ACQUIRE THE QUANTUM DRIVE HOLDING THE AXIOM PROTOCOLS BEFORE IT GOES ON SALE.
MOCKINGBIRD? MAY?
ALPHA UNIT?
FWIP FWIP
DOES ANYBODY COPY?
WE COPY, PHIL. WE WERE JUST A LITTLE BUSY.
ROGER. PROCEED TO PHASE TWO.

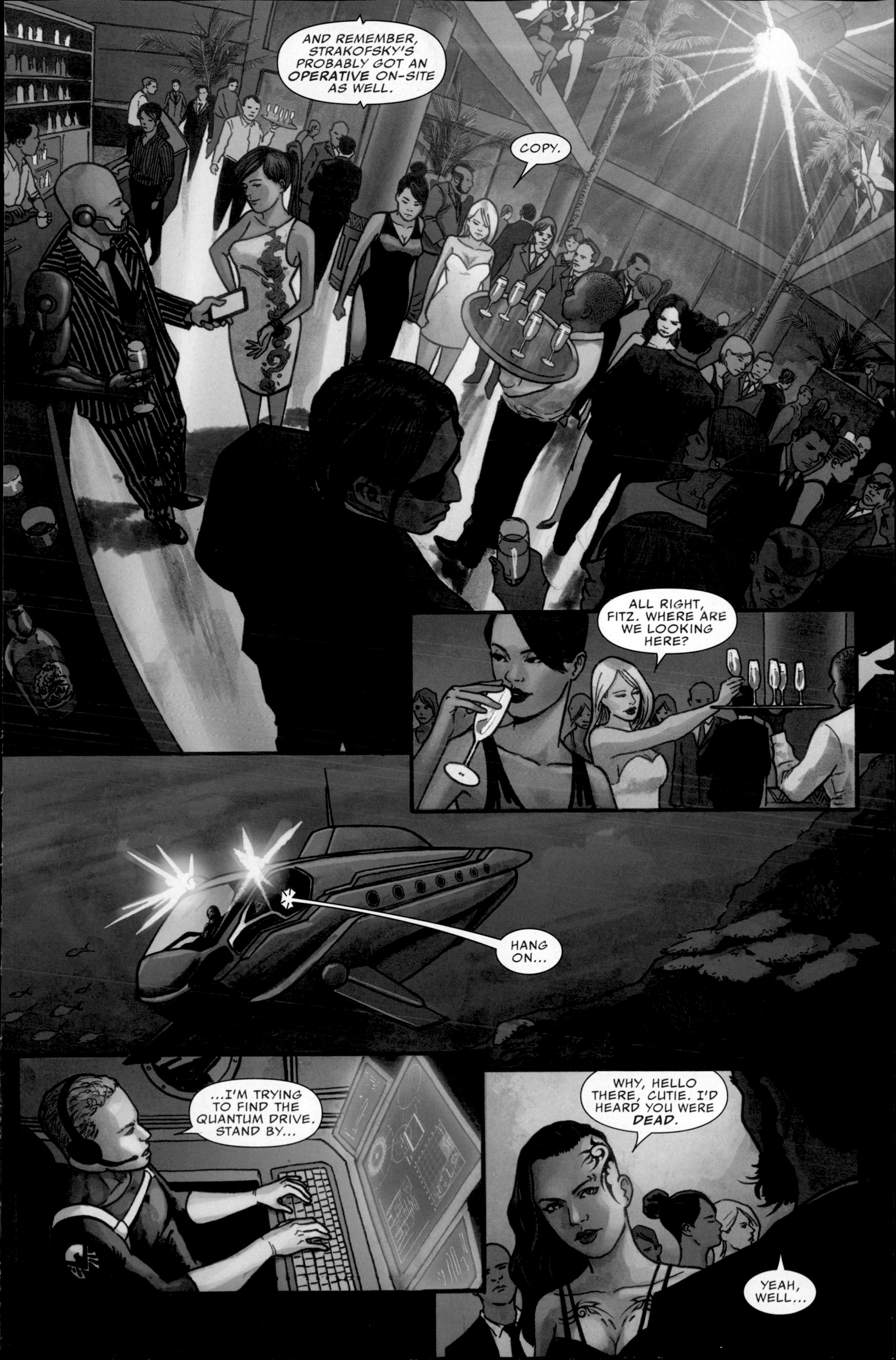
AND REMEMBER, STRAKOFSKY'S PROBABLY GOT AN OPERATIVE ON-SITE AS WELL.
COPY.
ALL RIGHT, FITZ. WHERE ARE WE LOOKING HERE?
HANG ON...
...I'M TRYING TO FIND THE QUANTUM DRIVE. STAND BY...
WHY, HELLO THERE, CUTIE. I'D HEARD YOU WERE DEAD.
YEAH, WELL...

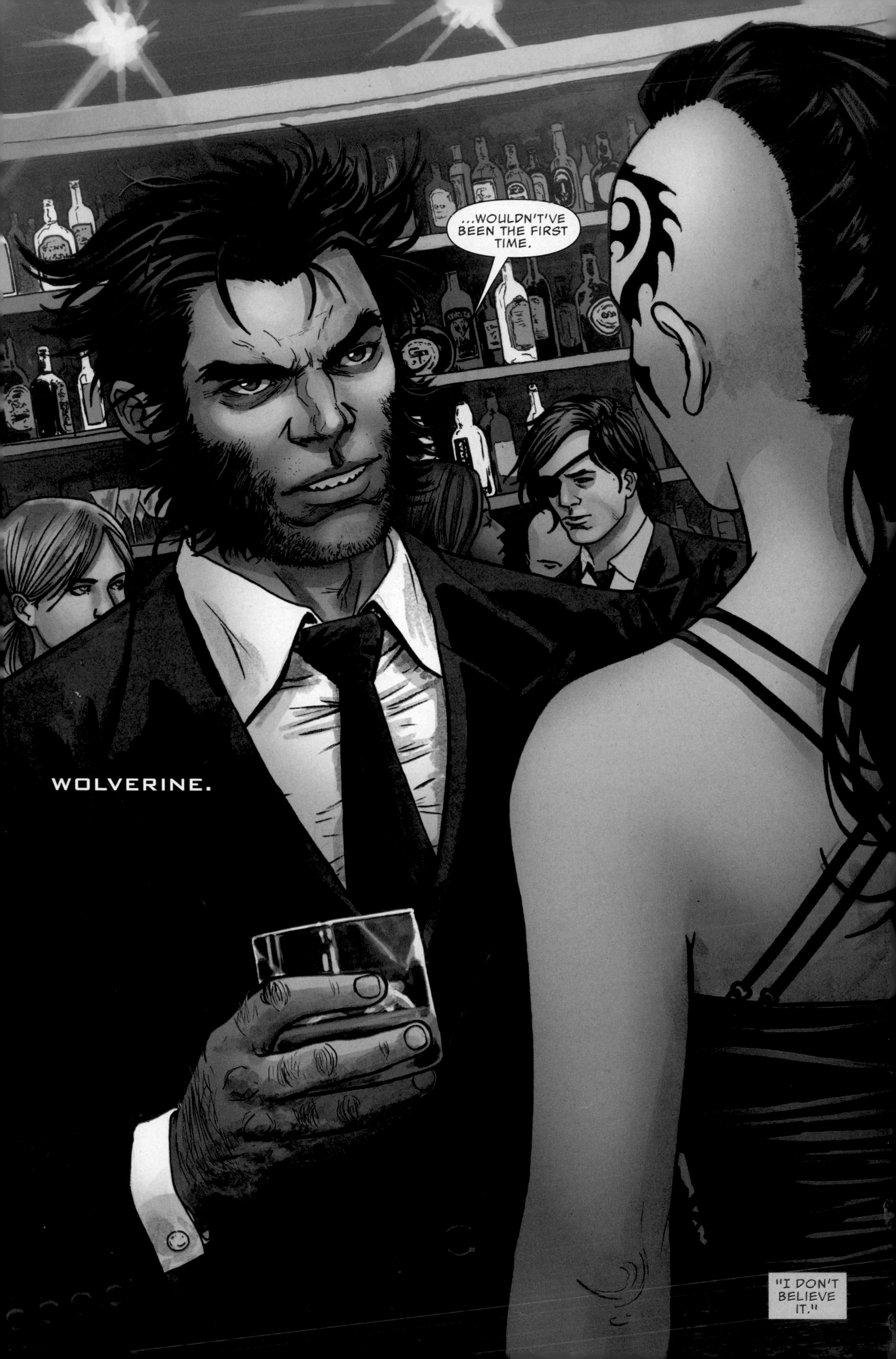
...WOULDN'T'VE BEEN THE FIRST TIME.
WOLVERINE.
"I DON'T BELIEVE IT."

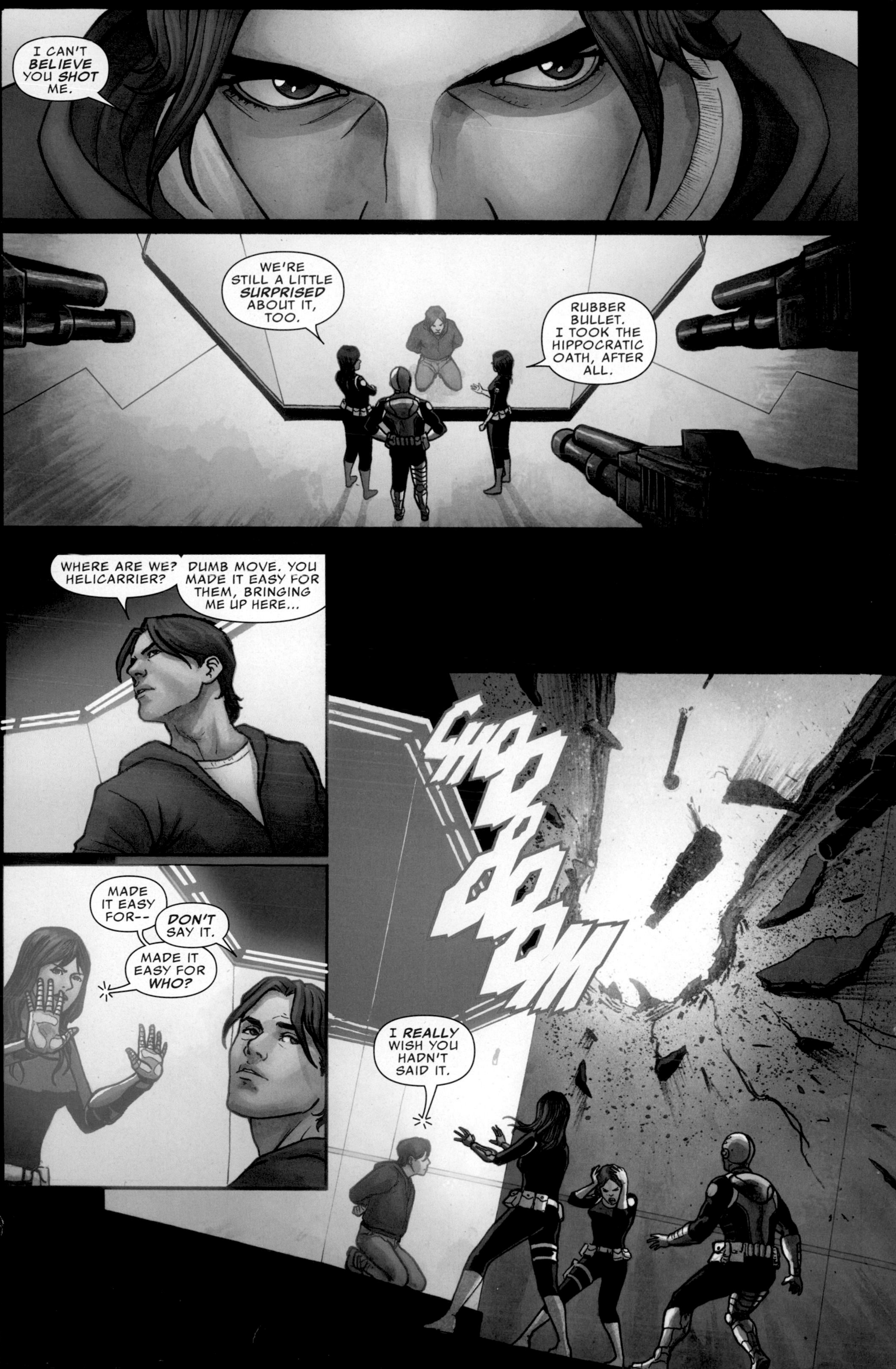
I CAN'T BELIEVE YOU SHOT ME.
WE'RE STILL A LITTLE SURPRISED ABOUT IT, TOO.
RUBBER BULLET. I TOOK THE HIPPOCRATIC OATH, AFTER ALL.
WHERE ARE WE? HELICARRIER?
DUMB MOVE. YOU MADE IT EASY FOR THEM, BRINGING ME UP HERE...
MADE IT EASY FOR--
DON'T SAY IT.
MADE IT EASY FOR WHO?
CHOOOOOOM
I REALLY WISH YOU HADN'T SAID IT.

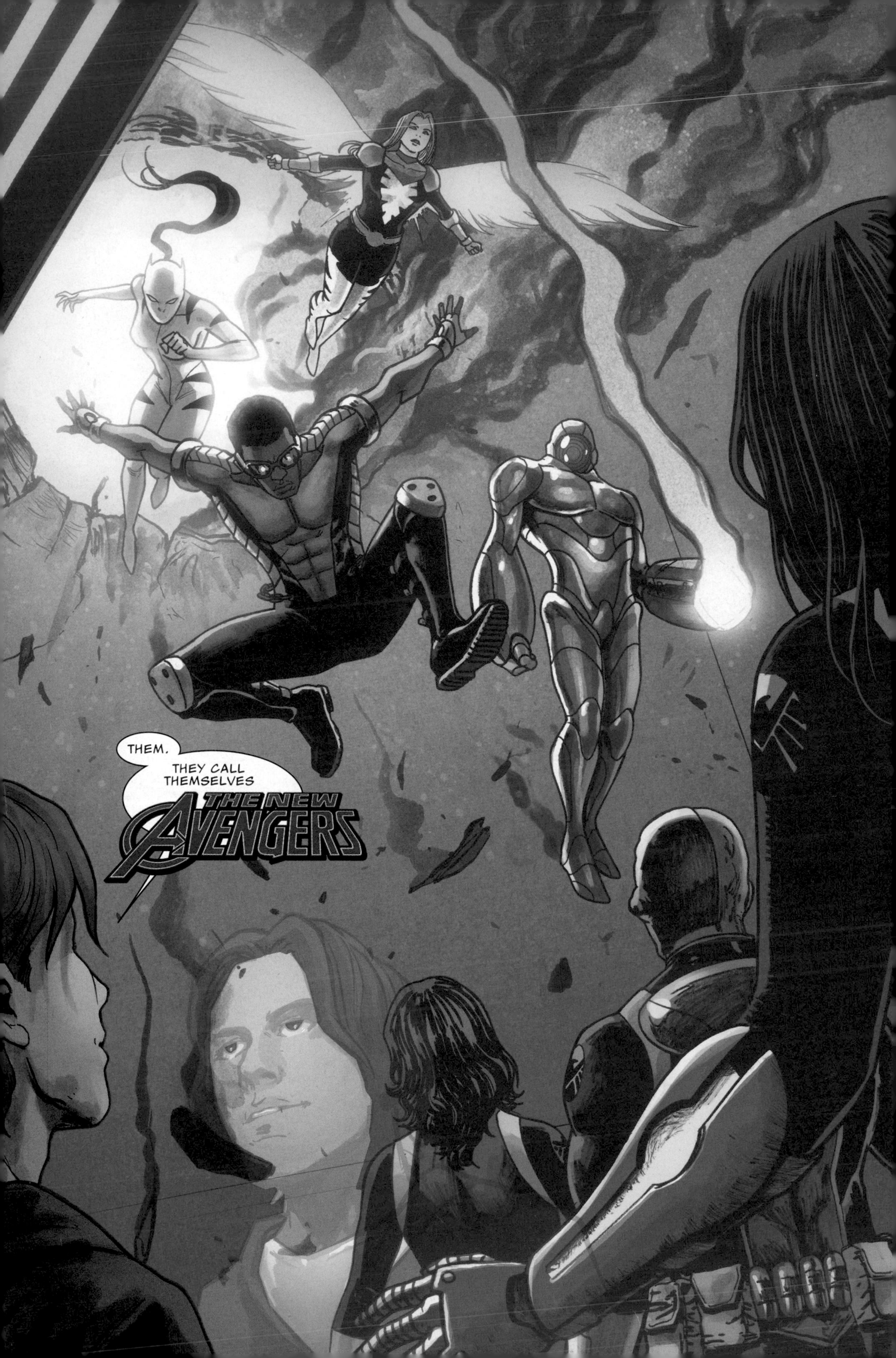
THEM.
THEY CALL THEMSELVES
THE NEW AVENGERS

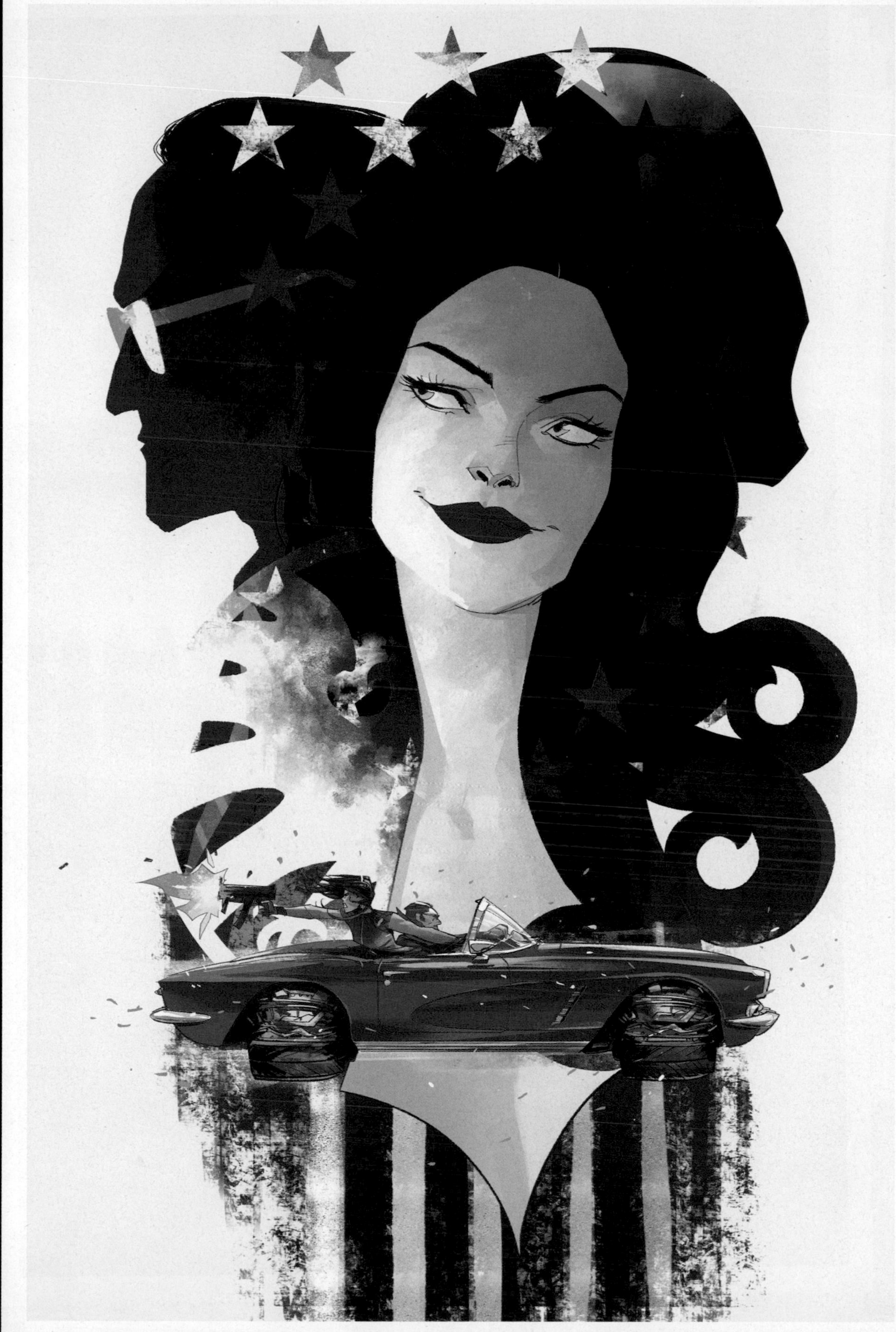

Agents of S.H.I.E.L.D. No. 3 variant by
OTTO SCHMIDT

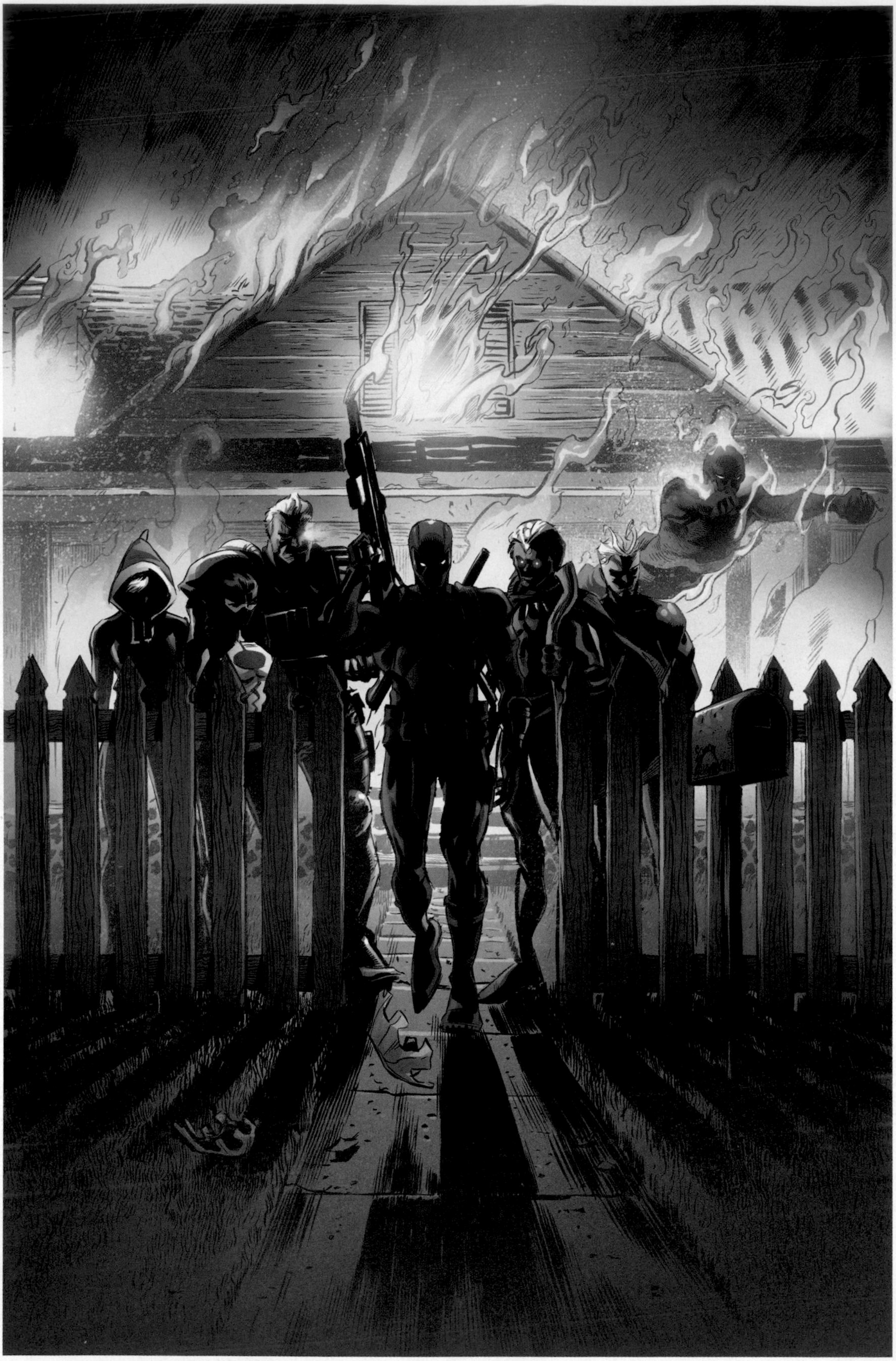

Uncanny Avengers No. 7

Mission Brief

To encourage peace after the war between the Avengers and the X-Men, the original Captain America, Steve Rogers, brought together members of both teams to form the Avengers Unity Squad. Now, to promote cooperation in the face of rising tensions, the Unity Squad has expanded to include a new faction: Inhumans.

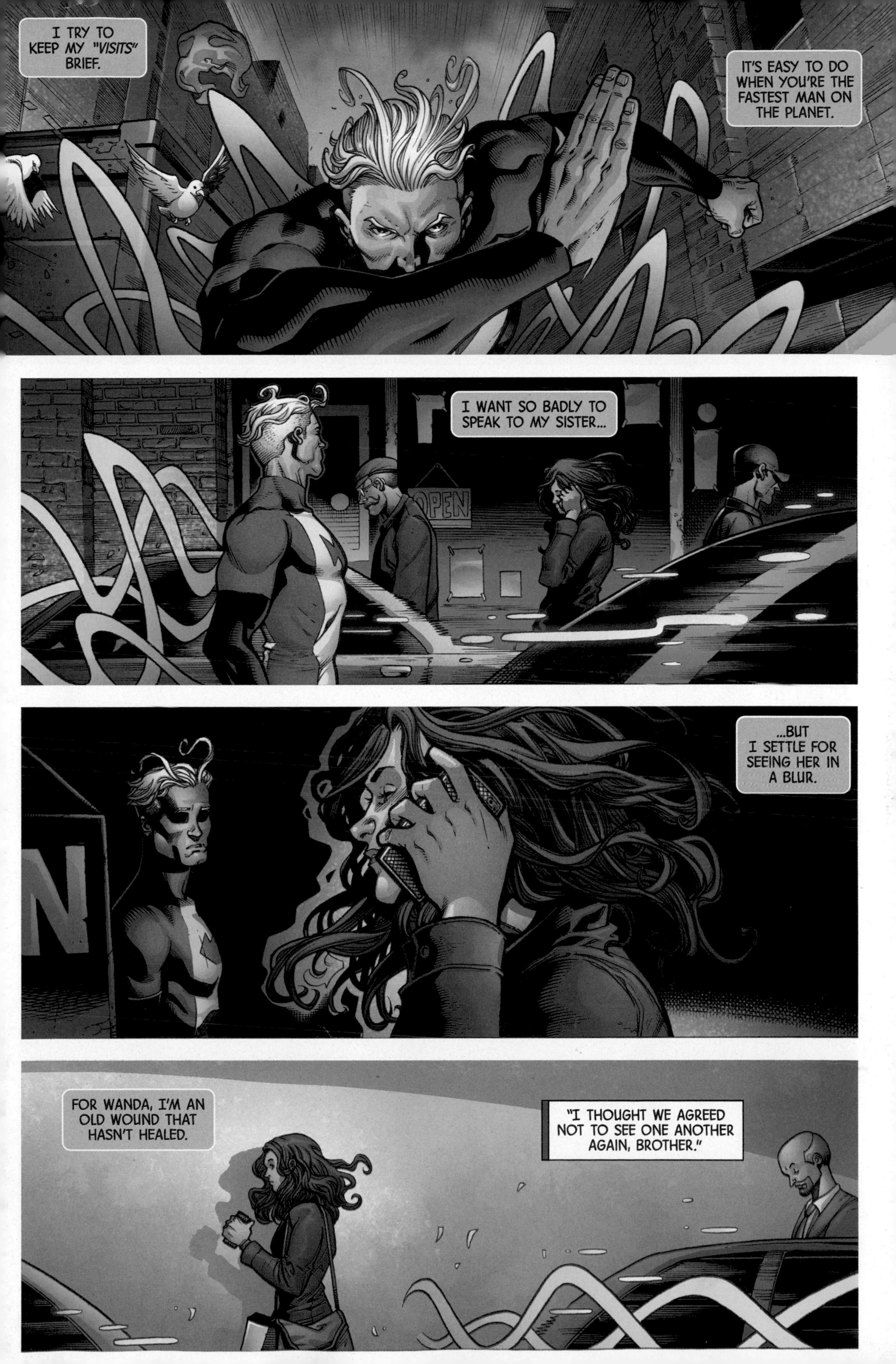

I TRY TO KEEP MY "VISITS" BRIEF.
IT'S EASY TO DO WHEN YOU'RE THE FASTEST MAN ON THE PLANET.
I WANT SO BADLY TO SPEAK TO MY SISTER...
OPEN
...BUT I SETTLE FOR SEEING HER IN A BLUR.
FOR WANDA, I'M AN OLD WOUND THAT HASN'T HEALED.
"I THOUGHT WE AGREED NOT TO SEE ONE ANOTHER AGAIN, BROTHER."

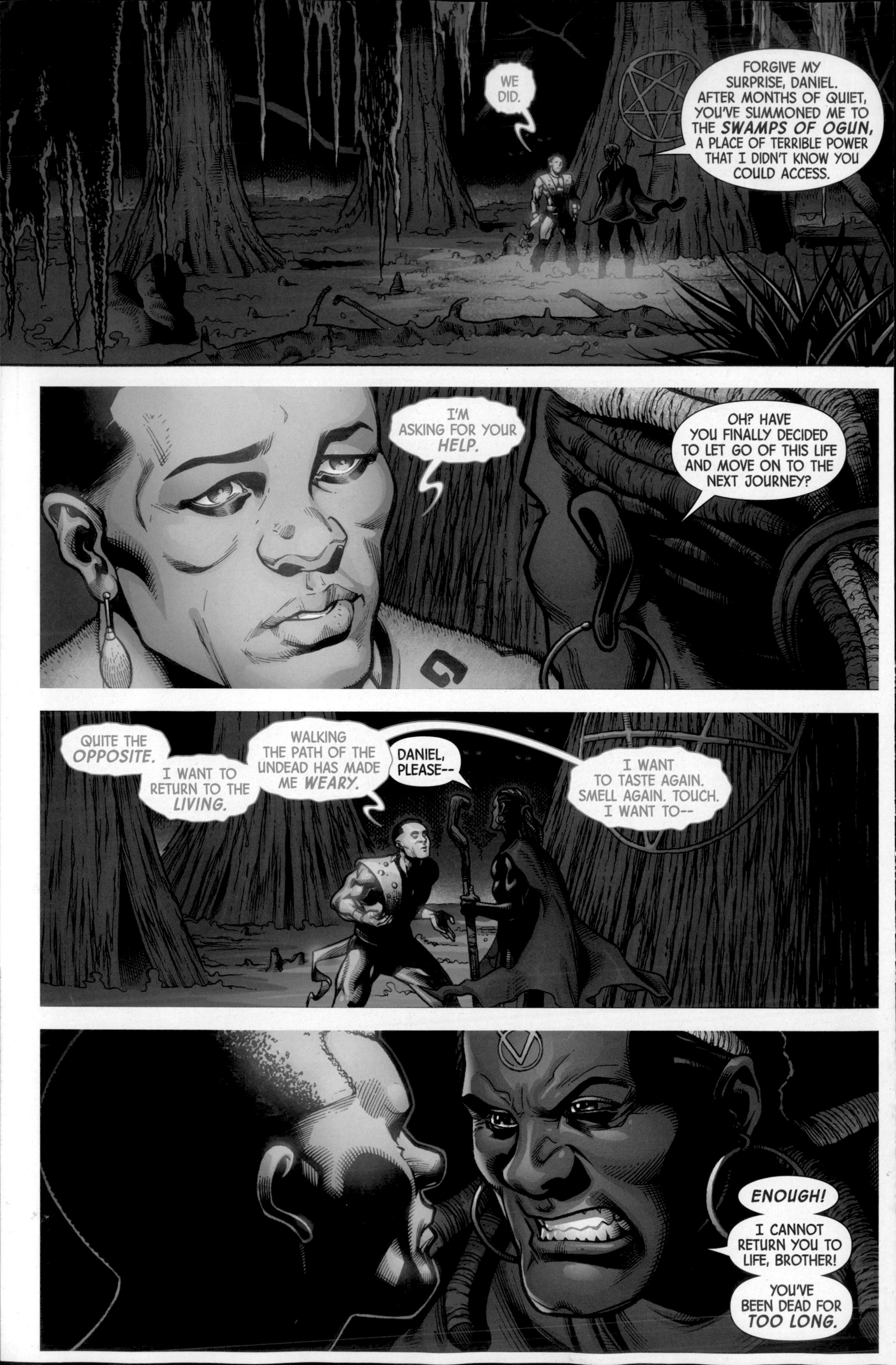
FORGIVE MY SURPRISE, DANIEL. AFTER MONTHS OF QUIET, YOU'VE SUMMONED ME TO THE SWAMPS OF OGUN, A PLACE OF TERRIBLE POWER THAT I DIDN'T KNOW YOU COULD ACCESS.
WE DID.
I'M ASKING FOR YOUR HELP.
OH? HAVE YOU FINALLY DECIDED TO LET GO OF THIS LIFE AND MOVE ON TO THE NEXT JOURNEY?
QUITE THE OPPOSITE.
I WANT TO RETURN TO THE LIVING.
WALKING THE PATH OF THE UNDEAD HAS MADE ME WEARY.
I WANT TO TASTE AGAIN. SMELL AGAIN. TOUCH. I WANT TO--
DANIEL, PLEASE--
ENOUGH!
I CANNOT RETURN YOU TO LIFE, BROTHER!
YOU'VE BEEN DEAD FOR TOO LONG.

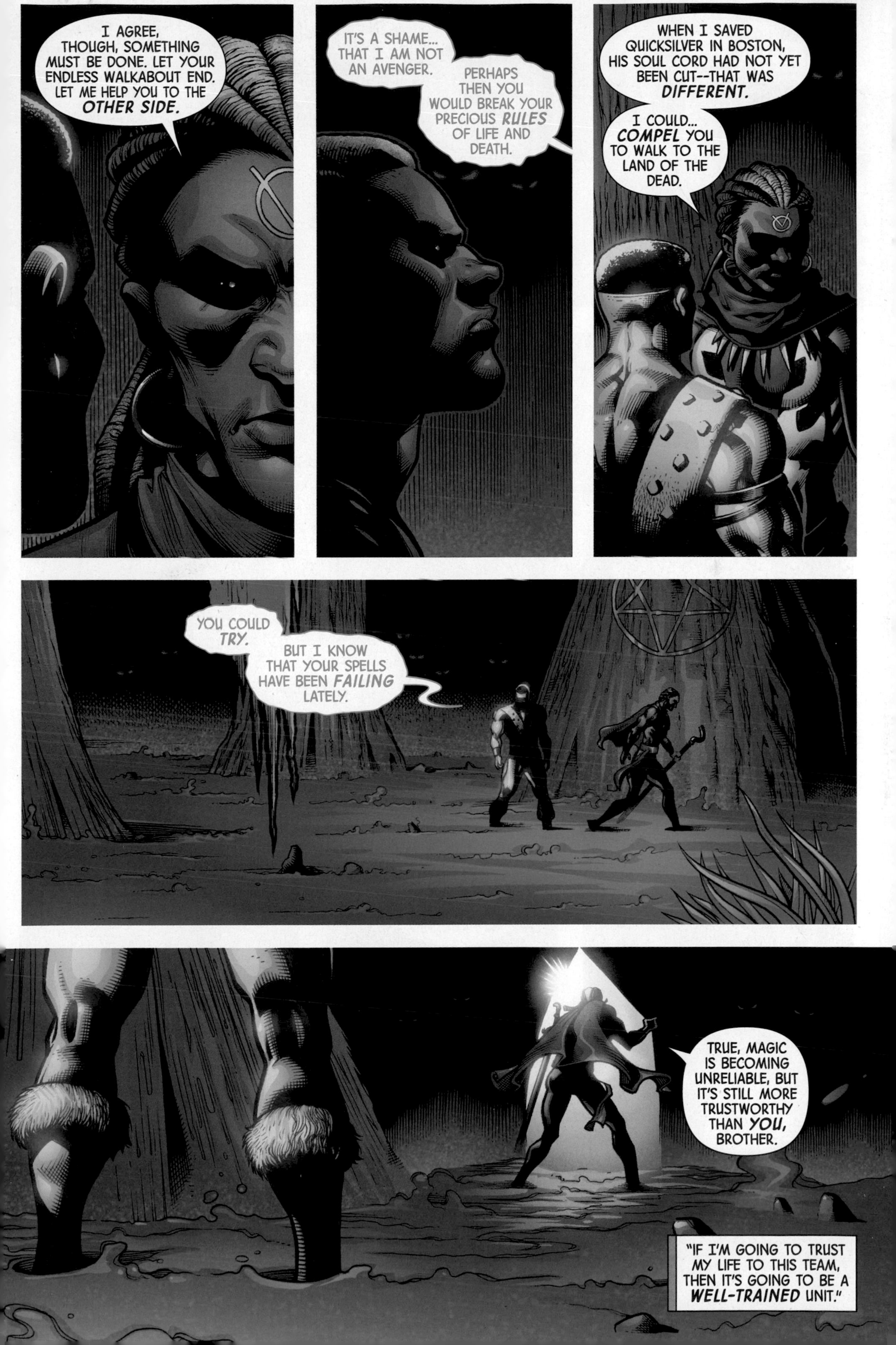

I AGREE, THOUGH, SOMETHING MUST BE DONE. LET YOUR ENDLESS WALKABOUT END. LET ME HELP YOU TO THE OTHER SIDE.
IT'S A SHAME... THAT I AM NOT AN AVENGER.
PERHAPS THEN YOU WOULD BREAK YOUR PRECIOUS RULES OF LIFE AND DEATH.
WHEN I SAVED QUICKSILVER IN BOSTON, HIS SOUL CORD HAD NOT YET BEEN CUT--THAT WAS DIFFERENT.
I COULD... COMPEL YOU TO WALK TO THE LAND OF THE DEAD.
YOU COULD TRY.
BUT I KNOW THAT YOUR SPELLS HAVE BEEN FAILING LATELY.
TRUE, MAGIC IS BECOMING UNRELIABLE, BUT IT'S STILL MORE TRUSTWORTHY THAN YOU, BROTHER.
"IF I'M GOING TO TRUST MY LIFE TO THIS TEAM, THEN IT'S GOING TO BE A WELL-TRAINED UNIT."

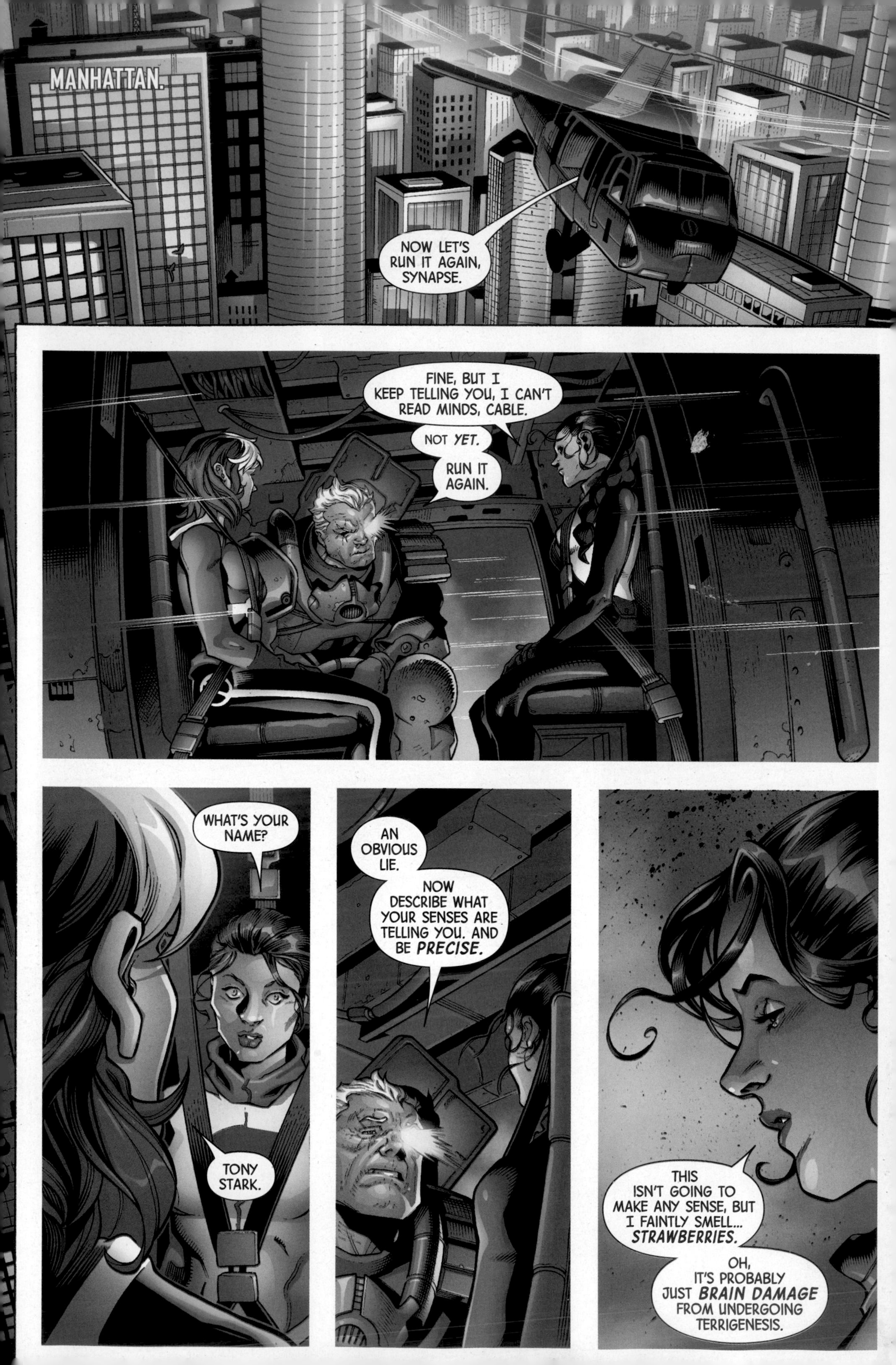
MANHATTAN.
NOW LET'S RUN IT AGAIN, SYNAPSE.
FINE, BUT I KEEP TELLING YOU, I CAN'T READ MINDS, CABLE.
NOT YET.
RUN IT AGAIN.
WHAT'S YOUR NAME?
TONY STARK.
AN OBVIOUS LIE.
NOW DESCRIBE WHAT YOUR SENSES ARE TELLING YOU. AND BE PRECISE.
THIS ISN'T GOING TO MAKE ANY SENSE, BUT I FAINTLY SMELL... STRAWBERRIES.
OH, IT'S PROBABLY JUST BRAIN DAMAGE FROM UNDERGOING TERRIGENESIS.

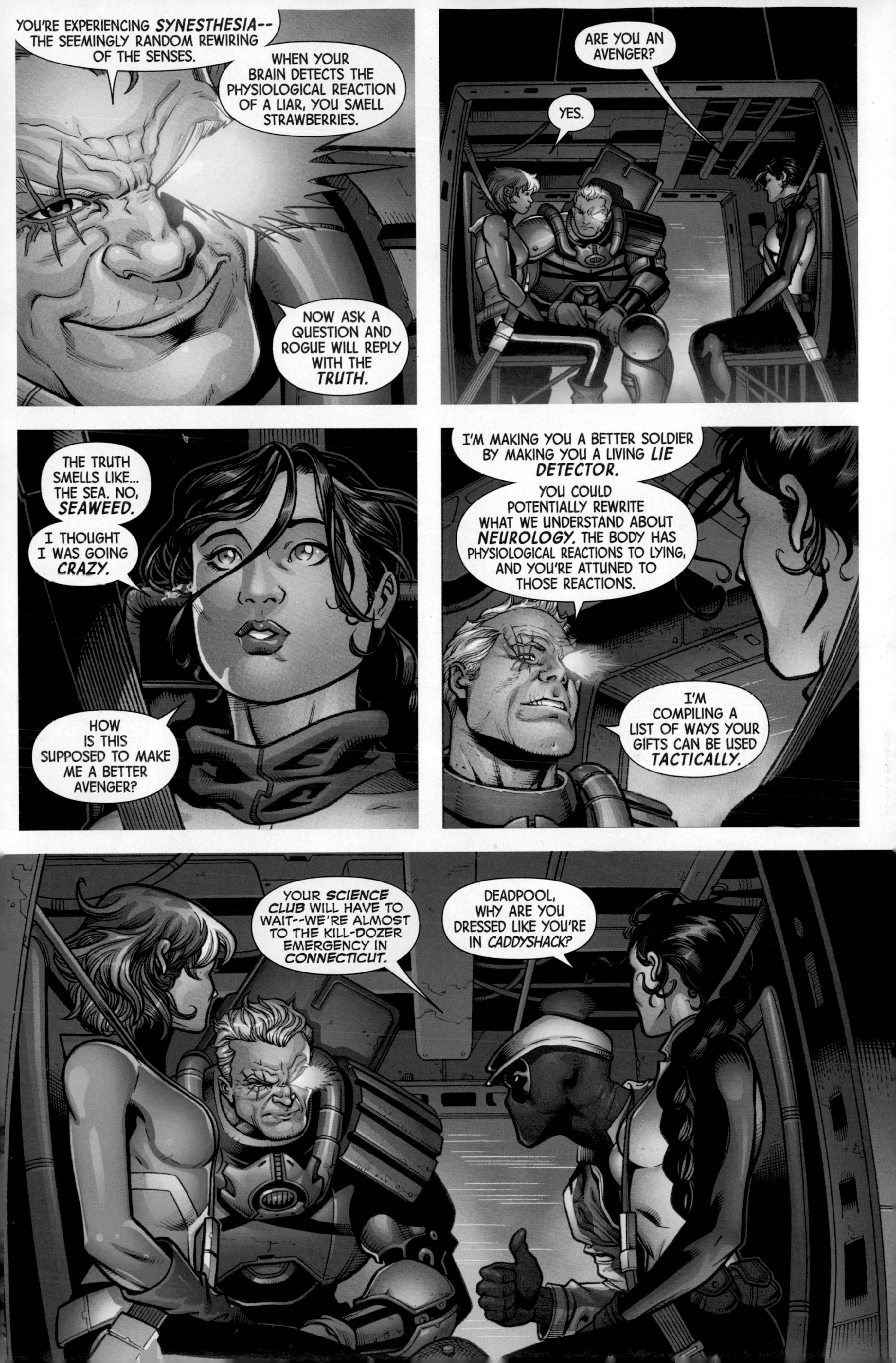
YOU'RE EXPERIENCING SYNESTHESIA-- THE SEEMINGLY RANDOM REWIRING OF THE SENSES.
WHEN YOUR BRAIN DETECTS THE PHYSIOLOGICAL REACTION OF A LIAR, YOU SMELL STRAWBERRIES.
NOW ASK A QUESTION AND ROGUE WILL REPLY WITH THE TRUTH.
ARE YOU AN AVENGER?
YES.
THE TRUTH SMELLS LIKE... THE SEA. NO, SEAWEED.
I THOUGHT I WAS GOING CRAZY.
HOW IS THIS SUPPOSED TO MAKE ME A BETTER AVENGER?
I'M MAKING YOU A BETTER SOLDIER BY MAKING YOU A LIVING LIE DETECTOR.
YOU COULD POTENTIALLY REWRITE WHAT WE UNDERSTAND ABOUT NEUROLOGY. THE BODY HAS PHYSIOLOGICAL REACTIONS TO LYING, AND YOU'RE ATTUNED TO THOSE REACTIONS.
I'M COMPILING A LIST OF WAYS YOUR GIFTS CAN BE USED TACTICALLY.
YOUR SCIENCE CLUB WILL HAVE TO WAIT--WE'RE ALMOST TO THE KILL-DOZER EMERGENCY IN CONNECTICUT.
DEADPOOL, WHY ARE YOU DRESSED LIKE YOU'RE IN CADDYSHACK?

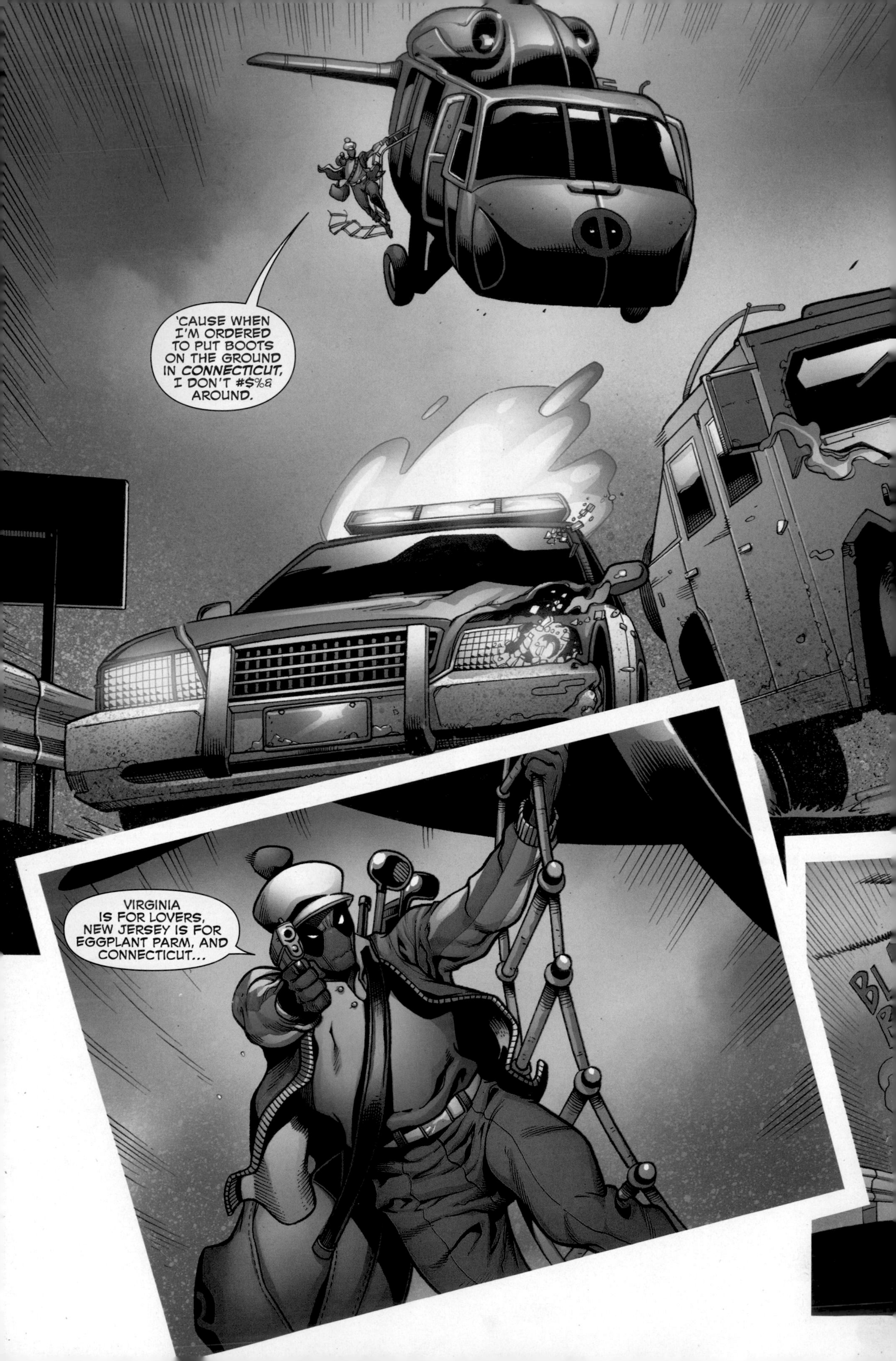
'CAUSE WHEN I'M ORDERED TO PUT BOOTS ON THE GROUND IN *CONNECTICUT*, I DON'T #$%& AROUND.
VIRGINIA IS FOR LOVERS, NEW JERSEY IS FOR EGGPLANT PARM, AND CONNECTICUT...

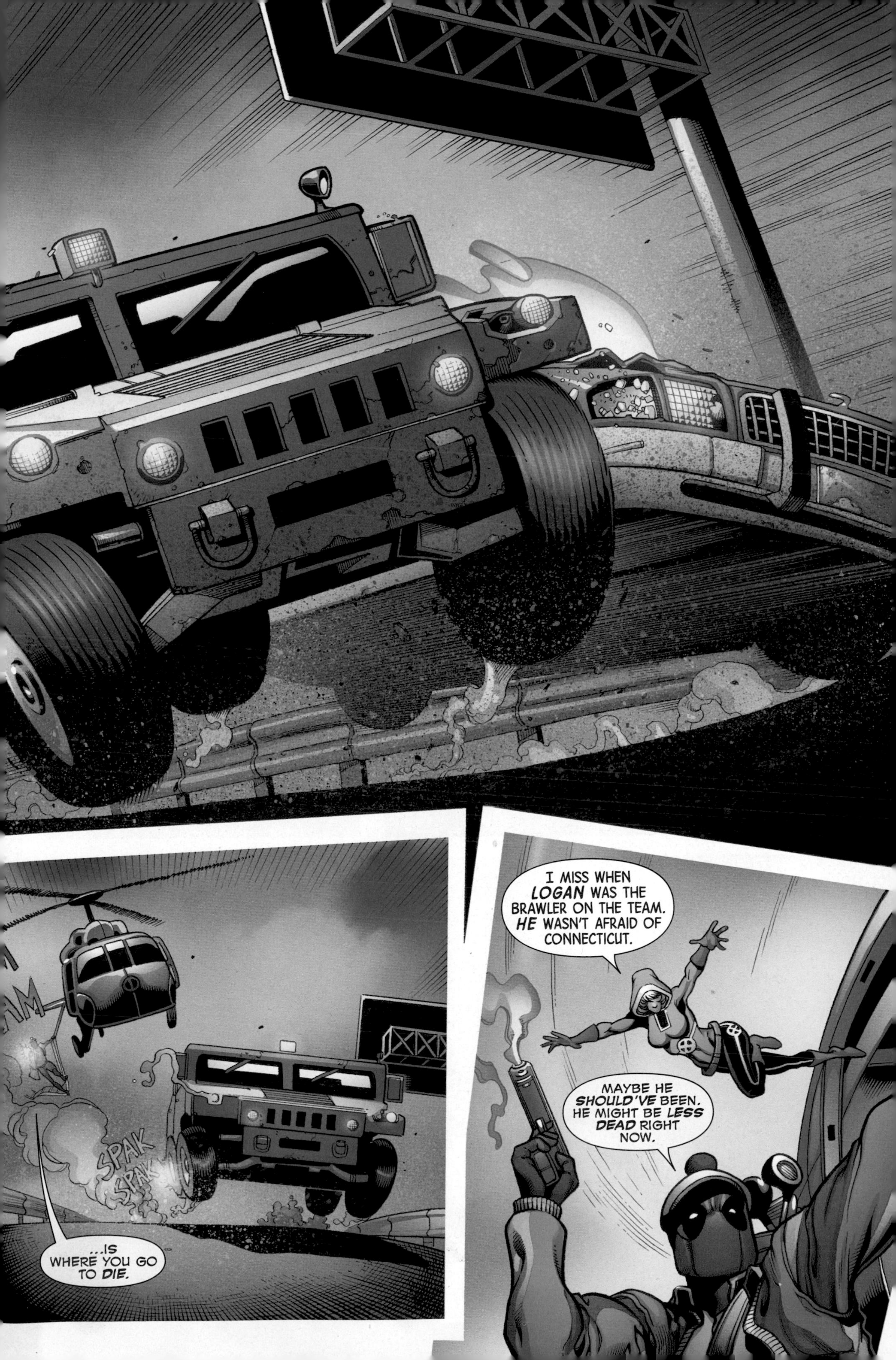
SPAK
SPAK
...IS WHERE YOU GO TO DIE.
I MISS WHEN LOGAN WAS THE BRAWLER ON THE TEAM. HE WASN'T AFRAID OF CONNECTICUT.
MAYBE HE SHOULD'VE BEEN. HE MIGHT BE LESS DEAD RIGHT NOW.

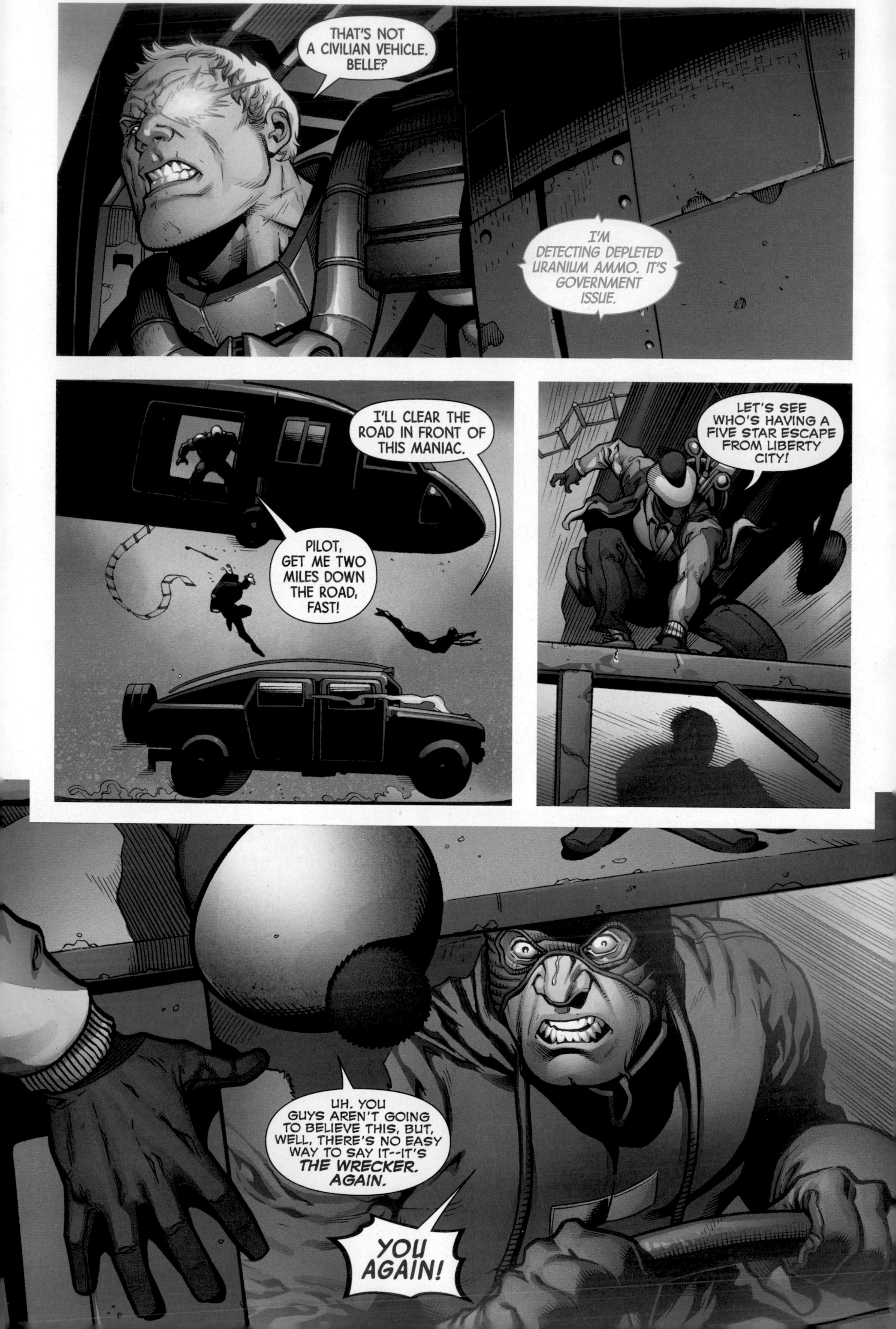
THAT'S NOT A CIVILIAN VEHICLE. BELLE?
I'M DETECTING DEPLETED URANIUM AMMO. IT'S GOVERNMENT ISSUE.
I'LL CLEAR THE ROAD IN FRONT OF THIS MANIAC.
PILOT, GET ME TWO MILES DOWN THE ROAD, FAST!
LET'S SEE WHO'S HAVING A FIVE STAR ESCAPE FROM LIBERTY CITY!
UH. YOU GUYS AREN'T GOING TO BELIEVE THIS, BUT, WELL, THERE'S NO EASY WAY TO SAY IT--IT'S *THE WRECKER.* *AGAIN.*
YOU AGAIN!

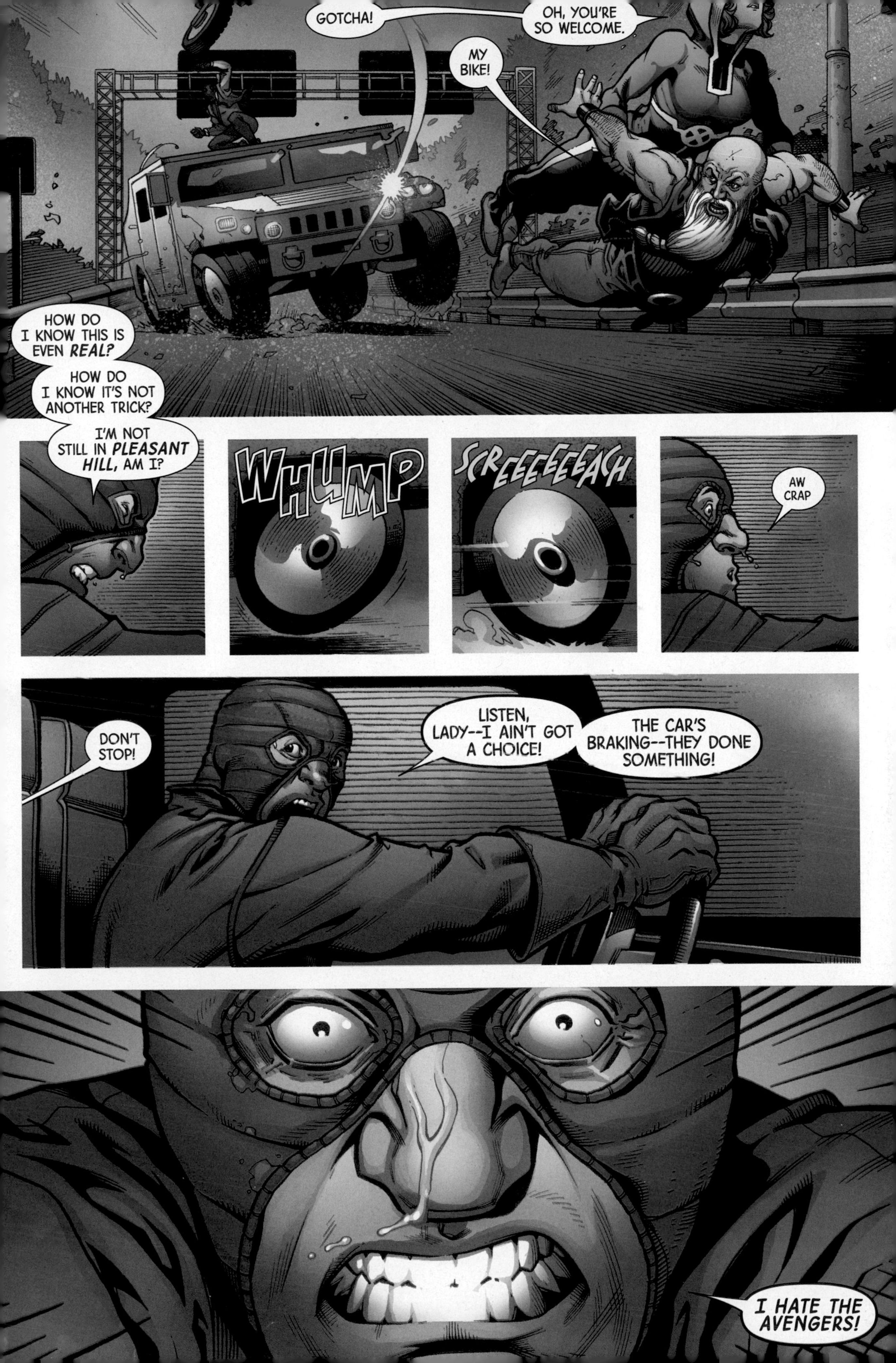
GOTCHA!
OH, YOU'RE SO WELCOME.
MY BIKE!
HOW DO I KNOW THIS IS EVEN *REAL?*
HOW DO I KNOW IT'S NOT ANOTHER TRICK?
I'M NOT STILL IN *PLEASANT HILL,* AM I?
WHUMP
SCREEEEEEACH
AW CRAP
DON'T STOP!
LISTEN, LADY--I AIN'T GOT A CHOICE!
THE CAR'S BRAKING--THEY DONE SOMETHING!
I HATE THE AVENGERS!

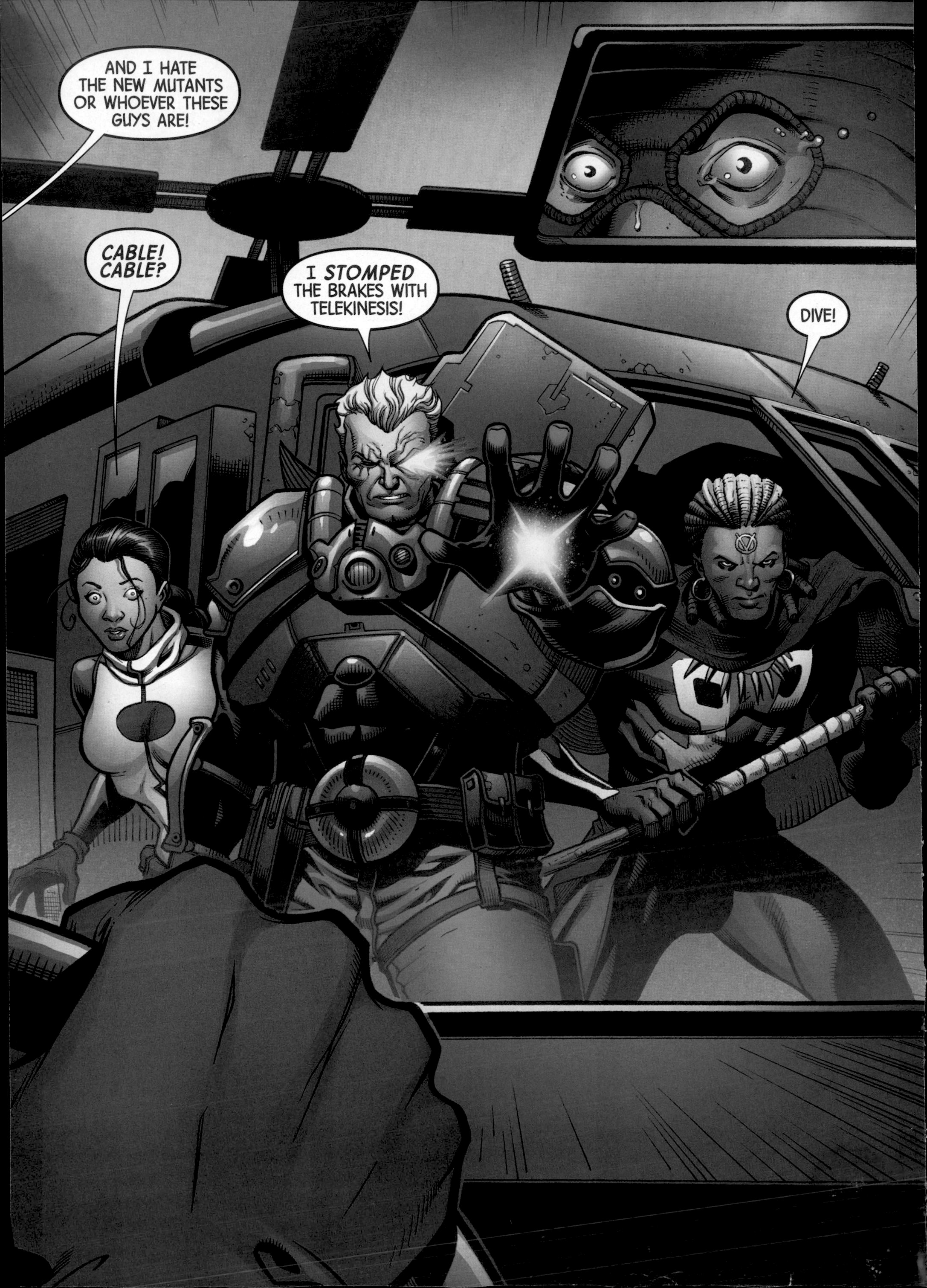
AND I HATE THE NEW MUTANTS OR WHOEVER THESE GUYS ARE!
CABLE! CABLE?
I STOMPED THE BRAKES WITH TELEKINESIS!
DIVE!

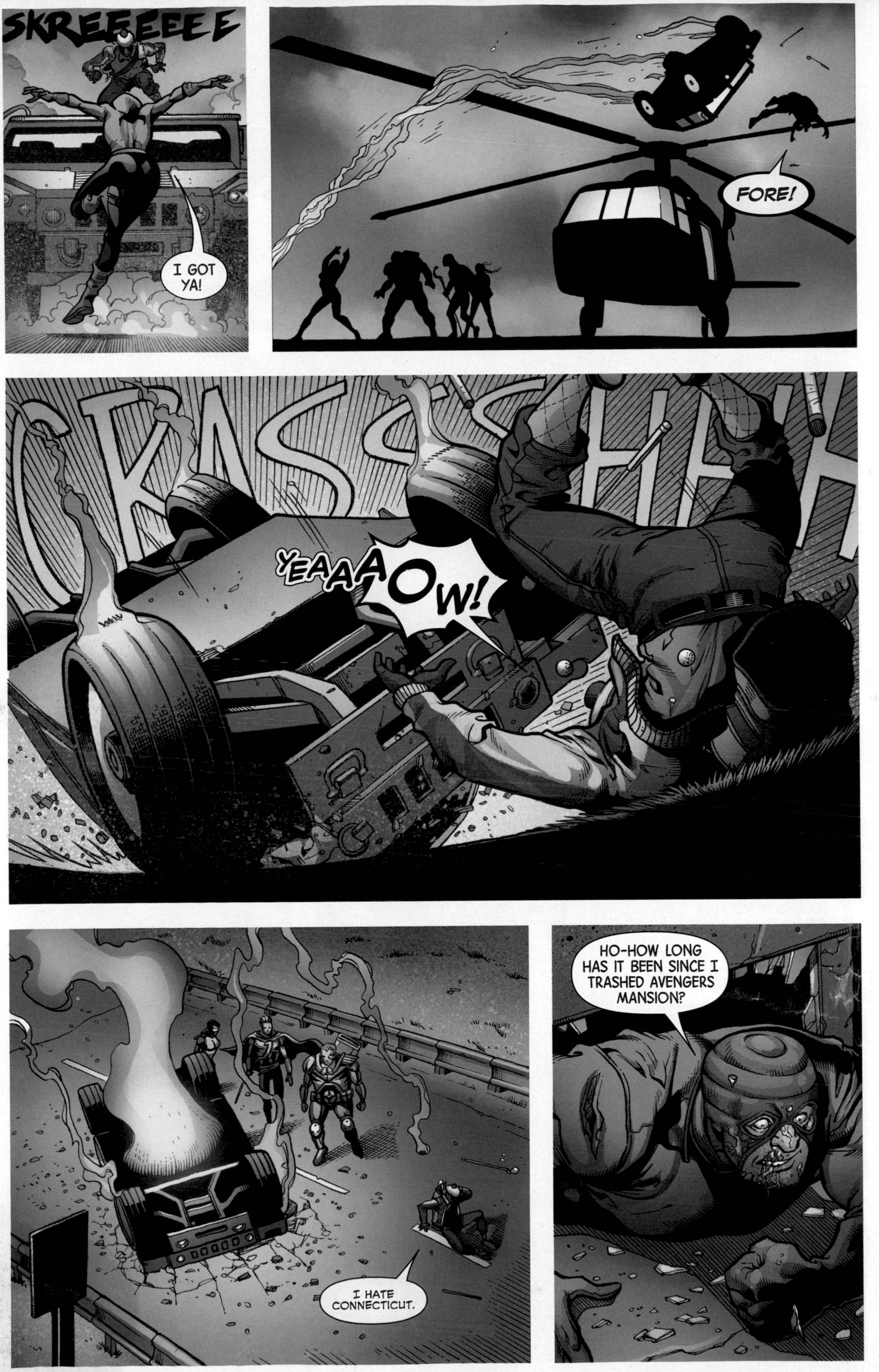
SKREEEEEE
I GOT YA!
FORE!
CRASSSHHH
YEAAAAOW!
I HATE CONNECTICUT.
HO-HOW LONG HAS IT BEEN SINCE I TRASHED AVENGERS MANSION?

I DUNNO-- A COUPLE OF WEEKS?

NO! JIM'S BEEN INSIDE ALONE!

WEREN'T YOU SUPPOSED TO BE LOOKING THROUGH THE UNDERWORLD FOR THE RED SKULL FOR ME?

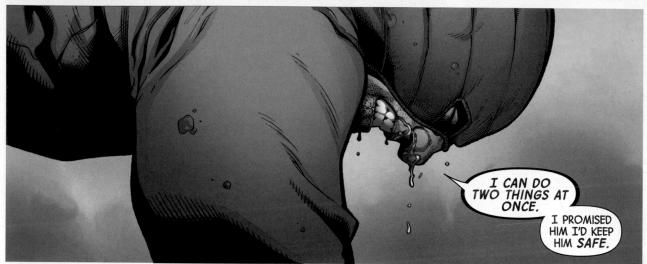

I CAN DO TWO THINGS AT ONCE.

I PROMISED HIM I'D KEEP HIM SAFE.

KEEP WHO SAFE?

I UNDERSTAND NOW.

YOU WANTED TO BE SENT BACK TO PRISON BECAUSE YOU WERE HELPING SOMEONE SURVIVE INSIDE.

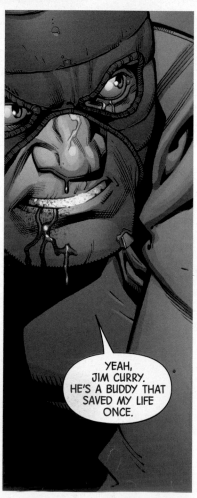

YEAH, JIM CURRY. HE'S A BUDDY THAT SAVED MY LIFE ONCE.

AH. YOU TRASHED AVENGERS MANSION FOR A QUICK RETURN TICKET. ONLY, YOU WEREN'T RETURNED TO JAIL, WERE YOU? THEY SENT YOU SOMEPLACE ELSE.

I'M SORRY TO TELL YOU THIS...

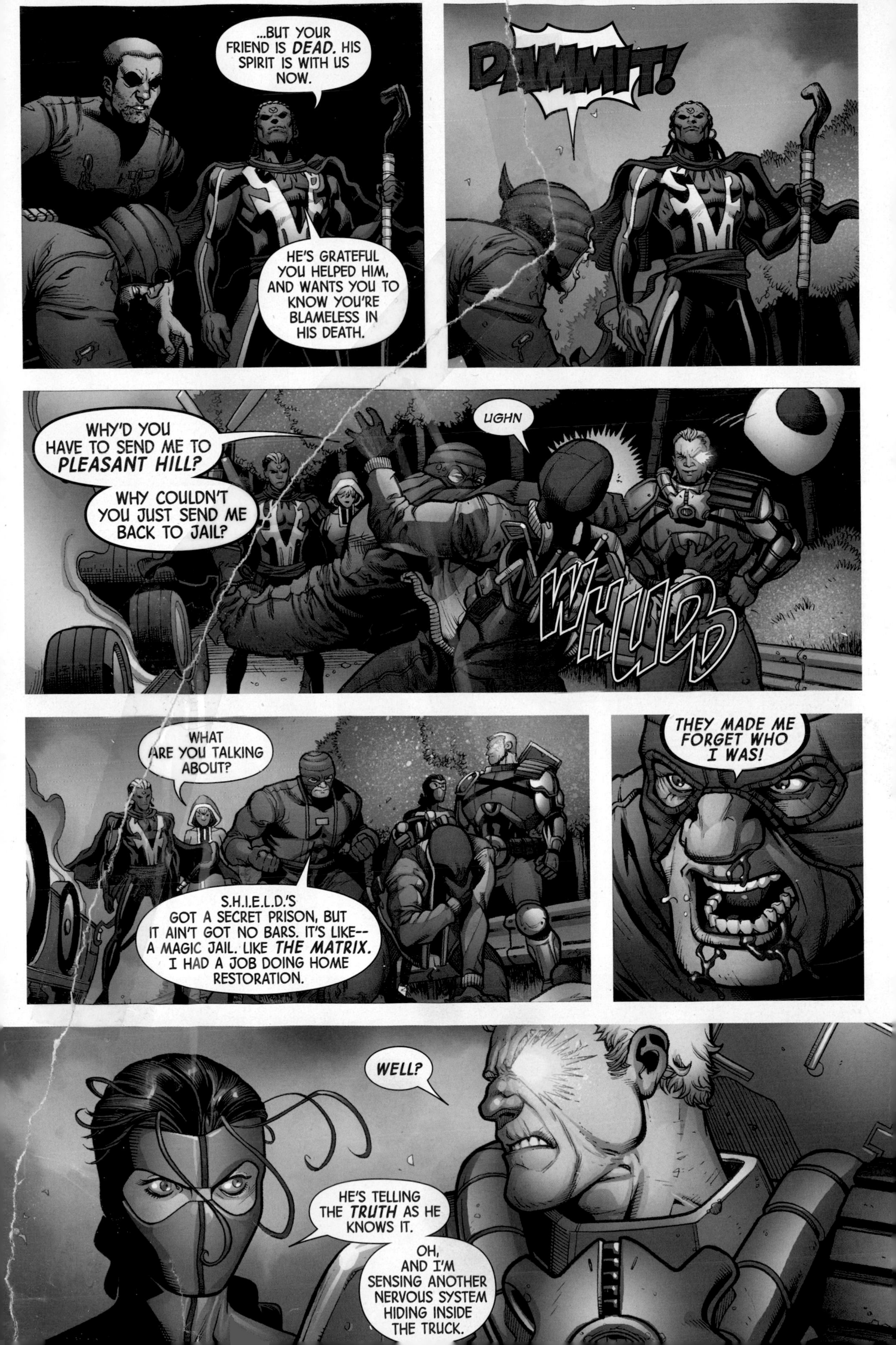
...BUT YOUR FRIEND IS DEAD. HIS SPIRIT IS WITH US NOW.
HE'S GRATEFUL YOU HELPED HIM, AND WANTS YOU TO KNOW YOU'RE BLAMELESS IN HIS DEATH.
DAMMIT!
WHY'D YOU HAVE TO SEND ME TO PLEASANT HILL?
WHY COULDN'T YOU JUST SEND ME BACK TO JAIL?
UGHN
WHUDD
WHAT ARE YOU TALKING ABOUT?
S.H.I.E.L.D.'S GOT A SECRET PRISON, BUT IT AIN'T GOT NO BARS. IT'S LIKE-- A MAGIC JAIL. LIKE THE MATRIX. I HAD A JOB DOING HOME RESTORATION.
THEY MADE ME FORGET WHO I WAS!
WELL?
HE'S TELLING THE TRUTH AS HE KNOWS IT.
OH, AND I'M SENSING ANOTHER NERVOUS SYSTEM HIDING INSIDE THE TRUCK.

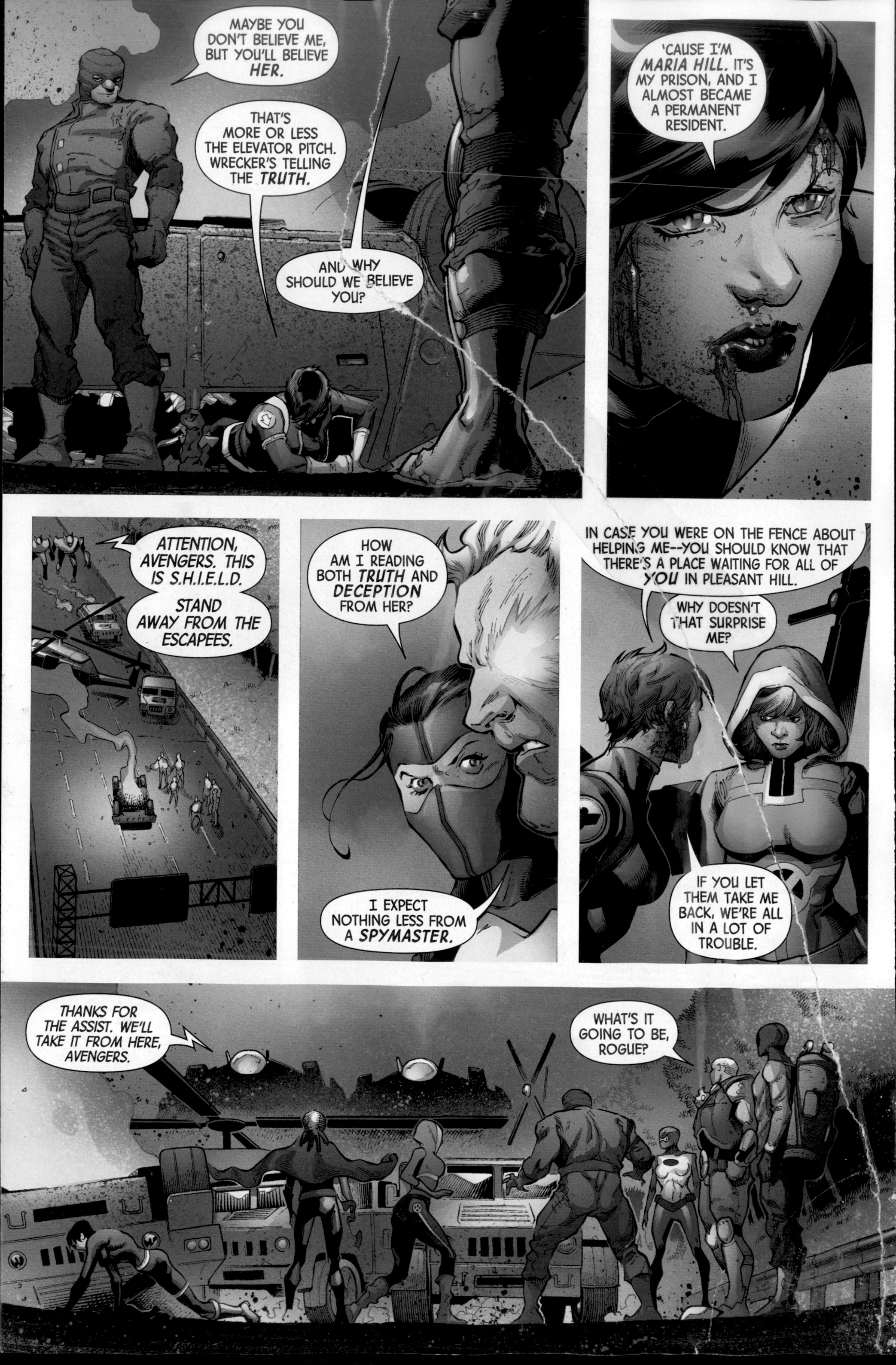
MAYBE YOU DON'T BELIEVE ME, BUT YOU'LL BELIEVE HER.
THAT'S MORE OR LESS THE ELEVATOR PITCH. WRECKER'S TELLING THE TRUTH.
AND WHY SHOULD WE BELIEVE YOU?
'CAUSE I'M MARIA HILL. IT'S MY PRISON, AND I ALMOST BECAME A PERMANENT RESIDENT.
ATTENTION, AVENGERS. THIS IS S.H.I.E.L.D.
STAND AWAY FROM THE ESCAPEES.
HOW AM I READING BOTH TRUTH AND DECEPTION FROM HER?
I EXPECT NOTHING LESS FROM A SPYMASTER.
IN CASE YOU WERE ON THE FENCE ABOUT HELPING ME--YOU SHOULD KNOW THAT THERE'S A PLACE WAITING FOR ALL OF YOU IN PLEASANT HILL.
WHY DOESN'T THAT SURPRISE ME?
IF YOU LET THEM TAKE ME BACK, WE'RE ALL IN A LOT OF TROUBLE.
THANKS FOR THE ASSIST. WE'LL TAKE IT FROM HERE, AVENGERS.
WHAT'S IT GOING TO BE, ROGUE?

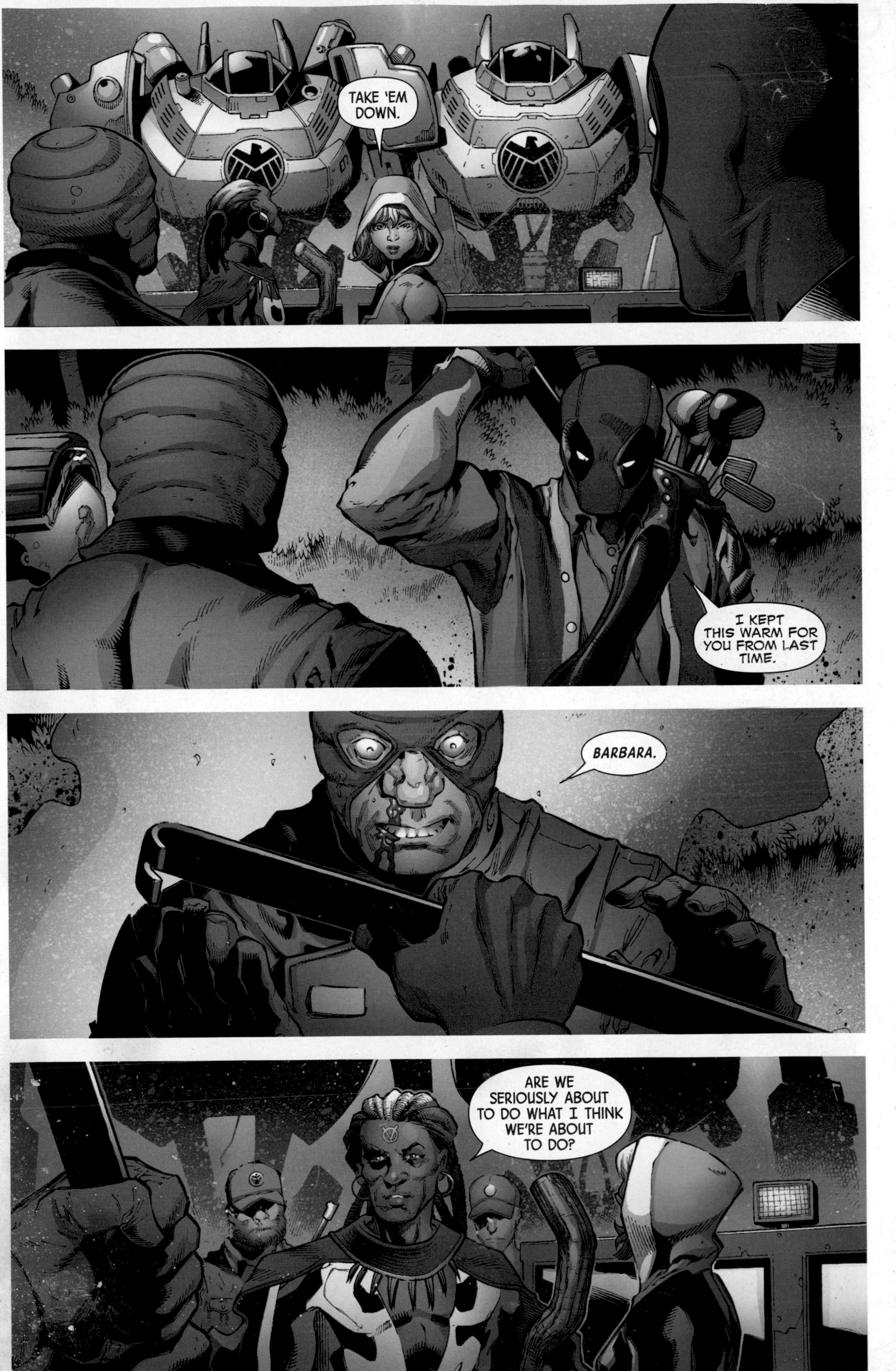
TAKE 'EM DOWN.
I KEPT THIS WARM FOR YOU FROM LAST TIME.
BARBARA.
ARE WE SERIOUSLY ABOUT TO DO WHAT I THINK WE'RE ABOUT TO DO?

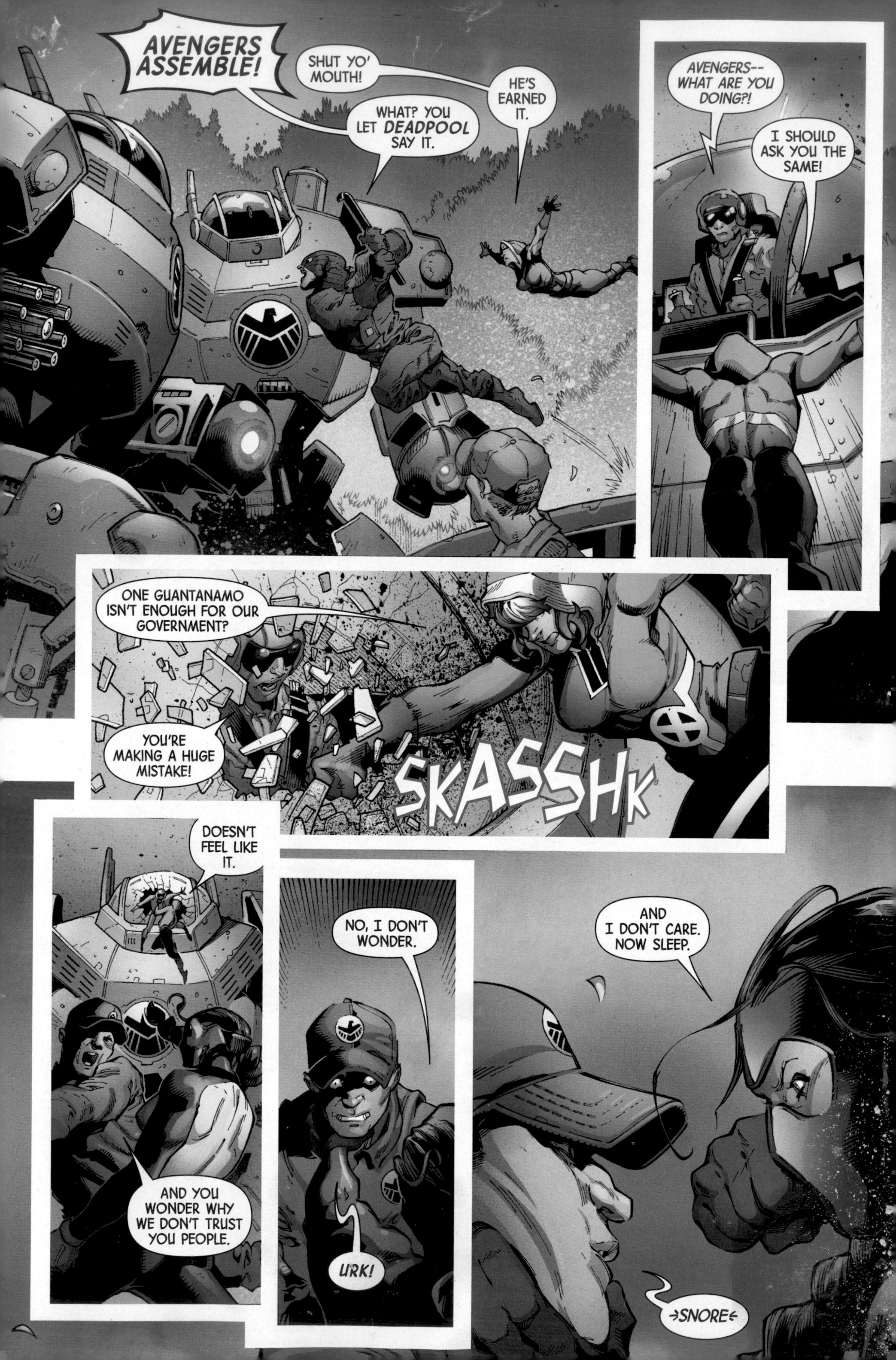
AVENGERS ASSEMBLE!
SHUT YO' MOUTH!
HE'S EARNED IT.
WHAT? YOU LET DEADPOOL SAY IT.
AVENGERS-- WHAT ARE YOU DOING?!
I SHOULD ASK YOU THE SAME!
ONE GUANTANAMO ISN'T ENOUGH FOR OUR GOVERNMENT?
YOU'RE MAKING A HUGE MISTAKE!
SKASSHK
DOESN'T FEEL LIKE IT.
AND YOU WONDER WHY WE DON'T TRUST YOU PEOPLE.
NO, I DON'T WONDER.
URK!
AND I DON'T CARE. NOW SLEEP.
SNORE

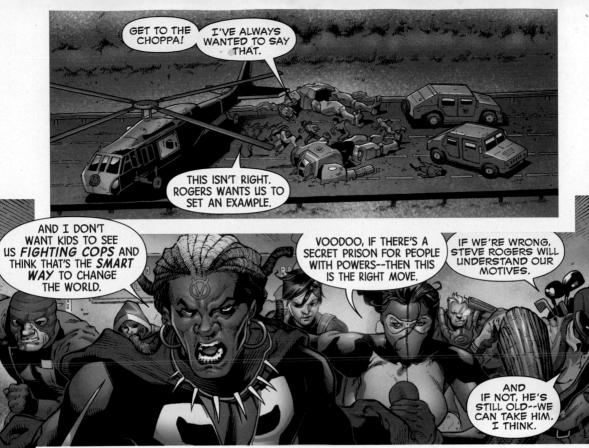

GET TO THE CHOPPA!

I'VE ALWAYS WANTED TO SAY THAT.

THIS ISN'T RIGHT. ROGERS WANTS US TO SET AN EXAMPLE.

AND I DON'T WANT KIDS TO SEE US *FIGHTING COPS* AND THINK THAT'S THE *SMART WAY* TO CHANGE THE WORLD.

VOODOO, IF THERE'S A SECRET PRISON FOR PEOPLE WITH POWERS--THEN THIS IS THE RIGHT MOVE.

IF WE'RE WRONG, STEVE ROGERS WILL UNDERSTAND OUR MOTIVES.

AND IF NOT, HE'S STILL OLD--WE CAN TAKE HIM. I THINK.

HEH. I'LL ADMIT, I THOUGHT THROWING IN WITH AN AVENGERS TEAM WOULD BORE THE PISS OUT OF ME...

...BUT THIS HAS BEEN *FUN.*

THANKS FOR BELIEVING ME--

--SO WHAT'S OUR NEXT MOVE?

ABOUT TWENTY FEET DOWN.

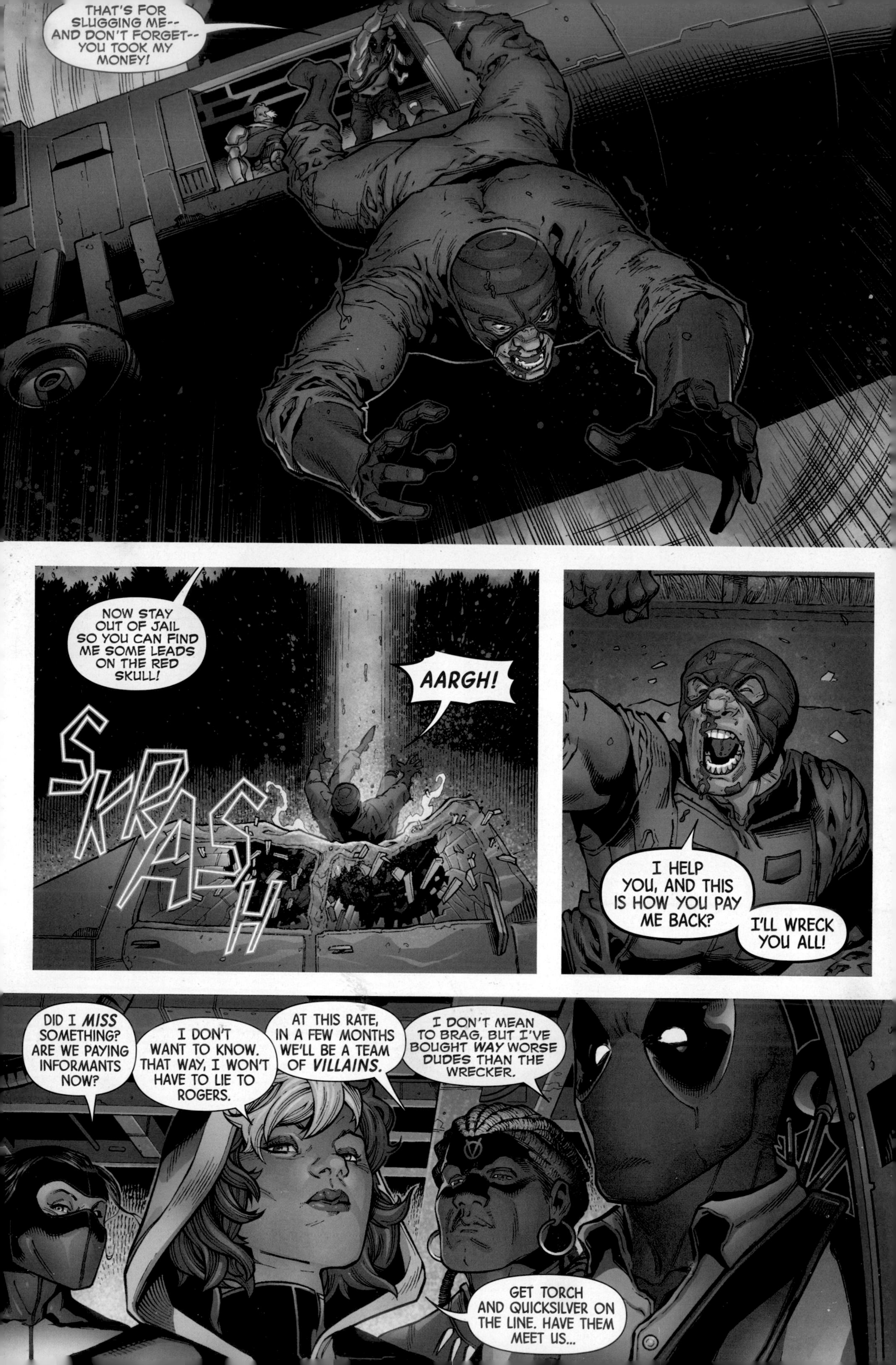
THAT'S FOR SLUGGING ME-- AND DON'T FORGET-- YOU TOOK MY MONEY!
NOW STAY OUT OF JAIL SO YOU CAN FIND ME SOME LEADS ON THE RED SKULL!
AARGH!
SKRASH
I HELP YOU, AND THIS IS HOW YOU PAY ME BACK?
I'LL WRECK YOU ALL!
DID I MISS SOMETHING? ARE WE PAYING INFORMANTS NOW?
I DON'T WANT TO KNOW. THAT WAY, I WON'T HAVE TO LIE TO ROGERS.
AT THIS RATE, IN A FEW MONTHS WE'LL BE A TEAM OF VILLAINS.
I DON'T MEAN TO BRAG, BUT I'VE BOUGHT WAY WORSE DUDES THAN THE WRECKER.
GET TORCH AND QUICKSILVER ON THE LINE. HAVE THEM MEET US...

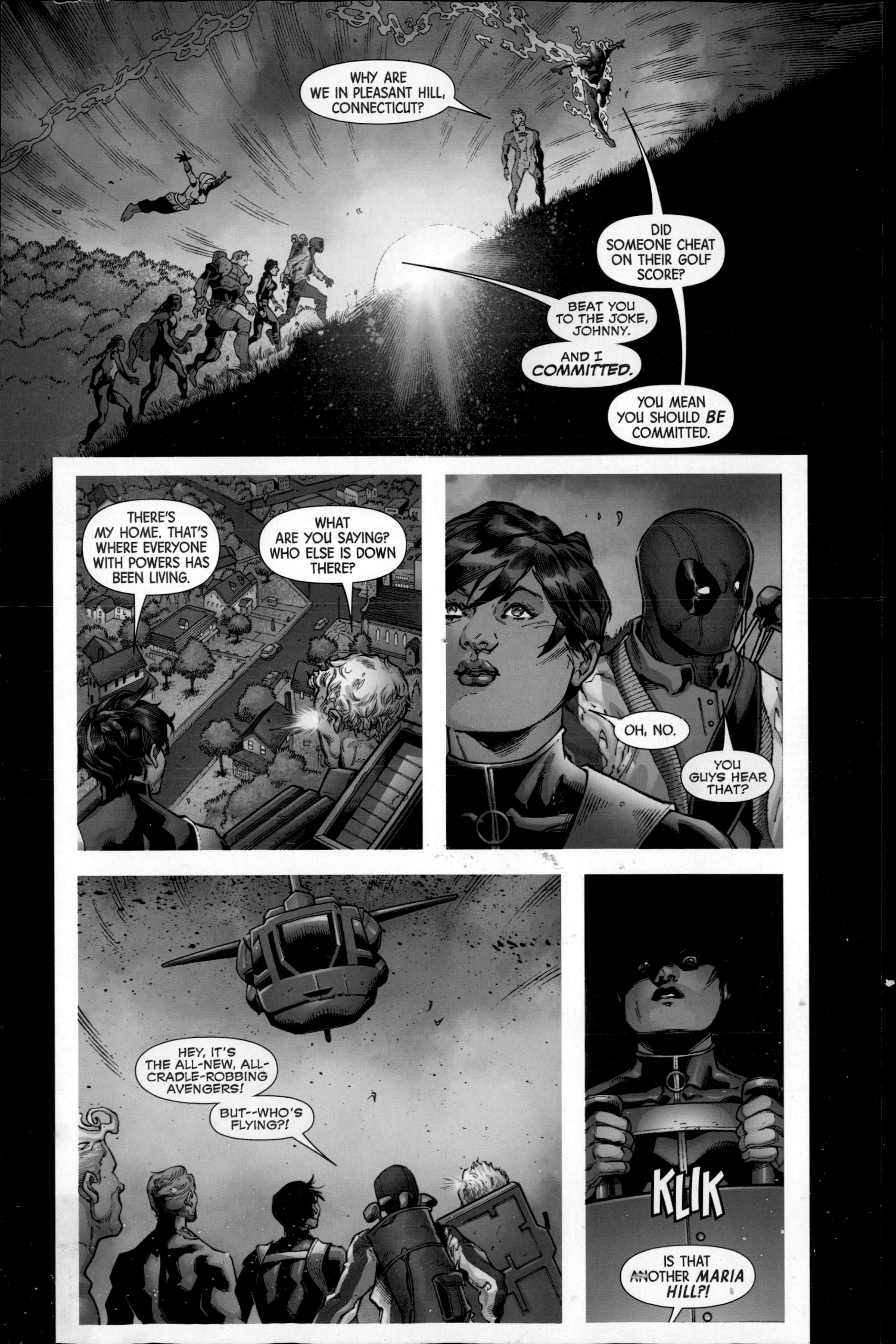
WHY ARE WE IN PLEASANT HILL, CONNECTICUT?
DID SOMEONE CHEAT ON THEIR GOLF SCORE?
BEAT YOU TO THE JOKE, JOHNNY.
AND I COMMITTED.
YOU MEAN YOU SHOULD BE COMMITTED.
THERE'S MY HOME. THAT'S WHERE EVERYONE WITH POWERS HAS BEEN LIVING.
WHAT ARE YOU SAYING? WHO ELSE IS DOWN THERE?
OH, NO.
YOU GUYS HEAR THAT?
HEY, IT'S THE ALL-NEW, ALL-CRADLE-ROBBING AVENGERS!
BUT--WHO'S FLYING?!
KLIK
IS THAT ANOTHER MARIA HILL?!

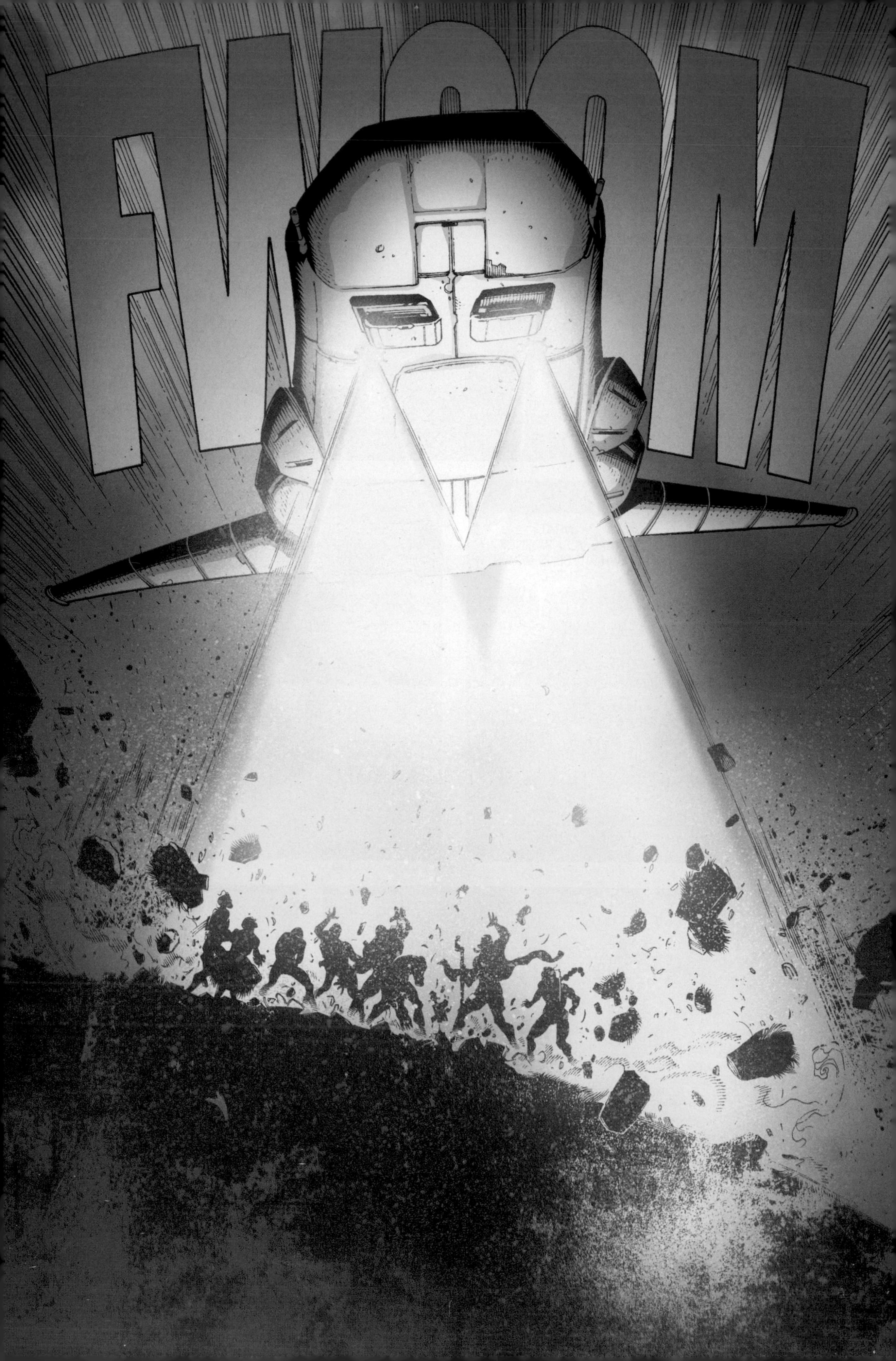
FWOOM

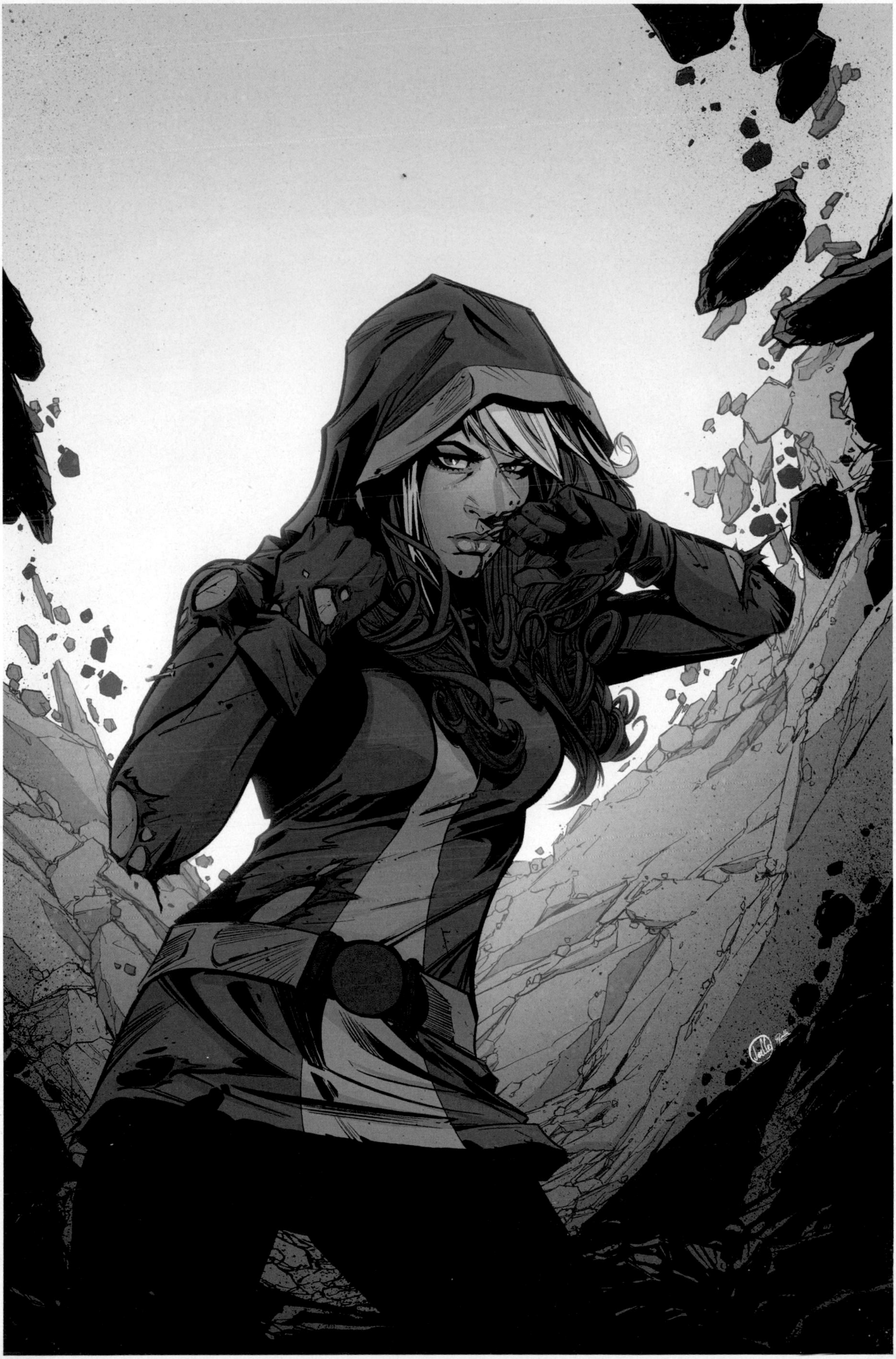

Uncanny Avengers No. 7 Women of Power variant by
JOËLLE JONES & RACHELLE ROSENBERG

All-New, All-Different Avengers No. 7

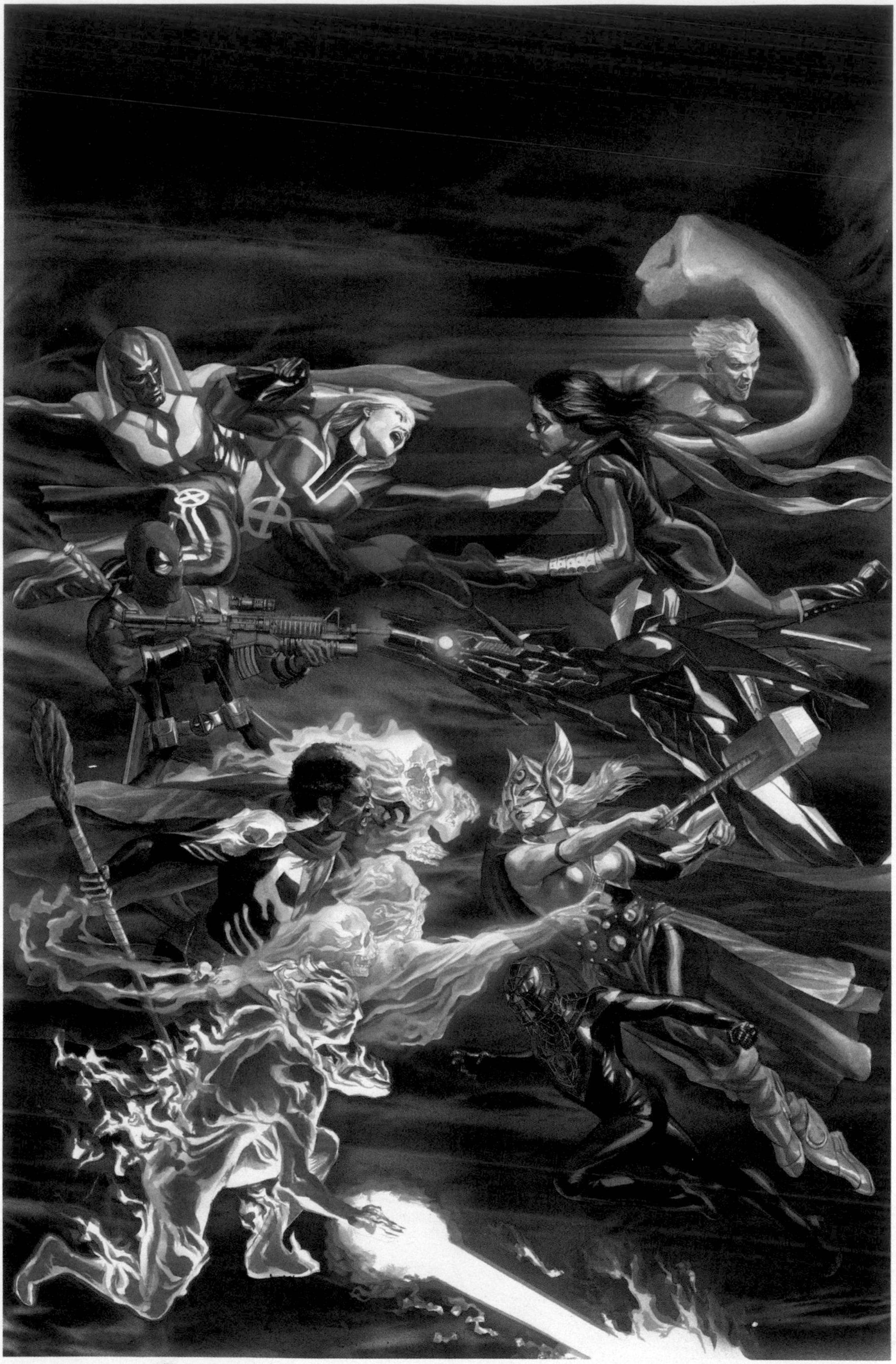

Mission Brief

And there came a day, a day unlike any other, when Earth's mightiest heroes (or the ones that were around that day, anyway) found themselves united against a common threat. On that day, the Avengers were born – to fight the foes no single super hero could withstand!

Now Captain America, Iron Man, Thor, Vision, Spider-Man, Ms. Marvel and Nova are the All-New, All-Different Avengers!

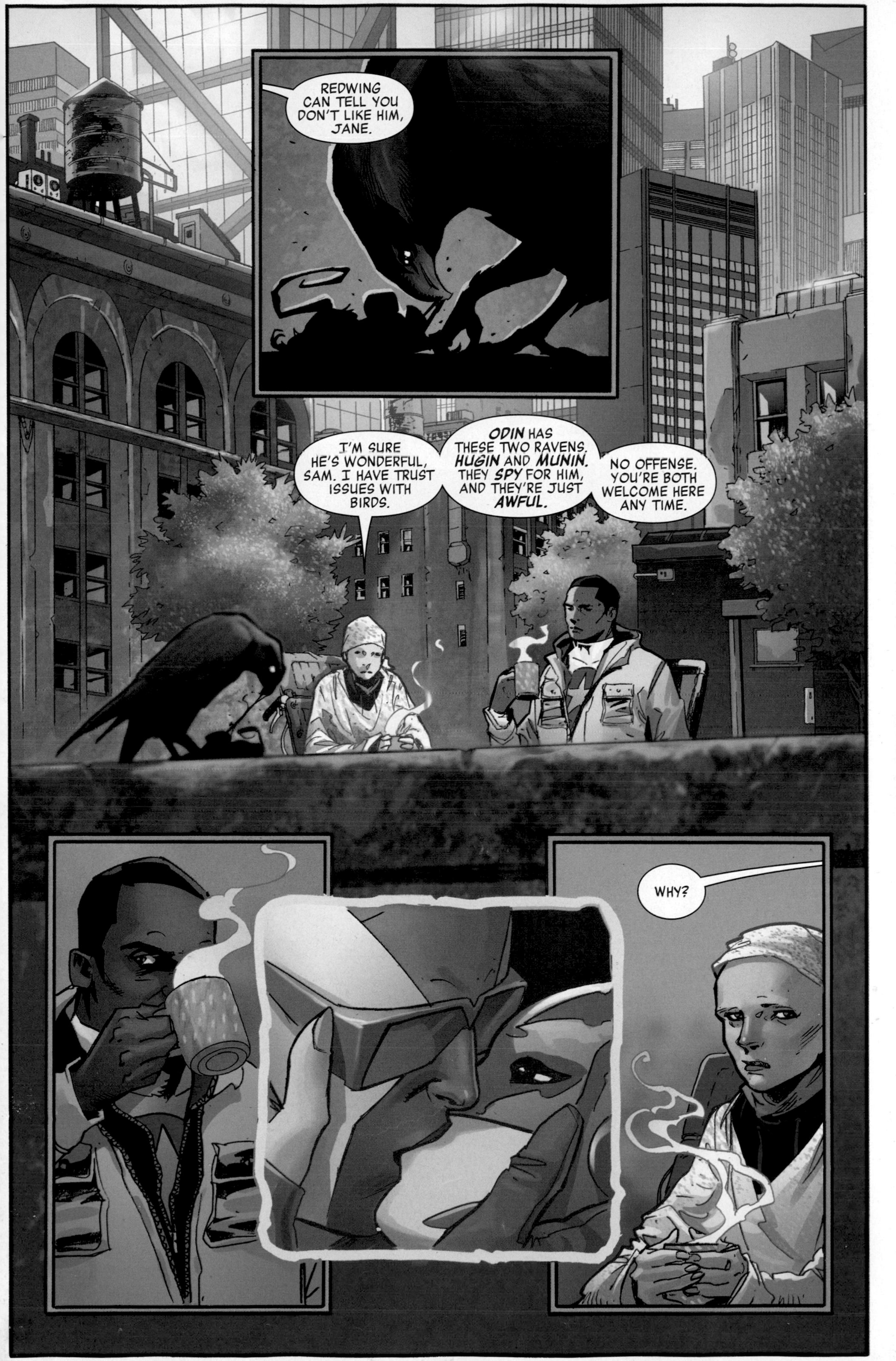
REDWING CAN TELL YOU DON'T LIKE HIM, JANE.
I'M SURE HE'S WONDERFUL, SAM. I HAVE TRUST ISSUES WITH BIRDS.
ODIN HAS THESE TWO RAVENS. HUGIN AND MUNIN. THEY SPY FOR HIM, AND THEY'RE JUST AWFUL.
NO OFFENSE. YOU'RE BOTH WELCOME HERE ANY TIME.
WHY?

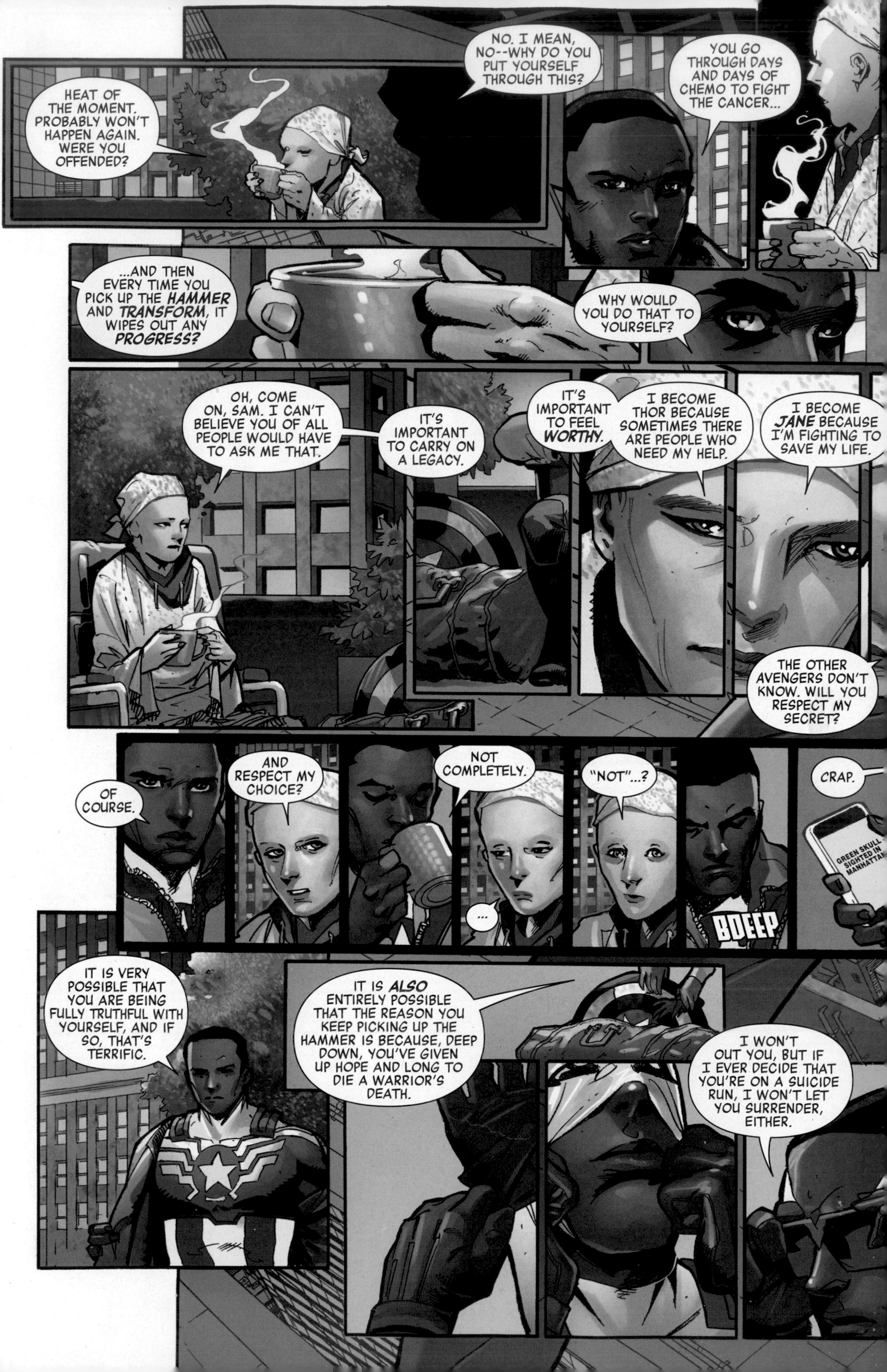
HEAT OF THE MOMENT. PROBABLY WON'T HAPPEN AGAIN. WERE YOU OFFENDED?
NO. I MEAN, NO--WHY DO YOU PUT YOURSELF THROUGH THIS?
YOU GO THROUGH DAYS AND DAYS OF CHEMO TO FIGHT THE CANCER...
...AND THEN EVERY TIME YOU PICK UP THE HAMMER AND TRANSFORM, IT WIPES OUT ANY PROGRESS?
WHY WOULD YOU DO THAT TO YOURSELF?
OH, COME ON, SAM. I CAN'T BELIEVE YOU OF ALL PEOPLE WOULD HAVE TO ASK ME THAT.
IT'S IMPORTANT TO CARRY ON A LEGACY.
IT'S IMPORTANT TO FEEL WORTHY.
I BECOME THOR BECAUSE SOMETIMES THERE ARE PEOPLE WHO NEED MY HELP.
I BECOME JANE BECAUSE I'M FIGHTING TO SAVE MY LIFE.
THE OTHER AVENGERS DON'T KNOW. WILL YOU RESPECT MY SECRET?
OF COURSE.
AND RESPECT MY CHOICE?
NOT COMPLETELY.
...
"NOT"...?
BDEEP
CRAP.
GREEN SKULL SIGHTED IN MANHATTAN
IT IS VERY POSSIBLE THAT YOU ARE BEING FULLY TRUTHFUL WITH YOURSELF, AND IF SO, THAT'S TERRIFIC.
IT IS ALSO ENTIRELY POSSIBLE THAT THE REASON YOU KEEP PICKING UP THE HAMMER IS BECAUSE, DEEP DOWN, YOU'VE GIVEN UP HOPE AND LONG TO DIE A WARRIOR'S DEATH.
I WON'T OUT YOU, BUT IF I EVER DECIDE THAT YOU'RE ON A SUICIDE RUN, I WON'T LET YOU SURRENDER, EITHER.

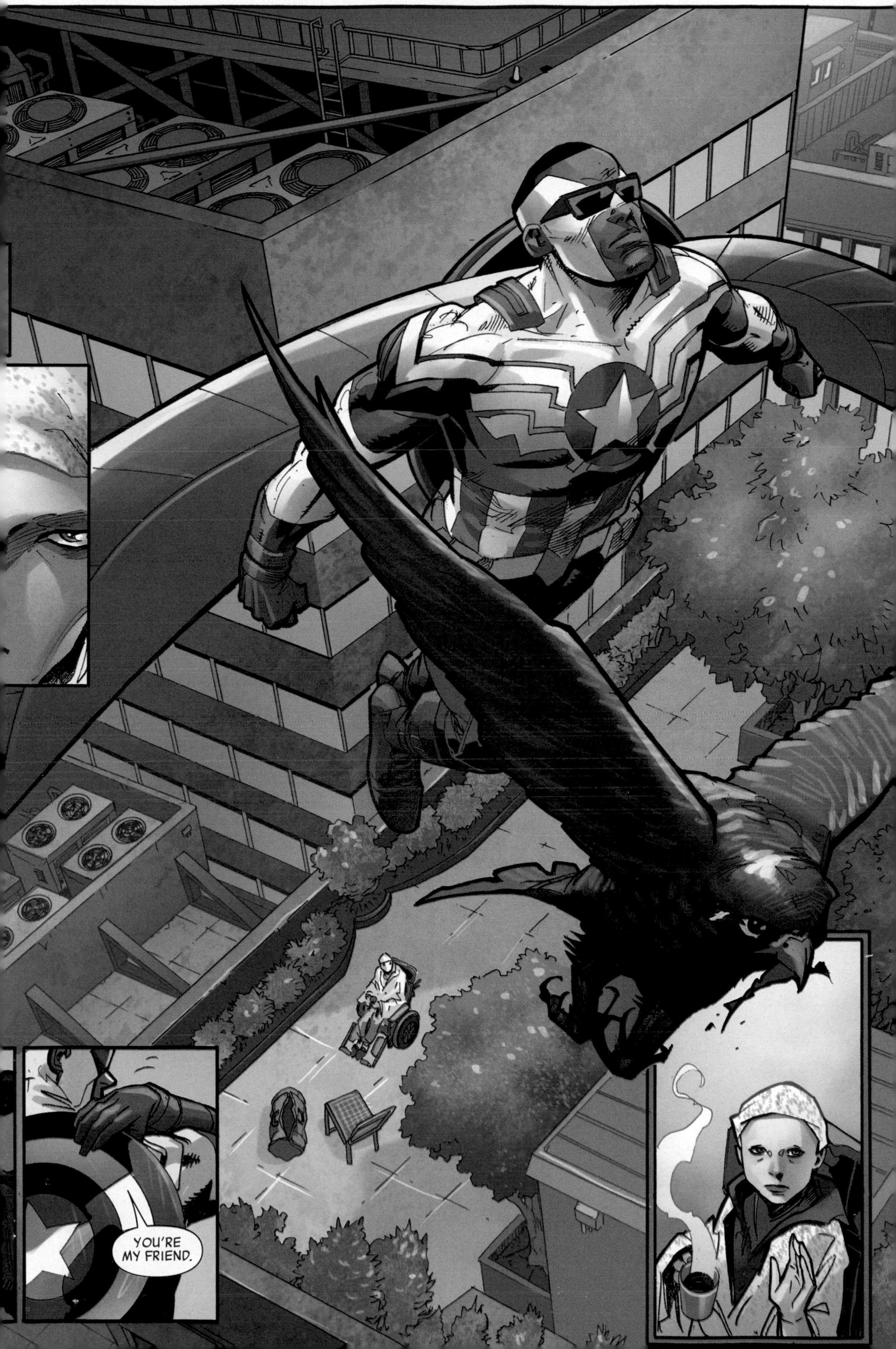
YOU'RE MY FRIEND.

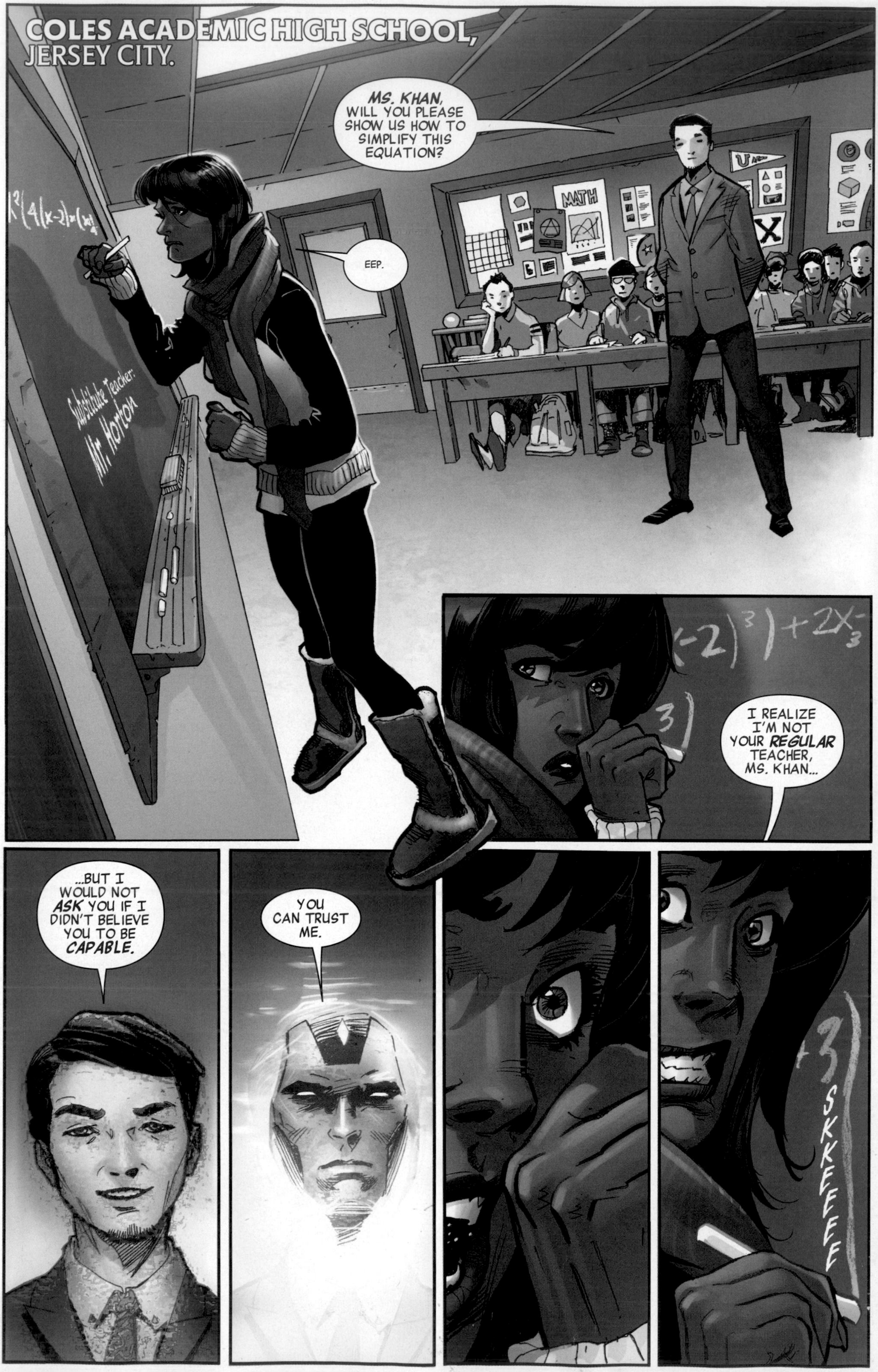
COLES ACADEMIC HIGH SCHOOL, JERSEY CITY.
MS. KHAN, WILL YOU PLEASE SHOW US HOW TO SIMPLIFY THIS EQUATION?
EEP.
Substitute Teacher: Mr. Horton
MATH
I REALIZE I'M NOT YOUR REGULAR TEACHER, MS. KHAN...
...BUT I WOULD NOT ASK YOU IF I DIDN'T BELIEVE YOU TO BE CAPABLE.
YOU CAN TRUST ME.
SKEEEE

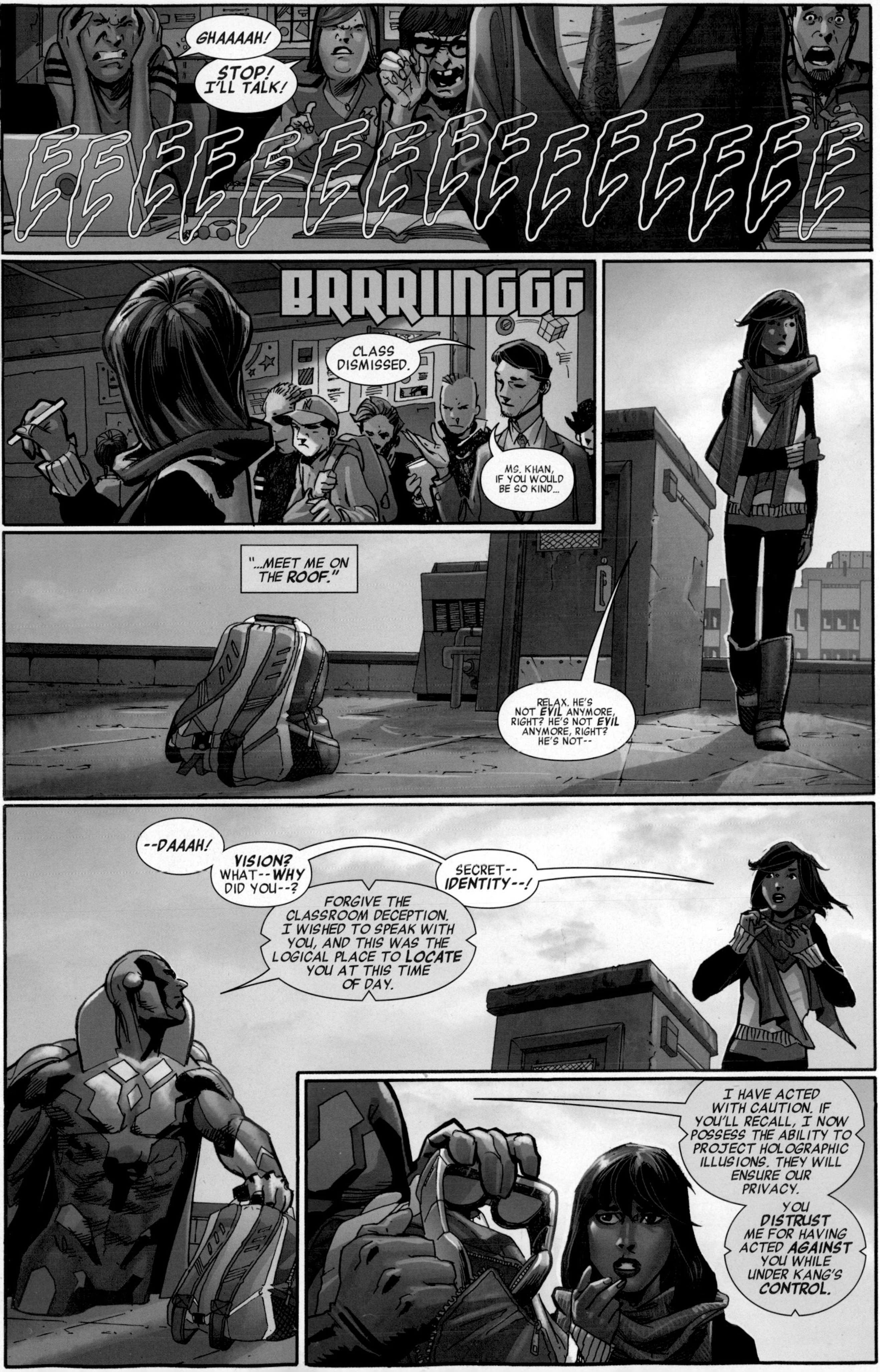
GHAAAAH!
STOP! I'LL TALK!
EEEEEEEEEEEEEEEEE
BRRRIINGGG
CLASS DISMISSED.
MS. KHAN, IF YOU WOULD BE SO KIND...
"...MEET ME ON THE ROOF."
RELAX. HE'S NOT EVIL ANYMORE, RIGHT? HE'S NOT EVIL ANYMORE, RIGHT? HE'S NOT--
--DAAAH!
VISION? WHAT--WHY DID YOU--?
SECRET-- IDENTITY--!
FORGIVE THE CLASSROOM DECEPTION. I WISHED TO SPEAK WITH YOU, AND THIS WAS THE LOGICAL PLACE TO LOCATE YOU AT THIS TIME OF DAY.
I HAVE ACTED WITH CAUTION. IF YOU'LL RECALL, I NOW POSSESS THE ABILITY TO PROJECT HOLOGRAPHIC ILLUSIONS. THEY WILL ENSURE OUR PRIVACY.
YOU DISTRUST ME FOR HAVING ACTED AGAINST YOU WHILE UNDER KANG'S CONTROL.

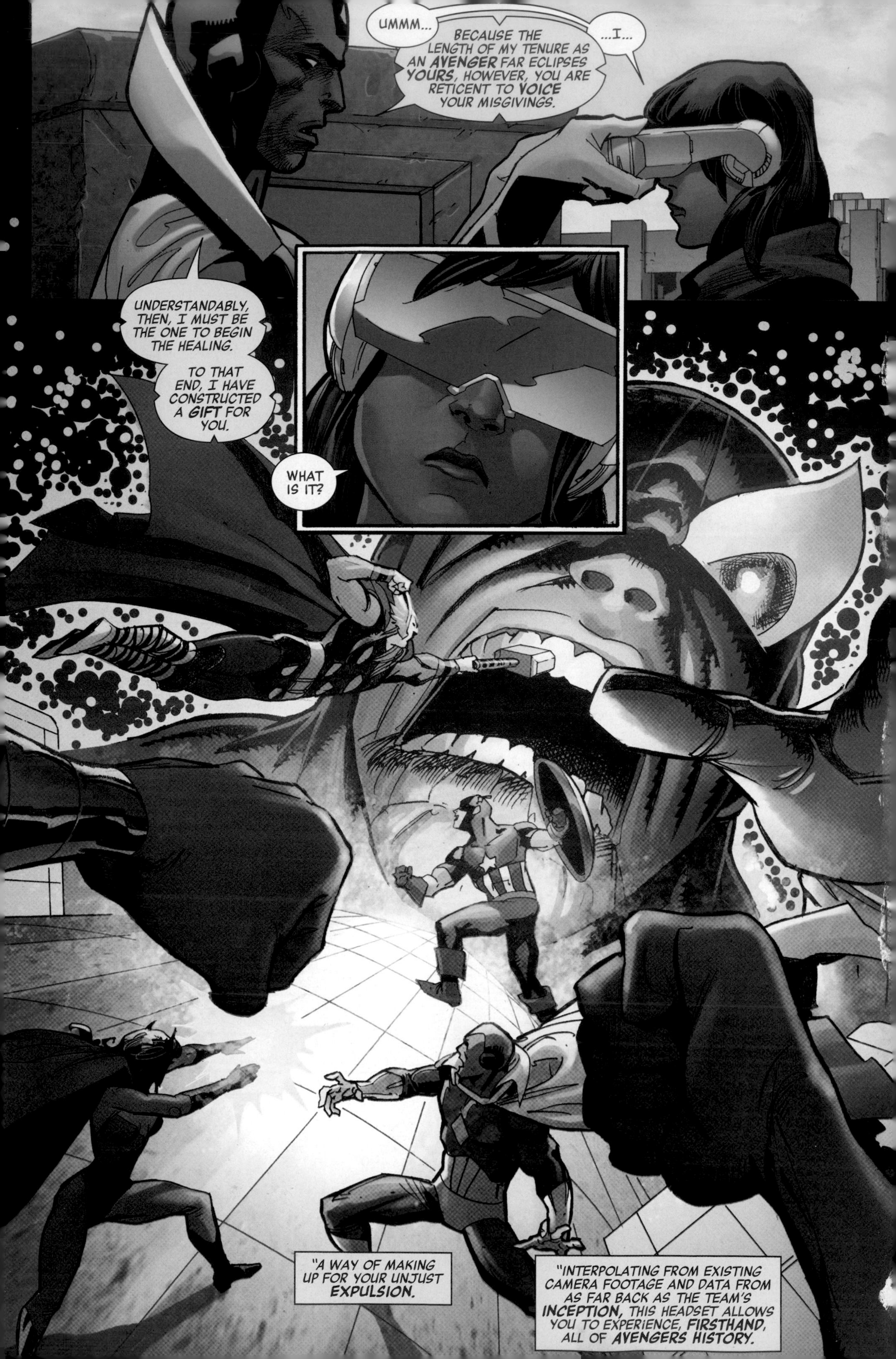

UMMM...
BECAUSE THE LENGTH OF MY TENURE AS AN AVENGER FAR ECLIPSES YOURS, HOWEVER, YOU ARE RETICENT TO VOICE YOUR MISGIVINGS.
...I...
UNDERSTANDABLY, THEN, I MUST BE THE ONE TO BEGIN THE HEALING.
TO THAT END, I HAVE CONSTRUCTED A GIFT FOR YOU.
WHAT IS IT?
"A WAY OF MAKING UP FOR YOUR UNJUST EXPULSION.
"INTERPOLATING FROM EXISTING CAMERA FOOTAGE AND DATA FROM AS FAR BACK AS THE TEAM'S INCEPTION, THIS HEADSET ALLOWS YOU TO EXPERIENCE, FIRSTHAND, ALL OF AVENGERS HISTORY.

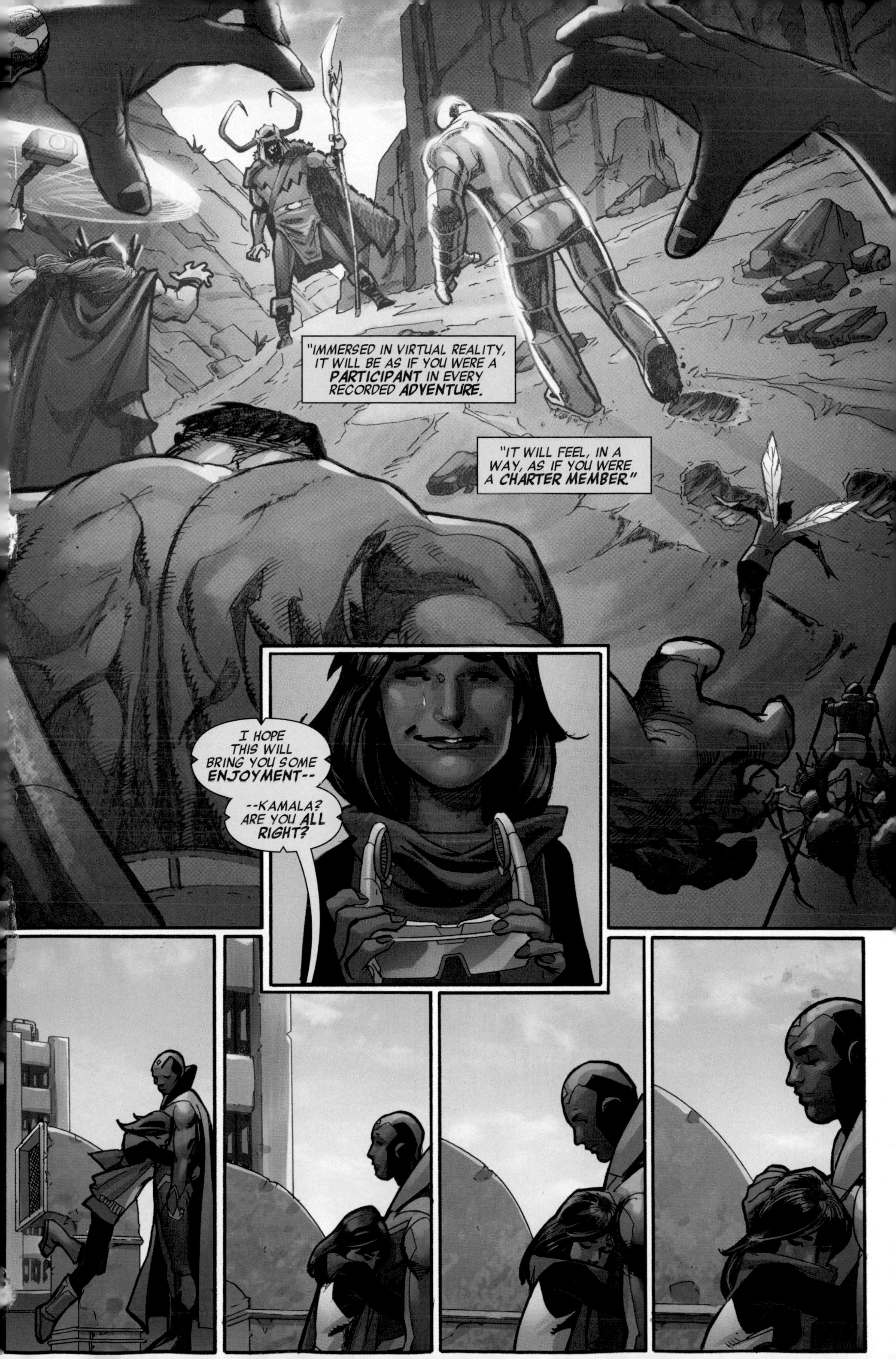
"IMMERSED IN VIRTUAL REALITY, IT WILL BE AS IF YOU WERE A PARTICIPANT IN EVERY RECORDED ADVENTURE.
"IT WILL FEEL, IN A WAY, AS IF YOU WERE A CHARTER MEMBER."
I HOPE THIS WILL BRING YOU SOME ENJOYMENT--
--KAMALA? ARE YOU ALL RIGHT?

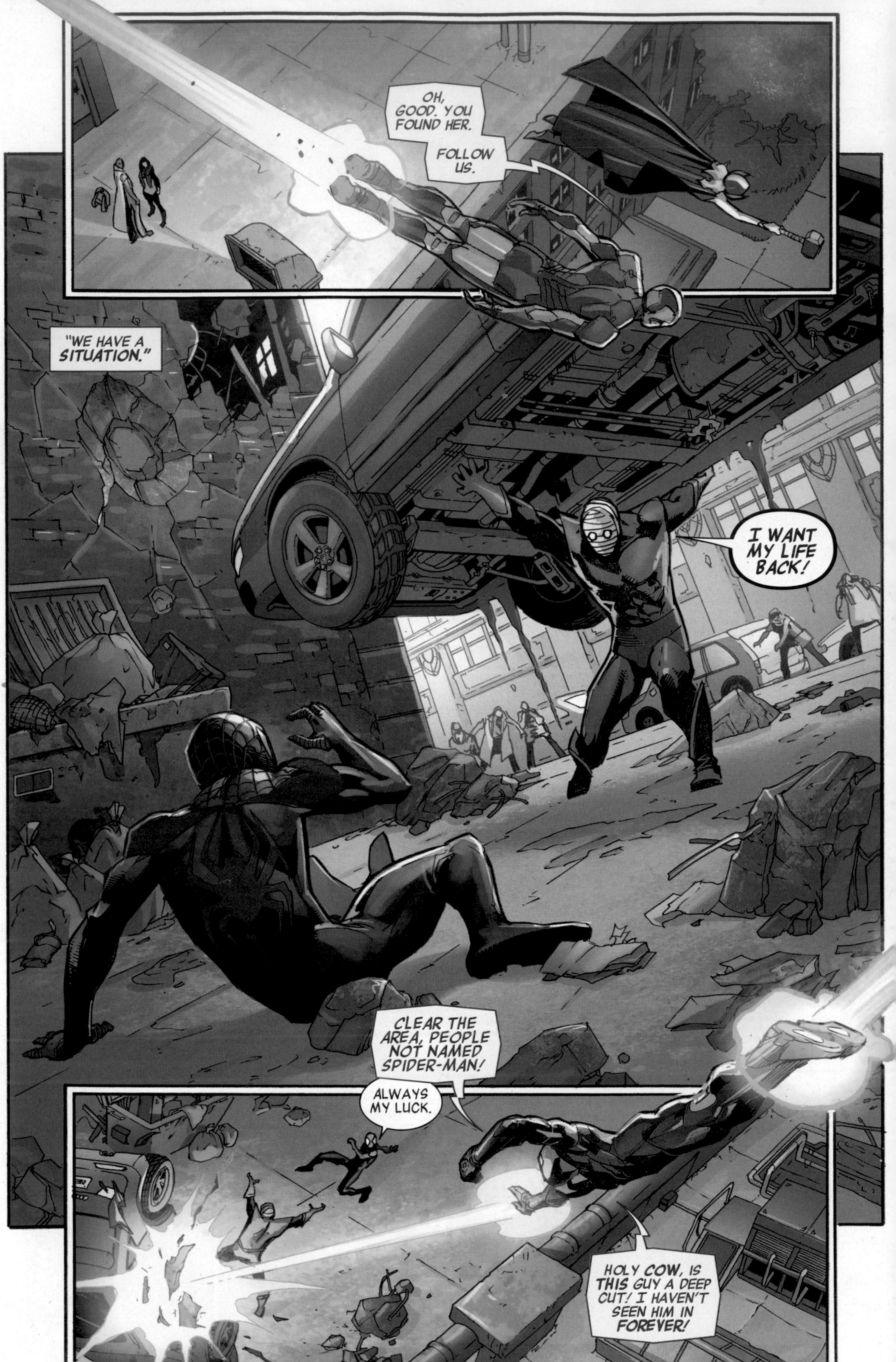
OH, GOOD. YOU FOUND HER.
FOLLOW US.
"WE HAVE A SITUATION."
I WANT MY LIFE BACK!
CLEAR THE AREA, PEOPLE NOT NAMED SPIDER-MAN!
ALWAYS MY LUCK.
HOLY COW, IS THIS GUY A DEEP CUT! I HAVEN'T SEEN HIM IN FOREVER!

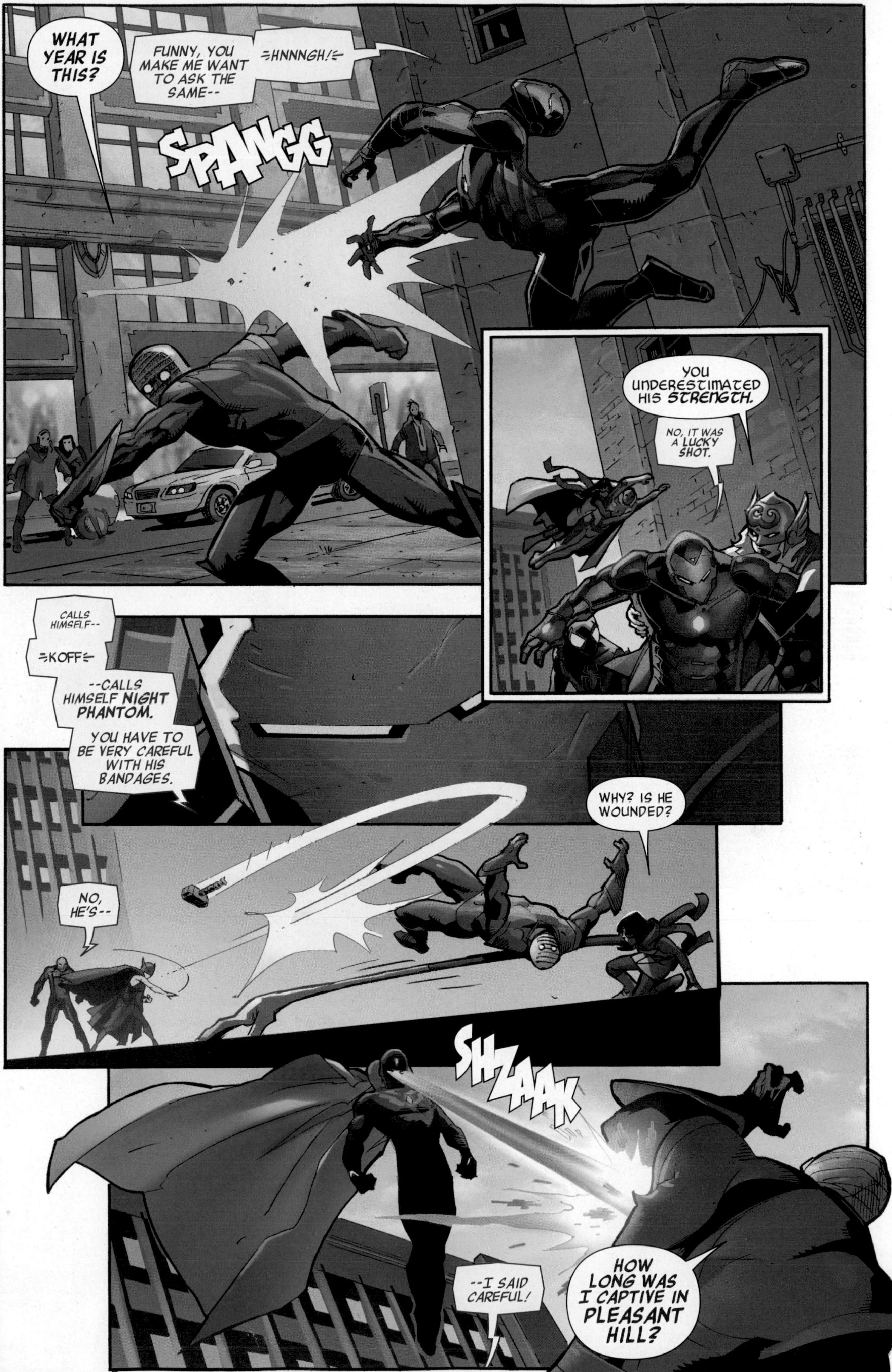

WHAT YEAR IS THIS?
FUNNY, YOU MAKE ME WANT TO ASK THE SAME--
HNNNGH!
SPANGG
YOU UNDERESTIMATED HIS STRENGTH.
NO, IT WAS A LUCKY SHOT.
CALLS HIMSELF--
KOFF
--CALLS HIMSELF NIGHT PHANTOM.
YOU HAVE TO BE VERY CAREFUL WITH HIS BANDAGES.
WHY? IS HE WOUNDED?
NO, HE'S--
SHZAAK
--I SAID CAREFUL!
HOW LONG WAS I CAPTIVE IN PLEASANT HILL?

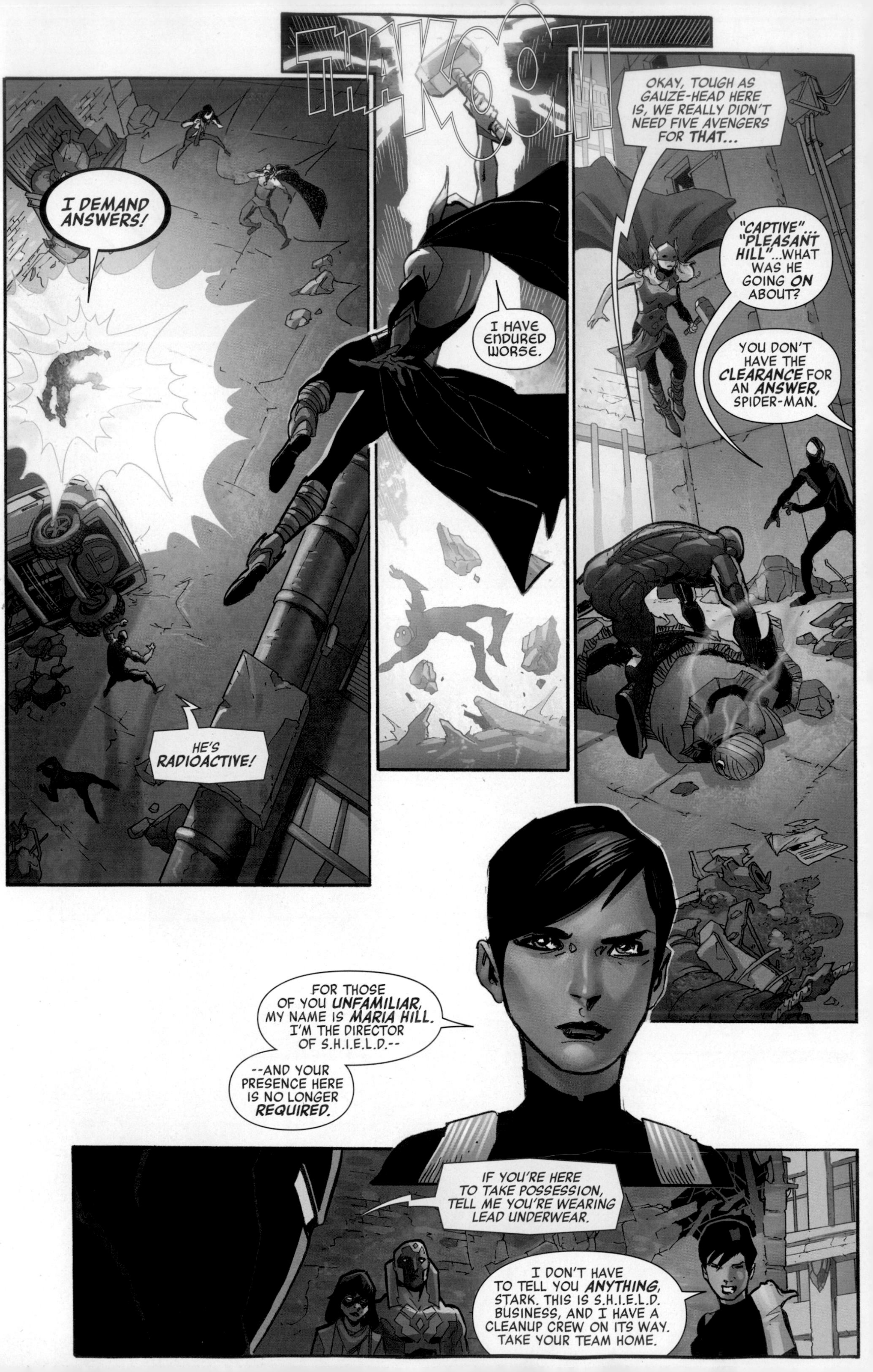
THAKOOM
I DEMAND ANSWERS!
HE'S RADIOACTIVE!
I HAVE ENDURED WORSE.
OKAY, TOUGH AS GAUZE-HEAD HERE IS, WE REALLY DIDN'T NEED FIVE AVENGERS FOR THAT...
"CAPTIVE"... "PLEASANT HILL"...WHAT WAS HE GOING ON ABOUT?
YOU DON'T HAVE THE CLEARANCE FOR AN ANSWER, SPIDER-MAN.
FOR THOSE OF YOU UNFAMILIAR, MY NAME IS MARIA HILL. I'M THE DIRECTOR OF S.H.I.E.L.D.--
--AND YOUR PRESENCE HERE IS NO LONGER REQUIRED.
IF YOU'RE HERE TO TAKE POSSESSION, TELL ME YOU'RE WEARING LEAD UNDERWEAR.
I DON'T HAVE TO TELL YOU ANYTHING, STARK. THIS IS S.H.I.E.L.D. BUSINESS, AND I HAVE A CLEANUP CREW ON ITS WAY. TAKE YOUR TEAM HOME.

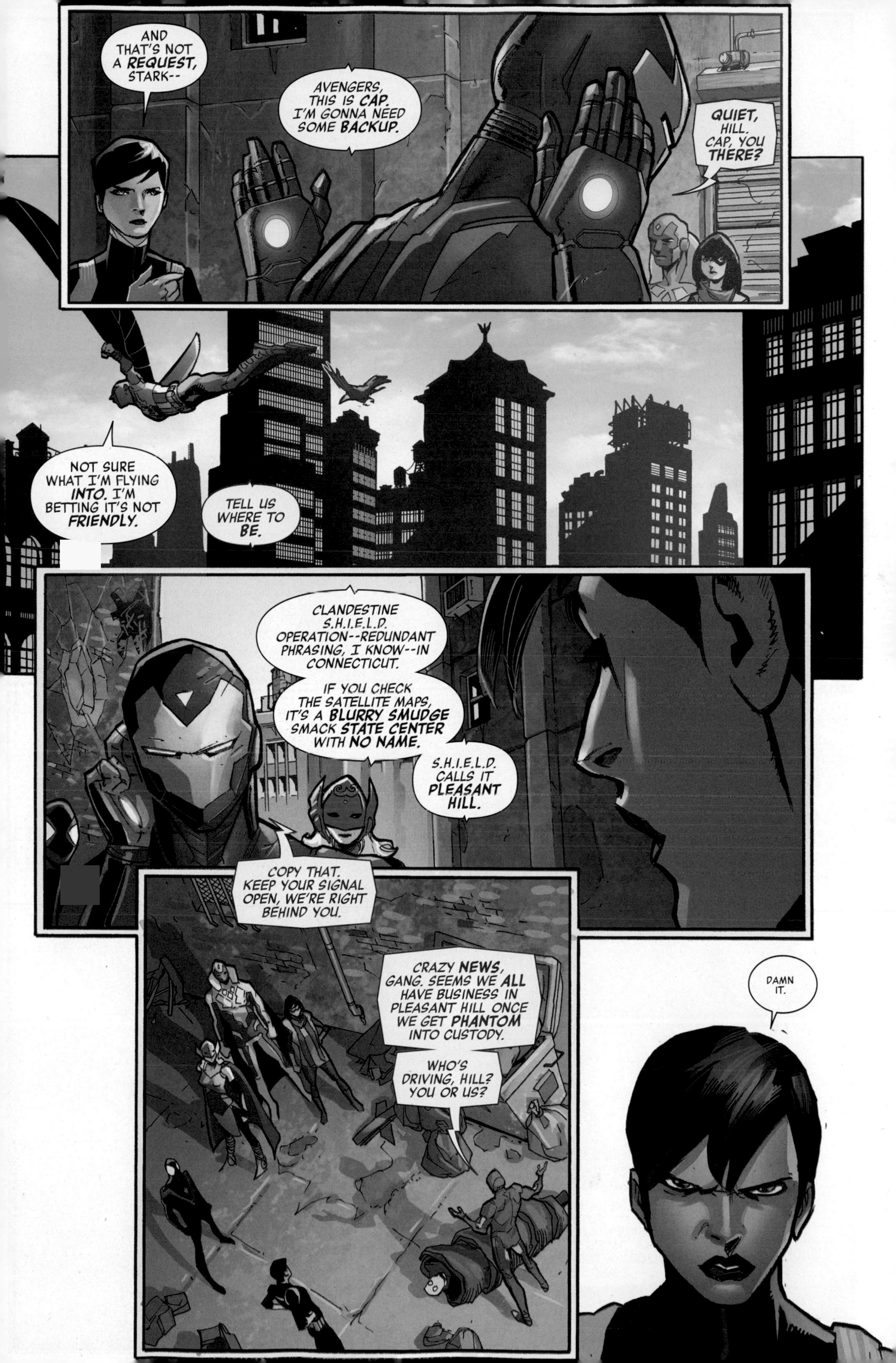
AND THAT'S NOT A **REQUEST**, STARK--
AVENGERS, THIS IS **CAP**. I'M GONNA NEED SOME **BACKUP**.
QUIET, HILL. CAP, YOU **THERE?**
NOT SURE WHAT I'M FLYING **INTO**. I'M BETTING IT'S NOT **FRIENDLY**.
TELL US WHERE TO **BE**.
CLANDESTINE S.H.I.E.L.D. OPERATION--REDUNDANT PHRASING, I KNOW--IN CONNECTICUT.
IF YOU CHECK THE SATELLITE MAPS, IT'S A **BLURRY SMUDGE** SMACK **STATE CENTER** WITH **NO NAME**.
S.H.I.E.L.D. CALLS IT **PLEASANT HILL**.
COPY THAT. KEEP YOUR SIGNAL OPEN, WE'RE RIGHT BEHIND YOU.
CRAZY **NEWS**, GANG. SEEMS WE **ALL** HAVE BUSINESS IN PLEASANT HILL ONCE WE GET **PHANTOM** INTO CUSTODY.
WHO'S DRIVING, HILL? YOU OR US?
DAMN IT.

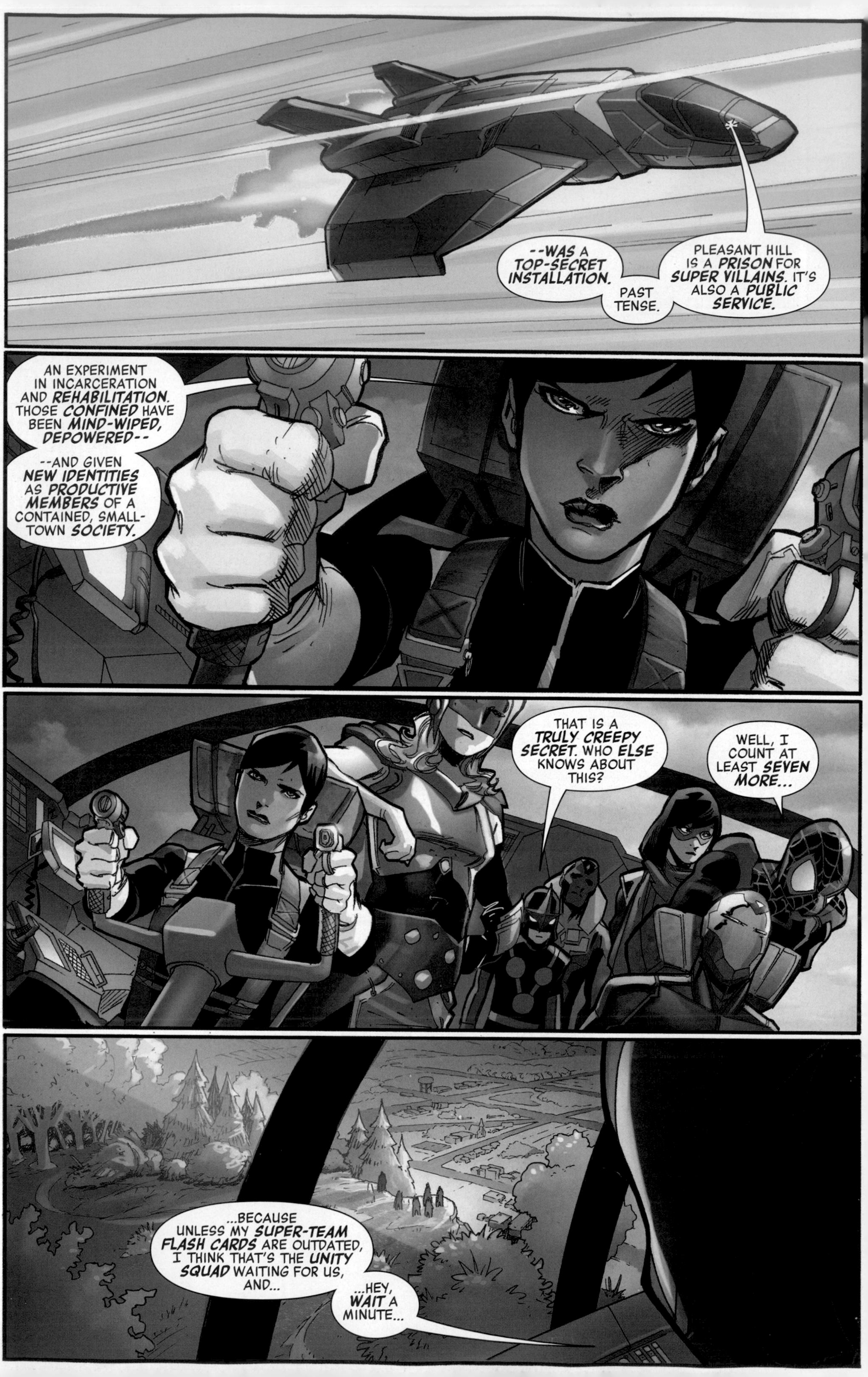
PLEASANT HILL IS A PRISON FOR SUPER VILLAINS. IT'S ALSO A PUBLIC SERVICE.
--WAS A TOP-SECRET INSTALLATION.
PAST TENSE.
AN EXPERIMENT IN INCARCERATION AND REHABILITATION. THOSE CONFINED HAVE BEEN MIND-WIPED, DEPOWERED--
--AND GIVEN NEW IDENTITIES AS PRODUCTIVE MEMBERS OF A CONTAINED, SMALL-TOWN SOCIETY.
THAT IS A TRULY CREEPY SECRET. WHO ELSE KNOWS ABOUT THIS?
WELL, I COUNT AT LEAST SEVEN MORE...
...BECAUSE UNLESS MY SUPER-TEAM FLASH CARDS ARE OUTDATED, I THINK THAT'S THE UNITY SQUAD WAITING FOR US, AND...
...HEY, WAIT A MINUTE...

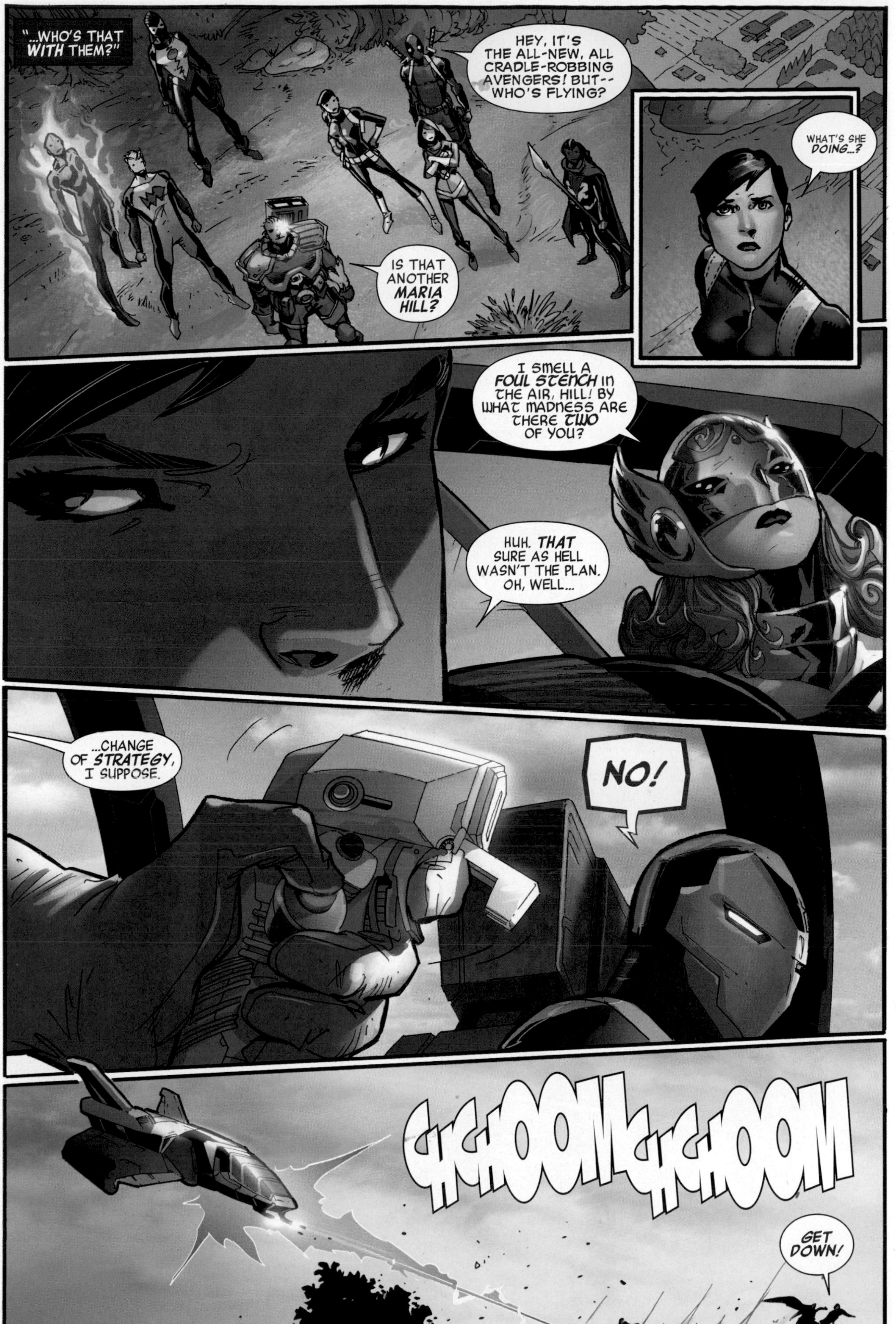
"...WHO'S THAT WITH THEM?"
HEY, IT'S THE ALL-NEW, ALL CRADLE-ROBBING AVENGERS! BUT--WHO'S FLYING?
IS THAT ANOTHER MARIA HILL?
WHAT'S SHE DOING...?
I SMELL A FOUL STENCH IN THE AIR, HILL! BY WHAT MADNESS ARE THERE TWO OF YOU?
HUH. THAT SURE AS HELL WASN'T THE PLAN. OH, WELL...
...CHANGE OF STRATEGY, I SUPPOSE.
NO!
CHCHOOM CHCHOOM
GET DOWN!

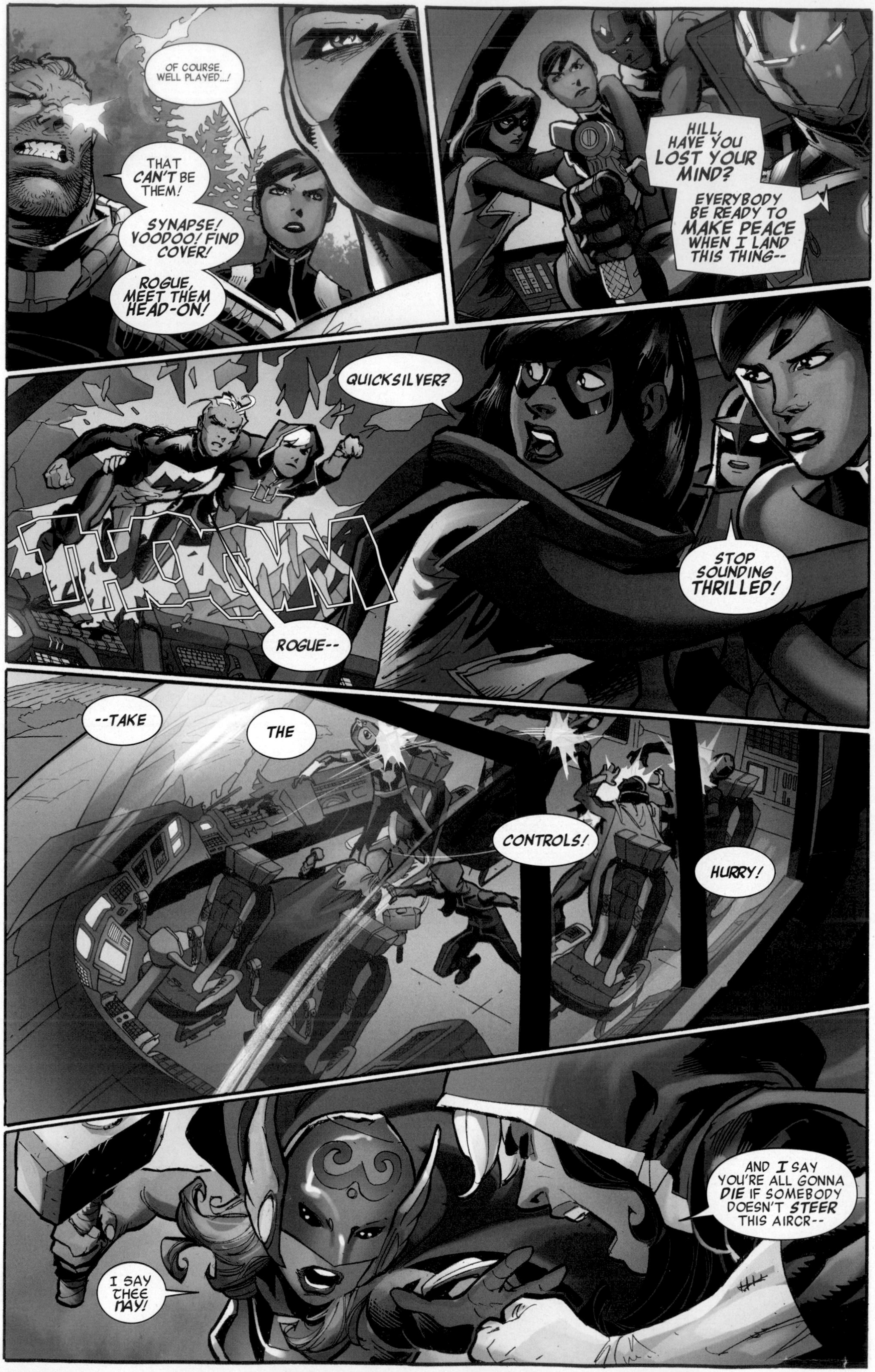
OF COURSE. WELL PLAYED...!
THAT CAN'T BE THEM!
SYNAPSE! VOODOO! FIND COVER!
ROGUE, MEET THEM HEAD-ON!
HILL, HAVE YOU LOST YOUR MIND?
EVERYBODY BE READY TO MAKE PEACE WHEN I LAND THIS THING--
QUICKSILVER?
STOP SOUNDING THRILLED!
ROGUE--
--TAKE
THE
CONTROLS!
HURRY!
AND I SAY YOU'RE ALL GONNA DIE IF SOMEBODY DOESN'T STEER THIS AIRCR--
I SAY THEE NAY!

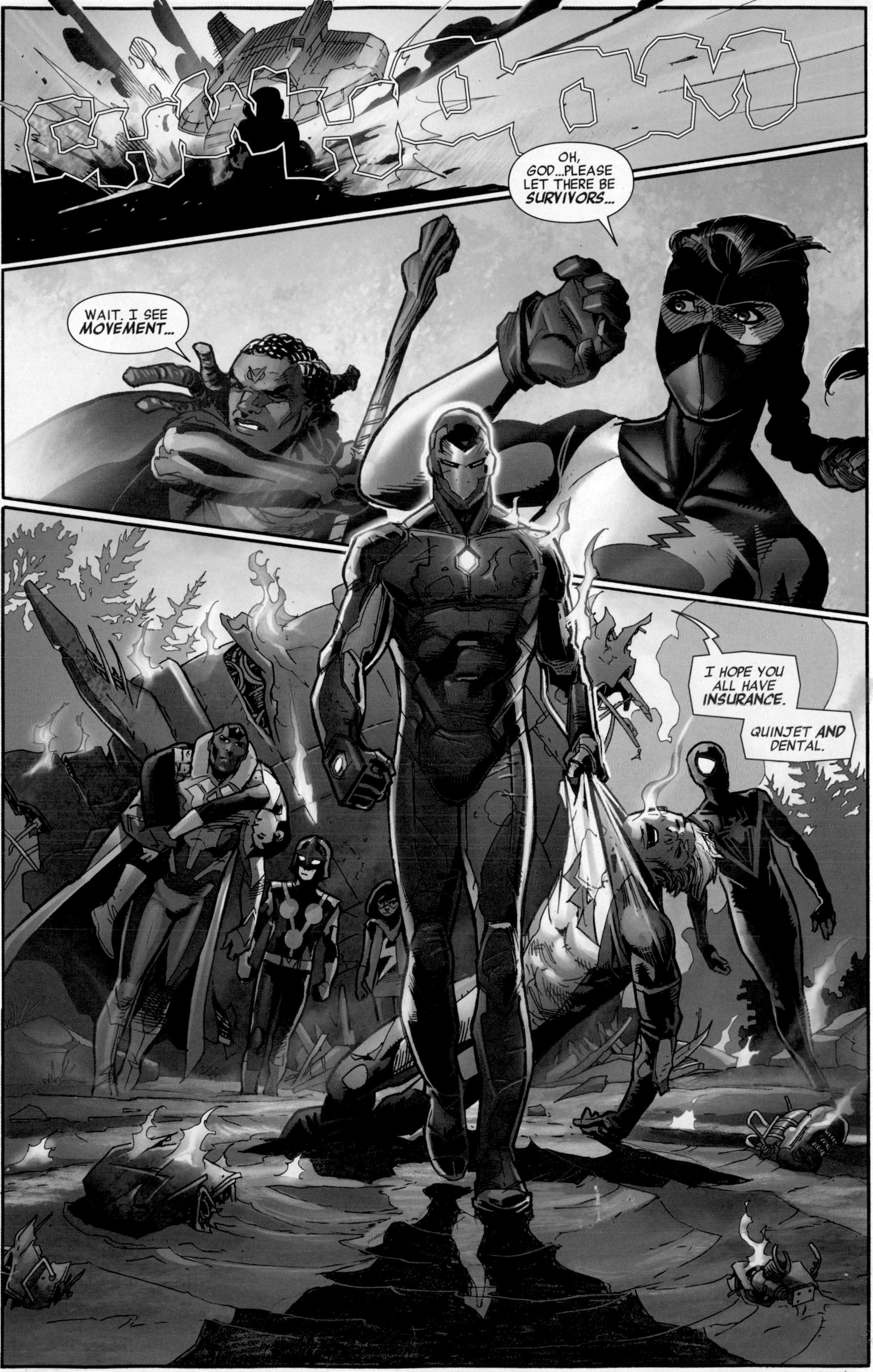
OH, GOD...PLEASE LET THERE BE SURVIVORS...
WAIT. I SEE MOVEMENT...
I HOPE YOU ALL HAVE INSURANCE.
QUINJET AND DENTAL.

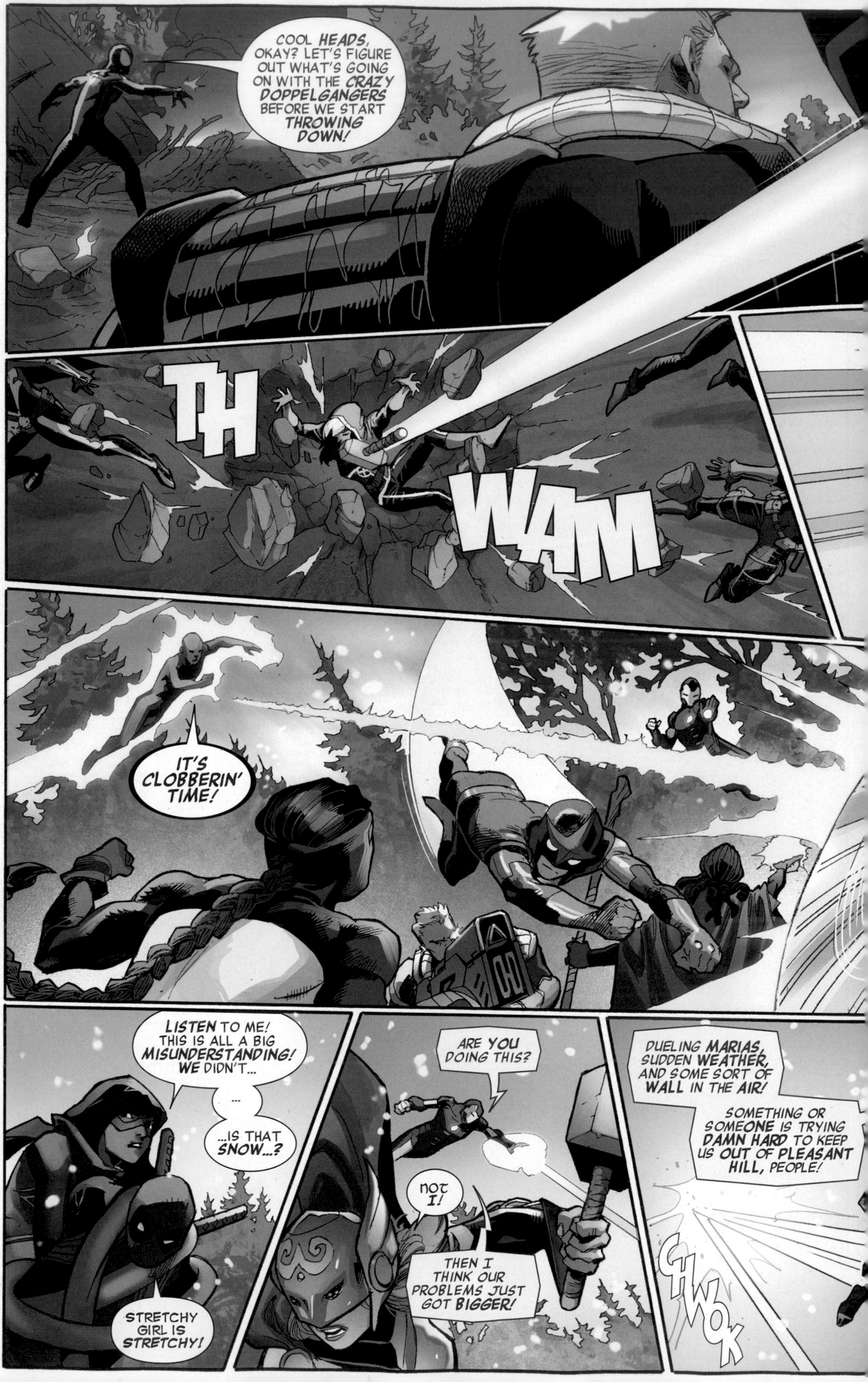
COOL HEADS, OKAY? LET'S FIGURE OUT WHAT'S GOING ON WITH THE CRAZY DOPPELGANGERS BEFORE WE START THROWING DOWN!
THWAM
IT'S CLOBBERIN' TIME!
LISTEN TO ME! THIS IS ALL A BIG MISUNDERSTANDING! WE DIDN'T...
...
...IS THAT SNOW...?
STRETCHY GIRL IS STRETCHY!
ARE YOU DOING THIS?
NOT I!
THEN I THINK OUR PROBLEMS JUST GOT BIGGER!
DUELING MARIAS, SUDDEN WEATHER, AND SOME SORT OF WALL IN THE AIR!
SOMETHING OR SOMEONE IS TRYING DAMN HARD TO KEEP US OUT OF PLEASANT HILL, PEOPLE!
CHWOK

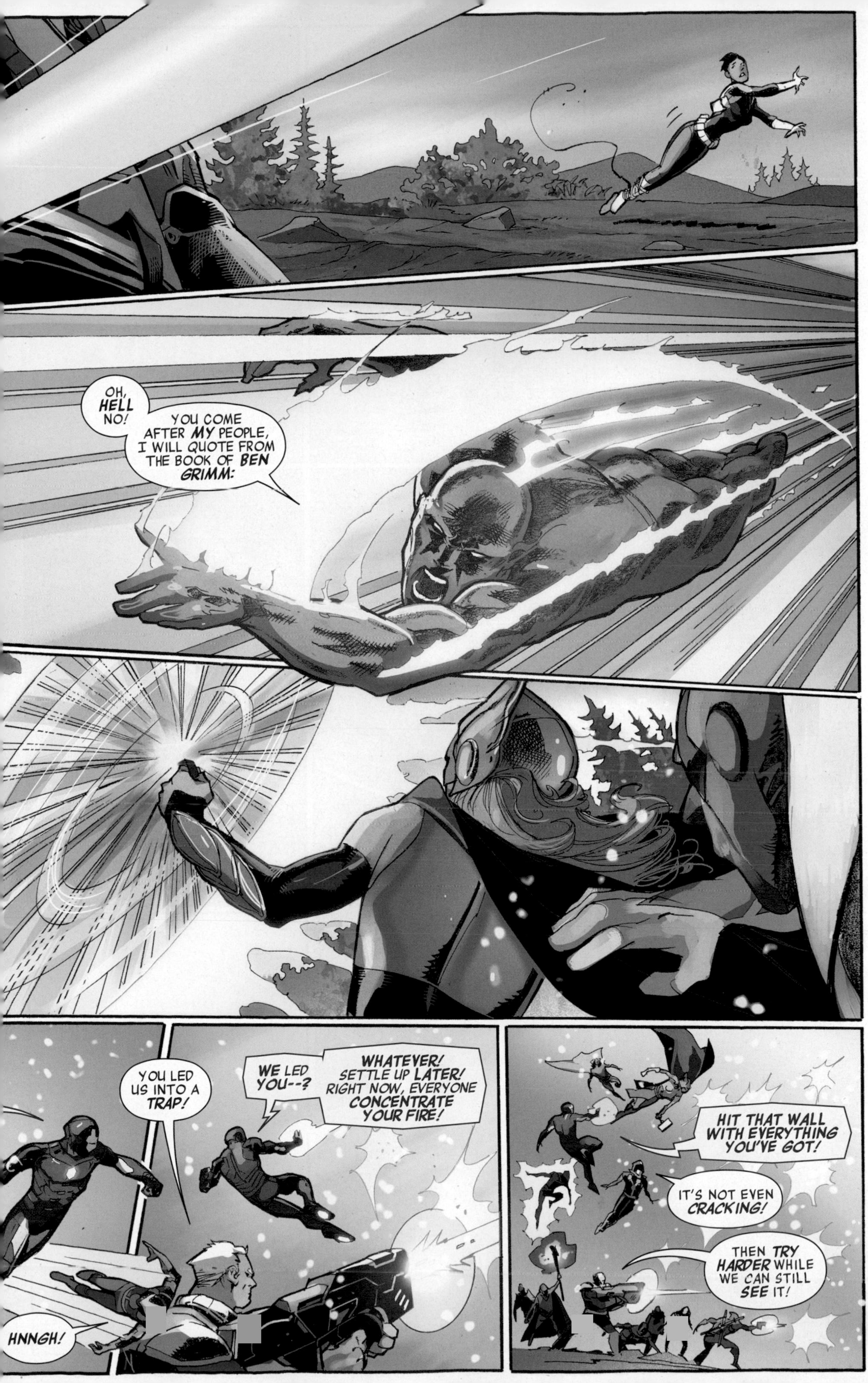
OH, HELL NO!
YOU COME AFTER MY PEOPLE, I WILL QUOTE FROM THE BOOK OF BEN GRIMM:
YOU LED US INTO A TRAP!
WE LED YOU--?
WHATEVER! SETTLE UP LATER! RIGHT NOW, EVERYONE CONCENTRATE YOUR FIRE!
HNNGH!
HIT THAT WALL WITH EVERYTHING YOU'VE GOT!
IT'S NOT EVEN CRACKING!
THEN TRY HARDER WHILE WE CAN STILL SEE IT!

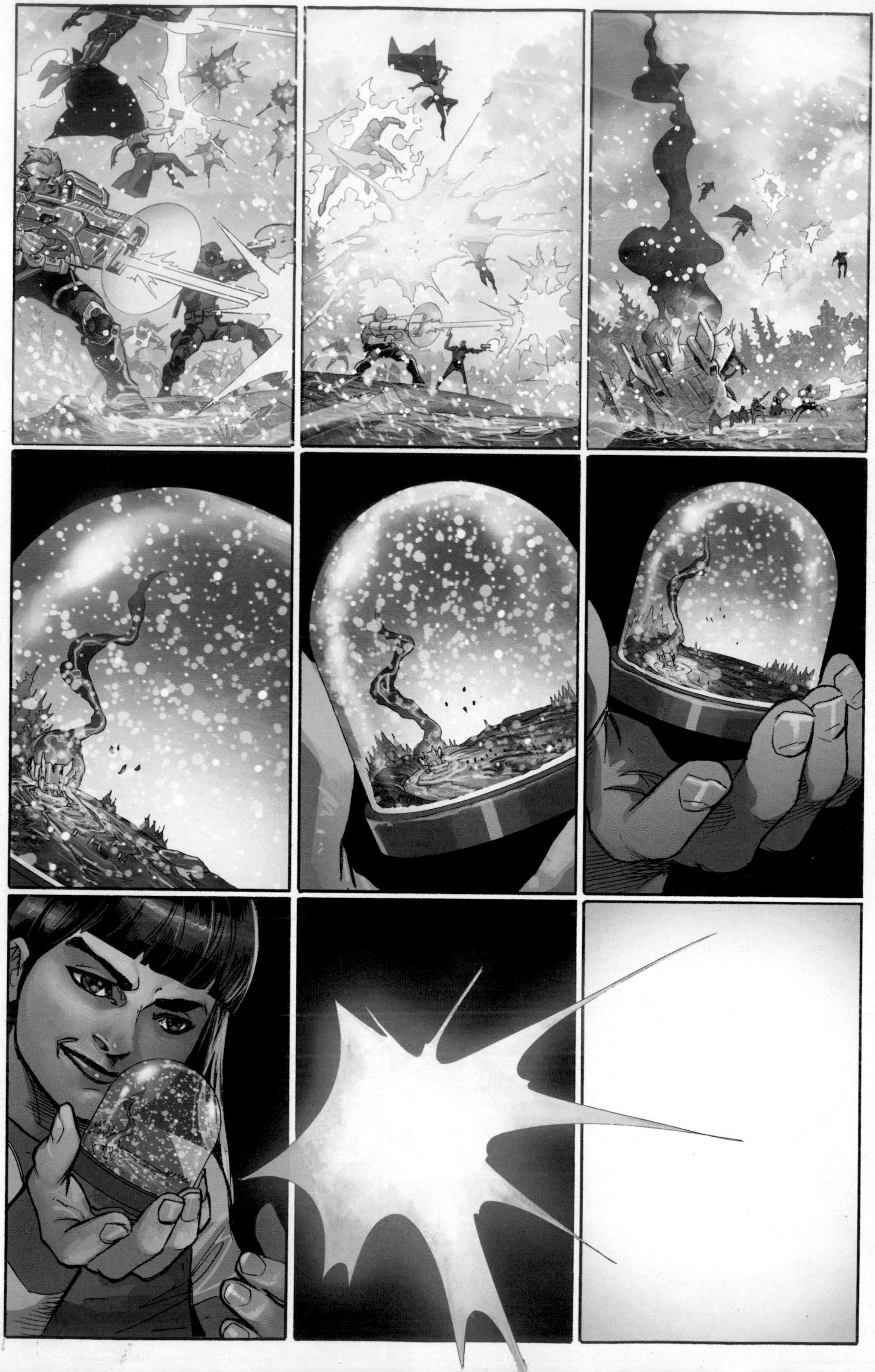

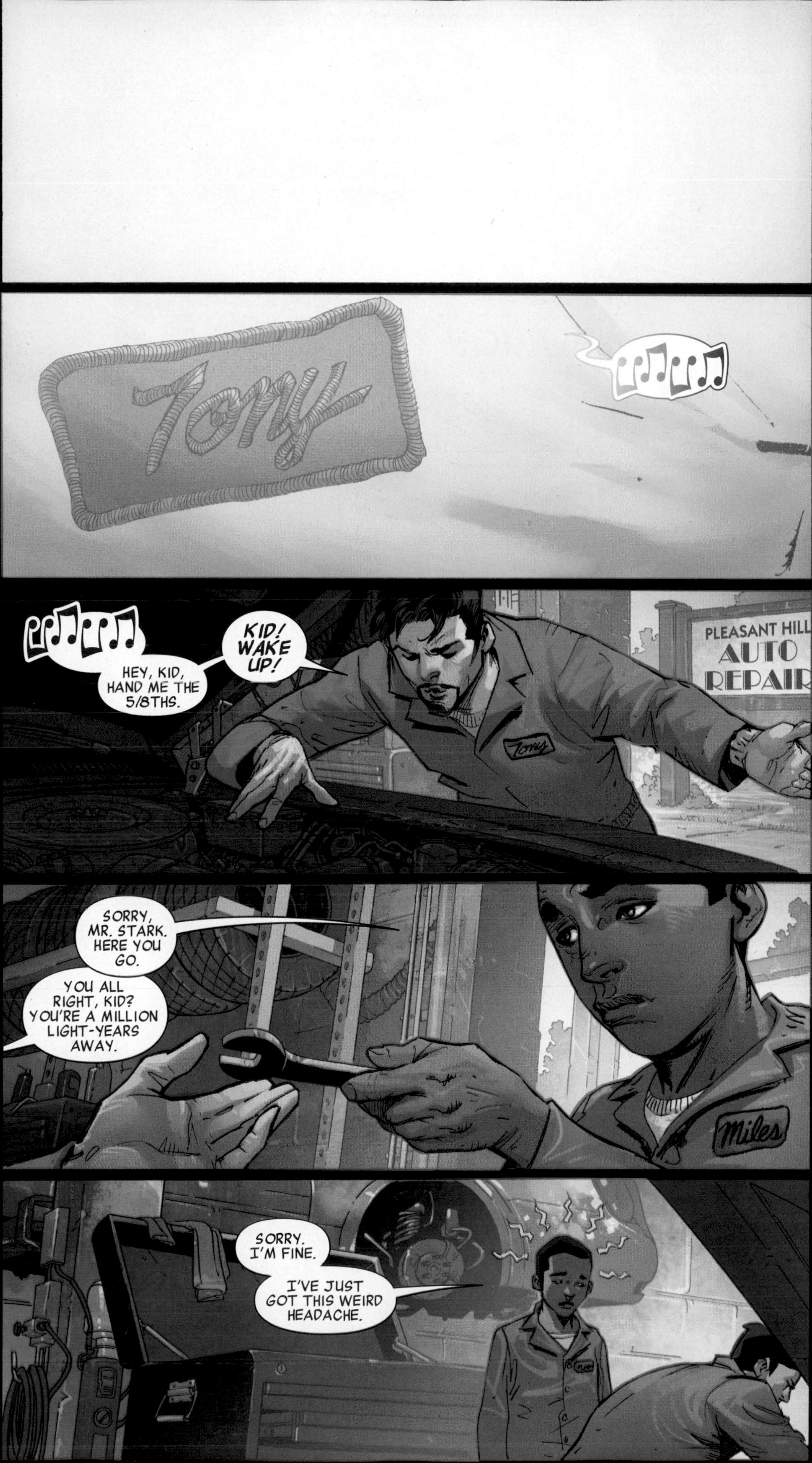
Tony
HEY, KID, HAND ME THE 5/8THS.
KID! WAKE UP!
PLEASANT HILL AUTO REPAIR
Tony
SORRY, MR. STARK. HERE YOU GO.
YOU ALL RIGHT, KID? YOU'RE A MILLION LIGHT-YEARS AWAY.
Miles
SORRY. I'M FINE.
I'VE JUST GOT THIS WEIRD HEADACHE.

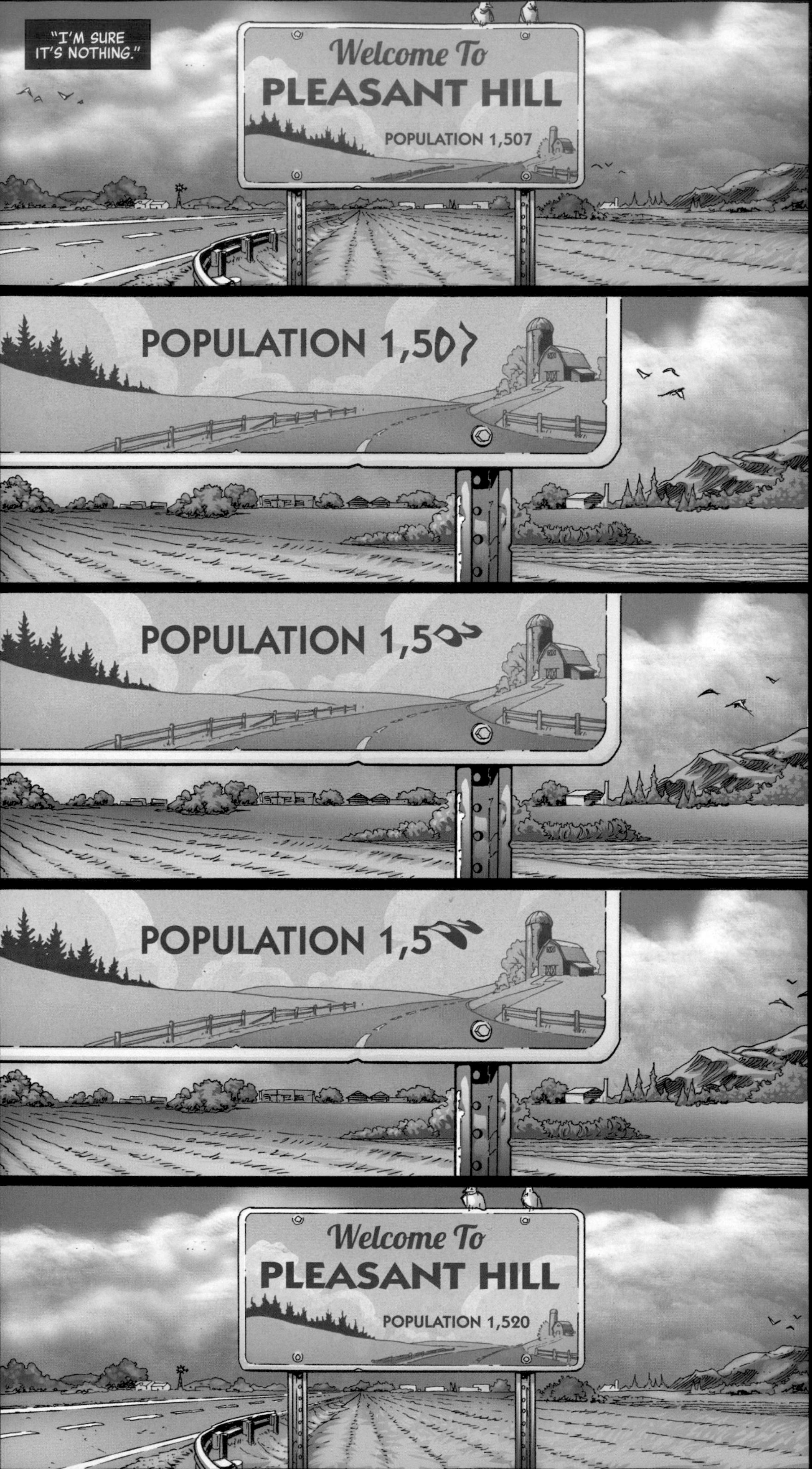
"I'M SURE IT'S NOTHING."
Welcome To
PLEASANT HILL
POPULATION 1,507
POPULATION 1,50
POPULATION 1,5
POPULATION 1,5
Welcome To
PLEASANT HILL
POPULATION 1,520

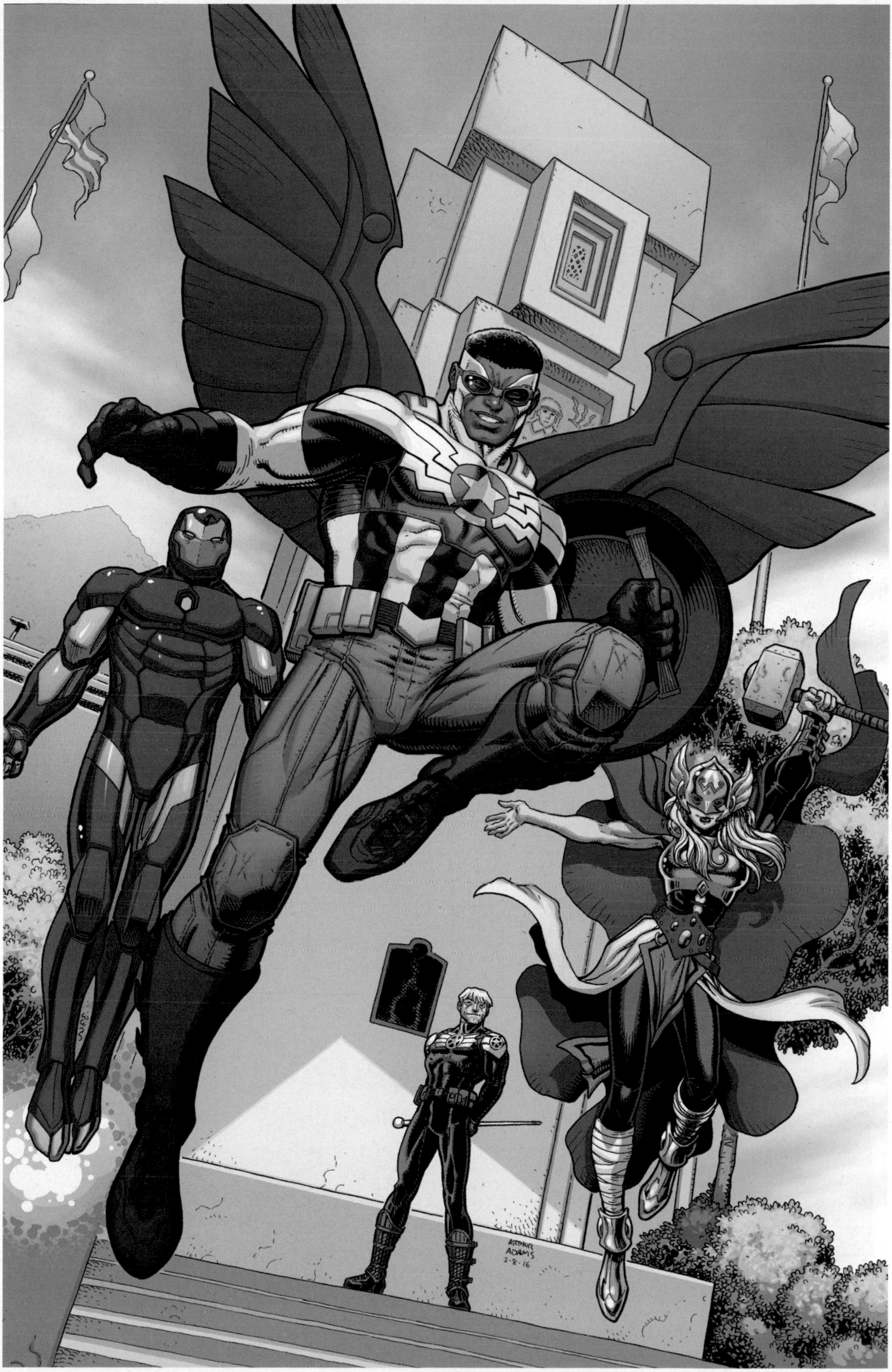
ARTHUR ADAMS 2-8-16

Avengers Standoff: Assault on Pleasant Hill Alpha variant by
ART ADAMS & DAVE McCAIG

New Avengers No. 8

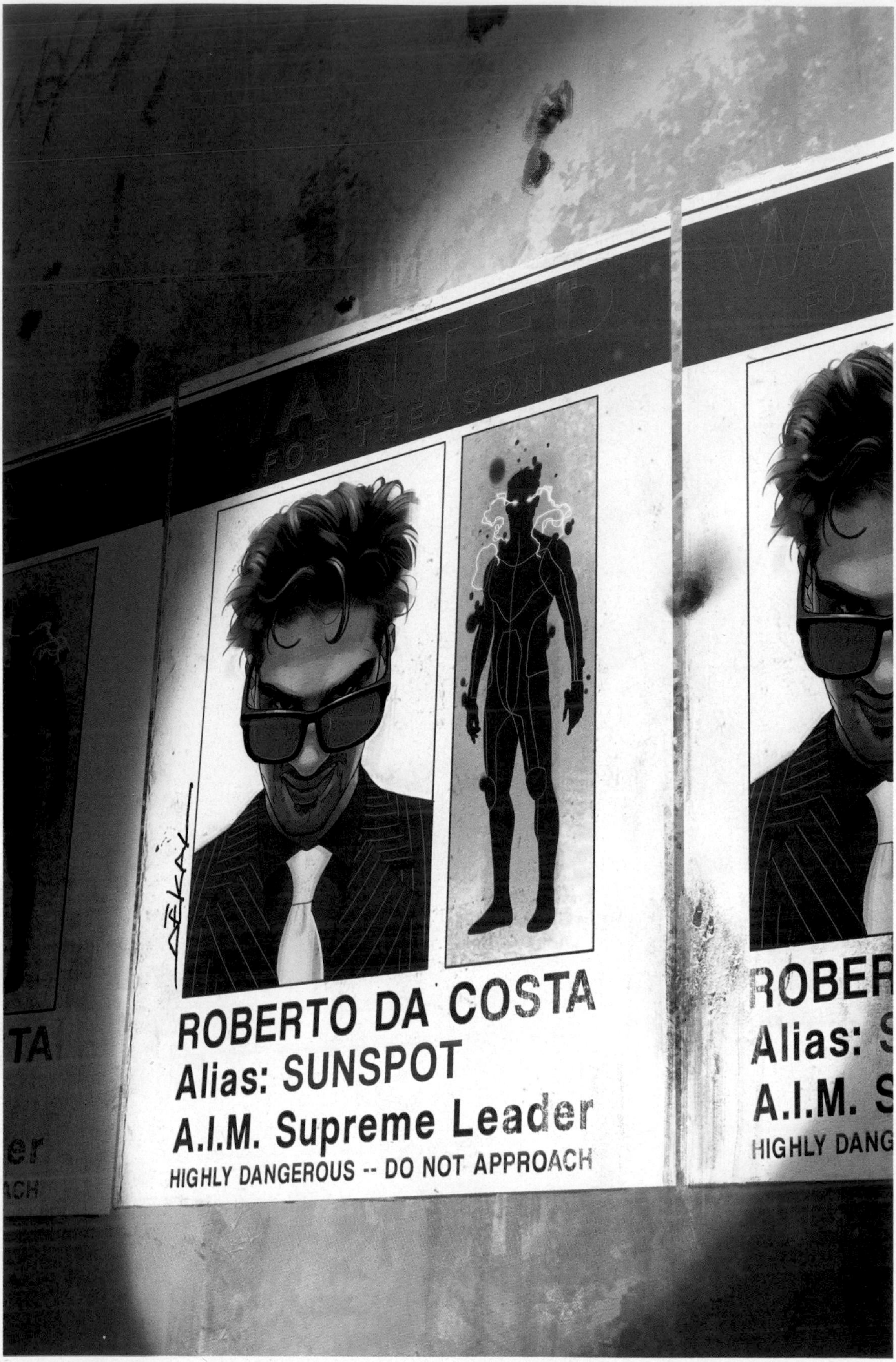
FOR TREASON
ROBERTO DA COSTA
Alias: SUNSPOT
A.I.M. Supreme Leader
HIGHLY DANGEROUS -- DO NOT APPROACH

Mission Brief

Roberto Da Costa bought the villainous organization A.I.M. and transformed it into Avengers Idea Mechanics, a group dedicated to international rescue operations. Backed by an army of the best scientists and engineers in the world, the New Avengers work to protect Earth from anything that threatens the peace – despite the disapproval of the U.S. government.

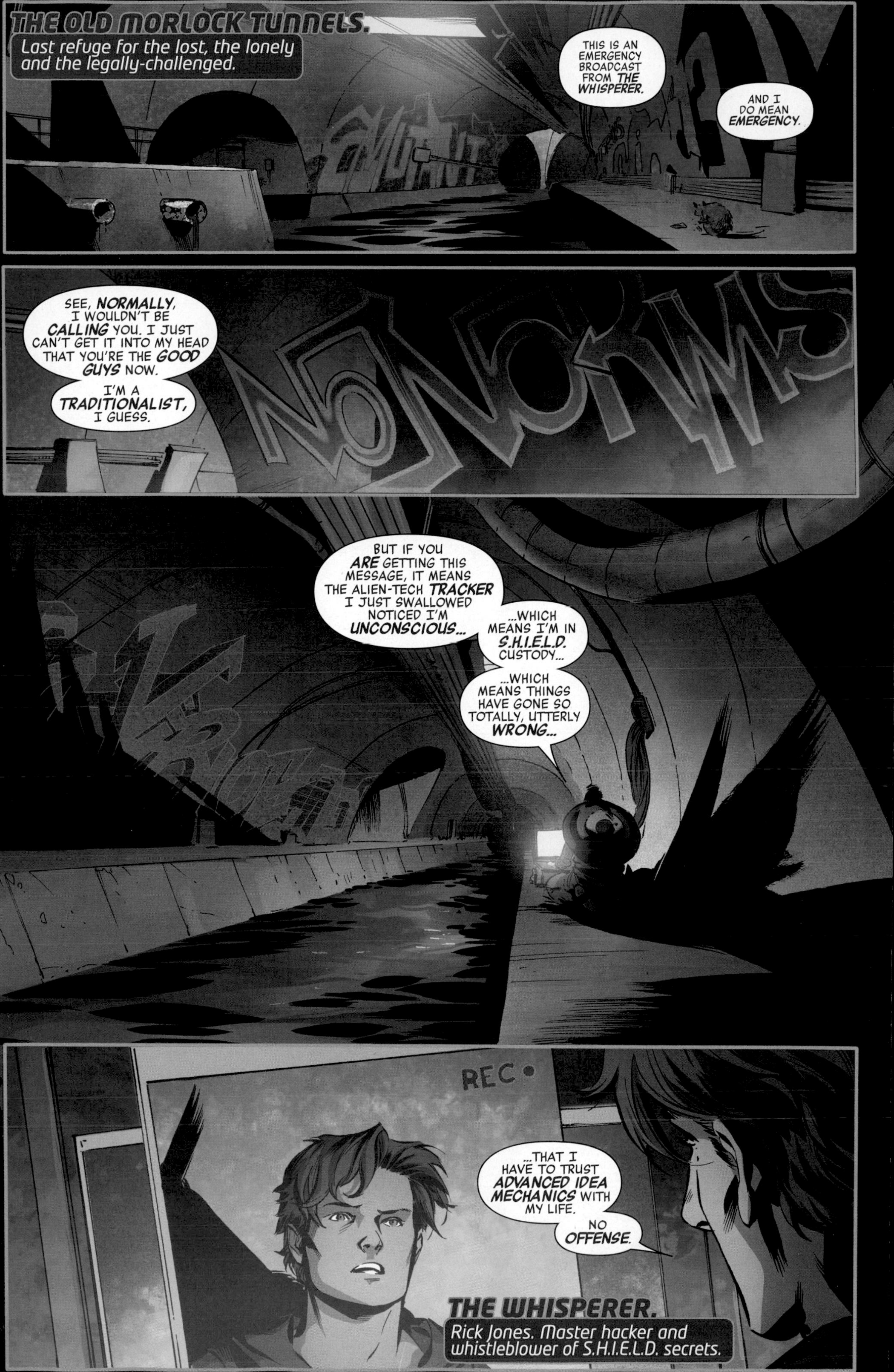
THE OLD MORLOCK TUNNELS.
Last refuge for the lost, the lonely and the legally-challenged.
THIS IS AN EMERGENCY BROADCAST FROM THE WHISPERER.
AND I DO MEAN EMERGENCY.
SEE, NORMALLY, I WOULDN'T BE CALLING YOU. I JUST CAN'T GET IT INTO MY HEAD THAT YOU'RE THE GOOD GUYS NOW.
I'M A TRADITIONALIST, I GUESS.
BUT IF YOU ARE GETTING THIS MESSAGE, IT MEANS THE ALIEN-TECH TRACKER I JUST SWALLOWED NOTICED I'M UNCONSCIOUS...
...WHICH MEANS I'M IN S.H.I.E.L.D. CUSTODY...
...WHICH MEANS THINGS HAVE GONE SO TOTALLY, UTTERLY WRONG...
REC
...THAT I HAVE TO TRUST ADVANCED IDEA MECHANICS WITH MY LIFE.
NO OFFENSE.
THE WHISPERER.
Rick Jones. Master hacker and whistleblower of S.H.I.E.L.D. secrets.

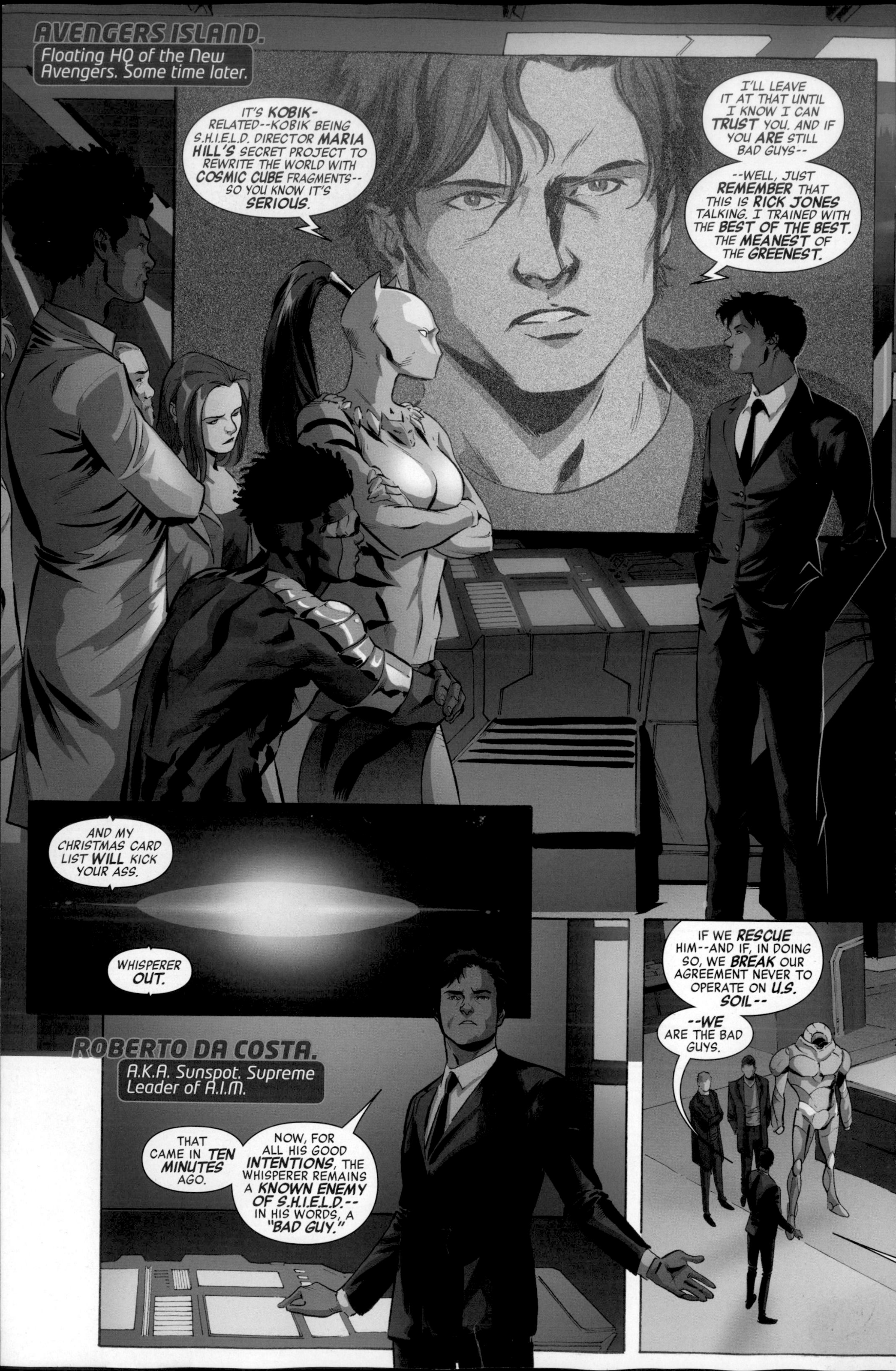
AVENGERS ISLAND.
Floating HQ of the New Avengers. Some time later.
IT'S KOBIK-RELATED--KOBIK BEING S.H.I.E.L.D. DIRECTOR MARIA HILL'S SECRET PROJECT TO REWRITE THE WORLD WITH COSMIC CUBE FRAGMENTS--SO YOU KNOW IT'S SERIOUS.
I'LL LEAVE IT AT THAT UNTIL I KNOW I CAN TRUST YOU. AND IF YOU ARE STILL BAD GUYS--
--WELL, JUST REMEMBER THAT THIS IS RICK JONES TALKING. I TRAINED WITH THE BEST OF THE BEST. THE MEANEST OF THE GREENEST.
AND MY CHRISTMAS CARD LIST WILL KICK YOUR ASS.
WHISPERER OUT.
ROBERTO DA COSTA.
A.K.A. Sunspot. Supreme Leader of A.I.M.
THAT CAME IN TEN MINUTES AGO.
NOW, FOR ALL HIS GOOD INTENTIONS, THE WHISPERER REMAINS A KNOWN ENEMY OF S.H.I.E.L.D.--IN HIS WORDS, A "BAD GUY."
IF WE RESCUE HIM--AND IF, IN DOING SO, WE BREAK OUR AGREEMENT NEVER TO OPERATE ON U.S. SOIL--
--WE ARE THE BAD GUYS.

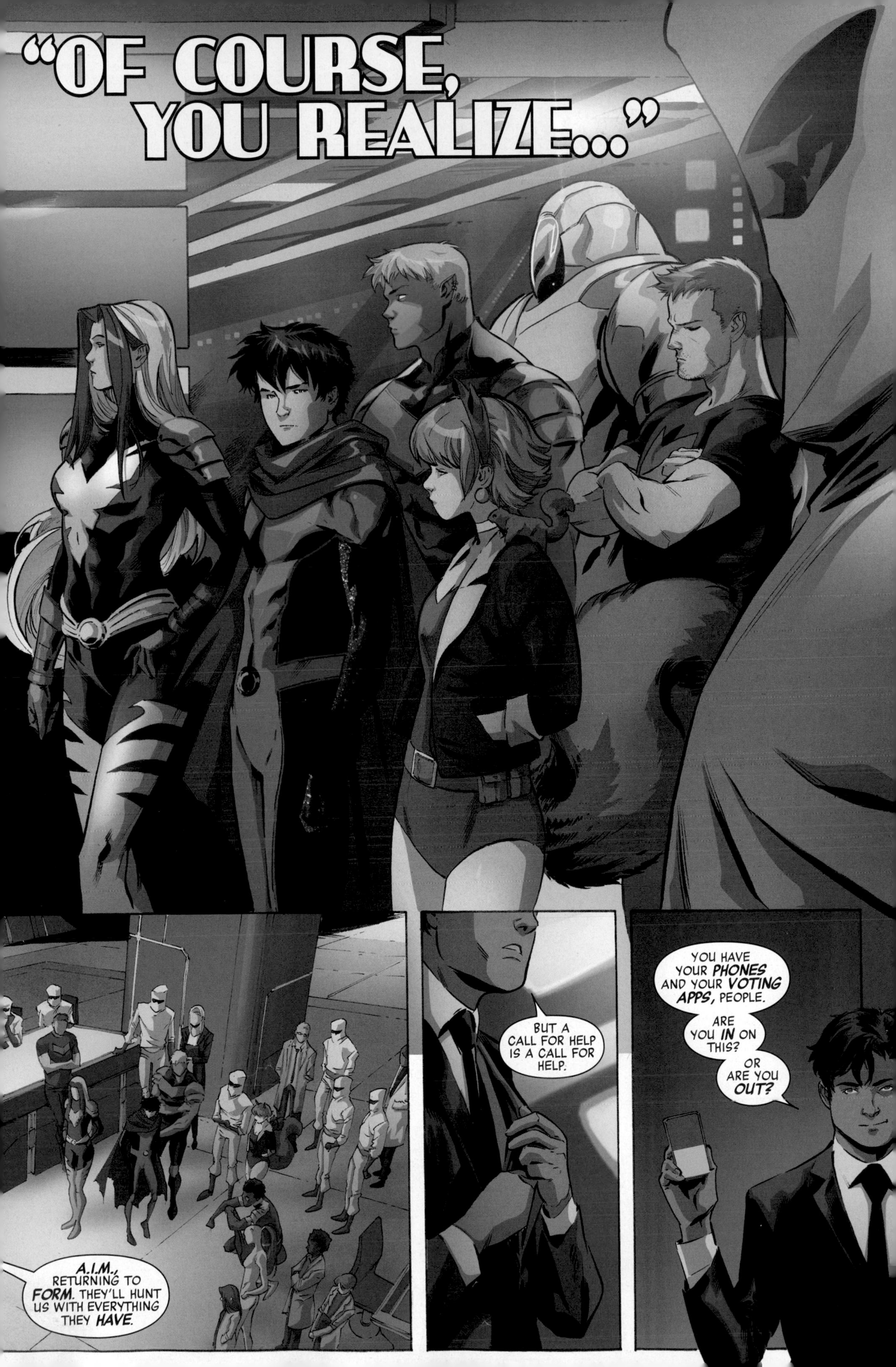
"OF COURSE, YOU REALIZE..."
A.I.M., RETURNING TO FORM. THEY'LL HUNT US WITH EVERYTHING THEY HAVE.
BUT A CALL FOR HELP IS A CALL FOR HELP.
YOU HAVE YOUR PHONES AND YOUR VOTING APPS, PEOPLE.
ARE YOU IN ON THIS?
OR ARE YOU OUT?

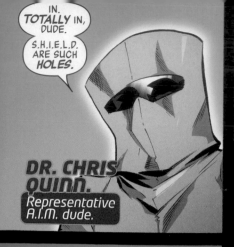

IN. **TOTALLY IN, DUDE.** S.H.I.E.L.D. ARE SUCH **HOLES.**

DR. CHRIS QUINN.
Representative A.I.M. dude.

THIS **KOBIK** STUFF... THEY'VE GONE **WAY** TOO FAR.

I'M **IN.**

POWER MAN.
Vic Alvarez. History-powered fighter.

IN.

POD.
Aikku Jokinen. Planetary defense mechanism.

... I'M IN TOO.

DR. TONI HO.
Head of Engineering.

WHY CAN'T WE JUST **TALK** TO THEM? AVA, BACK ME **UP--**

CHTT CHUK

SQUIRREL GIRL.
Doreen Green. Squirrel powers.

THEY DON'T TALK TO **US.** THEY TALK **AT** US.

AND THEY **LIE.**

I'M IN.

WHITE TIGER.
Ava Ayala. Normal human martial artist.

I DON'T **KNOW.** I'M NOT **COMFORTABLE** WITH THIS...

YEAH. I'M WITH **S.G.--**I SAY **TALK.**

WICCAN. DEMIURGE. ?????
Billy Kaplan. Reality warper.

HULKLING.
Teddy Altman. Super-strong shape-shifter.

WELL, **I'M** IN.

SONGBIRD.
Melissa Gold. Solid-sound manipulator.

BRING IT **ON.**

DR. MAX BRASHEAR.
Head of Theoretical Physics.

ALL RIGHT. HAWKEYE, YOU'RE A **S.H.I.E.L.D. AGENT,** SO I KNOW WHAT **YOU'RE--**

NO. YOU DON'T.

I'M IN.

HAWKEYE THE ARCHER.
Clint Barton. No longer a S.H.I.E.L.D. agent.

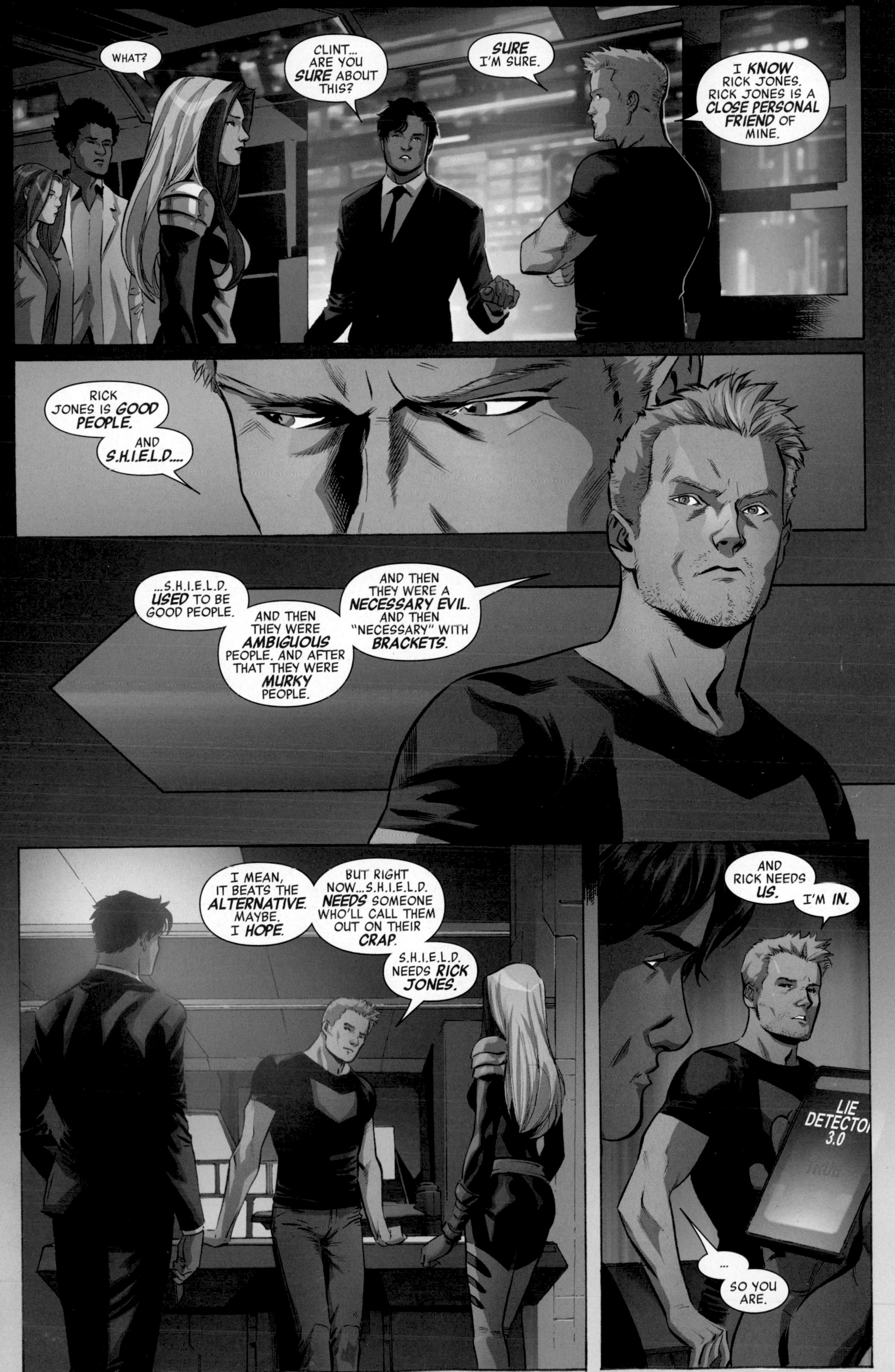
WHAT?
CLINT... ARE YOU SURE ABOUT THIS?
SURE I'M SURE.
I KNOW RICK JONES. RICK JONES IS A CLOSE PERSONAL FRIEND OF MINE.
RICK JONES IS GOOD PEOPLE.
AND S.H.I.E.L.D....
...S.H.I.E.L.D. USED TO BE GOOD PEOPLE.
AND THEN THEY WERE AMBIGUOUS PEOPLE. AND AFTER THAT THEY WERE MURKY PEOPLE.
AND THEN THEY WERE A NECESSARY EVIL. AND THEN "NECESSARY" WITH BRACKETS.
I MEAN, IT BEATS THE ALTERNATIVE. MAYBE. I HOPE.
BUT RIGHT NOW...S.H.I.E.L.D. NEEDS SOMEONE WHO'LL CALL THEM OUT ON THEIR CRAP.
S.H.I.E.L.D. NEEDS RICK JONES.
AND RICK NEEDS US.
I'M IN.
LIE DETECTOR 3.0
...
SO YOU ARE.

THAT CHECKS. I'M GLAD YOU'RE WITH US, CLINT.

MEANWHILE, JUDGING BY THE APP--OUT OF OVER TWO HUNDRED A.I.M. STAFF ACROSS THE ISLAND, WE HAVE... *FOUR* PEOPLE WHO DON'T WANT TO DO THIS.

UM. I ACCIDENTALLY TAPPED ON BOTH BUTTONS AT ONCE AND IT SAID "OUT" BUT I MEANT "IN."

SORRY.

DUDE, YOU'RE THE I.T. GUY--

I HAVE *FAT FINGERS!* I'M SORRY!

SO THAT'S TWO HUNDRED AND WHATEVER *FOR,* THREE *AGAINST.* MOTION *CARRIED.*

ALTHOUGH... IT WASN'T ACTUALLY A *VOTE.*

HUH? WHAT DO YOU--

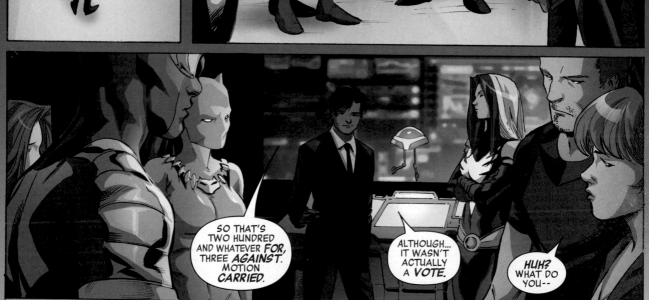

CHAMPAGNE ROBOT?

BOAT DRINKS.

VVVVWWWWWMMMM

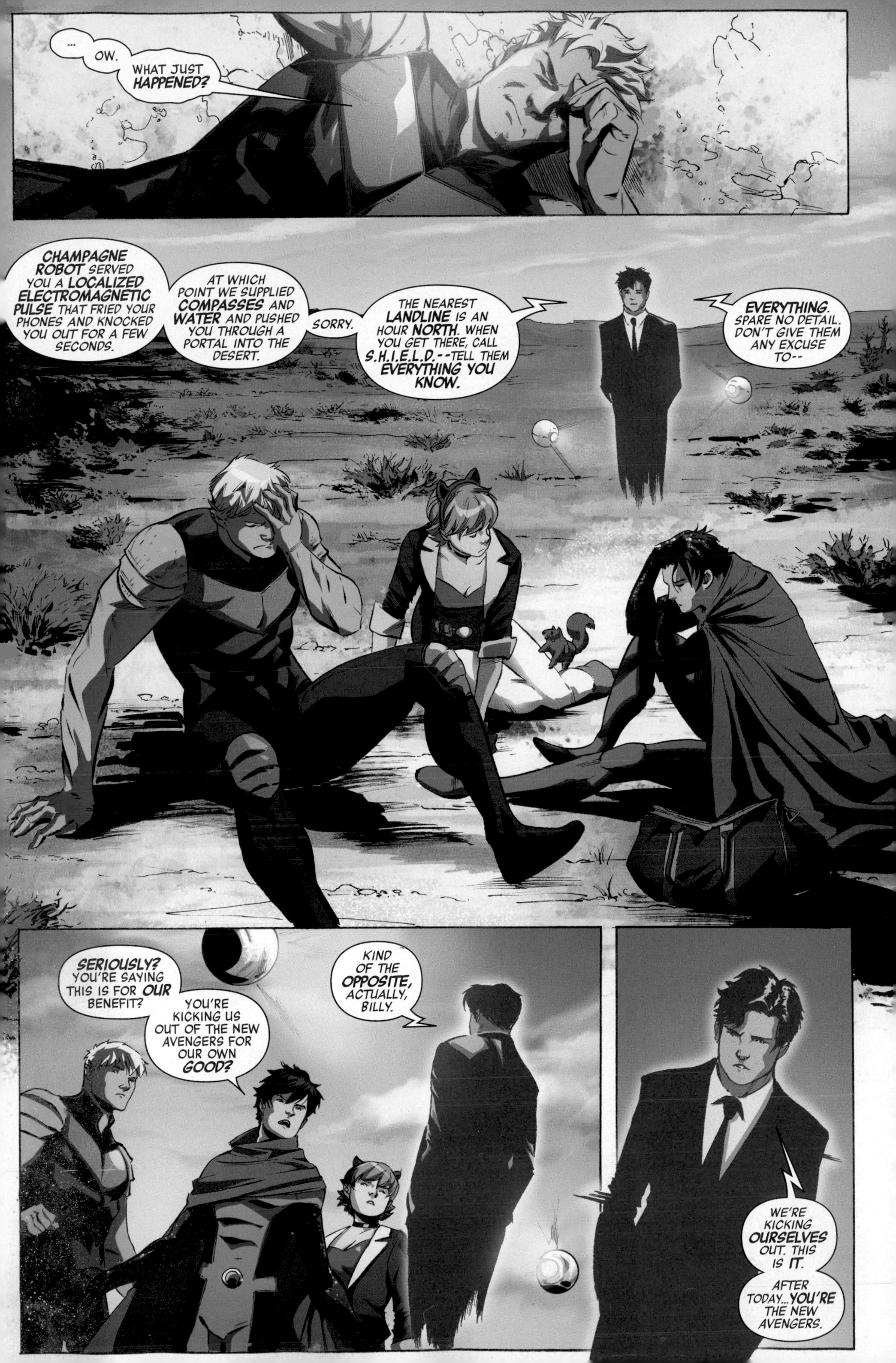
...
OW.
WHAT JUST HAPPENED?
CHAMPAGNE ROBOT SERVED YOU A LOCALIZED ELECTROMAGNETIC PULSE THAT FRIED YOUR PHONES AND KNOCKED YOU OUT FOR A FEW SECONDS.
AT WHICH POINT WE SUPPLIED COMPASSES AND WATER AND PUSHED YOU THROUGH A PORTAL INTO THE DESERT.
SORRY.
THE NEAREST LANDLINE IS AN HOUR NORTH. WHEN YOU GET THERE, CALL S.H.I.E.L.D.--TELL THEM EVERYTHING YOU KNOW.
EVERYTHING. SPARE NO DETAIL. DON'T GIVE THEM ANY EXCUSE TO--
SERIOUSLY? YOU'RE SAYING THIS IS FOR OUR BENEFIT?
YOU'RE KICKING US OUT OF THE NEW AVENGERS FOR OUR OWN GOOD?
KIND OF THE OPPOSITE, ACTUALLY, BILLY.
WE'RE KICKING OURSELVES OUT. THIS IS IT.
AFTER TODAY... YOU'RE THE NEW AVENGERS.

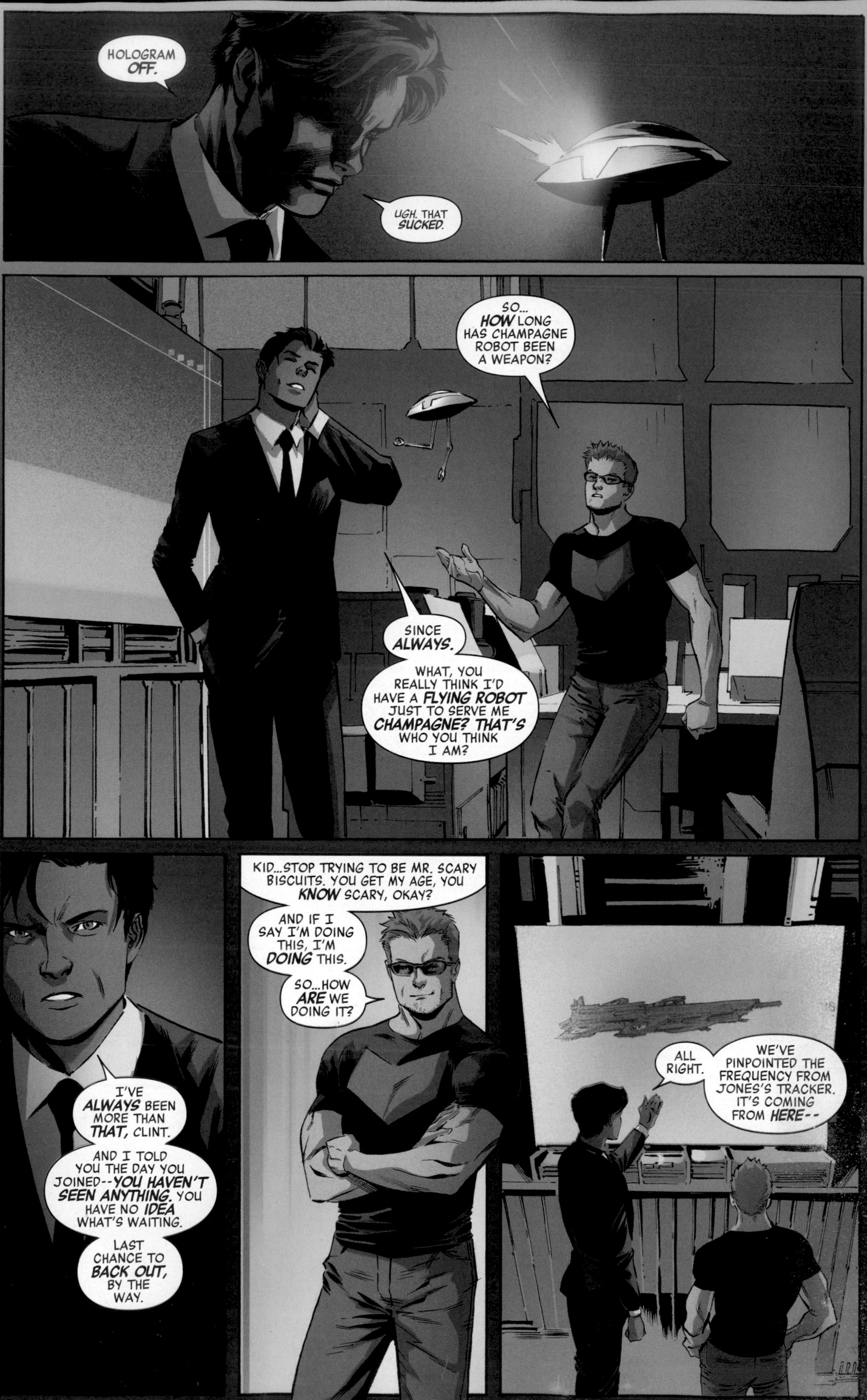
HOLOGRAM OFF.
UGH. THAT SUCKED.
SO... HOW LONG HAS CHAMPAGNE ROBOT BEEN A WEAPON?
SINCE ALWAYS.
WHAT, YOU REALLY THINK I'D HAVE A FLYING ROBOT JUST TO SERVE ME CHAMPAGNE? THAT'S WHO YOU THINK I AM?
I'VE ALWAYS BEEN MORE THAN THAT, CLINT.
AND I TOLD YOU THE DAY YOU JOINED--YOU HAVEN'T SEEN ANYTHING. YOU HAVE NO IDEA WHAT'S WAITING.
LAST CHANCE TO BACK OUT, BY THE WAY.
KID...STOP TRYING TO BE MR. SCARY BISCUITS. YOU GET MY AGE, YOU KNOW SCARY, OKAY?
AND IF I SAY I'M DOING THIS, I'M DOING THIS.
SO...HOW ARE WE DOING IT?
ALL RIGHT.
WE'VE PINPOINTED THE FREQUENCY FROM JONES'S TRACKER. IT'S COMING FROM HERE--

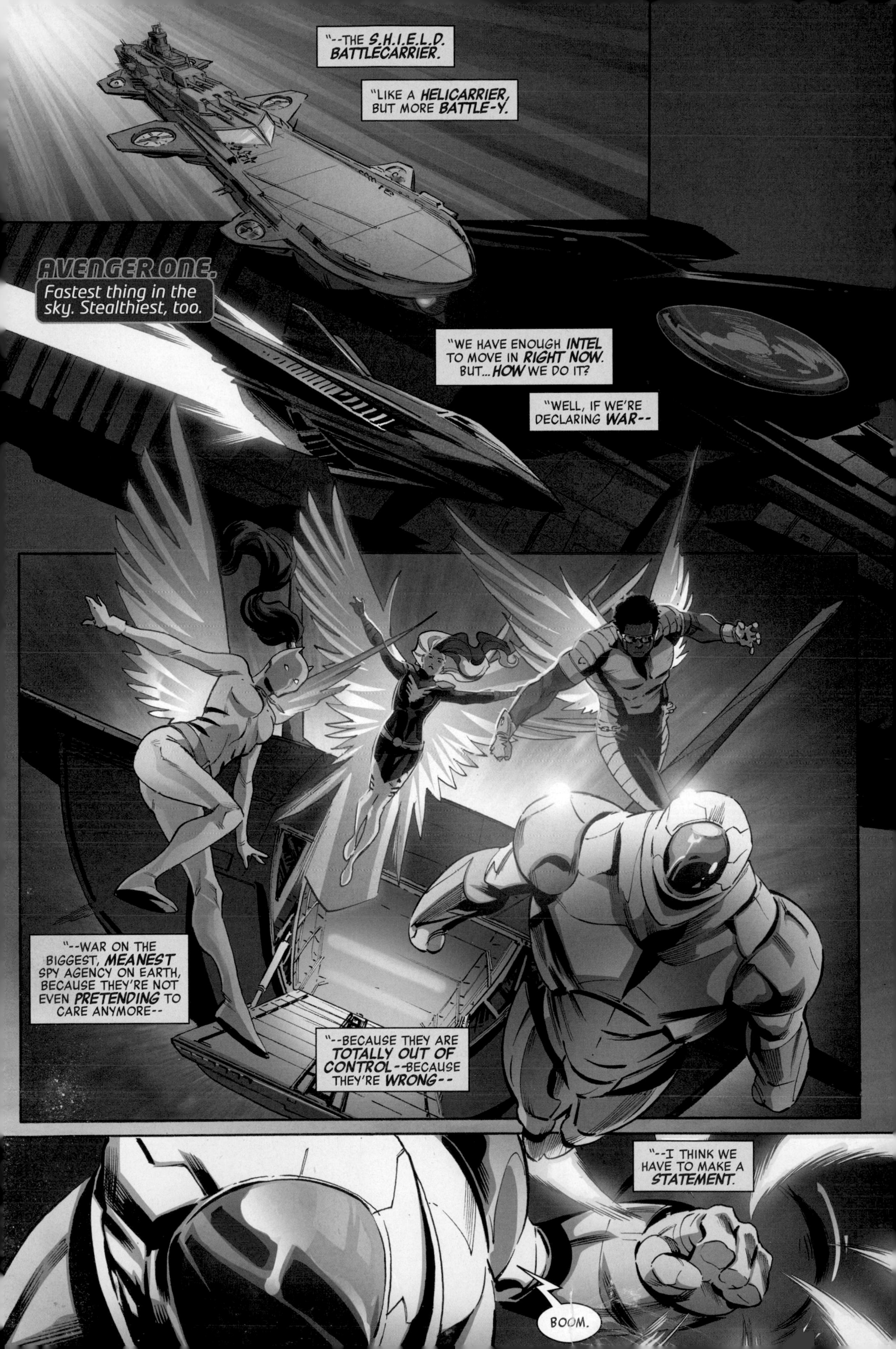

"--THE S.H.I.E.L.D. BATTLECARRIER.
"LIKE A HELICARRIER, BUT MORE BATTLE-Y.
AVENGER ONE.
Fastest thing in the sky. Stealthiest, too.
"WE HAVE ENOUGH INTEL TO MOVE IN RIGHT NOW. BUT... HOW WE DO IT?
"WELL, IF WE'RE DECLARING WAR--
"--WAR ON THE BIGGEST, MEANEST SPY AGENCY ON EARTH, BECAUSE THEY'RE NOT EVEN PRETENDING TO CARE ANYMORE--
"--BECAUSE THEY ARE TOTALLY OUT OF CONTROL--BECAUSE THEY'RE WRONG--
"--I THINK WE HAVE TO MAKE A STATEMENT.
BOOM.

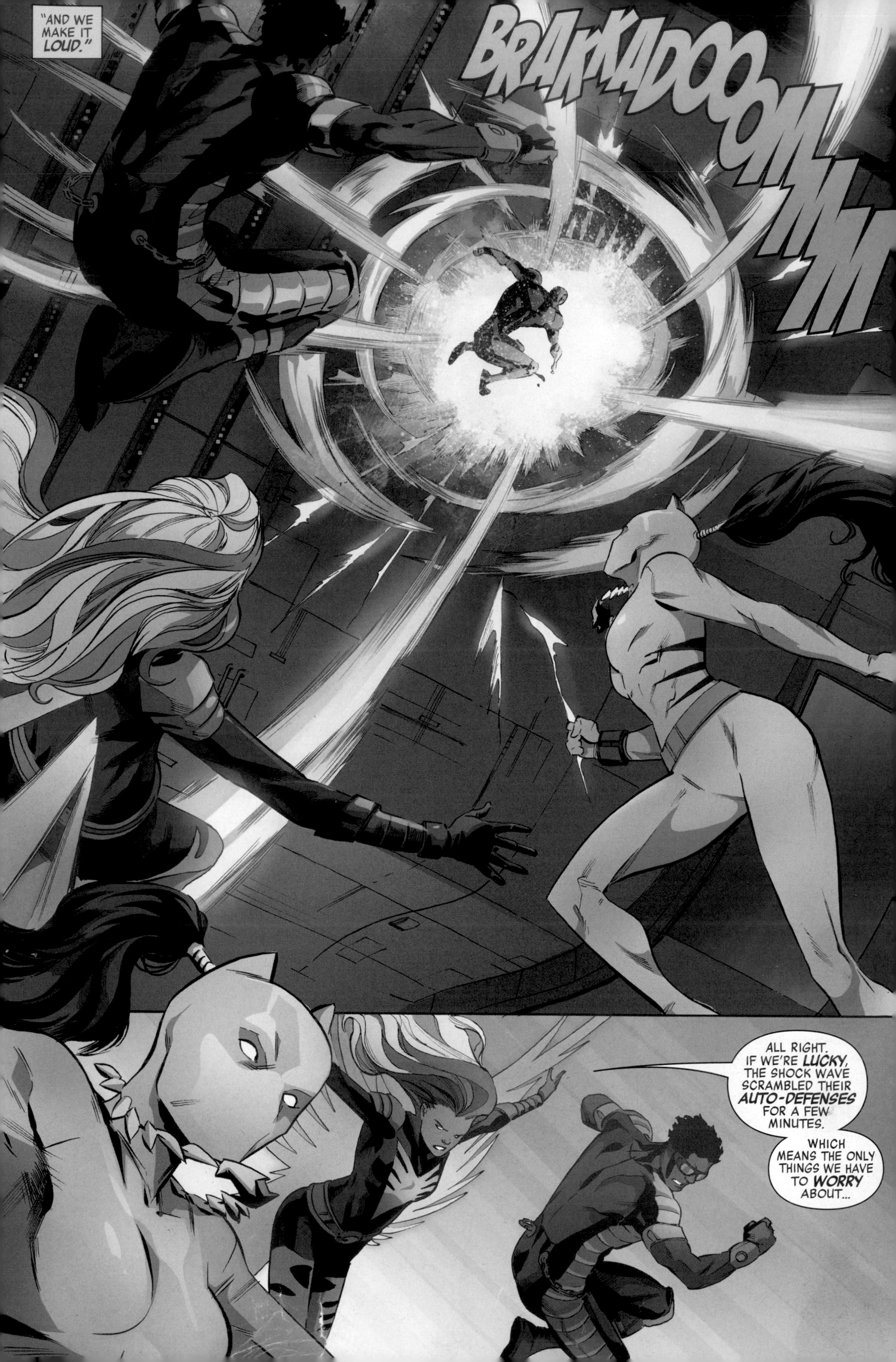
"AND WE MAKE IT LOUD."
BRAKADOOOMMM
ALL RIGHT. IF WE'RE LUCKY, THE SHOCK WAVE SCRAMBLED THEIR AUTO-DEFENSES FOR A FEW MINUTES.
WHICH MEANS THE ONLY THINGS WE HAVE TO WORRY ABOUT...

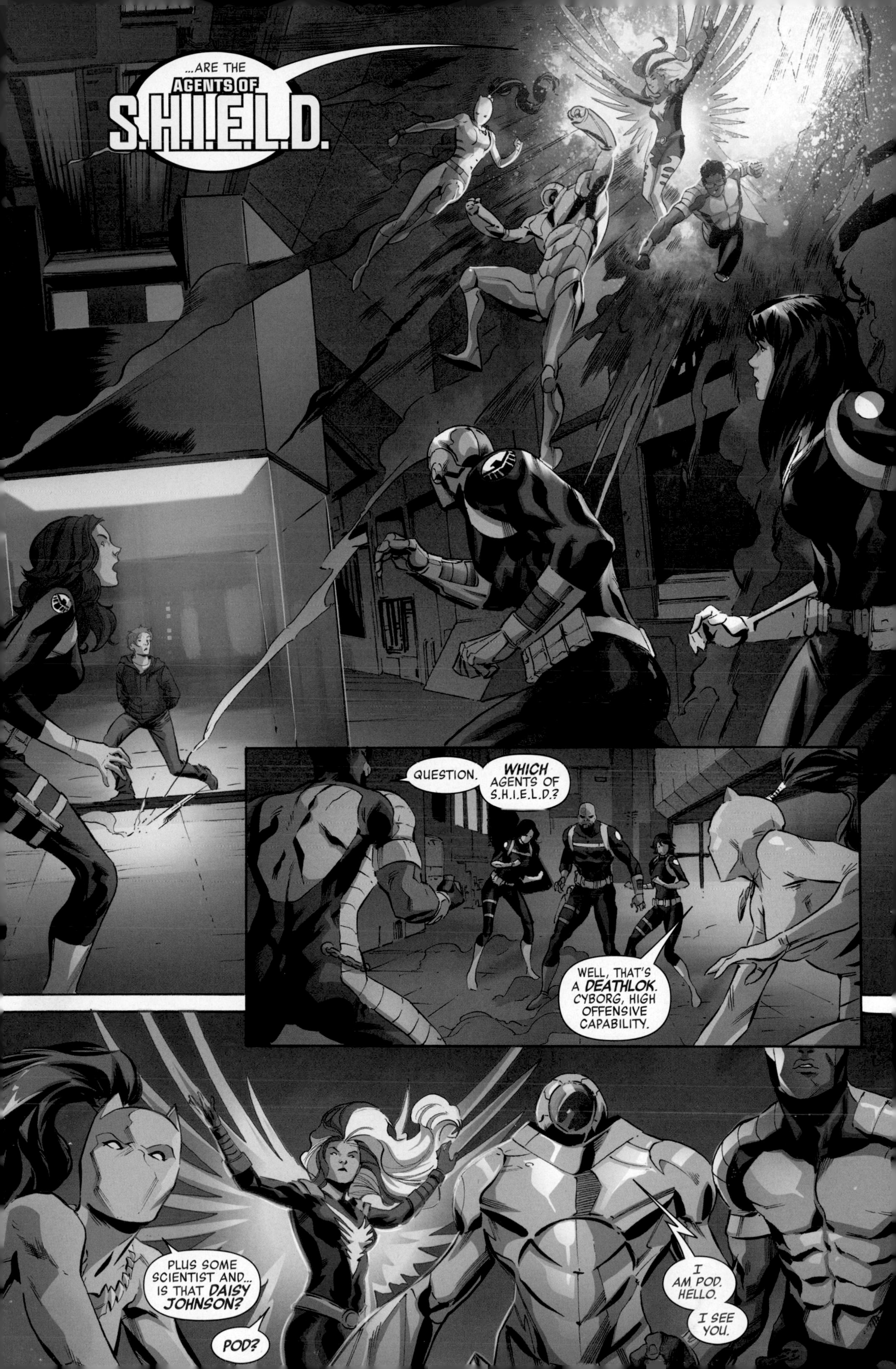
...ARE THE
AGENTS OF
S.H.I.E.L.D.
QUESTION.
WHICH AGENTS OF S.H.I.E.L.D.?
WELL, THAT'S A DEATHLOK. CYBORG, HIGH OFFENSIVE CAPABILITY.
PLUS SOME SCIENTIST AND... IS THAT DAISY JOHNSON?
POD?
I AM POD. HELLO.
I SEE YOU.

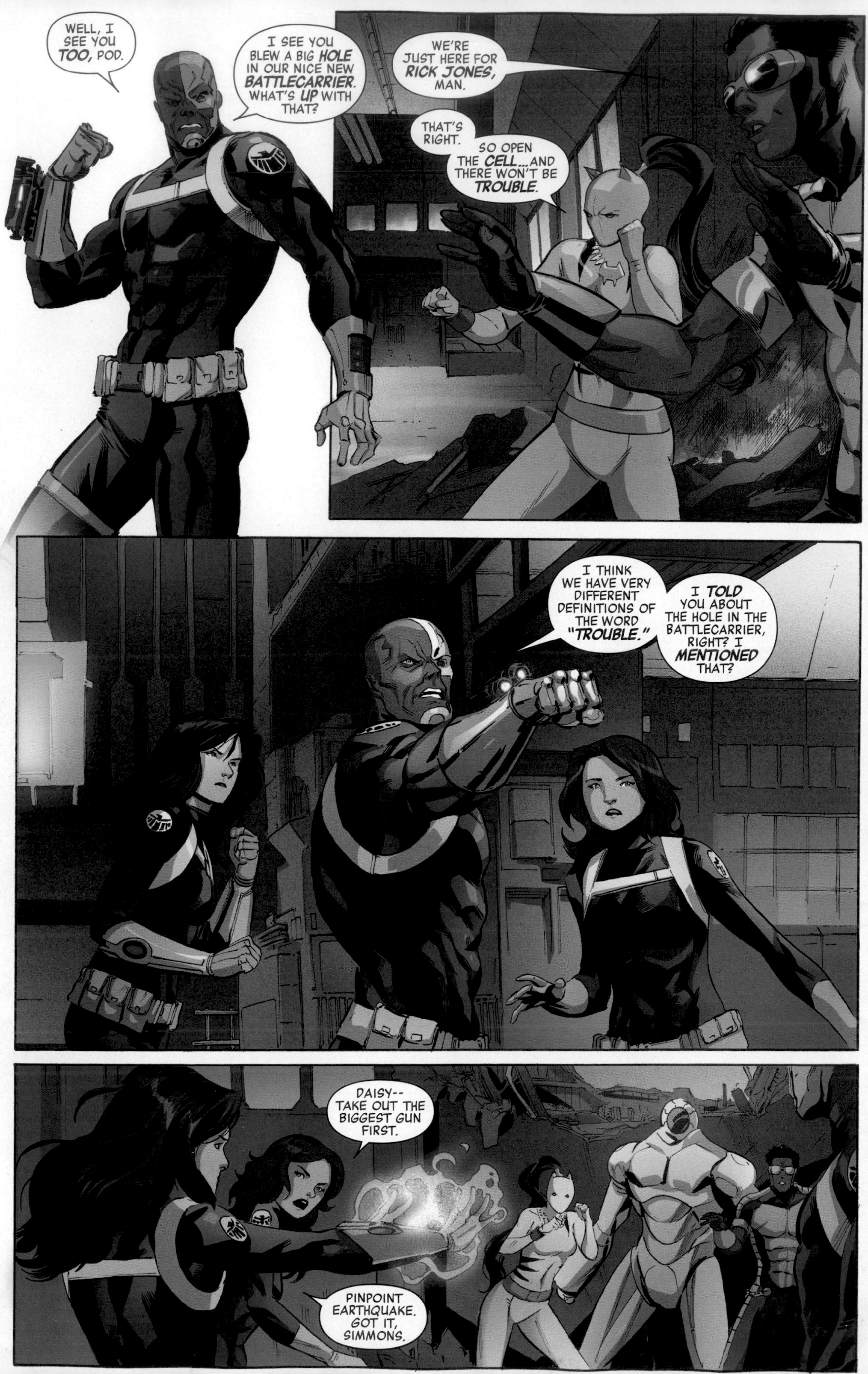
WELL, I SEE YOU TOO, POD.
I SEE YOU BLEW A BIG HOLE IN OUR NICE NEW BATTLECARRIER. WHAT'S UP WITH THAT?
WE'RE JUST HERE FOR RICK JONES, MAN.
THAT'S RIGHT.
SO OPEN THE CELL...AND THERE WON'T BE TROUBLE.
I THINK WE HAVE VERY DIFFERENT DEFINITIONS OF THE WORD "TROUBLE."
I TOLD YOU ABOUT THE HOLE IN THE BATTLECARRIER, RIGHT? I MENTIONED THAT?
DAISY-- TAKE OUT THE BIGGEST GUN FIRST.
PINPOINT EARTHQUAKE. GOT IT, SIMMONS.

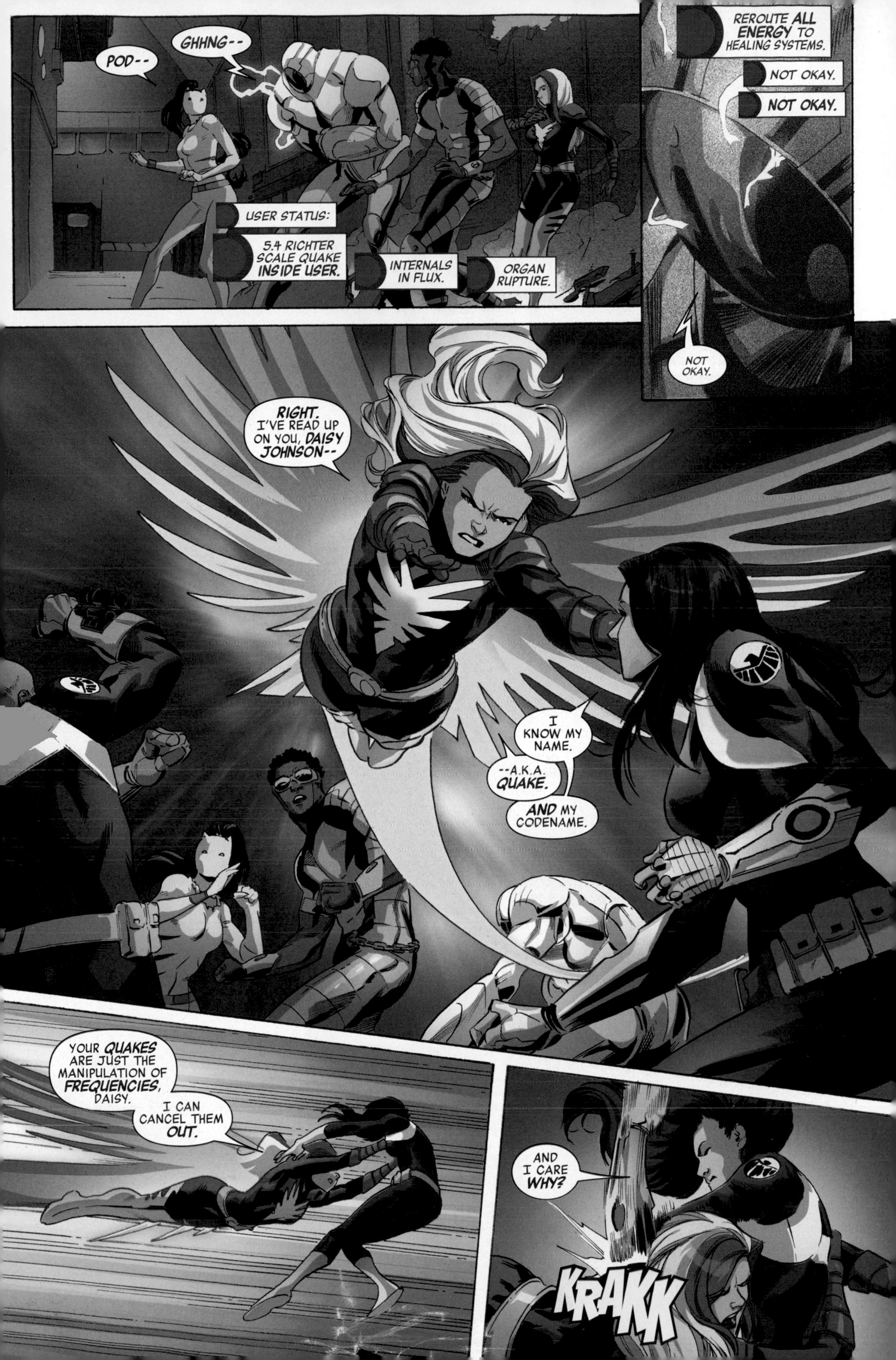

POD--
GHHNG--
USER STATUS:
5.4 RICHTER SCALE QUAKE INSIDE USER.
INTERNALS IN FLUX.
ORGAN RUPTURE.
REROUTE ALL ENERGY TO HEALING SYSTEMS.
NOT OKAY.
NOT OKAY.
NOT OKAY.
RIGHT. I'VE READ UP ON YOU, DAISY JOHNSON--
I KNOW MY NAME.
--A.K.A. QUAKE.
AND MY CODENAME.
YOUR QUAKES ARE JUST THE MANIPULATION OF FREQUENCIES, DAISY.
I CAN CANCEL THEM OUT.
AND I CARE WHY?
KRAKK

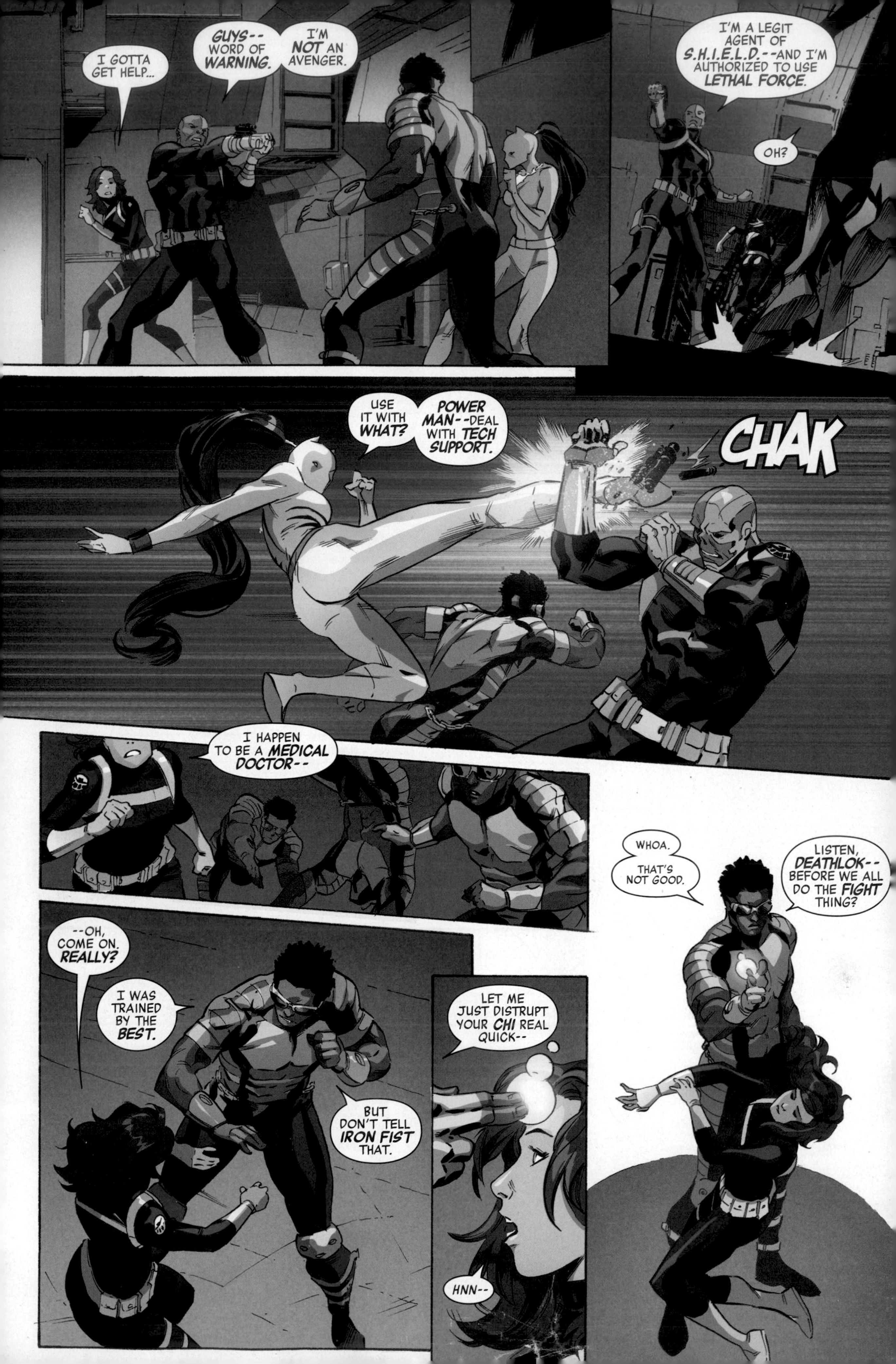
I GOTTA GET HELP...
GUYS-- WORD OF WARNING.
I'M NOT AN AVENGER.
I'M A LEGIT AGENT OF S.H.I.E.L.D.--AND I'M AUTHORIZED TO USE LETHAL FORCE.
OH?
USE IT WITH WHAT?
POWER MAN--DEAL WITH TECH SUPPORT.
CHAK
I HAPPEN TO BE A MEDICAL DOCTOR--
--OH, COME ON. REALLY?
I WAS TRAINED BY THE BEST.
BUT DON'T TELL IRON FIST THAT.
LET ME JUST DISTRUPT YOUR CHI REAL QUICK--
HNN--
WHOA.
THAT'S NOT GOOD.
LISTEN, DEATHLOK-- BEFORE WE ALL DO THE FIGHT THING?

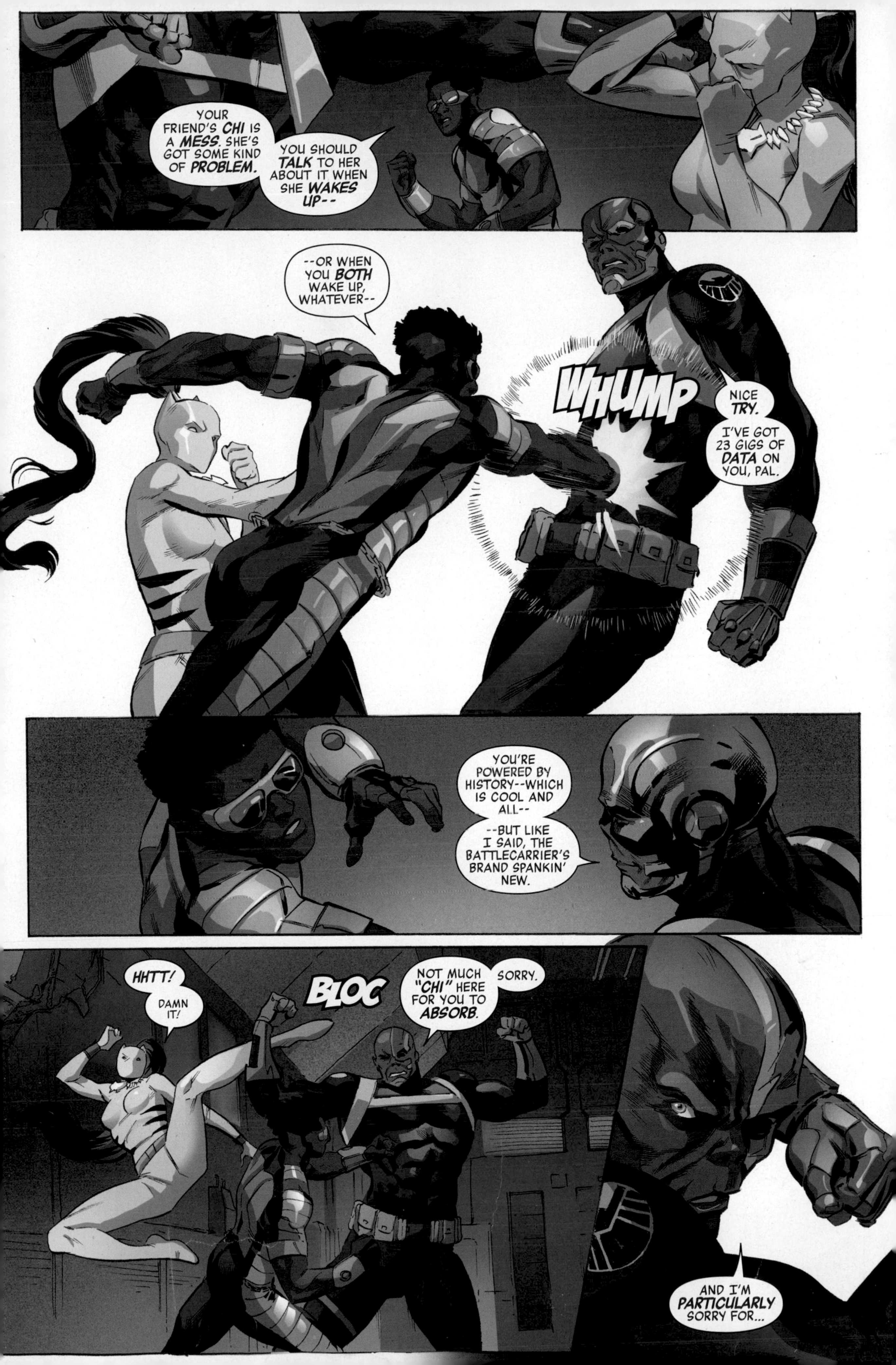
YOUR FRIEND'S CHI IS A MESS. SHE'S GOT SOME KIND OF PROBLEM.
YOU SHOULD TALK TO HER ABOUT IT WHEN SHE WAKES UP--
--OR WHEN YOU BOTH WAKE UP, WHATEVER--
WHUMP
NICE TRY.
I'VE GOT 23 GIGS OF DATA ON YOU, PAL.
YOU'RE POWERED BY HISTORY--WHICH IS COOL AND ALL--
--BUT LIKE I SAID, THE BATTLECARRIER'S BRAND SPANKIN' NEW.
HHTT!
DAMN IT!
BLOC
NOT MUCH "CHI" HERE FOR YOU TO ABSORB.
SORRY.
AND I'M PARTICULARLY SORRY FOR...

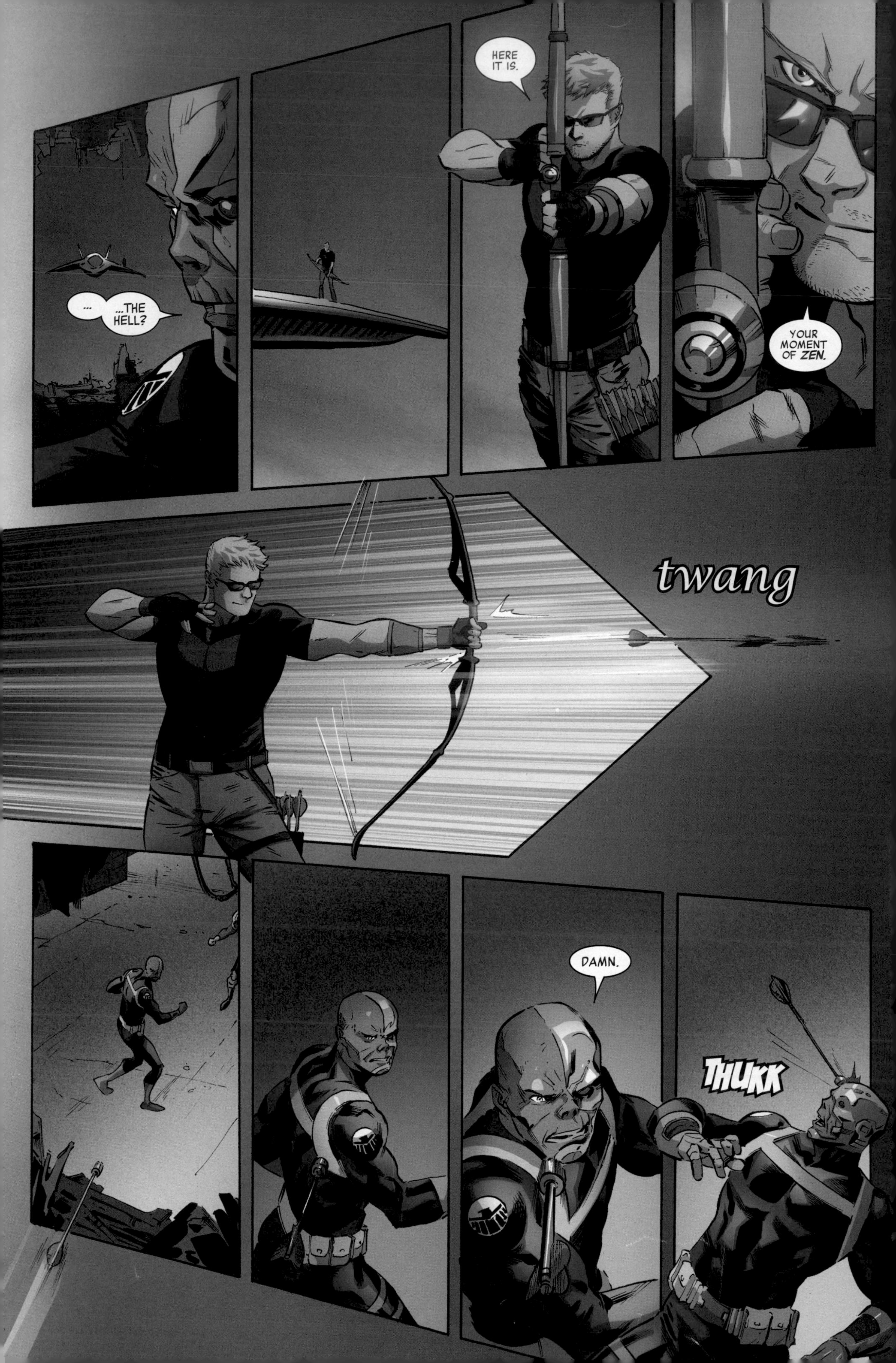
...
...THE HELL?
HERE IT IS.
YOUR MOMENT OF ZEN.
twang
DAMN.
THUKK

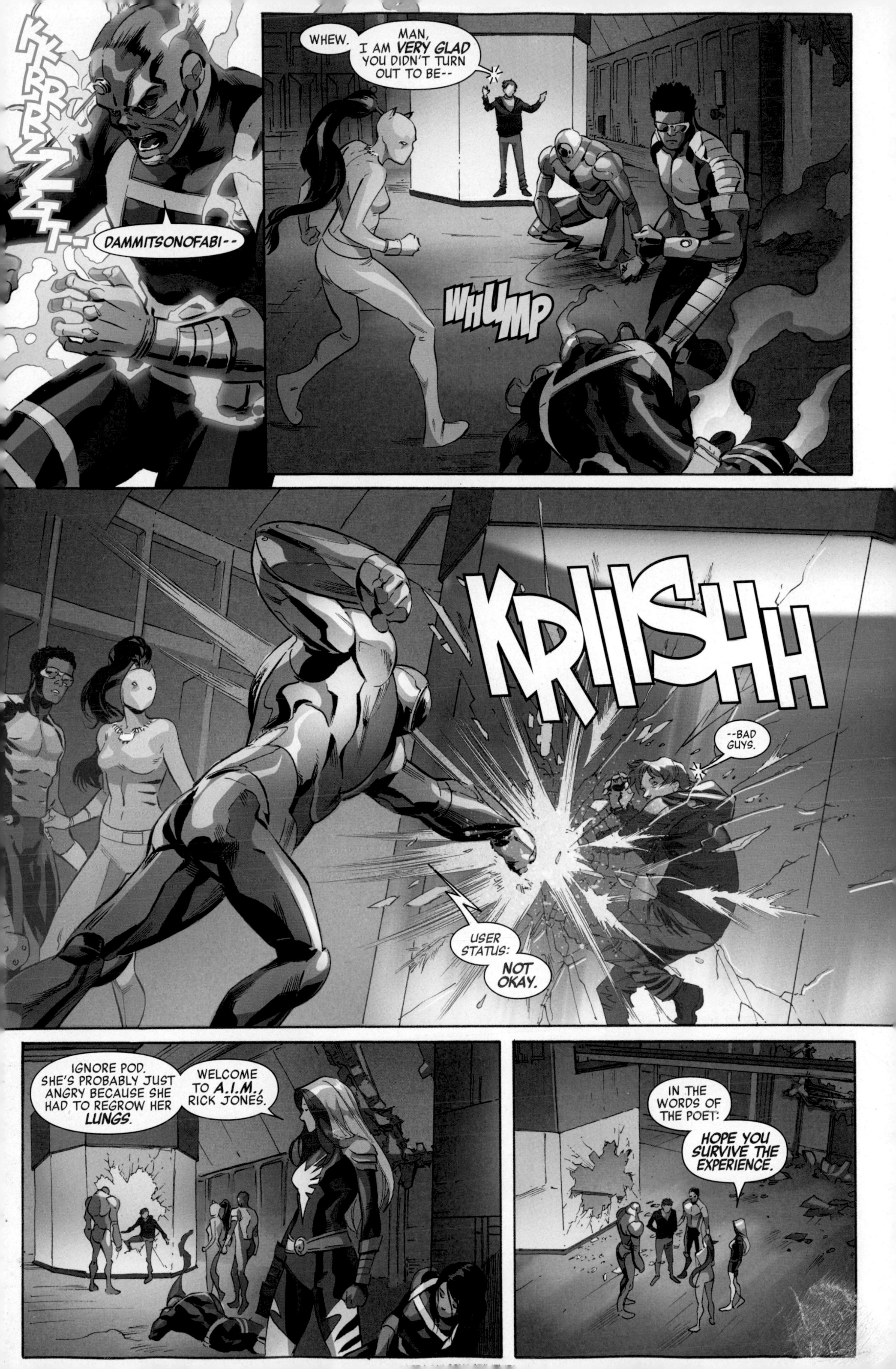
KKRRBZZZTT--
DAMMITSONOFABI--
WHEW.
MAN, I AM VERY GLAD YOU DIDN'T TURN OUT TO BE--
WHUMP
KRIIISHH
--BAD GUYS.
USER STATUS: NOT OKAY.
IGNORE POD. SHE'S PROBABLY JUST ANGRY BECAUSE SHE HAD TO REGROW HER LUNGS.
WELCOME TO A.I.M., RICK JONES.
IN THE WORDS OF THE POET:
HOPE YOU SURVIVE THE EXPERIENCE.

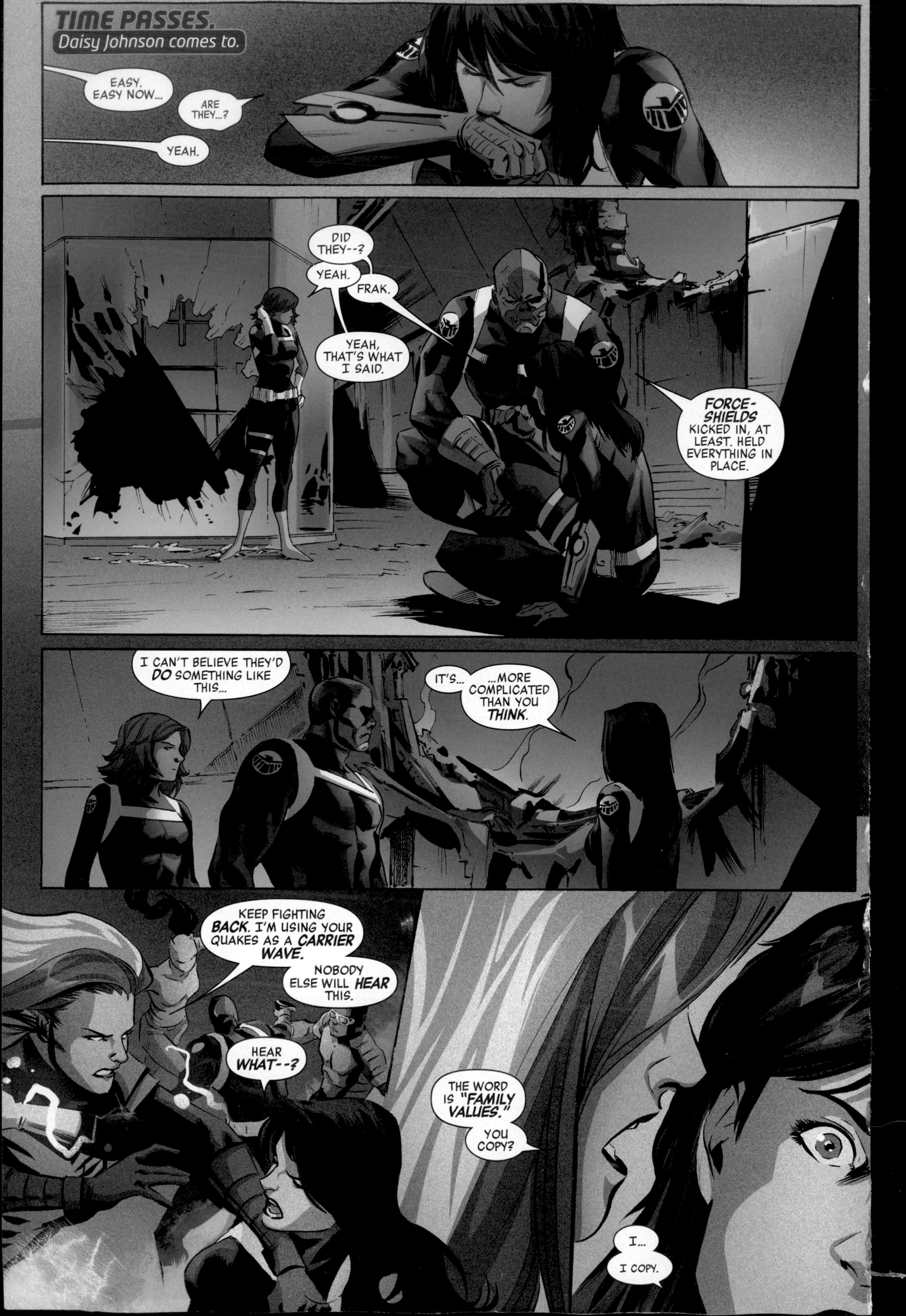
TIME PASSES.
Daisy Johnson comes to.
EASY. EASY NOW...
ARE THEY...?
YEAH.
DID THEY--?
YEAH.
FRAK.
YEAH, THAT'S WHAT I SAID.
FORCE-SHIELDS KICKED IN, AT LEAST. HELD EVERYTHING IN PLACE.
I CAN'T BELIEVE THEY'D DO SOMETHING LIKE THIS...
IT'S...
...MORE COMPLICATED THAN YOU THINK.
KEEP FIGHTING BACK. I'M USING YOUR QUAKES AS A CARRIER WAVE.
NOBODY ELSE WILL HEAR THIS.
HEAR WHAT--?
THE WORD IS "FAMILY VALUES."
YOU COPY?
I...
I COPY.

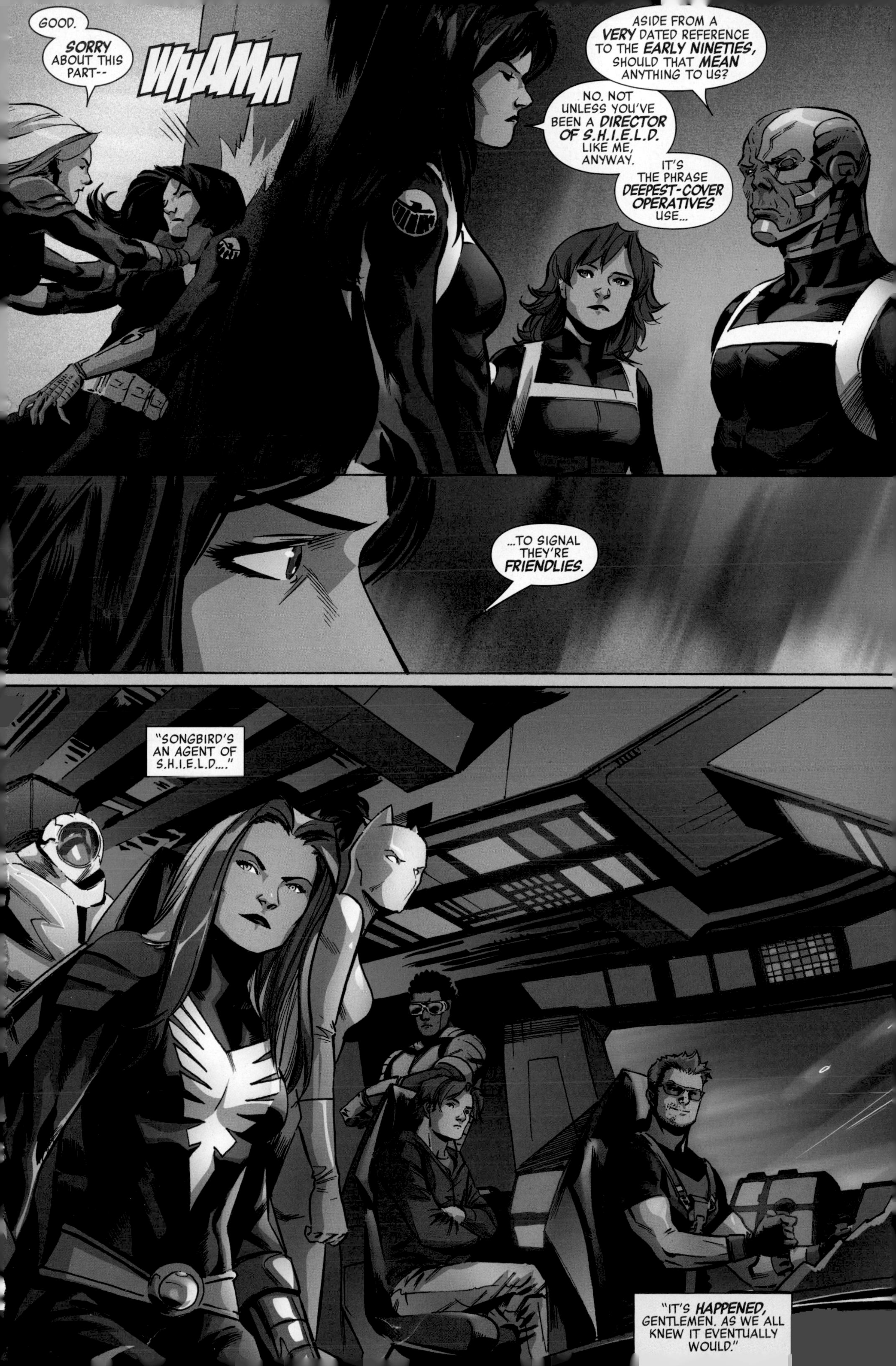
GOOD. SORRY ABOUT THIS PART--
WHAMM
ASIDE FROM A VERY DATED REFERENCE TO THE EARLY NINETIES, SHOULD THAT MEAN ANYTHING TO US?
NO. NOT UNLESS YOU'VE BEEN A DIRECTOR OF S.H.I.E.L.D. LIKE ME, ANYWAY.
IT'S THE PHRASE DEEPEST-COVER OPERATIVES USE...
...TO SIGNAL THEY'RE FRIENDLIES.
"SONGBIRD'S AN AGENT OF S.H.I.E.L.D...."
"IT'S HAPPENED, GENTLEMEN. AS WE ALL KNEW IT EVENTUALLY WOULD."

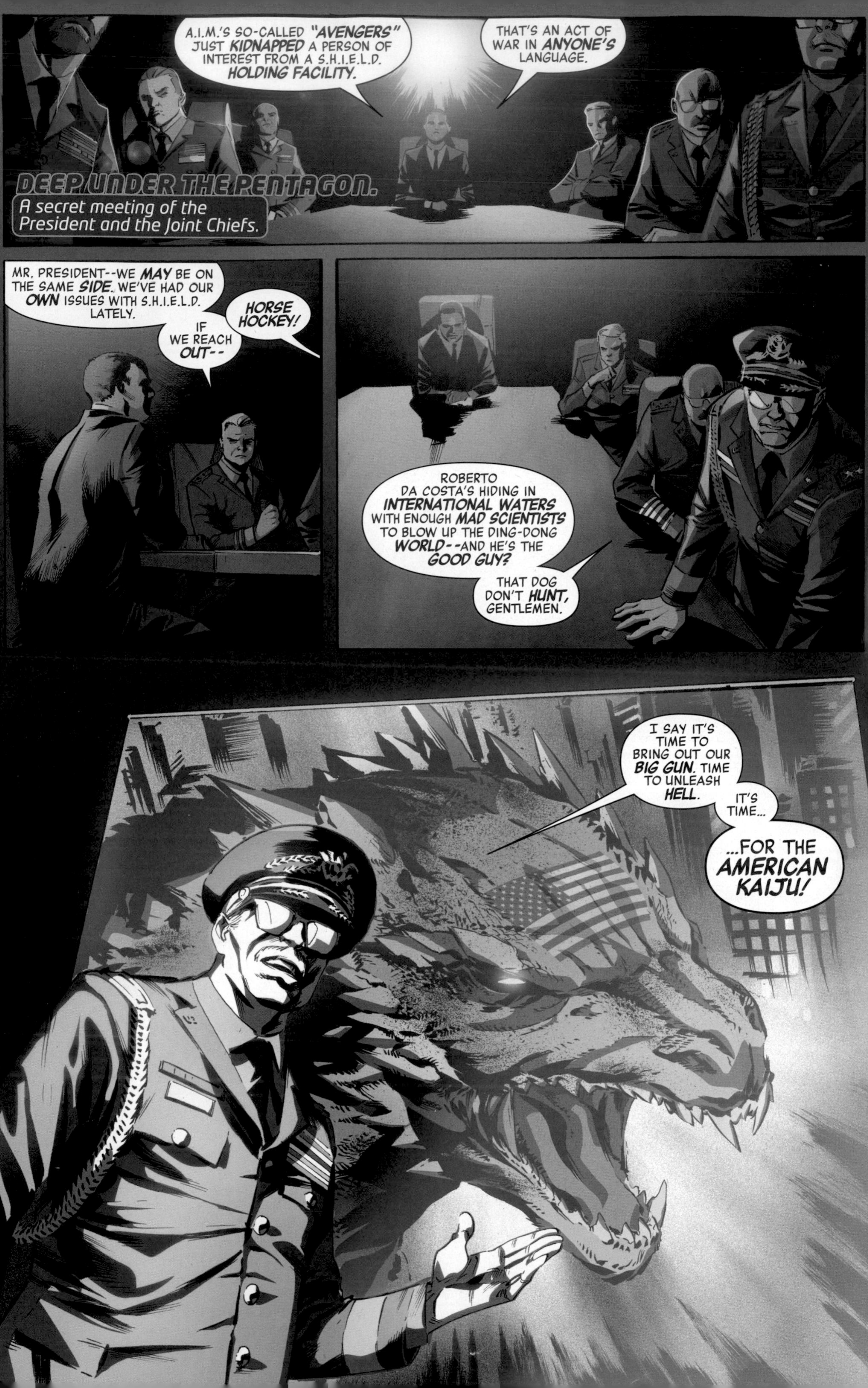
A.I.M.'S SO-CALLED "AVENGERS" JUST KIDNAPPED A PERSON OF INTEREST FROM A S.H.I.E.L.D. HOLDING FACILITY.
THAT'S AN ACT OF WAR IN ANYONE'S LANGUAGE.
DEEP UNDER THE PENTAGON.
A secret meeting of the President and the Joint Chiefs.
MR. PRESIDENT--WE MAY BE ON THE SAME SIDE. WE'VE HAD OUR OWN ISSUES WITH S.H.I.E.L.D. LATELY.
IF WE REACH OUT--
HORSE HOCKEY!
ROBERTO DA COSTA'S HIDING IN INTERNATIONAL WATERS WITH ENOUGH MAD SCIENTISTS TO BLOW UP THE DING-DONG WORLD--AND HE'S THE GOOD GUY?
THAT DOG DON'T HUNT, GENTLEMEN.
I SAY IT'S TIME TO BRING OUT OUR BIG GUN. TIME TO UNLEASH HELL.
IT'S TIME...
...FOR THE AMERICAN KAIJU!

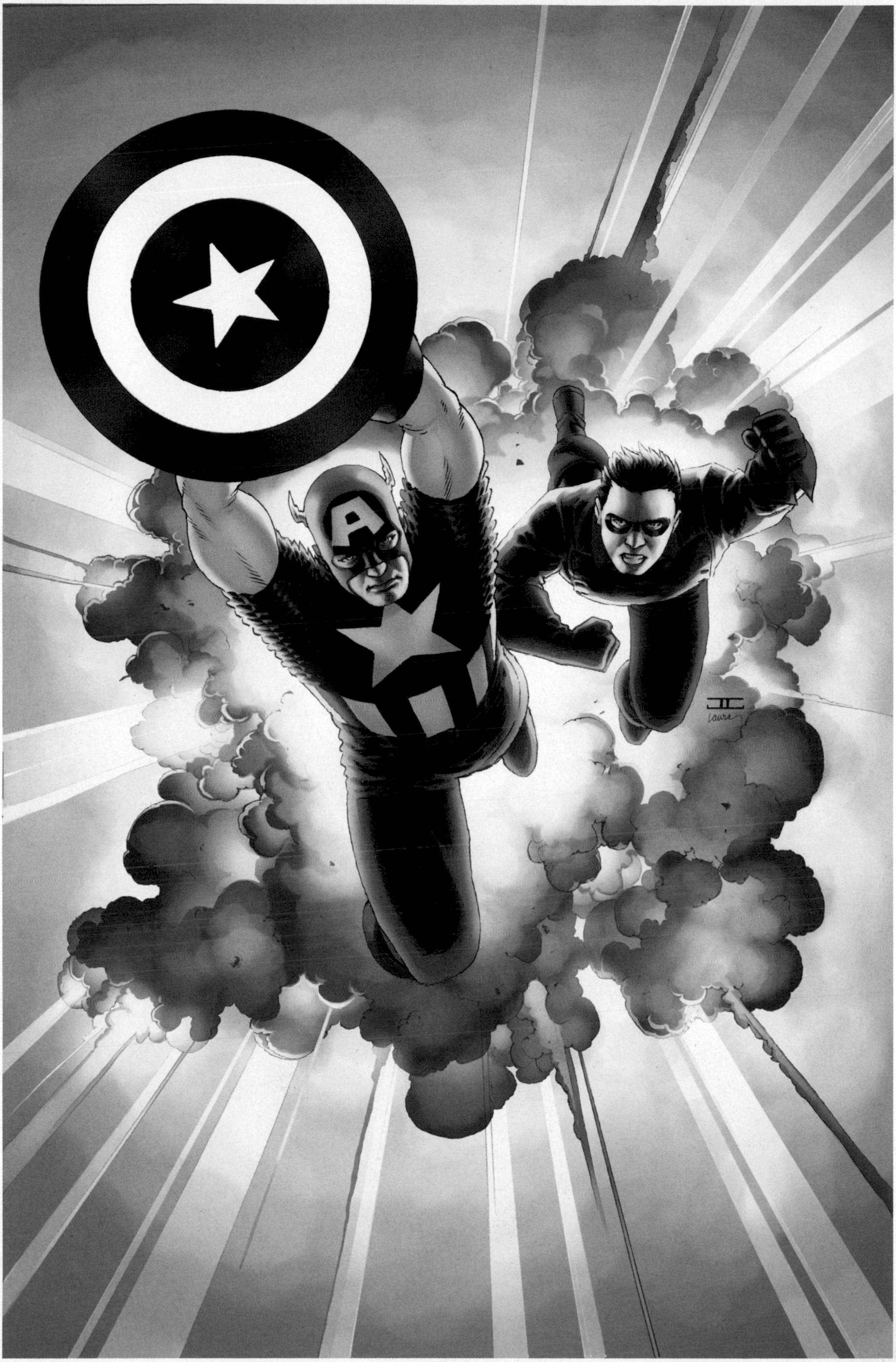

Captain America: Sam Wilson No. 7 variant by
JOHN CASSADAY & LAURA MARTIN

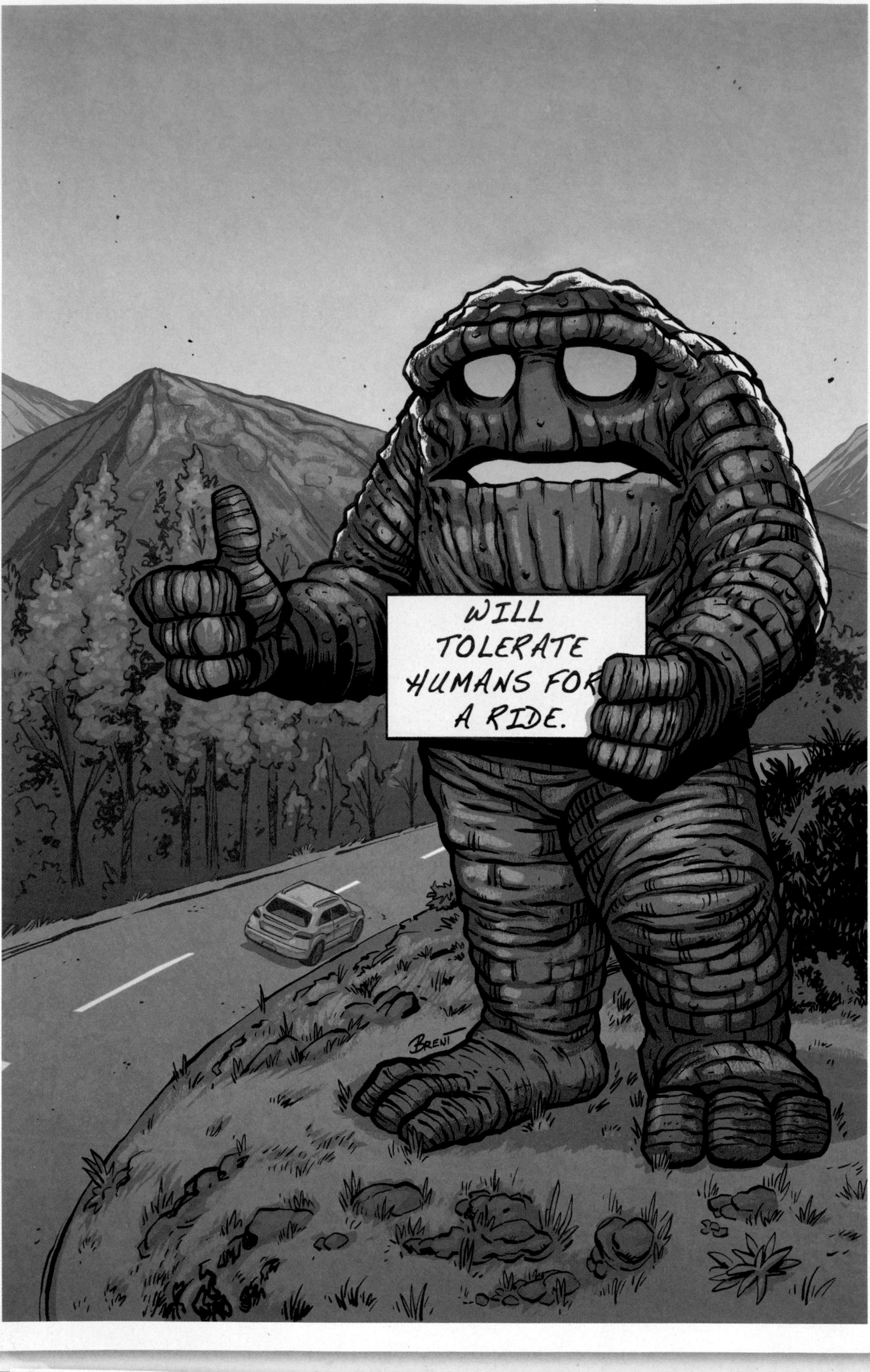
WILL TOLERATE HUMANS FOR A RIDE.
BRENT

Mission Brief

Dum Dum Dugan has been assigned to S.H.I.E.L.D.'s S.T.A.K.E. division and placed in charge of its field team, the Howling Commandos. The ragtag group of monsters had a rough beginning, but they thought all of that was behind them — until the team's communications expert, Orrgo, went missing...

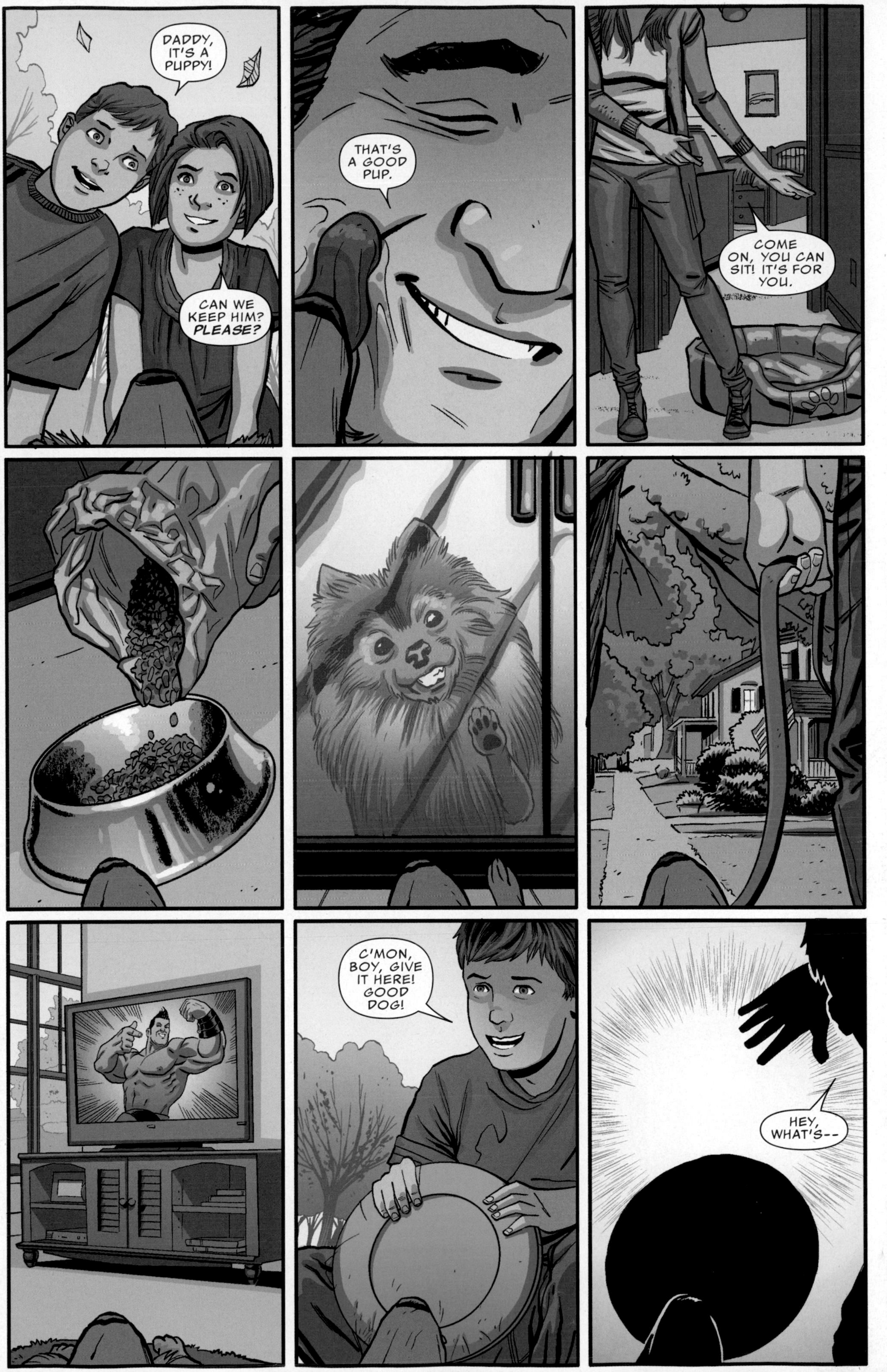
DADDY, IT'S A PUPPY!
CAN WE KEEP HIM? *PLEASE?*
THAT'S A GOOD PUP.
COME ON, YOU CAN SIT! IT'S FOR YOU.
C'MON, BOY, GIVE IT HERE! GOOD DOG!
HEY, WHAT'S--

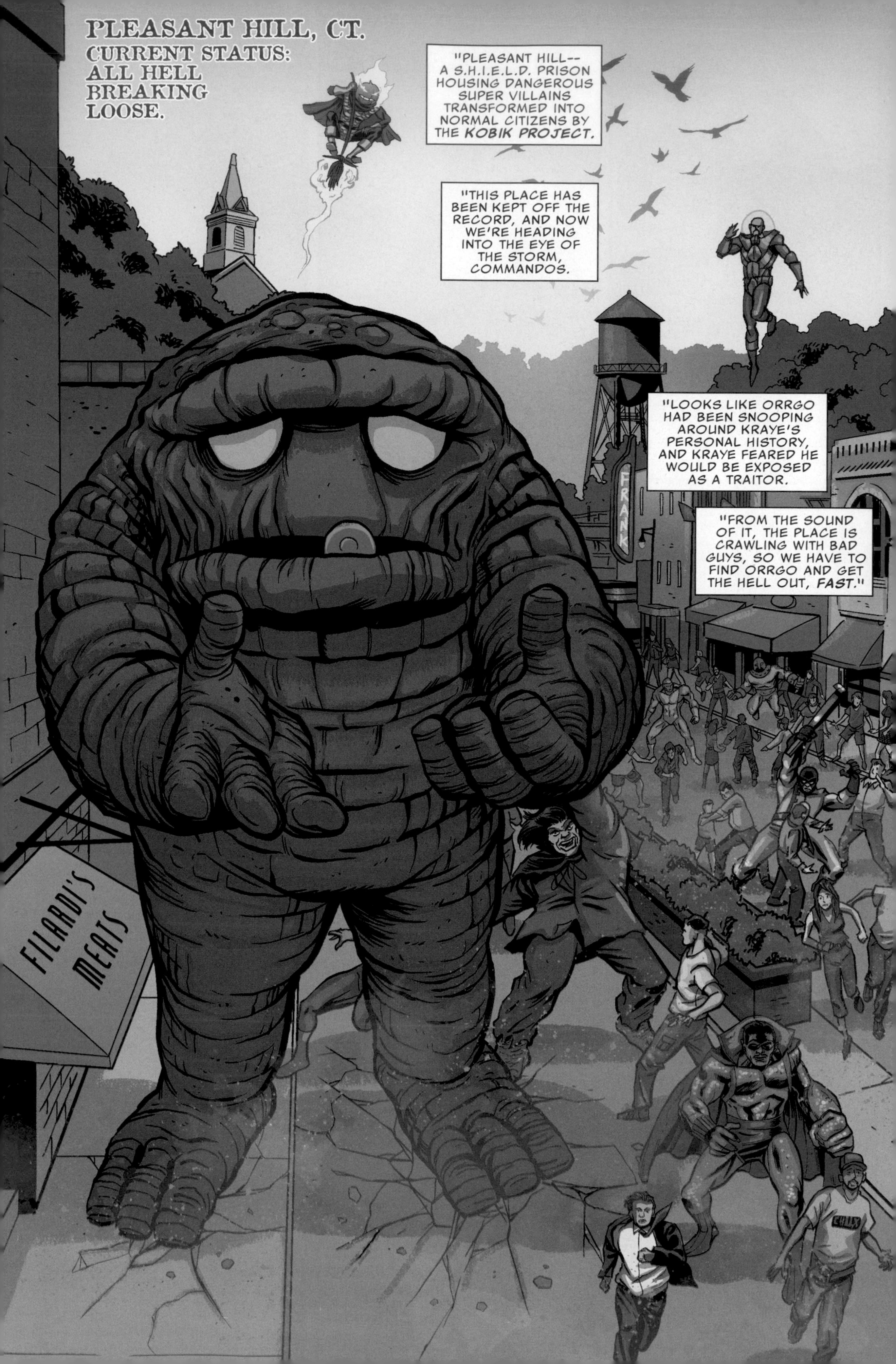
PLEASANT HILL, CT.
CURRENT STATUS: ALL HELL BREAKING LOOSE.
"PLEASANT HILL-- A S.H.I.E.L.D. PRISON HOUSING DANGEROUS SUPER VILLAINS TRANSFORMED INTO NORMAL CITIZENS BY THE KOBIK PROJECT.
"THIS PLACE HAS BEEN KEPT OFF THE RECORD, AND NOW WE'RE HEADING INTO THE EYE OF THE STORM, COMMANDOS.
"LOOKS LIKE ORRGO HAD BEEN SNOOPING AROUND KRAYE'S PERSONAL HISTORY, AND KRAYE FEARED HE WOULD BE EXPOSED AS A TRAITOR.
"FROM THE SOUND OF IT, THE PLACE IS CRAWLING WITH BAD GUYS, SO WE HAVE TO FIND ORRGO AND GET THE HELL OUT, FAST."
FRANK
FILARDI'S MEATS

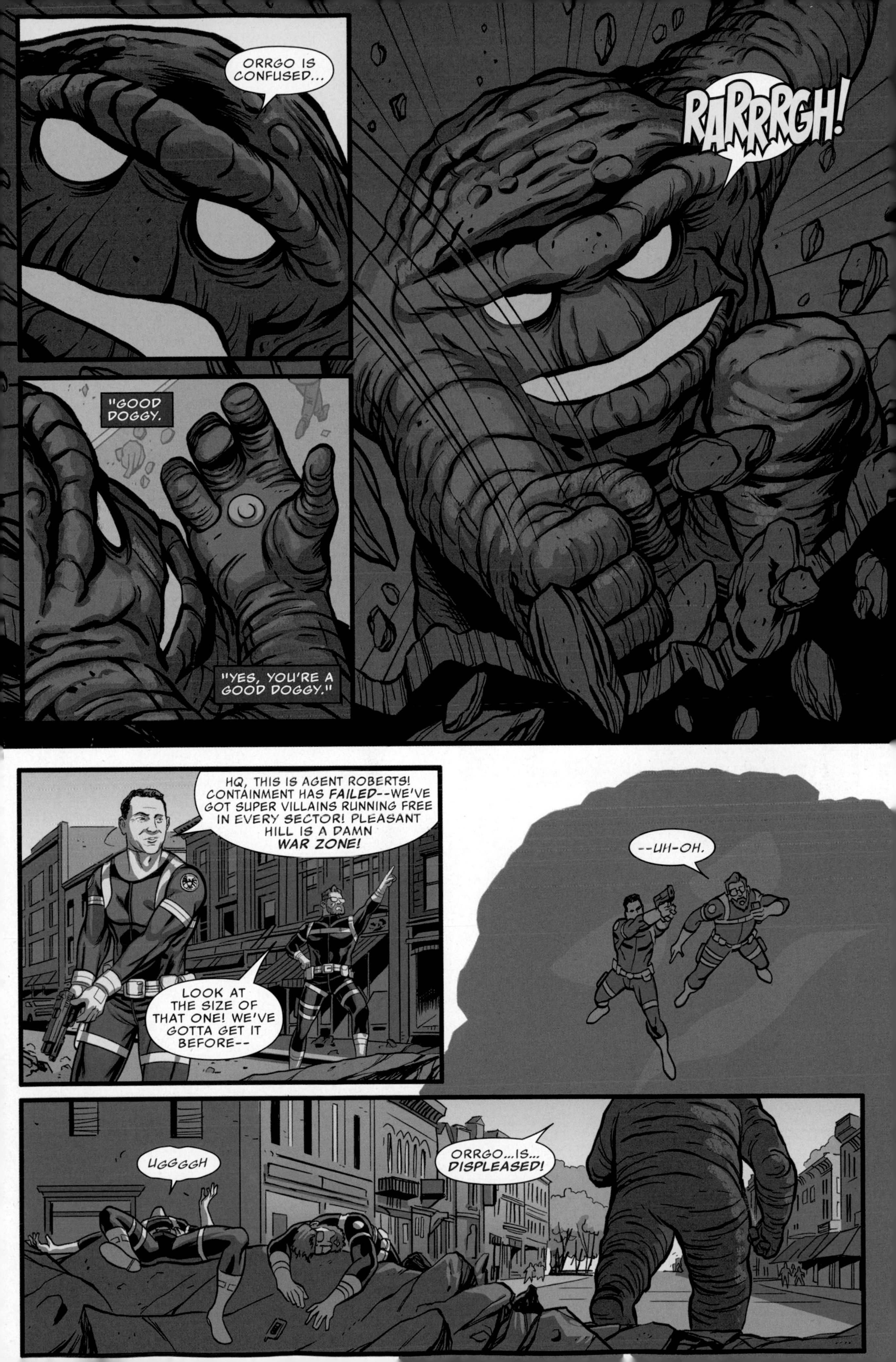
ORRGO IS CONFUSED...
"GOOD DOGGY.
"YES, YOU'RE A GOOD DOGGY."
RARRRGH!
HQ, THIS IS AGENT ROBERTS! CONTAINMENT HAS FAILED--WE'VE GOT SUPER VILLAINS RUNNING FREE IN EVERY SECTOR! PLEASANT HILL IS A DAMN WAR ZONE!
LOOK AT THE SIZE OF THAT ONE! WE'VE GOTTA GET IT BEFORE--
--UH-OH.
UGGGGH
ORRGO...IS... DISPLEASED!

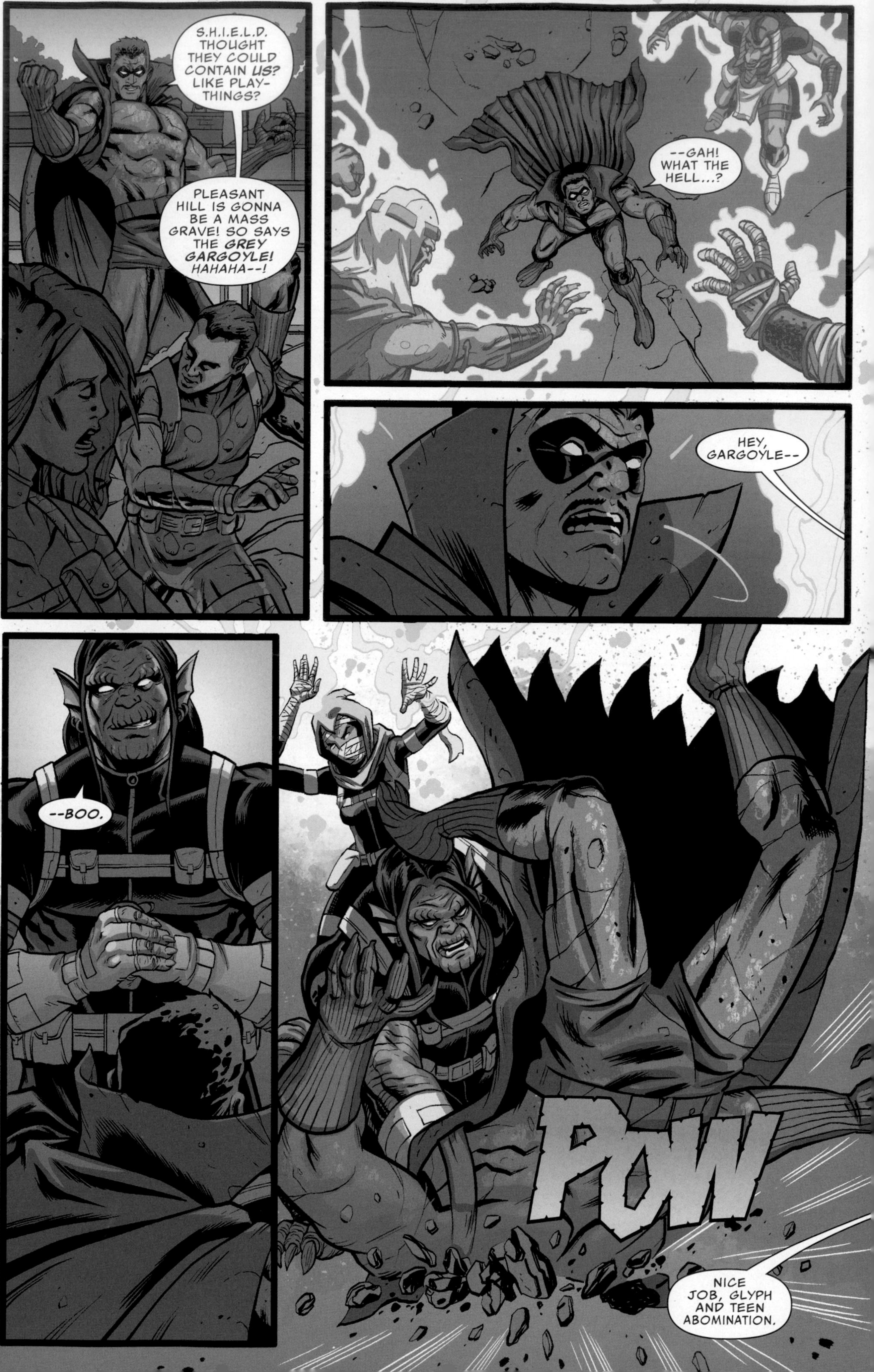
S.H.I.E.L.D. THOUGHT THEY COULD CONTAIN US? LIKE PLAY-THINGS?
PLEASANT HILL IS GONNA BE A MASS GRAVE! SO SAYS THE GREY GARGOYLE! HAHAHA--!
--GAH! WHAT THE HELL...?
HEY, GARGOYLE--
--BOO.
POW
NICE JOB, GLYPH AND TEEN ABOMINATION.

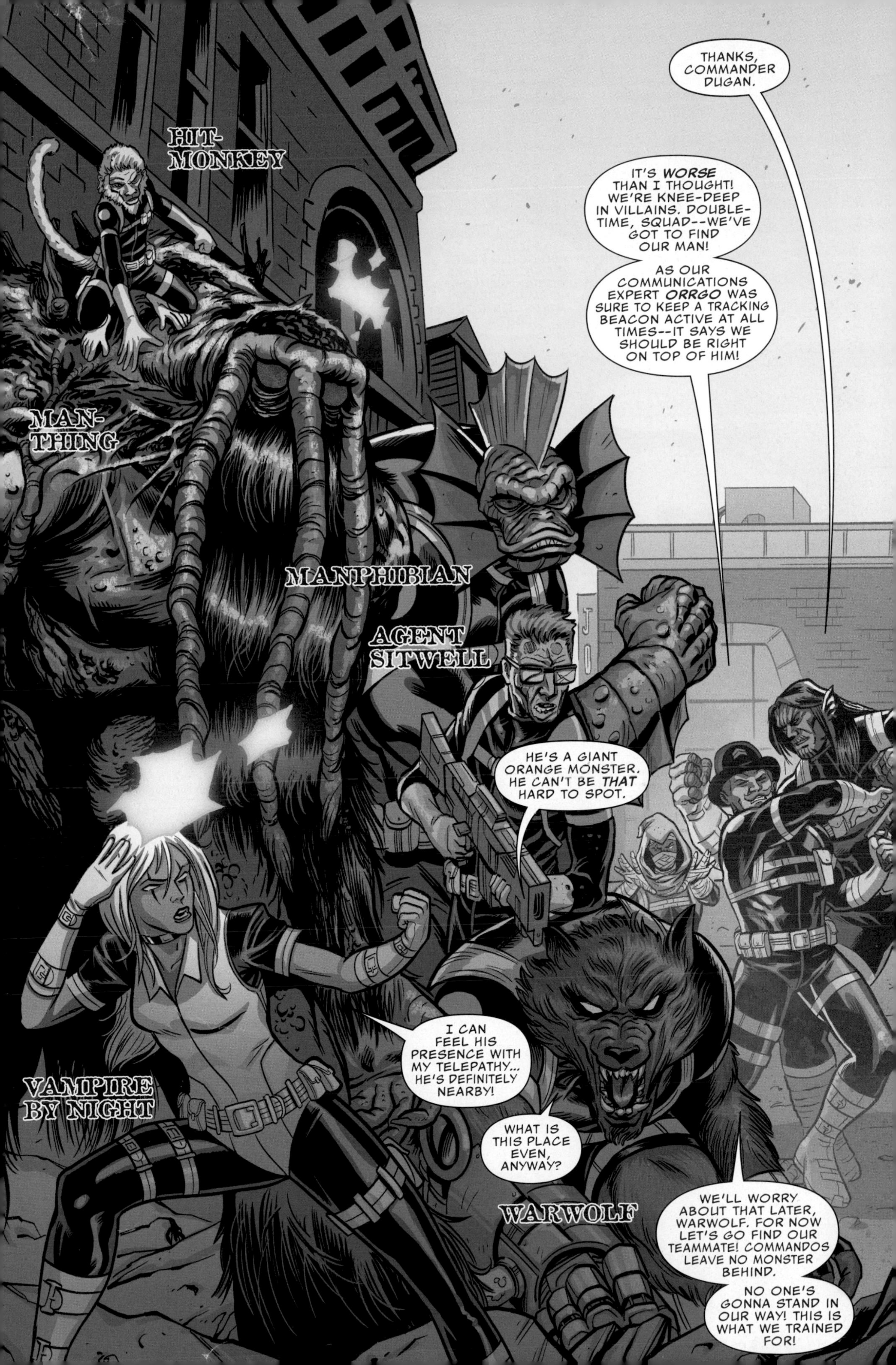
THANKS, COMMANDER DUGAN.
HIT-MONKEY
IT'S WORSE THAN I THOUGHT! WE'RE KNEE-DEEP IN VILLAINS. DOUBLE-TIME, SQUAD--WE'VE GOT TO FIND OUR MAN!
AS OUR COMMUNICATIONS EXPERT ORRGO WAS SURE TO KEEP A TRACKING BEACON ACTIVE AT ALL TIMES--IT SAYS WE SHOULD BE RIGHT ON TOP OF HIM!
MAN-THING
MANPHIBIAN
AGENT SITWELL
HE'S A GIANT ORANGE MONSTER. HE CAN'T BE THAT HARD TO SPOT.
I CAN FEEL HIS PRESENCE WITH MY TELEPATHY... HE'S DEFINITELY NEARBY!
VAMPIRE BY NIGHT
WHAT IS THIS PLACE EVEN, ANYWAY?
WARWOLF
WE'LL WORRY ABOUT THAT LATER, WARWOLF. FOR NOW LET'S GO FIND OUR TEAMMATE! COMMANDOS LEAVE NO MONSTER BEHIND.
NO ONE'S GONNA STAND IN OUR WAY! THIS IS WHAT WE TRAINED FOR!

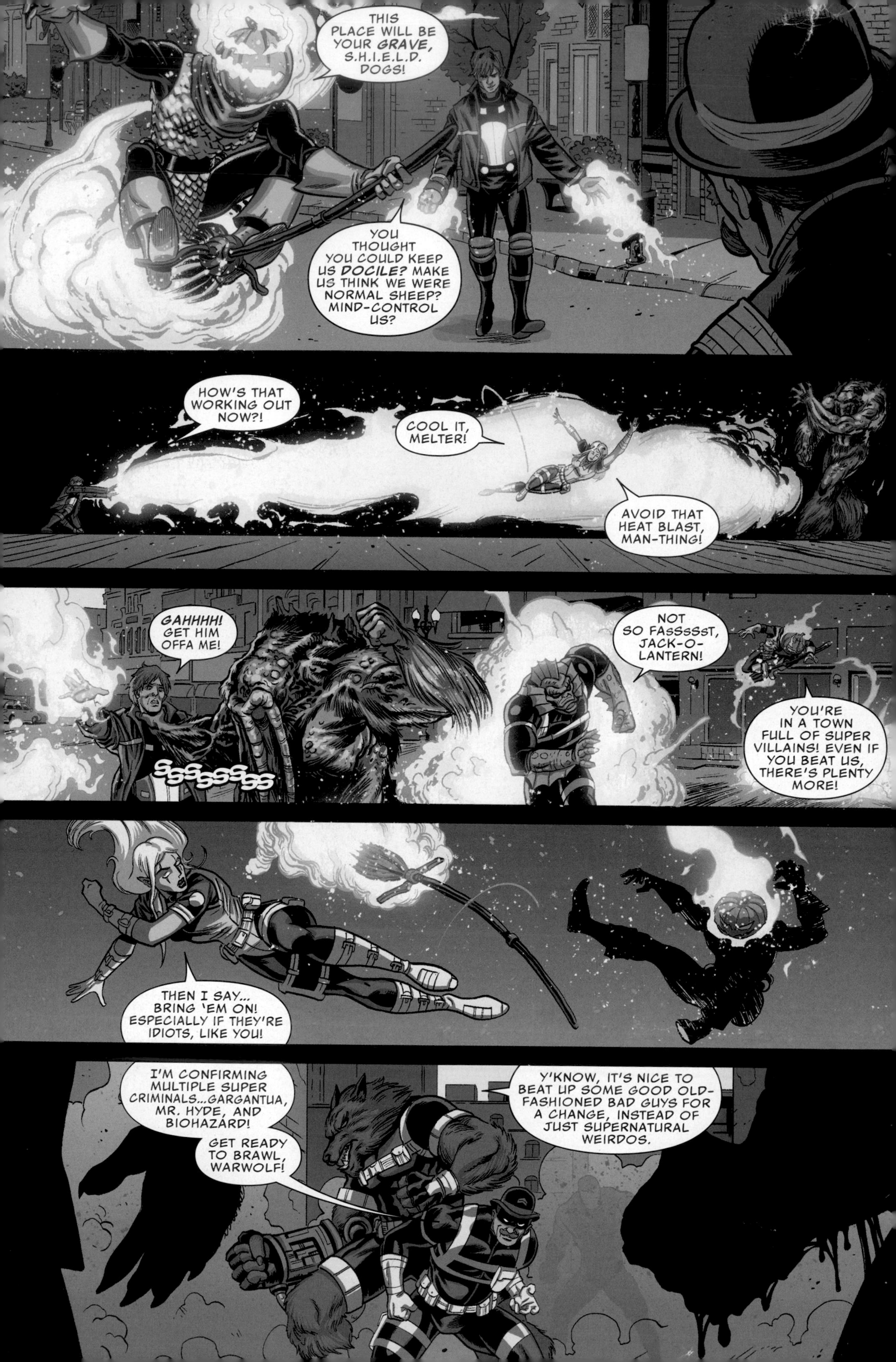
THIS PLACE WILL BE YOUR GRAVE, S.H.I.E.L.D. DOGS!
YOU THOUGHT YOU COULD KEEP US DOCILE? MAKE US THINK WE WERE NORMAL SHEEP? MIND-CONTROL US?
HOW'S THAT WORKING OUT NOW?!
COOL IT, MELTER!
AVOID THAT HEAT BLAST, MAN-THING!
GAHHHH! GET HIM OFFA ME!
SSSSSSSS
NOT SO FASSSSST, JACK-O-LANTERN!
YOU'RE IN A TOWN FULL OF SUPER VILLAINS! EVEN IF YOU BEAT US, THERE'S PLENTY MORE!
THEN I SAY... BRING 'EM ON! ESPECIALLY IF THEY'RE IDIOTS, LIKE YOU!
I'M CONFIRMING MULTIPLE SUPER CRIMINALS...GARGANTUA, MR. HYDE, AND BIOHAZARD!
GET READY TO BRAWL, WARWOLF!
Y'KNOW, IT'S NICE TO BEAT UP SOME GOOD OLD-FASHIONED BAD GUYS FOR A CHANGE, INSTEAD OF JUST SUPERNATURAL WEIRDOS.

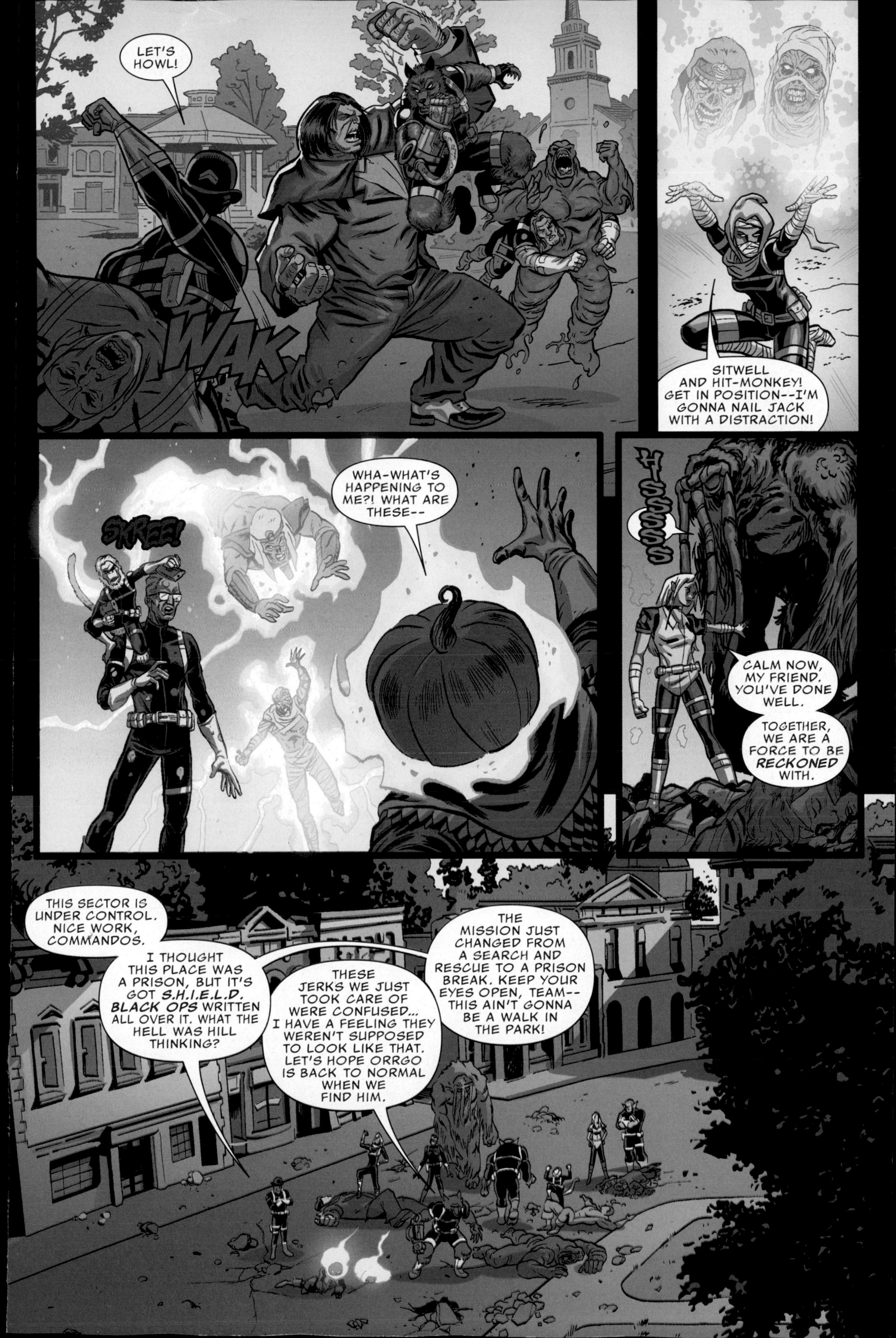

LET'S HOWL!
WAK
SITWELL AND HIT-MONKEY! GET IN POSITION--I'M GONNA NAIL JACK WITH A DISTRACTION!
SKREE!
WHA-WHAT'S HAPPENING TO ME?! WHAT ARE THESE--
HISSSSSS
CALM NOW, MY FRIEND. YOU'VE DONE WELL.
TOGETHER, WE ARE A FORCE TO BE RECKONED WITH.
THIS SECTOR IS UNDER CONTROL. NICE WORK, COMMANDOS.
I THOUGHT THIS PLACE WAS A PRISON, BUT IT'S GOT S.H.I.E.L.D. BLACK OPS WRITTEN ALL OVER IT. WHAT THE HELL WAS HILL THINKING?
THESE JERKS WE JUST TOOK CARE OF WERE CONFUSED... I HAVE A FEELING THEY WEREN'T SUPPOSED TO LOOK LIKE THAT. LET'S HOPE ORRGO IS BACK TO NORMAL WHEN WE FIND HIM.
THE MISSION JUST CHANGED FROM A SEARCH AND RESCUE TO A PRISON BREAK. KEEP YOUR EYES OPEN, TEAM--THIS AIN'T GONNA BE A WALK IN THE PARK!

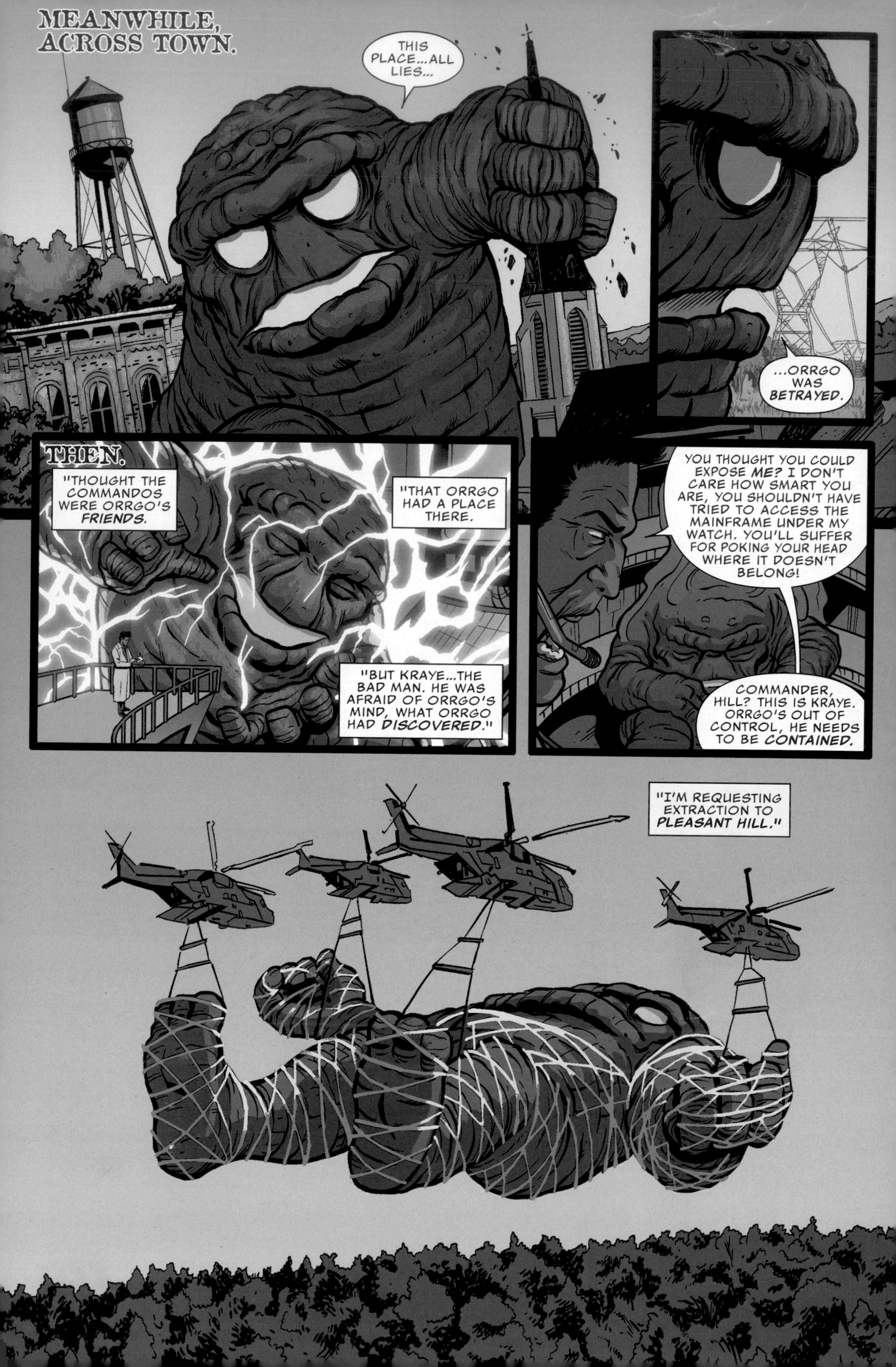
MEANWHILE, ACROSS TOWN.
THIS PLACE...ALL LIES...
...ORRGO WAS BETRAYED.
THEN.
"THOUGHT THE COMMANDOS WERE ORRGO'S FRIENDS.
"THAT ORRGO HAD A PLACE THERE.
"BUT KRAYE...THE BAD MAN. HE WAS AFRAID OF ORRGO'S MIND, WHAT ORRGO HAD DISCOVERED."
YOU THOUGHT YOU COULD EXPOSE ME? I DON'T CARE HOW SMART YOU ARE, YOU SHOULDN'T HAVE TRIED TO ACCESS THE MAINFRAME UNDER MY WATCH. YOU'LL SUFFER FOR POKING YOUR HEAD WHERE IT DOESN'T BELONG!
COMMANDER HILL? THIS IS KRAYE. ORRGO'S OUT OF CONTROL, HE NEEDS TO BE CONTAINED.
"I'M REQUESTING EXTRACTION TO PLEASANT HILL."

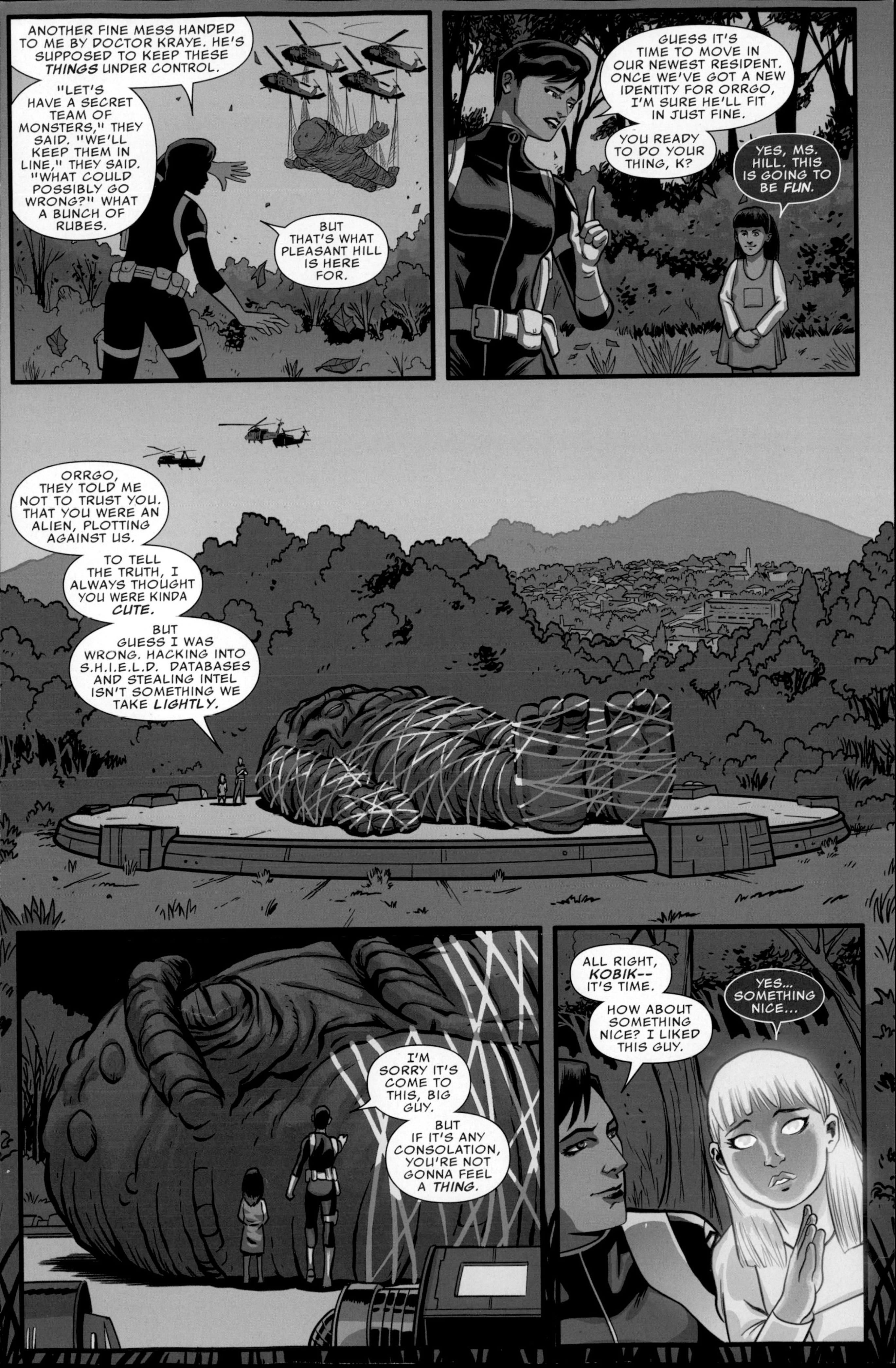
ANOTHER FINE MESS HANDED TO ME BY DOCTOR KRAYE. HE'S SUPPOSED TO KEEP THESE *THINGS* UNDER CONTROL.
"LET'S HAVE A SECRET TEAM OF MONSTERS," THEY SAID. "WE'LL KEEP THEM IN LINE," THEY SAID. "WHAT COULD POSSIBLY GO WRONG?" WHAT A BUNCH OF RUBES.
BUT THAT'S WHAT PLEASANT HILL IS HERE FOR.
GUESS IT'S TIME TO MOVE IN OUR NEWEST RESIDENT. ONCE WE'VE GOT A NEW IDENTITY FOR ORRGO, I'M SURE HE'LL FIT IN JUST FINE.
YOU READY TO DO YOUR THING, K?
YES, MS. HILL. THIS IS GOING TO BE *FUN*.
ORRGO, THEY TOLD ME NOT TO TRUST YOU. THAT YOU WERE AN ALIEN, PLOTTING AGAINST US.
TO TELL THE TRUTH, I ALWAYS THOUGHT YOU WERE KINDA *CUTE*.
BUT GUESS I WAS WRONG. HACKING INTO S.H.I.E.L.D. DATABASES AND STEALING INTEL ISN'T SOMETHING WE TAKE *LIGHTLY*.
I'M SORRY IT'S COME TO THIS, BIG GUY.
BUT IF IT'S ANY CONSOLATION, YOU'RE NOT GONNA FEEL A *THING*.
ALL RIGHT, *KOBIK*-- IT'S TIME.
HOW ABOUT SOMETHING NICE? I LIKED THIS GUY.
YES... SOMETHING NICE...

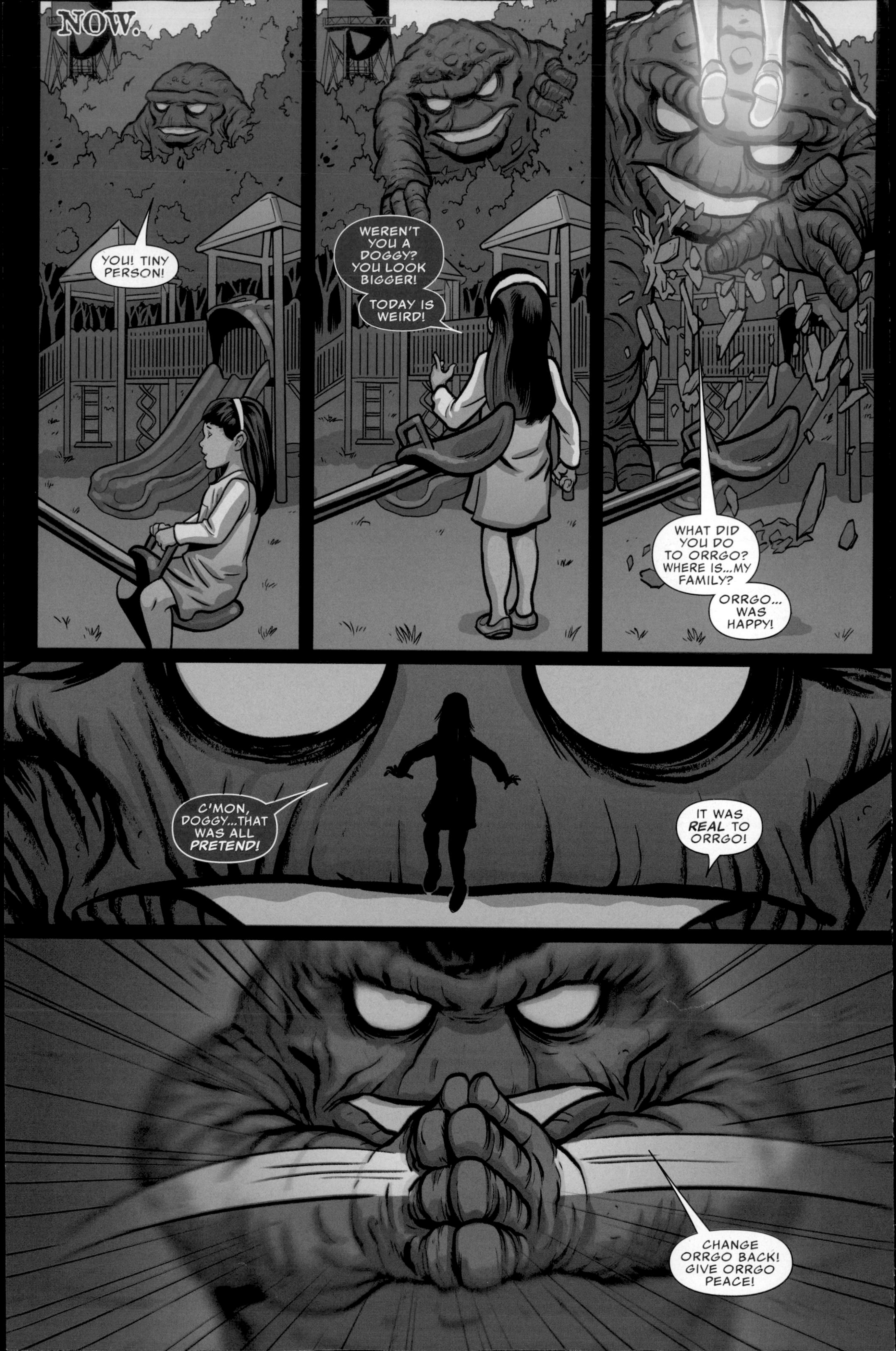
NOW.
YOU! TINY PERSON!
WEREN'T YOU A DOGGY? YOU LOOK BIGGER!
TODAY IS WEIRD!
WHAT DID YOU DO TO ORRGO? WHERE IS...MY FAMILY?
ORRGO... WAS HAPPY!
C'MON, DOGGY...THAT WAS ALL PRETEND!
IT WAS REAL TO ORRGO!
CHANGE ORRGO BACK! GIVE ORRGO PEACE!

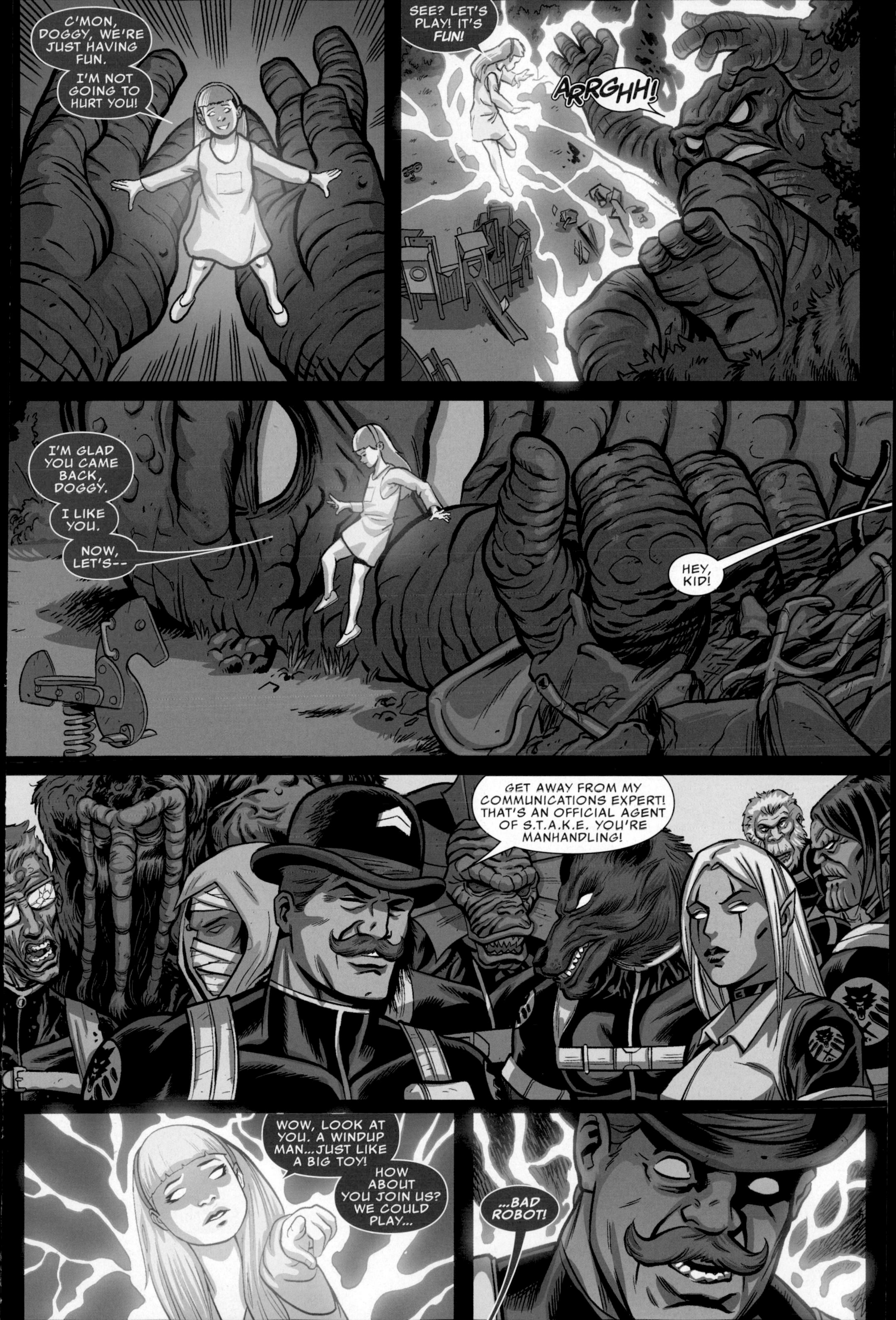
C'MON, DOGGY, WE'RE JUST HAVING FUN.
I'M NOT GOING TO HURT YOU!
SEE? LET'S PLAY! IT'S FUN!
ARRGHH!
I'M GLAD YOU CAME BACK, DOGGY.
I LIKE YOU.
NOW, LET'S--
HEY, KID!
GET AWAY FROM MY COMMUNICATIONS EXPERT! THAT'S AN OFFICIAL AGENT OF S.T.A.K.E. YOU'RE MANHANDLING!
WOW, LOOK AT YOU. A WINDUP MAN...JUST LIKE A BIG TOY!
HOW ABOUT YOU JOIN US? WE COULD PLAY...
...BAD ROBOT!

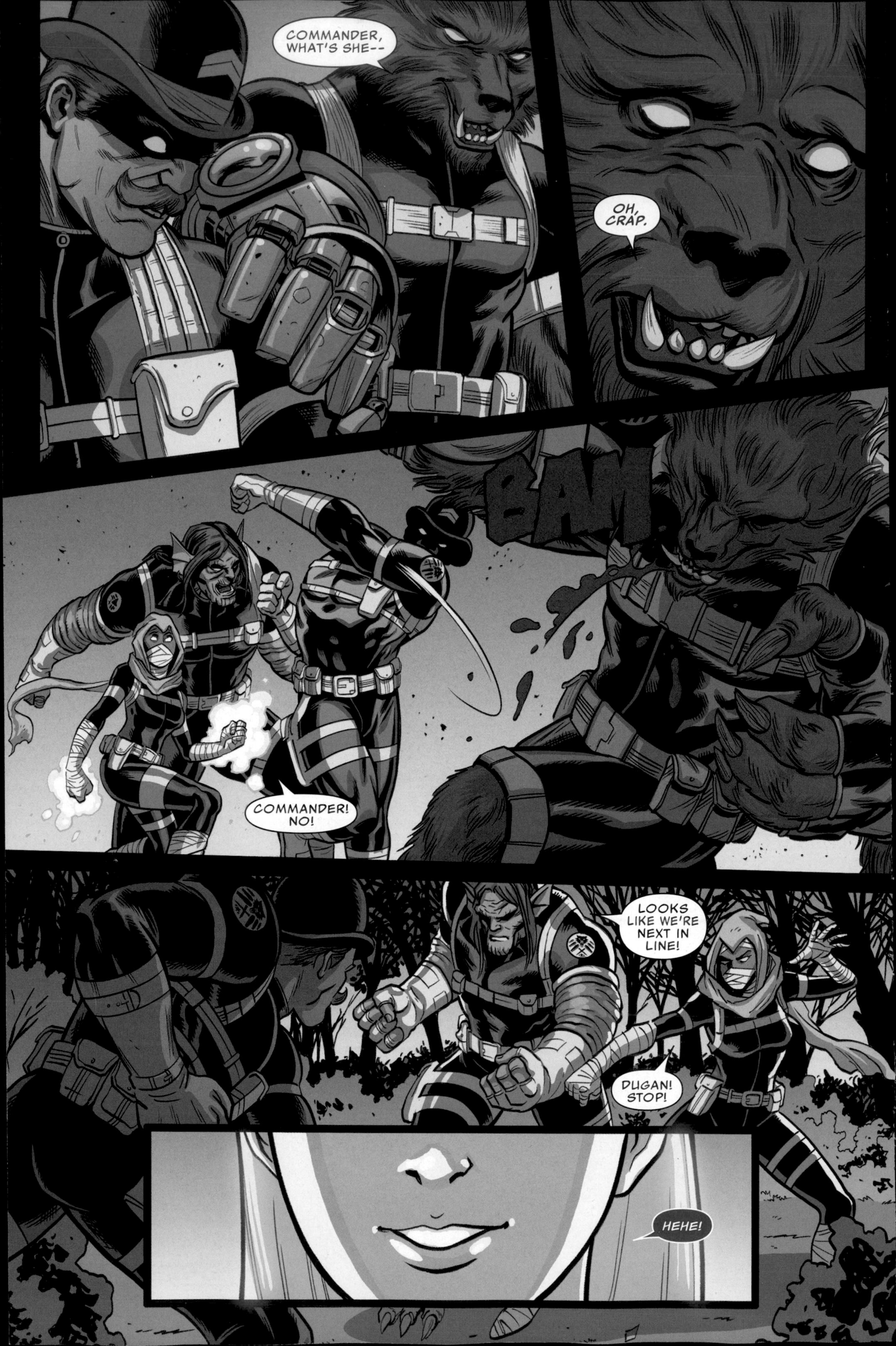
COMMANDER, WHAT'S SHE--
OH, CRAP.
BAM
COMMANDER! NO!
LOOKS LIKE WE'RE NEXT IN LINE!
DUGAN! STOP!
HEHE!

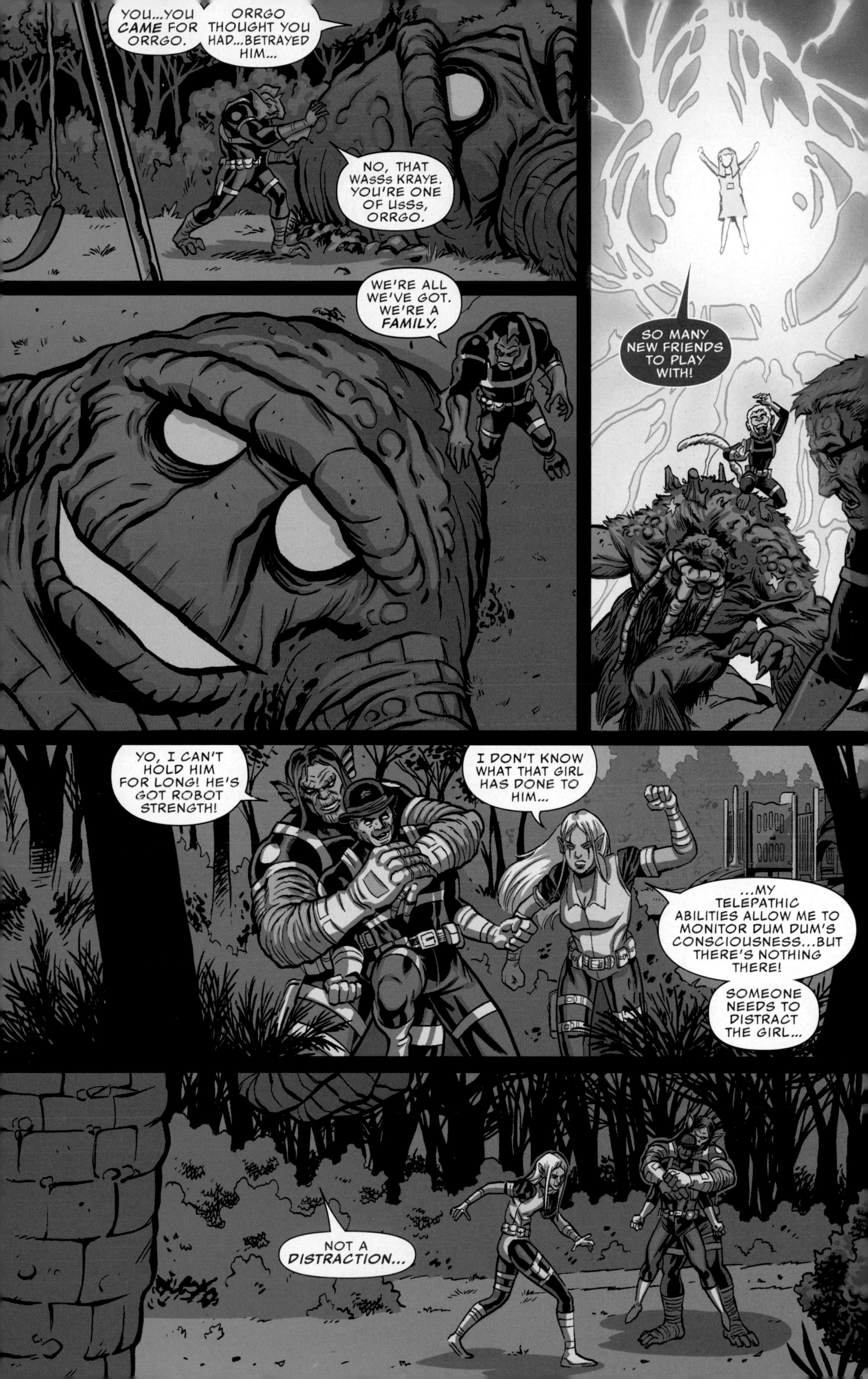
YOU...YOU CAME FOR ORRGO.
ORRGO THOUGHT YOU HAD...BETRAYED HIM...
NO, THAT WASSS KRAYE. YOU'RE ONE OF USSS, ORRGO.
WE'RE ALL WE'VE GOT. WE'RE A FAMILY.
SO MANY NEW FRIENDS TO PLAY WITH!
YO, I CAN'T HOLD HIM FOR LONG! HE'S GOT ROBOT STRENGTH!
I DON'T KNOW WHAT THAT GIRL HAS DONE TO HIM...
...MY TELEPATHIC ABILITIES ALLOW ME TO MONITOR DUM DUM'S CONSCIOUSNESS...BUT THERE'S NOTHING THERE!
SOMEONE NEEDS TO DISTRACT THE GIRL...
NOT A DISTRACTION...

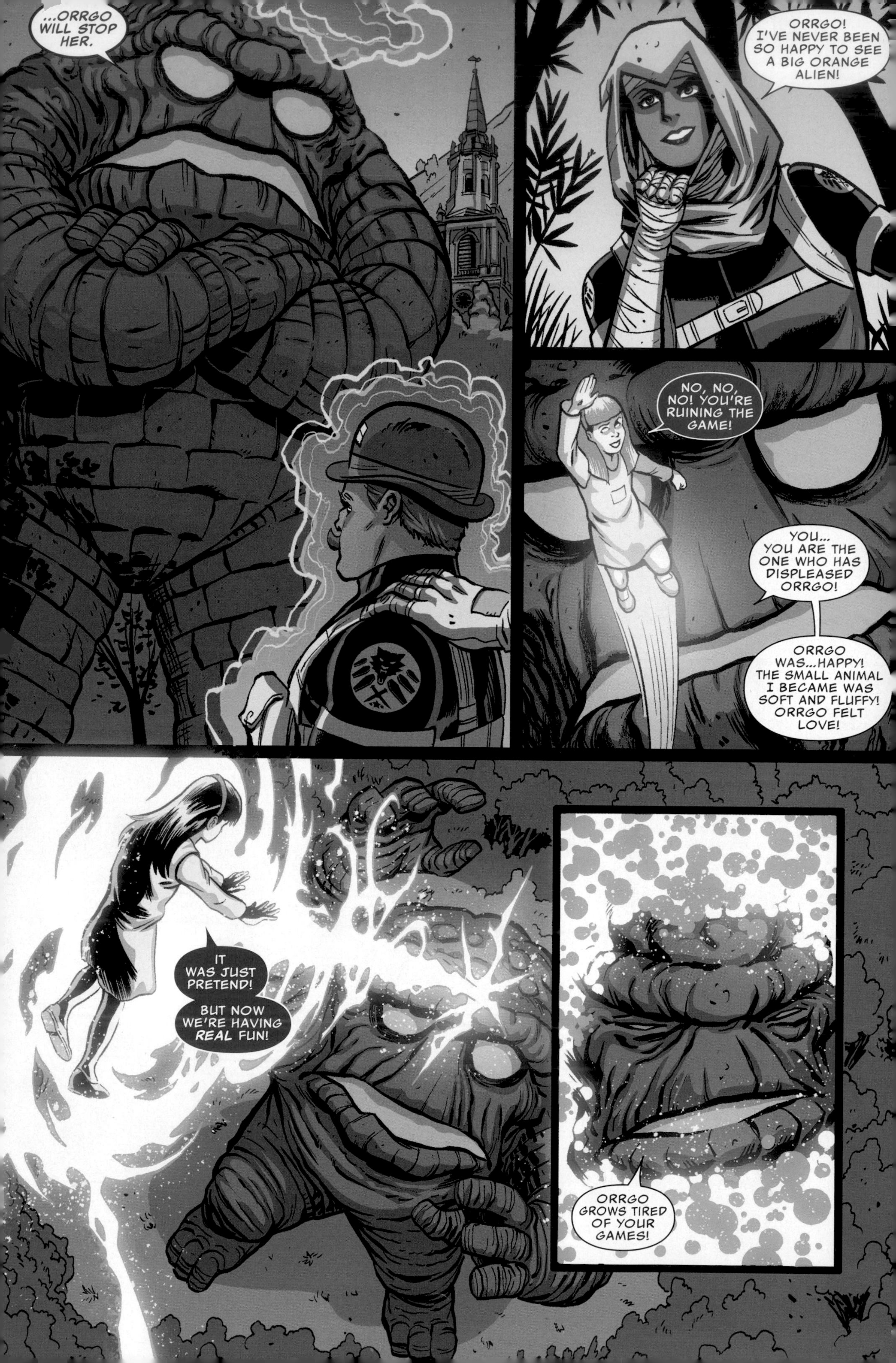
...ORRGO WILL STOP HER.
ORRGO! I'VE NEVER BEEN SO HAPPY TO SEE A BIG ORANGE ALIEN!
NO, NO, NO! YOU'RE RUINING THE GAME!
YOU... YOU ARE THE ONE WHO HAS DISPLEASED ORRGO!
ORRGO WAS...HAPPY! THE SMALL ANIMAL I BECAME WAS SOFT AND FLUFFY! ORRGO FELT LOVE!
IT WAS JUST PRETEND!
BUT NOW WE'RE HAVING REAL FUN!
ORRGO GROWS TIRED OF YOUR GAMES!

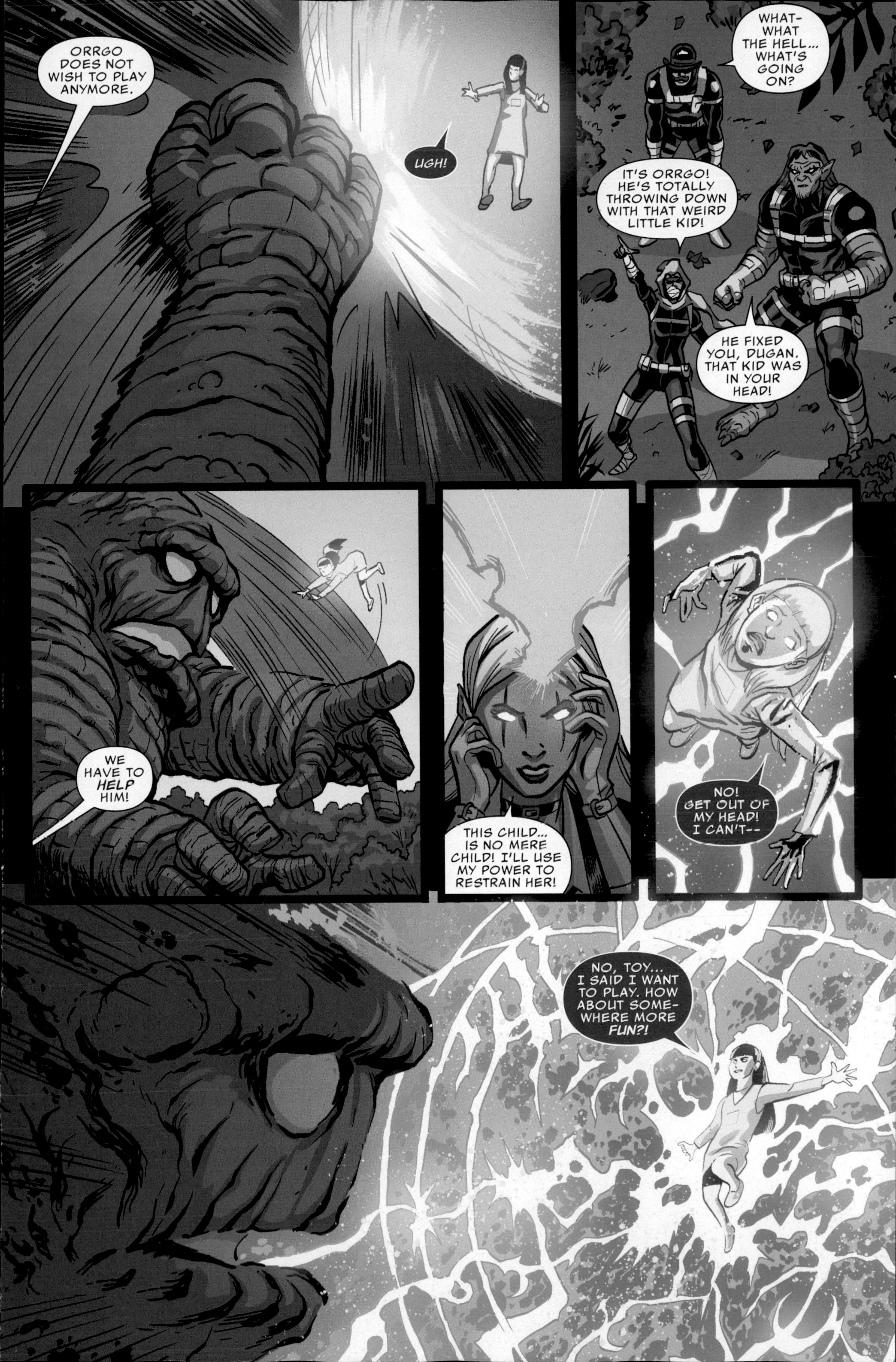
ORRGO DOES NOT WISH TO PLAY ANYMORE.
UGH!
WHAT-WHAT THE HELL... WHAT'S GOING ON?
IT'S ORRGO! HE'S TOTALLY THROWING DOWN WITH THAT WEIRD LITTLE KID!
HE FIXED YOU, DUGAN. THAT KID WAS IN YOUR HEAD!
WE HAVE TO HELP HIM!
THIS CHILD... IS NO MERE CHILD! I'LL USE MY POWER TO RESTRAIN HER!
NO! GET OUT OF MY HEAD! I CAN'T--
NO, TOY... I SAID I WANT TO PLAY. HOW ABOUT SOME-WHERE MORE FUN?!

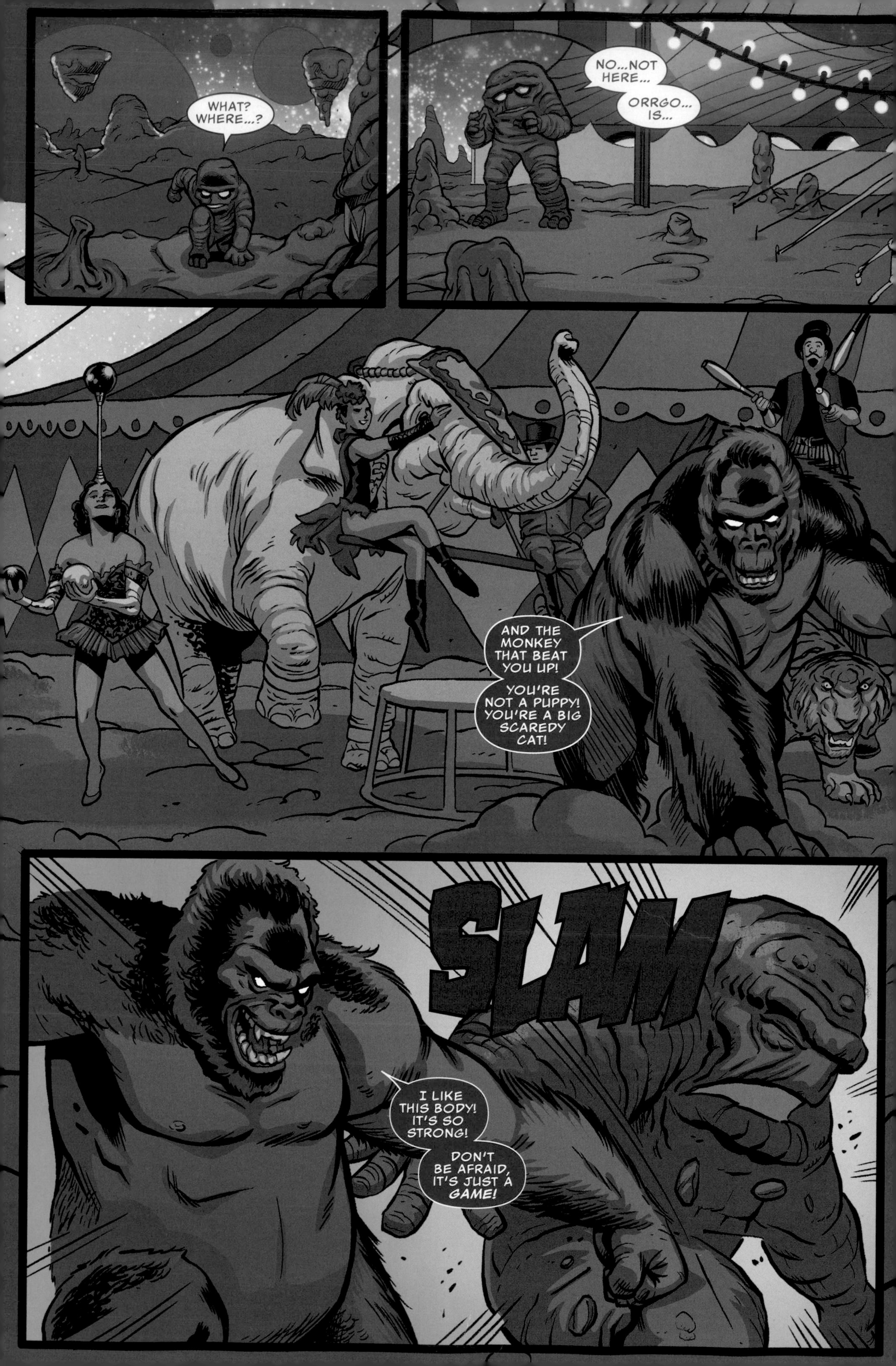
WHAT? WHERE...?
NO...NOT HERE...
ORRGO... IS...
AND THE MONKEY THAT BEAT YOU UP!
YOU'RE NOT A PUPPY! YOU'RE A BIG SCAREDY CAT!
SLAM
I LIKE THIS BODY! IT'S SO STRONG!
DON'T BE AFRAID, IT'S JUST A GAME!

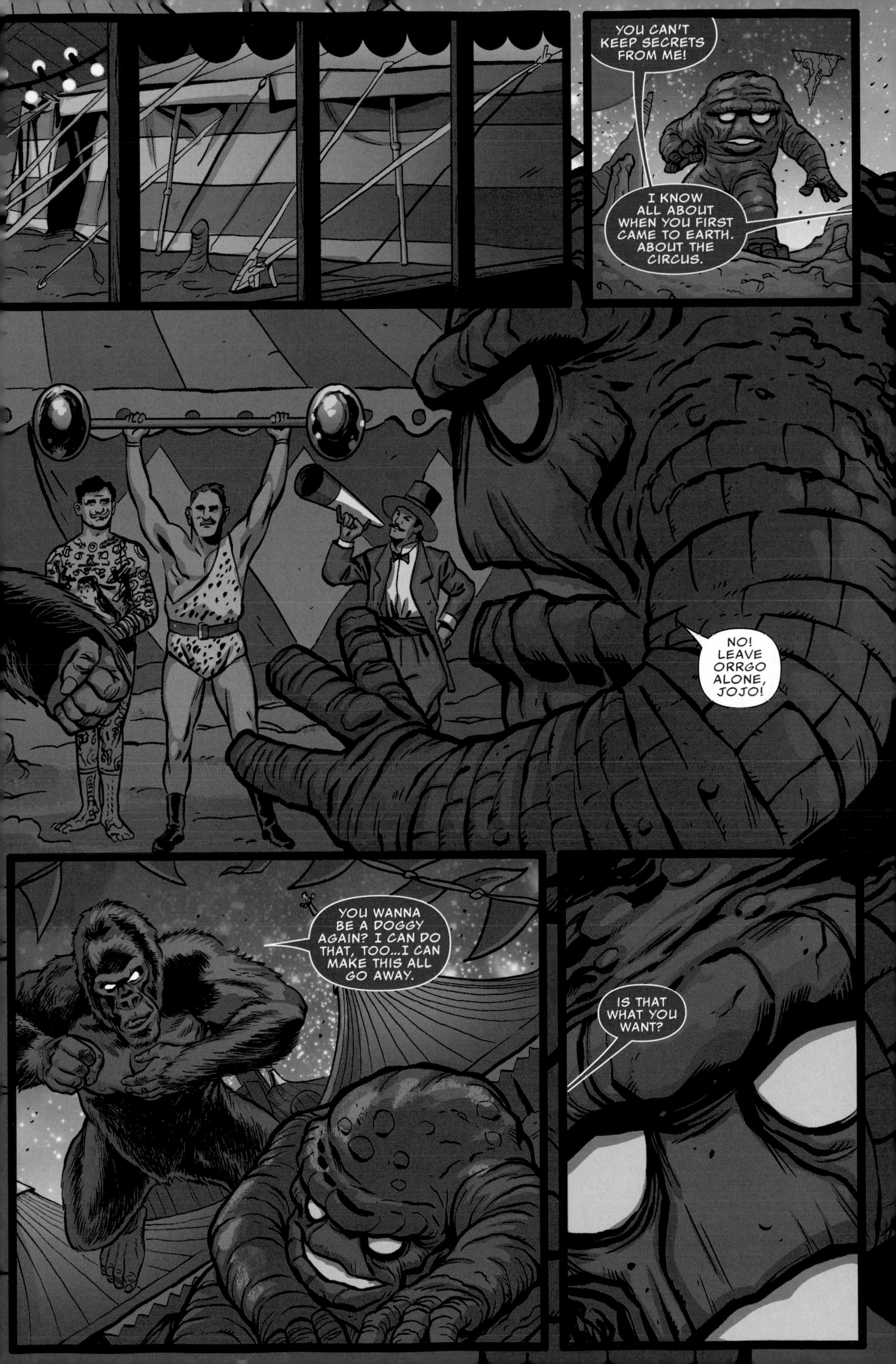
YOU CAN'T KEEP SECRETS FROM ME!
I KNOW ALL ABOUT WHEN YOU FIRST CAME TO EARTH. ABOUT THE CIRCUS.
NO! LEAVE ORRGO ALONE, JOJO!
YOU WANNA BE A DOGGY AGAIN? I CAN DO THAT, TOO...I CAN MAKE THIS ALL GO AWAY.
IS THAT WHAT YOU WANT?

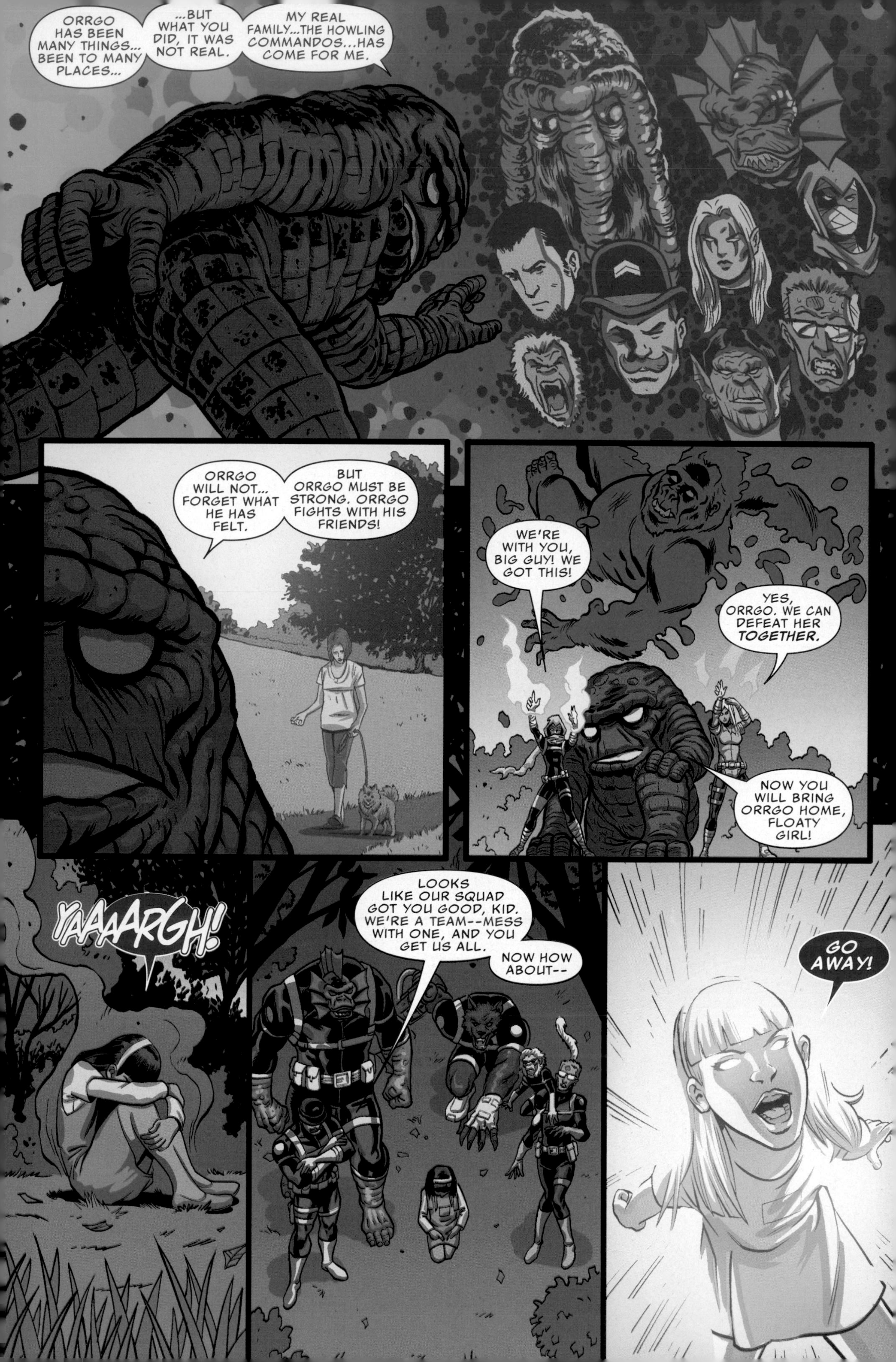
ORRGO HAS BEEN MANY THINGS... BEEN TO MANY PLACES...
...BUT WHAT YOU DID, IT WAS NOT REAL.
MY REAL FAMILY...THE HOWLING COMMANDOS...HAS COME FOR ME.
ORRGO WILL NOT... FORGET WHAT HE HAS FELT.
BUT ORRGO MUST BE STRONG. ORRGO FIGHTS WITH HIS FRIENDS!
WE'RE WITH YOU, BIG GUY! WE GOT THIS!
YES, ORRGO. WE CAN DEFEAT HER TOGETHER.
NOW YOU WILL BRING ORRGO HOME, FLOATY GIRL!
YAAAARGH!
LOOKS LIKE OUR SQUAD GOT YOU GOOD, KID. WE'RE A TEAM--MESS WITH ONE, AND YOU GET US ALL.
NOW HOW ABOUT--
GO AWAY!

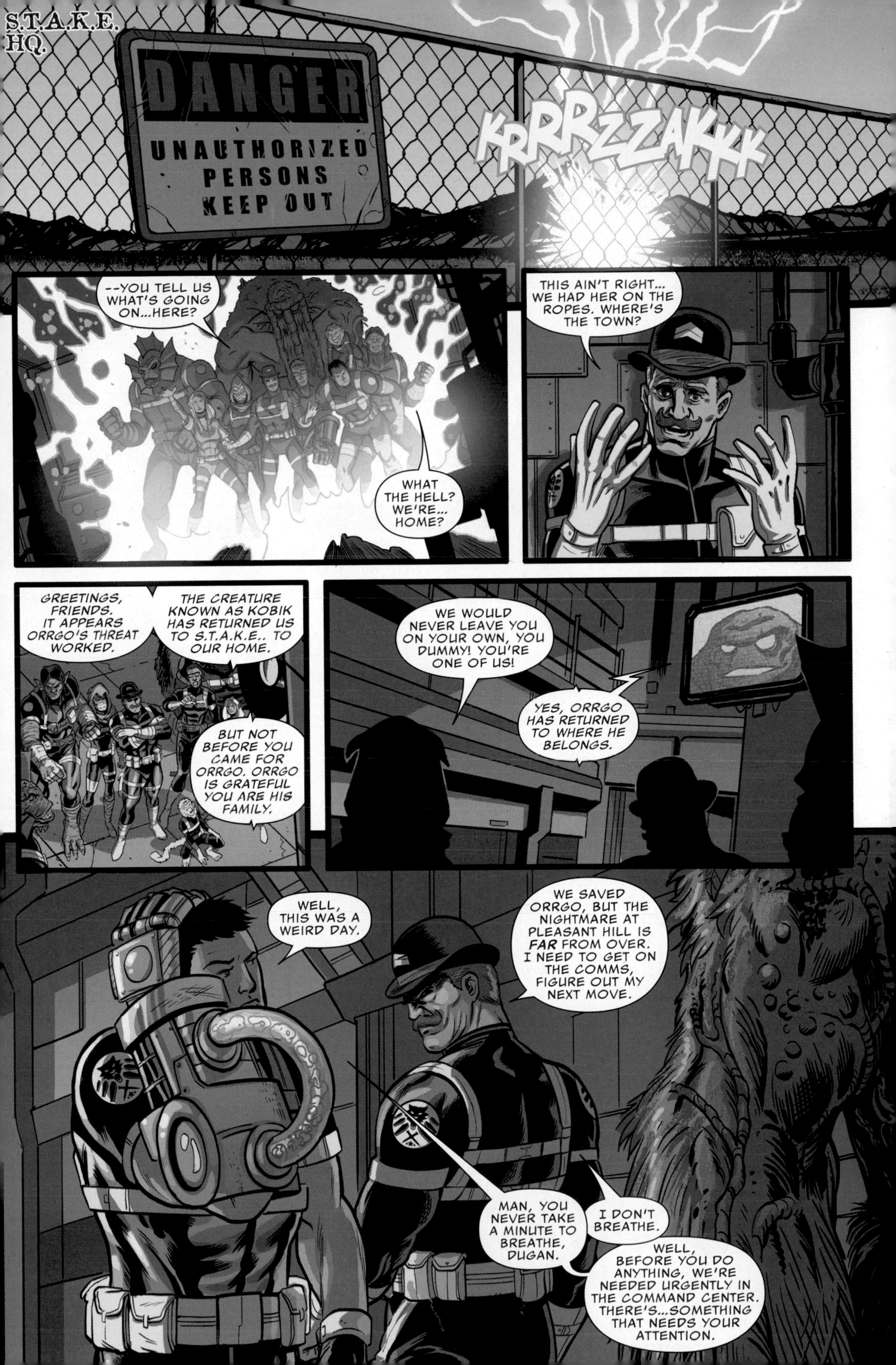
S.T.A.K.E. HQ.
DANGER
UNAUTHORIZED PERSONS KEEP OUT
KRRRZZZAKKK
--YOU TELL US WHAT'S GOING ON...HERE?
WHAT THE HELL? WE'RE... HOME?
THIS AIN'T RIGHT... WE HAD HER ON THE ROPES. WHERE'S THE TOWN?
GREETINGS, FRIENDS. IT APPEARS ORRGO'S THREAT WORKED.
THE CREATURE KNOWN AS KOBIK HAS RETURNED US TO S.T.A.K.E.. TO OUR HOME.
BUT NOT BEFORE YOU CAME FOR ORRGO. ORRGO IS GRATEFUL YOU ARE HIS FAMILY.
WE WOULD NEVER LEAVE YOU ON YOUR OWN, YOU DUMMY! YOU'RE ONE OF US!
YES, ORRGO HAS RETURNED TO WHERE HE BELONGS.
WELL, THIS WAS A WEIRD DAY.
WE SAVED ORRGO, BUT THE NIGHTMARE AT PLEASANT HILL IS FAR FROM OVER. I NEED TO GET ON THE COMMS, FIGURE OUT MY NEXT MOVE.
MAN, YOU NEVER TAKE A MINUTE TO BREATHE, DUGAN.
I DON'T BREATHE.
WELL, BEFORE YOU DO ANYTHING, WE'RE NEEDED URGENTLY IN THE COMMAND CENTER. THERE'S...SOMETHING THAT NEEDS YOUR ATTENTION.

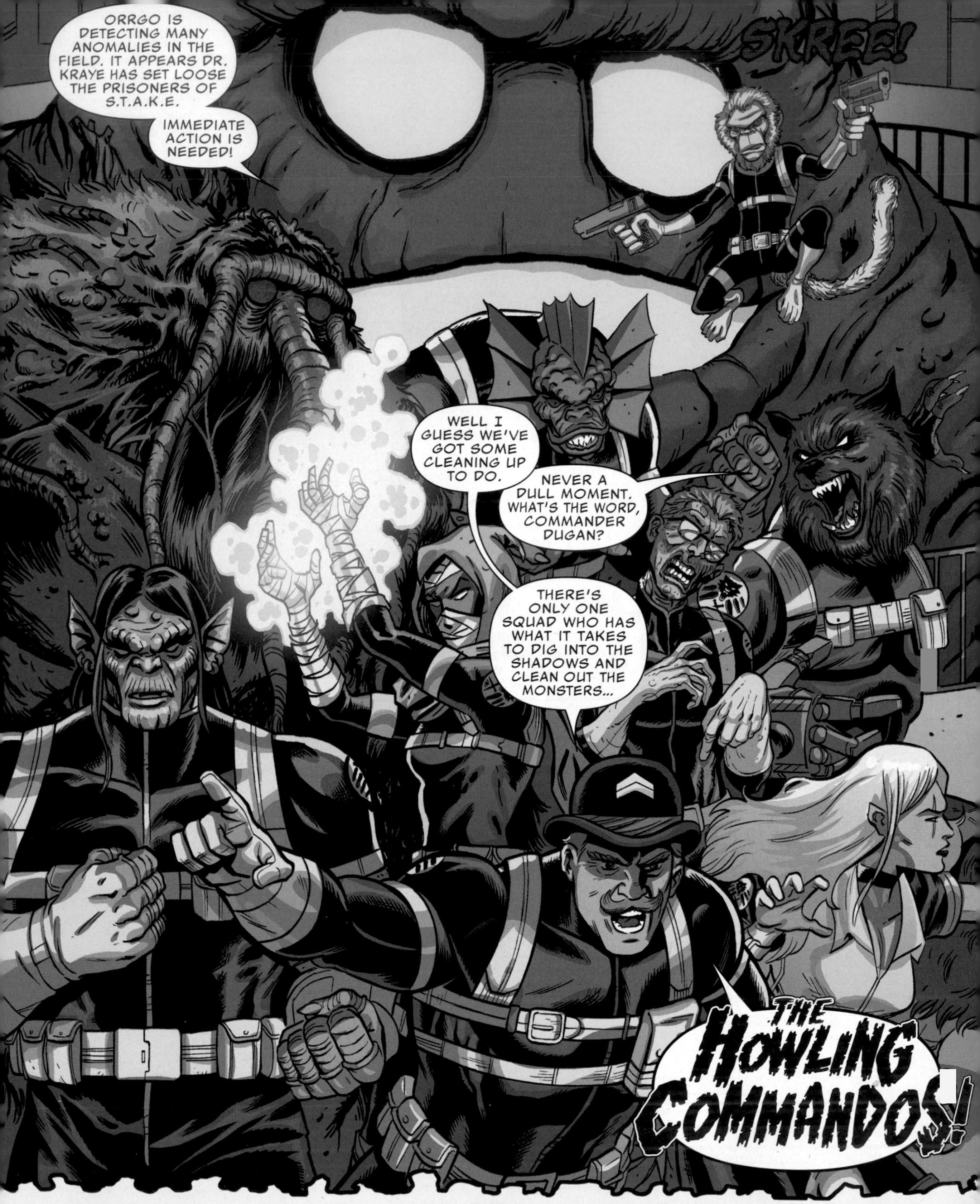
SKREE!
ORRGO IS DETECTING MANY ANOMALIES IN THE FIELD. IT APPEARS DR. KRAYE HAS SET LOOSE THE PRISONERS OF S.T.A.K.E.
IMMEDIATE ACTION IS NEEDED!
WELL I GUESS WE'VE GOT SOME CLEANING UP TO DO.
NEVER A DULL MOMENT. WHAT'S THE WORD, COMMANDER DUGAN?
THERE'S ONLY ONE SQUAD WHO HAS WHAT IT TAKES TO DIG INTO THE SHADOWS AND CLEAN OUT THE MONSTERS...
THE HOWLING COMMANDOS!

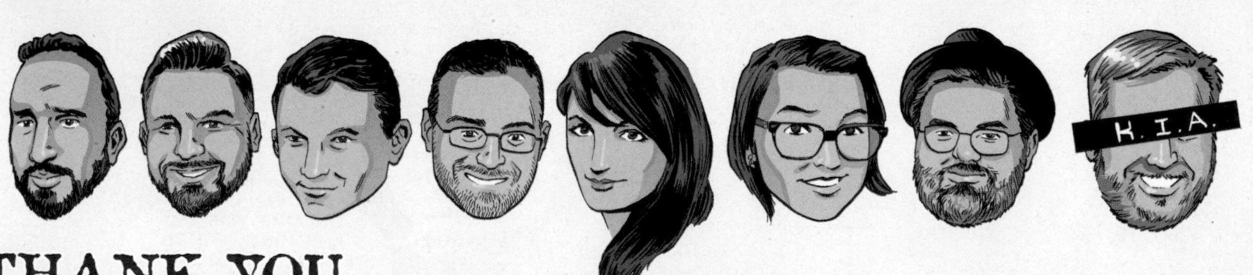
K.I.A.

THANK YOU

from the whole team at Howler HQ for joining us on this mission!
Until we meet again, stay away from things that go bump in the night!

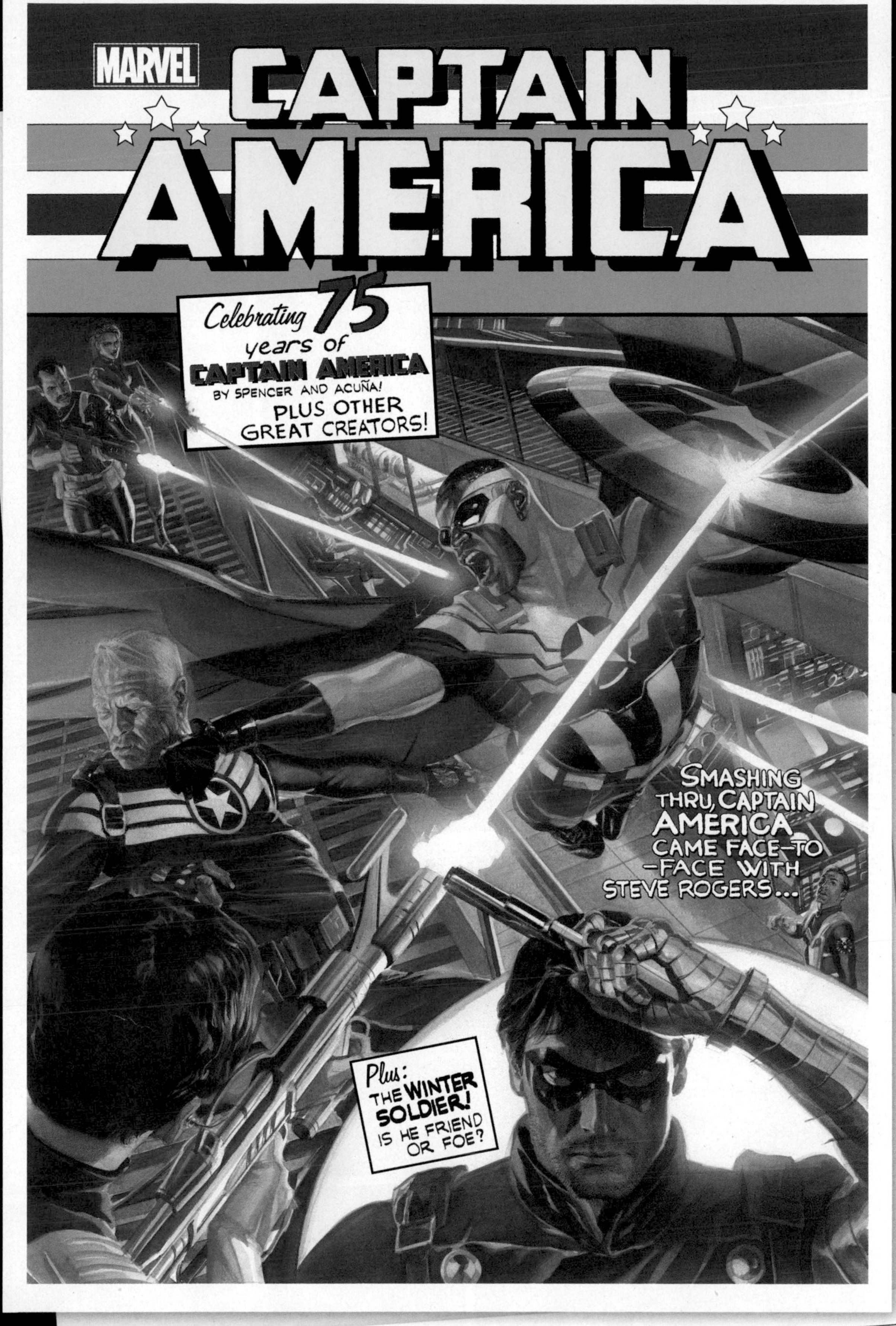
MARVEL
CAPTAIN AMERICA
Celebrating 75 years of CAPTAIN AMERICA
BY SPENCER AND ACUÑA!
PLUS OTHER GREAT CREATORS!
SMASHING THRU, CAPTAIN AMERICA CAME FACE-TO-FACE WITH STEVE ROGERS...
Plus: THE WINTER SOLDIER! IS HE FRIEND OR FOE?

Captain America: Sam Wilson No. 7

Mission Brief

After Steve Rogers was drained of the super-soldier serum that kept him young and strong, he passed his shield to his longtime ally Sam Wilson, A.K.A. The Falcon.

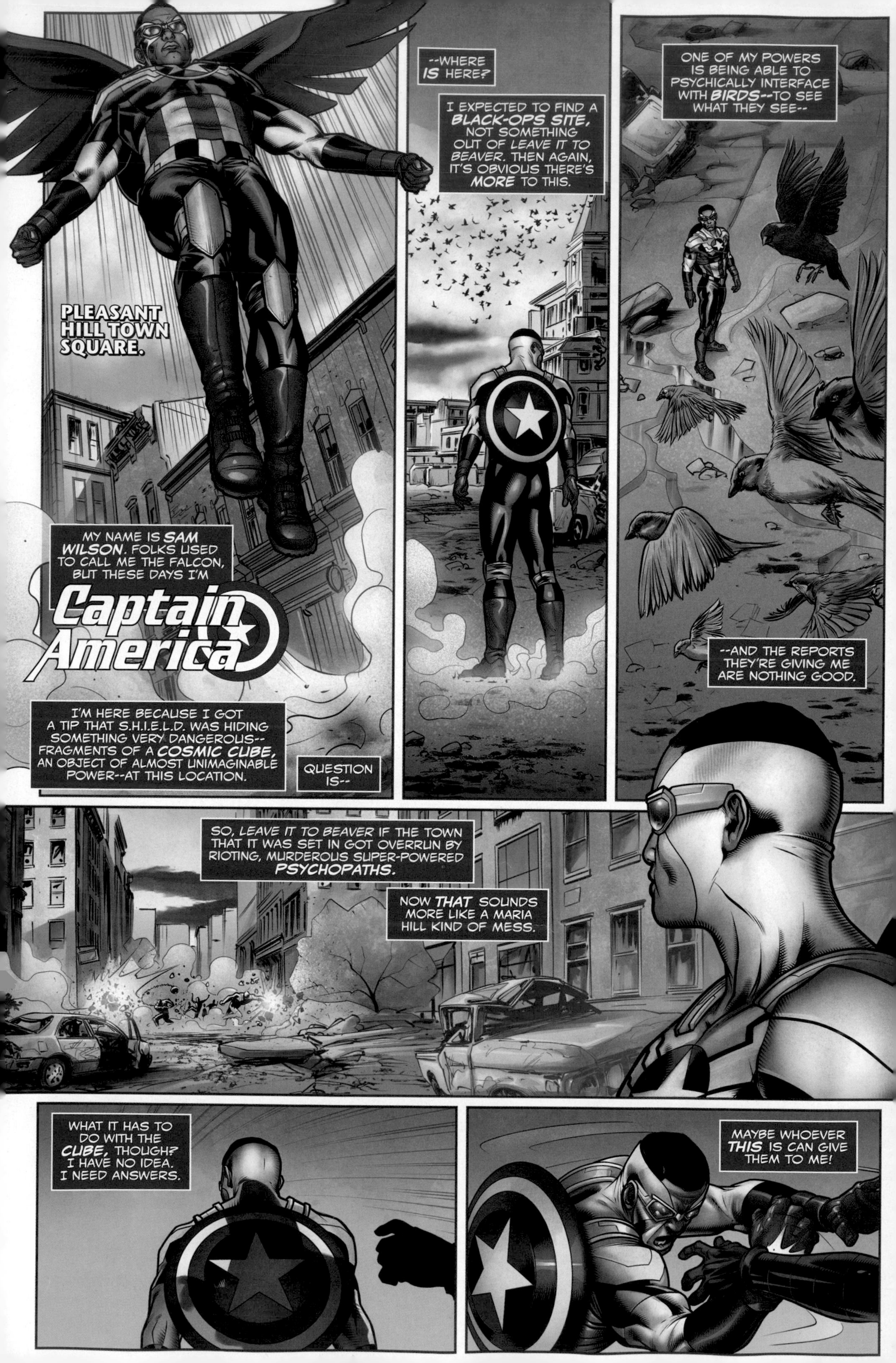
PLEASANT HILL TOWN SQUARE.
MY NAME IS SAM WILSON. FOLKS USED TO CALL ME THE FALCON, BUT THESE DAYS I'M
Captain America
I'M HERE BECAUSE I GOT A TIP THAT S.H.I.E.L.D. WAS HIDING SOMETHING VERY DANGEROUS--FRAGMENTS OF A COSMIC CUBE, AN OBJECT OF ALMOST UNIMAGINABLE POWER--AT THIS LOCATION.
QUESTION IS--
--WHERE IS HERE?
I EXPECTED TO FIND A BLACK-OPS SITE, NOT SOMETHING OUT OF LEAVE IT TO BEAVER. THEN AGAIN, IT'S OBVIOUS THERE'S MORE TO THIS.
ONE OF MY POWERS IS BEING ABLE TO PSYCHICALLY INTERFACE WITH BIRDS--TO SEE WHAT THEY SEE--
--AND THE REPORTS THEY'RE GIVING ME ARE NOTHING GOOD.
SO, LEAVE IT TO BEAVER IF THE TOWN THAT IT WAS SET IN GOT OVERRUN BY RIOTING, MURDEROUS SUPER-POWERED PSYCHOPATHS.
NOW THAT SOUNDS MORE LIKE A MARIA HILL KIND OF MESS.
WHAT IT HAS TO DO WITH THE CUBE, THOUGH? I HAVE NO IDEA. I NEED ANSWERS.
MAYBE WHOEVER THIS IS CAN GIVE THEM TO ME!

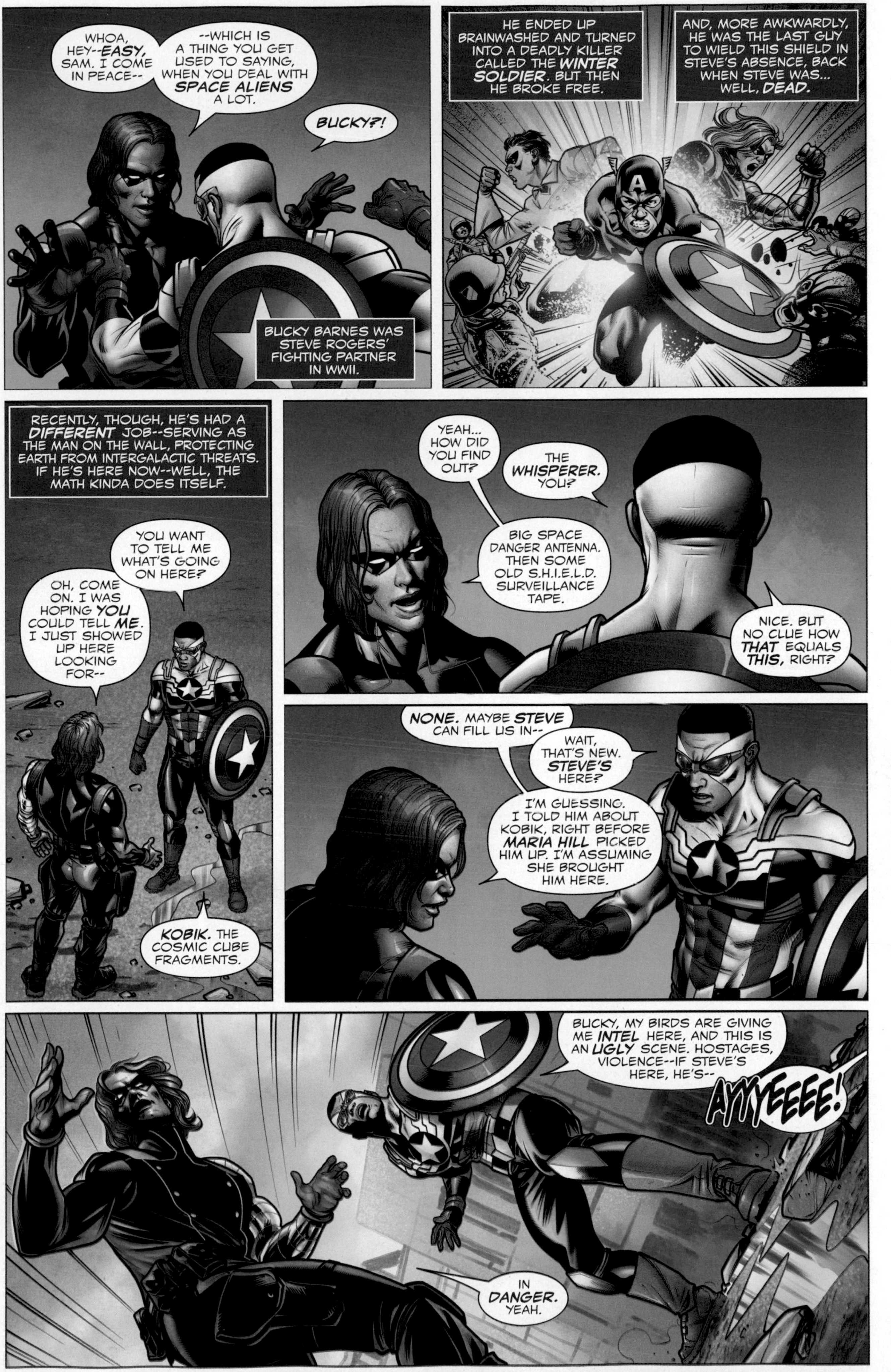

WHOA, HEY--EASY, SAM. I COME IN PEACE--
--WHICH IS A THING YOU GET USED TO SAYING, WHEN YOU DEAL WITH SPACE ALIENS A LOT.
BUCKY?!
BUCKY BARNES WAS STEVE ROGERS' FIGHTING PARTNER IN WWII.
HE ENDED UP BRAINWASHED AND TURNED INTO A DEADLY KILLER CALLED THE WINTER SOLDIER. BUT THEN HE BROKE FREE.
AND, MORE AWKWARDLY, HE WAS THE LAST GUY TO WIELD THIS SHIELD IN STEVE'S ABSENCE, BACK WHEN STEVE WAS... WELL, DEAD.
RECENTLY, THOUGH, HE'S HAD A DIFFERENT JOB--SERVING AS THE MAN ON THE WALL, PROTECTING EARTH FROM INTERGALACTIC THREATS. IF HE'S HERE NOW--WELL, THE MATH KINDA DOES ITSELF.
YOU WANT TO TELL ME WHAT'S GOING ON HERE?
OH, COME ON. I WAS HOPING YOU COULD TELL ME. I JUST SHOWED UP HERE LOOKING FOR--
KOBIK. THE COSMIC CUBE FRAGMENTS.
YEAH... HOW DID YOU FIND OUT?
THE WHISPERER. YOU?
BIG SPACE DANGER ANTENNA. THEN SOME OLD S.H.I.E.L.D. SURVEILLANCE TAPE.
NICE. BUT NO CLUE HOW THAT EQUALS THIS, RIGHT?
NONE. MAYBE STEVE CAN FILL US IN--
WAIT, THAT'S NEW. STEVE'S HERE?
I'M GUESSING. I TOLD HIM ABOUT KOBIK, RIGHT BEFORE MARIA HILL PICKED HIM UP. I'M ASSUMING SHE BROUGHT HIM HERE.
BUCKY, MY BIRDS ARE GIVING ME INTEL HERE, AND THIS IS AN UGLY SCENE. HOSTAGES, VIOLENCE--IF STEVE'S HERE, HE'S--
AYYEEEE!
IN DANGER. YEAH.

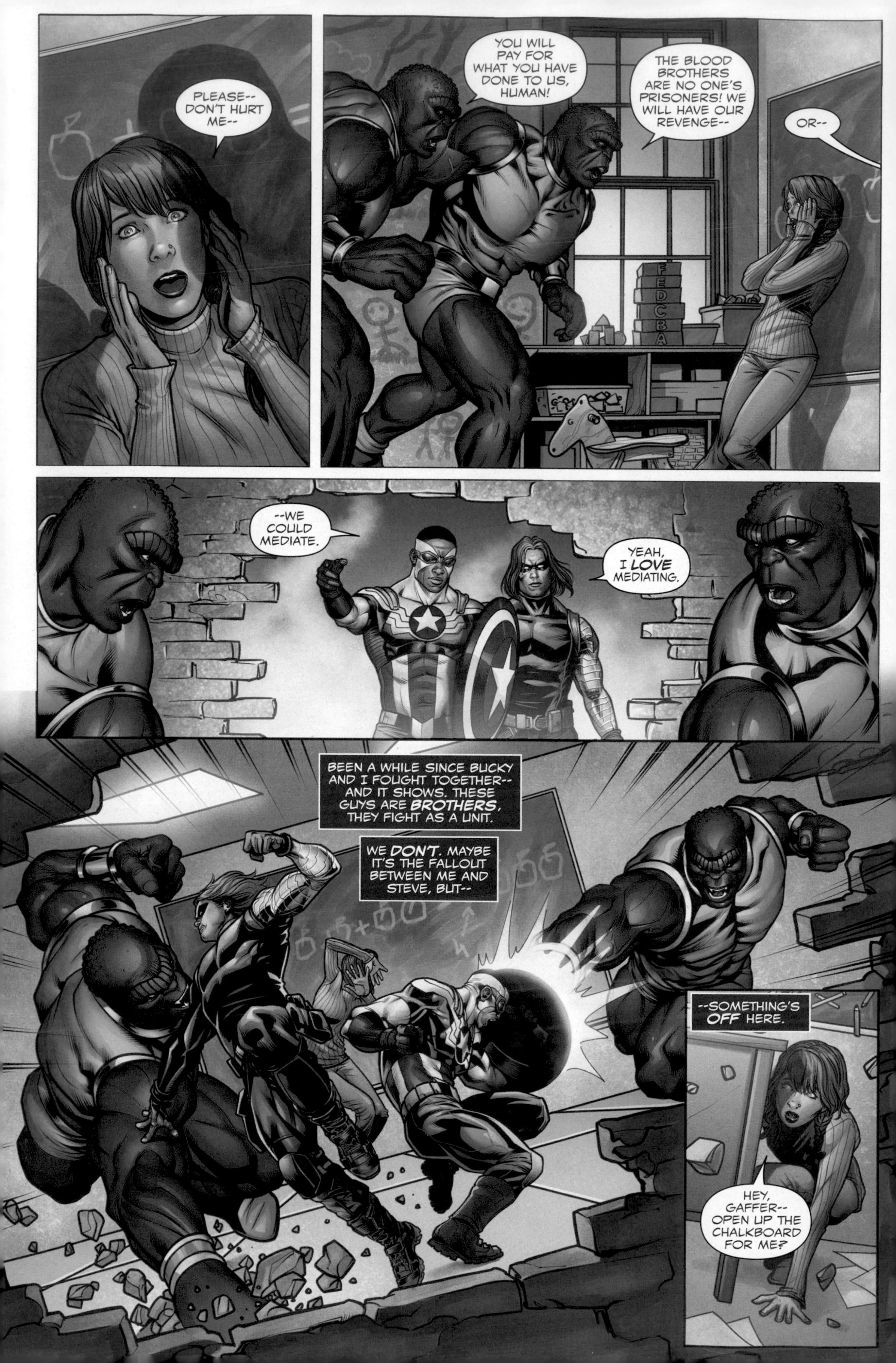
PLEASE--
DON'T HURT ME--
YOU WILL PAY FOR WHAT YOU HAVE DONE TO US, HUMAN!
THE BLOOD BROTHERS ARE NO ONE'S PRISONERS! WE WILL HAVE OUR REVENGE--
OR--
--WE COULD MEDIATE.
YEAH, I **LOVE** MEDIATING.
BEEN A WHILE SINCE BUCKY AND I FOUGHT TOGETHER--AND IT SHOWS. THESE GUYS ARE **BROTHERS**, THEY FIGHT AS A UNIT.
WE **DON'T**. MAYBE IT'S THE FALLOUT BETWEEN ME AND STEVE, BUT--
--SOMETHING'S **OFF** HERE.
HEY, GAFFER--OPEN UP THE CHALKBOARD FOR ME?

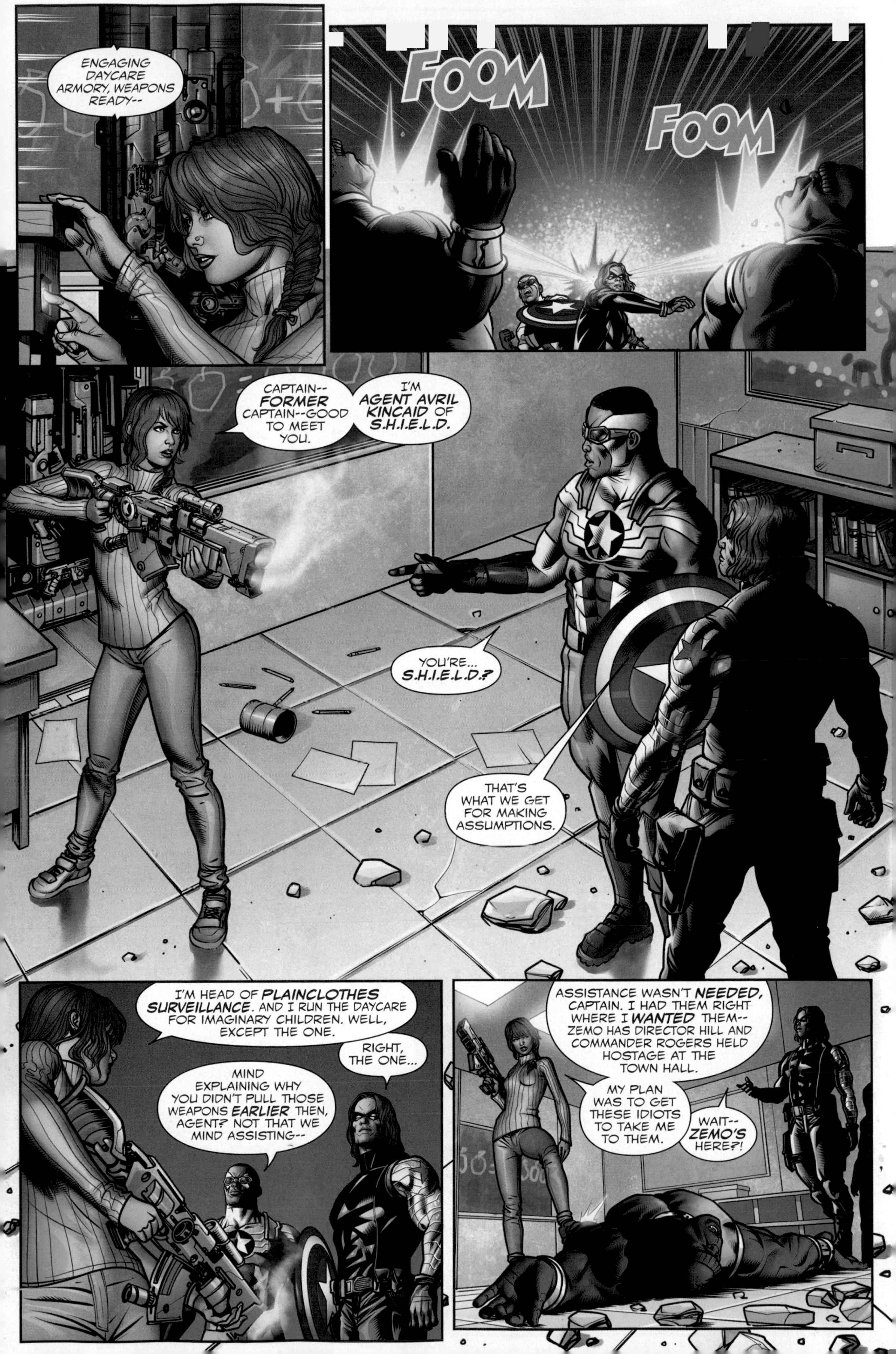
ENGAGING DAYCARE ARMORY, WEAPONS READY--
FOOM
FOOM
CAPTAIN-- FORMER CAPTAIN--GOOD TO MEET YOU.
I'M AGENT AVRIL KINCAID OF S.H.I.E.L.D.
YOU'RE... S.H.I.E.L.D.?
THAT'S WHAT WE GET FOR MAKING ASSUMPTIONS.
I'M HEAD OF PLAINCLOTHES SURVEILLANCE. AND I RUN THE DAYCARE FOR IMAGINARY CHILDREN. WELL, EXCEPT THE ONE.
RIGHT, THE ONE...
MIND EXPLAINING WHY YOU DIDN'T PULL THOSE WEAPONS EARLIER THEN, AGENT? NOT THAT WE MIND ASSISTING--
ASSISTANCE WASN'T NEEDED, CAPTAIN. I HAD THEM RIGHT WHERE I WANTED THEM--ZEMO HAS DIRECTOR HILL AND COMMANDER ROGERS HELD HOSTAGE AT THE TOWN HALL.
MY PLAN WAS TO GET THESE IDIOTS TO TAKE ME TO THEM.
WAIT-- ZEMO'S HERE?!

OH, GOD-- --YOU TWO HAVE NO CLUE WHAT'S GOING ON HERE, DO YOU?

MA'AM, WE'RE **SUPER HEROES.** OF COURSE WE KNOW WHAT'S GOING ON HERE.

BUT--WHY DON'T YOU TELL US EVERYTHING YOU KNOW, JUST SO WE'RE SURE WE'RE ALL ON THE SAME **PAGE.**

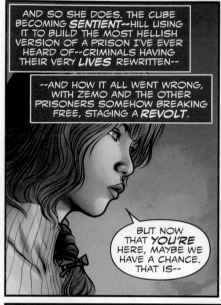

AND SO SHE DOES. THE CUBE BECOMING **SENTIENT**--HILL USING IT TO BUILD THE MOST HELLISH VERSION OF A PRISON I'VE EVER HEARD OF--CRIMINALS HAVING THEIR VERY **LIVES** REWRITTEN--

--AND HOW IT ALL WENT WRONG, WITH ZEMO AND THE OTHER PRISONERS SOMEHOW BREAKING FREE, STAGING A **REVOLT.**

BUT NOW THAT **YOU'RE** HERE, MAYBE WE HAVE A CHANCE. THAT IS--

--PRESUMING I DON'T ARREST **YOU.**

OKAY...MAYBE I ATTACKED A FEW S.H.I.E.L.D. INSTALLATIONS. HOW DO YOU THINK I FOUND OUT ABOUT THIS PLACE?

"SPACE DANGER ANTENNA," MY ASS.

AGENT-- I'LL VOUCH FOR **BARNES.**

AND I GET I'M NOT EXACTLY A FRIEND OF S.H.I.E.L.D.'S THESE DAYS EITHER, BUT, LOOKING AROUND, YOU SHOULD MAYBE TAKE THE HELP YOU CAN GET.

-:SIGH:- FINE-- --NOT LIKE I THOUGHT ANY OF THIS WAS A GOOD IDEA ANYWAY.

I'D ALREADY **ABANDONED** MY PLAN-A WHEN I COULDN'T MAKE CONTACT WITH ANYONE ELSE IN MY UNIT. THIS WOULD NEED TO BE A TWO-TEAM JOB, AFTER ALL--

WE'RE LISTENING.

"I NEED ACCESS TO THE **PLEASANT HILL MUSEUM.** THE DIRECTOR ISN'T JUST HIDING CRIMINALS AND TERRORISTS HERE--THERE'S AN **INVENTORY**--HIDDEN, TRANSFORMED BY KOBIK LIKE EVERYTHING ELSE--

"--AND THERE'S SOMETHING THERE--A **WEAPON**-- THAT I THINK I CAN USE TO TURN THE TIDE."

Pleasant Hill Museum

CAN'T WAIT TO HEAR THE CATCH.

THE CATCH IS IT'S ON A **TOP-LEVEL SECURITY LOCKDOWN.** AND THE ONLY WAY TO GET THROUGH IS TO SHUT THE SYSTEM DOWN AT A **REMOTE** STATION.

AND THAT STATION'S LOCATION?

WELL, YEAH...

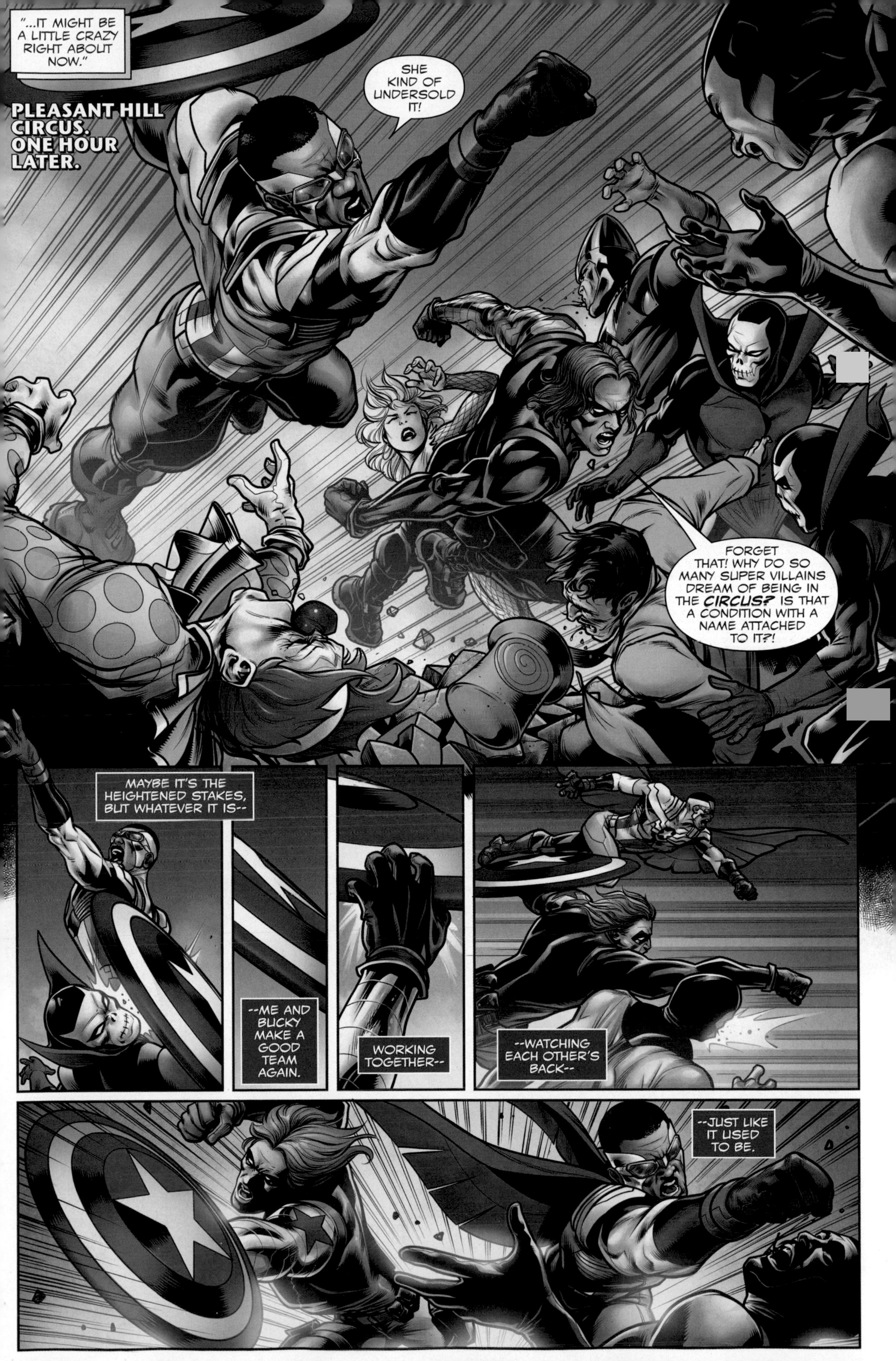
"...IT MIGHT BE A LITTLE CRAZY RIGHT ABOUT NOW."
PLEASANT HILL CIRCUS. ONE HOUR LATER.
SHE KIND OF UNDERSOLD IT!
FORGET THAT! WHY DO SO MANY SUPER VILLAINS DREAM OF BEING IN THE CIRCUS? IS THAT A CONDITION WITH A NAME ATTACHED TO IT?!
MAYBE IT'S THE HEIGHTENED STAKES, BUT WHATEVER IT IS--
--ME AND BUCKY MAKE A GOOD TEAM AGAIN.
WORKING TOGETHER--
--WATCHING EACH OTHER'S BACK--
--JUST LIKE IT USED TO BE.

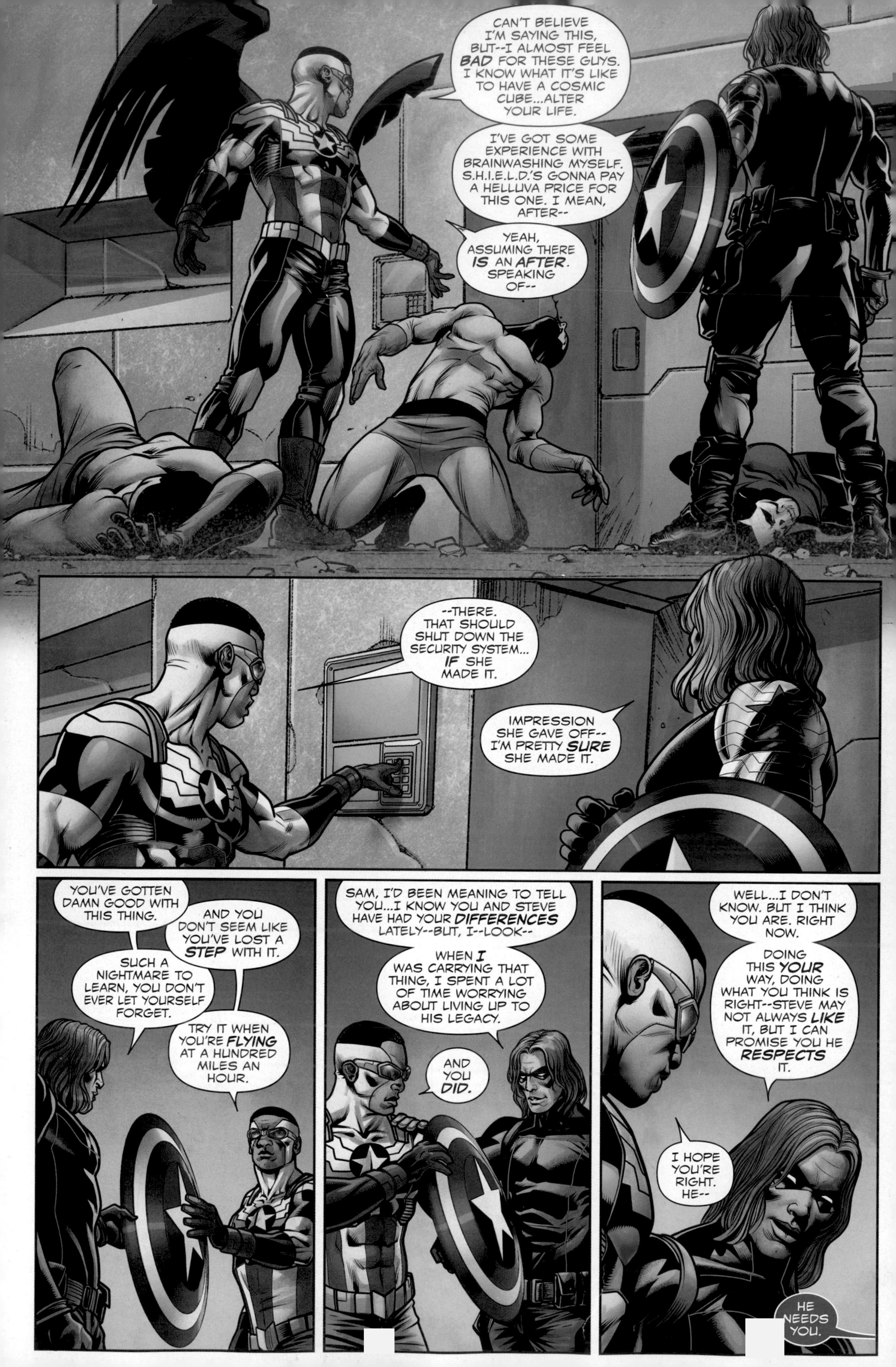
CAN'T BELIEVE I'M SAYING THIS, BUT--I ALMOST FEEL BAD FOR THESE GUYS. I KNOW WHAT IT'S LIKE TO HAVE A COSMIC CUBE...ALTER YOUR LIFE.
I'VE GOT SOME EXPERIENCE WITH BRAINWASHING MYSELF. S.H.I.E.L.D.'S GONNA PAY A HELLUVA PRICE FOR THIS ONE. I MEAN, AFTER--
YEAH, ASSUMING THERE IS AN AFTER. SPEAKING OF--
--THERE. THAT SHOULD SHUT DOWN THE SECURITY SYSTEM... IF SHE MADE IT.
IMPRESSION SHE GAVE OFF-- I'M PRETTY SURE SHE MADE IT.
YOU'VE GOTTEN DAMN GOOD WITH THIS THING.
AND YOU DON'T SEEM LIKE YOU'VE LOST A STEP WITH IT.
SUCH A NIGHTMARE TO LEARN, YOU DON'T EVER LET YOURSELF FORGET.
TRY IT WHEN YOU'RE FLYING AT A HUNDRED MILES AN HOUR.
SAM, I'D BEEN MEANING TO TELL YOU...I KNOW YOU AND STEVE HAVE HAD YOUR DIFFERENCES LATELY--BUT, I--LOOK--
WHEN I WAS CARRYING THAT THING, I SPENT A LOT OF TIME WORRYING ABOUT LIVING UP TO HIS LEGACY.
AND YOU DID.
WELL...I DON'T KNOW. BUT I THINK YOU ARE. RIGHT NOW.
DOING THIS YOUR WAY, DOING WHAT YOU THINK IS RIGHT--STEVE MAY NOT ALWAYS LIKE IT, BUT I CAN PROMISE YOU HE RESPECTS IT.
I HOPE YOU'RE RIGHT. HE--
HE NEEDS YOU.

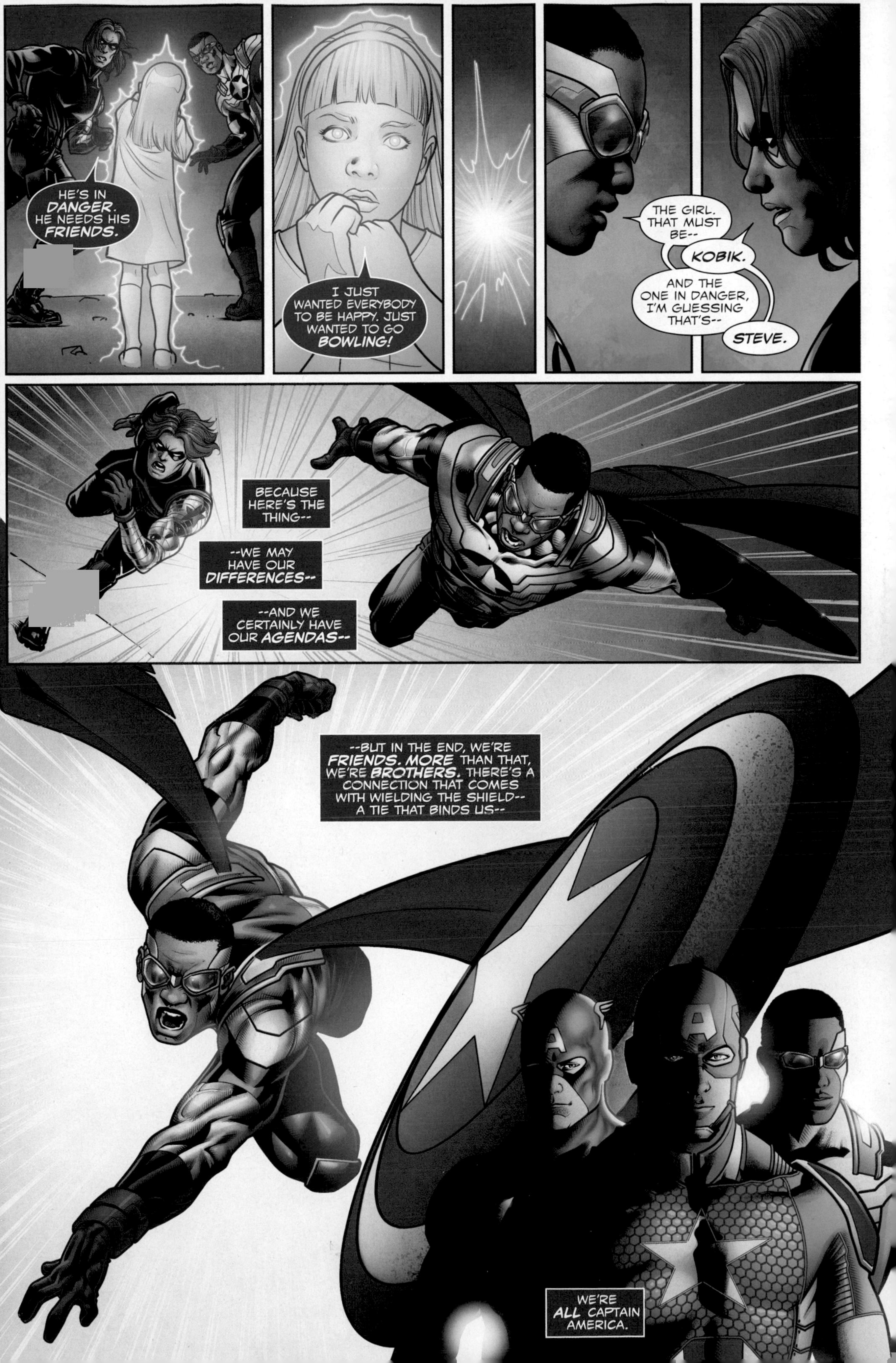
HE'S IN DANGER. HE NEEDS HIS FRIENDS.
I JUST WANTED EVERYBODY TO BE HAPPY. JUST WANTED TO GO BOWLING!
THE GIRL. THAT MUST BE--
KOBIK.
AND THE ONE IN DANGER, I'M GUESSING THAT'S--
STEVE.
BECAUSE HERE'S THE THING--
--WE MAY HAVE OUR DIFFERENCES--
--AND WE CERTAINLY HAVE OUR AGENDAS--
--BUT IN THE END, WE'RE FRIENDS. MORE THAN THAT, WE'RE BROTHERS. THERE'S A CONNECTION THAT COMES WITH WIELDING THE SHIELD-- A TIE THAT BINDS US--
WE'RE ALL CAPTAIN AMERICA.

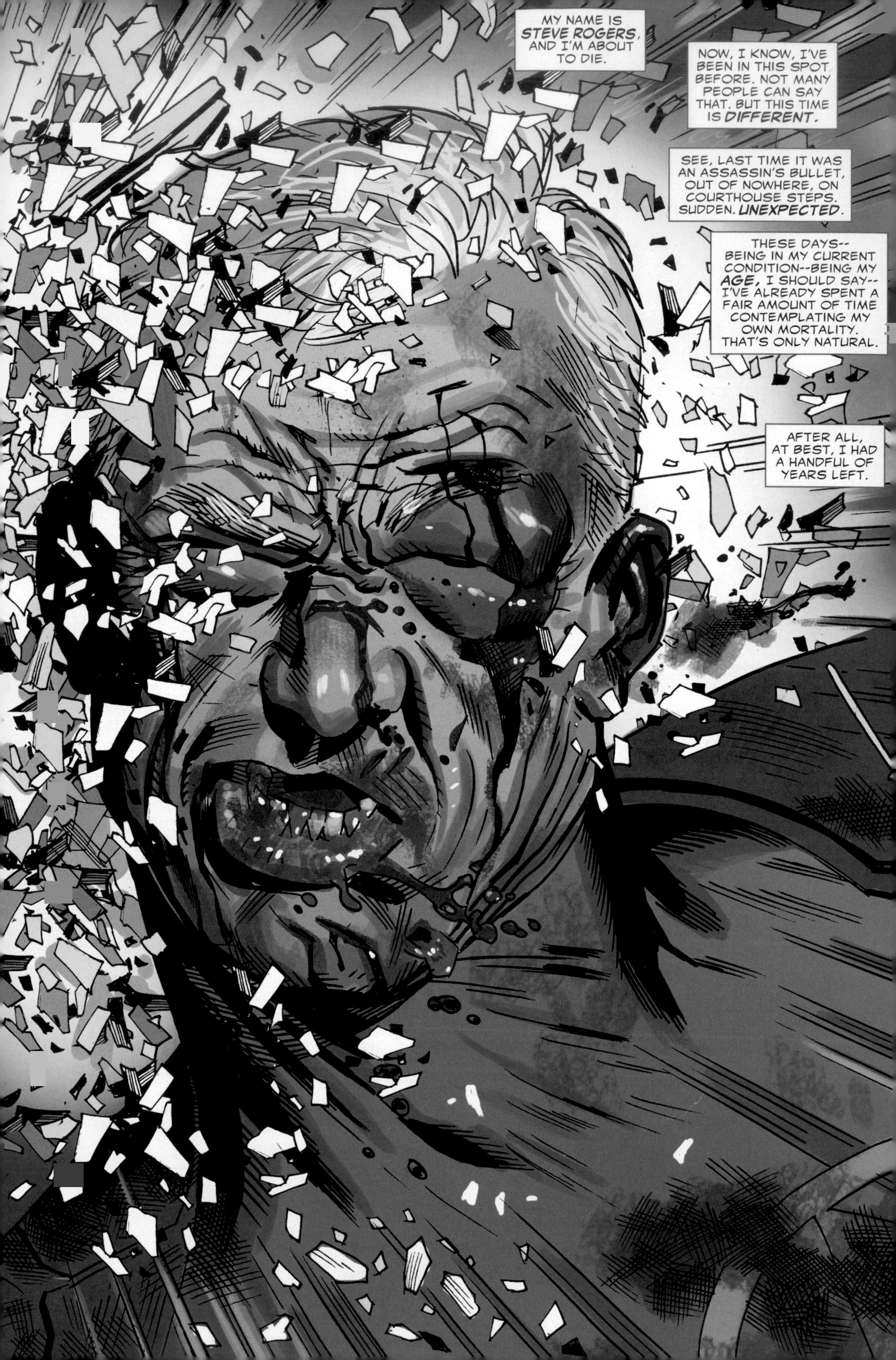
MY NAME IS STEVE ROGERS, AND I'M ABOUT TO DIE.
NOW, I KNOW, I'VE BEEN IN THIS SPOT BEFORE. NOT MANY PEOPLE CAN SAY THAT. BUT THIS TIME IS DIFFERENT.
SEE, LAST TIME IT WAS AN ASSASSIN'S BULLET, OUT OF NOWHERE, ON COURTHOUSE STEPS. SUDDEN. UNEXPECTED.
THESE DAYS-- BEING IN MY CURRENT CONDITION--BEING MY AGE, I SHOULD SAY-- I'VE ALREADY SPENT A FAIR AMOUNT OF TIME CONTEMPLATING MY OWN MORTALITY. THAT'S ONLY NATURAL.
AFTER ALL, AT BEST, I HAD A HANDFUL OF YEARS LEFT.

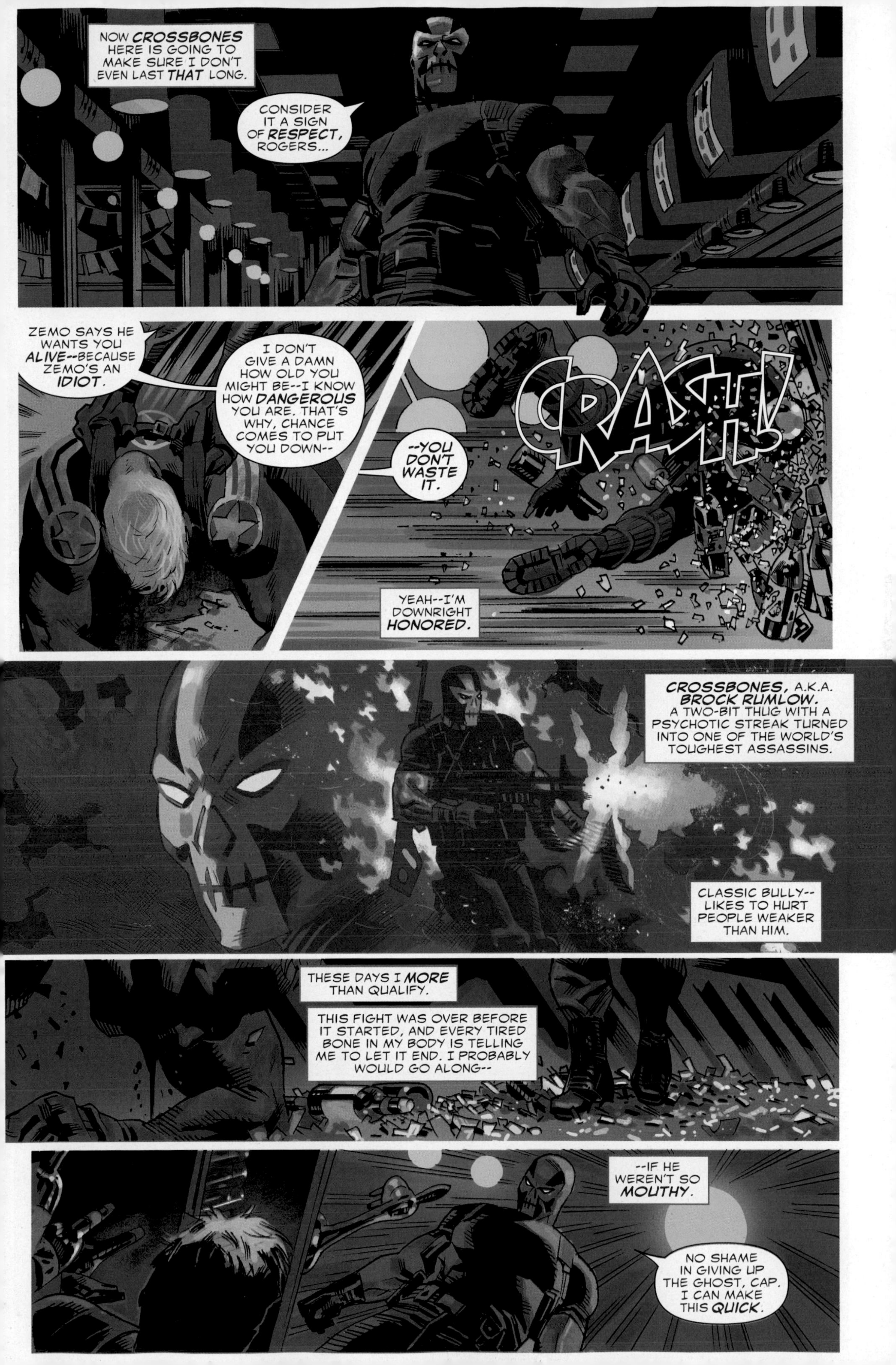

NOW CROSSBONES HERE IS GOING TO MAKE SURE I DON'T EVEN LAST THAT LONG.
CONSIDER IT A SIGN OF RESPECT, ROGERS...
ZEMO SAYS HE WANTS YOU ALIVE--BECAUSE ZEMO'S AN IDIOT.
I DON'T GIVE A DAMN HOW OLD YOU MIGHT BE--I KNOW HOW DANGEROUS YOU ARE. THAT'S WHY, CHANCE COMES TO PUT YOU DOWN--
--YOU DON'T WASTE IT.
CRASH!
YEAH--I'M DOWNRIGHT HONORED.
CROSSBONES, A.K.A. BROCK RUMLOW. A TWO-BIT THUG WITH A PSYCHOTIC STREAK TURNED INTO ONE OF THE WORLD'S TOUGHEST ASSASSINS.
CLASSIC BULLY--LIKES TO HURT PEOPLE WEAKER THAN HIM.
THESE DAYS I MORE THAN QUALIFY.
THIS FIGHT WAS OVER BEFORE IT STARTED, AND EVERY TIRED BONE IN MY BODY IS TELLING ME TO LET IT END. I PROBABLY WOULD GO ALONG--
--IF HE WEREN'T SO MOUTHY.
NO SHAME IN GIVING UP THE GHOST, CAP. I CAN MAKE THIS QUICK.

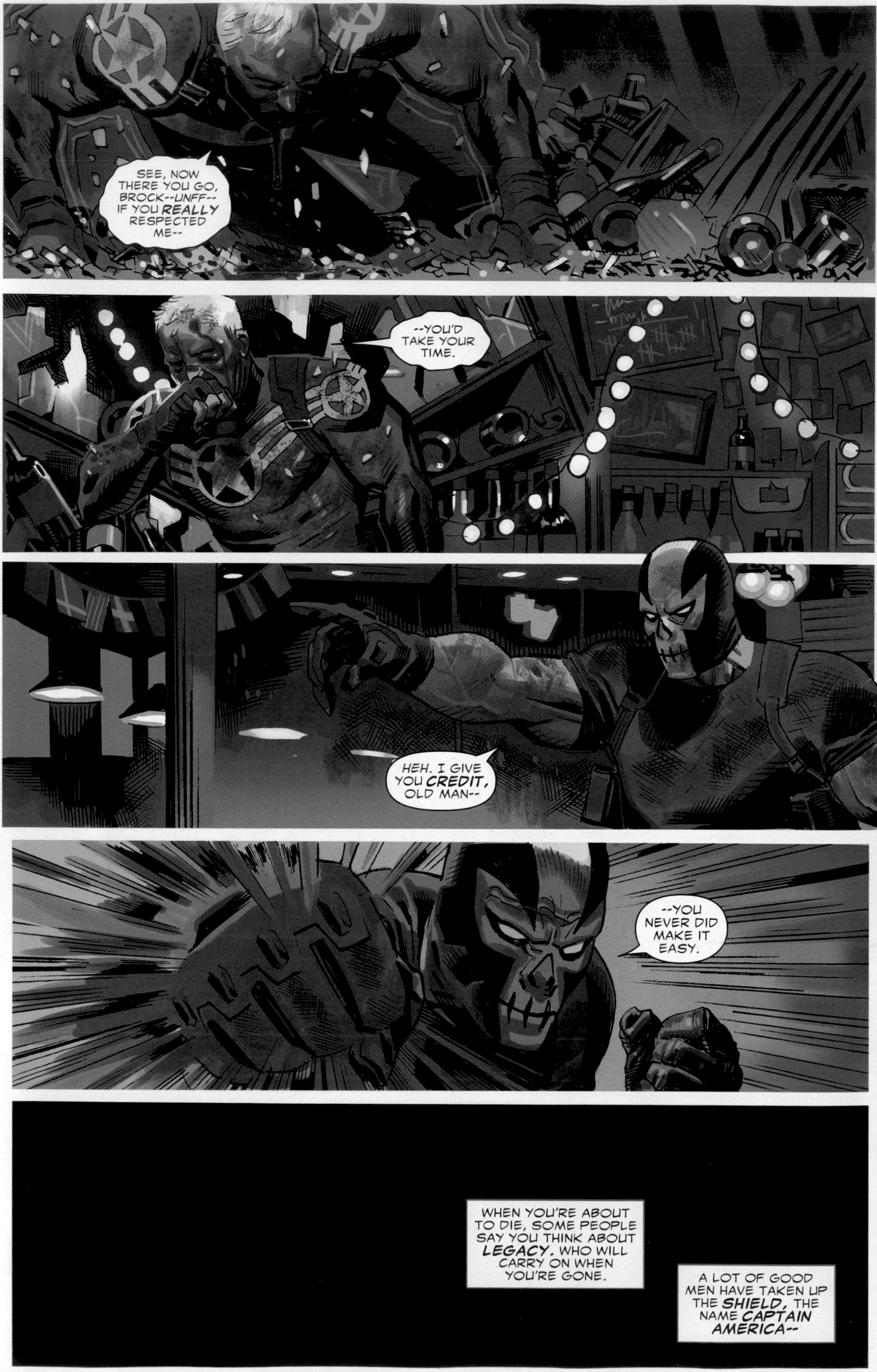
SEE, NOW THERE YOU GO, BROCK--UNFF-- IF YOU REALLY RESPECTED ME--
--YOU'D TAKE YOUR TIME.
HEH. I GIVE YOU CREDIT, OLD MAN--
--YOU NEVER DID MAKE IT EASY.
WHEN YOU'RE ABOUT TO DIE, SOME PEOPLE SAY YOU THINK ABOUT LEGACY. WHO WILL CARRY ON WHEN YOU'RE GONE.
A LOT OF GOOD MEN HAVE TAKEN UP THE SHIELD, THE NAME CAPTAIN AMERICA--

SAM WILSON. A SOCIAL WORKER AND COMMUNITY ORGANIZER IN HARLEM--

--WHO BECAME THE HIGH-FLYING HERO KNOWN AS THE *FALCON*.

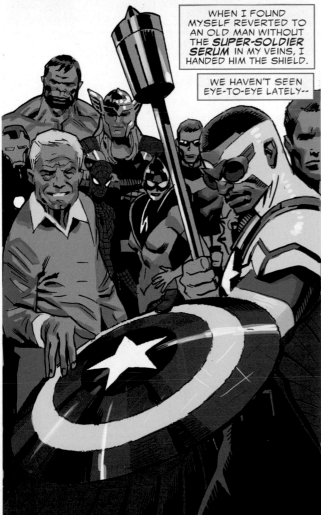

WHEN I FOUND MYSELF REVERTED TO AN OLD MAN WITHOUT THE *SUPER-SOLDIER SERUM* IN MY VEINS, I HANDED HIM THE SHIELD.

WE HAVEN'T SEEN EYE-TO-EYE LATELY--

--BUT I HOPE HE KNOWS I'M STILL HIS *FRIEND*.

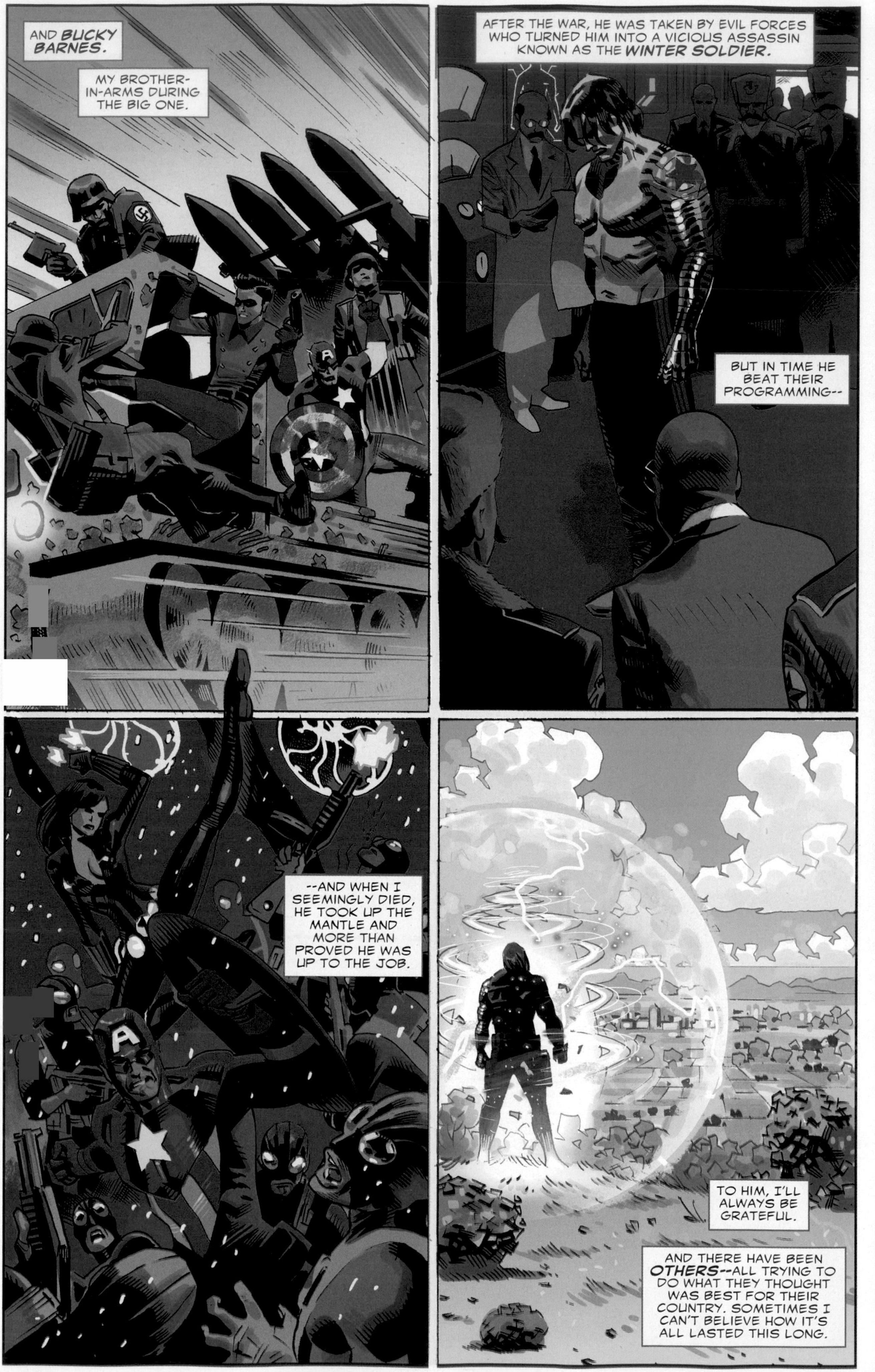
AND **BUCKY BARNES.**
MY BROTHER-IN-ARMS DURING THE BIG ONE.
AFTER THE WAR, HE WAS TAKEN BY EVIL FORCES WHO TURNED HIM INTO A VICIOUS ASSASSIN KNOWN AS THE **WINTER SOLDIER.**
BUT IN TIME HE BEAT THEIR PROGRAMMING--
--AND WHEN I SEEMINGLY DIED, HE TOOK UP THE MANTLE AND MORE THAN PROVED HE WAS UP TO THE JOB.
TO HIM, I'LL ALWAYS BE GRATEFUL.
AND THERE HAVE BEEN **OTHERS**--ALL TRYING TO DO WHAT THEY THOUGHT WAS BEST FOR THEIR COUNTRY. SOMETIMES I CAN'T BELIEVE HOW IT'S ALL LASTED THIS LONG.

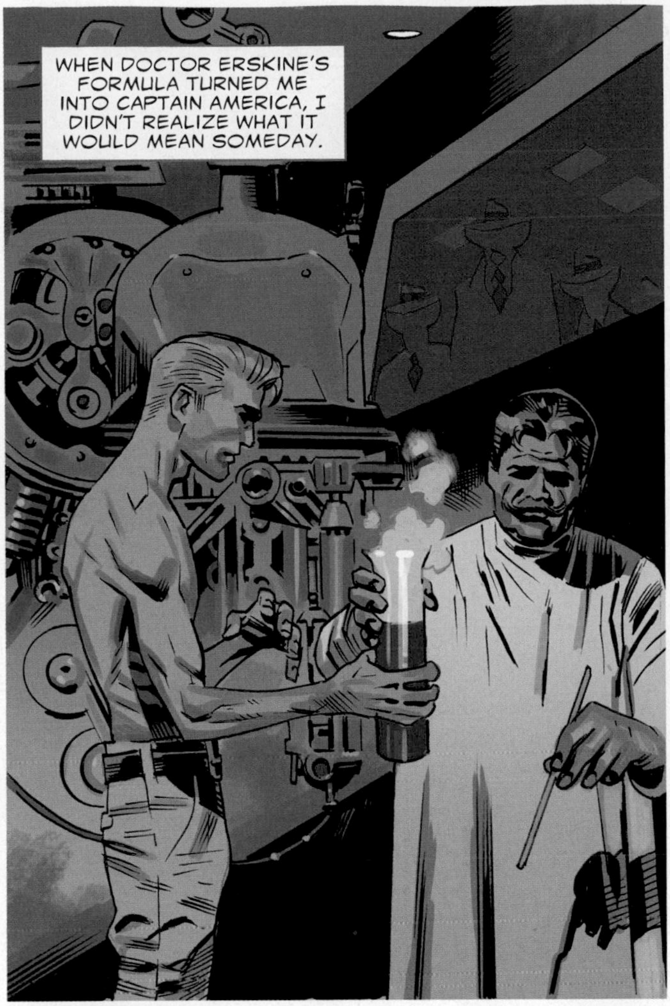
WHEN DOCTOR ERSKINE'S FORMULA TURNED ME INTO CAPTAIN AMERICA, I DIDN'T REALIZE WHAT IT WOULD MEAN SOMEDAY.

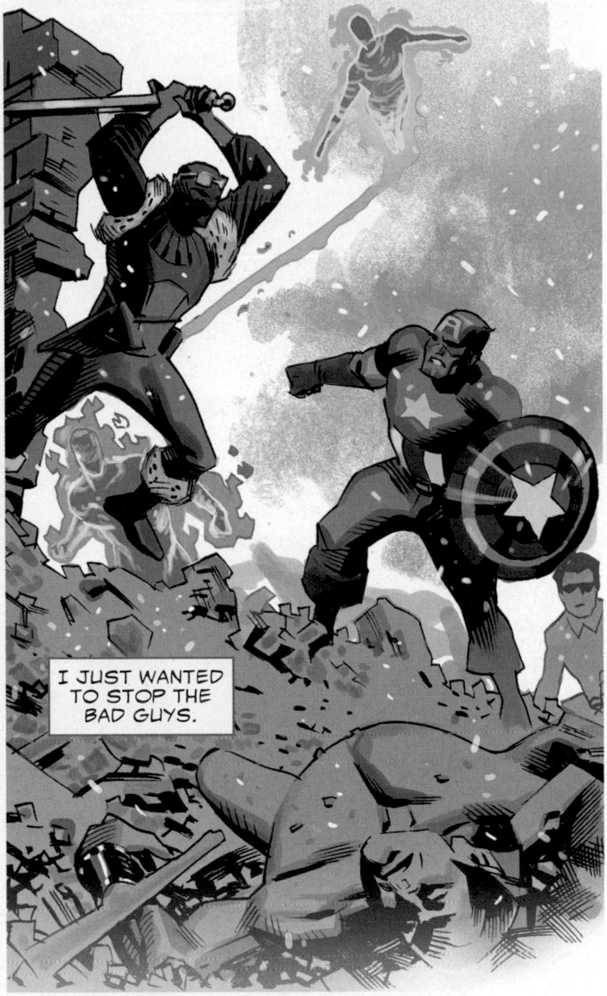
I JUST WANTED TO STOP THE BAD GUYS.

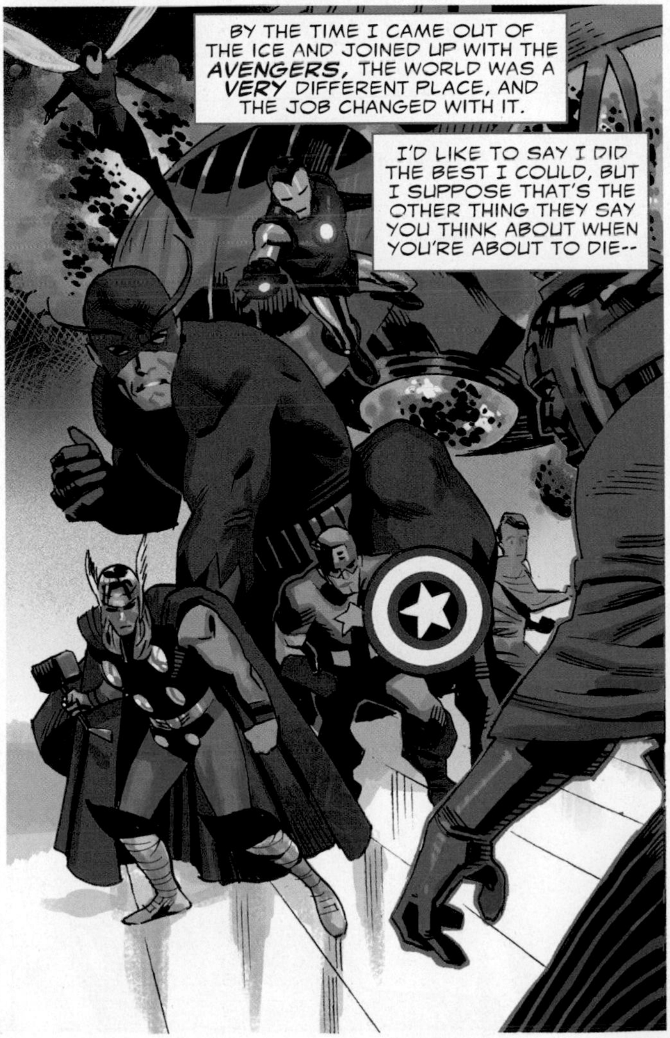
BY THE TIME I CAME OUT OF THE ICE AND JOINED UP WITH THE AVENGERS, THE WORLD WAS A VERY DIFFERENT PLACE, AND THE JOB CHANGED WITH IT.
I'D LIKE TO SAY I DID THE BEST I COULD, BUT I SUPPOSE THAT'S THE OTHER THING THEY SAY YOU THINK ABOUT WHEN YOU'RE ABOUT TO DIE--

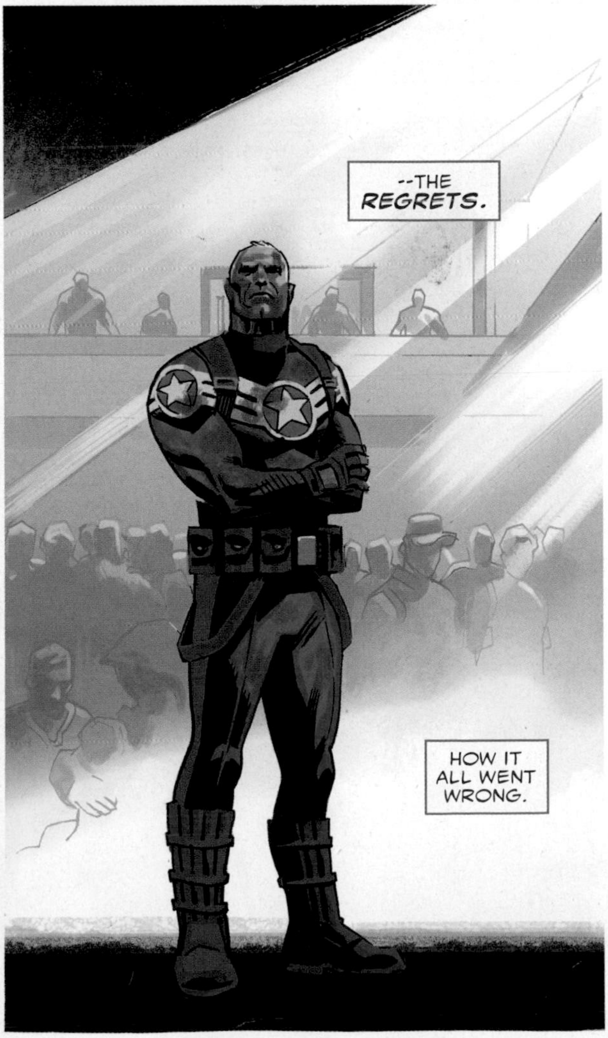
--THE REGRETS.
HOW IT ALL WENT WRONG.

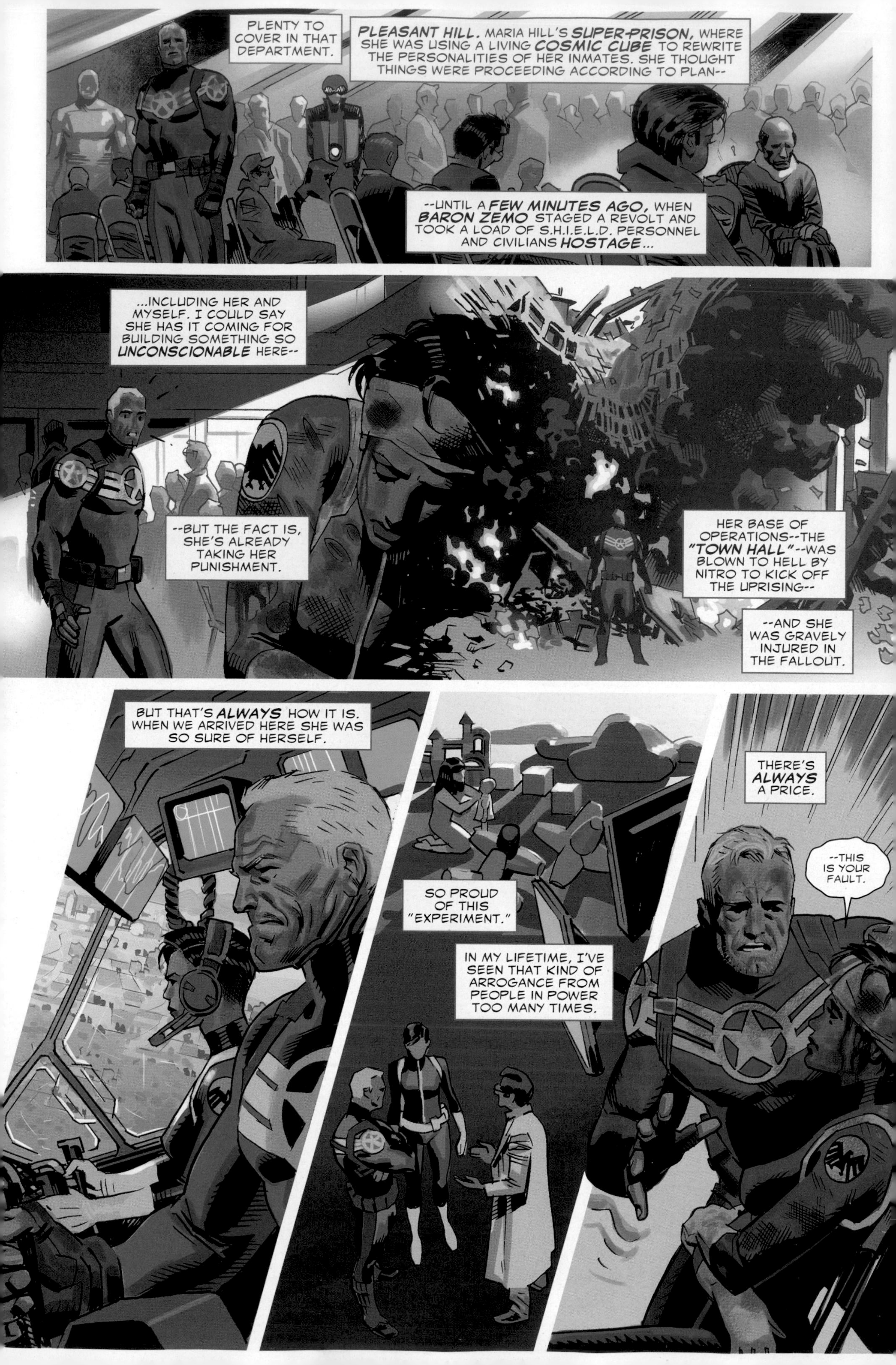

PLENTY TO COVER IN THAT DEPARTMENT.
PLEASANT HILL. MARIA HILL'S SUPER-PRISON, WHERE SHE WAS USING A LIVING COSMIC CUBE TO REWRITE THE PERSONALITIES OF HER INMATES. SHE THOUGHT THINGS WERE PROCEEDING ACCORDING TO PLAN--
--UNTIL A FEW MINUTES AGO, WHEN BARON ZEMO STAGED A REVOLT AND TOOK A LOAD OF S.H.I.E.L.D. PERSONNEL AND CIVILIANS HOSTAGE...
...INCLUDING HER AND MYSELF. I COULD SAY SHE HAS IT COMING FOR BUILDING SOMETHING SO UNCONSCIONABLE HERE--
--BUT THE FACT IS, SHE'S ALREADY TAKING HER PUNISHMENT.
HER BASE OF OPERATIONS--THE "TOWN HALL"--WAS BLOWN TO HELL BY NITRO TO KICK OFF THE UPRISING--
--AND SHE WAS GRAVELY INJURED IN THE FALLOUT.
BUT THAT'S ALWAYS HOW IT IS. WHEN WE ARRIVED HERE SHE WAS SO SURE OF HERSELF.
SO PROUD OF THIS "EXPERIMENT."
IN MY LIFETIME, I'VE SEEN THAT KIND OF ARROGANCE FROM PEOPLE IN POWER TOO MANY TIMES.
THERE'S ALWAYS A PRICE.
--THIS IS YOUR FAULT.

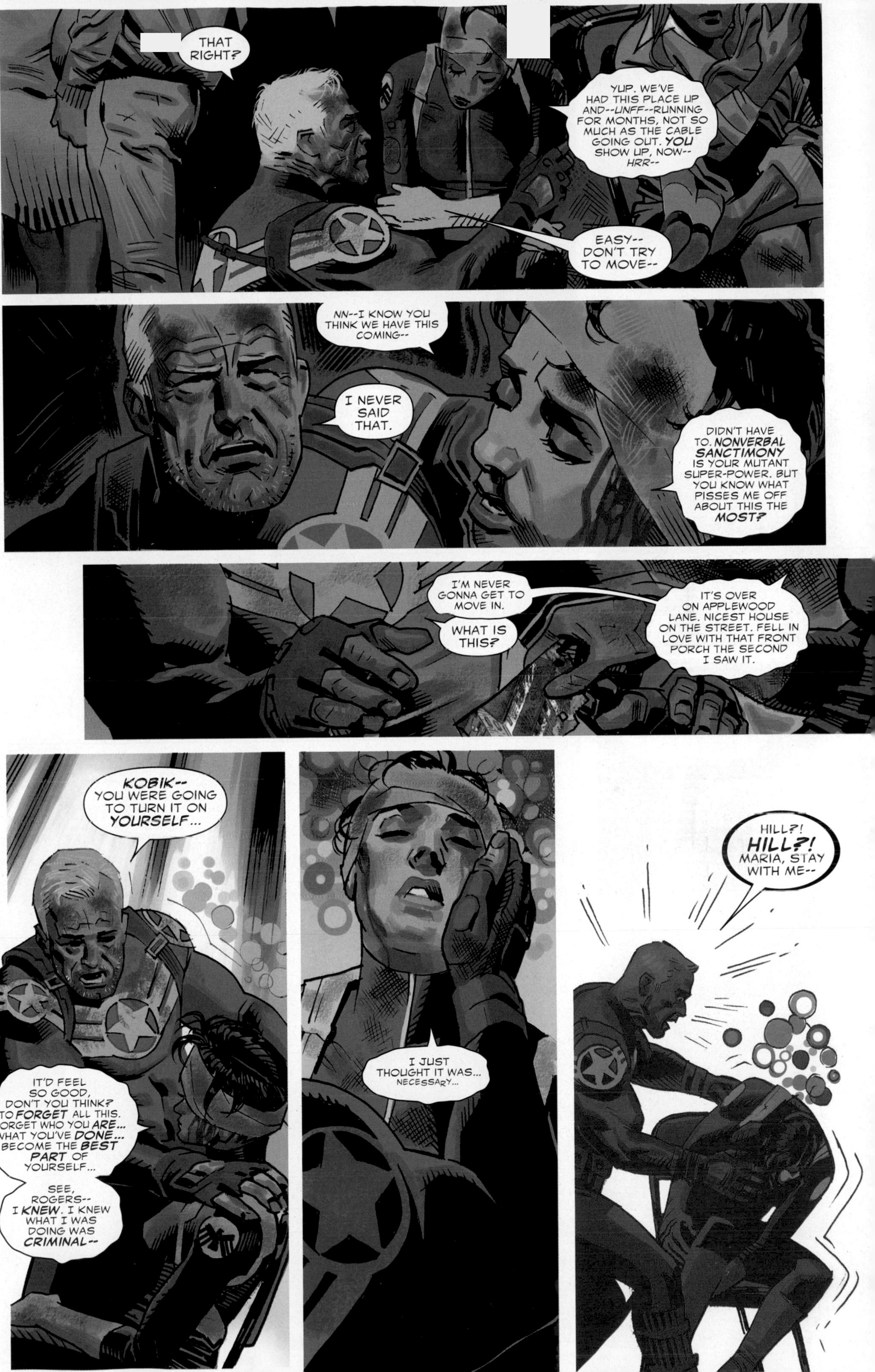
THAT RIGHT?
YUP. WE'VE HAD THIS PLACE UP AND--UNFF--RUNNING FOR MONTHS, NOT SO MUCH AS THE CABLE GOING OUT. YOU SHOW UP, NOW-- HRR--
EASY-- DON'T TRY TO MOVE--
NN--I KNOW YOU THINK WE HAVE THIS COMING--
I NEVER SAID THAT.
DIDN'T HAVE TO. NONVERBAL SANCTIMONY IS YOUR MUTANT SUPER-POWER. BUT YOU KNOW WHAT PISSES ME OFF ABOUT THIS THE MOST?
I'M NEVER GONNA GET TO MOVE IN.
IT'S OVER ON APPLEWOOD LANE. NICEST HOUSE ON THE STREET. FELL IN LOVE WITH THAT FRONT PORCH THE SECOND I SAW IT.
WHAT IS THIS?
KOBIK-- YOU WERE GOING TO TURN IT ON YOURSELF...
IT'D FEEL SO GOOD, DON'T YOU THINK? TO FORGET ALL THIS. FORGET WHO YOU ARE... WHAT YOU'VE DONE... BECOME THE BEST PART OF YOURSELF...
SEE, ROGERS-- I KNEW. I KNEW WHAT I WAS DOING WAS CRIMINAL--
I JUST THOUGHT IT WAS... NECESSARY...
HILL?! HILL?! MARIA, STAY WITH ME--

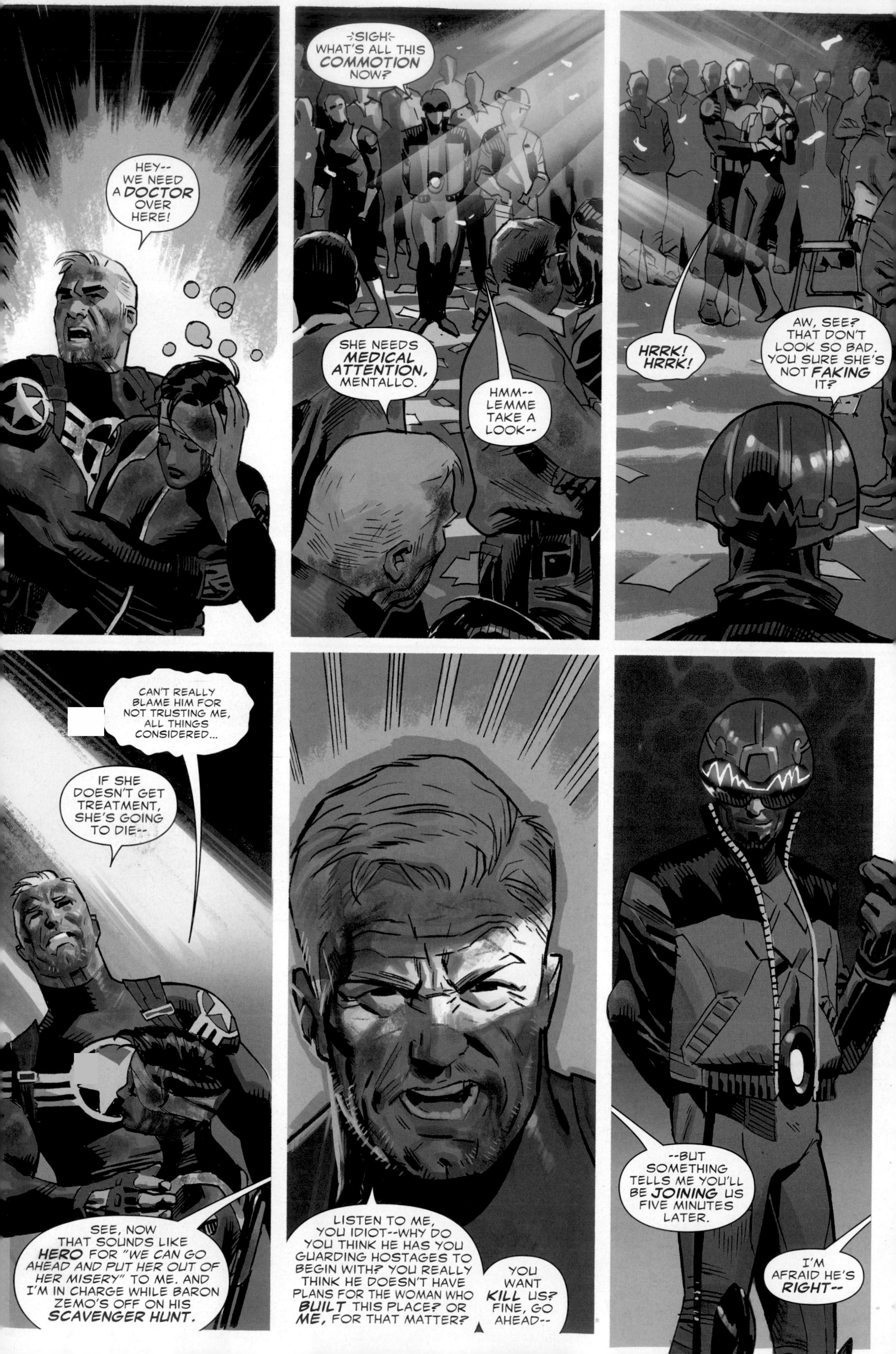
HEY-- WE NEED A DOCTOR OVER HERE!
-SIGH- WHAT'S ALL THIS COMMOTION NOW?
SHE NEEDS MEDICAL ATTENTION, MENTALLO.
HMM-- LEMME TAKE A LOOK--
HRRK! HRRK!
AW, SEE? THAT DON'T LOOK SO BAD. YOU SURE SHE'S NOT FAKING IT?
CAN'T REALLY BLAME HIM FOR NOT TRUSTING ME, ALL THINGS CONSIDERED...
IF SHE DOESN'T GET TREATMENT, SHE'S GOING TO DIE--
SEE, NOW THAT SOUNDS LIKE HERO FOR "WE CAN GO AHEAD AND PUT HER OUT OF HER MISERY" TO ME. AND I'M IN CHARGE WHILE BARON ZEMO'S OFF ON HIS SCAVENGER HUNT.
LISTEN TO ME, YOU IDIOT--WHY DO YOU THINK HE HAS YOU GUARDING HOSTAGES TO BEGIN WITH? YOU REALLY THINK HE DOESN'T HAVE PLANS FOR THE WOMAN WHO BUILT THIS PLACE? OR ME, FOR THAT MATTER?
YOU WANT KILL US? FINE, GO AHEAD--
I'M AFRAID HE'S RIGHT--
--BUT SOMETHING TELLS ME YOU'LL BE JOINING US FIVE MINUTES LATER.

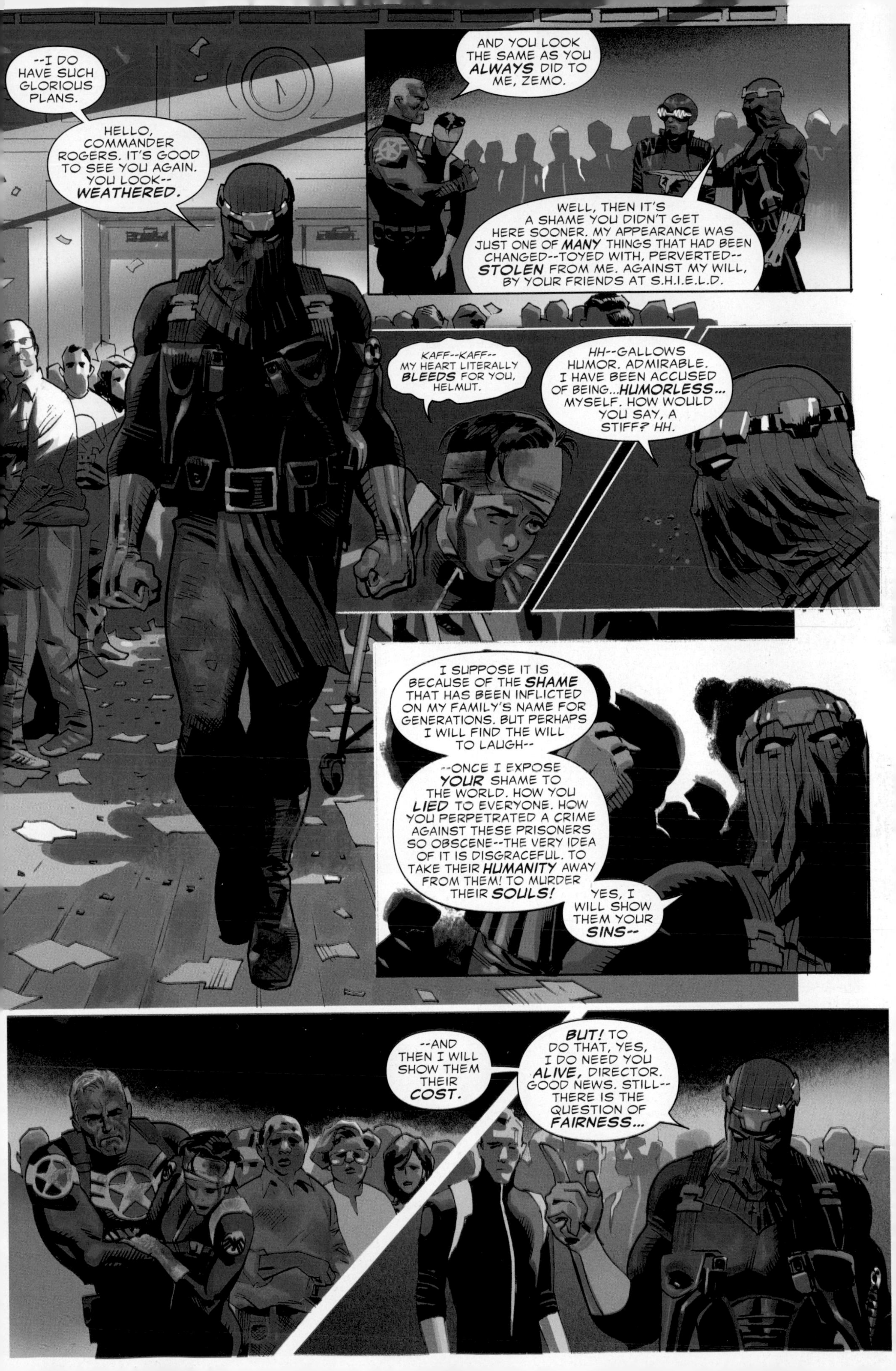
--I DO HAVE SUCH GLORIOUS PLANS.
HELLO, COMMANDER ROGERS. IT'S GOOD TO SEE YOU AGAIN. YOU LOOK-- WEATHERED.
AND YOU LOOK THE SAME AS YOU ALWAYS DID TO ME, ZEMO.
WELL, THEN IT'S A SHAME YOU DIDN'T GET HERE SOONER. MY APPEARANCE WAS JUST ONE OF MANY THINGS THAT HAD BEEN CHANGED--TOYED WITH, PERVERTED-- STOLEN FROM ME. AGAINST MY WILL, BY YOUR FRIENDS AT S.H.I.E.L.D.
KAFF--KAFF-- MY HEART LITERALLY BLEEDS FOR YOU, HELMUT.
HH--GALLOWS HUMOR. ADMIRABLE. I HAVE BEEN ACCUSED OF BEING...HUMORLESS... MYSELF. HOW WOULD YOU SAY, A STIFF? HH.
I SUPPOSE IT IS BECAUSE OF THE SHAME THAT HAS BEEN INFLICTED ON MY FAMILY'S NAME FOR GENERATIONS. BUT PERHAPS I WILL FIND THE WILL TO LAUGH--
--ONCE I EXPOSE YOUR SHAME TO THE WORLD. HOW YOU LIED TO EVERYONE. HOW YOU PERPETRATED A CRIME AGAINST THESE PRISONERS SO OBSCENE--THE VERY IDEA OF IT IS DISGRACEFUL. TO TAKE THEIR HUMANITY AWAY FROM THEM! TO MURDER THEIR SOULS!
YES, I WILL SHOW THEM YOUR SINS--
--AND THEN I WILL SHOW THEM THEIR COST.
BUT! TO DO THAT, YES, I DO NEED YOU ALIVE, DIRECTOR. GOOD NEWS. STILL-- THERE IS THE QUESTION OF FAIRNESS...

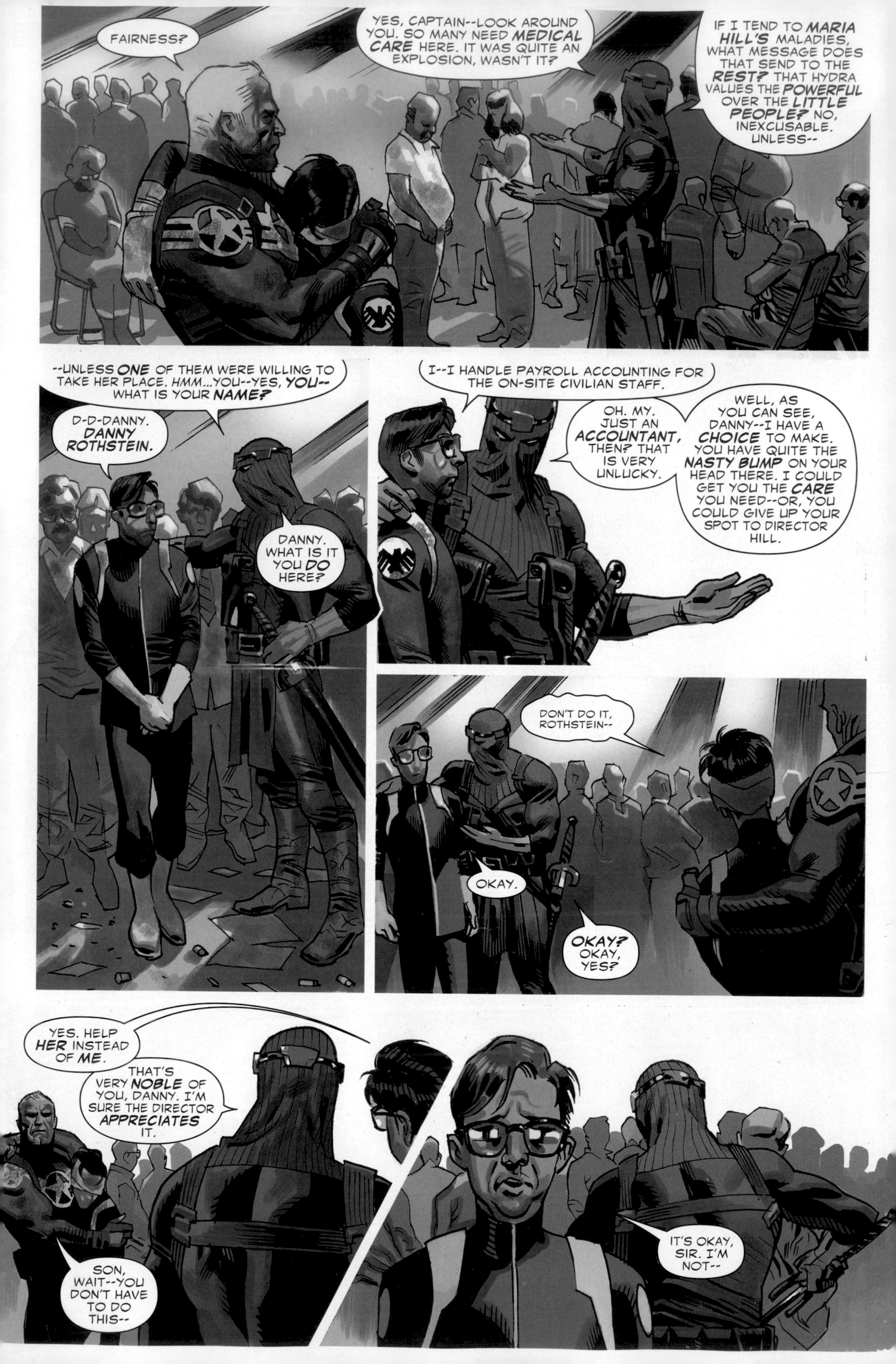
FAIRNESS?
YES, CAPTAIN--LOOK AROUND YOU. SO MANY NEED MEDICAL CARE HERE. IT WAS QUITE AN EXPLOSION, WASN'T IT?
IF I TEND TO MARIA HILL'S MALADIES, WHAT MESSAGE DOES THAT SEND TO THE REST? THAT HYDRA VALUES THE POWERFUL OVER THE LITTLE PEOPLE? NO, INEXCUSABLE. UNLESS--
--UNLESS ONE OF THEM WERE WILLING TO TAKE HER PLACE. HMM...YOU--YES, YOU-- WHAT IS YOUR NAME?
D-D-DANNY. DANNY ROTHSTEIN.
DANNY. WHAT IS IT YOU DO HERE?
I--I HANDLE PAYROLL ACCOUNTING FOR THE ON-SITE CIVILIAN STAFF.
OH. MY. JUST AN ACCOUNTANT, THEN? THAT IS VERY UNLUCKY.
WELL, AS YOU CAN SEE, DANNY--I HAVE A CHOICE TO MAKE. YOU HAVE QUITE THE NASTY BUMP ON YOUR HEAD THERE. I COULD GET YOU THE CARE YOU NEED--OR, YOU COULD GIVE UP YOUR SPOT TO DIRECTOR HILL.
DON'T DO IT, ROTHSTEIN--
OKAY.
OKAY? OKAY, YES?
YES. HELP HER INSTEAD OF ME.
THAT'S VERY NOBLE OF YOU, DANNY. I'M SURE THE DIRECTOR APPRECIATES IT.
SON, WAIT--YOU DON'T HAVE TO DO THIS--
IT'S OKAY, SIR. I'M NOT--

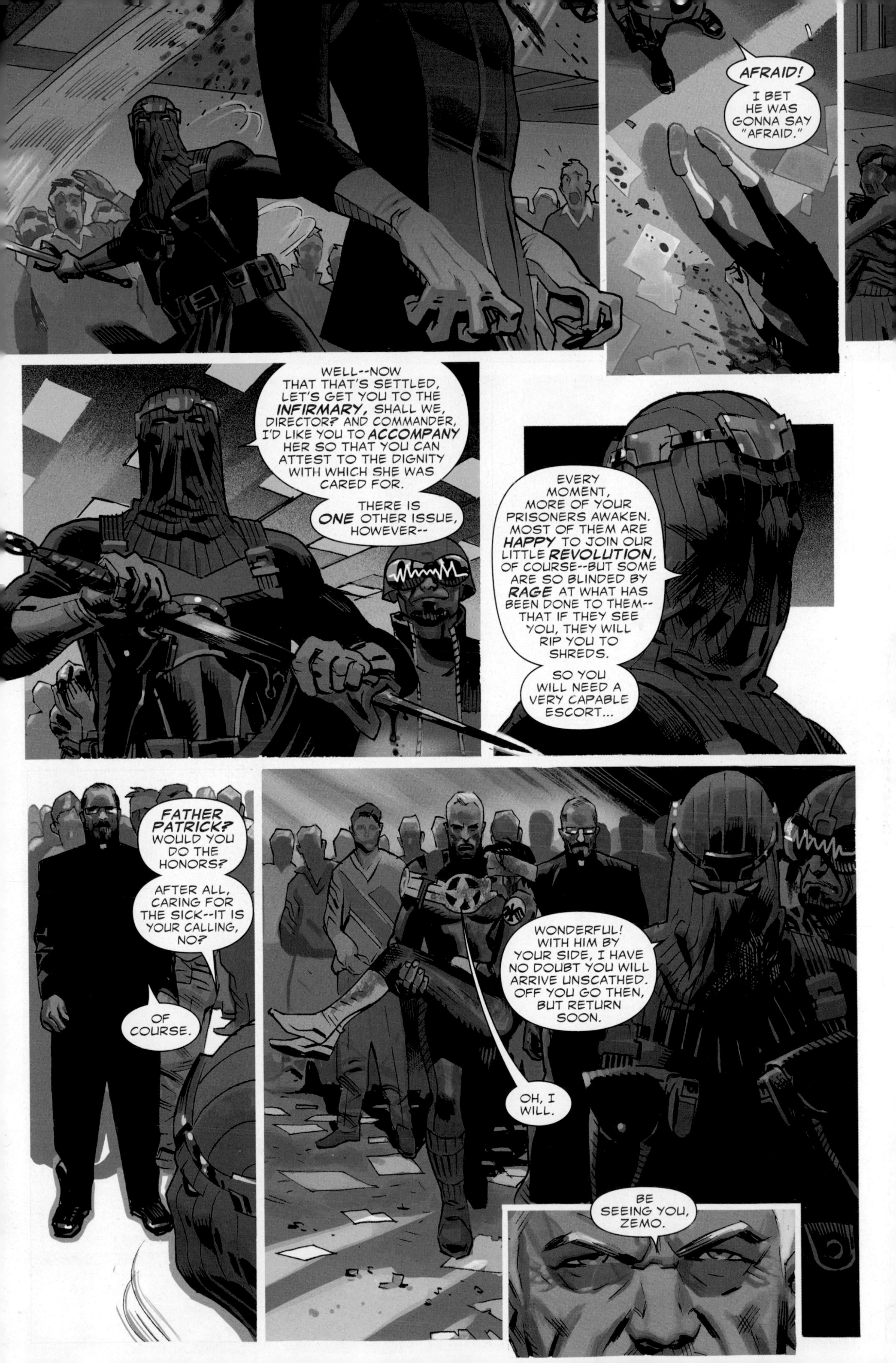

AFRAID! I BET HE WAS GONNA SAY "AFRAID."
WELL--NOW THAT THAT'S SETTLED, LET'S GET YOU TO THE INFIRMARY, SHALL WE, DIRECTOR? AND COMMANDER, I'D LIKE YOU TO ACCOMPANY HER SO THAT YOU CAN ATTEST TO THE DIGNITY WITH WHICH SHE WAS CARED FOR.
THERE IS ONE OTHER ISSUE, HOWEVER--
EVERY MOMENT, MORE OF YOUR PRISONERS AWAKEN. MOST OF THEM ARE HAPPY TO JOIN OUR LITTLE REVOLUTION, OF COURSE--BUT SOME ARE SO BLINDED BY RAGE AT WHAT HAS BEEN DONE TO THEM--THAT IF THEY SEE YOU, THEY WILL RIP YOU TO SHREDS.
SO YOU WILL NEED A VERY CAPABLE ESCORT...
FATHER PATRICK? WOULD YOU DO THE HONORS?
AFTER ALL, CARING FOR THE SICK--IT IS YOUR CALLING, NO?
OF COURSE.
WONDERFUL! WITH HIM BY YOUR SIDE, I HAVE NO DOUBT YOU WILL ARRIVE UNSCATHED. OFF YOU GO THEN, BUT RETURN SOON.
OH, I WILL.
BE SEEING YOU, ZEMO.

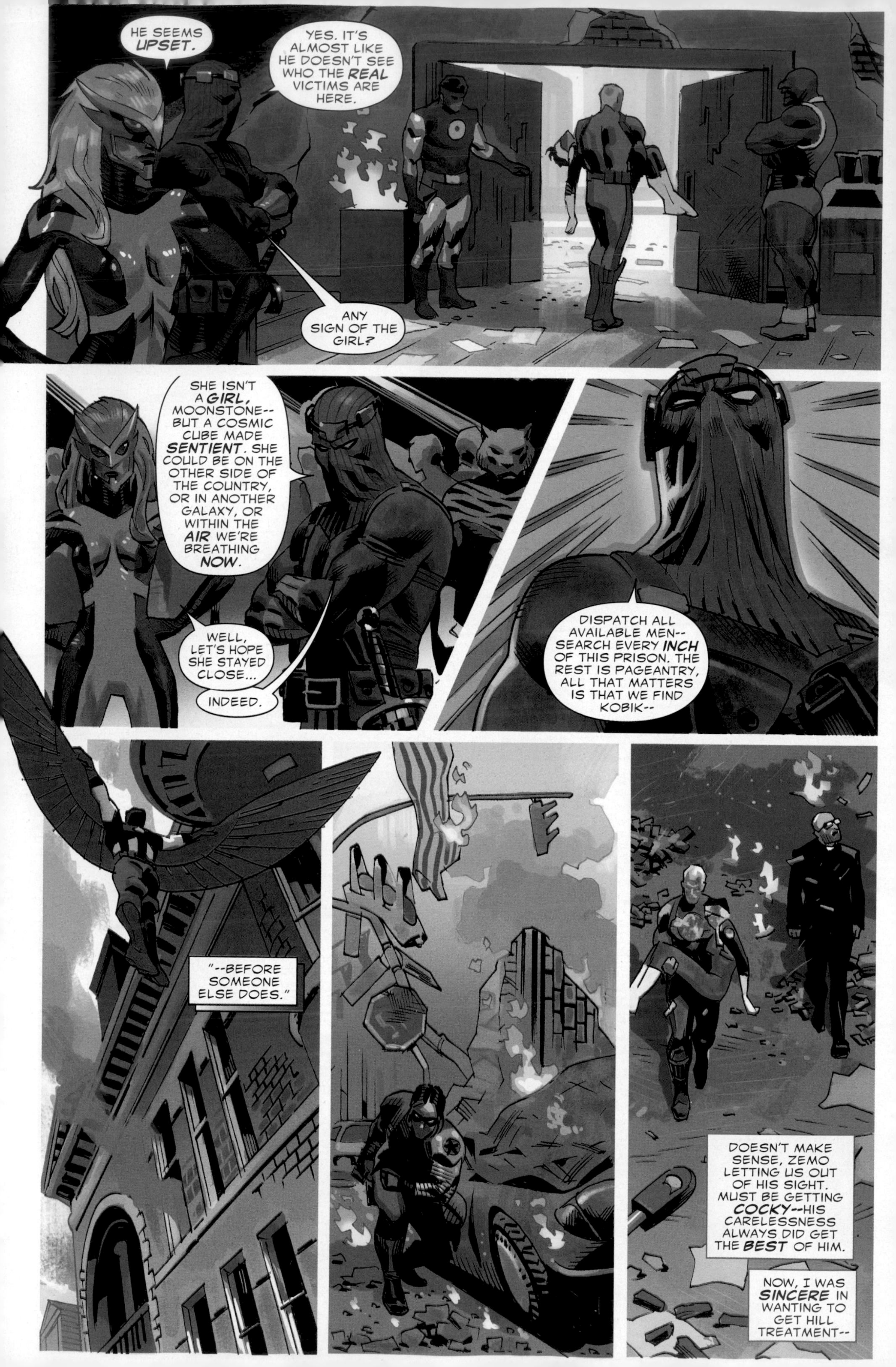

HE SEEMS UPSET.
YES. IT'S ALMOST LIKE HE DOESN'T SEE WHO THE REAL VICTIMS ARE HERE.
ANY SIGN OF THE GIRL?
SHE ISN'T A GIRL, MOONSTONE-- BUT A COSMIC CUBE MADE SENTIENT. SHE COULD BE ON THE OTHER SIDE OF THE COUNTRY, OR IN ANOTHER GALAXY, OR WITHIN THE AIR WE'RE BREATHING NOW.
WELL, LET'S HOPE SHE STAYED CLOSE...
INDEED.
DISPATCH ALL AVAILABLE MEN-- SEARCH EVERY INCH OF THIS PRISON. THE REST IS PAGEANTRY, ALL THAT MATTERS IS THAT WE FIND KOBIK--
"--BEFORE SOMEONE ELSE DOES."
DOESN'T MAKE SENSE, ZEMO LETTING US OUT OF HIS SIGHT. MUST BE GETTING COCKY--HIS CARELESSNESS ALWAYS DID GET THE BEST OF HIM.
NOW, I WAS SINCERE IN WANTING TO GET HILL TREATMENT--

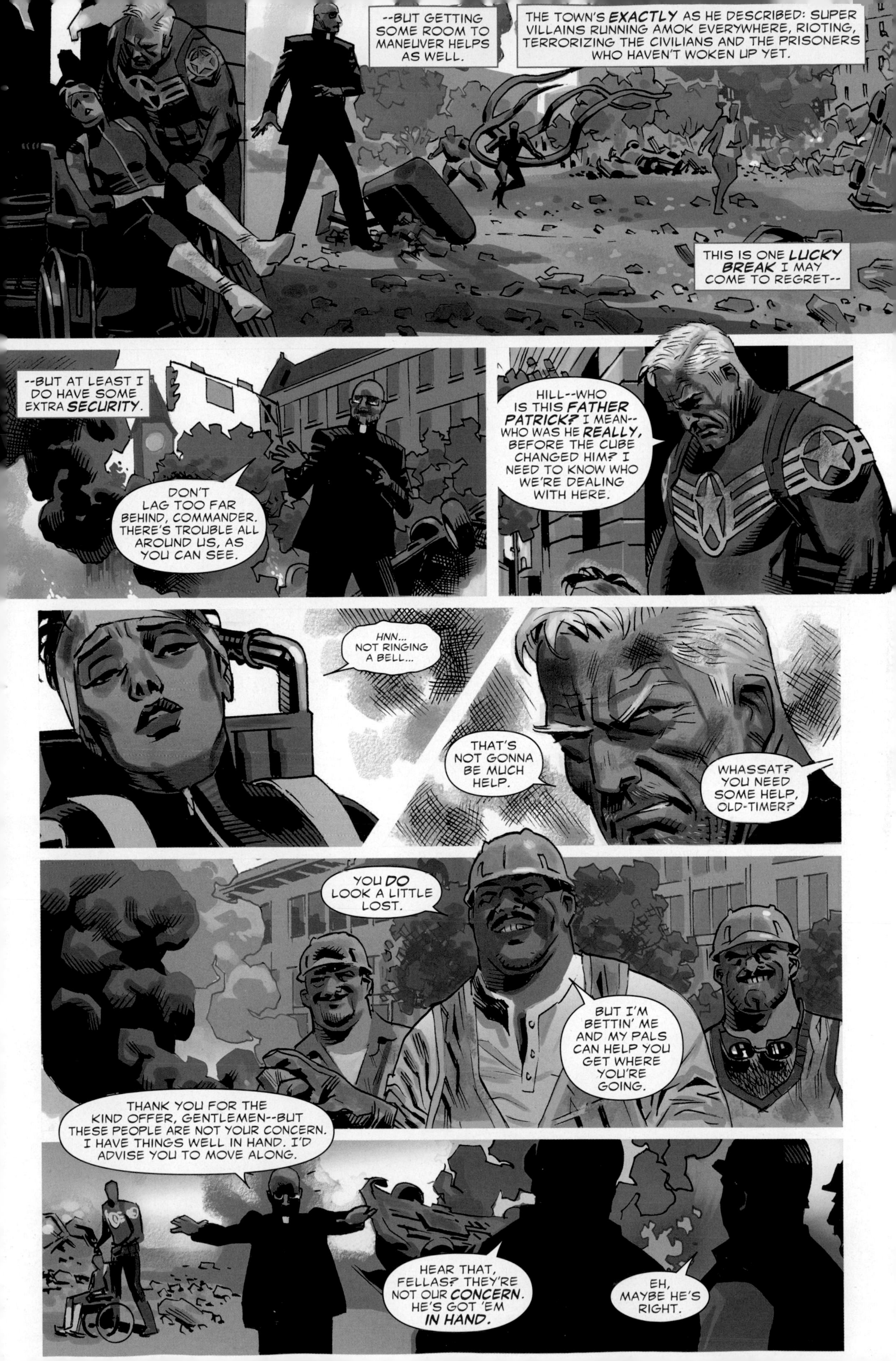
--BUT GETTING SOME ROOM TO MANEUVER HELPS AS WELL.
THE TOWN'S EXACTLY AS HE DESCRIBED: SUPER VILLAINS RUNNING AMOK EVERYWHERE, RIOTING, TERRORIZING THE CIVILIANS AND THE PRISONERS WHO HAVEN'T WOKEN UP YET.
THIS IS ONE LUCKY BREAK I MAY COME TO REGRET--
--BUT AT LEAST I DO HAVE SOME EXTRA SECURITY.
DON'T LAG TOO FAR BEHIND, COMMANDER. THERE'S TROUBLE ALL AROUND US, AS YOU CAN SEE.
HILL--WHO IS THIS FATHER PATRICK? I MEAN--WHO WAS HE REALLY, BEFORE THE CUBE CHANGED HIM? I NEED TO KNOW WHO WE'RE DEALING WITH HERE.
HNN... NOT RINGING A BELL...
THAT'S NOT GONNA BE MUCH HELP.
WHASSAT? YOU NEED SOME HELP, OLD-TIMER?
YOU DO LOOK A LITTLE LOST.
BUT I'M BETTIN' ME AND MY PALS CAN HELP YOU GET WHERE YOU'RE GOING.
THANK YOU FOR THE KIND OFFER, GENTLEMEN--BUT THESE PEOPLE ARE NOT YOUR CONCERN. I HAVE THINGS WELL IN HAND. I'D ADVISE YOU TO MOVE ALONG.
HEAR THAT, FELLAS? THEY'RE NOT OUR CONCERN. HE'S GOT 'EM IN HAND.
EH, MAYBE HE'S RIGHT.

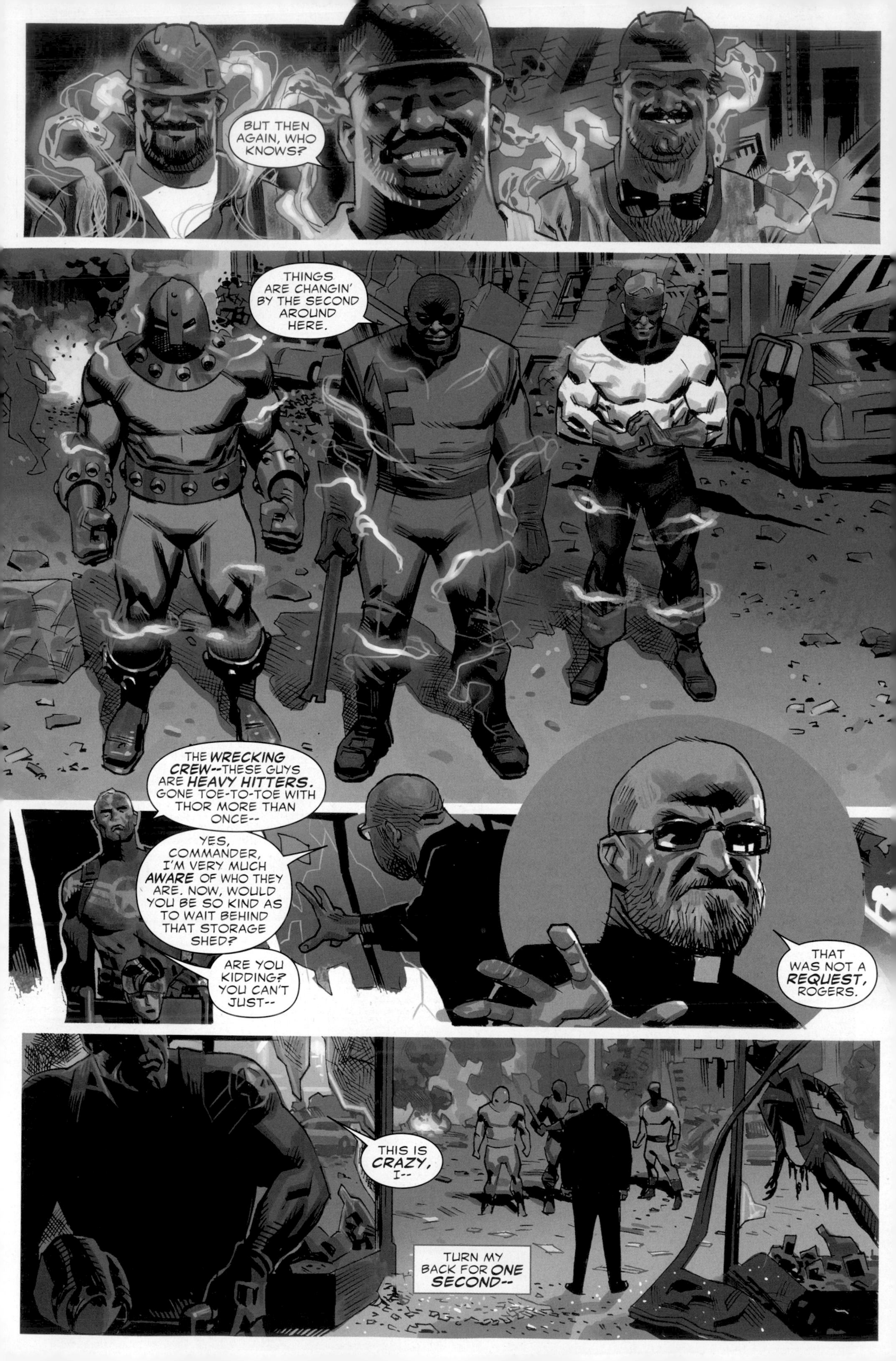
BUT THEN AGAIN, WHO KNOWS?
THINGS ARE CHANGIN' BY THE SECOND AROUND HERE.
THE WRECKING CREW--THESE GUYS ARE HEAVY HITTERS. GONE TOE-TO-TOE WITH THOR MORE THAN ONCE--
YES, COMMANDER, I'M VERY MUCH AWARE OF WHO THEY ARE. NOW, WOULD YOU BE SO KIND AS TO WAIT BEHIND THAT STORAGE SHED?
ARE YOU KIDDING? YOU CAN'T JUST--
THAT WAS NOT A REQUEST, ROGERS.
THIS IS CRAZY, I--
TURN MY BACK FOR ONE SECOND--

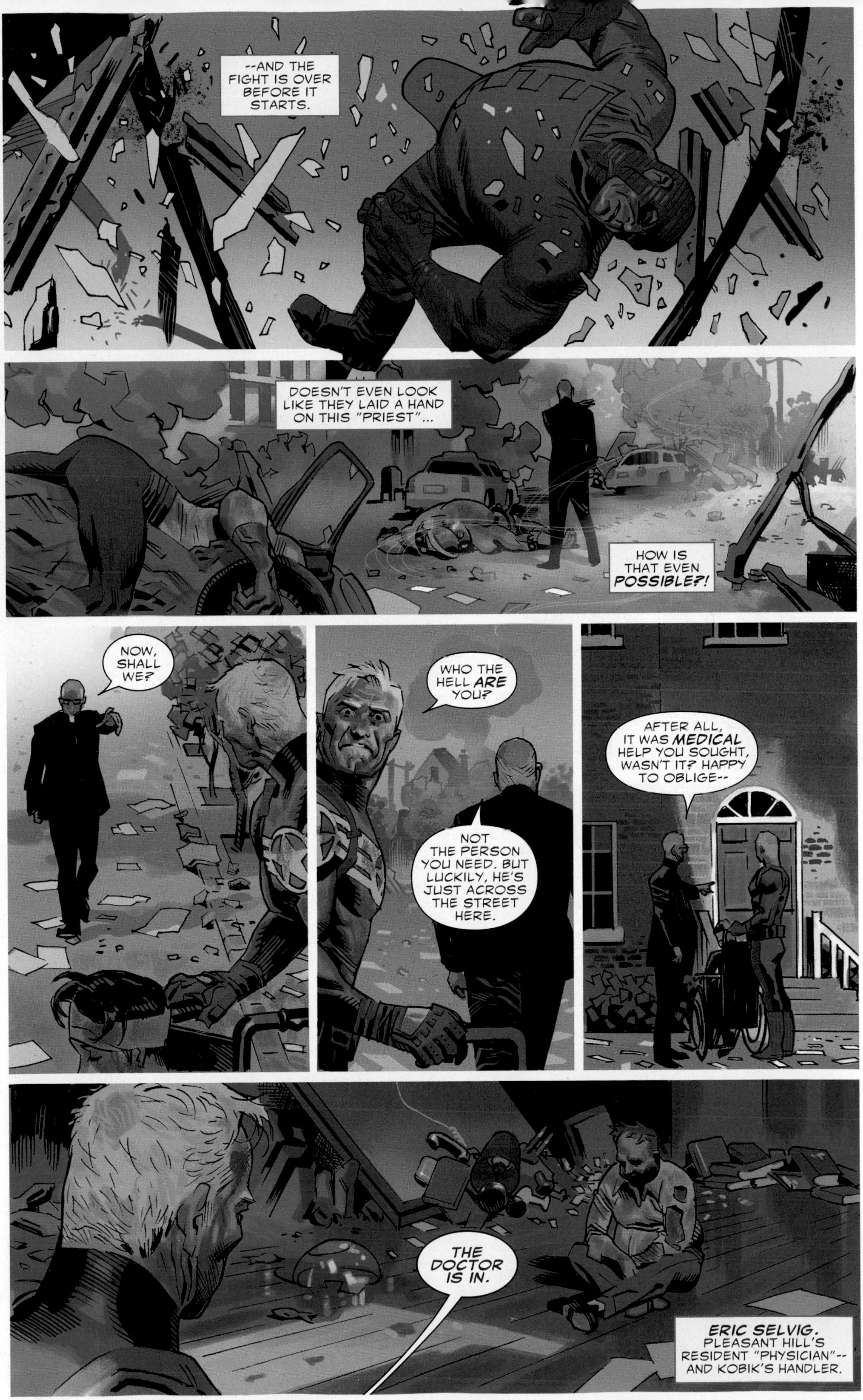
--AND THE FIGHT IS OVER BEFORE IT STARTS.
DOESN'T EVEN LOOK LIKE THEY LAID A HAND ON THIS "PRIEST"...
HOW IS THAT EVEN POSSIBLE?!
NOW, SHALL WE?
WHO THE HELL ARE YOU?
NOT THE PERSON YOU NEED. BUT LUCKILY, HE'S JUST ACROSS THE STREET HERE.
AFTER ALL, IT WAS MEDICAL HELP YOU SOUGHT, WASN'T IT? HAPPY TO OBLIGE--
THE DOCTOR IS IN.
ERIC SELVIG. PLEASANT HILL'S RESIDENT "PHYSICIAN"-- AND KOBIK'S HANDLER.

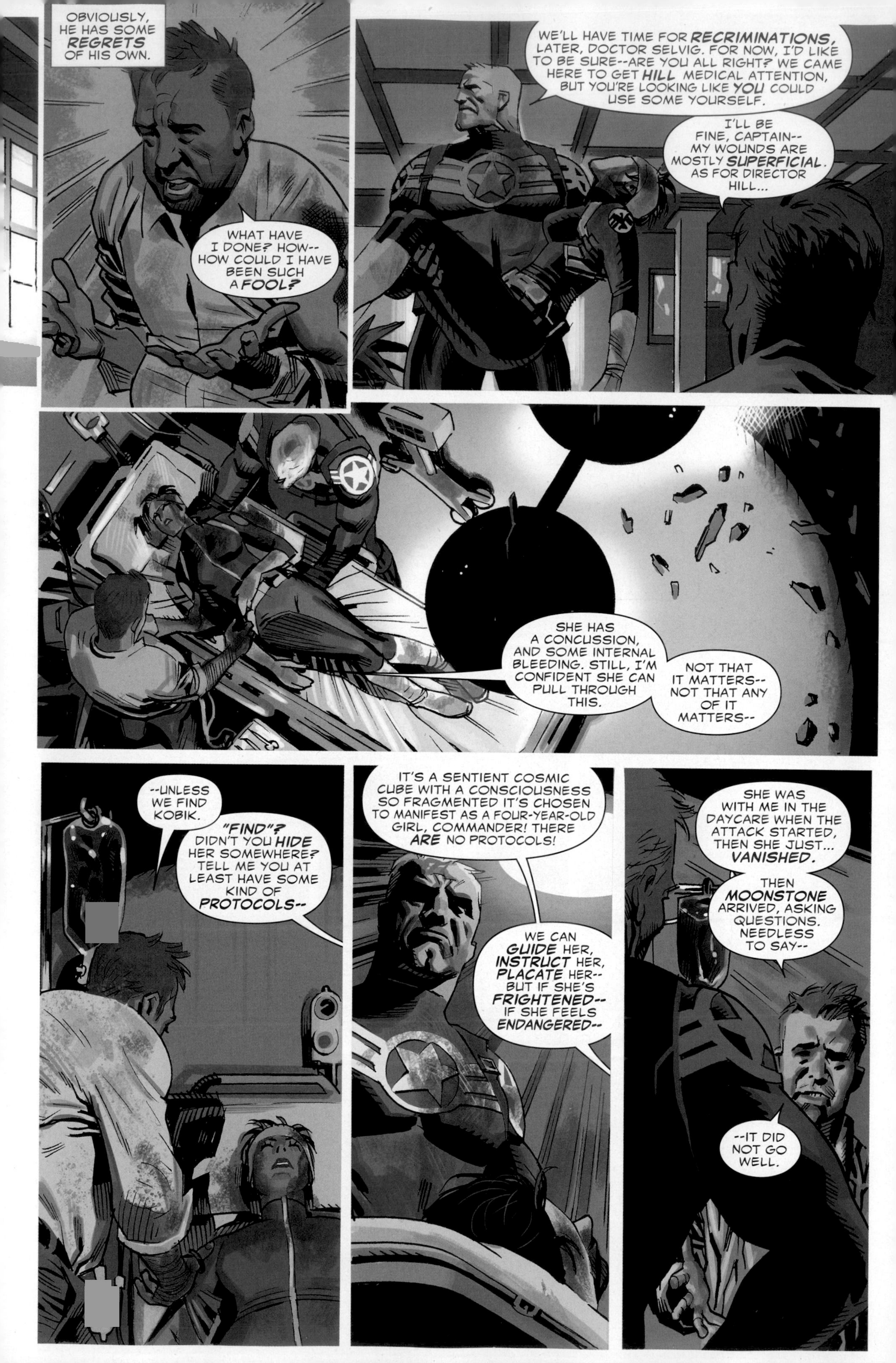
OBVIOUSLY, HE HAS SOME REGRETS OF HIS OWN.
WHAT HAVE I DONE? HOW-- HOW COULD I HAVE BEEN SUCH A FOOL?
WE'LL HAVE TIME FOR RECRIMINATIONS, LATER, DOCTOR SELVIG. FOR NOW, I'D LIKE TO BE SURE--ARE YOU ALL RIGHT? WE CAME HERE TO GET HILL MEDICAL ATTENTION, BUT YOU'RE LOOKING LIKE YOU COULD USE SOME YOURSELF.
I'LL BE FINE, CAPTAIN-- MY WOUNDS ARE MOSTLY SUPERFICIAL. AS FOR DIRECTOR HILL...
SHE HAS A CONCUSSION, AND SOME INTERNAL BLEEDING. STILL, I'M CONFIDENT SHE CAN PULL THROUGH THIS.
NOT THAT IT MATTERS-- NOT THAT ANY OF IT MATTERS--
--UNLESS WE FIND KOBIK.
"FIND"? DIDN'T YOU HIDE HER SOMEWHERE? TELL ME YOU AT LEAST HAVE SOME KIND OF PROTOCOLS--
IT'S A SENTIENT COSMIC CUBE WITH A CONSCIOUSNESS SO FRAGMENTED IT'S CHOSEN TO MANIFEST AS A FOUR-YEAR-OLD GIRL, COMMANDER! THERE ARE NO PROTOCOLS!
WE CAN GUIDE HER, INSTRUCT HER, PLACATE HER-- BUT IF SHE'S FRIGHTENED-- IF SHE FEELS ENDANGERED--
SHE WAS WITH ME IN THE DAYCARE WHEN THE ATTACK STARTED, THEN SHE JUST... VANISHED.
THEN MOONSTONE ARRIVED, ASKING QUESTIONS. NEEDLESS TO SAY--
--IT DID NOT GO WELL.

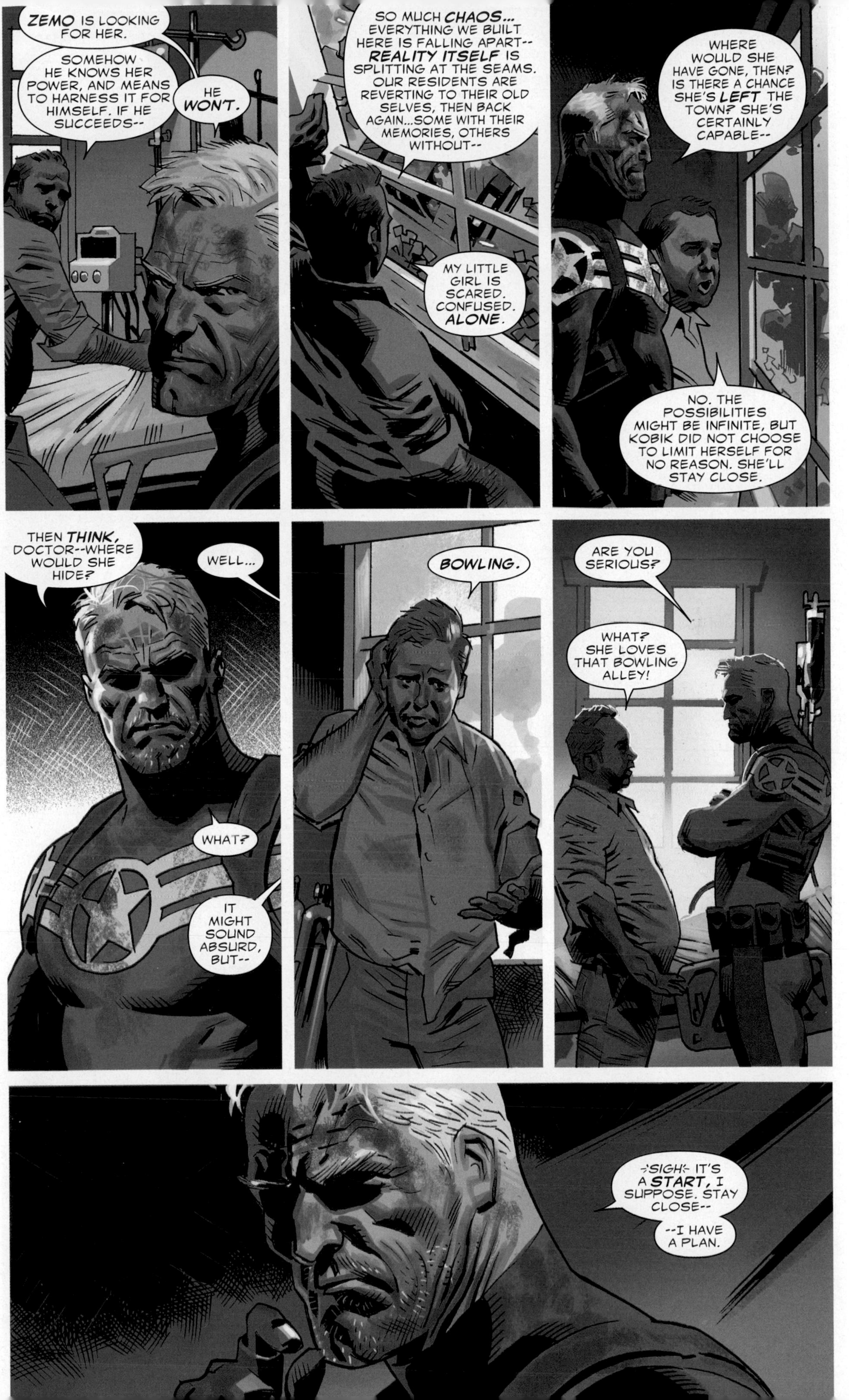
ZEMO IS LOOKING FOR HER.
SOMEHOW HE KNOWS HER POWER, AND MEANS TO HARNESS IT FOR HIMSELF. IF HE SUCCEEDS--
HE WON'T.
SO MUCH CHAOS... EVERYTHING WE BUILT HERE IS FALLING APART-- REALITY ITSELF IS SPLITTING AT THE SEAMS. OUR RESIDENTS ARE REVERTING TO THEIR OLD SELVES, THEN BACK AGAIN...SOME WITH THEIR MEMORIES, OTHERS WITHOUT--
MY LITTLE GIRL IS SCARED. CONFUSED. ALONE.
WHERE WOULD SHE HAVE GONE, THEN? IS THERE A CHANCE SHE'S LEFT THE TOWN? SHE'S CERTAINLY CAPABLE--
NO. THE POSSIBILITIES MIGHT BE INFINITE, BUT KOBIK DID NOT CHOOSE TO LIMIT HERSELF FOR NO REASON. SHE'LL STAY CLOSE.
THEN THINK, DOCTOR--WHERE WOULD SHE HIDE?
WELL...
WHAT?
IT MIGHT SOUND ABSURD, BUT--
BOWLING.
ARE YOU SERIOUS?
WHAT? SHE LOVES THAT BOWLING ALLEY!
-SIGH- IT'S A START, I SUPPOSE. STAY CLOSE--
--I HAVE A PLAN.

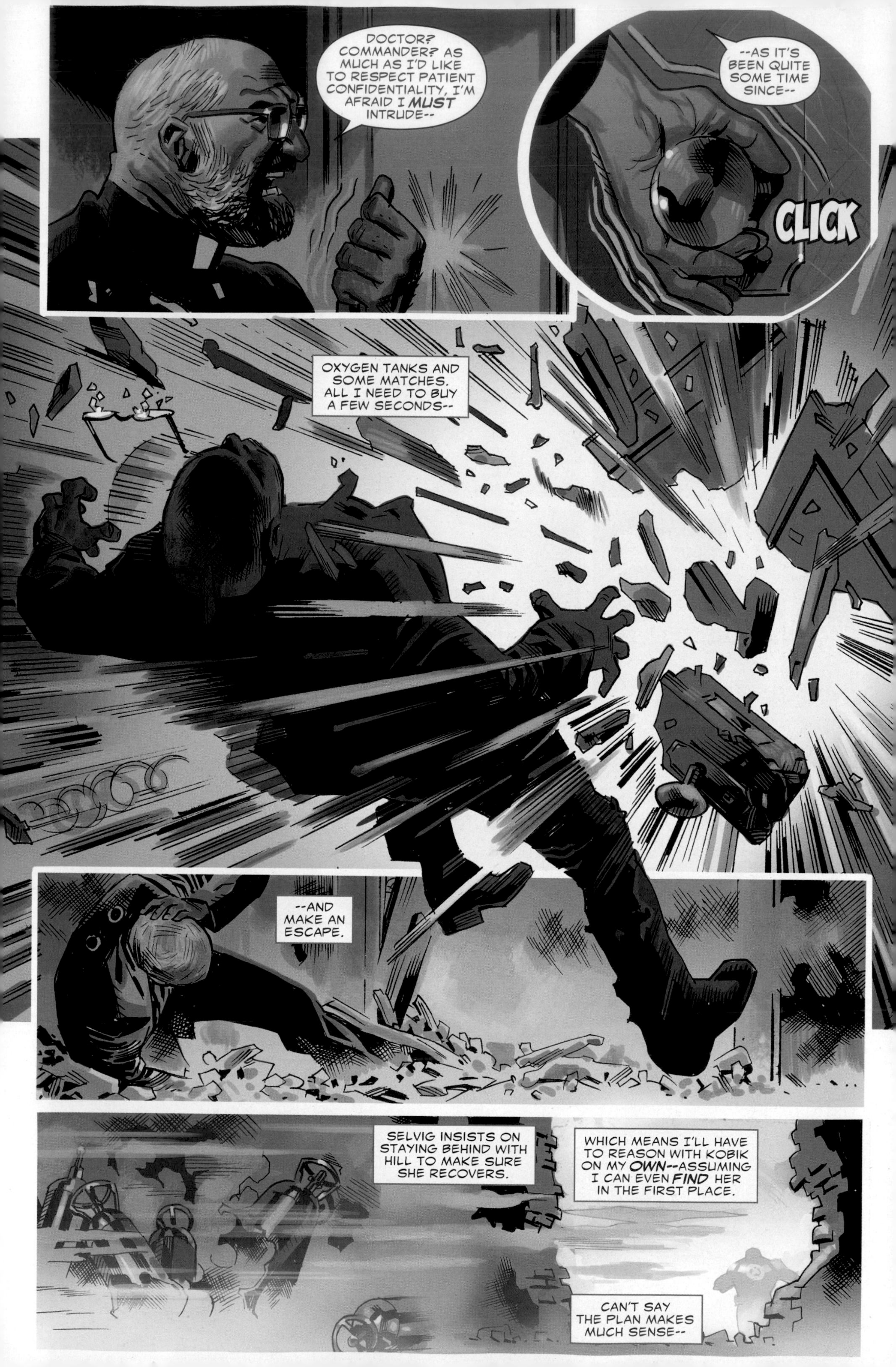
DOCTOR? COMMANDER? AS MUCH AS I'D LIKE TO RESPECT PATIENT CONFIDENTIALITY, I'M AFRAID I MUST INTRUDE--
--AS IT'S BEEN QUITE SOME TIME SINCE--
CLICK
OXYGEN TANKS AND SOME MATCHES. ALL I NEED TO BUY A FEW SECONDS--
--AND MAKE AN ESCAPE.
SELVIG INSISTS ON STAYING BEHIND WITH HILL TO MAKE SURE SHE RECOVERS.
WHICH MEANS I'LL HAVE TO REASON WITH KOBIK ON MY OWN--ASSUMING I CAN EVEN FIND HER IN THE FIRST PLACE.
CAN'T SAY THE PLAN MAKES MUCH SENSE--

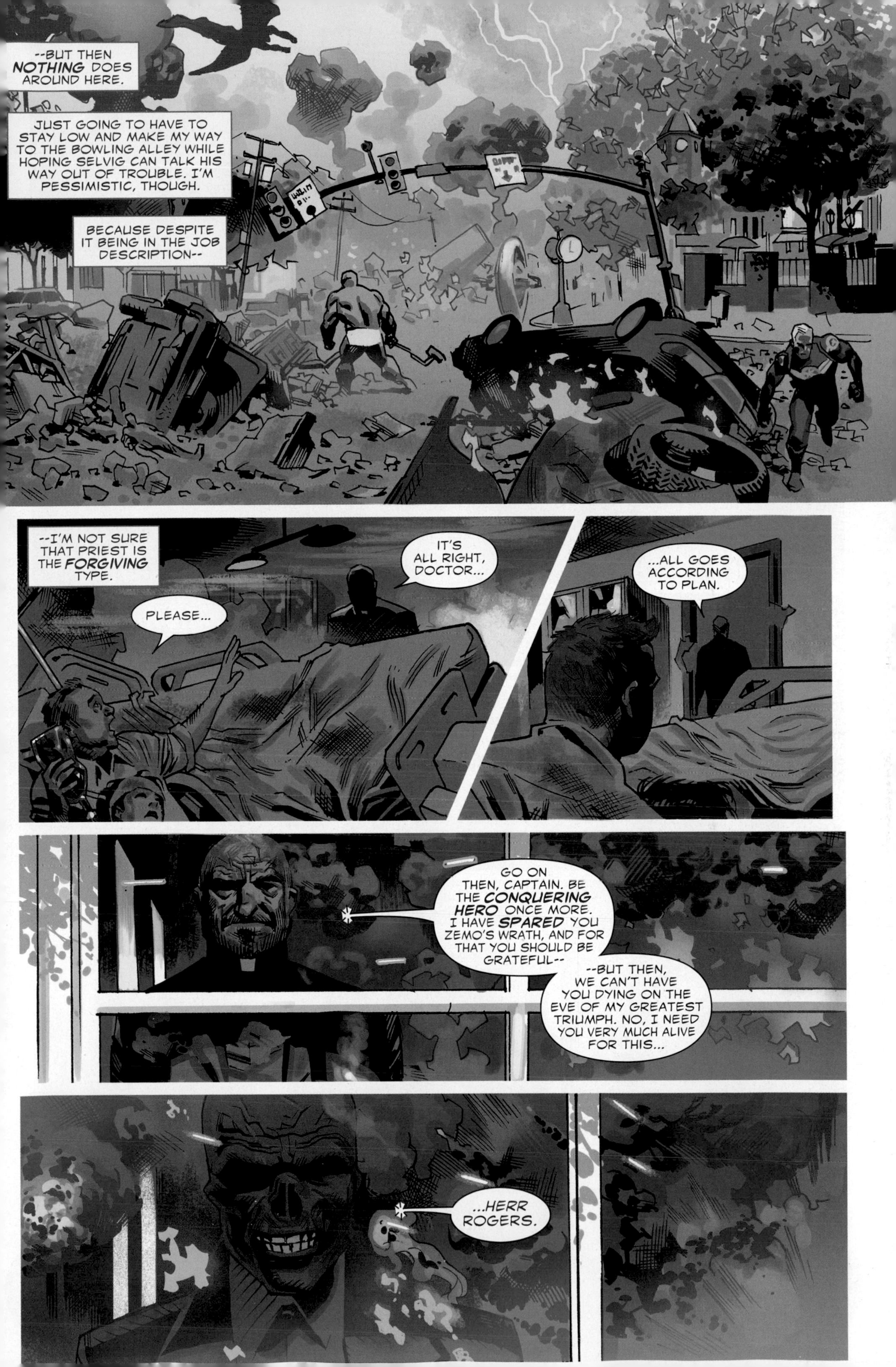
--BUT THEN NOTHING DOES AROUND HERE.
JUST GOING TO HAVE TO STAY LOW AND MAKE MY WAY TO THE BOWLING ALLEY WHILE HOPING SELVIG CAN TALK HIS WAY OUT OF TROUBLE. I'M PESSIMISTIC, THOUGH.
BECAUSE DESPITE IT BEING IN THE JOB DESCRIPTION--
--I'M NOT SURE THAT PRIEST IS THE FORGIVING TYPE.
PLEASE...
IT'S ALL RIGHT, DOCTOR...
...ALL GOES ACCORDING TO PLAN.
GO ON THEN, CAPTAIN. BE THE CONQUERING HERO ONCE MORE. I HAVE SPARED YOU ZEMO'S WRATH, AND FOR THAT YOU SHOULD BE GRATEFUL--
--BUT THEN, WE CAN'T HAVE YOU DYING ON THE EVE OF MY GREATEST TRIUMPH. NO, I NEED YOU VERY MUCH ALIVE FOR THIS...
...HERR ROGERS.

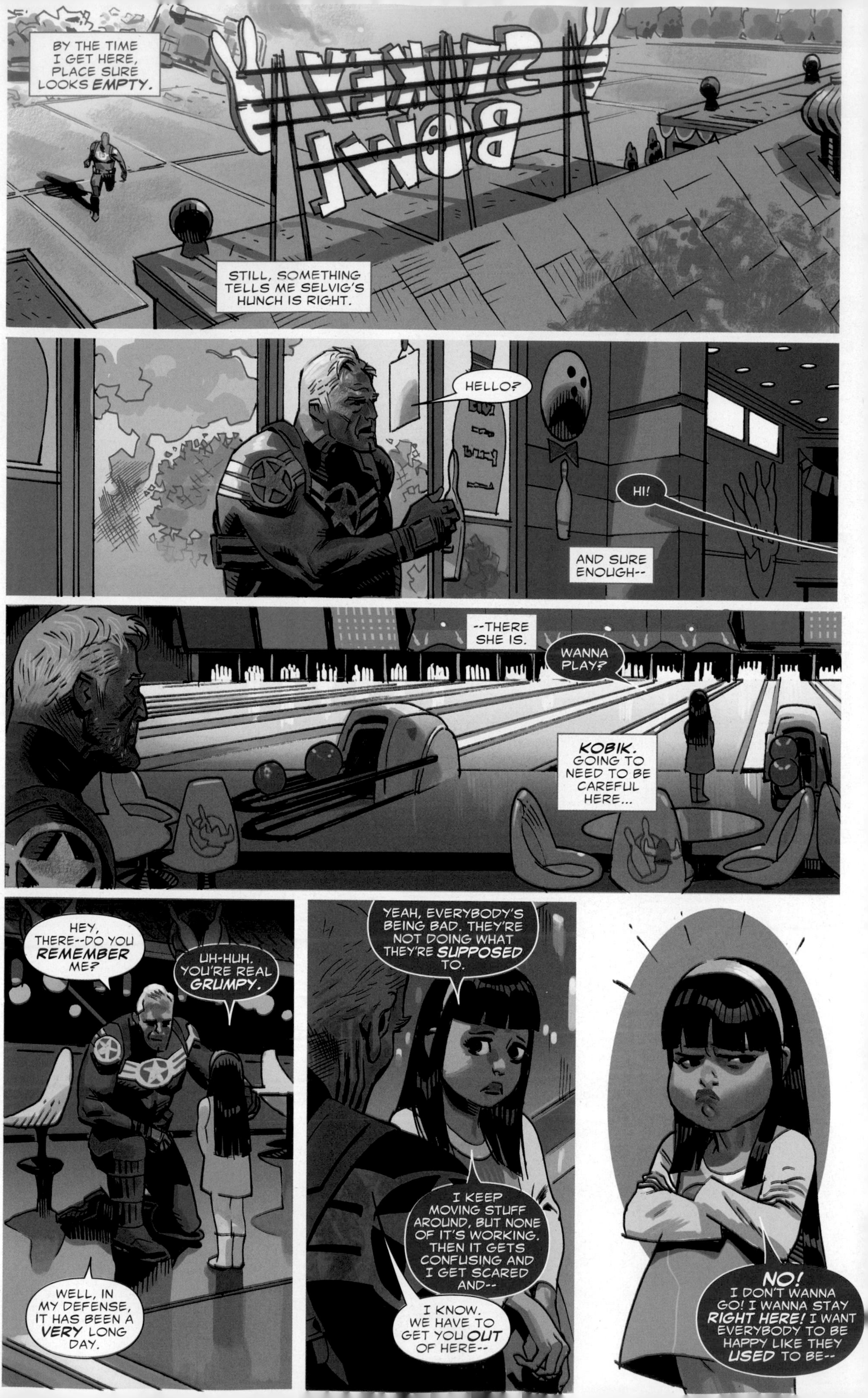

BY THE TIME I GET HERE, PLACE SURE LOOKS **EMPTY.**
STILL, SOMETHING TELLS ME SELVIG'S HUNCH IS RIGHT.
HELLO?
HI!
AND SURE ENOUGH--
--THERE SHE IS.
WANNA PLAY?
KOBIK. GOING TO NEED TO BE CAREFUL HERE...
HEY, THERE--DO YOU **REMEMBER** ME?
UH-HUH. YOU'RE REAL **GRUMPY.**
WELL, IN MY DEFENSE, IT HAS BEEN A **VERY** LONG DAY.
YEAH, EVERYBODY'S BEING BAD. THEY'RE NOT DOING WHAT THEY'RE **SUPPOSED** TO.
I KEEP MOVING STUFF AROUND, BUT NONE OF IT'S WORKING. THEN IT GETS CONFUSING AND I GET SCARED AND--
I KNOW. WE HAVE TO GET YOU **OUT** OF HERE--
NO! I DON'T WANNA GO! I WANNA STAY **RIGHT HERE!** I WANT EVERYBODY TO BE HAPPY LIKE THEY **USED** TO BE--

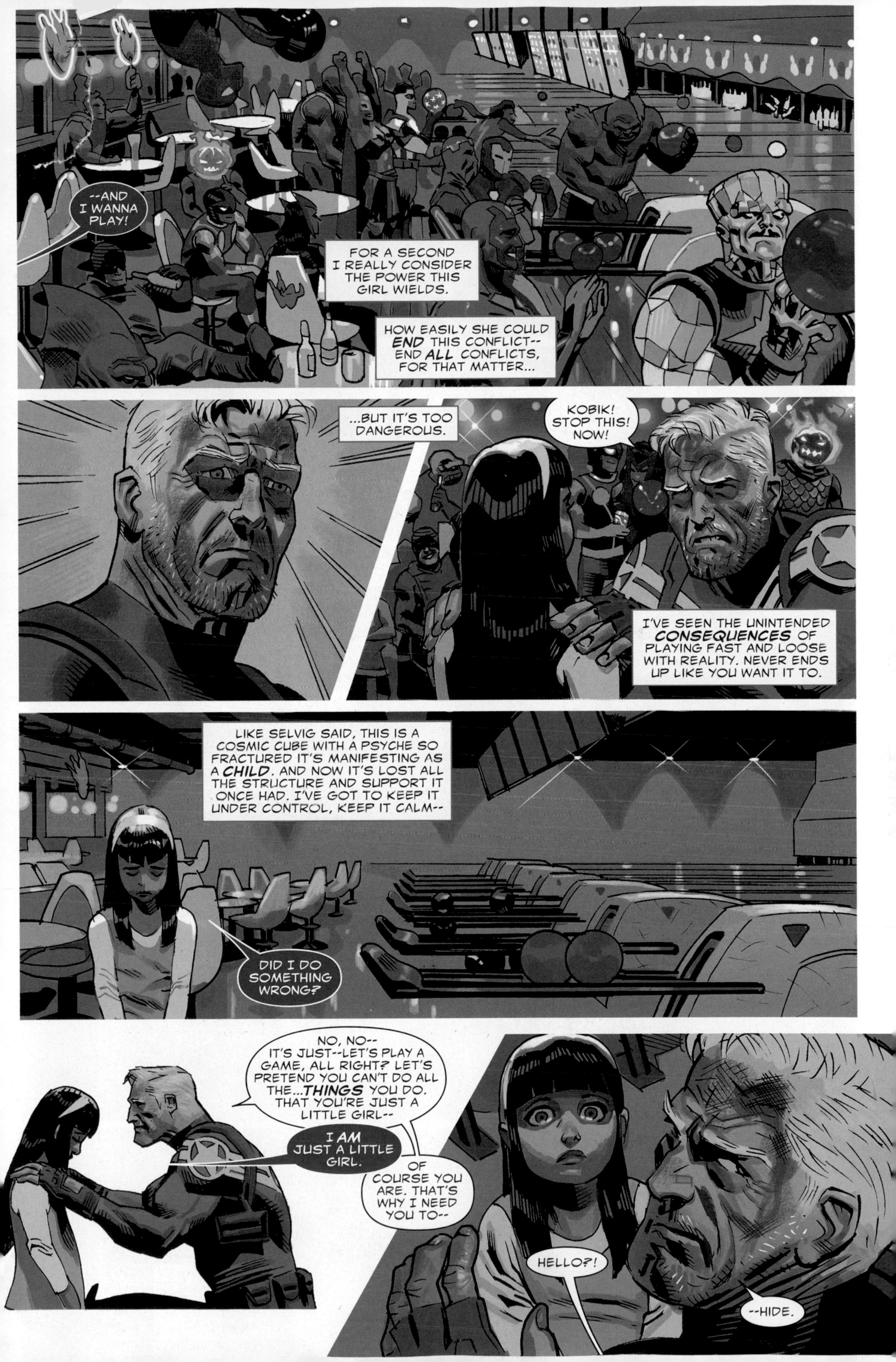

--AND I WANNA PLAY!
FOR A SECOND I REALLY CONSIDER THE POWER THIS GIRL WIELDS.
HOW EASILY SHE COULD END THIS CONFLICT-- END ALL CONFLICTS, FOR THAT MATTER...
...BUT IT'S TOO DANGEROUS.
KOBIK! STOP THIS! NOW!
I'VE SEEN THE UNINTENDED CONSEQUENCES OF PLAYING FAST AND LOOSE WITH REALITY. NEVER ENDS UP LIKE YOU WANT IT TO.
LIKE SELVIG SAID, THIS IS A COSMIC CUBE WITH A PSYCHE SO FRACTURED IT'S MANIFESTING AS A CHILD. AND NOW IT'S LOST ALL THE STRUCTURE AND SUPPORT IT ONCE HAD. I'VE GOT TO KEEP IT UNDER CONTROL, KEEP IT CALM--
DID I DO SOMETHING WRONG?
NO, NO-- IT'S JUST--LET'S PLAY A GAME, ALL RIGHT? LET'S PRETEND YOU CAN'T DO ALL THE...THINGS YOU DO. THAT YOU'RE JUST A LITTLE GIRL--
I AM JUST A LITTLE GIRL.
OF COURSE YOU ARE. THAT'S WHY I NEED YOU TO--
HELLO?!
--HIDE.

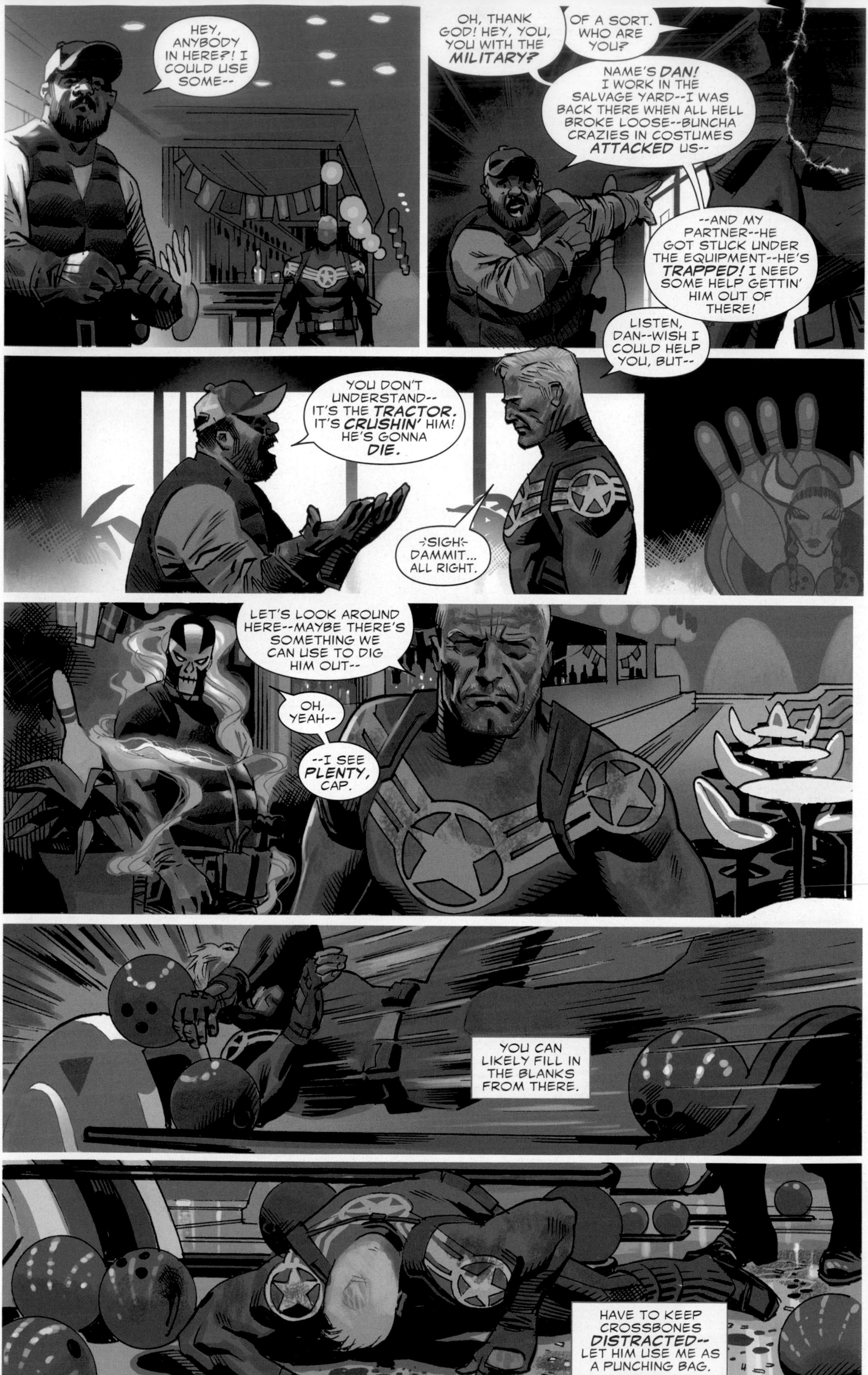
HEY, ANYBODY IN HERE?! I COULD USE SOME--
OH, THANK GOD! HEY, YOU, YOU WITH THE MILITARY?
OF A SORT. WHO ARE YOU?
NAME'S DAN! I WORK IN THE SALVAGE YARD--I WAS BACK THERE WHEN ALL HELL BROKE LOOSE--BUNCHA CRAZIES IN COSTUMES ATTACKED US--
--AND MY PARTNER--HE GOT STUCK UNDER THE EQUIPMENT--HE'S TRAPPED! I NEED SOME HELP GETTIN' HIM OUT OF THERE!
LISTEN, DAN--WISH I COULD HELP YOU, BUT--
YOU DON'T UNDERSTAND-- IT'S THE TRACTOR. IT'S CRUSHIN' HIM! HE'S GONNA DIE.
-SIGH- DAMMIT... ALL RIGHT.
LET'S LOOK AROUND HERE--MAYBE THERE'S SOMETHING WE CAN USE TO DIG HIM OUT--
OH, YEAH--
--I SEE PLENTY, CAP.
YOU CAN LIKELY FILL IN THE BLANKS FROM THERE.
HAVE TO KEEP CROSSBONES DISTRACTED-- LET HIM USE ME AS A PUNCHING BAG.

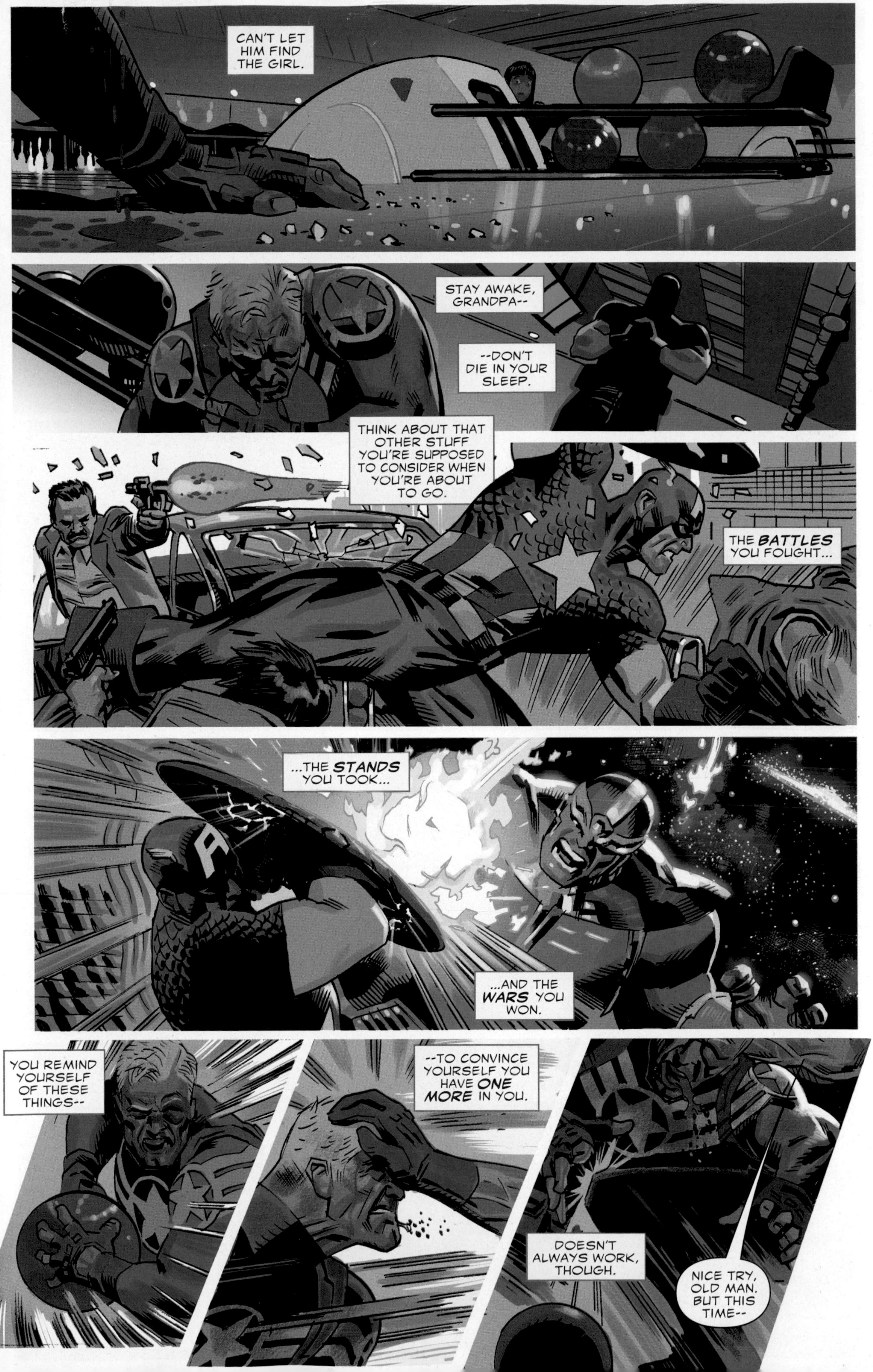

CAN'T LET HIM FIND THE GIRL.
STAY AWAKE, GRANDPA--
--DON'T DIE IN YOUR SLEEP.
THINK ABOUT THAT OTHER STUFF YOU'RE SUPPOSED TO CONSIDER WHEN YOU'RE ABOUT TO GO.
THE BATTLES YOU FOUGHT...
...THE STANDS YOU TOOK...
...AND THE WARS YOU WON.
YOU REMIND YOURSELF OF THESE THINGS--
--TO CONVINCE YOURSELF YOU HAVE ONE MORE IN YOU.
DOESN'T ALWAYS WORK, THOUGH.
NICE TRY, OLD MAN. BUT THIS TIME--

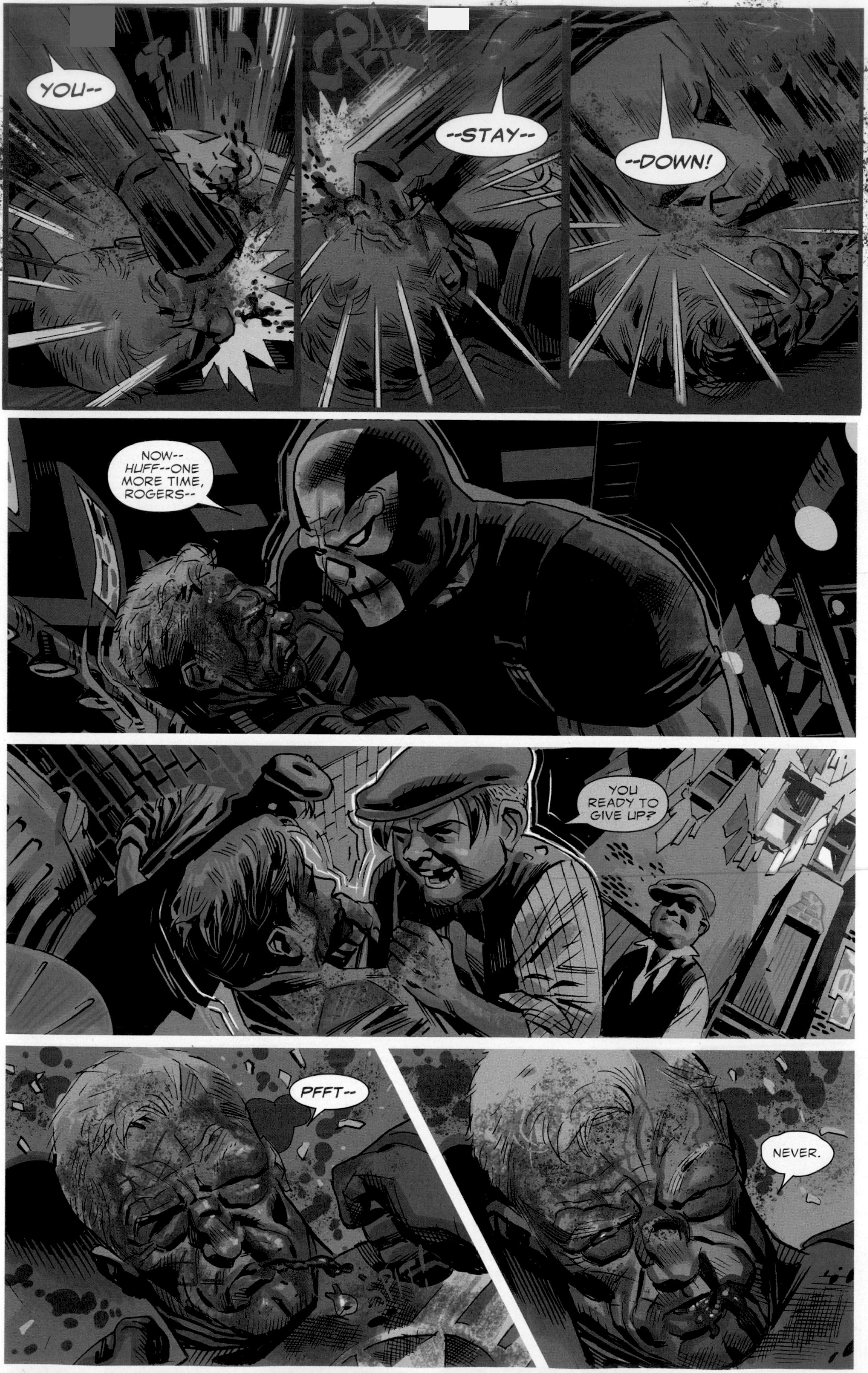
YOU--
--STAY--
--DOWN!
NOW--
HUFF--ONE
MORE TIME,
ROGERS--
YOU
READY TO
GIVE UP?
PFFT--
NEVER.

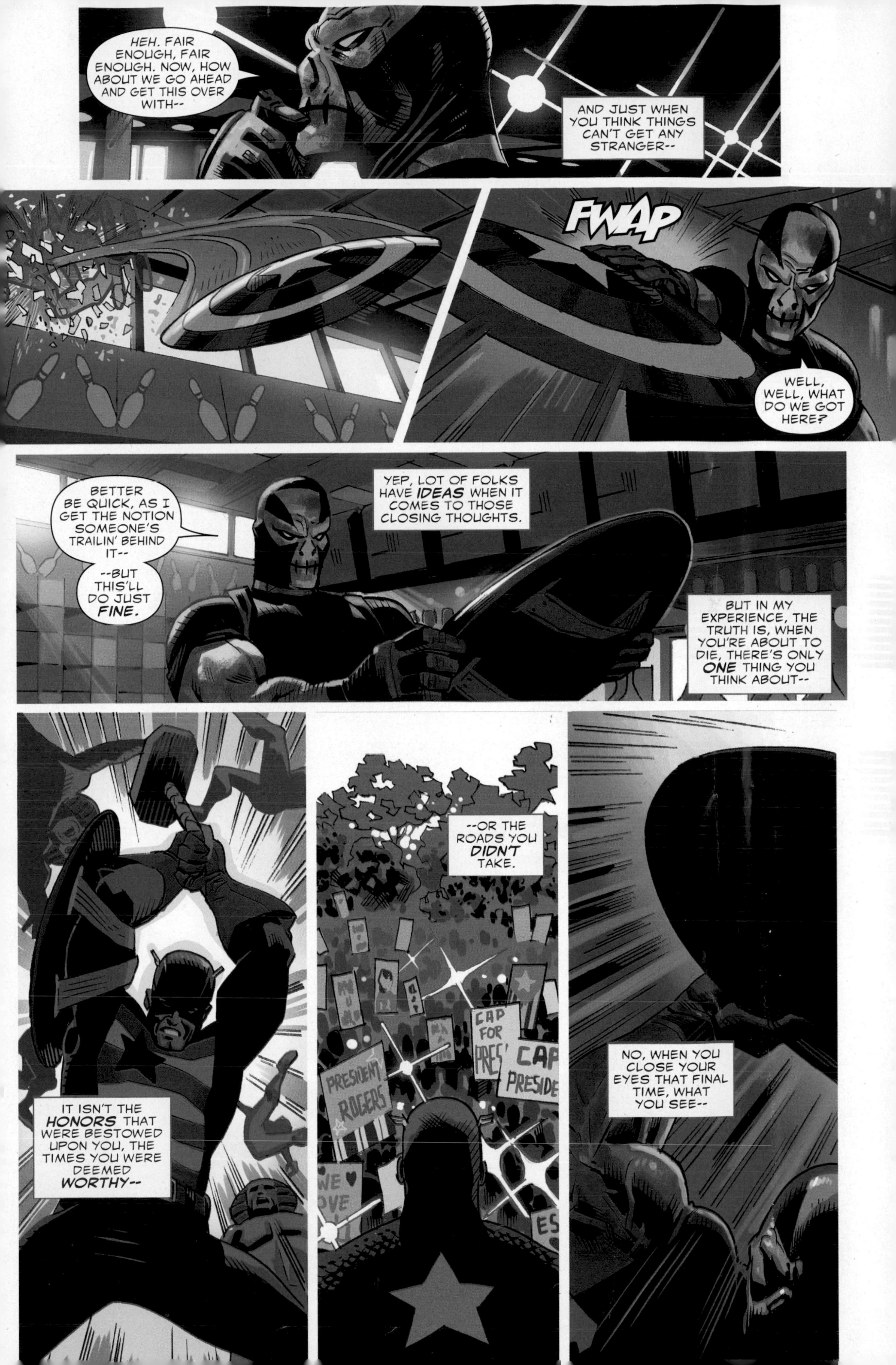
HEH. FAIR ENOUGH, FAIR ENOUGH. NOW, HOW ABOUT WE GO AHEAD AND GET THIS OVER WITH--
AND JUST WHEN YOU THINK THINGS CAN'T GET ANY STRANGER--
FWAP
WELL, WELL, WHAT DO WE GOT HERE?
BETTER BE QUICK, AS I GET THE NOTION SOMEONE'S TRAILIN' BEHIND IT--
--BUT THIS'LL DO JUST FINE.
YEP, LOT OF FOLKS HAVE IDEAS WHEN IT COMES TO THOSE CLOSING THOUGHTS.
BUT IN MY EXPERIENCE, THE TRUTH IS, WHEN YOU'RE ABOUT TO DIE, THERE'S ONLY ONE THING YOU THINK ABOUT--
IT ISN'T THE HONORS THAT WERE BESTOWED UPON YOU, THE TIMES YOU WERE DEEMED WORTHY--
--OR THE ROADS YOU DIDN'T TAKE.
CAP FOR PRES'
CAP PRESIDE
PRESIDENT ROGERS
NO, WHEN YOU CLOSE YOUR EYES THAT FINAL TIME, WHAT YOU SEE--

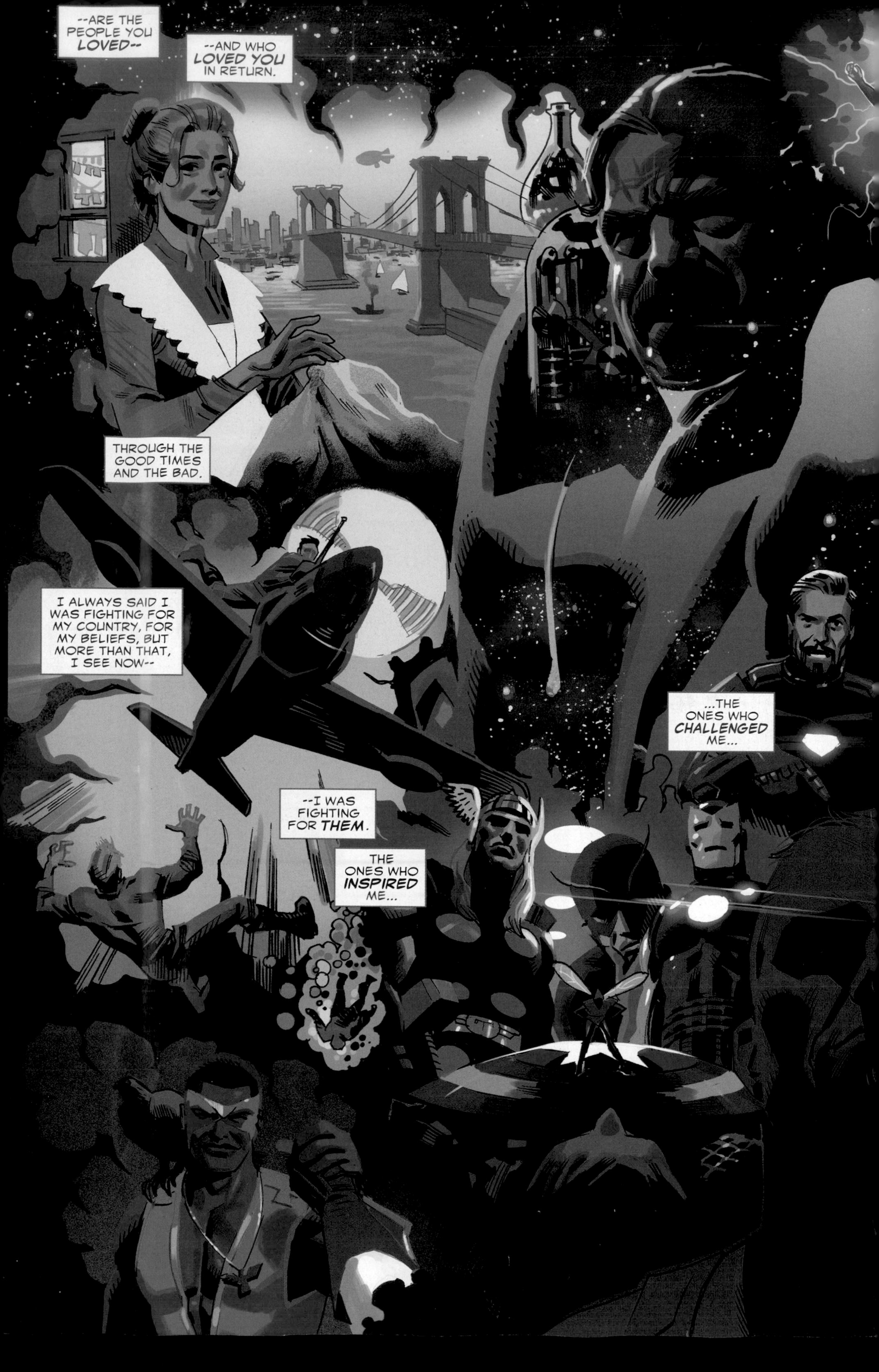
--ARE THE PEOPLE YOU LOVED--
--AND WHO LOVED YOU IN RETURN.
THROUGH THE GOOD TIMES AND THE BAD.
I ALWAYS SAID I WAS FIGHTING FOR MY COUNTRY, FOR MY BELIEFS, BUT MORE THAN THAT, I SEE NOW--
--I WAS FIGHTING FOR THEM.
THE ONES WHO INSPIRED ME...
...THE ONES WHO CHALLENGED ME...

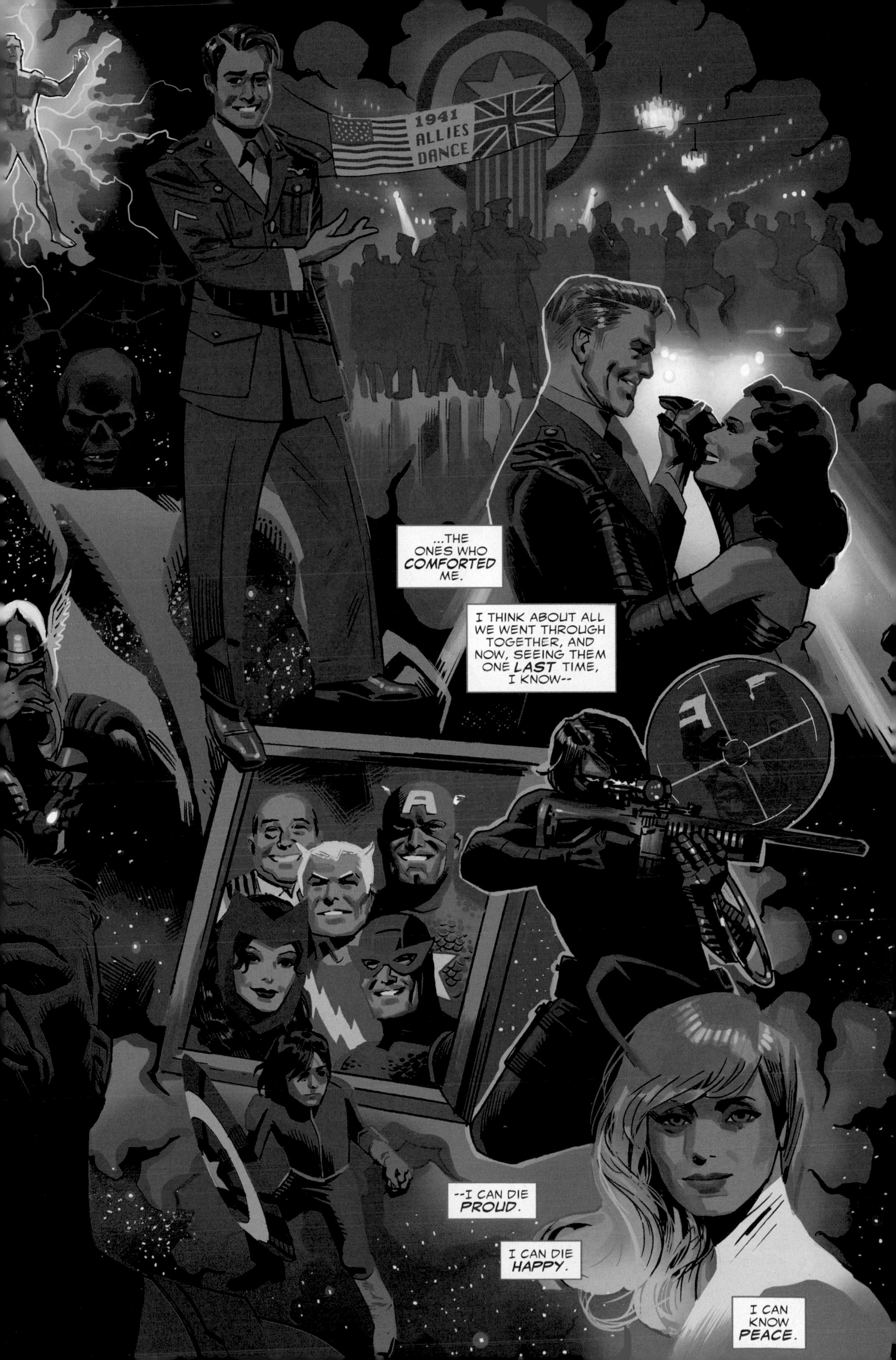
1941 ALLIES DANCE
...THE ONES WHO COMFORTED ME.
I THINK ABOUT ALL WE WENT THROUGH TOGETHER, AND NOW, SEEING THEM ONE LAST TIME, I KNOW--
--I CAN DIE PROUD.
I CAN DIE HAPPY.
I CAN KNOW PEACE.

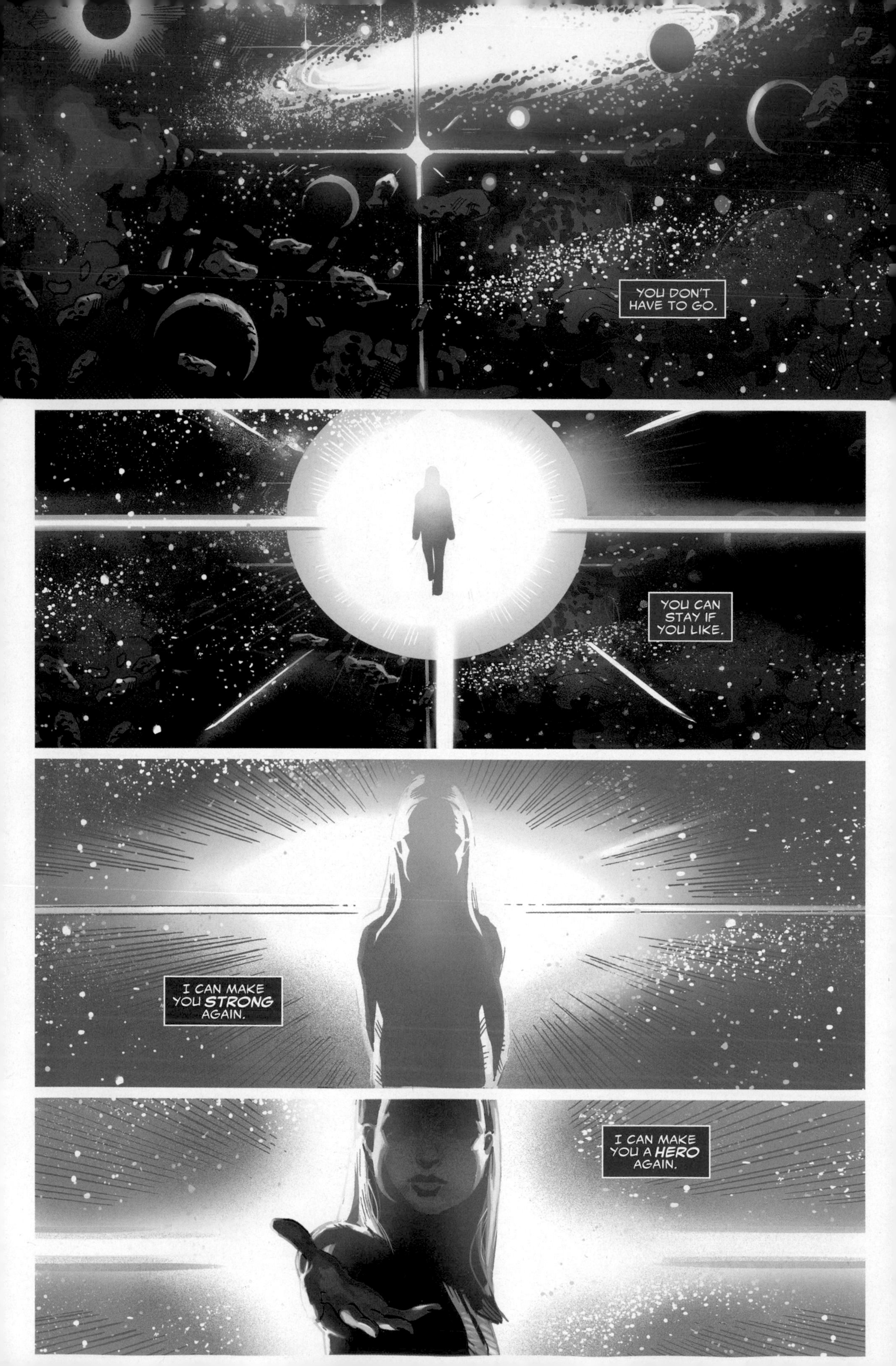
YOU DON'T HAVE TO GO.
YOU CAN STAY IF YOU LIKE.
I CAN MAKE YOU **STRONG** AGAIN.
I CAN MAKE YOU A **HERO** AGAIN.

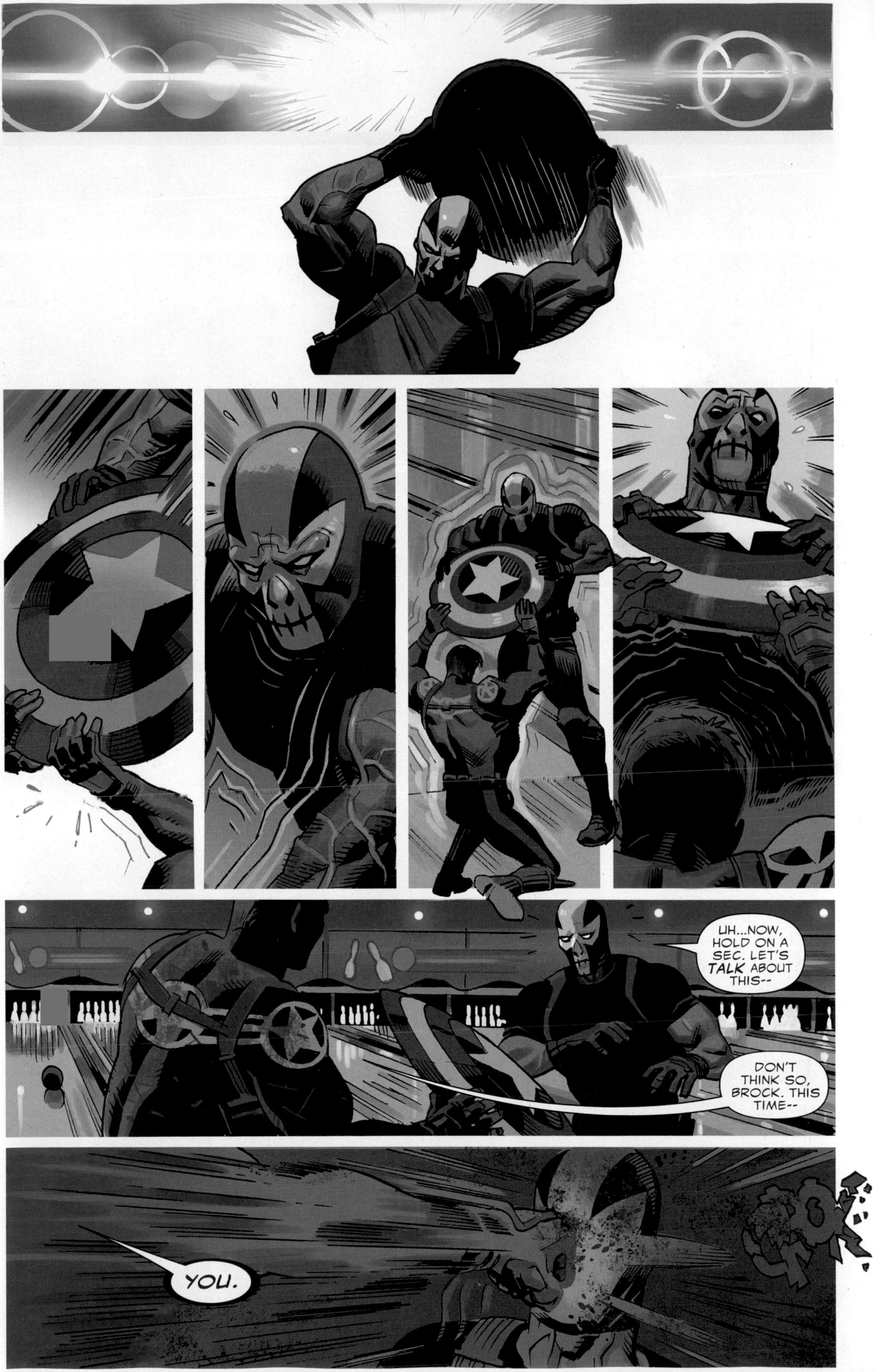
UH...NOW, HOLD ON A SEC. LET'S TALK ABOUT THIS--
DON'T THINK SO, BROCK. THIS TIME--
YOU.

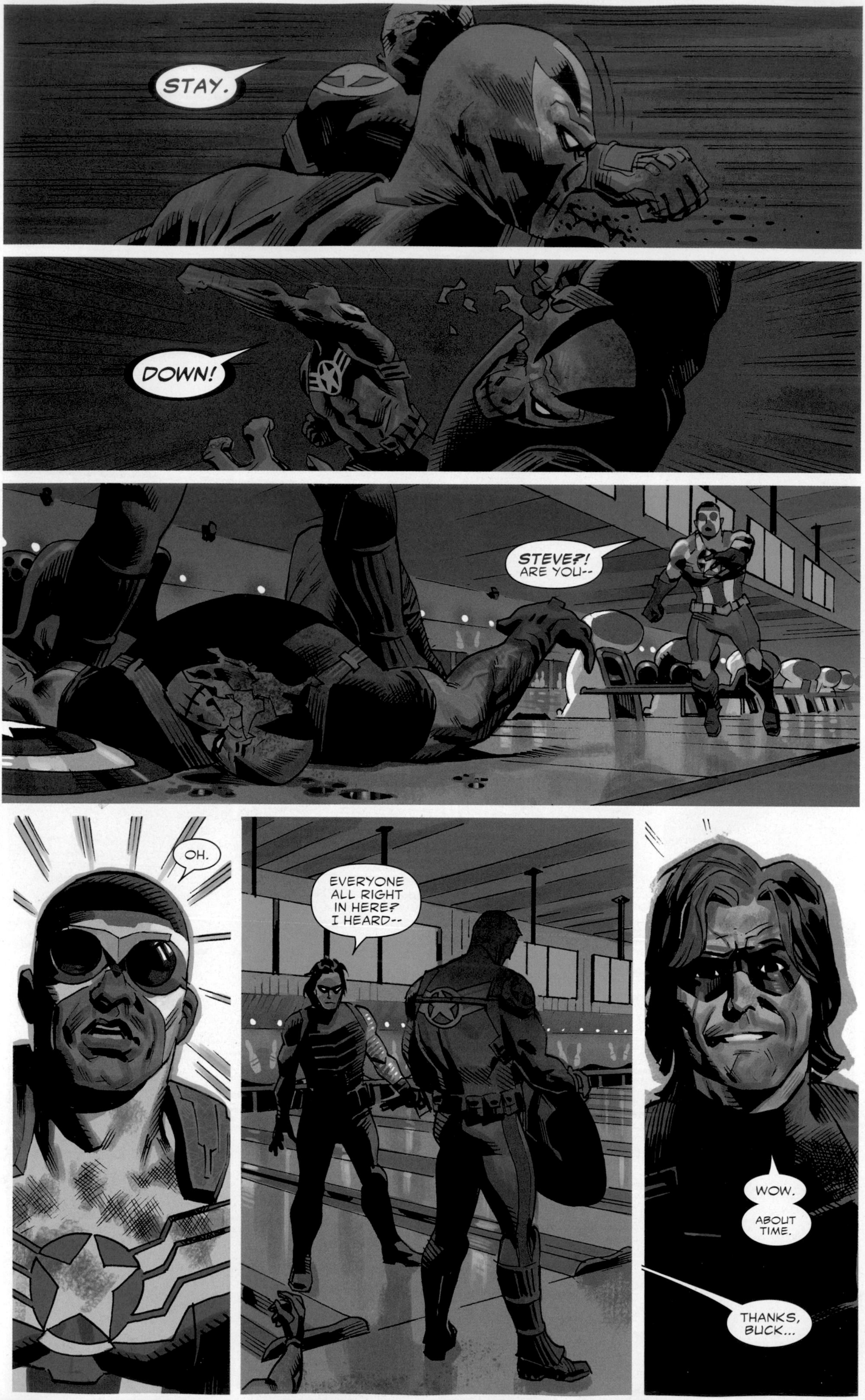
STAY.
DOWN!
STEVE?! ARE YOU--
OH.
EVERYONE ALL RIGHT IN HERE? I HEARD--
WOW.
ABOUT TIME.
THANKS, BUCK...

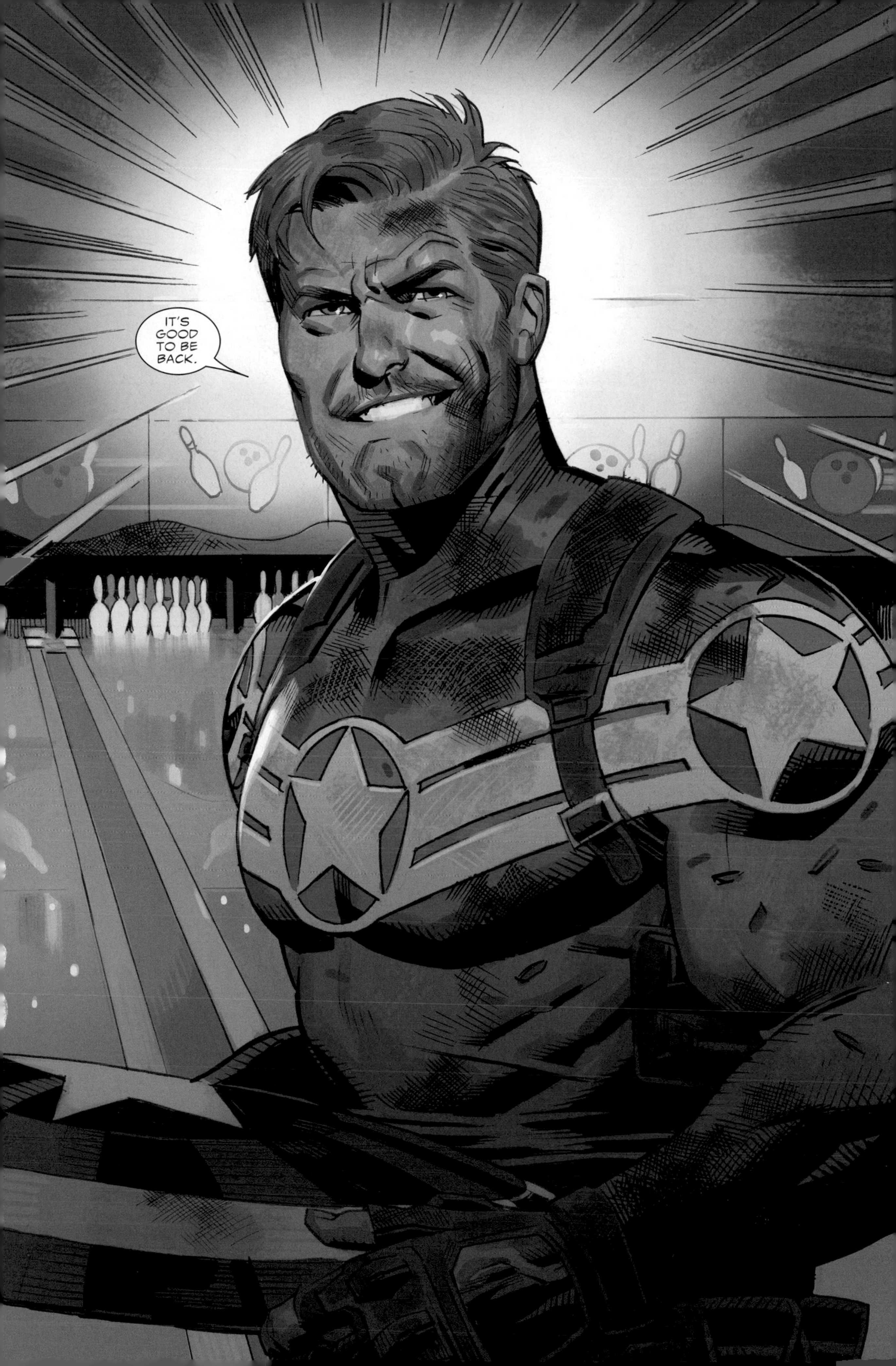
IT'S GOOD TO BE BACK.

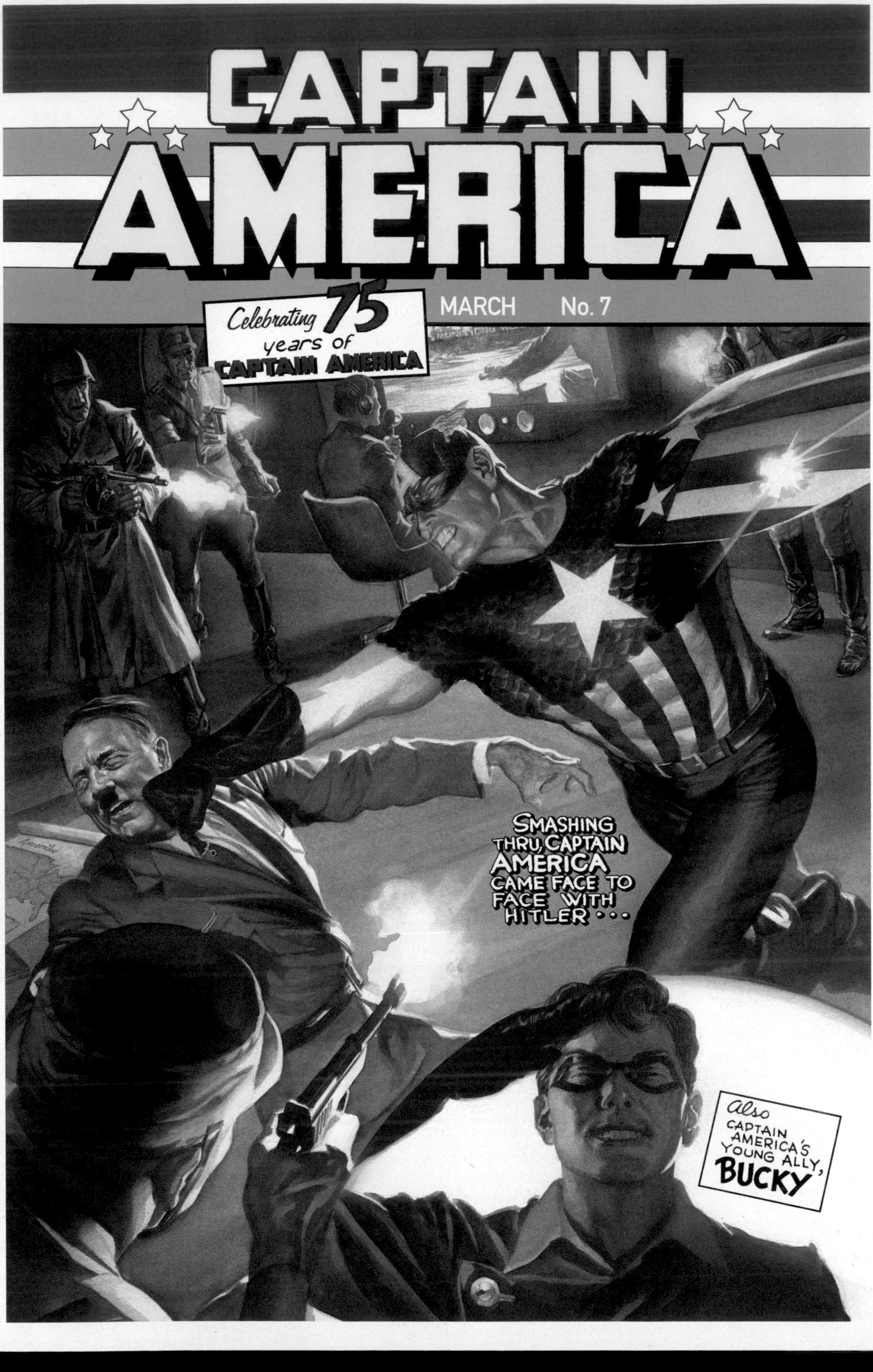
CAPTAIN AMERICA
Celebrating 75 years of CAPTAIN AMERICA
MARCH No. 7
SMASHING THRU, CAPTAIN AMERICA CAME FACE TO FACE WITH HITLER...
Also CAPTAIN AMERICA'S YOUNG ALLY, BUCKY

Captain America: Sam Wilson No. 7 variant by

ALEX ROSS

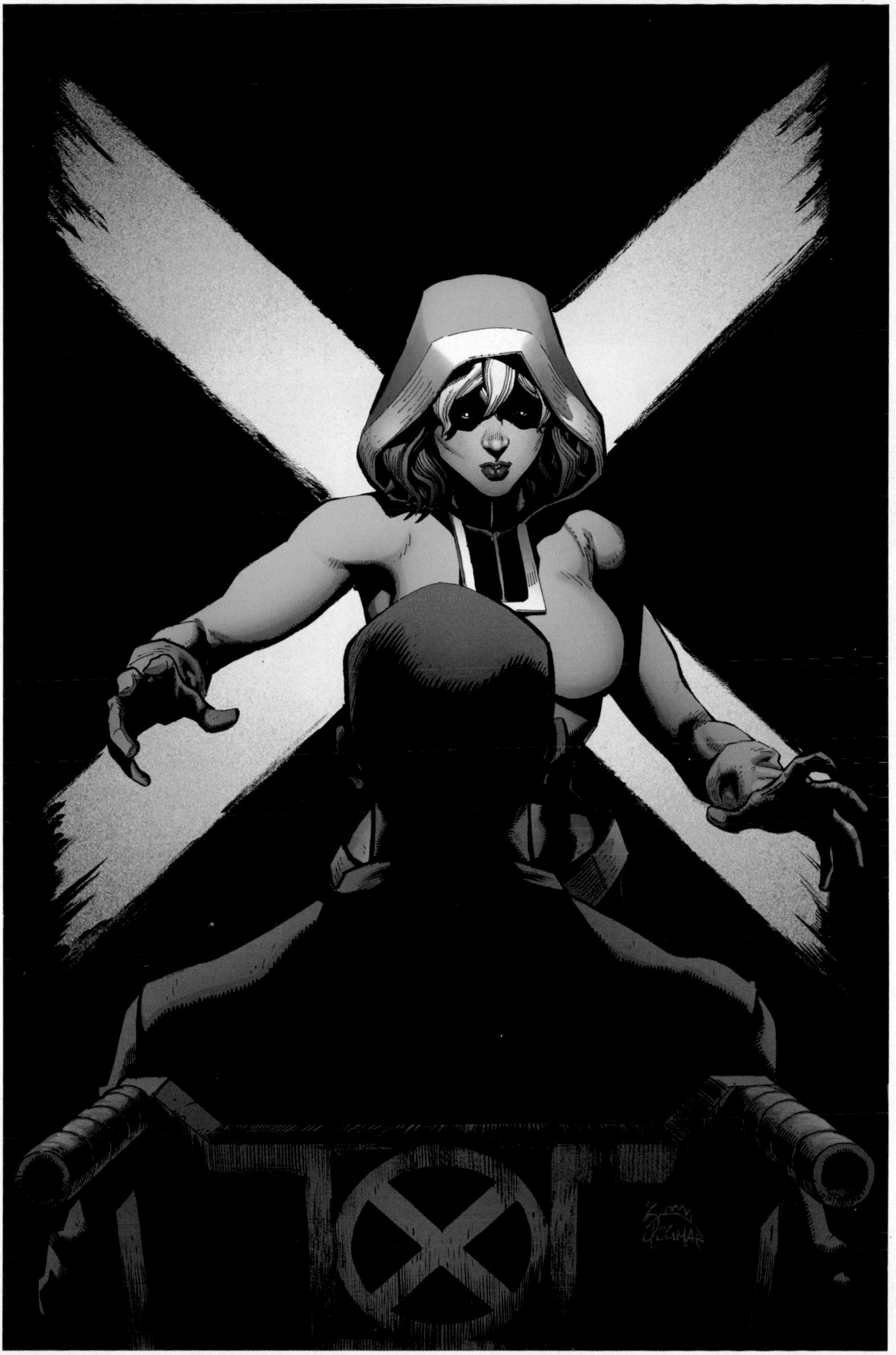

Uncanny Avengers No. 8

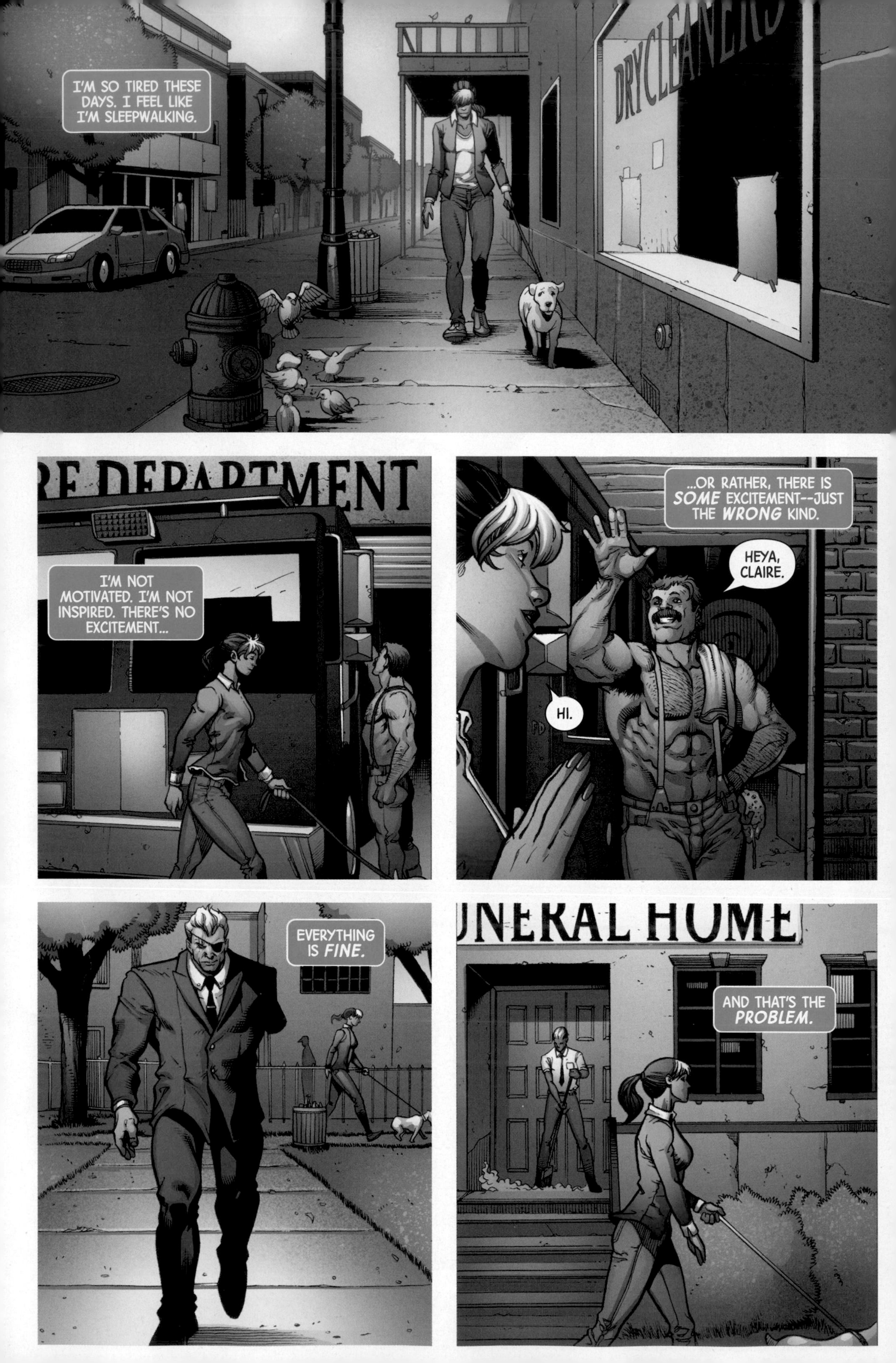
DRYCLEANERS
I'M SO TIRED THESE DAYS. I FEEL LIKE I'M SLEEPWALKING.
RE DEPARTMENT
I'M NOT MOTIVATED. I'M NOT INSPIRED. THERE'S NO EXCITEMENT...
...OR RATHER, THERE IS SOME EXCITEMENT--JUST THE WRONG KIND.
HEYA, CLAIRE.
HI.
EVERYTHING IS FINE.
UNERAL HOME
AND THAT'S THE PROBLEM.

PLEASANT HILL IS ALMOST *INSIPIDLY* PLEASANT.

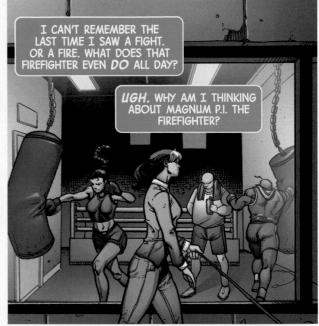

I CAN'T REMEMBER THE LAST TIME I SAW A FIGHT. OR A FIRE. WHAT DOES THAT FIREFIGHTER EVEN *DO* ALL DAY?

UGH. WHY AM I THINKING ABOUT MAGNUM P.I. THE FIREFIGHTER?

THERE IS ONE *UNPLEASANT* THING IN MY LIFE NOWADAYS.

IF THAT WEIRDO WHO'S BEEN HARASSING ME CALLS AGAIN, I'M *NOT* ANSWERING.

DAMMIT, I'M NOT ANSWERING THE PHONE TODAY!

DEET DEET DEET

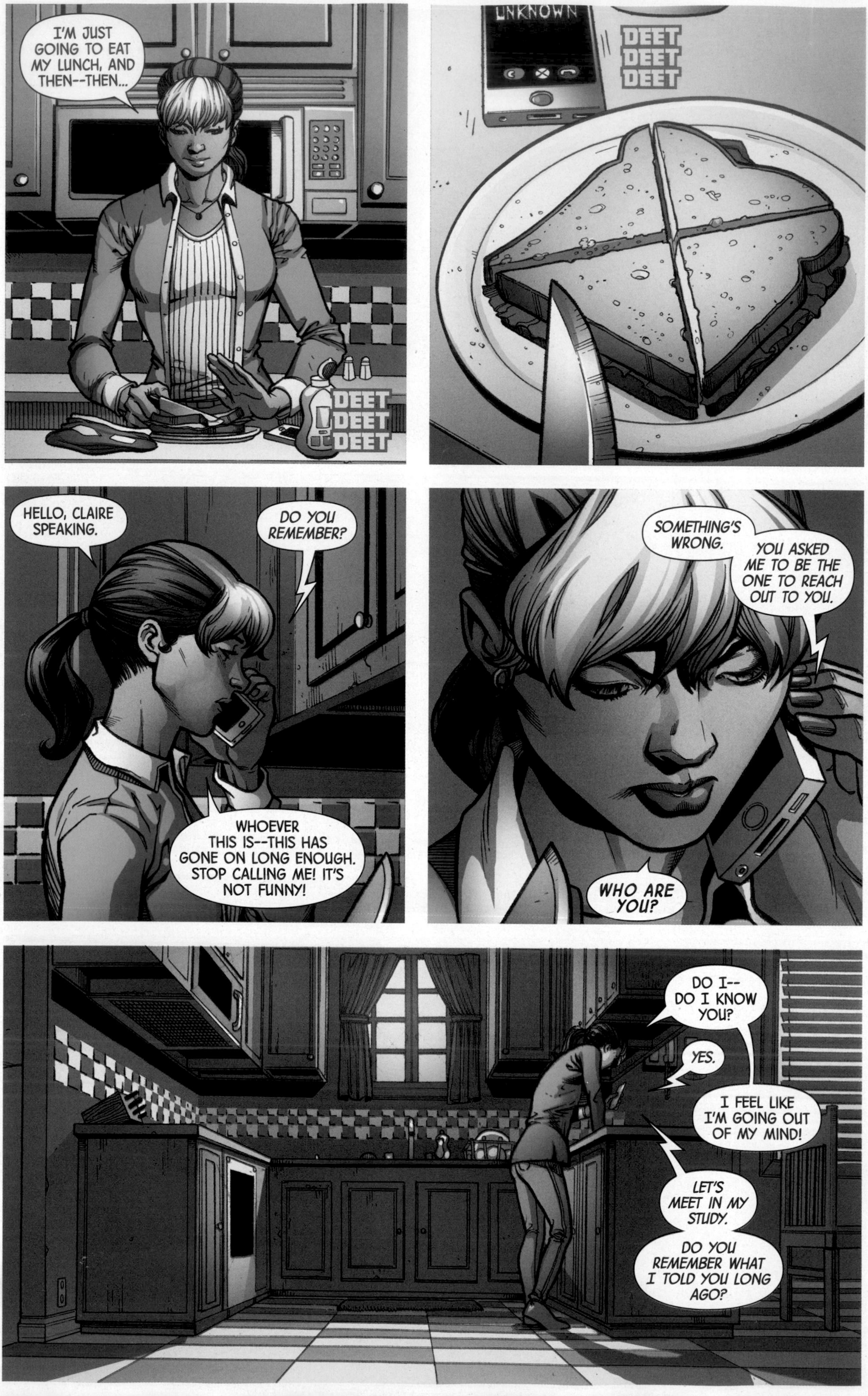

I'M JUST GOING TO EAT MY LUNCH, AND THEN--THEN...
DEET DEET DEET
UNKNOWN
DEET DEET DEET
HELLO, CLAIRE SPEAKING.
DO YOU REMEMBER?
WHOEVER THIS IS--THIS HAS GONE ON LONG ENOUGH. STOP CALLING ME! IT'S NOT FUNNY!
SOMETHING'S WRONG.
YOU ASKED ME TO BE THE ONE TO REACH OUT TO YOU.
WHO ARE YOU?
DO I-- DO I KNOW YOU?
YES.
I FEEL LIKE I'M GOING OUT OF MY MIND!
LET'S MEET IN MY STUDY.
DO YOU REMEMBER WHAT I TOLD YOU LONG AGO?

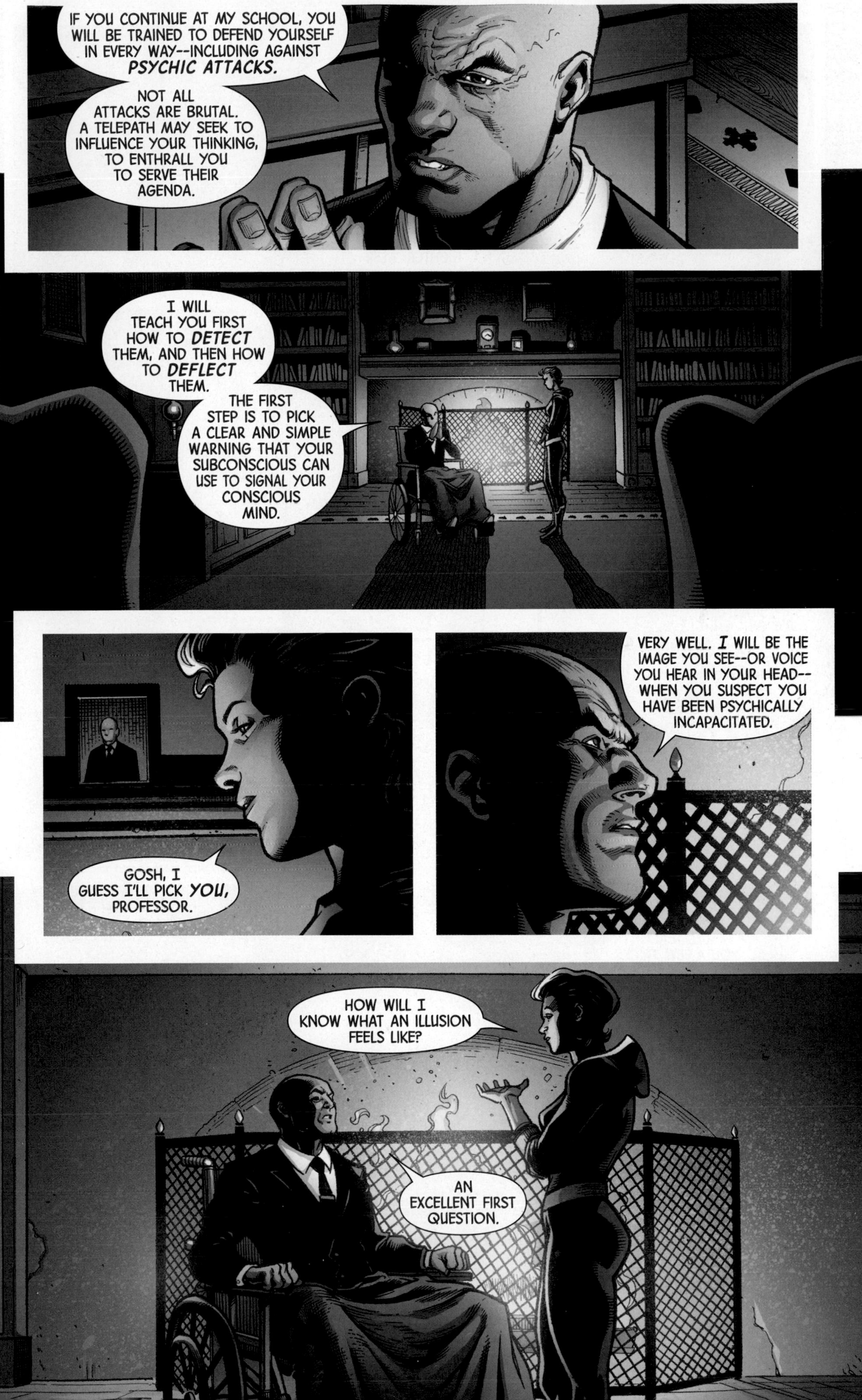
IF YOU CONTINUE AT MY SCHOOL, YOU WILL BE TRAINED TO DEFEND YOURSELF IN EVERY WAY--INCLUDING AGAINST PSYCHIC ATTACKS.
NOT ALL ATTACKS ARE BRUTAL. A TELEPATH MAY SEEK TO INFLUENCE YOUR THINKING, TO ENTHRALL YOU TO SERVE THEIR AGENDA.
I WILL TEACH YOU FIRST HOW TO DETECT THEM, AND THEN HOW TO DEFLECT THEM.
THE FIRST STEP IS TO PICK A CLEAR AND SIMPLE WARNING THAT YOUR SUBCONSCIOUS CAN USE TO SIGNAL YOUR CONSCIOUS MIND.
GOSH, I GUESS I'LL PICK YOU, PROFESSOR.
VERY WELL. I WILL BE THE IMAGE YOU SEE--OR VOICE YOU HEAR IN YOUR HEAD--WHEN YOU SUSPECT YOU HAVE BEEN PSYCHICALLY INCAPACITATED.
HOW WILL I KNOW WHAT AN ILLUSION FEELS LIKE?
AN EXCELLENT FIRST QUESTION.

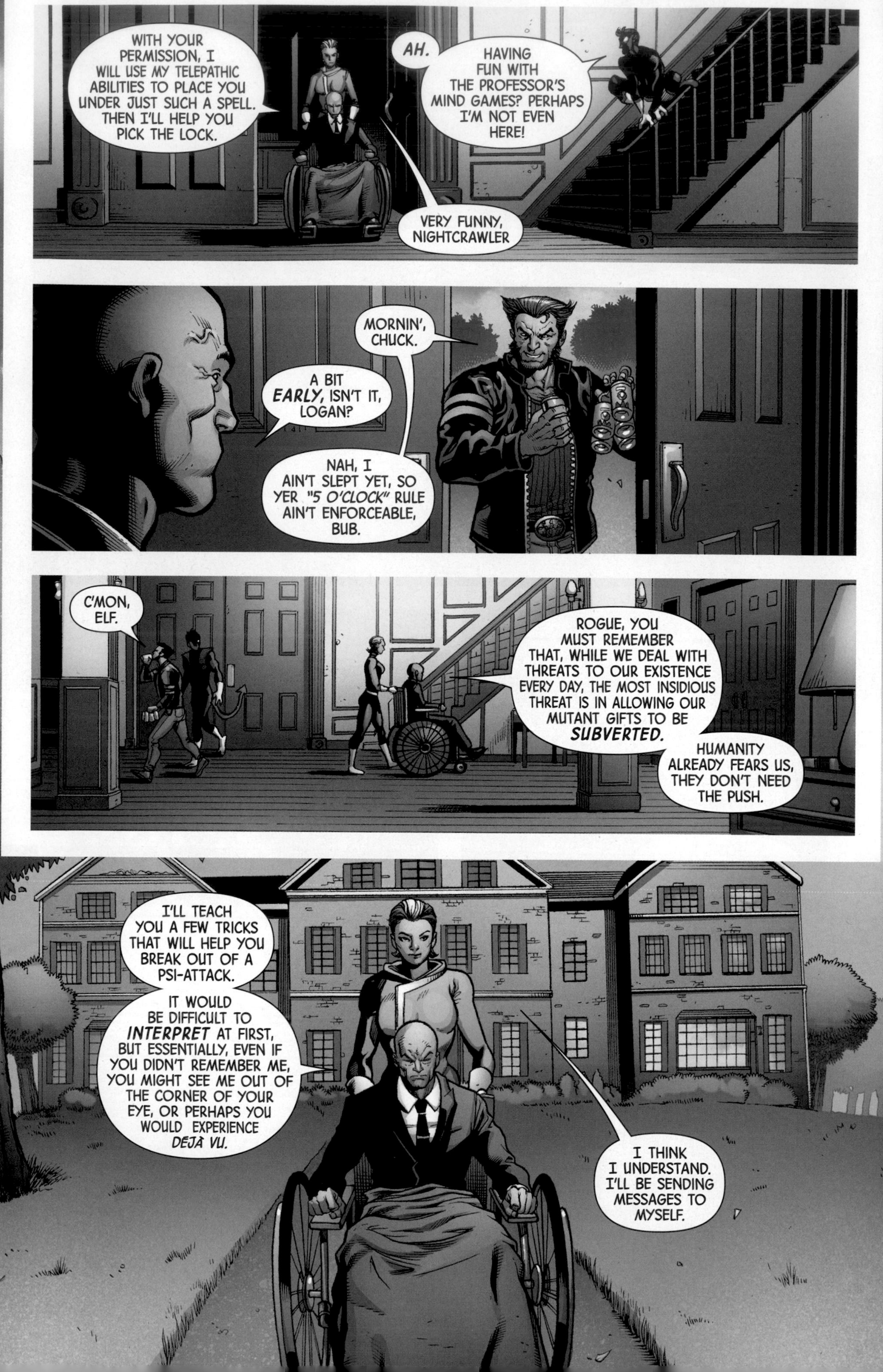

WITH YOUR PERMISSION, I WILL USE MY TELEPATHIC ABILITIES TO PLACE YOU UNDER JUST SUCH A SPELL. THEN I'LL HELP YOU PICK THE LOCK.
AH.
HAVING FUN WITH THE PROFESSOR'S MIND GAMES? PERHAPS I'M NOT EVEN HERE!
VERY FUNNY, NIGHTCRAWLER
MORNIN', CHUCK.
A BIT *EARLY,* ISN'T IT, LOGAN?
NAH, I AIN'T SLEPT YET, SO YER *"5 O'CLOCK"* RULE AIN'T ENFORCEABLE, BUB.
C'MON, ELF.
ROGUE, YOU MUST REMEMBER THAT, WHILE WE DEAL WITH THREATS TO OUR EXISTENCE EVERY DAY, THE MOST INSIDIOUS THREAT IS IN ALLOWING OUR MUTANT GIFTS TO BE ***SUBVERTED.***
HUMANITY ALREADY FEARS US, THEY DON'T NEED THE PUSH.
I'LL TEACH YOU A FEW TRICKS THAT WILL HELP YOU BREAK OUT OF A PSI-ATTACK.
IT WOULD BE DIFFICULT TO ***INTERPRET*** AT FIRST, BUT ESSENTIALLY, EVEN IF YOU DIDN'T REMEMBER ME, YOU MIGHT SEE ME OUT OF THE CORNER OF YOUR EYE, OR PERHAPS YOU WOULD EXPERIENCE *DEJÀ VU.*
I THINK I UNDERSTAND. I'LL BE SENDING MESSAGES TO MYSELF.

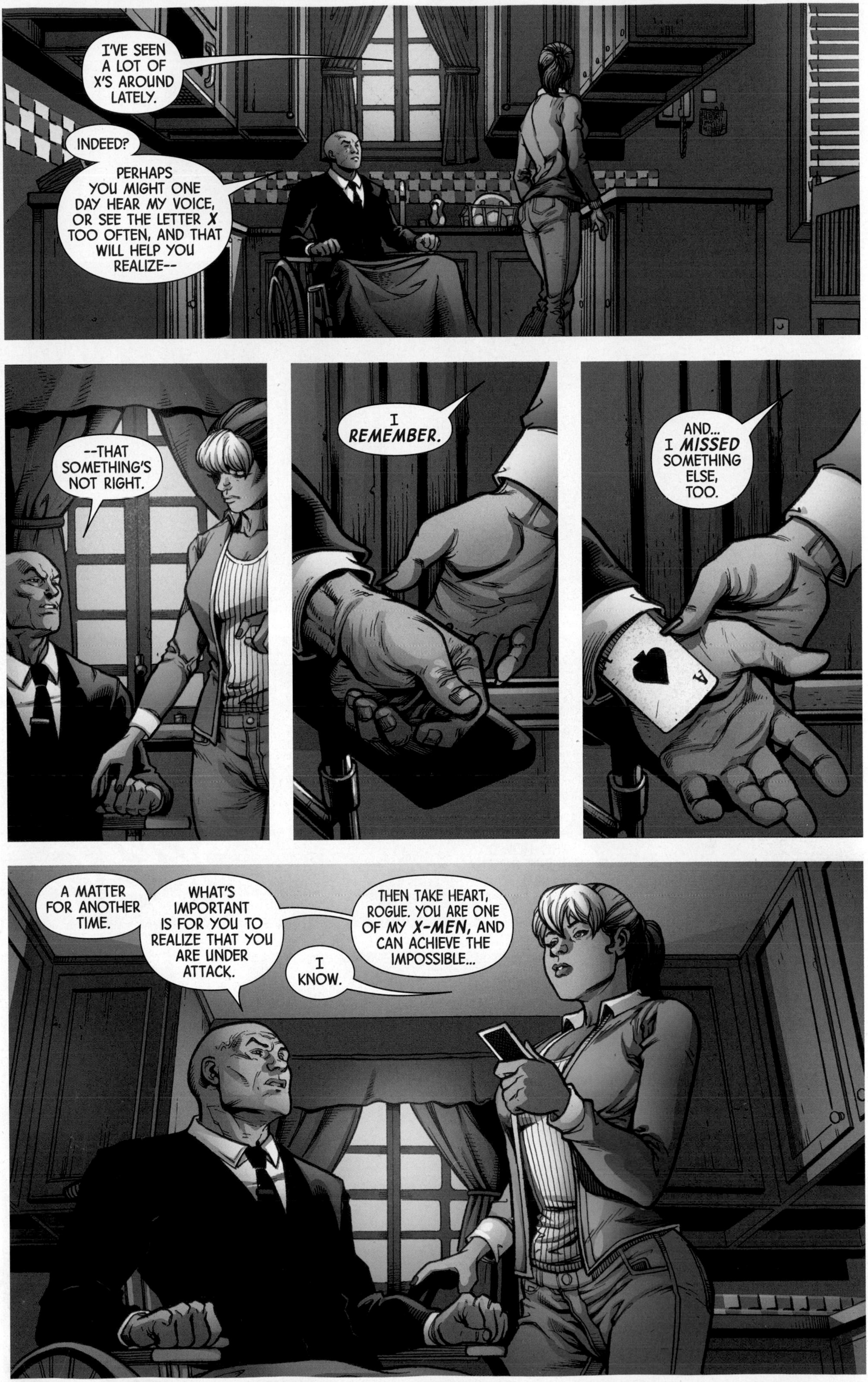
I'VE SEEN A LOT OF X'S AROUND LATELY.
INDEED?
PERHAPS YOU MIGHT ONE DAY HEAR MY VOICE, OR SEE THE LETTER X TOO OFTEN, AND THAT WILL HELP YOU REALIZE--
--THAT SOMETHING'S NOT RIGHT.
I REMEMBER.
AND... I MISSED SOMETHING ELSE, TOO.
A MATTER FOR ANOTHER TIME.
WHAT'S IMPORTANT IS FOR YOU TO REALIZE THAT YOU ARE UNDER ATTACK.
I KNOW.
THEN TAKE HEART, ROGUE. YOU ARE ONE OF MY X-MEN, AND CAN ACHIEVE THE IMPOSSIBLE...

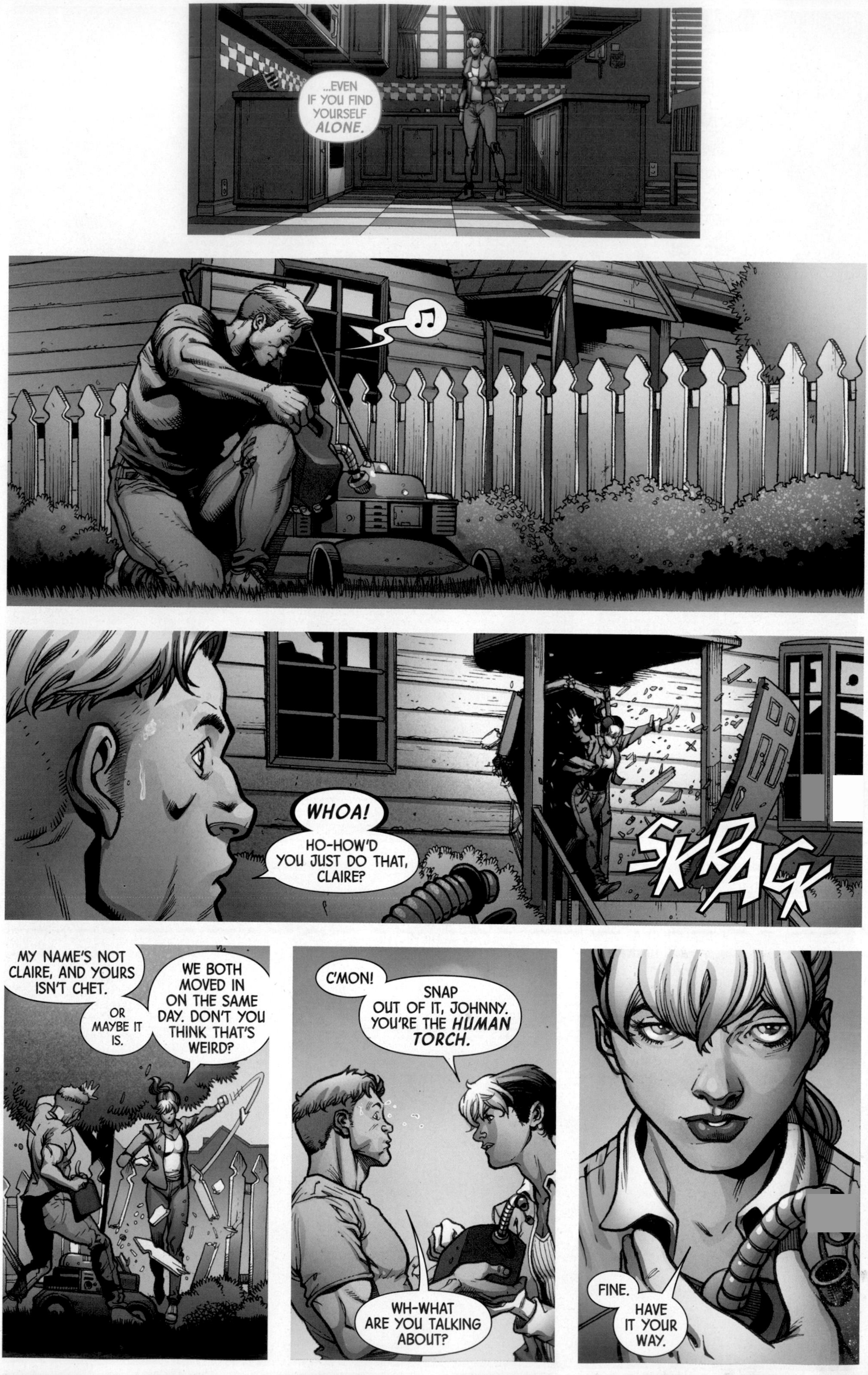

...EVEN IF YOU FIND YOURSELF ALONE.
♫
WHOA!
HO-HOW'D YOU JUST DO THAT, CLAIRE?
SKRACK
MY NAME'S NOT CLAIRE, AND YOURS ISN'T CHET.
OR MAYBE IT IS.
WE BOTH MOVED IN ON THE SAME DAY. DON'T YOU THINK THAT'S WEIRD?
C'MON!
SNAP OUT OF IT, JOHNNY. YOU'RE THE HUMAN TORCH.
WH-WHAT ARE YOU TALKING ABOUT?
FINE.
HAVE IT YOUR WAY.

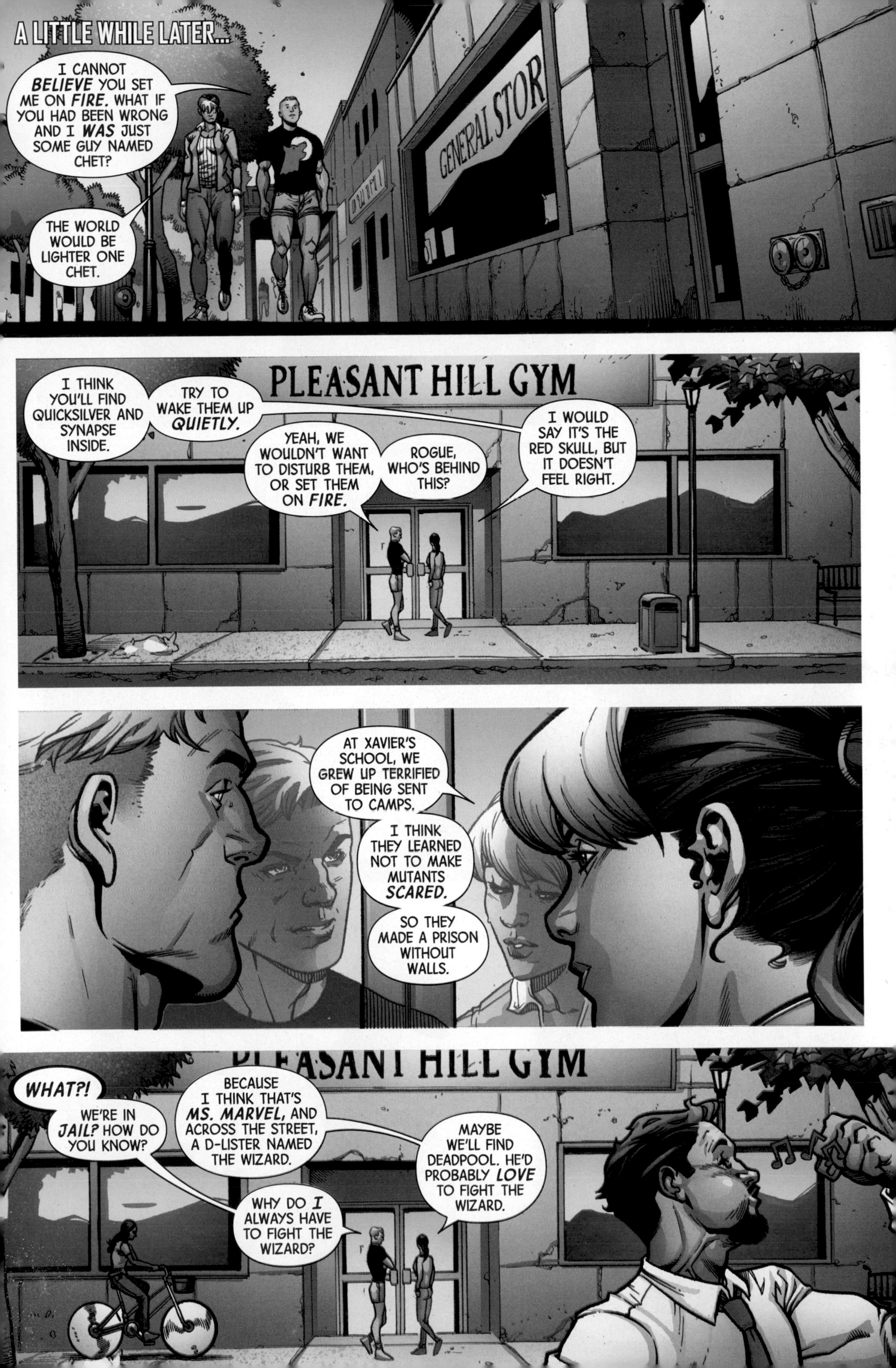
A LITTLE WHILE LATER...
I CANNOT BELIEVE YOU SET ME ON FIRE. WHAT IF YOU HAD BEEN WRONG AND I WAS JUST SOME GUY NAMED CHET?
THE WORLD WOULD BE LIGHTER ONE CHET.
GENERAL STOR
PLEASANT HILL GYM
I THINK YOU'LL FIND QUICKSILVER AND SYNAPSE INSIDE.
TRY TO WAKE THEM UP QUIETLY.
YEAH, WE WOULDN'T WANT TO DISTURB THEM, OR SET THEM ON FIRE.
ROGUE, WHO'S BEHIND THIS?
I WOULD SAY IT'S THE RED SKULL, BUT IT DOESN'T FEEL RIGHT.
AT XAVIER'S SCHOOL, WE GREW UP TERRIFIED OF BEING SENT TO CAMPS.
I THINK THEY LEARNED NOT TO MAKE MUTANTS SCARED.
SO THEY MADE A PRISON WITHOUT WALLS.
PLEASANT HILL GYM
WHAT?!
WE'RE IN JAIL? HOW DO YOU KNOW?
BECAUSE I THINK THAT'S MS. MARVEL, AND ACROSS THE STREET, A D-LISTER NAMED THE WIZARD.
MAYBE WE'LL FIND DEADPOOL. HE'D PROBABLY LOVE TO FIGHT THE WIZARD.
WHY DO I ALWAYS HAVE TO FIGHT THE WIZARD?

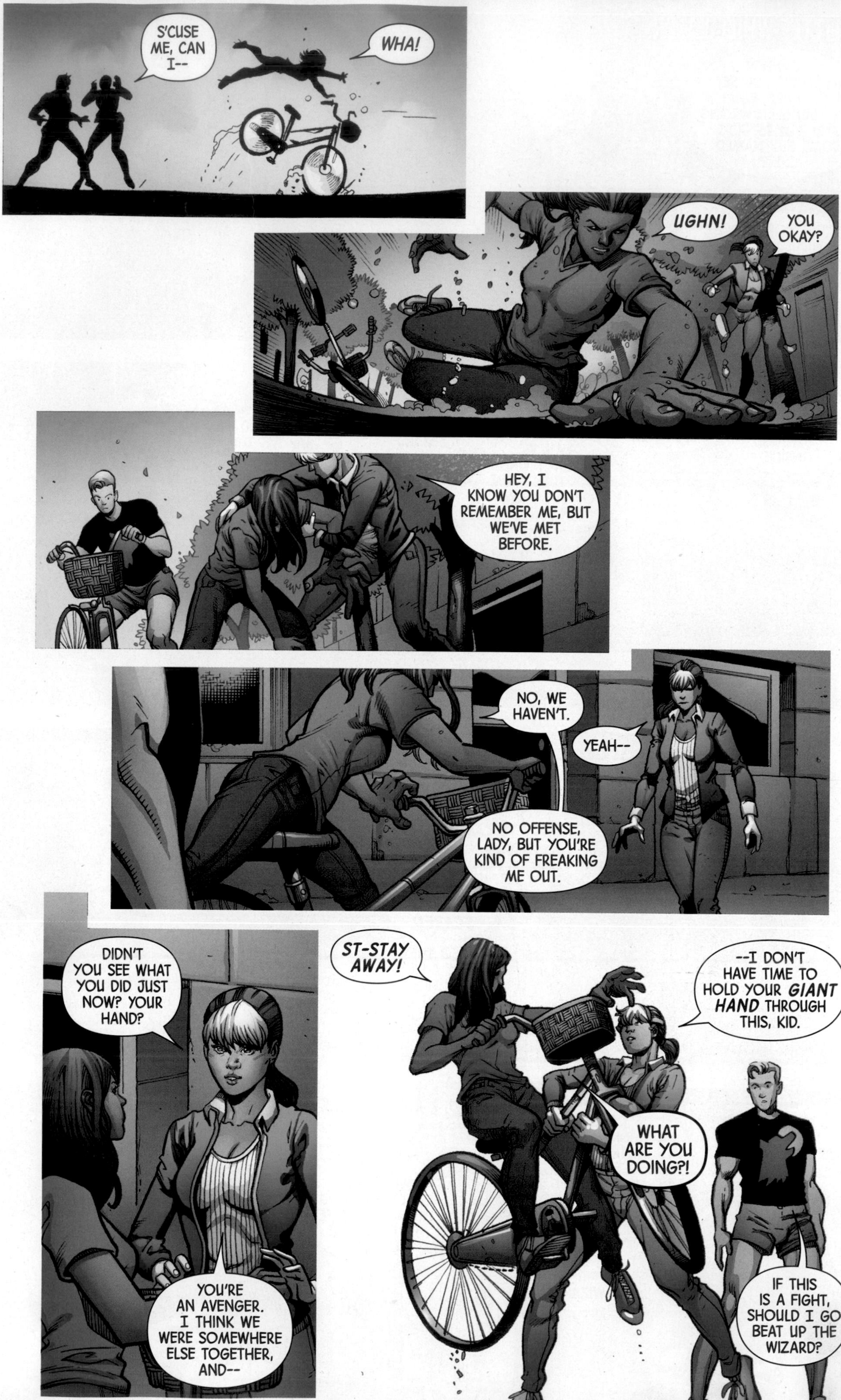
S'CUSE ME, CAN I--
WHA!
UGHN!
YOU OKAY?
HEY, I KNOW YOU DON'T REMEMBER ME, BUT WE'VE MET BEFORE.
NO, WE HAVEN'T.
YEAH--
NO OFFENSE, LADY, BUT YOU'RE KIND OF FREAKING ME OUT.
DIDN'T YOU SEE WHAT YOU DID JUST NOW? YOUR HAND?
YOU'RE AN AVENGER. I THINK WE WERE SOMEWHERE ELSE TOGETHER, AND--
ST-STAY AWAY!
--I DON'T HAVE TIME TO HOLD YOUR GIANT HAND THROUGH THIS, KID.
WHAT ARE YOU DOING?!
IF THIS IS A FIGHT, SHOULD I GO BEAT UP THE WIZARD?

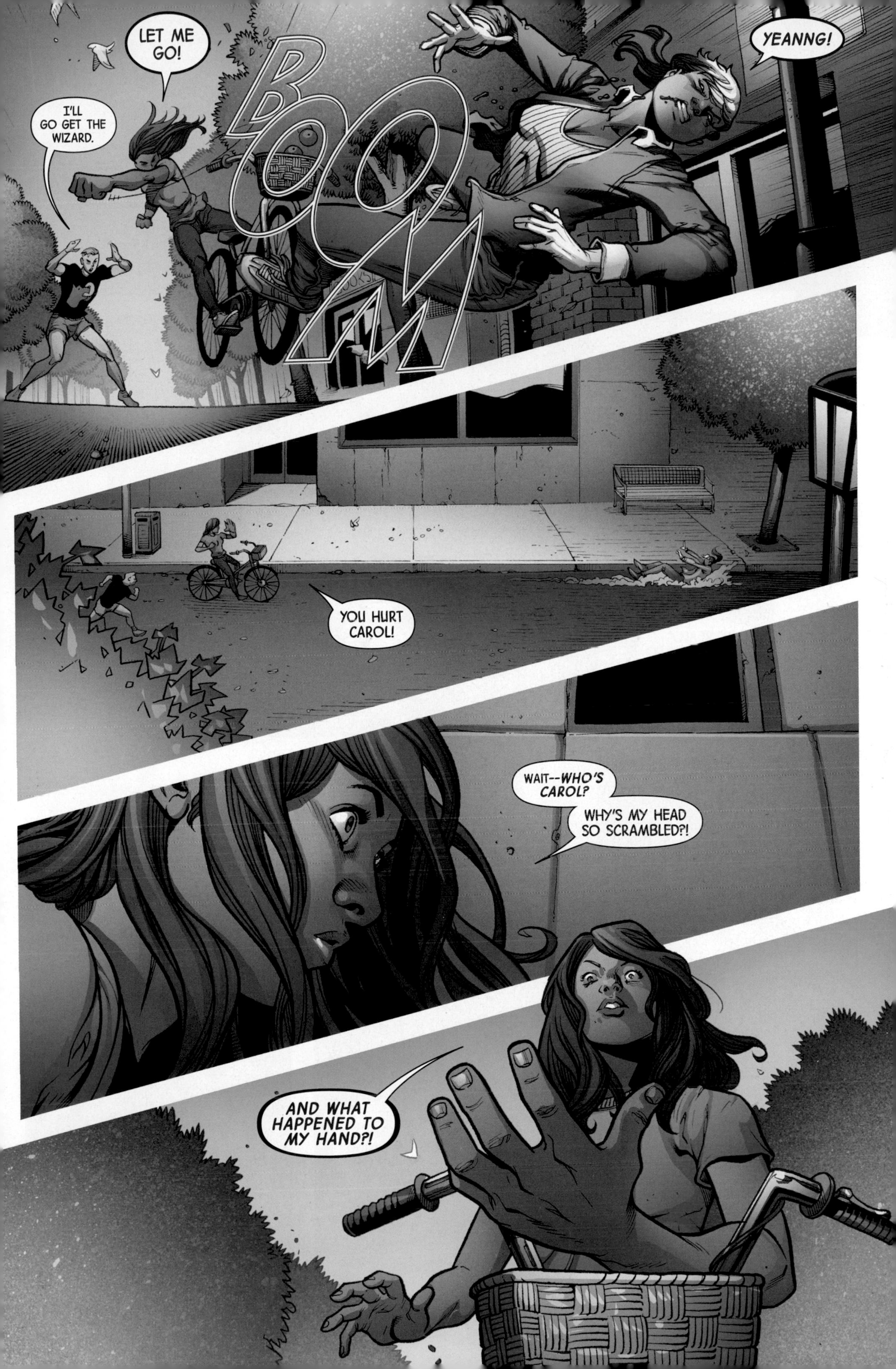
LET ME GO!
I'LL GO GET THE WIZARD.
BOOM
YEANNG!
YOU HURT CAROL!
WAIT--WHO'S CAROL?
WHY'S MY HEAD SO SCRAMBLED?!
AND WHAT HAPPENED TO MY HAND?!

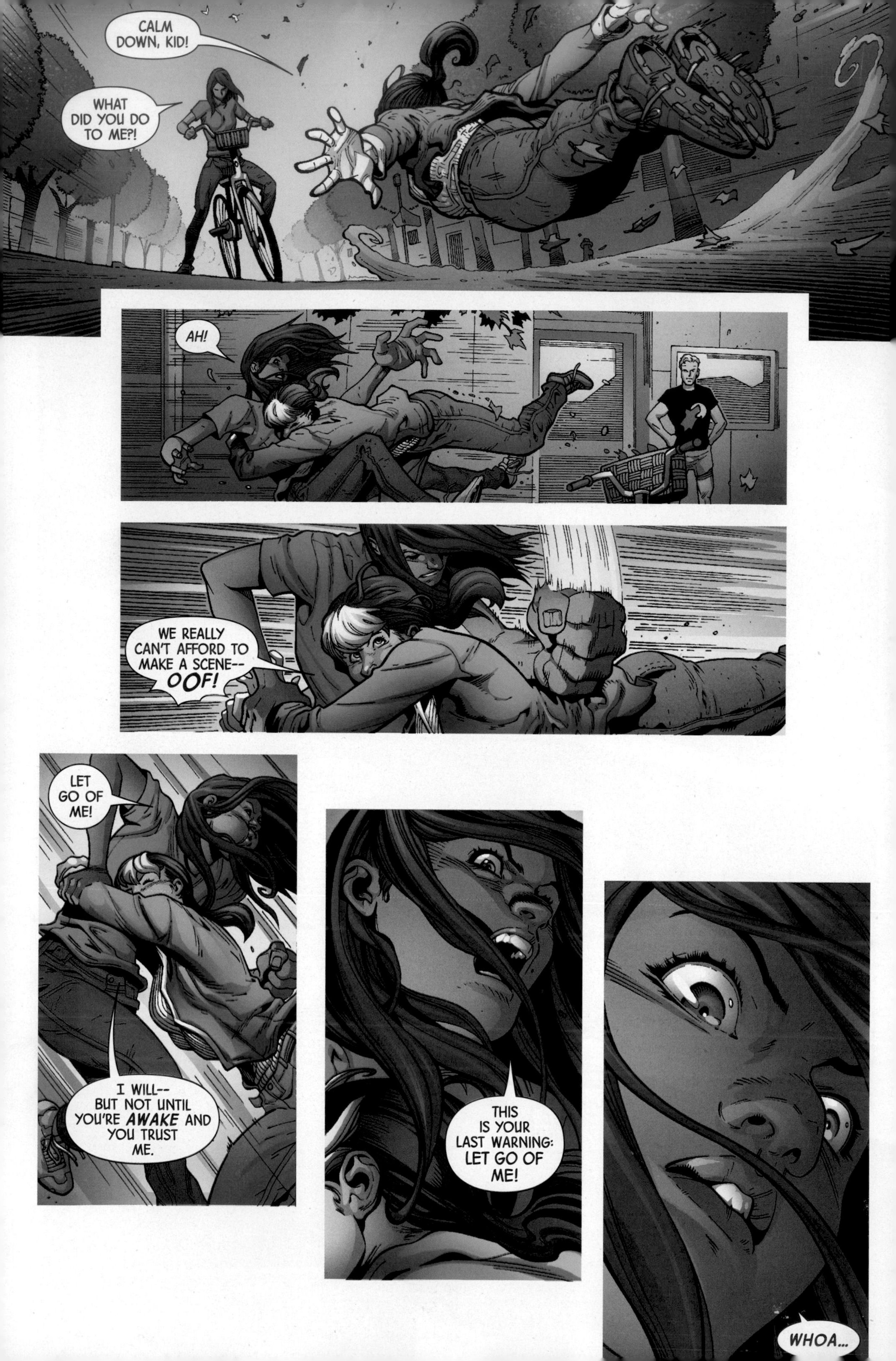

CALM DOWN, KID!
WHAT DID YOU DO TO ME?!
AH!
WE REALLY CAN'T AFFORD TO MAKE A SCENE-- OOF!
LET GO OF ME!
I WILL-- BUT NOT UNTIL YOU'RE *AWAKE* AND YOU TRUST ME.
THIS IS YOUR LAST WARNING: LET GO OF ME!
WHOA...

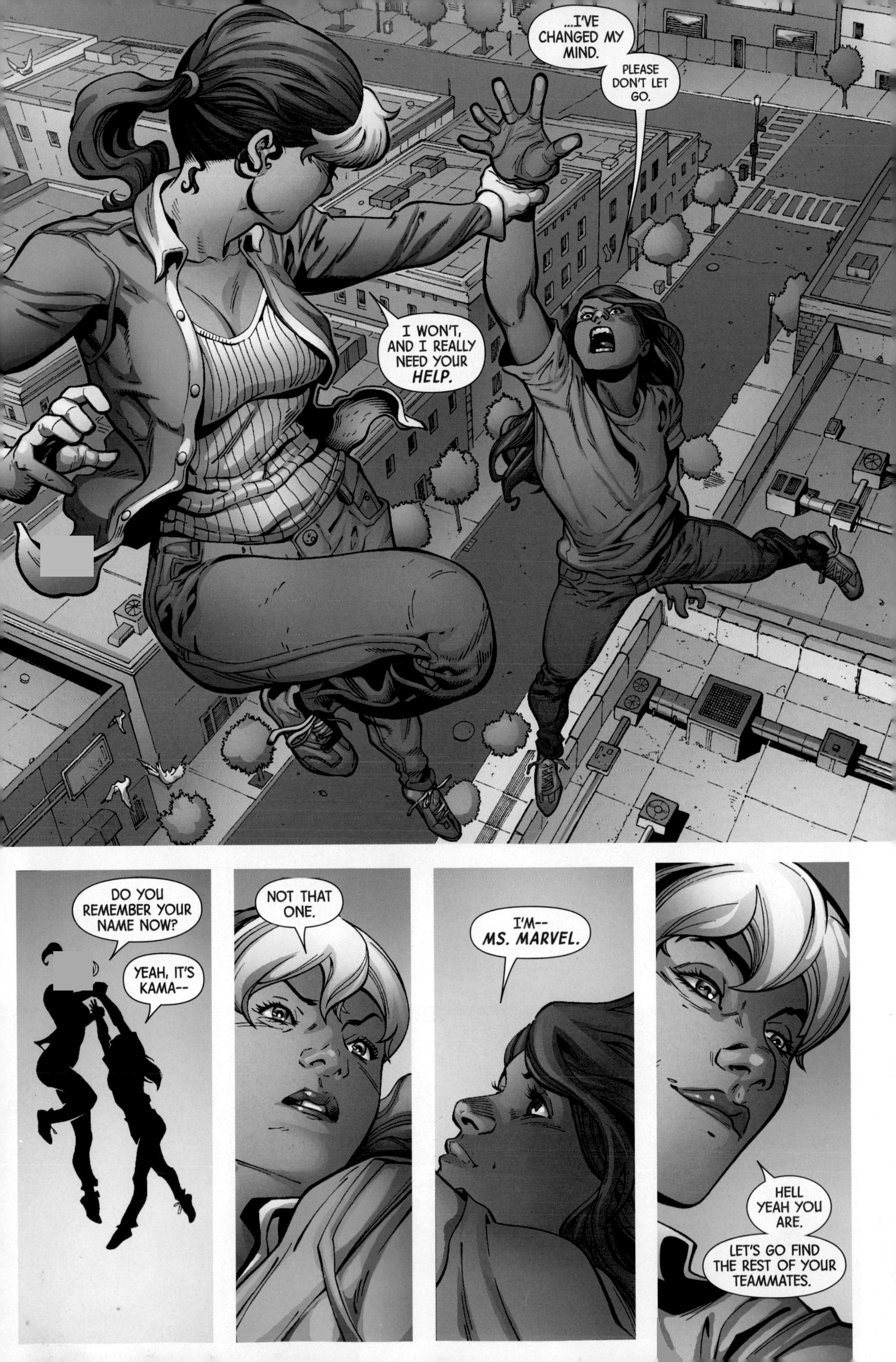
...I'VE CHANGED MY MIND.
PLEASE DON'T LET GO.
I WON'T, AND I REALLY NEED YOUR *HELP.*
DO YOU REMEMBER YOUR NAME NOW?
YEAH, IT'S KAMA--
NOT THAT ONE.
I'M-- *MS. MARVEL.*
HELL YEAH YOU ARE.
LET'S GO FIND THE REST OF YOUR TEAMMATES.

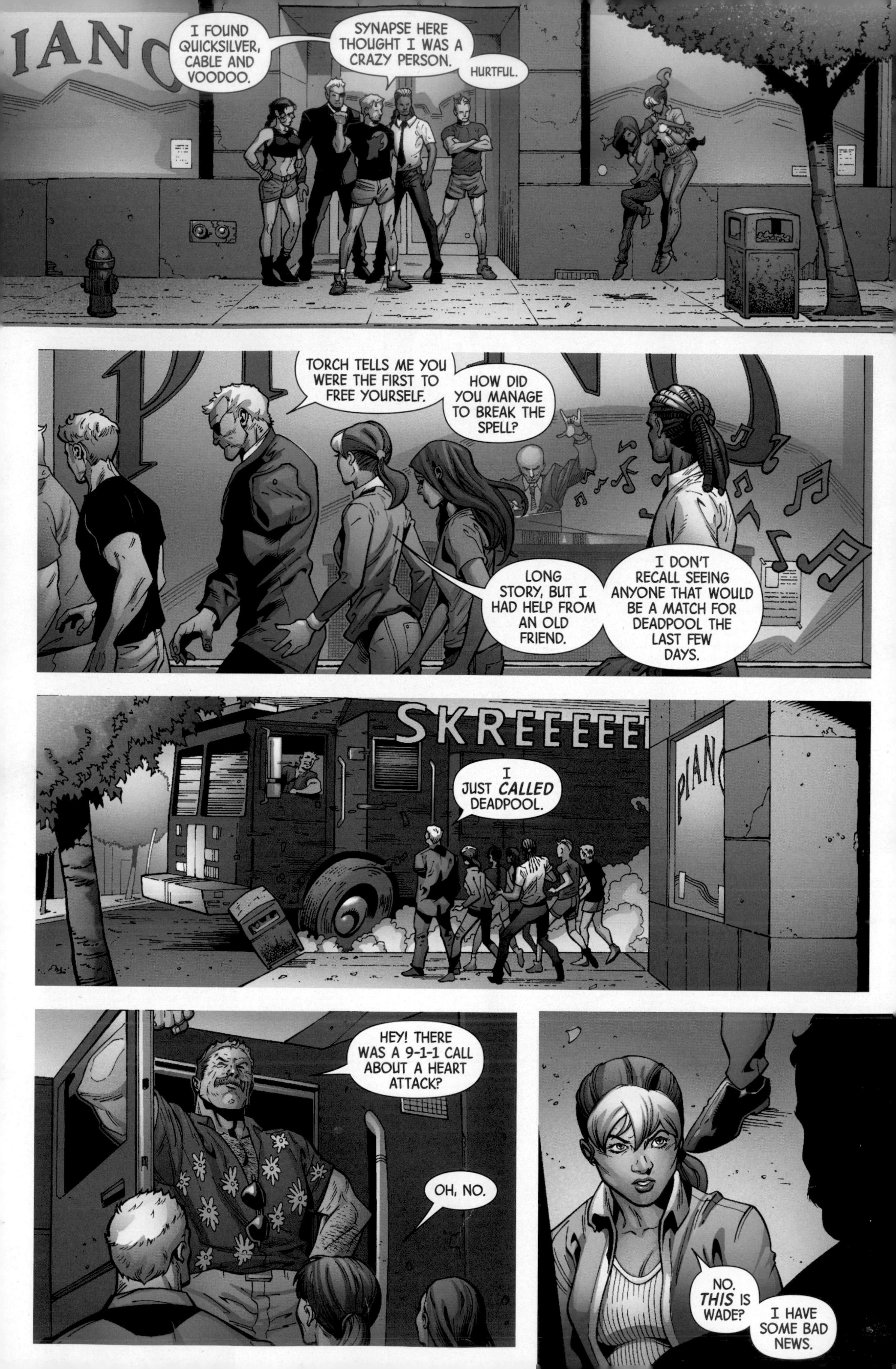
PIANO
I FOUND QUICKSILVER, CABLE AND VOODOO.
SYNAPSE HERE THOUGHT I WAS A CRAZY PERSON.
HURTFUL.
TORCH TELLS ME YOU WERE THE FIRST TO FREE YOURSELF.
HOW DID YOU MANAGE TO BREAK THE SPELL?
LONG STORY, BUT I HAD HELP FROM AN OLD FRIEND.
I DON'T RECALL SEEING ANYONE THAT WOULD BE A MATCH FOR DEADPOOL THE LAST FEW DAYS.
SKREEEEEE
I JUST *CALLED* DEADPOOL.
PIANO
HEY! THERE WAS A 9-1-1 CALL ABOUT A HEART ATTACK?
OH, NO.
NO. *THIS* IS WADE?
I HAVE SOME BAD NEWS.

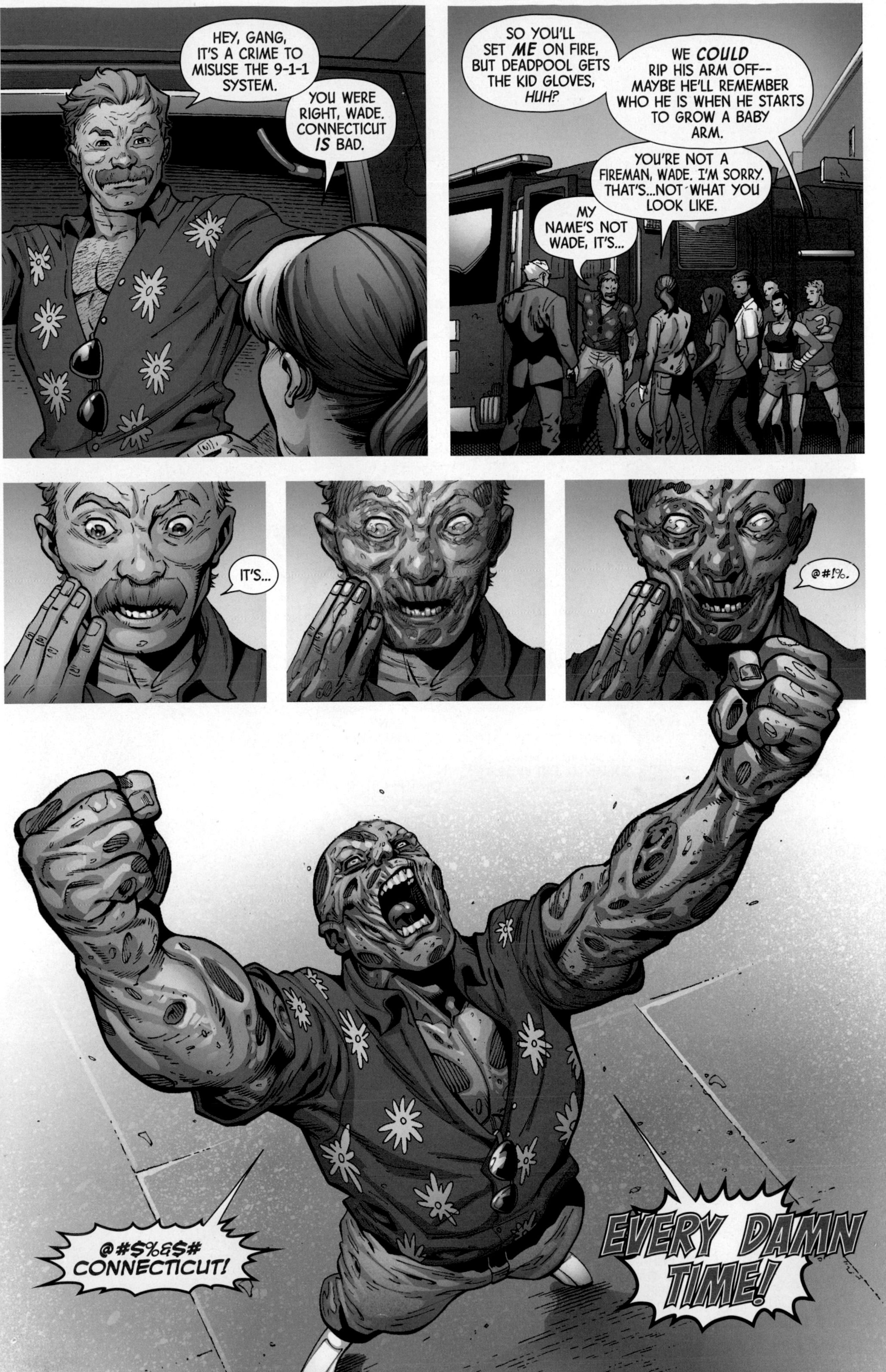

HEY, GANG, IT'S A CRIME TO MISUSE THE 9-1-1 SYSTEM.
YOU WERE RIGHT, WADE. CONNECTICUT *IS* BAD.
SO YOU'LL SET *ME* ON FIRE, BUT DEADPOOL GETS THE KID GLOVES, *HUH?*
WE *COULD* RIP HIS ARM OFF-- MAYBE HE'LL REMEMBER WHO HE IS WHEN HE STARTS TO GROW A BABY ARM.
YOU'RE NOT A FIREMAN, WADE. I'M SORRY. THAT'S...NOT WHAT YOU LOOK LIKE.
MY NAME'S NOT WADE, IT'S...
IT'S...
@#!%.
@#$%&$# CONNECTICUT!
EVERY DAMN TIME!

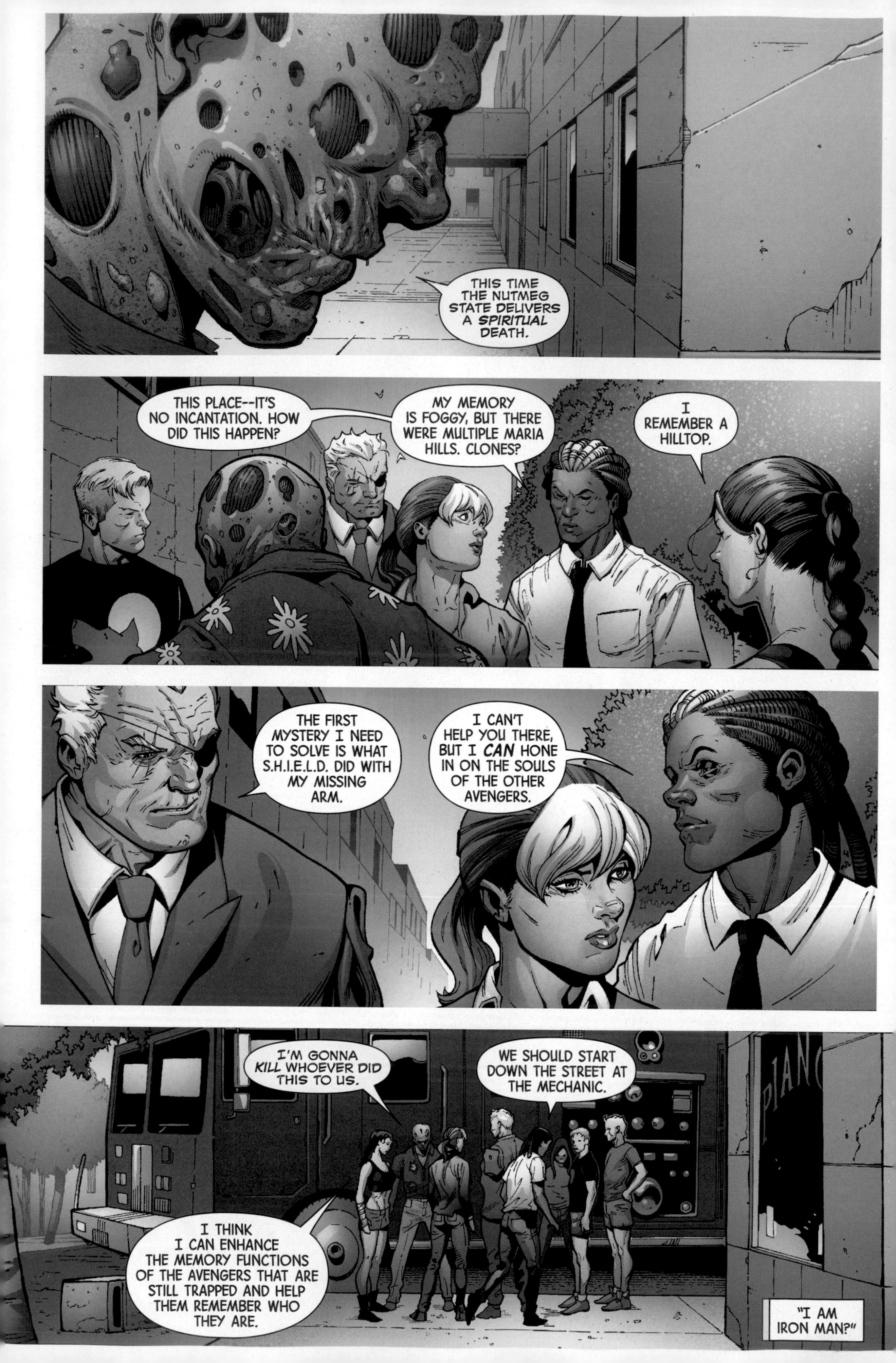

THIS TIME THE NUTMEG STATE DELIVERS A SPIRITUAL DEATH.
THIS PLACE--IT'S NO INCANTATION. HOW DID THIS HAPPEN?
MY MEMORY IS FOGGY, BUT THERE WERE MULTIPLE MARIA HILLS. CLONES?
I REMEMBER A HILLTOP.
THE FIRST MYSTERY I NEED TO SOLVE IS WHAT S.H.I.E.L.D. DID WITH MY MISSING ARM.
I CAN'T HELP YOU THERE, BUT I CAN HONE IN ON THE SOULS OF THE OTHER AVENGERS.
I'M GONNA KILL WHOEVER DID THIS TO US.
WE SHOULD START DOWN THE STREET AT THE MECHANIC.
I THINK I CAN ENHANCE THE MEMORY FUNCTIONS OF THE AVENGERS THAT ARE STILL TRAPPED AND HELP THEM REMEMBER WHO THEY ARE.
"I AM IRON MAN?"

I THOUGHT THIS DAY WAS WEIRD ENOUGH.
DID I MAKE MYSELF A MECHANIC? OR DID THEY? AND WHO'S "THEY"?
I REMEMBER SOMETHING ABOUT A GIRL.
TOUCHÉ.
YOU'RE GOING TO NEED TO BE A LITTLE MORE SPECIFIC.
I REMEMBER A GIRL, TOO.
UNTIL WE KNOW WHAT WE'RE UP AGAINST, LET'S PLAY IT SLOW. NO REASON TO LET ANYONE KNOW THAT WE'RE AWAKE.
I SENT QUICKSILVER OUT ON RECON. WE'RE SURROUNDED BY SOME KIND OF FORCE-FIELD.
GARAGE
DAMMIT. WHERE'S MY ARMOR?
WHERE'S MY ARM?
Tony
I THINK MARIA HILL LURED US RIGHT INTO THIS TRAP.
WHERE ARE SAM WILSON AND STEVE ROGERS? HAVE THEY BEEN HIT WITH THE WHAMMY STICK, TOO?
AT LEAST IF STEVE WERE BRAINWASHED IT WOULD EXPLAIN WHY HE MADE YOU AN AVENGER.
THAT WAS NEVER ABOUT ME. IT WAS ABOUT ALL OF YOU.
I'M SORRY?
ROGERS TOLD ME I WAS AROUND TO REMIND ALL OF YOU ALL THAT NOT EVERYONE IS A GOD.
Tony

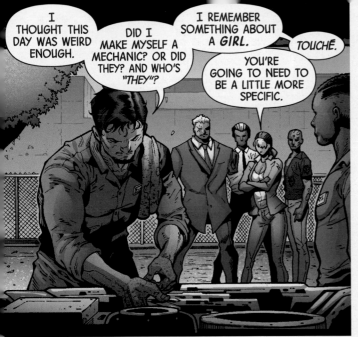

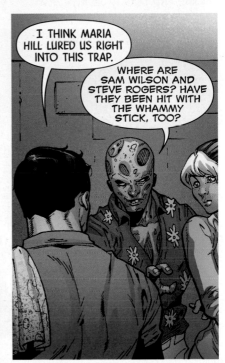

I'M *FINISHED* APOLOGIZING FOR BEING AN AVENGER. THE DECISION WAS MADE *FOR* ME BY STEVE ROGERS. YOU GOT A PROBLEM WITH IT, HEAD ON OVER TO THE PLEASANT HILL NURSING HOME AND TAKE IT UP WITH *HIM*.

BUT WHILE WE'RE ON THE SUBJECT OF QUESTIONABLE ROSTERS, MAYBE FORMING THE *"TINY TONY URBAN ACHIEVERS"*--YES, AND PROUD WE ARE OF ALL OF *THEM*--WASN'T YOUR FINEST HOUR, MAN.

GARAG

WELL-- HE SHUT *ME* UP.

LET'S FIND WHERE MY ARMOR IS STOWED. NOVA'S HELMET. JOHNNY'S ASBESTOS PAJAMAS.

I COULD TELEPORT US AWAY SO WE CAN REGROUP.

THAT'LL BE OUR BACKUP PLAN. LET'S NOT GIVE UP THE ELEMENT OF SURPRISE.

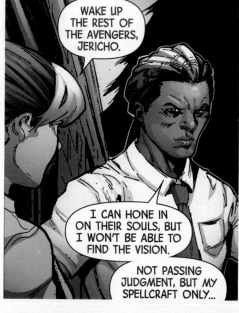

WAKE UP THE REST OF THE AVENGERS, JERICHO.

I CAN HONE IN ON THEIR SOULS, BUT I WON'T BE ABLE TO FIND THE VISION.

NOT PASSING JUDGMENT, BUT MY SPELLCRAFT ONLY...

I THINK I KNOW WHERE TO FIND HIM. MEET ME AT THE MUSIC STORE WHEN YOU'RE DONE.

MS. MARVEL, WOULD YOU JOIN ME?

"LET'S SAY FOR THE SAKE OF ARGUMENT THAT I BELIEVE YOU..."

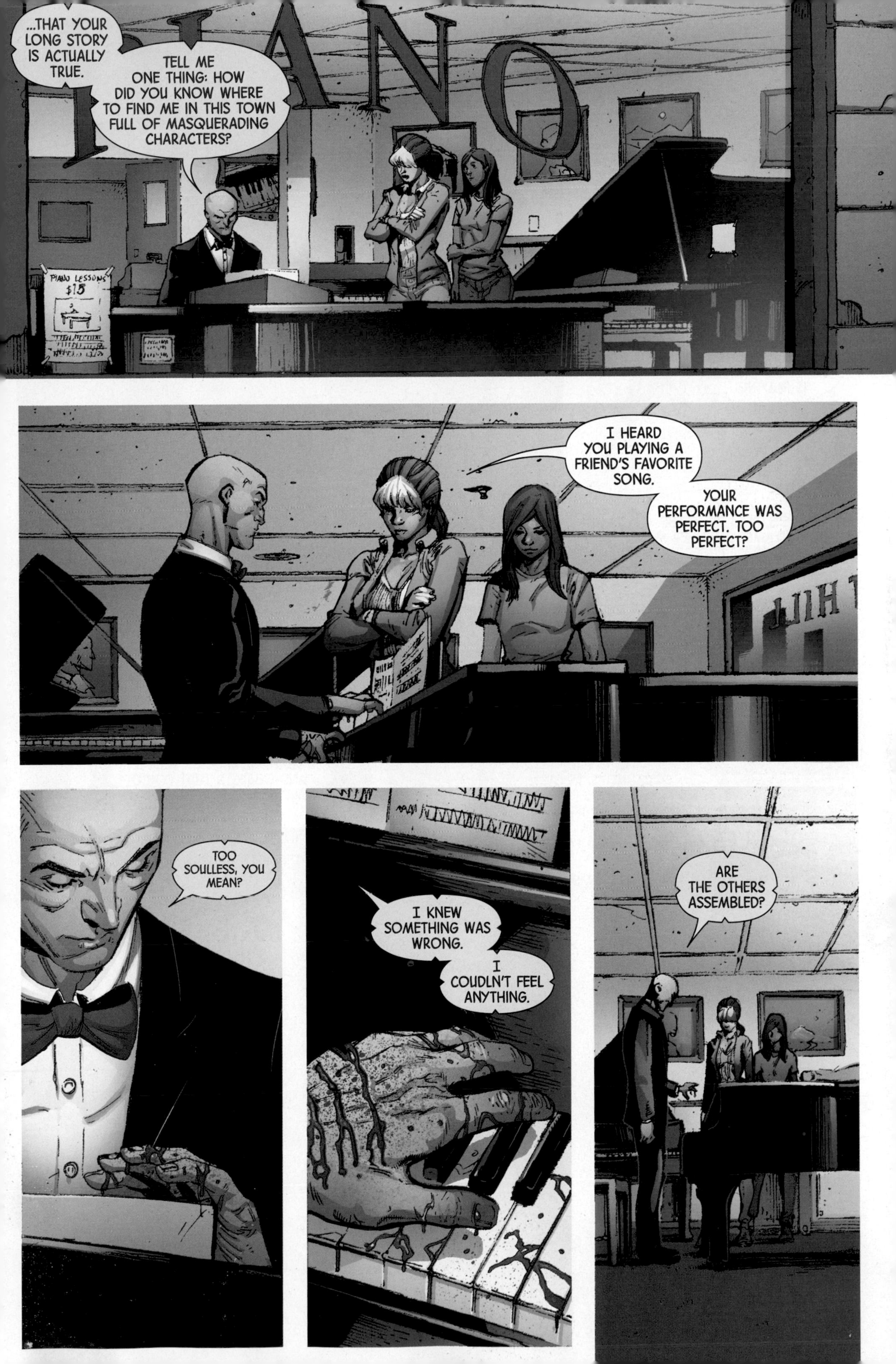
...THAT YOUR LONG STORY IS ACTUALLY TRUE.
TELL ME ONE THING: HOW DID YOU KNOW WHERE TO FIND ME IN THIS TOWN FULL OF MASQUERADING CHARACTERS?
PIANO LESSONS $15
I HEARD YOU PLAYING A FRIEND'S FAVORITE SONG.
YOUR PERFORMANCE WAS PERFECT. TOO PERFECT?
TOO SOULLESS, YOU MEAN?
I KNEW SOMETHING WAS WRONG.
I COUDLN'T FEEL ANYTHING.
ARE THE OTHERS ASSEMBLED?

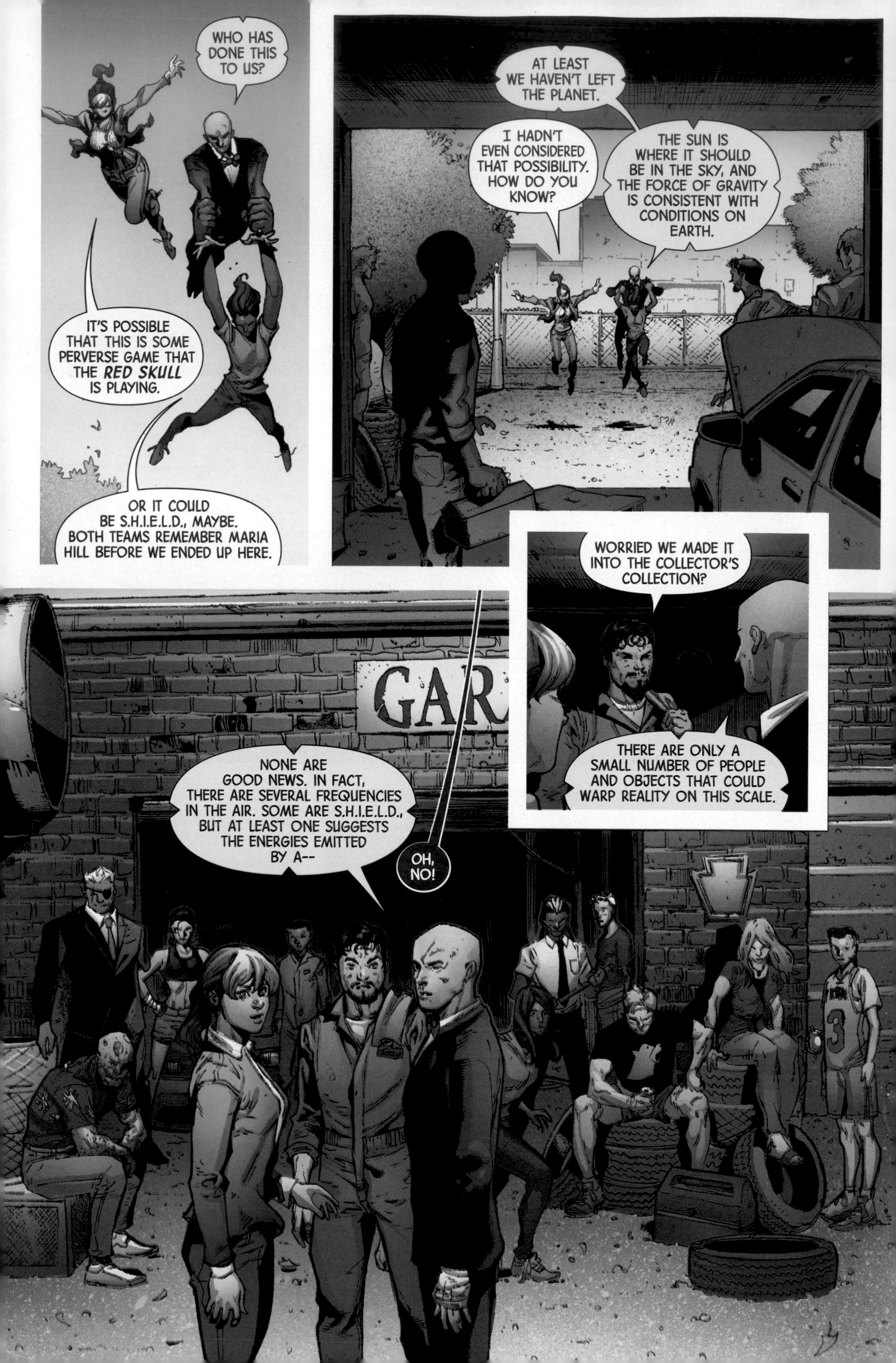
WHO HAS DONE THIS TO US?
IT'S POSSIBLE THAT THIS IS SOME PERVERSE GAME THAT THE **RED SKULL** IS PLAYING.
OR IT COULD BE S.H.I.E.L.D., MAYBE. BOTH TEAMS REMEMBER MARIA HILL BEFORE WE ENDED UP HERE.
AT LEAST WE HAVEN'T LEFT THE PLANET.
I HADN'T EVEN CONSIDERED THAT POSSIBILITY. HOW DO YOU KNOW?
THE SUN IS WHERE IT SHOULD BE IN THE SKY, AND THE FORCE OF GRAVITY IS CONSISTENT WITH CONDITIONS ON EARTH.
WORRIED WE MADE IT INTO THE COLLECTOR'S COLLECTION?
THERE ARE ONLY A SMALL NUMBER OF PEOPLE AND OBJECTS THAT COULD WARP REALITY ON THIS SCALE.
GAR
NONE ARE GOOD NEWS. IN FACT, THERE ARE SEVERAL FREQUENCIES IN THE AIR. SOME ARE S.H.I.E.L.D., BUT AT LEAST ONE SUGGESTS THE ENERGIES EMITTED BY A--
OH, NO!

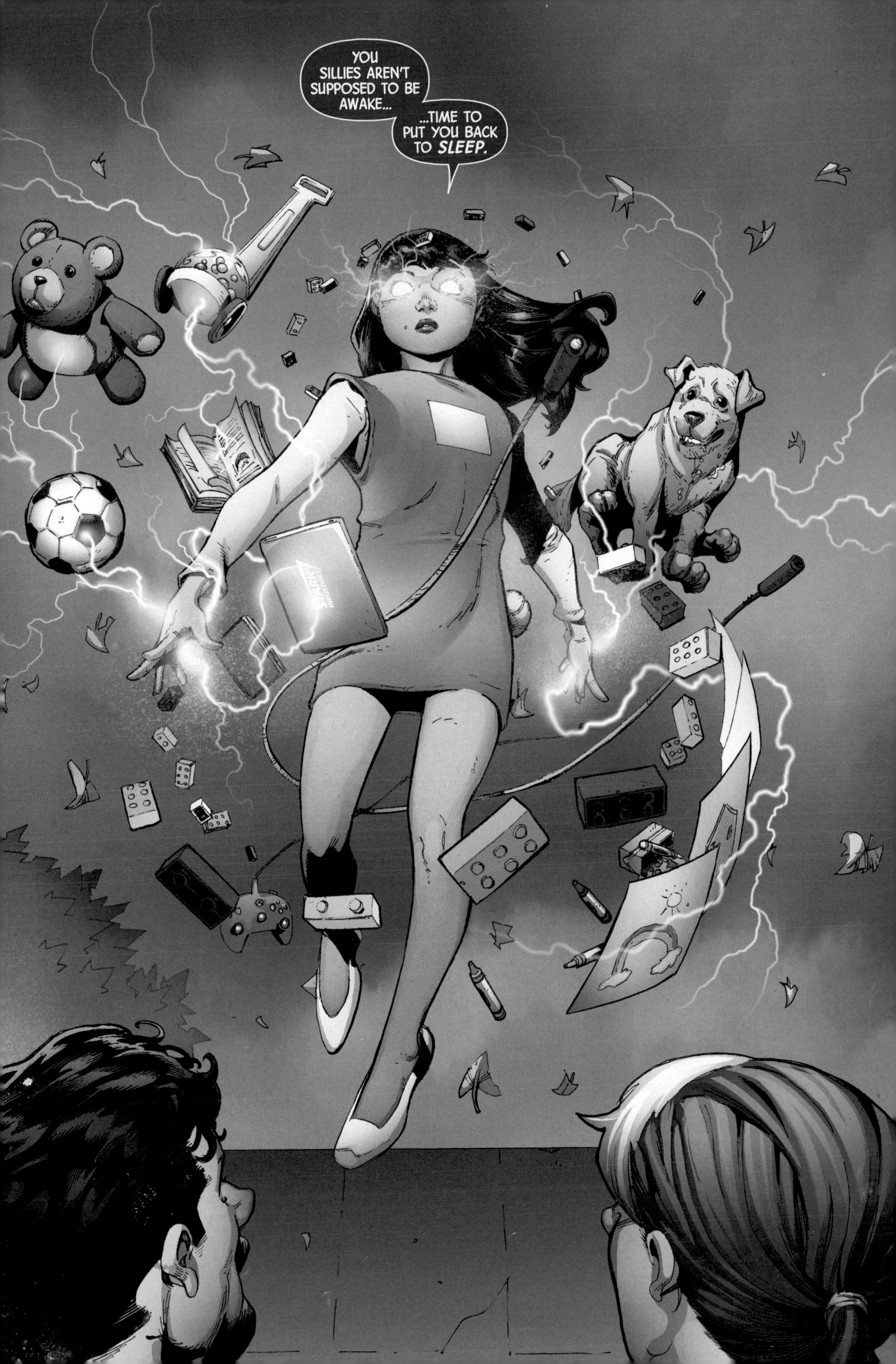
YOU SILLIES AREN'T SUPPOSED TO BE AWAKE...
...TIME TO PUT YOU BACK TO SLEEP.
STARK INDUSTRIES

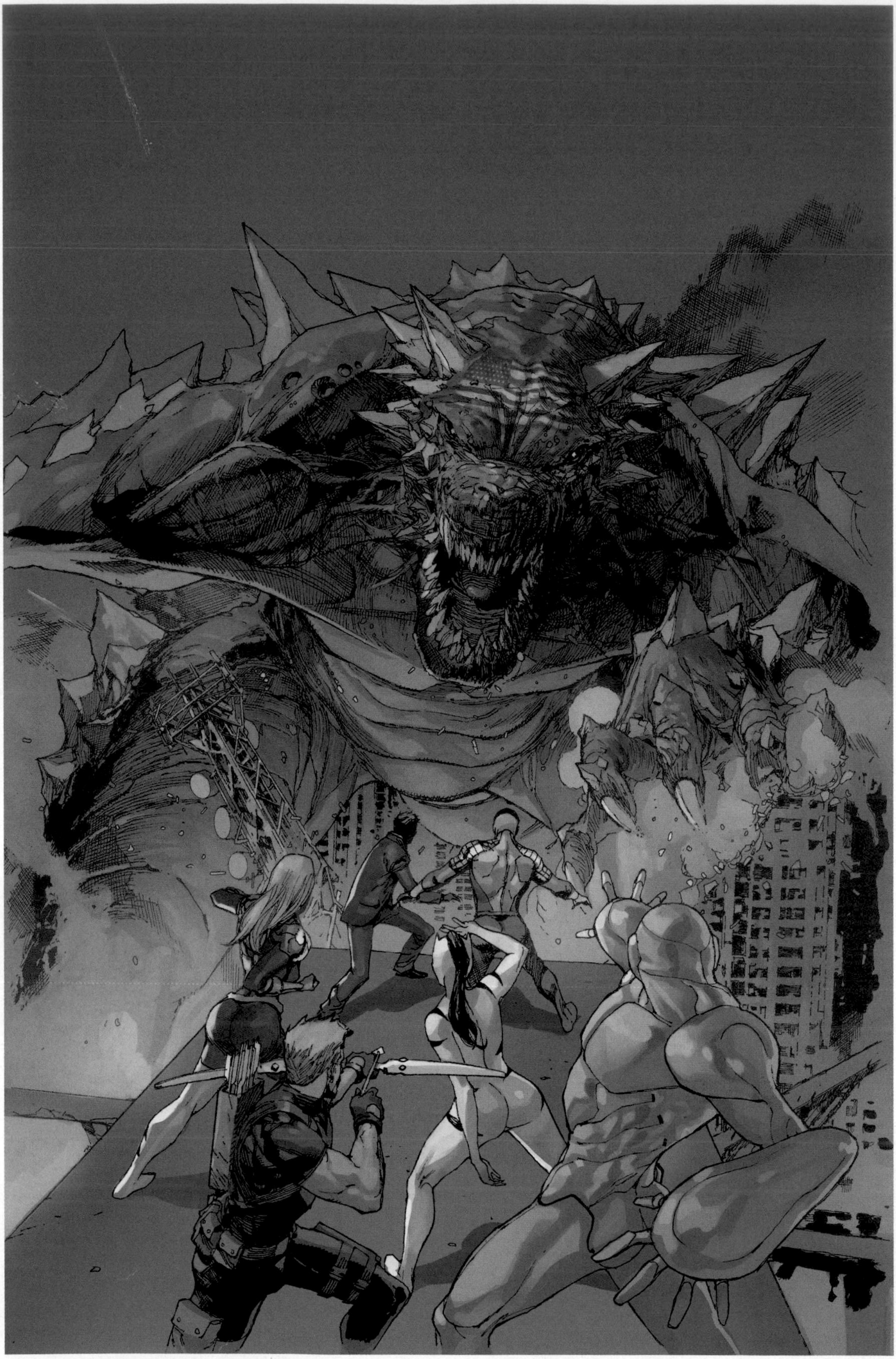

New Avengers No. 9

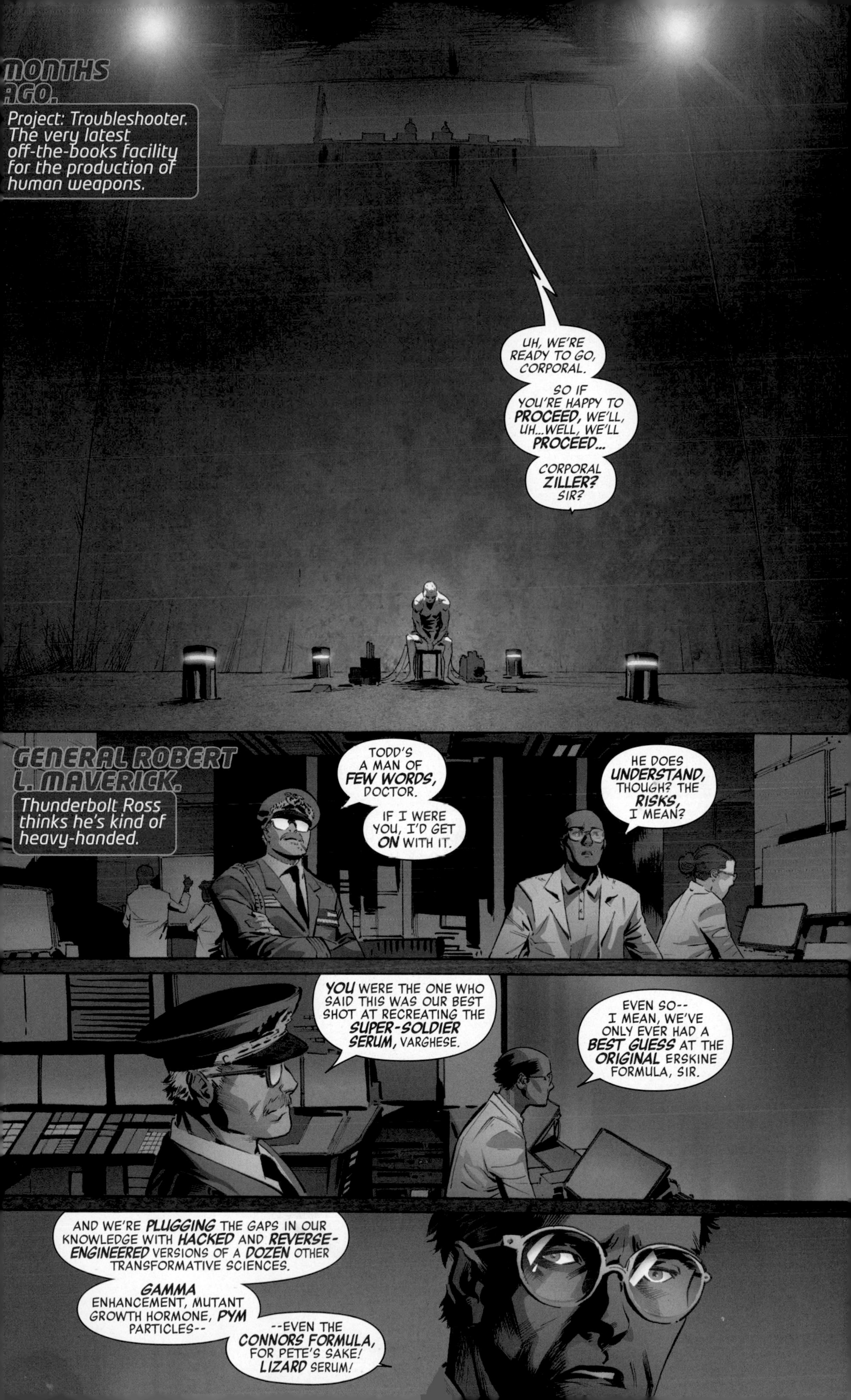
MONTHS AGO.
Project: Troubleshooter. The very latest off-the-books facility for the production of human weapons.
UH, WE'RE READY TO GO, CORPORAL.
SO IF YOU'RE HAPPY TO PROCEED, WE'LL, UH...WELL, WE'LL PROCEED...
CORPORAL ZILLER? SIR?
GENERAL ROBERT L. MAVERICK.
Thunderbolt Ross thinks he's kind of heavy-handed.
TODD'S A MAN OF FEW WORDS, DOCTOR.
IF I WERE YOU, I'D GET ON WITH IT.
HE DOES UNDERSTAND, THOUGH? THE RISKS, I MEAN?
YOU WERE THE ONE WHO SAID THIS WAS OUR BEST SHOT AT RECREATING THE SUPER-SOLDIER SERUM, VARGHESE.
EVEN SO-- I MEAN, WE'VE ONLY EVER HAD A BEST GUESS AT THE ORIGINAL ERSKINE FORMULA, SIR.
AND WE'RE PLUGGING THE GAPS IN OUR KNOWLEDGE WITH HACKED AND REVERSE-ENGINEERED VERSIONS OF A DOZEN OTHER TRANSFORMATIVE SCIENCES.
GAMMA ENHANCEMENT, MUTANT GROWTH HORMONE, PYM PARTICLES--
--EVEN THE CONNORS FORMULA, FOR PETE'S SAKE! LIZARD SERUM!

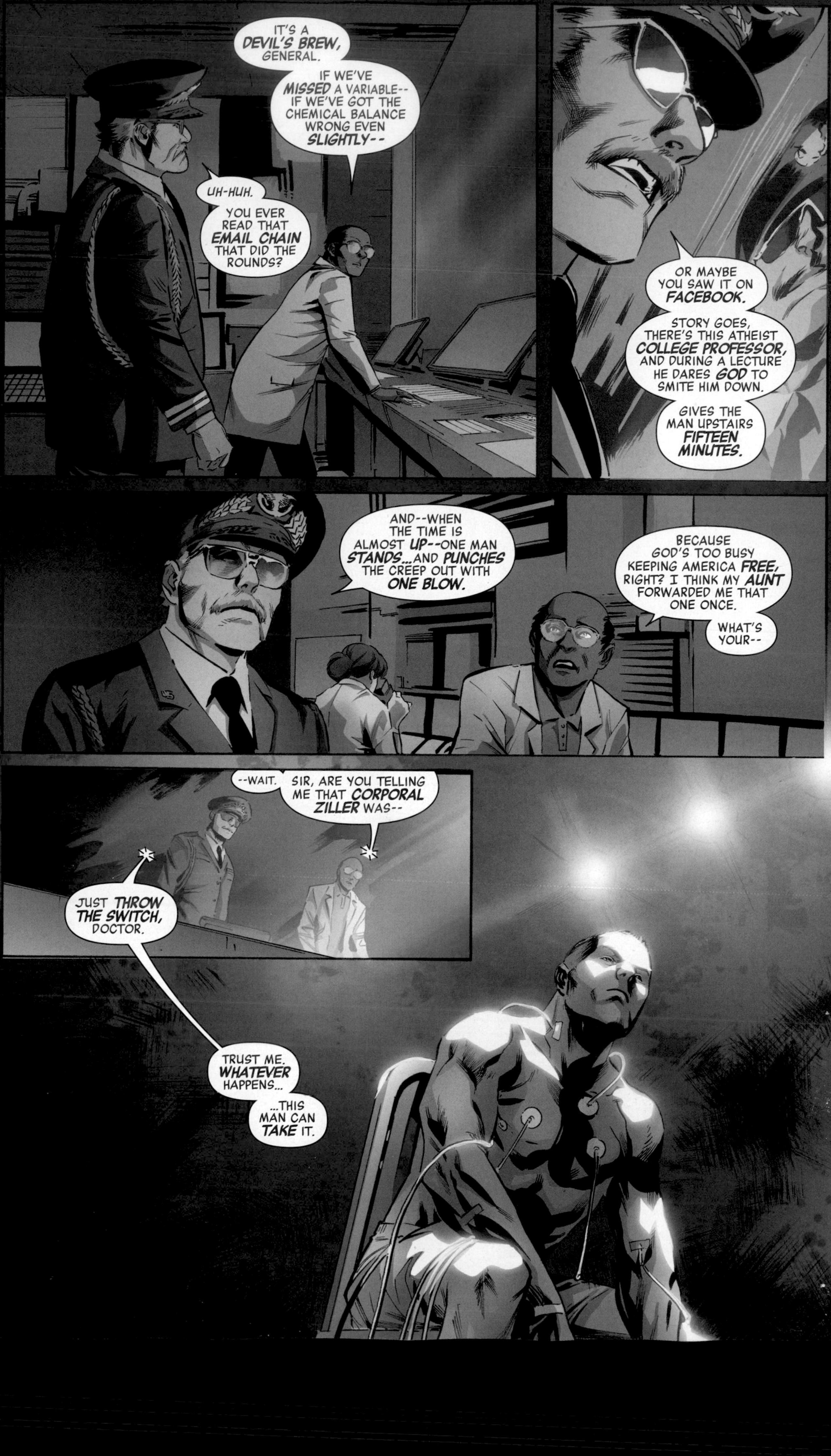
IT'S A DEVIL'S BREW, GENERAL.
IF WE'VE MISSED A VARIABLE-- IF WE'VE GOT THE CHEMICAL BALANCE WRONG EVEN SLIGHTLY--
UH-HUH.
YOU EVER READ THAT EMAIL CHAIN THAT DID THE ROUNDS?
OR MAYBE YOU SAW IT ON FACEBOOK.
STORY GOES, THERE'S THIS ATHEIST COLLEGE PROFESSOR, AND DURING A LECTURE HE DARES GOD TO SMITE HIM DOWN.
GIVES THE MAN UPSTAIRS FIFTEEN MINUTES.
AND--WHEN THE TIME IS ALMOST UP--ONE MAN STANDS...AND PUNCHES THE CREEP OUT WITH ONE BLOW.
BECAUSE GOD'S TOO BUSY KEEPING AMERICA FREE, RIGHT? I THINK MY AUNT FORWARDED ME THAT ONE ONCE.
WHAT'S YOUR--
--WAIT.
SIR, ARE YOU TELLING ME THAT CORPORAL ZILLER WAS--
JUST THROW THE SWITCH, DOCTOR.
TRUST ME. WHATEVER HAPPENS...
...THIS MAN CAN TAKE IT.

A-ALL RIGHT, SIR. SYSTEMS **ON.** HERE'S HOPING...

VVVRRZZZ

HRRRRH--

RRAAARH--

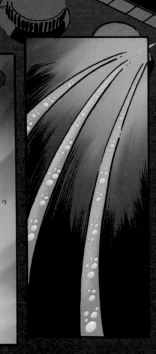

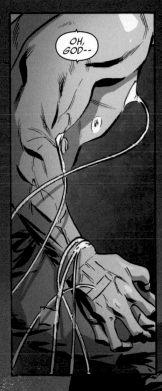

OH, GOD--

ABORT!

ABORT, I SAID!

ABORT THE TEST! SOMEONE!

OH, GOD-- I'M--I'M SORRY, I'M SO SORRY--

WHAT ARE YOU **WHINING** ABOUT, VARGHESE?

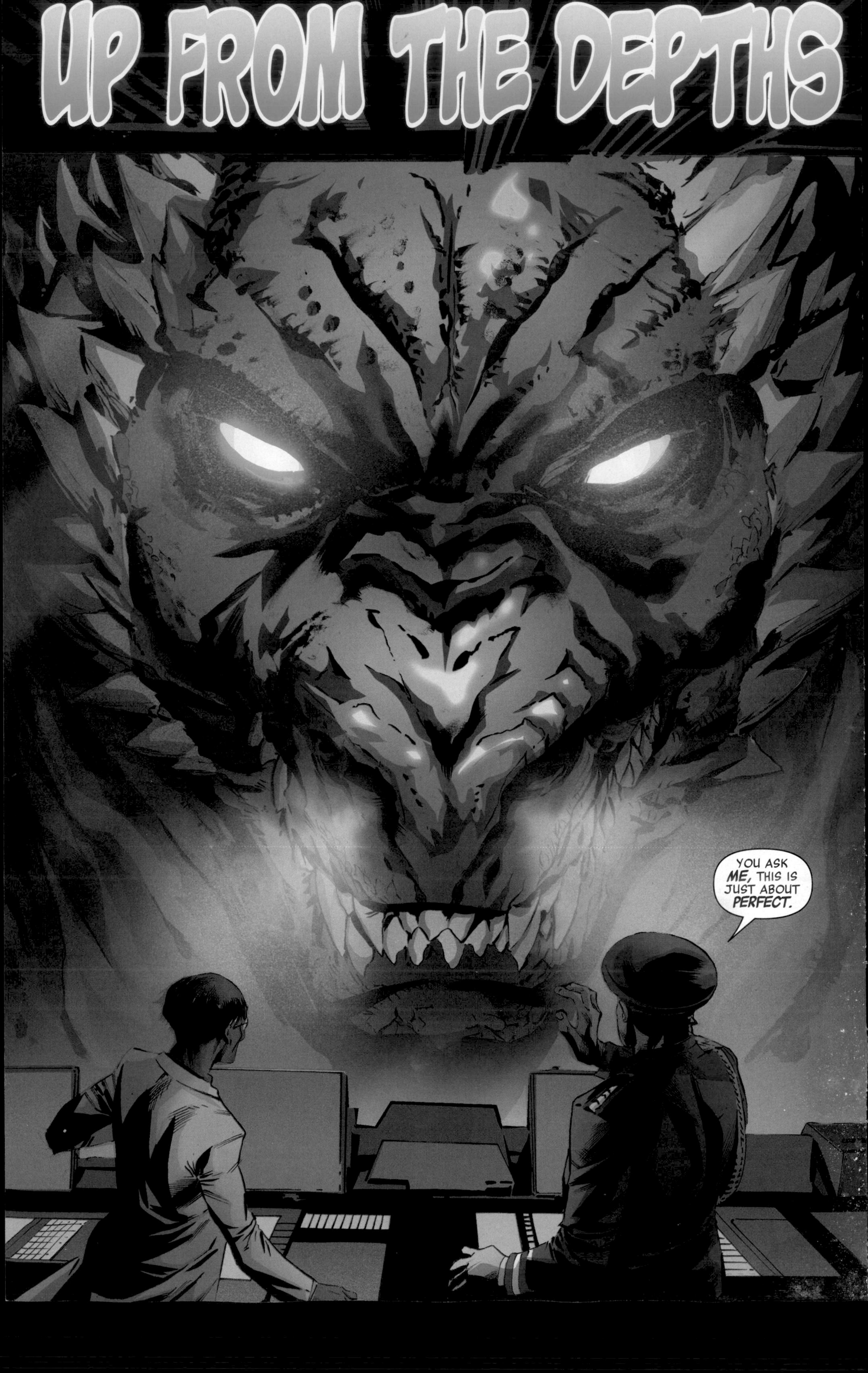
UP FROM THE DEPTHS
YOU ASK ME, THIS IS JUST ABOUT PERFECT.

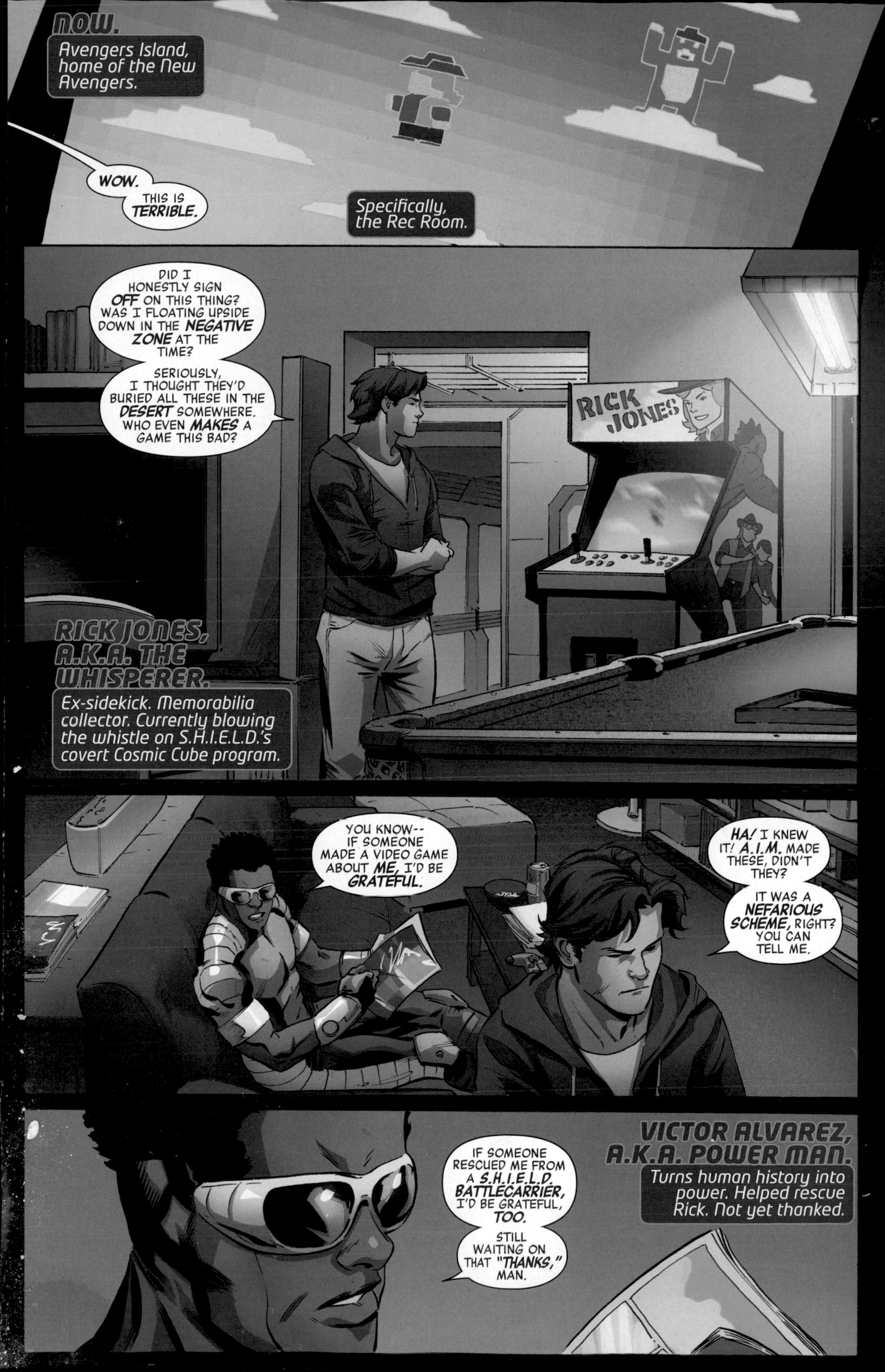

NOW.
Avengers Island, home of the New Avengers.
WOW. THIS IS TERRIBLE.
Specifically, the Rec Room.
DID I HONESTLY SIGN OFF ON THIS THING? WAS I FLOATING UPSIDE DOWN IN THE NEGATIVE ZONE AT THE TIME?
SERIOUSLY, I THOUGHT THEY'D BURIED ALL THESE IN THE DESERT SOMEWHERE. WHO EVEN MAKES A GAME THIS BAD?
RICK JONES
RICK JONES, A.K.A. THE WHISPERER.
Ex-sidekick. Memorabilia collector. Currently blowing the whistle on S.H.I.E.L.D.'s covert Cosmic Cube program.
YOU KNOW-- IF SOMEONE MADE A VIDEO GAME ABOUT ME, I'D BE GRATEFUL.
HA! I KNEW IT! A.I.M. MADE THESE, DIDN'T THEY?
IT WAS A NEFARIOUS SCHEME, RIGHT? YOU CAN TELL ME.
VICTOR ALVAREZ, A.K.A. POWER MAN.
Turns human history into power. Helped rescue Rick. Not yet thanked.
IF SOMEONE RESCUED ME FROM A S.H.I.E.L.D. BATTLECARRIER, I'D BE GRATEFUL, TOO.
STILL WAITING ON THAT "THANKS," MAN.

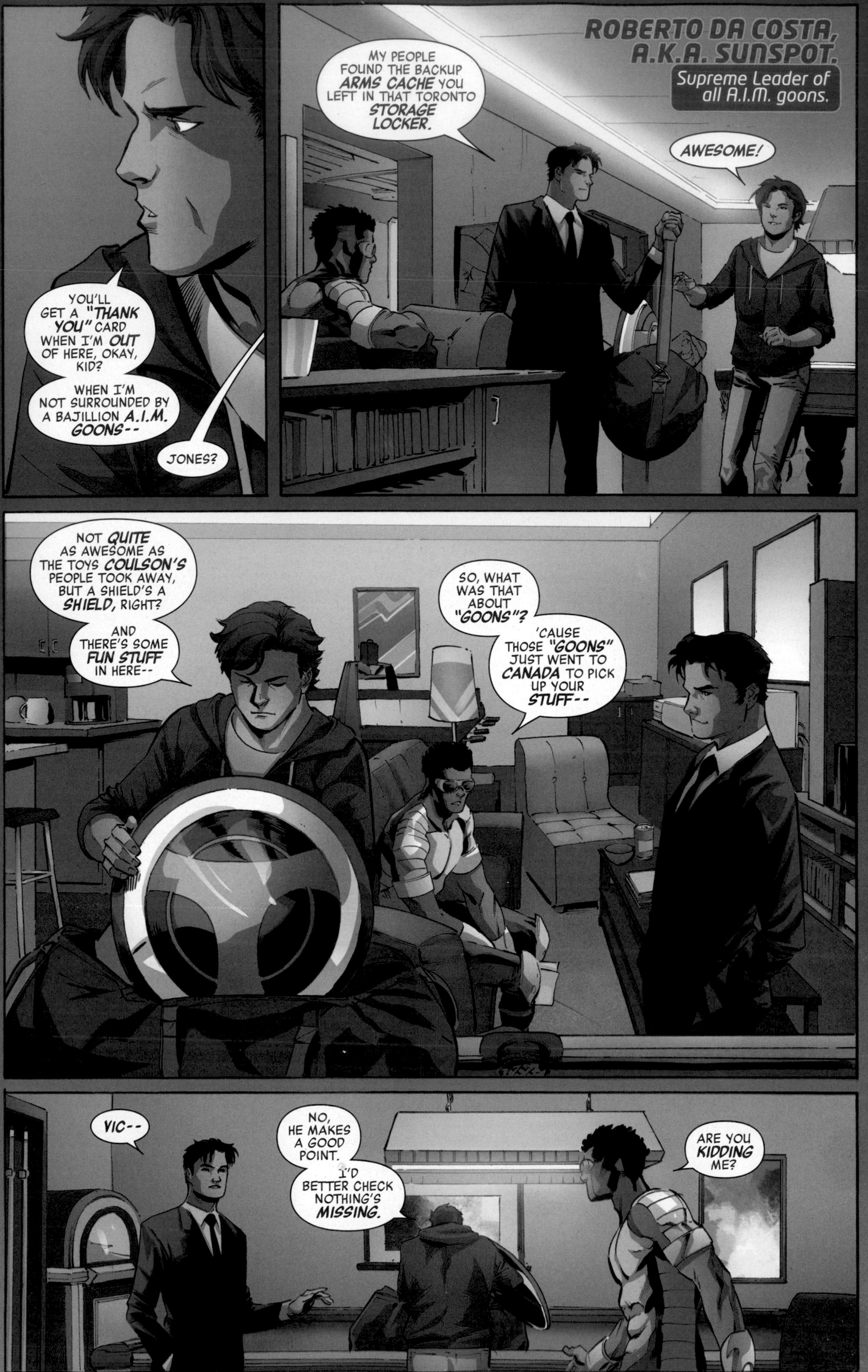
ROBERTO DA COSTA, A.K.A. SUNSPOT.
Supreme Leader of all A.I.M. goons.
MY PEOPLE FOUND THE BACKUP ARMS CACHE YOU LEFT IN THAT TORONTO STORAGE LOCKER.
AWESOME!
YOU'LL GET A "THANK YOU" CARD WHEN I'M OUT OF HERE, OKAY, KID?
WHEN I'M NOT SURROUNDED BY A BAJILLION A.I.M. GOONS--
JONES?
NOT QUITE AS AWESOME AS THE TOYS COULSON'S PEOPLE TOOK AWAY, BUT A SHIELD'S A SHIELD, RIGHT?
AND THERE'S SOME FUN STUFF IN HERE--
SO, WHAT WAS THAT ABOUT "GOONS"?
'CAUSE THOSE "GOONS" JUST WENT TO CANADA TO PICK UP YOUR STUFF--
VIC--
NO, HE MAKES A GOOD POINT.
I'D BETTER CHECK NOTHING'S MISSING.
ARE YOU KIDDING ME?

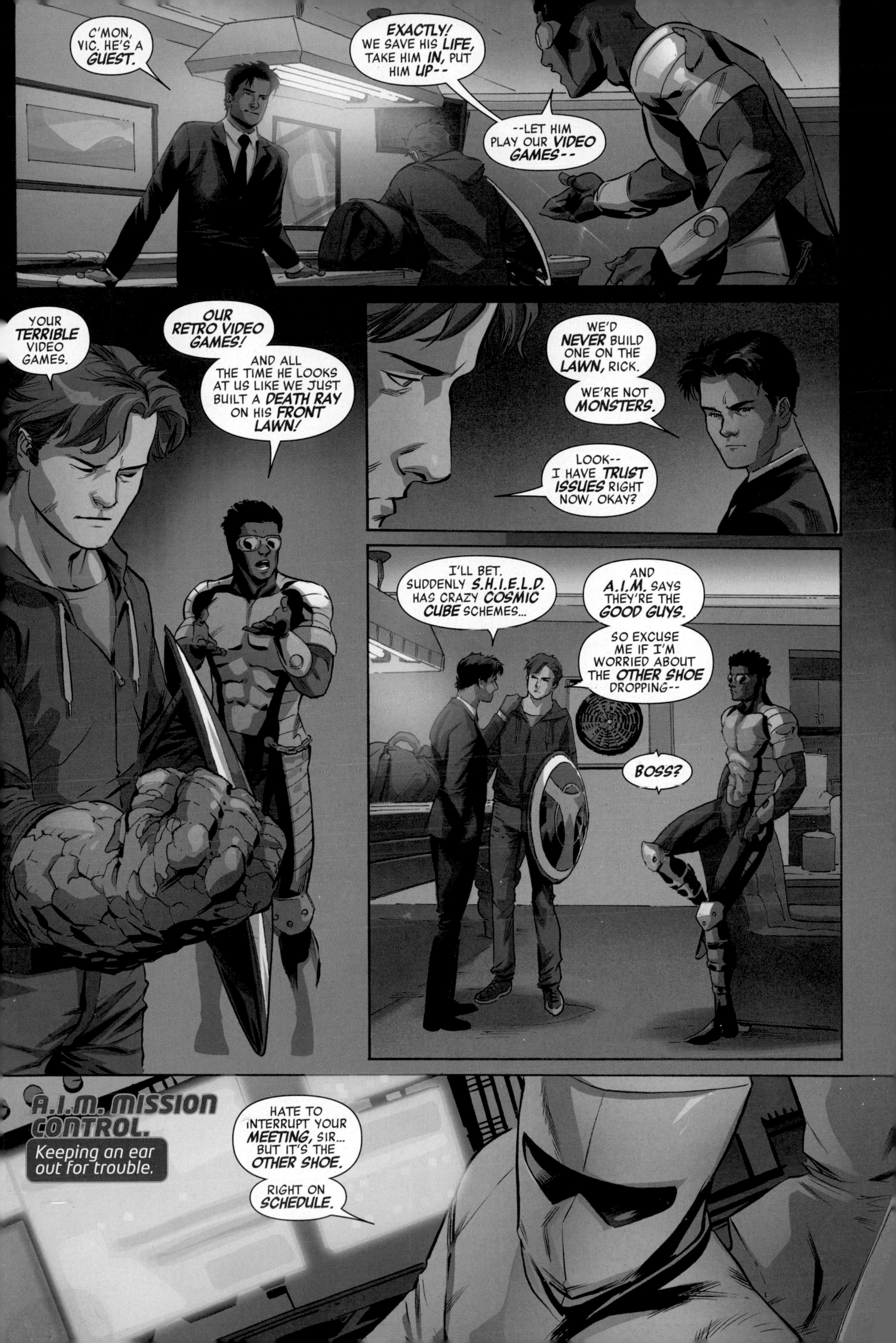
C'MON, VIC. HE'S A GUEST.
EXACTLY! WE SAVE HIS LIFE, TAKE HIM IN, PUT HIM UP--
--LET HIM PLAY OUR VIDEO GAMES--
YOUR TERRIBLE VIDEO GAMES.
OUR RETRO VIDEO GAMES!
AND ALL THE TIME HE LOOKS AT US LIKE WE JUST BUILT A DEATH RAY ON HIS FRONT LAWN!
WE'D NEVER BUILD ONE ON THE LAWN, RICK.
WE'RE NOT MONSTERS.
LOOK-- I HAVE TRUST ISSUES RIGHT NOW, OKAY?
I'LL BET. SUDDENLY S.H.I.E.L.D. HAS CRAZY COSMIC CUBE SCHEMES...
AND A.I.M. SAYS THEY'RE THE GOOD GUYS.
SO EXCUSE ME IF I'M WORRIED ABOUT THE OTHER SHOE DROPPING--
BOSS?
A.I.M. MISSION CONTROL.
Keeping an ear out for trouble.
HATE TO INTERRUPT YOUR MEETING, SIR... BUT IT'S THE OTHER SHOE.
RIGHT ON SCHEDULE.

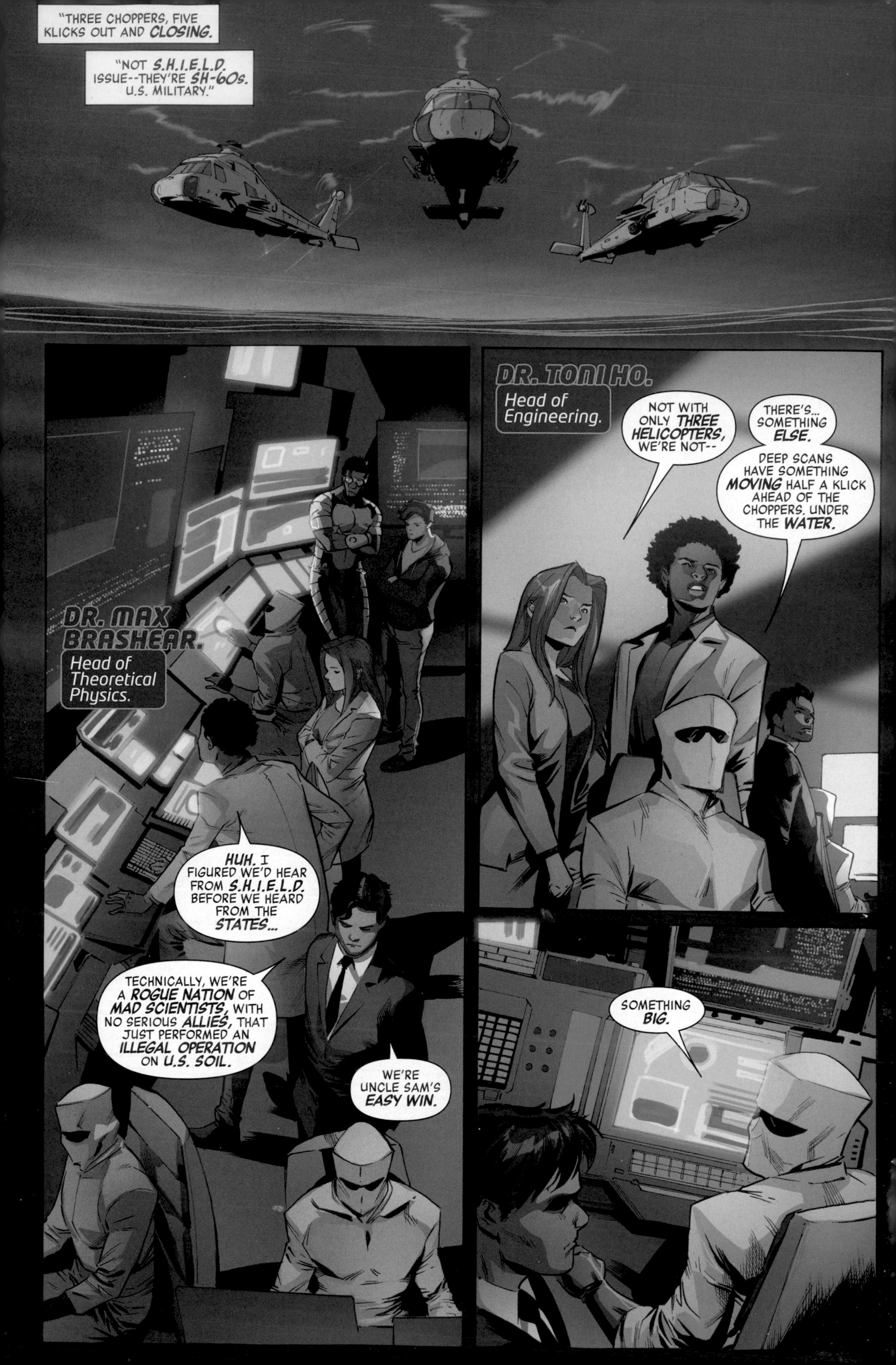
"THREE CHOPPERS, FIVE KLICKS OUT AND CLOSING.
"NOT S.H.I.E.L.D. ISSUE--THEY'RE SH-60s. U.S. MILITARY."
DR. MAX BRASHEAR.
Head of Theoretical Physics.
HUH. I FIGURED WE'D HEAR FROM S.H.I.E.L.D. BEFORE WE HEARD FROM THE STATES...
TECHNICALLY, WE'RE A ROGUE NATION OF MAD SCIENTISTS, WITH NO SERIOUS ALLIES, THAT JUST PERFORMED AN ILLEGAL OPERATION ON U.S. SOIL.
WE'RE UNCLE SAM'S EASY WIN.
DR. TONI HO.
Head of Engineering.
NOT WITH ONLY THREE HELICOPTERS, WE'RE NOT--
THERE'S... SOMETHING ELSE.
DEEP SCANS HAVE SOMETHING MOVING HALF A KLICK AHEAD OF THE CHOPPERS. UNDER THE WATER.
SOMETHING BIG.

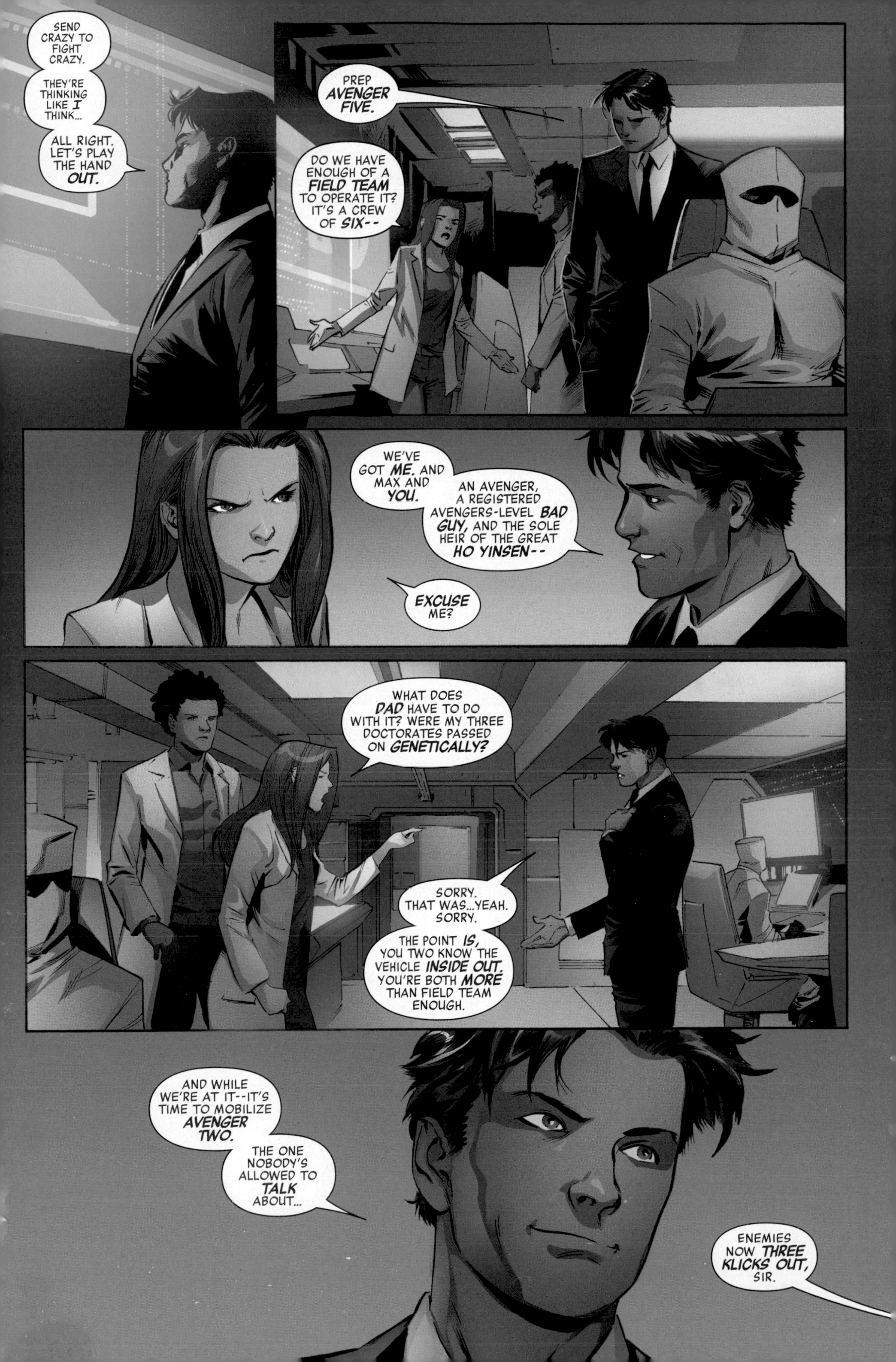
SEND CRAZY TO FIGHT CRAZY.
THEY'RE THINKING LIKE I THINK...
ALL RIGHT. LET'S PLAY THE HAND OUT.
PREP AVENGER FIVE.
DO WE HAVE ENOUGH OF A FIELD TEAM TO OPERATE IT? IT'S A CREW OF SIX--
WE'VE GOT ME. AND MAX AND YOU.
AN AVENGER, A REGISTERED AVENGERS-LEVEL BAD GUY, AND THE SOLE HEIR OF THE GREAT HO YINSEN--
EXCUSE ME?
WHAT DOES DAD HAVE TO DO WITH IT? WERE MY THREE DOCTORATES PASSED ON GENETICALLY?
SORRY. THAT WAS...YEAH. SORRY.
THE POINT IS, YOU TWO KNOW THE VEHICLE INSIDE OUT. YOU'RE BOTH MORE THAN FIELD TEAM ENOUGH.
AND WHILE WE'RE AT IT--IT'S TIME TO MOBILIZE AVENGER TWO.
THE ONE NOBODY'S ALLOWED TO TALK ABOUT...
ENEMIES NOW THREE KLICKS OUT, SIR.

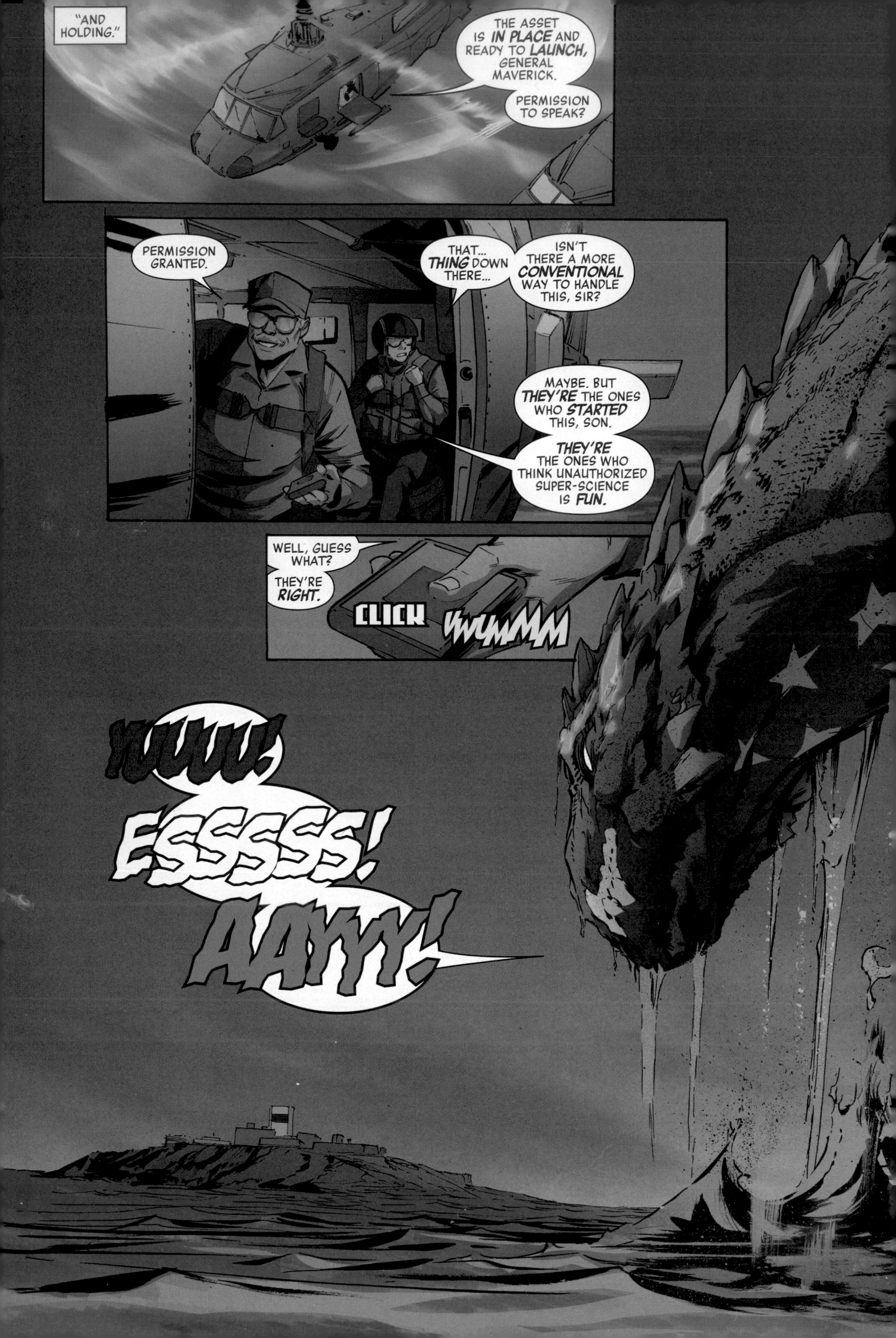
"AND HOLDING."
THE ASSET IS IN PLACE AND READY TO LAUNCH, GENERAL MAVERICK.
PERMISSION TO SPEAK?
PERMISSION GRANTED.
THAT... THING DOWN THERE...
ISN'T THERE A MORE CONVENTIONAL WAY TO HANDLE THIS, SIR?
MAYBE. BUT THEY'RE THE ONES WHO STARTED THIS, SON.
THEY'RE THE ONES WHO THINK UNAUTHORIZED SUPER-SCIENCE IS FUN.
WELL, GUESS WHAT?
THEY'RE RIGHT.
CLICK
VWUMMM
YUUU!
ESSSSS!
AAYYY!

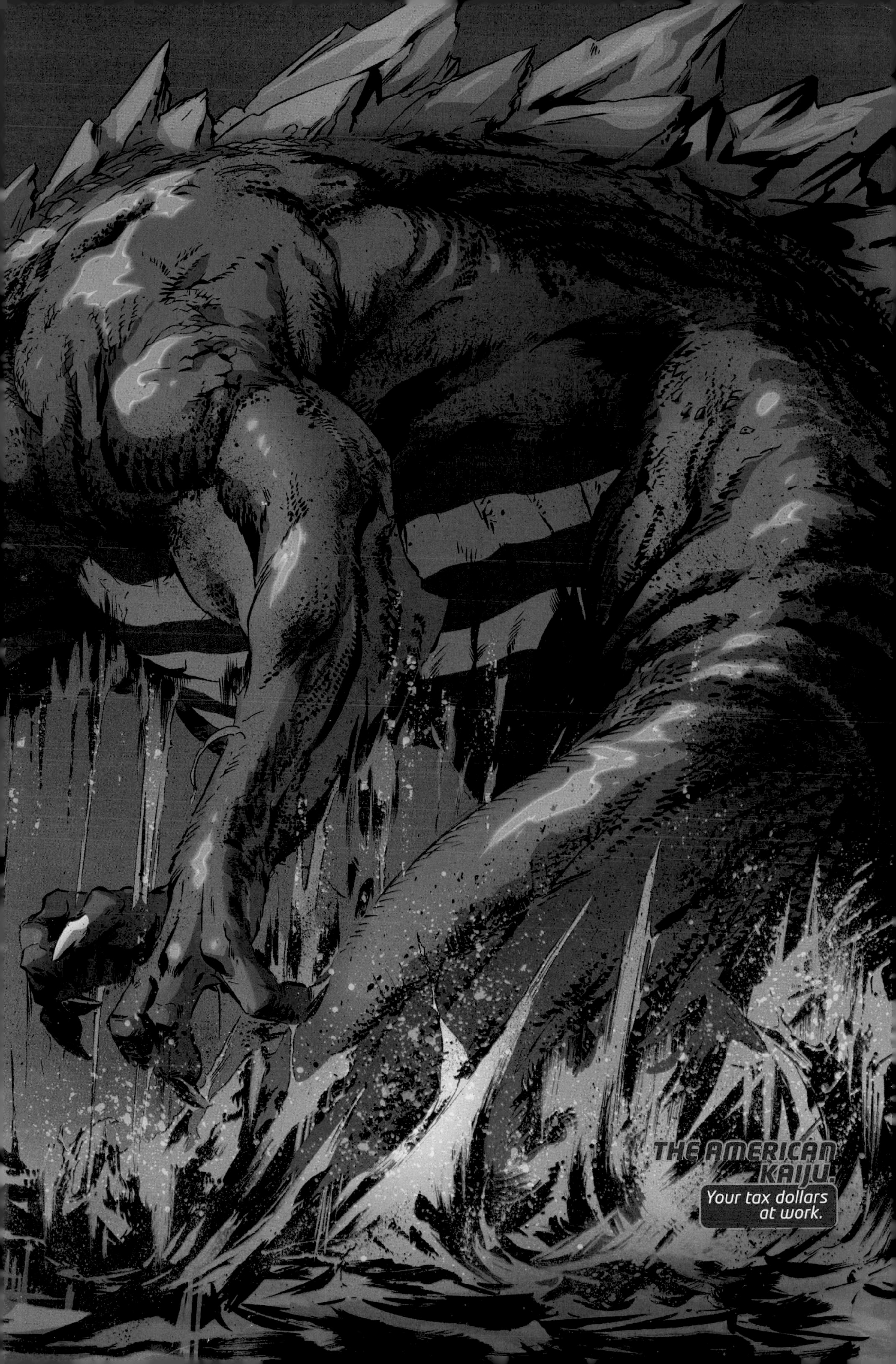
THE AMERICAN KAIJU.
Your tax dollars at work.

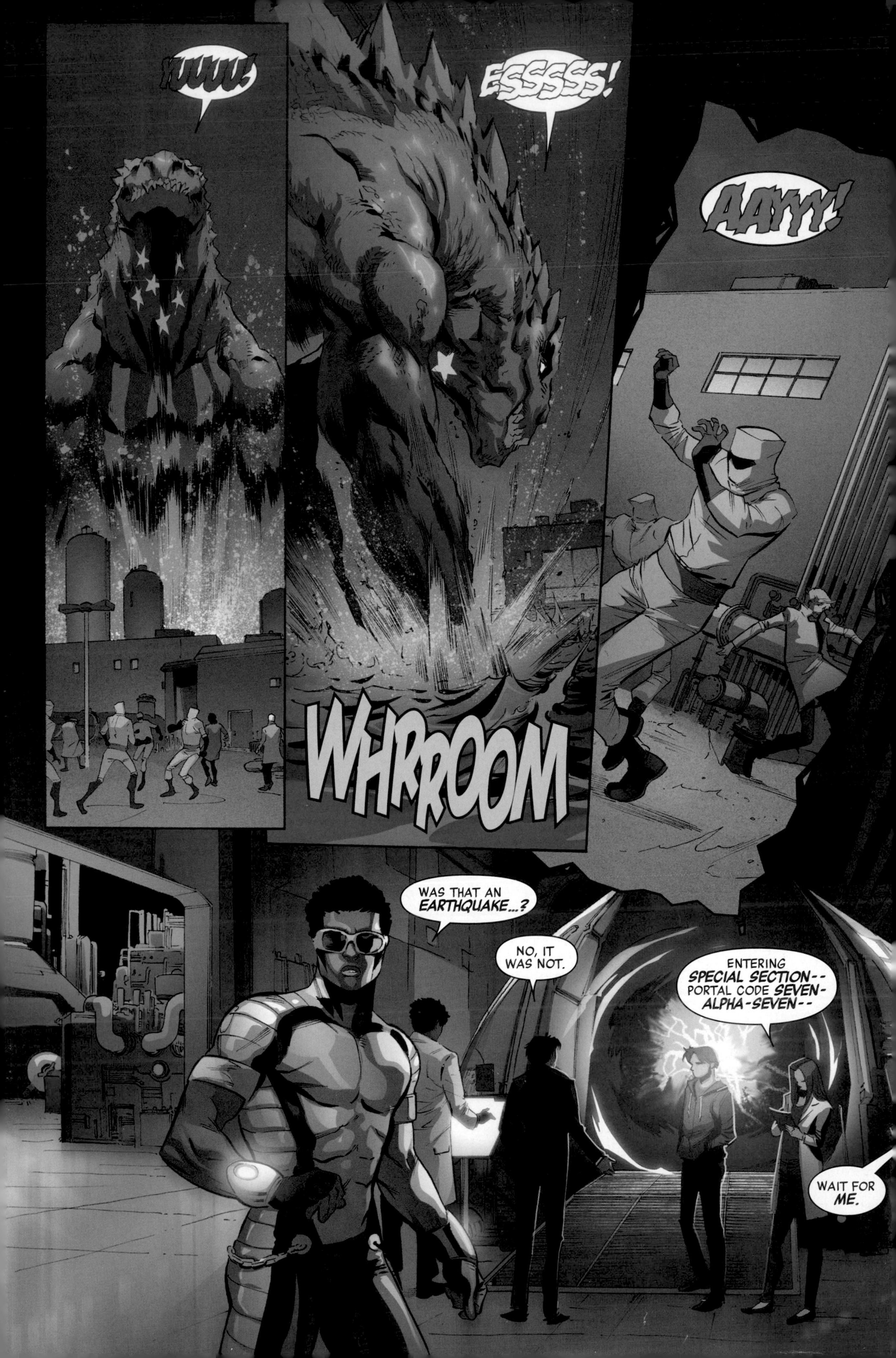
YUUUU!
ESSSSS!
AAYYY!
WHRROOM
WAS THAT AN EARTHQUAKE...?
NO, IT WAS NOT.
ENTERING SPECIAL SECTION-- PORTAL CODE SEVEN-ALPHA-SEVEN--
WAIT FOR ME.

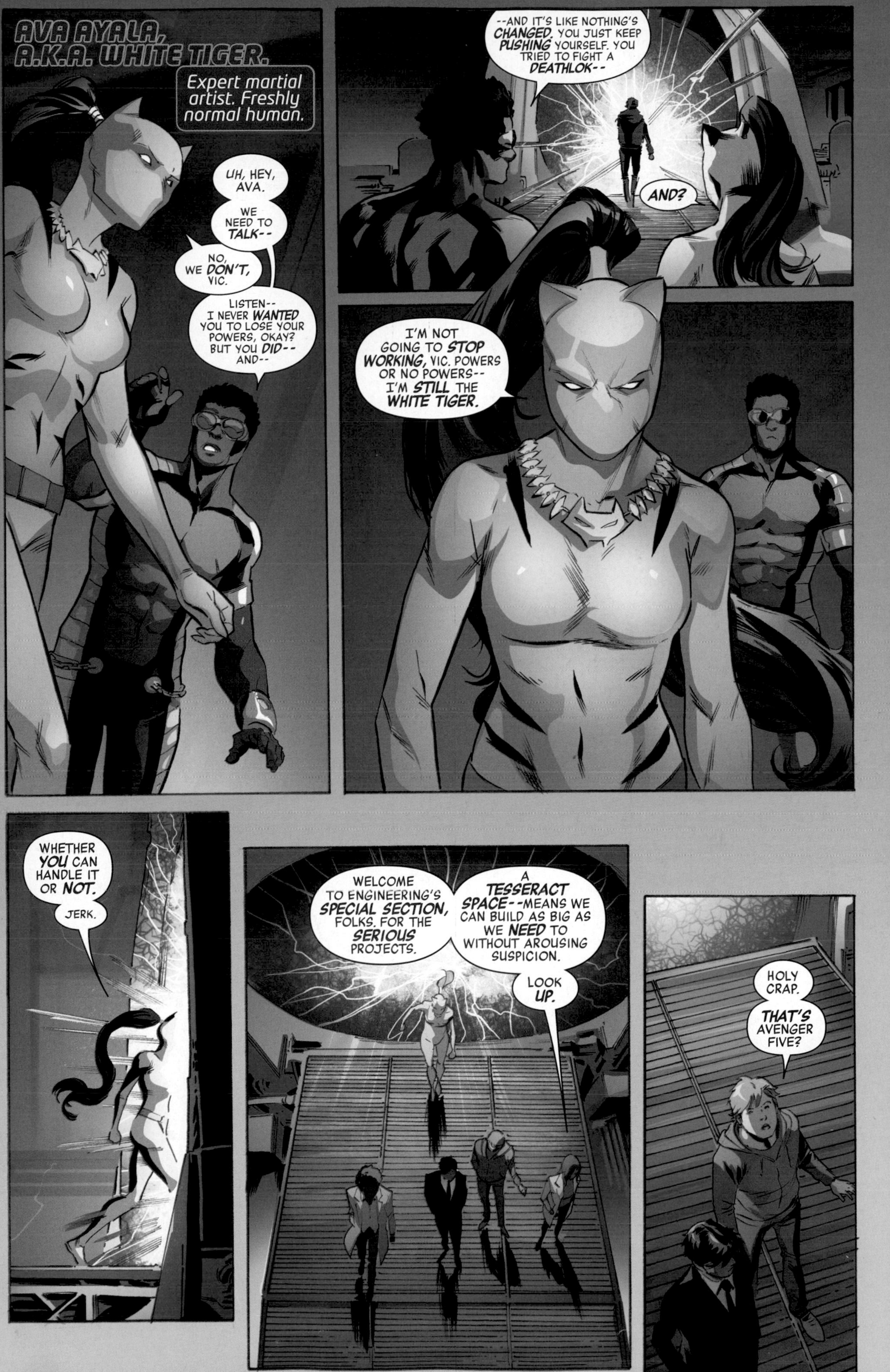
AVA AYALA, A.K.A. WHITE TIGER.
Expert martial artist. Freshly normal human.
UH, HEY, AVA.
WE NEED TO TALK--
NO, WE DON'T, VIC.
LISTEN-- I NEVER WANTED YOU TO LOSE YOUR POWERS, OKAY? BUT YOU DID-- AND--
--AND IT'S LIKE NOTHING'S CHANGED. YOU JUST KEEP PUSHING YOURSELF. YOU TRIED TO FIGHT A DEATHLOK--
AND?
I'M NOT GOING TO STOP WORKING, VIC. POWERS OR NO POWERS-- I'M STILL THE WHITE TIGER.
WHETHER YOU CAN HANDLE IT OR NOT.
JERK.
WELCOME TO ENGINEERING'S SPECIAL SECTION, FOLKS. FOR THE SERIOUS PROJECTS.
A TESSERACT SPACE--MEANS WE CAN BUILD AS BIG AS WE NEED TO WITHOUT AROUSING SUSPICION.
LOOK UP.
HOLY CRAP.
THAT'S AVENGER FIVE?

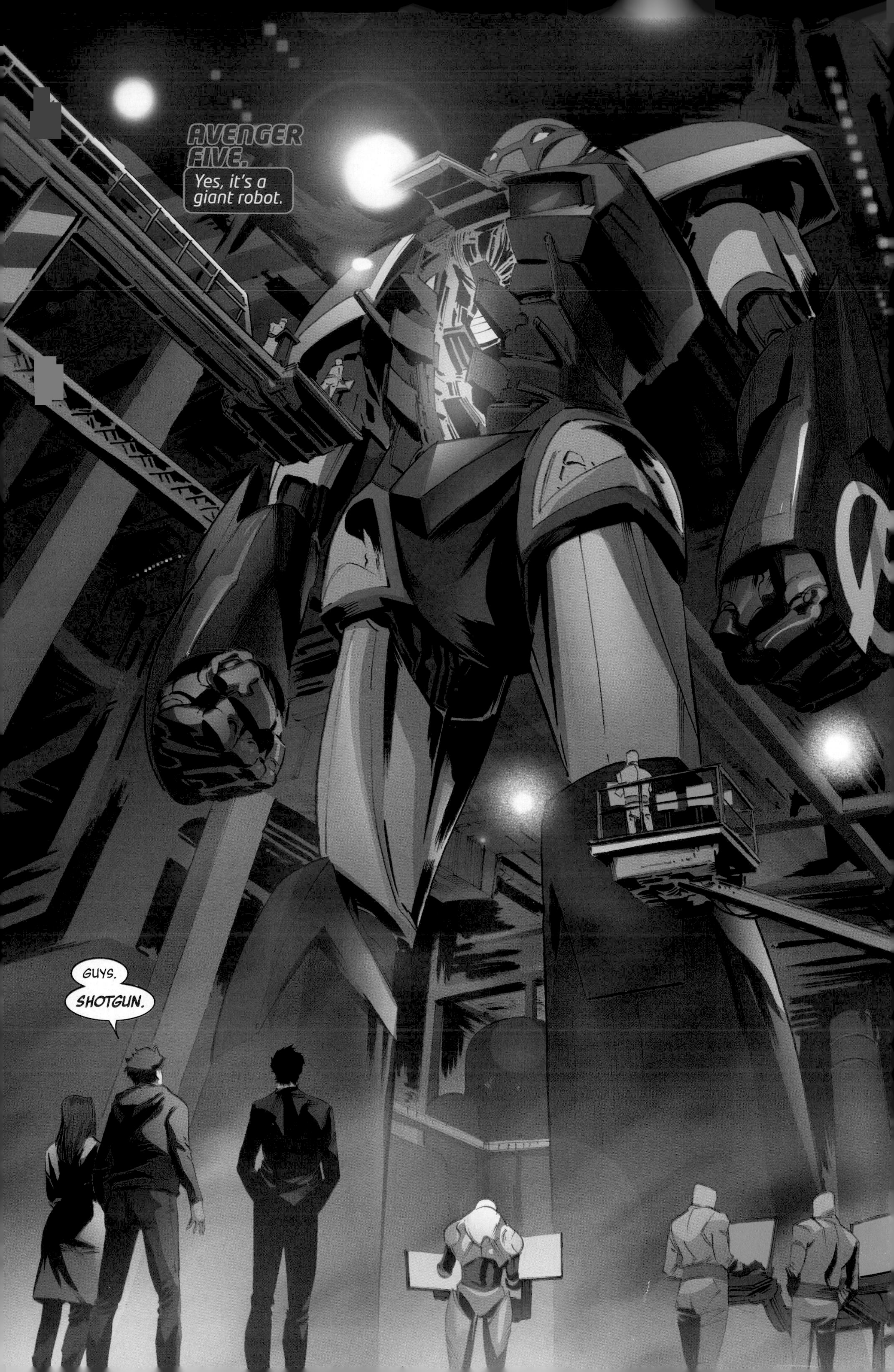
AVENGER FIVE.
Yes, it's a giant robot.
GUYS. SHOTGUN.

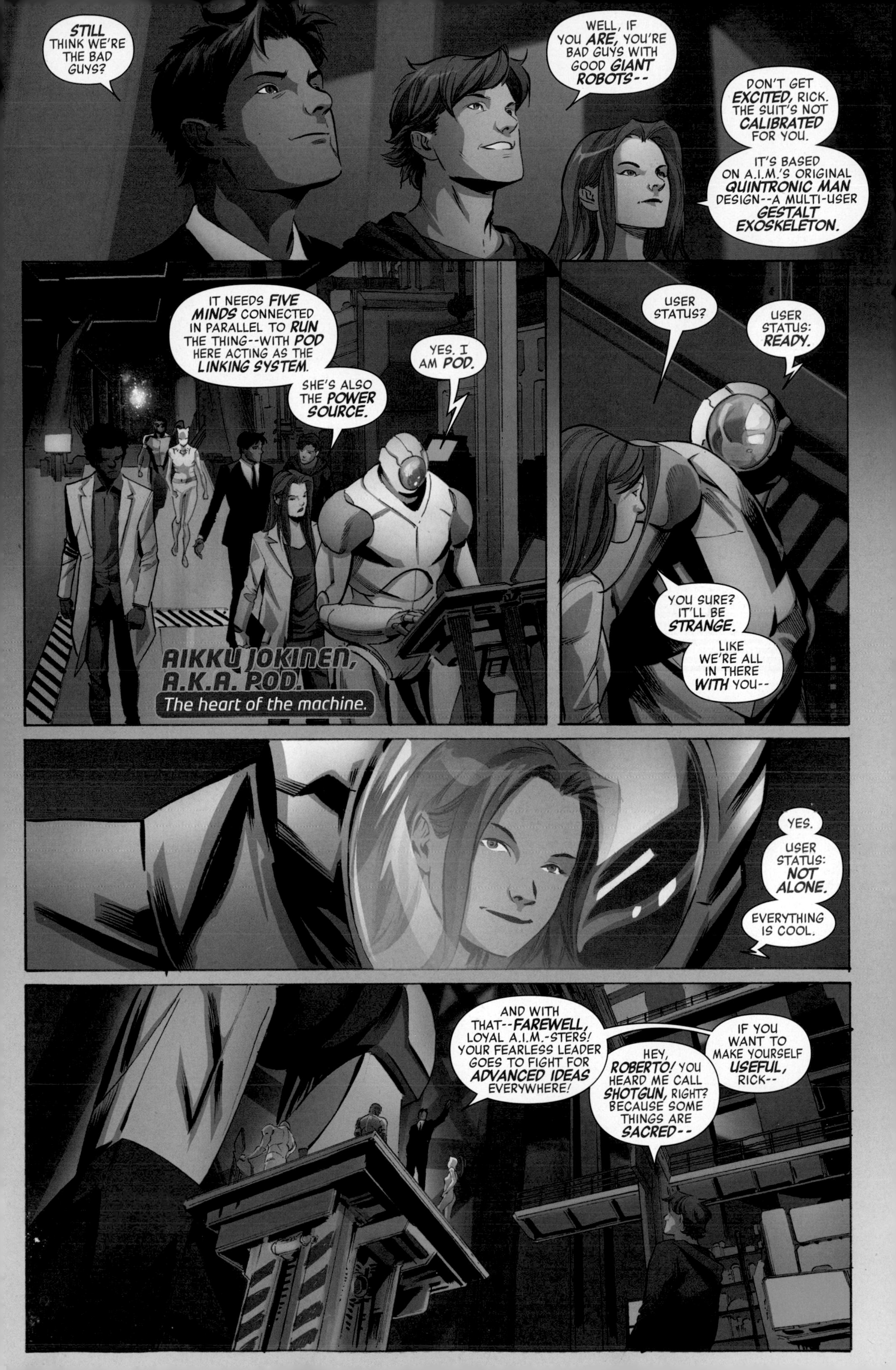
STILL THINK WE'RE THE BAD GUYS?
WELL, IF YOU ARE, YOU'RE BAD GUYS WITH GOOD GIANT ROBOTS--
DON'T GET EXCITED, RICK. THE SUIT'S NOT CALIBRATED FOR YOU.
IT'S BASED ON A.I.M.'S ORIGINAL QUINTRONIC MAN DESIGN--A MULTI-USER GESTALT EXOSKELETON.
IT NEEDS FIVE MINDS CONNECTED IN PARALLEL TO RUN THE THING--WITH POD HERE ACTING AS THE LINKING SYSTEM.
SHE'S ALSO THE POWER SOURCE.
YES. I AM POD.
AIKKU JOKINEN, A.K.A. POD.
The heart of the machine.
USER STATUS?
USER STATUS: READY.
YOU SURE? IT'LL BE STRANGE.
LIKE WE'RE ALL IN THERE WITH YOU--
YES.
USER STATUS: NOT ALONE.
EVERYTHING IS COOL.
AND WITH THAT--FAREWELL, LOYAL A.I.M.-STERS! YOUR FEARLESS LEADER GOES TO FIGHT FOR ADVANCED IDEAS EVERYWHERE!
IF YOU WANT TO MAKE YOURSELF USEFUL, RICK--
HEY, ROBERTO! YOU HEARD ME CALL SHOTGUN, RIGHT? BECAUSE SOME THINGS ARE SACRED--

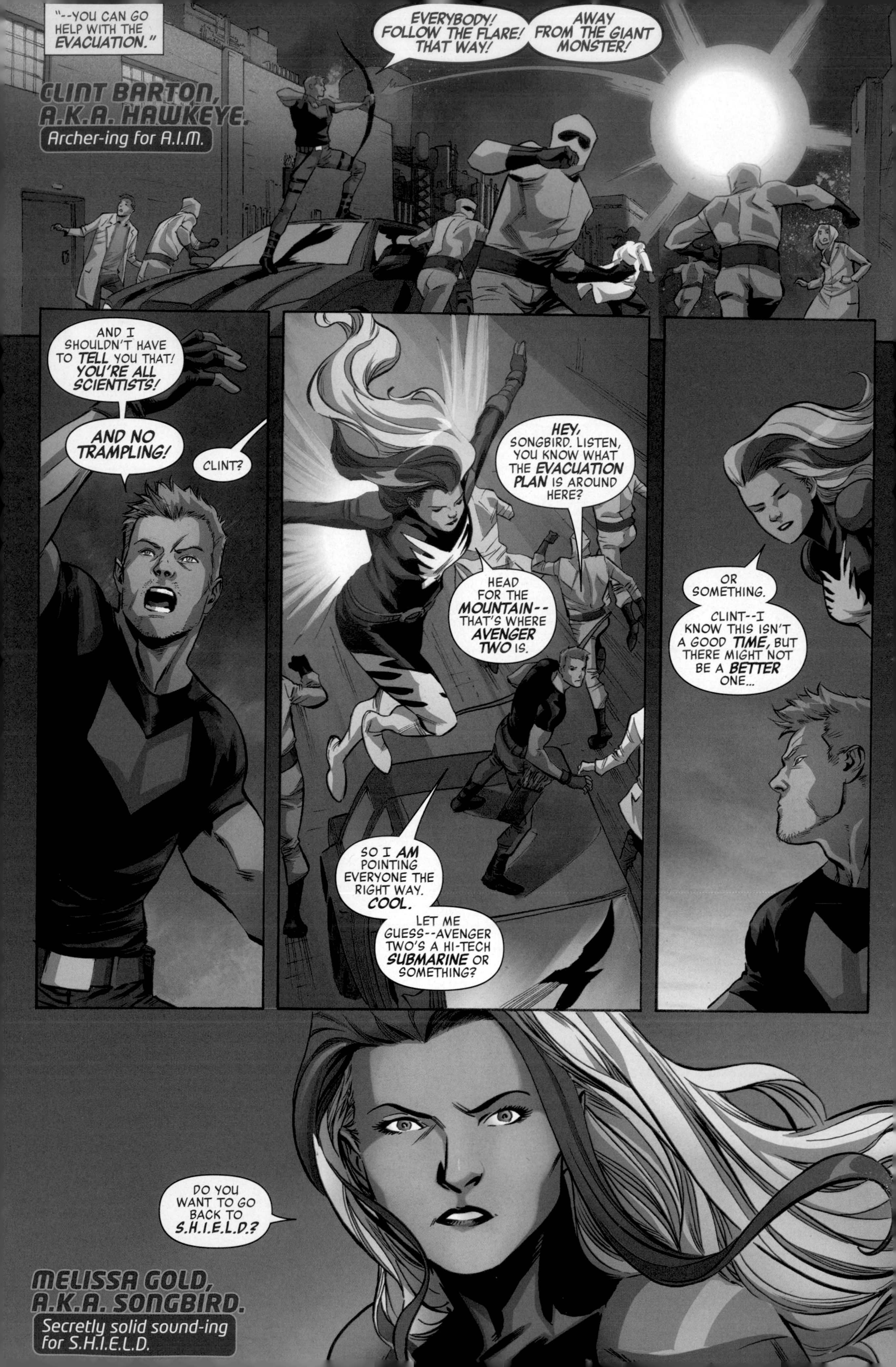
"--YOU CAN GO HELP WITH THE EVACUATION."
EVERYBODY! FOLLOW THE FLARE! THAT WAY!
AWAY FROM THE GIANT MONSTER!
CLINT BARTON, A.K.A. HAWKEYE.
Archer-ing for A.I.M.
AND I SHOULDN'T HAVE TO TELL YOU THAT! YOU'RE ALL SCIENTISTS!
AND NO TRAMPLING!
CLINT?
HEY, SONGBIRD. LISTEN, YOU KNOW WHAT THE EVACUATION PLAN IS AROUND HERE?
HEAD FOR THE MOUNTAIN--THAT'S WHERE AVENGER TWO IS.
SO I AM POINTING EVERYONE THE RIGHT WAY. COOL.
LET ME GUESS--AVENGER TWO'S A HI-TECH SUBMARINE OR SOMETHING?
OR SOMETHING.
CLINT--I KNOW THIS ISN'T A GOOD TIME, BUT THERE MIGHT NOT BE A BETTER ONE...
DO YOU WANT TO GO BACK TO S.H.I.E.L.D.?
MELISSA GOLD, A.K.A. SONGBIRD.
Secretly solid sound-ing for S.H.I.E.L.D.

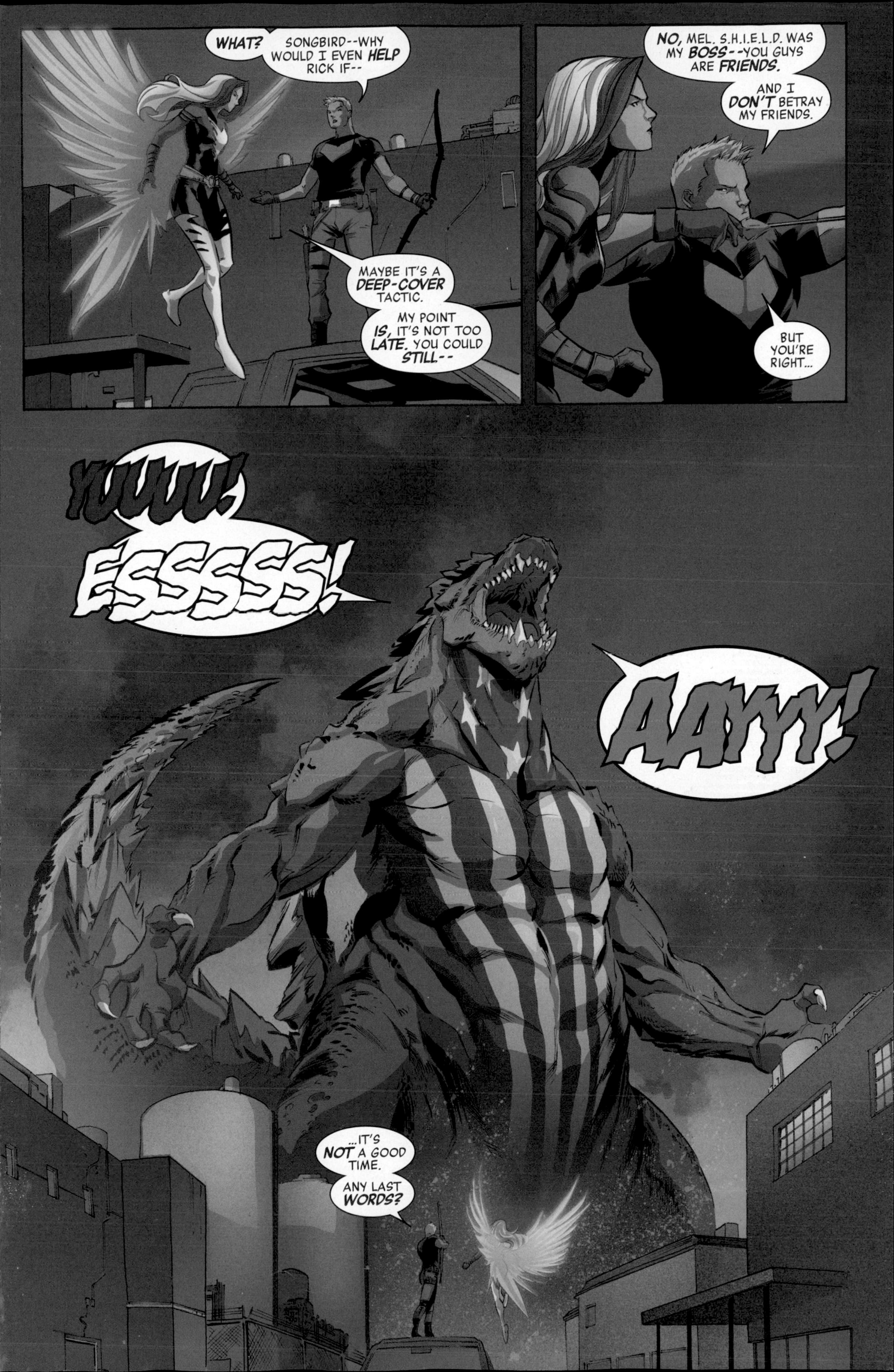
WHAT?
SONGBIRD--WHY WOULD I EVEN HELP RICK IF--
MAYBE IT'S A DEEP-COVER TACTIC.
MY POINT IS, IT'S NOT TOO LATE. YOU COULD STILL--
NO, MEL. S.H.I.E.L.D. WAS MY BOSS--YOU GUYS ARE FRIENDS.
AND I DON'T BETRAY MY FRIENDS.
BUT YOU'RE RIGHT...
YUUUU!
ESSSSS!
AAYYY!
...IT'S NOT A GOOD TIME.
ANY LAST WORDS?

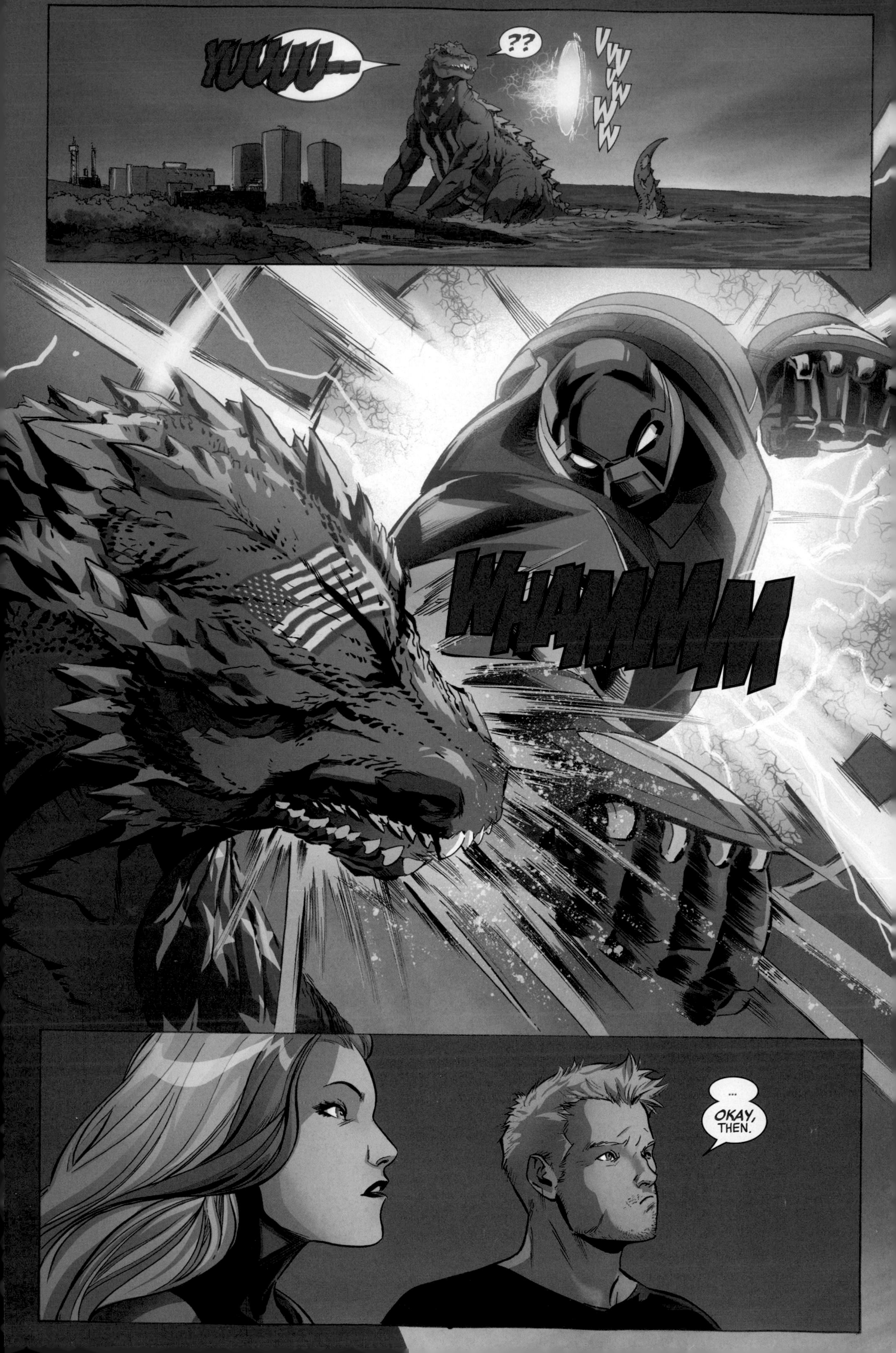
YUUUU--
??
VVVWWWW
WHAMMMM
...
OKAY, THEN.

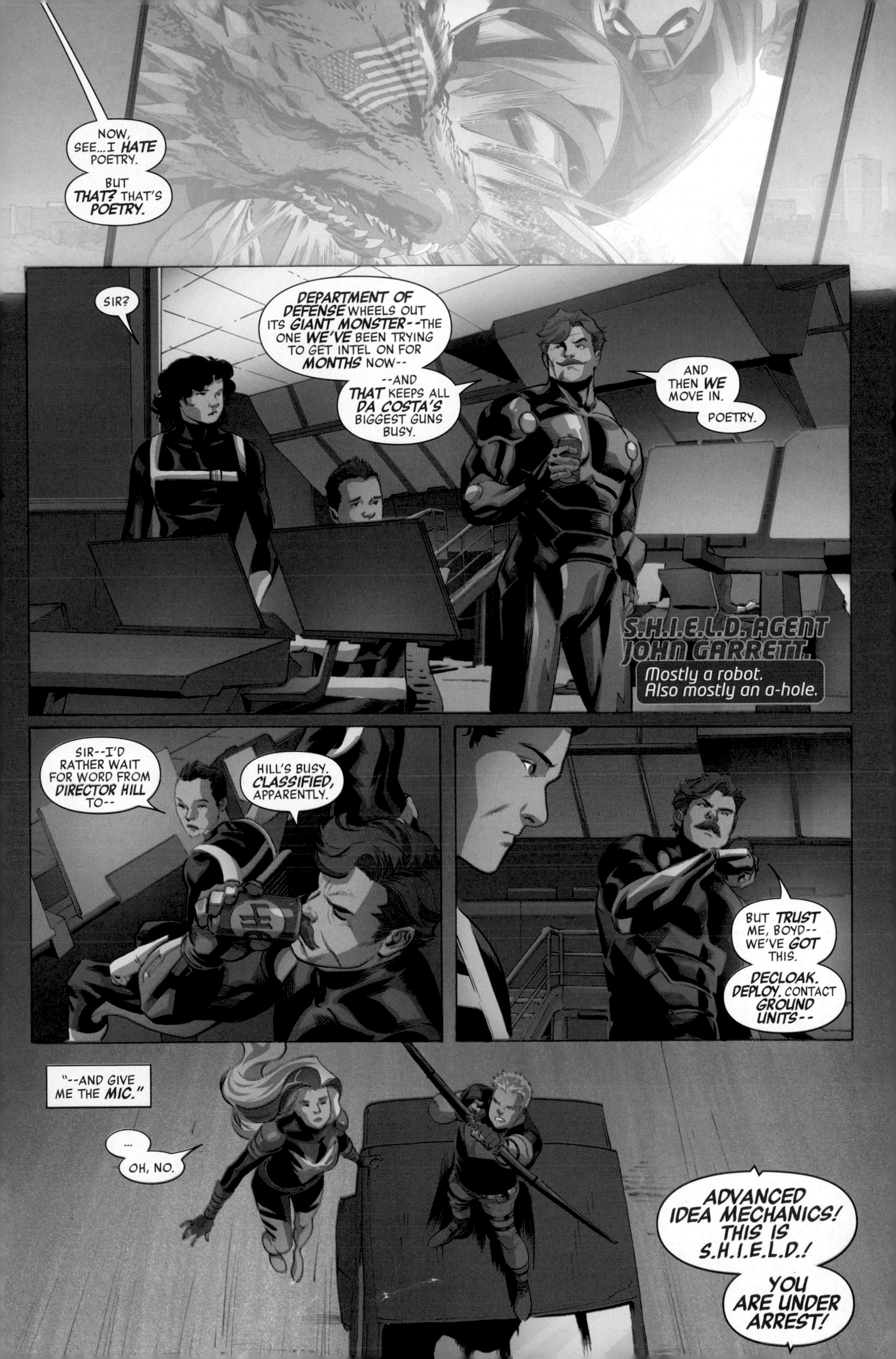
NOW, SEE...I HATE POETRY.
BUT THAT? THAT'S POETRY.
SIR?
DEPARTMENT OF DEFENSE WHEELS OUT ITS GIANT MONSTER--THE ONE WE'VE BEEN TRYING TO GET INTEL ON FOR MONTHS NOW--
--AND THAT KEEPS ALL DA COSTA'S BIGGEST GUNS BUSY.
AND THEN WE MOVE IN.
POETRY.
S.H.I.E.L.D. AGENT JOHN GARRETT.
Mostly a robot. Also mostly an a-hole.
SIR--I'D RATHER WAIT FOR WORD FROM DIRECTOR HILL TO--
HILL'S BUSY. CLASSIFIED, APPARENTLY.
BUT TRUST ME, BOYD-- WE'VE GOT THIS.
DECLOAK. DEPLOY. CONTACT GROUND UNITS--
"--AND GIVE ME THE MIC."
...
OH, NO.
ADVANCED IDEA MECHANICS! THIS IS S.H.I.E.L.D.!
YOU ARE UNDER ARREST!

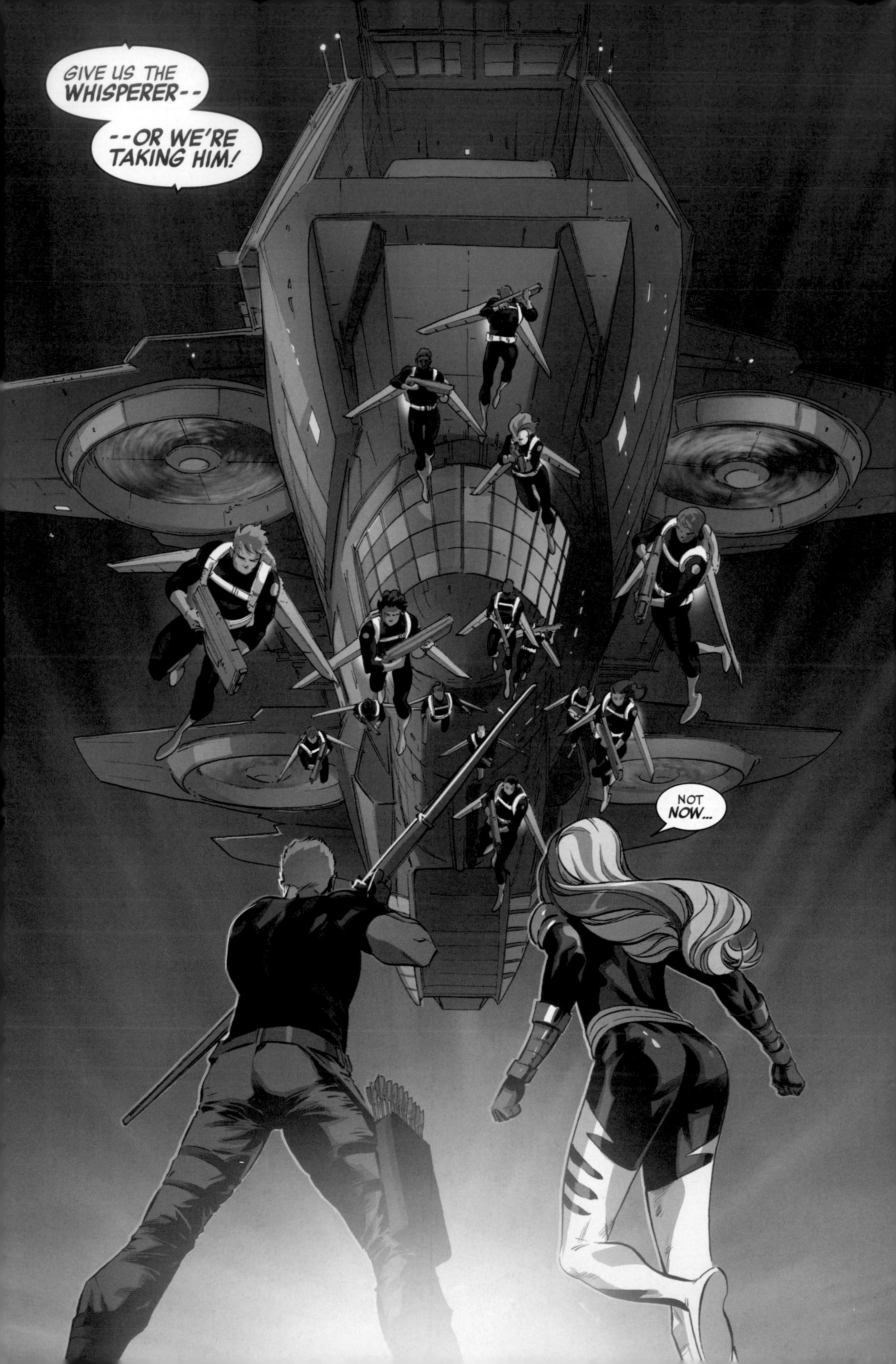
GIVE US THE WHISPERER--
--OR WE'RE TAKING HIM!
NOT NOW...

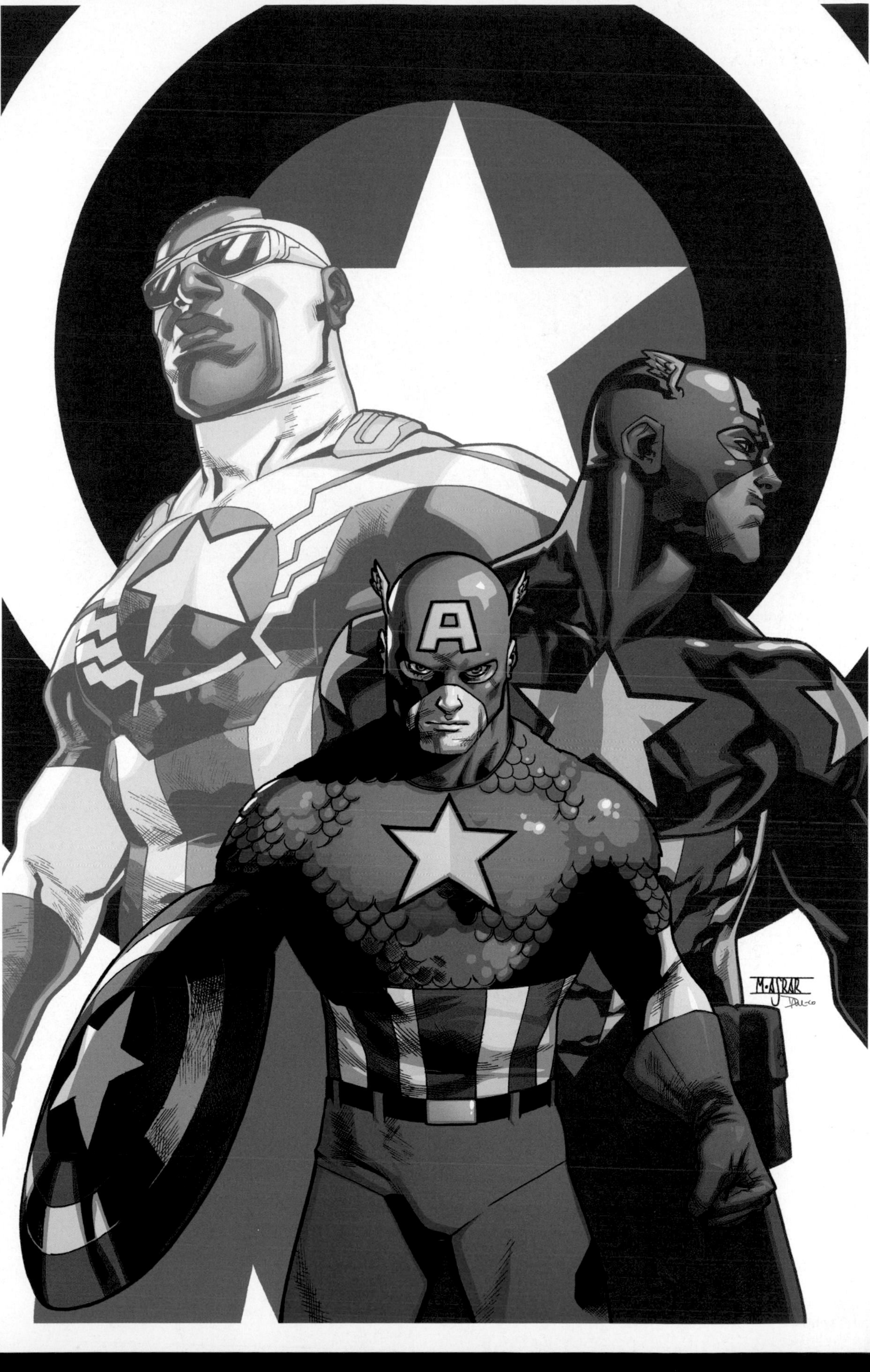

Captain America: Sam Wilson No. 7 variant by
MAHMUD ASRAR & DAVE McCAIG

Illuminati No. 6

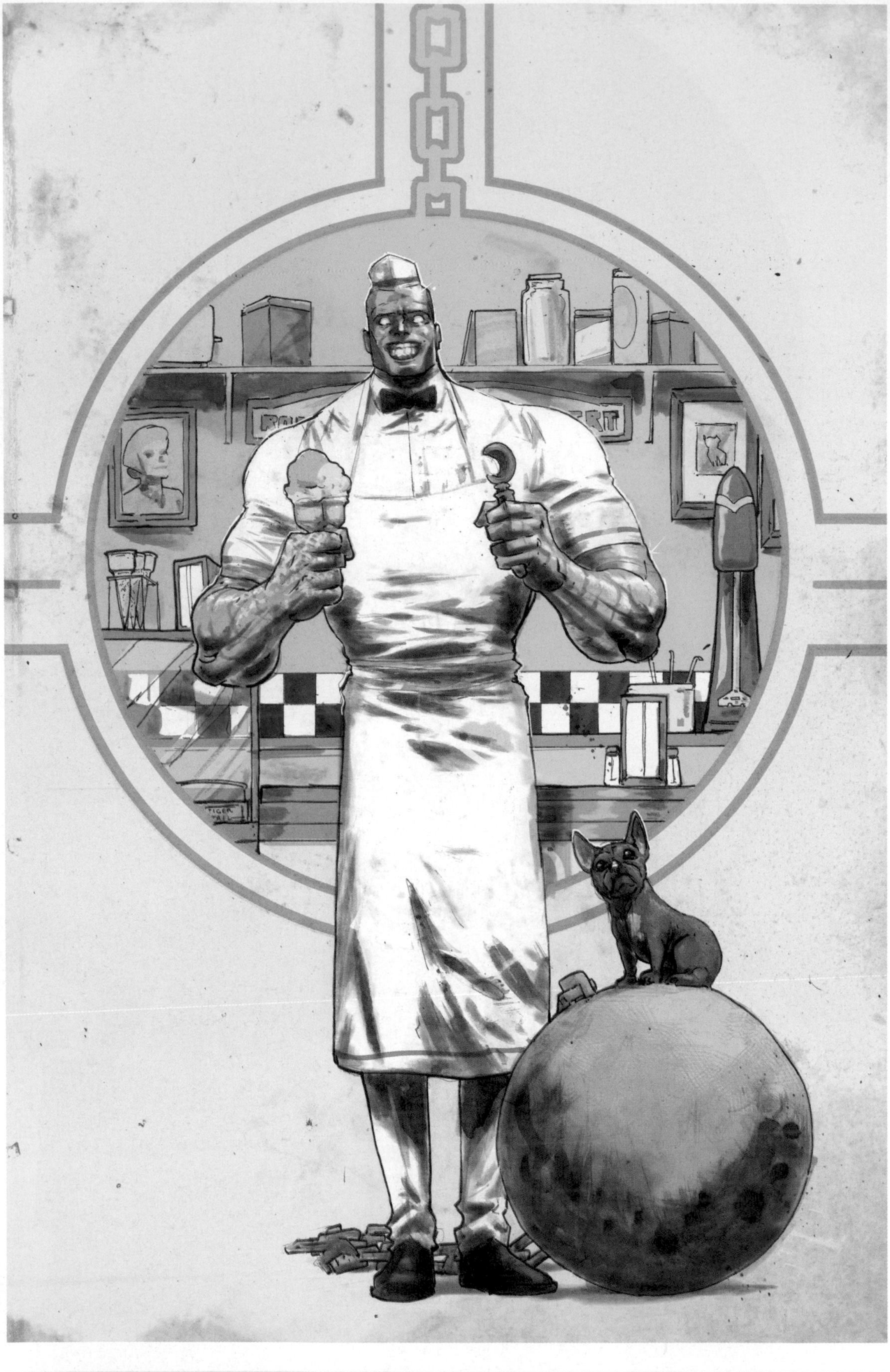

Mission Brief

Parker Robbins, a.k.a. the Hood, promised Titania he'd help her husband, the Absorbing Man, break out of prison. The only problem is that the Absorbing Man has been locked up in some fancy prison called Pleasant Hill...

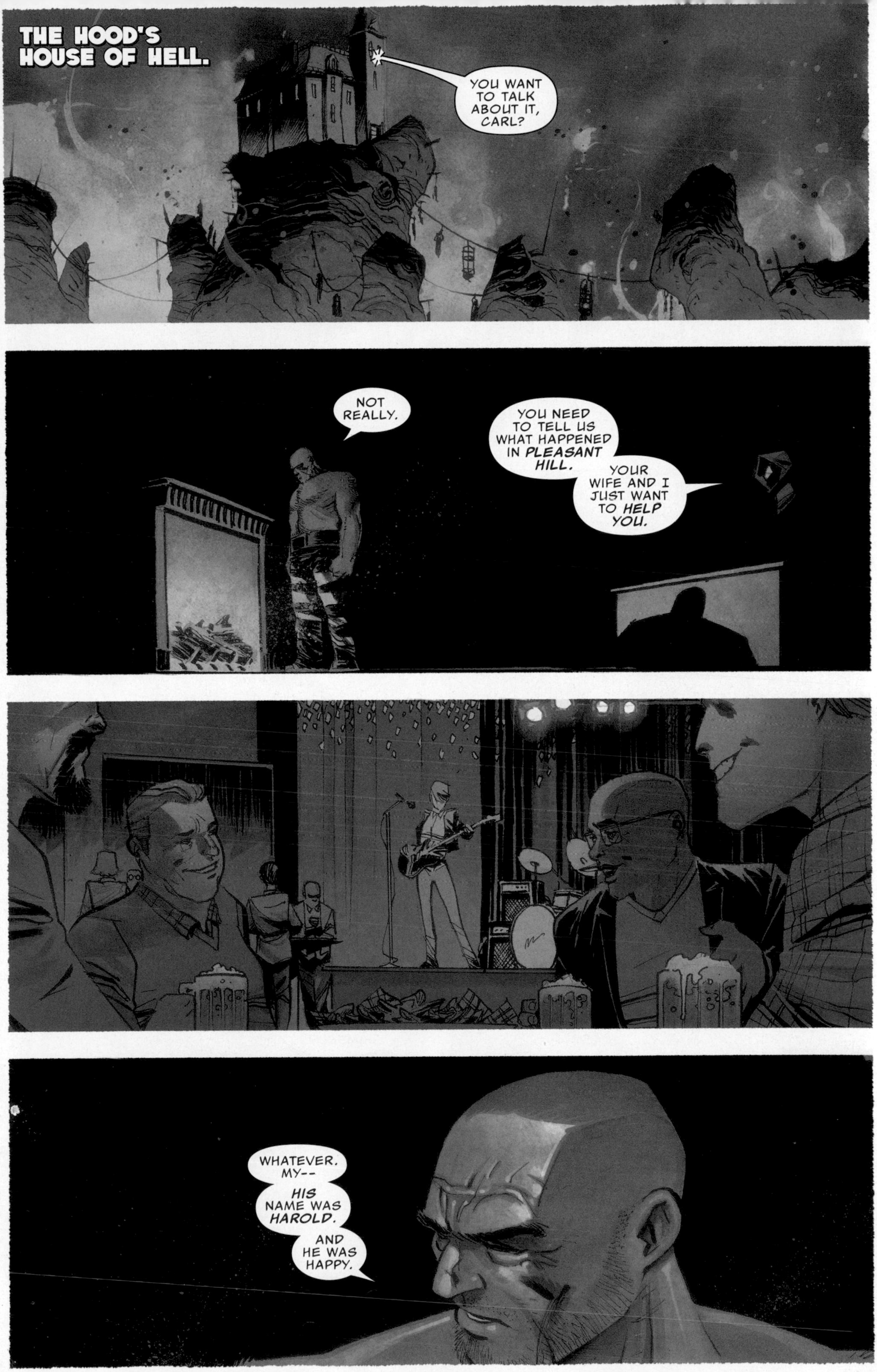
THE HOOD'S HOUSE OF HELL.
YOU WANT TO TALK ABOUT IT, CARL?
NOT REALLY.
YOU NEED TO TELL US WHAT HAPPENED IN PLEASANT HILL.
YOUR WIFE AND I JUST WANT TO HELP YOU.
WHATEVER. MY--
HIS NAME WAS HAROLD.
AND HE WAS HAPPY.

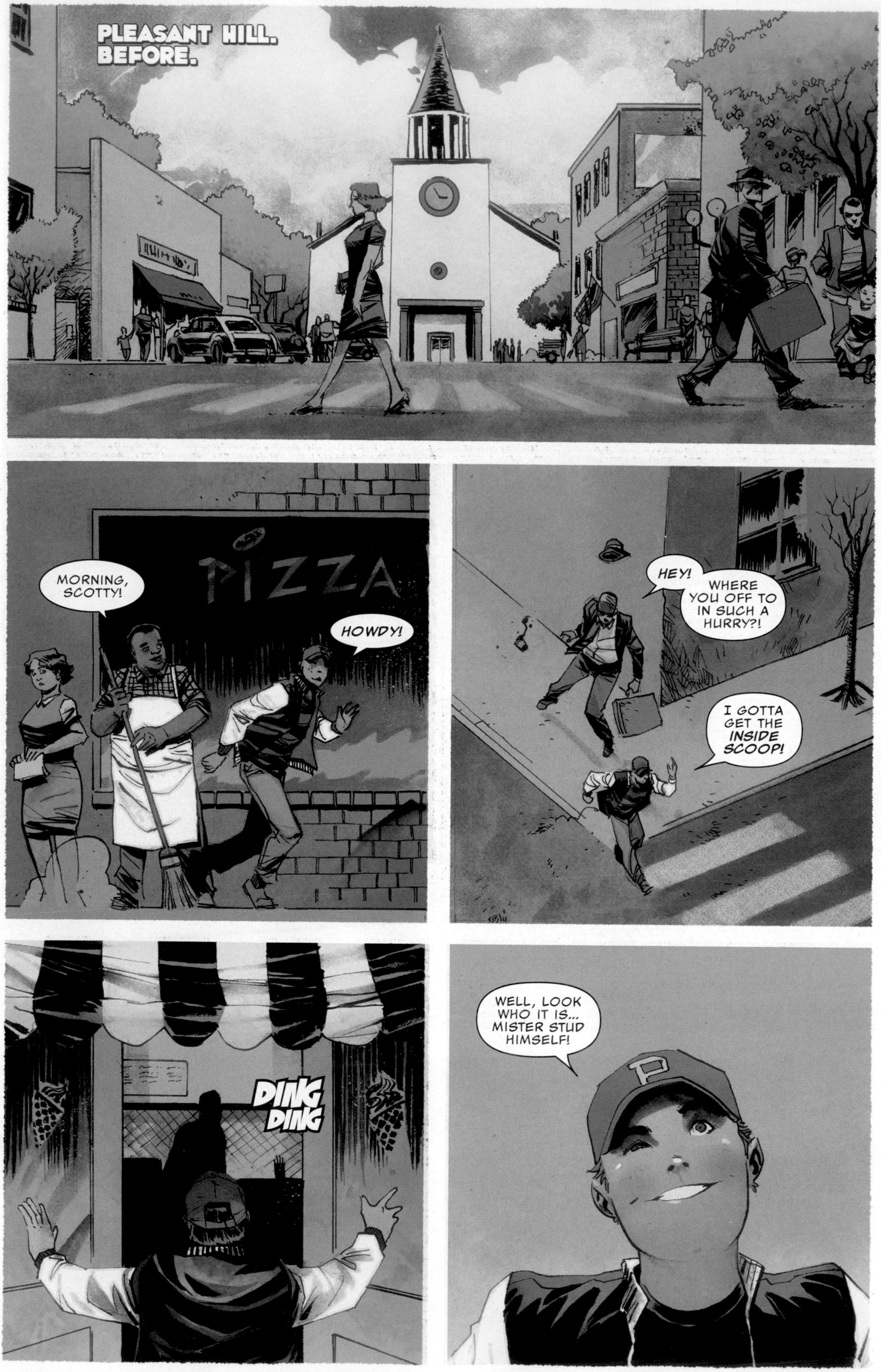
PLEASANT HILL. BEFORE.
MORNING, SCOTTY!
HOWDY!
HEY!
WHERE YOU OFF TO IN SUCH A HURRY?!
I GOTTA GET THE INSIDE SCOOP!
DING DING
WELL, LOOK WHO IT IS... MISTER STUD HIMSELF!

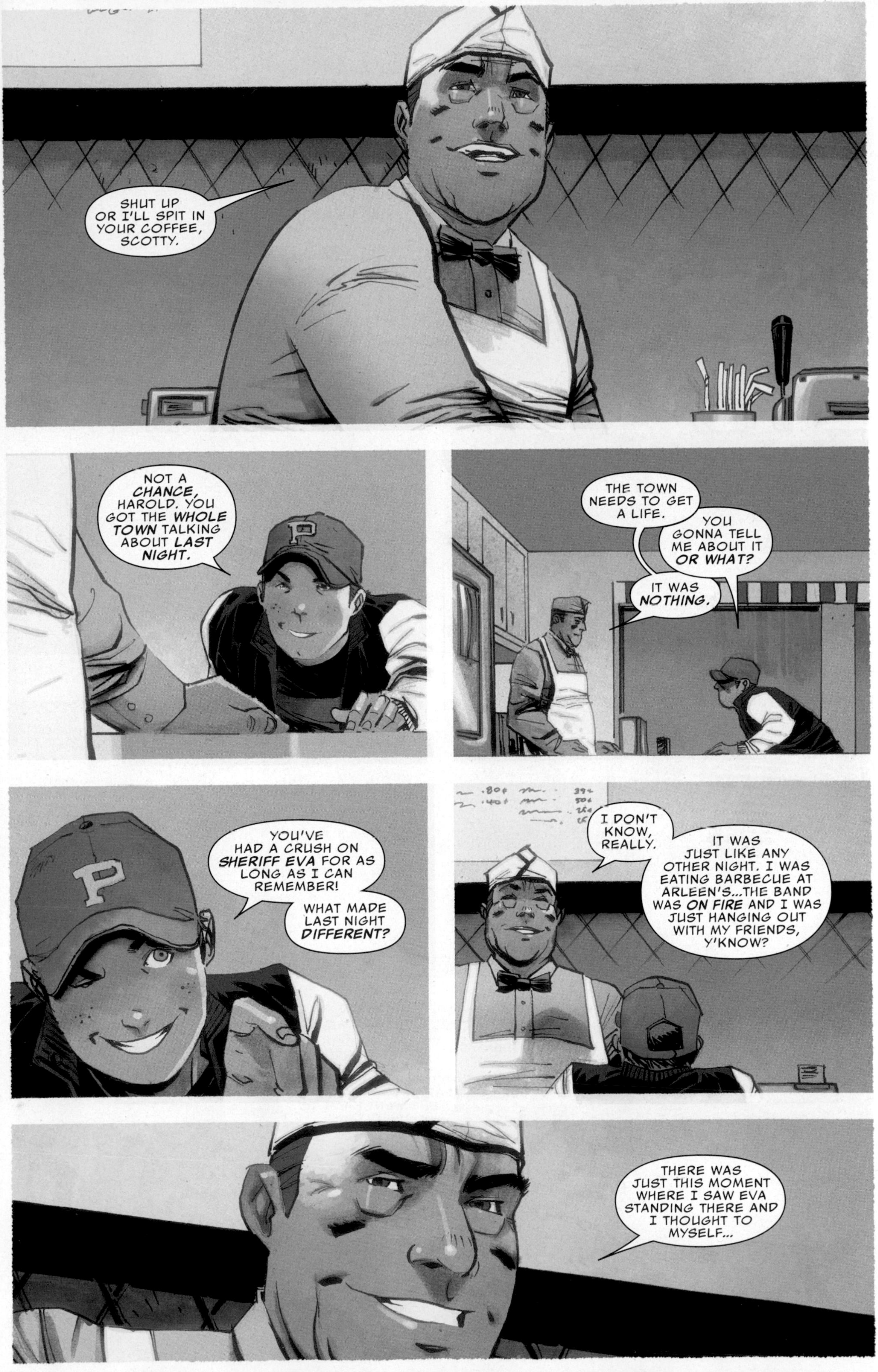
SHUT UP OR I'LL SPIT IN YOUR COFFEE, SCOTTY.
NOT A CHANCE, HAROLD. YOU GOT THE WHOLE TOWN TALKING ABOUT LAST NIGHT.
THE TOWN NEEDS TO GET A LIFE.
YOU GONNA TELL ME ABOUT IT OR WHAT?
IT WAS NOTHING.
YOU'VE HAD A CRUSH ON SHERIFF EVA FOR AS LONG AS I CAN REMEMBER!
WHAT MADE LAST NIGHT DIFFERENT?
I DON'T KNOW, REALLY.
IT WAS JUST LIKE ANY OTHER NIGHT. I WAS EATING BARBECUE AT ARLEEN'S...THE BAND WAS ON FIRE AND I WAS JUST HANGING OUT WITH MY FRIENDS, Y'KNOW?
THERE WAS JUST THIS MOMENT WHERE I SAW EVA STANDING THERE AND I THOUGHT TO MYSELF...

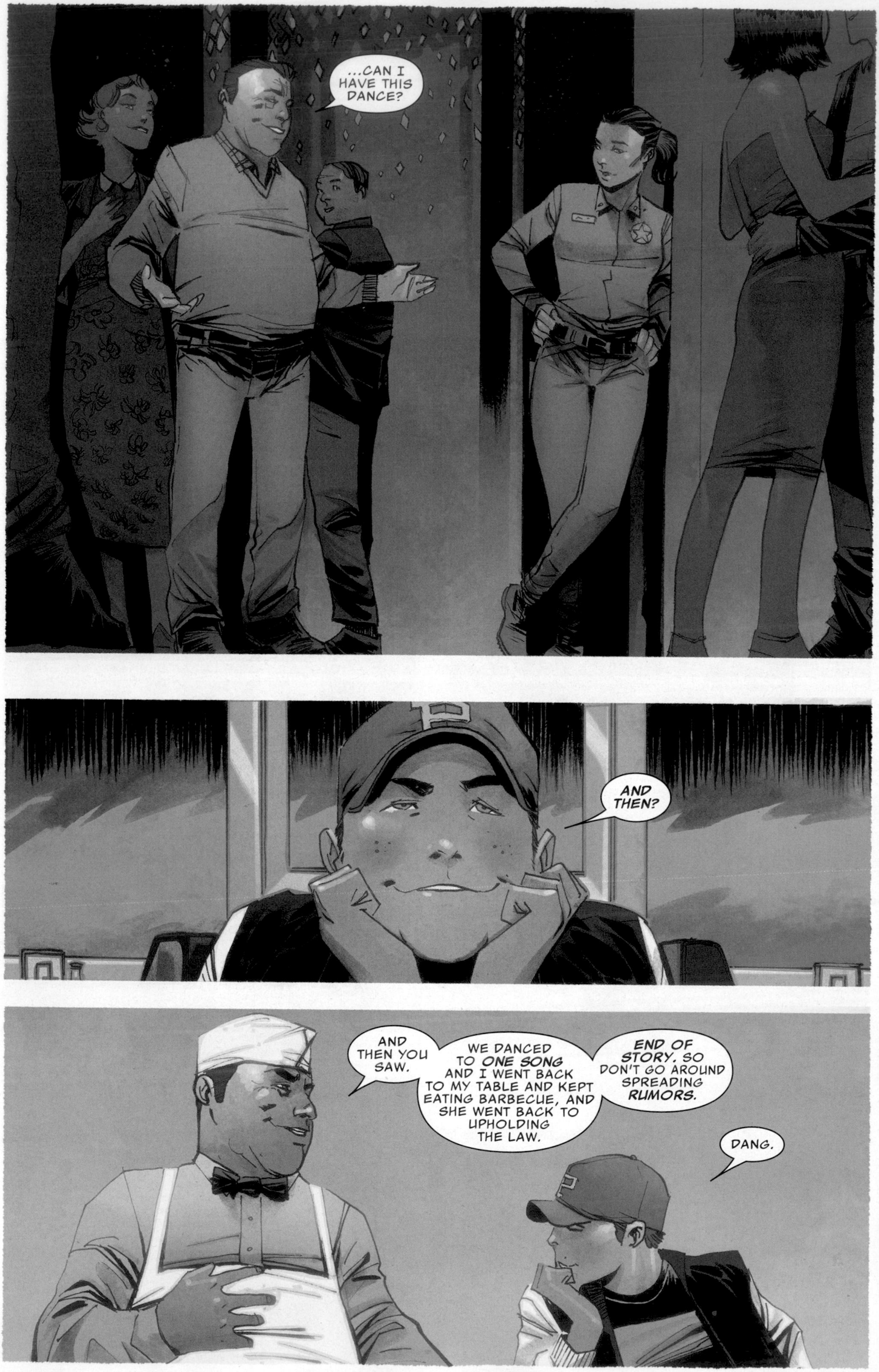
...CAN I HAVE THIS DANCE?
AND THEN?
AND THEN YOU SAW.
WE DANCED TO ONE SONG AND I WENT BACK TO MY TABLE AND KEPT EATING BARBECUE, AND SHE WENT BACK TO UPHOLDING THE LAW.
END OF STORY. SO DON'T GO AROUND SPREADING RUMORS.
DANG.

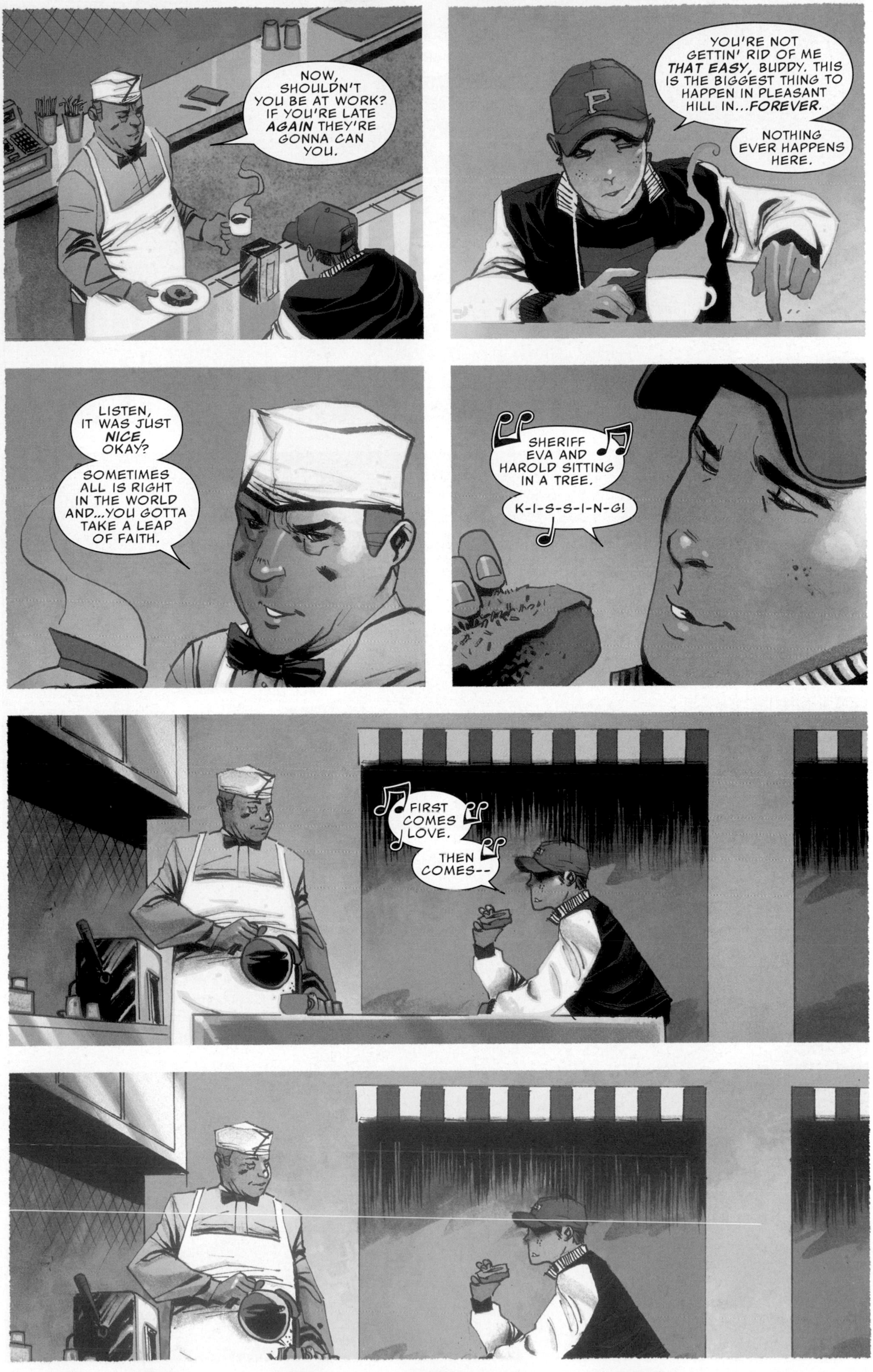
NOW, SHOULDN'T YOU BE AT WORK? IF YOU'RE LATE AGAIN THEY'RE GONNA CAN YOU.
YOU'RE NOT GETTIN' RID OF ME THAT EASY, BUDDY. THIS IS THE BIGGEST THING TO HAPPEN IN PLEASANT HILL IN...FOREVER.
NOTHING EVER HAPPENS HERE.
LISTEN, IT WAS JUST NICE, OKAY?
SOMETIMES ALL IS RIGHT IN THE WORLD AND...YOU GOTTA TAKE A LEAP OF FAITH.
SHERIFF EVA AND HAROLD SITTING IN A TREE.
K-I-S-S-I-N-G!
FIRST COMES LOVE.
THEN COMES--

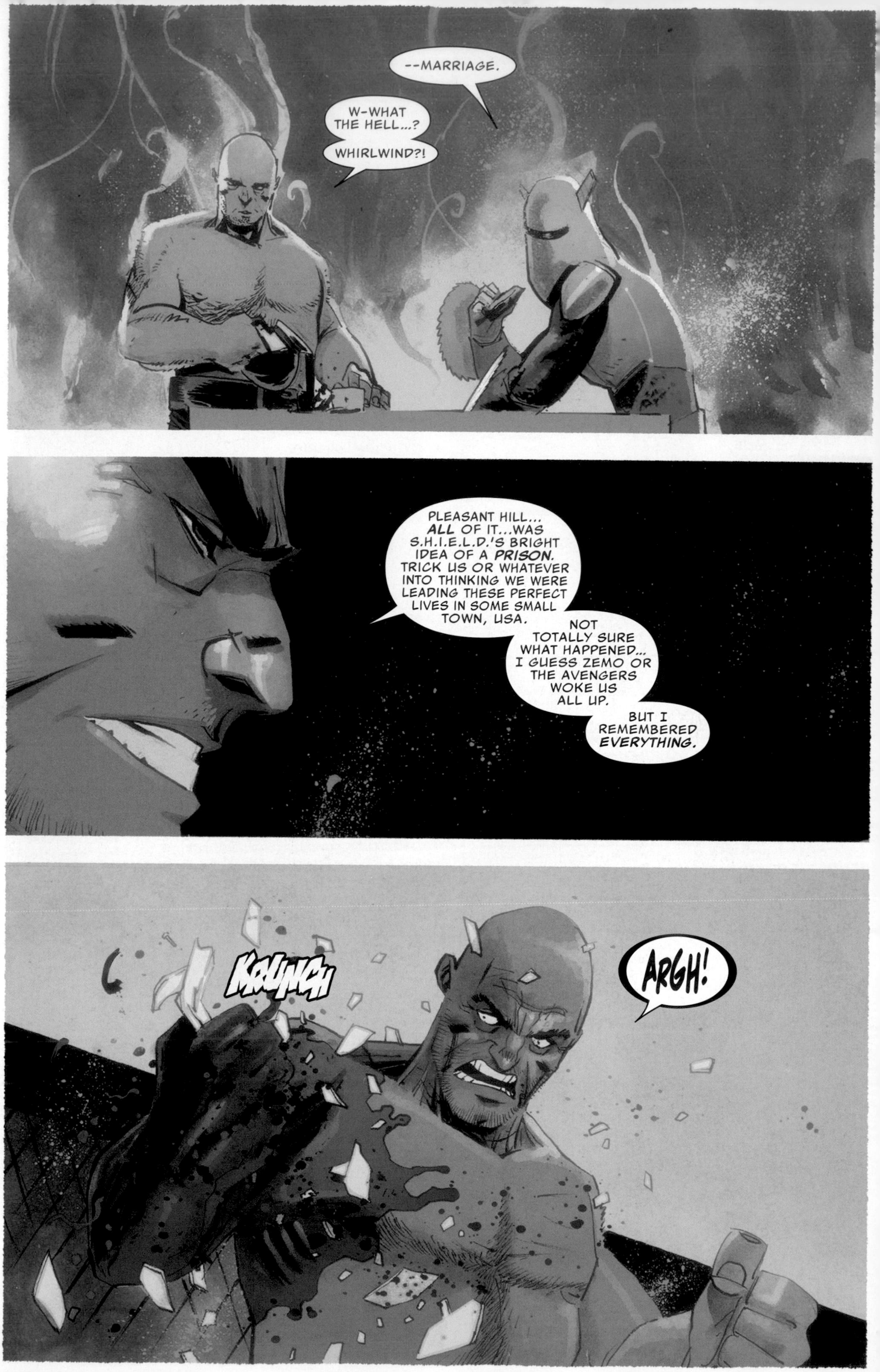
W-WHAT THE HELL...?
WHIRLWIND?!
--MARRIAGE.
PLEASANT HILL... ALL OF IT...WAS S.H.I.E.L.D.'S BRIGHT IDEA OF A PRISON. TRICK US OR WHATEVER INTO THINKING WE WERE LEADING THESE PERFECT LIVES IN SOME SMALL TOWN, USA.
NOT TOTALLY SURE WHAT HAPPENED... I GUESS ZEMO OR THE AVENGERS WOKE US ALL UP.
BUT I REMEMBERED EVERYTHING.
KRUNCH
ARGH!

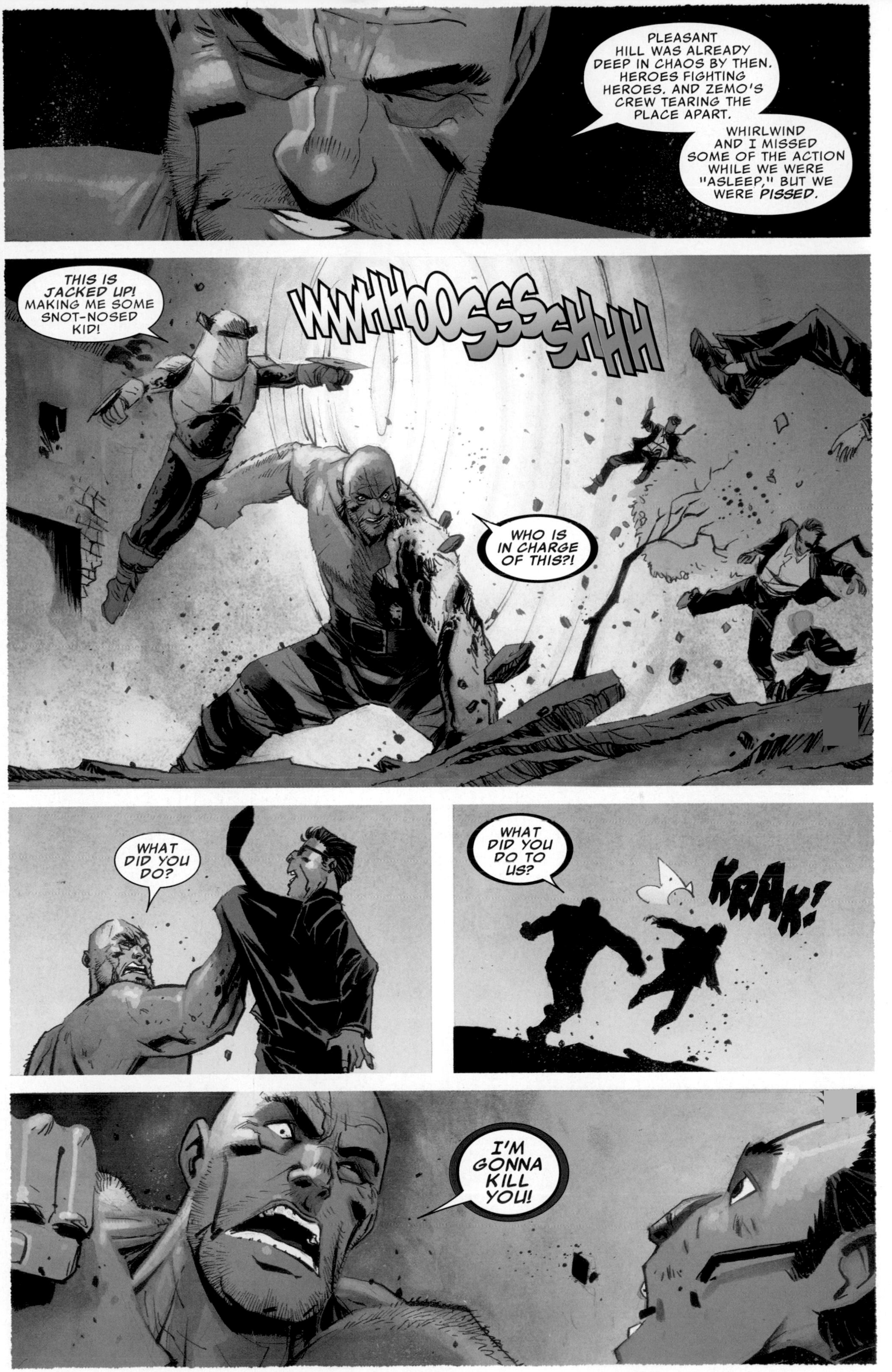
PLEASANT HILL WAS ALREADY DEEP IN CHAOS BY THEN. HEROES FIGHTING HEROES. AND ZEMO'S CREW TEARING THE PLACE APART.
WHIRLWIND AND I MISSED SOME OF THE ACTION WHILE WE WERE "ASLEEP," BUT WE WERE PISSED.
THIS IS JACKED UP! MAKING ME SOME SNOT-NOSED KID!
WWHHOOSSSSHHH
WHO IS IN CHARGE OF THIS?!
WHAT DID YOU DO?
WHAT DID YOU DO TO US?
KRAK!
I'M GONNA KILL YOU!

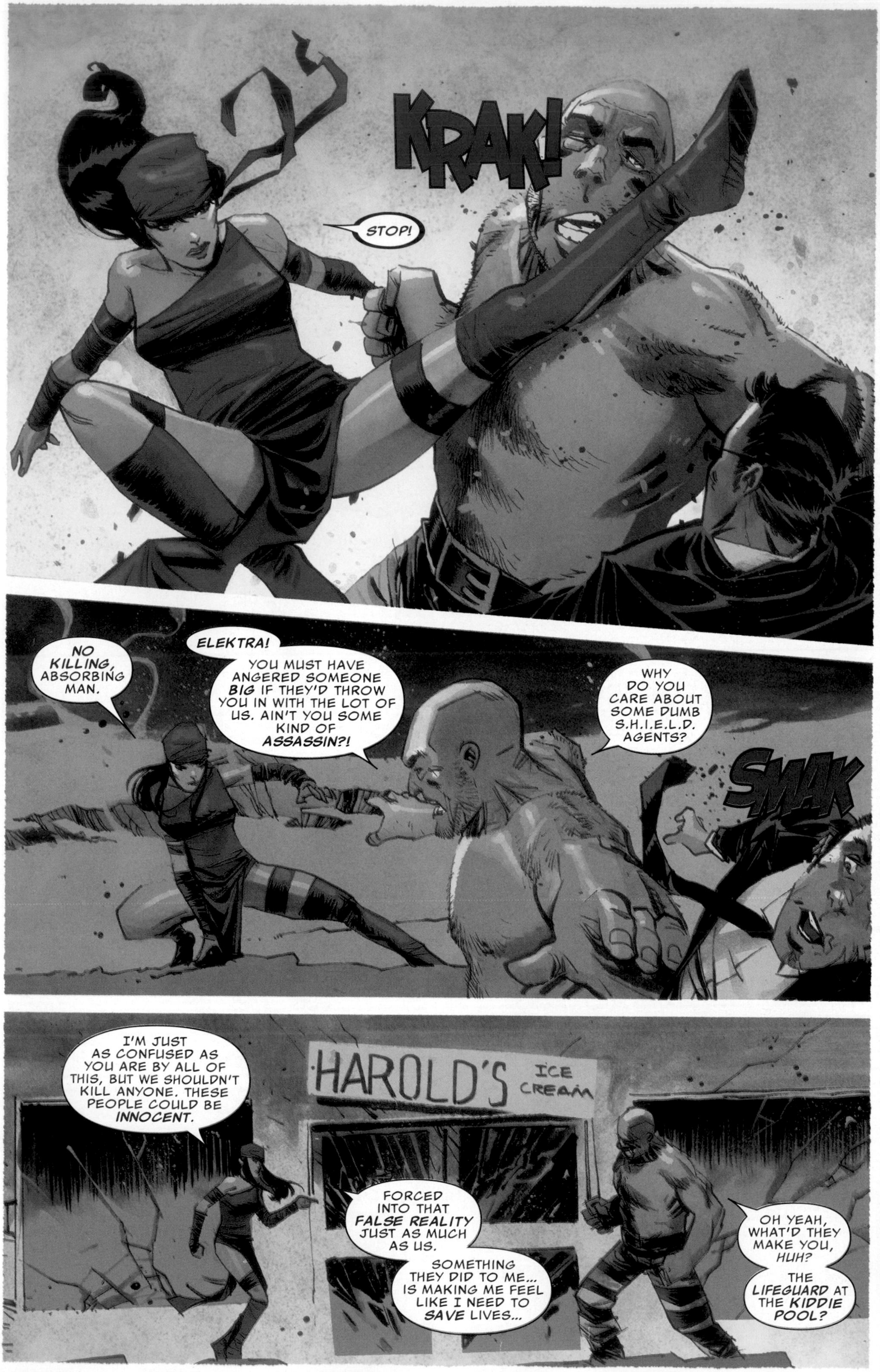
KRAK!
STOP!
NO KILLING, ABSORBING MAN.
ELEKTRA!
YOU MUST HAVE ANGERED SOMEONE BIG IF THEY'D THROW YOU IN WITH THE LOT OF US. AIN'T YOU SOME KIND OF ASSASSIN?!
WHY DO YOU CARE ABOUT SOME DUMB S.H.I.E.L.D. AGENTS?
SMAK
I'M JUST AS CONFUSED AS YOU ARE BY ALL OF THIS, BUT WE SHOULDN'T KILL ANYONE. THESE PEOPLE COULD BE INNOCENT.
HAROLD'S ICE CREAM
FORCED INTO THAT FALSE REALITY JUST AS MUCH AS US.
SOMETHING THEY DID TO ME... IS MAKING ME FEEL LIKE I NEED TO SAVE LIVES...
OH YEAH, WHAT'D THEY MAKE YOU, HUH?
THE LIFEGUARD AT THE KIDDIE POOL?

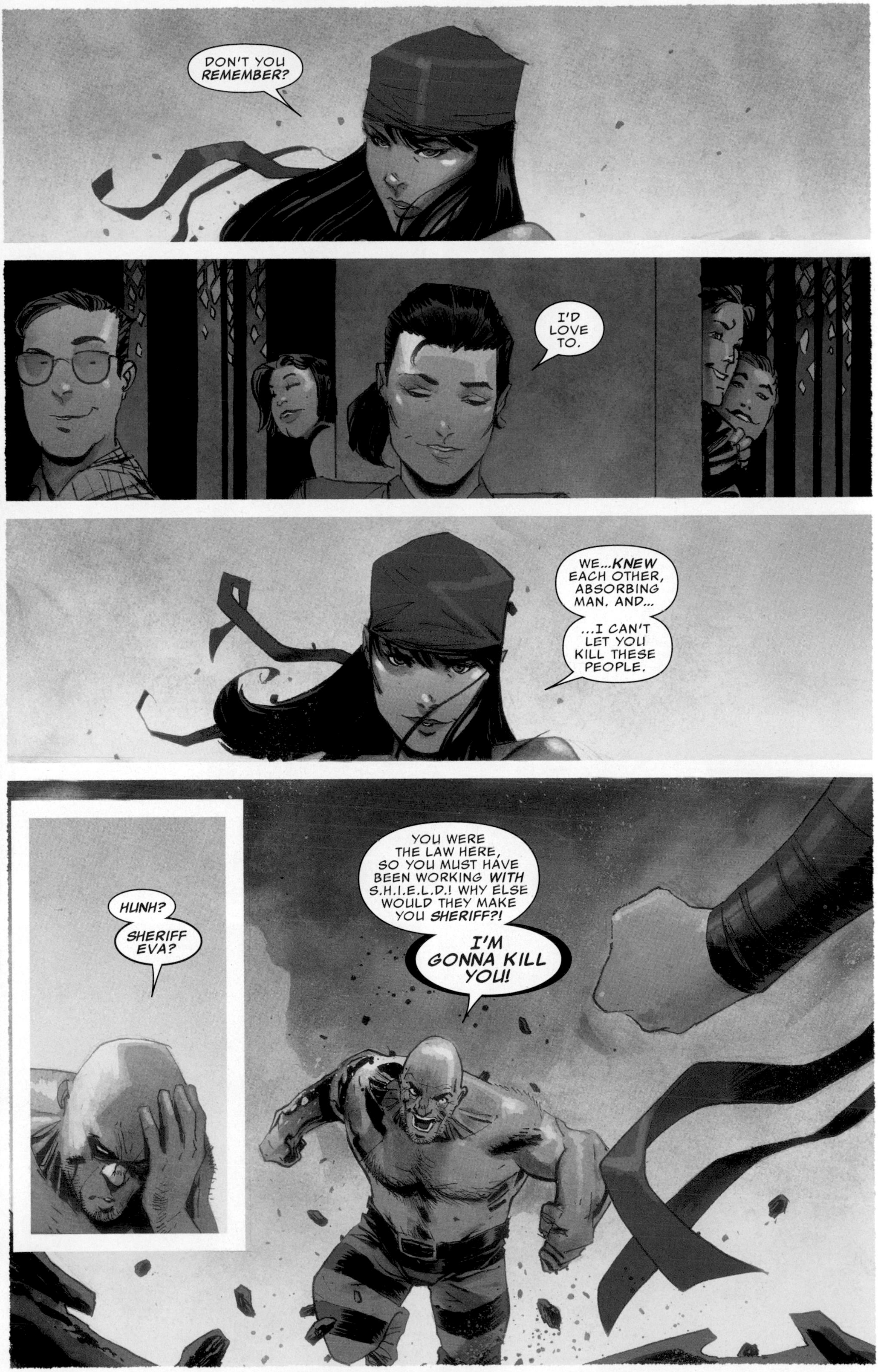
DON'T YOU REMEMBER?
I'D LOVE TO.
WE...KNEW EACH OTHER, ABSORBING MAN. AND...
...I CAN'T LET YOU KILL THESE PEOPLE.
HUNH?
SHERIFF EVA?
YOU WERE THE LAW HERE, SO YOU MUST HAVE BEEN WORKING WITH S.H.I.E.L.D.! WHY ELSE WOULD THEY MAKE YOU SHERIFF?!
I'M GONNA KILL YOU!

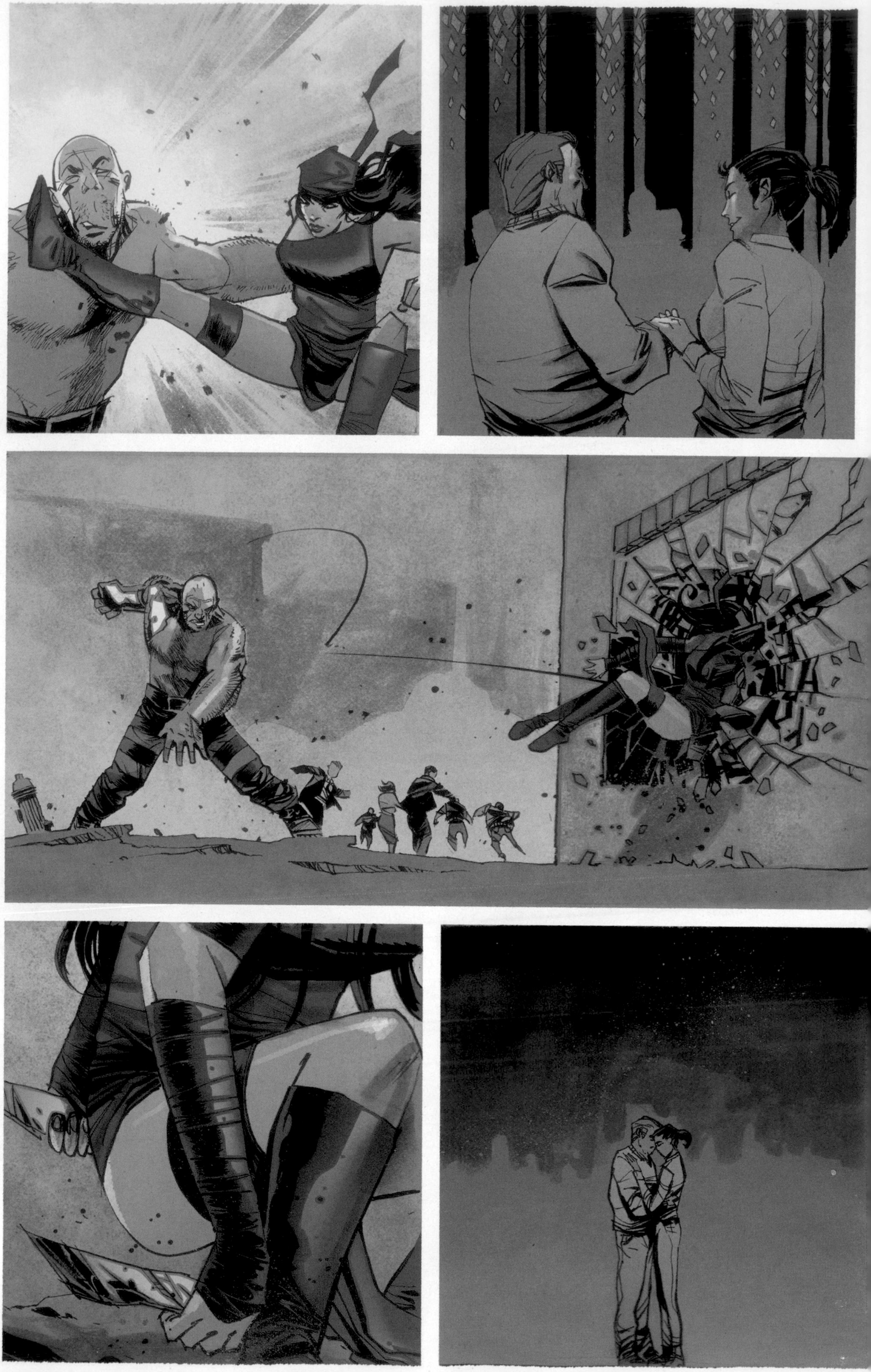

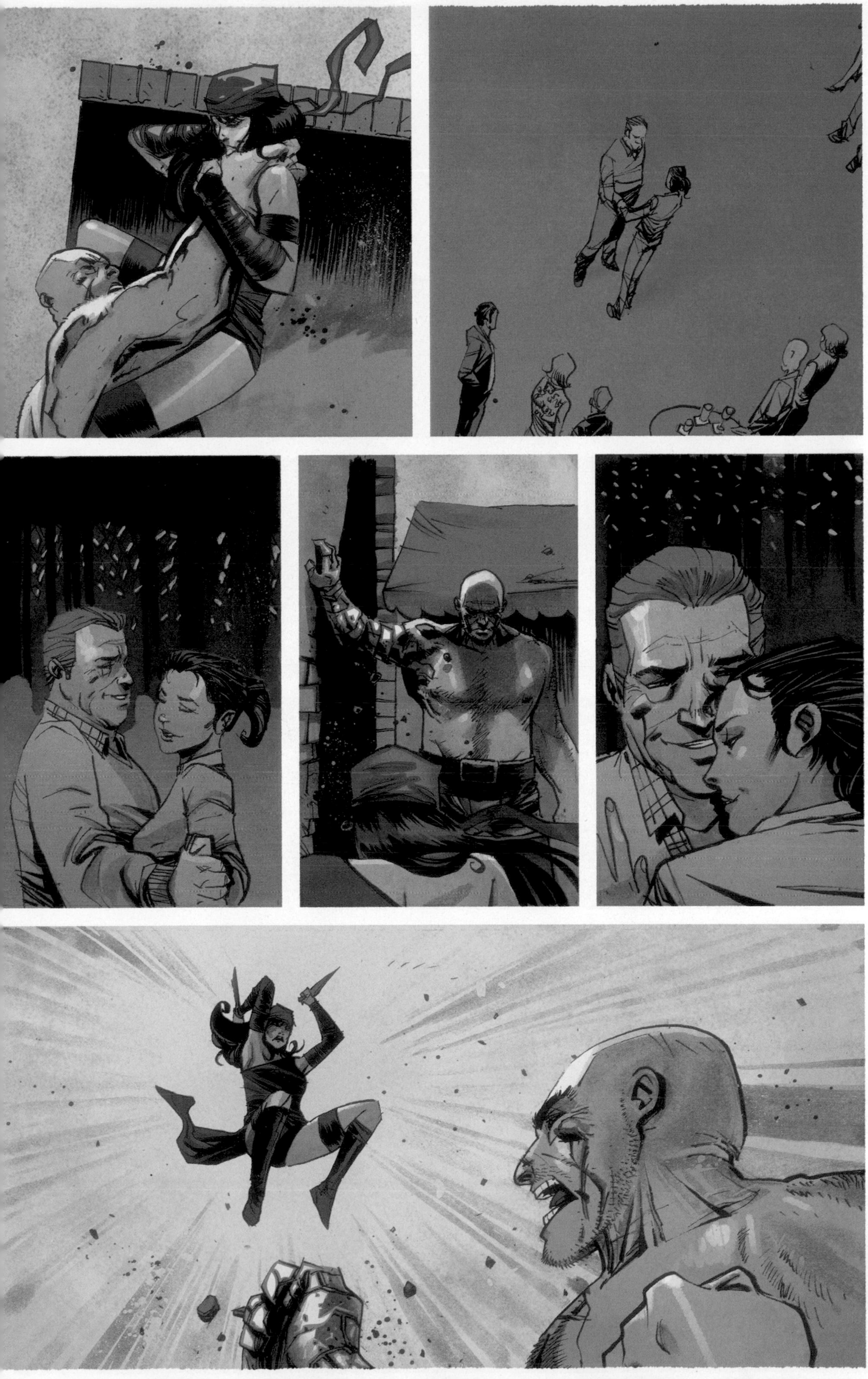

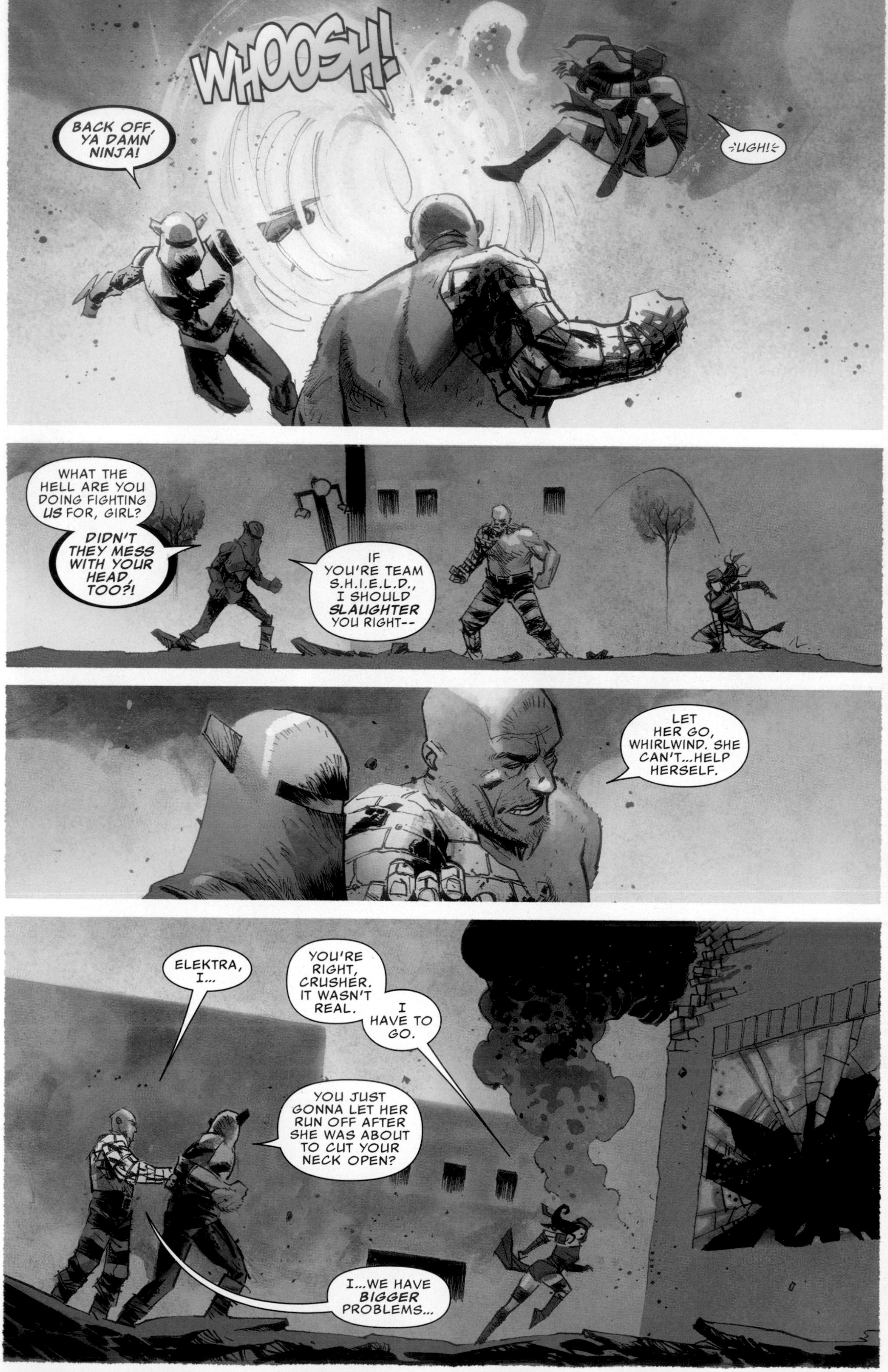
WHOOSH!
BACK OFF, YA DAMN' NINJA!
UGH!
WHAT THE HELL ARE YOU DOING FIGHTING US FOR, GIRL?
DIDN'T THEY MESS WITH YOUR HEAD, TOO?!
IF YOU'RE TEAM S.H.I.E.L.D., I SHOULD SLAUGHTER YOU RIGHT--
LET HER GO, WHIRLWIND. SHE CAN'T...HELP HERSELF.
ELEKTRA, I...
YOU'RE RIGHT, CRUSHER. IT WASN'T REAL.
I HAVE TO GO.
YOU JUST GONNA LET HER RUN OFF AFTER SHE WAS ABOUT TO CUT YOUR NECK OPEN?
I...WE HAVE BIGGER PROBLEMS...

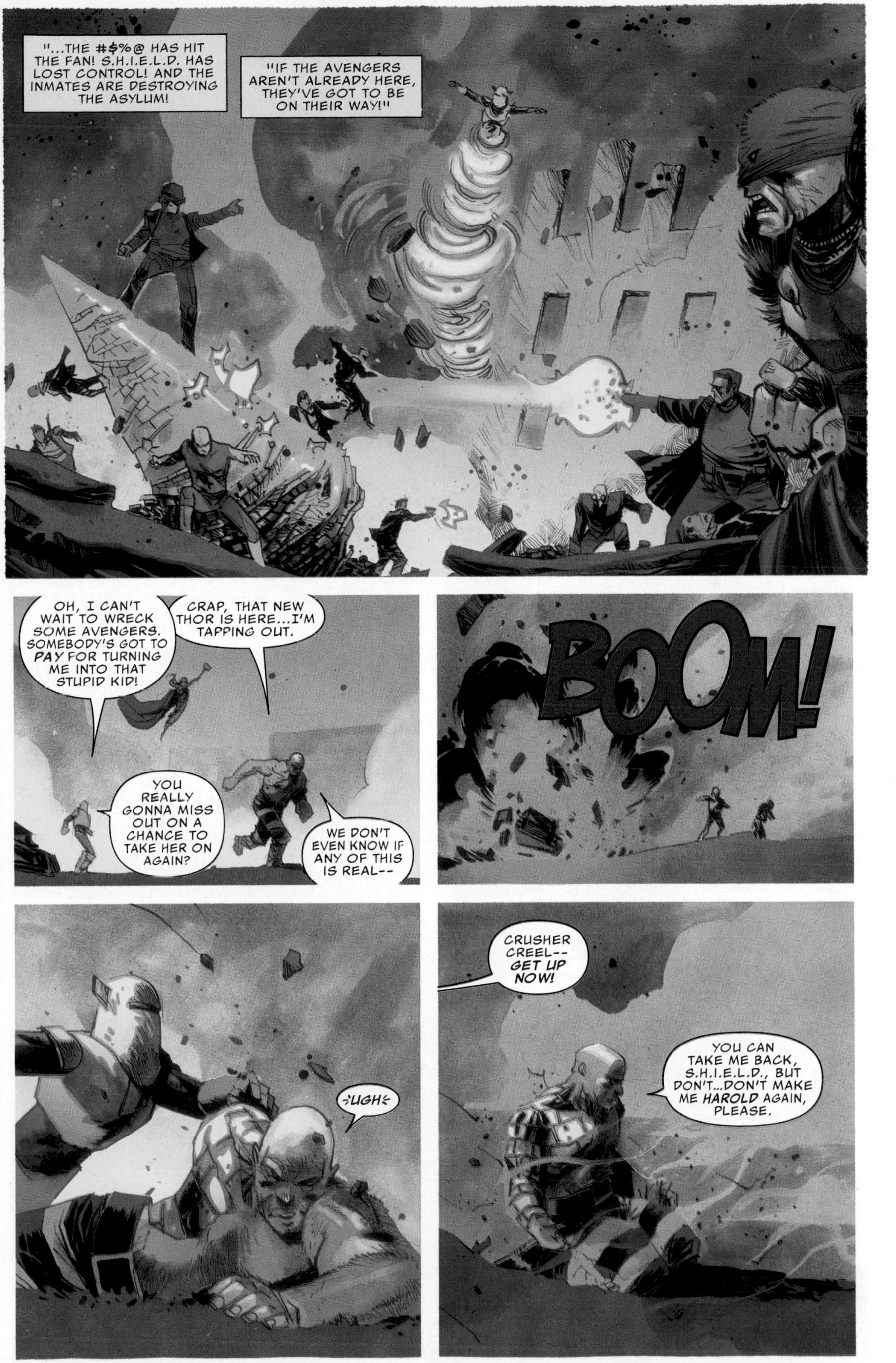
"...THE #$%@ HAS HIT THE FAN! S.H.I.E.L.D. HAS LOST CONTROL! AND THE INMATES ARE DESTROYING THE ASYLUM!
"IF THE AVENGERS AREN'T ALREADY HERE, THEY'VE GOT TO BE ON THEIR WAY!"
OH, I CAN'T WAIT TO WRECK SOME AVENGERS. SOMEBODY'S GOT TO PAY FOR TURNING ME INTO THAT STUPID KID!
CRAP, THAT NEW THOR IS HERE...I'M TAPPING OUT.
YOU REALLY GONNA MISS OUT ON A CHANCE TO TAKE HER ON AGAIN?
WE DON'T EVEN KNOW IF ANY OF THIS IS REAL--
BOOM!
UGH
CRUSHER CREEL-- GET UP NOW!
YOU CAN TAKE ME BACK, S.H.I.E.L.D., BUT DON'T...DON'T MAKE ME HAROLD AGAIN, PLEASE.

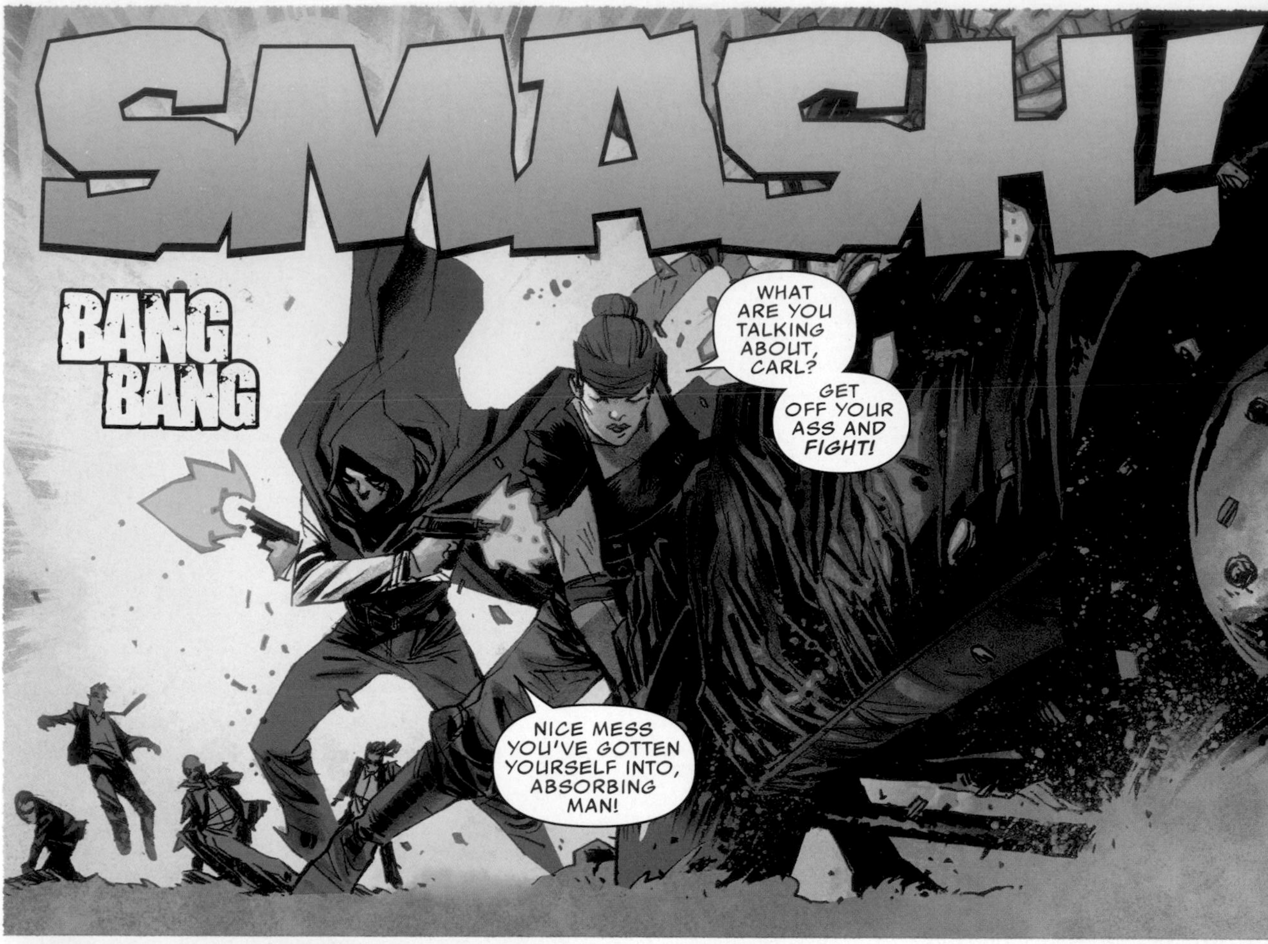
SMASH!
BANG BANG
WHAT ARE YOU TALKING ABOUT, CARL?
GET OFF YOUR ASS AND FIGHT!
NICE MESS YOU'VE GOTTEN YOURSELF INTO, ABSORBING MAN!

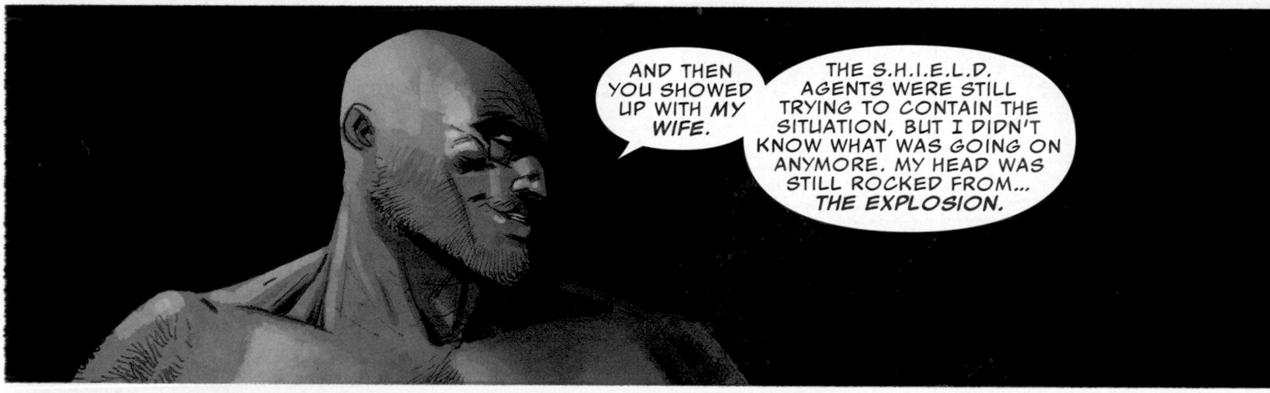
AND THEN YOU SHOWED UP WITH MY WIFE.
THE S.H.I.E.L.D. AGENTS WERE STILL TRYING TO CONTAIN THE SITUATION, BUT I DIDN'T KNOW WHAT WAS GOING ON ANYMORE. MY HEAD WAS STILL ROCKED FROM... THE EXPLOSION.

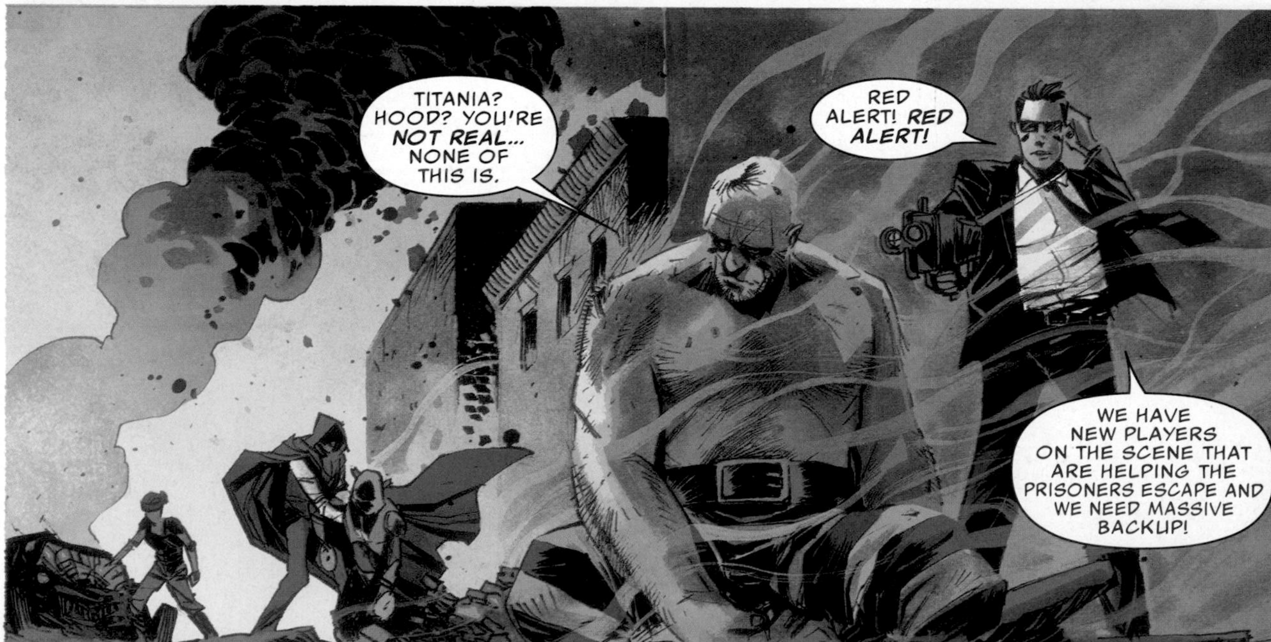
TITANIA? HOOD? YOU'RE NOT REAL... NONE OF THIS IS.
RED ALERT! RED ALERT!
WE HAVE NEW PLAYERS ON THE SCENE THAT ARE HELPING THE PRISONERS ESCAPE AND WE NEED MASSIVE BACKUP!

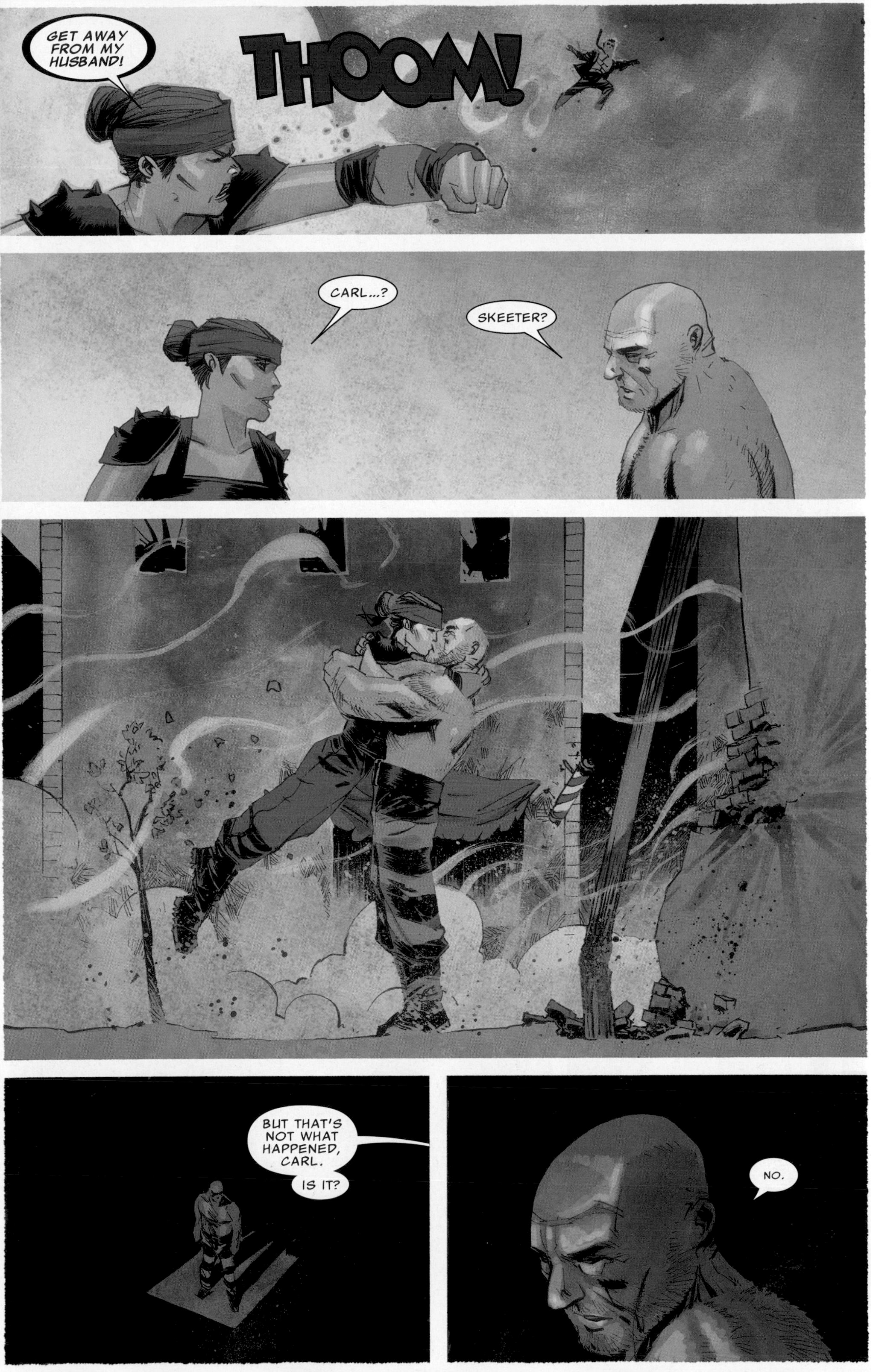
GET AWAY FROM MY HUSBAND!
THOOM!
CARL...?
SKEETER?
BUT THAT'S NOT WHAT HAPPENED, CARL.
IS IT?
NO.

CARL...?

SKEETER...? I CAN'T...I JUST CAN'T.

WAIT... WHAT?

GET ME THE HELL OUTTA HERE.

DONE.

DOORS OF DORMAMMU.

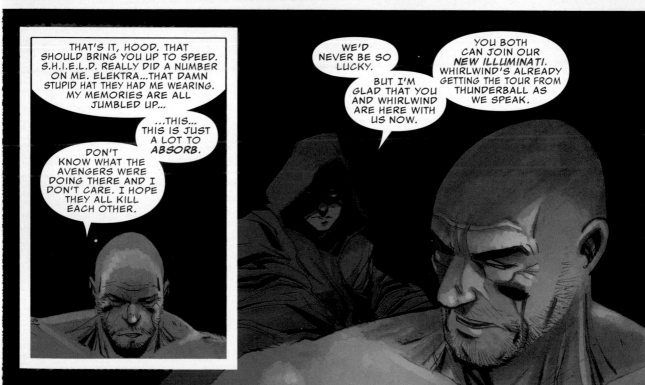

THAT'S IT, HOOD. THAT SHOULD BRING YOU UP TO SPEED. S.H.I.E.L.D. REALLY DID A NUMBER ON ME. ELEKTRA...THAT DAMN STUPID HAT THEY HAD ME WEARING. MY MEMORIES ARE ALL JUMBLED UP...

...THIS... THIS IS JUST A LOT TO ABSORB.

DON'T KNOW WHAT THE AVENGERS WERE DOING THERE AND I DON'T CARE. I HOPE THEY ALL KILL EACH OTHER.

WE'D NEVER BE SO LUCKY.

BUT I'M GLAD THAT YOU AND WHIRLWIND ARE HERE WITH US NOW.

YOU BOTH CAN JOIN OUR NEW ILLUMINATI. WHIRLWIND'S ALREADY GETTING THE TOUR FROM THUNDERBALL AS WE SPEAK.

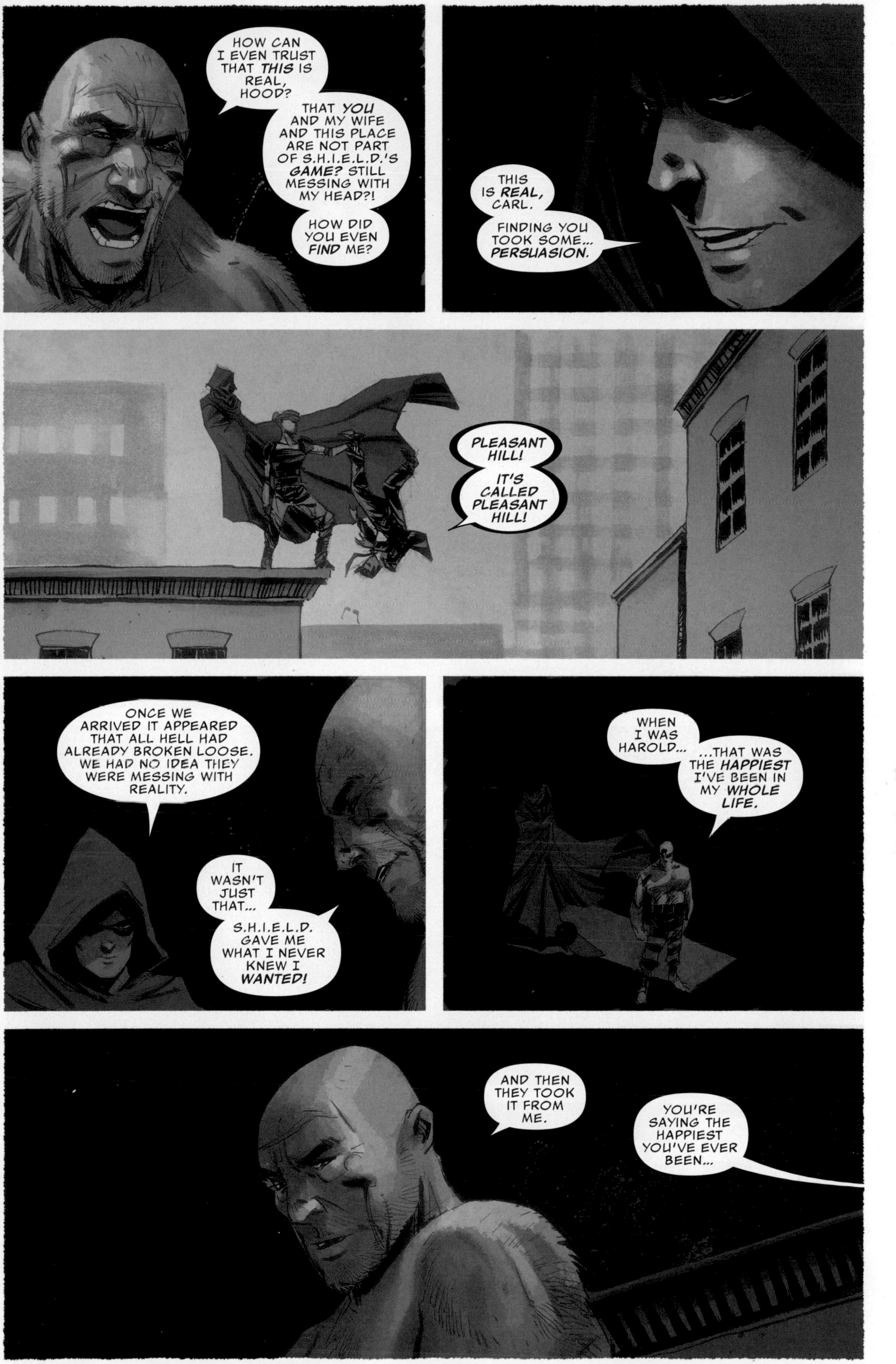
HOW CAN I EVEN TRUST THAT THIS IS REAL, HOOD?
THAT YOU AND MY WIFE AND THIS PLACE ARE NOT PART OF S.H.I.E.L.D.'S GAME? STILL MESSING WITH MY HEAD?!
HOW DID YOU EVEN FIND ME?
THIS IS REAL, CARL.
FINDING YOU TOOK SOME... PERSUASION.
PLEASANT HILL!
IT'S CALLED PLEASANT HILL!
ONCE WE ARRIVED IT APPEARED THAT ALL HELL HAD ALREADY BROKEN LOOSE. WE HAD NO IDEA THEY WERE MESSING WITH REALITY.
IT WASN'T JUST THAT...
S.H.I.E.L.D. GAVE ME WHAT I NEVER KNEW I WANTED!
WHEN I WAS HAROLD...
...THAT WAS THE HAPPIEST I'VE BEEN IN MY WHOLE LIFE.
AND THEN THEY TOOK IT FROM ME.
YOU'RE SAYING THE HAPPIEST YOU'VE EVER BEEN...

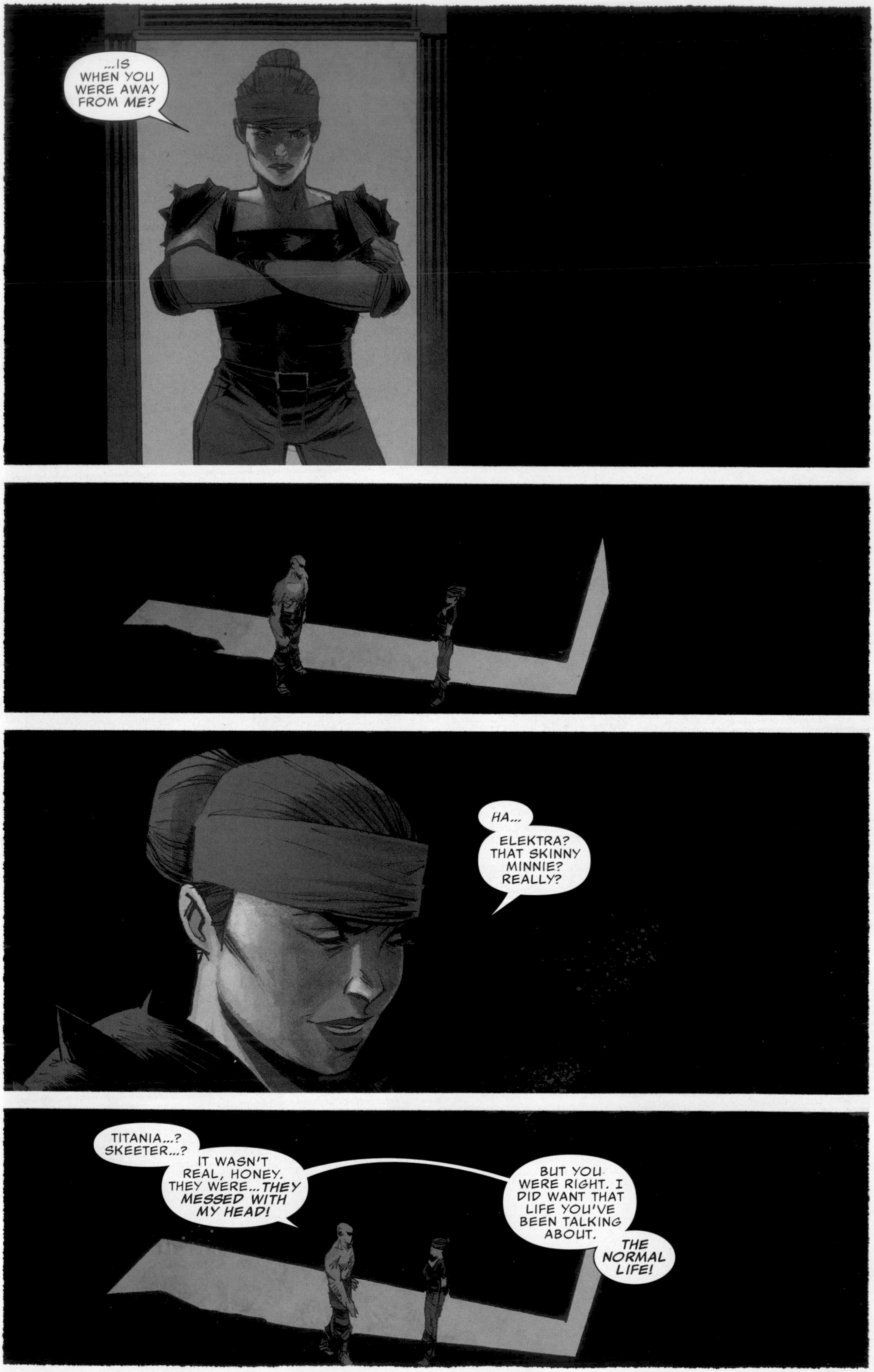

...IS WHEN YOU WERE AWAY FROM ME?
HA...
ELEKTRA? THAT SKINNY MINNIE? REALLY?
TITANIA...? SKEETER...?
IT WASN'T REAL, HONEY. THEY WERE... THEY MESSED WITH MY HEAD!
BUT YOU WERE RIGHT. I DID WANT THAT LIFE YOU'VE BEEN TALKING ABOUT.
THE NORMAL LIFE!

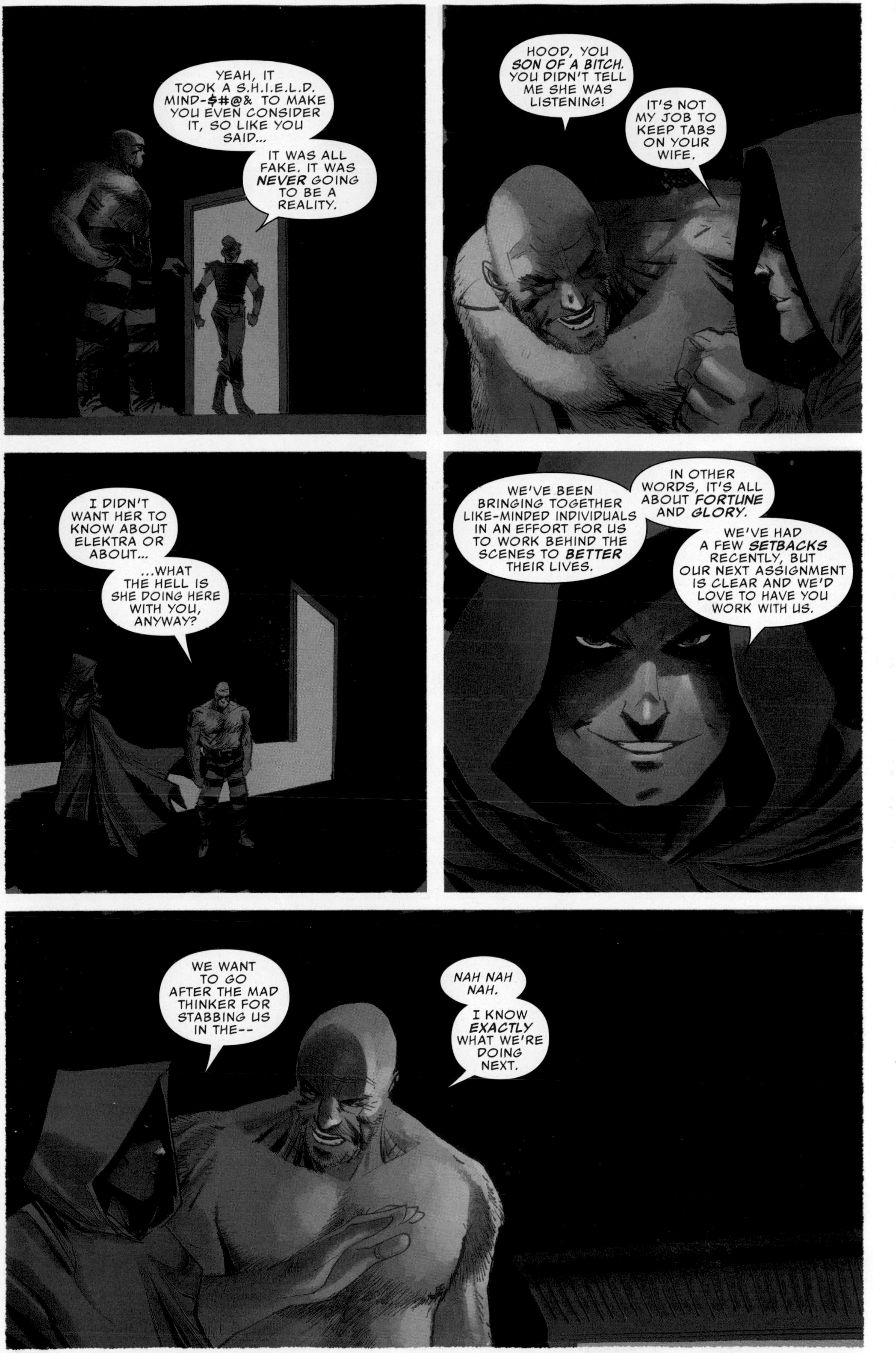

YEAH, IT TOOK A S.H.I.E.L.D. MIND-$#@& TO MAKE YOU EVEN CONSIDER IT, SO LIKE YOU SAID...
IT WAS ALL FAKE. IT WAS NEVER GOING TO BE A REALITY.
HOOD, YOU SON OF A BITCH. YOU DIDN'T TELL ME SHE WAS LISTENING!
IT'S NOT MY JOB TO KEEP TABS ON YOUR WIFE.
I DIDN'T WANT HER TO KNOW ABOUT ELEKTRA OR ABOUT...
...WHAT THE HELL IS SHE DOING HERE WITH YOU, ANYWAY?
WE'VE BEEN BRINGING TOGETHER LIKE-MINDED INDIVIDUALS IN AN EFFORT FOR US TO WORK BEHIND THE SCENES TO BETTER THEIR LIVES.
IN OTHER WORDS, IT'S ALL ABOUT FORTUNE AND GLORY.
WE'VE HAD A FEW SETBACKS RECENTLY, BUT OUR NEXT ASSIGNMENT IS CLEAR AND WE'D LOVE TO HAVE YOU WORK WITH US.
WE WANT TO GO AFTER THE MAD THINKER FOR STABBING US IN THE--
NAH NAH NAH.
I KNOW EXACTLY WHAT WE'RE DOING NEXT.

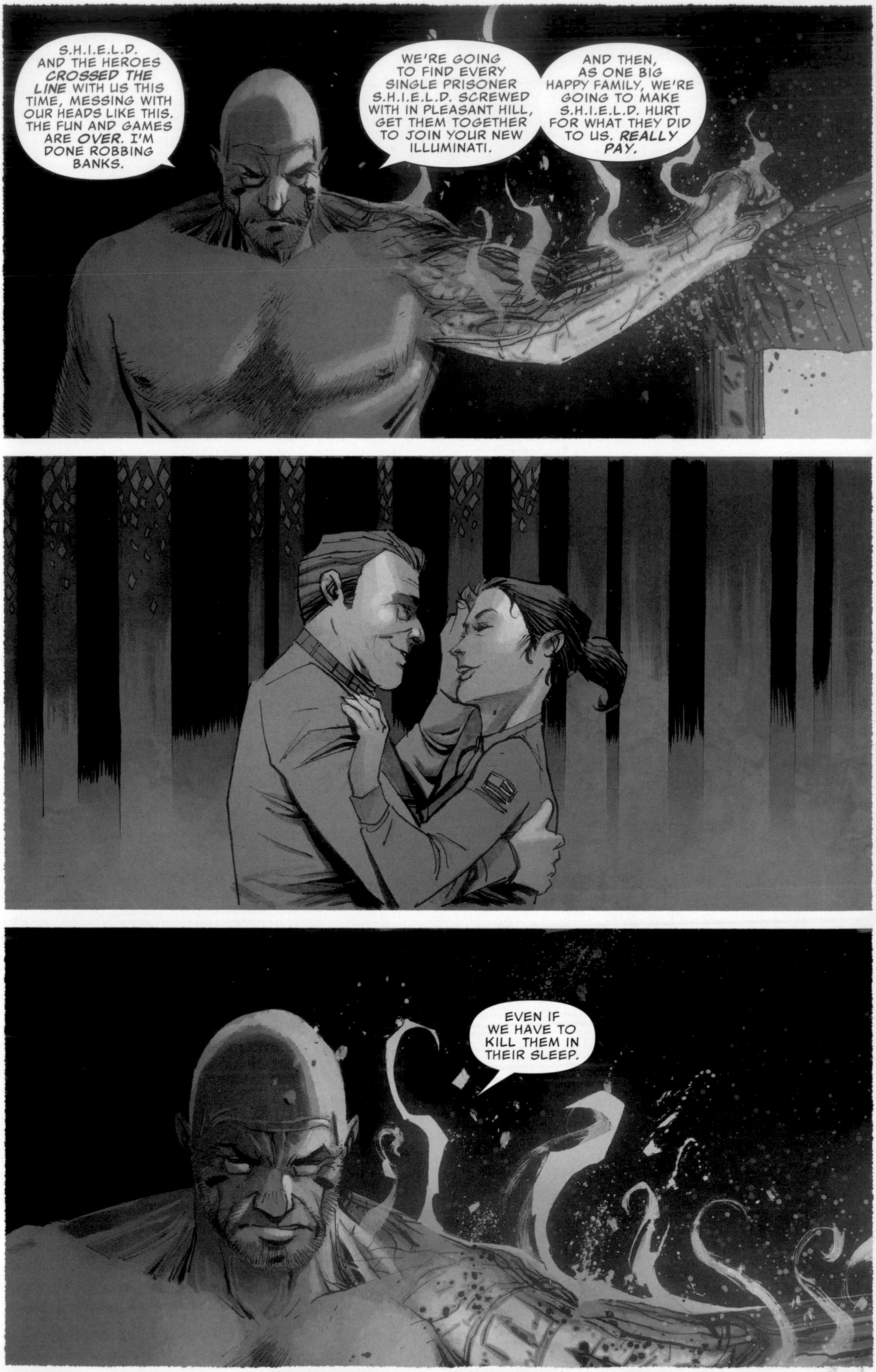
S.H.I.E.L.D. AND THE HEROES CROSSED THE LINE WITH US THIS TIME, MESSING WITH OUR HEADS LIKE THIS. THE FUN AND GAMES ARE OVER. I'M DONE ROBBING BANKS.
WE'RE GOING TO FIND EVERY SINGLE PRISONER S.H.I.E.L.D. SCREWED WITH IN PLEASANT HILL, GET THEM TOGETHER TO JOIN YOUR NEW ILLUMINATI.
AND THEN, AS ONE BIG HAPPY FAMILY, WE'RE GOING TO MAKE S.H.I.E.L.D. HURT FOR WHAT THEY DID TO US. REALLY PAY.
EVEN IF WE HAVE TO KILL THEM IN THEIR SLEEP.

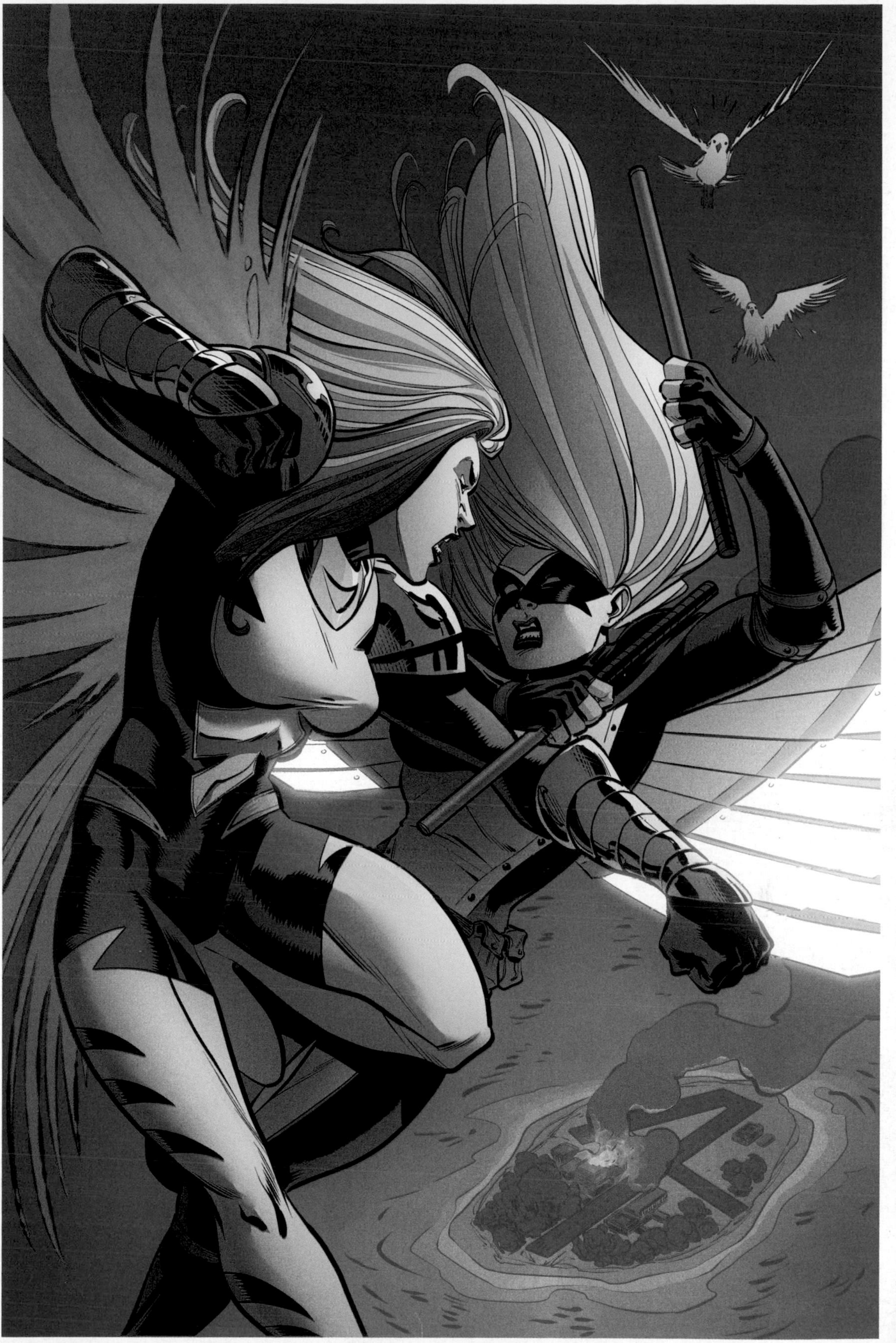

Agents of S.H.I.E.L.D. No. 4

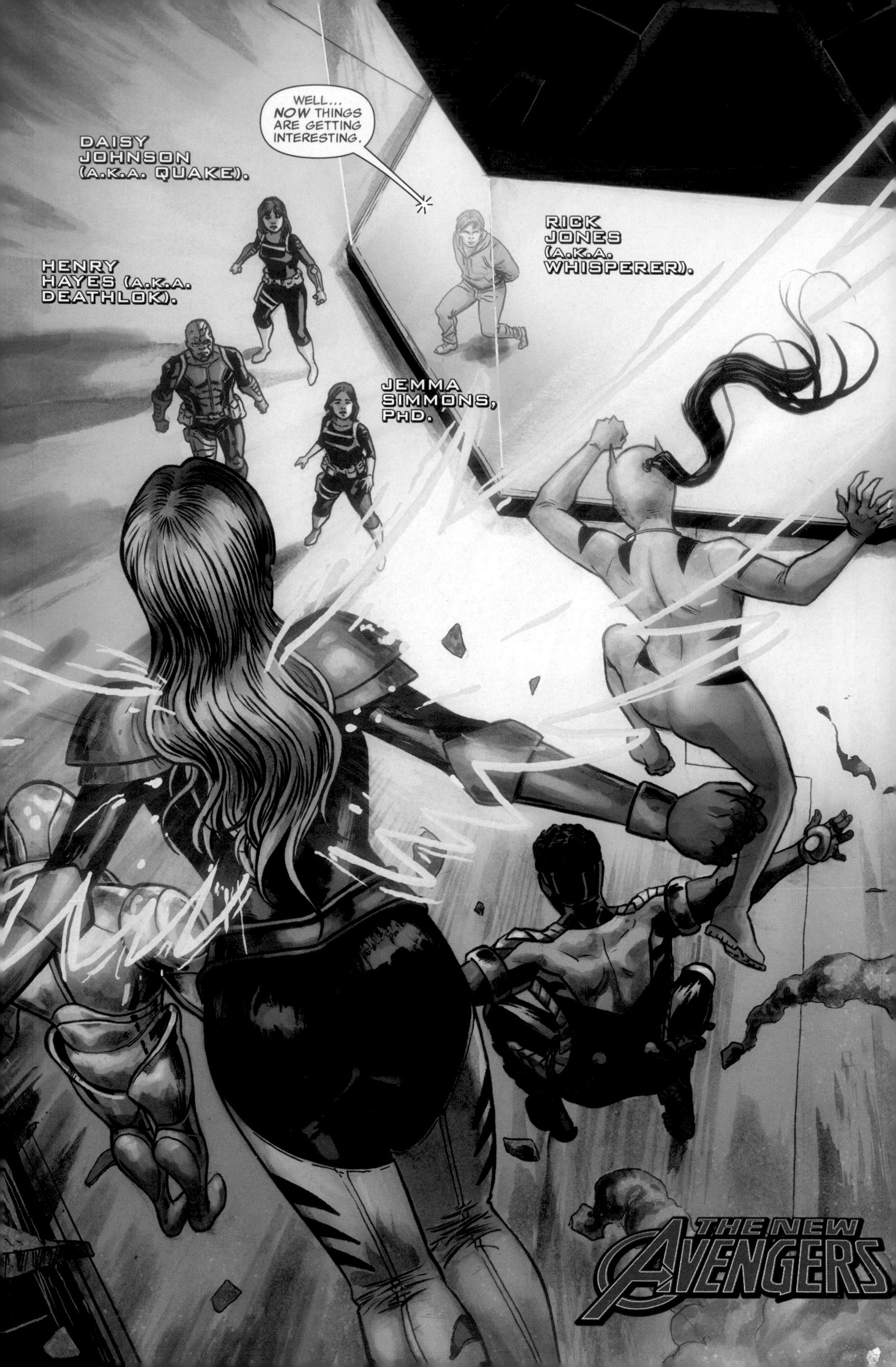

DAISY JOHNSON (A.K.A. QUAKE).
WELL... NOW THINGS ARE GETTING INTERESTING.
RICK JONES (A.K.A. WHISPERER).
HENRY HAYES (A.K.A. DEATHLOK).
JEMMA SIMMONS, PHD.
THE NEW AVENGERS

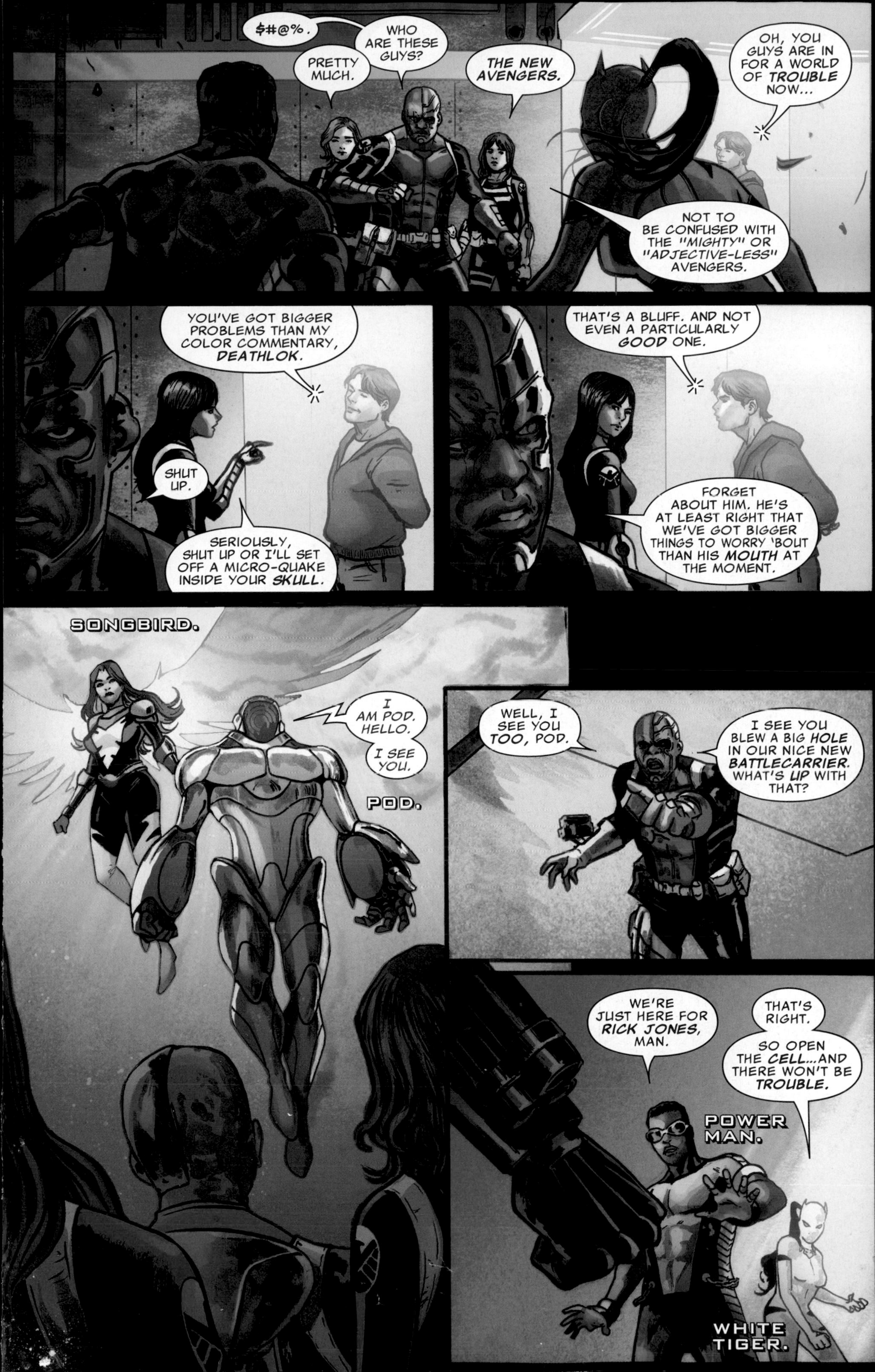
$#@%.
WHO ARE THESE GUYS?
PRETTY MUCH.
THE NEW AVENGERS.
OH, YOU GUYS ARE IN FOR A WORLD OF TROUBLE NOW...
NOT TO BE CONFUSED WITH THE "MIGHTY" OR "ADJECTIVE-LESS" AVENGERS.
YOU'VE GOT BIGGER PROBLEMS THAN MY COLOR COMMENTARY, DEATHLOK.
SHUT UP.
SERIOUSLY, SHUT UP OR I'LL SET OFF A MICRO-QUAKE INSIDE YOUR SKULL.
THAT'S A BLUFF. AND NOT EVEN A PARTICULARLY GOOD ONE.
FORGET ABOUT HIM. HE'S AT LEAST RIGHT THAT WE'VE GOT BIGGER THINGS TO WORRY 'BOUT THAN HIS MOUTH AT THE MOMENT.
SONGBIRD.
I AM POD. HELLO.
I SEE YOU.
POD.
WELL, I SEE YOU TOO, POD.
I SEE YOU BLEW A BIG HOLE IN OUR NICE NEW BATTLECARRIER. WHAT'S UP WITH THAT?
WE'RE JUST HERE FOR RICK JONES, MAN.
THAT'S RIGHT.
SO OPEN THE CELL...AND THERE WON'T BE TROUBLE.
POWER MAN.
WHITE TIGER.

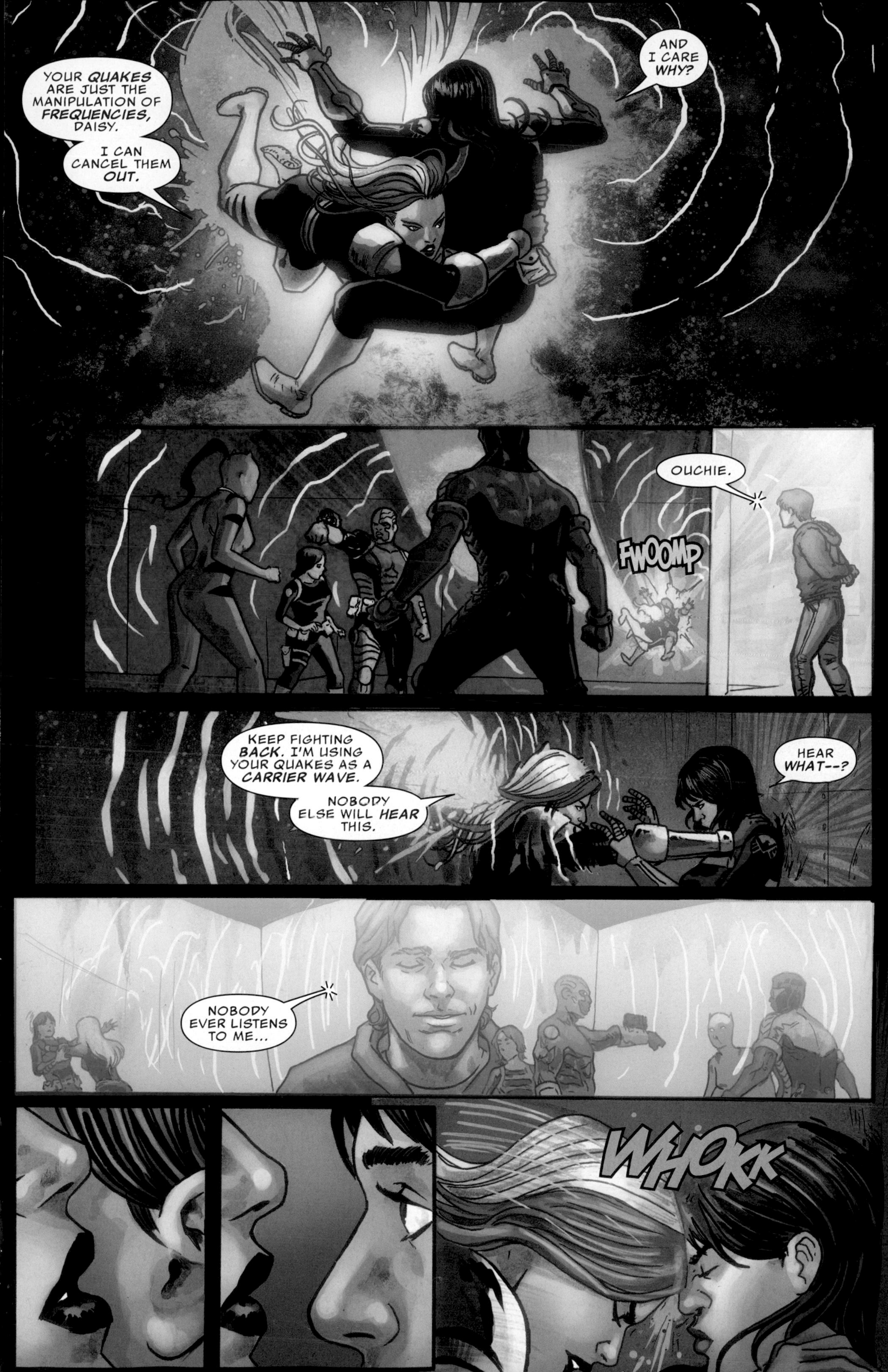
YOUR QUAKES ARE JUST THE MANIPULATION OF FREQUENCIES, DAISY.
I CAN CANCEL THEM OUT.
AND I CARE WHY?
OUCHIE.
FWOOMP
KEEP FIGHTING BACK. I'M USING YOUR QUAKES AS A CARRIER WAVE.
NOBODY ELSE WILL HEAR THIS.
HEAR WHAT--?
NOBODY EVER LISTENS TO ME...
WHOKK

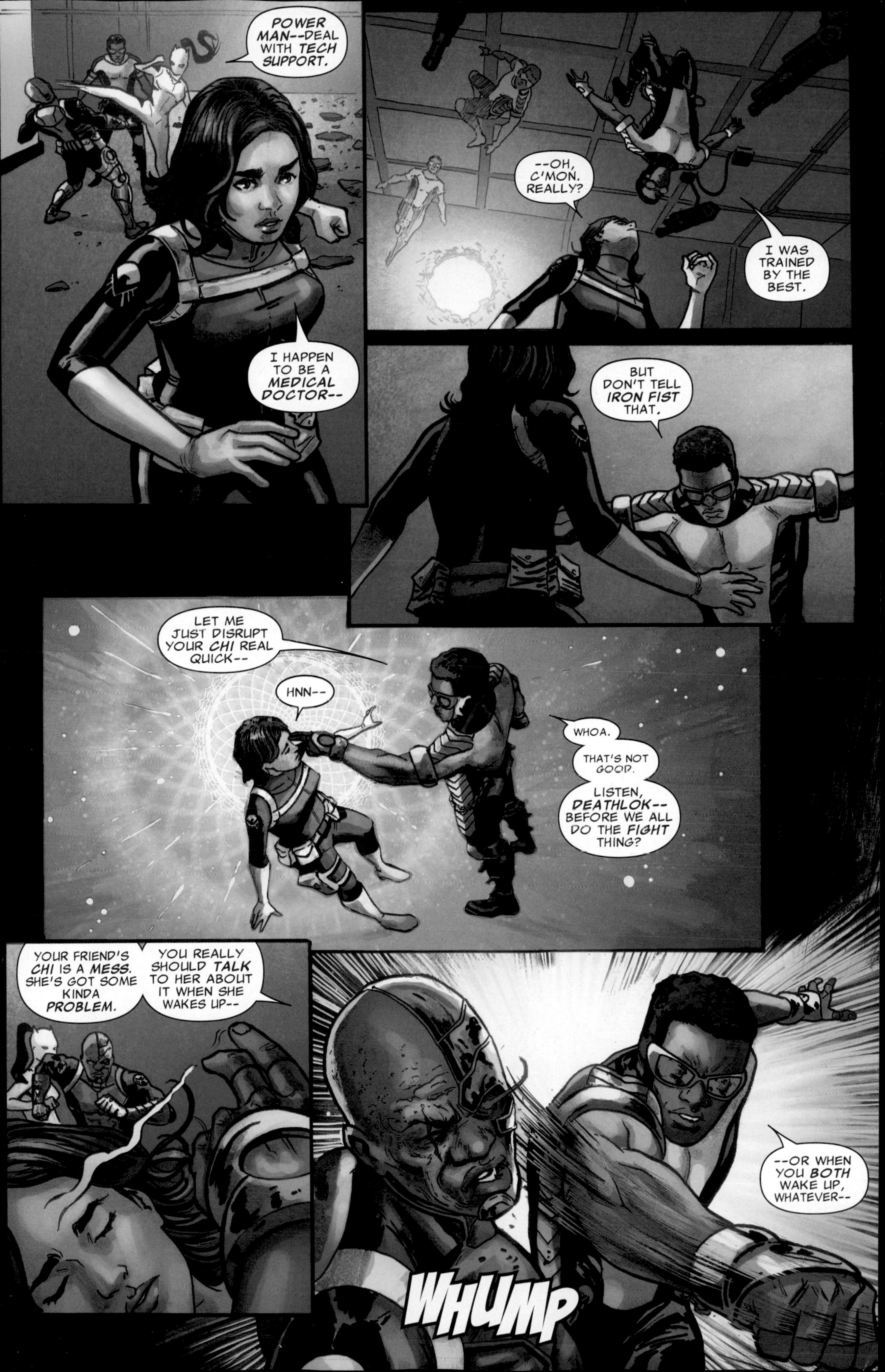
POWER MAN--DEAL WITH TECH SUPPORT.
I HAPPEN TO BE A MEDICAL DOCTOR--
--OH, C'MON. REALLY?
I WAS TRAINED BY THE BEST.
BUT DON'T TELL IRON FIST THAT.
LET ME JUST DISRUPT YOUR CHI REAL QUICK--
HNN--
WHOA.
THAT'S NOT GOOD.
LISTEN, DEATHLOK--BEFORE WE ALL DO THE FIGHT THING?
YOUR FRIEND'S CHI IS A MESS. SHE'S GOT SOME KINDA PROBLEM.
YOU REALLY SHOULD TALK TO HER ABOUT IT WHEN SHE WAKES UP--
--OR WHEN YOU BOTH WAKE UP, WHATEVER--
WHUMP

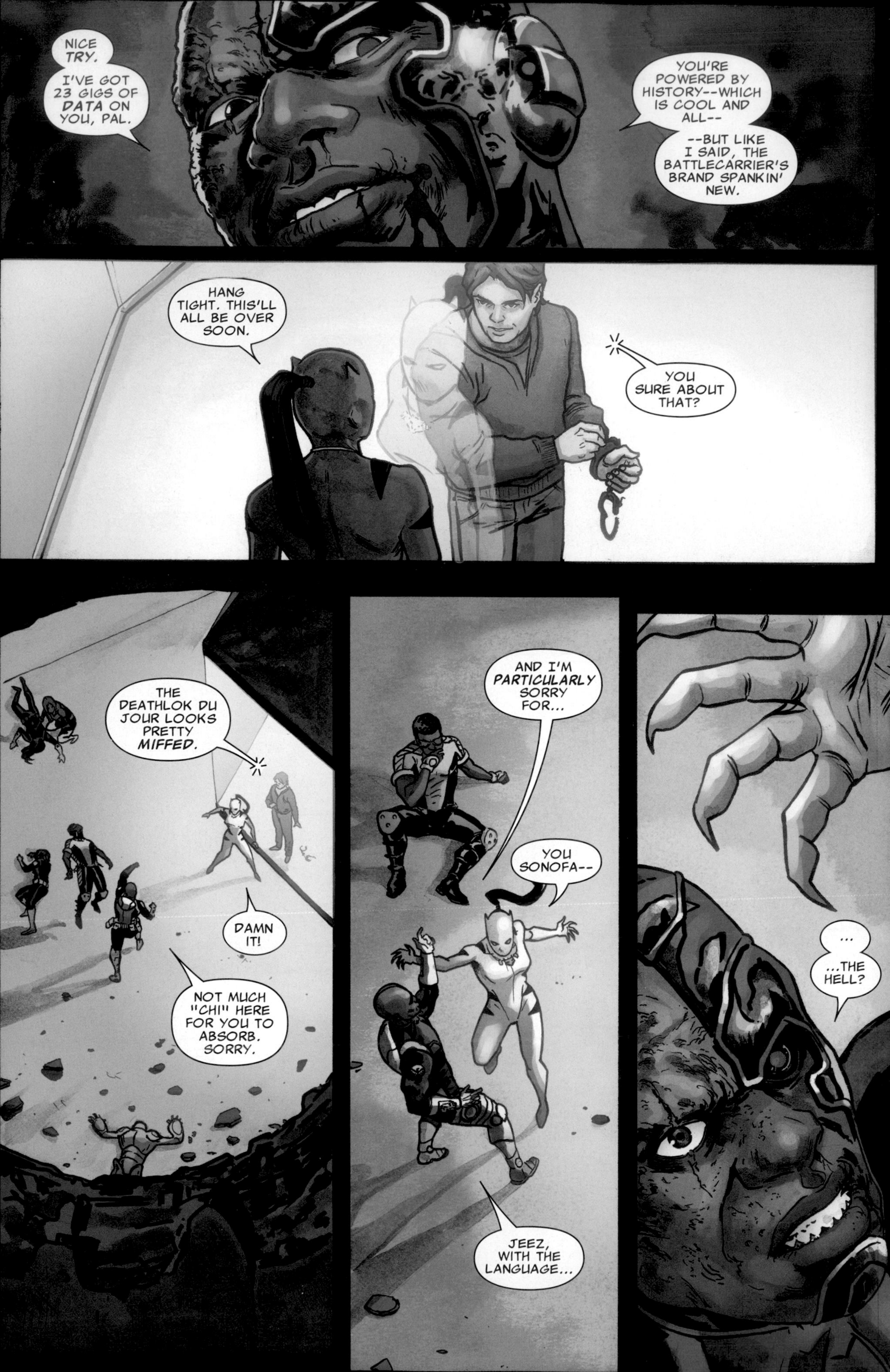
NICE TRY.
I'VE GOT 23 GIGS OF DATA ON YOU, PAL.
YOU'RE POWERED BY HISTORY--WHICH IS COOL AND ALL--
--BUT LIKE I SAID, THE BATTLECARRIER'S BRAND SPANKIN' NEW.
HANG TIGHT. THIS'LL ALL BE OVER SOON.
YOU SURE ABOUT THAT?
THE DEATHLOK DU JOUR LOOKS PRETTY MIFFED.
DAMN IT!
NOT MUCH "CHI" HERE FOR YOU TO ABSORB. SORRY.
AND I'M PARTICULARLY SORRY FOR...
YOU SONOFA--
JEEZ, WITH THE LANGUAGE...
...
...THE HELL?

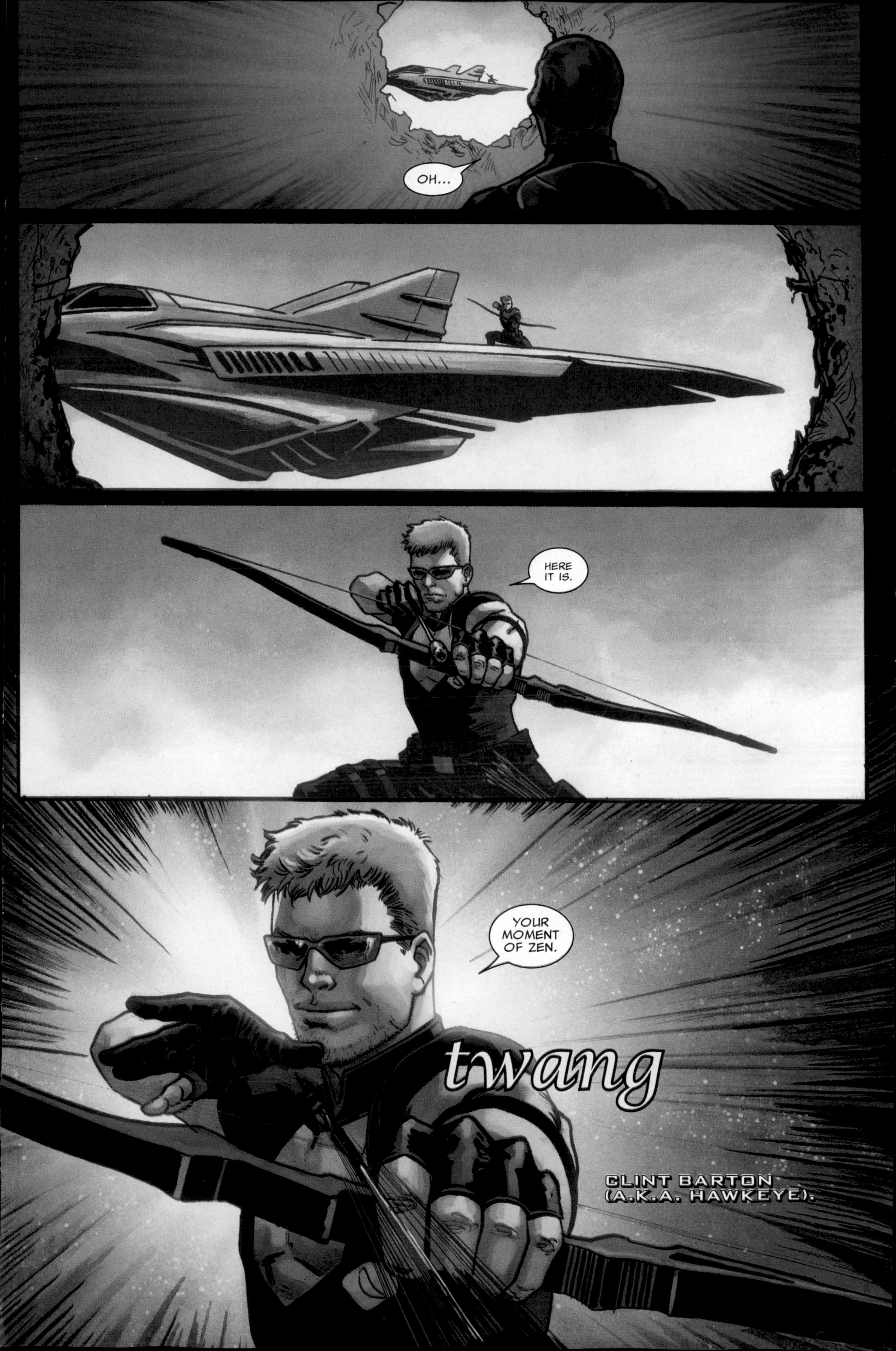
OH...
HERE IT IS.
YOUR MOMENT OF ZEN.
twang
CLINT BARTON (A.K.A. HAWKEYE).

THUKK

KKRRRZZZTT--

DAMMITSONOFABI--

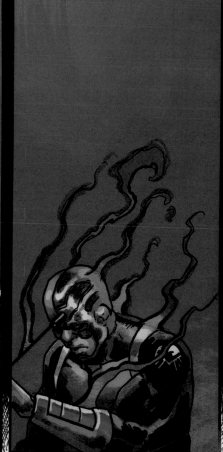

WHEW. MAN, I AM VERY GLAD YOU DIDN'T TURN OUT TO BE--

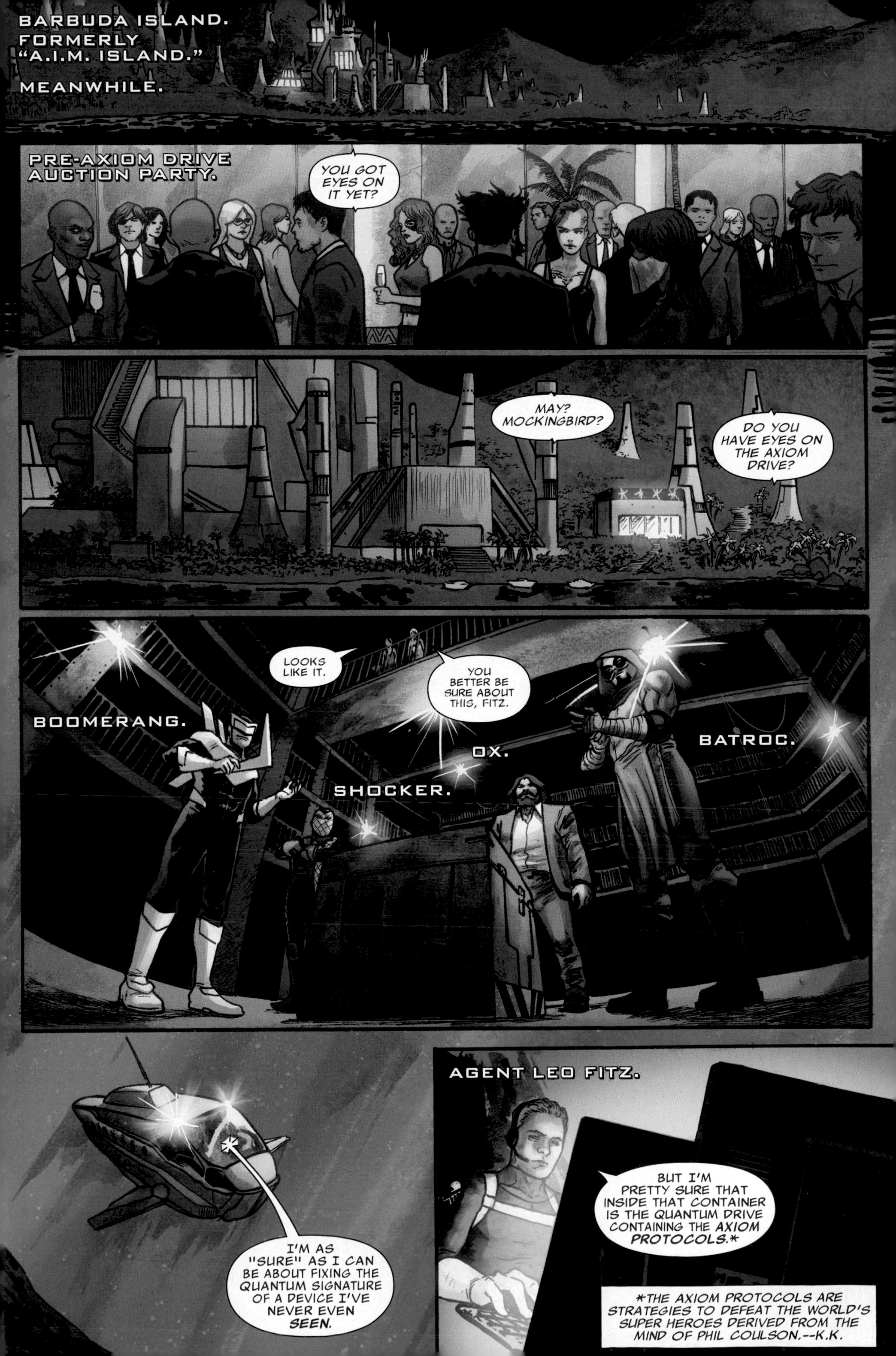
BARBUDA ISLAND.
FORMERLY
"A.I.M. ISLAND."
MEANWHILE.
PRE-AXIOM DRIVE
AUCTION PARTY.
YOU GOT EYES ON IT YET?
MAY? MOCKINGBIRD?
DO YOU HAVE EYES ON THE AXIOM DRIVE?
LOOKS LIKE IT.
YOU BETTER BE SURE ABOUT THIS, FITZ.
BOOMERANG.
SHOCKER.
OX.
BATROC.
I'M AS "SURE" AS I CAN BE ABOUT FIXING THE QUANTUM SIGNATURE OF A DEVICE I'VE NEVER EVEN SEEN.
AGENT LEO FITZ.
BUT I'M PRETTY SURE THAT INSIDE THAT CONTAINER IS THE QUANTUM DRIVE CONTAINING THE AXIOM PROTOCOLS.*
*THE AXIOM PROTOCOLS ARE STRATEGIES TO DEFEAT THE WORLD'S SUPER HEROES DERIVED FROM THE MIND OF PHIL COULSON.--K.K.

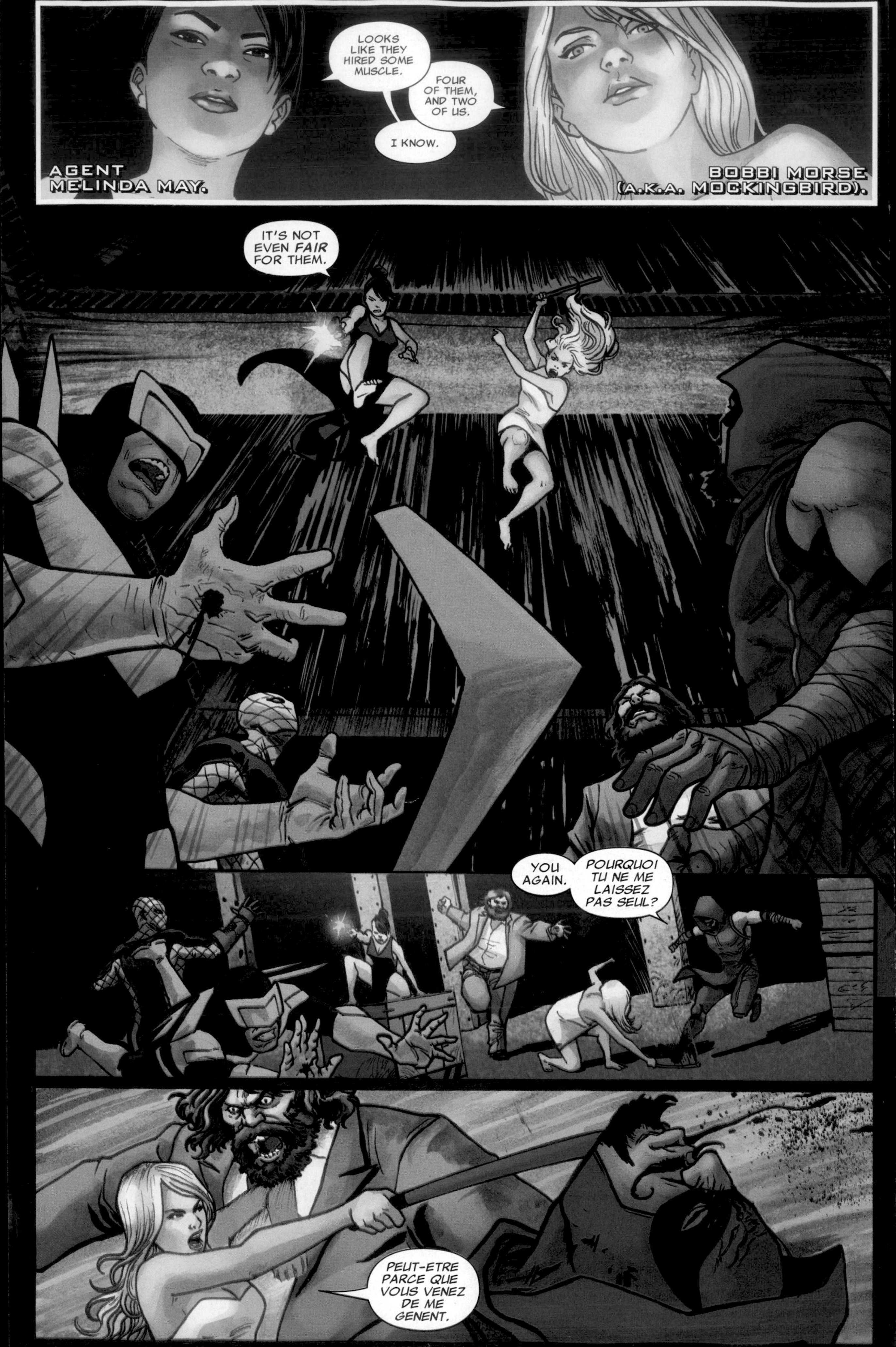
LOOKS LIKE THEY HIRED SOME MUSCLE.
FOUR OF THEM, AND TWO OF US.
I KNOW.
AGENT MELINDA MAY.
BOBBI MORSE (A.K.A. MOCKINGBIRD).
IT'S NOT EVEN FAIR FOR THEM.
YOU AGAIN.
POURQUOI TU NE ME LAISSEZ PAS SEUL?
PEUT-ETRE PARCE QUE VOUS VENEZ DE ME GENENT.

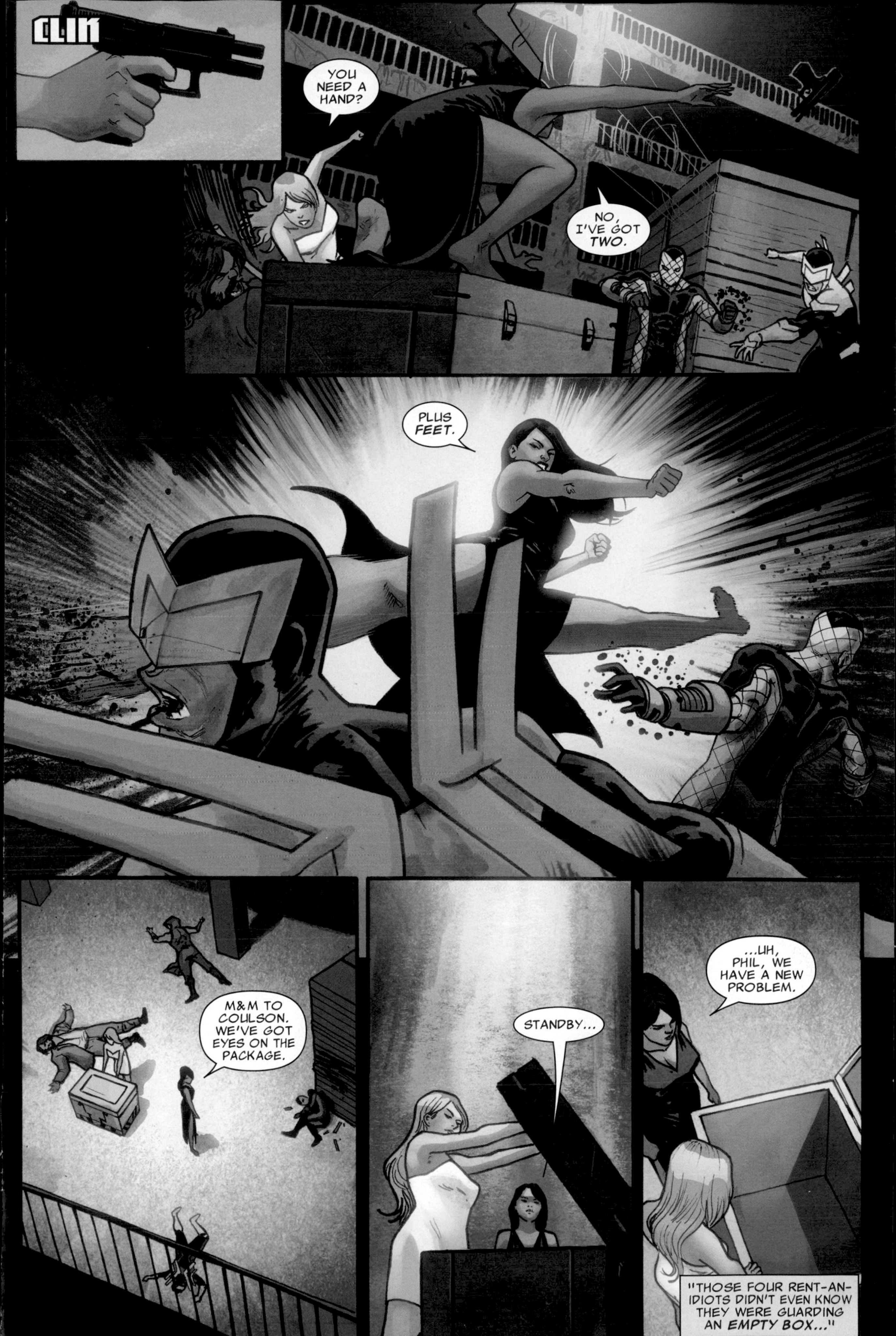
CLIK
YOU NEED A HAND?
NO, I'VE GOT TWO.
PLUS FEET.
M&M TO COULSON. WE'VE GOT EYES ON THE PACKAGE.
STANDBY...
...UH, PHIL, WE HAVE A NEW PROBLEM.
"THOSE FOUR RENT-AN-IDIOTS DIDN'T EVEN KNOW THEY WERE GUARDING AN EMPTY BOX..."

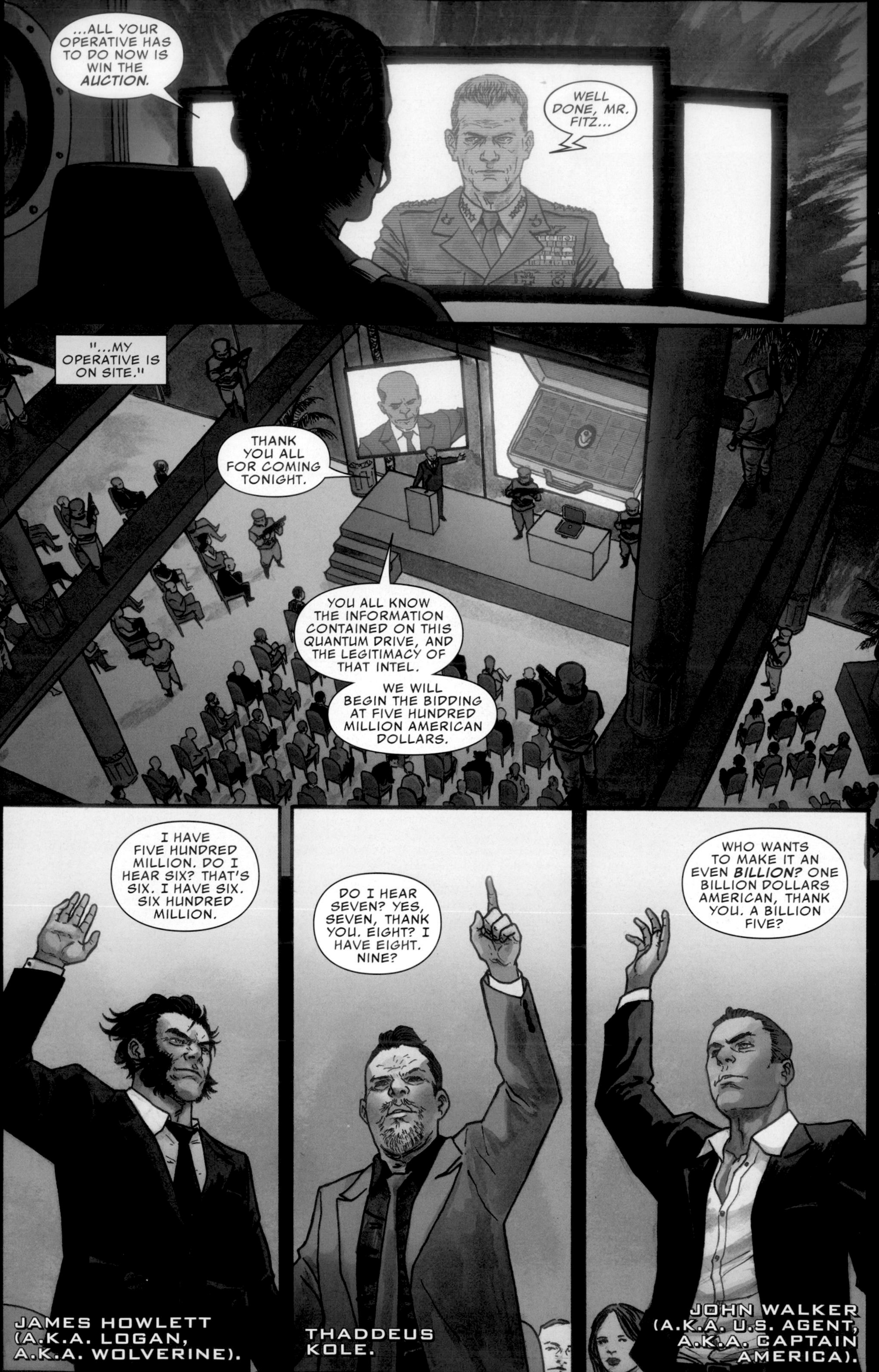

...ALL YOUR OPERATIVE HAS TO DO NOW IS WIN THE AUCTION.
WELL DONE, MR. FITZ...
"...MY OPERATIVE IS ON SITE."
THANK YOU ALL FOR COMING TONIGHT.
YOU ALL KNOW THE INFORMATION CONTAINED ON THIS QUANTUM DRIVE, AND THE LEGITIMACY OF THAT INTEL.
WE WILL BEGIN THE BIDDING AT FIVE HUNDRED MILLION AMERICAN DOLLARS.
I HAVE FIVE HUNDRED MILLION. DO I HEAR SIX? THAT'S SIX. I HAVE SIX. SIX HUNDRED MILLION.
JAMES HOWLETT (A.K.A. LOGAN, A.K.A. WOLVERINE).
DO I HEAR SEVEN? YES, SEVEN, THANK YOU. EIGHT? I HAVE EIGHT. NINE?
THADDEUS KOLE.
WHO WANTS TO MAKE IT AN EVEN BILLION? ONE BILLION DOLLARS AMERICAN, THANK YOU. A BILLION FIVE?
JOHN WALKER (A.K.A. U.S. AGENT, A.K.A. CAPTAIN AMERICA).

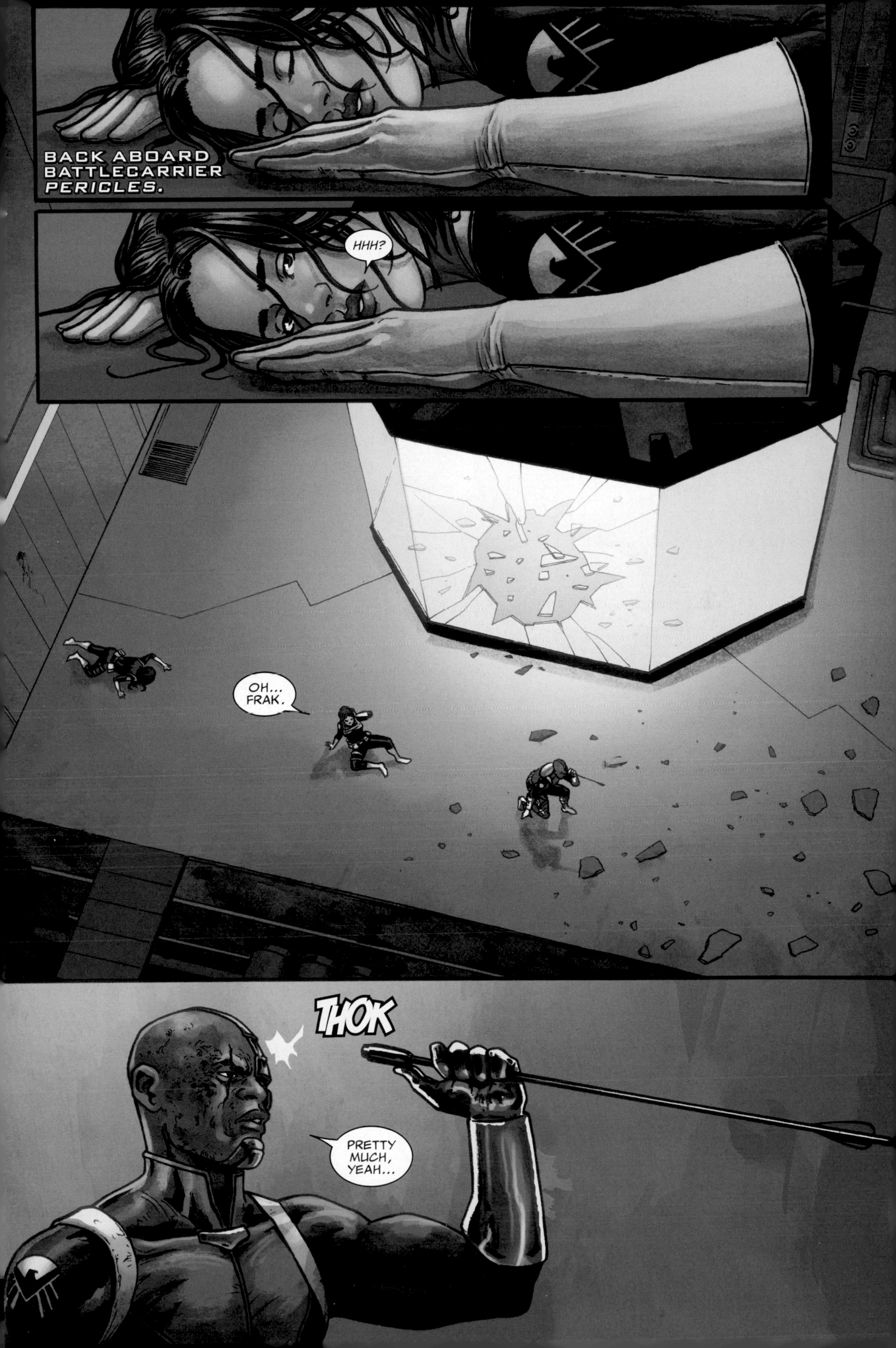
BACK ABOARD BATTLECARRIER PERICLES.
HHH?
OH... FRAK.
THOK
PRETTY MUCH, YEAH...

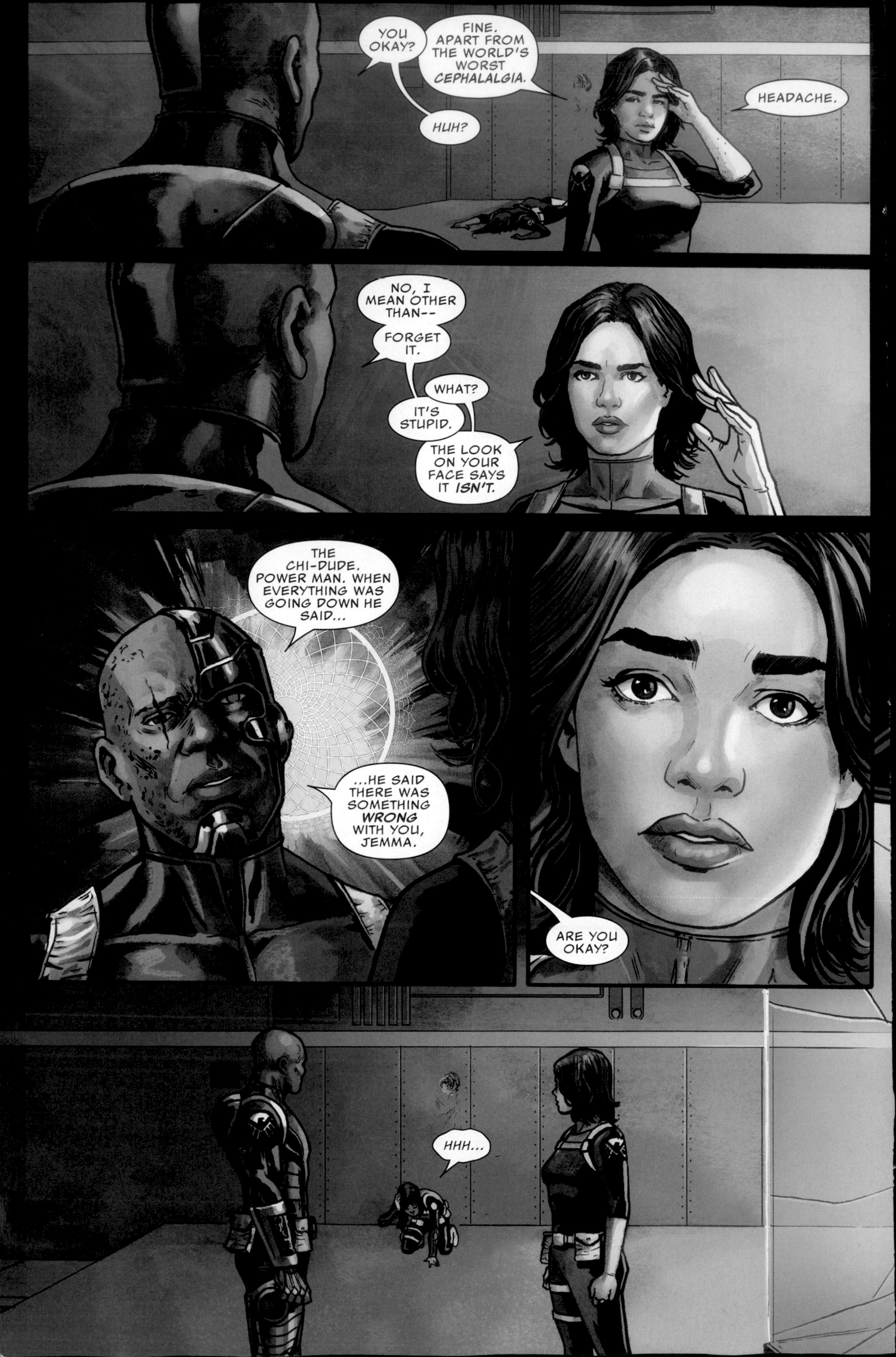

YOU OKAY?
FINE. APART FROM THE WORLD'S WORST *CEPHALALGIA.*
HUH?
HEADACHE.
NO, I MEAN OTHER THAN--
FORGET IT.
WHAT?
IT'S STUPID.
THE LOOK ON YOUR FACE SAYS IT ***ISN'T.***
THE CHI-DUDE. POWER MAN. WHEN EVERYTHING WAS GOING DOWN HE SAID...
...HE SAID THERE WAS SOMETHING ***WRONG*** WITH YOU, JEMMA.
ARE YOU OKAY?
HHH...

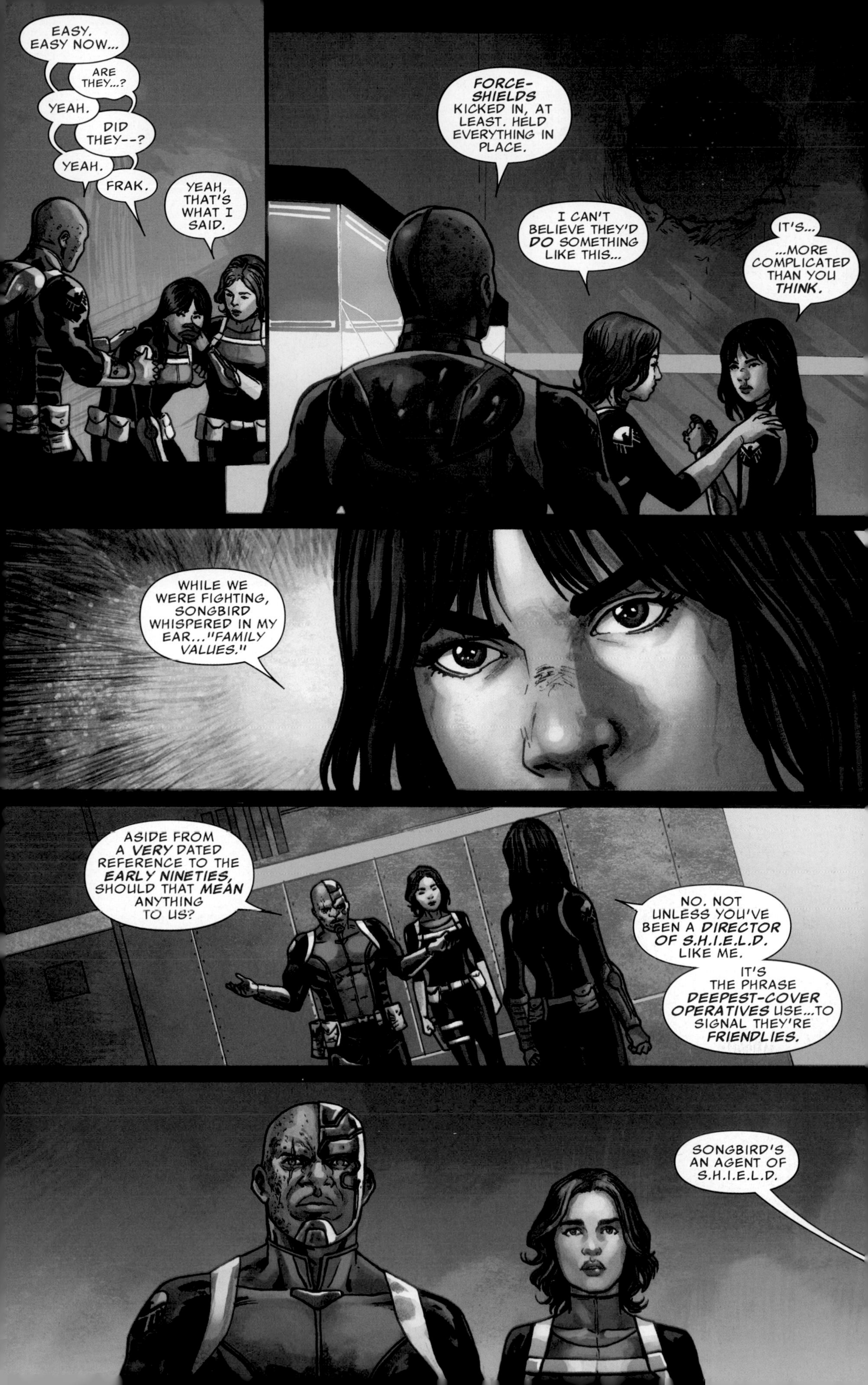
EASY. EASY NOW...
ARE THEY...?
YEAH.
DID THEY--?
YEAH.
FRAK.
YEAH, THAT'S WHAT I SAID.
FORCE-SHIELDS KICKED IN, AT LEAST. HELD EVERYTHING IN PLACE.
I CAN'T BELIEVE THEY'D DO SOMETHING LIKE THIS...
IT'S...
...MORE COMPLICATED THAN YOU THINK.
WHILE WE WERE FIGHTING, SONGBIRD WHISPERED IN MY EAR..."FAMILY VALUES."
ASIDE FROM A VERY DATED REFERENCE TO THE EARLY NINETIES, SHOULD THAT MEAN ANYTHING TO US?
NO. NOT UNLESS YOU'VE BEEN A DIRECTOR OF S.H.I.E.L.D. LIKE ME.
IT'S THE PHRASE DEEPEST-COVER OPERATIVES USE...TO SIGNAL THEY'RE FRIENDLIES.
SONGBIRD'S AN AGENT OF S.H.I.E.L.D.

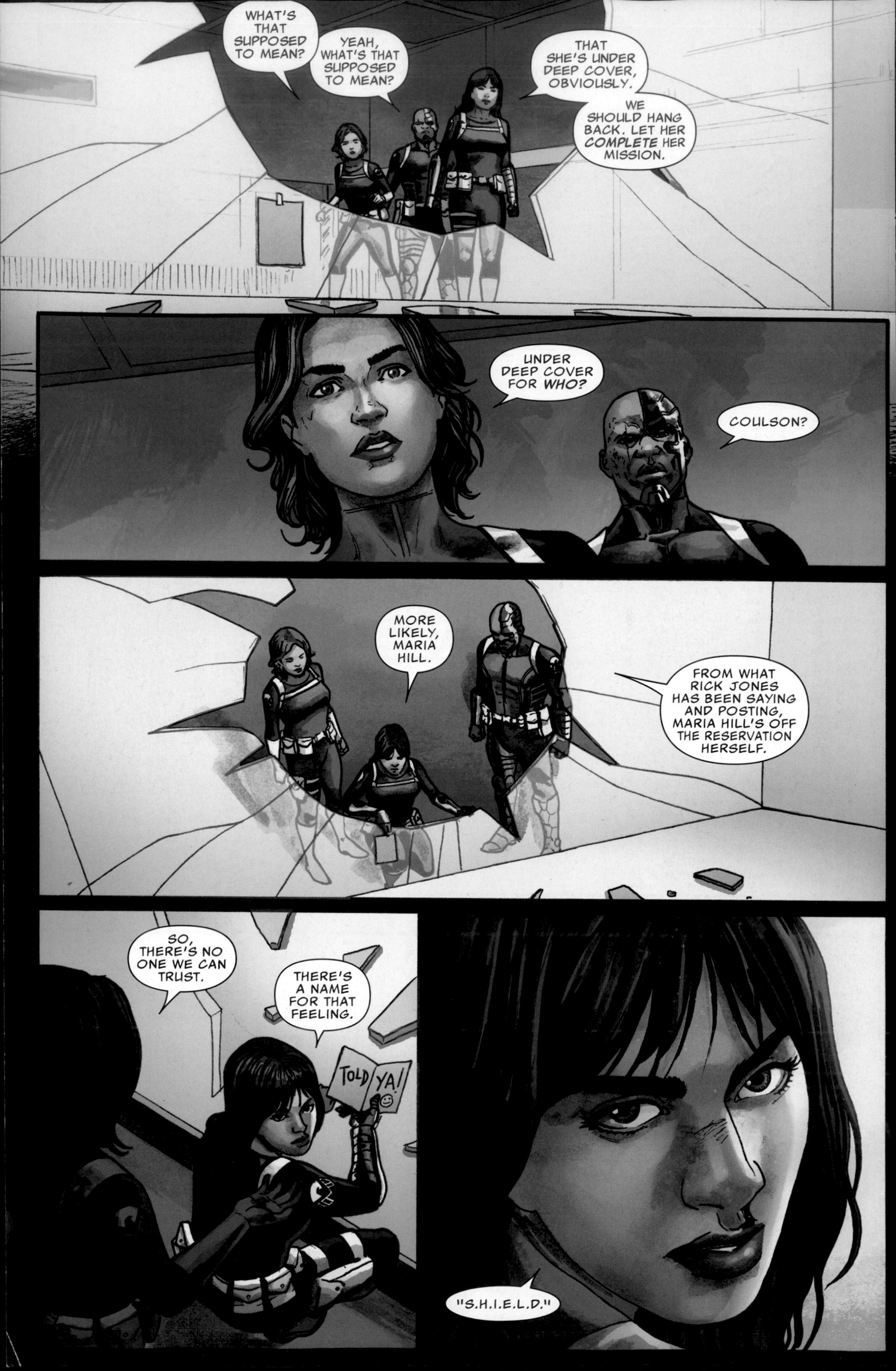
WHAT'S THAT SUPPOSED TO MEAN?
YEAH, WHAT'S THAT SUPPOSED TO MEAN?
THAT SHE'S UNDER DEEP COVER, OBVIOUSLY.
WE SHOULD HANG BACK. LET HER COMPLETE HER MISSION.
UNDER DEEP COVER FOR WHO?
COULSON?
MORE LIKELY, MARIA HILL.
FROM WHAT RICK JONES HAS BEEN SAYING AND POSTING, MARIA HILL'S OFF THE RESERVATION HERSELF.
SO, THERE'S NO ONE WE CAN TRUST.
THERE'S A NAME FOR THAT FEELING.
TOLD YA!
"S.H.I.E.L.D."

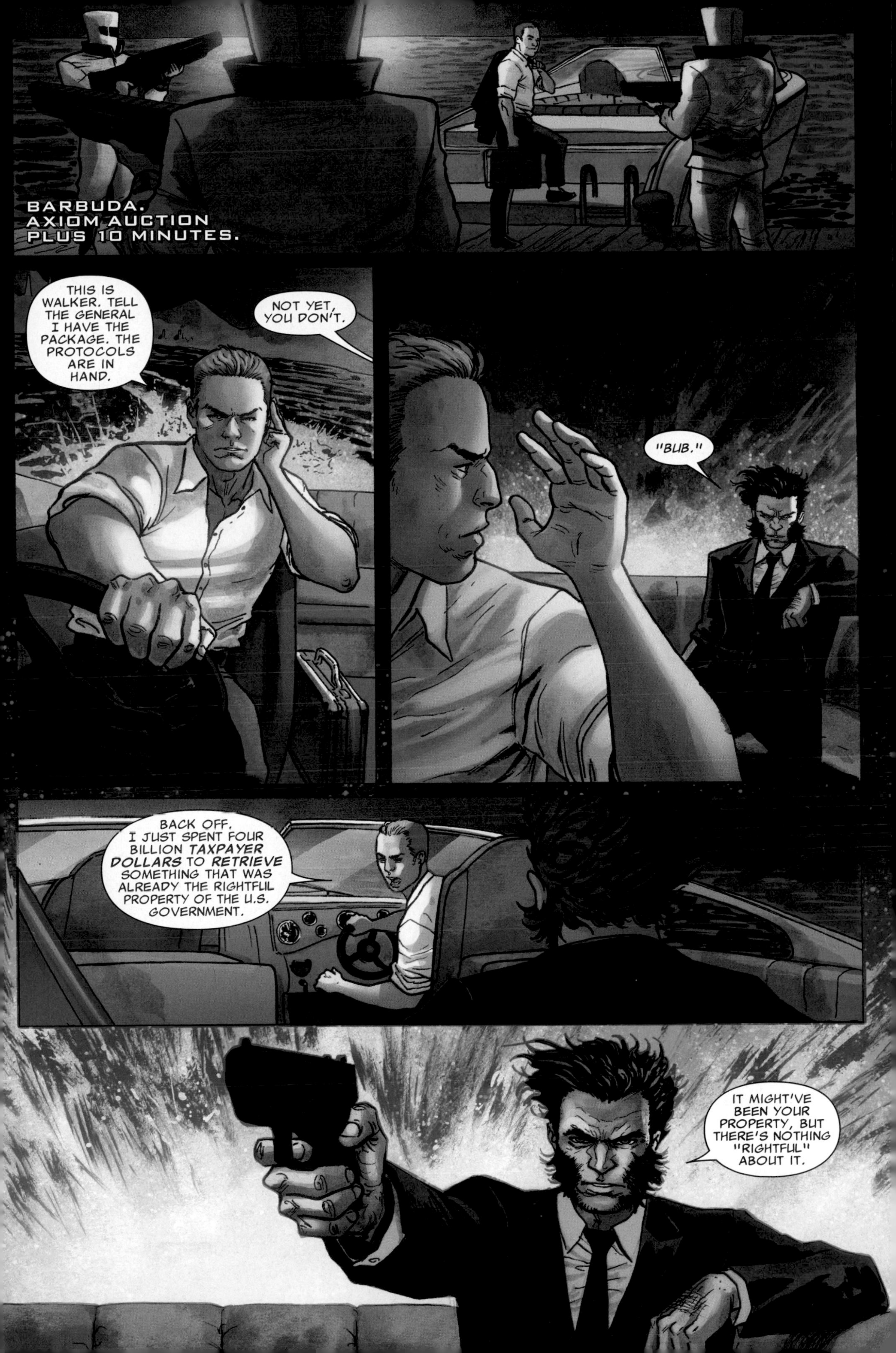
BARBUDA. AXIOM AUCTION PLUS 10 MINUTES.
THIS IS WALKER. TELL THE GENERAL I HAVE THE PACKAGE. THE PROTOCOLS ARE IN HAND.
NOT YET, YOU DON'T.
"BUB."
BACK OFF. I JUST SPENT FOUR BILLION TAXPAYER DOLLARS TO RETRIEVE SOMETHING THAT WAS ALREADY THE RIGHTFUL PROPERTY OF THE U.S. GOVERNMENT.
IT MIGHT'VE BEEN YOUR PROPERTY, BUT THERE'S NOTHING "RIGHTFUL" ABOUT IT.

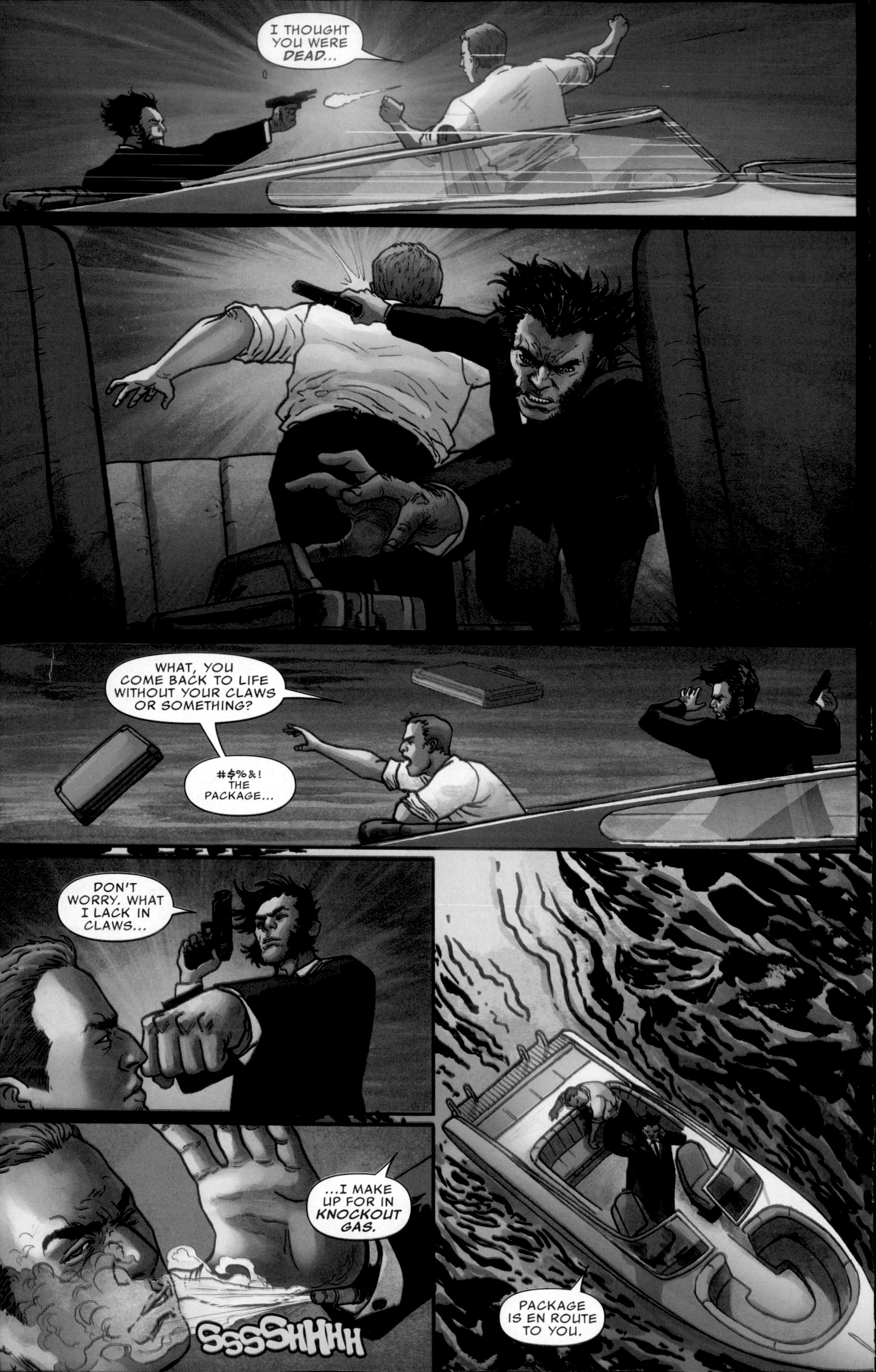
I THOUGHT YOU WERE DEAD...
WHAT, YOU COME BACK TO LIFE WITHOUT YOUR CLAWS OR SOMETHING?
#$%&! THE PACKAGE...
DON'T WORRY. WHAT I LACK IN CLAWS...
...I MAKE UP FOR IN KNOCKOUT GAS.
SSSSHHHH
PACKAGE IS EN ROUTE TO YOU.

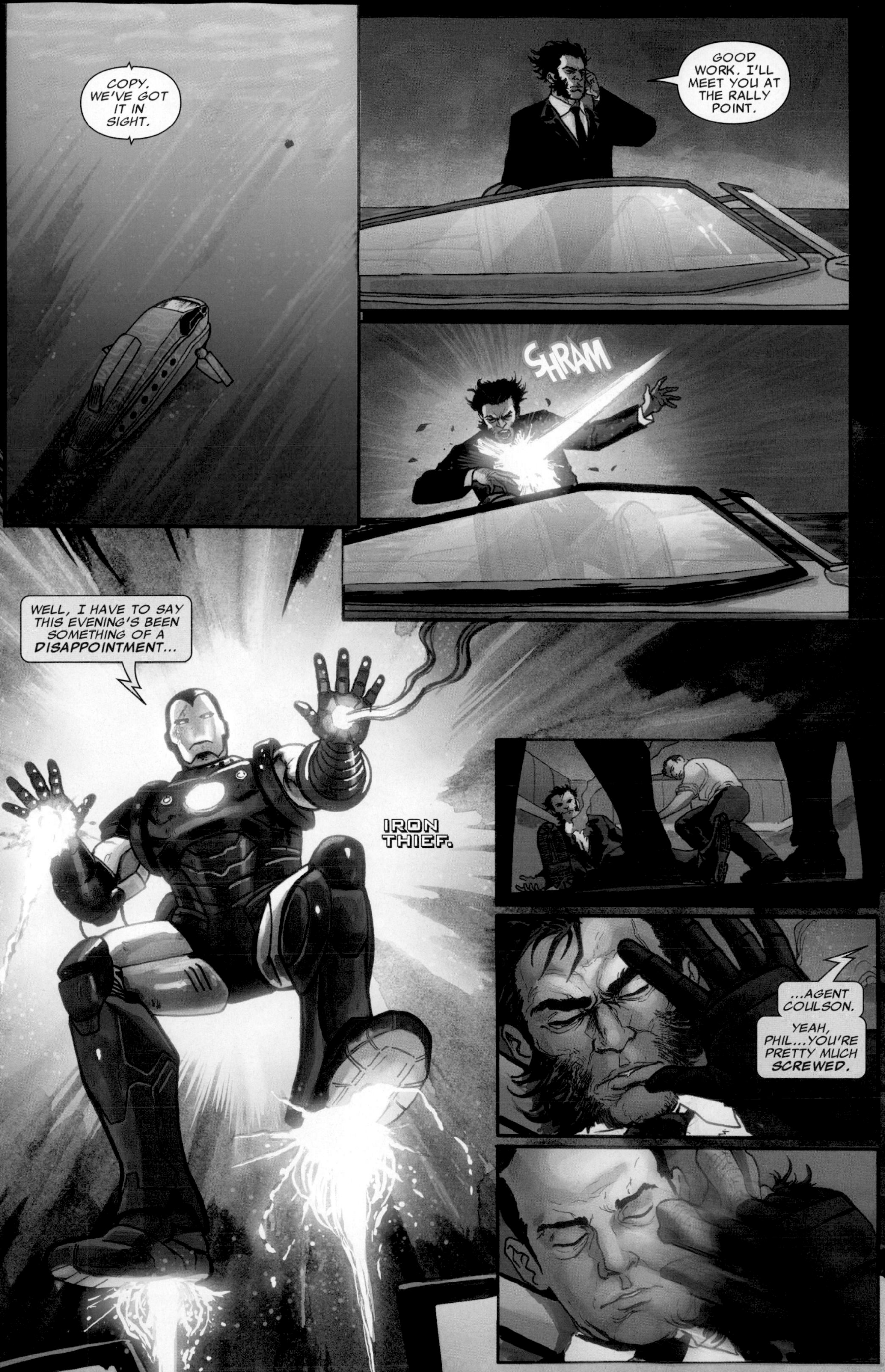
COPY. WE'VE GOT IT IN SIGHT.
GOOD WORK. I'LL MEET YOU AT THE RALLY POINT.
SHRAM
WELL, I HAVE TO SAY THIS EVENING'S BEEN SOMETHING OF A DISAPPOINTMENT...
IRON THIEF.
...AGENT COULSON.
YEAH, PHIL...YOU'RE PRETTY MUCH SCREWED.

All-New, All-Different Avengers No. 8

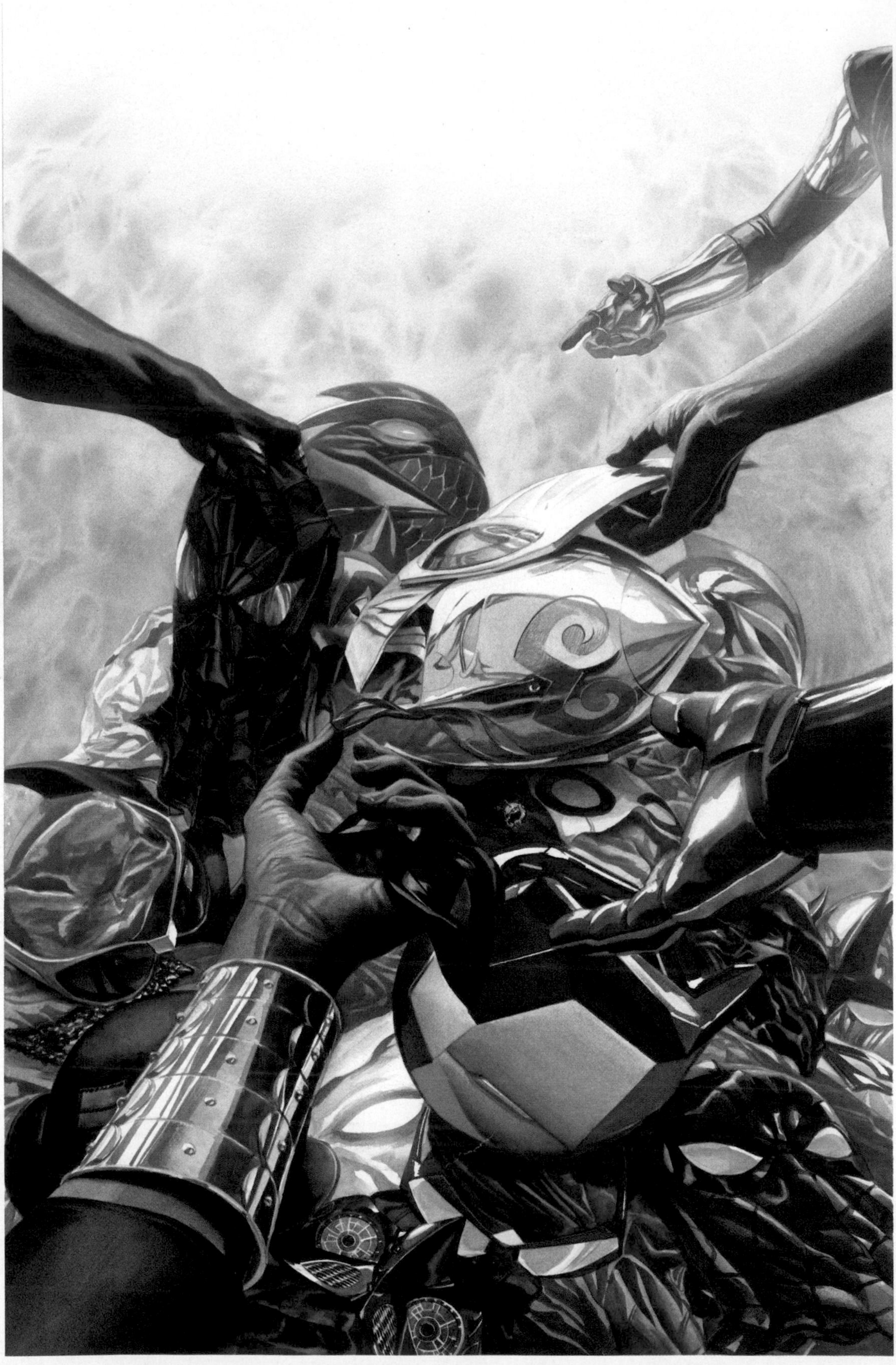

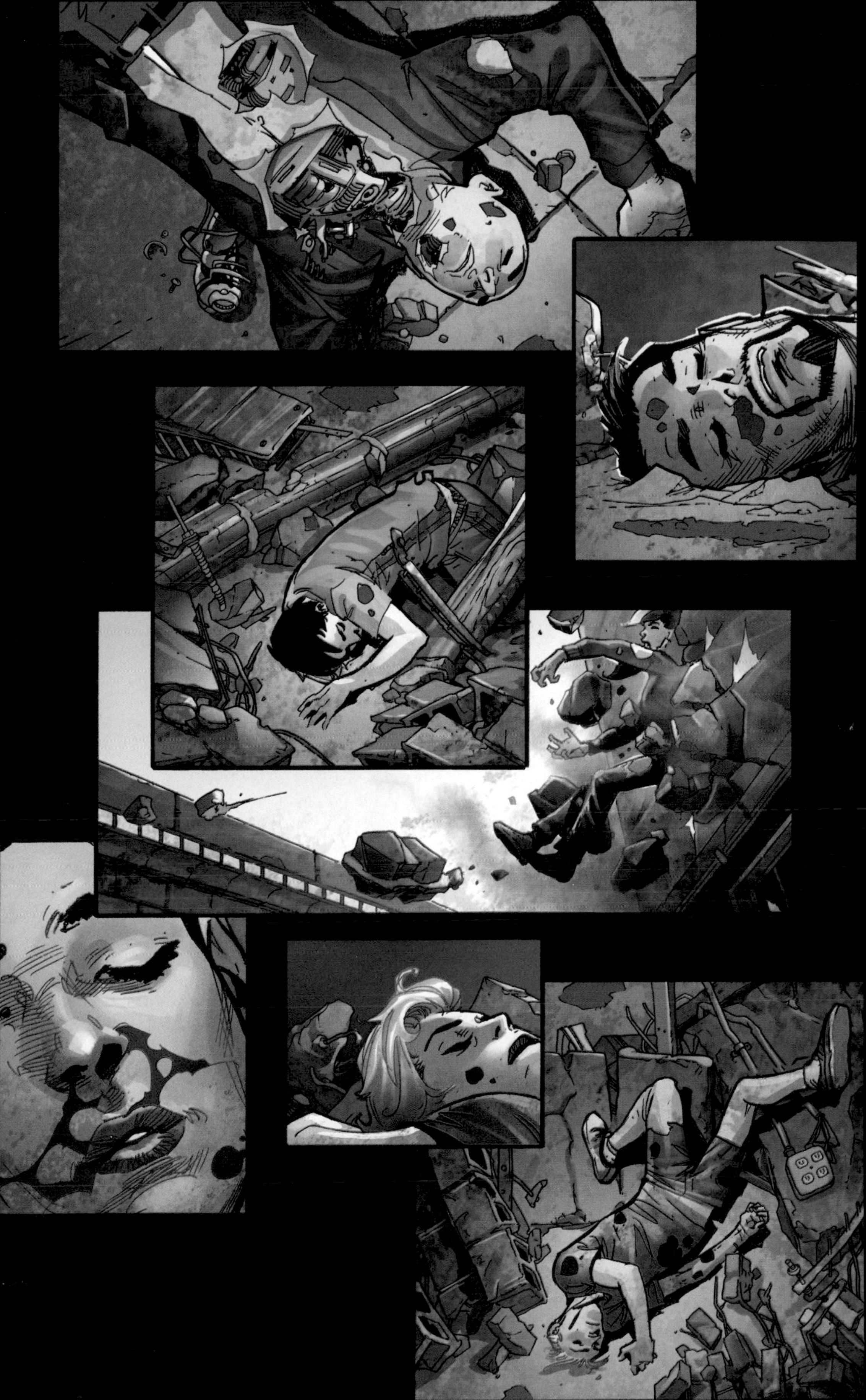

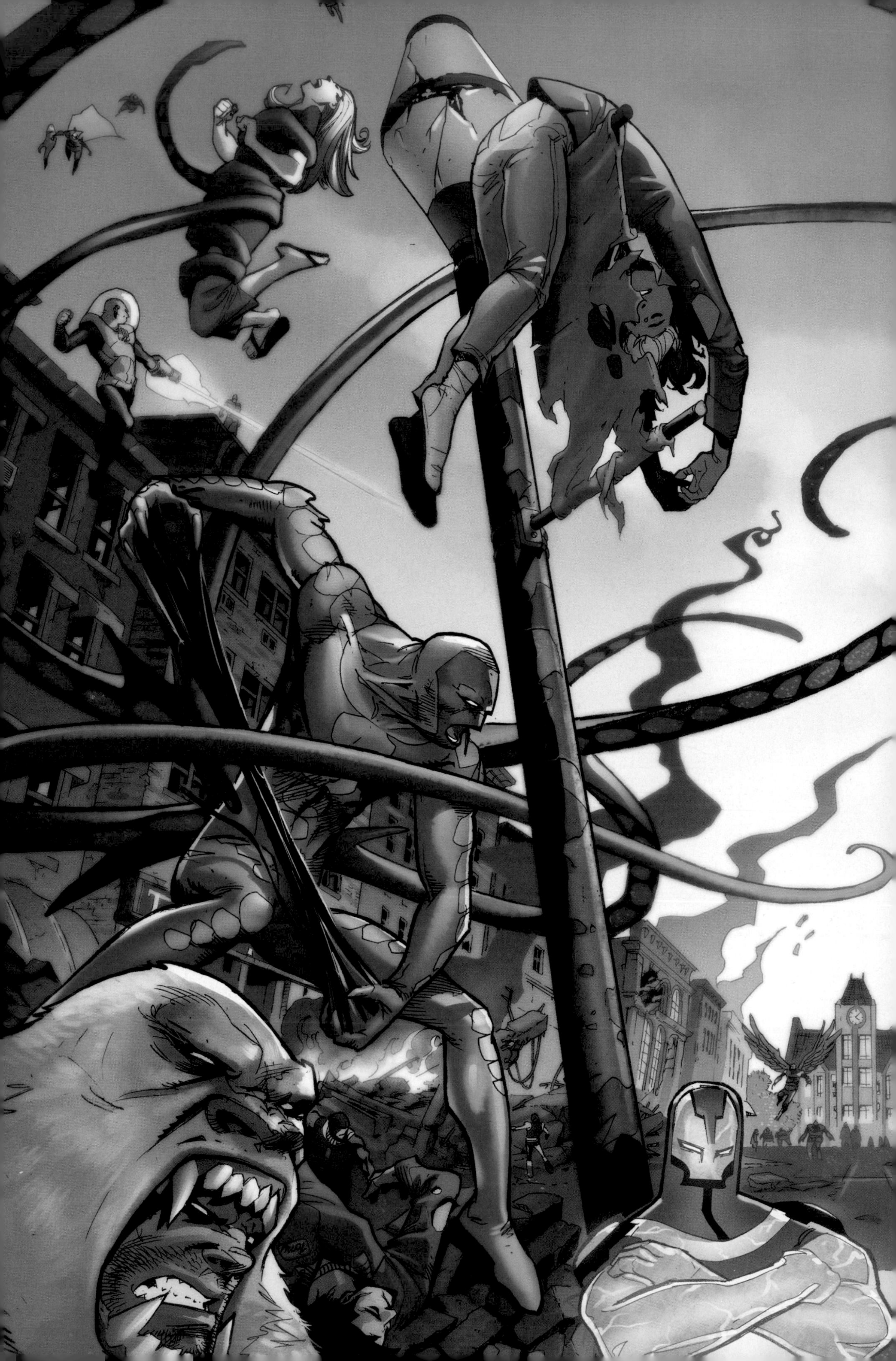

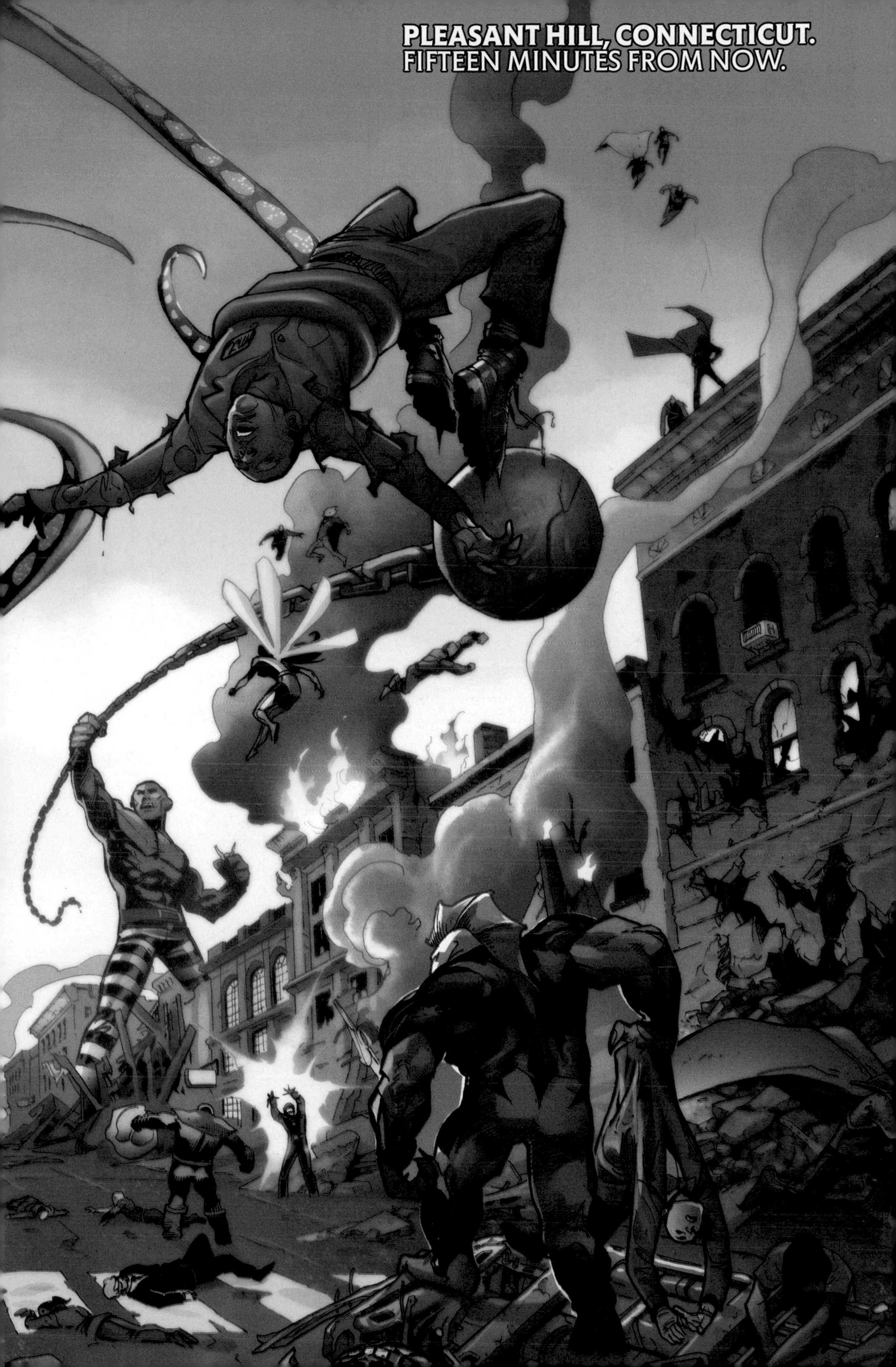
PLEASANT HILL, CONNECTICUT.
FIFTEEN MINUTES FROM NOW.

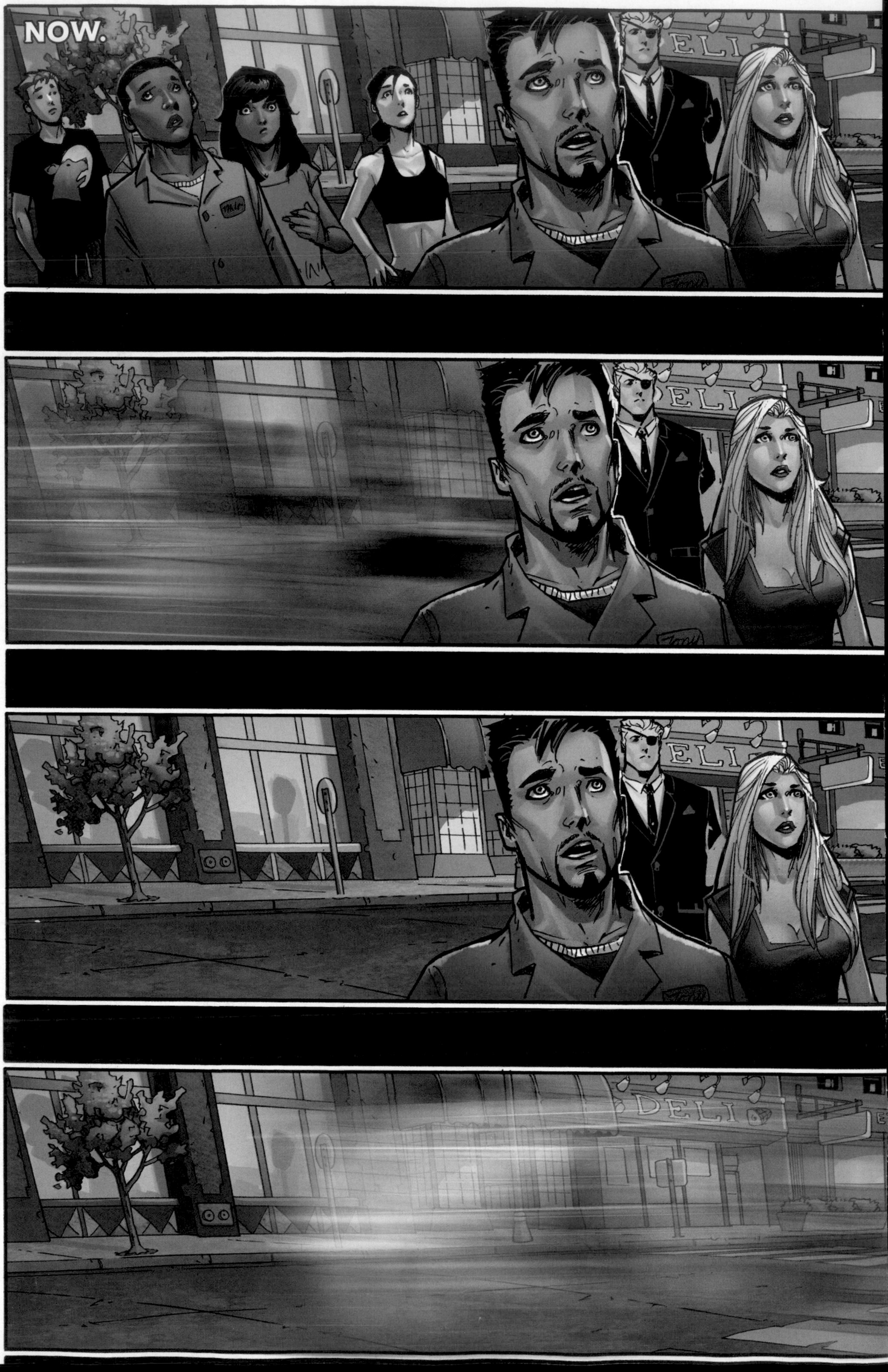
NOW.
DELI

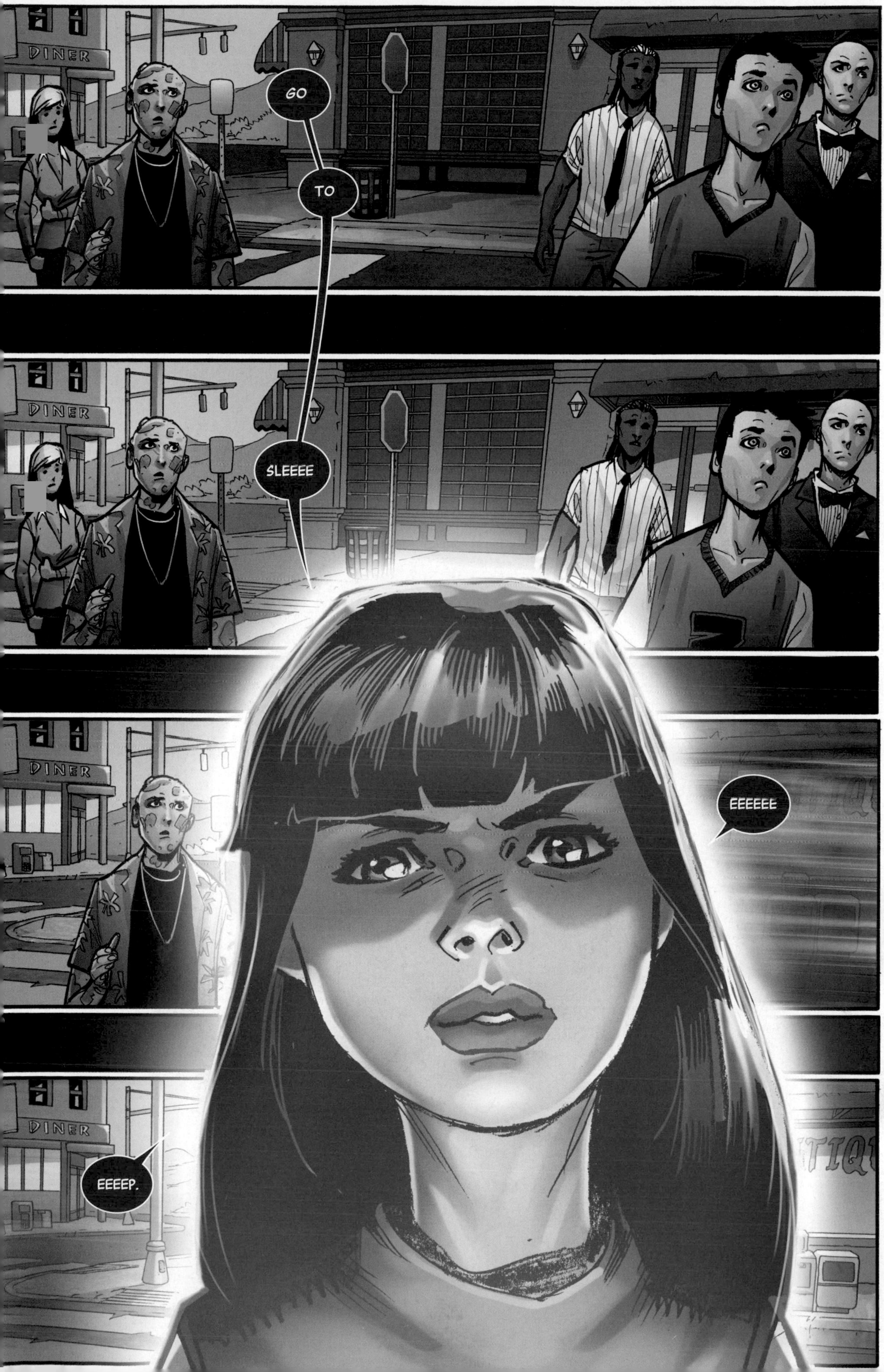

DINER
GO
TO
SLEEEE
EEEEEE
EEEEP.

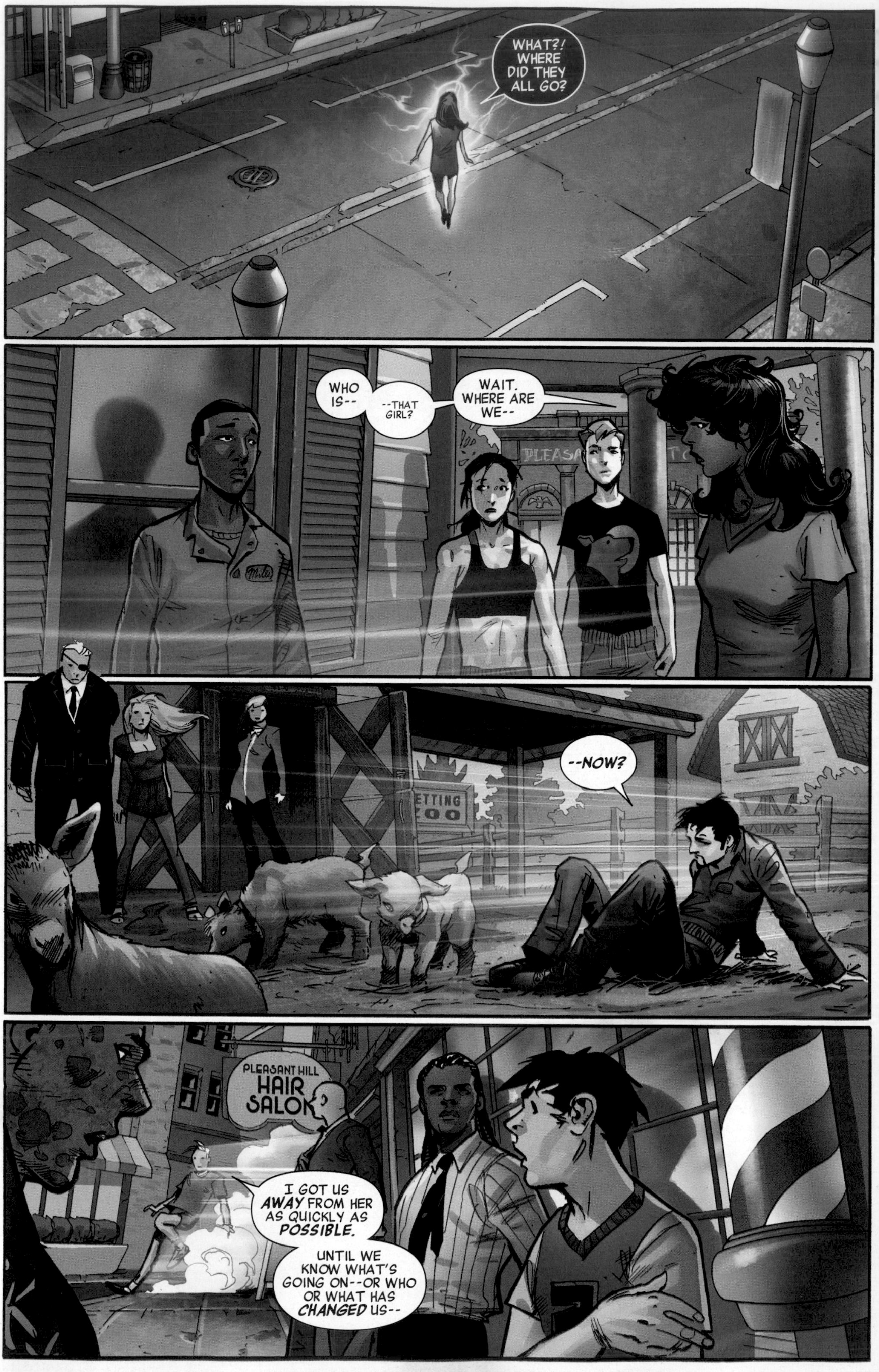
WHAT?! WHERE DID THEY ALL GO?
WHO IS--
--THAT GIRL?
WAIT. WHERE ARE WE--
--NOW?
PLEASANT HILL
HAIR
I GOT US AWAY FROM HER AS QUICKLY AS POSSIBLE.
UNTIL WE KNOW WHAT'S GOING ON--OR WHO OR WHAT HAS CHANGED US--

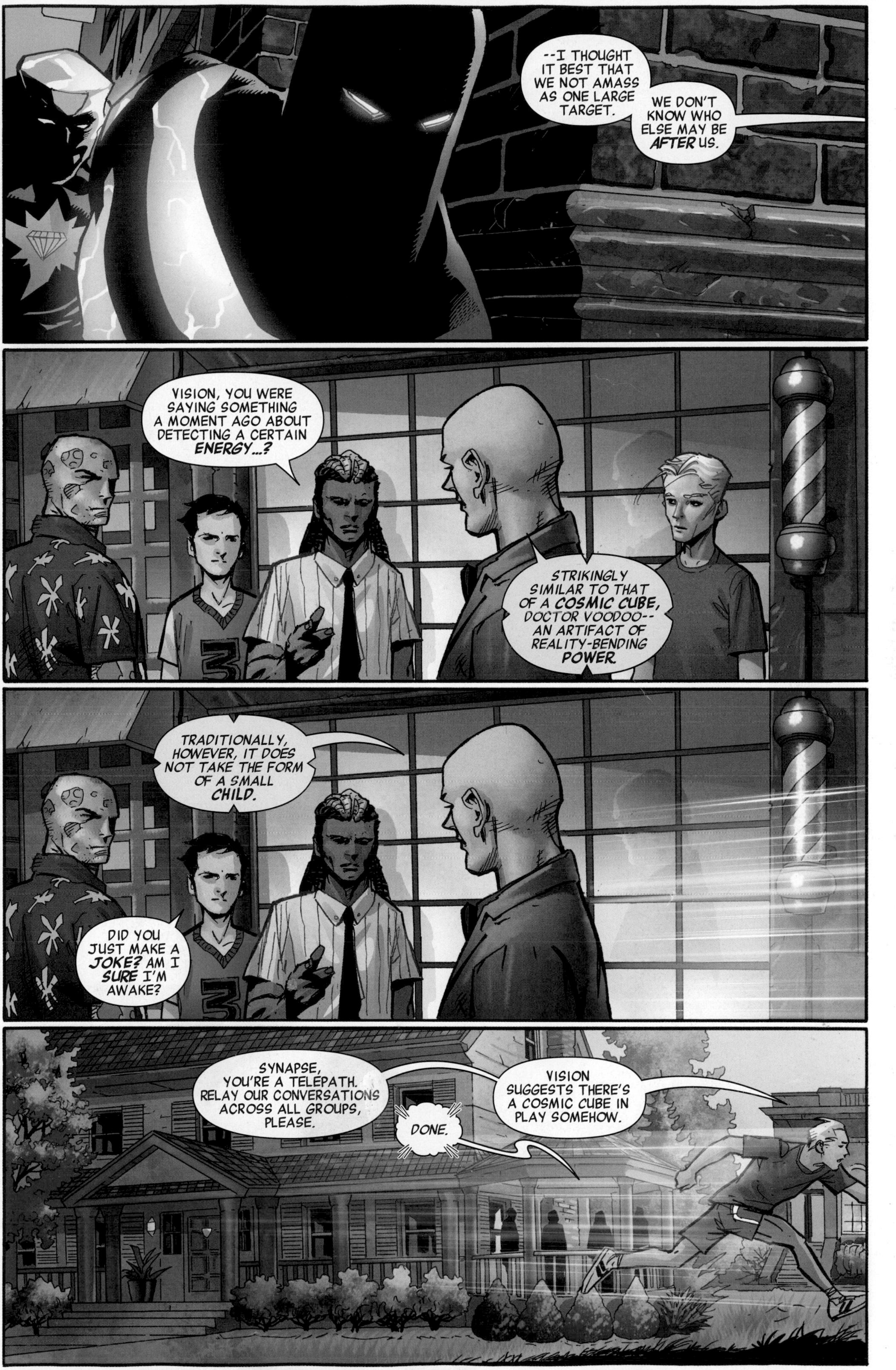
--I THOUGHT IT BEST THAT WE NOT AMASS AS ONE LARGE TARGET.
WE DON'T KNOW WHO ELSE MAY BE AFTER US.
VISION, YOU WERE SAYING SOMETHING A MOMENT AGO ABOUT DETECTING A CERTAIN ENERGY...?
STRIKINGLY SIMILAR TO THAT OF A COSMIC CUBE, DOCTOR VOODOO--AN ARTIFACT OF REALITY-BENDING POWER.
TRADITIONALLY, HOWEVER, IT DOES NOT TAKE THE FORM OF A SMALL CHILD.
DID YOU JUST MAKE A JOKE? AM I SURE I'M AWAKE?
SYNAPSE, YOU'RE A TELEPATH. RELAY OUR CONVERSATIONS ACROSS ALL GROUPS, PLEASE.
VISION SUGGESTS THERE'S A COSMIC CUBE IN PLAY SOMEHOW.
DONE.

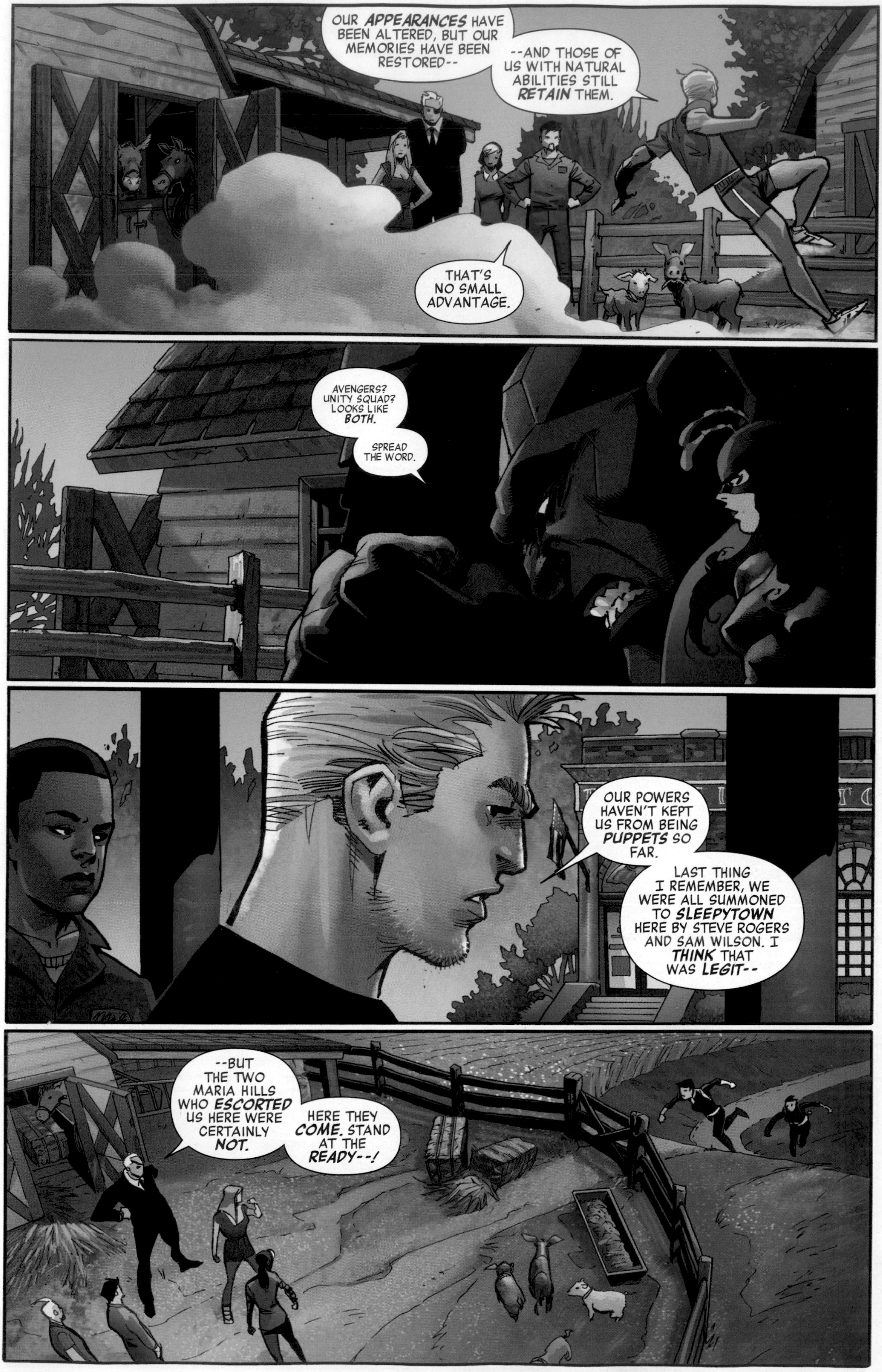
OUR APPEARANCES HAVE BEEN ALTERED, BUT OUR MEMORIES HAVE BEEN RESTORED--
--AND THOSE OF US WITH NATURAL ABILITIES STILL RETAIN THEM.
THAT'S NO SMALL ADVANTAGE.
AVENGERS? UNITY SQUAD? LOOKS LIKE BOTH.
SPREAD THE WORD.
OUR POWERS HAVEN'T KEPT US FROM BEING PUPPETS SO FAR.
LAST THING I REMEMBER, WE WERE ALL SUMMONED TO SLEEPYTOWN HERE BY STEVE ROGERS AND SAM WILSON. I THINK THAT WAS LEGIT--
--BUT THE TWO MARIA HILLS WHO ESCORTED US HERE WERE CERTAINLY NOT.
HERE THEY COME. STAND AT THE READY--!

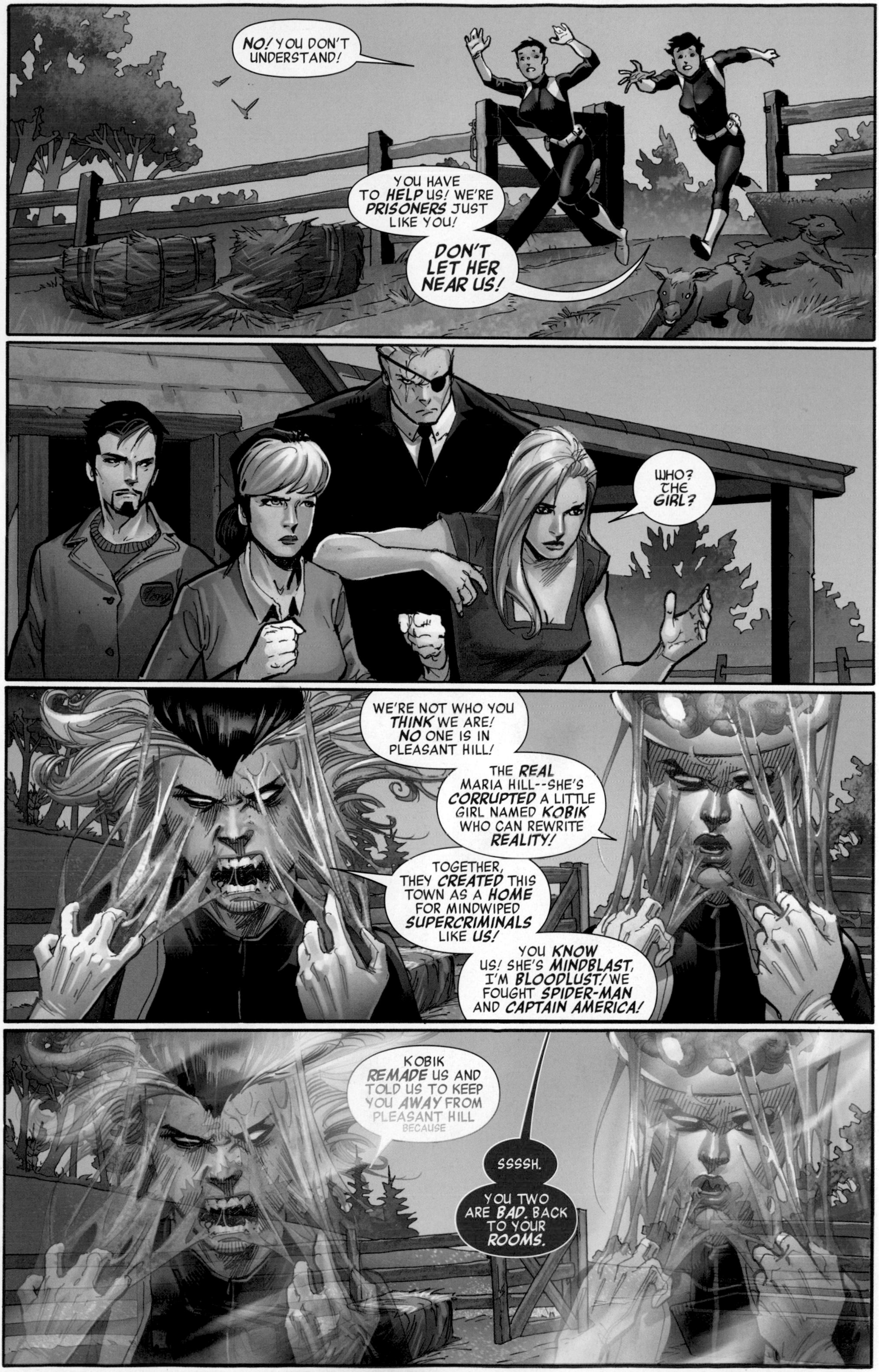

NO! YOU DON'T UNDERSTAND!
YOU HAVE TO HELP US! WE'RE PRISONERS JUST LIKE YOU!
DON'T LET HER NEAR US!
WHO? THE GIRL?
WE'RE NOT WHO YOU THINK WE ARE! NO ONE IS IN PLEASANT HILL!
THE REAL MARIA HILL--SHE'S CORRUPTED A LITTLE GIRL NAMED KOBIK WHO CAN REWRITE REALITY!
TOGETHER, THEY CREATED THIS TOWN AS A HOME FOR MINDWIPED SUPERCRIMINALS LIKE US!
YOU KNOW US! SHE'S MINDBLAST, I'M BLOODLUST! WE FOUGHT SPIDER-MAN AND CAPTAIN AMERICA!
KOBIK REMADE US AND TOLD US TO KEEP YOU AWAY FROM PLEASANT HILL BECAUSE
SSSSH.
YOU TWO ARE BAD. BACK TO YOUR ROOMS.

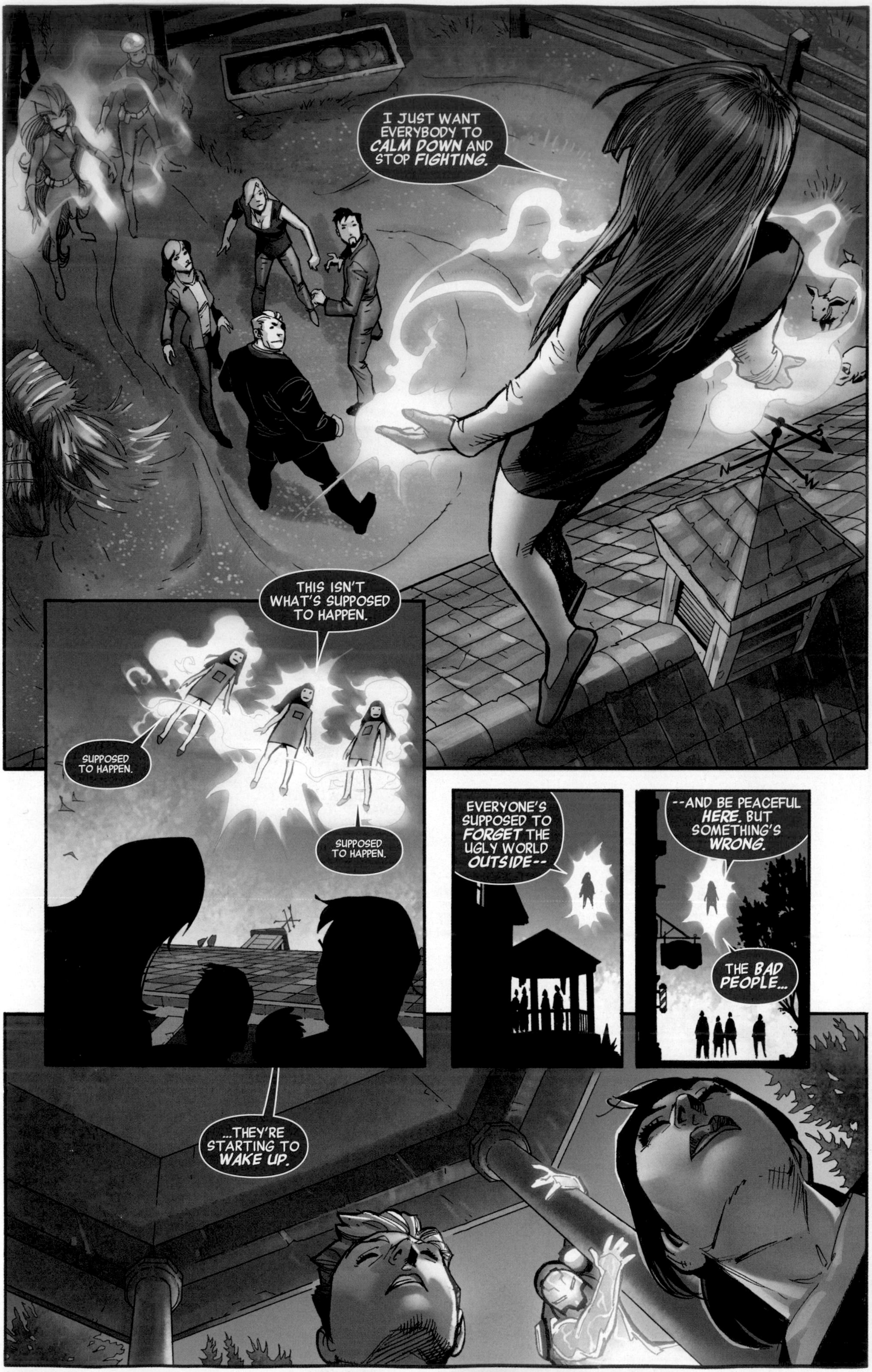
I JUST WANT EVERYBODY TO CALM DOWN AND STOP FIGHTING.
THIS ISN'T WHAT'S SUPPOSED TO HAPPEN.
SUPPOSED TO HAPPEN.
SUPPOSED TO HAPPEN.
EVERYONE'S SUPPOSED TO FORGET THE UGLY WORLD OUTSIDE--
--AND BE PEACEFUL HERE. BUT SOMETHING'S WRONG.
THE BAD PEOPLE...
...THEY'RE STARTING TO WAKE UP.

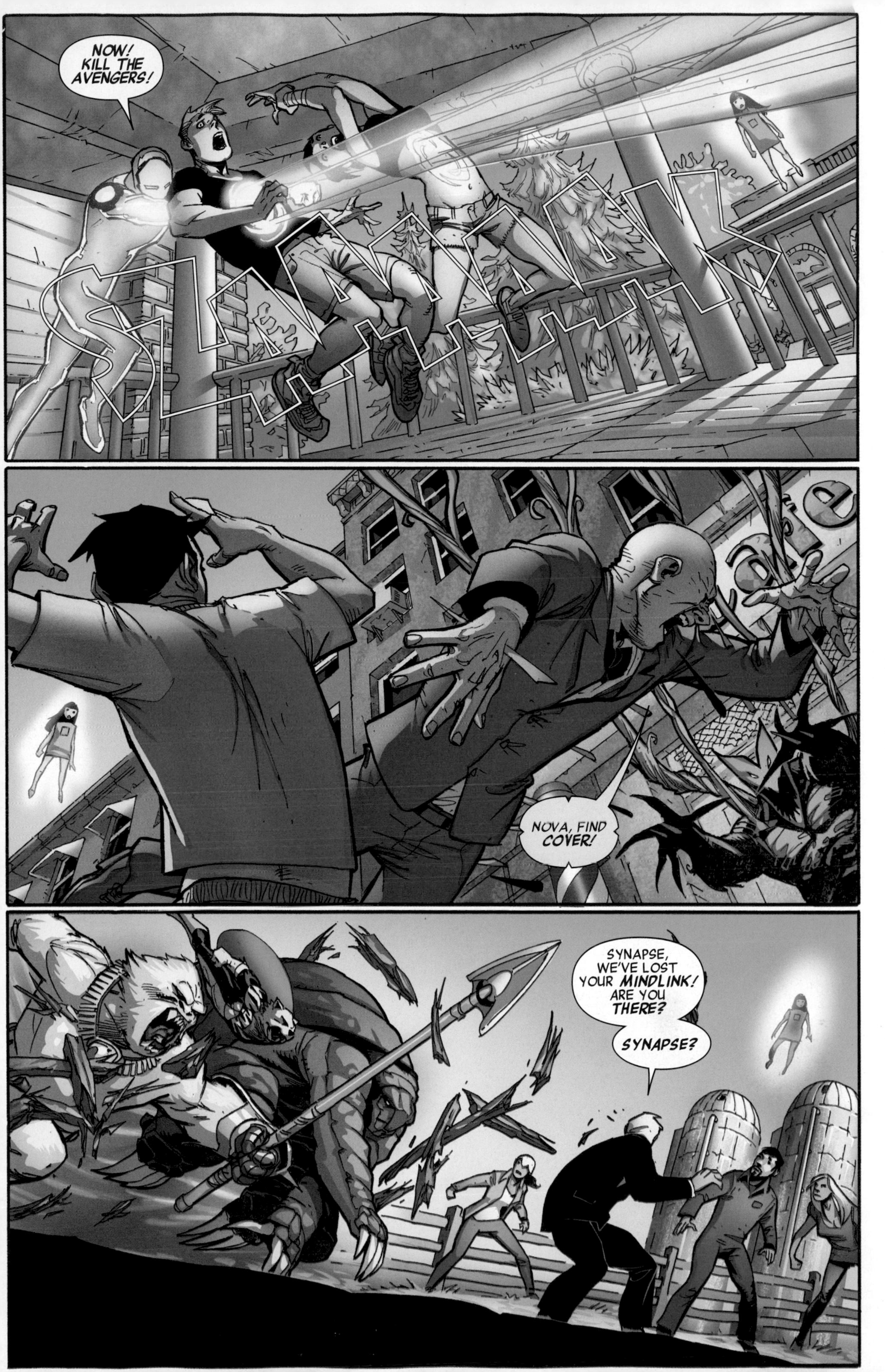
NOW! KILL THE AVENGERS!
NOVA, FIND COVER!
SYNAPSE, WE'VE LOST YOUR MINDLINK! ARE YOU THERE?
SYNAPSE?

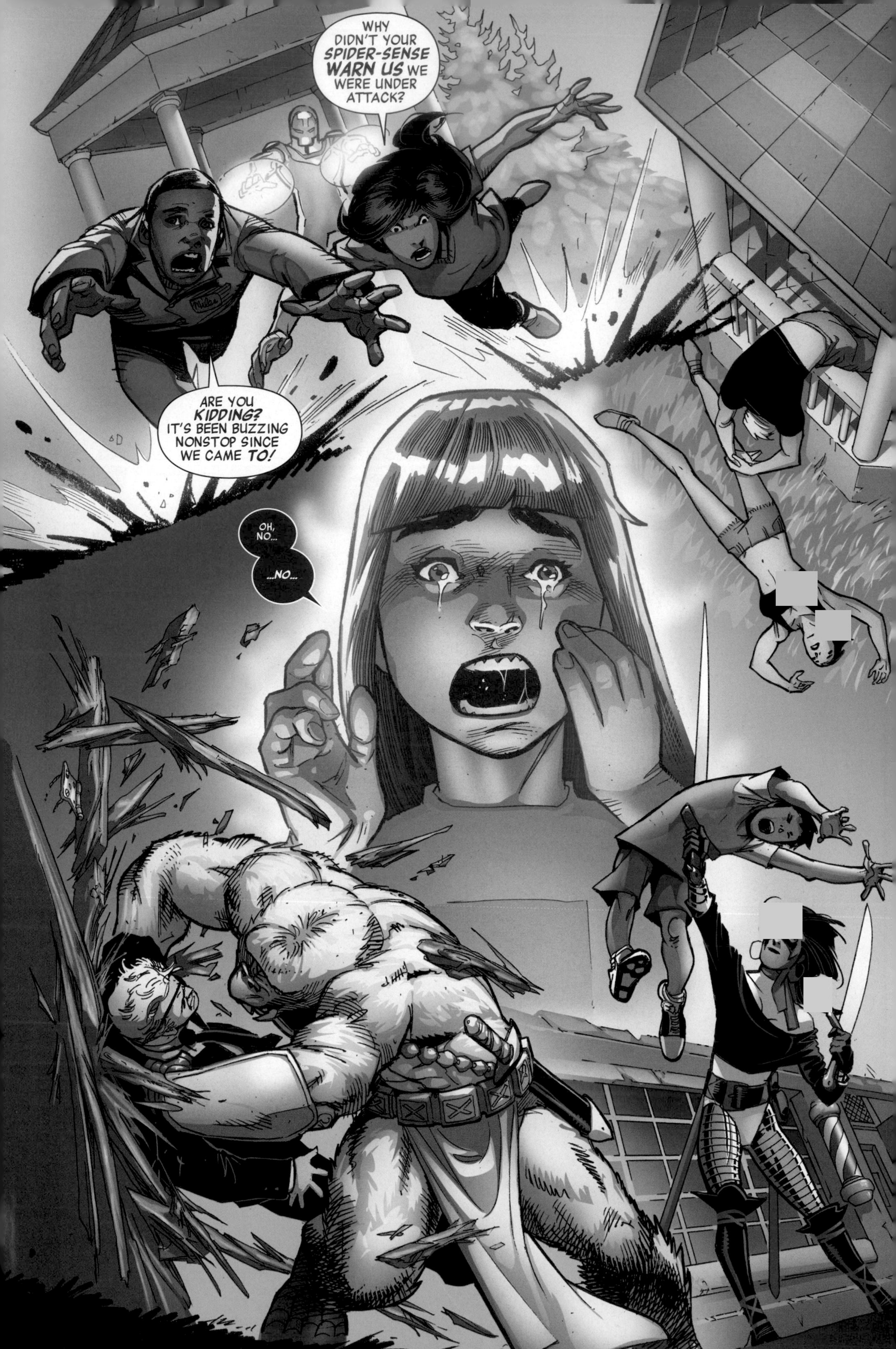
WHY DIDN'T YOUR SPIDER-SENSE WARN US WE WERE UNDER ATTACK?
ARE YOU KIDDING? IT'S BEEN BUZZING NONSTOP SINCE WE CAME TO!
OH, NO...
...NO...

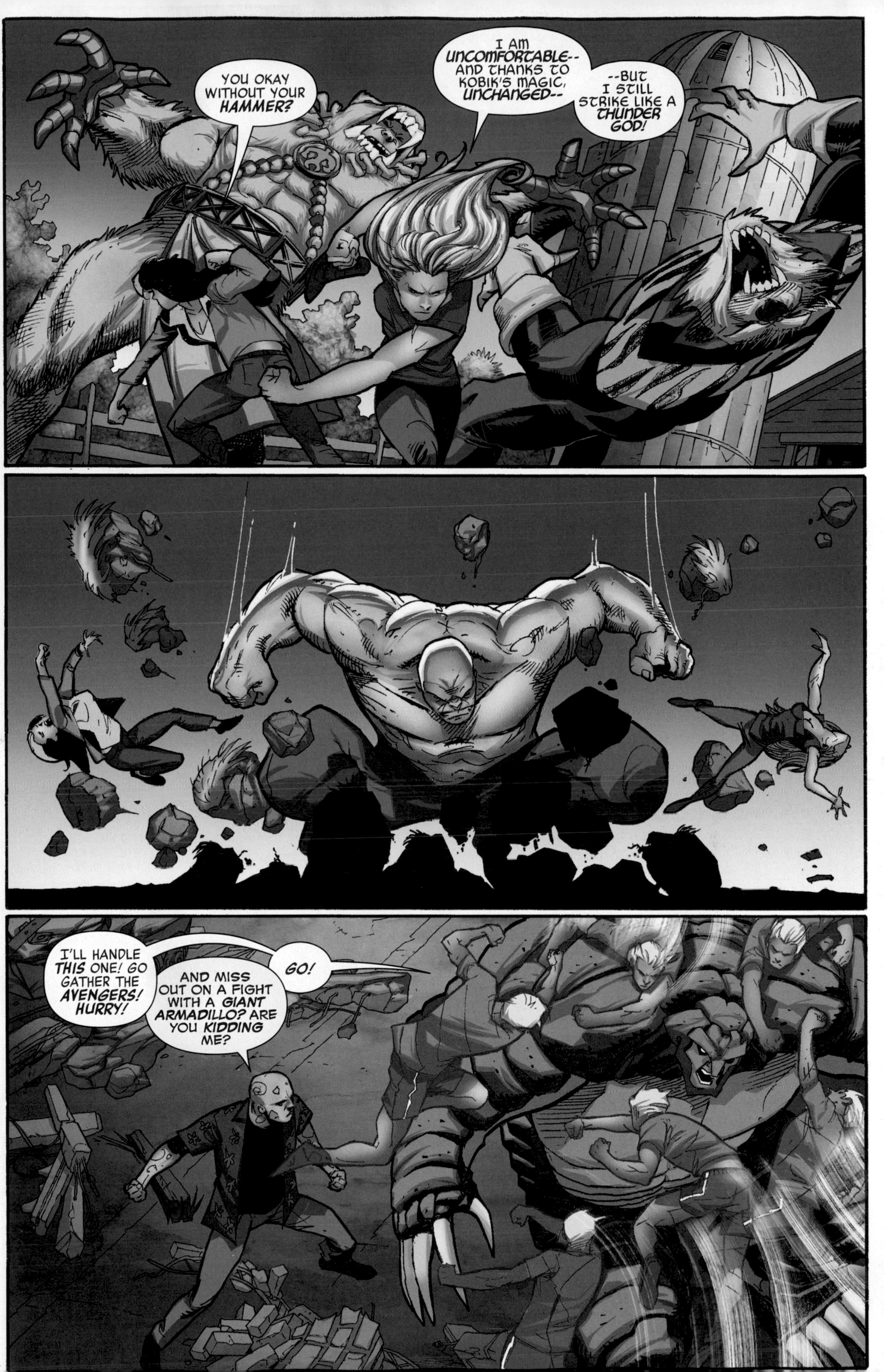
YOU OKAY WITHOUT YOUR HAMMER?
I AM UNCOMFORTABLE-- AND THANKS TO KOBIK'S MAGIC, UNCHANGED--
--BUT I STILL STRIKE LIKE A THUNDER GOD!
I'LL HANDLE THIS ONE! GO GATHER THE AVENGERS! HURRY!
AND MISS OUT ON A FIGHT WITH A GIANT ARMADILLO? ARE YOU KIDDING ME?
GO!

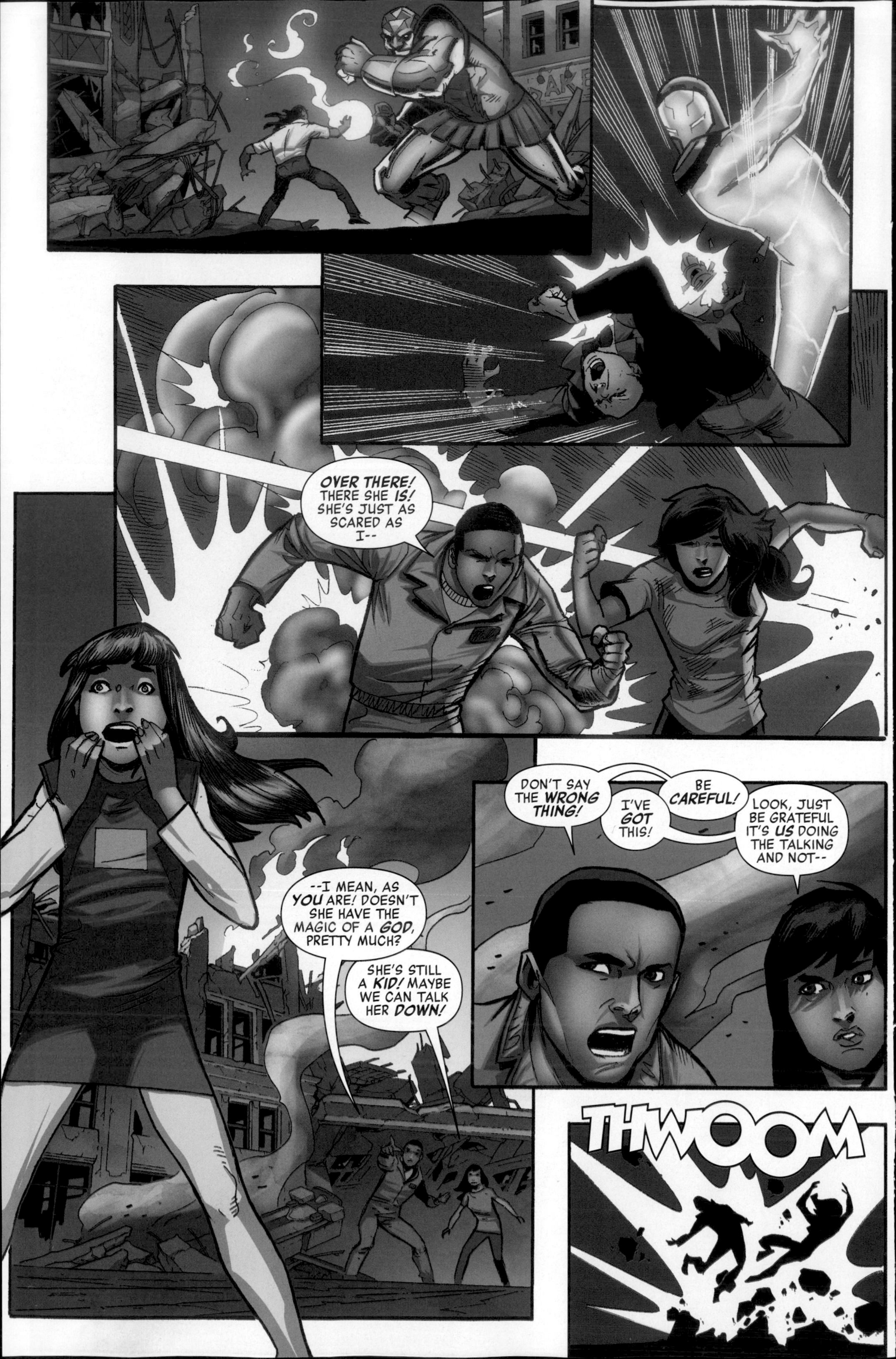
OVER THERE! THERE SHE IS! SHE'S JUST AS SCARED AS I--
--I MEAN, AS YOU ARE! DOESN'T SHE HAVE THE MAGIC OF A GOD, PRETTY MUCH?
SHE'S STILL A KID! MAYBE WE CAN TALK HER DOWN!
DON'T SAY THE WRONG THING!
I'VE GOT THIS!
BE CAREFUL!
LOOK, JUST BE GRATEFUL IT'S US DOING THE TALKING AND NOT--
THWOOM

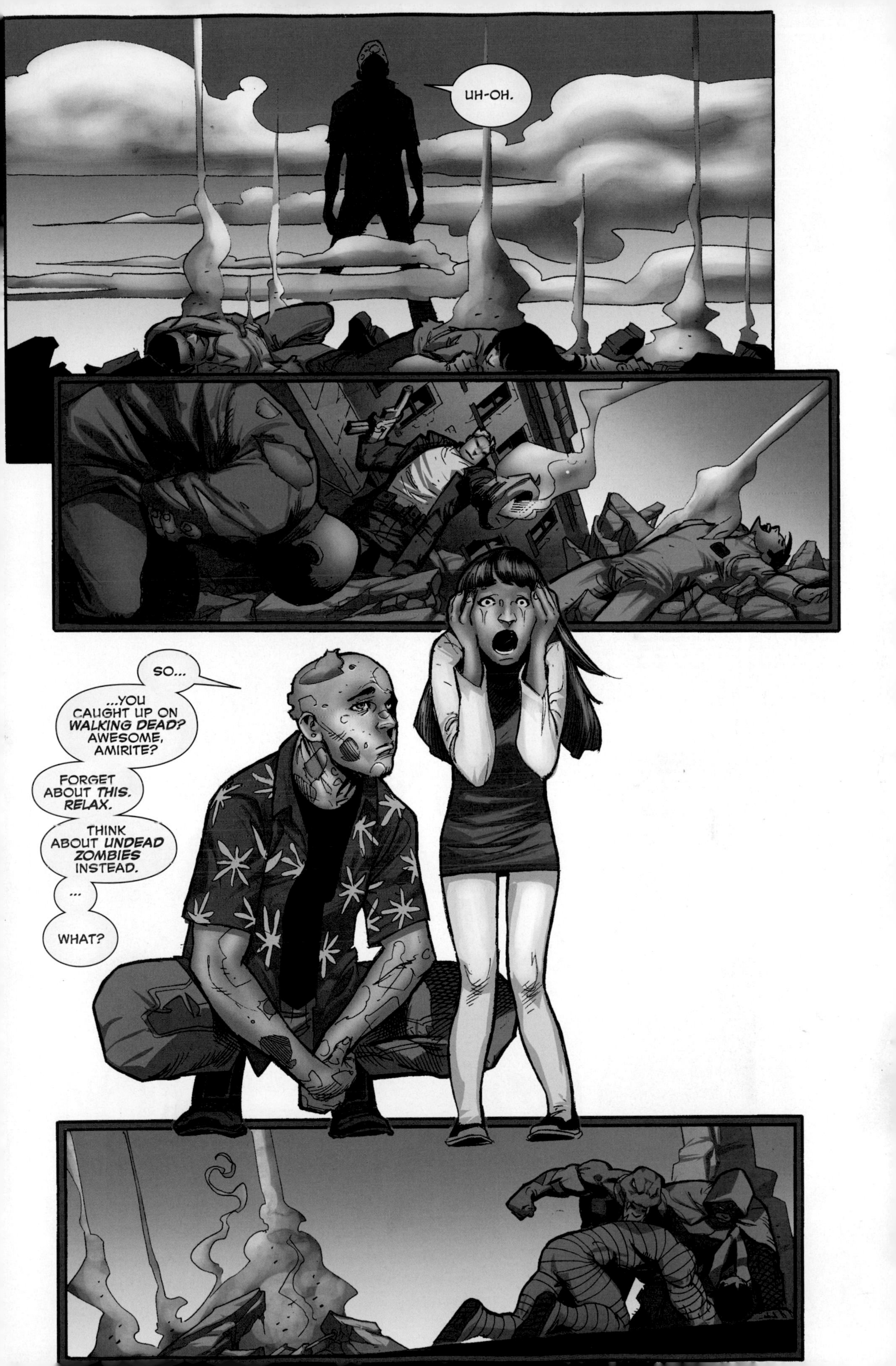
UH-OH.
SO...
...YOU CAUGHT UP ON *WALKING DEAD?* AWESOME, AMIRITE?
FORGET ABOUT *THIS. RELAX.*
THINK ABOUT *UNDEAD ZOMBIES* INSTEAD.
...
WHAT?

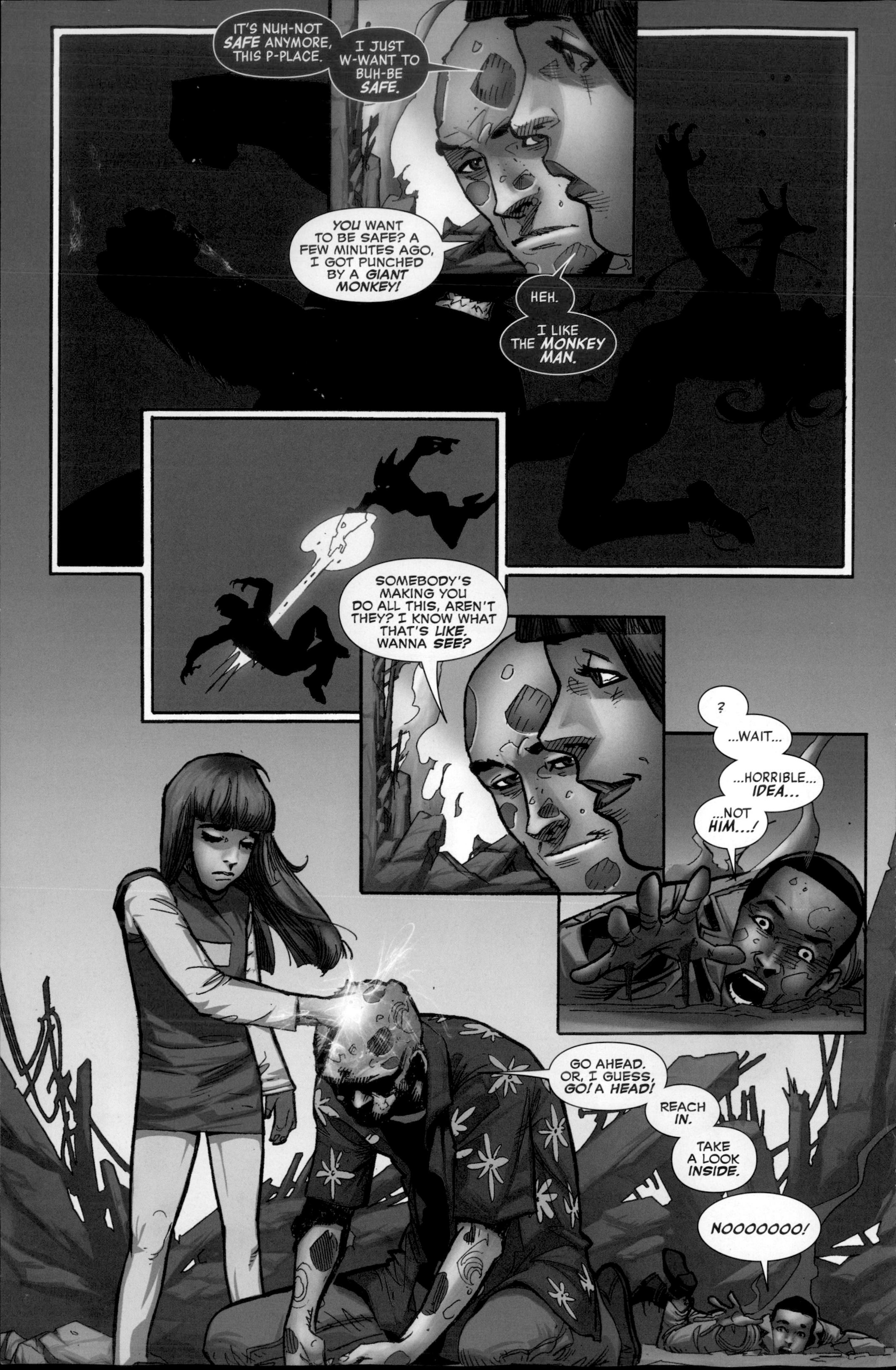
IT'S NUH-NOT SAFE ANYMORE, THIS P-PLACE.
I JUST W-WANT TO BUH-BE SAFE.
YOU WANT TO BE SAFE? A FEW MINUTES AGO, I GOT PUNCHED BY A GIANT MONKEY!
HEH.
I LIKE THE MONKEY MAN.
SOMEBODY'S MAKING YOU DO ALL THIS, AREN'T THEY? I KNOW WHAT THAT'S LIKE. WANNA SEE?
?
...WAIT...
...HORRIBLE... IDEA...
...NOT HIM...!
GO AHEAD. OR, I GUESS, GO! A HEAD!
REACH IN.
TAKE A LOOK INSIDE.
NOOOOOOO!

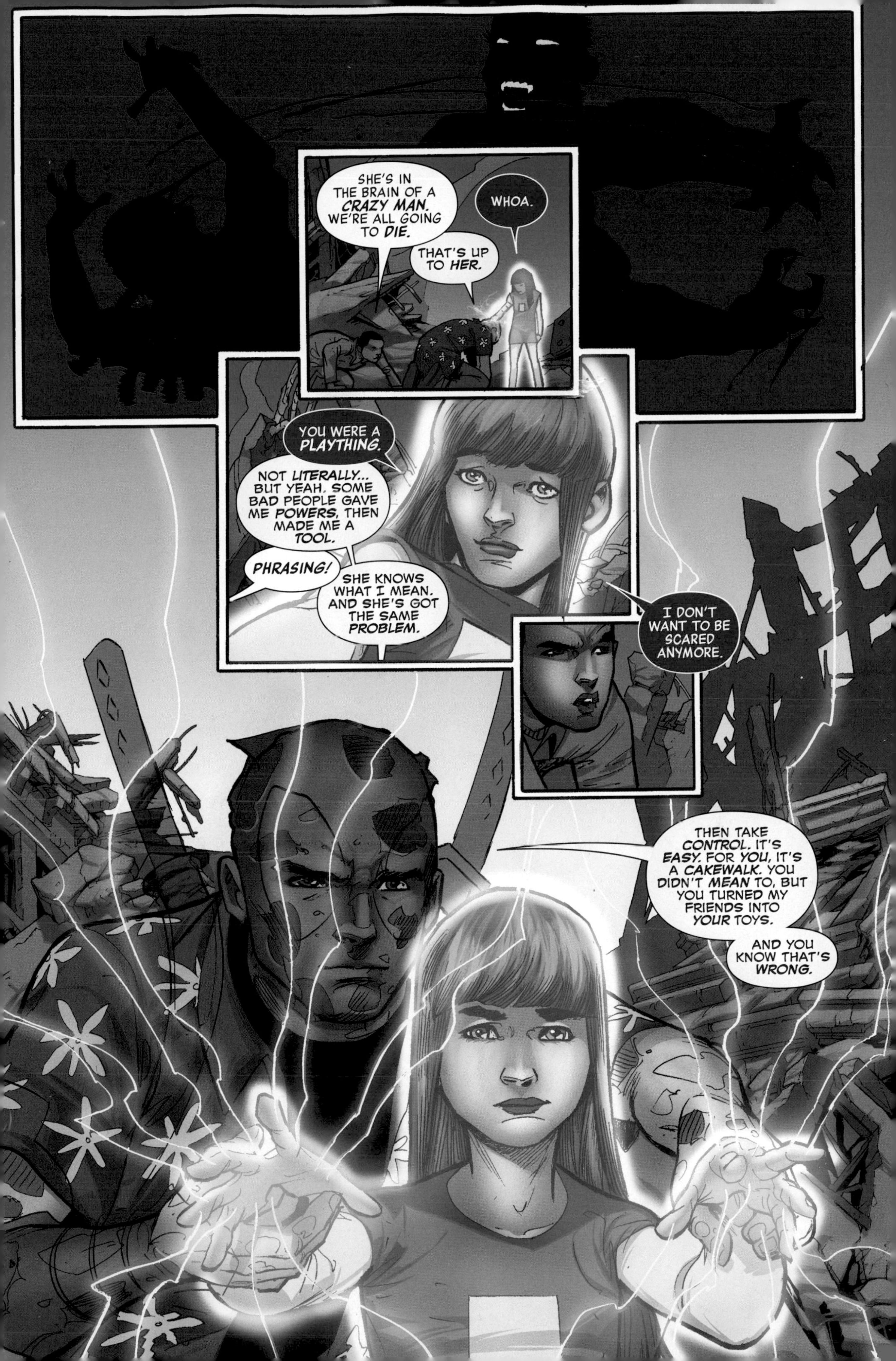
SHE'S IN THE BRAIN OF A CRAZY MAN. WE'RE ALL GOING TO DIE.
WHOA.
THAT'S UP TO HER.
YOU WERE A PLAYTHING.
NOT LITERALLY... BUT YEAH. SOME BAD PEOPLE GAVE ME POWERS, THEN MADE ME A TOOL.
PHRASING!
SHE KNOWS WHAT I MEAN. AND SHE'S GOT THE SAME PROBLEM.
I DON'T WANT TO BE SCARED ANYMORE.
THEN TAKE CONTROL. IT'S EASY. FOR YOU, IT'S A CAKEWALK. YOU DIDN'T MEAN TO, BUT YOU TURNED MY FRIENDS INTO YOUR TOYS.
AND YOU KNOW THAT'S WRONG.

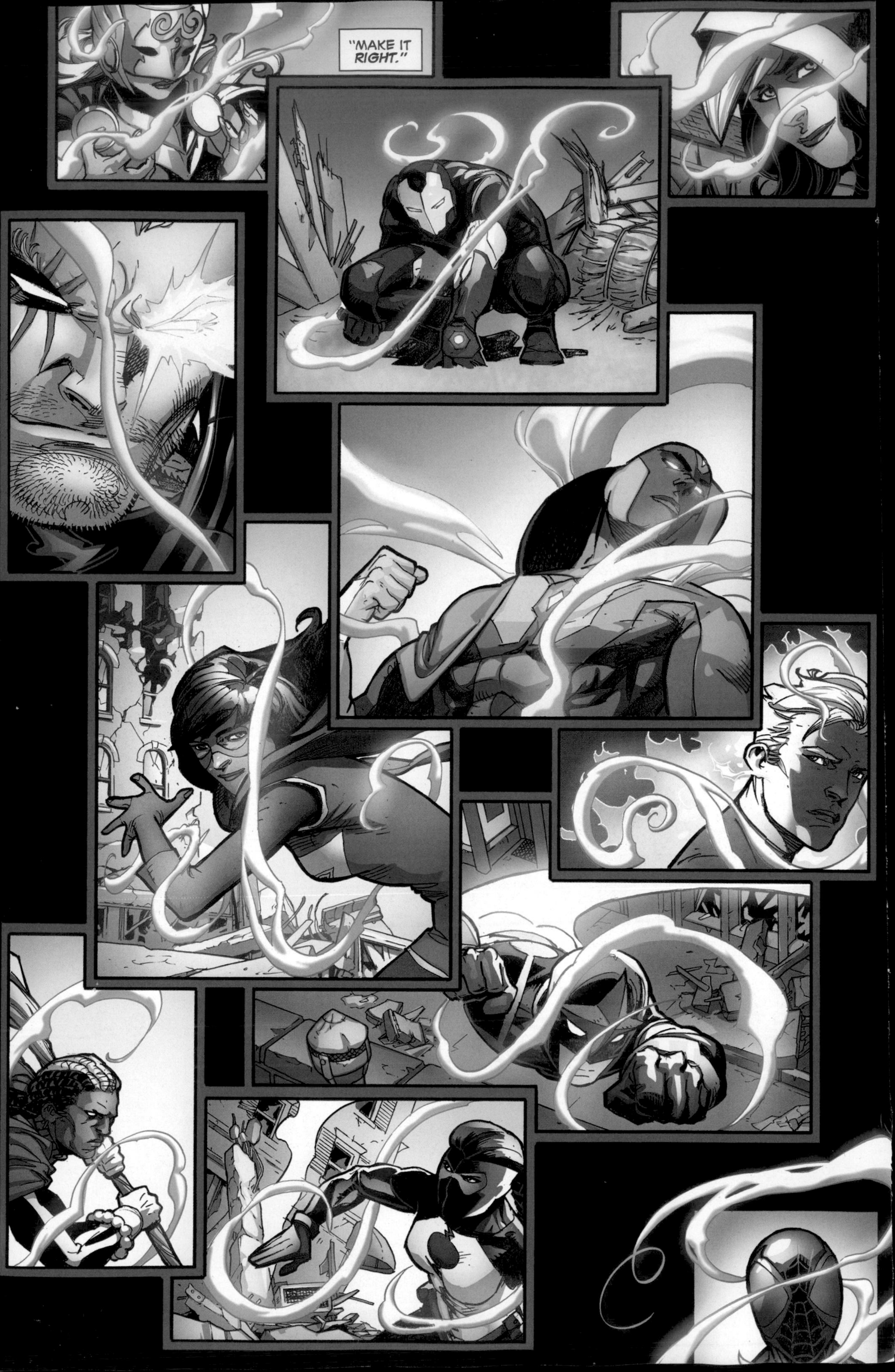
"MAKE IT RIGHT."

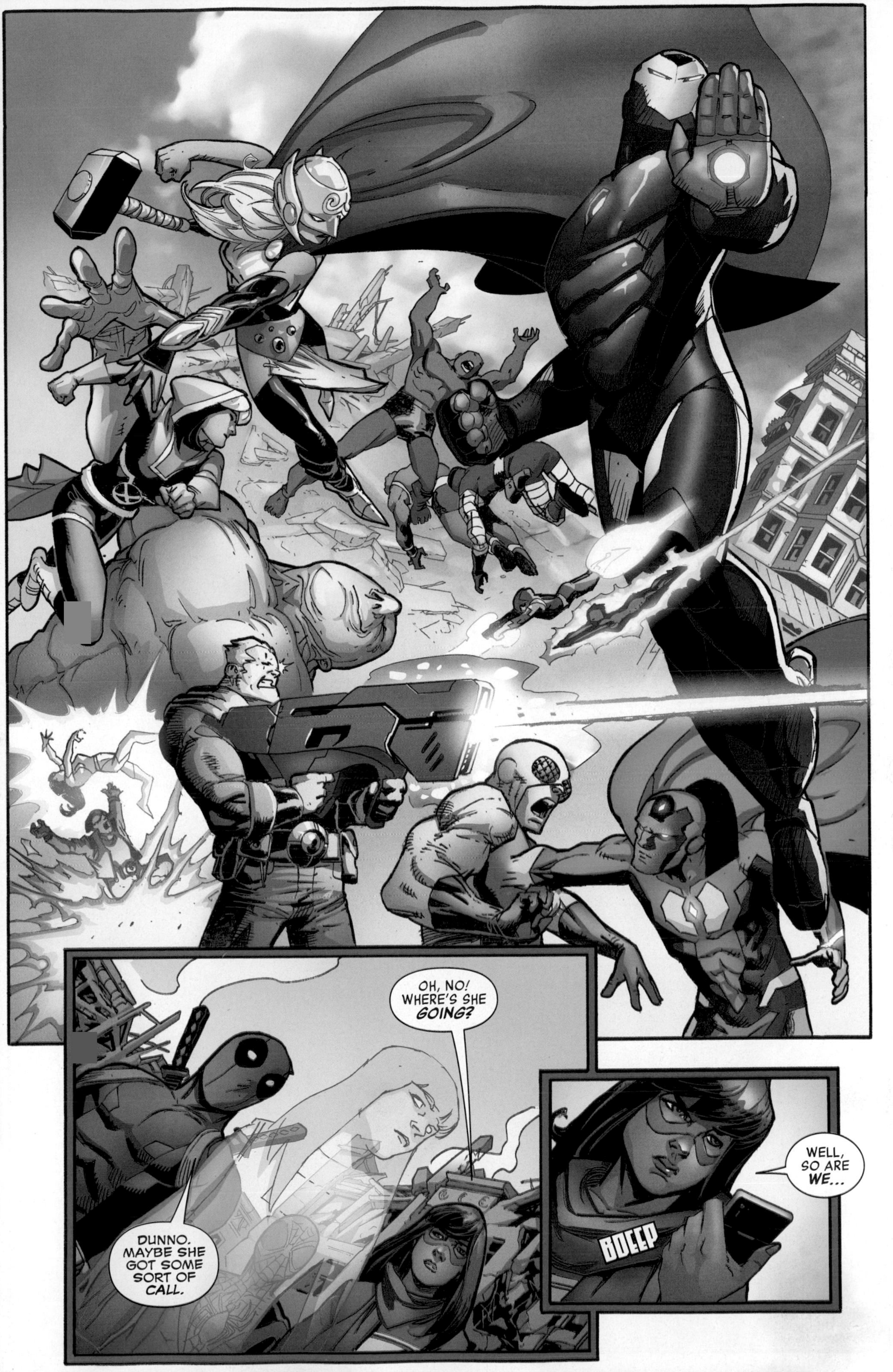
OH, NO! WHERE'S SHE GOING?
DUNNO. MAYBE SHE GOT SOME SORT OF CALL.
BDEEP
WELL, SO ARE WE...

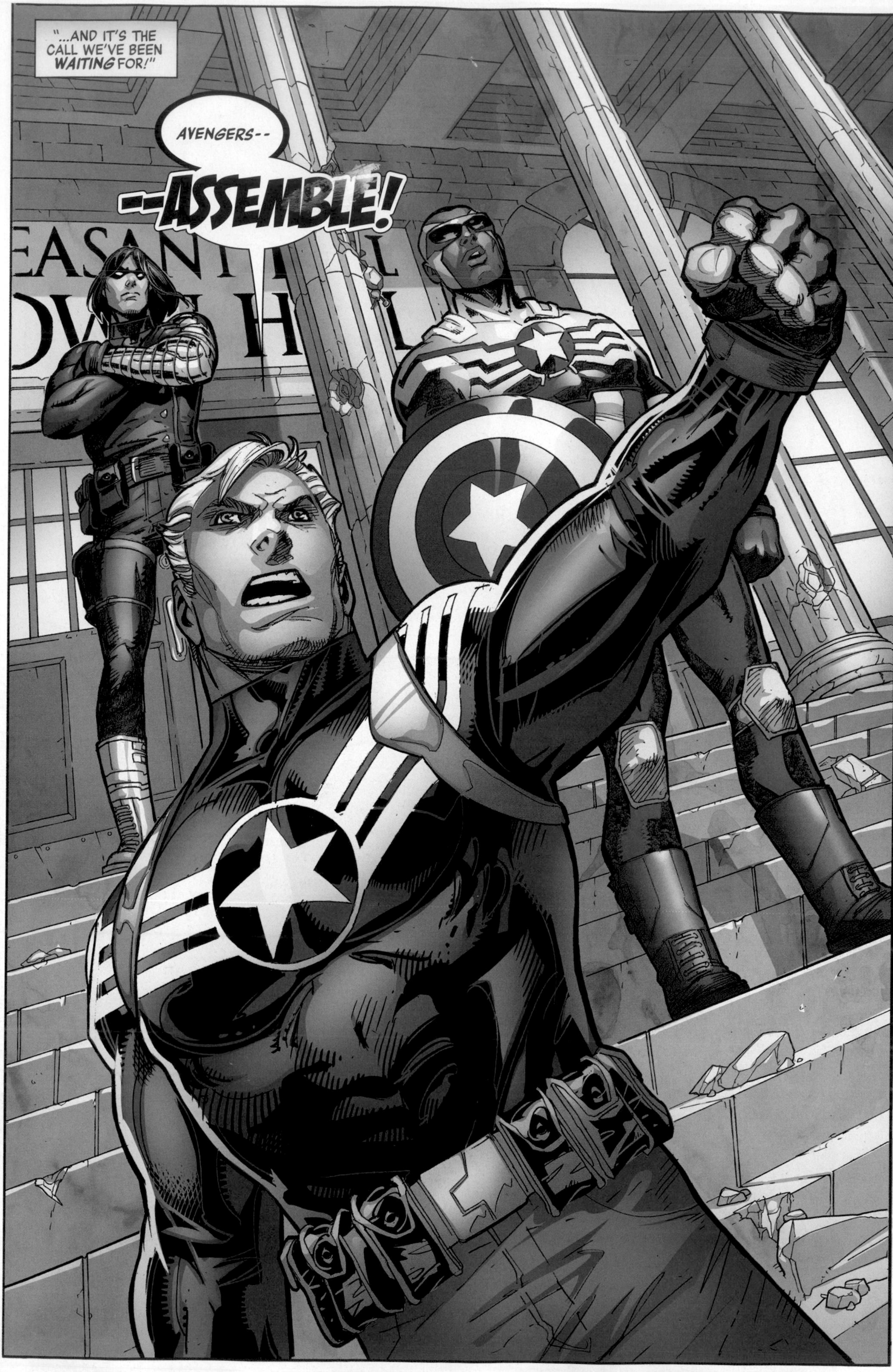
"...AND IT'S THE CALL WE'VE BEEN WAITING FOR!"
AVENGERS--
--ASSEMBLE!

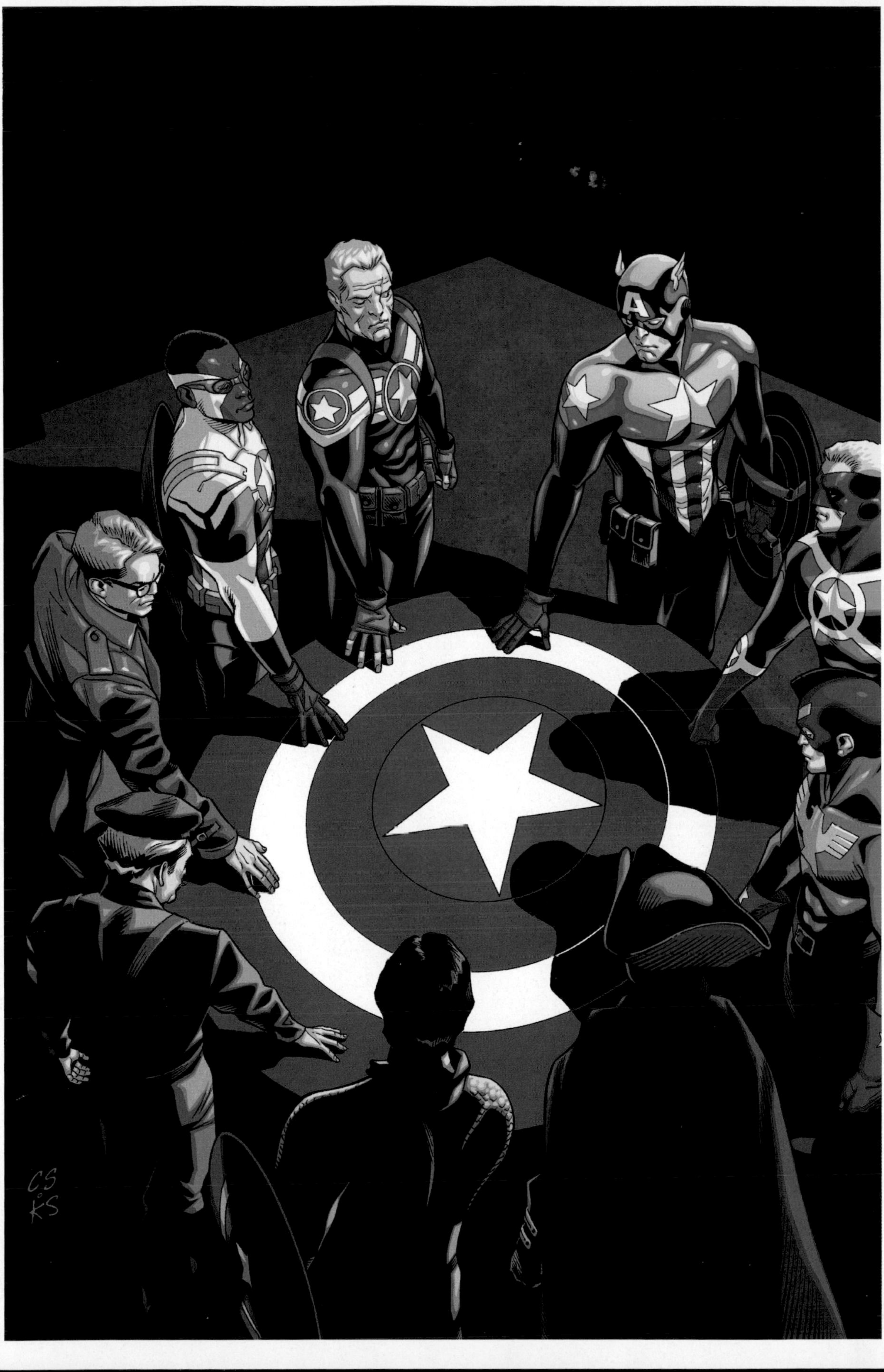
CS
KS

Captain America: Sam Wilson No. 7 variant by

CHRIS SPROUSE, KARL STORY & DAVE McCAIG

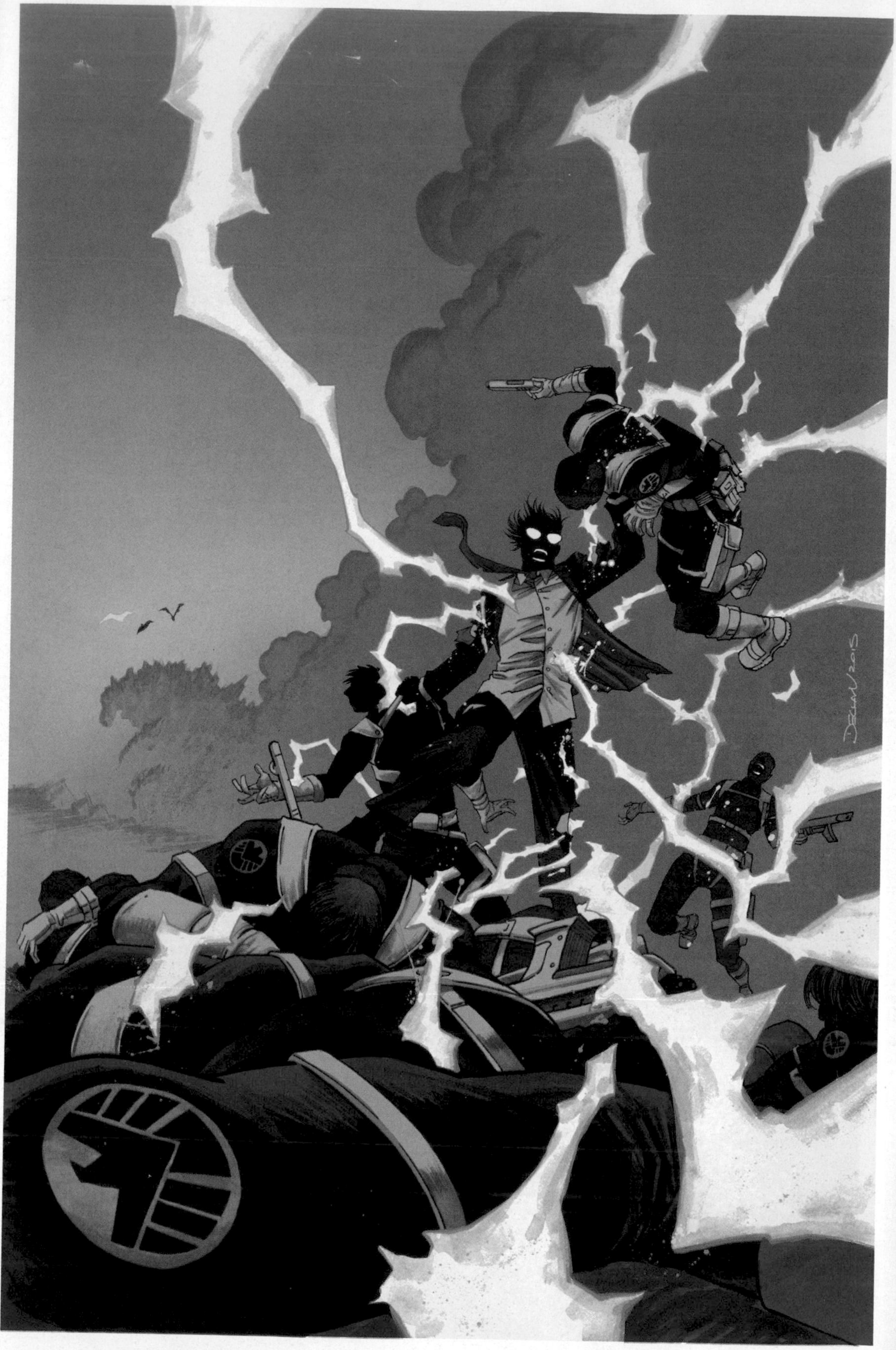

New Avengers No. 10

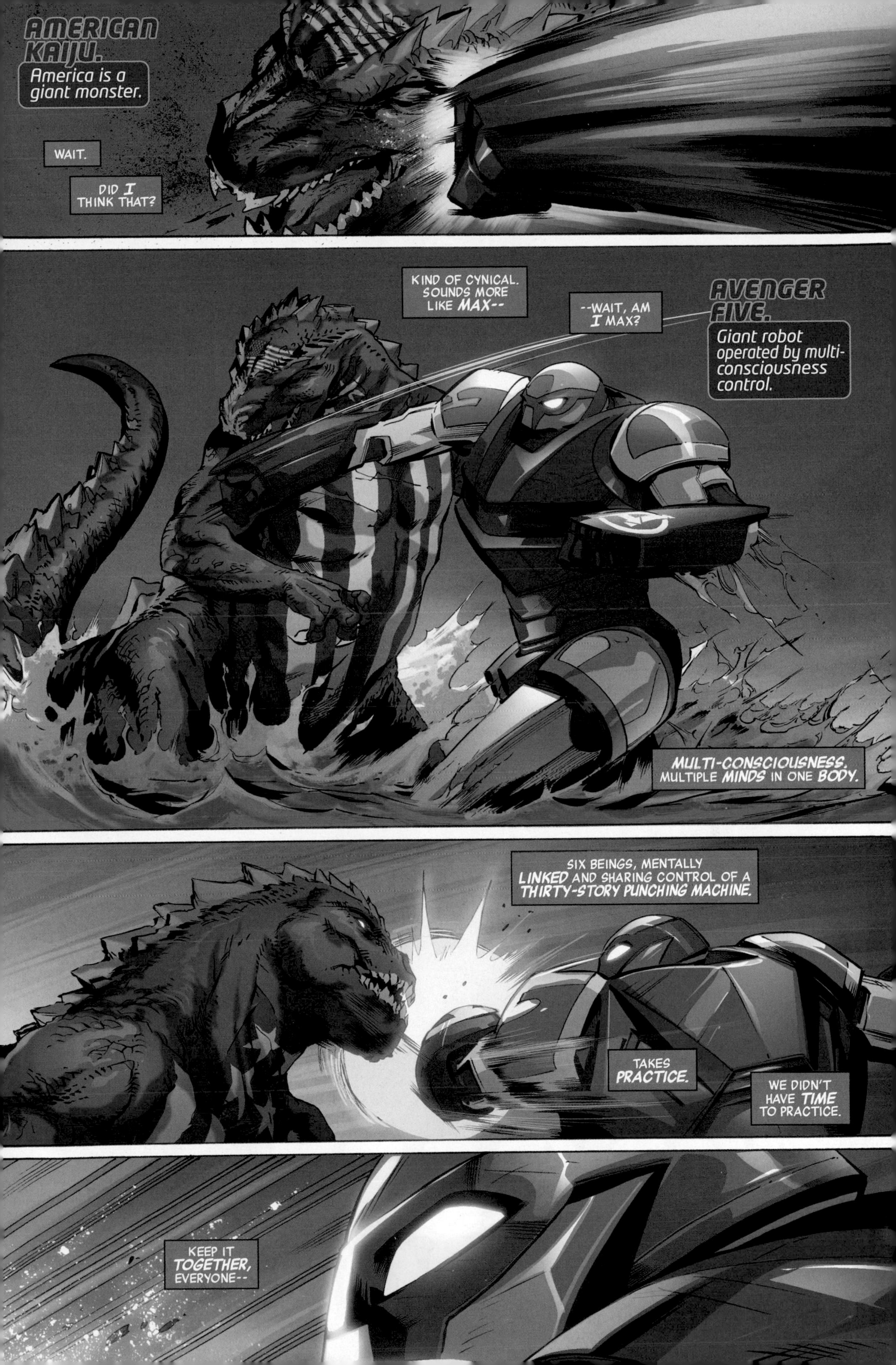
AMERICAN KAIJU.
America is a giant monster.
WAIT.
DID I THINK THAT?
KIND OF CYNICAL. SOUNDS MORE LIKE MAX--
--WAIT, AM I MAX?
AVENGER FIVE.
Giant robot operated by multi-consciousness control.
MULTI-CONSCIOUSNESS. MULTIPLE MINDS IN ONE BODY.
SIX BEINGS, MENTALLY LINKED AND SHARING CONTROL OF A THIRTY-STORY PUNCHING MACHINE.
TAKES PRACTICE.
WE DIDN'T HAVE TIME TO PRACTICE.
KEEP IT TOGETHER, EVERYONE--

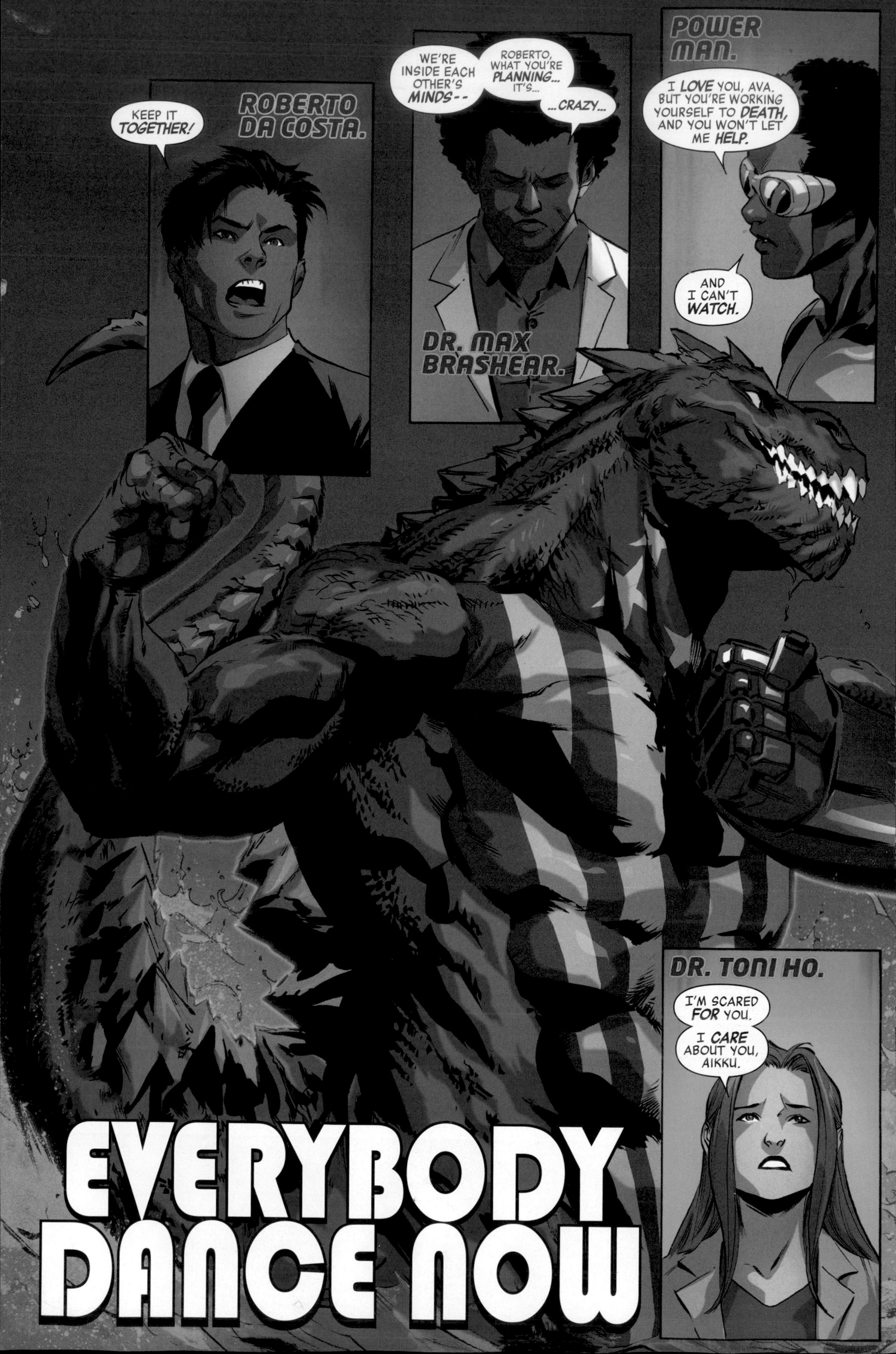
ROBERTO DA COSTA.
KEEP IT TOGETHER!
WE'RE INSIDE EACH OTHER'S MINDS--
ROBERTO, WHAT YOU'RE PLANNING... IT'S...
...CRAZY...
DR. MAX BRASHEAR.
POWER MAN.
I LOVE YOU, AVA. BUT YOU'RE WORKING YOURSELF TO DEATH, AND YOU WON'T LET ME HELP.
AND I CAN'T WATCH.
DR. TONI HO.
I'M SCARED FOR YOU.
I CARE ABOUT YOU, AIKKU.
EVERYBODY DANCE NOW

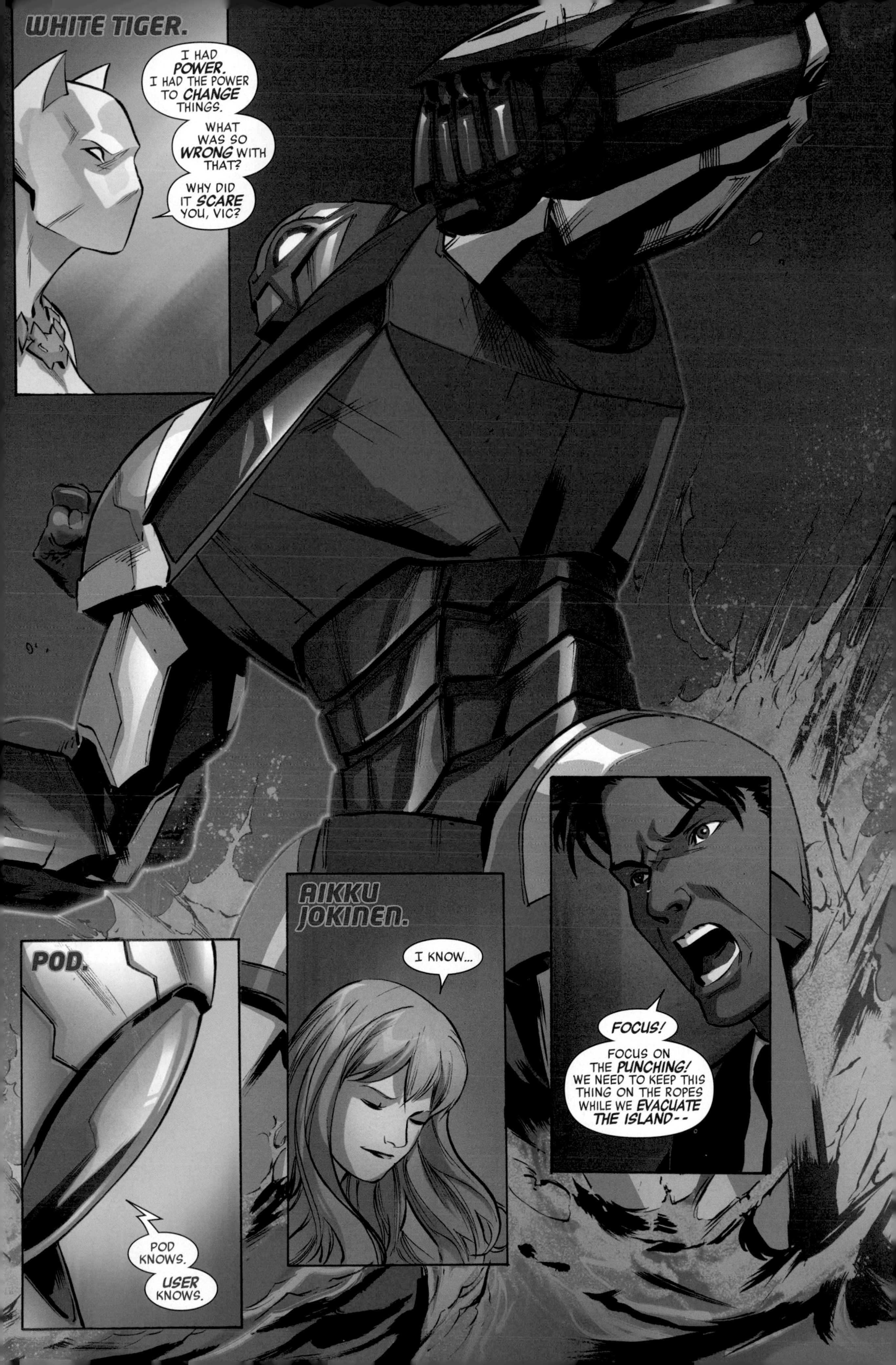
WHITE TIGER.
I HAD POWER. I HAD THE POWER TO CHANGE THINGS.
WHAT WAS SO WRONG WITH THAT?
WHY DID IT SCARE YOU, VIC?
POD.
POD KNOWS.
USER KNOWS.
AIKKU JOKINEN.
I KNOW...
FOCUS!
FOCUS ON THE PUNCHING! WE NEED TO KEEP THIS THING ON THE ROPES WHILE WE EVACUATE THE ISLAND--

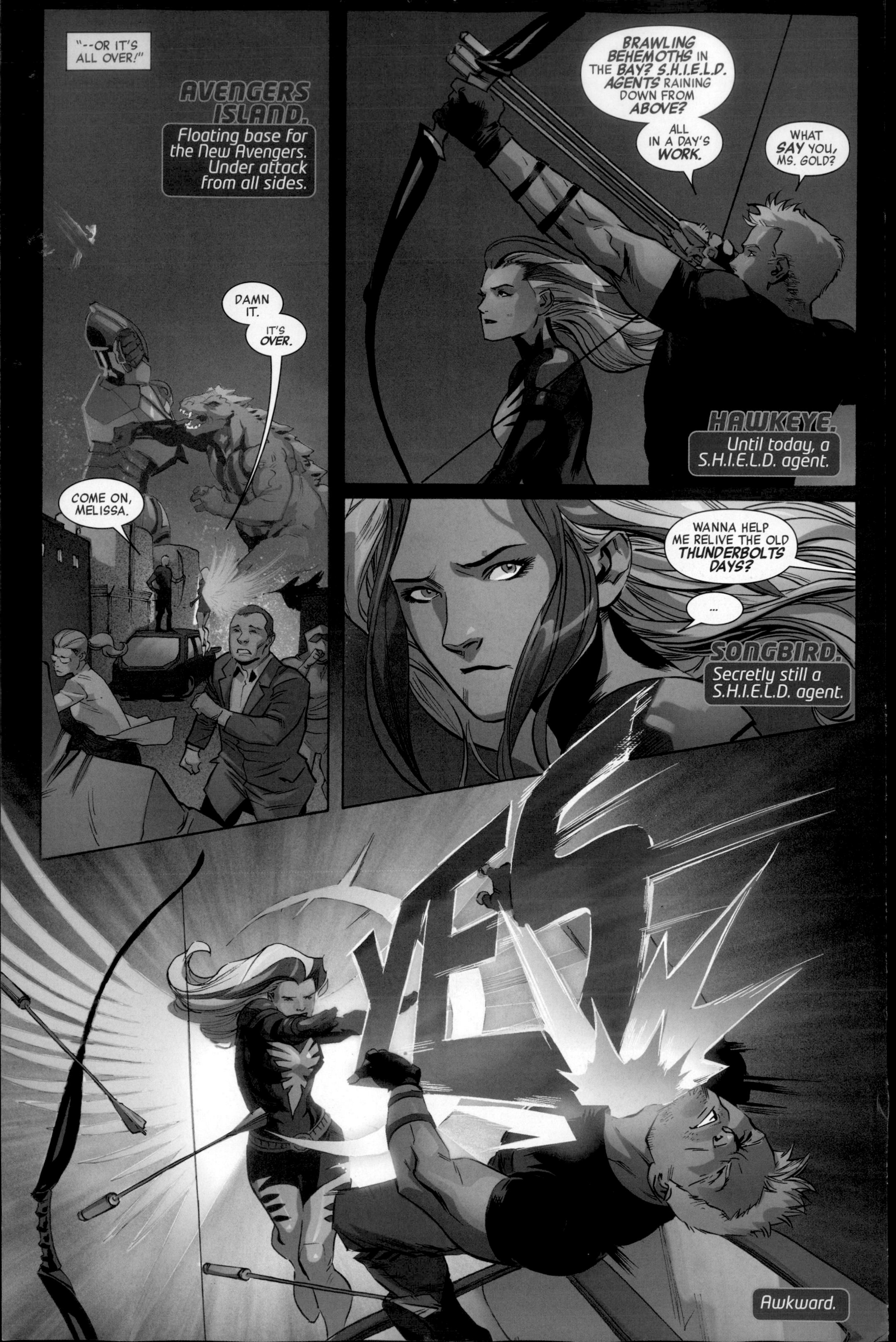

"--OR IT'S ALL OVER!"
AVENGERS ISLAND.
Floating base for the New Avengers. Under attack from all sides.
DAMN IT.
IT'S OVER.
COME ON, MELISSA.
BRAWLING BEHEMOTHS IN THE BAY? S.H.I.E.L.D. AGENTS RAINING DOWN FROM ABOVE?
ALL IN A DAY'S WORK.
WHAT SAY YOU, MS. GOLD?
HAWKEYE.
Until today, a S.H.I.E.L.D. agent.
WANNA HELP ME RELIVE THE OLD THUNDERBOLTS DAYS?
...
SONGBIRD.
Secretly still a S.H.I.E.L.D. agent.
YES!
Awkward.

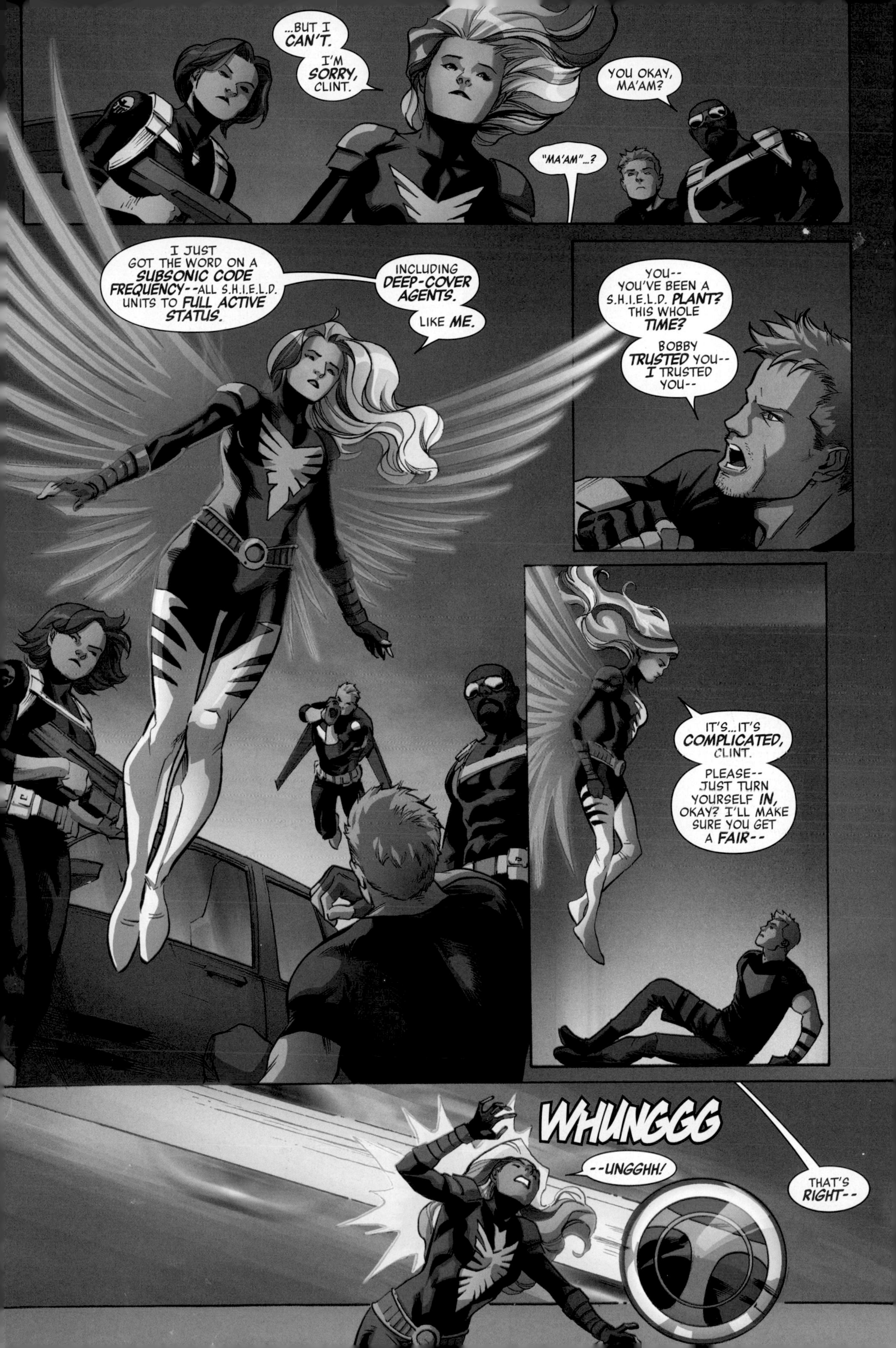
...BUT I CAN'T.
I'M SORRY, CLINT.
YOU OKAY, MA'AM?
"MA'AM"...?
I JUST GOT THE WORD ON A SUBSONIC CODE FREQUENCY--ALL S.H.I.E.L.D. UNITS TO FULL ACTIVE STATUS.
INCLUDING DEEP-COVER AGENTS.
LIKE ME.
YOU-- YOU'VE BEEN A S.H.I.E.L.D. PLANT? THIS WHOLE TIME?
BOBBY TRUSTED YOU-- I TRUSTED YOU--
IT'S...IT'S COMPLICATED, CLINT.
PLEASE-- JUST TURN YOURSELF IN, OKAY? I'LL MAKE SURE YOU GET A FAIR--
WHUNGGG
--UNGGHH!
THAT'S RIGHT--

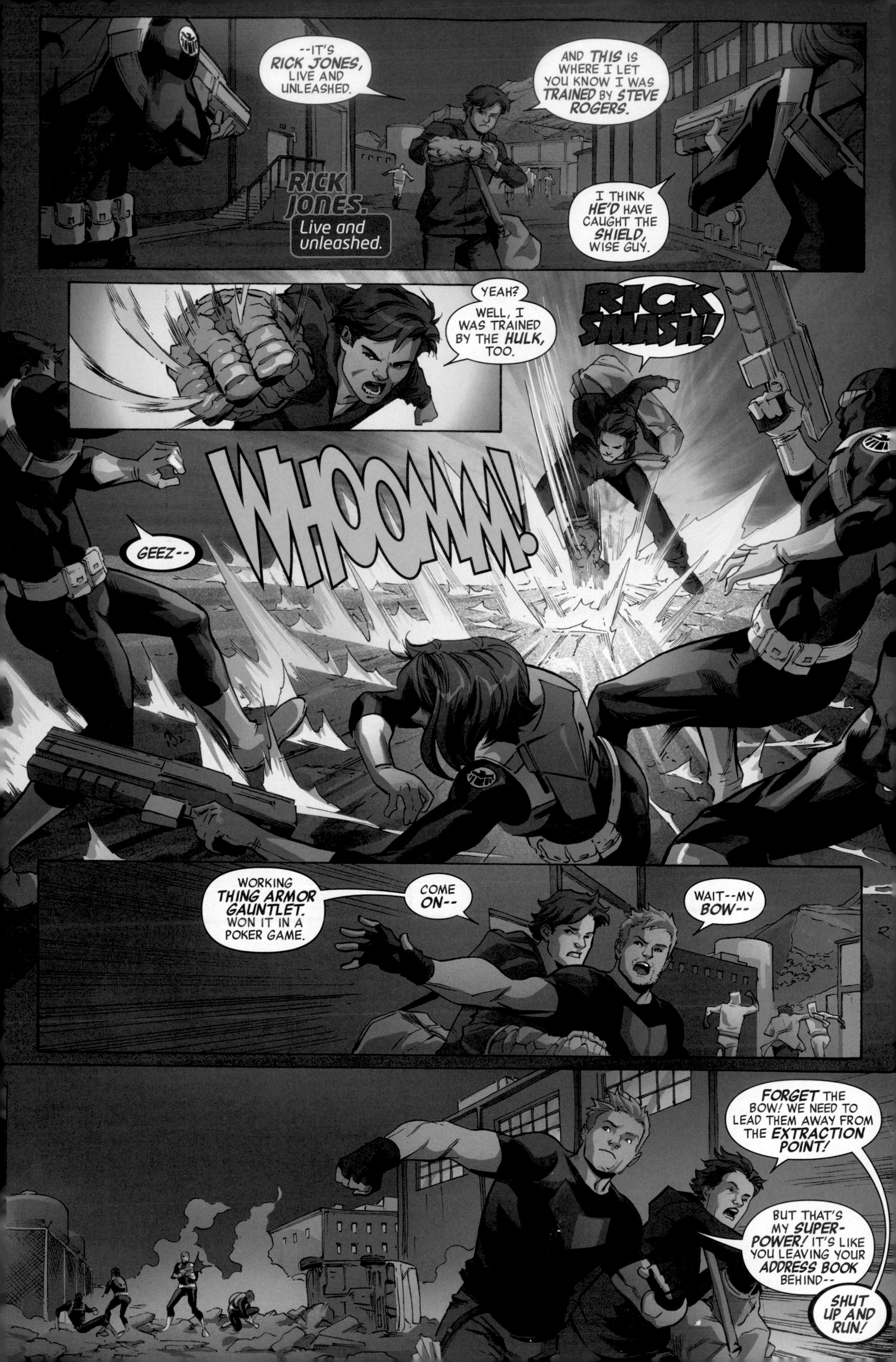
--IT'S RICK JONES, LIVE AND UNLEASHED.
AND THIS IS WHERE I LET YOU KNOW I WAS TRAINED BY STEVE ROGERS.
RICK JONES.
Live and unleashed.
I THINK HE'D HAVE CAUGHT THE SHIELD, WISE GUY.
YEAH?
WELL, I WAS TRAINED BY THE HULK, TOO.
RICK SMASH!
WHOOMM!
GEEZ--
WORKING THING ARMOR GAUNTLET. WON IT IN A POKER GAME.
COME ON--
WAIT--MY BOW--
FORGET THE BOW! WE NEED TO LEAD THEM AWAY FROM THE EXTRACTION POINT!
BUT THAT'S MY SUPER-POWER! IT'S LIKE YOU LEAVING YOUR ADDRESS BOOK BEHIND--
SHUT UP AND RUN!

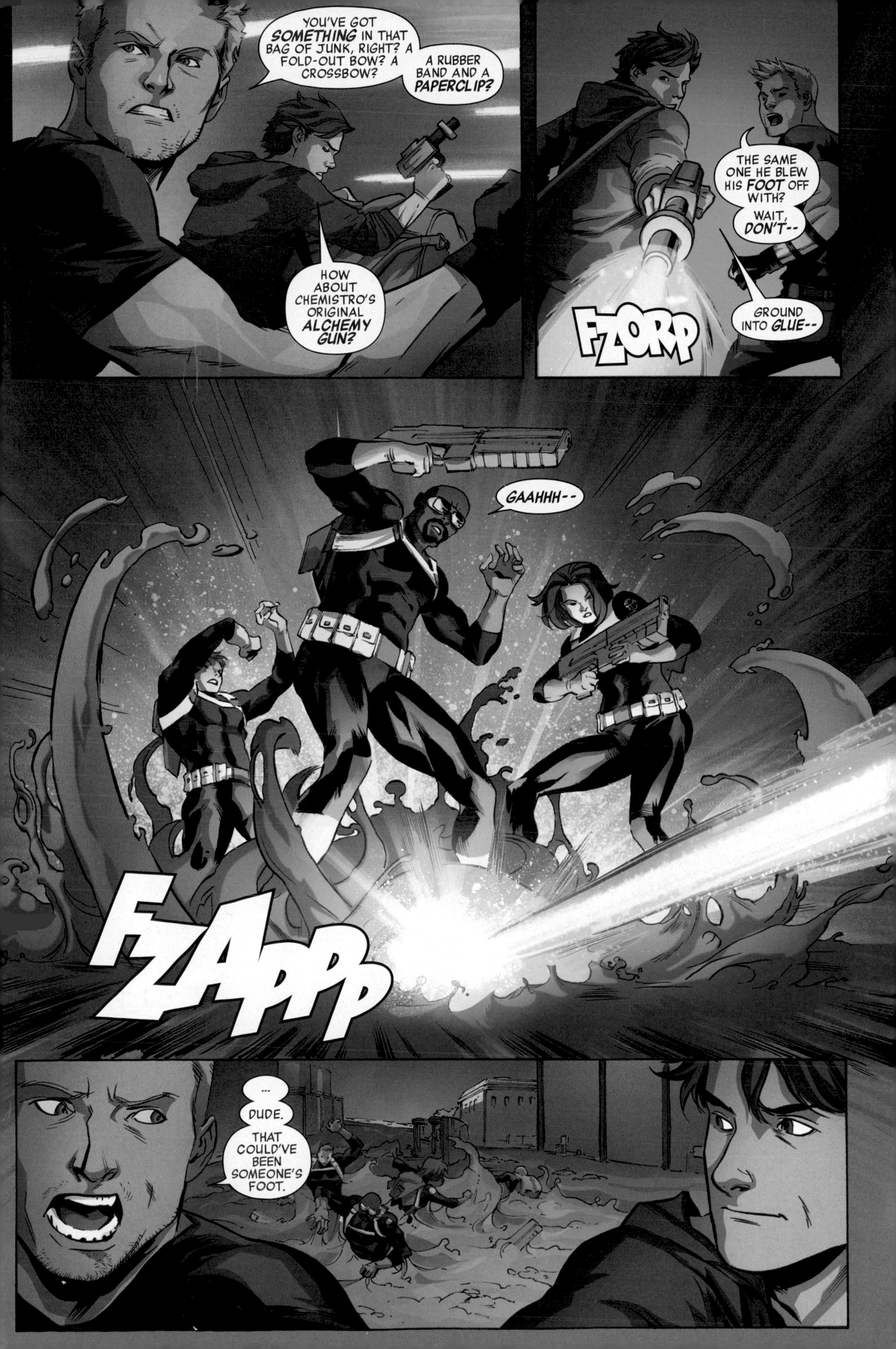
YOU'VE GOT SOMETHING IN THAT BAG OF JUNK, RIGHT? A FOLD-OUT BOW? A CROSSBOW?
A RUBBER BAND AND A PAPERCLIP?
HOW ABOUT CHEMISTRO'S ORIGINAL ALCHEMY GUN?
THE SAME ONE HE BLEW HIS FOOT OFF WITH?
WAIT, DON'T--
FZORP
GROUND INTO GLUE--
GAAHHH--
FZAPPP
...
DUDE.
THAT COULD'VE BEEN SOMEONE'S FOOT.

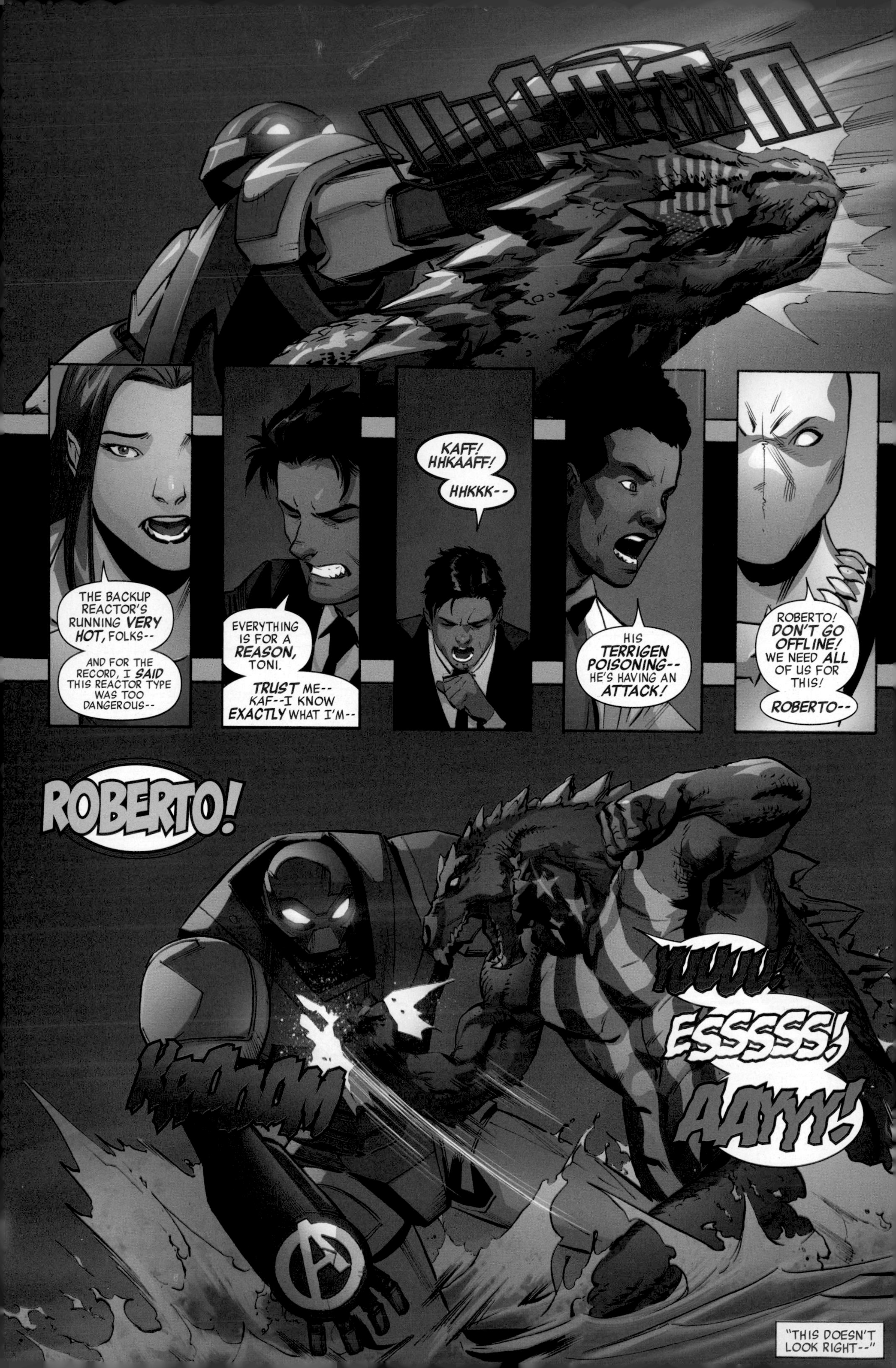
THE BACKUP REACTOR'S RUNNING VERY HOT, FOLKS--
AND FOR THE RECORD, I SAID THIS REACTOR TYPE WAS TOO DANGEROUS--
EVERYTHING IS FOR A REASON, TONI.
TRUST ME--KAF--I KNOW EXACTLY WHAT I'M--
KAFF! HHKAAFF!
HHKKK--
HIS TERRIGEN POISONING--HE'S HAVING AN ATTACK!
ROBERTO! DON'T GO OFFLINE! WE NEED ALL OF US FOR THIS!
ROBERTO--
ROBERTO!
ESSSSS!
AAYYY!
"THIS DOESN'T LOOK RIGHT--"

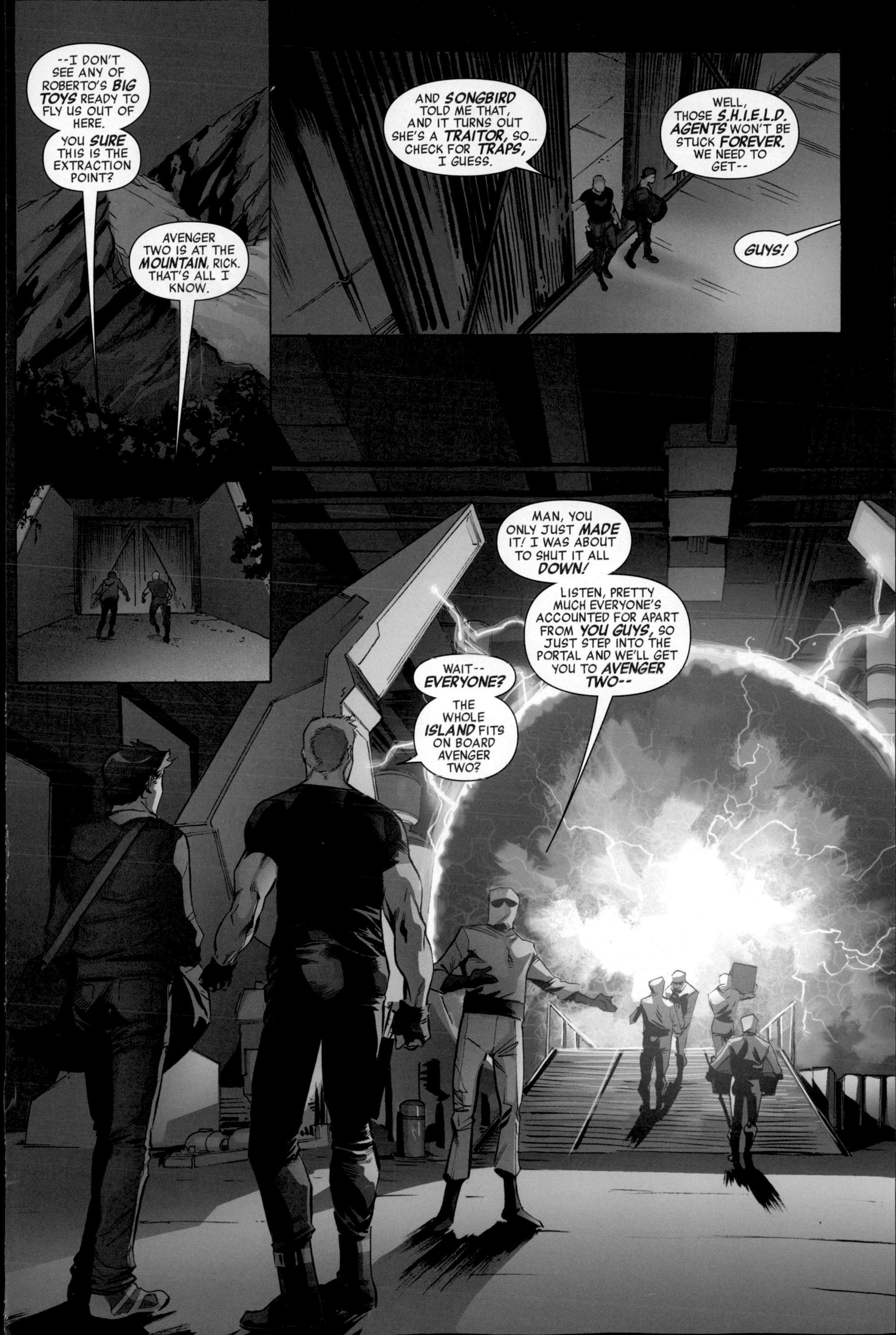
--I DON'T SEE ANY OF ROBERTO'S BIG TOYS READY TO FLY US OUT OF HERE.
YOU SURE THIS IS THE EXTRACTION POINT?
AVENGER TWO IS AT THE MOUNTAIN, RICK. THAT'S ALL I KNOW.
AND SONGBIRD TOLD ME THAT, AND IT TURNS OUT SHE'S A TRAITOR, SO... CHECK FOR TRAPS, I GUESS.
WELL, THOSE S.H.I.E.L.D. AGENTS WON'T BE STUCK FOREVER. WE NEED TO GET--
GUYS!
MAN, YOU ONLY JUST MADE IT! I WAS ABOUT TO SHUT IT ALL DOWN!
LISTEN, PRETTY MUCH EVERYONE'S ACCOUNTED FOR APART FROM YOU GUYS, SO JUST STEP INTO THE PORTAL AND WE'LL GET YOU TO AVENGER TWO--
WAIT-- EVERYONE?
THE WHOLE ISLAND FITS ON BOARD AVENGER TWO?

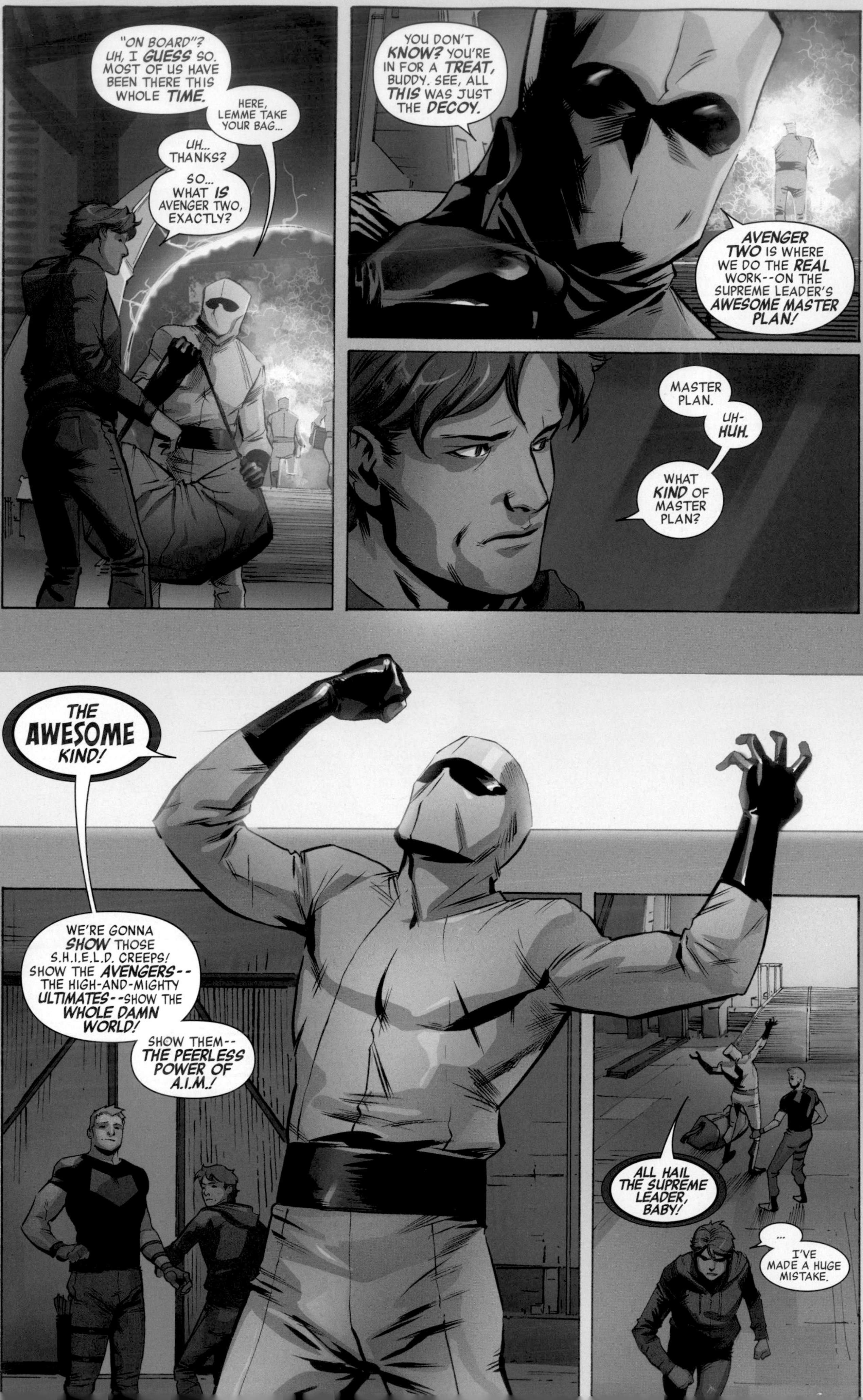
"ON BOARD"? UH, I GUESS SO. MOST OF US HAVE BEEN THERE THIS WHOLE TIME.
HERE, LEMME TAKE YOUR BAG...
UH... THANKS?
SO... WHAT IS AVENGER TWO, EXACTLY?
YOU DON'T KNOW? YOU'RE IN FOR A TREAT, BUDDY. SEE, ALL THIS WAS JUST THE DECOY.
AVENGER TWO IS WHERE WE DO THE REAL WORK--ON THE SUPREME LEADER'S AWESOME MASTER PLAN!
MASTER PLAN.
UH-HUH.
WHAT KIND OF MASTER PLAN?
THE AWESOME KIND!
WE'RE GONNA SHOW THOSE S.H.I.E.L.D. CREEPS! SHOW THE AVENGERS--THE HIGH-AND-MIGHTY ULTIMATES--SHOW THE WHOLE DAMN WORLD!
SHOW THEM--THE PEERLESS POWER OF A.I.M.!
ALL HAIL THE SUPREME LEADER, BABY!
...
I'VE MADE A HUGE MISTAKE.

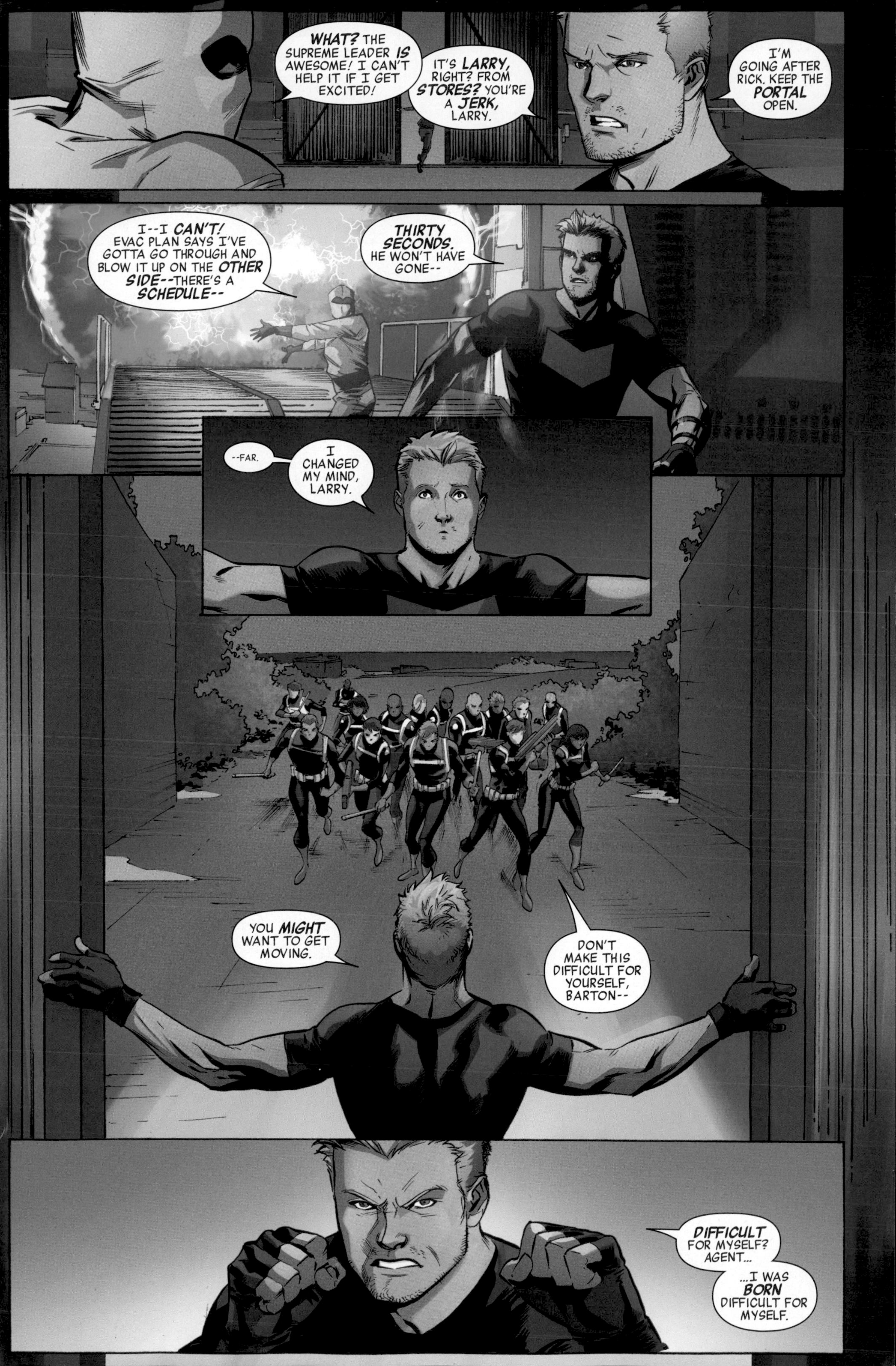
WHAT? THE SUPREME LEADER IS AWESOME! I CAN'T HELP IT IF I GET EXCITED!
IT'S LARRY, RIGHT? FROM STORES? YOU'RE A JERK, LARRY.
I'M GOING AFTER RICK. KEEP THE PORTAL OPEN.
I--I CAN'T! EVAC PLAN SAYS I'VE GOTTA GO THROUGH AND BLOW IT UP ON THE OTHER SIDE--THERE'S A SCHEDULE--
THIRTY SECONDS. HE WON'T HAVE GONE--
--FAR.
I CHANGED MY MIND, LARRY.
YOU MIGHT WANT TO GET MOVING.
DON'T MAKE THIS DIFFICULT FOR YOURSELF, BARTON--
DIFFICULT FOR MYSELF? AGENT...
...I WAS BORN DIFFICULT FOR MYSELF.

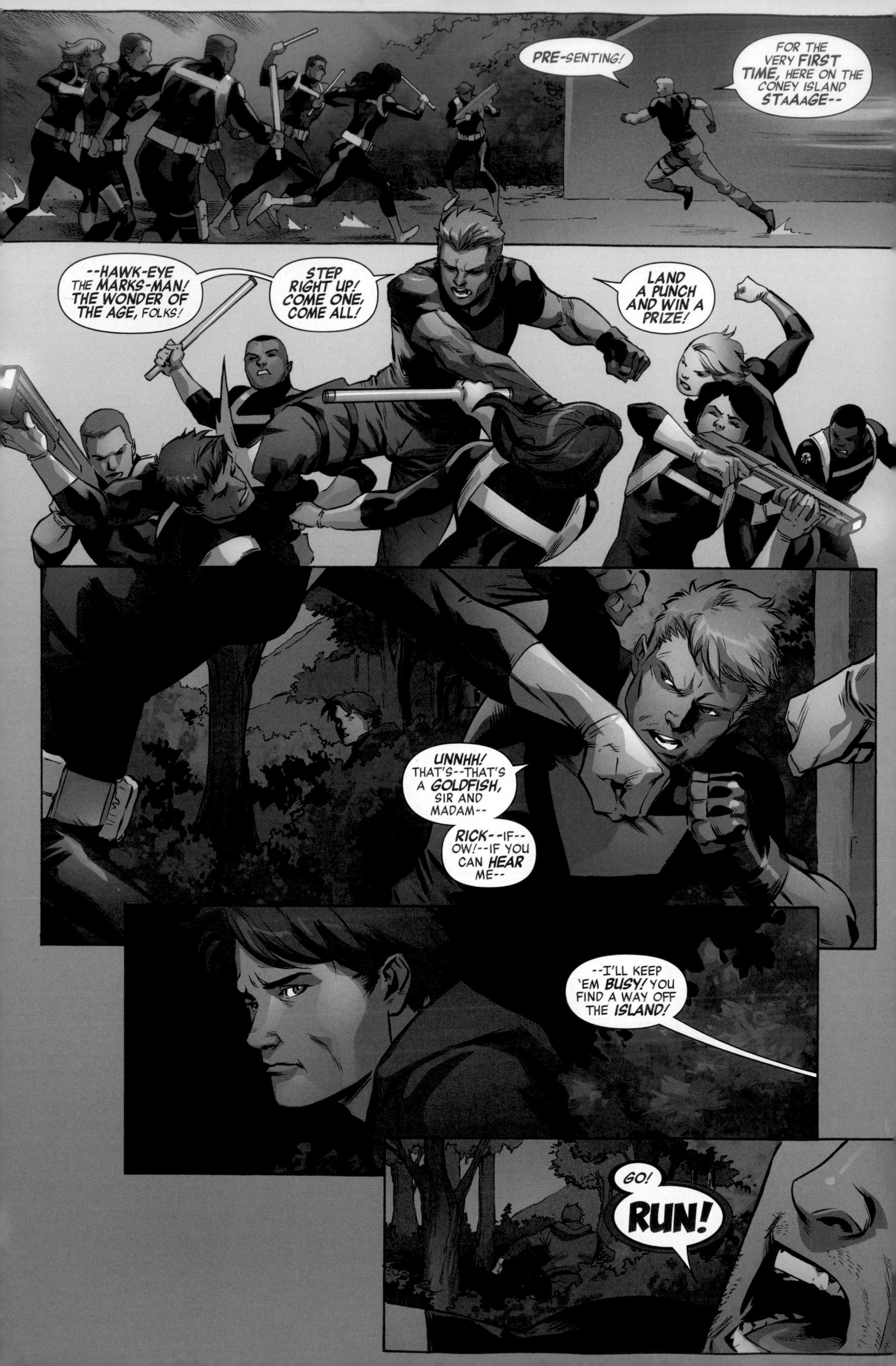
PRE-SENTING!
FOR THE VERY FIRST TIME, HERE ON THE CONEY ISLAND STAAAGE--
--HAWK-EYE THE MARKS-MAN! THE WONDER OF THE AGE, FOLKS!
STEP RIGHT UP! COME ONE, COME ALL!
LAND A PUNCH AND WIN A PRIZE!
UNNHH! THAT'S--THAT'S A GOLDFISH, SIR AND MADAM--
RICK--IF--OW!--IF YOU CAN HEAR ME--
--I'LL KEEP 'EM BUSY! YOU FIND A WAY OFF THE ISLAND!
GO!
RUN!

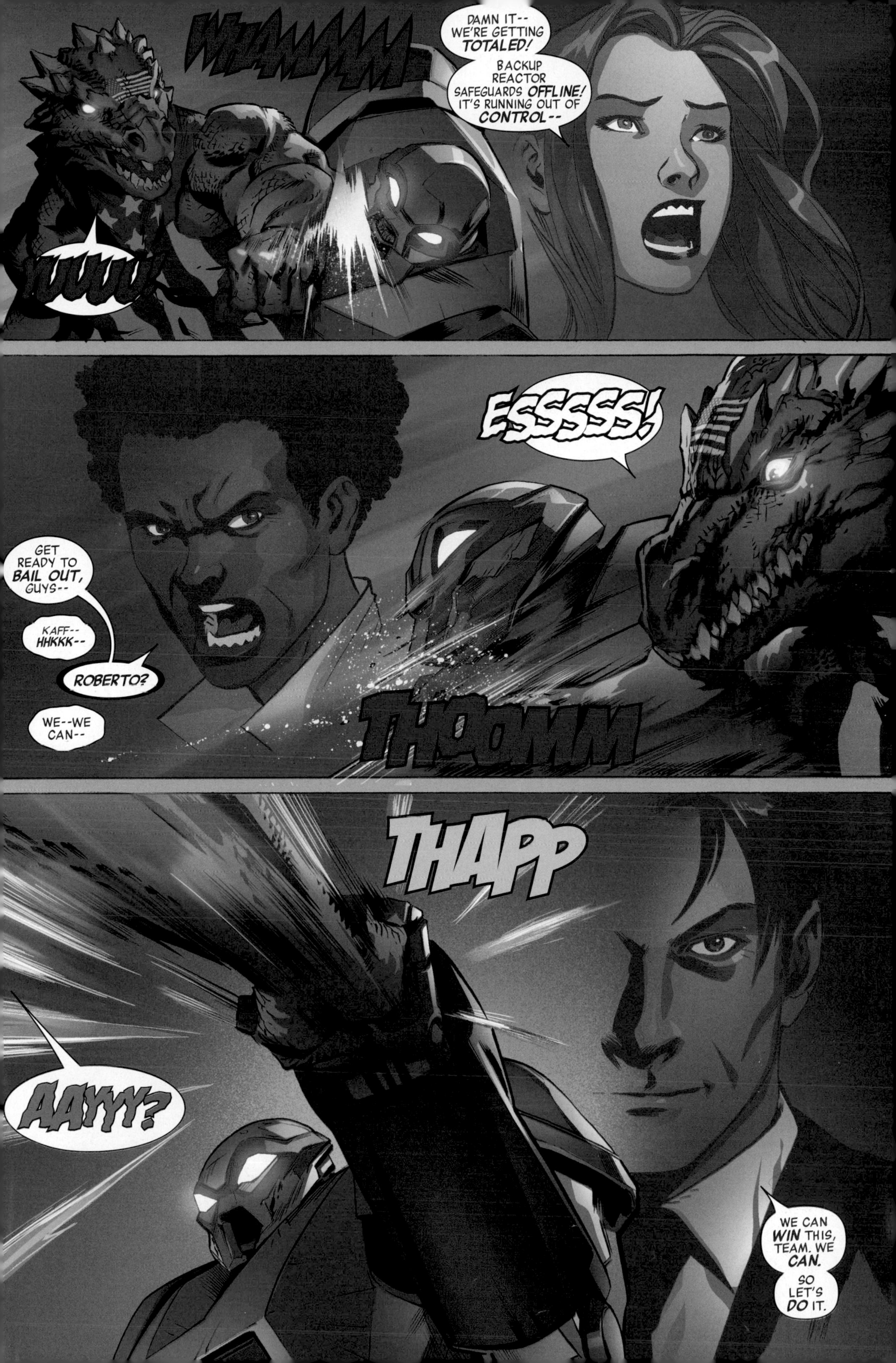
WHAAAAAM
DAMN IT-- WE'RE GETTING TOTALED!
BACKUP REACTOR SAFEGUARDS OFFLINE! IT'S RUNNING OUT OF CONTROL--
ESSSSS!
GET READY TO BAIL OUT, GUYS--
KAFF-- HHKKK--
ROBERTO?
WE--WE CAN--
THOOMM
THAPP
AAYYY?
WE CAN WIN THIS, TEAM. WE CAN.
SO LET'S DO IT.

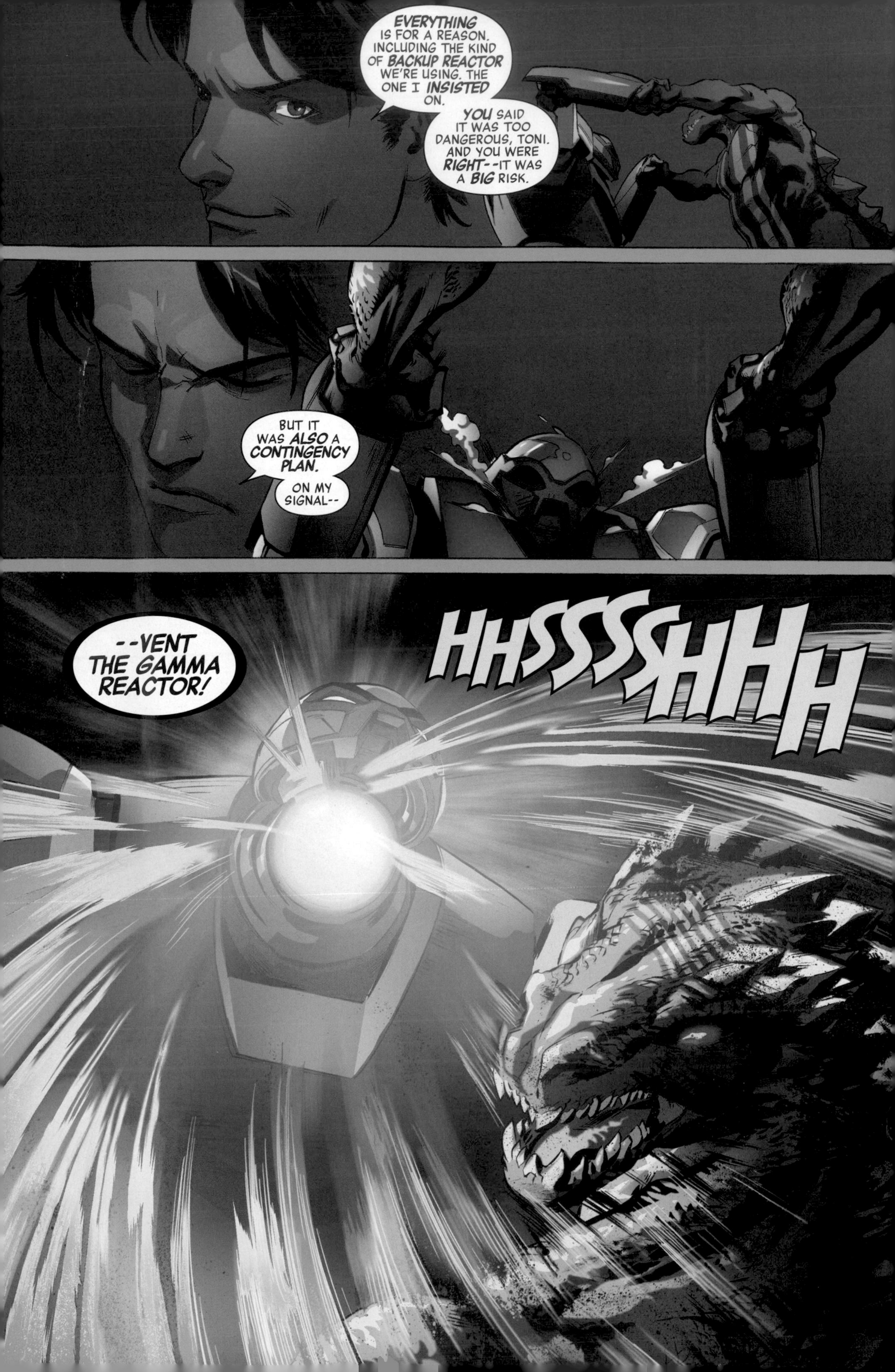
EVERYTHING IS FOR A REASON. INCLUDING THE KIND OF BACKUP REACTOR WE'RE USING. THE ONE I INSISTED ON.
YOU SAID IT WAS TOO DANGEROUS, TONI. AND YOU WERE RIGHT--IT WAS A BIG RISK.
BUT IT WAS ALSO A CONTINGENCY PLAN.
ON MY SIGNAL--
--VENT THE GAMMA REACTOR!
HHSSSSHHHH

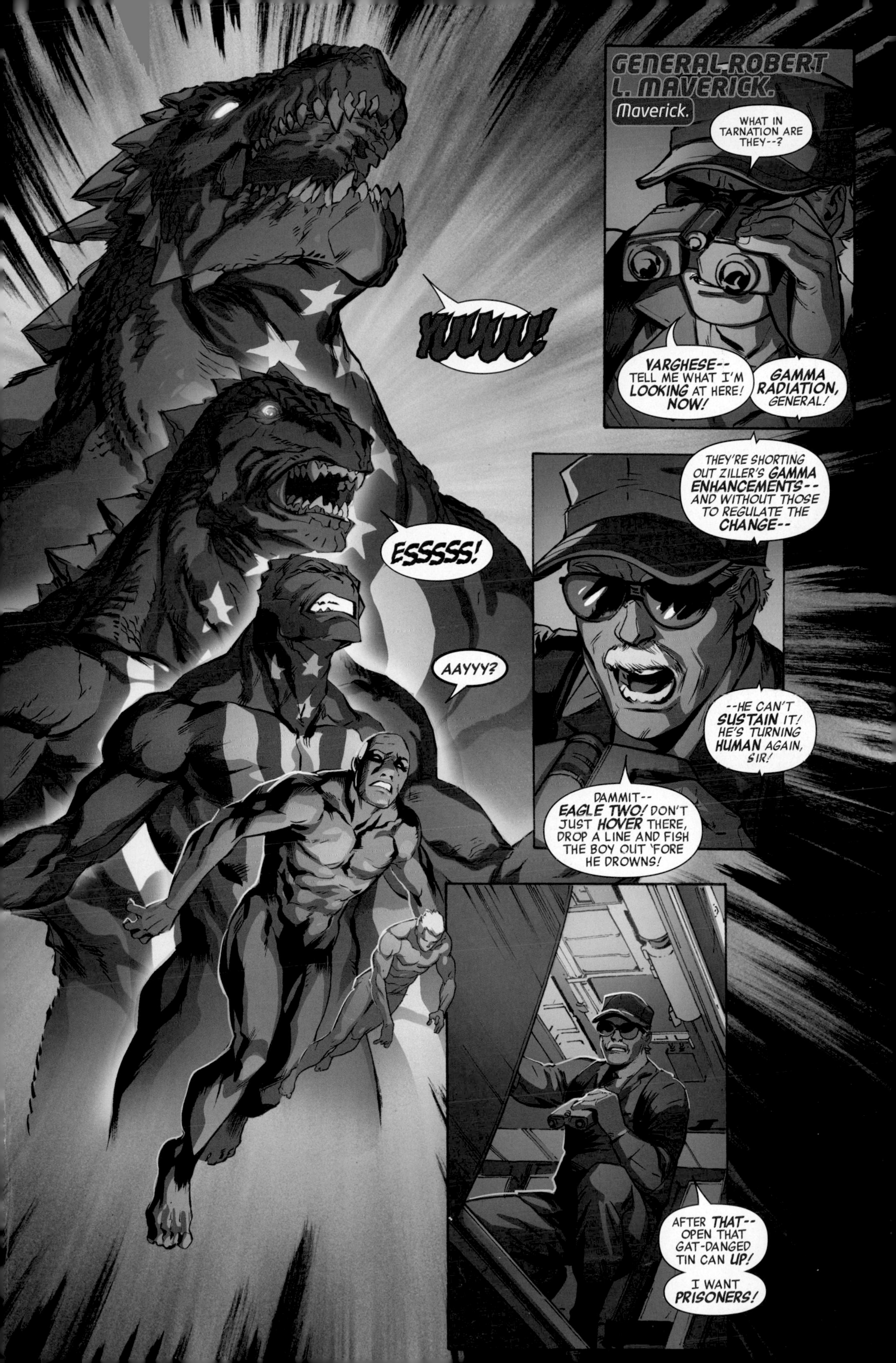
GENERAL ROBERT L. MAVERICK.
Maverick.
WHAT IN TARNATION ARE THEY--?
YUUUU!
VARGHESE-- TELL ME WHAT I'M LOOKING AT HERE! NOW!
GAMMA RADIATION, GENERAL!
ESSSSS!
AAYYY?
THEY'RE SHORTING OUT ZILLER'S GAMMA ENHANCEMENTS-- AND WITHOUT THOSE TO REGULATE THE CHANGE--
--HE CAN'T SUSTAIN IT! HE'S TURNING HUMAN AGAIN, SIR!
DAMMIT-- EAGLE TWO! DON'T JUST HOVER THERE, DROP A LINE AND FISH THE BOY OUT 'FORE HE DROWNS!
AFTER THAT-- OPEN THAT GAT-DANGED TIN CAN UP!
I WANT PRISONERS!

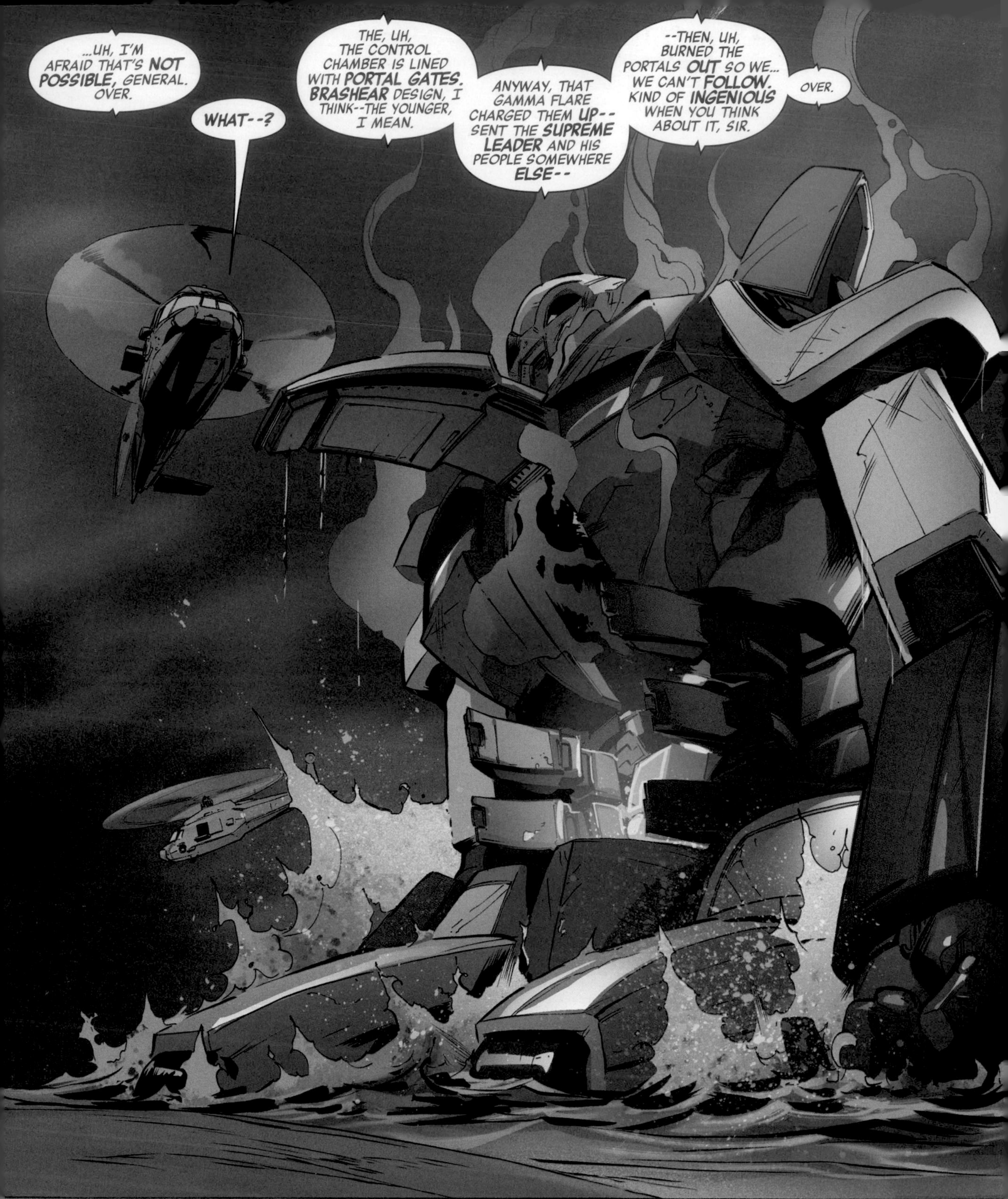
...UH, I'M AFRAID THAT'S NOT POSSIBLE, GENERAL. OVER.
WHAT--?
THE, UH, THE CONTROL CHAMBER IS LINED WITH PORTAL GATES. BRASHEAR DESIGN, I THINK--THE YOUNGER, I MEAN.
ANYWAY, THAT GAMMA FLARE CHARGED THEM UP--SENT THE SUPREME LEADER AND HIS PEOPLE SOMEWHERE ELSE--
--THEN, UH, BURNED THE PORTALS OUT SO WE... WE CAN'T FOLLOW. KIND OF INGENIOUS WHEN YOU THINK ABOUT IT, SIR.
OVER.

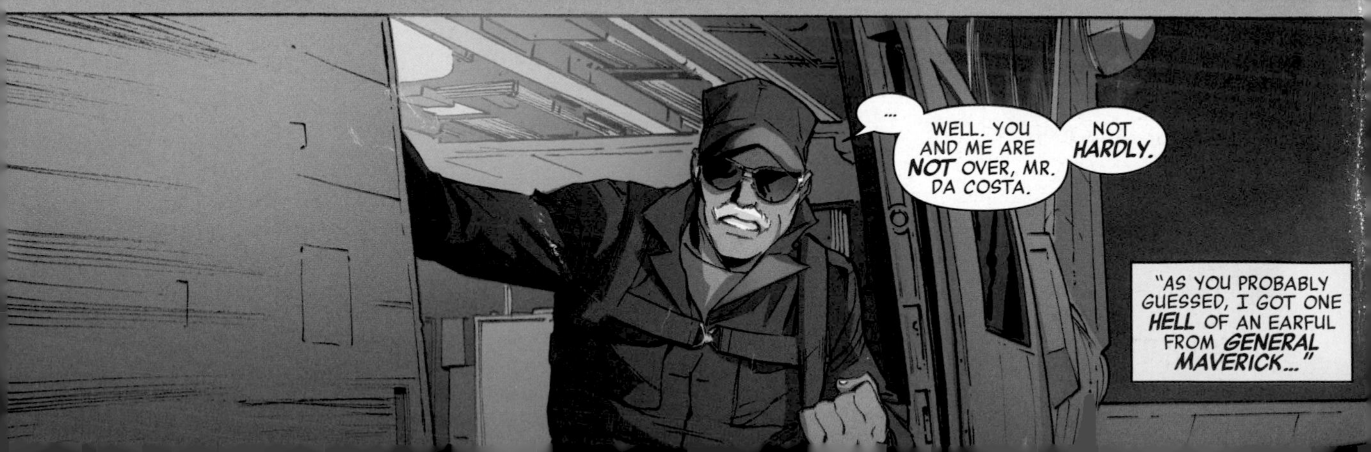
...
WELL. YOU AND ME ARE NOT OVER, MR. DA COSTA.
NOT HARDLY.
"AS YOU PROBABLY GUESSED, I GOT ONE HELL OF AN EARFUL FROM GENERAL MAVERICK..."

LATER.

...AND ON A *NORMAL* DAY, I'D KINDA *ENJOY* THAT.

HELL, ON A *NORMAL* DAY, I'D SHAKE YOUR *HAND.* I UNDERSTAND *PRINCIPLE,* SON.

DUM DUM DUGAN.
S.H.I.E.L.D. officer. Robot.

YOU'RE PROBABLY EXPECTING ME TO TEAR YOU A *NEW ONE,* AGENT. AND NORMALLY, MAYBE I *WOULD.*

MISSION'S *FAILED,* AFTER ALL.

JOHN GARRETT.
S.H.I.E.L.D. agent. Mostly robot.

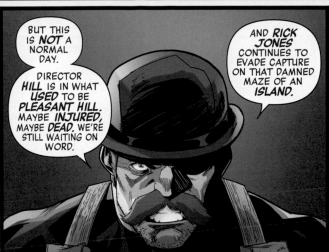

BUT THIS IS *NOT* A *NORMAL* DAY.

DIRECTOR *HILL* IS IN WHAT *USED* TO BE *PLEASANT HILL.* MAYBE *INJURED,* MAYBE *DEAD.* WE'RE STILL WAITING ON WORD.

AND *RICK JONES* CONTINUES TO EVADE CAPTURE ON THAT DAMNED MAZE OF AN *ISLAND.*

ROBERTO DA COSTA IS OUT IN THE *WILD,* ALONG WITH ALL HIS TOP *LIEUTENANTS,* PLANNING *WHO KNOWS WHAT.*

BAD DAY.

AND THE *ROUGH* PART IS...

SO, *TODAY* WAS NOT THE DAY FOR YOUR *CRAP,* BARTON.

...IT WAS *OUR* SCREWUP, AGENT GOLD.

YOU'LL BE *DETAINED ON STATION* UNTIL THE DIRECTOR RETURNS-- AND YOU HAD BEST *PRAY* THAT SHE *DOES--*

--AND THEN *SHE'LL* DECIDE WHAT WE *DO* WITH YOU.

I GAVE A BLANKET ORDER TO *EXIT COVER.* IF I *HADN'T,* YOU'D BE WITH *DA COSTA* AND WE'D KNOW WHERE HE *WAS.*

SO...YEAH. *HILL* WILL DECIDE YOUR NEXT MOVE ON THIS, IF--*WHEN*-- SHE GETS BACK.

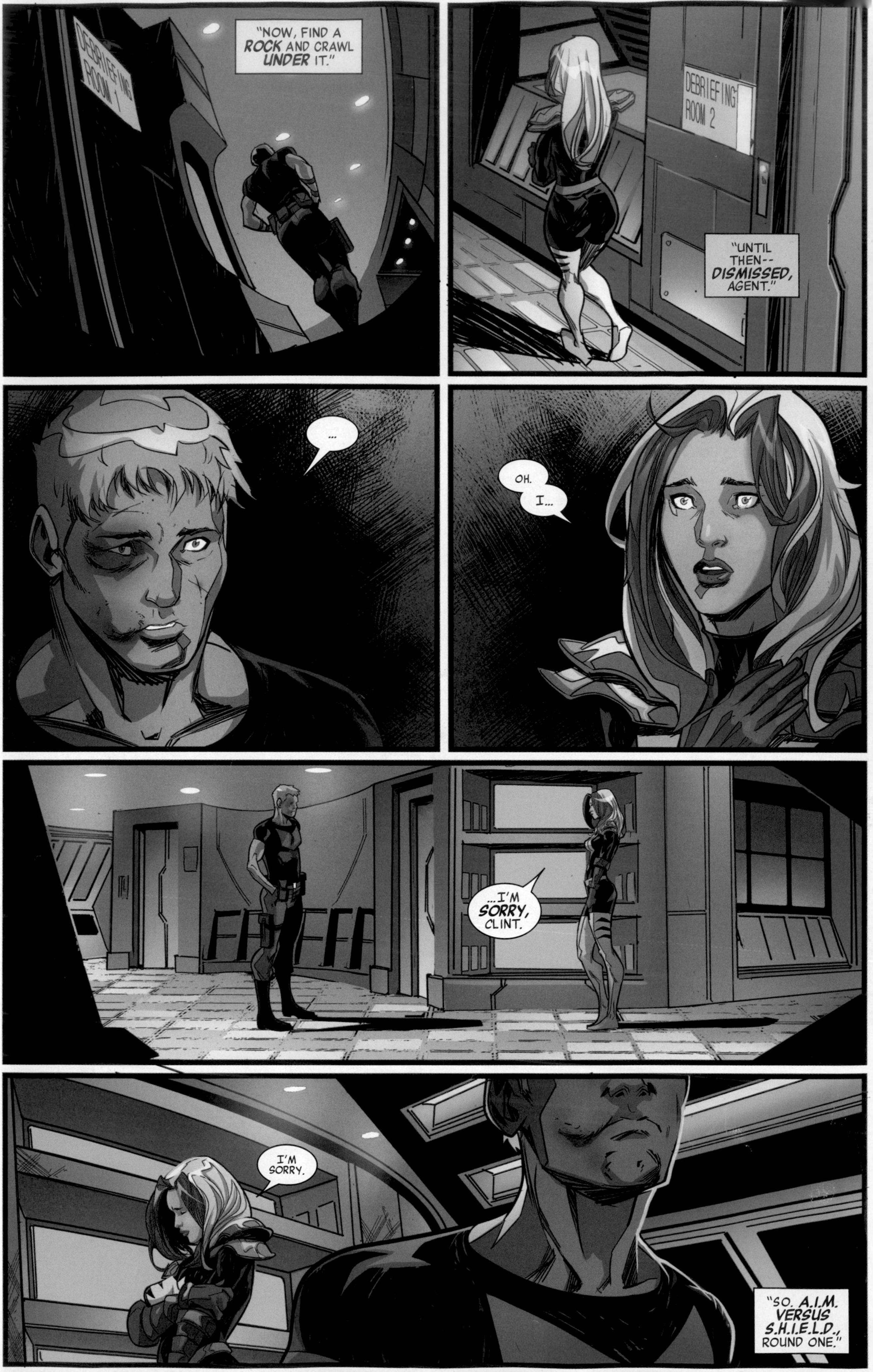
DEBRIEFING ROOM 1
"NOW, FIND A ROCK AND CRAWL UNDER IT."
DEBRIEFING ROOM 2
"UNTIL THEN-- DISMISSED, AGENT."
...
OH.
I...
...I'M SORRY, CLINT.
I'M SORRY.
"SO. A.I.M. VERSUS S.H.I.E.L.D., ROUND ONE."

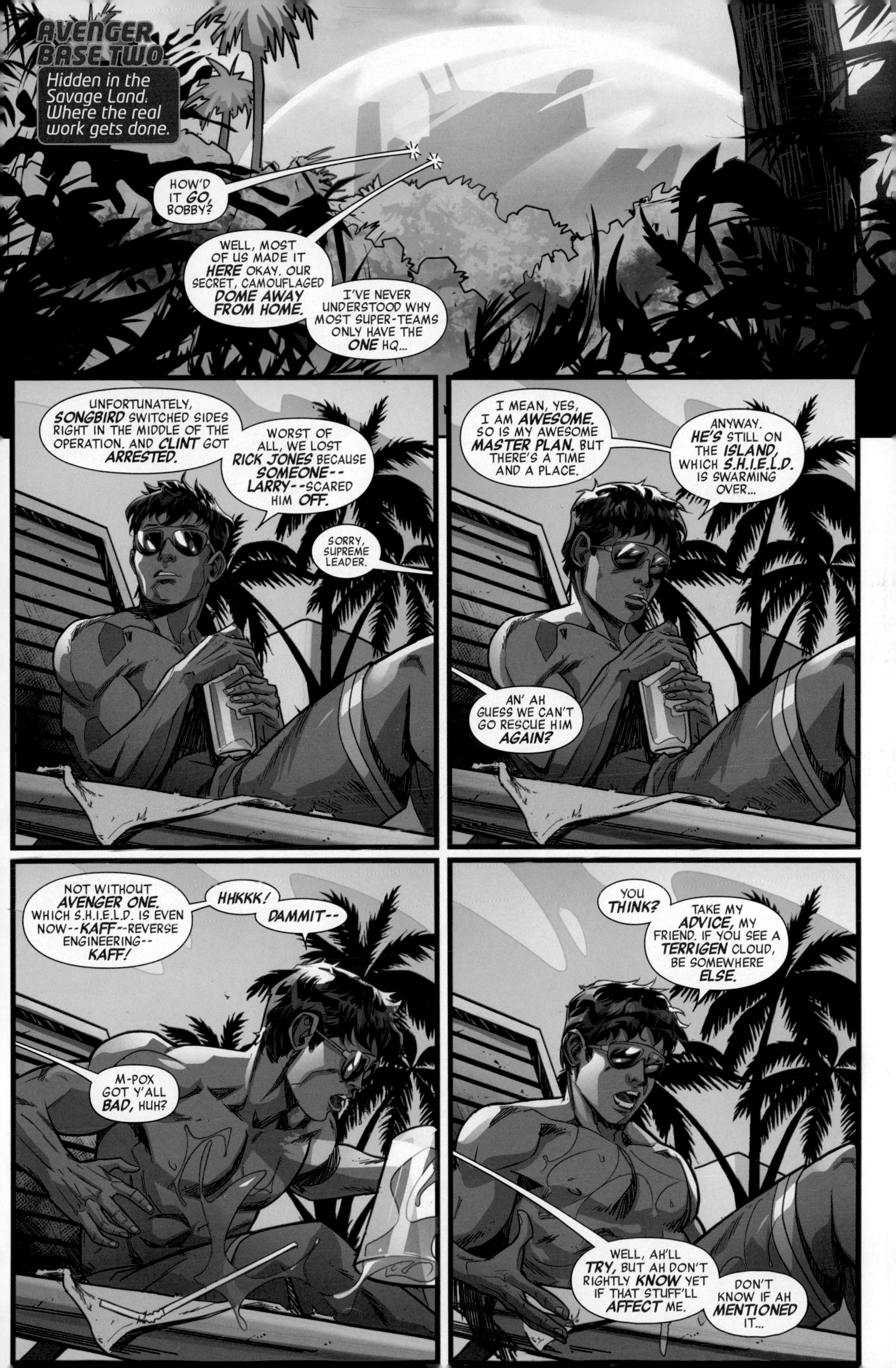
AVENGER BASE TWO.
Hidden in the Savage Land. Where the real work gets done.
HOW'D IT GO, BOBBY?
WELL, MOST OF US MADE IT HERE OKAY. OUR SECRET, CAMOUFLAGED DOME AWAY FROM HOME.
I'VE NEVER UNDERSTOOD WHY MOST SUPER-TEAMS ONLY HAVE THE ONE HQ...
UNFORTUNATELY, SONGBIRD SWITCHED SIDES RIGHT IN THE MIDDLE OF THE OPERATION. AND CLINT GOT ARRESTED.
WORST OF ALL, WE LOST RICK JONES BECAUSE SOMEONE-- LARRY--SCARED HIM OFF.
SORRY, SUPREME LEADER.
I MEAN, YES, I AM AWESOME. SO IS MY AWESOME MASTER PLAN. BUT THERE'S A TIME AND A PLACE.
ANYWAY. HE'S STILL ON THE ISLAND, WHICH S.H.I.E.L.D. IS SWARMING OVER...
AN' AH GUESS WE CAN'T GO RESCUE HIM AGAIN?
NOT WITHOUT AVENGER ONE. WHICH S.H.I.E.L.D. IS EVEN NOW--KAFF--REVERSE ENGINEERING-- KAFF!
HHKKK!
DAMMIT--
M-POX GOT Y'ALL BAD, HUH?
YOU THINK?
TAKE MY ADVICE, MY FRIEND. IF YOU SEE A TERRIGEN CLOUD, BE SOMEWHERE ELSE.
WELL, AH'LL TRY, BUT AH DON'T RIGHTLY KNOW YET IF THAT STUFF'LL AFFECT ME.
DON'T KNOW IF AH MENTIONED IT...

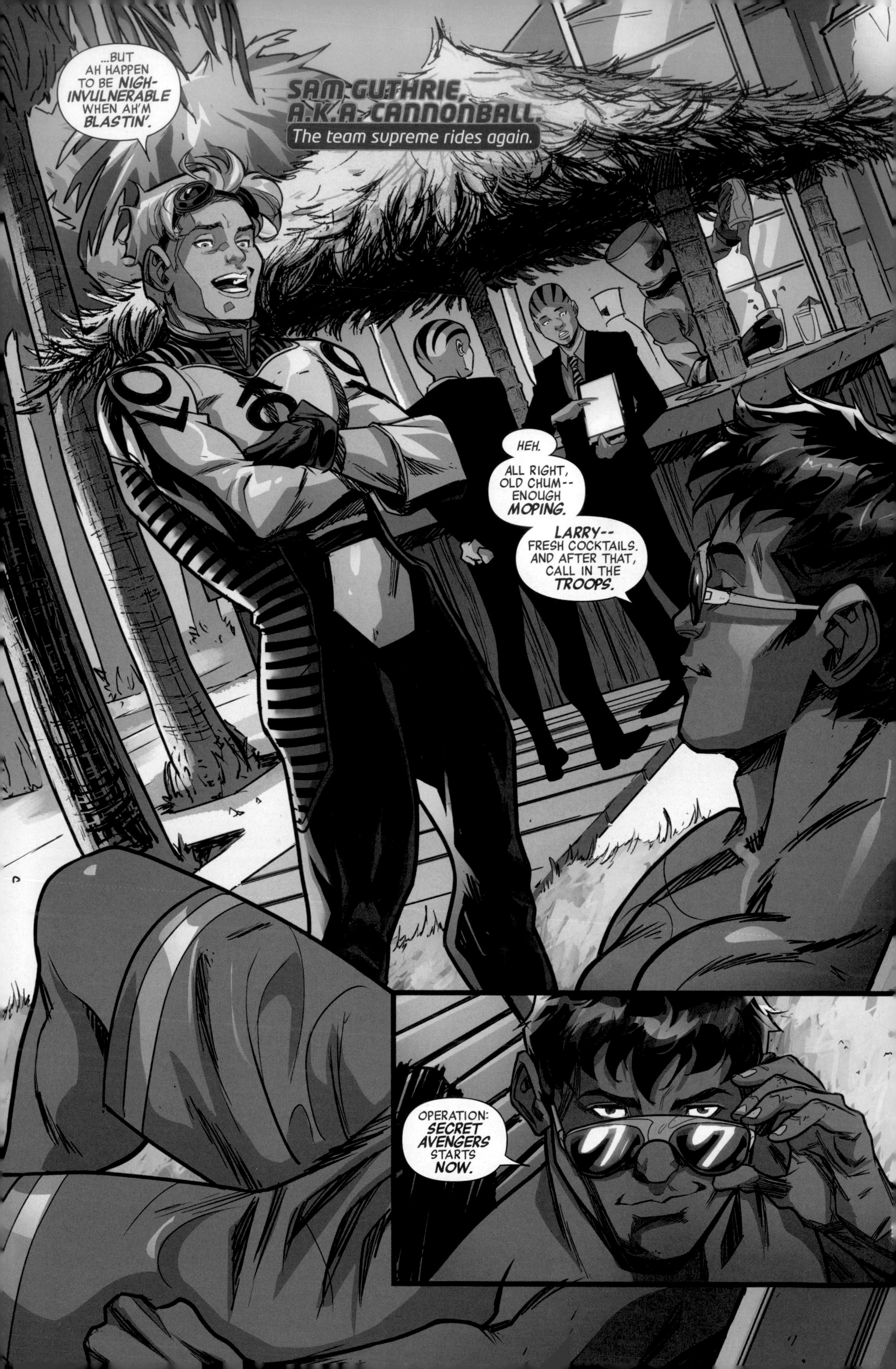
...BUT AH HAPPEN TO BE NIGH-INVULNERABLE WHEN AH'M BLASTIN'.
SAM GUTHRIE, A.K.A. CANNONBALL.
The team supreme rides again.
HEH.
ALL RIGHT, OLD CHUM-- ENOUGH MOPING.
LARRY-- FRESH COCKTAILS. AND AFTER THAT, CALL IN THE TROOPS.
OPERATION: SECRET AVENGERS STARTS NOW.

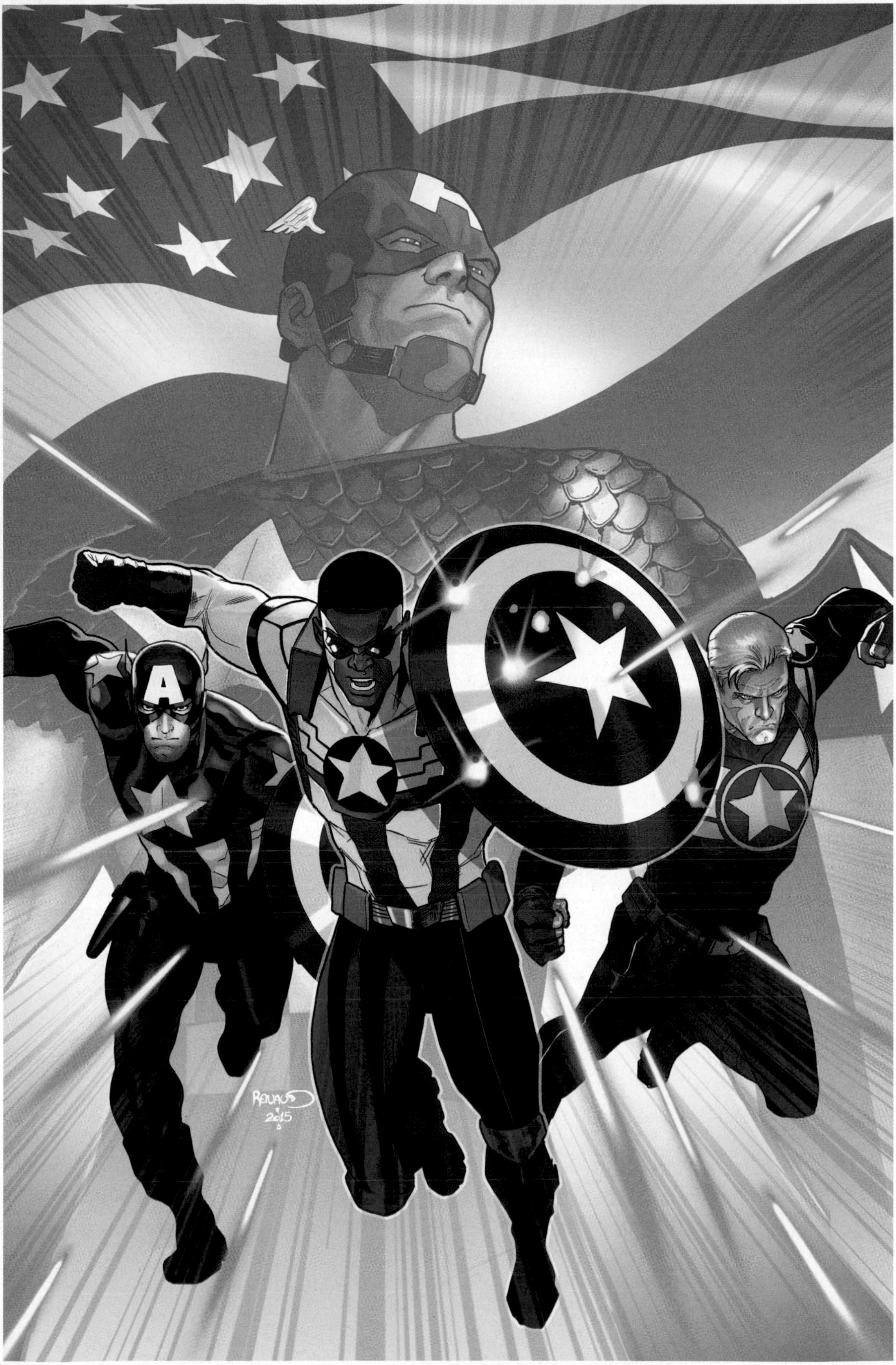

Captain America: Sam Wilson No. 8

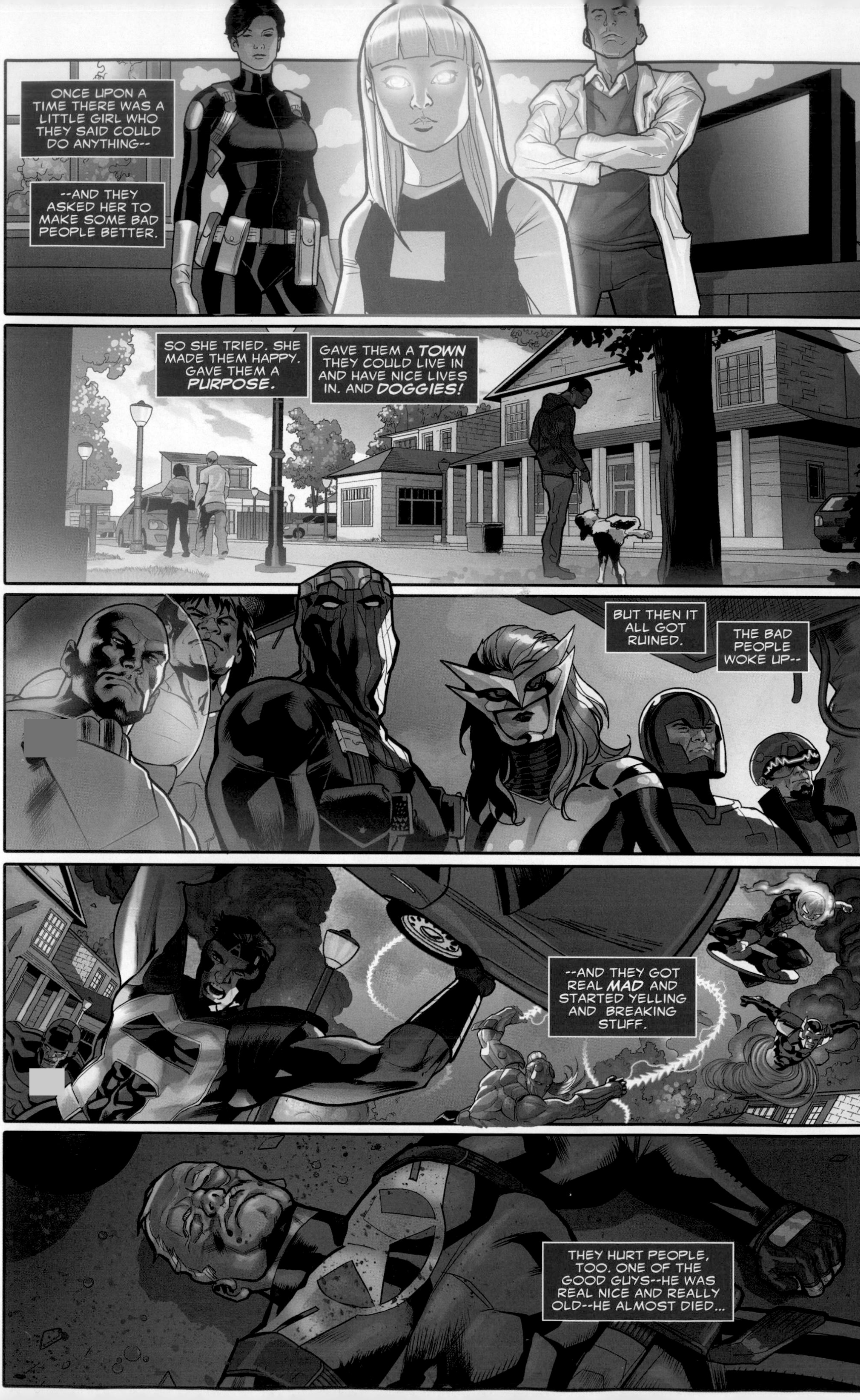
ONCE UPON A TIME THERE WAS A LITTLE GIRL WHO THEY SAID COULD DO ANYTHING--
--AND THEY ASKED HER TO MAKE SOME BAD PEOPLE BETTER.
SO SHE TRIED. SHE MADE THEM HAPPY. GAVE THEM A PURPOSE.
GAVE THEM A TOWN THEY COULD LIVE IN AND HAVE NICE LIVES IN. AND DOGGIES!
BUT THEN IT ALL GOT RUINED.
THE BAD PEOPLE WOKE UP--
--AND THEY GOT REAL MAD AND STARTED YELLING AND BREAKING STUFF.
THEY HURT PEOPLE, TOO. ONE OF THE GOOD GUYS--HE WAS REAL NICE AND REALLY OLD--HE ALMOST DIED...

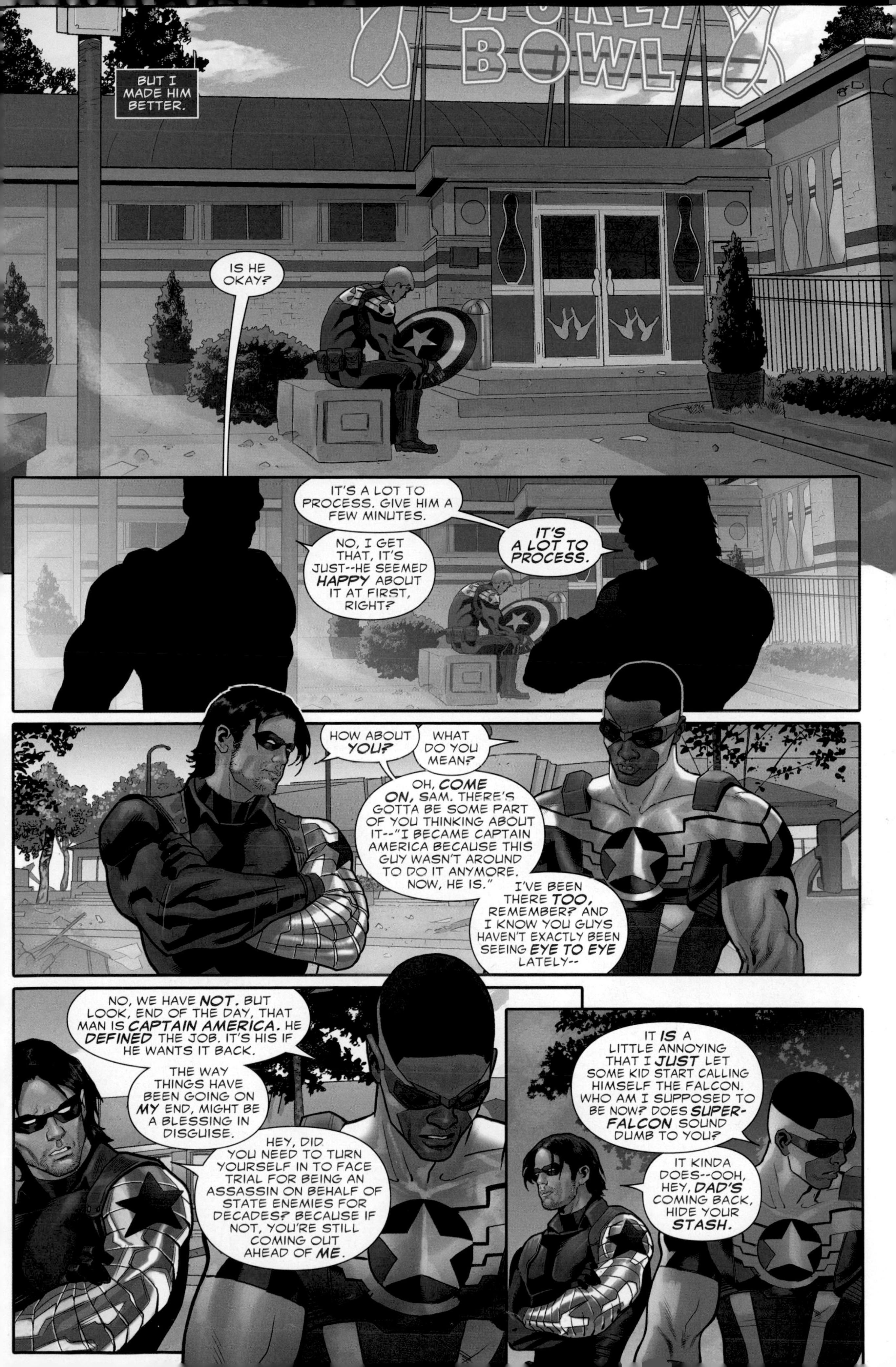

BOWL
BUT I MADE HIM BETTER.
IS HE OKAY?
IT'S A LOT TO PROCESS. GIVE HIM A FEW MINUTES.
NO, I GET THAT, IT'S JUST--HE SEEMED HAPPY ABOUT IT AT FIRST, RIGHT?
IT'S A LOT TO PROCESS.
HOW ABOUT YOU?
WHAT DO YOU MEAN?
OH, COME ON, SAM. THERE'S GOTTA BE SOME PART OF YOU THINKING ABOUT IT--"I BECAME CAPTAIN AMERICA BECAUSE THIS GUY WASN'T AROUND TO DO IT ANYMORE. NOW, HE IS."
I'VE BEEN THERE TOO, REMEMBER? AND I KNOW YOU GUYS HAVEN'T EXACTLY BEEN SEEING EYE TO EYE LATELY--
NO, WE HAVE NOT. BUT LOOK, END OF THE DAY, THAT MAN IS CAPTAIN AMERICA. HE DEFINED THE JOB. IT'S HIS IF HE WANTS IT BACK.
THE WAY THINGS HAVE BEEN GOING ON MY END, MIGHT BE A BLESSING IN DISGUISE.
HEY, DID YOU NEED TO TURN YOURSELF IN TO FACE TRIAL FOR BEING AN ASSASSIN ON BEHALF OF STATE ENEMIES FOR DECADES? BECAUSE IF NOT, YOU'RE STILL COMING OUT AHEAD OF ME.
IT IS A LITTLE ANNOYING THAT I JUST LET SOME KID START CALLING HIMSELF THE FALCON. WHO AM I SUPPOSED TO BE NOW? DOES SUPER-FALCON SOUND DUMB TO YOU?
IT KINDA DOES--OOH, HEY, DAD'S COMING BACK, HIDE YOUR STASH.

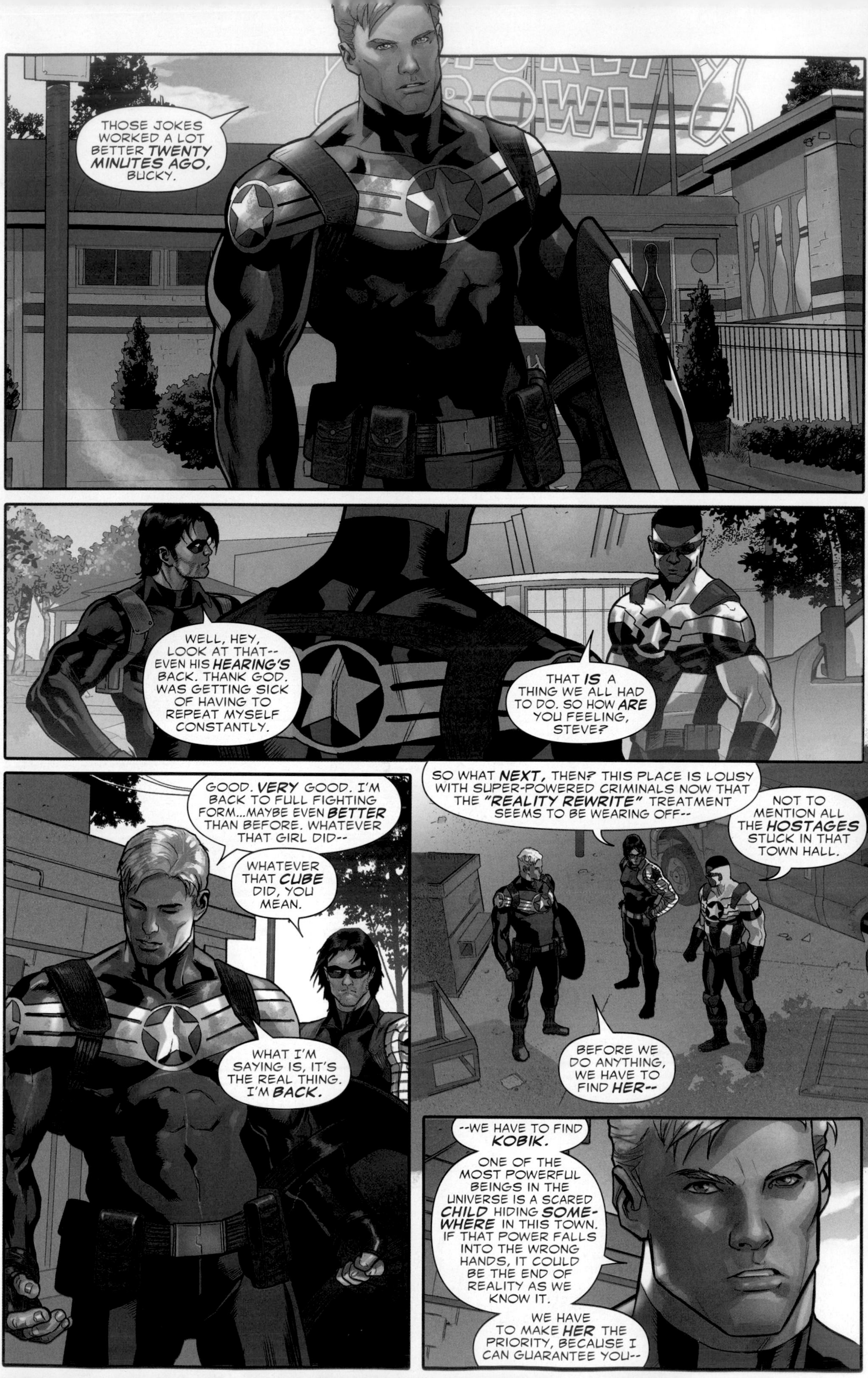

THOSE JOKES WORKED A LOT BETTER TWENTY MINUTES AGO, BUCKY.
BOWL
WELL, HEY, LOOK AT THAT-- EVEN HIS HEARING'S BACK. THANK GOD. WAS GETTING SICK OF HAVING TO REPEAT MYSELF CONSTANTLY.
THAT IS A THING WE ALL HAD TO DO. SO HOW ARE YOU FEELING, STEVE?
GOOD. VERY GOOD. I'M BACK TO FULL FIGHTING FORM...MAYBE EVEN BETTER THAN BEFORE. WHATEVER THAT GIRL DID--
WHATEVER THAT CUBE DID, YOU MEAN.
WHAT I'M SAYING IS, IT'S THE REAL THING. I'M BACK.
SO WHAT NEXT, THEN? THIS PLACE IS LOUSY WITH SUPER-POWERED CRIMINALS NOW THAT THE "REALITY REWRITE" TREATMENT SEEMS TO BE WEARING OFF--
NOT TO MENTION ALL THE HOSTAGES STUCK IN THAT TOWN HALL.
BEFORE WE DO ANYTHING, WE HAVE TO FIND HER--
--WE HAVE TO FIND KOBIK.
ONE OF THE MOST POWERFUL BEINGS IN THE UNIVERSE IS A SCARED CHILD HIDING SOME-WHERE IN THIS TOWN. IF THAT POWER FALLS INTO THE WRONG HANDS, IT COULD BE THE END OF REALITY AS WE KNOW IT.
WE HAVE TO MAKE HER THE PRIORITY, BECAUSE I CAN GUARANTEE YOU--

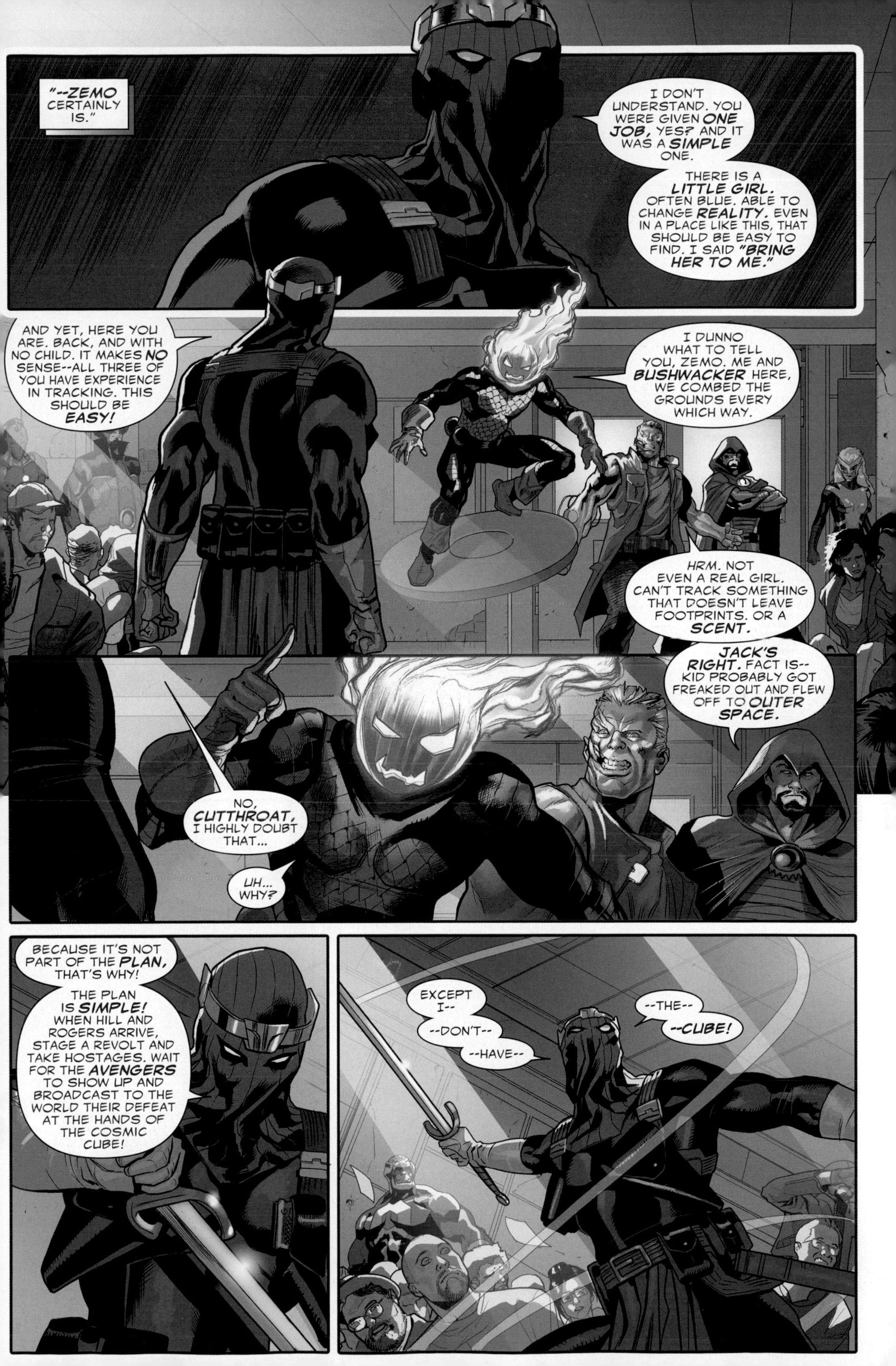
"--ZEMO CERTAINLY IS."
I DON'T UNDERSTAND. YOU WERE GIVEN ONE JOB, YES? AND IT WAS A SIMPLE ONE.
THERE IS A LITTLE GIRL. OFTEN BLUE. ABLE TO CHANGE REALITY. EVEN IN A PLACE LIKE THIS, THAT SHOULD BE EASY TO FIND. I SAID "BRING HER TO ME."
AND YET, HERE YOU ARE. BACK, AND WITH NO CHILD. IT MAKES NO SENSE--ALL THREE OF YOU HAVE EXPERIENCE IN TRACKING. THIS SHOULD BE EASY!
I DUNNO WHAT TO TELL YOU, ZEMO. ME AND BUSHWACKER HERE, WE COMBED THE GROUNDS EVERY WHICH WAY.
HRM. NOT EVEN A REAL GIRL. CAN'T TRACK SOMETHING THAT DOESN'T LEAVE FOOTPRINTS. OR A SCENT.
JACK'S RIGHT. FACT IS--KID PROBABLY GOT FREAKED OUT AND FLEW OFF TO OUTER SPACE.
NO, CUTTHROAT, I HIGHLY DOUBT THAT...
UH... WHY?
BECAUSE IT'S NOT PART OF THE PLAN, THAT'S WHY!
THE PLAN IS SIMPLE! WHEN HILL AND ROGERS ARRIVE, STAGE A REVOLT AND TAKE HOSTAGES. WAIT FOR THE AVENGERS TO SHOW UP AND BROADCAST TO THE WORLD THEIR DEFEAT AT THE HANDS OF THE COSMIC CUBE!
EXCEPT I--
--DON'T--
--HAVE--
--THE--
--CUBE!

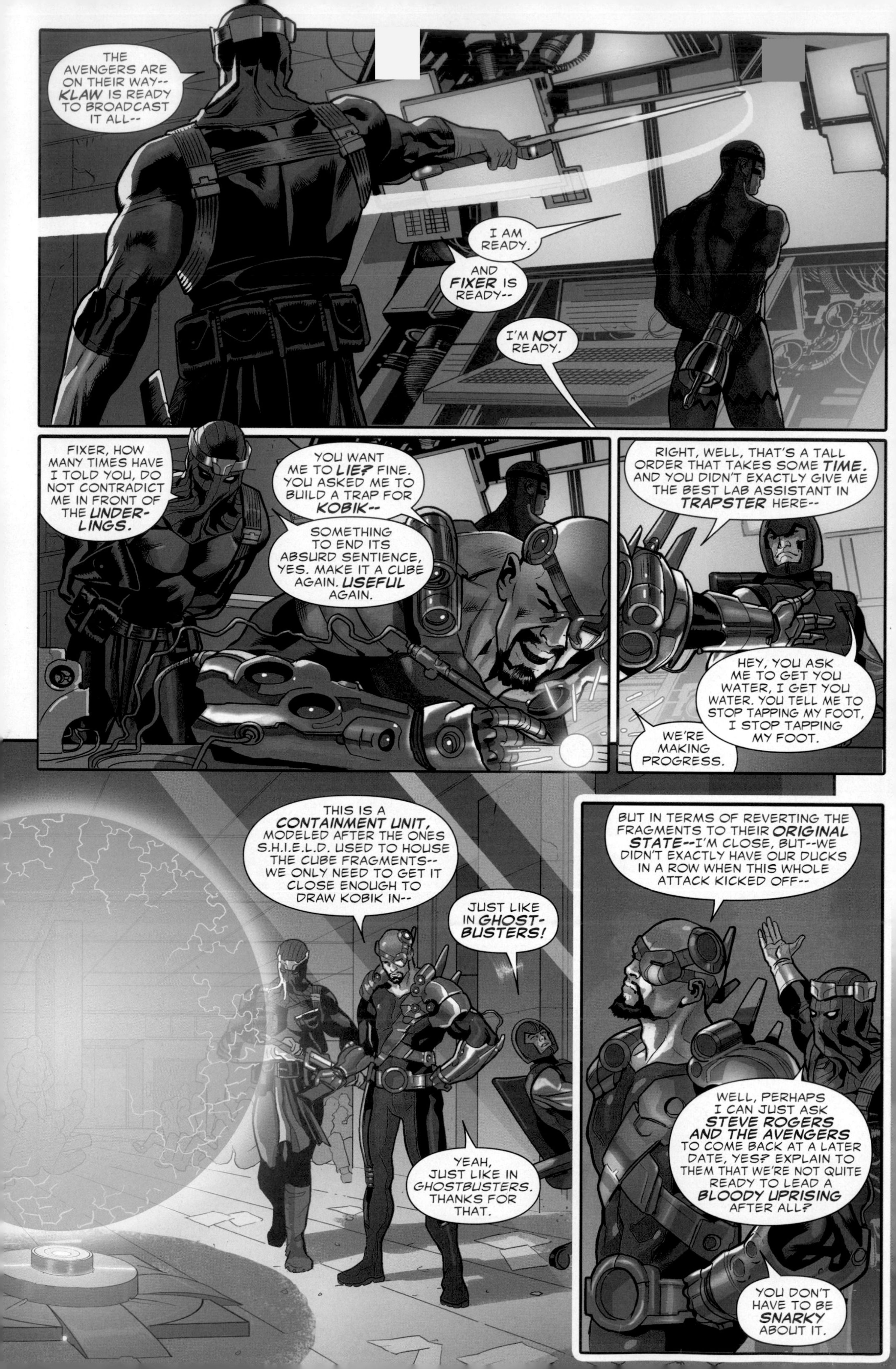
THE AVENGERS ARE ON THEIR WAY-- KLAW IS READY TO BROADCAST IT ALL--
I AM READY.
AND FIXER IS READY--
I'M NOT READY.
FIXER, HOW MANY TIMES HAVE I TOLD YOU, DO NOT CONTRADICT ME IN FRONT OF THE UNDER-LINGS.
YOU WANT ME TO LIE? FINE. YOU ASKED ME TO BUILD A TRAP FOR KOBIK--
SOMETHING TO END ITS ABSURD SENTIENCE, YES. MAKE IT A CUBE AGAIN. USEFUL AGAIN.
RIGHT, WELL, THAT'S A TALL ORDER THAT TAKES SOME TIME. AND YOU DIDN'T EXACTLY GIVE ME THE BEST LAB ASSISTANT IN TRAPSTER HERE--
HEY, YOU ASK ME TO GET YOU WATER, I GET YOU WATER. YOU TELL ME TO STOP TAPPING MY FOOT, I STOP TAPPING MY FOOT.
WE'RE MAKING PROGRESS.
THIS IS A CONTAINMENT UNIT, MODELED AFTER THE ONES S.H.I.E.L.D. USED TO HOUSE THE CUBE FRAGMENTS-- WE ONLY NEED TO GET IT CLOSE ENOUGH TO DRAW KOBIK IN--
JUST LIKE IN GHOST-BUSTERS!
YEAH, JUST LIKE IN GHOSTBUSTERS. THANKS FOR THAT.
BUT IN TERMS OF REVERTING THE FRAGMENTS TO THEIR ORIGINAL STATE--I'M CLOSE, BUT--WE DIDN'T EXACTLY HAVE OUR DUCKS IN A ROW WHEN THIS WHOLE ATTACK KICKED OFF--
WELL, PERHAPS I CAN JUST ASK STEVE ROGERS AND THE AVENGERS TO COME BACK AT A LATER DATE, YES? EXPLAIN TO THEM THAT WE'RE NOT QUITE READY TO LEAD A BLOODY UPRISING AFTER ALL?
YOU DON'T HAVE TO BE SNARKY ABOUT IT.

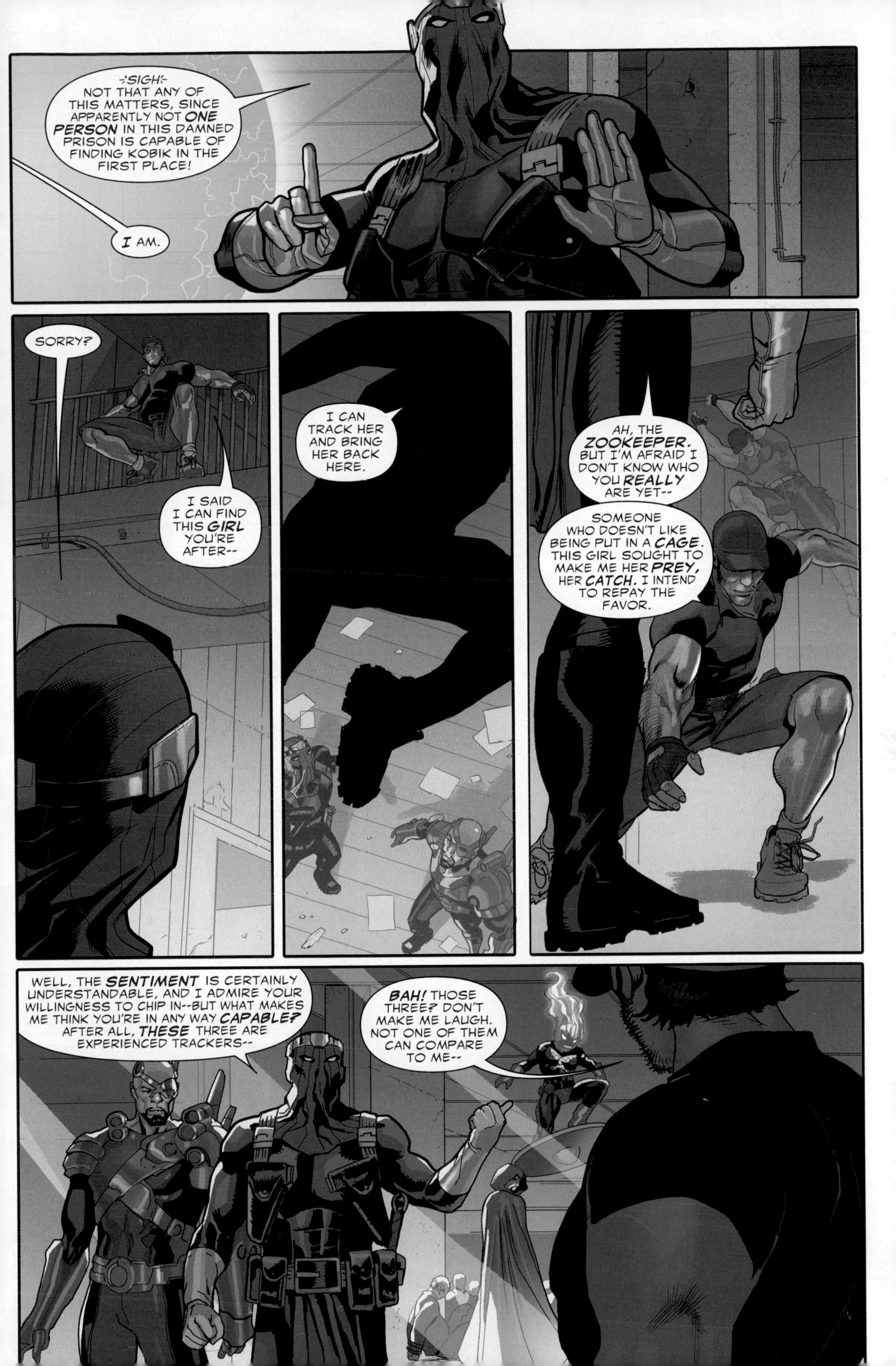
-SIGH-
NOT THAT ANY OF THIS MATTERS, SINCE APPARENTLY NOT ONE PERSON IN THIS DAMNED PRISON IS CAPABLE OF FINDING KOBIK IN THE FIRST PLACE!
I AM.
SORRY?
I SAID I CAN FIND THIS GIRL YOU'RE AFTER--
I CAN TRACK HER AND BRING HER BACK HERE.
AH, THE ZOOKEEPER. BUT I'M AFRAID I DON'T KNOW WHO YOU REALLY ARE YET--
SOMEONE WHO DOESN'T LIKE BEING PUT IN A CAGE. THIS GIRL SOUGHT TO MAKE ME HER PREY, HER CATCH. I INTEND TO REPAY THE FAVOR.
WELL, THE SENTIMENT IS CERTAINLY UNDERSTANDABLE, AND I ADMIRE YOUR WILLINGNESS TO CHIP IN--BUT WHAT MAKES ME THINK YOU'RE IN ANY WAY CAPABLE? AFTER ALL, THESE THREE ARE EXPERIENCED TRACKERS--
BAH! THOSE THREE? DON'T MAKE ME LAUGH. NOT ONE OF THEM CAN COMPARE TO ME--

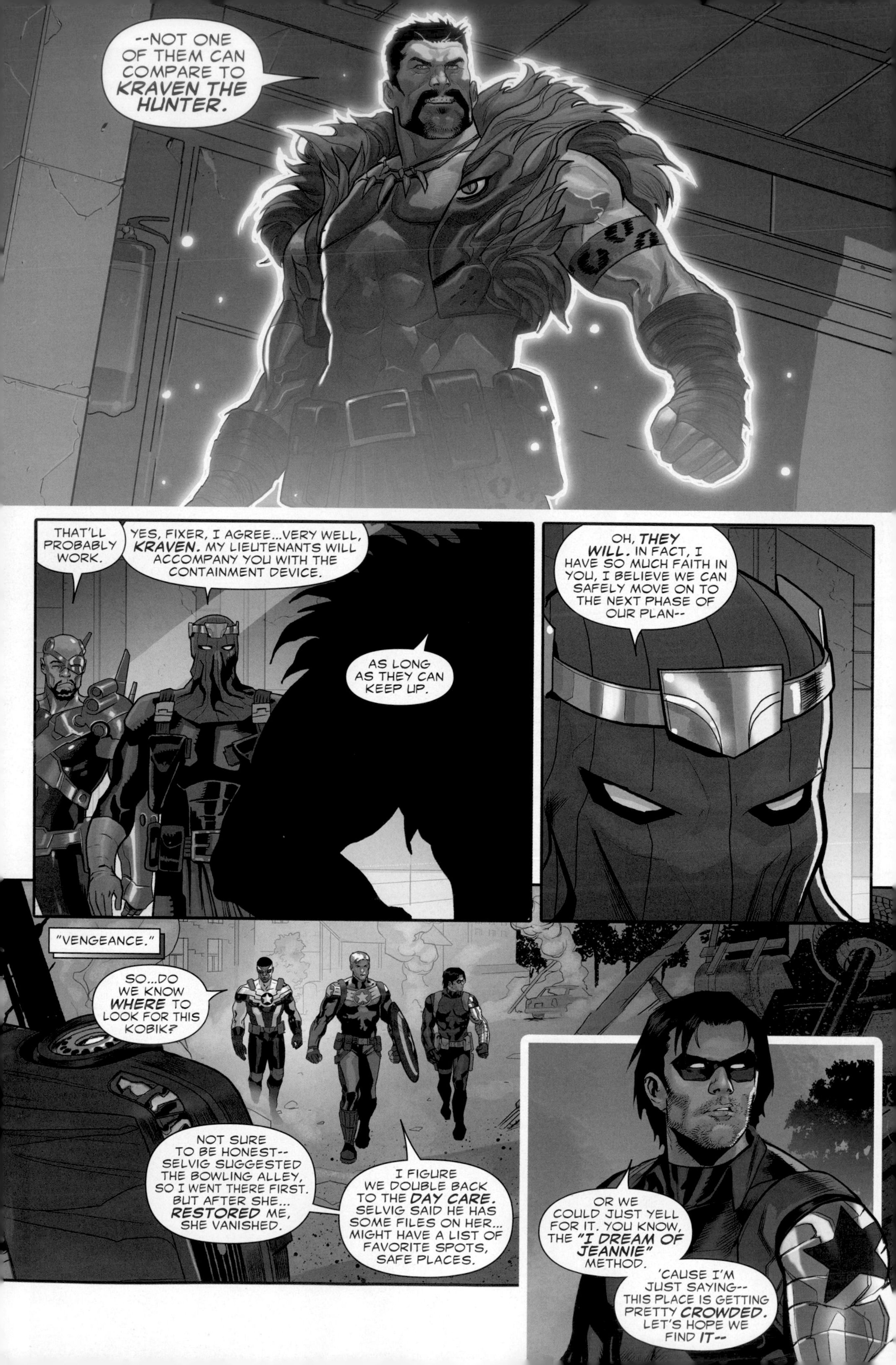
--NOT ONE OF THEM CAN COMPARE TO KRAVEN THE HUNTER.
THAT'LL PROBABLY WORK.
YES, FIXER, I AGREE...VERY WELL, KRAVEN. MY LIEUTENANTS WILL ACCOMPANY YOU WITH THE CONTAINMENT DEVICE.
AS LONG AS THEY CAN KEEP UP.
OH, THEY WILL. IN FACT, I HAVE SO MUCH FAITH IN YOU, I BELIEVE WE CAN SAFELY MOVE ON TO THE NEXT PHASE OF OUR PLAN--
"VENGEANCE."
SO...DO WE KNOW WHERE TO LOOK FOR THIS KOBIK?
NOT SURE TO BE HONEST--SELVIG SUGGESTED THE BOWLING ALLEY, SO I WENT THERE FIRST. BUT AFTER SHE... RESTORED ME, SHE VANISHED.
I FIGURE WE DOUBLE BACK TO THE DAY CARE. SELVIG SAID HE HAS SOME FILES ON HER... MIGHT HAVE A LIST OF FAVORITE SPOTS, SAFE PLACES.
OR WE COULD JUST YELL FOR IT. YOU KNOW, THE "I DREAM OF JEANNIE" METHOD.
'CAUSE I'M JUST SAYING--THIS PLACE IS GETTING PRETTY CROWDED. LET'S HOPE WE FIND IT--

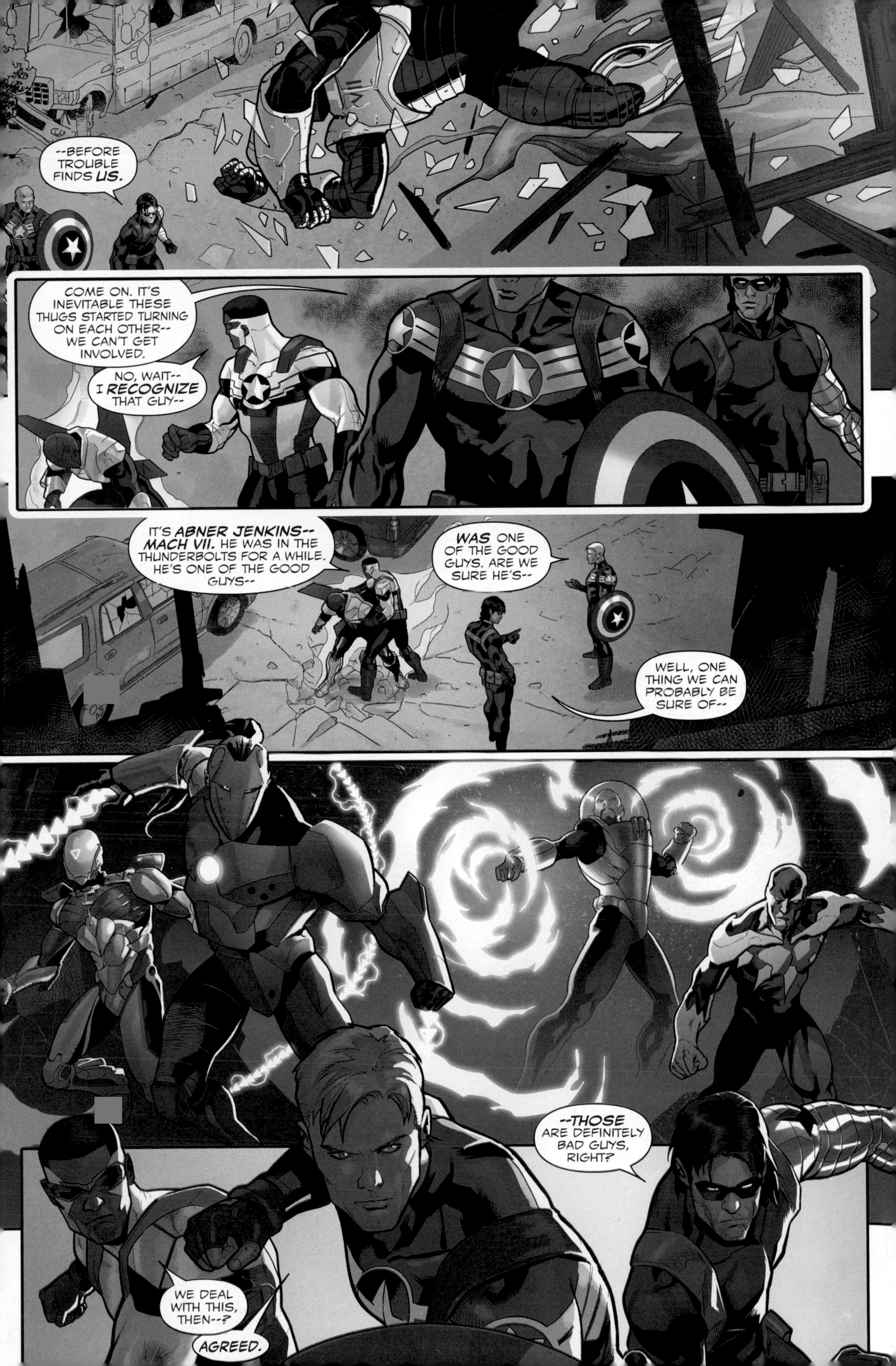
--BEFORE TROUBLE FINDS US.
COME ON. IT'S INEVITABLE THESE THUGS STARTED TURNING ON EACH OTHER-- WE CAN'T GET INVOLVED.
NO, WAIT-- I RECOGNIZE THAT GUY--
IT'S ABNER JENKINS-- MACH VII. HE WAS IN THE THUNDERBOLTS FOR A WHILE. HE'S ONE OF THE GOOD GUYS--
WAS ONE OF THE GOOD GUYS. ARE WE SURE HE'S--
WELL, ONE THING WE CAN PROBABLY BE SURE OF--
--THOSE ARE DEFINITELY BAD GUYS, RIGHT?
WE DEAL WITH THIS, THEN--?
AGREED.

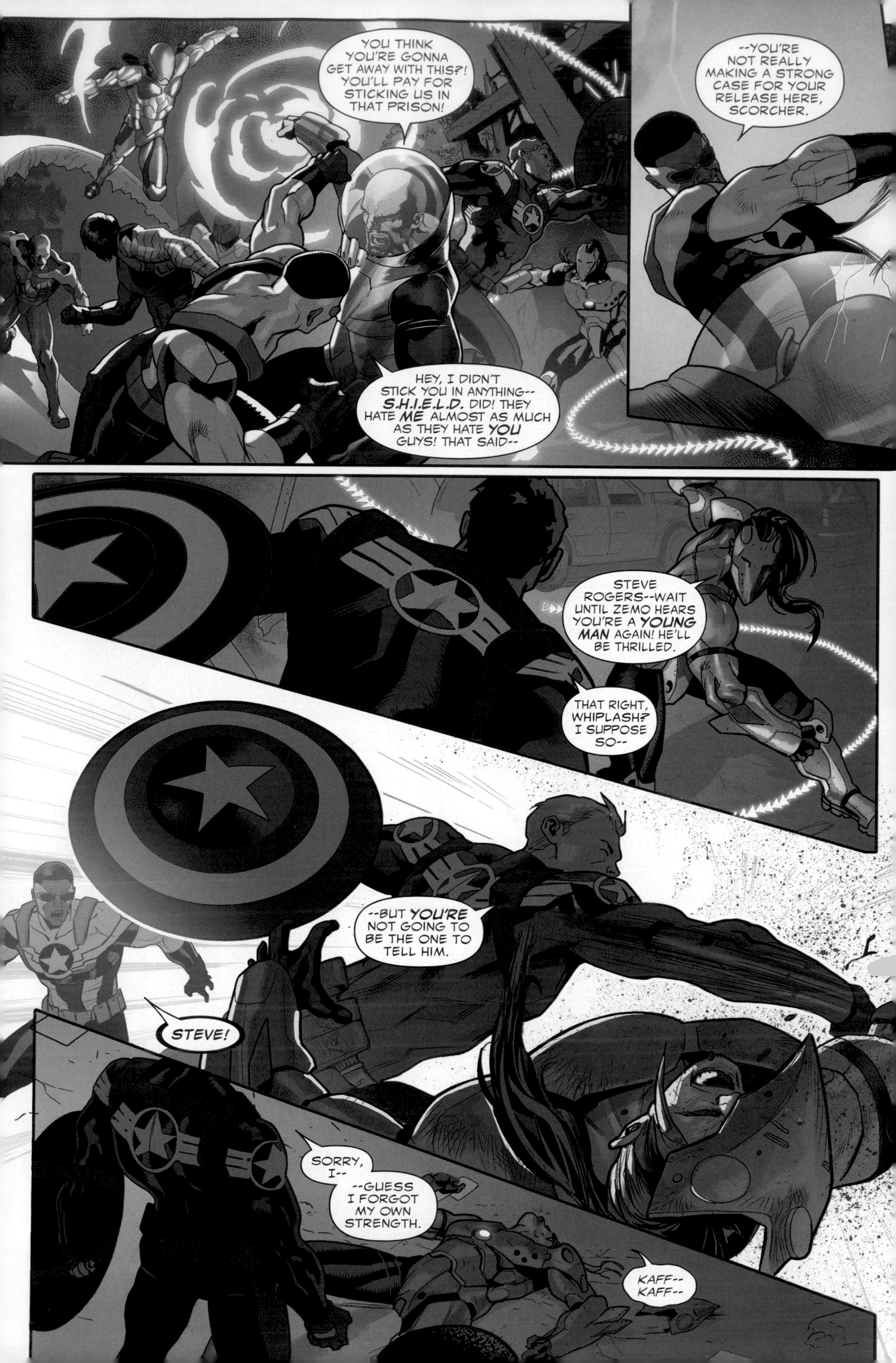
YOU THINK YOU'RE GONNA GET AWAY WITH THIS?! YOU'LL PAY FOR STICKING US IN THAT PRISON!
HEY, I DIDN'T STICK YOU IN ANYTHING-- S.H.I.E.L.D. DID! THEY HATE ME ALMOST AS MUCH AS THEY HATE YOU GUYS! THAT SAID--
--YOU'RE NOT REALLY MAKING A STRONG CASE FOR YOUR RELEASE HERE, SCORCHER.
STEVE ROGERS--WAIT UNTIL ZEMO HEARS YOU'RE A YOUNG MAN AGAIN! HE'LL BE THRILLED.
THAT RIGHT, WHIPLASH? I SUPPOSE SO--
--BUT YOU'RE NOT GOING TO BE THE ONE TO TELL HIM.
STEVE!
SORRY, I--
--GUESS I FORGOT MY OWN STRENGTH.
KAFF-- KAFF--

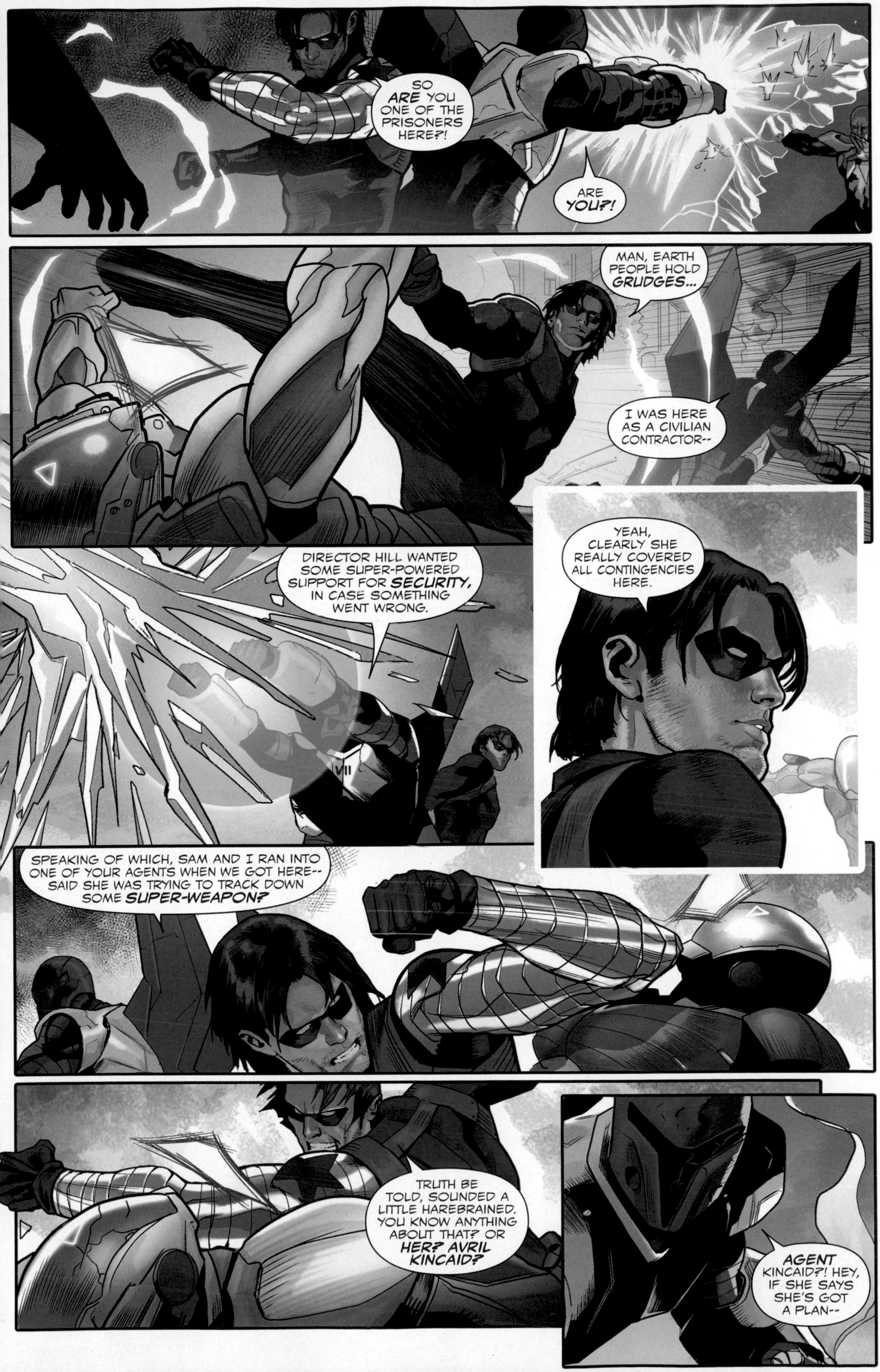
SO ARE YOU ONE OF THE PRISONERS HERE?!
ARE YOU?!
MAN, EARTH PEOPLE HOLD GRUDGES...
I WAS HERE AS A CIVILIAN CONTRACTOR--
DIRECTOR HILL WANTED SOME SUPER-POWERED SUPPORT FOR SECURITY, IN CASE SOMETHING WENT WRONG.
YEAH, CLEARLY SHE REALLY COVERED ALL CONTINGENCIES HERE.
SPEAKING OF WHICH, SAM AND I RAN INTO ONE OF YOUR AGENTS WHEN WE GOT HERE-- SAID SHE WAS TRYING TO TRACK DOWN SOME SUPER-WEAPON?
TRUTH BE TOLD, SOUNDED A LITTLE HAREBRAINED. YOU KNOW ANYTHING ABOUT THAT? OR HER? AVRIL KINCAID?
AGENT KINCAID?! HEY, IF SHE SAYS SHE'S GOT A PLAN--

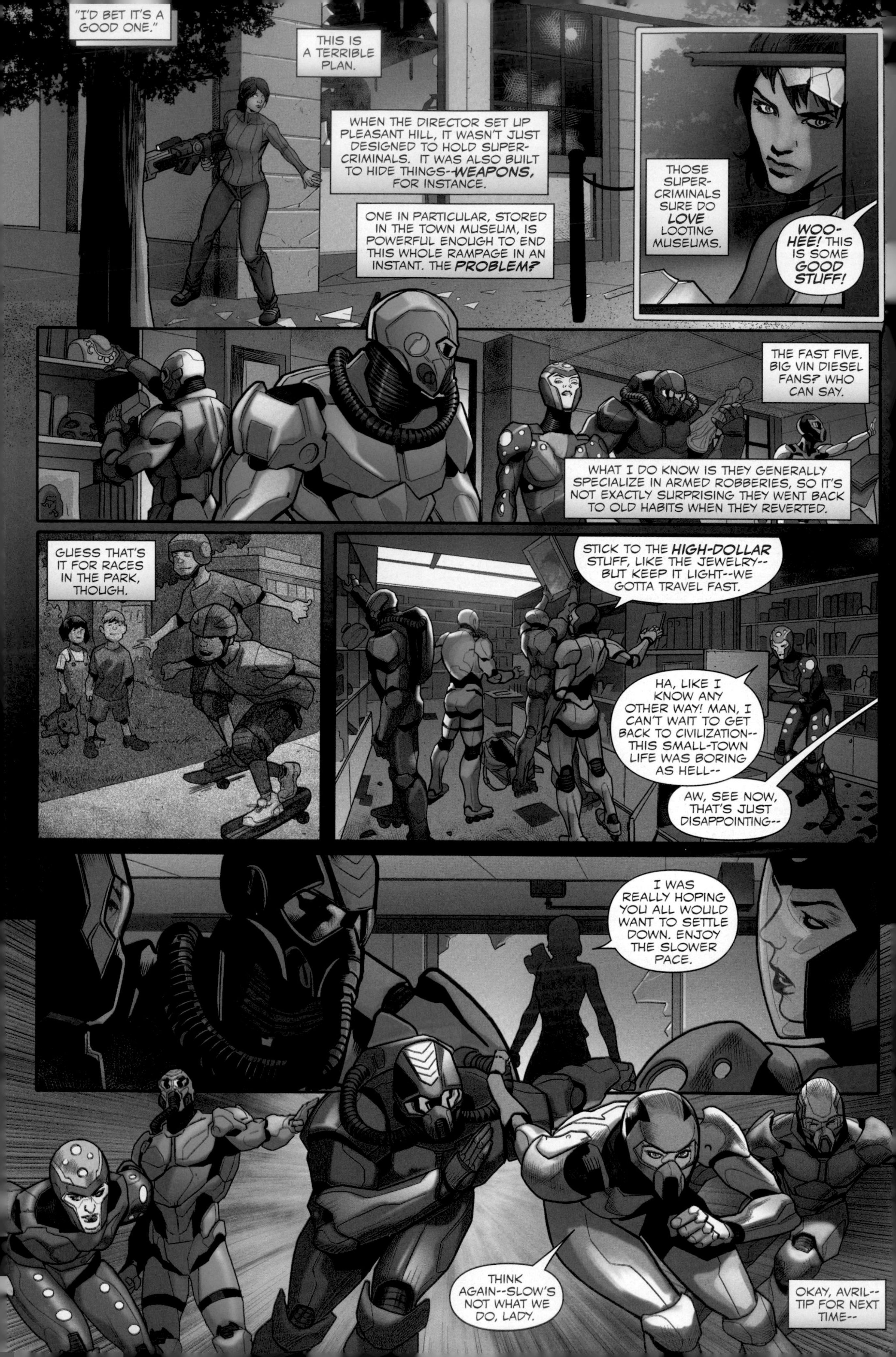
"I'D BET IT'S A GOOD ONE."
THIS IS A TERRIBLE PLAN.
WHEN THE DIRECTOR SET UP PLEASANT HILL, IT WASN'T JUST DESIGNED TO HOLD SUPER-CRIMINALS. IT WAS ALSO BUILT TO HIDE THINGS--WEAPONS, FOR INSTANCE.
ONE IN PARTICULAR, STORED IN THE TOWN MUSEUM, IS POWERFUL ENOUGH TO END THIS WHOLE RAMPAGE IN AN INSTANT. THE PROBLEM?
THOSE SUPER-CRIMINALS SURE DO LOVE LOOTING MUSEUMS.
WOO-HEE! THIS IS SOME GOOD STUFF!
THE FAST FIVE. BIG VIN DIESEL FANS? WHO CAN SAY.
WHAT I DO KNOW IS THEY GENERALLY SPECIALIZE IN ARMED ROBBERIES, SO IT'S NOT EXACTLY SURPRISING THEY WENT BACK TO OLD HABITS WHEN THEY REVERTED.
GUESS THAT'S IT FOR RACES IN THE PARK, THOUGH.
STICK TO THE HIGH-DOLLAR STUFF, LIKE THE JEWELRY--BUT KEEP IT LIGHT--WE GOTTA TRAVEL FAST.
HA, LIKE I KNOW ANY OTHER WAY! MAN, I CAN'T WAIT TO GET BACK TO CIVILIZATION--THIS SMALL-TOWN LIFE WAS BORING AS HELL--
AW, SEE NOW, THAT'S JUST DISAPPOINTING--
I WAS REALLY HOPING YOU ALL WOULD WANT TO SETTLE DOWN. ENJOY THE SLOWER PACE.
THINK AGAIN--SLOW'S NOT WHAT WE DO, LADY.
OKAY, AVRIL--TIP FOR NEXT TIME--

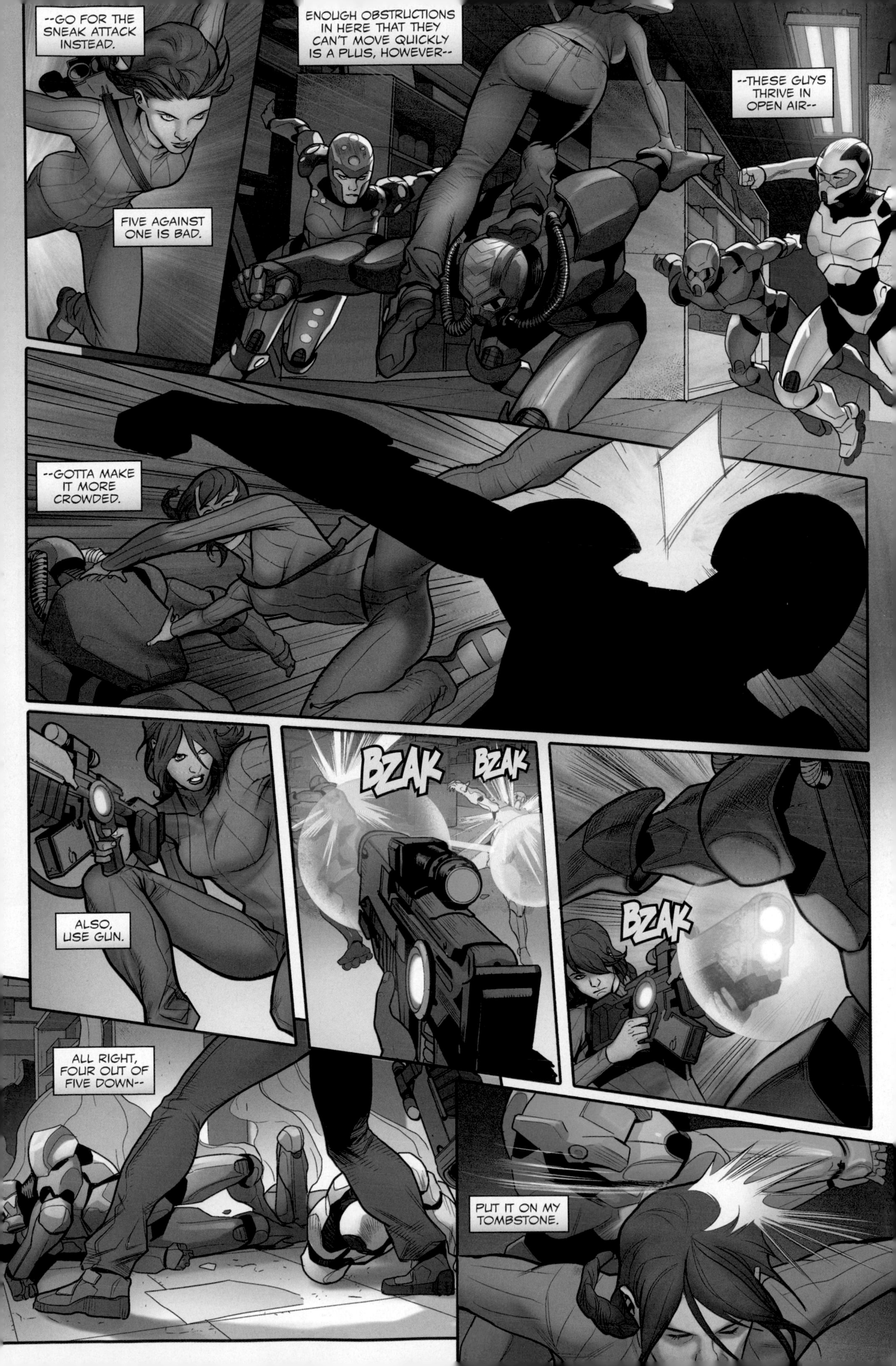
--GO FOR THE SNEAK ATTACK INSTEAD.
ENOUGH OBSTRUCTIONS IN HERE THAT THEY CAN'T MOVE QUICKLY IS A PLUS, HOWEVER--
--THESE GUYS THRIVE IN OPEN AIR--
FIVE AGAINST ONE IS BAD.
--GOTTA MAKE IT MORE CROWDED.
ALSO, USE GUN.
BZAK
BZAK
BZAK
ALL RIGHT, FOUR OUT OF FIVE DOWN--
PUT IT ON MY TOMBSTONE.

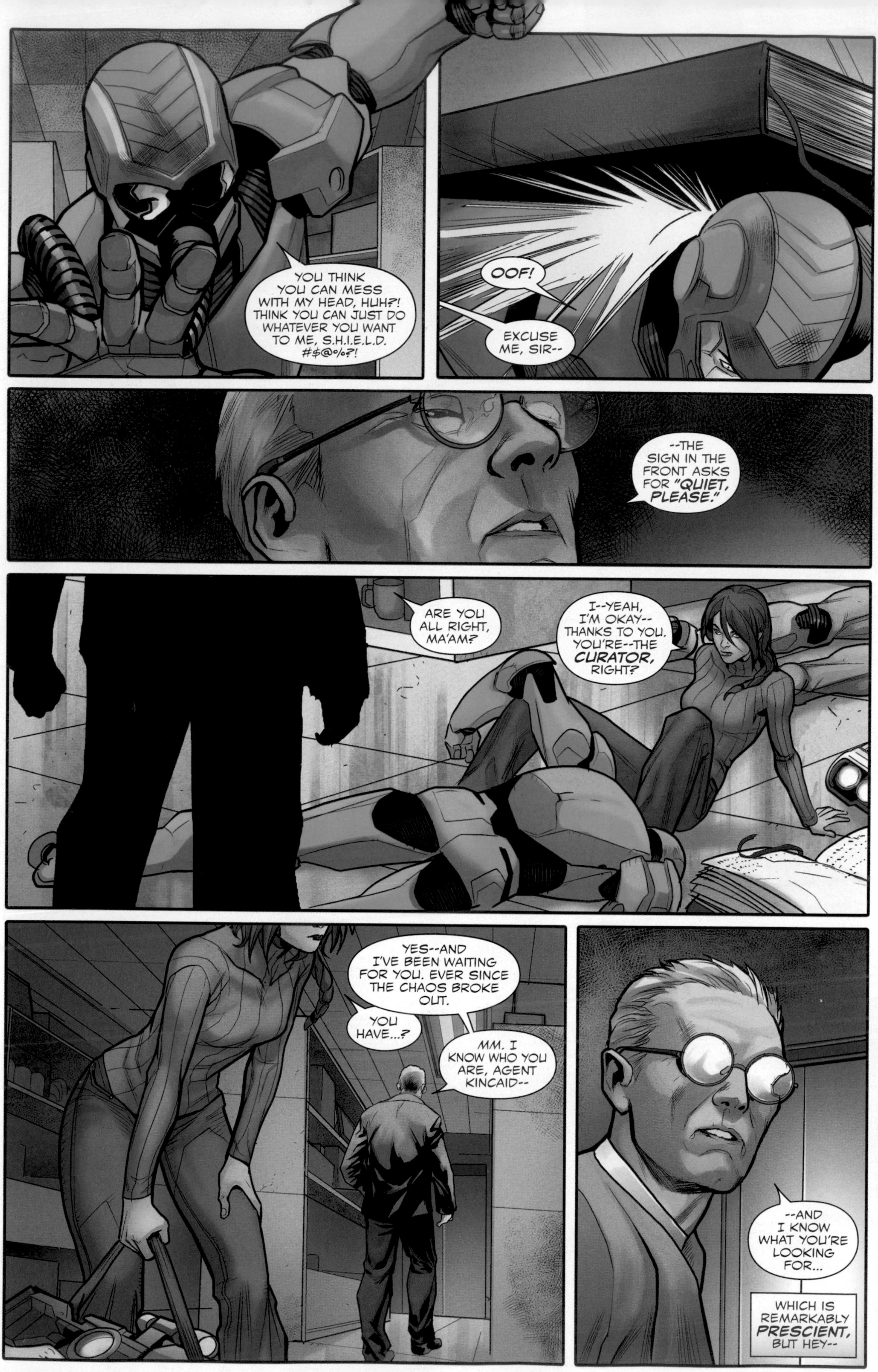

YOU THINK YOU CAN MESS WITH MY HEAD, HUH?! THINK YOU CAN JUST DO WHATEVER YOU WANT TO ME, S.H.I.E.L.D. #$@%?!
OOF!
EXCUSE ME, SIR--
--THE SIGN IN THE FRONT ASKS FOR "QUIET, PLEASE."
ARE YOU ALL RIGHT, MA'AM?
I--YEAH, I'M OKAY--THANKS TO YOU. YOU'RE--THE CURATOR, RIGHT?
YES--AND I'VE BEEN WAITING FOR YOU. EVER SINCE THE CHAOS BROKE OUT.
YOU HAVE...?
MM. I KNOW WHO YOU ARE, AGENT KINCAID--
--AND I KNOW WHAT YOU'RE LOOKING FOR...
WHICH IS REMARKABLY PRESCIENT, BUT HEY--

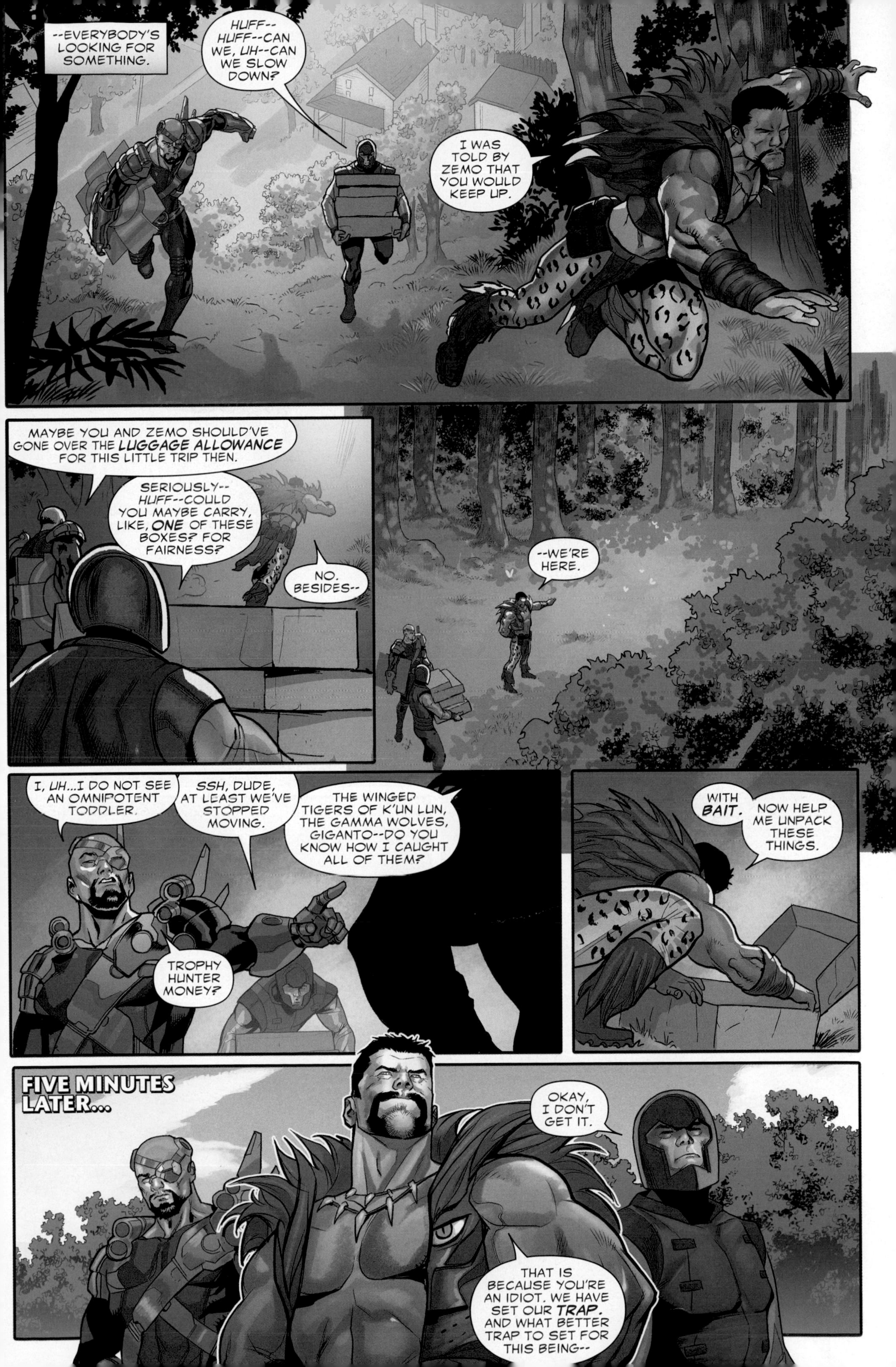
--EVERYBODY'S LOOKING FOR SOMETHING.
HUFF--HUFF--CAN WE, UH--CAN WE SLOW DOWN?
I WAS TOLD BY ZEMO THAT YOU WOULD KEEP UP.
MAYBE YOU AND ZEMO SHOULD'VE GONE OVER THE LUGGAGE ALLOWANCE FOR THIS LITTLE TRIP THEN.
SERIOUSLY--HUFF--COULD YOU MAYBE CARRY, LIKE, ONE OF THESE BOXES? FOR FAIRNESS?
NO. BESIDES--
--WE'RE HERE.
I, UH...I DO NOT SEE AN OMNIPOTENT TODDLER.
SSH, DUDE, AT LEAST WE'VE STOPPED MOVING.
THE WINGED TIGERS OF K'UN LUN, THE GAMMA WOLVES, GIGANTO--DO YOU KNOW HOW I CAUGHT ALL OF THEM?
TROPHY HUNTER MONEY?
WITH BAIT.
NOW HELP ME UNPACK THESE THINGS.
FIVE MINUTES LATER...
OKAY, I DON'T GET IT.
THAT IS BECAUSE YOU'RE AN IDIOT. WE HAVE SET OUR TRAP. AND WHAT BETTER TRAP TO SET FOR THIS BEING--

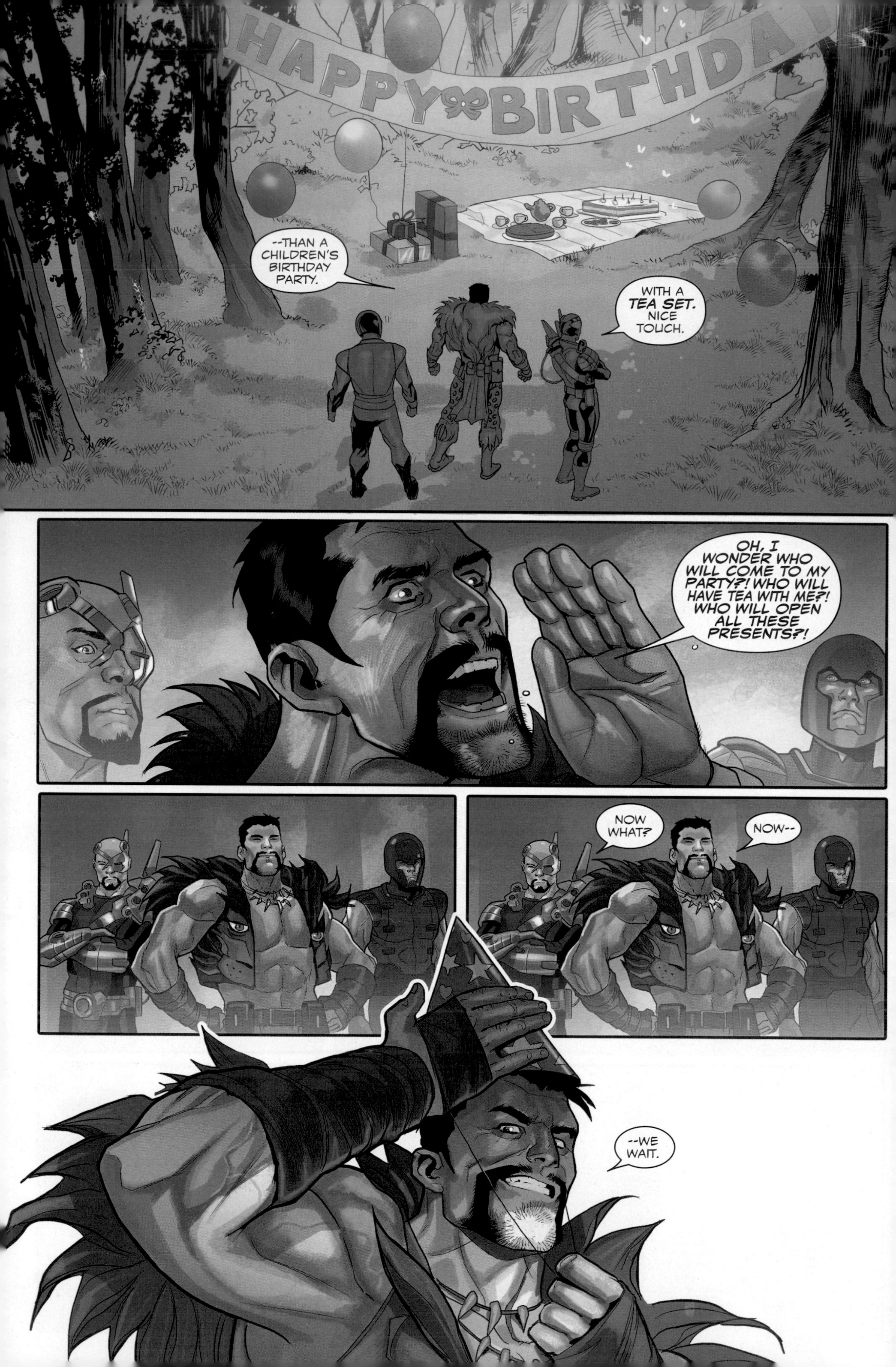
HAPPY BIRTHDAY
--THAN A CHILDREN'S BIRTHDAY PARTY.
WITH A TEA SET. NICE TOUCH.
OH, I WONDER WHO WILL COME TO MY PARTY?! WHO WILL HAVE TEA WITH ME?! WHO WILL OPEN ALL THESE PRESENTS?!
NOW WHAT?
NOW--
--WE WAIT.

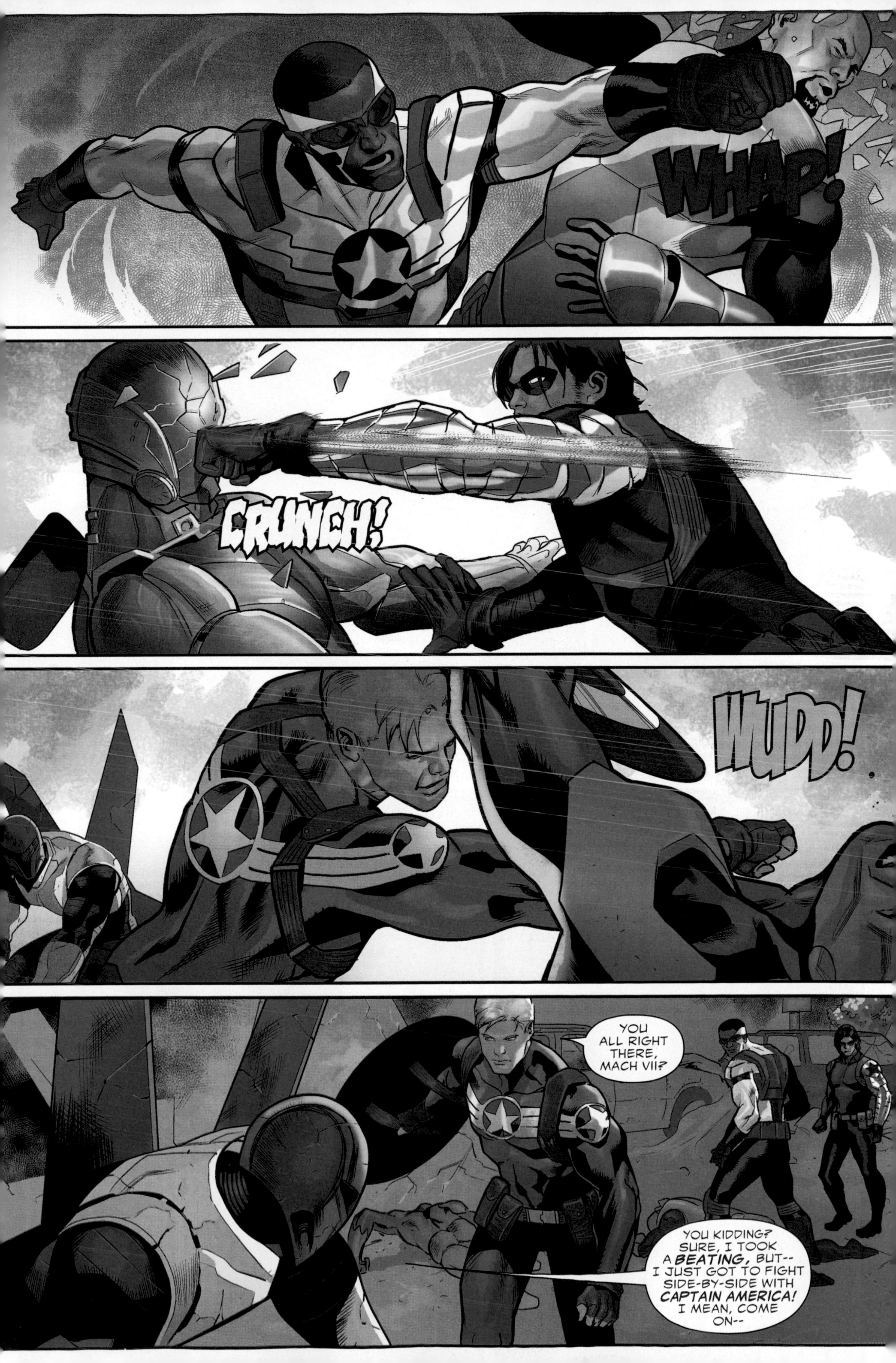
WHAP!
CRUNCH!
WUDD!
YOU ALL RIGHT THERE, MACH VII?
YOU KIDDING? SURE, I TOOK A BEATING, BUT-- I JUST GOT TO FIGHT SIDE-BY-SIDE WITH CAPTAIN AMERICA! I MEAN, COME ON--

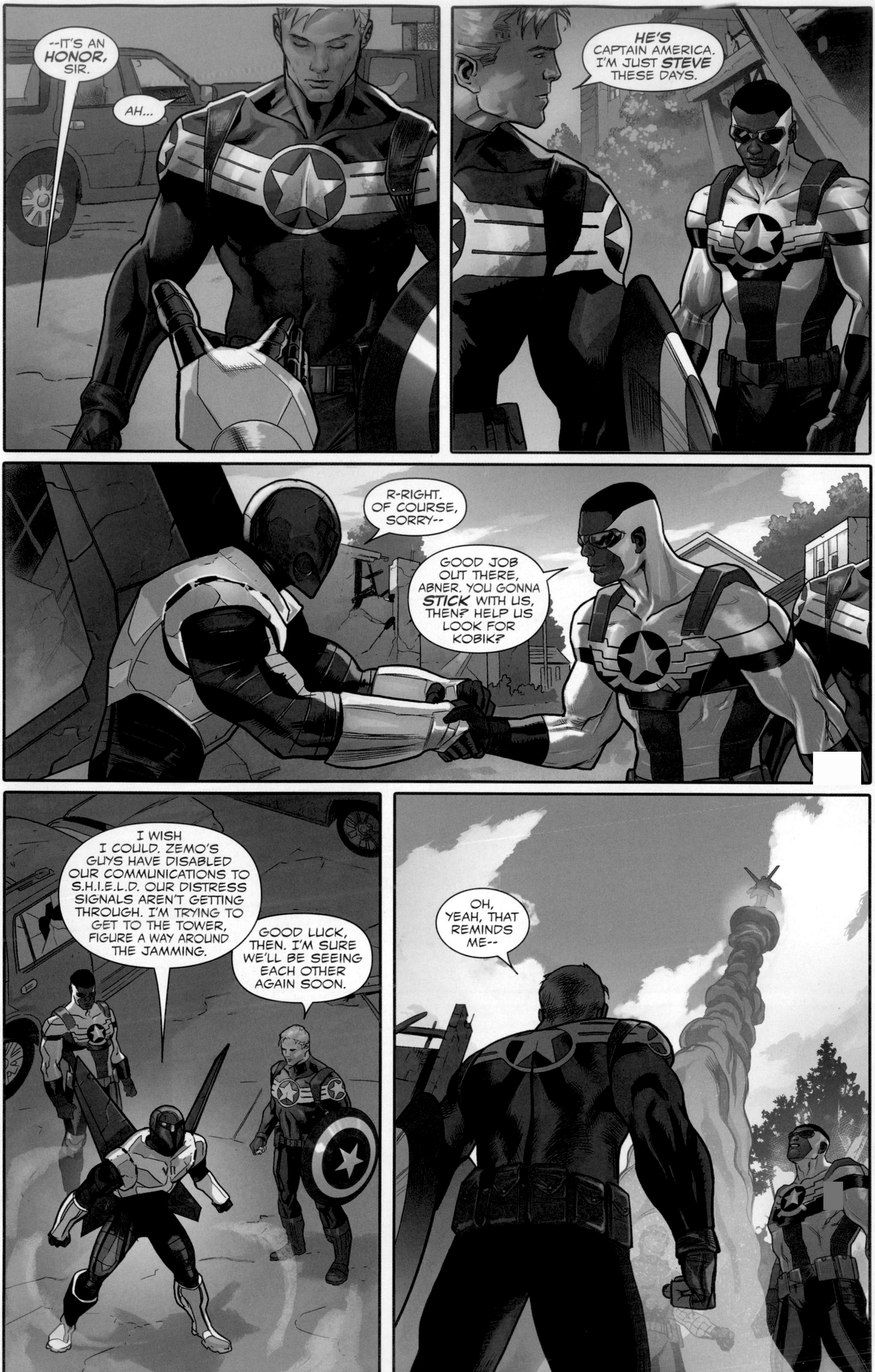
--IT'S AN HONOR, SIR.
AH...
HE'S CAPTAIN AMERICA. I'M JUST STEVE THESE DAYS.
R-RIGHT. OF COURSE, SORRY--
GOOD JOB OUT THERE, ABNER. YOU GONNA STICK WITH US, THEN? HELP US LOOK FOR KOBIK?
I WISH I COULD. ZEMO'S GUYS HAVE DISABLED OUR COMMUNICATIONS TO S.H.I.E.L.D. OUR DISTRESS SIGNALS AREN'T GETTING THROUGH. I'M TRYING TO GET TO THE TOWER, FIGURE A WAY AROUND THE JAMMING.
GOOD LUCK, THEN. I'M SURE WE'LL BE SEEING EACH OTHER AGAIN SOON.
OH, YEAH, THAT REMINDS ME--

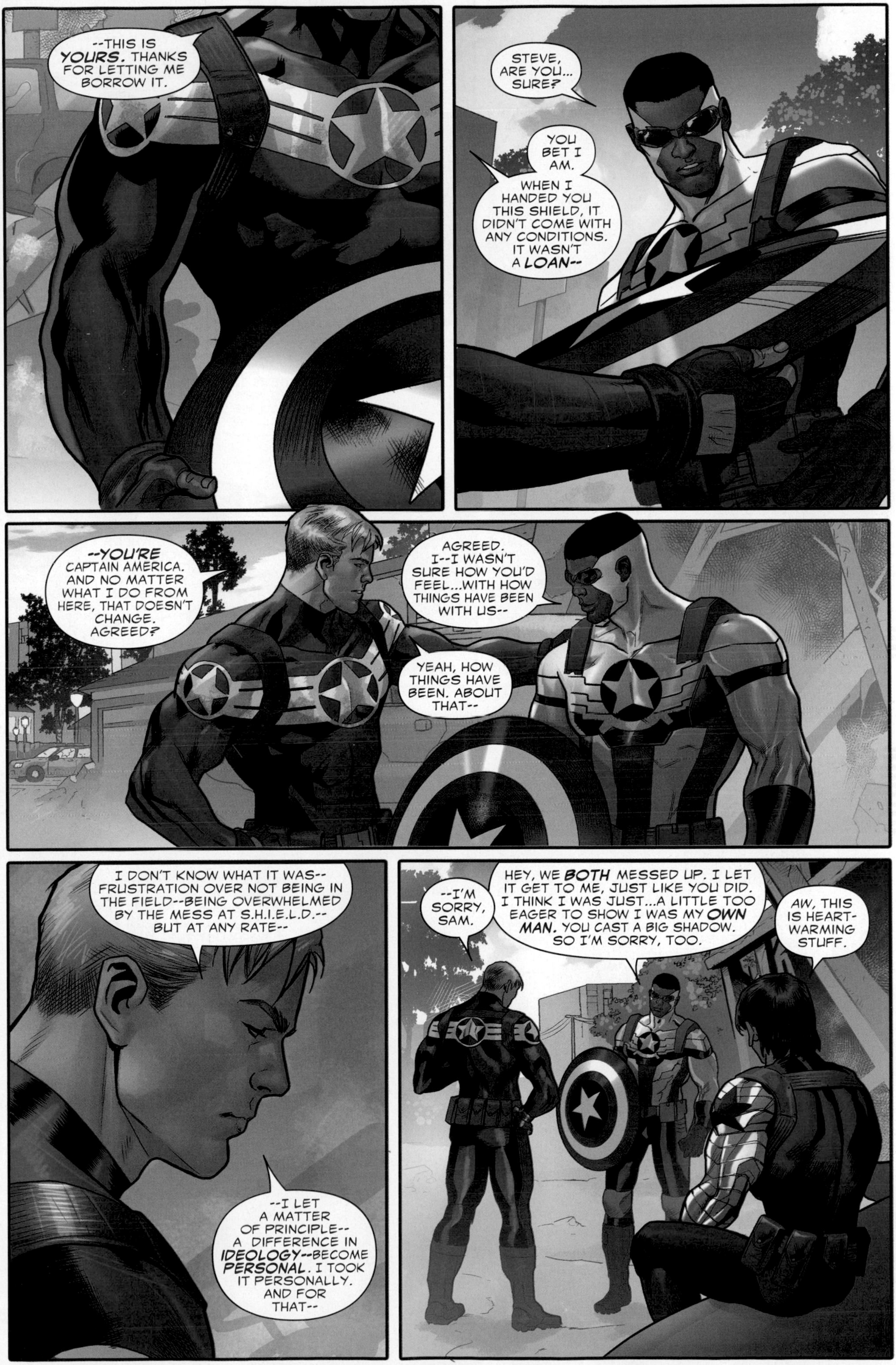
--THIS IS YOURS. THANKS FOR LETTING ME BORROW IT.
STEVE, ARE YOU... SURE?
YOU BET I AM.
WHEN I HANDED YOU THIS SHIELD, IT DIDN'T COME WITH ANY CONDITIONS. IT WASN'T A LOAN--
--YOU'RE CAPTAIN AMERICA. AND NO MATTER WHAT I DO FROM HERE, THAT DOESN'T CHANGE. AGREED?
AGREED. I--I WASN'T SURE HOW YOU'D FEEL...WITH HOW THINGS HAVE BEEN WITH US--
YEAH, HOW THINGS HAVE BEEN. ABOUT THAT--
I DON'T KNOW WHAT IT WAS-- FRUSTRATION OVER NOT BEING IN THE FIELD--BEING OVERWHELMED BY THE MESS AT S.H.I.E.L.D.-- BUT AT ANY RATE--
--I LET A MATTER OF PRINCIPLE-- A DIFFERENCE IN IDEOLOGY--BECOME PERSONAL. I TOOK IT PERSONALLY. AND FOR THAT--
--I'M SORRY, SAM.
HEY, WE BOTH MESSED UP. I LET IT GET TO ME, JUST LIKE YOU DID. I THINK I WAS JUST...A LITTLE TOO EAGER TO SHOW I WAS MY OWN MAN. YOU CAST A BIG SHADOW. SO I'M SORRY, TOO.
AW, THIS IS HEART-WARMING STUFF.

AND I APOLOGIZE TO YOU, TOO, BUCK--

--THERE'S LETTING FRIENDSHIPS GET TORN APART, THEN THERE'S LETTING THEM DRIFT AWAY.

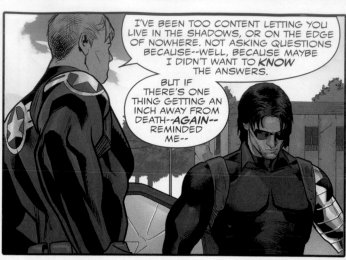

I'VE BEEN TOO CONTENT LETTING YOU LIVE IN THE SHADOWS, OR ON THE EDGE OF NOWHERE. NOT ASKING QUESTIONS BECAUSE--WELL, BECAUSE MAYBE I DIDN'T WANT TO KNOW THE ANSWERS.

BUT IF THERE'S ONE THING GETTING AN INCH AWAY FROM DEATH--AGAIN-- REMINDED ME--

--IT'S THAT WE'RE AT OUR STRONGEST WHEN WE'RE TOGETHER. THAT'S WHY, FROM NOW ON, WE STICK CLOSE.

HEY, WHERE WOULD I BE WITHOUT MY BEST PAL, RIGHT? QUESTION IS--

WHAT DO WE DO FROM HERE? AS FAR AS FINDING KOBIK--

SLIGHT CHANGE OF PLAN. IF WE CAN'T FIND HER, THEN WE AT LEAST MAKE SURE NOBODY ELSE IS LOOKING. WE STOP ZEMO'S REVOLT.

PRETTY TALL ORDER FOR JUST THE THREE OF US, STEVE. HE HAS A WHOLE ARMY.

IT'S NOT GOING TO BE JUST US, SAM--

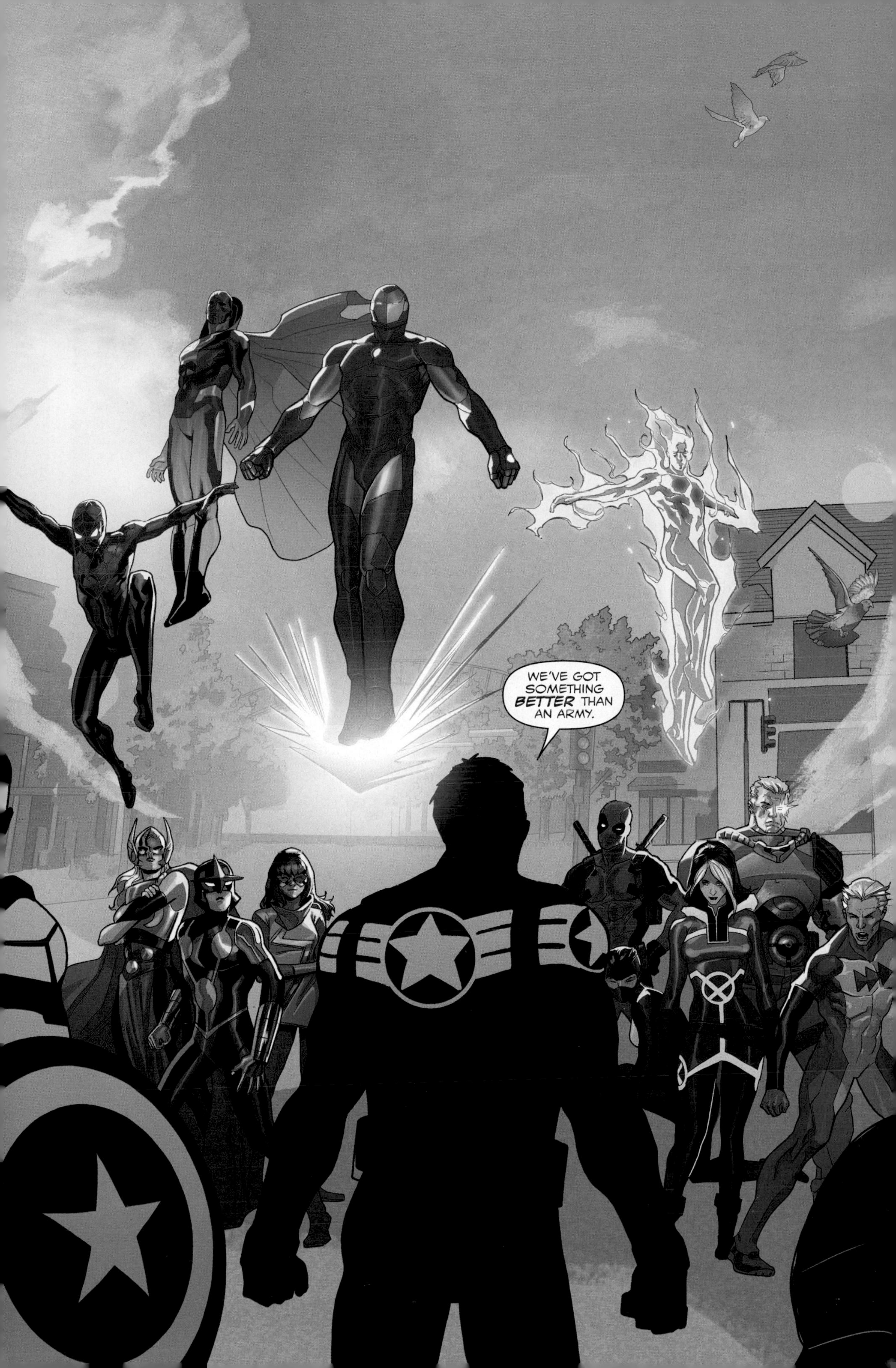
WE'VE GOT SOMETHING BETTER THAN AN ARMY.

Avengers Standoff:
Assault on Pleasant Hill Omega

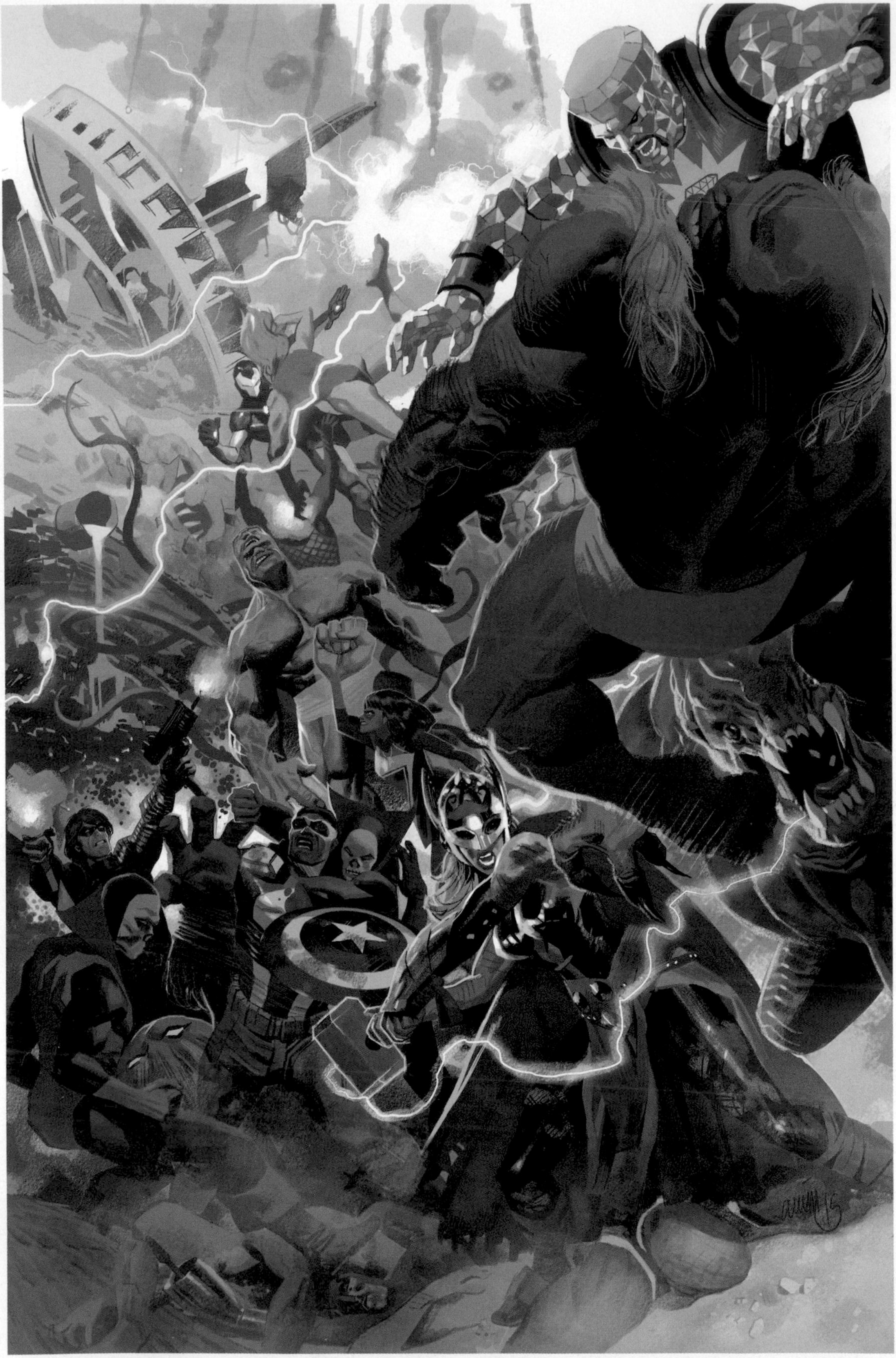

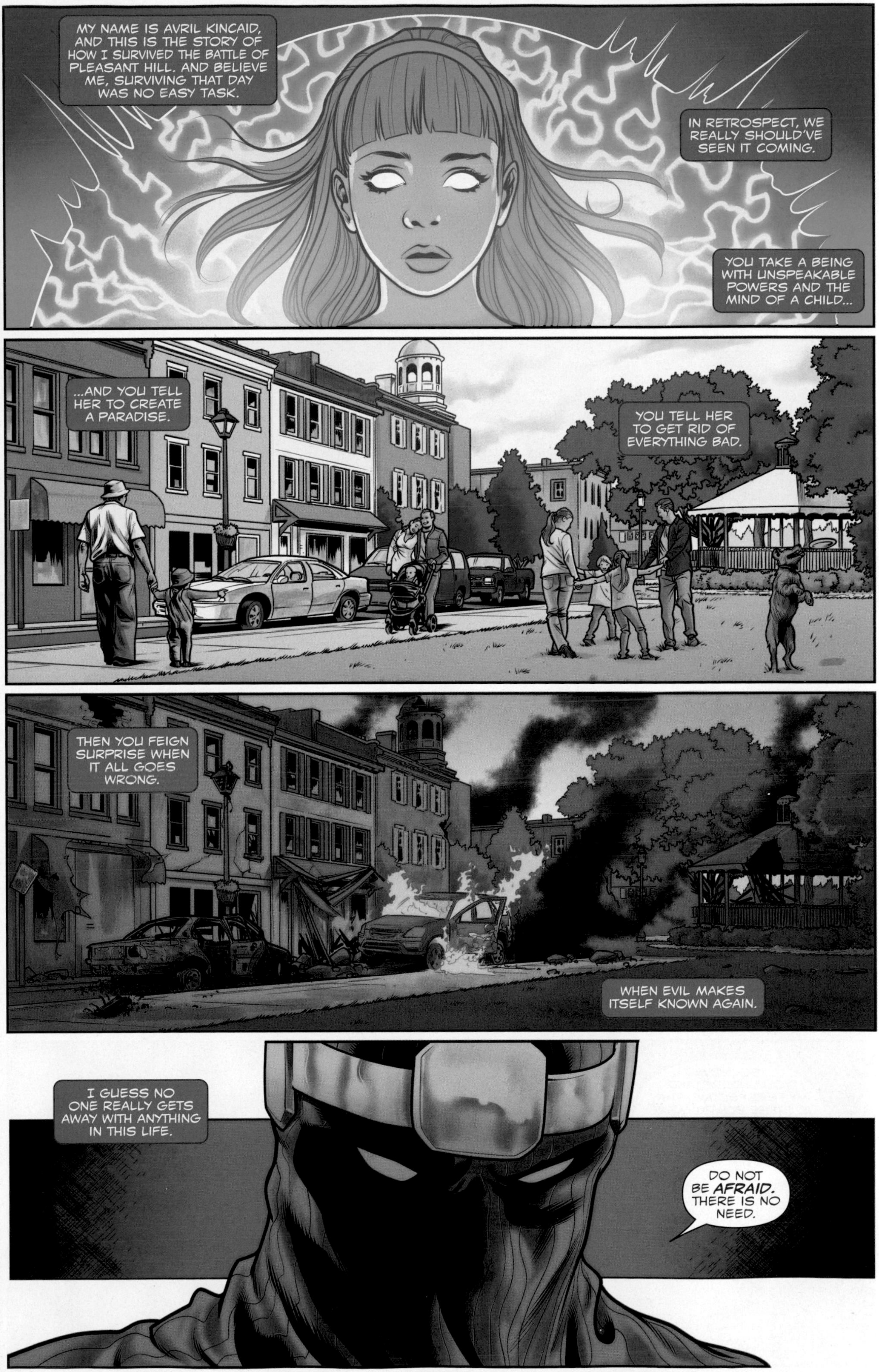
MY NAME IS AVRIL KINCAID, AND THIS IS THE STORY OF HOW I SURVIVED THE BATTLE OF PLEASANT HILL. AND BELIEVE ME, SURVIVING THAT DAY WAS NO EASY TASK.
IN RETROSPECT, WE REALLY SHOULD'VE SEEN IT COMING.
YOU TAKE A BEING WITH UNSPEAKABLE POWERS AND THE MIND OF A CHILD...
...AND YOU TELL HER TO CREATE A PARADISE.
YOU TELL HER TO GET RID OF EVERYTHING BAD.
THEN YOU FEIGN SURPRISE WHEN IT ALL GOES WRONG.
WHEN EVIL MAKES ITSELF KNOWN AGAIN.
I GUESS NO ONE REALLY GETS AWAY WITH ANYTHING IN THIS LIFE.
DO NOT BE *AFRAID.* THERE IS NO NEED.

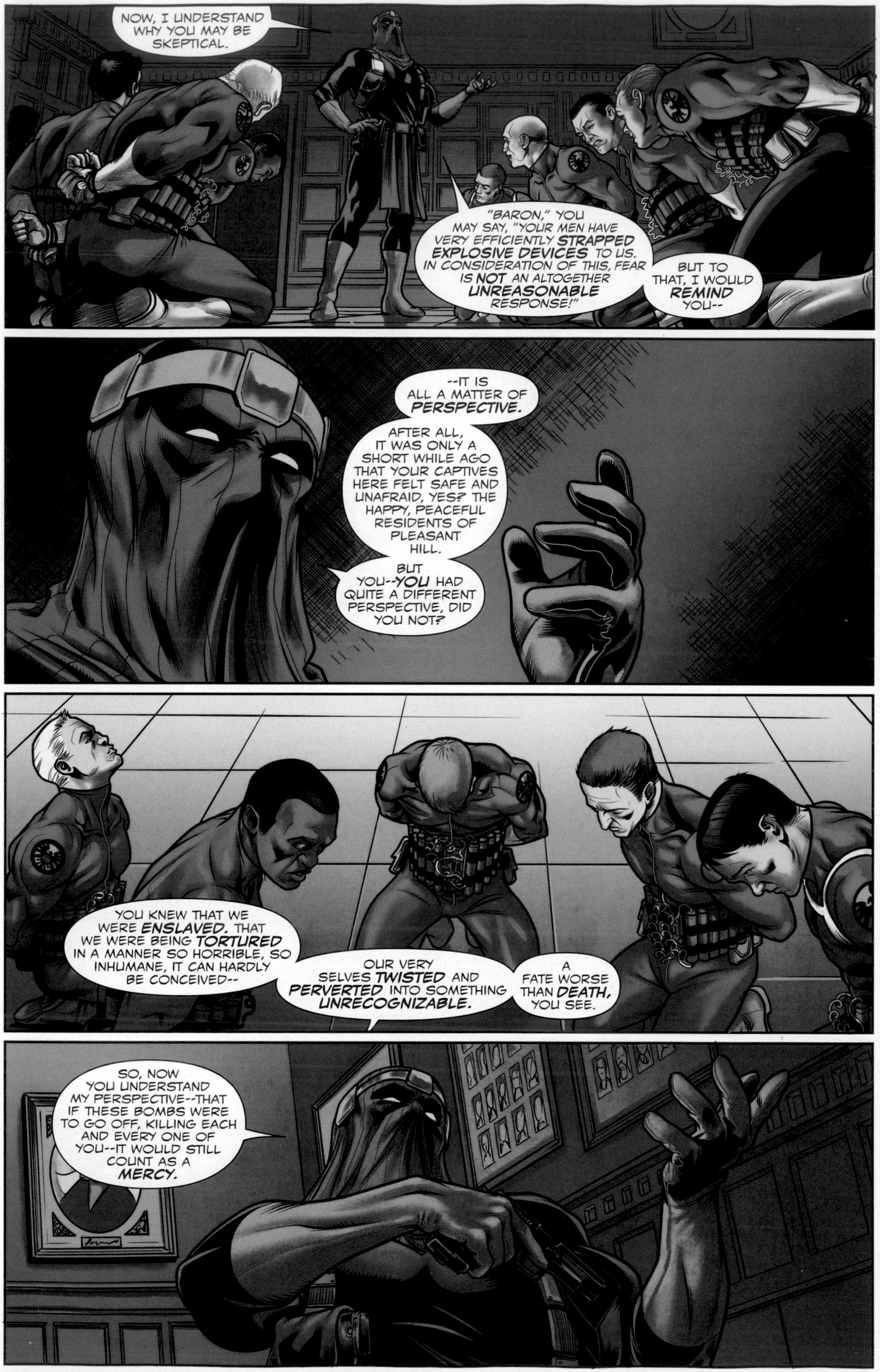
NOW, I UNDERSTAND WHY YOU MAY BE SKEPTICAL.
"BARON," YOU MAY SAY, "YOUR MEN HAVE VERY EFFICIENTLY STRAPPED EXPLOSIVE DEVICES TO US. IN CONSIDERATION OF THIS, FEAR IS NOT AN ALTOGETHER UNREASONABLE RESPONSE!"
BUT TO THAT, I WOULD REMIND YOU--
--IT IS ALL A MATTER OF PERSPECTIVE.
AFTER ALL, IT WAS ONLY A SHORT WHILE AGO THAT YOUR CAPTIVES HERE FELT SAFE AND UNAFRAID, YES? THE HAPPY, PEACEFUL RESIDENTS OF PLEASANT HILL.
BUT YOU--YOU HAD QUITE A DIFFERENT PERSPECTIVE, DID YOU NOT?
YOU KNEW THAT WE WERE ENSLAVED. THAT WE WERE BEING TORTURED IN A MANNER SO HORRIBLE, SO INHUMANE, IT CAN HARDLY BE CONCEIVED--
OUR VERY SELVES TWISTED AND PERVERTED INTO SOMETHING UNRECOGNIZABLE.
A FATE WORSE THAN DEATH, YOU SEE.
SO, NOW YOU UNDERSTAND MY PERSPECTIVE--THAT IF THESE BOMBS WERE TO GO OFF, KILLING EACH AND EVERY ONE OF YOU--IT WOULD STILL COUNT AS A MERCY.

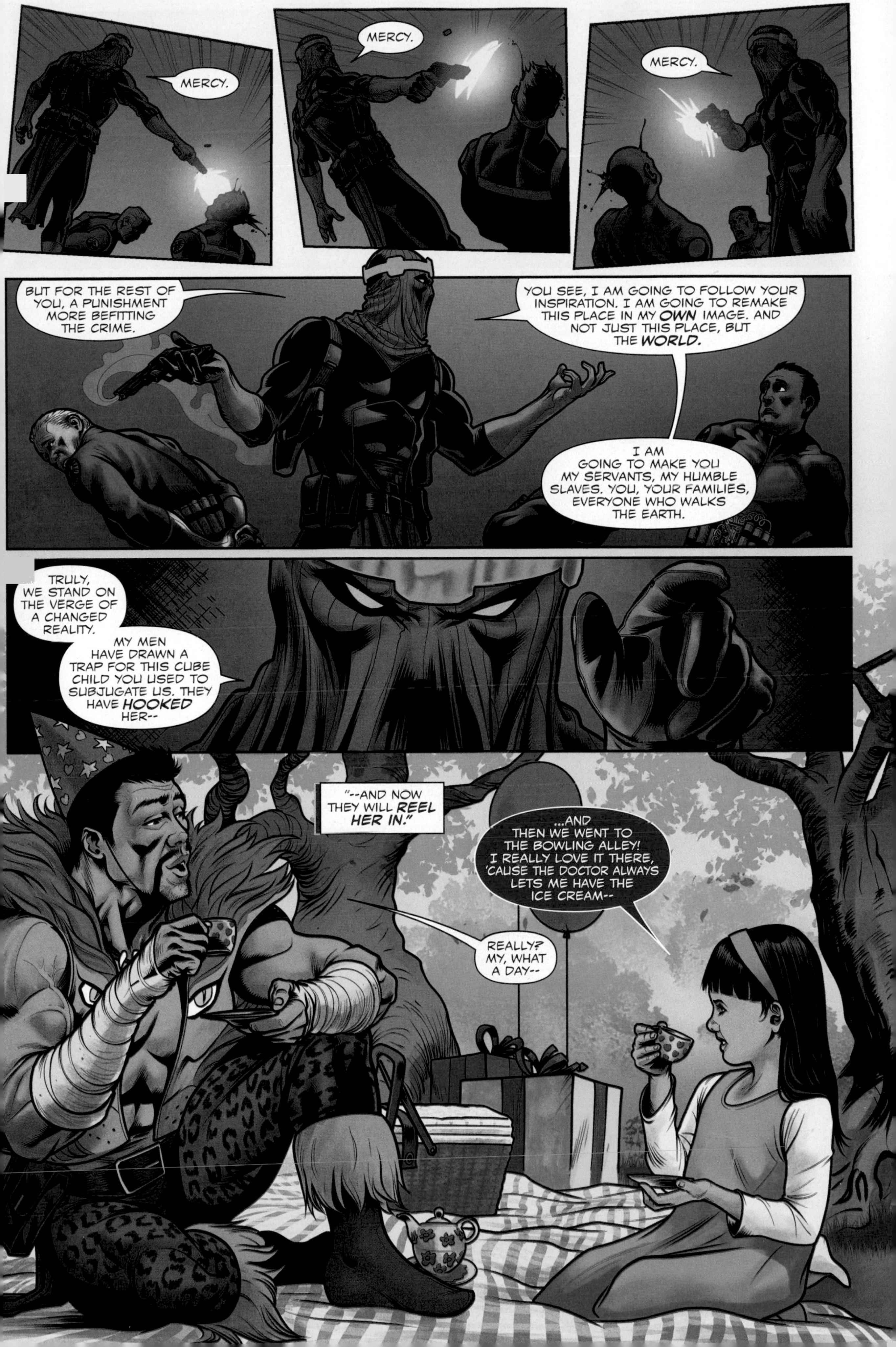
MERCY.
MERCY.
MERCY.
BUT FOR THE REST OF YOU, A PUNISHMENT MORE BEFITTING THE CRIME.
YOU SEE, I AM GOING TO FOLLOW YOUR INSPIRATION. I AM GOING TO REMAKE THIS PLACE IN MY OWN IMAGE. AND NOT JUST THIS PLACE, BUT THE WORLD.
I AM GOING TO MAKE YOU MY SERVANTS, MY HUMBLE SLAVES. YOU, YOUR FAMILIES, EVERYONE WHO WALKS THE EARTH.
TRULY, WE STAND ON THE VERGE OF A CHANGED REALITY.
MY MEN HAVE DRAWN A TRAP FOR THIS CUBE CHILD YOU USED TO SUBJUGATE US. THEY HAVE HOOKED HER--
"--AND NOW THEY WILL REEL HER IN."
...AND THEN WE WENT TO THE BOWLING ALLEY! I REALLY LOVE IT THERE, 'CAUSE THE DOCTOR ALWAYS LETS ME HAVE THE ICE CREAM--
REALLY? MY, WHAT A DAY--

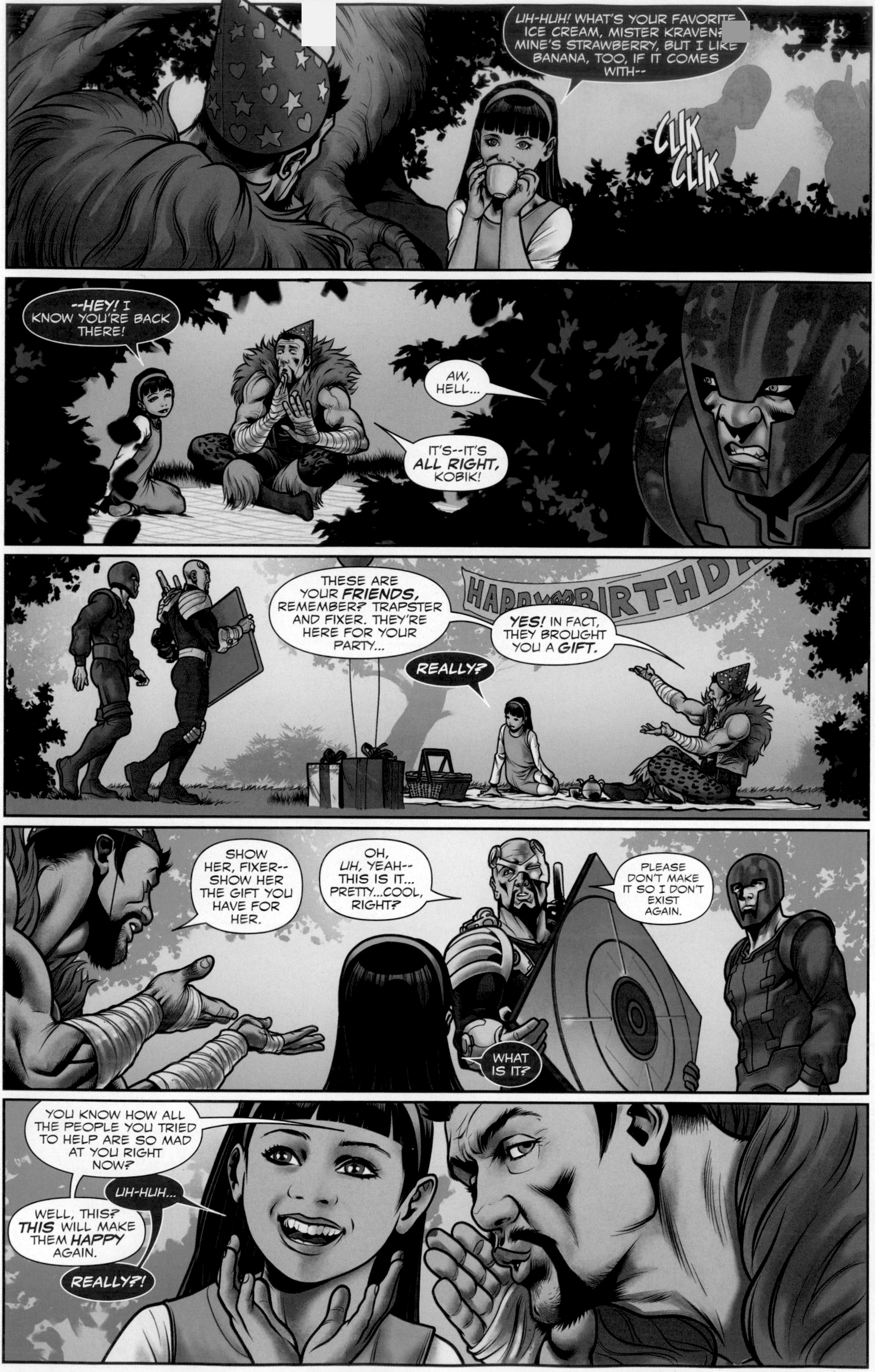

UH-HUH! WHAT'S YOUR FAVORITE ICE CREAM, MISTER KRAVEN? MINE'S STRAWBERRY, BUT I LIKE BANANA, TOO, IF IT COMES WITH--
CLIK CLIK
--HEY! I KNOW YOU'RE BACK THERE!
AW, HELL...
IT'S--IT'S ALL RIGHT, KOBIK!
THESE ARE YOUR FRIENDS, REMEMBER? TRAPSTER AND FIXER. THEY'RE HERE FOR YOUR PARTY...
REALLY?
YES! IN FACT, THEY BROUGHT YOU A GIFT.
HAPPY BIRTHD
SHOW HER, FIXER--SHOW HER THE GIFT YOU HAVE FOR HER.
OH, UH, YEAH--THIS IS IT... PRETTY...COOL, RIGHT?
PLEASE DON'T MAKE IT SO I DON'T EXIST AGAIN.
WHAT IS IT?
YOU KNOW HOW ALL THE PEOPLE YOU TRIED TO HELP ARE SO MAD AT YOU RIGHT NOW?
UH-HUH...
WELL, THIS? THIS WILL MAKE THEM HAPPY AGAIN.
REALLY?!

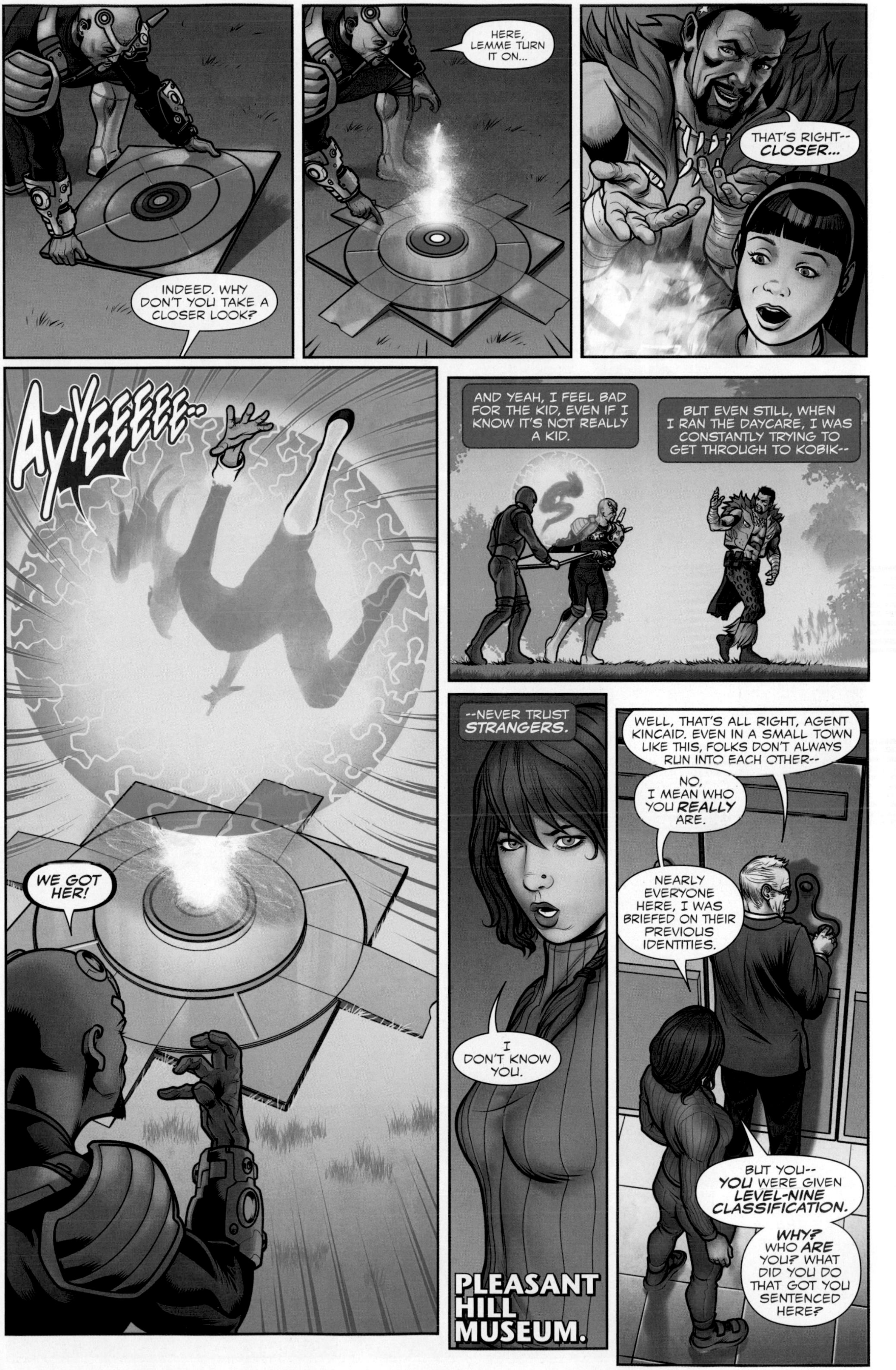
INDEED. WHY DON'T YOU TAKE A CLOSER LOOK?
HERE, LEMME TURN IT ON...
THAT'S RIGHT-- CLOSER...
AyYEEEEE..
WE GOT HER!
AND YEAH, I FEEL BAD FOR THE KID, EVEN IF I KNOW IT'S NOT REALLY A KID.
BUT EVEN STILL, WHEN I RAN THE DAYCARE, I WAS CONSTANTLY TRYING TO GET THROUGH TO KOBIK--
--NEVER TRUST STRANGERS.
PLEASANT HILL MUSEUM.
WELL, THAT'S ALL RIGHT, AGENT KINCAID. EVEN IN A SMALL TOWN LIKE THIS, FOLKS DON'T ALWAYS RUN INTO EACH OTHER--
NO, I MEAN WHO YOU REALLY ARE.
NEARLY EVERYONE HERE, I WAS BRIEFED ON THEIR PREVIOUS IDENTITIES.
I DON'T KNOW YOU.
BUT YOU-- YOU WERE GIVEN LEVEL-NINE CLASSIFICATION.
WHY? WHO ARE YOU? WHAT DID YOU DO THAT GOT YOU SENTENCED HERE?

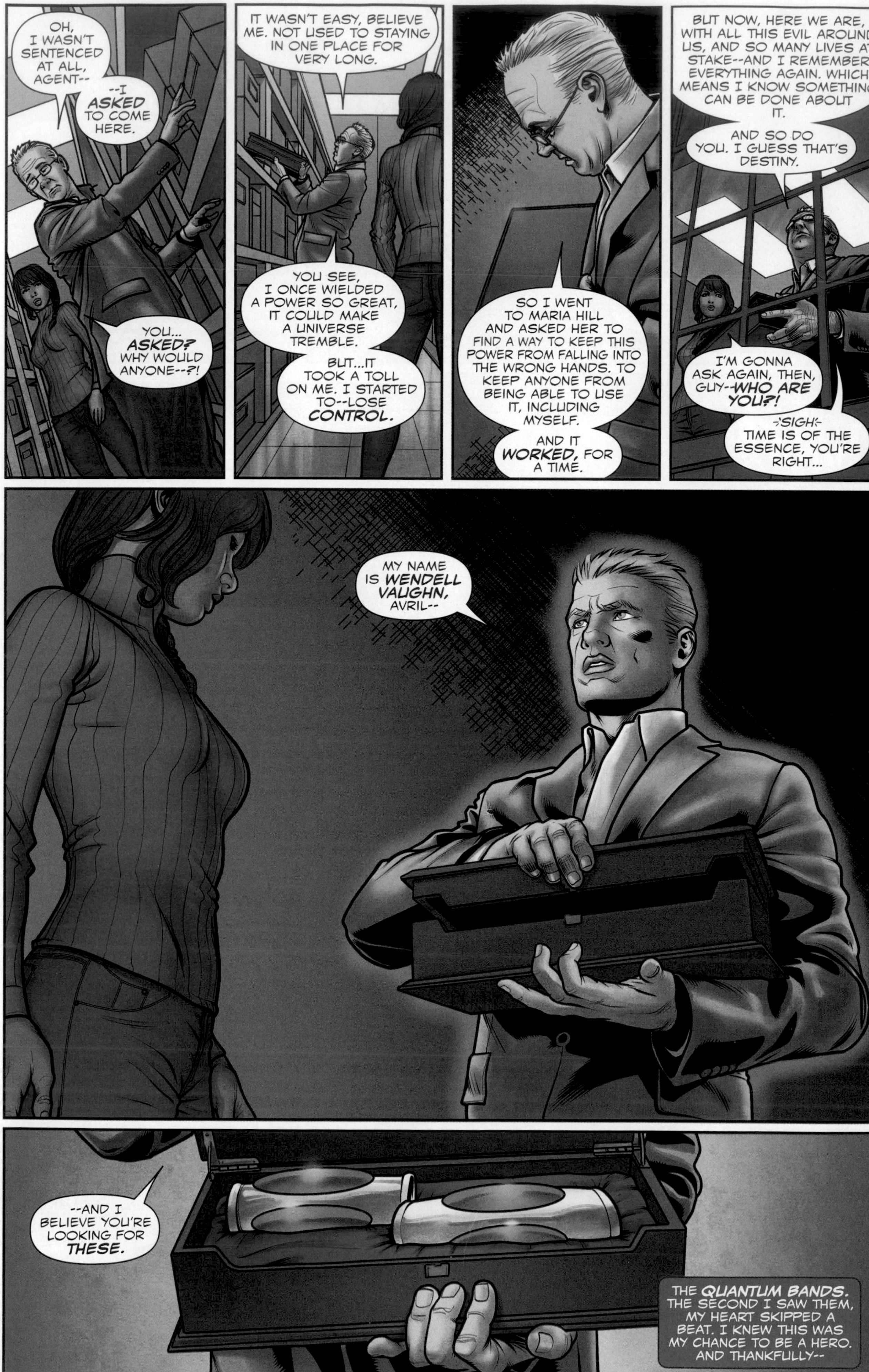
OH, I WASN'T SENTENCED AT ALL, AGENT--
--I *ASKED* TO COME HERE.
YOU... *ASKED?* WHY WOULD ANYONE--?!
IT WASN'T EASY, BELIEVE ME. NOT USED TO STAYING IN ONE PLACE FOR VERY LONG.
YOU SEE, I ONCE WIELDED A POWER SO GREAT, IT COULD MAKE A UNIVERSE TREMBLE.
BUT...IT TOOK A TOLL ON ME. I STARTED TO--LOSE *CONTROL.*
SO I WENT TO MARIA HILL AND ASKED HER TO FIND A WAY TO KEEP THIS POWER FROM FALLING INTO THE WRONG HANDS. TO KEEP ANYONE FROM BEING ABLE TO USE IT, INCLUDING MYSELF.
AND IT *WORKED,* FOR A TIME.
BUT NOW, HERE WE ARE, WITH ALL THIS EVIL AROUND US, AND SO MANY LIVES AT STAKE--AND I REMEMBER EVERYTHING AGAIN. WHICH MEANS I KNOW SOMETHING CAN BE DONE ABOUT IT.
AND SO DO YOU. I GUESS THAT'S DESTINY.
I'M GONNA ASK AGAIN, THEN, GUY--*WHO ARE YOU?!*
SIGH TIME IS OF THE ESSENCE, YOU'RE RIGHT...
MY NAME IS *WENDELL VAUGHN,* AVRIL--
--AND I BELIEVE YOU'RE LOOKING FOR *THESE.*
THE *QUANTUM BANDS.* THE SECOND I SAW THEM, MY HEART SKIPPED A BEAT. I KNEW THIS WAS MY CHANCE TO BE A HERO. AND THANKFULLY--

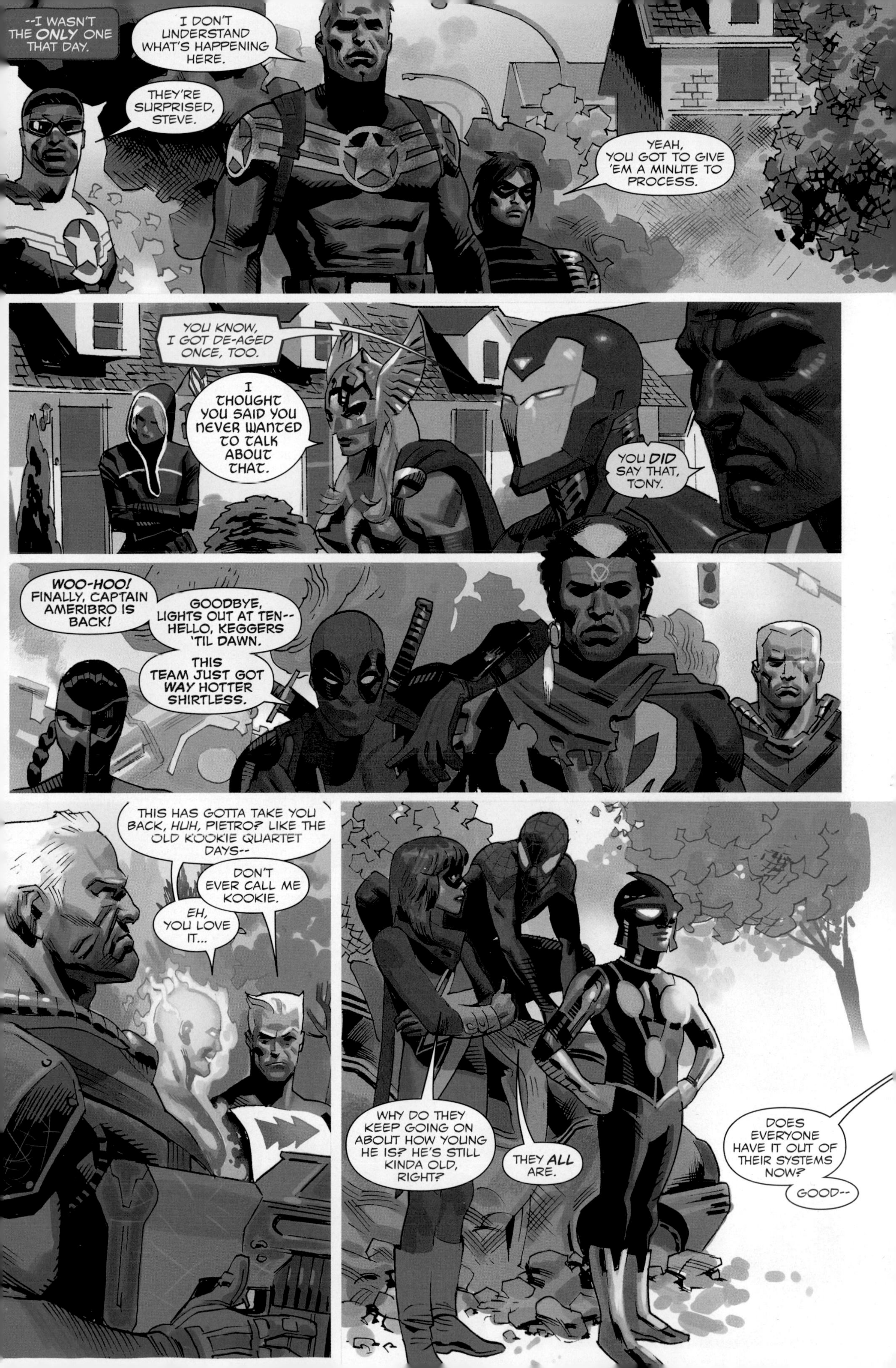
--I WASN'T THE ONLY ONE THAT DAY.
I DON'T UNDERSTAND WHAT'S HAPPENING HERE.
THEY'RE SURPRISED, STEVE.
YEAH, YOU GOT TO GIVE 'EM A MINUTE TO PROCESS.
YOU KNOW, I GOT DE-AGED ONCE, TOO.
I THOUGHT YOU SAID YOU NEVER WANTED TO TALK ABOUT THAT.
YOU DID SAY THAT, TONY.
WOO-HOO! FINALLY, CAPTAIN AMERIBRO IS BACK!
GOODBYE, LIGHTS OUT AT TEN-- HELLO, KEGGERS 'TIL DAWN.
THIS TEAM JUST GOT WAY HOTTER SHIRTLESS.
THIS HAS GOTTA TAKE YOU BACK, HUH, PIETRO? LIKE THE OLD KOOKIE QUARTET DAYS--
DON'T EVER CALL ME KOOKIE.
EH, YOU LOVE IT...
WHY DO THEY KEEP GOING ON ABOUT HOW YOUNG HE IS? HE'S STILL KINDA OLD, RIGHT?
THEY ALL ARE.
DOES EVERYONE HAVE IT OUT OF THEIR SYSTEMS NOW?
GOOD--

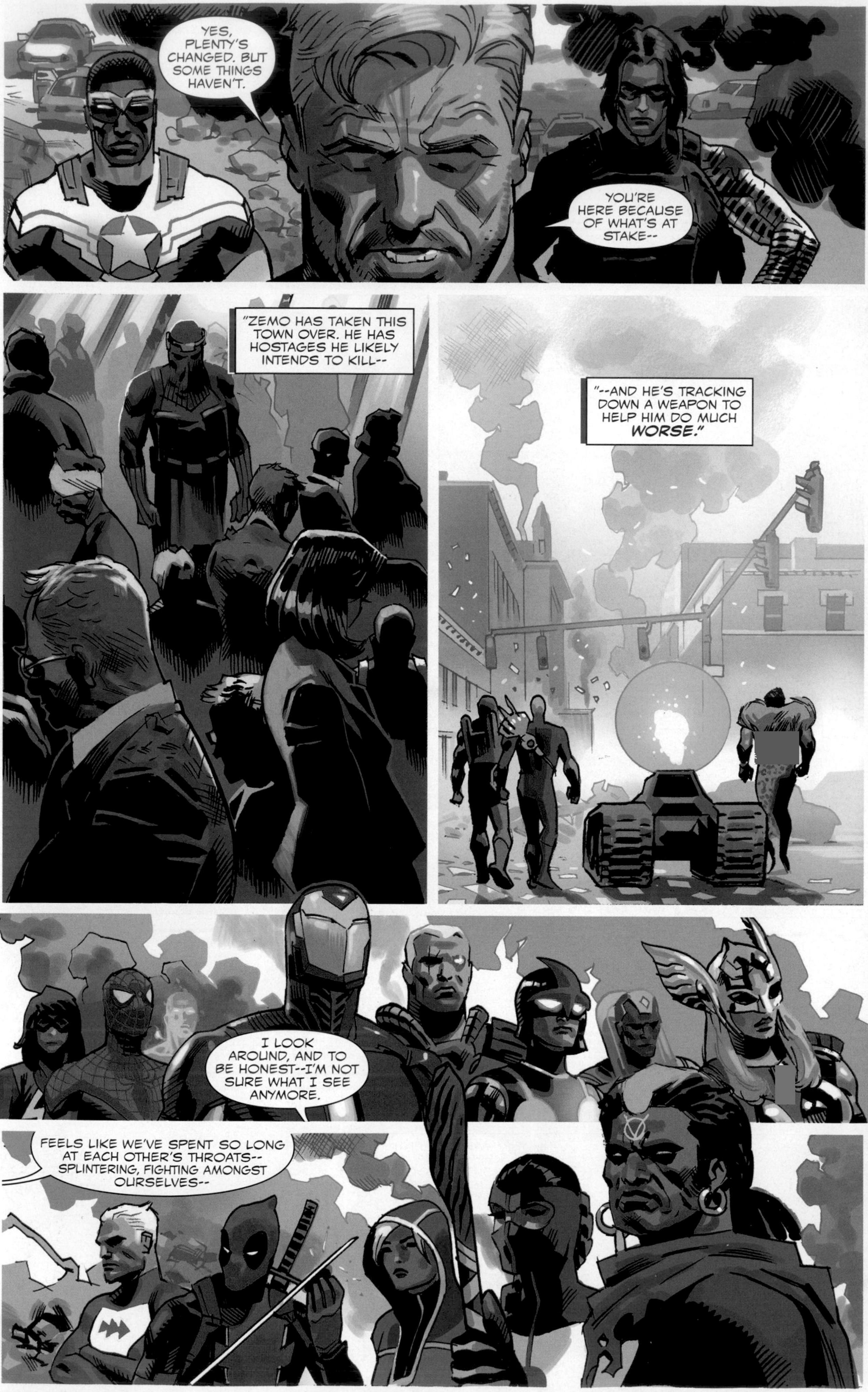
YES, PLENTY'S CHANGED. BUT SOME THINGS HAVEN'T.
YOU'RE HERE BECAUSE OF WHAT'S AT STAKE--
"ZEMO HAS TAKEN THIS TOWN OVER. HE HAS HOSTAGES HE LIKELY INTENDS TO KILL--
"--AND HE'S TRACKING DOWN A WEAPON TO HELP HIM DO MUCH WORSE."
I LOOK AROUND, AND TO BE HONEST--I'M NOT SURE WHAT I SEE ANYMORE.
FEELS LIKE WE'VE SPENT SO LONG AT EACH OTHER'S THROATS--SPLINTERING, FIGHTING AMONGST OURSELVES--

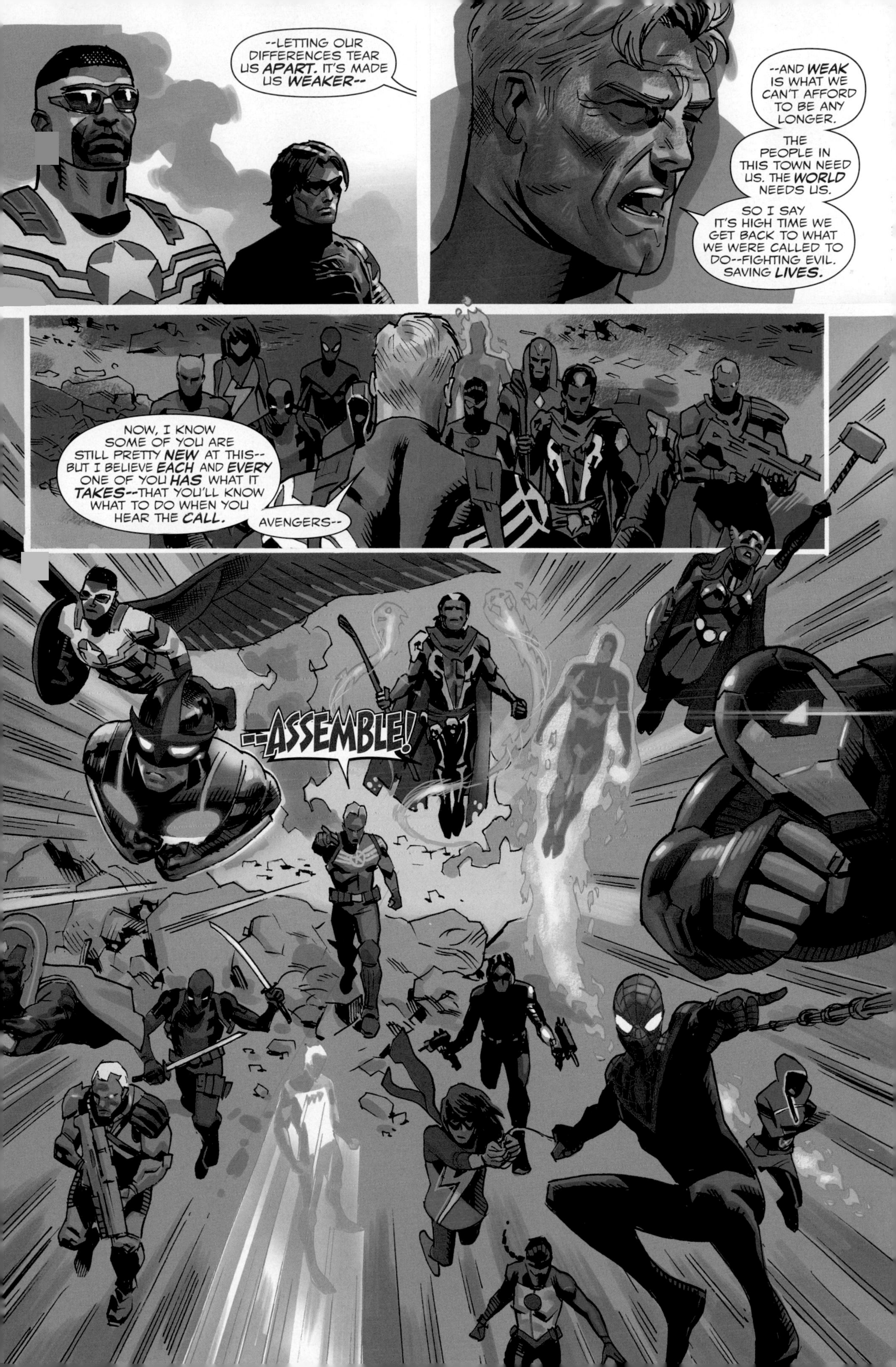
--LETTING OUR DIFFERENCES TEAR US APART. IT'S MADE US WEAKER--
--AND WEAK IS WHAT WE CAN'T AFFORD TO BE ANY LONGER.
THE PEOPLE IN THIS TOWN NEED US. THE WORLD NEEDS US.
SO I SAY IT'S HIGH TIME WE GET BACK TO WHAT WE WERE CALLED TO DO--FIGHTING EVIL. SAVING LIVES.
NOW, I KNOW SOME OF YOU ARE STILL PRETTY NEW AT THIS--BUT I BELIEVE EACH AND EVERY ONE OF YOU HAS WHAT IT TAKES--THAT YOU'LL KNOW WHAT TO DO WHEN YOU HEAR THE CALL.
AVENGERS--
--ASSEMBLE!

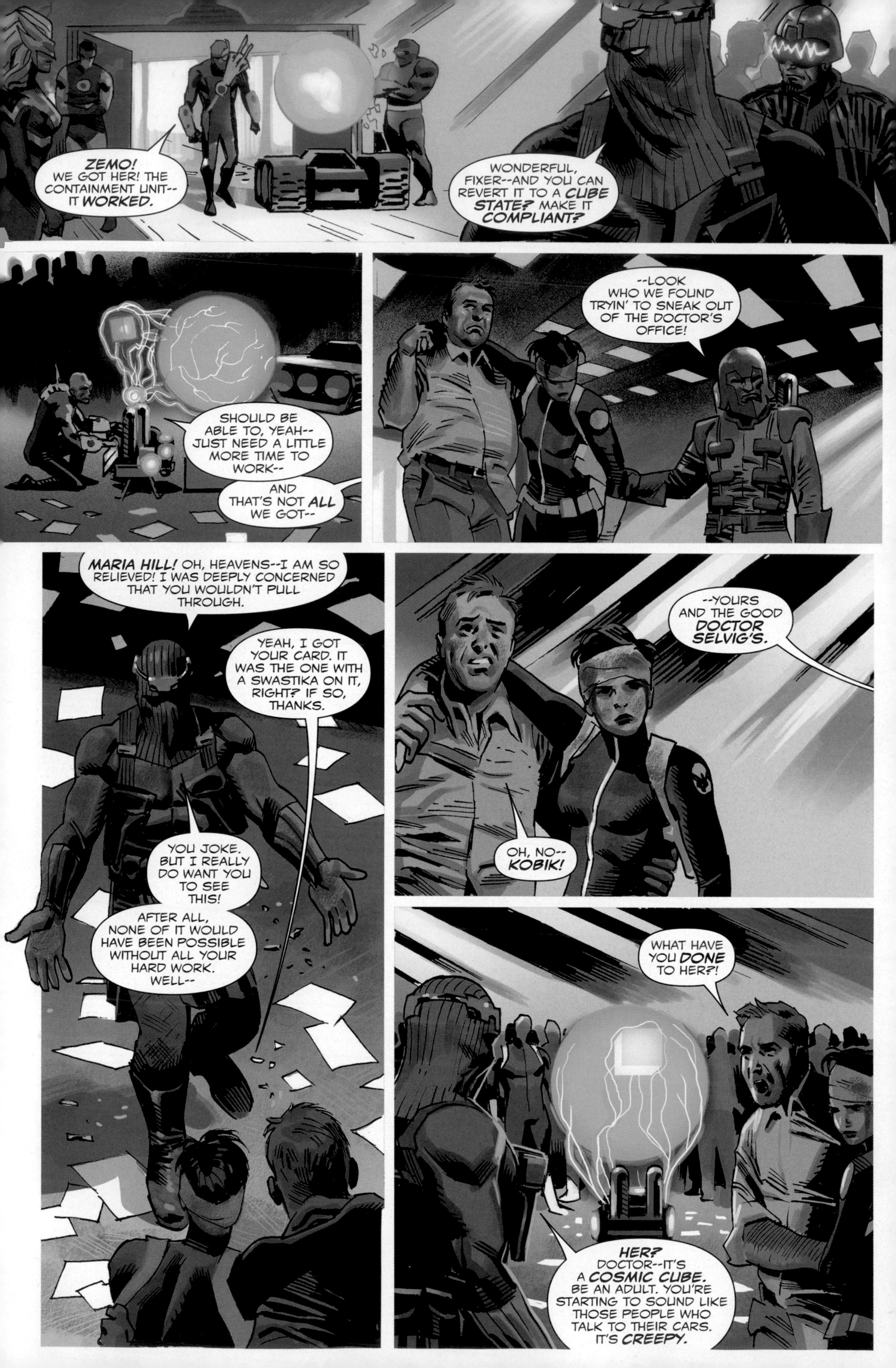
ZEMO! WE GOT HER! THE CONTAINMENT UNIT-- IT WORKED.
WONDERFUL, FIXER--AND YOU CAN REVERT IT TO A CUBE STATE? MAKE IT COMPLIANT?
SHOULD BE ABLE TO, YEAH-- JUST NEED A LITTLE MORE TIME TO WORK--
AND THAT'S NOT ALL WE GOT--
--LOOK WHO WE FOUND TRYIN' TO SNEAK OUT OF THE DOCTOR'S OFFICE!
MARIA HILL! OH, HEAVENS--I AM SO RELIEVED! I WAS DEEPLY CONCERNED THAT YOU WOULDN'T PULL THROUGH.
YEAH, I GOT YOUR CARD. IT WAS THE ONE WITH A SWASTIKA ON IT, RIGHT? IF SO, THANKS.
YOU JOKE. BUT I REALLY DO WANT YOU TO SEE THIS!
AFTER ALL, NONE OF IT WOULD HAVE BEEN POSSIBLE WITHOUT ALL YOUR HARD WORK. WELL--
--YOURS AND THE GOOD DOCTOR SELVIG'S.
OH, NO-- KOBIK!
WHAT HAVE YOU DONE TO HER?!
HER? DOCTOR--IT'S A COSMIC CUBE. BE AN ADULT. YOU'RE STARTING TO SOUND LIKE THOSE PEOPLE WHO TALK TO THEIR CARS. IT'S CREEPY.

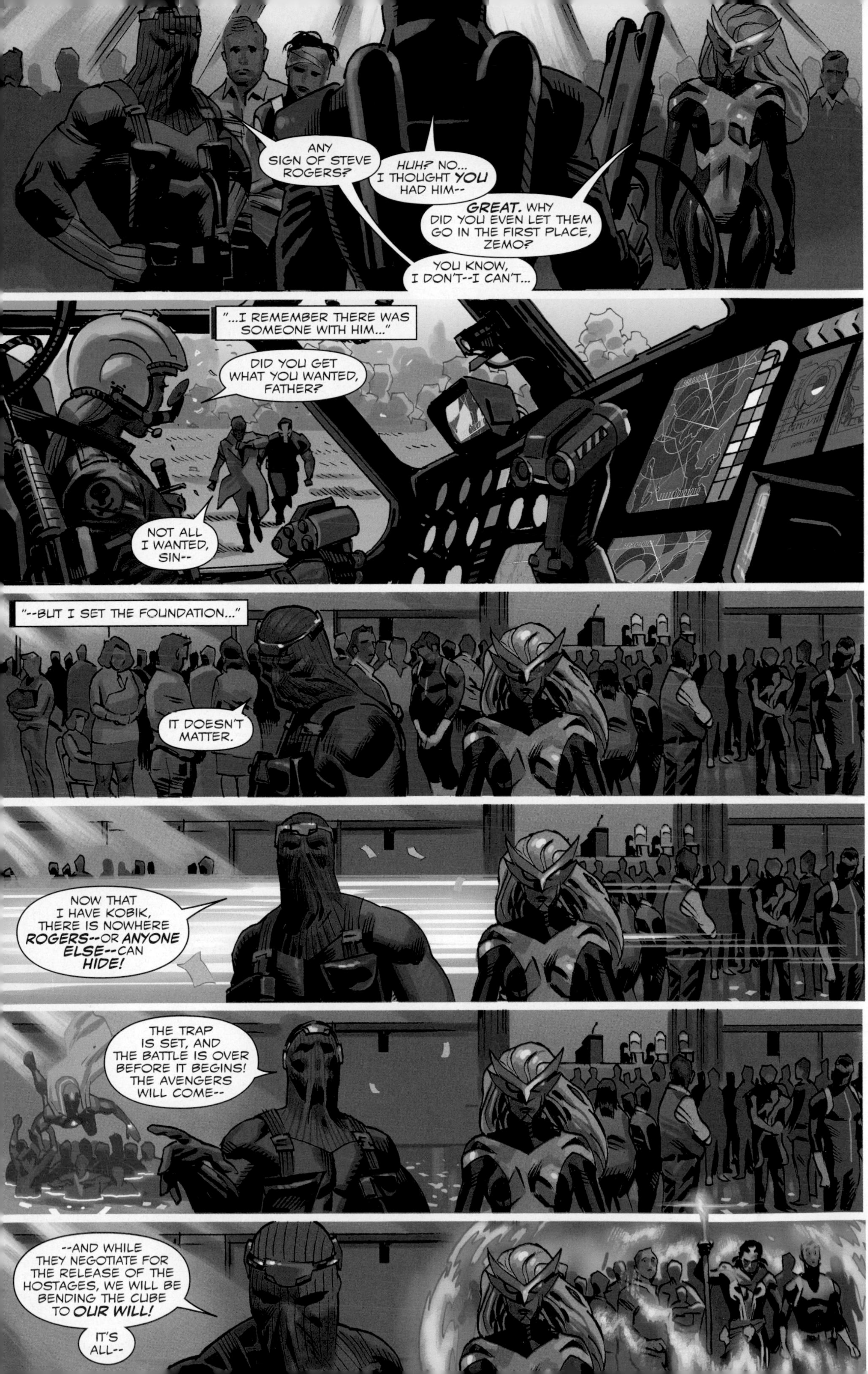
ANY SIGN OF STEVE ROGERS?
HUH? NO... I THOUGHT YOU HAD HIM--
GREAT. WHY DID YOU EVEN LET THEM GO IN THE FIRST PLACE, ZEMO?
YOU KNOW, I DON'T--I CAN'T...
"...I REMEMBER THERE WAS SOMEONE WITH HIM..."
DID YOU GET WHAT YOU WANTED, FATHER?
NOT ALL I WANTED, SIN--
"--BUT I SET THE FOUNDATION..."
IT DOESN'T MATTER.
NOW THAT I HAVE KOBIK, THERE IS NOWHERE ROGERS--OR ANYONE ELSE--CAN HIDE!
THE TRAP IS SET, AND THE BATTLE IS OVER BEFORE IT BEGINS! THE AVENGERS WILL COME--
--AND WHILE THEY NEGOTIATE FOR THE RELEASE OF THE HOSTAGES, WE WILL BE BENDING THE CUBE TO OUR WILL!
IT'S ALL--

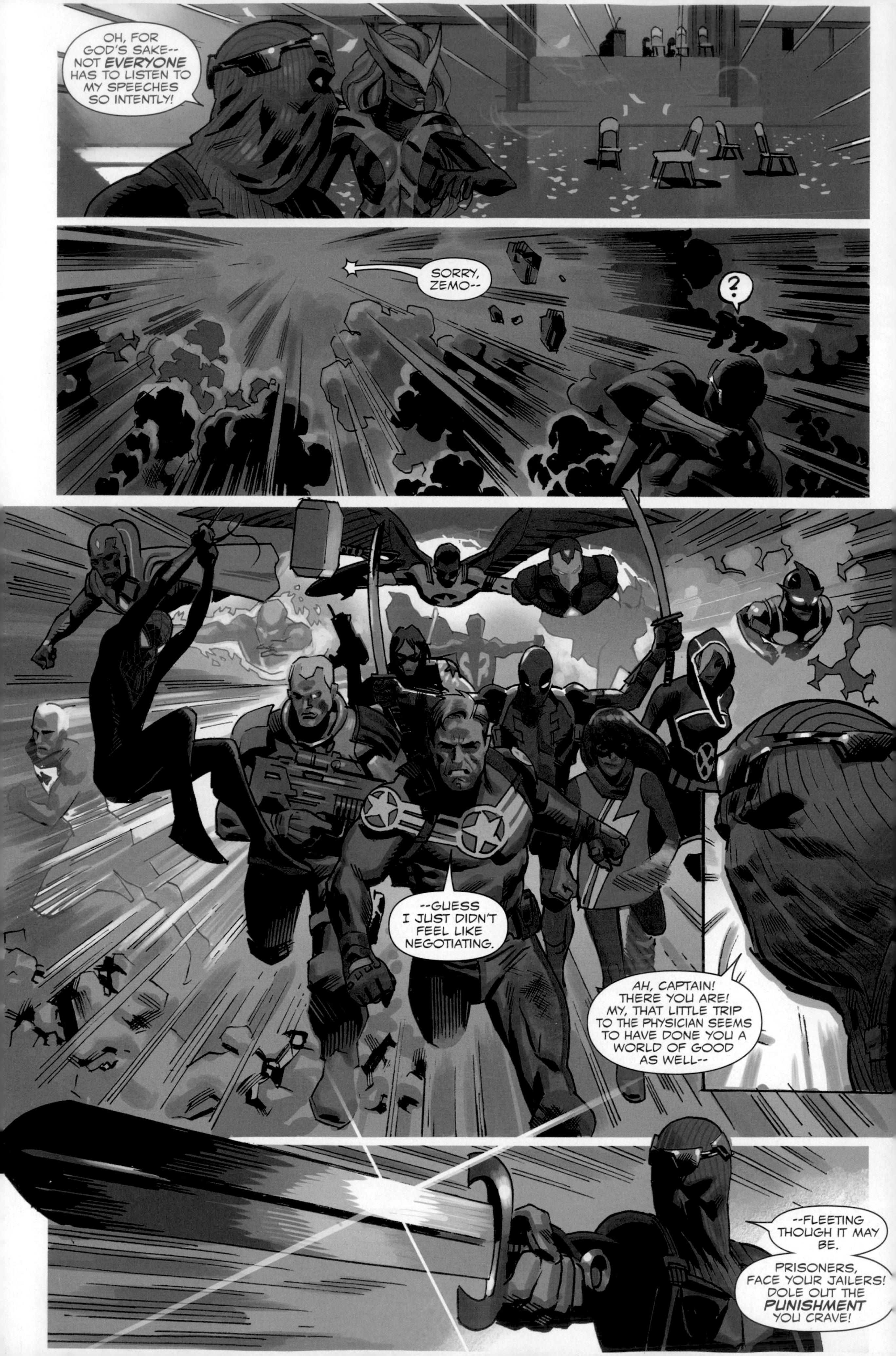

OH, FOR GOD'S SAKE-- NOT **EVERYONE** HAS TO LISTEN TO MY SPEECHES SO INTENTLY!
SORRY, ZEMO--
?
--GUESS I JUST DIDN'T FEEL LIKE NEGOTIATING.
AH, CAPTAIN! THERE YOU ARE! MY, THAT LITTLE TRIP TO THE PHYSICIAN SEEMS TO HAVE DONE YOU A WORLD OF GOOD AS WELL--
--FLEETING THOUGH IT MAY BE.
PRISONERS, FACE YOUR JAILERS! DOLE OUT THE **PUNISHMENT** YOU CRAVE!

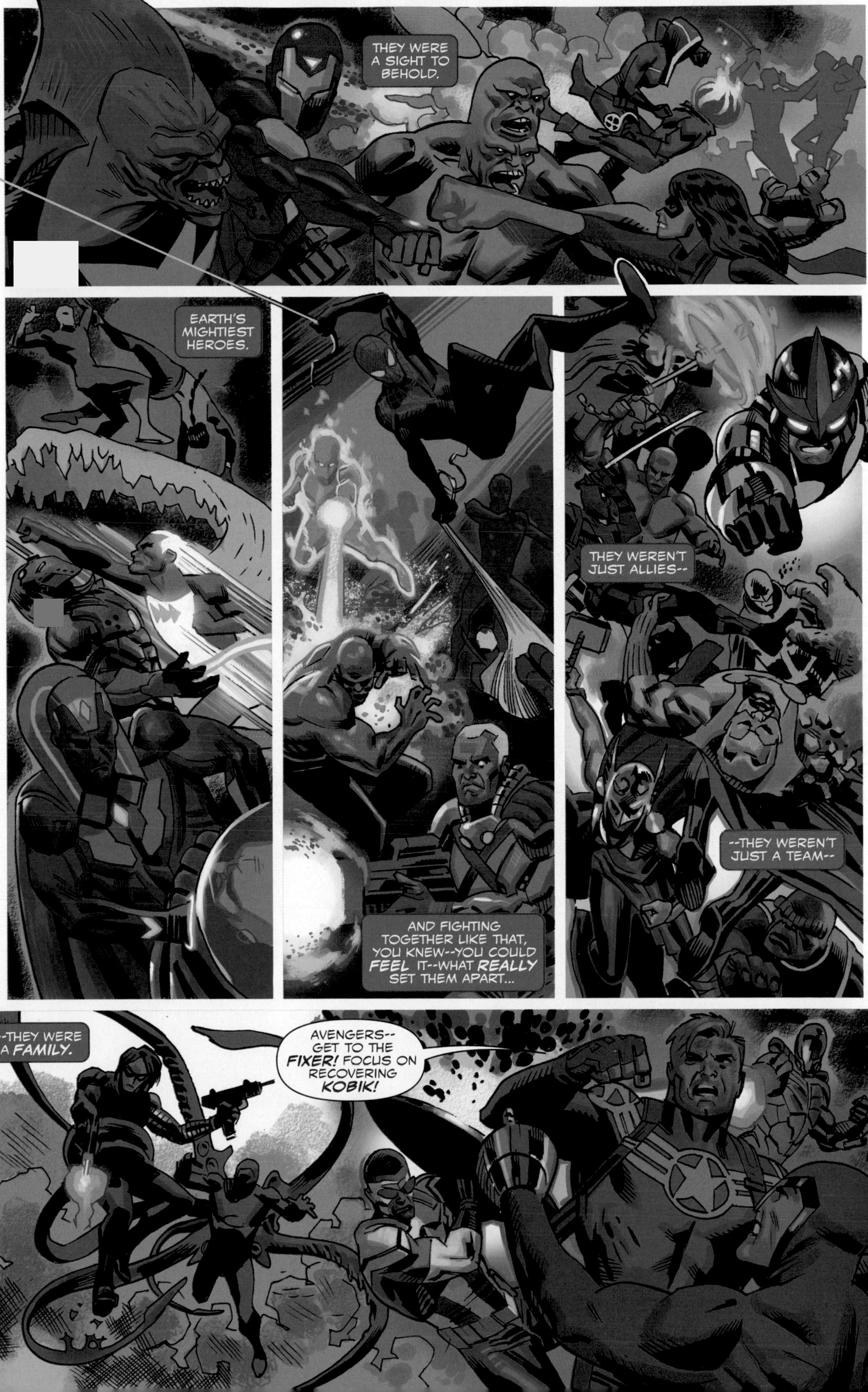
THEY WERE A SIGHT TO BEHOLD.
EARTH'S MIGHTIEST HEROES.
AND FIGHTING TOGETHER LIKE THAT, YOU KNEW--YOU COULD FEEL IT--WHAT REALLY SET THEM APART...
THEY WEREN'T JUST ALLIES--
--THEY WEREN'T JUST A TEAM--
--THEY WERE A FAMILY.
AVENGERS-- GET TO THE FIXER! FOCUS ON RECOVERING KOBIK!

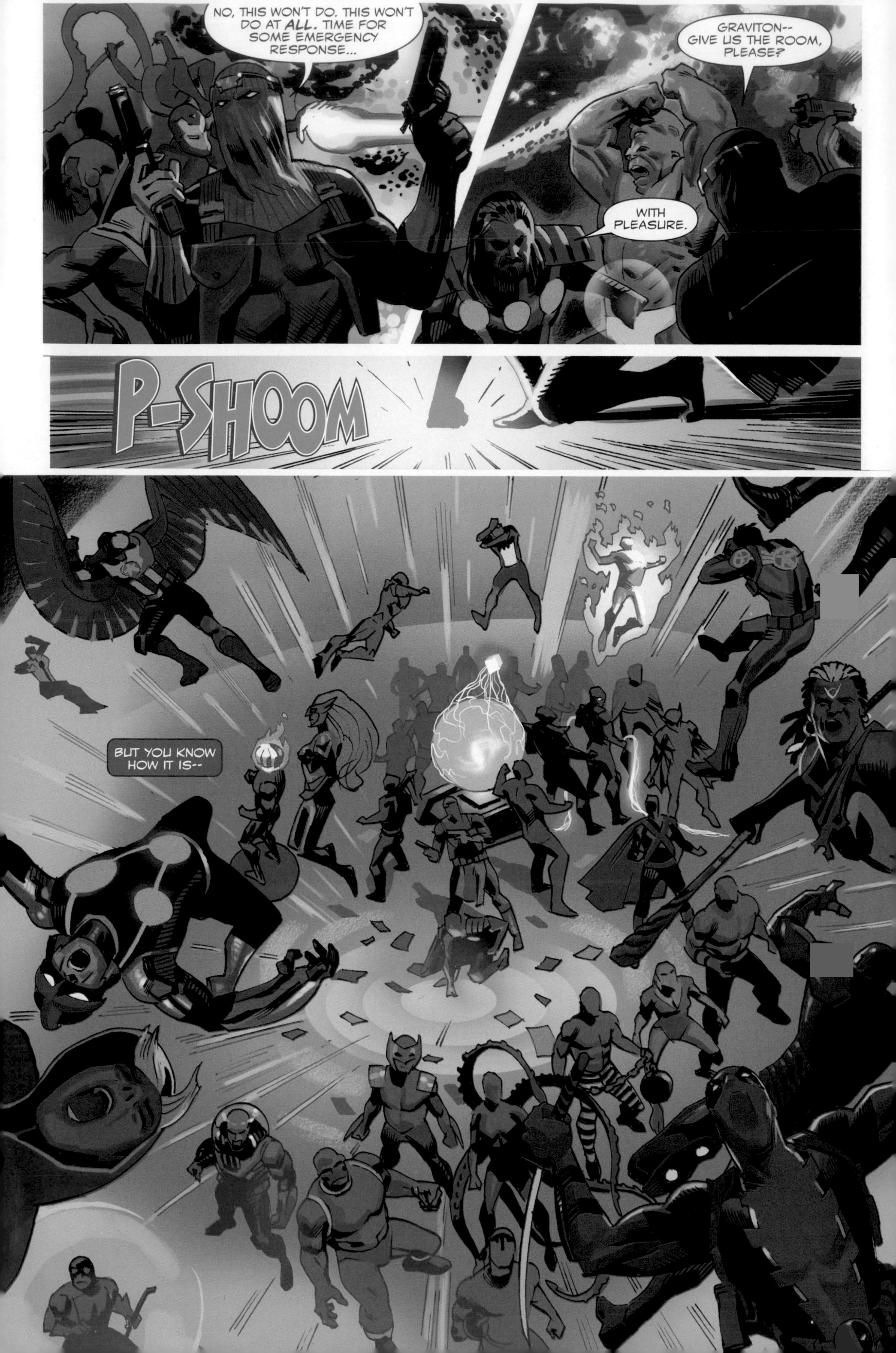
NO, THIS WON'T DO. THIS WON'T DO AT ALL. TIME FOR SOME EMERGENCY RESPONSE...
GRAVITON-- GIVE US THE ROOM, PLEASE?
WITH PLEASURE.
P-SHOOM
BUT YOU KNOW HOW IT IS--

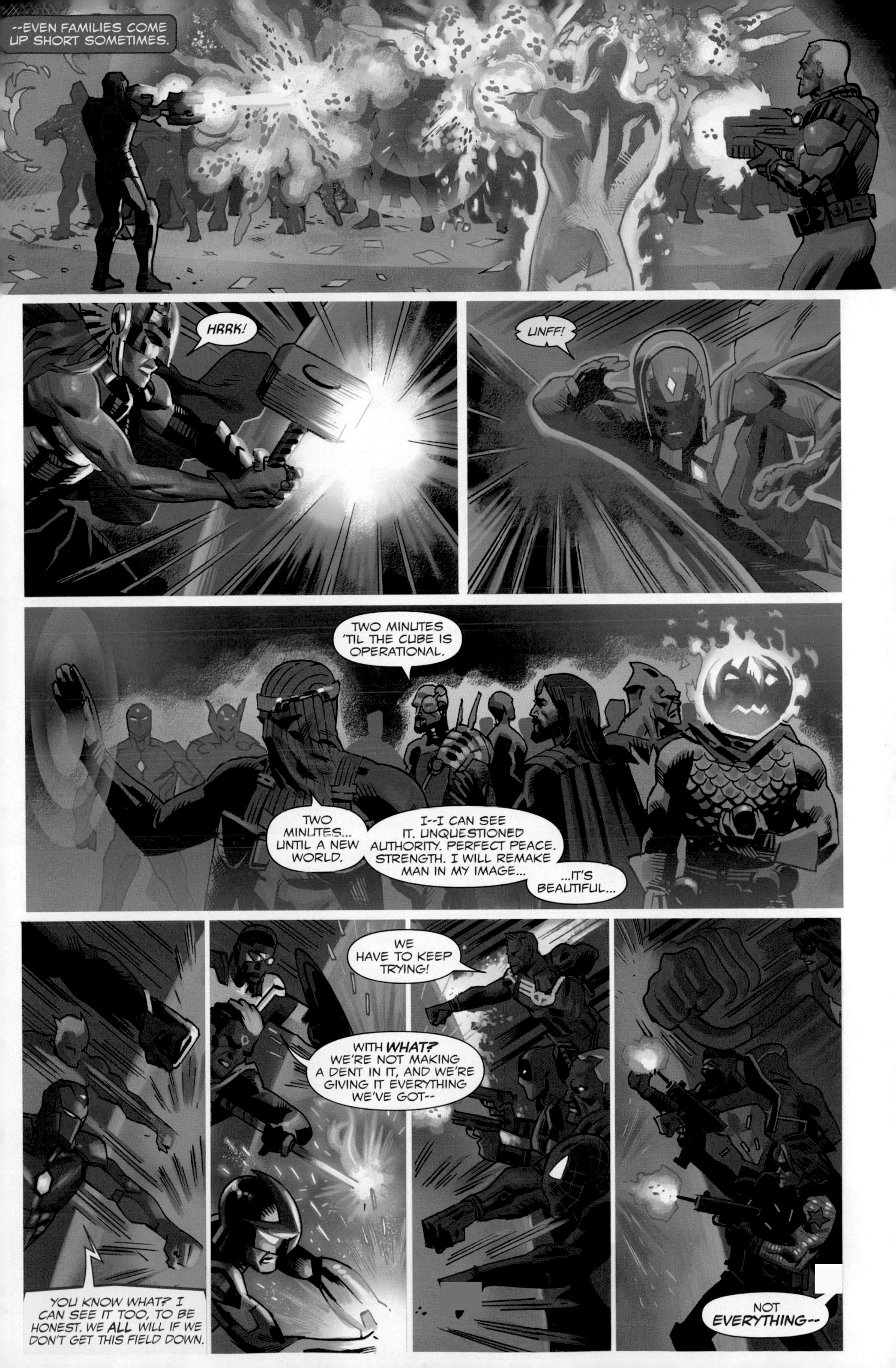
--EVEN FAMILIES COME UP SHORT SOMETIMES.
HRRK!
UNFF!
TWO MINUTES 'TIL THE CUBE IS OPERATIONAL.
TWO MINUTES... UNTIL A NEW WORLD.
I--I CAN SEE IT. UNQUESTIONED AUTHORITY. PERFECT PEACE. STRENGTH. I WILL REMAKE MAN IN MY IMAGE...
...IT'S BEAUTIFUL...
YOU KNOW WHAT? I CAN SEE IT TOO, TO BE HONEST. WE ALL WILL IF WE DON'T GET THIS FIELD DOWN.
WE HAVE TO KEEP TRYING!
WITH WHAT? WE'RE NOT MAKING A DENT IN IT, AND WE'RE GIVING IT EVERYTHING WE'VE GOT--
NOT EVERYTHING--

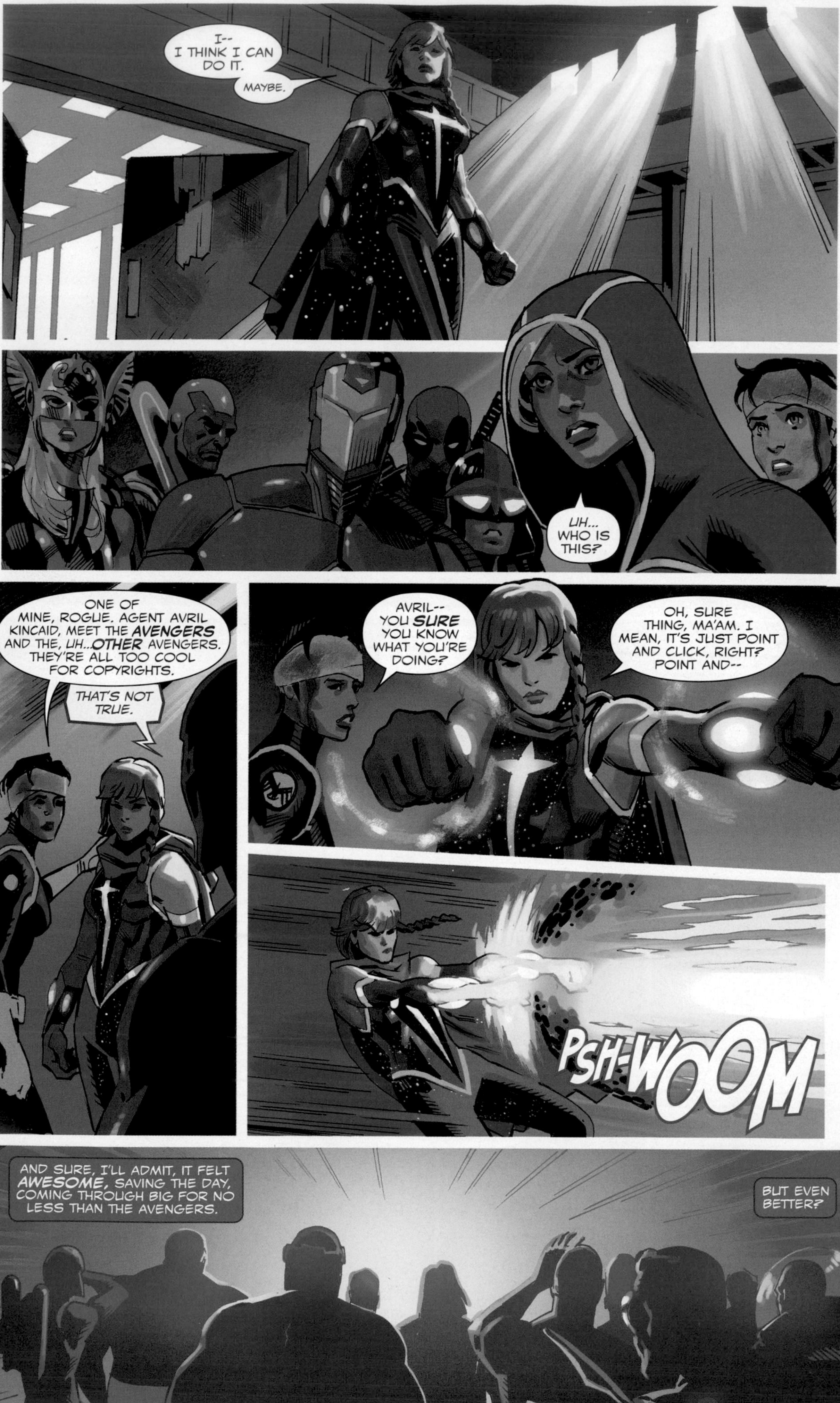
I-- I THINK I CAN DO IT.
MAYBE.
UH... WHO IS THIS?
ONE OF MINE, ROGUE. AGENT AVRIL KINCAID, MEET THE AVENGERS AND THE, UH...OTHER AVENGERS. THEY'RE ALL TOO COOL FOR COPYRIGHTS.
THAT'S NOT TRUE.
AVRIL-- YOU SURE YOU KNOW WHAT YOU'RE DOING?
OH, SURE THING, MA'AM. I MEAN, IT'S JUST POINT AND CLICK, RIGHT? POINT AND--
PSH-WOOM
AND SURE, I'LL ADMIT, IT FELT AWESOME, SAVING THE DAY, COMING THROUGH BIG FOR NO LESS THAN THE AVENGERS.
BUT EVEN BETTER?

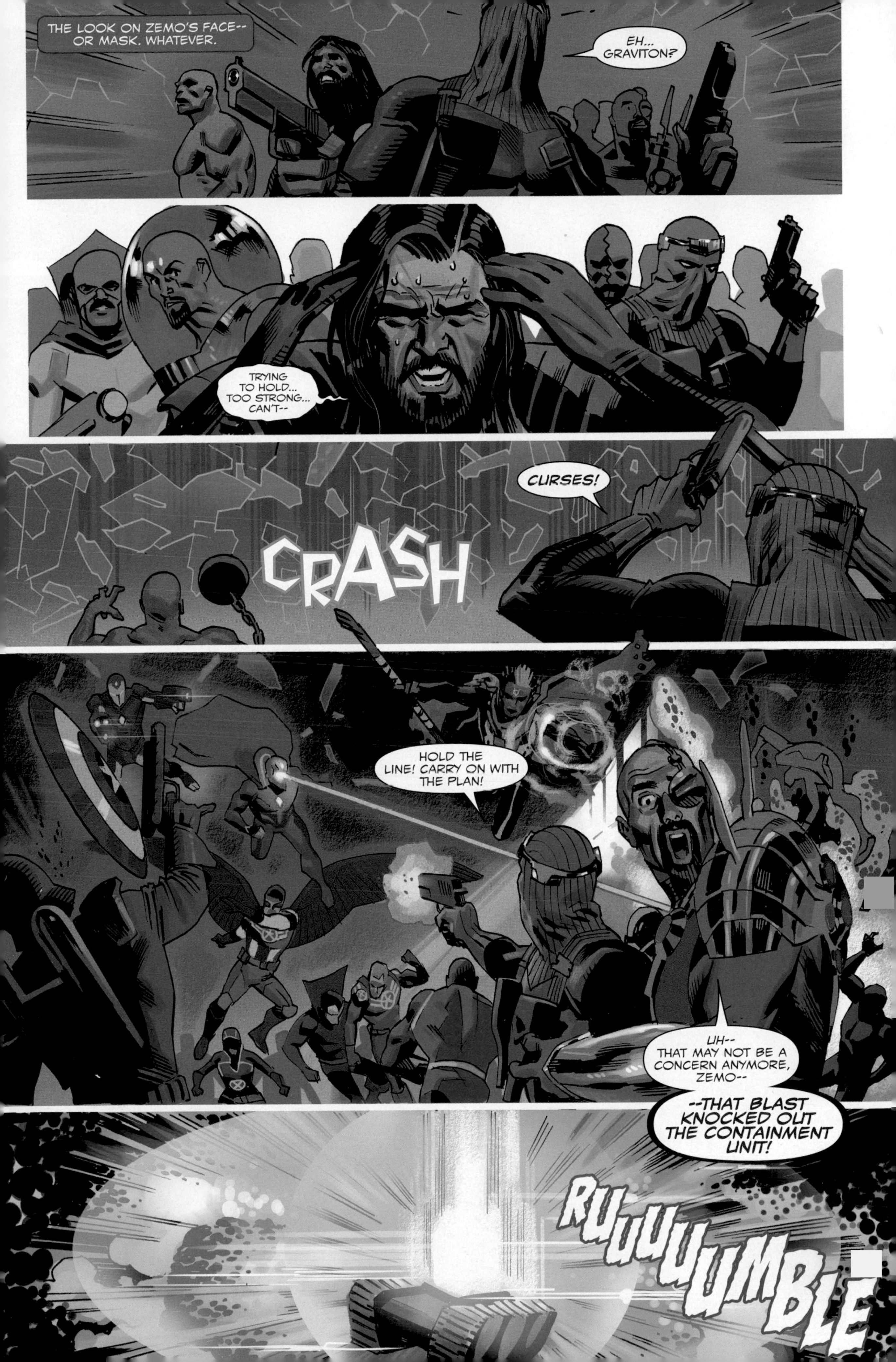
THE LOOK ON ZEMO'S FACE-- OR MASK. WHATEVER.
EH... GRAVITON?
TRYING TO HOLD... TOO STRONG... CAN'T--
CURSES!
CRASH
HOLD THE LINE! CARRY ON WITH THE PLAN!
UH-- THAT MAY NOT BE A CONCERN ANYMORE, ZEMO--
--THAT BLAST KNOCKED OUT THE CONTAINMENT UNIT!
RUUUUUMBLE

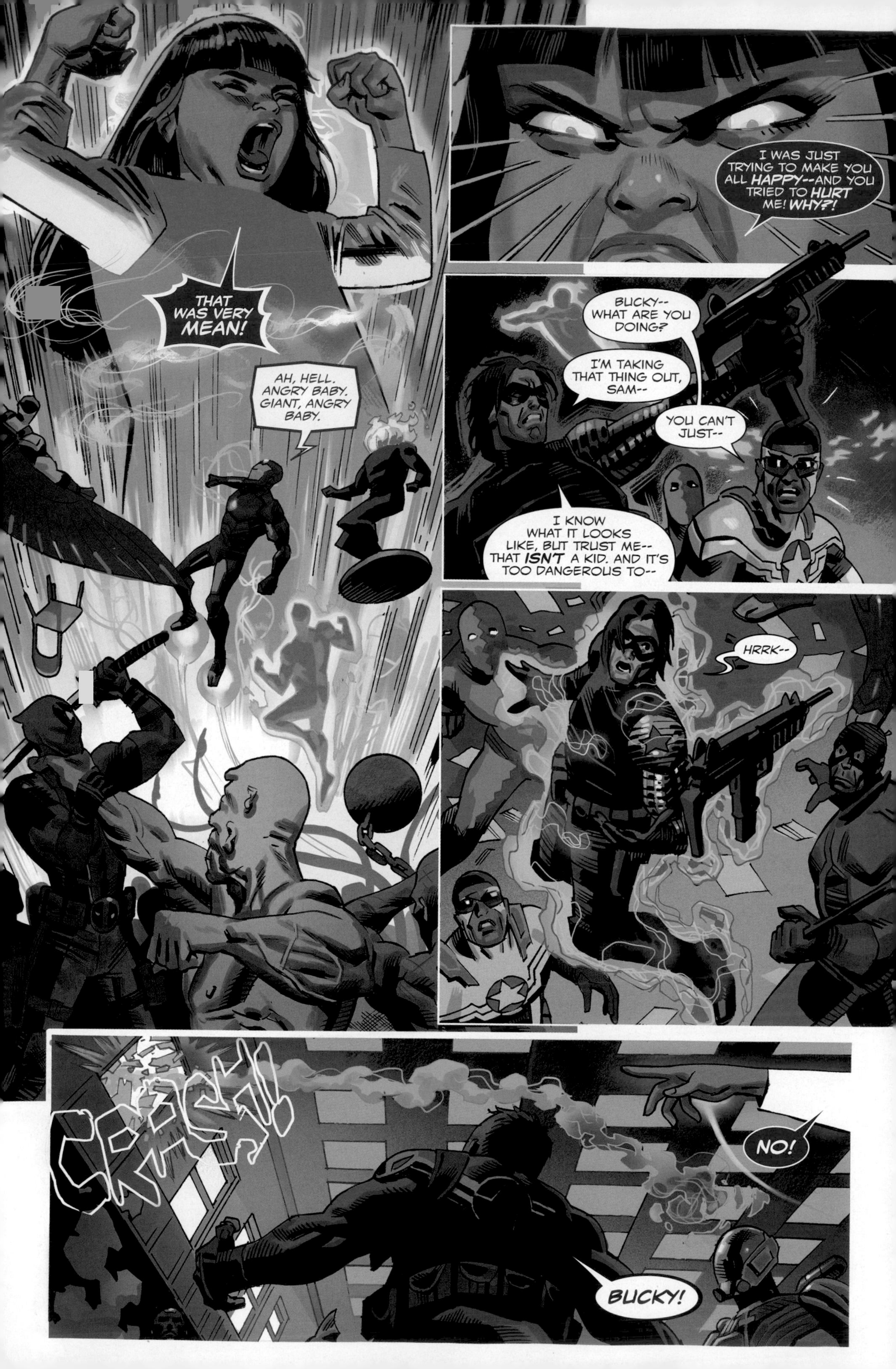
THAT WAS VERY MEAN!
AH, HELL. ANGRY BABY. GIANT, ANGRY BABY.
I WAS JUST TRYING TO MAKE YOU ALL HAPPY--AND YOU TRIED TO HURT ME! WHY?!
BUCKY-- WHAT ARE YOU DOING?
I'M TAKING THAT THING OUT, SAM--
YOU CAN'T JUST--
I KNOW WHAT IT LOOKS LIKE, BUT TRUST ME-- THAT ISN'T A KID. AND IT'S TOO DANGEROUS TO--
HRRK--
CRASH!!
NO!
BUCKY!

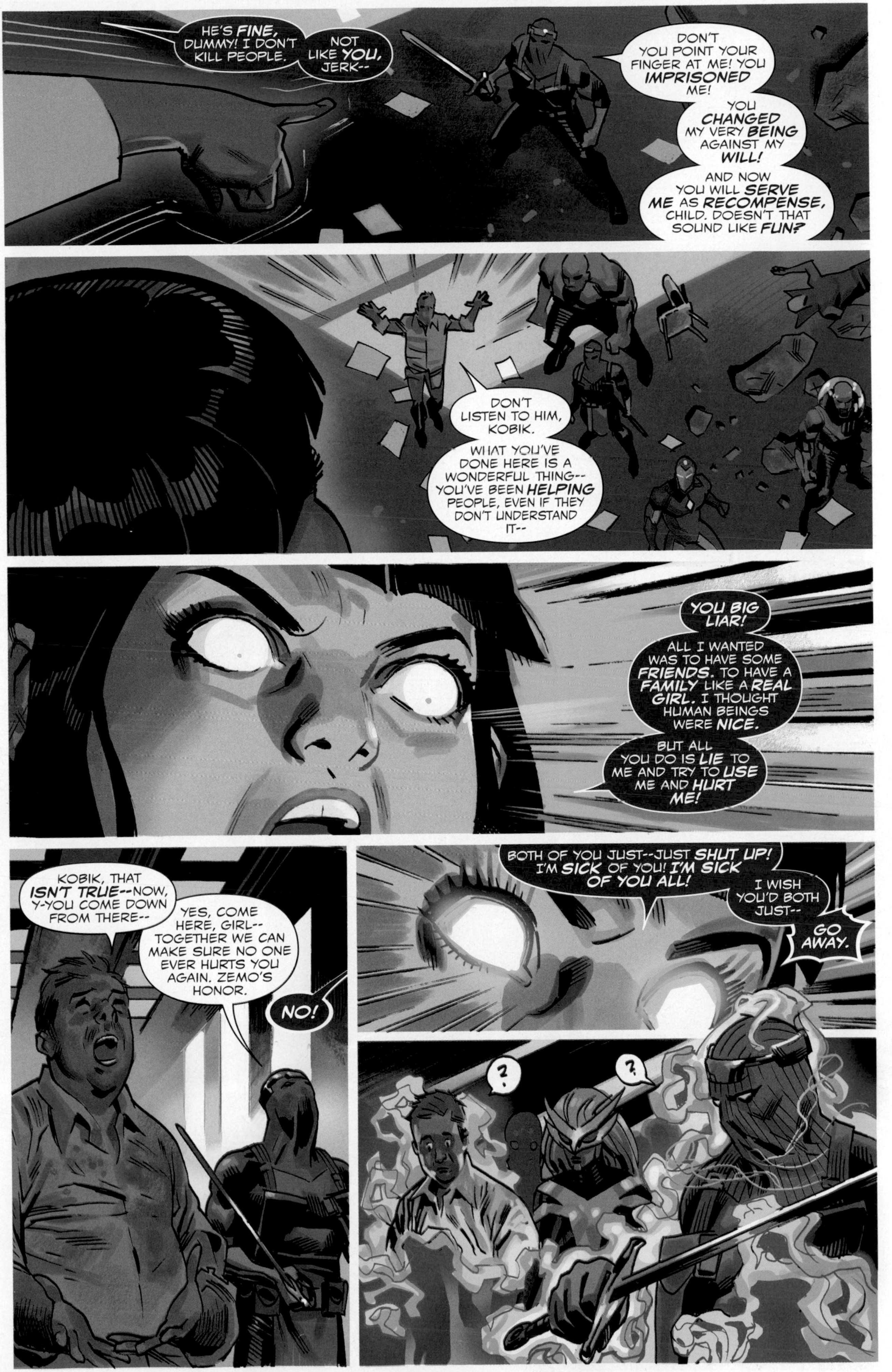
HE'S FINE, DUMMY! I DON'T KILL PEOPLE.
NOT LIKE YOU, JERK--
DON'T YOU POINT YOUR FINGER AT ME! YOU IMPRISONED ME!
YOU CHANGED MY VERY BEING AGAINST MY WILL!
AND NOW YOU WILL SERVE ME AS RECOMPENSE, CHILD. DOESN'T THAT SOUND LIKE FUN?
DON'T LISTEN TO HIM, KOBIK.
WHAT YOU'VE DONE HERE IS A WONDERFUL THING-- YOU'VE BEEN HELPING PEOPLE, EVEN IF THEY DON'T UNDERSTAND IT--
YOU BIG LIAR!
ALL I WANTED WAS TO HAVE SOME FRIENDS. TO HAVE A FAMILY LIKE A REAL GIRL. I THOUGHT HUMAN BEINGS WERE NICE.
BUT ALL YOU DO IS LIE TO ME AND TRY TO USE ME AND HURT ME!
KOBIK, THAT ISN'T TRUE--NOW, Y-YOU COME DOWN FROM THERE--
YES, COME HERE, GIRL-- TOGETHER WE CAN MAKE SURE NO ONE EVER HURTS YOU AGAIN. ZEMO'S HONOR.
NO!
BOTH OF YOU JUST--JUST SHUT UP! I'M SICK OF YOU! I'M SICK OF YOU ALL!
I WISH YOU'D BOTH JUST--
GO AWAY.
?
?

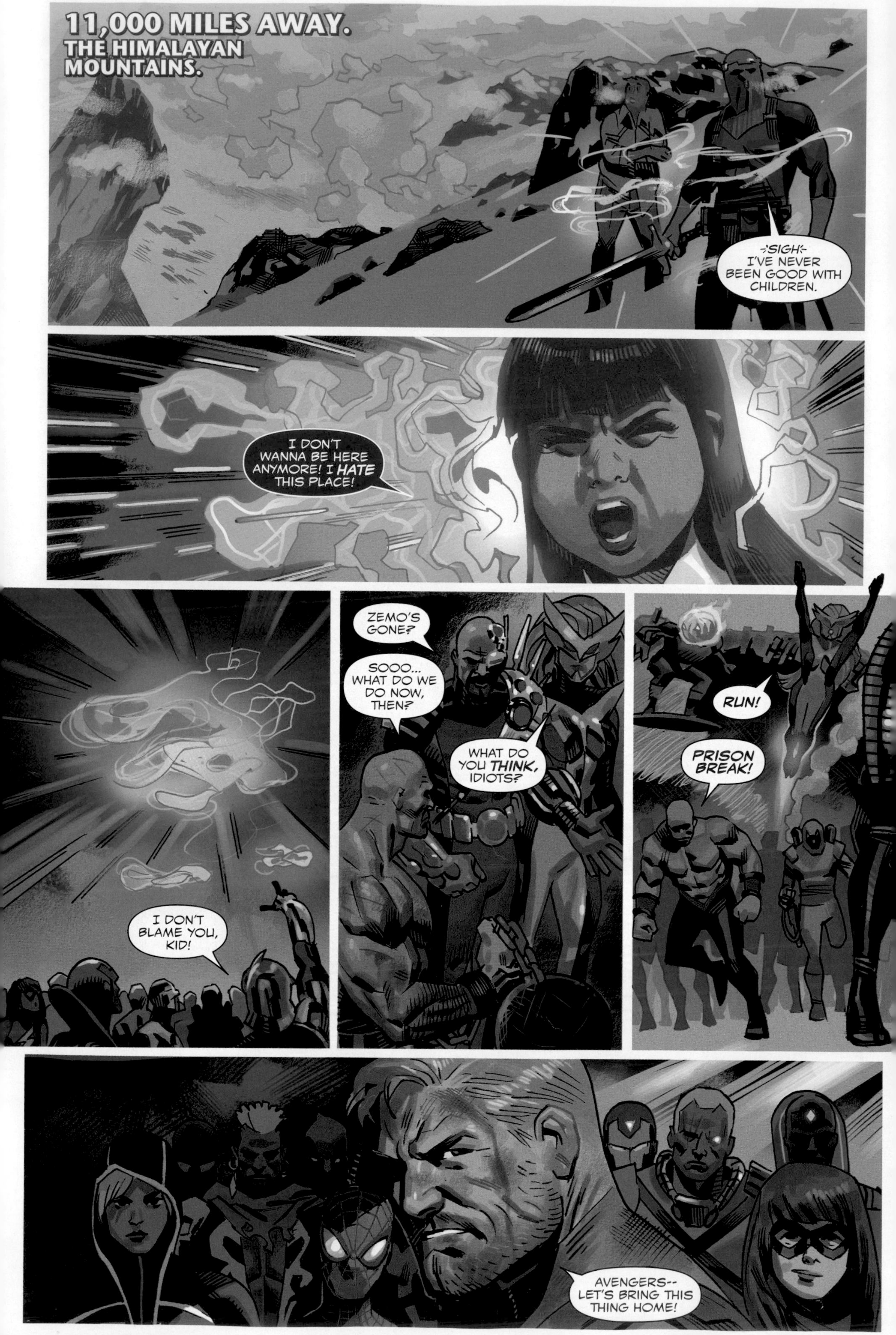
11,000 MILES AWAY.
THE HIMALAYAN MOUNTAINS.
-SIGH- I'VE NEVER BEEN GOOD WITH CHILDREN.
I DON'T WANNA BE HERE ANYMORE! I HATE THIS PLACE!
I DON'T BLAME YOU, KID!
ZEMO'S GONE?
SOOO... WHAT DO WE DO NOW, THEN?
WHAT DO YOU THINK, IDIOTS?
RUN!
PRISON BREAK!
AVENGERS-- LET'S BRING THIS THING HOME!

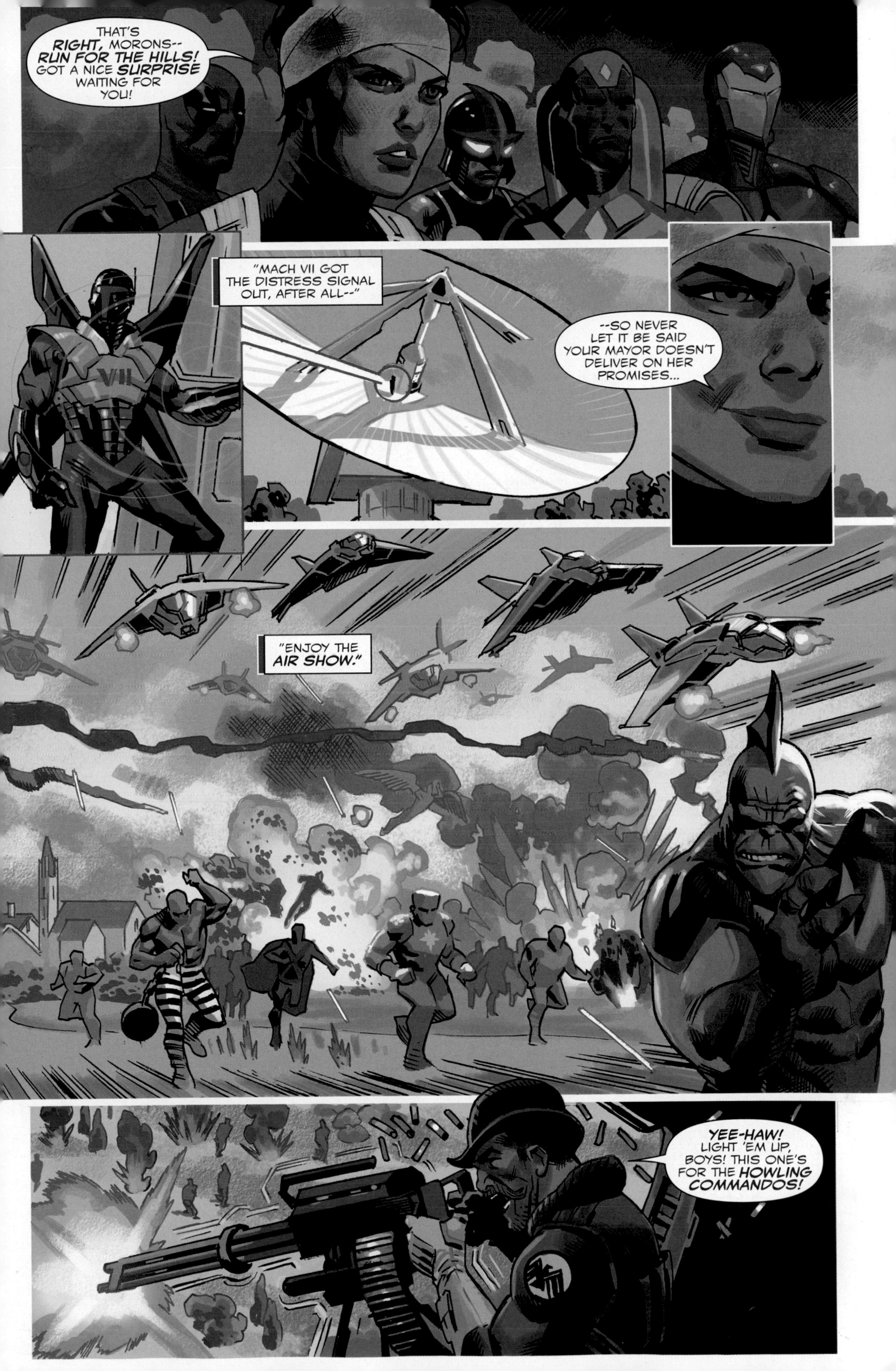
THAT'S RIGHT, MORONS-- RUN FOR THE HILLS! GOT A NICE SURPRISE WAITING FOR YOU!
"MACH VII GOT THE DISTRESS SIGNAL OUT, AFTER ALL--"
VII
--SO NEVER LET IT BE SAID YOUR MAYOR DOESN'T DELIVER ON HER PROMISES...
"ENJOY THE AIR SHOW."
YEE-HAW! LIGHT 'EM UP, BOYS! THIS ONE'S FOR THE HOWLING COMMANDOS!

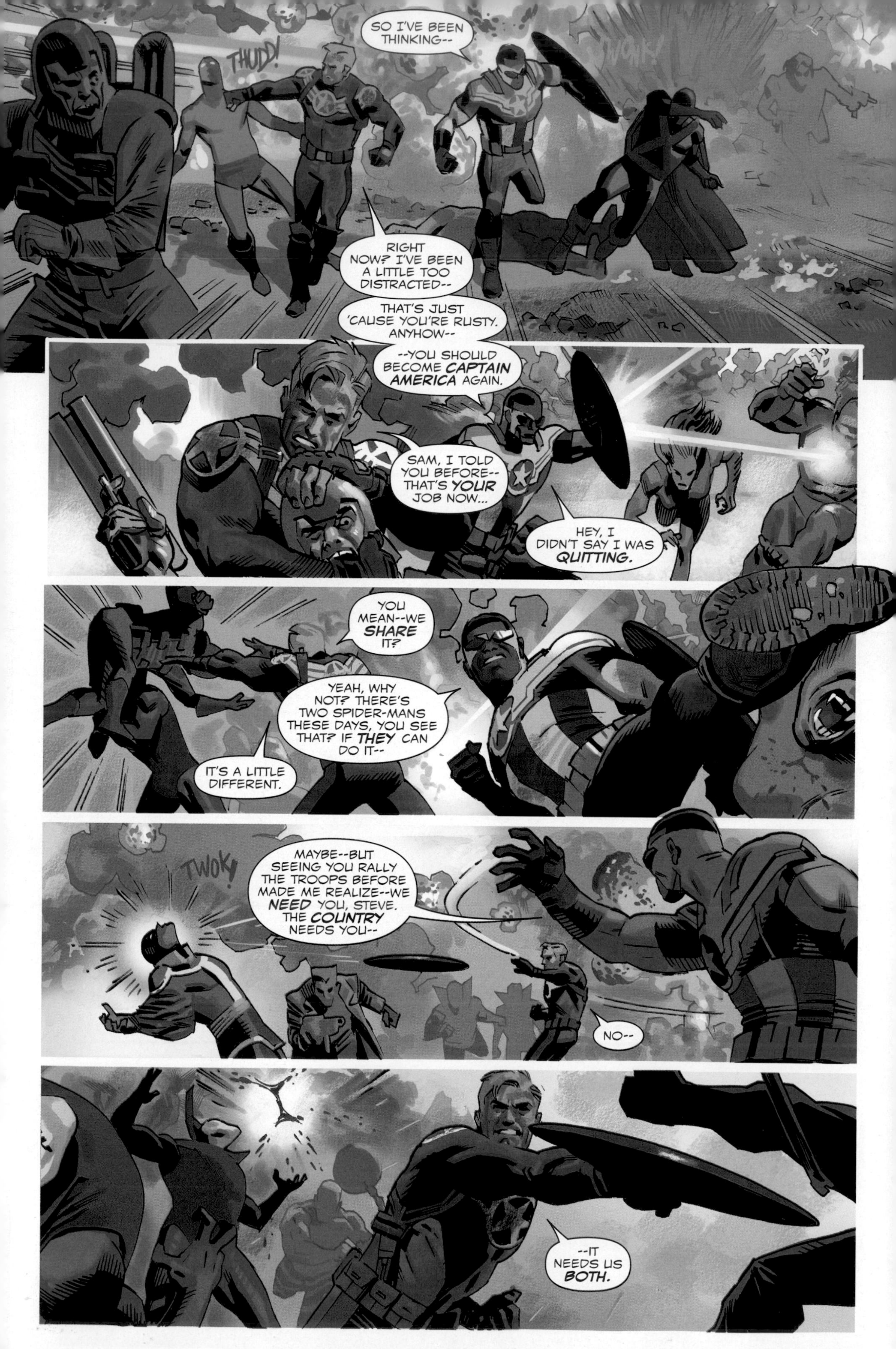
THUDD!
SO I'VE BEEN THINKING--
TWOK!
RIGHT NOW? I'VE BEEN A LITTLE TOO DISTRACTED--
THAT'S JUST 'CAUSE YOU'RE RUSTY. ANYHOW--
--YOU SHOULD BECOME CAPTAIN AMERICA AGAIN.
SAM, I TOLD YOU BEFORE--THAT'S YOUR JOB NOW...
HEY, I DIDN'T SAY I WAS QUITTING.
YOU MEAN--WE SHARE IT?
YEAH, WHY NOT? THERE'S TWO SPIDER-MANS THESE DAYS, YOU SEE THAT? IF THEY CAN DO IT--
IT'S A LITTLE DIFFERENT.
TWOK!
MAYBE--BUT SEEING YOU RALLY THE TROOPS BEFORE MADE ME REALIZE--WE NEED YOU, STEVE. THE COUNTRY NEEDS YOU--
NO--
--IT NEEDS US BOTH.

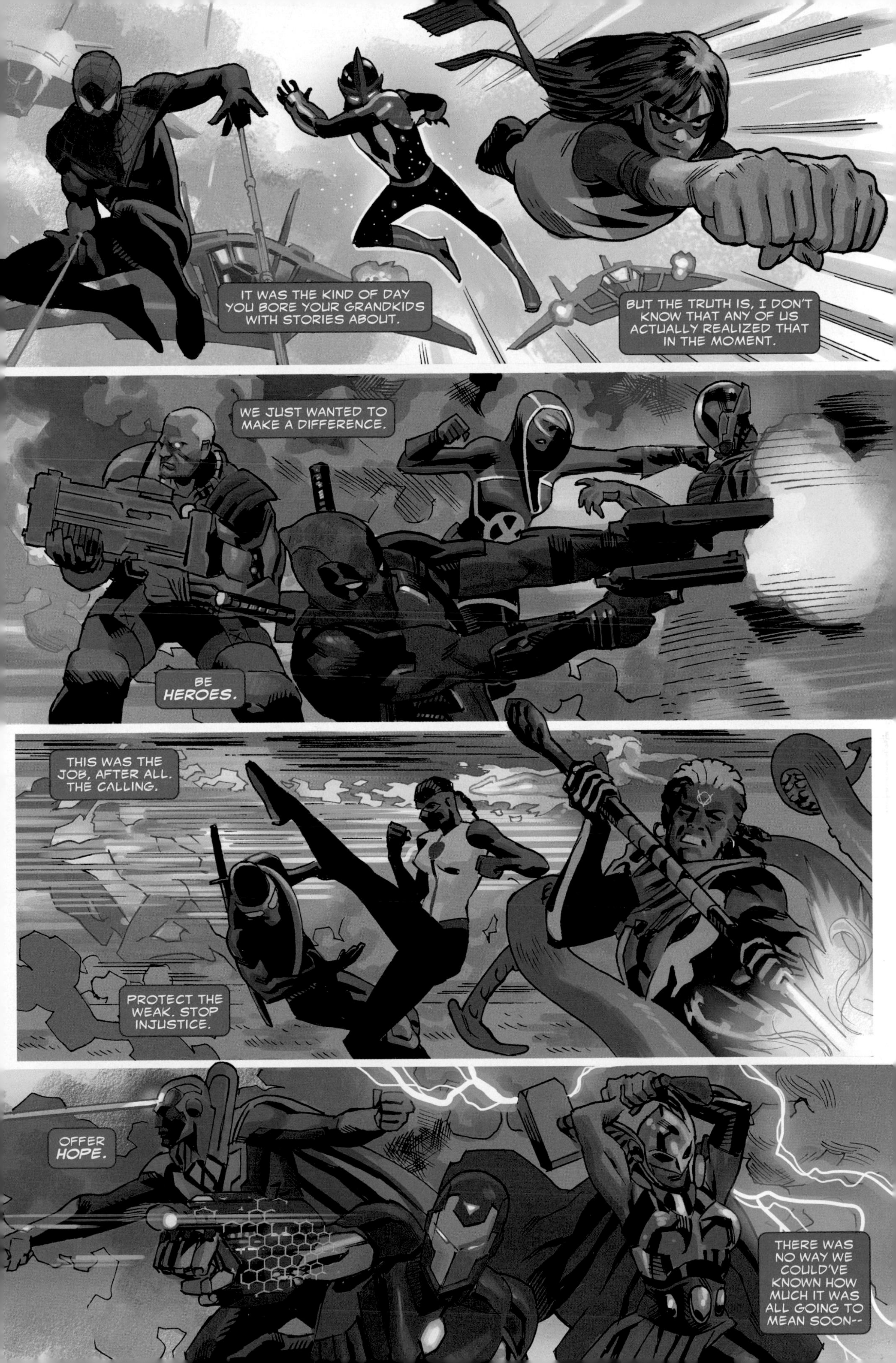
IT WAS THE KIND OF DAY YOU BORE YOUR GRANDKIDS WITH STORIES ABOUT.
BUT THE TRUTH IS, I DON'T KNOW THAT ANY OF US ACTUALLY REALIZED THAT IN THE MOMENT.
WE JUST WANTED TO MAKE A DIFFERENCE.
BE *HEROES.*
THIS WAS THE JOB, AFTER ALL. THE CALLING.
PROTECT THE WEAK. STOP INJUSTICE.
OFFER *HOPE.*
THERE WAS NO WAY WE COULD'VE KNOWN HOW MUCH IT WAS ALL GOING TO MEAN SOON--

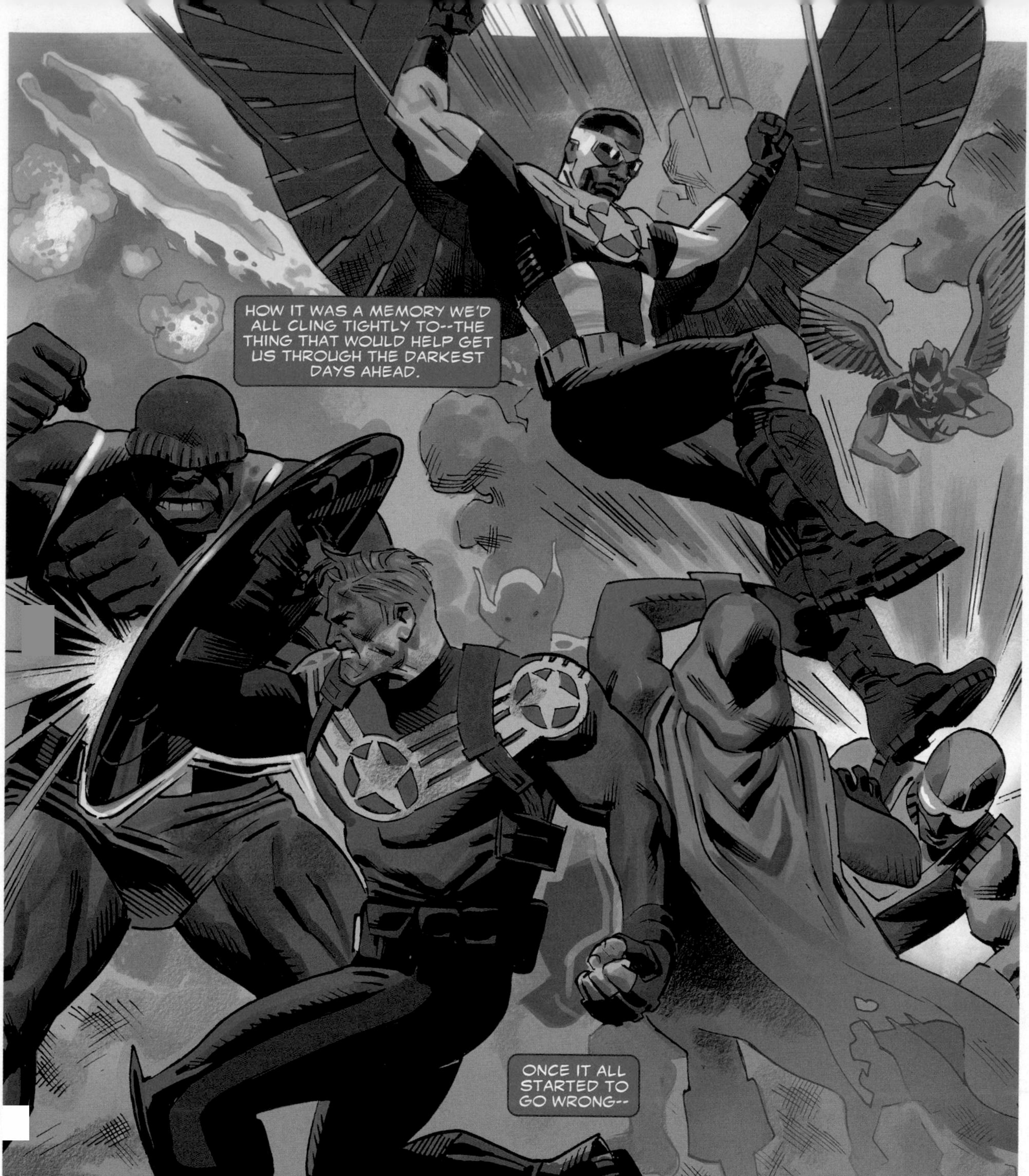
HOW IT WAS A MEMORY WE'D ALL CLING TIGHTLY TO--THE THING THAT WOULD HELP GET US THROUGH THE DARKEST DAYS AHEAD.
ONCE IT ALL STARTED TO GO WRONG--
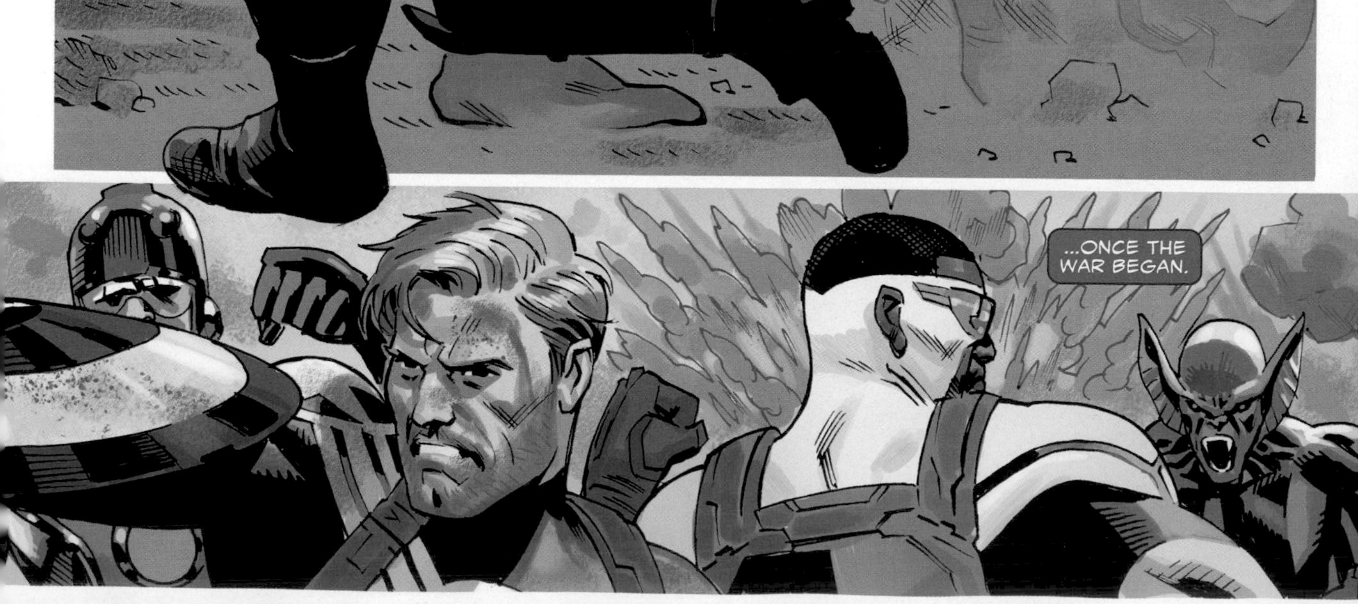
...ONCE THE WAR BEGAN.

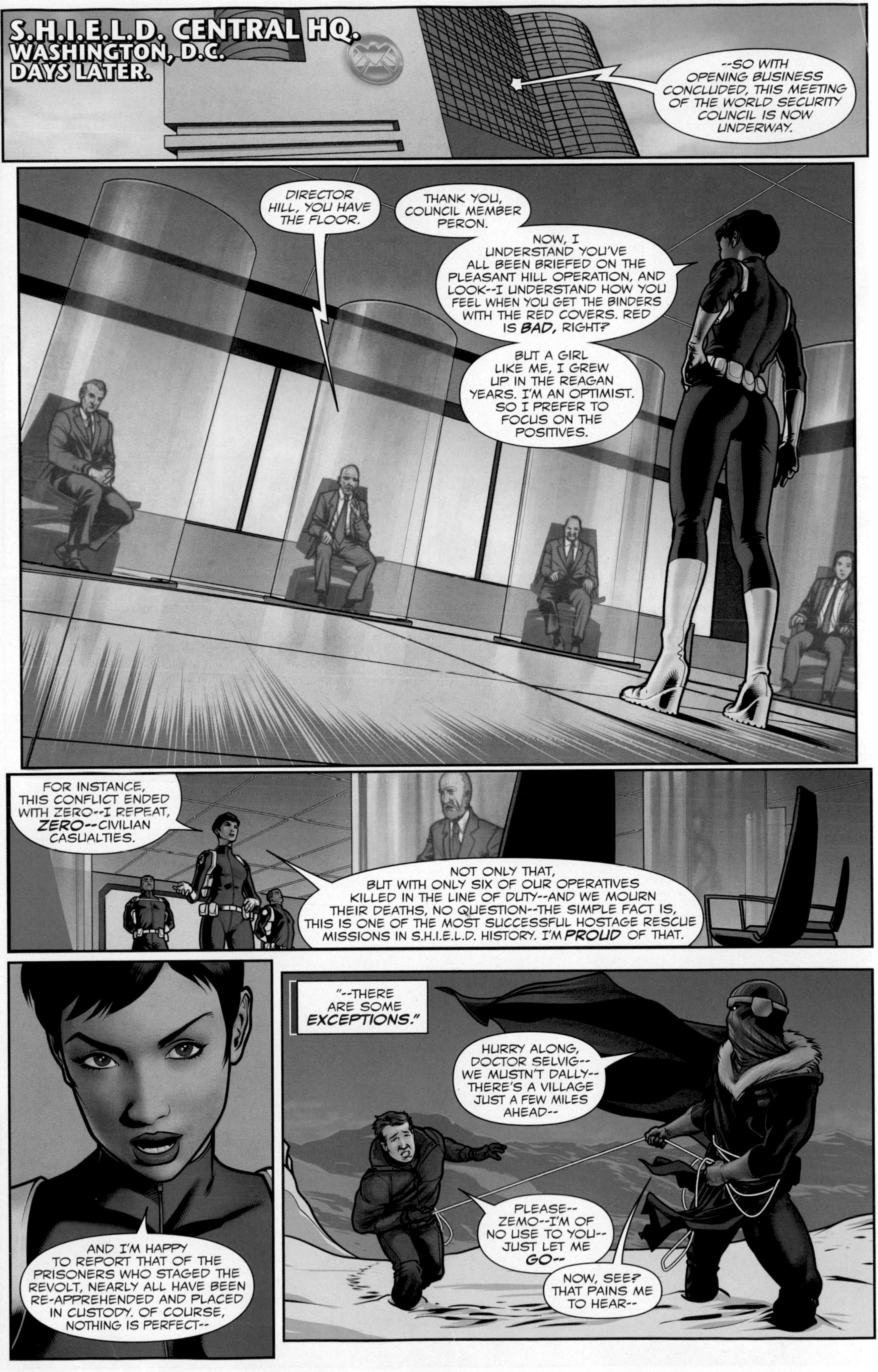
S.H.I.E.L.D. CENTRAL HQ. WASHINGTON, D.C. DAYS LATER.
--SO WITH OPENING BUSINESS CONCLUDED, THIS MEETING OF THE WORLD SECURITY COUNCIL IS NOW UNDERWAY.
DIRECTOR HILL, YOU HAVE THE FLOOR.
THANK YOU, COUNCIL MEMBER PERON.
NOW, I UNDERSTAND YOU'VE ALL BEEN BRIEFED ON THE PLEASANT HILL OPERATION, AND LOOK--I UNDERSTAND HOW YOU FEEL WHEN YOU GET THE BINDERS WITH THE RED COVERS. RED IS BAD, RIGHT?
BUT A GIRL LIKE ME, I GREW UP IN THE REAGAN YEARS. I'M AN OPTIMIST. SO I PREFER TO FOCUS ON THE POSITIVES.
FOR INSTANCE, THIS CONFLICT ENDED WITH ZERO--I REPEAT, ZERO--CIVILIAN CASUALTIES.
NOT ONLY THAT, BUT WITH ONLY SIX OF OUR OPERATIVES KILLED IN THE LINE OF DUTY--AND WE MOURN THEIR DEATHS, NO QUESTION--THE SIMPLE FACT IS, THIS IS ONE OF THE MOST SUCCESSFUL HOSTAGE RESCUE MISSIONS IN S.H.I.E.L.D. HISTORY. I'M PROUD OF THAT.
AND I'M HAPPY TO REPORT THAT OF THE PRISONERS WHO STAGED THE REVOLT, NEARLY ALL HAVE BEEN RE-APPREHENDED AND PLACED IN CUSTODY. OF COURSE, NOTHING IS PERFECT--
"--THERE ARE SOME EXCEPTIONS."
HURRY ALONG, DOCTOR SELVIG--WE MUSTN'T DALLY--THERE'S A VILLAGE JUST A FEW MILES AHEAD--
PLEASE--ZEMO--I'M OF NO USE TO YOU--JUST LET ME GO--
NOW, SEE? THAT PAINS ME TO HEAR--

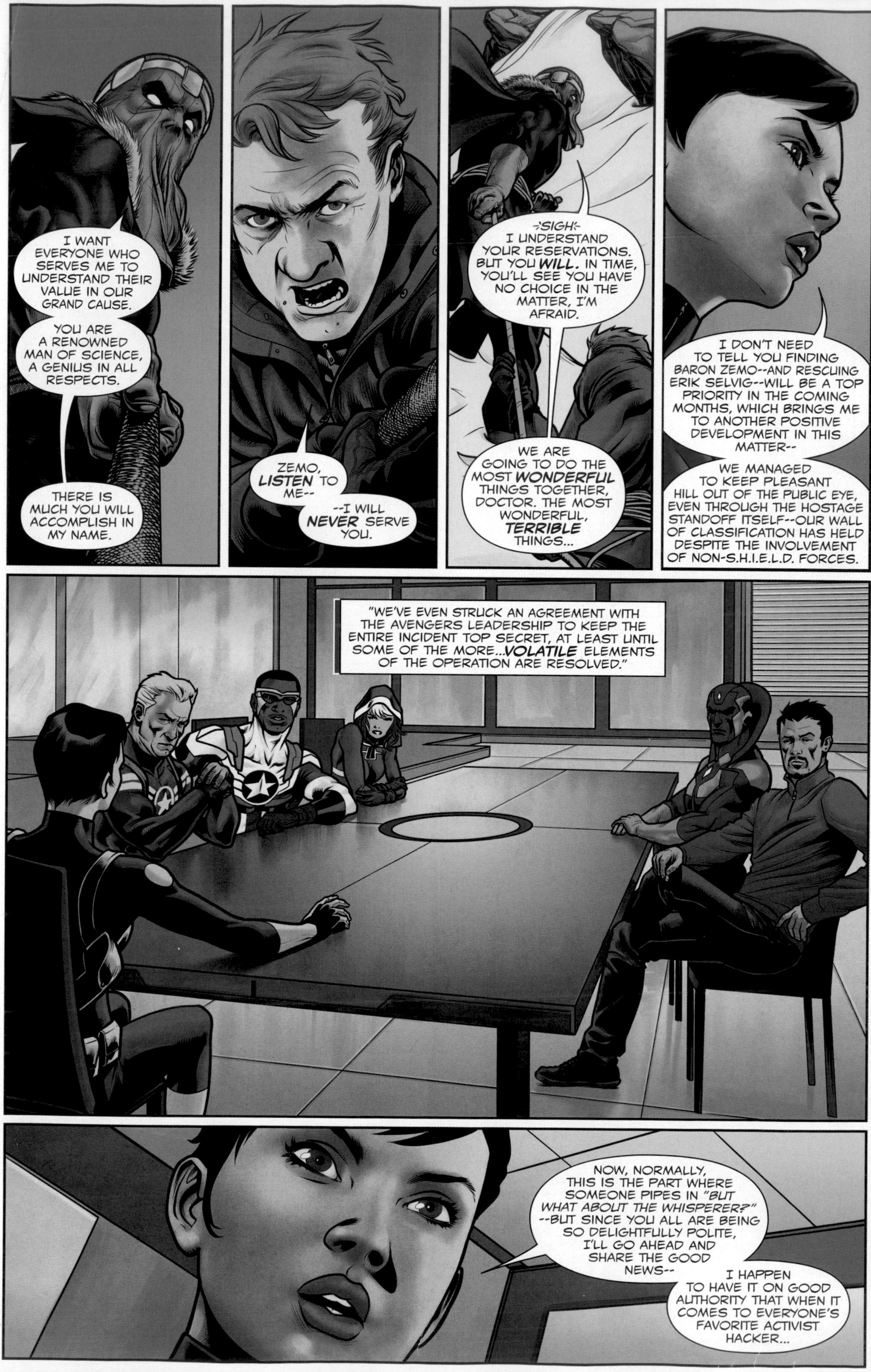

I WANT EVERYONE WHO SERVES ME TO UNDERSTAND THEIR VALUE IN OUR GRAND CAUSE.
YOU ARE A RENOWNED MAN OF SCIENCE, A GENIUS IN ALL RESPECTS.
THERE IS MUCH YOU WILL ACCOMPLISH IN MY NAME.
ZEMO, **LISTEN** TO ME--
--I WILL **NEVER** SERVE YOU.
SIGH I UNDERSTAND YOUR RESERVATIONS. BUT YOU **WILL.** IN TIME, YOU'LL SEE YOU HAVE NO CHOICE IN THE MATTER, I'M AFRAID.
WE ARE GOING TO DO THE MOST **WONDERFUL** THINGS TOGETHER, DOCTOR. THE MOST WONDERFUL, **TERRIBLE** THINGS...
I DON'T NEED TO TELL YOU FINDING BARON ZEMO--AND RESCUING ERIK SELVIG--WILL BE A TOP PRIORITY IN THE COMING MONTHS, WHICH BRINGS ME TO ANOTHER POSITIVE DEVELOPMENT IN THIS MATTER--
WE MANAGED TO KEEP PLEASANT HILL OUT OF THE PUBLIC EYE, EVEN THROUGH THE HOSTAGE STANDOFF ITSELF--OUR WALL OF CLASSIFICATION HAS HELD DESPITE THE INVOLVEMENT OF NON-S.H.I.E.L.D. FORCES.
"WE'VE EVEN STRUCK AN AGREEMENT WITH THE AVENGERS LEADERSHIP TO KEEP THE ENTIRE INCIDENT TOP SECRET, AT LEAST UNTIL SOME OF THE MORE...**VOLATILE** ELEMENTS OF THE OPERATION ARE RESOLVED."
NOW, NORMALLY, THIS IS THE PART WHERE SOMEONE PIPES IN *"BUT WHAT ABOUT THE WHISPERER?"* --BUT SINCE YOU ALL ARE BEING SO DELIGHTFULLY POLITE, I'LL GO AHEAD AND SHARE THE GOOD NEWS--
I HAPPEN TO HAVE IT ON GOOD AUTHORITY THAT WHEN IT COMES TO EVERYONE'S FAVORITE ACTIVIST HACKER...

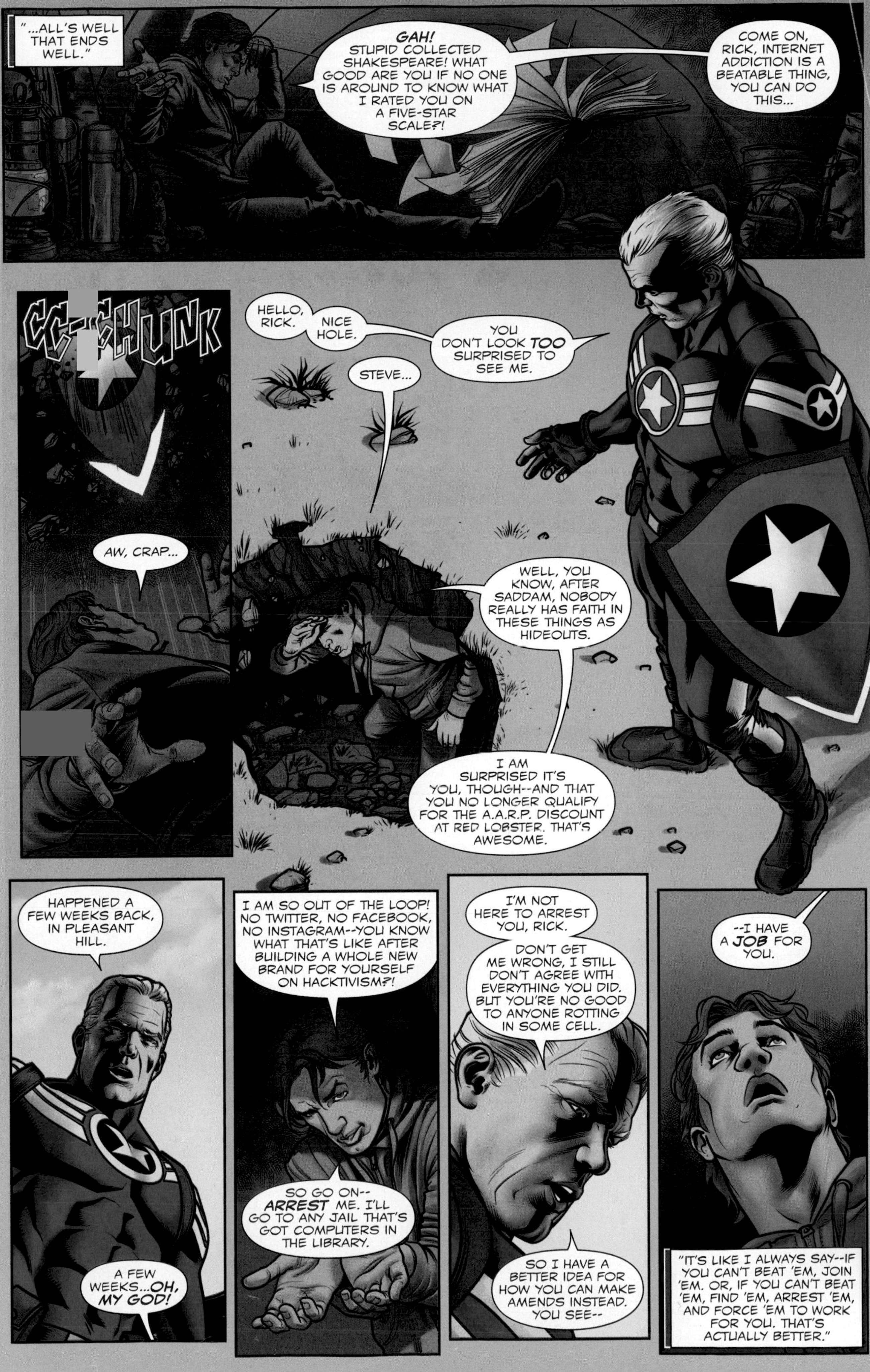
"...ALL'S WELL THAT ENDS WELL."
GAH! STUPID COLLECTED SHAKESPEARE! WHAT GOOD ARE YOU IF NO ONE IS AROUND TO KNOW WHAT I RATED YOU ON A FIVE-STAR SCALE?!
COME ON, RICK, INTERNET ADDICTION IS A BEATABLE THING, YOU CAN DO THIS...
CC-CHUNK
AW, CRAP...
HELLO, RICK.
NICE HOLE.
STEVE...
YOU DON'T LOOK TOO SURPRISED TO SEE ME.
WELL, YOU KNOW, AFTER SADDAM, NOBODY REALLY HAS FAITH IN THESE THINGS AS HIDEOUTS.
I AM SURPRISED IT'S YOU, THOUGH--AND THAT YOU NO LONGER QUALIFY FOR THE A.A.R.P. DISCOUNT AT RED LOBSTER. THAT'S AWESOME.
HAPPENED A FEW WEEKS BACK, IN PLEASANT HILL.
A FEW WEEKS...OH, MY GOD!
I AM SO OUT OF THE LOOP! NO TWITTER, NO FACEBOOK, NO INSTAGRAM--YOU KNOW WHAT THAT'S LIKE AFTER BUILDING A WHOLE NEW BRAND FOR YOURSELF ON HACKTIVISM?!
SO GO ON--ARREST ME. I'LL GO TO ANY JAIL THAT'S GOT COMPUTERS IN THE LIBRARY.
I'M NOT HERE TO ARREST YOU, RICK.
DON'T GET ME WRONG, I STILL DON'T AGREE WITH EVERYTHING YOU DID. BUT YOU'RE NO GOOD TO ANYONE ROTTING IN SOME CELL.
SO I HAVE A BETTER IDEA FOR HOW YOU CAN MAKE AMENDS INSTEAD. YOU SEE--
--I HAVE A JOB FOR YOU.
"IT'S LIKE I ALWAYS SAY--IF YOU CAN'T BEAT 'EM, JOIN 'EM. OR, IF YOU CAN'T BEAT 'EM, FIND 'EM, ARREST 'EM, AND FORCE 'EM TO WORK FOR YOU. THAT'S ACTUALLY BETTER."

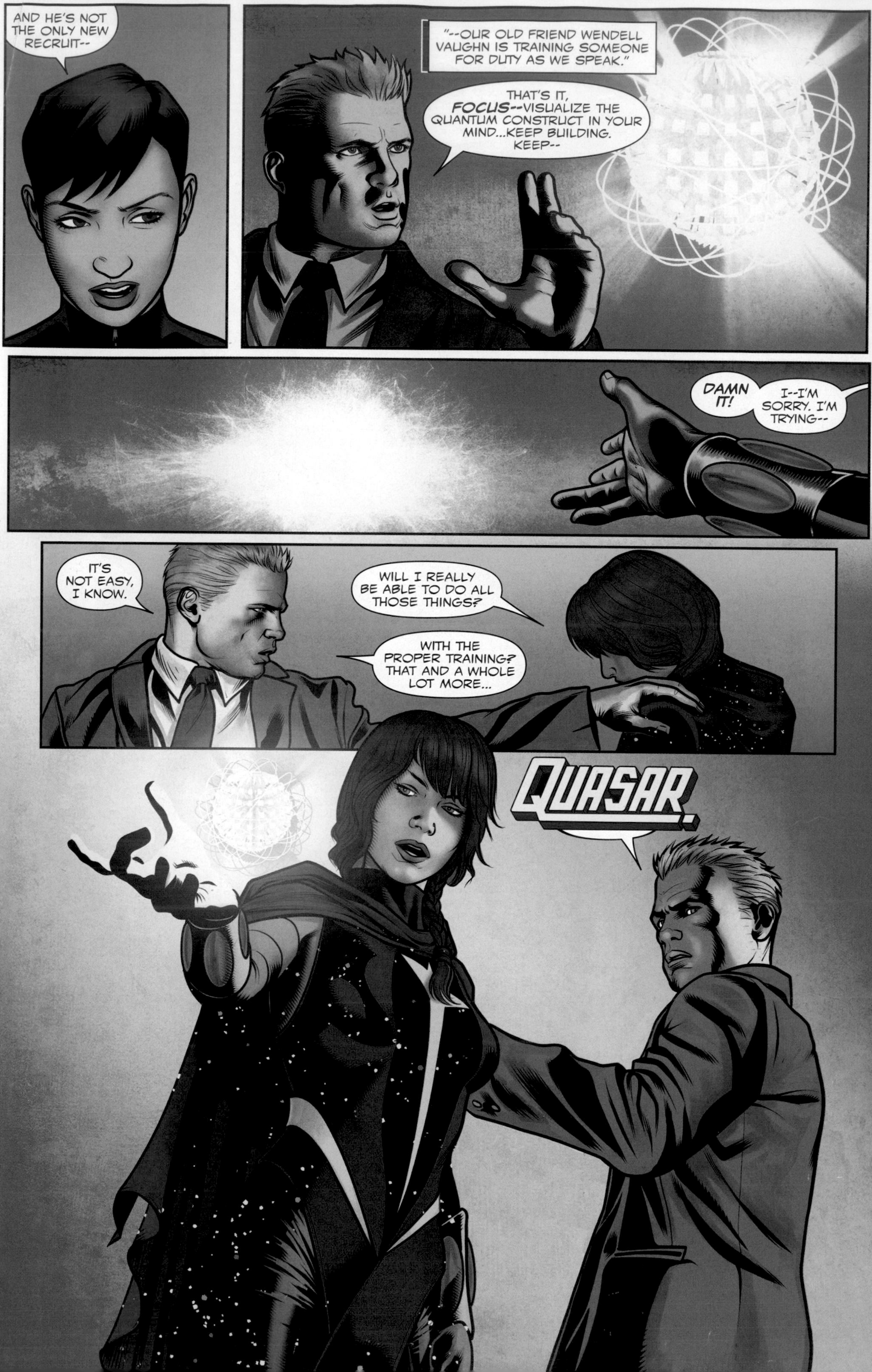
AND HE'S NOT THE ONLY NEW RECRUIT--
"--OUR OLD FRIEND WENDELL VAUGHN IS TRAINING SOMEONE FOR DUTY AS WE SPEAK."
THAT'S IT, FOCUS--VISUALIZE THE QUANTUM CONSTRUCT IN YOUR MIND...KEEP BUILDING. KEEP--
DAMN IT!
I--I'M SORRY. I'M TRYING--
IT'S NOT EASY, I KNOW.
WILL I REALLY BE ABLE TO DO ALL THOSE THINGS?
WITH THE PROPER TRAINING? THAT AND A WHOLE LOT MORE...
QUASAR.

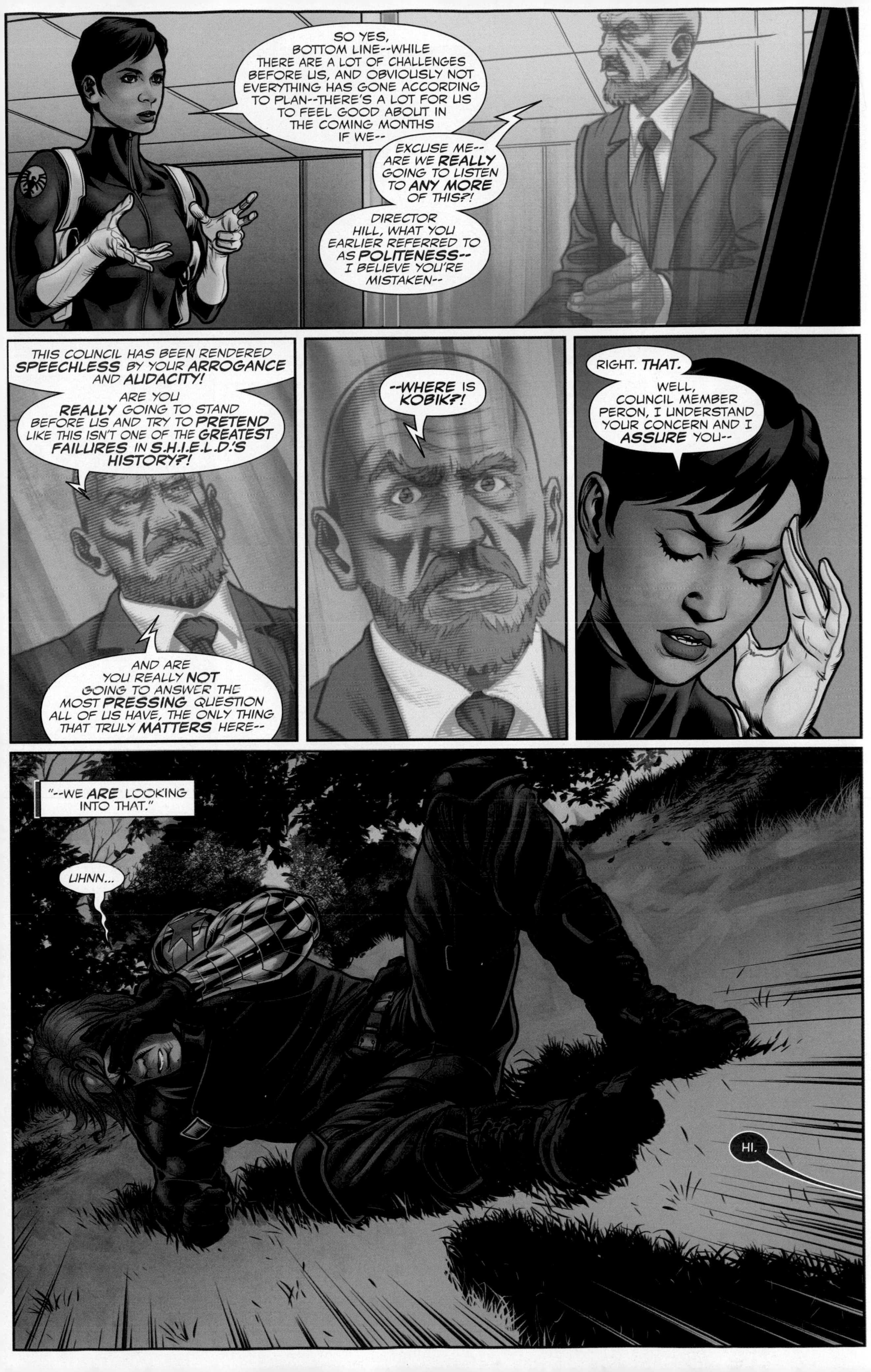
SO YES, BOTTOM LINE--WHILE THERE ARE A LOT OF CHALLENGES BEFORE US, AND OBVIOUSLY NOT EVERYTHING HAS GONE ACCORDING TO PLAN--THERE'S A LOT FOR US TO FEEL GOOD ABOUT IN THE COMING MONTHS IF WE--
EXCUSE ME--ARE WE REALLY GOING TO LISTEN TO ANY MORE OF THIS?!
DIRECTOR HILL, WHAT YOU EARLIER REFERRED TO AS POLITENESS--I BELIEVE YOU'RE MISTAKEN--
THIS COUNCIL HAS BEEN RENDERED SPEECHLESS BY YOUR ARROGANCE AND AUDACITY!
ARE YOU REALLY GOING TO STAND BEFORE US AND TRY TO PRETEND LIKE THIS ISN'T ONE OF THE GREATEST FAILURES IN S.H.I.E.L.D.'S HISTORY?!
AND ARE YOU REALLY NOT GOING TO ANSWER THE MOST PRESSING QUESTION ALL OF US HAVE, THE ONLY THING THAT TRULY MATTERS HERE--
--WHERE IS KOBIK?!
RIGHT. THAT.
WELL, COUNCIL MEMBER PERON, I UNDERSTAND YOUR CONCERN AND I ASSURE YOU--
"--WE ARE LOOKING INTO THAT."
UHNN...
HI.

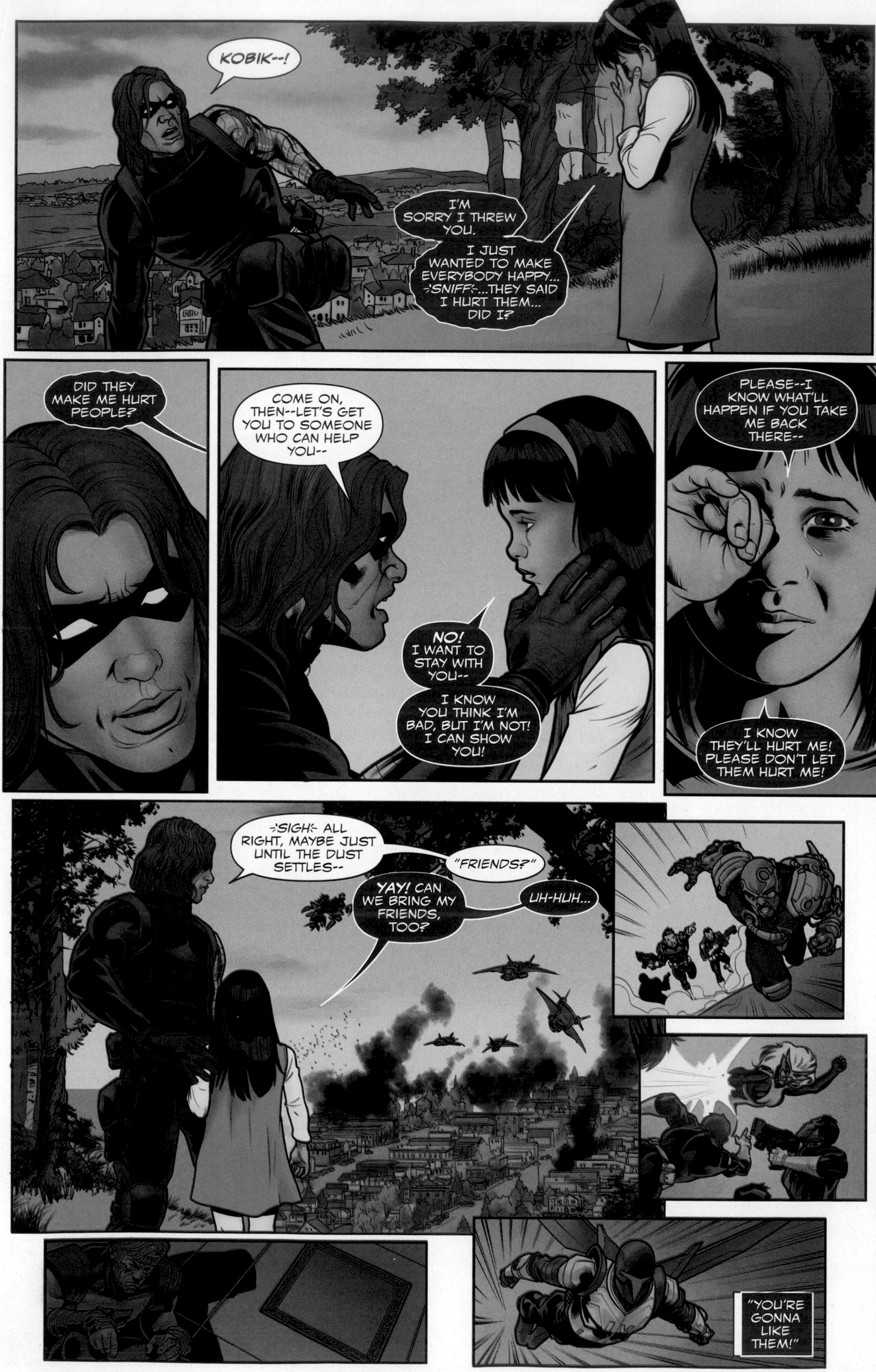
KOBIK--!
I'M SORRY I THREW YOU.
I JUST WANTED TO MAKE EVERYBODY HAPPY... -SNIFF- ...THEY SAID I HURT THEM... DID I?
DID THEY MAKE ME HURT PEOPLE?
COME ON, THEN--LET'S GET YOU TO SOMEONE WHO CAN HELP YOU--
NO! I WANT TO STAY WITH YOU--
I KNOW YOU THINK I'M BAD, BUT I'M NOT! I CAN SHOW YOU!
PLEASE--I KNOW WHAT'LL HAPPEN IF YOU TAKE ME BACK THERE--
I KNOW THEY'LL HURT ME! PLEASE DON'T LET THEM HURT ME!
-SIGH- ALL RIGHT, MAYBE JUST UNTIL THE DUST SETTLES--
YAY! CAN WE BRING MY FRIENDS, TOO?
UH-HUH...
"FRIENDS?"
"YOU'RE GONNA LIKE THEM!"

YOU'RE "LOOKING INTO IT"?! LOOKING INTO IT **AGGRESSIVELY.** HOW'S **THAT?** IN FACT--

--AS **MUCH** AS I LOVE THESE LITTLE CONFERENCES-- AS THEY GIVE ME A FEW MINUTES' BREAK FROM DOING THINGS THAT ACTUALLY MAKE THE WORLD **SAFER--**

--I SHOULD PROBABLY GET BACK TO IT.

WHAT THE--?

I'M SORRY, MA'AM. COUNCIL'S ORDERS.

NOT SO FAST, DIRECTOR--

IT'S BAD ENOUGH THAT YOUR ARROGANCE PUT US IN THIS SPOT TO BEGIN WITH--BUT NOW--TO NOT GET SO MUCH AS AN **APOLOGY** FROM YOU--

COUNCIL MEMBER PERON IS **RIGHT,** MARIA. THE BLAME FOR ALL THIS RESTS SQUARELY ON YOUR SHOULDERS. THE KOBIK INITIATIVE WAS **YOUR** IDEA, AFTER ALL.

AND EVEN AFTER IT WAS OUTED BY THE WHISPERER, YOU PRESSED AHEAD, INSISTING THIS PLEASANT HILL NONSENSE WAS FOOLPROOF--AND NOW HERE WE SIT, ALL FOOLS.

YOU HAVE ENDANGERED THE ENTIRE **PLANET**--PERHAPS EVEN THE ENTIRE **UNIVERSE!** YOU CREATED A WEAPON OF **UNLIMITED, UNIMAGINABLE POWER**-- WIELDED IT **CARELESSLY**-- AND THEN YOU **LOST** IT!

AND THAT'S NOT EVEN MENTIONING ZEMO'S **ESCAPE,** OR THE HUNDREDS OF LIVES THAT COULD'VE BEEN **LOST** IN THE REVOLT--

BUT **WEREN'T.** LOOK, I UNDERSTAND YOUR ANGER--I CARRY IT AROUND EVERY DAY, BELIEVE ME--

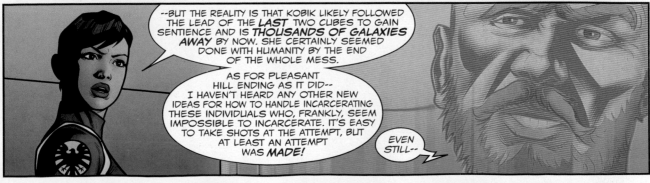

--BUT THE REALITY IS THAT KOBIK LIKELY FOLLOWED THE LEAD OF THE **LAST** TWO CUBES TO GAIN SENTIENCE AND IS **THOUSANDS OF GALAXIES AWAY** BY NOW. SHE CERTAINLY SEEMED DONE WITH HUMANITY BY THE END OF THE WHOLE MESS.

AS FOR PLEASANT HILL ENDING AS IT DID-- I HAVEN'T HEARD ANY OTHER NEW IDEAS FOR HOW TO HANDLE INCARCERATING THESE INDIVIDUALS WHO, FRANKLY, SEEM IMPOSSIBLE TO INCARCERATE. IT'S EASY TO TAKE SHOTS AT THE ATTEMPT, BUT AT LEAST AN ATTEMPT WAS **MADE!**

EVEN STILL--

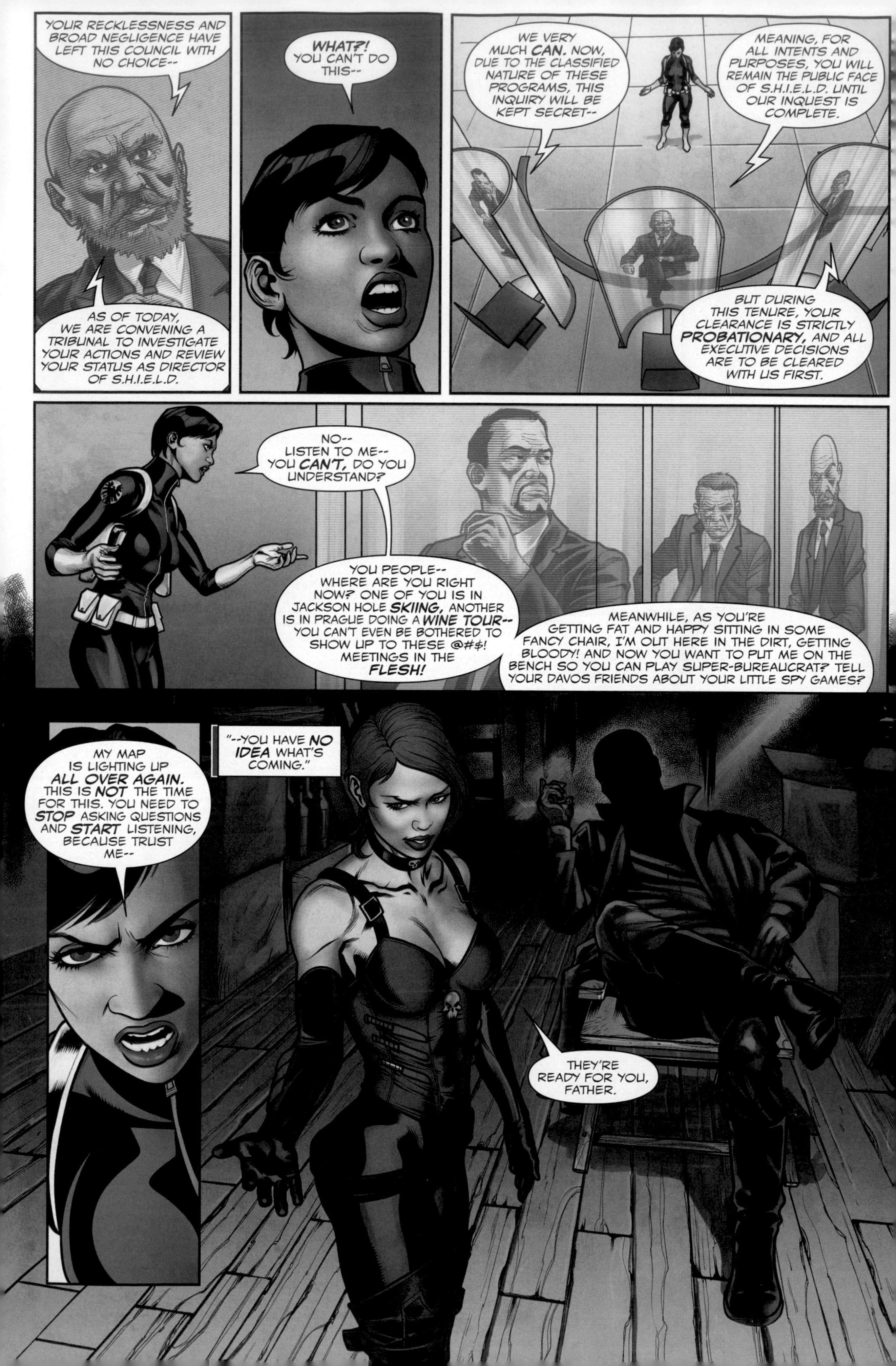
YOUR RECKLESSNESS AND BROAD NEGLIGENCE HAVE LEFT THIS COUNCIL WITH NO CHOICE--
AS OF TODAY, WE ARE CONVENING A TRIBUNAL TO INVESTIGATE YOUR ACTIONS AND REVIEW YOUR STATUS AS DIRECTOR OF S.H.I.E.L.D.
WHAT?! YOU CAN'T DO THIS--
WE VERY MUCH CAN. NOW, DUE TO THE CLASSIFIED NATURE OF THESE PROGRAMS, THIS INQUIRY WILL BE KEPT SECRET--
MEANING, FOR ALL INTENTS AND PURPOSES, YOU WILL REMAIN THE PUBLIC FACE OF S.H.I.E.L.D. UNTIL OUR INQUEST IS COMPLETE.
BUT DURING THIS TENURE, YOUR CLEARANCE IS STRICTLY PROBATIONARY, AND ALL EXECUTIVE DECISIONS ARE TO BE CLEARED WITH US FIRST.
NO-- LISTEN TO ME-- YOU CAN'T, DO YOU UNDERSTAND?
YOU PEOPLE-- WHERE ARE YOU RIGHT NOW? ONE OF YOU IS IN JACKSON HOLE SKIING, ANOTHER IS IN PRAGUE DOING A WINE TOUR-- YOU CAN'T EVEN BE BOTHERED TO SHOW UP TO THESE @#$! MEETINGS IN THE FLESH!
MEANWHILE, AS YOU'RE GETTING FAT AND HAPPY SITTING IN SOME FANCY CHAIR, I'M OUT HERE IN THE DIRT, GETTING BLOODY! AND NOW YOU WANT TO PUT ME ON THE BENCH SO YOU CAN PLAY SUPER-BUREAUCRAT? TELL YOUR DAVOS FRIENDS ABOUT YOUR LITTLE SPY GAMES?
MY MAP IS LIGHTING UP ALL OVER AGAIN. THIS IS NOT THE TIME FOR THIS. YOU NEED TO STOP ASKING QUESTIONS AND START LISTENING, BECAUSE TRUST ME--
"--YOU HAVE NO IDEA WHAT'S COMING."
THEY'RE READY FOR YOU, FATHER.

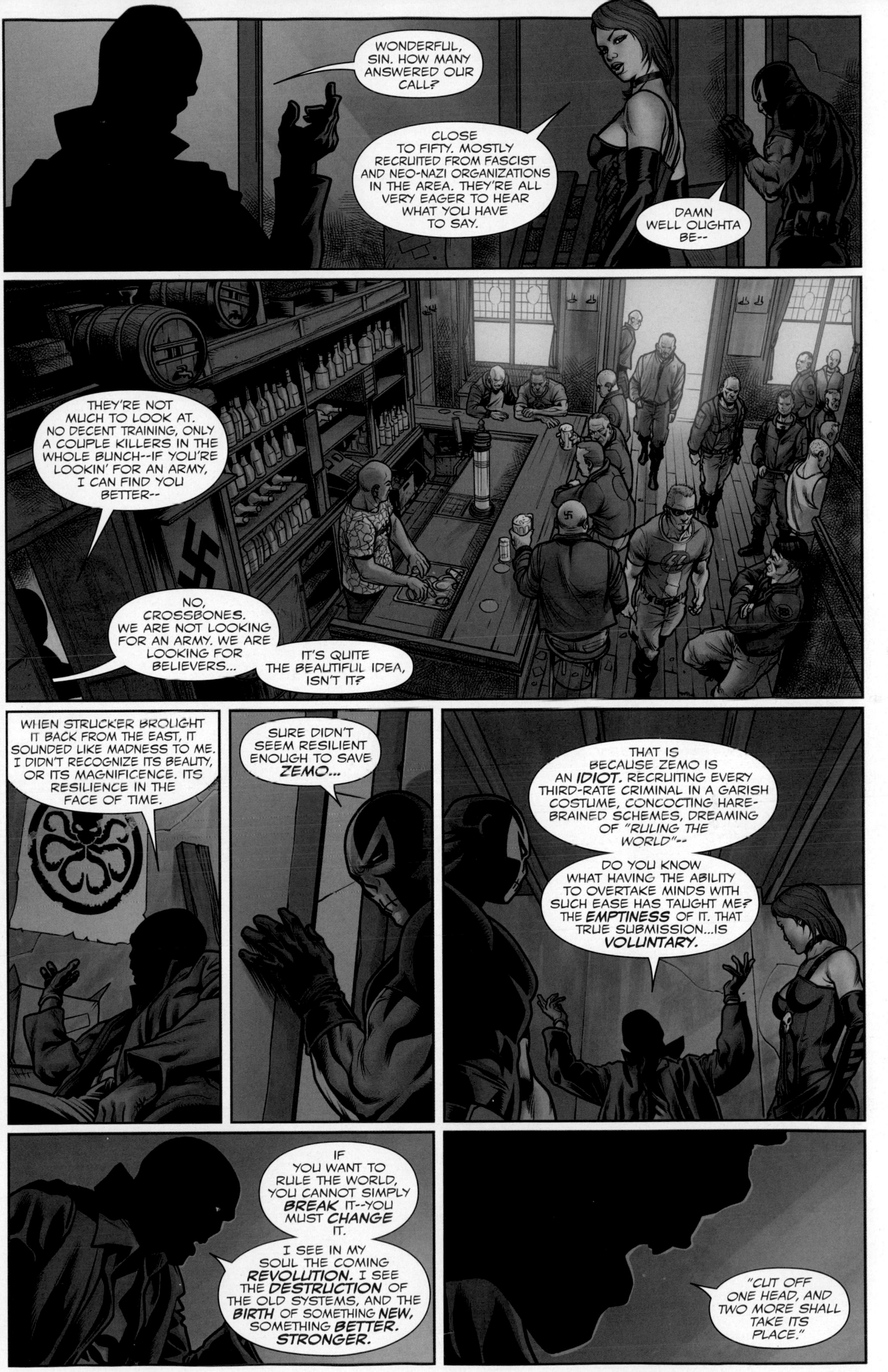

WONDERFUL, SIN. HOW MANY ANSWERED OUR CALL?
CLOSE TO FIFTY. MOSTLY RECRUITED FROM FASCIST AND NEO-NAZI ORGANIZATIONS IN THE AREA. THEY'RE ALL VERY EAGER TO HEAR WHAT YOU HAVE TO SAY.
DAMN WELL OUGHTA BE--
THEY'RE NOT MUCH TO LOOK AT. NO DECENT TRAINING, ONLY A COUPLE KILLERS IN THE WHOLE BUNCH--IF YOU'RE LOOKIN' FOR AN ARMY, I CAN FIND YOU BETTER--
NO, CROSSBONES. WE ARE NOT LOOKING FOR AN ARMY. WE ARE LOOKING FOR BELIEVERS...
IT'S QUITE THE BEAUTIFUL IDEA, ISN'T IT?
WHEN STRUCKER BROUGHT IT BACK FROM THE EAST, IT SOUNDED LIKE MADNESS TO ME. I DIDN'T RECOGNIZE ITS BEAUTY, OR ITS MAGNIFICENCE. ITS RESILIENCE IN THE FACE OF TIME.
SURE DIDN'T SEEM RESILIENT ENOUGH TO SAVE **ZEMO...**
THAT IS BECAUSE ZEMO IS AN **IDIOT.** RECRUITING EVERY THIRD-RATE CRIMINAL IN A GARISH COSTUME, CONCOCTING HARE-BRAINED SCHEMES, DREAMING OF *"RULING THE WORLD"*--
DO YOU KNOW WHAT HAVING THE ABILITY TO OVERTAKE MINDS WITH SUCH EASE HAS TAUGHT ME? THE **EMPTINESS** OF IT. THAT TRUE SUBMISSION...IS **VOLUNTARY.**
IF YOU WANT TO RULE THE WORLD, YOU CANNOT SIMPLY **BREAK** IT--YOU MUST **CHANGE** IT.
I SEE IN MY SOUL THE COMING **REVOLUTION.** I SEE THE **DESTRUCTION** OF THE OLD SYSTEMS, AND THE **BIRTH** OF SOMETHING **NEW,** SOMETHING **BETTER. STRONGER.**
"CUT OFF ONE HEAD, AND TWO MORE SHALL TAKE ITS PLACE."

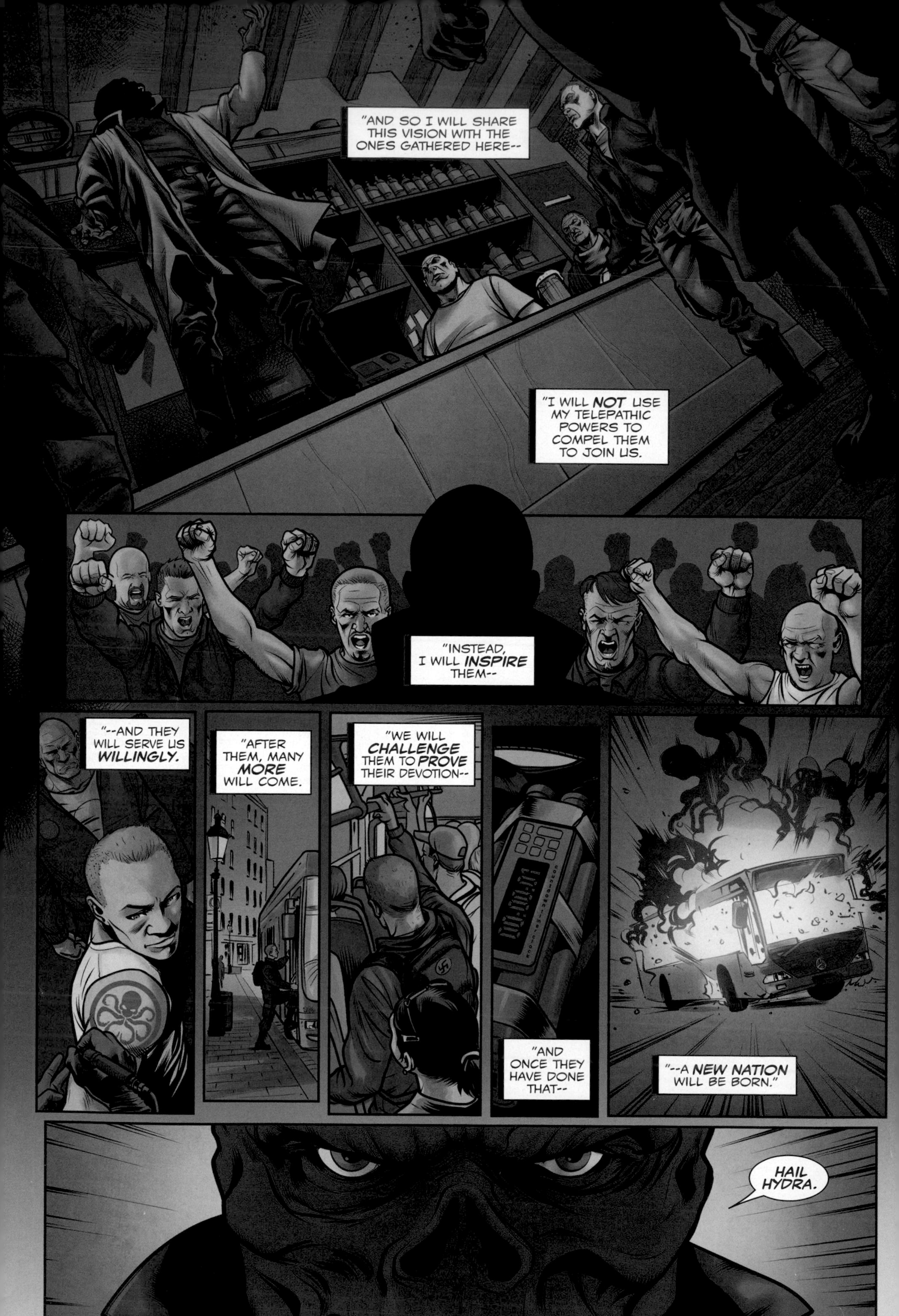
"AND SO I WILL SHARE THIS VISION WITH THE ONES GATHERED HERE--
"I WILL NOT USE MY TELEPATHIC POWERS TO COMPEL THEM TO JOIN US.
"INSTEAD, I WILL INSPIRE THEM--
"--AND THEY WILL SERVE US WILLINGLY.
"AFTER THEM, MANY MORE WILL COME.
"WE WILL CHALLENGE THEM TO PROVE THEIR DEVOTION--
"AND ONCE THEY HAVE DONE THAT--
"--A NEW NATION WILL BE BORN."
HAIL HYDRA.
THE END.

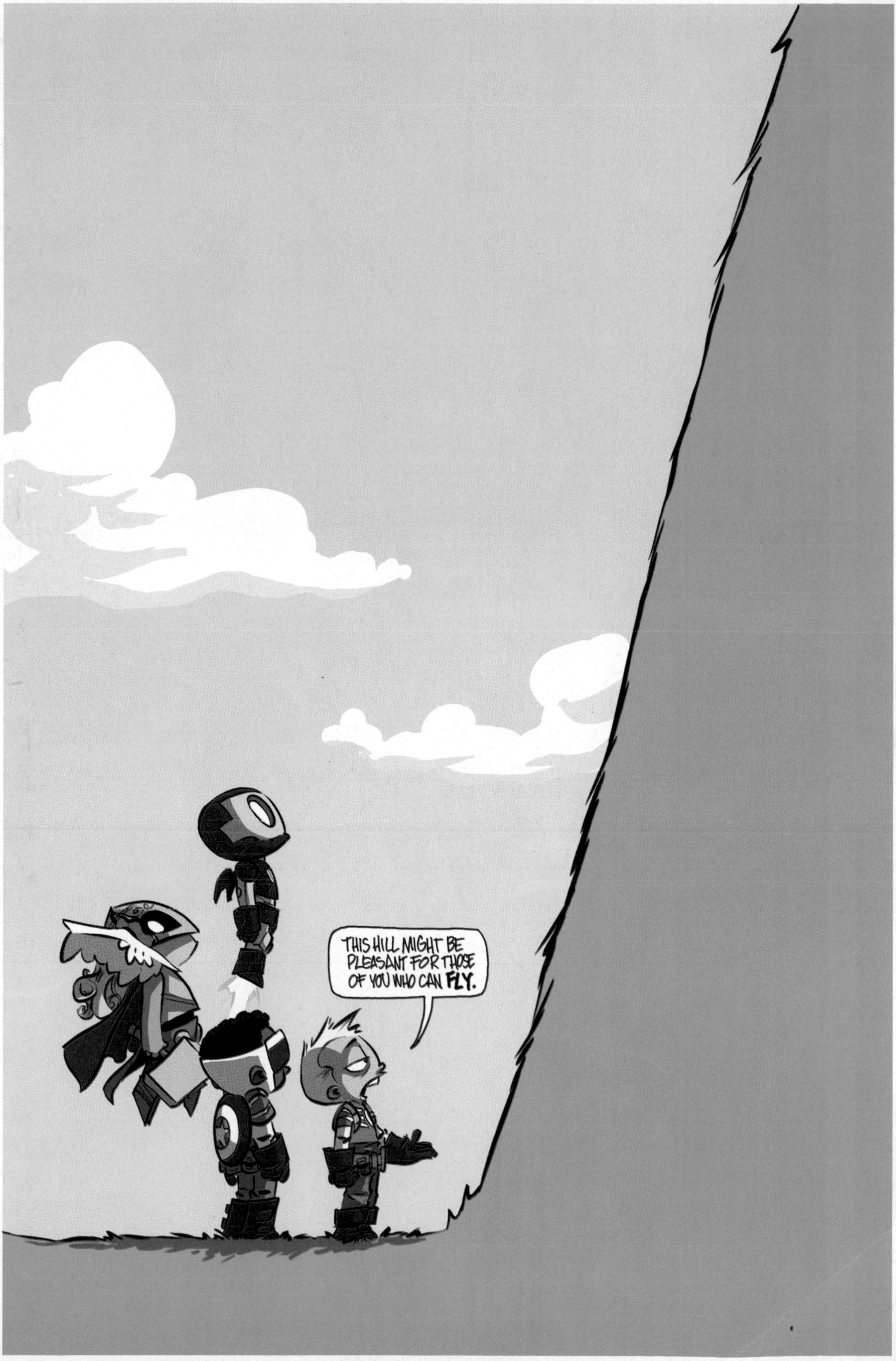
THIS HILL MIGHT BE PLEASANT FOR THOSE OF YOU WHO CAN FLY.

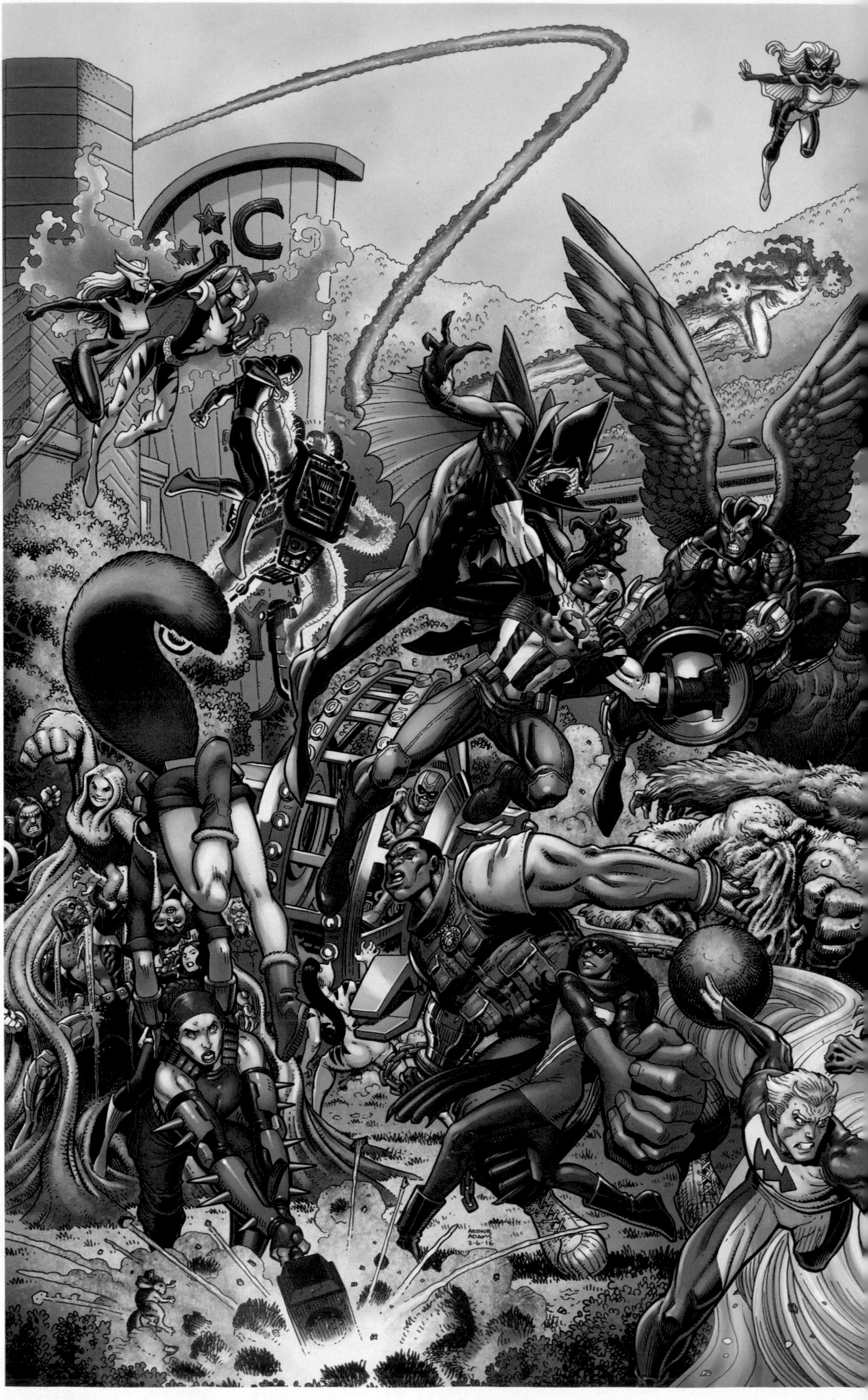
ARTHUR ADAMS 2-6-16

Avengers Standoff: Assault on Pleasant Hill Alpha & Omega connecting variants by **ART ADAMS & CHRIS SOTOMAYOR**

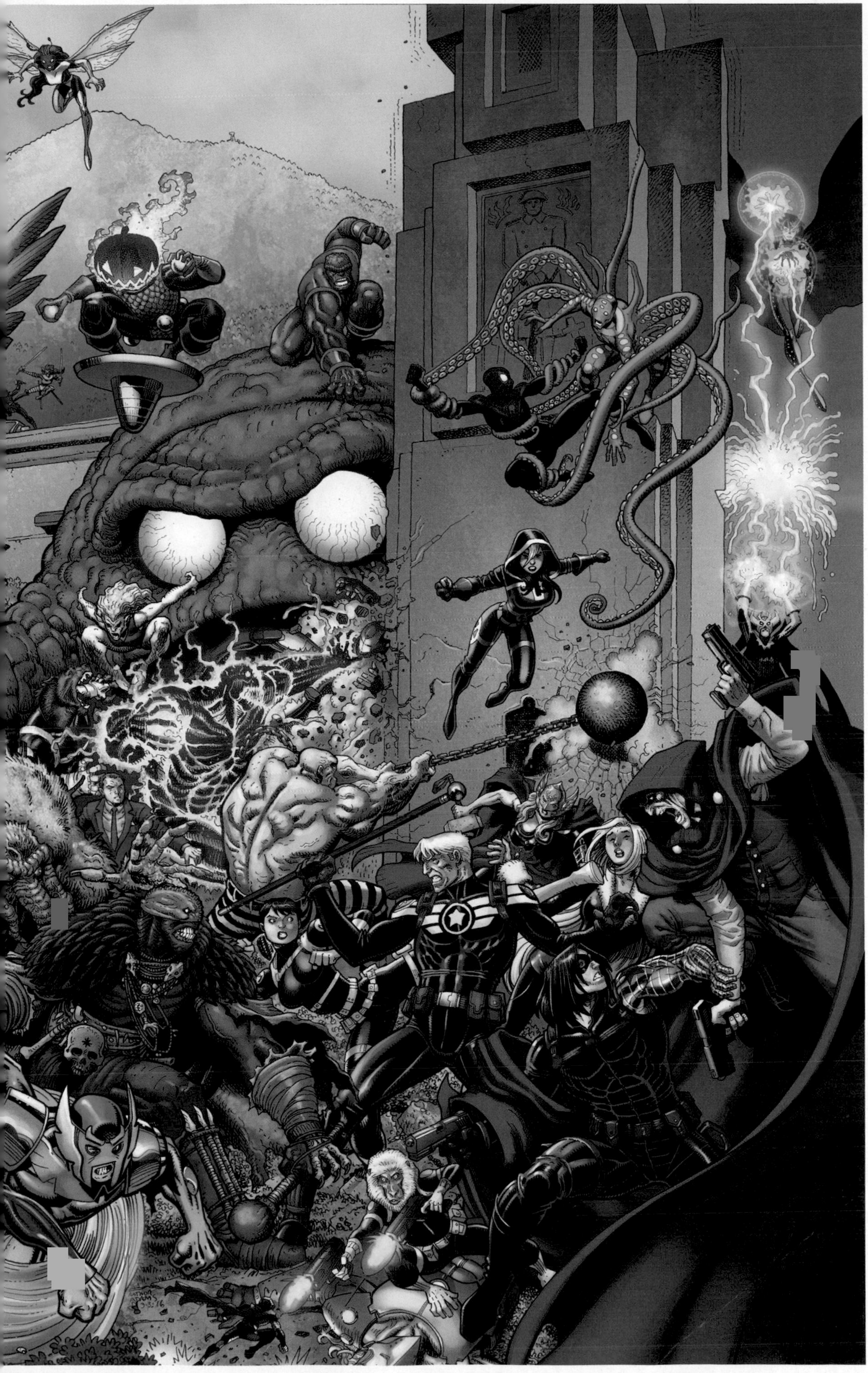

Avengers Standoff:
Assault on Pleasant Hill Omega variant by
JIM STERANKO

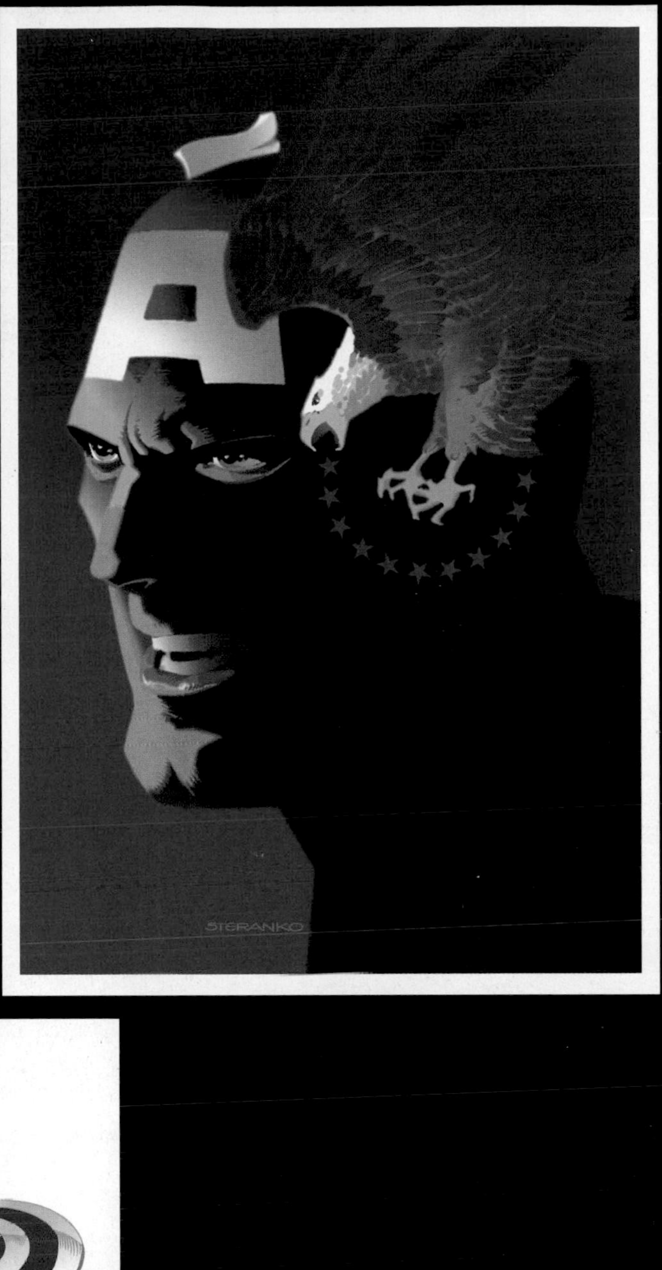
STERANKO

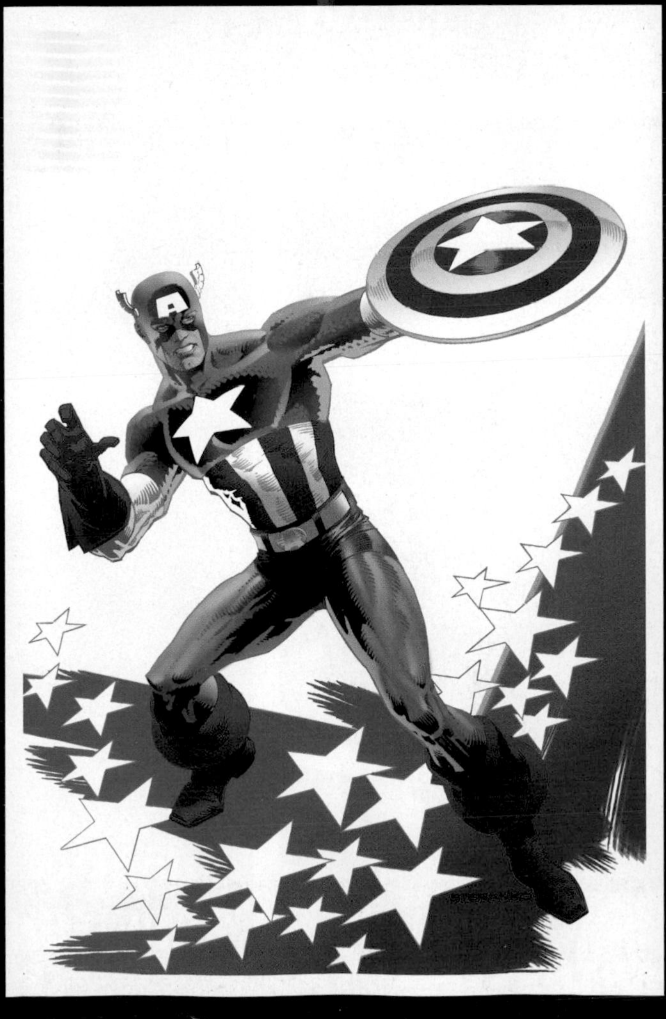

Captain America:
Sam Wilson No. 7 variant by
JIM STERANKO

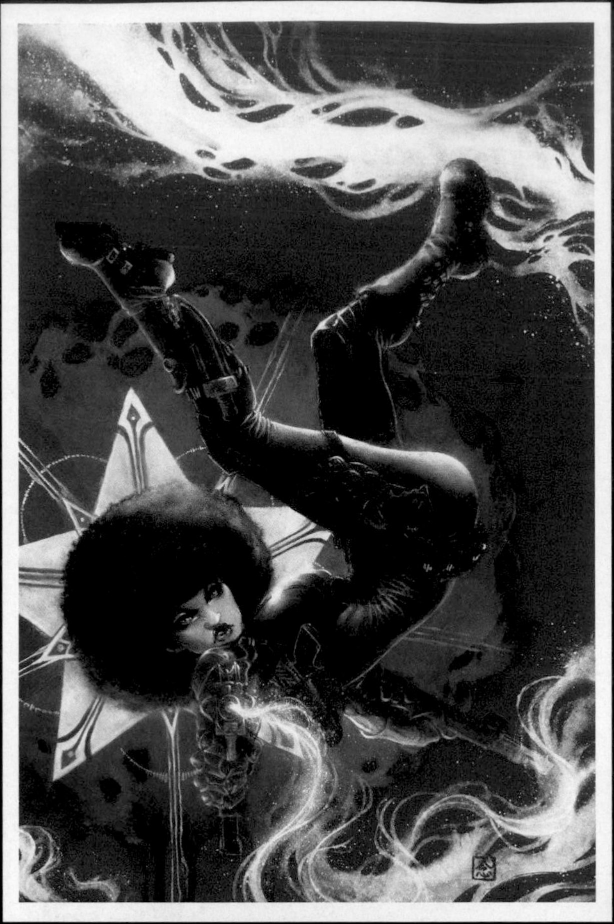

Captain America: Sam Wilson No. 7
Women of Power variant by

NEN CHANG

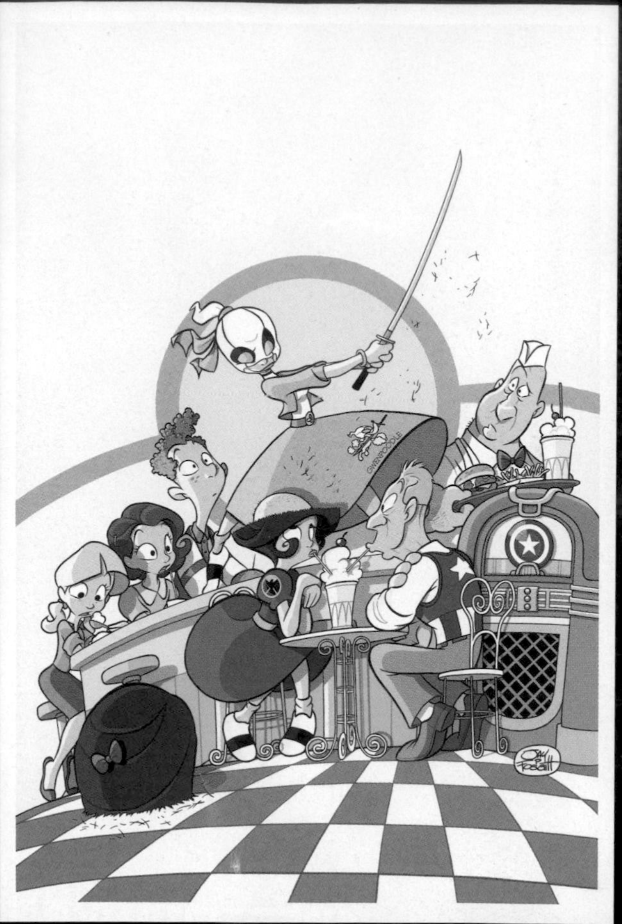

Avengers Standoff: Assault on Pleasant Hill
Alpha Gwenpool Party variant by

JAY FOSGITT

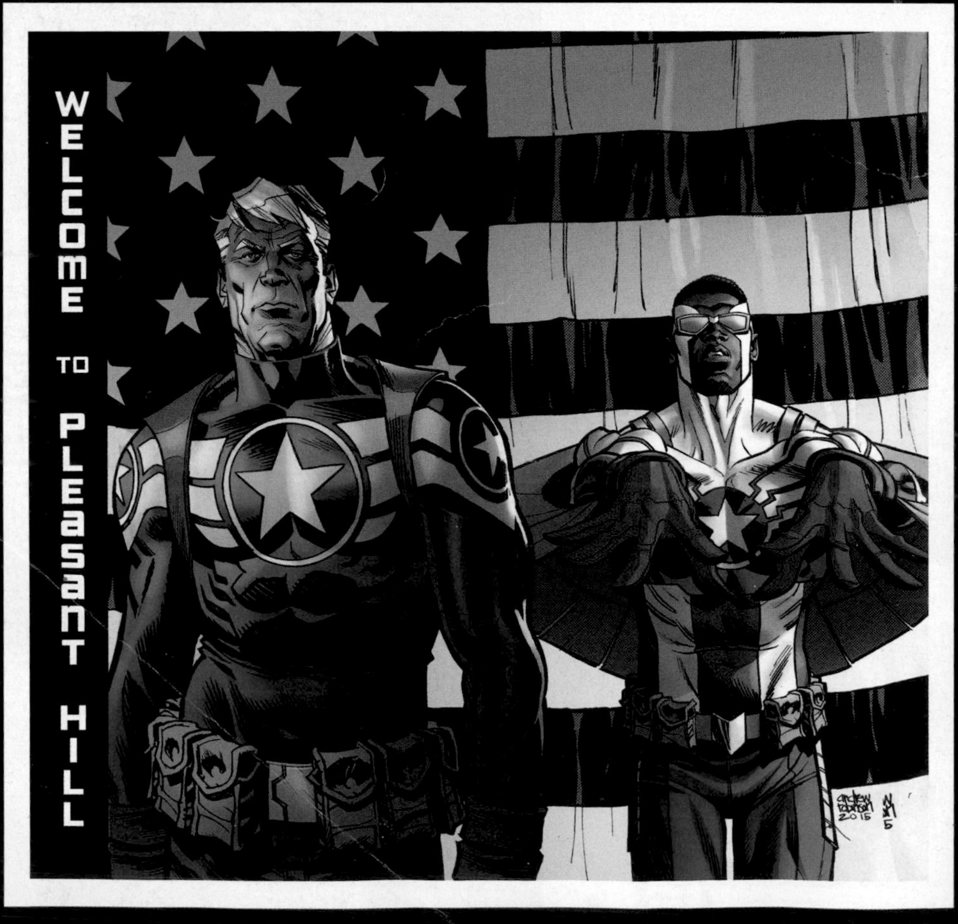
WELCOME TO PLEASANT HILL

Avengers Standoff:
Welcome to Pleasant
Hill Hip-Hop
variant by

ANDREW ROBINSON